BENSON and HEDGES
CRICKET YEAR
THIRTEENTH EDITION

Life assurance and pension products are provided by National Westminster Life Assurance Limited, whose investment Business is regulated by the SIB. National Westminster Bank Plc. Member of the NatWest Life and NatWest Unit Trust Marketing Group. Registered Number 929027 England. Registered Office: 41 Lothbury, London EC2P 2BP Member of IMRO.

Life assurance, yawn. Pensions, zzzzzz.

From hundreds of policy options (snore) we've designed 12 products to protect you and your family, all your life.

For details call in at a branch or dial 0800 200 400. We have over 1500 Personal Financial Advisers at your disposal.

National Westminster Bank
We're here to make life easier

BENSON and HEDGES
CRICKET YEAR

THIRTEENTH EDITION
SEPTEMBER 1993 to SEPTEMBER 1994

EDITOR – DAVID LEMMON
FOREWORD by MIKE ATHERTON

HEADLINE

Editor's note

The aim of *Benson and Hedges Cricket Year* is to give the cricket enthusiast an opportunity to read through the happenings in world cricket from each October until the following September (the end of the English season). Form charts are printed for first-class matches, and a player's every appearance will be given in these charts; the date and place allow these appearances to be quickly identified in the text. For the first time, the statistics of limited-over cricket are presented in a more compact and readily accessible way.

The symbol * indicates 'not out' or 'wicket-keeper' according to the context.

The editor would like to express his deepest thanks to Sudhir Vaidya, Anthony Lalley, John R. Ward, Ian Smith, Qamar Ahmed, Richard Lockwood, Philip Bailey, Les Hatton, Andrew Samson and, in particular, Brian Croudy for their untiring help and encouragement throughout the year.

First published in 1994
by HEADLINE BOOK PUBLISHING

10 9 8 7 6 5 4 3 2 1

A CIP catalogue record for this book is available from the British Library

ISBN 0-7472-1148-5

Designed and produced by Book Production Consultants Plc, 25–27 High Street, Chesterton, Cambridge CB4 1ND

Printed and bound in Great Britain by Butler & Tanner Ltd.

HEADLINE BOOK PUBLISHING
A division of Hodder Headline PLC
338 Euston Road
London NW1 3BH

CONTENTS

Sponsor's message

Welcome to the *Benson and Hedges Cricket Year* – the 13th of its kind – and one that spans a memorable chapter in the history of the game. When the great Viv Richards retired from the first-class scene in 1993, many predicted that a vacuum would long be felt in the West Indian batting line-up. They were wrong. If proof were needed, the West Indies once again demonstrated its remarkable propensity for producing world-class cricketers.

In the Antigua Test against England in April of this year, Brian Lara hit a stylish, powerful and masterly 375. By doing so he assumed Sir Garry Sobers' crown as the scorer of the highest individual innings in a Test match. A couple of months later, Lara was in among the records again with his 501 not out for Warwickshire against Durham.

More history was made when a South African touring side played Test cricket in England for the first time since 1965. Their highly competitive, 'Go for it!' attitude made the three-match series splendidly entertaining. And, in deference to the symbolic significance of South Africa's return to the fold, even the English weather behaved itself.

It was a great summer – as Warwickshire would undoubtedly agree. Thanks to a potent blending of experience, talent, fine captaincy from Dermot Reeve, strong team spirit – and the presence of Mr Lara – Warwickshire reserved 1994 for itself.

The county took the 23rd Benson and Hedges Cup at Lord's in July; the AXA Equity and Law League title; almost clinched the NatWest Trophy final; and won the Britannic Assurance County Championship. An incredible performance.

As the sponsor of longest standing in cricket competition, Benson and Hedges is pleased to enjoy an excellent relationship with the MCC and the Test and County Cricket Board. Their continued support is much appreciated.

Thanks mixed with admiration go to David Lemmon, his team and everyone involved in the compilation of this book. How they manage to produce so comprehensive a record of the past year in cricket worldwide – just a few weeks after the close of the England season – is mystifying.

This edition of the *Benson and Hedges Cricket Year* is packed to the gunnels with facts, figures, match results and fine photography – all in sufficient helpings to satisfy the most carnivorous of cricket appetites. Adding spice to the feast, I'm delighted that England captain Mike Atherton has been kind enough to pen the foreword. We wish him and the team every success on the forthcoming Ashes tour.

PHIL TRITTON
Marketing Manager,
Benson and Hedges

Comment

Cricket was graced by several memorable achievements in 1994. Firstly, of course, there was Brian Lara and his 375 against England in Antigua followed a few weeks later by his run of centuries in the county championship and his 501 not out for Warwickshire against Durham. As a team, Warwickshire enhanced the year with their vibrant spirit and positive cricket. They were joyful and committed in all they did, and the paying customers responded to them. Under Atherton, England captured something of this spirit and attitude. There was the brave win in Barbados after the humiliation at Port of Spain, and there was the vigorous victory over South Africa at The Oval where Devon Malcolm touched unexpected heights, Gough and DeFreitas battled thrillingly, and Graeme Hick confirmed that he was a born-again cricketer. Yet these memorable delights must not be allowed to obscure the problems that confound the game.

After just two seasons of the 'radical reforms' which were to transform the domestic pattern of cricket in England, two of the reforms have been jettisoned; the Sunday League has quickly reverted to 40 overs and a 2 p.m. start while next season the Benson and Hedges Cup returns to its group structure for the qualifying rounds. As yet, coloured clothing and the four-day game survive although neither has anything to commend it.

Coloured clothing came into being as part of floodlit cricket in Australia. We do not have this form of cricket in England, and the thought of cricketers in blue, green, yellow or red garb on a dull afternoon in Bristol or Derby borders on the ludicrous. The sale of shirts in county club shops has, of course, brought in revenue, but this will not continue unless, like soccer clubs, counties change their shirt design every three or four years to trap more buyers. One fears that they will.

The four-day game has done nothing to improve the standard of cricket. Indeed, the general opinion is that the standard has dropped quite dramatically at county level. One thing is certain, and that is that the four-day programme is sapping the soul of the domestic game. One can do no better than draw attention to the views of the England captain. 'I fear for the paying spectator too; four-day cricket on bland wickets does little for the imagination, and the game is poorer without the variety that different conditions, such as festival weeks and uncovered wickets, would bring.'

The greatest cricketers that this country has produced were nurtured on uncovered wickets in three-day matches. Techniques were honed and tested, characters developed; and people came to watch.

Television, of course, has a far greater influence on people's lives today than it had in those days. The guardians of the game have recently negotiated a deal with television companies that will bring millions of pounds into cricket in the next few years. If the money is used wisely on the game at all levels, this is a marvellous achievement, but we must not make too great a god of television. There are the gravest dangers in abnegating too much responsibility to the camera, the company and the commentator. The camera has become umpire and referee. Where once a difference of opinion or the interpretation of a shake of the head was discussed in the privacy of a dressing room or with the conviviality of a pint of beer, the nuances of a facial expression have now become commentators' fodder for the rest of the week and the source of endless video replays.

But if one carries fears for the professional game, one remains ever confident of the indestructibility of the game itself. Some of my greatest joys from the past year go unreported in this volume: the Mobil Matchplay at Chelmsford with its scores of under-11s in happy competition in the morning, and the keenly fought under-16 final in the afternoon; the Abbot Ale National Club final at Lord's, a glorious day's cricket, with a large crowd and the Chorley Girls urging their side to victory all day long; and, eight days later, Ealing, beaten finalists at Lord's, gaining compensation with victory over Spencer in the *Evening Standard* Greater London Club final at The Oval. Another good crowd saw 534 runs scored and the match decided on the last ball.

As Bob Willis made the presentation, my West Indian companion said, 'There was only one winner, man, cricket. It's always the same.'

Thankfully, he is right.

DAVID LEMMON

Benson and Hedges Cricket Year World XI, 1994

The World XI is chosen by the editor and reflects the performance of players, mostly at international level, during the period covered by this book. The figures in brackets are the standings of the players in the Coopers and Lybrand ratings. Haynes and Richardson still hold high places in those ratings although both appear to have lost form at Test level in the past twelve months. Atherton, on the other hand, has risen dramatically during that period with fine performances in three series for England, against West Indies, New Zealand and South Africa. Coopers and Lybrand have no ratings for wicket-keepers, and Ian Healy seems to have no serious challenger in this position at present.

M.A. Atherton (11)
D.C. Boon (3)
B.C. Lara (1)
S.R. Tendulkar (2)
S.R. Waugh (5)
Wasim Akram (5)
*I.A. Healy
A.R. Kumble (4)
S.K. Warne (3)
C.E.L. Ambrose (1)
Waqar Younis (2)

The ratings for Wasim Akram, A.R. Kumble, S.K. Warne, C.E.L. Ambrose and Waqar Younis are for bowling; the remainder are for batting. Boon, Lara, Tendulkar, Healy, Kumble, Warne, Ambrose and Waqar Younis were in the eleven last year. Martin Crowe has more than earned a place as twelfth man.

Foreword

by Mike Atherton

It has, as the Queen might say, been a turbulent year. Forty-six all out in Trinidad, two awful performances at Headquarters and my various contretemps with ICC referee Peter Burge have been among the lows. Counter-balancing these was the momentous victory at Barbados and, on the first anniversary of my first win as England captain, the way the England team fought back to level the Test series against South Africa, playing some stunning cricket in the process.

Without resorting to hyperbole, it is fair to say that we have made real progress this year. Much of it has coincided with the appointment of Raymond Illingworth as Chairman of Selectors. While the media endeavoured to drive a wedge between captain and chairman, I would like to say, on record, that the relationship is a harmonious one and has prospered. Certainly, I have appreciated his support during the difficult times this summer. Perhaps the best sign of progress is that of expectation: for England's first international match of 1994 (which we won) there was no expectation of success; while the last (to date) victory was roundly expected. As I ponder, on the verge of an Ashes adventure, an England side playing with real character, spirit and pride is surely what we all want to see.

On the domestic front, some of the concerns expressed by Graham Gooch in last year's foreword remain. The general standard of county cricket remains too low, with too few players who would be deemed good enough to play first-class cricket elsewhere, and too few whose aspirations are loftier than the county scene. It is to be hoped that the four-day structure will gradually improve the standard. I have my doubts; too many counties, too many players, too little competitiveness are inherent weaknesses which a facelift will do little to change. I fear for the paying spectator too; four-day cricket on bland wickets does little for the imagination, and the game is poorer without the variety that different conditions, such as festival weeks, which have been reduced in number over the years, and uncovered wickets, would bring.

But enough of my tale of woe, and heartiest congratulations to Warwickshire. Undoubtedly the team of the year, they became the first county to win three of the four major competitions in one season – the Benson and Hedges Cup, the Britannic Assurance County Championship, and the AXA Equity and Law League – and only narrowly missed the clean sweep by losing to Worcestershire in the NatWest Trophy final. In Dermot Reeve, they have a captain of flair and enterprise who has led a side, unhindered by international calls, whose ability to fight their way out of situations has been as impressive as anything in their marvellous year. While only the churlish would say they were a one-man team, they did have the good fortune (and being present in Antigua when the deed was done, it was certainly good fortune) to have the services of the Cricketer of the Year,

Brian Lara. Special mention must be made of his record Test score, and record first-class score. One can only hope his star continues to burn brightly in the face of an exhausting cricket schedule, and accompanying hype.

It would seem strange, therefore, that while extolling the virtues of one overseas player and the effect on his county, the TCCB is considering the future of overseas players in this country. In particular it is strange that it is Lancashire, a county with a strong tradition of overseas players, who are forwarding the proposals. My views on this are ambiguous: from a county viewpoint the overseas player brings flair and entertainment and provides a stiff challenge for home-grown talent. However, as a member of the national side it is irritating to see the improvement of such players after a season in England. For example, Cameron Cuffy (this year of Surrey) could well return to England with the West Indies next year with greater success than may have been otherwise possible. It seems to me that the feeling around the counties is not yet strong enough to end our association with overseas players for good; yet this may well be an issue where the counties should bow to the needs of the national side. After all, who finances the county programme?

One group of overseas players it was a delight to see here this summer were the touring South Africans, whose return to Test cricket in England was a momentous occasion. Amazingly, the Proteas played with such professionalism and nous that one would scarcely have known of their absence from the international stage. None felt their absence more than the 'lost' generation of cricketers, such as Barry Richards and Graeme Pollock. As a present player, blessed with the opportunity of playing Test cricket, it was a privilege to see one such player, Mike Procter, enjoying the moment of victory of his young, and not so young, charges without any hint of bitterness or remorse.

Last year saw the retirement of many of the great names of cricket such as Richards, Botham and Gower. This year, one retirement has stood out, that of Allan Border. As a 'Pom' who has suffered, it is only fitting to record his phenomenal achievements: only the second member of the 10,000 Test run club and a successful leader who transformed his side into a combative and successful unit. Let us hope Australia misses him!

Dare I say it, his retirement has coincided with a significant attempt to clean up the game's image. From the Australian Cricket Board's clampdown on Hughes and Warne to 'Burge's Purge' this summer, there is a clear message from the authorities that lapses in behaviour will not be tolerated. Everybody, I am sure, wants to see the ideals of the game upheld. It is to be remembered, however, that it is precisely the emotion and passion that make Test cricket, in particular, a great game. As such, players and referees alike must attempt to strike a balance between commitment and fair play.

SECTION A
Australia
Sheffield Shield
Mercantile Mutual Cup
Test series, Australia *v.* New Zealand; Australia *v.* South Africa
Benson and Hedges World Series – Australia, New Zealand and South Africa
Form charts
First-class averages

Matthew Hayden – seven centuries in the Sheffield Shield for Queensland,
and 1,136 runs, average 126.22. (Ben Radford/Allsport)

'Aussies on Fire', proclaimed Australia's leading cricket magazine when Border's side returned from England where they had been triumphant by four Tests to one in the Ashes series. There was just cause for the enthusiasm and the optimism for, as the *Australian Cricketer* pointed out, the success in England was based to a large extent on young players like Warne and Slater, and other young cricketers like Hayden, Martyn, Bevan and Ponting were pressing their claims strongly.

There were fewer moves between states before the start of the 1993–4 season than there had been in recent years. The most significant changes were in Victoria who saw Lehmann and Nobes return to South Australia, and Maxwell to New South Wales. Victoria could not balance their losses with new imports, and they had further worries in that Merv Hughes was to begin the season in hospital for further treatment on a knee injury.

South Australia could only feel strengthened by the return of Lehmann and Nobes while Western Australia had lost only Terry Alderman to retirement. Queensland welcomed the return of Peter McPhee from Tasmania who had gained Steve Herzberg from Western Australia for whom he had played very little.

Like Alderman, New South Wales' Steve Small had retired, but Maxwell had returned, and there was so much talent available to the reigning champions that they started as firm favourites to retain the Shield.

 ## MERCANTILE MUTUAL CUP

9 October 1993 *at WACA Ground, Perth*

Western Australia 281 for 4 (M.W. McPhee 99, G.R. March 55, D.R. Martyn 54)
South Australia 260 for 9 (P.C. Nobes 60)
Western Australia (2 pts.) won by 21 runs

10 October 1993 *at Woolloongabba, Brisbane*

New South Wales 278 for 4 (M.J. Slater 96, S.R. Waugh 59, M.A. Taylor 55)
Queensland 151 (G.D. McGrath 4 for 17)
New South Wales (2 pts.) won by 127 runs

15 October 1993 *at WACA Ground, Perth*

Tasmania 208 for 6 (D.F. Hills 68)
Western Australia 209 for 8 (G.R. Marsh 56)
Western Australia (2 pts.) won by 2 wickets

17 October 1993 *at MCG, Melbourne*

Victoria 224 for 4 (D.J. Ramshaw 82, D.M. Jones 68)

Darren Webber hit 176, the highest score of his career, for South Australia against Queensland at Brisbane, but lost form later in the season. (Stephen Laffer/Sports-Line)

Queensland 225 for 3 (S.G. Law 107 not out, D.M. Wellham 70)
Queensland (2 pts.) won by 7 wickets

24 October 1993 *at North Sydney Oval*

New South Wales 307 for 7 (M.E. Waugh 68, R. Chee Quee 56)
Tasmania 248 for 8 (D.F. Hills 59, D.C. Boon 52)
New South Wales (2 pts.) won by 59 runs

31 October 1993 *at Adelaide Oval*

South Australia 226 for 4 (J.D. Siddons 90 not out)
Victoria 227 for 3 (D.M. Jones 95 not out)
Victoria (2 pts.) won by 7 wickets

In Australia's one-day competition, each side met the other once. The state that topped the league won an automatic place in the final while the teams finishing second and third met for the right to meet them. As has become customary, the first rounds of the tournament were played during the first month of the season with the last of the qualifying matches being played in February. Holders New South Wales began well, winning their first two matches, as did Western Australia.

Queensland welcomed back Craig McDermott, and although he took no wickets against New South Wales, the Australian selectors breathed a sigh of relief. There

was interest in the performance of the New South Wales pace bowler McGrath who took four good wickets in 10 overs for 17 runs and gave early notice that he could be the replacement for the injured Merv Hughes. Law hit a spectacular century to take Queensland to victory over Victoria with 21 balls to spare, and there was a run feast at North Sydney where Holdsworth took the individual performance for a blazing 49 not out. His runs came out of 56 for the unbroken eighth-wicket stand with Emery.

19 October 1993 *at Lilac Hill*

New Zealanders 189 (B.A. Pocock 68, W. Watson 57 not out)

Australian Cricket Board Chairman's XI 192 for 4 (D.R. Martyn 81 not out)

ACB Chairman's XI won by 6 wickets

21, 22, 23 and 24 October 1993 *at WACA Ground, Perth*

New Zealanders 149 (J. Angel 5 for 32) and 350 (A.H. Jones 67, K.R. Rutherford 51, D.N. Patel 50, J. Angel 5 for 108)

Western Australia 508 (T.M. Moody 110, T.J. Zoehrer 83, D.R. Martyn 80, J.L. Langer 71, B.P. Julian 59, M.L. Su'a 4 for 84)

Western Australia won by an innings and 9 runs

at Woolloongabba, Brisbane

South Australia 522 (D.S. Webber 176, D.S. Lehmann 128, J.C. Scuderi 54, S.P. George 50, P.W. Jackson 4 for 90, C.J. McDermott 4 for 111)

Queensland 352 (M.L. Hayden 125, T.B.A. May 4 for 112) and 416 for 4 (A.R. Border 125 not out, T.J. Barsby 116, S.G. Law 100, M.L. Love 56 not out)

Match drawn

South Australia 2 pts., Queensland 0 pts.

The New Zealanders had a less than happy start to their tour of Australia. In Lilac Hill, they did not manage to bat out their 50 overs against an attack which included Richard Hadlee, Dennis Lillee and Jeff Thomson. If the veteran trio could no longer command the pace of yesteryear, they still had the control over accuracy, and the tourists' attack could have learned much from them.

In their opening first-class match, the New Zealanders were heavily beaten by Western Australia, and they also lost Greatbatch with an injury. Bowled out by Angel and Atkinson on the first day, they were savaged by the Western Australian middle order on the second. Tom Moody led the assault with 110 off 175 balls, and he and Martyn added 185 for the fifth wicket. The tourists offered spirited resistance in their second innings, but Angel completed his first ten-wicket haul in first-class cricket and bowled his side to victory.

In the first Sheffield Shield match of the new campaign, Queensland had early encouragement from Craig

McDermott who helped reduce South Australia to 76 for 4, but Lehmann and Webber then added 160. Lehmann celebrated his return to South Australia with 128 off 133 balls while Webber hit the second and higher century of his career. George scored a maiden fifty off 44 balls, and Queensland faced a formidable task.

Hayden continued in the manner in which he had batted in England, and reached 2,000 runs in Sheffield Shield cricket, but he could not prevent Queensland from being forced to follow-on. Three second innings centuries, including the 67th of Border's career, determined that the game would be drawn.

27 October 1993 *at North Sydney Oval*

Australian Cricket Academy 241 (J. Arnberger 79, C.L. Cairns 4 for 39)

New Zealanders 131

Australian Cricket Academy won by 110 runs

The New Zealanders suffered further discomfort when they were overwhelmed by Australia's future cricketers who plundered 241 runs in 49.1 overs. The New Zealanders were out in 42.2 overs against an attack that had variety and the desire to succeed. Jason Arnberger of New South Wales was top scorer in the match.

27, 28, 29 and 30 October 1993 *at Adelaide Oval*

Victoria 357 for 9 dec. (W.N. Phillips 60, D.J. Ramshaw 58, M.T.G. Elliott 54, A.I.C. Dodemaide 52, P.E. McIntyre 4 for 101) and 198 (M.T.G. Elliott 99, P.E. McIntyre 5 for 61, T.B.A. May 5 for 80)

South Australia 430 (P.C. Nobes 141, J.A. Brayshaw 134, S.H. Cook 5 for 114, S.K. Warne 4 for 119) and 127 for 1 (P.C. Nobes 63 not out, J.A. Brayshaw 54 not out)

South Australia won by 9 wickets

South Australia 6 pts., Victoria 0 pts.

29, 30, 31 October and 1 November 1993 *at WACA Ground, Perth*

Western Australia 211 (J.L. Langer 65, D.R. Martyn 59, C.J. McDermott 5 for 62) and 373 (J.L. Langer 96, T.J. Zoehrer 57, D.R. Martyn 56, C.G. Rackemann 6 for 93)

Queensland 430 (T.J. Barsby 82, I.A. Healy 79, A.R. Border 65, C.J. McDermott 61) and 158 for 1 (M.L. Hayden 96 not out)

Queensland won by 9 wickets

Queensland 6 pts., Western Australia 0 pts.

at Newcastle Sports Ground

New South Wales 299 (S.R. Waugh 88, M.E. Waugh 63, M.G. Bevan 55, D.N. Patel 6 for 87) and 109 (D.K. Morrison 6 for 54)

New Zealanders 163 (K.R. Rutherford 65,
   G.R.J. Matthews 4 for 52) and 247 for 7
New Zealanders won by 3 wickets

South Australia confirmed an impressive start to the season with a crushing win over Victoria. A consistent batting display took the visitors to 332 for 8 at the close of the first day, and Jones declared when Dodemaide was run out by May on the second morning. Blewett was caught behind off Cook at 60, but South Australia did not lose another wicket during the day and finished on 286. The following morning, Nobes and Brayshaw, who made the highest score of his career, extended their partnership to 232 before Nobes was caught behind off Shane Warne. The later batsmen hit briskly, and South Australia led by 73 on the first innings. Batting a second time, Victoria crumbled before the leg-spin of Peter McIntyre and the off-spin of Tim May. Opener Elliott was the only one to offer serious resistance, batting 267 minutes for the highest score of his career and being ninth out. Nobes and Brayshaw shared their second century stand of the match and took South Australia to an easy win.

Queensland, too, were comfortable winners. Healy won the toss, asked Western Australia to bat and saw his decision to field justified when McDermott and Rackemann bowled out the home state for 211. Healy was to play a major part in the Queensland success, for his side were 167 for 5 and had lost Law retired hurt when he came to the wicket. He and Border added 129 in two hours and two minutes, and with McDermott blasting 61 off 59 balls, Queensland took control. There was some determined second innings resistance from Western Australia, but the veteran Rackemann broke them down.

Hayden led the charge to victory with 96 not out in just over two hours. Western Australia included Kent fast bowler Duncan Spencer in their side.

There was cheer for the New Zealanders as the first Test approached. In spite of Patel's bowling and Rutherford's heroics with the bat, they trailed New South Wales by 136 runs on the first innings. Danny Morrison brought the tourists back into contention with four wickets in 35 balls at the end of the second day, and he and Patel completed the rout of New South Wales, who were without the injured Whitney, on the second morning. Pocock was out early, but steady and consistent batting took the New Zealanders to victory on the last day.

4, 5, 6 and 7 November 1993 *at Woolloongabba, Brisbane*

Queensland 257 (A.R. Border 85, P.J.S. Alley 4 for 45)
   and 281 (M.L. Hayden 173 not out)
New South Wales 382 (G.R. Robertson 85, M.E. Waugh
   61, P.W. Jackson 4 for 86) and 157 for 2
   (M.E. Waugh 85)
New South Wales won by 8 wickets
New South Wales 6 pts., Queensland 0 pts.

at MCG, Melbourne

Western Australia 322 (J.L. Langer 144,
   A.I.C. Dodemaide 5 for 85) and 185 (D.R. Martyn 89
   not out, S.K. Warne 6 for 42)
Victoria 230 (B.J. Hodge 95) and 278 for 4
   (M.T.G. Elliott 175 not out)
Victoria won by 6 wickets
Victoria 6 pts., Western Australia 2 pts.

at NTCA Ground, Launceston

Tasmania 306 for 9 dec. (S. Young 77, M.N. Atkinson
   69, C.L. Cairns 5 for 105) and 207 for 6 dec.
   (R.T. Ponting 54)
New Zealanders 215 for 7 dec. (A.H. Jones 67) and 247
   for 7 (M.D. Crowe 105, A.H. Jones 60)
Match drawn

In spite of omitting Greg Matthews for disciplinary reasons, New South Wales proved too good for Queensland. A ninth-wicket stand of 72 in 61 minutes between Robertson and Holdsworth took New South Wales to a surprisingly substantial first innings lead. Queensland had been roused from the depths of 150 for 7 by Allan Border who reached 25,000 runs in first-class cricket, but in their second innings, they owed survival entirely to Matthew Hayden who carried his bat for 390 minutes, faced 338 balls and hit 4 sixes and 13 fours in the highest score of his career. Needing to score at nearly four an over to win the match, New South Wales opened with Mark Waugh, and he responded with 85 off 88 balls.

Australia's new pace bowler Glenn McGrath of New South Wales who made his Test debut against New Zealand at Perth. (Stephen Laffer/Sports-Line)

Ian Healy hit a fine century for Australia against New Zealand in the first Test match and kept wicket admirably throughout the season. (Joe Mann/Allsport)

Western Australia, thanks to Langer's patient 144, led Victoria by 92 runs on the first innings. Hodge made the highest score of his career for the home side, and when Western Australia batted again Shane Warne bowled Victoria back into the game with his best bowling performance in Shield cricket. Needing 278 to win, and with most of the last day in which to score the runs, Victoria lost Phillips and Jones for 'ducks', but Elliott was magnificent. He hit 15 fours in what was the first century of his career and faced 240 balls for his 175. His innings brought his side victory.

On a slow pitch in Launceston, the New Zealanders could take comfort from a drawn match through the second innings of Martin Crowe. He found form with 105 off 137 balls, including 9 fours.

11, 12, 13 and **14 November 1993** *at Bellerive Oval, Hobart*

Western Australia 473 for 5 dec. (J.L. Langer 135, D.R. Martyn 100, M.R.J. Veletta 65 not out, T.M. Moody 65) and 56 for 2
Tasmania 514 (M.J. DiVenuto 125, R.T. Ponting 105, S. Young 63)
Match drawn
Tasmania 2 pts., Western Australia 0 pts.

Century stands between Marsh and Langer, and Langer and Martyn took Western Australia to an impressive score by the end of the first day, but they were outshone by the two Tasmanian youngsters, DiVenuto and Ponting. They established a third-wicket record for the island against Western Australia with a partnership of 207, both batsmen scoring centuries. It was DiVenuto's first in first-class cricket. Young and Herzberg also established a record with 70 for the ninth wicket, and a high-scoring match was, inevitably, drawn.

 ## FIRST TEST MATCH
AUSTRALIA *v.* NEW ZEALAND, at Perth

Two new caps were on show for the first Test match between Australia and New Zealand. New South Wales' pace bowler Glenn McGrath came in for the injured Merv Hughes, and Blair Pocock was chosen to open the New Zealand innings. Australia also welcomed back Craig McDermott. Crowe won the toss and asked Australia to bat.

Crowe's decision certainly seemed justified at the end of the first day when Australia were 229 for 6. Rain delayed the start for 80 minutes and then, under a sultry sky, the greenish pitch appeared sluggish. Cairns was overpitching, but in his sixth over, he dismissed Slater with a ball that cut back and which the batsman lobbed to square-leg. The next ball had Boon caught at slip off the shoulder of the bat, and New Zealand had seized a huge advantage.

Mark Taylor was becalmed, but Mark Waugh was in his customary attacking mood and, for a time, Australia moved along happily. The reintroduction of Morrison accounted for Waugh, leg before to a skimming off-cutter, and tea was taken at 115 for 3. Border slashed at Morrison shortly after the break, and Rutherford held a stinging catch at second slip.

Taylor's four-hour innings ended when he chopped a ball from Cairns onto his stumps, and Steve Waugh, who had batted sensibly, was out 34 runs later as he drove loosely at Patel and was caught behind. This was the first wicket to be taken by a spinner in a Test match at the WACA for five years.

Healy and Reiffel had added 31 before the close, and on the second morning they prospered, extending their partnership to 93 in 102 minutes. Reiffel faced 65 balls and reached his first Test fifty, but the real hero of the day was Ian Healy who made his second Test century. It was an emotional occasion for Healy, whose grandfather had died on the previous day, and he dedicated his innings to his father who had nursed the grandfather for the last two years of his life.

Healy has never received the praise due to him from critics outside Australia, but he remains the most consistent of Test wicket-keepers and, with his batting skills developing with every match, he has virtually no rival as the world's number one. With McDermott, who hit 35 off 33 balls, he added 69 for the ninth wicket, and in all he batted for 262 minutes, faced 181 deliveries and hit 11 fours.

New Zealand batted most sensibly. They lost Greatbatch to a catch behind which gave McGrath his first Test

FIRST TEST MATCH – AUSTRALIA v. NEW ZEALAND
12, 13, 14, 15 and 16 November 1993 at WACA Ground, Perth

AUSTRALIA

	FIRST INNINGS		SECOND INNINGS	
M.A. Taylor	b Cairns	64	(2) not out	142
M.J. Slater	c Patel, b Cairns	10	(1) c Blain, b Patel	99
D.C. Boon	c Rutherford, b Cairns	0	not out	67
M.E. Waugh	lbw, b Morrison	36		
A.R. Border (capt)	c Rutherford, b Morrison	16		
S.R. Waugh	c Blain, b Patel	44		
*I.A. Healy	not out	113		
P.R. Reiffel	c Jones, b Watson	51		
S.K. Warne	c Patel, b Cairns	11		
C.J. McDermott	b Su'a	35		
G.D. McGrath	lbw, b Su'a	0		
Extras	b 4, lb 7, nb 7	18	lb 6, nb 9	15
		398	(for 1 wicket, dec.)	**323**

NEW ZEALAND

	FIRST INNINGS		SECOND INNINGS	
M.J. Greatbatch	c Healy, b McGrath	18	c Healy, b McDermott	0
B.A. Pocock	c Boon, b McDermott	34	c Healy, b McGrath	28
A.H. Jones	c Healy, b M. Waugh	143	lbw, b M. Waugh	45
M.D. Crowe (capt)	c Taylor, b Reiffel	42	not out	31
K.R. Rutherford	c Healy, b McDermott	17	lbw, b S. Waugh	39
D.N. Patel	c S. Waugh, b Reiffel	20	not out	18
C.L. Cairns	b Warne	78		
*T.E. Blain	lbw, b McDermott	36		
M.L. Su'a	not out	14		
D.K. Morrison	lbw, b McGrath	0		
W. Watson	not out	0		
Extras	b 1, lb 6, nb 10	17	lb 1, nb 4	5
	(for 9 wickets, dec.)	**419**	(for 4 wickets)	**166**

	O	M	R	W	O	M	R	W		O	M	R	W	O	M	R	W
Morrison	35	4	113	2	25	5	80	–	McDermott	40	10	127	3	13	3	40	1
Cairns	28	4	113	4	1	–	12	–	McGrath	39	12	92	2	16	6	50	1
Watson	24	11	52	1					Reiffel	24	2	75	2	7	2	25	–
Su'a	19.5	2	72	2	20	–	71	–	Warne	37.1	6	90	1	13	6	23	–
Patel	8	–	37	1	39	4	144	1	M.E. Waugh	13	5	18	1	6	4	17	1
Pocock					2	–	10	–	S.R. Waugh	4	–	10	–	7	2	10	1
									Border	2	2	0	–				

FALL OF WICKETS
1–37, 2–37, 3–100, 4–129, 5–164, 6–198, 7–291, 8–329, 9–398
1–198

FALL OF WICKETS
1–25, 2–100, 3–199, 4–239, 5–275, 6–292, 7–394, 8–413, 9–418
1–0, 2–66, 3–85, 4–145

Umpires: D.B. Hair & A.J. McQuillan

Match drawn

wicket, and Pocock was brilliantly caught at short-leg after 157 minutes of dogged batting. New Zealand closed on 100 for 2.

On the third day, Andrew Jones hit his seventh Test century, batting 351 minutes for his 143 and facing 283 balls. He hit 11 fours. There was good support from Crowe, and towards the close, there was some excellent batting by Cairns and Blain, but with the score on 390 for 6 a draw loomed as inevitable. When McDermott had Rutherford caught behind he claimed his 200th Test wicket, a feat denied him when he was taken ill in England.

Lacking Cairns, who had a bruised heel, and Watson, who tore a hamstring while batting although he did not face a ball, New Zealand opened their attack with Patel and Morrison, who had a confident appeal for leg before against Taylor rejected. Taylor also survived an appeal for a bat/pad catch, and Jones was reprimanded for his reaction.

Cairns bowled one over in which Slater hit 3 fours, and the New South Wales right-hander hit 9 other fours on his way to 99 in 243 minutes. He and Taylor shared an opening stand of 198, a record for Australia against New Zealand. On the last day, Taylor became the first player to make centuries on each of Australia's six current grounds. He batted for six hours and hit 8 fours in his 142.

New Zealand lost Greatbatch to the first ball of their second innings, and at tea, they were 105 for 3. Martin Crowe endured for more than 2½ hours to end any thought of defeat, but it was his last innings of the tour. He had rested his injured right knee in an attempt to avoid surgery, but the injury had reasserted itself, and Crowe was forced to return to New Zealand. Rutherford took over the captaincy.

Andrew Jones was named Man of the Match.

19, 20, 21 and 22 November 1993 *at MCG, Melbourne*

New South Wales 227 (M.J. Slater 77, M.E. Waugh 58, S.K. Warne 4 for 72) and 268 for 7 dec. (S.R. Waugh 122, M.A. Taylor 50, P.R. Reiffel 5 for 73)

Victoria 233 (D.J. Ramshaw 85, B.J. Hodge 54, B.E. McNamara 6 for 43) and 263 for 9 (B.J. Hodge 92, D.M. Jones 72)

Victoria won by 1 wicket

Victoria 6 pts., New South Wales 0 pts.

at Adelaide Oval

South Australia 158 (J.C. Scuderi 51, S.B. Doull 6 for 55) and 260 for 9 dec. (J.A. Brayshaw 94)

New Zealanders 276 (K.R. Rutherford 76, M.J.
Greatbatch 65, M.L. Su'a 56, D.A. Reeves 4 for 62)
and 143 for 3 (M.J. Greatbatch 64, B.A. Pocock 60)
New Zealanders won by 7 wickets

The revitalised Victoria side, sparked by the attacking
enthusiasm of skipper Dean Jones, recorded their second
win in succession, an exciting victory over Shield-holders
New South Wales. The left-handed Matthew Elliott, who
had scored a match-winning century against Western
Australia, was absent with disc problems, and fast bowler
Fleming was still not considered fully fit, but there was
much confidence in the Victorian side. Rain restricted the
first day and New South Wales, who chose to bat when
they won the toss, finished on 58 for 2. The third-wicket
stand between Slater and Mark Waugh was worth 108,
but thereafter the batting was very uneven. The Victorian
innings followed a similar pattern with Darren Ramshaw
and Brad Hodge adding 139 after two wickets had fallen
for 19. Warren Ayres batted 108 minutes for 23 to offer
stability, but it was left to the last-wicket pair of Howard
and Cook to snatch first-innings points. They defied the
medium pace of Brad McNamara who took five wickets
in an innings for the first time. Steve Waugh hit a fine
hundred to set up a declaration, and Victoria went in
search of 263 for victory. Jones gave the innings early
sparkle, and there was another fine knock from the 18-
year-old Brad Hodge who hit a six and 8 fours in his 143-
ball innings. He was seventh out with Victoria still 17
short of victory. Reiffel was bowled by Holdsworth at 259,
and two runs later Warne was run out by Bevan. In a
tense finish, Holdsworth was no-balled for over-
stepping, and the two runs gave Victoria an exciting win.

The New Zealanders gained an encouraging victory
over South Australia who lost Peter McIntyre with a
chipped bone in his right hand. As South Australia were
leading the Sheffield Shield table, and as the tourists had
beaten New South Wales and performed creditably in the
first Test, there was every hope that they would do well in
the two remaining Tests. Their woes, however, were
compounded when it was learned that Willie Watson was
out of the rest of the tour. Chris Harris and Richard de
Groen joined the party as replacements, and de Groen
played a leading part in the victory over South Australia
with match figures of 5 for 80. Simon Doull took 9 for 109,
and Pocock and Greatbatch began the second innings
chase for victory with 131 in 128 minutes.

 MERCANTILE MUTUAL CUP

21 November 1993 *at Woolloongabba, Brisbane*

Queensland 320 for 4 (S.G. Law 159, M.L. Hayden 100)
Tasmania 228 for 7 (D.J. Buckingham 61, D.C. Boon
56)
Queensland (2 pts.) won by 92 runs

25, 26, 27 and **28** November 1993 *at SCG, Sydney*

New South Wales 353 for 5 dec. (M.G. Bevan 141,
R. Chee Quee 69, G.R.J. Matthews 55 not out) and
274 for 9 dec. (R.J. Davison 133 not out, S. Herzberg
4 for 82)
Tasmania 343 (D.F. Hills 88, N.C.P. Courtney 55,
M.J. DiVenuto 53, S. Young 52 not out,
G.R.J. Matthews 7 for 99) and 215 (A.E. Tucker 4 for
64, G.R.J. Matthews 4 for 82)
New South Wales won by 69 runs
New South Wales 6 pts., Tasmania 0 pts.

at Adelaide Oval

Queensland 330 (M.L. Hayden 165, T.J. Barsby 79) and
351 for 4 dec. (T.J. Barsby 129, M.L. Hayden 116)
South Australia 420 (P.C. Nobes 140, D.S. Webber 100)
and 262 for 5 (P.C. Nobes 106, D.S. Lehmann 50)
South Australia won by 5 wickets
South Australia 6 pts., Queensland 0 pts.

*A brilliant start to the season for Greg Matthews, 11 wickets and 55
not out for New South Wales against Tasmania in Sydney, but then
came the injury in Perth which was to bring an abrupt end to his
season. (Joe Mann/Allsport)*

Andrew Jones under fire in the second Test match, Australia v. New Zealand in Hobart. (Ben Radford/Allsport)

with Tucker, bowled New South Wales to victory on the last afternoon. Matthews' match figures of 11 for 181 gave him 10 or more wickets in a match for the fifth time, and as he also scored 55 not out and 40, he enjoyed a splendid all-round match.

Meanwhile, South Australia maintained their excellent form with a good win over Queensland in a match dominated by batsmen. Matthew Hayden and Trevor Barsby shared opening stands of 183 and 243 for Queensland, and Hayden strengthened his Test claims with a century in each innings. Nobes did the same for South Australia, and this was the first time for 20 years that a player from each side had scored a century in each innings of a Shield match. Webber again proved his worth, and Lehmann, promoted to open in the second South Australian innings, sparked off the run chase with 50 off 55 balls.

 ## SECOND TEST MATCH
AUSTRALIA *v.* NEW ZEALAND, at Hobart

The optimism engendered by the New Zealanders' victory over South Australia quickly disappeared at the Bellerive Oval. Doull and de Groen came into the side as replacements for Crowe and Watson while Harris also

New South Wales reasserted themselves with a fine victory over Tasmania. Deprived of their Test players, the reigning champions introduced the 24-year-old Rodney Davison to first-class cricket. A short, neat, compact opener, who spent a season with Ealing in the Middlesex League, Davison hit 133 not out off 233 balls in 270 minutes in his second innings, and made it possible for Emery to declare. Earlier Bevan, with his 11th first-class hundred, and Chee Quee had given the New South Wales first innings substance. Tasmania responded with consistent application. Courtney and Hills began with a partnership of 107, and Michael DiVenuto again caught the eye. Eager to attack – he had reached his maiden century against Western Australia with a six – DiVenuto joins Ponting as one of Australia's most promising young batting prospects. It was an older player who blighted Tasmania's hopes of claiming first-innings points. Greg Matthews took 7 for 99, his 19th five-wicket haul, and,

Captain courageous Ken Rutherford sets an example to his ailing New Zealand side in the second Test match. (Ben Radford/Allsport)

SECOND TEST MATCH – AUSTRALIA v. NEW ZEALAND
26, 27, 28, 29 and 30 November 1993 at Bellerive Oval, Hobart

AUSTRALIA

FIRST INNINGS

M.A. Taylor	c Jones, b Su'a	27
M.J. Slater	c Morrison, b Patel	168
D.C. Boon	c Jones, b Doull	106
M.E. Waugh	c Doull, b de Groen	111
A.R. Border (capt)	c and b Morrison	60
S.R. Waugh	not out	25
*I.A. Healy	c Doull, b de Groen	1
P.R. Reiffel	not out	23
S.K. Warne		
C.J. McDermott		
T.B.A. May		
Extras	b 7, lb 2, nb 14	23
	(for 6 wickets, dec.)	544

NEW ZEALAND

		FIRST INNINGS		SECOND INNINGS	
M.J. Greatbatch	c May, b McDermott	12	c M. Waugh, b McDermott	0
B.A. Pocock	lbw, b M. Waugh	9	st Healy, b Warne	15
A.H. Jones	c Healy, b May	47	c Border, b M. Waugh	18
K.R. Rutherford (capt)	c Taylor, b May	17	b Warne	55
D.N. Patel	c Taylor, b Warne	18	lbw, b May	16
C.Z. Harris	c M. Waugh, b May	0	b May	4
*T.E. Blain	c Warne, b May	40	c and b Warne	29
M.L. Su'a	c Taylor, b Warne	6	b Warne	5
D.K. Morrison	c M. Waugh, b May	0	b Warne	0
S.B. Doull	lbw, b Warne	0	c May, b Warne	1
R.P. de Groen	not out	0	not out	3
Extras	b 2, lb 1, nb 9	12	b 2, lb 5, nb 8	15
		161		161

	O	M	R	W
Morrison	33	4	125	1
Su'a	24	3	102	1
Doull	21	–	99	1
de Groen	36	9	113	2
Patel	23	3	78	1
Harris	2	–	18	–

	O	M	R	W	O	M	R	W
McDermott	15	3	29	1	17	8	42	1
Reiffel	5	1	13	–	12	1	28	–
S.R. Waugh	4	1	8	–				
M.E. Waugh	9	4	7	1	4	–	8	1
May	31.3	10	65	5	25	13	45	2
Warne	18	5	36	3	19.5	9	31	6

FALL OF WICKETS

1–65, 2–300, 3–335, 4–485, 5–501, 6–502

FALL OF WICKETS

1–15, 2–47, 3–84, 4–105, 5–107, 6–117, 7–137, 8–138, 9–139

1–1, 2–29, 3–84, 4–103, 5–111, 6–133, 7–149, 8–149, 9–158

Umpires: D.B. Hair & W.P. Sheahan

Australia won by an innings and 222 runs

played when, to the consternation of captain and management, Cairns declined to appear simply as a batsman because of his bruised heel. Trouble followed trouble when Border won the toss, and Australia who had brought in May for McGrath batted.

The first day was one of total disaster for New Zealand. Morrison saw both openers dropped at slip off his bowling, and by the time Taylor drove into the hands of gully, 65 runs had been scored in 66 minutes. The hundred was on the board before lunch, and in the afternoon session, Boon began to square-cut and straight-drive with relish. A limp attack, with Su'a below par and de Groen making his Test debut, was ill-served in the field. The New Zealand out-cricket was quite dreadful, and it did not improve. Boon should have been stumped off Patel on 65, and on 99 Slater was left stranded only to be saved from being run out by a wild throw.

To his credit, Slater played some magnificent shots and reached his century off 162 deliveries. At tea, Australia were 211 for 1, having scored 107 runs in the afternoon session, and after the break, Slater became even more expansive, crashing the ball through the covers and scoring all round the wicket. He finally fell to a fine catch by Morrison as he attempted another massive off-drive. He had hit 17 fours and faced 235 balls for his highest score in first-class cricket. He and Boon had added 235, an

Australian second-wicket record against New Zealand. Boon reached his 18th Test century shortly before the close, and during the course of his innings, he had become only the fifth Australian to surpass 6,000 runs in Test cricket. Australia closed on 329 for 2.

Boon, who hit 9 fours and faced 242 balls, added only one to his overnight score before falling to Doull, but there was to be no respite for the New Zealand bowlers. Morrison, the best of the New Zealand attack, suffered another dropped catch, and the escapee, Border, set about him with a relish to give able assistance to Mark Waugh in a stand of 150. Mark Waugh was at his mightiest, hitting 15 fours in his 111 which came off only 139 balls. The New Zealanders were battered into submission, and Border thankfully declared just before tea. By the close, both New Zealand openers were gone, and 81 runs were on the board.

On the third day, New Zealand lost 13 wickets and any faint hope they might have had of saving the match. Tim May was the master, far too thoughtful and with far too many variations in flight, dip and length for the inexperienced New Zealanders, many of whom seemed quite out of their depth. Jones, Rutherford and Blain alone showed the necessary application, and the last eight wickets fell for 77 runs.

The follow-on allowed no improvement. Greatbatch

drove without moving his feet, and Jones hooked a bouncer to square-leg. Pocock battled bravely for two hours before being beaten and stranded by Warne's superb leg-break. Rutherford intimated what could be done until he swept at Warne and was bowled behind his pads. Patel never suggested permanence, and New Zealand ended the day at 127 for 5.

Tony Blain lasted 81 minutes on the final morning, and he showed both character and ability. For the rest, Harris was bowled as he cut at May; Su'a played on; Morrison heaved across the line and was bowled for his 18th 'duck' in 32 Tests – and he was at number nine; and Doull clouted to mid-on shortly after Blain had been caught and bowled by Shane Warne off a fierce return. Warne took the last four wickets for three runs in 14 balls.

Mark Waugh was named Man of the Match as New Zealand suffered their worst defeat in Test history. Ken Rutherford was, rightly, severely critical of his team's performance, and of the lack of guts and determination. The gap between the two sides was a vast one.

2 December 1993 *at Manuka Oval, Canberra*

Prime Minister's XI 156 for 8
South Africans 152 (W.J. Cronje 60)

Prime Minister's XI won by 4 runs

While the New Zealanders were still recovering from shell-shock the South Africans warmed up for their forthcoming ventures with defeat in a 42-over game in Canberra. Four of the South African batsmen were run out.

THIRD TEST MATCH
AUSTRALIA *v.* NEW ZEALAND
at Brisbane

Australia brought back McGrath in place of Reiffel, and after the debacle of Hobart, New Zealand saw the return of the reluctant Cairns and gave a first Test cap to Bryan Young. Su'a and Harris stood down. Rutherford won the toss, and New Zealand batted.

Pocock perished in the fifth over when he played down the wrong line and gave a diving catch to Healy. Young and Jones showed commendable determination, however, and added 94, taking the innings into the afternoon before Jones was bowled by a devastating flipper from Warne. In the next over, Young, who had batted for more than three hours, mis-hooked Mark Waugh and top-edged to Healy who enjoyed a fine match.

Rutherford and Greatbatch took the score to 147 at tea, but the last session was a disaster for the visitors. Rutherford was splendidly caught at short-leg by Boon, diving to his left, and in his next over, McDermott had Greatbatch caught behind. Patel was taken at short-leg off a poor shot. Cairns was adjudged caught and bowled, and Morrison caught behind, although both seemed to be unfortunate, and when Doull fenced at McDermott to

give Healy his fifth catch of the innings New Zealand were in the deepest trouble.

They closed on 208 for 9, and, thanks to Blain, who hit 6 fours, they reached 233 the next morning. The New Zealand bowling was better than it had been at Hobart, but only marginally, and on a true pitch the visitors spilled more vital catches. Mark Waugh, who hit a six and 8 fours in his 96-ball innings, was missed before he scored, and two more chances were put down. Slater, in rather circumspect mood, and Taylor began with 80 in 91 minutes, and runs flowed at three an over throughout the day which ended with Australia eight runs ahead and three wickets down.

On a cloudy third day, Australia moved to an impregnable 300-run lead. Boon went to Doull's out-swinger with the new ball, having scored 1,216 Test runs in 1993, and Border and Steve Waugh then engaged in a partnership of 159 which ground down the New Zealanders. In his 150th Test match, Allan Border hit 105 off 193 balls before slogging de Groen to long-on. It was his 27th Test century, and the runs were acquired with the usual dash, many of them coming square of the wicket on either side. The crowd rose to him, for his reign as Australia's captain, glorious as it had been, was close to an end.

There was a relentlessness about the Australian batting, with 93 runs coming in the first session, and 96 and 103 in the second and third. Healy was run out in going for a risky single, but Steve Waugh, more sedate than his captain, was 113 not out by the end of the day when Australia were 533 for 6. Waugh might have been stumped when he was 44, but generally he was very comfortable, and in reaching his sixth Test hundred he became only the second Australian to score 3,000 runs and take 50 wickets in Test cricket. It also meant that, as in England the previous summer, the first seven Australian batsmen had all scored centuries in the series, and that is a formidable achievement.

The fourth day was again cloudy, and for New Zealand the gloom was unabating. Warne hit the highest score of his career. He and Steve Waugh, who batted for 380 minutes and hit 15 fours, shared an unbroken partnership of 142. When Border declared at lunch, after brief interruptions for rain, Australia had reached their highest score in a Test match against New Zealand.

Batting a second time, New Zealand lost Pocock after an hour, but Young batted with more vigour than in his first innings. He and Jones looked to be settling, but, as in the first innings, both men fell in quick succession. Jones clouted to mid-wicket, and Young was bowled round his legs by Warne on whose bowling one can lavish nothing but praise and wonder. McDermott was recalled to account for Greatbatch, and Cairns resisted for 68 minutes before driving extravagantly at McGrath and being caught behind. Blain and Rutherford held firm until drizzle and bad light ended play with New Zealand 158 for 5.

Rain delayed the start on the last day and offered New Zealand their only hope of survival, but Blain was bowled by a lively straight ball from McGrath, and Patel, after a series of kicks and lunges, offered no shot at Warne and was bowled. Rutherford had set an impressive example

THIRD TEST MATCH – AUSTRALIA v. NEW ZEALAND
3, 4, 5, 6 and 7 December 1993 at Woolloongabba, Brisbane

NEW ZEALAND

	FIRST INNINGS		SECOND INNINGS	
B.A. Pocock	c Healy, b McDermott	0	(2) c Healy, b McDermott	11
B.A. Young	c Healy, b M. Waugh	38	(1) b Warne	53
A.H. Jones	b Warne	56	c Border, b Warne	15
K.R. Rutherford (capt)	c Boon, b McDermott	36	c Warne, b McGrath	86
M.J. Greatbatch	c Healy, b McDermott	35	lbw, b McDermott	2
C.L. Cairns	c and b Warne	5	c Healy, b McGrath	16
D.N. Patel	c Boon, b May	1	(8) b Warne	3
*T.E. Blain	not out	42	(7) b McGrath	18
D.K. Morrison	c Healy, b Warne	0	not out	20
S.B. Doull	c Healy, b McDermott	10	c Taylor, b Warne	24
R.P. de Groen	c Border, b Warne	3	b May	6
Extras	b 2, lb 3, nb 2	7	b 7, lb 12, nb 5	24
		233		**278**

AUSTRALIA

	FIRST INNINGS	
M.J. Slater	c Blain, b Patel	28
M.A. Taylor	c Pocock, b Doull	53
D.C. Boon	c Blain, b Doull	89
M.E. Waugh	c Greatbatch, b Cairns	68
A.R. Border (capt)	c Patel, b de Groen	105
S.R. Waugh	not out	147
*I.A. Healy	run out	15
S.K. Warne	not out	74
C.J. McDermott		
T.B.A. May		
G.D. McGrath		
Extras	b 6, lb 13, nb 9	28
	(for 6 wickets, dec.)	**607**

	O	M	R	W	O	M	R	W
McDermott	23	11	39	4	25	4	63	2
McGrath	20	7	45	–	21	1	66	3
S.R. Waugh	3	–	13	–				
M.E. Waugh	10	4	14	1	6	1	30	–
May	21	7	51	1	16	3	41	1
Warne	28.3	12	66	4	35	11	59	4

	O	M	R	W
Morrison	33	3	104	–
Cairns	36	7	128	1
Doull	33	5	105	2
de Groen	46	14	120	1
Patel	33	4	125	1
Jones	2	–	6	–

FALL OF WICKETS

1–2, 2–96, 3–98, 4–167, 5–170, 6–174, 7–174, 8–178, 9–193

1–34, 2–80, 3–81, 4–84, 5–138, 6–187, 7–218, 8–230, 9–265

FALL OF WICKETS

1–80, 2–102, 3–227, 4–277, 5–436, 6–465

Umpires: P.D. Parker & S.G. Randell

Australia won by an innings and 96 runs

to his side, and he batted for 201 minutes in a brave effort to save the game, but when he hooked McGrath to Warne New Zealand were 230 for 8 and the end was nigh. Morrison, who had not scored in four previous innings in the series, and Doull offered some clouts, but, in truth, New Zealand had offered no real opposition to Australia.

Shane Warne, with a record 18 wickets in the series, was named Man of the Match.

4, 5, 6 and 7 December 1993 *at MCG, Melbourne*

South Africans 261 (B.M. McMillan 55, D.W. Fleming 6 for 86) and 178 (J.N. Rhodes 59, C. Howard 5 for 42)

Victoria 330 for 8 dec. (B.J. Hodge 80, D.J. Ramshaw 71, D.W. Fleming 54 not out) and 110 for 4

Victoria won by 6 wickets

For the South Africans, the match against Victoria was a total disaster. Brian McMillan developed a knee ligament injury which brought an end to his tour. He was replaced by the left-handed Gary Kirsten, who is also a useful off-spinner. The tourists were also well beaten by Victoria who were well served by Fleming and Howard. The pair shared an unbroken stand of 101 for the ninth wicket, and

Fleming took six wickets in the South Africans' first innings while Howard took five in the second. Howard, 41 not out and 5 for 42, had career bests in both batting and bowling, and as he is a leg-spinner, this did not bode well for South Africa in the Tests against Warne. Hodge continued his run of success by taking a wicket, that of Callaghan, with his first ball in first-class cricket.

10, 11, 12 and 13 December 1993 *at Bellerive Oval, Hobart*

Tasmania 328 (R.J. Tucker 107, D.F. Hills 71, S.H. Cook 4 for 84) and 308 for 6 dec. (R.T. Ponting 66, D.F. Hills 59, C. Howard 5 for 112)

Victoria 329 for 3 dec. (D.M. Jones 158 not out, B.J. Hodge 106) and 267 for 8 (D.M. Jones 60, D.J. Ramshaw 53)

Match drawn

Victoria 2 pts., Tasmania 0 pts.

at WACA Ground, Perth

Western Australia 503 for 8 dec. (D.R. Martyn 197, G.R. Marsh 128, T.M. Moody 68, P.J.S. Alley 5 for 101)

Jonty Rhodes of South Africa, an exciting batsman and wonderful fielder, particularly effective in the one-day game. (Joe Mann/Allsport)

New South Wales 73 (B.P. Julian 5 for 34) and 177
  (M.G. Bevan 50, J. Angel 5 for 57)

Western Australia won by an innings and 253 runs

Western Australia 6 pts., New South Wales −0.2 pts.

The Tasmanian captain Rod Tucker rallied his side with 107 off 151 balls after five wickets had gone for 115 runs. The left-hander hit 15 fours and shared a seventh-wicket stand of 82 with wicket-keeper Atkinson. A second day on which little more than an hour's play was possible made a draw inevitable, but Jones and Hodge added 201 in 160 minutes for Victoria's third wicket to keep the match alive. Howard took five wickets in a Shield match for the first time, and Tucker left Victoria 70 overs in which to score 308 to win. Jones and Ramshaw hit well, but Herzberg and Tucker himself posed problems, and Garlick, on his debut, and Howard were content to bat out the last half hour to draw the match.

The match between New South Wales and Western Australia in Perth provided the sensation of the season. Following an incident in a night-club, New South Wales were without Greg Matthews. Emery won the toss and asked Western Australia to bat. Veletta and Langer were out for 36, but Marsh and Martyn added 271 in 319 minutes. Martyn, who hit a six and 22 fours, made the highest score of his career. By the end of the first day, the home side were 438 for 4, and Marsh declared half an hour before lunch on the second. In two hours 12 minutes, New South Wales were bowled out for 71 and, following-on, they were bowled out in 175 minutes so suffering the indignity of being bowled out twice in a day for the first time since 1883. The match became the first Shield game to be finished in two days since 1976. New South Wales were humiliated. Julian had match figures of 8 for 79, and Angel had 8 for 82.

 BENSON AND HEDGES WORLD SERIES
Phase One – Matches One to Six

South Africa enjoyed a fine start to the limited-over competition with a decisive win over the host country. Slater had given Australia an excellent start with 73 off 69 balls. Playing his first one-day international, Slater hit 9 fours and put on 105 for the first wicket with Taylor, but once he was out the impetus to the innings was lost. Rhodes put great pressure on the Australians with his outstanding fielding which saw him run out both Boon and Steve Waugh with direct hits from the covers.

McGrath, playing in his first one-day international, was economical but, following the early loss of Hudson, Wessels and Cronje added 140. Cronje batted with great control and steered his side to victory with eight balls to spare.

Rain prevented any play in the second match in the series which was due to be staged in Adelaide and involved South Africa and New Zealand. When New Zealand did take the field against Australia the following day they were soundly beaten. They were 77 for 3 from 29 overs before Warne joined the Australian attack. With wickets in his fourth, fifth and sixth overs, he left the New Zealand innings in tatters. Slater was leg before to Pringle at the start of the Australian reply, and Mark Waugh was insanely run out in attempting a fourth run, but Hayden and Boon moved serenely to victory with more than 11 overs to spare.

The Australians moved to the top of the table when they crushed South Africa in the day/night game in Sydney. On a grassy pitch, Australia struggled for runs, but a stand of 68 between Healy and Reiffel proved to be invaluable. South Africa suffered a severe blow when Jonty Rhodes broke a finger while fielding. The Australian seam bowlers maintained accuracy and allowed the pitch to do the rest. Reiffel found his line after beginning with three wides and tore the heart out of the middle order. He also brought about an astonishing run out when he hit the stumps with his throw to dismiss de Villiers.

Australia consolidated their position as the leaders in the competition when they narrowly beat New Zealand in

Melbourne. Mark Taylor batted through 47 overs and faced 130 balls to hold the Australian innings together. The sparks were provided by the Waugh twins but, having hit 25 off 28 balls, Steve Waugh tore a hamstring and was forced to retire. New Zealand were well served by their one-day recruits, Latham, Larsen, Pringle and Thomson, and it was Latham who helped resurrect their innings by adding 66 with Rutherford after Young had fallen third ball. Unfortunately for New Zealand, wickets fell at crucial times. Warne was fortunate to get an l.b.w. decision against Greatbatch, but the leg-spinner bowled splendidly to take 4 for 19 in his 10 overs. New Zealand arrived at the last over needing 11 to win, but Pringle was run out going for a suicidal second run, and Morrison's attempts to baseball hit the last ball for six were to no avail.

New Zealand did manage victory in the last match of phase one, and this brought them level on points with South Africa. Gavin Larsen's splendidly economic bowling gave New Zealand a strangle-hold on the South African innings, and only Richardson threatened to loosen the grip. Tony Blain's four catches equalled the New Zealand record for a one-day international. Bryan Young hit 74 from 116 balls, and when he was dismissed the score was 112 for 4. Chris Cairns brought about the expected result although Matthews posed problems.

BENSON AND HEDGES WORLD SERIES – MATCH ONE – AUSTRALIA *v.* SOUTH AFRICA
9 December 1993 at MCG, Melbourne

AUSTRALIA

M.A. Taylor	b Cronje	30
M.J. Slater	c and b Symcox	73
D.C. Boon	run out	1
M.E. Waugh	c Symcox, b Cronje	8
S.R. Waugh	run out	33
A.R. Border (capt)	b Snell	11
*I.A. Healy	not out	21
S.K. Warne	run out	3
P.R. Reiffel	lbw, b de Villiers	0
C.J. McDermott	c Richardson, b de Villiers	5
G.D. McGrath	b de Villiers	0
Extras	lb 2, w 2	4
		—
(45.5 overs)		189

SOUTH AFRICA

A.C. Hudson	c Taylor, b McDermott	4
K.C. Wessels (capt)	b McDermott	70
W.J. Cronje	not out	91
D.J. Cullinan	b Warne	0
J.N. Rhodes	not out	20
D.J. Callaghan		
*D.J. Richardson		
R.P. Snell		
P.L. Symcox		
P.S. de Villiers		
A.A. Donald		
Extras	lb 2, w 1, nb 2	5
		—
(48.4 overs)	(for 3 wickets)	190

	O	M	R	W
Donald	10	1	32	–
de Villiers	7.5	–	30	3
Snell	8	–	43	1
Cronje	10	–	42	2
Symcox	10	–	40	1

	O	M	R	W
McDermott	10	1	31	2
McGrath	8.4	1	28	–
Reiffel	4	–	19	–
S.R. Waugh	10	–	37	–
Border	3	–	15	–
Warne	10	–	43	1
M.E. Waugh	3	–	15	–

FALL OF WICKETS
1–105, **2**–106, **3**–106, **4**–119, **5**–151, **6**–166, **7**–180, **8**–181, **9**–189.

FALL OF WICKETS
1–4, **2**–144, **3**–149

Umpires: T.A. Prue & W.P. Sheahan   *Man of the Match:* W.J. Cronje   *South Africa won by 7 wickets*

BENSON AND HEDGES WORLD SERIES – MATCH THREE – AUSTRALIA *v.* NEW ZEALAND
12 December 1993 at Adelaide Oval

NEW ZEALAND

B.A. Young	b Reiffel	18
R.T. Latham	c M.E. Waugh, b McGrath	1
K.R. Rutherford (capt)	c Reiffel, b McGrath	15
M.J. Greatbatch	lbw, b Warne	28
C.L. Cairns	c Border, b Warne	31
C.Z. Harris	c and b Warne	4
*T.E. Blain	not out	9
D.N. Patel	c Healy, b McDermott	1
G.R. Larsen	c Reiffel, b Warne	8
C. Pringle	c Border, b McGrath	4
D.K. Morrison	c Healy, b McGrath	3
Extras	lb 8, w 3, nb 2	13
(48.2 overs)		135

AUSTRALIA

M.J. Slater	lbw, b Pringle	8
M.L. Hayden	not out	50
M.E. Waugh	run out	21
D.C. Boon	not out	51
S.R. Waugh		
A.R. Border (capt)		
*I.A. Healy		
P.R. Reiffel		
S.K. Warne		
C.J. McDermott		
G.D. McGrath		
Extras	lb 4, w 1, nb 1	6
(38.5 overs)	(for 2 wickets)	136

	O	M	R	W
McDermott	10	2	15	1
McGrath	8.2	2	32	4
Reiffel	8	2	20	1
S.R. Waugh	7	–	16	–
M.W. Waugh	5	–	19	–
Warne	10	1	25	4

	O	M	R	W
Morrison	8	2	31	–
Pringle	8	3	18	1
Cairns	9.5	–	27	–
Larsen	9	–	37	–
Patel	4	–	19	–

FALL OF WICKETS

1–6, 2–33, 3–45, 4–104, 5–109, 6–112, 7–113, 8–124, 9–132.

FALL OF WICKETS

1–16, 2–42

Umpires: A.J. McQuillan & W.P. Sheahan   *Man of the Match:* S.K. Warne   *Australia won by 8 wickets*

BENSON AND HEDGES WORLD SERIES – MATCH FOUR – AUSTRALIA *v.* SOUTH AFRICA
14 December 1993 at SCG, Sydney

AUSTRALIA

M.A. Taylor	run out	11
M.J. Slater	c Rhodes, b de Villiers	10
M.E. Waugh	c Kirsten, b Matthews	36
D.C. Boon	c Richardson, b Matthews	4
S.R. Waugh	c Richardson, b Cronje	13
A.R. Border (capt)	c de Villiers, b Matthews	8
*I.A. Healy	c Cronje, b Donald	38
P.R. Reiffel	not out	29
S.K. Warne	c Cullinan, b de Villiers	0
C.J. McDermott	c Cronje, b de Villiers	3
G.D. McGrath		
Extras	b 1, lb 4, w 7, nb 8	20
(50 overs)	(for 9 wickets)	172

SOUTH AFRICA

A.C. Hudson	c Reiffel, b McDermott	0
G. Kirsten	c Healy, b McGrath	4
K.C. Wessels (capt)	lbw, b Reiffel	19
W.J. Cronje	c Healy, b Reiffel	20
D.J. Cullinan	c S.R. Waugh, b McGrath	1
*D.J. Richardson	c Healy, b Reiffel	1
R.P. Snell	b Reiffel	0
C.R. Matthews	c Reiffel, b S.R. Waugh	7
J.N. Rhodes	not out	4
P.S. de Villiers	run out	0
A.A. Donald	b S.R. Waugh	0
Extras	lb 3, w 8, nb 2	13
(28 overs)		69

	O	M	R	W
Donald	10	1	49	1
de Villiers	10	–	37	3
Matthews	10	–	23	3
Snell	10	–	44	–
Cronje	10	4	14	1

	O	M	R	W
McDermott	6	2	8	1
McGrath	8	–	25	2
Reiffel	8	4	13	4
S.R. Waugh	6	–	20	2

FALL OF WICKETS

1–28, 2–30, 3–44, 4–76, 5–95, 6–96, 7–164, 8–164, 9–172

FALL OF WICKETS

1–0, 2–23, 3–34, 4–38, 5–47, 6–48, 7–59, 8–65, 9–69

Umpires: D.B. Hair & P.D. Parker   *Man of the Match:* P.R. Reiffel   *Australia won by 103 runs*

BENSON AND HEDGES WORLD SERIES – MATCH FIVE – AUSTRALIA *v.* NEW ZEALAND
16 December 1993 at MCG, Melbourne

AUSTRALIA

M.L. Hayden	c Cairns, **b** Pringle		5
M.A. Taylor	c Blain, **b** Cairns		81
M.E. Waugh	c Rutherford, **b** de Groen		53
D.C. Boon	c Morrison, **b** de Groen		14
S.R. Waugh	retired hurt		25
A.R. Border (capt)	run out		9
*I.A. Healy	not out		5
P.R. Reiffel			
S.K. Warne			
T.B.A. May			
C.J. McDermott			
Extras	lb **7**, w **3**		10
(50 overs)	(for 5 wickets)		202

NEW ZEALAND

B.A. Young	lbw, **b** McDermott		0
R.T. Latham	st Healy, **b** Warne		39
K.R. Rutherford (capt)	**b** M.E. Waugh		39
M.J. Greatbatch	lbw, **b** Warne		41
C.L. Cairns	c Healy, **b** Warne		5
S.A. Thomson	c Border, **b** McDermott		42
*T.E. Blain	c Border, **b** Warne		1
G.R. Larsen	**b** M.E. Waugh		17
C. Pringle	run out		4
D.K. Morrison	not out		2
R.P. de Groen	not out		2
Extras	b **1**, lb **5**, w **1**		7
(50 overs)	(for 9 wickets)		199

	O	M	R	W
Pringle	9	1	26	1
Morrison	7	2	17	–
Cairns	7	–	33	1
de Groen	10	–	40	2
Larsen	10	–	57	–
Thomson	7	–	22	–

	O	M	R	W
McDermott	9	1	40	2
Reiffel	10	1	44	–
M.E. Waugh	9	–	42	2
May	10	–	35	–
Warne	10	1	19	4
Border	2	–	13	–

FALL OF WICKETS

1–8, **2**–97, **3**–131, 4–183, **5**–202

FALL OF WICKETS

1–0, **2**–66, **3**–99, 4–109, **5**–146, **6**–154, **7**–187, **8**–193, **9**–194

Umpires: L.J. King & A.J. McQuillan   *Man of the Match:* S.K. Warne   *Australia won by 3 runs*

BENSON AND HEDGES WORLD SERIES – MATCH SIX – SOUTH AFRICA *v.* NEW ZEALAND
18 December 1993 at Bellerive Oval, Hobart

SOUTH AFRICA

A.C. Hudson	c Blain, **b** Pringle		8
G. Kirsten	c Young, **b** Pringle		7
K.C. Wessels (capt)	c Blain, **b** Larsen		15
W.J. Cronje	c Morrison, **b** Larsen		18
D.J. Cullinan	c Blain, **b** Thomson		8
D.J. Callaghan	**b** Pringle		25
*D.J. Richardson	not out		38
P.L. Symcox	c Blain, **b** Cairns		8
R.P. Snell	not out		13
C.R. Matthews			
P.S. de Villiers			
Extras	lb **4**, w **3**		7
(50 overs)	(for 7 wickets)		147

NEW ZEALAND

B.A. Young	lbw, **b** Matthews		74
R.T. Latham	c Wessels, **b** Matthews		7
K.R. Rutherford (capt)	run out		9
M.J. Greatbatch	run out		8
C.L. Cairns	not out		30
S.A. Thomson	**b** Matthews		9
*T.E. Blain	c Richardson, **b** Matthews		5
G.R. Larsen	not out		4
D.N. Patel			
C. Pringle			
D.K. Morrison			
Extras	w **1**, nb **1**		2
(44.1 overs)	(for 6 wickets)		148

	O	M	R	W
Pringle	10	1	28	3
Morrison	8	1	32	–
Larsen	10	5	12	2
Patel	10	2	25	–
Thomson	5	–	19	1
Cairns	7	–	27	1

	O	M	R	W
Matthews	10	1	38	4
de Villiers	9.1	1	23	–
Snell	10	2	29	–
Symcox	10	–	25	–
Cronje	5	–	33	–

FALL OF WICKETS

1–15, **2**–22, 3–50, 4–53, **5**–66, **6**–101, **7**–119

FALL OF WICKETS

1–22, **2**–54, **3**–66, 4–112, **5**–132, **6**–142

Umpires: S.J. Davis & S.G. Randell   *Man of the Match:* G.R. Larsen   *New Zealand won by 4 wickets*

18, 19, 20 and 21 December 1993 *at WACA Ground, Perth*

South Australia 179 (D.S. Webber 58, T.M. Moody 4 for 43) and 283 (J.D. Siddons 129, J. Angel 5 for 59)

Western Australia 304 (T.M. Moody 65) and 160 for 1 (J.L. Langer 90 not out, G.R. Marsh 62 not out)

Western Australia won by 9 wickets

Western Australia 6 pts., South Australia 0 pts.

at SCG, Sydney

Victoria 264 (W.N. Phillips 57, B.J. Hodge 57, G.D. McGrath 4 for 60) and 324 for 6 dec. (D.M. Jones 155, D.J. Ramshaw 80)

New South Wales 283 (M.E. Waugh 119, S.K. Warne 5 for 77) and 275 for 9 (M.G. Bevan 81, R. Chee Quee 76, P.R. Reiffel 4 for 68)

Match drawn

New South Wales 2 pts., Victoria 0 pts.

The major force of the Western Australian attack – Joe Angel. (Stephen Laffer/Sports-Line)

Allan Donald appeals unsuccessfully for leg before against Mark Taylor in the rain-ruined first Test, Australia v. South Africa. (Ben Radford/Allsport)

Western Australia maintained their impressive form by beating South Australia inside three days. Moody enjoyed a good all-round match, and the bowling of Angel was once more a prime force in the home state's victory. He finished with match figures of 8 for 89.

In contrast, New South Wales had to settle for a draw against Victoria. Mark Waugh's patient century took the home state to first-innings points, but Jones and Ramshaw revitalised Victoria with a 175-run fourth-wicket partnership which enabled Jones to declare and set New South Wales the task of scoring 306 in 74 overs to win. They began slowly and lost three wickets for 79 runs, but Bevan and Chee Quee added 114. The run rate was never in keeping with what was required, however, and McGrath eventually had to survive the last ball to save the match.

20, 21, 22 and **23** December 1993 *at Woolloongabba, Brisbane*

South Africans 335 for 7 dec. (W.J. Cronje 145, D.J. Cullinan 113, M.S. Kasprowicz 5 for 92) and 224 for 8 dec. (A.C. Hudson 105)
Queensland 183 (S.G. Law 56) and 268 for 5 (T.J. Barsby 99, J.P. Maher 50 not out)

Match drawn

On the eve of the first Test match, the South Africans gained some encouragement from their draw with Queensland. They won the toss, batted and found themselves reduced to 38 for 3. Cronje and Cullinan then added 242, a fourth-wicket record for South Africa in Australia. Matthews, Rundle and de Villiers dismissed Queensland cheaply, and Gary Kirsten claimed two of the last three wickets. Hudson hit 105 in 321 minutes, and Wessels declared shortly after he was out. Barsby and Foley began Queensland's second innings with a partnership of 116, and Maher gave further immunity to defeat.

FIRST TEST MATCH
AUSTRALIA *v.* SOUTH AFRICA,
at Melbourne

The much-awaited clash between Australia and South Africa was completely ruined by rain. South Africa gave first Test caps to de Villiers and Gary Kirsten, but, like the other players, they had to wait until five o'clock on the first day before seeing any action. Australia won the toss and batted, with Martyn replacing the injured Steve Waugh and Reiffel preferred to McGrath.

There was quite a lively start. Donald had a vehement appeal for leg before against Taylor rejected, and Slater edged the ball over the slips and then into and out of Cullinan's hands at second slip. Slater finally lobbed a

FIRST TEST MATCH – AUSTRALIA *v.* SOUTH AFRICA
26, 27, 28, 29 and 30 December 1993 at MCG, Melbourne

AUSTRALIA

FIRST INNINGS

M.A. Taylor	b Symcox	170
M.J. Slater	c Kirsten, b Donald	32
S.K. Warne	lbw, b de Villiers	0
D.C. Boon	b Matthews	25
M.E. Waugh	lbw, b Matthews	84
A.R. Border (capt)	c Richardson, b Matthews	2
D.R. Martyn	b Symcox	8
*I.A. Healy	not out	7
P.R. Reiffel		
C.J. McDermott		
T.B.A. May		
Extras	b 2, lb 7, nb 5	14
	(for 7 wickets, dec.)	342

SOUTH AFRICA

FIRST INNINGS

A.C. Hudson	retired hurt	64
G. Kirsten	c Taylor, b M. Waugh	16
W.J. Cronje	c Boon, b Warne	71
D.J. Cullinan	c Border, b McDermott	0
J.N. Rhodes	not out	35
K.C. Wessels (capt)	not out	63
*D.J. Richardson		
C.R. Matthews		
P.L. Symcox		
A.A. Donald		
P.S. de Villiers		
Extras	lb 2, nb 7	9
	(for 3 wickets)	258

	O	M	R	W
Donald	30	4	108	1
de Villiers	32	6	83	1
Matthews	24	5	68	3
Cronje	13	4	25	–
Symcox	16.5	3	49	2

	O	M	R	W
McDermott	23	5	60	1
Reiffel	21	4	55	–
M.E. Waugh	12	3	20	1
May	28	7	58	–
Warne	31	8	63	1

FALL OF WICKETS
1–57, 2–58, 3–127, 4–296, 5–300, 6–327, 7–342

FALL OF WICKETS
1–49, 2–157, 3–157

Umpires: D.B. Hair & T.A. Prue

Match drawn

catch to short-leg and night-watchman Warne was leg before, second ball.

There was no play at all on the second day, and the third day was restricted to the pre-lunch session and 29 minutes towards the end of the day after a four-hour stoppage. During this time, Australia moved from 71 for 2 to 140 for 3, Boon having played on to Matthews.

With a draw inevitable, Mark Taylor became the first player to score a century on debut against four countries, adding South Africa to his achievements against Pakistan, England and Sri Lanka. Cullinan at second slip missed both Mark Waugh and Taylor during the course of their record 169-run stand, and when Taylor was out, having batted 495 minutes, faced 349 balls and hit 12 fours, Border declared.

Wessels was off the field for much of the time with an injured knee, and McMillan, also suffering knee trouble, substituted for him. At the end of the fourth day, South Africa were 59 for the loss of Gary Kirsten.

Hudson was hit on the forearm, and the arm stiffened so that he retired shortly after lunch on the last day with the score on 152. Cullinan completed a miserable match by being out first ball, and Cronje left at the same score after which Rhodes and Wessels played out time.

both played well, but in the end, it was an unbroken stand of 59 in 94 minutes between Tucker and Atkinson which saved the day.

Unfit for the Test match, Steve Waugh led New South Wales in Adelaide and added 105 with Davison after Chee Quee had gone for 0. Bevan hit 103 off 128 balls before becoming Marsh's first wicket in first-class cricket, and with Maxwell hitting well, Steve Waugh was able to declare at 395 for 9. Without the injured Matthews and their Test players, New South Wales found it hard to break down South Australia. Blewett and Nobes began with a stand of 181, and Siddons and Lehmann put on 121 for the fourth wicket so that the home state took a lead of 70. Bevan again batted well, and with McNamara, he added 134 for the fourth wicket in New South Wales' second innings. There was also solid support from Chee Quee, Steve Waugh and Maxwell, and South Australia were left to score 268 to win. The first three wickets went down for 44, and there was no effective recovery as the off-breaks of Gavin Robertson took their toll.

31 December 1993 and **1, 2** and **3** January 1994

at Woolloongabba, Brisbane

Queensland 245 and 399 for 6 dec. (M.L. Love 138,
M.L. Hayden 121 not out)

Tasmania 190 (S. Young 55, M.S. Kasprowicz 4 for 56)
and 329 for 7 (D.J. Buckingham 77, R.T. Ponting 64)

Match drawn

Queensland 2 pts., Tasmania 0 pts.

at Adelaide Oval

New South Wales 395 for 9 dec. (M.G. Bevan 103,
S.R. Waugh 73, N.D. Maxwell 61, R.J. Davison 56,
S.P. George 5 for 102) and 337 (M.G. Bevan 89)

South Australia 465 for 8 dec. (G.S. Blewett 93,
D.S. Lehmann 85, P.C. Nobes 78, J.D. Siddons 64)
and 158 (G.R. Robertson 5 for 43)

New South Wales won by 109 runs

New South Wales 6 pts., South Australia 2 pts.

Put in to bat, Queensland did so with consistency rather than flair to reach 245 against Tasmania, but this score took on massive proportions when Kasprowicz dismissed Courtney and Cooley with only two scored. Early next morning he claimed Hills, and Tasmania were 9 for 3. They slipped into deeper trouble at 68 for 6, but they were well served by their tail. Hayden dropped down to number six for Queensland in the second innings and shared a fifth-wicket stand of 218 with Love which enabled Law to declare and leave Tasmania more than a day in which to survive or score 395 to win. They closed on 42 for 3, and defeat looked certain. Ponting and Buckingham

Gavin Robertson – a driving force with his off-spin in New South Wales' triumphant season. (Stephen Laffer/Sports-Line)

SECOND TEST MATCH
AUSTRALIA *v.* SOUTH AFRICA, at Sydney

Australia brought back McGrath in place of Reiffel while South Africa were unchanged. Wessels won the toss, and South Africa batted. Hudson was soon out, rather unfortunately adjudged to be leg before, but Kirsten and Cronje added 90 in 152 minutes, attempting to play positively against the spinners. Cronje was out when he was caught in the gully by the leaping Mark Waugh. Cullinan hit Warne for 2 fours before being bowled by the 'flipper', a dismissal which was accompanied by unnecessary remarks and gestures from the bowler. Warne was now in full flow and he beat Rhodes with another 'flipper'. Kirsten's 218-minute innings ended when he was drawn forward and beaten by the ball which turned away from the left-hander. Richardson was taken at slip, and Wessels drove a full toss back to the bowler. At tea South Africa were 142 for 7 and five of the wickets had gone to Warne who quickly extended his run to 5 for 5 in 22 balls when he had Matthews caught at slip. Symcox was bowled behind his legs by a mighty leg-break,

Warne's seventh victim, and McDermott ended de Villiers' resistance. Warne led a triumphant Australia from the field.

Taylor was caught behind off Donald's away swinger, but Slater and Boon moved to the close on 20 for 1. Batting was not easy on a pitch which offered uneven bounce, but Slater played with great concentration and maturity. Boon played on to de Villiers, and Mark Waugh tried too much too soon against the off-spinner Symcox who bowled a long spell, but Border stayed with Slater to add 104 in 242 minutes. The Australian captain was out when he edged high to Richardson. Slater went without addition to the score. He batted for 380 minutes, faced 262 balls and hit 5 fours. His dedication deserved the highest praise, and he had put Australia in a good position. Wessels dropped Healy at slip off de Villiers and broke a finger into the bargain. Australia ended the day on 200 for 5.

A sensible innings from Martyn helped Australia to a first-innings lead of 123. Both Donald and de Villiers finished with four wickets, but McDermott was equally lively and accounted for Hudson and Kirsten before the close which ended with South Africa still 29 runs adrift.

On the fourth morning, McDermott bowled Cronje

SECOND TEST MATCH – AUSTRALIA *v.* SOUTH AFRICA
2, 3, 4, 5 and 6 January 1994 at SCG, Sydney

SOUTH AFRICA

	FIRST INNINGS		SECOND INNINGS	
A.C. Hudson	lbw, b McGrath	0	c Healy, b McDermott	1
G. Kirsten	st Healy, b Warne	67	b McDermott	41
W.J. Cronje	c Waugh, b McDermott	41	b McDermott	38
D.J. Cullinan	b Warne	9	(5) lbw, b Warne	2
J.N. Rhodes	lbw, b Warne	4	(6) not out	76
K.C. Wessels (capt)	c and b Warne	3	(4) b Warne	18
*D.J. Richardson	c Taylor, b Warne	4	lbw, b McGrath	24
P.L. Symcox	b Warne	7	c Healy, b McDermott	4
C.R. Matthews	c Taylor, b Warne	0	c Waugh, b Warne	4
P.S. de Villiers	c Waugh, b McDermott	18	lbw, b Warne	2
A.A. Donald	not out	0	c Healy, b Warne	10
Extras	b 1, lb 4, nb 11	16	b 13, lb 1, nb 5	19
		169		**239**

AUSTRALIA

	FIRST INNINGS		SECOND INNINGS	
M.J. Slater	b Donald	92	(2) b de Villiers	1
M.A. Taylor	c Richardson, b Donald	7	(1) c Richardson, b de Villiers	27
D.C. Boon	b de Villiers	19	c Kirsten, b de Villiers	24
M.E. Waugh	lbw, b Symcox	7	(5) lbw, b Donald	11
A.R. Border (capt)	c Richardson, b de Villiers	49	(6) b Donald	7
D.R. Martyn	c Richardson, b de Villiers	59	(7) c Hudson, b Donald	6
*I.A. Healy	c Richardson, b Donald	19	b de Villiers	1
S.K. Warne	c Rhodes, b Symcox	11	(9) run out	1
C.J. McDermott	c Cronje, b de Villiers	6	(10) not out	29
T.B.A. May	not out	8	(4) lbw, b de Villiers	0
G.D. McGrath	b Donald	9	c and b de Villiers	1
Extras	b 1, lb 2, nb 3	6	lb 3	3
		292		**111**

	O	M	R	W	O	M	R	W		O	M	R	W	O	M	R	W
McDermott	18.1	2	42	2	28	9	62	4	Donald	31.2	8	83	4	17	5	34	3
McGrath	19	5	32	1	14	3	30	1	de Villiers	36	12	80	4	23.3	8	43	6
Warne	27	8	56	7	42	17	72	5	Matthews	28	11	44	–	6	5	9	–
May	10	1	34	–	22	4	53	–	Symcox	46	11	82	2	10	3	22	–
Border					3	1	8	–									

FALL OF WICKETS

1–1, 2–91, 3–110, 4–133, 5–134, 6–141, 7–142, 8–142, 9–152
1–2, 2–75, 3–101, 4–107, 5–110, 6–182, 7–188, 8–197, 9–203

FALL OF WICKETS

1–10, 2–58, 3–75, 4–179, 5–179, 6–229, 7–250, 8–266, 9–281
1–4, 2–51, 3–51, 4–56, 5–63, 6–72, 7–73, 8–75, 9–110

Umpires: S.G. Randell & W.P. Sheahan

South Africa won by 5 runs

Warne ran himself out, beaten by Cronje's throw from mid-off. Australia were now 75 for 8, and for the first time in the match, South Africa were on top.

Craig McDermott led the counter attack. He hit the first ball he received through the covers for four, and three more boundaries saw Australia reach 100. Martyn, however, the last front-line batsman was becalmed. In 106 minutes, off 59 balls, he hit six singles. A more positive approach might well have brought better results, but, through McDermott's aggression, Australia reached 110 for 8. Then Martyn hit Donald lamely into the hands of cover. McGrath survived and took a single to third man, but this meant that he had to face an over from Man of the Match de Villiers while McDermott, the potential match-winner, could only look on helpless. McGrath negotiated two deliveries, and the third he hit softly back to the bowler. South Africa had won an extraordinary victory by five runs.

An emotional Ali Bacher believed it was their greatest achievement ever. It was certainly an heroic one.

Border is bowled by Donald, and South Africa are on the brink of victory. (Ben Radford/Allsport)

between bat and pad, and Warne began to wreak havoc again, bowling Wessels and beating Cullinan with his 'flipper' for the second time in the match. At 110 for 5, South Africa were still 13 runs short of making Australia bat again. Rhodes and Richardson took their side into a slender lead, but Richardson fell to McGrath, and Warne then had Matthews caught off a huge leg-break. This was the first time that Warne had taken 10 wickets in a match, and he made it 11 when he trapped de Villiers leg before. At this stage, South Africa led by 80, but Rhodes now decided to attack. He pulled McDermott for six, and then hit the 5th and 6th fours of his innings. He and Donald added 36 in 42 minutes before Warne had Donald caught behind to finish with match figures of 12 for 128.

Needing 117 to win, Australia had 33 overs and a day in which to score them. Slater played across an outswinger, but Donald failed to take a return catch offered by Boon, and the fifty was passed before the same batsman chipped the ball to short-leg. Sent in as night-watchman, May was out first ball, and when Taylor edged to the keeper Australia were 56 for 4. Mark Waugh and Border added seven before the close. 'Fanie' de Villiers had taken all four wickets.

So Australia began the last day needing 54 to win, with six wickets in hand, and Border and Mark Waugh at the crease. An Australian victory looked certain, yet there were seeds of doubt. Those doubts increased when, with the fourth ball of the morning, Donald clipped Border's off stump. Nine runs later, Mark Waugh was leg before to Donald's yorker. Healy played on to de Villiers, and

Shane Warne in celebratory mood in the second Test match. Warne took 12 for 128 but finished on the losing side. (Ben Radford/Allsport)

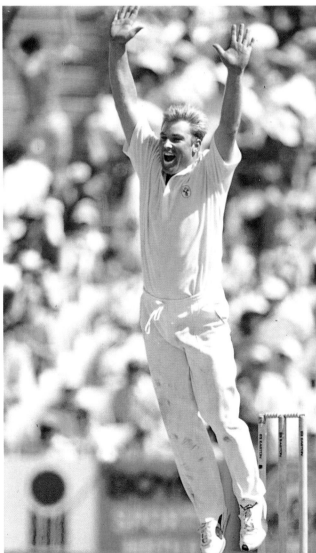

ABOVE: *Man of the Match Fanie de Villiers traps night-watchman Tim May leg before and heralds South Africa's famous victory. (Ben Radford/Allsport)*

BELOW: *Darren Lehmann returned to South Australia from Victoria and enjoyed an outstanding season. Against Western Australia at Adelaide, he hit 200 off 212 balls. (Stephen Laffer/Sports-Line)*

7, 8, 9 and **10** January 1994 *at Bellerive Oval, Hobart*

New South Wales 398 (S.R. Waugh 190 not out, M.G. Bevan 71, C.R. Miller 7 for 83) and 296 for 4 dec. (M.G. Bevan 117 not out, M.J. Slater 107)

Tasmania 401 for 6 dec. (D.F. Hills 158 not out, D.J. Buckingham 52) and 294 for 6 (D.J. Buckingham 88 not out, D.F. Hills 68)

Tasmania won by 4 wickets

Tasmania 6 pts., New South Wales 0 pts.

at Adelaide Oval

Western Australia 446 for 7 dec. (G.R. Marsh 98, J.L. Langer 96, M.R.J. Veletta 75, T.M. Moody 58) and 174 for 3 (J.L. Langer 56 not out)

South Australia 437 (D.S. Lehmann 200, J.A. Brayshaw 146, B.P. Julian 4 for 108, D.J. Spencer 4 for 85)

Match drawn

Western Australia 1.8 pts., South Australia 0 pts.

Tasmania strengthened their claims for a place in the Sheffield Shield final with an unexpected and resounding victory over New South Wales. Steve Waugh displayed how much Australia had missed him in the Sydney Test with a significant 190 not out. His runs were made out of 392, and he hit 22 fours and 2 sixes. He and Bevan, who was enjoying a fine season, put on 156 for the third wicket, but medium-pacer Colin Miller restricted the visitors with the best bowling performance of his career. Dene Hills threw off his recent run of bad form with the highest score of his career which took Tasmania to first-innings points. Still the runs flowed as Slater and Bevan put on 129 for New South Wales' third wicket when they batted again. Bevan's 117 came off 126 balls, and Slater's 107 off 138 balls. The rate of scoring enabled Steve Waugh to declare and ask Tasmania to score 294 to win at nearly four runs an over. They began briskly, but lost six wickets for 193 runs. Atkinson then joined Buckingham and in 70 minutes they hit the remaining 101 runs needed for victory.

Little play was possible on the first day at Adelaide, and the Western Australian innings extended into the third morning. It was marked by its consistency, the first four batsmen passing fifty. South Australia were 60 for 3 in reply, but Lehmann and Brayshaw then engaged in an astonishing stand of 318 in 261 minutes. Lehmann hit a hundred between lunch and tea, and his 200 came from 212 balls and included a six and 30 fours. Brayshaw, who made his highest score in first-class cricket, was more circumspect, facing 275 balls and hitting 17 fours. In spite of their efforts, South Australia failed to take first-innings points, the later batsmen succumbing to the Kent bowler Spencer. Western Australia lost 0.2 points for a slow over rate.

13, 14, 15 and 16 January 1994 *at Woolloongabba, Brisbane*

Queensland 347 (M.L. Hayden 126, J.P. Maher 70, M.L. Love 50, M.G. Hughes 5 for 70) and 331 for 6 dec. (M.L. Hayden 155, S.G. Law 76, T.J. Barsby 58)

Victoria 272 (G.J. Allardice 86, A.J. Bichel 4 for 69, M.S. Kasprowicz 4 for 76) and 212 (B.J. Hodge 64, C.G. Rackemann 5 for 32)

Queensland won by 194 runs

Queensland 6 pts., Victoria 0 pts.

Queensland's victory over Victoria was yet another triumph for Matthew Hayden. The left-hander hit a century in each innings, and his sixth century in seven innings established a record for the Shield by an Australian player. He also passed 1,000 runs for the season and set a new record for runs in a Shield season for Queensland. The other encouraging aspects of the game for Queensland were the continued good form of pace bowler Kasprowicz and the unflagging zest of the veteran Carl Rackemann. For Victoria, Merv Hughes signalled his return to fitness with five wickets on the first day.

 BENSON AND HEDGES WORLD SERIES
Phase Two – Matches Seven to Twelve

With Wessels having returned to South Africa to receive treatment on his various injuries, Hansie Cronje took over the captaincy of South Africa and, when the World Series resumed, asked New Zealand to bat when he won the toss in Brisbane. His decision appeared to be correct as New Zealand slumped to 86 for 5 after 27 overs. Chris Cairns, 70 off 54 balls, and Shane Thomson revitalised the innings in a partnership of 111, and Tony Blain hit 36 off 23 deliveries to consolidate their work. Rain reduced South Africa's target to 229 off 39 overs and Peter Kirsten, who had arrived in Australia as a replacement for the injured Wessels, hit 97 off 108 balls, but he received scant support and South Africa fell short of their target.

The following day, Dean Jones, returning to the Australian side, hit 98 off 124 balls to set up victory over South Africa for whom debutant Dave Rundle was the most impressive bowler. There was considerable surprise that Australia omitted Slater to accommodate Martyn, but the home side still made sufficient runs, and McGrath confirmed his growing maturity with another good bowling display.

New Zealand became favourites to meet Australia when they played with considerable verve to beat the hosts in Sydney. At 40 for 3, New Zealand were struggling, but Rutherford and Greatbatch added 89, and the eventual total of 198 looked defendable. McGrath was again the most impressive of the Australian bowlers. The early running out of Mark Taylor gave New Zealand the encouragement they needed, and Pringle and de Groen bowled well to reduce Australia to 87 for 5. Healy and Boon added 77 before Healy was caught behind off de Groen, and when Boon edged a ball from Pringle into his stumps Australia lost control.

Victory over South Africa in Perth would have put New Zealand into the finals, but they slumped badly against the pace of Donald, de Villiers and McMillan and were 84 for 6 after 25 overs. There was brave batting from Cairns, Harris and Blain, but 150 never looked like being a winning score, and so it proved. The Kirstens gave South Africa a fine start, and although Chris Pringle produced another good spell, the Springboks won with nearly 20 overs to spare.

South Africa now asserted their claim to a place in the final by routing Australia two days later. Put in to bat, South Africa made 208. They then bowled with hostility and accuracy to shoot out an Australian side who were resting some key players and for whom Fleming was making his debut.

Border and Healy returned for the final preliminary round match, but neither was called upon to do much as Boon and Jones shared a second-wicket stand of 121. New Zealand bowled well, and Australia's 217 was by no means a daunting score. Once again, however, the batsmen disappointed, and New Zealand lost their chance to win a place in the finals. They had fought bravely in the second half of the competition, but the absence of Crowe and Morrison had proved too great a loss.

BENSON AND HEDGES WORLD SERIES – MATCH SEVEN – NEW ZEALAND *v.* SOUTH AFRICA
8 January 1994 at Woolloongabba, Brisbane

NEW ZEALAND

B.A. Young	c Cullinan, b McMillan	28
R.T. Latham	c McMillan, b Donald	11
A.H. Jones	c Kirsten, b Matthews	9
K.R. Rutherford (capt)	b McMillan	1
M.J. Greatbatch	c Rhodes, b Donald	21
S.A. Thomson	c Donald, b Cronje	68
C.L. Cairns	run out	70
*T.E. Blain	not out	36
G.R. Larsen	not out	6
C. Pringle		
R.P. de Groen		
Extras	lb 2, w 2, nb 2	6
(50 overs)	(for 7 wickets)	256

SOUTH AFRICA

A.C. Hudson	c Thomson, b Pringle	14
P.N. Kirsten	c Jones, b Cairns	97
*E.L.R. Stewart	c and b Thomson	19
W.J. Cronje (capt)	c Greatbatch, b Thomson	19
D.J. Cullinan	c Greatbatch, b de Groen	37
J.N. Rhodes	c Blain, b Cairns	21
B.M. McMillan	b Pringle	0
P.L. Symcox	not out	4
C.R. Matthews	c Latham, b Pringle	1
P.S. de Villiers	not out	0
A.A. Donald		
Extras	lb 4, w 2, nb 1	7
(39 overs)	(for 8 wickets)	219

	O	M	R	W
Donald	8	–	38	2
de Villiers	10	2	40	–
McMillan	10	–	59	2
Matthews	10	2	52	1
Symcox	7	1	26	–
Cronje	5	–	39	1

	O	M	R	W
Pringle	8	1	38	3
Cairns	8	1	44	2
de Groen	7	–	41	1
Thomson	6	–	38	2
Larsen	8	–	42	–
Latham	2	–	12	–

FALL OF WICKETS
1–33, 2–47, 3–52, 4–55, 5–86, 6–197, 7–221

FALL OF WICKETS
1–24, 2–62, 3–96, 4–181, 5–207, 6–213, 7–215, 8–217

Umpires: I.S. Thomas & C.D. Timmins   *Man of the Match:* P.N. Kirsten   *New Zealand won on faster scoring rate*

BENSON AND HEDGES WORLD SERIES – MATCH EIGHT – AUSTRALIA *v.* SOUTH AFRICA
9 January 1994 at Woolloongabba, Brisbane

AUSTRALIA

D.C. Boon	c Rundle, b McMillan	45
M.A. Taylor	b de Villiers	12
D.M. Jones	b Rundle	98
M.E. Waugh	c Cullinan, b Symcox	10
D.R. Martyn	c Cronje, b Rundle	23
A.R. Border (capt)	c Kirsten, b Rundle	15
*I.A. Healy	c and b Rundle	0
C.J. McDermott	run out	2
P.R. Reiffel	run out	9
T.B.A. May	not out	5
G.D. McGrath		
Extras	lb 4, w 6, nb 1	11
(50 overs)	(for 9 wickets)	230

SOUTH AFRICA

W.J. Cronje (capt)	c Healy, b Reiffel	17
G. Kirsten	c Healy, b Waugh	51
D.J. Cullinan	c Reiffel, b Border	27
J.N. Rhodes	c Healy, b May	46
D.J. Callaghan	run out	1
B.M. McMillan	c and b Border	6
*D.J. Richardson	lbw, b McGrath	15
P.L. Symcox	lbw, b McGrath	0
R.P. Snell	c Martyn, b McGrath	9
D.B. Rundle	c Border, b McGrath	0
P.S. de Villiers	not out	1
Extras	lb 6, w 2, nb 1	9
(46.5 overs)		182

	O	M	R	W
de Villiers	10	–	28	1
Snell	8	–	36	–
McMillan	10	2	42	1
Cronje	5	–	31	–
Symcox	8	–	47	1
Rundle	9	–	42	4

	O	M	R	W
McDermott	5	–	14	–
McGrath	8.5	–	24	4
Reiffel	7	–	24	1
May	9	–	45	1
Waugh	7	–	29	1
Border	10	–	40	2

FALL OF WICKETS
1–20, 2–108, 3–127, 4–180, 5–205, 6–208, 7–211, 8–214, 9–230

FALL OF WICKETS
1–33, 2–88, 3–116, 4–119, 5–138, 6–168, 7–168, 8–175, 9–181

Umpires: D.B. Hair & A.J. McQuillan   *Man of the Match:* D.M. Jones   *Australia won by 48 runs*

BENSON AND HEDGES WORLD SERIES – MATCH NINE – AUSTRALIA v. NEW ZEALAND
11 January 1994 at SCG Sydney

NEW ZEALAND

B.A. Young	b Waugh	19
R.T. Latham	c Taylor, b Reiffel	0
A.H. Jones	lbw, b McGrath	6
K.R. Rutherford (capt)	c Healy, b Border	65
M.J. Greatbatch	lbw, b Warne	50
S.A. Thomson	st Healy, b Warne	1
C.L. Cairns	c Healy, b McGrath	16
*T.E. Blain	c and b Border	0
G.R. Larsen	not out	29
C. Pringle	b McGrath	1
R.P. de Groen	not out	7
Extras	b 3, lb 1	4
(50 overs)	(for 9 wickets)	198

AUSTRALIA

M.A. Taylor	run out	1
D.C. Boon	b Pringle	67
D.M. Jones	c Pringle, b de Groen	21
M.E. Waugh	b Pringle	15
D.R. Martyn	run out	7
A.R. Border (capt)	b Thomson	1
*I.A. Healy	c Blain, b de Groen	48
P.R. Reiffel	lbw, b Pringle	3
S.K. Warne	b Cairns	9
T.B.A. May	not out	4
G.D. McGrath	b Pringle	4
Extras	w 4, nb 1	5
(48.3 overs)		185

	O	M	R	W
McGrath	10	3	29	3
Reiffel	9	–	33	1
Waugh	7	–	38	1
May	10	1	43	–
Warne	10	1	27	2
Border	4	–	24	2

	O	M	R	W
de Groen	10	–	34	2
Pringle	9.3	–	40	4
Cairns	9	2	18	1
Thomson	9	–	40	1
Latham	2	–	10	–
Larsen	9	–	43	–

FALL OF WICKETS

1–4, 2–13, 3–40, 4–129, 5–131, 6–152, 7–152, 8–164, 9–168

FALL OF WICKETS

1–1, 2–38, 3–76, 4–86, 5–87, 6–164, 7–166, 8–171, 9–180

Umpires: S.J. Davis & S.G. Randell   *Man of the Match:* C. Pringle   *New Zealand won by 13 runs*

BENSON AND HEDGES WORLD SERIES – MATCH TEN – NEW ZEALAND v. SOUTH AFRICA
14 January 1994 at WACA Ground, Perth

NEW ZEALAND

B.A. Young	c Richardson, b de Villiers	2
A.H. Jones	lbw, b Donald	0
K.R. Rutherford (capt)	b McMillan	25
M.J. Greatbatch	c Richardson, b Matthews	16
S.A. Thomson	c Richardson, b McMillan	0
C.L. Cairns	c Richardson, b Callaghan	29
C.Z. Harris	not out	29
*T.E. Blain	run out	32
G.R. Larsen	c Matthews, b, McMillan	2
C. Pringle	b Donald	1
R.P. de Groen	c Cullinan, b Donald	0
Extras	lb 7, w 6, nb 1	14
(44.2 overs)		150

SOUTH AFRICA

P.N. Kirsten	run out	50
G. Kirsten	c Blain, b Pringle	31
W.J. Cronje (capt)	c sub (Latham), b Thomson	40
J.N. Rhodes	c de Groen, b Pringle	3
D.J. Cullinan	not out	5
D.J. Callaghan	c Rutherford, b Pringle	2
B.M. McMillan	not out	1
*D.J. Richardson		
C.R. Matthews		
P.S. de Villiers		
A.A. Donald		
Extras	lb 10, w 8, nb 1	19
(30.3 overs)	(for 5 wickets)	151

	O	M	R	W
Donald	8.2	3	15	3
de Villiers	8	–	15	1
Matthews	10	1	46	1
McMillan	10	2	39	3
Callaghan	5	1	15	1
Cronje	3	–	13	–

	O	M	R	W
Pringle	8.3	–	24	3
de Groen	5	–	30	–
Cairns	7	–	32	–
Larsen	8	–	36	–
Thomson	2	–	19	1

FALL OF WICKETS

1–1, 2–3, 3–45, 4–46, 5–58, 6–84, 7–133, 8–145, 9–148

FALL OF WICKETS

1–80, 2–117, 3–139, 4–141, 5–148

Umpires: R.J. Evans & D.J. Harper   *Man of the Match:* A.A. Donald   *South Africa won by 5 wickets*

BENSON AND HEDGES WORLD SERIES – MATCH ELEVEN – AUSTRALIA *v.* SOUTH AFRICA
16 January 1994 at WACA Ground, Perth

SOUTH AFRICA

P.N. Kirsten	retired hurt	5
G. Kirsten	c Zoehrer, b M.E. Waugh	55
W.J. Cronje (capt)	c Warne, b Reiffel	11
J.N. Rhodes	run out	14
D.J. Cullinan	c Warne, b M.E. Waugh	34
D.J. Callaghan	lbw, b Warne	26
*D.J. Richardson	run out	25
R.P. Snell	not out	20
C.R. Matthews	st Zoehrer, b Warne	0
P.S. de Villiers	not out	0
A.A. Donald		
Extras	b 1, lb 8, w 9	18
		—
(50 overs)	(for 7 wickets)	208

AUSTRALIA

D.C. Boon	c sub (McMillan), b Snell	11
M.A. Taylor	c Richardson, b Snell	29
D.M. Jones	c sub (McMillan), b Matthews	10
M.E. Waugh	c sub (McMillan), b Callaghan	14
S.R. Waugh	c Richardson, b Callaghan	25
D.R. Martyn	c Richardson, b Cronje	0
*T.J. Zoehrer	lbw, b de Villiers	9
P.R. Reiffel	not out	10
S.K. Warne	run out	1
D.W. Fleming	lbw, b Matthews	2
G.D. McGrath	b Snell	4
Extras	lb 9, w 1, nb 1	11
		—
(41 overs)		126

	O	M	R	W
McGrath	10	1	38	–
Reiffel	10	2	25	1
Fleming	7	–	42	–
S.R. Waugh	6	–	32	–
Warne	10	–	36	2
M.E. Waugh	7	–	26	2

	O	M	R	W
Donald	8	–	20	–
de Villiers	8	2	19	1
Snell	7	–	26	3
Matthews	7	1	20	2
Cronje	6	1	17	1
Callaghan	5	1	15	2

FALL OF WICKETS

1–27, 2–69, 3–133, 4–133, 5–175, 6–196, 7–196

FALL OF WICKETS

1–22, 2–49, 3–57, 4–92, 5–93, 6–93, 7–109, 8–110, 9–121

Umpires: T.A. Prue & W.P. Sheahan   *Man of the Match:* D.J. Callaghan   *South Africa won by 82 runs*

BENSON AND HEDGES WORLD SERIES – MATCH TWELVE – AUSTRALIA *v.* NEW ZEALAND
19 January 1994 at MCG, Melbourne

AUSTRALIA

M.L. Hayden	c Blain, b Watson	13
D.C. Boon	c Rutherford, b Cairns	65
D.M. Jones	c Cairns, b Pringle	82
M.E. Waugh	not out	45
S.R. Waugh	not out	0
A.R. Border (capt)		
*I.A. Healy		
P.R. Reiffel		
S.K. Warne		
D.W. Fleming		
G.D. McGrath		
Extras	lb 12	12
		—
(50 overs)	(for 3 wickets)	217

NEW ZEALAND

B.A. Young	b Warne	43
R.T. Latham	c Warne, b Reiffel	10
A.H. Jones	lbw, b Fleming	9
K.R. Rutherford (capt)	run out	0
M.J. Greatbatch	c Reiffel, b Warne	13
S.A. Thomson	lbw, b McGrath	12
C.L. Cairns	lbw, b Fleming	39
*T.E. Blain	c Hayden, b Warne	4
G.R. Larsen	not out	17
C. Pringle	b Reiffel	6
W. Watson	c Healy, b Reiffel	0
Extras	lb 4, w 8, nb 1	13
		—
(47.5 overs)		166

	O	M	R	W
Pringle	10	–	45	1
Watson	10	2	33	1
Cairns	10	–	53	1
Larsen	10	1	23	–
Thomson	4	–	27	–
Latham	6	–	24	–

	O	M	R	W
McGrath	9	1	48	1
Reiffel	9.5	2	35	3
Fleming	9	2	15	2
S.R. Waugh	10	–	36	–
Warne	10	1	28	3

FALL OF WICKETS

1–15, 2–136, 3–214

FALL OF WICKETS

1–37, 2–60, 3–64, 4–80, 5–82, 6 107, 7–124, 8–147, 9–166

Umpires: P.D. Parker & S.G. Randell   *Man of the Match:* D.M. Jones   *Australia won by 51 runs*

BENSON AND HEDGES WORLD SERIES – FINAL TABLE

	P	W	L	Ab.	Pts.	Net R/R
Australia	8	5	3	–	10	0.37
South Africa	8	3	4	1	7	−0.07
New Zealand	8	3	4	1	7	−0.40

18 January 1994 *at SCG, Sydney*

South Africans 247 for 5 (D.J. Cullinan 95 not out,
  D.J. Callaghan 50)
New South Wales Invitation XI 228 (M.E. Waugh 59,
  S.R. Waugh 53, R.P. Snell 4 for 22)

South Africans won by 19 runs

18, 19, 20 and **21** January 1994 *at Bellerive Oval, Hobart*

South Australia 519 (J.D. Siddons 161, D.S. Lehmann
  137, G.S. Blewett 51, C.R. Miller 4 for 108) and 209
  for 3 dec. (J.D. Siddons 89 not out)
Tasmania 401 for 8 dec. (S. Young 124 not out,
  D.F. Hills 63, D.J. Buckingham 57) and 329 for 6
  (M.J. DiVenuto 112)

Tasmania won by 4 wickets

Tasmania 6 pts., South Australia 2 pts.

19, 20, 21 and **22** January 1994 *at Woolloongabba, Brisbane*

Queensland 244 (S.G. Law 118, J. Angel 4 for 64) and
  375 for 8 (J.P. Maher 122, M.L. Love 112)
Western Australia 413 (J.L. Langer 89, M.R.J. Veletta 80
  retired hurt, T.J. Zoehrer 69, J. Angel 52)

Match drawn

Western Australia 2 pts., Queensland 0 pts.

The South Africans met a New South Wales Invitation XI
in a 50-over match played in aid of the victims of the bush
fire which had swept through the area around Sydney.

Tasmania moved a step closer to qualifying for the
Sheffield Shield final with another fine victory. Batting
first, South Australia established a massive score thanks
mainly to a fourth-wicket partnership of 277 in 281
minutes between Siddons and Lehmann. Miller was
again the best of the Tasmanian bowlers. At 172 for 5,
Tasmania were in danger of having to follow-on, but the
left-hander Shaun Young hit a maiden first-class hundred and shared century stands with Buckingham and
Atkinson so that Tucker was able to declare on the third
afternoon. Siddons' eventual declaration left Tasmania to
score 328 at nearly four runs an over. They were 44 for 2,
but DiVenuto displayed his exciting talent with his
second century of the season, hitting 112 off 169 balls, and
with Ponting, Buckingham, Young and Tucker all making
fine contributions, victory came with four wickets to
spare.

There was no such success for either side in Brisbane
where Angel continued his excellent bowling form and
skipper Law held the Queensland first innings together.
Consistent batting gave Western Australia first innings
points but, as much time had been lost on the first day, a
result never looked likely. Love and Maher, who hit the
highest score of his career, put on 189 for Queensland's
fifth wicket in the second innings.

 ## MERCANTILE MUTUAL CUP

22 January 1994 *at Bellerive Oval, Hobart*

Tasmania 240 for 6 (D.F. Hills 64)
South Australia 243 for 6 (P.C. Nobes 64)

South Australia (2 pts.) won by 4 wickets

23 January 1994 *at Woolloongabba, Brisbane*

Queensland 283 for 6 (S.G. Law 114, J.M. Thomas 71)
Western Australia 254 (G.R. Marsh 95, D.R. Martyn 53,
  S.G. Law 4 for 33)

Queensland (2 pts.) won by 29 runs

Stuart Law, the acting-captain of Queensland, established a record for the one-day competition with his third
consecutive century. He also created a new record for
runs in a season in the Mercantile Mutual Cup. He and
Jeff Thomas hit 187 from 194 balls against Western Australia.

 ## BENSON AND HEDGES WORLD SERIES
The Finals

Australia won the World Series Cup, but they had a hard
struggle, for they were soundly beaten in the opening
match in Melbourne. South Africa won the toss, and the
Kirstens opened. Peter was dropped at slip early in his
innings by Shane Warne, and from that moment, South
Africa always had the edge. The opening partnership
realised 53, and Cronje then joined Gary Kirsten in a
stand of 90. The left-hander Gary Kirsten again proved
his worth. He batted throughout the 50 overs to score his
first one-day international century. Australia never recovered from the loss of Hayden and Jones in quick
succession although Border did his best to resuscitate his
side with 42 off 43 balls. Border was bowled by Snell who
became the only bowler in the competition to take five
wickets in a match during the season.

Border was happier winning the toss in the second
match and so allowing his team to bat first and establish a
formidable target, their preferred plan of play. The plan
did not go well at first as both openers were out with only

Gary Kirsten during his innings of 112 not out in the first World Series final. (Joe Mann/Allsport)

Mark Waugh, Man of the Finals, during his dashing innings of 60 in the third match. (Joe Mann/Allsport)

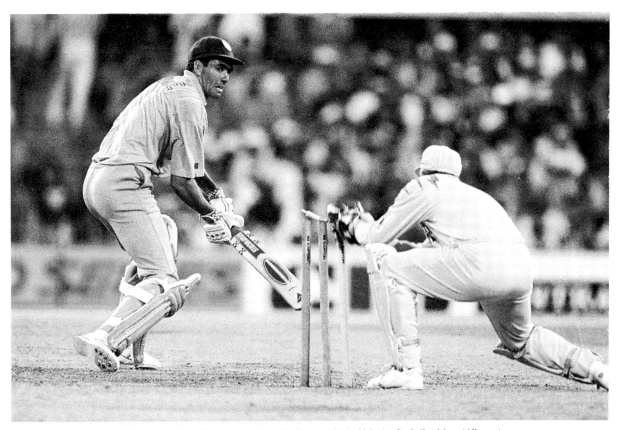

Ian Healy stumps Cronje off Warne as Australia move to victory in the second World Series final. (Joe Mann/Allsport)

35 scored, but Jones and Mark Waugh batted magnificently. Jones attacked from the start, and Waugh was soon in his stride so that 175 runs came in 34 overs of electric batting. With the Australian spinners keeping a tight hold and Steve Waugh bowling five mean overs, South Africa never suggested that they would approach their target of 248.

The same pattern unfolded in the deciding game when Border again won the toss. There was a stable start by Boon and Hayden, and Boon's 64 off 98 balls gave the innings substance. Dean Jones, with 25 off 29 balls, and Mark Waugh, 60 off 53 balls, were once more the swashbucklers, and Allan Border hit 30 off 26 balls just when it seemed the innings might melt away. Australia finished short of their total in the second match, but South Africa still faced a daunting task. When they slipped to 51 for 4 with two insane run outs, the visitors virtually surrendered the match. Warne ended Rhodes' resistance, and the last over of the tournament was bowled by Border who received an emotional and rapturous reception.

Mark Waugh was named Man of the Finals, and Shane Warne took the individual award for the preliminary rounds.

Border is held aloft as Australia win the Benson and Hedges World Series. (Joe Mann/Allsport)

BENSON AND HEDGES WORLD SERIES – FIRST FINAL – AUSTRALIA v. SOUTH AFRICA
21 January 1994 at MCG, Melbourne

SOUTH AFRICA

P.N. Kirsten	c Healy, b S.R. Waugh	28
G. Kirsten	not out	112
W.J. Cronje (capt)	c Jones, b Warne	40
J.N. Rhodes	c Healy, b McGrath	31
D.J. Cullinan	c Hayden, b McDermott	7
R.P. Snell	c Jones, b McGrath	3
D.J. Callaghan	not out	3
B.M. McMillan		
*D.J. Richardson		
P.S. de Villiers		
A.A. Donald		
Extras	lb 2, w 3, nb 1	6
(50 overs)	(for 5 wickets)	230

AUSTRALIA

D.C. Boon	run out	45
M.L. Hayden	b Snell	20
D.M. Jones	c Cronje, b McMillan	3
M.E. Waugh	c Richardson, b Donald	36
S.R. Waugh	c P.N. Kirsten, b Snell	27
A.R. Border (capt)	b Snell	42
*I.A. Healy	c P.N. Kirsten, b de Villiers	0
P.R. Reiffel	b Snell	18
S.K. Warne	c McMillan, b de Villiers	1
C.J. McDermott	b Snell	1
G.D. McGrath	not out	5
Extras	lb 1, w 3	4
(48.5 overs)		202

	O	M	R	W
McDermott	10	1	40	1
McGrath	9	–	52	2
Reiffel	7	2	23	–
S.R. Waugh	7	–	27	1
Warne	10	1	45	1
M.E. Waugh	3	–	15	–
Border	4	–	26	–

	O	M	R	W
Donald	10	–	48	1
de Villiers	9	1	26	2
Snell	9.5	–	40	5
McMillan	10	2	38	1
Callaghan	5	–	27	–
Cronje	5	–	22	–

FALL OF WICKETS

1–53, 2–143, 3–196, 4–217, 5–223

FALL OF WICKETS

1–41, 2–53, 3–84, 4–128, 5–150, 6–150, 7–192, 8–195, 9–197

Umpires: T.A. Prue & W.P. Sheahan

South Africa won by 28 runs

BENSON AND HEDGES WORLD SERIES – SECOND FINAL – AUSTRALIA *v.* SOUTH AFRICA
23 January 1994 at SCG, Sydney

AUSTRALIA

M.L. Hayden	c Snell, b Donald	16
D.C. Boon	c Rhodes, b Donald	14
D.M. Jones	c Cronje, b Donald	79
M.E. Waugh	c G. Kirsten, b de Villiers	107
S.R. Waugh	b Donald	1
A.R. Border (capt)	c Richardson, b de Villiers	6
*I.A. Healy	not out	10
P.R. Reiffel	not out	5
S.K. Warne		
C.J. McDermott		
T.B.A. May		
Extras	lb 5, w 3, nb 1	9
(50 overs)	(for 6 wickets)	247

SOUTH AFRICA

P.N. Kirsten	run out	11
G. Kirsten	c Boon, b May	42
W.J. Cronje (capt)	st Healy, b Warne	28
J.N. Rhodes	b McDermott	52
D.J. Cullinan	c S.R. Waugh, b Warne	3
B.M. McMillan	lbw, b Warne	0
*D.J. Richardson	b Border	16
R.P. Snell	b McDermott	6
P.L. Symcox	run out	12
P.S. de Villiers	not out	0
A.A. Donald	c and b McDermott	0
Extras	lb 7, nb 1	8
(45.5 overs)		178

	O	M	R	W
Donald	10	–	40	4
de Villiers	10	2	39	2
Snell	10	–	59	–
McMillan	7	–	40	–
Symcox	6	–	26	–
Cronje	7	–	38	–

	O	M	R	W
McDermott	8.5	–	39	3
Reiffel	8	–	23	–
S.R. Waugh	5	–	11	–
May	10	1	35	1
Warne	10	–	42	3
Border	4	–	21	1

FALL OF WICKETS
1–33, 2–35, 3–210, 4–221, 5–227, 6–241

FALL OF WICKETS
1–50, 2–74, 3–102, 4–106, 5–107, 6–156, 7–160, 8–174, 9–178

Umpires: D.B. Hair & S.G. Randell   *Australia won by 69 runs*

BENSON AND HEDGES WORLD SERIES – THIRD FINAL – AUSTRALIA *v.* SOUTH AFRICA
25 January 1994 at SCG, Sydney

AUSTRALIA

D.C. Boon	c Rhodes, b de Villiers	64
M.L. Hayden	st Richardson, b Rundle	20
D.M. Jones	c Rundle, b Donald	25
M.E. Waugh	run out	60
S.R. Waugh	b Cronje	17
A.R. Border (capt)	b de Villiers	30
*I.A. Healy	run out	0
P.R. Reiffel	run out	2
S.K. Warne	run out	1
C.J. McDermott		
T.B.A. May		
Extras	lb 3, w 1	4
(50 overs)	(for 8 wickets)	223

SOUTH AFRICA

P.N. Kirsten	run out	14
G. Kirsten	c M.E. Waugh, b Reiffel	10
W.J. Cronje (capt)	run out	0
J.N. Rhodes	c Healy, b Warne	43
E.L.R. Stewart	b Warne	13
D.J. Callaghan	c Healy, b McDermott	30
*D.J. Richardson	not out	38
R.P. Snell	run out	6
D.B. Rundle	lbw, b May	6
P.S. de Villiers	b S.R. Waugh	15
A.A. Donald	not out	7
Extras	b 1, lb 2, w 3	6
(50 overs)	(for 9 wickets)	188

	O	M	R	W
Donald	10	1	40	1
de Villiers	10	2	41	2
Snell	10	1	34	–
Cronje	10	–	35	1
Rundle	7	–	53	1
Callaghan	3	–	17	–

	O	M	R	W
McDermott	10	1	41	1
Reiffel	9	–	32	1
S.R. Waugh	10	2	39	1
Warne	10	–	36	2
May	10	–	31	1
Border	1	–	6	–

FALL OF WICKETS
1–62, 2–112, 3–114 4–150, 5–218, 6–220, 7–221, 8–223

FALL OF WICKETS
1–21, 2 23, 3–26, 4–51, 5–110, 6–117, 7–124, 8–136, 9–166

Umpires: D.B. Hair & S.G. Randell   *Man of the Finals:* M.E. Waugh   *Australia won by 35 runs*

28, 29, 30 and 31 January 1994 *at MCG, Melbourne*

Victoria 377 for 9 dec. (D.M. Jones 145, M.T.G. Elliott
72) and 337 for 1 dec. (W.N. Phillips 156 not out,
D.M. Jones 152 not out)

South Australia 499 (G.S. Blewett 268, D.S. Lehmann
86, D.W. Fleming 4 for 130, C. Howard 4 for 144)
and 177 for 8 (D.S. Lehmann 67, D.W. Fleming 4 for
65)

Match drawn

South Australia 2 pts., Victoria 0 pts.

Dean Jones celebrated his selection for the Australian
party to tour South Africa with a century in each innings
against South Australia. He and Elliott scored 182 for the
second wicket after Victoria had won the toss, and Jones
declared on the second morning. Greg Blewett
batted throughout the South Australian innings, reaching the third century of his career and going on to make
his first double century. His 268 came from 389 balls,
included 38 fours and occupied 496 minutes. He hit a
hundred between lunch and tea on the third day, and he
and Lehmann hit 136 in 94 minutes for the fourth wicket.
Victoria responded through Jones and Phillips who
shared an unbeaten second-wicket partnership of 311 in
277 minutes. Jones' declaration allowed South Australia
142 minutes in which to score 216, a rate of 6½ an over.
Lehmann and Blewett opened, and Lehmann hit 67 off as
many deliveries. Webber followed with 35 off 28 balls but,
eventually, South Australia were happy to survive.

 THIRD TEST MATCH
AUSTRALIA v. SOUTH AFRICA,
at Adelaide

Unexpectedly finding themselves one down in the three-
match series, Australia brought back Steve Waugh for
Martyn and recalled Reiffel in place of McGrath. Neither
change was surprising. South Africa adopted a safety-
first policy, leaving out both spinners and packing their
side with batsmen. It was a tactic that deserved to fail in
the way it did.

Border won the toss, and Australia batted. The
approach was positive, and 83 came at just over a run a
minute before Slater deflected a ball from Donald onto his
helmet from where it looped to point. The dismissal was
accompanied by unnecessary gestures from the bowler.
Boon and Taylor offered their usual solidity, and Cronje
was forced to turn to the occasional off-spin of Gary
Kirsten. With his ninth ball, he claimed his first Test
wicket, and half an hour later, Boon fell to Donald. By
then Mark Waugh had gone, and Australia were in some
difficulties at 183 for 4. Steve Waugh joined Border in a
decisive partnership. By the end of the day, the score was
240, and on the second day, the pair advanced their stand
to a record 208. The previous fifth-wicket record for
Australia against South Africa had stood for 83 years, and

*Michael Slater drives through the covers in the third Test match
against South Africa. (Joe Mann/Allsport)*

the holders had been two of the great men of Australian
cricket, Victor Trumper and Warwick Armstrong.

Border had struggled for 328 minutes and hit only 3
fours, but his innings was of immense value. Steve Waugh
was at his most fluent, and his 164 came off 276 balls and
included 19 fours. Border's declaration left South Africa
an uncomfortable hour at the end of the day, but Hudson
and Gary Kirsten scored 39 without too much trouble.

The partnership was extended to exactly 100 the next
morning before the left-handed Kirsten fell to McDermott. Cronje batted painfully for a quarter of an hour
before being caught behind off Reiffel, but Peter Kirsten
joined Hudson in a grim stand which halted the Australian advance.

*Steve Waugh in all his glory – 164 in the third Test. (Joe Mann/
Allsport)*

THIRD TEST MATCH – AUSTRALIA v. SOUTH AFRICA
28, 29, 30 and 31 January, 1 February 1994 at Adelaide Oval, Adelaide

AUSTRALIA

	FIRST INNINGS		SECOND INNINGS	
M.A. Taylor	b G. Kirsten	62	(2) b Snell	38
M.J. Slater	c Rhodes, b Donald	53	(1) lbw, b Donald	7
D.C. Boon	c de Villiers, b Donald	50	c Hudson, b McMillan	38
M.E. Waugh	c Snell, b McMillan	2	c Richardson, b Donald	12
A.R. Border (capt)	c Richardson,		run out	4
	b McMillan	84		
S.R. Waugh	c Richardson, b Donald	164	c Richardson, b Snell	1
*I.A. Healy	c Rhodes, b McMillan	0	not out	14
P.R. Reiffel	not out	32	not out	2
S.K. Warne	not out	4		
C.J. McDermott				
T.B.A. May				
Extras	lb 9, nb 9	18	lb 7, nb 1	8
	(for 7 wickets, dec.)	469	(for 6 wickets, dec.)	124

SOUTH AFRICA

	FIRST INNINGS		SECOND INNINGS	
A.C. Hudson	lbw, b S. Waugh	90	(2) c S. Waugh,	
			b McDermott	2
G. Kirsten	c May, b McDermott	43	(1) b Warne	7
W.J. Cronje (capt)	c Healy, b Reiffel	0	lbw, b Warne	3
P.N. Kirsten	c M. Waugh, b Warne	79	lbw, b McDermott	42
J.N. Rhodes	b S. Waugh	5	(6) lbw, b May	4
D.J. Cullinan	b S. Waugh	10	(7) c Healy,	
			b McDermott	5
B.M. McMillan	lbw, b S. Waugh	2	(8) lbw, b Warne	4
*D.J. Richardson	lbw, b McDermott	6	(9) c Taylor, b May	10
R.P. Snell	c Healy, b McDermott	10	(10) c and b Warne	1
P.S. de Villiers	run out	4	(5) c Reiffel,	
			b McDermott	30
A.A. Donald	not out	1	not out	0
Extras	b 3, lb 10, w 1, nb 9	23	b 9, lb 7, w 2, nb 3	21
		273		129

	O	M	R	W	O	M	R	W
Donald	38	7	122	3	11	2	26	2
de Villiers	41	11	105	–				
Snell	19	6	44	–	12	3	38	2
McMillan	30	3	89	3	11	–	33	1
Cronje	9	3	21	–	6	1	20	–
G. Kirsten	23	8	62	1				
P.N. Kirsten	4	–	17	–				

	O	M	R	W	O	M	R	W
McDermott	27	9	49	3	19	8	33	4
Reiffel	15	4	36	1	11	4	15	–
May	25	9	57	–	32	20	26	2
Warne	44.2	15	85	1	30.5	15	31	4
M.E. Waugh	3	1	7	–	3	2	3	–
S.R. Waugh	18	7	26	4	6	3	4	–
Border					4	3	1	–

FALL OF WICKETS

1–83, 2–152, 3–159, 4–183, 5–391, 6–391, 7–464
1–23, 2–79, 3–91, 4–99, 5–103, 6–109

FALL OF WICKETS

1–100, 2–103, 3–173, 4–179, 5–195, 6–203, 7–222, 8–243, 9–270
1–12, 2–17, 3–18, 4–100, 5–105, 6–113, 7–116, 8–128, 9–128

Umpires: D.B. Hair & T.A. Prue

Australia won by 191 runs

Border called upon Steve Waugh as his sixth bowler, and the all-rounder immediately had Hudson leg before. He then bowled Rhodes and Cullinan and had McMillan leg before. Richardson also went leg before, to McDermott, and Peter Kirsten exchanged words with umpire Hair regarding the leg before decisions. He was fined 25% of his match fee, and he lost another 40% when he questioned the decision against himself in the second innings.

South Africa ended the third day on 235 for 7, and they soon lost Snell on the fourth morning. They had just edged past the follow-on figure when Peter Kirsten, having faced 235 balls and hit 9 fours, became Warne's only victim of the innings. The end came quickly, and Australia led by 196 runs. They sacrificed wickets in the pursuit of quick runs. It was not a particularly successful pursuit, 124 runs coming in 168 minutes from 40 overs for the loss of six wickets, but it sufficed.

Border congratulates Warne as Australia win the third Test and level the series. (Joe Mann/Allsport)

Border's declaration left South Africa 7½ hours in which to score 321, but any hopes of victory that the visitors might have had were swept away in the last 22 overs of the fourth day. After half an hour, Hudson was caught off McDermott. The last nine overs produced only one run. Gary Kirsten was strokeless before Warne bowled him with a leg-break which turned sharply, and the same bowler had Cronje leg before. South Africa tottered to the close of play at 18 for 3.

Peter Kirsten and Fanie de Villiers, who was batting with a broken thumb, played a brave rearguard action on the final day. In all, they batted for 198 minutes and scored 82, with de Villiers escaping a chance to Boon at short-leg and surviving an appeal for stumping when no television replay was available. The heroics came to an end when de Villiers drove loosely to mid-off. The walls of the South African innings now crumbled. Rhodes was adjudged leg before, and Peter Kirsten fell to McDermott and, as we have noted, left complaining. Cullinan ducked at a bouncer from McDermott but left his bat in the air and touched the ball to the wicket-keeper. It was Healy's 200th Test dismissal. McMillan fell to Warne's 'flipper', the leg-spinner's 100th Test wicket, and Richardson had already been taken at slip. Snell gave Warne a return catch so that seven wickets had gone down for 29 runs, and Australia were victors by 191 runs.

Steve Waugh was, not surprisingly, named Man of the Match.

Australia's win had earned them a draw in a series which, on reflection, they should have won with some ease.

Michael Bevan, 203 not out for New South Wales against Western Australia in Sydney and the heart of the champions' batting throughout the season. (Stephen Laffer/Sports-Line)

2, 3, 4 and 5 February 1994 *at SCG, Sydney*

Western Australia 379 (T.M. Moody 115, J. Angel 84 not out, M.R.J. Veletta 71) and 135 (G.R. Robertson 5 for 71)

New South Wales 409 (M.G. Bevan 203 not out, R.J. Davison 56, P.A. Emery 50, W.K. Wishart 4 for 90) and 106 for 1 (R. Chee Quee 50)

New South Wales won by 9 wickets

New South Wales 6 pts., Western Australia 0 pts.

New South Wales gained ample revenge for the humiliation they had suffered in Perth earlier in the season when they routed Western Australia on the last day of the return match in Sydney. Batting first, Western Australia were well served by Tom Moody who hit 115 in 237 minutes. On the second morning, Angel, who was enjoying a fine season with the ball, reached the highest score of his career, but all was overshadowed by the batting of Bevan who hit his highest first-class score, facing 409 balls and hitting 17 fours. The value of his innings was immense, for New South Wales lost their first five wickets for 180 runs before Bevan and Emery added 143. Bevan reached 1,000 runs for the season. There seemed no time left for New South Wales to force victory, but Maxwell and Robertson combined to bowl out the visitors in 208 minutes on the last day, and the Blues romped to the win

which gave them a narrow lead at the top of the Shield table.

 MERCANTILE MUTUAL CUP

5 February 1994 *at Bellerive Oval, Hobart*

Victoria 162 (C.D. Matthews 4 for 31)
Tasmania 164 for 3

Tasmania (2 pts.) won by 7 wickets

6 February 1994 *at SCG, Sydney*

Western Australia 162
New South Wales 163 for 4 (R. Chee Quee 66, M.G. Bevan 64 not out)

New South Wales (2 pts.) won by 6 wickets

at Adelaide Oval

Queensland 119
South Australia 120 for 0 (D.S. Lehmann 76 not out)

South Australia (2 pts.) won by 10 wickets

11 February 1994 *at MCG, Melbourne*

Western Australia 173 for 7
Victoria 123 (D.J. Ramshaw 52)

Western Australia (2 pts.) won by 50 runs

13 February 1994 *at MCG, Melbourne*

Victoria 183
New South Wales 184 for 6 (R.J. Davison 51)

New South Wales (2 pts.) won by 4 wickets

20 February 1994 *at SCG, Sydney*

New South Wales 225 for 8 (R. Chee Quee 55)
South Australia 218 for 7 (G.S. Blewett 80 not out)

South Australia (2 pts.) won on faster scoring rate

New South Wales sailed into the final of the Mercantile Mutual Cup when they won their first four matches with ease. It had looked as if Queensland would be their closest challengers, but they lost heavily to South Australia. Stuart Law had scored three centuries in succession, had made the fastest fifty and, with seven wickets to his credit, was the outstanding player in the competition, but he was out for a 'duck' against South Australia as Queensland took 40.3 overs to score 119. South Australia reached their target in 28 overs. Two weeks later, in Sydney, South Australia faced a score of 225, but rain reduced their target to 218 in 45 overs. They won with four balls to spare and so climbed above Queensland and Western Australia on run rate.

QUALIFYING TABLE

	P	W	L	Pts.
New South Wales	5	4	1	8
South Australia	5	3	2	6
Western Australia	5	3	2	6
Queensland	5	3	2	6
Victoria	5	1	4	2
Tasmania	5	1	4	2

10, 11, 12 and **13** February 1994 *at Bellerive Oval, Hobart*

Queensland 339 (A.J. Bichel 61 not out, G.I. Foley 52) and 208 for 9 dec. (J.P. Maher 89, C.R. Miller 4 for 56)
Tasmania 248 (S. Young 68, D. Tazelaar 5 for 49) and 293 for 6 (D.F. Hills 91, J. Cox 81, C.G. Rackemann 4 for 72)

Match drawn

Queensland 2 pts., Tasmania 0 pts.

In a spirited contest in Hobart, Tasmania narrowly failed in a brave bid to beat Queensland. Set to make 300 to win in 68 overs, Tasmania were given a roaring start by Cox

and Hills who put on 162 for the first wicket. The loss of four wickets to Rackemann, all caught behind by Seccombe, halted the progress, and although Tucker and Atkinson battled fiercely, they failed to reach the target by seven runs.

16, 17, 18 and **19** February 1994 *at SCG, Sydney*

New South Wales 391 (N.D. Maxwell 75, M.G. Bevan 67, B.E. McNamara 59, R. Chee Quee 58, S.P. George 4 for 88)
South Australia 123 (N.D. Maxwell 4 for 31) and 198 (G.S. Blewett 90, G.R. Robertson 6 for 54)

New South Wales won by an innings and 70 runs

New South Wales 6 pts., South Australia 0 pts.

17, 18, 19 and **20** February 1994 *at MCG, Melbourne*

Tasmania 444 for 9 dec. (M.J. DiVenuto 89, C.D. Matthews 75, D.J. Buckingham 71, R.J. Tucker 57, S.H. Cook 4 for 114) and 213 for 2 dec. (J. Cox 103 not out, D.F. Hills 52)
Victoria 331 (W.N. Phillips 130, B.J. Hodge 62, R.J. Tucker 4 for 56, S. Young 4 for 85) and 236 for 9 (B.J. Hodge 72, G.J. Allardice 65, S. Herzberg 4 for 66)

Match drawn

Tasmania 2 pts., Victoria 0 pts.

New South Wales assured themselves of a place in the Sheffield Shield final when they crushed South Australia in Sydney. A consistent batting performance in which Bevan reached 1,000 runs in the Shield for the season and Maxwell and McNamara added 132 for the sixth wicket put the home state in a strong position. Maxwell's 75 was his highest score in first-class cricket, and he then bowled admirably as South Australia were tumbled out for 123. Forced to follow-on, the visitors were only saved from complete indignity by Greg Blewett who hit 90 out of 178 and was sixth out. The second-innings damage was caused by Robertson who returned the best bowling figures of his career.

Tasmania kept alive their slim hopes of reaching the final by taking first-innings points against Victoria, but it was a game that they should have won. In spite of DiVenuto's innings, which included 12 fours, Tasmania lost half their side for 183, but the next three wickets realised 242 runs. Matthews and Atkinson added 110 in 113 minutes for the eighth wicket, and the left-handed Chris Matthews made 75 of the runs, the highest score of his career. The Victorian innings was a tale of two captains. Rod Tucker had the best bowling performance of his career, and Wayne Phillips, one of three men to captain Victoria during the season and leading the state for the first time, hit 130. He and Hodge, continuing to enjoy a fine debut season, put on 127 for the third wicket, but Victoria lost their last seven wickets for 50 runs, and Tasmania led by 113 runs. An opening stand of 123 between Cox and Hills consolidated Tasmania's strong position, and Cox reached the seventh century of his career off 140 balls. Tucker might have declared earlier, but he set Victoria a target of 327 in 67 overs. Only when Allardice and Hodge were sharing a third-wicket partnership of 94 did Victoria appear to have any chance of success. Once again there was a collapse, and it was left to Cook and Fleming to hold out for the last 18 minutes to save the game. Victoria introduced Steve McCooke, a right-handed batsman and off-break bowler, 34 years old, to first-class cricket.

24, 25, 26 and 27 February 1994 *at MCG, Melbourne*

Victoria 242 (I.A. Wrigglesworth 58) and 250
 (M.T.G. Elliott 113, C.G. Rackemann 4 for 38)
Queensland 275 (W.A. Seccombe 95, G.I. Foley 89,
 D.W. Fleming 5 for 61) and 214 (J.P. Maher 90,
 S.G. Law 58, S.M. McCooke 6 for 35)

Victoria won by 3 runs

Victoria 5.6 pts., Queensland 2 pts.

at WACA Ground, Perth

Western Australia 454 (J.L. Langer 233, M.R.J. Veletta
 66, M.W. Ridgway 4 for 127) and 286 for 6 dec.
 (G.R. Marsh 81, D.R. Martyn 58)

Tasmania 487 for 4 dec. (J. Cox 129, R.T. Ponting 101,
 D.J. Buckingham 100 not out) and 53 for 1

Match drawn

Tasmania 2 pts., Western Australia 0 pts.

The off-breaks of Steve McCooke brought Victoria a sensational victory over Queensland for whom the season was falling apart. Put in to bat, Victoria struggled against a varied attack in which Tazelaar and Bichel were again preferred to Kasprowicz. They were saved to some extent by Ian Wrigglesworth, a left-handed batsman and right-arm medium-pace bowler, who hit 6 fours and a six in an innings of 58 on his debut. Queensland lost their first five wickets for 79 runs before Foley and Seccombe added 183. Reserve keeper Seccombe hit a six and 12 fours in what was the highest score of his career. Both men were dismissed by Wrigglesworth who took 3 for 72 while Fleming had five wickets in an innings for the fifth time. This could not prevent Queensland from taking a first-innings lead of 33. Elliott's second century and Rackemann's 500th first-class wicket were the main features of Victoria's second innings, and it seemed that Queensland had a comfortable task in being left more than a day in which to score 218 to win. At 134 for 3, with Law and Maher batting comfortably, a Queensland victory seemed assured. Then Berry stumped Law off McCooke, and 14 runs later Foley suffered the same fate. McCooke had Seccombe caught, and Hodge ran out Bichel. Tazelaar was stumped, Jackson caught, and when Rackemann joined Maher 15 were still needed. Eleven had been scored, nine of them by Maher, before McCooke ended Maher's 244-minute innings by bowling him with a well flighted off-break.

In Perth, Western Australia failed to take a point against Tasmania in spite of the fact that Justin Langer hit the highest score of his career, 233 off 314 balls in 408 minutes. The left-handed Langer, chosen for Australia's squad to go to Sharjah, hit a six and 27 fours. He shared a second-wicket stand of 142 with Veletta and reached 1,000 runs for the season. Medium-pace bowler Mark Ridgway had the best figures of his brief career with Tasmania who were 92 for 2 in reply to the home state's 454. Cox and Ponting then added 181 for the third wicket, and with Young and Buckingham sharing an unbroken partnership of 163 for the fifth wicket, Tasmania took first-innings points, and the game moved inevitably to a draw.

 MERCANTILE MUTUAL CUP QUALIFYING FINAL

5 March 1994 *at Adelaide Oval*

Western Australia 248 for 7 (T.M. Moody 69, D.R.
 Martyn 50 not out)
South Australia 197

Western Australia won by 51 runs

Man of the Match in the Mercantile Mutual Cup final – Richard Chee Quee. (Stephen Laffer/Sports-Line)

MERCANTILE MUTUAL CUP FINAL – NEW SOUTH WALES *v.* WESTERN AUSTRALIA
12 March 1994 at SCG, Sydney

NEW SOUTH WALES			WESTERN AUSTRALIA		
R. Chee Quee	b Martyn	131	T.M. Moody	c Alley, b Maxwell	12
M.T. Haywood	run out	4	G.R. Marsh (capt)	lbw, b Holdsworth	11
M.G. Bevan	c Martyn, b Angel	77	J.L. Langer	c Maxwell, b Lee	65
T.H. Bayliss	not out	36	D.R. Martyn	c McNamara, b Alley	0
S. Lee	b Martyn	4	M.R.J. Veletta	lbw, b McNamara	1
N.D. Maxwell	not out	7	G.B. Hogg	run out	5
B.E. McNamara			B.P. Julian	c Lee, b Robertson	19
*P.A. Emery (capt)			*T.J. Zoehrer	b McNamara	61
G.R. Robertson			M.P. Atkinson	c Maxwell, b Robertson	10
P.J.S. Alley			J. Angel	not out	19
W.J. Holdsworth			J. Stewart	not out	1
Extras	lb 5	5	Extras	lb 9, w 1, nb 4	14
(50 overs)	(for 4 wickets)	264	(49 overs)	(for 9 wickets)	218

	O	M	R	W		O	M	R	W
Angel	10	–	40	1	Holdsworth	10	–	39	1
Atkinson	10	–	47	–	Maxwell	6	–	23	1
Julian	10	–	42	–	McNamara	10	–	39	2
Moody	6	–	46	–	Alley	10	–	34	1
Stewart	10	–	53	–	Robertson	10	–	56	2
Martyn	4	–	31	2	Lee	3	–	18	1

FALL OF WICKETS
1–13, 2–212, 3–226, 4–242

FALL OF WICKETS
1–16, 2–39, 3–43, 4–52, 5–73, 6–109, 7–126, 8–172, 9–209.

Umpires: D.B. Hair & S.G. Randell   *Man of the Match:* R. Chee Quee   *New South Wales won on faster scoring rate*

From the point when Marsh and Moody began the Western Australia innings with a partnership of 91, there only looked to be one winner in the match to see who would play New South Wales in the final. The nearest Western Australia came to disaster was when four wickets fell in quick succession towards the end of their 50 overs. Lehmann began with a furious burst of scoring, 20 out of 23, but once he had fallen to Angel, and Blewett and Nobes had gone within 12 runs of each other, the contest was over. Moody took the individual award, taking 1 for 33 as well as scoring 69.

MERCANTILE MUTUAL CUP FINAL
NEW SOUTH WALES *v.* WESTERN
AUSTRALIA, at Sydney

New South Wales outplayed Western Australia in the final to retain the trophy. Dropped twice, Richard Chee Quee hit 131 off 146 balls to set his side on a rate of scoring which Western Australia could never hope to emulate. The visitors were destroyed by the right-hand/left-hand combination of Chee Quee and Bevan which produced 199 for the second wicket. Bevan hit 77 from 104 deliveries, and 57 of his runs came in singles which caused havoc among the Western Australian fielders.

Langer and, belatedly, Zoehrer were the only Western Australian batsmen to suggest that they could reach the run rate of more than five an over. A brief shower reduced Western's target to 262 in 49 overs.

17, 18, 19 and **20** March 1994 *at WACA Ground, Perth*

Victoria 118 and 155 (G.J. Allardice 53, B.A. Reid 5 for 34)

Western Australia 112 (D.W. Fleming 5 for 34, S.H. Cook 4 for 41) and 162 for 7 (S.H. Cook 4 for 43)

Western Australia won by 3 wickets

Western Australia 6 pts., Victoria 1.4 pts.

at SCG, Sydney

New South Wales 412 for 6 dec. (S. Lee 104 not out, R. J. Davison 81, B.E. McNamara 51, D.A. Freedman 50, M.G. Bevan 50) and 207 for 4 dec. (M.G. Bevan 69 not out)

Queensland 200 (N.D. Maxwell 4 for 45) and 368 (S.G. Law 108, G.I. Foley 68)

New South Wales won by 51 runs

New South Wales 6 pts., Queensland 0 pts.

at Adelaide Oval

South Australia 489 (G.S. Blewett 214, D.S. Lehmann
157, P.C. Nobes 54, C.R. Miller 5 for 82) and 246 for
6 dec. (G.S. Blewett 80, M.P. Faull 66)

Tasmania 370 for 5 dec. (D.F. Hills 114, J. Cox 98,
R.T. Ponting 84 not out) and 366 for 6 (R.T. Ponting
161, D.F. Hills 126, P.E. McIntyre 4 for 97)

Tasmania won by 4 wickets

Tasmania 6 pts., South Australia 2 pts.

The last round of matches in the Sheffield Shield arrived
with any one of the other five states still finding it possible
to qualify to meet New South Wales in the final. Western
Australia became the first to stake their claim when they
beat Victoria inside three days on a WACA pitch far different from the one on which they had played Tasmania.
In his 100th Shield match, Geoff Marsh won the toss and
asked Victoria to bat. The first day, in fact, saw both sides
complete their first innings with the pace men revelling in
the conditions. Hodge (43), Marsh (42), and Angel (24 not
out) were the only batsmen to reach 20. Leading by six
runs on the first innings, Victoria were boosted by a
second-wicket stand of 73 between Phillips and Allardice
when they batted again. When Ramshaw was out at 124,
however, Reid took over, capturing the last five wickets
as 31 runs were scored. For the tall left-arm bowler, the
season ended on a note of hope that he could be on the
way to a full recovery after his constant back problems.
Needing 162 to win, Western Australia ended the second
day on 119 for 5. Angel and Zoehrer went quickly the next
morning, but Julian adopted the belligerent approach,
hitting 21 off 22 balls and, with Hogg, he took the home
state to victory. They could only rue the penalty points
that had been deducted from them for their slow over rate
against South Australia in the drawn game at Adelaide.

Not unexpectedly, New South Wales crushed Queensland and condemned them to bottom place. Chee Quee
went early, but Davison and Bevan added 100, and then
Lee, who hit a maiden first-class century, and Freedman,
his first fifty in first-class cricket coming in two hours, put
on 116 for the sixth wicket. Queensland were bowled out
by the end of the second day, but Emery did not enforce
the follow-on. Law hit a defiant century when Queensland went in search of 420 for victory, but Maxwell, seven
wickets in the match, and the spinners were always on
top.

The most dramatic events occurred in Adelaide.
Siddons won the toss, and South Australia batted. Greg
Blewett hit his second double century in three matches,
reached 1,000 runs for the season, and, with Darren
Lehmann, who also reached 1,000 runs, he established a
new third-wicket Sheffield Shield record for South
Australia of 286, the runs coming at one a minute. Miller,
who had been unable to command a regular place earlier
in the season, bowled manfully, but the South Australian
innings did not end until the second afternoon. Tasmania responded with panache, for both sides needed a
maximum six points to have any hope of qualifying for

*Outstanding all-round cricket from Neil Maxwell was an important
reason for New South Wales' dominance of domestic competitions in
Australia. (Stephen Laffer/Sports-Line)*

the final. By the end of the second day, they were 209
without loss, and although Cox added only one to his
overnight score before being bowled by McIntyre, Tasmania continued to attack, and Tucker declared 119 runs
in arrears.

In three hours, in under 50 overs, South Australia hit
246 for 6, and Siddons' declaration left Tasmania the last
day in which to score 366 or, more positively, his own
bowlers a day in which to bowl their side into the
Sheffield Shield final. When Cox went at 2, and DiVenuto
at 35, it seemed that South Australia would win. By lunch,
Ponting and Hills had taken the score to 112. Between
lunch and tea, they added another 153, and when Ponting was finally caught off McIntyre for 161, the highest
score of his career, the partnership was worth 290, a
Tasmanian record for any wicket. The runs had come in
243 minutes. Only 13 runs were scored as Young, Tucker
and Hills followed Ponting back to the pavilion, but
Atkinson found a good partner in Farrell, and it was
Farrell who made the winning hit to bring an historic
victory with 4.3 overs remaining.

SHEFFIELD SHIELD – FINAL TABLE

	P	W	L	D	Pts.
New South Wales	10	6	3	1	37.8
Tasmania	10	3	1	6	24
Western Australia	10	3	3	4	23.8
South Australia	10	2	5	3	22
Victoria	10	3	3	4	21
Queensland	10	2	4	4	18

SHEFFIELD SHIELD FINAL
NEW SOUTH WALES v. TASMANIA,
at Sydney

Tasmania's feat in reaching the final for the first time was a mighty one, but the final itself was disappointingly one-sided with Tasmania unable to find the inspiration that had carried them through the season with such energy and enthusiasm. They were not aided, perhaps, by their selection decision. Still in a state of euphoria over the great win against South Australia, they chose an unchanged side. This meant that Brian Robinson, an off-break bowler and left-handed batsman, who made his first-class debut against South Australia was picked ahead of Scott Herzberg who had enjoyed several successes during the season and, more significantly, that no place was found for the reliable Danny Buckingham. Buckingham had missed the game in Adelaide through injury, but he had proved his fitness in a club game, and his omission was surely an error of judgement.

Choosing to bat first, Tasmania were quickly struggling at 52 for 4. Young, who batted for 3¼ hours, and Tucker repaired some of the damage, and at the close, they were 230 for 6. The innings was soon ended on the second morning, and New South Wales then began their long grinding innings. There was polish in the batting of Bevan and Haywood, but McNamara's maiden first-class hundred occupied a minute under seven hours, and he faced 339 balls for his 128. New South Wales batted until the fourth morning although it must be granted that time was lost to rain. Tired and dispirited, Tasmania were bowled out in 3¾ hours, and New South Wales were Sheffield Shield champions for the 42nd time.

A condemnation of first-class cricket in Australia is that David Boon, Tasmania's elected captain, was not available for a single Shield match because of international commitments. This cannot be offered as an excuse for their failure, for the strength of New South Wales is awesome. Five of their players, Taylor, Slater, the Waugh twins and McGrath, were on tour with the Australian side in South Africa and were therefore unavailable for the later stages of the competition. Holdsworth, the leading wicket-taker of the previous season, had lost form and was twelfth man. Greg Matthews had been out of favour since the night-club incident in Perth which had put him in hospital, and Mike Whitney had retired after one match at the beginning of the season. Only three players who had appeared in the Shield final in 1993 were in the side which won the Shield final in 1994. In the words of Greg Baum of the Australian *Cricketer*, 'It is time to recognise New South Wales as the most durable phenomenon in Australian sport.'

SHEFFIELD SHIELD FINAL – NEW SOUTH WALES v. TASMANIA
25, 26, 27, 28 and 29 March 1994 at SCG, Sydney

TASMANIA

	FIRST INNINGS		SECOND INNINGS	
D.F. Hills	c Emery, b McNamara	20	c Chee Quee,	
			b Robertson	17
J. Cox	c McNamara, b Maxwell	23	lbw, b Maxwell	11
M.J. DiVenuto	c Emery, b Maxwell	4	b Alley	27
R.T. Ponting	b McNamara	1	c Davison, b Alley	28
S. Young	b Alley	62	b Maxwell	9
R.J. Tucker (capt)	run out	49	(7) c Emery, b Alley	2
*M.N. Atkinson	run out	44	(8) not out	3
M.G. Farrell	c Maxwell, b McNamara	18	(9) c McNamara,	
			b Maxwell	1
C.D. Matthews	c Emery, b Maxwell	0	(10) b Alley	5
B. Robinson	not out	1	(6) c Emery, b Maxwell	0
C.R. Miller	c Bevan, b McNamara	4	c McNamara, b Alley	10
Extras	b 4, lb 5, w 8, nb 12	29	b 2, lb 1, w 8, nb 2	13
		255		126

NEW SOUTH WALES

	FIRST INNINGS	
R. Chee Quee	c Ponting, b Tucker	43
R.J. Davison	c Atkinson, b Matthews	5
M.G. Bevan	b Young	113
M.T. Haywood	c Cox, b Matthews	73
S. Lee	c DiVenuto, b Young	0
B.E. McNamara	lbw, b Robinson	128
N.D. Maxwell	c Ponting, b Young	15
*P.A. Emery (capt)	c Atkinson, b Tucker	2
G.R. Robertson	b Robinson	5
D.A. Freedman	run out	5
P.J.S. Alley	not out	17
Extras	b 4, lb 15, w 1, nb 16	36
		442

	O	M	R	W	O	M	R	W
Alley	19	3	51	1	12.2	4	24	5
Lee	10	1	49	–				
Maxwell	32	12	61	3	21	3	50	4
McNamara	24.2	13	24	4	8	4	15	–
Robertson	20	6	42	–	16	5	34	1
Freedman	6	–	19	–				

	O	M	R	W
Miller	36	10	99	–
Matthews	40	12	99	2
Young	36	14	65	3
Tucker	28	13	47	2
Robinson	44.3	19	84	2
Farrell	12	3	26	–
Ponting	1	–	3	–

FALL OF WICKETS
1–47, 2–51, 3–52, 4–52, 5–152, 6–201, 7–243, 8–246, 9–249
1–17, 2–43, 3–80, 4–89, 5–92, 6–103, 7–105, 8–107, 9–116

FALL OF WICKETS
1–30, 2–77, 3–229, 4–233, 5–269, 6–311, 7–337, 8–360, 9–383

Umpires: D.B. Hair, T.A. Prue & S.G. Randell

New South Wales won by an innings and 61 runs

NEW SOUTH WALES
FIRST-CLASS MATCHES 1993–4

BATTING

	v. New Zealanders (Newcastle) 29 Oct.–1 Nov. 1993	v. Queensland (Brisbane) 4–7 November 1993	v. Victoria (Melbourne) 19–22 November 1993	v. Tasmania (Sydney) 25–8 November 1993	v. Western Australia (Perth) 10–11 December 1993	v. Victoria (Sydney) 18–21 December 1993	v. South Australia (Adelaide) 31 Dec. 1993–3 Jan. 1994	v. Tasmania (Hobart) 7–10 January 1994	v. Western Australia (Sydney) 2–5 February 1994	v. South Australia (Sydney) 16–19 February 1994
M.A. Taylor	26 30	19 –	6 50			28 14				
M.J. Slater	16 19	17 28	77 4			1 19		24 107		
S.R. Waugh	88 4	43 11*	1 122				73 46	190* 17		
M.E. Waugh	63 1	61 85	58 24			119 23				
M.G. Bevan	55 17	20 29*	0 9	141 14	11 50	2 81	103 89	71 117*	203* 1*	67
G.R.J. Matthews	31* 7		2 30*	55* 40						
B.E. McNamara	9 7	40 –	28 0	10 18	0 6	44 7	12 47		0 –	59 –
P.A. Emery	0 2	30 –	8 –	24* 13	4 33*	31 3	35 4	4 –	50 –	2 –
P.J.S. Alley	3 19	0 –			– –	0 1	0 3*	8 –		19 –
G.D. McGrath	3* 0*	6* –	0 –			0 0*				
M.R. Whitney	– –									
G.R. Robertson		85 –			18* 6	14 0	28* 8	42 –	24 –	18*
W.J. Holdsworth		34 –	23 5	– 0	7 6	3 21	5* 1	1 –	0 –	1 –
D.A. Freedman			12* –						5 –	1 –
R. Chee Quee				69 17	17 0	8 76	0 47	1 6	32 50	58 –
R.J. Davison				18 133*	0 21		56 5		56 49*	16 –
A.C. Gilchrist				0 19	1 20				3 –	
N.D. Maxwell				– 0	8 0		61 42	35 30*	0 –	75 –
A.E. Tucker				– 7		25* 19*		8 36	0 –	
R.J. Green					4 32			8 15		17 –
S. Lee									7 –	
M.T. Haywood										39 –
Byes		1	2 11	1 6		4 4	4 2	1	14 4	6
Leg-byes	3 3	19 3	6 3	5 3	1	1	4 6	6 1	2 2	4
Wides			2			1	2 1	1 1	1	2
No-balls	2	8	4 8	30 4	2 2	4 6	4	6 2	12	8
Total	299 109	382 157	227 268	353 274	73 177	283 275	395 337	398 296	409 106	391
Wickets	8 9†	10 2	10 9	5 9	10 10	10 9	9 10	10 4	10 1	10
Result	L	W	L	W	L	D	W	L	W	W
Points		6	0	6	−0.2	2	6	0	6	6

† M.R. Whitney absent injured

BOWLING

	G.D. McGrath	M.R. Whitney	B.E. McNamara	P.J.S. Alley	M.E. Waugh	G.R.J. Matthews	S.R. Waugh	M.G. Bevan
v. New Zealanders (Newcastle) 29 October–1 November 1993	18-8-26-1, 24.2-6-53-2	6-4-4-1	14-5-29-3, 16-6-37-2	9-2-43-0, 24-4-62-0	2-0-2-0, 13.5-6-20-1	15.5-4-52-4, 28.1-5-67-2	5-1-6-0	1-0-3-0
v. Queensland (Brisbane) 4–7 November 1993	28-13-50-2, 21-5-54-2		5.1-0-29-1, 8-3-17-0	18-5-45-4, 13-4-38-1			4-1-15-1, 15-5-40-1	
v. Victoria (Melbourne) 19–22 November 1993	14-3-27-0, 19-4-46-2		18-6-43-6, 17-4-46-0		13.4-4-24-2, 9-3-17-1	19.3-5-59-1, 18-2-53-1	3-0-15-0, 5-2-5-0	
v. Tasmania (Sydney) 25–8 November 1993			8-2-18-0	21-4-66-0, 5-0-21-1	11-4-20-1	50.5-16-99-7, 28-8-82-4		
v. Western Australia (Perth) 10–11 December 1993			4-1-12-0	24-4-101-5				4-2-22-0
v. Victoria (Sydney) 18–21 December 1993	21-7-60-4, 27-8-59-2				7-3-16-0, 12-1-38-1			5-1-10-0
v. South Australia (Adelaide) 31 December 1993–3 January 1994				16-1-82-1, 14-2-64-1				
v. Tasmania (Hobart) 7–10 January 1994				27-3-84-3, 14-1-71-1			4-0-26-0, 2-0-12-0	14-2-44-1, 1-0-7-0
v. Western Australia (Sydney) 2–5 February 1994			13-2-27-0, 4-3-5-0					
v. South Australia (Sydney) 16–19 February 1994			3-0-9-1, 8-4-10-0	13-5-45-3, 16-6-39-2				
v. Queensland (Sydney) 17–20 March 1994			15-4-42-1, 24.2-13-24-4	16-5-51-2, 17-3-57-0				4-0-16-0
v. Tasmania (Sydney) 25–9 March 1994			8-4-15-0	19-3-51-1, 12.2-4-24-5				
Bowler's average	172.2-54-375-15, 25.00	6-4-4-1, 4.00	165.3-57-363-18, 20.16	278.2-56-944-30, 31.46	68.3-21-137-6, 22.83	160.2-40-412-19, 21.68	38-9-119-2, 59.50	29-5-102-1, 102.00

Batting

v. Queensland (Sydney) 17–20 March 1994		v. Tasmania (Sydney) 25–9 March 1994		M	Inns	NO	Runs	HS	Av
				4	7	–	173	50	24.71
				5	10	–	312	107	31.20
				5	10	2	595	190*	74.37
				4	8	–	434	119	54.25
50	69*	113	–	12	22	5	1312	203*	77.17
				3	6	3	165	55*	55.00
51	10	128	–	11	18	–	476	128	26.44
–	13*	2	–	12	17	3	258	50	18.42
–	–	17*	–	9	10	2	70	19	8.75
				4	6	4	9	6*	4.50
				1					–
–	–	5	–	9	11	3	248	85	31.00
				8	12	1	106	34	9.63
50	–	5	–	5	5	1	73	50	18.25
6	40	43	–	9	16	–	470	76	29.37
81	42	5	–	7	12	2	482	133*	48.20
				3	5	–	43	20	8.60
12*	4	15	–	8	12	2	282	75	28.20
				4	6	2	95	36	23.75
				2	4	–	59	32	14.75
104*	17*	0	–	4	5	2	145	104*	48.33
29	–	73	–	3	3	–	141	73	47.00
1		4							
5	4	15							
1		1							
22	8	16							
412	207	442							
6	4	10							
W		W							
6		–							

FIELDING FIGURES

43 – P.A. Emery (ct 39/st 4)
10 – R.J. Davison and N.D. Maxwell
9 – P.J.S. Alley
8 – R. Chee Quee
6 – M.A. Taylor, M.G. Bevan, G.R.J. Matthews and B.E. McNamara (plus one as sub)
4 – M.J. Slater
3 – S.R. Waugh, M.E. Waugh, G.R. Robertson and W.J. Holdsworth (plus one as sub)
2 – G.D. McGrath, A.C. Gilchrist and S. Lee
1 – A.E. Tucker

Bowling

W.J. Holdsworth	G.R. Robertson	D.A. Freedman	N.D. Maxwell	A.E. Tucker	R.J. Green	S. Lee	Byes	Leg-byes	Wides	No-balls	Total	Wkts
								1	1	5	163	10
							1	4		5	247	7
20–4–69–1	12–1–45–1						1	3	18	2	257	10
15–3–39–2	23–8–59–1						1	9		14	281	10
19–5–39–2		6–0–22–0					5	6	1	6	233	10
15.3–1–59–2		6–0–19–2					5	10	1	2	263	9
22–3–68–1			6–2–21–0	25–9–62–1			4	5		10	343	10
9–1–36–1			2–0–3–0	21.5–4–64–4			2	7		4	215	10
29.4–3–142–1	28–2–119–0		22–2–77–1				14	16	1	22	503	8
18.5–5–73–3	16–3–36–1			25–9–71–2			1	7		6	264	10
18–4–57–2	19–4–67–0			19–2–82–1			9	2	1		324	6
28–5–127–2	31–9–83–3		22–5–82–1	19–4–81–0			4	6		32	465	8
5–1–18–1	26.5–12–43–5		8–3–27–3				4	2	2	20	158	10
23–7–67–0	20–9–35–0		25.5–7–82–2	13–3–39–0	1–1–0–0		7	17	3	14	401	6
5–0–39–0	30–8–68–2		3–0–20–0	21–3–74–2				3		6	294	6
28–8–62–2	35–8–103–1	26–3–47–3	17.3–3–47–3			18–1–54–1		3	2	16	379	10
4.2–1–6–0	27–6–71–5		14–8–21–3			5–1–21–1	5	6		4	135	10
	2–0–11–0		8–0–31–4			6–0–26–2		1	1	14	123	10
	23.4–4–54–6	19–5–49–2	12–4–20–0			5–1–23–0	2	1		10	198	10
	11–3–17–1	15.2–5–39–2	11–0–45–4			9–1–43–1		5	1	18	200	10
	39–5–111–3	16.4–3–48–1	17–3–54–3			7–2–29–0	5	6	4	8	368	10
	20–6–42–0	6–0–19–0	32–12–61–3			10–1–49–0	4	5	8	12	255	10
	16–5–34–1		21–3–50–4				2	1	6	2	126	10
260.2–51–901–20 45.05	379.3–93–998–30 33.26	95–16–279–8 34.87	221.2–52–641–31 20.67	143.5–34–473–10 47.30	1–1–0–0 –	60–7–245–5 49.00						

QUEENSLAND FIRST-CLASS MATCHES 1993-4

BATTING

	v. South Australia (Brisbane) 21-4 October 1993		v. Western Australia (Perth) 29 Oct.-1 Nov. 1993		v. New South Wales (Brisbane) 4-7 November 1993		v. South Australia (Adelaide) 25-8 November 1993		v. South Africans (Brisbane) 20-3 December 1993		v. Tasmania (Brisbane) 31 Dec. 1993-3 Jan 1994		v. Victoria (Brisbane) 13-16 January 1994		v. Western Australia (Brisbane) 19-22 January 1994		v. Tasmania (Hobart) 10-13 February 1994		v. Victoria (Melbourne) 24-7 February 1994	
T.J. Barsby	10	116	82	34	46	12	79	129	15	99	10	17	44	58	46	0	4	4	29	15
M.L. Hayden	125	1	23	96*	9	173*	165	116			26	121*	126	155						
D.M. Wellham	34	1	20	18*	21	2														
S.G. Law	24	100	33	–	3	1	5	38	56	33	43	6	4	76	118	1	2	24	5	58
A.R. Border	10	125*	65	–	85	11			6	–										
M.L. Love	18	56*	0	–	11	29			5	6	20	138	50	28	21	119	27	0		
I.A. Healy	46	–	79	–	6	21			41	5*										
C.J. McDermott	28	–	61	–	11	3			16	–										
M.S. Kasprowicz	14	–	20	–			0	–	2	–	35	–	0	–	7	33				
P.W. Jackson	3	–	0	–	5	0	19	–	1*	–	16*	3	19	–	4*	4*	0	–	0	0
C.G. Rackemann	20*	–	4*	–	13*	0	0*	–			20	–	4*	–	1	–	33	0	0*	2*
G.J. Rowell					23	5	1		17	16	2	–								
G.I. Foley							9	43*	18	39	10	45	0	2	12	6	52	31	89	5
J.P. Maher							19	5	1	50*	19	2	70	1	1	122	43	89	1	90
D.R. Kingdon							3	4*												
P.W. Anderson							0	–												
S.C. Storey																				
W.A. Seccombe											11	–	3	5*	3	1*	37	28	95	6
A.J. Bichel													6	–	3	37	61*	6	4	0
J.M. Thomas															19	30	38	18	34	19
D. Tazelaar																	11	2*	0	6
T.J. Dixon																			6	3
Byes	5	1			1	1				4	4				8	1	7	2	4	4
Leg-byes	7	4	12	2	3	9	4	9	2	9	9	3	7	5	2	5	7	6	2	6
Wides		2	1		2				1						1		6		4	
No-balls	8	10	30	8	18	14	26	2	3	7	24	4	6		6	10	16		2	
Total	352	416	430	158	257	281	330	351	183	268	245	339	347	331	244	375	339	208	275	214
Wickets	10	4	10	1	10	10	10	4	10	5	10	6	10	6	10	8	10	9	10	10
Result	D		W		L		L		D		D		W		D		D		L	
Points	0		6		0		0		–		2		6		0		2		2	

BOWLING

	C.J. McDermott	M.S. Kasprowicz	C.G. Rackemann	S.G. Law	P.W. Jackson	A.R. Border	G.J. Rowell	A.J. Bichel
v. South Australia (Brisbane) 21-4 October 1993	41-15-111-4	33-8-125-1	36-7-106-0	15-5-58-1	39-10-90-4	7-1-24-0		
v. Western Australia (Perth) 29 October-1 November 1993	22-6-62-5	13-1-40-0	15-4-57-3	9-2-25-0		8.5-1-24-1		
	33-7-96-2	31-9-84-0	36-11-93-6		34.3-13-61-1	15-5-33-1		
v. New South Wales (Brisbane) 4-7 November 1993	38-15-86-2		30-7-91-1	1-0-3-0	38.2-10-86-4	18-9-22-1	29-10-75-2	
	9-0-35-1		3-0-18-0	3.5-0-16-0	7-1-31-1	3-0-21-0	6-1-32-0	
v. South Australia (Adelaide) 25-8 November 1993		30-7-92-2	28-7-71-0	7-1-16-2	41-16-89-2	3-0-21-0	26-3-101-2	
		9.4-1-39-1	6-0-35-0	17-3-42-3	8-0-50-0		6-0-29-0	
v. South Africans (Brisbane) 20-3 December 1993	24-4-58-0	26-6-92-5		6-3-17-0	22-3-72-1		24-2-81-1	
	9-2-26-1	10-1-42-2		7-0-22-1	26-8-67-2	17-6-23-1	15-4-30-0	
v. Tasmania (Brisbane) 31 December 1993-3 January 1994		21-6-56-4	17-5-37-2	3-1-10-0	12-3-35-1		21-6-44-1	
		24-3-80-0	27-5-81-3	3-0-20-0	38-15-55-1		16-3-65-1	
v. Victoria (Brisbane) 13-16 January 1994		22-3-76-4	19-5-50-1	2.5-1-2-1	24-7-53-0			25-6-69-4
		16-3-49-1	11.5-3-32-5	6-1-12-1	15-1-56-2			10-3-50-1
v. Western Australia (Brisbane) 19-22 January 1994		27-7-69-0	25-6-59-2	5-1-13-0	40.2-9-118-3			17-3-86-1
v. Tasmania (Hobart) 10-13 February 1994			26-8-67-1	1-0-9-0	29-8-61-1			13-5-31-3
			19-3-72-4	10-2-44-0	12-1-53-1			8-3-31-0
v. Victoria (Melbourne) 24-7 February 1994			19-5-57-3	5-1-12-0	27-5-75-3			18-7-52-2
			16.3-6-38-4	10-2-23-1	17-3-49-0			20-7-62-0
v. New South Wales (Sydney) 17-20 March, 1994			32-5-94-2	4-0-27-0	27-10-83-0			26-5-89-3
			13-3-39-1	8-1-20-0	8-2-12-0			12-1-29-1
Bowler's average	176-49-474-15 31.60	262.4-55-844-20 42.40	379.2-90-1097-38 28.86	123.4-24-391-10 39.10	474-126-1220-28 43.57	60-21-123-3 41.00	143-29-457-7 65.28	149-40-499-15 33.26

A   M.R.J. Veletta retired hurt

v. New South Wales (Sydney) 17–20 March 1994		M	Inns	NO	Runs	HS	Av
15	36	11	22	–	900	129	40.90
		6	12	3	1136	173*	126.22
		3	6	1	96	34	19.20
9	108	11	21	–	747	118	35.57
		4	6	1	302	125*	60.40
19	24	9	17	1	571	138	35.68
		4	6	1	198	79	39.60
		4	5	–	119	61	23.80
		7	8	–	111	35	13.87
2	18*	11	16	5	94	19	8.54
13	26	10	14	7	136	33	19.42
		4	6	–	64	23	10.66
15	68	8	16	1	444	89	29.60
0	44	8	16	1	557	122	37.13
		1	2	1	7	4*	7.00
		1	1	–	0	0	0.00
0	0	1	2	–	0	0	0.00
37	4	6	11	2	230	95	25.55
47	17	5	9	1	181	61*	22.62
		3	6	–	158	38	26.33
19*	0	3	6	2	38	19*	9.50
		1	2	–	9	6	4.50
	5						
5	6						
1	4						
18	8						
200	368						
10	10						
L							
0							

FIELDING FIGURES

30 – W.A. Seccombe (ct 29/st 1)
14 – I.A. Healy (ct 12/st 2)
11 – S.G. Law
10 – M.L. Love
7 – J.P. Maher and T.J. Barsby
6 – M.L. Hayden and G.I. Foley
5 – G.J. Rowell (plus one as sub)
4 – A.J. Bichel
3 – P.W. Jackson, P.W. Anderson and J.M. Thomas
2 – D.M. Wellham, A.R. Border and M.S. Kasprowicz
1 – C.J. McDermott, D.R. Kingdon and D. Tazelaar

G.I. Foley	J.P. Maher	D. Tazelaar	S.C. Storey	Byes	Leg-byes	Wides	No-balls	Total	Wkts	
				6	2		20	522	10	
				1	2		20	211	10	
					6		49	373	10	
					19		8	382	10	
				1	3			157	2	
7.4–1–28–2				14	9	1	16	420	10	
10–0–49–1				3	15		6	262	5	
1–0–4–0	3–0–10–0				1		12	335	7	
4–1–10–1					4		7	224	8	
2–1–7–1					1		18	190	7	
9–4–18–0				1	9		22	329	7	
5–2–14–0				2	6		14	272	10	
				2	11	1	12	212	10	
21–3–64–3					4	1	14	413	9	A
11–2–17–0		29.2–12–49–5		11	3		18	248	10	
2–0–18–0		17–5–63–1		3	9	2	8	293	6	
1–0–5–0		17.4–7–36–2		3	2	1	16	242	10	
7–2–17–1		24–7–54–3		2	5	1	14	250	10	
6–0–23–1		28–9–63–0	7–0–27–0	1	5	1	22	412	6	
10–2–44–1		12–2–28–0	9–0–31–1		4		8	207	4	
96.4–18–	3–0–	128–42–	16–0–							
318–11	10–0	293–11	58–1							
28.90	–	26.63	58.00							

SOUTH AUSTRALIA — FIRST-CLASS MATCHES 1993-4

BATTING

	v. Queensland (Brisbane) 21-4 October 1993		v. Victoria (Adelaide) 27-30 October 1993		v. New Zealanders (Adelaide) 19-22 November 1993		v. Queensland (Adelaide) 25-8 November 1993		v. Western Australia (Perth) 18-20 December 1993		v. New South Wales (Adelaide) 31 Dec. 1993-3 Jan. 1994		v. Western Australia (Adelaide) 7-10 January 1994		v. Tasmania (Hobart) 18-21 January 1994		v. Victoria (Melbourne) 28-31 January 1994		v. New South Wales (Sydney) 16-19 February 1994	
G.S. Blewett	4	–	34	7	47	49	8	21*	23	0	93	26	0	–	51	–	268	14	7	90
P.C. Nobes	7	–	141	63*	0	17	140	106	2	7	78	0	18	–	16	18	43	8	25	18
J.A. Brayshaw	29	–	134	54*	16	94	9	7	0	39	36	16	146	–	47	37	21	15	7	37
J.D. Siddons	4	–	5	–			46	8	20	129	64	31	11	–	161	89*	46	5	10	0
D.S. Lehmann	128	–	1	–	6	16	38	50	20	7	85	15	200	–	137	18	86	67	6	13
D.S. Webber	176	–	47	–	3	10	100	29	58	23	2	30	7	–	7	44*	8	35	2	0
T.J. Nielsen	26	–	18	–	17	8	15	17*	4	33	34*	0	0	–	3	–	2	18	29	8
J.C. Scuderi	54	–			51	0													2	7
T.B.A. May	13*	–	8	–	3	13			0	2										
S.P. George	50	–	0	–			4	–	9	1	1	0	1	–	30	–	0*	–	17	7
B.N. Wigney	3	–	13*	–	0	7	0	–	0*	0*	3*	0							1*	1*
P.E. McIntyre			4	–	3*	–	6*	–			–	12*	19*	–	0	–	0	4*	1	4
D.A. Reeves					5	40*	14	–	21	27					5	–	16	0		
D.J. Marsh											27	0	22	–	48*	–	0	0*		
M.A. Harrity																				
M.P. Faull																				
M.J. Minigall																				
Byes	6						14	3	2	5	4	4	1		4		3			2
Leg-byes	2		9	1	2	3	9	15	2	6	6	2	4		7	3	4	11	1	1
Wides					2		1		4				2		3		1			
No-balls	20		16	2	3	3	16	6	14	4	32	20	8				2		14	10
Total	522		430	127	158	260	420	262	179	283	465	158	437		519	209	499	177	123	198
Wickets	10		10	1	10	9	10	5	10	10	8	10	10		10	3	10	8	10	10
Result	D		W		L		W		L		L		D		L		D		L	
Points	2		6		–		6		0		2		0		2		2		0	

BOWLING

	S.P. George	B.N. Wigney	T.B.A. May	J.C. Scuderi	D.S. Lehmann	G.S. Blewett	J.A. Brayshaw	P.C. Nobes
v. Queensland (Brisbane) 21-4 October 1993	27-4-106-2 / 13-3-63-0	26.1-7-95-3 / 14-2-45-1	42-10-112-4 / 33-10-94-1	5-2-13-0 / 26-4-121-1	4-0-14-0 / 8-1-32-0	10-4-31-1	7-1-22-0	1-0-3-0
v. Victoria (Adelaide) 27-30 October 1993	21.2-4-73-3 / 4-1-20-0	19-3-62-0 / 8-1-28-0	32-6-94-1 / 44.3-14-80-5			1-1-0-0	3-0-14-0	
v. New Zealanders (Adelaide) 19-22 November 1993		22-4-58-0 / 10-3-24-2	19-7-37-0 / 17-3-49-0	21-7-55-2 / 8-0-24-0	4-0-22-0 / 3-1-4-0	12-2-35-0		
v. Queensland (Adelaide) 25-8 November 1993	21-4-75-1 / 22-5-58-1	20-6-78-3 / 17-3-64-1			4-1-9-0 / 18-3-58-1	3-0-14-0		
v. Western Australia (Perth) 18-20 December 1993	18.4-5-54-3 / 5-0-15-0	27-8-57-2 / 10-0-33-1	30-5-96-3 / 9-2-23-0			10-4-21-2 / 7-0-37-0		
v. New South Wales (Adelaide) 31 December 1993-3 January 1994	28-6-102-5 / 9.3-1-31-3	27-3-95-0 / 14-3-52-1			5-1-9-0	6-2-20-0	11-3-21-1	
v. Western Australia (Adelaide) 7-10 January 1994	44-13-120-3 / 20-4-48-2					5-1-9-0	13-3-24-0	1-0-2-0
v. Tasmania (Hobart) 18-21 January 1994	31-9-96-3 / 20-3-92-1				9-1-25-0	0.3-0-5-0	6-0-14-0	
v. Victoria (Melbourne) 29-31 January 1994	30-10-38-3 / 13-4-27-0				4-2-10-0 / 9-0-32-0	20-7-34-1 / 6-3-14-0	4.3-1-15-2	
v. New South Wales (Sydney) 16-19 February 1994	30-5-88-4	24-2-91-0		19-4-48-2	9-3-20-0	6-2-11-0		
v. Tasmania (Adelaide) 17-20 March 1994	15-2-62-0 / 12-1-53-0				6-3-14-0 / 3-0-12-0	3-1-3-0 / 9-1-25-1	5-1-12-1 / 5-0-22-0	
Bowler's average	384.3-84-1221-34 — 35.91	238.1-45-782-14 — 55.85	226.3-57-585-14 — 41.78	79-17-261-5 — 52.20	86-16-262-1 — 262.00	98.3-28-259-5 — 51.80	54.3-9-144-4 — 36.00	2-0-5-0 — –

		v. Tasmania (Adelaide) 17–20 March 1994		M	Inns	NO	Runs	HS	Av
214	80			11	19	1	1036	268	57.55
54	35			11	20	1	796	141	41.89
16	6			11	20	1	766	146	40.31
4	7			10	17	1	640	161	40.00
157	37			11	19	–	1087	200	57.21
				10	17	–	581	176	36.31
18	2*			11	18	3	252	34*	16.80
				3	5	–	114	54	22.80
				4	6	1	39	13*	7.80
4	–			10	13	1	124	50	10.33
				7	11	6	28	13*	5.60
1	–			9	11	5	54	19*	9.00
				5	8	1	128	40*	18.28
				4	6	2	97	48*	24.25
0*	–			2	2	1	0	0*	0.00
8	66			1	2	–	74	66	37.00
3	–			1	1	–	3	3	3.00
1									
4	5								
3									
2	8								
489	246								
10	6								
L									
2									

FIELDING FIGURES

35 – T.J. Nielsen (ct 30/st 5)
11 – P.C. Nobes and J.D. Siddons
10 – D.S. Webber
6 – D.S. Lehmann
3 – J.A. Brayshaw, T.B.A. May, S.P. George and P.E. McIntyre
1 – G.S. Blewett, J.C. Scuderi (plus one as sub), D.A. Reeves
     (plus one as sub), D.J. Marsh, M.A. Harrity and sub (D. Jacobs)

P.E. McIntyre	D.A. Reeves	T.J. Nielsen	D.S. Webber	D.J. Marsh	M.A. Harrity	M.J. Mingall	J.D. Siddons	Byes	Leg-byes	Wides	No-balls	Total	Wkts
								5	7		8	352	10
								1	4	2	10	416	4
31–4–101–4									13		12	357	9
39–10–61–5								3	6		8	198	10
	19–2–62–4								7		5	276	6
8–3–11–0	6–1–19–0	3–2–2–1	0.5–0–3–0						7	1		143	3
34–5–112–2	11–1–52–3								4		26	330	10
19–0–96–0	18–4–47–1							4	9	1	2	351	4
	13–0–64–0								12	3	20	304	10
	7–0–33–0		0.1–0–4–0						6		2	160	1
36–5–119–2				17–4–51–1				4	4	2	4	395	9
40–4–128–3				32–4–97–1				2	6	1		337	10
52–14–135–1				21.3–5–65–3	26–2–92–0				1		8	446	3
29–6–75–0			3–0–7–0	12–1–27–0				2	13		4	174	3
40–9–132–1	26–5–113–2			13.1–3–35–1				5	6	1	16	401	8
24–4–86–0	8–1–35–2			22–4–74–3				9	3			329	6
34–6–142–1	20–4–64–0			23–5–64–1					10			377	9
21–3–79–0	19–1–102–1			20.2–1–67–0				12	4			337	1
42–8–123–3								6	4	2	8	391	10
28–5–75–3					22–4–79–1	32–3–102–0	3–0–14–0		9	3	6	370	5
33–5–97–4		8–0–44–0			12–2–41–1	13.3–2–60–0		8	4	6	10	366	6
510–91–	147–19–	11–2–	4–0–	161–27–	60–8–	45.3–5–	3–0–						
1572–29	591–13	46–1	14–0	480–10	212–2	162–0	14–0						
54.20	45.46	46.00	–	48.00	106.00	–	–						

TASMANIA FIRST-CLASS MATCHES 1993–4

BATTING

Player	v. New Zealanders (Launceston) 4–7 Nov 1993		v. Western Australia (Hobart) 11–14 Nov 1993		v. New South Wales (Sydney) 25–8 Nov 1993		v. Victoria (Hobart) 10–13 Dec 1993		v. Queensland (Brisbane) 31 Dec 1993–3 Jan 1994		v. New South Wales (Hobart) 7–10 Jan 1994		v. South Australia (Hobart) 18–21 Jan 1994		v. Queensland (Hobart) 10–13 Feb 1994		v. Victoria (Melbourne) 17–20 Feb 1994		v. Western Australia (Perth) 24–7 Feb 1994	
D.F. Hills	27	26	43	–	88	4	71	59	0	0	158*	68	63	16	0	91	2	52	10	13
N.C.P. Courtney	20	31	41	–	55	23	0	28	0	14	1	31								
D.C. Boon	2	21																		
R.T. Ponting	15	54	105	–	15	35	23	66	12	64	3	13	16	40	49	18	42	20*	101	–
D.J. Buckingham	18	47			16	6	18	14	13	77	52	88*	57	37	0	13	71	–	100*	–
R.J. Tucker	36	6	26	–	0	1	107	32*	41	44*	42	11	2	33*	28	23*	57	–	–	–
S. Young	77	12*	63	–	52*	42	6	49	55	31	18	21	124*	48	68	3	0	–	73*	–
M.N. Atkinson	69	3*	0	–	21	49	47	18*	12	40*	44*	40*	45	7*	25*	8*	43*	–		
C.D. Matthews	21	–	13	–	19	2	23	–	12	0	–	–	28	–	–	–	75	–		
S. Herzberg	5*	–	25	–	4	14	2	–			–	–	–	–	–	–				
T.J. Cooley	1*	–					15*	–	2	–										
M.J. DiVenuto			125		53	11			24	27	42	13	11	112	26	34	89	25	31	–
J. Cox			26				4	27	0*				27	24	10	81	32	103*	129	35*
C.R. Miller			6*						0*		–	–	–	–	0	–	17	–	–	–
M.W. Ridgway					1	15*									0	–			–	–
M.G. Farrell															10	–				
A.R.J. Humphreys																			–	1*
B.A. Robinson																				
Byes			1		4	2	4		1		7		5	9	11	3	2		2	
Leg-byes		3	11		5	7	4	6	1	9	17	3	6	3	3	9	6	6	9	2
Wides			1				1				3		1		2		6	1	2	
No-balls	15	4	28		10	4	8	4	18	22	14	6	16		18	8	4	4	30	2
Total	306	207	514		343	215	328	308	190	329	401	294	401	329	248	293	444	213	487	53
Wickets	9	6	10		10	10	10	6	10	7	6	6	8	6	10	6	9	2	4	1
Result	D		D		L		D		D		W		W		D		D		D	
Points	–		2		0		0		0		6		6		0		2		2	

BOWLING

	T.J. Cooley	C.D. Matthews	S. Young	S. Herzberg	R.J. Tucker	D.J. Buckingham	B.A. Robinson	C.R. Miller
v. New Zealanders (Launceston) 4–7 November 1993	25–6–61–1 / 13–4–33–2	19–6–37–2 / 14–2–43–2	17–7–33–1 / 14–3–42–0	25–6–63–2 / 25–5–79–2	5–1–10–0 / 9–1–34–1	2–0–8–0		
v. Western Australia (Hobart) 11–14 November 1993		34–8–98–1	36.5–6–104–1 / 5–3–4–0	48–14–98–1 / 10–3–16–1	20–4–55–2			27–7–78–0 / 12–7–24–1
v. New South Wales (Sydney) 25–8 November 1993		26–3–98–0 / 12–0–43–1	17–4–44–1 / 15.5–2–68–3	25–2–77–2 / 28.2–5–82–4	13–3–39–1 / 9–1–27–1			
v. Victoria (Hobart) 10–13 December 1993	21–2–89–1 / 4–0–23–0	16.4–4–62–0 / 31–5–110–2	21–6–74–1 / 11–2–37–0	16–4–45–1 / 15–2–47–2	8–0–34–0 / 14–2–38–2	3–0–17–0		
v. Queensland (Brisbane) 31 December 1993–3 January 1994	11–0–57–1 / 4–0–21–0	19–4–71–2 / 21.5–5–73–2	20.4–10–38–3 / 20–3–72–0		15–6–29–1 / 13–5–27–0			20–6–41–3 / 22–4–82–2
v. New South Wales (Hobart) 7–10 January 1994		26–4–115–0 / 13–2–56–2	26–5–77–2 / 3–0–12–0	15–1–66–0 / 10–1–57–0	12–1–31–0 / 14–2–67–0	2–0–14–0		31.5–9–83–7 / 13–3–70–1
v. South Australia (Hobart) 18–21 January 1994		33–6–103–2 / 5–0–28–0	22–4–86–0 / 1–1–0–0	39.3–6–133–3 / 10–1–56–0	18–4–73–1 / 1–0–10–0	6–0–54–0		40–11–108–4 / 8–2–22–2
v. Queensland (Hobart) 10–13 February 1994			26.3–9–66–3 / 22–6–48–2		18–6–37–0 / 16–6–31–1			23–6–69–2 / 18.2–2–56–4
v. Victoria (Melbourne) 17–20 February 1994		18–3–62–0 / 10–2–45–1	33.1–7–85–4 / 9–3–41–0	24–1–57–0 / 27–6–66–4	23–7–56–4 / 5–1–33–0			21–4–62–1 / 16–3–44–3
v. Western Australia (Perth) 24–7 February 1994			22–2–85–0 / 21–7–51–1		17–3–51–0 / 12–3–24–1			26–3–87–3 / 27–6–76–2
v. South Australia (Adelaide) 17–20 March 1994		24–4–102–0 / 10–2–47–0	24–5–97–1 / 7–0–29–2		13–2–51–1 / 5–0–30–0		11–2–44–0 / 14.1–1–75–3	22.3–3–82–5 / 13–1–60–0
v. New South Wales 25–9 March 1994		40–12–99–2	36–14–65–3		28–13–47–2		44.3–19–84–2	36–10–99–0
Totals	78–12–284–5	372.3–72–1292–19	431–109–1258–28	317.5–57–942–22	288–71–834–18	13–0–93–0	69.4–22–203–5	376.4–87–1143–40
Bowler's average	56.80	68.00	44.92	42.81	46.33	–	40.60	28.57

A   D.C. Boon 1–0–1–0

v. South Australia (Adelaide) 17–20 March 1994		v. New South Wales (Sydney) 25–9 March 1994		M	Inns	NO	Runs	HS	Av
114	126	20	17	12	23	1	1068	158*	48.54
				6	11	–	244	55	22.18
				1	2	–	23	21	11.50
84*	161	1	28	12	22	2	965	161	48.25
				9	16	2	627	100*	44.78
17	1	49	2	12	20	4	558	107	34.87
29	0	62	9	12	21	4	842	124*	49.52
1*	15*	44	3*	12	20	12	534	69	66.75
–	–	0	5	10	11	–	198	75	18.00
				7	5	1	50	25	12.50
				3	3	2	18	15*	18.00
9	15	4	27	10	18	–	678	125	37.66
98	0	23	11	8	15	2	630	129	48.46
–	–	4	10	9	6	2	37	17	9.25
				3	3	1	16	15*	8.00
–	20*	18	1	3	4	1	49	20*	16.33
				1	1	1	1	1*	–
–	–	1*	0	2	2	1	1	1*	1.00
	8	4	2						
9	4	5	1						
3	6	8	8						
6	10	12	2						
370	366	255	126						
5	6	10	10						
W		L							
6		–							

FIELDING FIGURES

44 – M.N. Atkinson (ct 40/st 4)
13 – R.T. Ponting
12 – S. Young
10 – D.F. Hills
 7 – R.J. Tucker
 6 – D.J. Buckingham
 5 – M.J. DiVenuto
 4 – J. Cox
 3 – N.C.P. Courtney, C.R. Miller and M.G. Farrell
 2 – S. Herzberg
 1 – T.J. Cooley and A.R.J. Humphreys

M.J. DiVenuto	N.C.P. Courtney	R.T. Ponting	M.W. Ridgway	D.F. Hills	J. Cox	M.G. Farrell	A.R.J. Humphreys	Byes	Leg-byes	Wides	No-balls	Total	Wkts
								2	9	1	4	215	7
									7	1	3	247	7
7–2–27–0	2–0–10–0	1–0–1–0						2	11	1		473	5
									1		4	56	2
			19–3–89–1					1	5		30	353	5
6–0–29–0			4.1–1–16–0					6	3		4	274	9
				1–0–1–0				2	5		20	329	3
								3	9		10	267	8
									9		24	245	10
	9–0–31–1	7–1–30–0							3		4	339	6
	2–0–19–1							1	6	1	6	398	10
	6–1–19–0								1	1	2	296	4
3–1–5–0								4	7	3		519	10
									3			209	3
		3–1–7–1				3–0–29–0		2	7	6	16	339	10
			29–5–109–2			23–6–49–2			6			208	9
			19–2–50–2			10–2–17–0		5	4	6	2	331	10
									7	1	2	236	9
		7–0–32–1	27–4–127–4				13–1–57–1	4	11	1	14	454	10
			18–2–67–0				16.3–3–63–2		5	2	2	286	6
		6–3–15–0				28–1–93–3		1	4	3	2	489	10
									5		8	246	6
		1–0–3–0				12–3–26–0		4	15	1	16	442	10
16–3– 61–0 –	19–1– 79–2 39.50	25–5– 88–2 44.00	116.1–17– 458–9 50.88	1–0– 1–0 –	3–0– 29–0 –	73–12– 185–5 37.00	29.3–4– 120–3 40.00						

VICTORIA
FIRST-CLASS MATCHES 1993–4
BATTING

	v. South Australia (Adelaide) 27–30 October 1993	v. Western Australia (Melbourne) 4–7 November 1993	v. New South Wales (Melbourne) 19–22 November 1993	v. South Africans (Melbourne) 4–7 December 1993	v. Tasmania (Hobart) 10–13 December 1993	v. New South Wales (Sydney) 18–21 December 1993	v. Queensland (Brisbane) 13–16 January 1994	v. South Australia (Melbourne) 28–31 January 1994	v. Tasmania (Melbourne) 17–20 February 1994	v. Queensland (Melbourne) 24–7 February 1994
W.N. Phillips	60 28	13 0	12 28	7 4		57 22	47 1	10 156*	130 10	41 15
M.T.G. Elliott	54 99	4 175*					5 23	72 13	11 19	30 113
D.M. Jones	33 10	47 0	0 72	38 34	158* 60	14 155		145 152*		
B.J. Hodge	27 5	95 25	54 92	80 8*	106 38	57 33	16 64	49 –	62 72	25 32
D.J. Ramshaw	58 4	0 43	85 7	71 41	5 53	40 80	41 5	11 –		33 24
A.I.C. Dodemaide	52 3	1 13*	6 0	2 –	– 32		34 35	33 –		
D.S. Berry	33 0	38* –	1 4	0 –	– 3	11* 8*	6 3	5 –	16* 28	6 0
P.R. Reiffel	0 2	11 –	0 17			17 –				
S.K. Warne	0 18	1 –	16 8			7 –				
C. Howard	15* 10	1 –	13 0*	41* –	– 6*	6 –	7 18	– –	8 0	
S.H. Cook	– 2*	2 –	5* 0*	– –	– –		0* 3*		5 1*	0 0*
W.G. Ayres			23 17	9 0						
R.S. Herman				1 4*						
D.W. Fleming				54* –	– 12	4		1* –	9 20*	2* 4
K.J. Neville					21 19					
G.J. Allardice					12* 14		86 13	41 –	42 65	8 1
P.A. Garlick					– 8*					
R.A. Bartlett						0 7				
I.J. Harvey						37 7	6 13		5 9	
M.G. Hughes							2 8	0 –		
D.A. Harris									22 0	2 9
S.M. McCooke									4 2	15 2
I.W. Wrigglesworth										58 28
Byes	3		5 5	7 10	2 3	1 9	2 2	12	5	3 2
Leg-byes	13 6	9 4	6 10	17 5	5 9	7 2	6 11	10 4	4 7	2 5
Wides		2	1 1	1		1		1	6 1	1 1
No-balls	12 8	6 18	6 2	3 3	20 10	6		14 12	2 2	16 14
Total	357 198	230 278	233 263	330 110	329 267	264 324	272 212	377 337	331 236	242 250
Wickets	9 10	10 4	10 9	8 4	3 8	10 6	10 10	9 1	10 9	10 10
Result	L	W	W	W	D	D	L	D	D	W
Points	0	6	6	–	2	0	0	0	0	5.6

BOWLING

	P.R. Reiffel	S.H. Cook	S.K. Warne	A.I.C. Dodemaide	C. Howard	D.M. Jones	W.G. Ayres	D.W. Fleming
v. South Australia (Adelaide) 27–30 October 1993	27–5–67–1 / 6–0–21–1	27.3–3–114–5 / 4–0–13–0	43–11–119–4 / 11–1–48–0	21–5–43–0 / 4–1–10–0	13–0–68–0 / 4–0–22–0	5–1–10–0 / 0.5–0–12–0		
v. Western Australia (Melbourne) 4–7 November 1993	26–7–73–1 / 21–5–54–1	17–6–43–0 / 9–2–38–3	36–9–92–3 / 29.4–12–42–6	37.5–13–85–5 / 3–2–6–0	9–1–19–1 / 15–4–44–0			
v. New South Wales (Melbourne) 19–22 November 1993	22–10–39–2 / 28.3–5–73–5	15–4–40–1 / 5–0–21–0	31–9–72–4 / 29–1–103–2	18–5–44–1 / 7–0–29–0	33.3–8–24–1 / 5–1–17–0		2–0–11–0	
v. South Africans (Melbourne) 4–7 December 1993		15–3–43–2 / 11–1–36–0		15–3–47–1 / 12–4–34–1	32–10–79–1 / 24.5–9–42–5			28–4–86–6 / 18–8–31–2
v. Tasmania (Hobart) 10–13 December 1993		18.4–2–84–4 / 11–2–30–0		23–6–77–2 / 31–8–83–1	23–5–68–0 / 29–5–112–5			19–2–77–3 / 11.1–2–45–0
v. New South Wales (Sydney) 18–21 December 1993	17.3–7–44–1 / 18–2–68–4		40–14–77–5 / 28–7–90–3		30–7–90–1 / 11–5–42–0			20–4–63–3 / 16–1–61–2
v. Queensland (Brisbane) 13–16 January 1994		11–0–68–0 / 4–0–22–0		21–5–74–3 / 22–4–73–0	18–1–73–0 / 13–2–79–1			
v. South Australia 28–31 January 1994				13–3–81–0 / 6–0–30–1	35.5–8–144–4 / 2–1–4–2	3–0–21–0		37–7–130–4 / 16–2–65–4
v. Tasmania (Melbourne) 17–20 February 1994		29–6–114–4 / 10–1–26–0			27–3–91–1 / 7–1–28–0			39–10–96–2 / 13–3–37–0
v. Queensland 24–7 February 1994		19–5–50–1 / 23–3–59–2						23.3–7–61–5 / 25–5–78–1
v. Western Australia (Perth) 17–19 March 1994		9.4–2–41–4 / 16–5–43–4		6–1–20–1 / 8–2–30–1				15–6–34–5 / 18–8–39–1
	166–41–439–16	254.5–45–885–30	247.4–64–643–27	247.5–62–766–17	312.1–71–1046–22	8.5–1–43–0	2–0–11–0	298.4–69–903–38
Bowler's average	27.43	29.50	23.81	45.05	47.54	–	–	23.76

v. Western Australia (Perth) 17–19 March 1994		M	Inns	NO	Runs	HS	Av
4	29	10	20	1	674	156*	35.47
2	1	7	14	1	621	175*	47.76
		7	14	2	918	158*	76.50
43*	8	11	21	2	991	106	52.15
1	12	10	19	–	614	85	32.31
0	3	8	13	1	214	52	17.83
13	9*	11	18	5	184	38*	14.15
		4	6	–	47	17	7.83
		4	6	–	50	18	8.33
		9	12	4	125	41*	15.62
9	0	9	12	7	27	9	5.40
		2	4	–	49	23	24.50
		1	2	1	5	4*	5.00
10	0	7	10	4	116	54*	19.33
		1	2	–	40	21	20.00
16	53	6	11	1	351	86	35.10
		1	1	1	8	8*	–
		1	2	–	7	7	3.50
		3	6	–	77	37	12.83
		2	3	–	10	8	3.33
		2	4	–	33	22	8.25
0	0	3	6	–	23	15	3.83
0	19	2	4	–	105	58	26.25
	1						
4	6						
16	14						
118	155						
10	10						
L							
1.4							

R.S. Herman	B.J. Hodge	P.A. Garlick	I.J. Harvey	M.G. Hughes	S.M. McCooke	I.A. Wrigglesworth	Byes	Leg-byes	Wides	No-balls	Total	Wkts
								9		16	430	10
								1		2	127	1
							3	7		12	322	10
								1		12	185	10
							2	6		4	227	10
							11	3	2	8	268	7
							2	4			261	10
8–2–24–0	2–0–2–1						4	5		1	178	10
		4–0–18–0						4		8	328	10
		7–1–28–0					4	6	1	4	308	6
			2–1–5–0				4			4	283	10
			1–0–9–0				4	1	1	6	275	9
			16–1–47–1	18.4–1–70–5			8	7		6	347	10
	3.4–0–29–1		18–5–57–1	10–1–66–0				5	1		331	6
				39–13–116–2			3	4		2	499	10
				9–0–67–0				11			177	8
			21–6–72–0		33.1–11–65–2			6	4	4	444	9
	1–0–3–0–		10–0–55–0		11–1–56–2		2	6	1	4	213	2
	3–0–19–0				21–5–67–1	21–3–72–3	4	2	4	2	275	10
					23.3–8–35–6	13–4–32–0	4	6			214	10
					11–6–13–0		2	2		4	112	10
						10–3–45–1		5	1	8	162	7
8–2– −	9.4–0–	11–1–	68–13–	76.4–15–	88.4–25–	55–16–						
24–0	53–2	46–0	245–2	319–7	223–11	162–4						
–	26.50	–	122.50	45.57	20.27	40.50						

WESTERN AUSTRALIA — FIRST-CLASS MATCHES 1993–4

BATTING

BATTING	v. New Zealanders (Perth) 21–4 October 1993		v. Queensland (Perth) 20 Oct.–1 Nov. 1993		v. Victoria (Melbourne) 4–7 November 1993		v. Tasmania (Hobart) 11–14 November 1993		v. New South Wales (Perth) 10–11 December 1993		v. South Australia (Perth) 18–20 December 1993		v. South Australia (Adelaide) 7–10 January 1994		v. Queensland (Brisbane) 19–22 January 1994		v. New South Wales (Sydney) 2–5 February 1994		v. Tasmania (Perth) 24–7 February 1994	
M.W. McPhee	7	–	17	29																
G.R. Marsh	16	–	15	24	6	0	43	20*	128	–	14	62*	98	32	0	–	10	11	1	81
J.L. Langer	61	–	65	96	144	16	135	5	9	–	34	90*	96	56*	89	–	26	4	233	5
B.P. Julian	59	–	13	4	27	9	–	–	12	–	17	–	15	–	19	–	3	36	0	25*
D.R. Martyn	80	–	59	56	4	89*	100	9*	197	–	20	–			30	–	6	0	41	58
T.M. Moody	110	–	0	24	33	37	65	–	68	–	65	–	58	38	15	–	115	33	22	39
M.R.J. Veletta	11	–	0	13	2	6	65*	–	4	–	40	0	75	12	80*	–	71	6	66	21
T.J. Zoehrer	83	–	18	57	22	5	44*	–	12*	–	30	–	37*	–	69	–	6	8	12	15
M.P. Atkinson	39	–	0	2*																
J. Angel	8*	–			0	1	–	–	0*	–	16*	–			52	–	84*	5	1	–
J. Stewart	6	–																		
C.E. Coulson			1	10																
D.J. Spencer			0*	3	16	0	–	–	18	–	0	–	–	–	38	–			0	–
M.P. Lavender					31	9	7	17												
W.K. Wishart					15*	0	–	–			–	–	10	–			6	0		
D.A. Fitzgerald									2	–	23	–	35	17*						
R.S. Russell													23	–						
B.A. Reid															2*	–			4*	–
G.B. Hogg																	22	15	44	33*
S.C.G. MacGill																	9	2*		
Byes	1		1		3		2		14				2				5		4	
Leg-byes	8		2	6	7	1	11	1	16		12	6	1	13	4		3	6	11	5
Wides							1		1		3				1		2		1	2
No-balls	19		20	49	12	12		4	22		20	2	8	4	14		16	4	14	2
Total	508		211	373	322	185	473	56	503		304	160	446	174	413		379	135	454	286
Wickets	10		10	10	10	10	5	2	8		10	1	7	3	9†		10	10	10	6
Result	W		L		L		D		W		W		D		D		L		D	
Points	–		0		2		0		6		6		1.8		2		0		0	

† M.R.J. Veletta retired hurt

BOWLING

BOWLING	J. Angel	M.P. Atkinson	T.M. Moody	B.P. Julian	J. Stewart	T.J. Zoehrer	D.J. Spencer	C.E. Coulson
v. New Zealanders (Perth) 21–4 October 1993	20.1–7–32–5 34–7–108–5	18–4–46–3 22–6–61–2	9–5–8–1 11–4–16–0	14–5–38–1 29–7–81–0	15–5–22–0 22.4–3–70–1	7–2–9–0		
v. Queensland (Perth) 29 October–1 November 1993		21–1–97–1 5–1–28–0	8.5–1–42–2 6–2–15–0	27–6–81–2 4–0–22–0		4–1–23–0	20–3–88–1 6–0–36–1	23–6–78–2 7.4–8–40–0
v. Victoria (Melbourne) 4–7 November 1993	25.3–10–38–3 7–1–37–1		7–2–16–0 23–8–47–1	22–12–31–2 19–5–54–2		3–0–20–0 5–0–27–0	15–1–66–3 11.1–0–65–0	
v. Tasmania (Hobart) 11–14 November 1993	43–13–118–3		16–8–27–1	19–3–74–1		22–2–77–1	18.1–0–91–2	
v. New South Wales (Perth) 10–11 December 1993	9.1–4–25–3 12.1–1–57–5		10–4–13–2 12–4–35–0	13–4–34–5 12–2–45–3			7–0–35–2	
v. South Australia (Perth) 18–20 December 1993	11.1–1–30–3 20.4–7–59–5		18–5–43–4 3.4–0–21–0	12–1–65–1 17–4–49–1			11–3–37–2 21–3–80–1	
v. South Australia (Adelaide) 7–10 January 1994	20–5–71–1			30–6–108–4			23.5–1–85–4	
v. Queensland (Brisbane) 19–24 January 1994	16.2–2–64–4 25–7–54–1		1–0–2–0 11–0–58–2			16–0–52–3 20–5–55–0	12–2–47–1 14–3–57–1	
v. New South Wales (Sydney) 2–5 February 1994	31.4–7–87–3 9–3–21–0		8–1–26–0 6–1–28–0			29–7–86–2 7–0–24–1		
v. Tasmania (Perth) 24–7 February 1994	27–3–134–1 10–3–14–0		26–5–75–2 8–4–13–0	21–3–90–1 6–0–11–0		10–1–34–0	24–4–63–1	
v. Victoria (Perth) 17–19 March 1994	9–2–28–1 17–7–47–3		16.5–5–32–3 4–1–7–2	21–9–53–2 3–1–14–0				
Bowler's average	347.5–90–1024–47 21.78	66–12–232–6 38.66	222.2–68–570–20 28.50	324–72–1021–30 34.03	37.4–8–92–1 92.00	51–6–190–1 190.00	183.1–20–750–20 37.50	30.4–9–118–2 59.00

A   M.J. Greatbatch absent hurt

v. Victoria (Perth) 17–19 March 1994		M	Inns	NO	Runs	HS	Av
		2	3	–	53	29	17.66
42	12	11	19	2	615	128	36.17
0	34	11	19	2	1198	233	70.47
2	21*	11	15	2	262	59	20.15
10	23	10	16	2	782	197	55.85
0	19	11	17	–	741	115	43.58
7	7	11	18	2	486	80*	30.37
0	4	11	16	3	422	83	32.46
		2	3	1	41	39	20.50
24*	1	10	11	5	192	84*	32.00
13	–	2	2	–	19	13	9.50
		1	2	–	11	10	5.50
		8	8	1	75	38	10.71
		2	4	–	64	31	16.00
		7	6	1	31	15*	6.20
		3	4	1	77	35	25.66
		1	1	–	23	23	23.00
6	–	3	3	2	12	6	12.00
0	27*	3	6	2	141	44	35.25
		1	2	1	11	9	11.00

2	
2	5
1	
4	8
112	162
10	7
W	
6	

FIELDING FIGURES

38 – T.J. Zoehrer (ct 37/st 1)
20 – M.R.J. Veletta (ct 19/st 1)
13 – T.M. Moody
11 – B.P. Julian
7 – D.R. Martyn and D.J. Spencer
5 – J.L. Langer
3 – D.A. Fitzgerald and G.R. Marsh
2 – M.P. Atkinson, M.P. Lavender, G.B. Hogg and W.K. Wishart
1 – M.W. McPhee, J. Angel and C.E. Coulson

D.R. Martyn	W.K. Wishart	R.S. Russell	B.A. Reid	J.L. Langer	S.C.G. MacGill	G.B. Hogg	Byes	Leg-byes	Wides	No-balls	Total	Wkts
								3		5	149	10
							1	4	4		350	9
3–0–9–0								12	1	30	430	10
6–2–15–0								2		8	158	1
	18–3–50–2							9	2	6	230	10
	12–1–44–0							4		18	278	4
3–0–14–0	68–27–101–2						1	11	1	28	514	10
								1		2	73	10
1–0–5–0										2	177	10
							2	2	4	14	179	10
12–5–29–3	14–4–34–0						5	6		4	283	10
	31–6–102–1	14–5–66–0					1	4		8	437	10
	13–2–43–0		12–2–33–1				1	2		6	244	10
9–1–26–1	24–8–60–2		15–4–48–1	1–0–5–0			7	5		10	375	8
2–0–13–0	56–19–90–4				29–4–91–0		14	2	1	12	409	10
	9–2–27–0						4	2			106	1
2–1–4–0			27–5–76–0				2	9	2	30	487	4
8–3–12–1				1–1–0–0		1–0–1–0		2		2	53	1
8–5–13–1			12–3–34–3					4		16	118	10
			11.4–5–34–5				1	6		14	155	10
54–17–	245–72–	14–5–	77.4–19–	2–1–	29–4–	1–0–						
140–6	551–11	66–0	225–10	5–0	91–0	1–0						
23.33	50.09	–	22.50	–	–	–						

A

TEST MATCH AVERAGES – AUSTRALIA *v.* NEW ZEALAND

AUSTRALIA BATTING

	M	Inns	NO	Runs	HS	Av	100s	50s
S.R. Waugh	3	3	3	216	147*	216.00	1	–
M.A. Taylor	3	4	1	286	142*	95.33	1	2
D.C. Boon	3	4	1	262	106	87.33	1	2
S.K. Warne	3	2	1	85	74*	85.00	–	1
M.J. Slater	3	4	–	305	168	76.25	1	1
P.R. Reiffel	2	2	1	74	51	74.00	–	1
M.E. Waugh	3	3	–	215	111	71.66	1	1
I.A. Healy	3	3	1	129	115	64.50	1	–
A.R. Border	3	3	–	181	105	60.33	1	1

Played in three Tests: C.J. McDermott 35
Played in two Tests: G.D. McGrath 0; T.B.A. May did not bat

AUSTRALIA BOWLING

	Overs	Mds	Runs	Wkts	Av	Best	5/inn
S.K. Warne	151.3	49	305	18	16.94	6-31	1
M.E. Waugh	48	18	94	5	18.80	1-7	–
T.B.A. May	93.3	33	202	9	22.44	5-65	1
C.J. McDermott	133	39	340	12	28.33	4-39	–
S.R. Waugh	18	3	41	1	41.00	1-10	–
G.D. McGrath	96	26	253	6	42.16	3-66	–
P.R. Reiffel	48	6	141	2	70.50	2-75	–

Bowled in one innings: A.R. Border 2–2–0–0

AUSTRALIA FIELDING FIGURES
14 – I.A. Healy (ct 13/st 1); 5 – M.A. Taylor; 4 – S.K. Warne; 3 – D.C. Boon, M.E. Waugh and A.R. Border; 2 – T.B.A. May; 1 – S.R. Waugh

NEW ZEALAND BATTING

	M	Inns	NO	Runs	HS	Av	100s	50s
A.H. Jones	3	6	–	324	143	54.00	1	1
K.R. Rutherford	3	6	–	250	86	41.66	–	2
T.E. Blain	3	5	1	165	42*	41.25	–	–
C.L. Cairns	2	3	–	99	78	33.00	–	1
B.A. Pocock	3	6	–	97	34	16.16	–	–
D.N. Patel	3	6	1	76	20	15.20	–	–
M.L. Su'a	2	3	1	25	14*	12.50	–	–
M.J. Greatbatch	3	6	–	67	35	11.16	–	–
S.B. Doull	2	4	–	35	24	8.75	–	–
R.P. De Groen	2	4	2	12	6	6.00	–	–
D.K. Morrison	3	5	1	20	20*	5.00	–	–

Played in one Test: M.D. Crowe 42 & 31*; W. Watson 0*; B.A. Young 38 & 53; C.Z. Harris 0 & 4

NEW ZEALAND BOWLING

	Overs	Mds	Runs	Wkts	Av	Best	5/inn
C.L. Cairns	65	11	253	5	50.60	4-113	–
S.B. Doull	54	5	204	3	68.00	2-105	–
R.P. de Groen	82	23	233	3	77.66	2-113	–
M.L. Su'a	63.5	5	245	3	81.66	2-72	–
D.N. Patel	103	11	384	4	96.00	1-37	–
D.K. Morrison	126	16	422	3	140.66	2-113	–

Bowled in one innings: A.H. Jones 2–0–6–0; C.Z. Harris 2–0–18–0; B.A. Pocock 2–0–10–0; W. Watson 24–11–52–1

NEW ZEALAND FIELDING FIGURES
4 – T.E. Blain; 3 – A.H. Jones and D.N. Patel; 2 – K.R. Rutherford, D.K. Morrison and S.B. Doull; 1 – M.J. Greatbatch and B.A. Pocock

---

TEST MATCH AVERAGES – AUSTRALIA *v.* SOUTH AFRICA

AUSTRALIA BATTING

	M	Inns	NO	Runs	HS	Av	100s	50s
M.A. Taylor	3	5	–	304	170	60.80	1	1
M.J. Slater	3	5	–	185	92	37.00	–	2
C.J. McDermott	3	2	1	35	29*	35.00	–	–
D.C. Boon	3	5	–	156	50	31.20	–	1
A.R. Border	3	5	–	146	84	29.20	–	1
D.R. Martyn	2	3	–	73	59	24.33	–	1
M.E. Waugh	3	5	–	116	84	23.20	–	1
I.A. Healy	3	5	2	41	19	13.66	–	–
T.B.A. May	3	2	1	8	8*	8.00	–	–
S.K. Warne	3	4	1	16	11	5.33	–	–

Played in two Tests: P.R. Reiffel 32* & 2*
Played in one Test: S.R. Waugh 164 & 1; G.D. McGrath 9 & 1

AUSTRALIA BOWLING

	Overs	Mds	Runs	Wkts	Av	Best	10/m	5/inn
S.R. Waugh	24	10	30	4	7.50	4-26	–	–
S.K. Warne	175.1	63	307	18	17.05	7-36	1	2
C.J. McDermott	115.1	33	246	14	17.57	4-33	–	–
M.E. Waugh	18	6	30	1	30.00	1-20	–	–
G.D. McGrath	33	8	62	2	31.00	1-30	–	–
P.R. Reiffel	47	12	106	1	106.00	1-36	–	–
T.B.A. May	117	41	228	2	114.00	2-26	–	–
A.R. Border	7	4	9	–	–	–	–	–

AUSTRALIA FIELDING FIGURES
7 – I.A. Healy (ct 6/st 1); 4 – M.E. Waugh and M.A. Taylor; 2 – S.K. Warne; 1 – D.C. Boon, A.R. Border, S.R. Waugh, P.R. Reiffel and T.B.A. May

SOUTH AFRICA BATTING

	M	Inns	NO	Runs	HS	Av	100s	50s
K.C. Wessels	2	3	1	84	63*	42.00	–	1
J.N. Rhodes	3	5	2	124	76*	41.33	–	1
A.C. Hudson	3	5	1	157	90	39.25	–	2
G. Kirsten	3	5	–	174	67	34.80	–	1
W.J. Cronje	3	5	–	153	71	30.60	–	1
P.S. de Villiers	3	4	–	54	30	13.50	–	–
D.J. Richardson	3	4	–	44	24	11.00	–	–
A.A. Donald	3	4	3	11	10	11.00	–	–
P.L. Symcox	2	2	–	11	7	5.50	–	–
D.J. Cullinan	3	5	–	26	10	5.20	–	–
C.R. Matthews	2	2	–	4	4	2.00	–	–

Played in one Test: P.N. Kirsten 79 & 42; B.M. McMillan 2 & 4; R.P. Snell 10 & 1

SOUTH AFRICA BOWLING

	Overs	Mds	Runs	Wkts	Av	Best	10/m	5/inn
P.S. de Villiers	132.3	37	311	11	28.27	6-43	1	1
A.A. Donald	127.2	26	373	13	28.69	4-83	–	–
B.M. McMillan	41	3	122	4	30.50	3-89	–	–
P.L. Symcox	72.5	17	153	4	38.25	2-49	–	–
C.R. Matthews	58	21	121	3	40.33	3-68	–	–
R.P. Snell	31	9	82	2	41.00	2-38	–	–
W.J. Cronje	28	8	66	–	–	–	–	–

Bowled in one innings: G. Kirsten 23–8–62–1; P.N. Kirsten 4–0–17–0

SOUTH AFRICA FIELDING FIGURES
10 – D.J. Richardson; 3 – J.N. Rhodes; 2 – A.C. Hudson, G. Kirsten and P.S. de Villiers; 1 – W.J. Cronje and R.P. Snell

BENSON AND HEDGES WORLD SERIES AVERAGES

AUSTRALIA BATTING

	M	Inns	NO	Runs	HS	Av	100s	50s
D.M. Jones	7	7	–	318	98	45.42	–	3
M.E. Waugh	11	11	1	405	107	40.50	1	2
D.C. Boon	11	11	1	381	67	38.10	–	4
M.J. Slater	3	3	–	91	73	30.33	–	1
M.A. Taylor	6	6	–	164	81	27.33	–	1
M.L. Hayden	6	6	1	124	50*	24.80	–	1
I.A. Healy	10	8	3	122	48	24.40	–	–
S.R. Waugh	9	8	2	141	33	23.50	–	–
A.R. Border	10	8	–	122	42	15.25	–	–
P.R. Reiffel	11	8	3	76	29*	15.20	–	–
D.R. Martyn	3	3	–	30	23	10.00	–	–
C.D. McGrath	7	4	1	13	5*	4.33	–	–
S.K. Warne	10	6	1	15	9	3.00	–	–
C.J. McDermott	8	4	–	11	5	2.75	–	–

Played in five matches: T.B.A. May 4* & 5*
Played in two matches: D.W. Fleming 2
Played in one match: T.J. Zoehrer 9

AUSTRALIA BOWLING

	Overs	Mds	Runs	Wkts	Av	Best
S.K. Warne	90	5	301	22	13.68	4-19
G.D. McGrath	71.5	8	276	16	17.25	4-24
C.J. McDermott	68.5	8	228	11	20.72	3-39
P.R. Reiffel	89.5	13	291	12	24.25	4-13
D.W. Fleming	16	2	57	2	28.50	2-15
A.R. Border	28	–	145	5	29.00	2-24
M.E. Waugh	41	–	184	6	30.66	2-26
S.R. Waugh	61	2	218	4	54.50	2-20
T.B.A. May	49	2	189	3	63.00	1-31

AUSTRALIA FIELDING FIGURES

19 – I.A. Healy (ct 16/st 3); 7 – A.R. Border; 6 – P.R. Reiffel; 4 – S.K. Warne; 2 – M.L. Hayden, D.M. Jones, M.E. Waugh, S.R. Waugh, M.A. Taylor and T.J. Zoehrer (ct 1/st 1); 1 – D.C. Boon, C.J. McDermott and D.R. Martyn

SOUTH AFRICA BATTING

	M	Inns	NO	Runs	HS	Av	100s	50s
G. Kirsten	8	8	1	312	112*	44.57	1	2
P.N. Kirsten	6	6	1	205	97	41.00	–	2
K.C. Wessels	3	3	–	104	70	34.66	–	1
J.N. Rhodes	9	9	2	234	52	33.42	–	1
D.J. Richardson	9	6	2	133	38*	33.25	–	–
W.J. Cronje	10	10	1	284	91*	31.55	–	1
D.J. Callaghan	7	6	1	87	30	17.40	–	–
E.L.R. Stewart	2	2	–	32	19	16.00	–	–
D.J. Cullinan	9	9	1	122	37	15.25	–	–
R.P. Snell	8	7	2	57	20*	11.40	–	–
P.L. Symcox	5	4	1	24	12	8.00	–	–
P.S. de Villiers	10	6	4	16	15	8.00	–	–
A.C. Hudson	4	4	–	26	14	6.50	–	–
A.A. Donald	8	3	1	7	7*	3.50	–	–
D.B. Rundle	2	2	–	6	6	3.00	–	–
C.R. Matthews	5	3	–	8	7	2.66	–	–
B.M. McMillan	5	4	1	7	6	2.33	–	–

SOUTH AFRICA BOWLING

	Overs	Mds	Runs	Wkts	Av	Best	5/inn
C.R. Matthews	47	5	179	11	16.27	4-38	–
D.B. Rundle	16	–	95	5	19.00	4-42	–
P.S. de Villiers	92	10	298	15	19.86	3-30	–
A.A. Donald	74.2	6	282	12	23.50	4-40	–
D.J. Callaghan	18	2	74	3	24.66	2-15	–
B.M. McMillan	47	6	218	7	31.14	3-39	–
R.P. Snell	72.5	3	311	9	34.55	5-40	1
W.J. Cronje	66	5	284	6	47.33	2-42	–
P.L. Symcox	41	1	164	2	82.00	1-40	–

SOUTH AFRICA FIELDING FIGURES

14 – D.J. Richardson (ct 13/st 1); 4 – W.J. Cronje, J.N. Rhodes and D.J. Cullinan; 3 – P.N. Kirsten, G. Kirsten, D.B. Rundle and B.M. McMillan (plus 3 as sub); 2 – P.L. Symcox; 1 – R.P. Snell, P.S. de Villiers, A.A. Donald, C.R. Matthews and K.C. Wessels

NEW ZEALAND BATTING

	M	Inns	NO	Runs	HS	Av	100s	50s
C.L. Cairns	7	7	1	220	70	36.66	–	1
C.Z. Harris	2	2	1	33	29*	33.00	–	–
G.R. Larsen	7	7	4	83	29*	27.66	–	–
B.A. Young	7	7	–	184	74	26.28	–	1
M.A. Greatbatch	7	7	–	177	50	25.28	–	1
S.A. Thomson	6	6	–	132	68	22.00	–	1
K.R. Rutherford	7	7	–	154	65	22.00	–	1
T.E. Blain	7	7	2	87	36*	17.40	–	–
R.T. Latham	6	6	–	68	39	11.33	–	–
R.P. de Groen	4	3	2	9	7*	9.00	–	–
A.H. Jones	4	4	–	24	9	6.00	–	–
D.K. Morrison	3	2	1	5	3	5.00	–	–
C. Pringle	7	5	–	16	6	3.20	–	–

Played in two matches: D.N. Patel 1
Played in one match: W. Watson 0

NEW ZEALAND BOWLING

	Overs	Mds	Runs	Wkts	Av	Best
C. Pringle	63	6	219	16	13.68	4-40
R.P. de Groen	32	–	145	5	29.00	2-34
S.A. Thomson	33	–	165	5	33.00	2-38
C.L. Cairns	57.5	3	234	6	39.00	2-44
G.R. Larsen	64	6	250	2	125.00	2-12
D.N. Patel	14	2	44	–	–	–
R.T. Latham	10	–	46	–	–	–
D.K. Morrison	23	5	80	–	–	–

Bowled in one match: W. Watson 10–2–33–1

NEW ZEALAND FIELDING FIGURES

9 – T.E. Blain; 3 – K.R. Rutherford; 2 – M.J. Greatbatch, C.L. Cairns, S.A. Thomson and D.K. Morrison; 1 – B.A. Young, A.H. Jones, C. Pringle, R.P. de Groen and R.T. Latham (plus one as sub)

FIRST-CLASS AVERAGES

BATTING

	M	Inns	NO	Runs	HS	Av	100s	50s
M.L. Hayden	6	12	3	1136	173*	126.22	7	1
S.R. Waugh	9	15	4	976	190*	88.72	4	2
M.G. Bevan	12	22	5	1312	203*	77.17	5	8
D.M. Jones	7	14	2	918	158*	76.50	4	2
J.L. Langer	11	19	2	1198	233	70.47	3	7
M.N. Atkinson	12	20	12	534	69	66.75	–	1
G.S. Blewett	11	19	1	1036	268	57.55	2	4
D.S. Lehmann	11	19	–	1087	200	57.21	4	4
G.R.J. Matthews	3	6	3	165	55*	55.00	–	1
B.J. Hodge	11	21	2	991	166	52.15	1	8
M.A. Taylor	10	16	1	763	170	50.86	2	4
D.R. Martyn	12	19	2	855	197	50.29	2	6
S. Young	12	21	4	842	124*	49.52	1	7
D.F. Hills	12	23	1	1068	158*	48.54	3	7
J. Cox	8	15	2	630	129	48.46	2	2
A.R. Border	10	14	1	629	125*	48.38	2	4
S. Lee	4	5	2	145	104*	48.33	1	–
R.T. Ponting	12	22	2	965	161	48.25	3	4
R.J. Davison	7	12	2	482	133*	48.20	1	3
M.E. Waugh	10	16	–	765	119	47.81	2	6
M.T.G. Elliott	7	14	1	621	175*	47.76	2	3
M.T. Haywood	3	3	–	141	73	47.00	–	1
D.J. Buckingham	9	16	2	627	100*	44.78	1	5
D.C. Boon	7	11	1	441	106	44.10	1	3
T.M. Moody	11	17	–	741	115	43.58	2	4
M.J. Slater	11	19	–	802	168	42.21	2	4
P.C. Nobes	11	20	1	796	141	41.89	3	3
T.J. Barsby	11	22	–	900	129	40.90	2	4
J.A. Brayshaw	11	20	1	766	146	40.31	2	2
J.D. Siddons	10	17	1	640	161	40.00	2	2
M.J. DiVenuto	10	18	–	678	125	37.66	2	2
J.P. Maher	8	16	1	557	122	37.13	1	4
I.A. Healy	10	14	4	368	113*	36.80	1	1
D.S. Webber	10	17	1	581	176	36.31	2	1
G.R. Marsh	11	19	2	615	128	36.17	1	3
M.L. Love	9	17	1	571	138	35.68	2	2
S.G. Law	11	21	–	747	118	35.57	3	3
W.N. Phillips	10	20	1	674	156*	35.47	2	2
C.B. Hogg	3	6	2	141	44	35.25	–	–
G.J. Allardice	6	11	1	351	86	35.10	–	3
R.J. Tucker	12	20	4	558	107	34.87	1	1
T.J. Zoehrer	11	16	3	422	83	32.46	–	3
D.J. Ramshaw	10	19	–	614	85	32.31	–	5
J. Angel	10	11	5	192	84*	32.00	–	2
G.R. Robertson	9	11	3	248	85	31.00	–	1
M.R.J. Veletta	11	18	2	486	80*	30.37	–	5
G.I. Foley	8	16	1	444	89	29.60	–	3
R. Chee Quee	9	16	–	470	76	29.37	–	4
N.D. Maxwell	8	12	2	282	75	28.20	–	2
C.J. McDermott	10	8	1	189	61	27.00	–	1
B.E. McNamara	11	18	–	476	128	26.44	1	2
J.M. Thomas	3	6	–	158	38	26.33	–	–
I.W. Wrigglesworth	2	4	–	105	58	26.25	–	1
W.A. Seccombe	6	11	2	230	95	25.55	–	1
J.C. Scuderi	3	5	–	114	54	22.80	–	2
A.J. Bichel	5	9	1	181	61*	22.62	–	1
P.R. Reiffel	8	10	3	155	51	22.14	–	1
N.C.P. Courtney	6	11	–	244	55	22.18	–	1
B.P. Julian	11	15	2	262	59	20.15	–	1
C.G. Rackemann	10	14	7	136	33	19.42	–	–
D.W. Fleming	7	10	4	116	54*	19.33	–	1
P.E. Emery	12	17	3	258	50	18.42	–	1
D.A. Reeves	5	8	1	128	40*	18.28	–	–
C.D. Matthews	10	11	–	198	75	18.00	–	1

	M	Inns	NO	Runs	HS	Av	100s	50s
A.I.C. Dodemaide	8	13	1	214	52	17.83	–	1
T.J. Nielsen	11	18	3	252	34*	16.80	–	–
C. Howard	9	12	4	125	41*	15.62	–	–
S.K. Warne	10	12	2	151	74*	15.10	–	1
D.S. Berry	11	18	5	184	38*	14.15	–	–
M.S. Kasprowicz	7	8	–	111	35	13.87	–	–
S.P. George	10	13	1	124	50	10.33	–	1

(Qualification – 100 runs, average 10.00)

BOWLING

	Overs	Mds	Runs	Wkts	Av	Best	10/m	5/inn
S.K. Warne	574.2	176	1255	63	19.92	7-56	1	5
B.E. McNamara	165.3	57	363	18	20.16	6-43	–	1
S.M. McCooke	88.4	25	223	11	20.27	6-35	–	1
N.D. Maxwell	221.2	52	641	31	20.67	4-31	–	–
G.R.J. Matthews	160.2	40	412	19	21.68	7-99	1	1
M.E. Waugh	134.3	45	261	12	21.75	2-24	–	–
J. Angel	347.5	90	1024	47	21.78	5-32	1	3
B.A. Reid	77.4	19	225	10	22.50	5-34	–	1
D.W. Fleming	298.4	69	903	38	23.76	6-86	–	3
C.J. McDermott	424.1	121	1060	41	25.85	5-62	–	1
D. Tazelaar	128	42	293	11	26.63	5-49	–	1
T.M. Moody	222.2	68	570	20	28.50	4-43	–	–
C.R. Miller	376.4	87	1143	40	28.57	7-83	–	2
C.G. Rackemann	379.2	90	1097	38	28.86	6-93	–	2
G.I. Foley	96.4	18	318	11	28.90	3-64	–	–
S.H. Cook	254.5	45	885	30	29.50	5-114	–	1
G.D. McGrath	301.2	88	690	23	30.00	4-60	–	–
P.J.S. Alley	278.2	56	944	30	31.46	5-24	–	2
G.R. Robertson	379.3	93	998	30	33.26	6-54	–	3
A.J. Bichel	149	40	499	15	33.26	4-69	–	–
B.P. Julian	324	72	1021	30	34.03	5-34	–	1
S.P. George	384.3	84	1221	34	35.91	5-102	–	1
P.R. Reiffel	261	59	686	19	36.10	5-73	–	1
D.J. Spencer	183.1	20	750	20	37.50	4-85	–	–
S.G. Law	123.4	24	391	10	39.10	3-42	–	–
T.B.A. May	437	131	1015	25	40.60	5-65	–	2
M.S. Kasprowicz	262.4	55	844	20	42.20	5-92	–	1
S. Herzberg	317.5	57	942	22	42.81	4-66	–	–
P.W. Jackson	474	126	1220	28	43.57	4-66	–	–
S. Young	431	109	1258	28	44.92	4-85	–	–
W.J. Holdsworth	260.2	51	901	20	45.05	3-73	–	–
A.I.C. Dodemaide	247.5	62	766	17	45.05	5-85	–	1
D.A. Reeves	147	19	591	13	45.46	4-62	–	–
R.J. Tucker	288	71	834	18	46.33	4-56	–	–
A.E. Tucker	143.5	34	473	10	47.30	4-64	–	–
C. Howard	312.1	71	1046	22	47.54	5-42	–	2
D.J. Marsh	161	27	480	10	48.00	3-65	–	–
W.K. Wishart	245	72	551	11	50.09	4-90	–	–
P.E. McIntyre	510	91	1572	29	54.20	5-61	–	1
B.N. Wigney	238.1	45	782	14	55.85	3-78	–	–
C.D. Matthews	372.3	72	1292	19	68.00	2-37	–	–

(Qualification – 10 wickets)

LEADING FIELDERS

44 – M.N. Atkinson (ct 40/st 4); 43 – D.S. Berry (ct 37/st 6) and P.A. Emery (ct 39/st 4); 38 – T.J. Zoehrer (ct 37/st 1); 35 – I.A. Healy (ct 31/st 4) and T.J. Nielsen (ct 30/st 5); 30 – W.A. Seccombe (ct 29/st 1); 20 – M.R.J. Veletta (ct 19/st 1); 15 – M.A. Taylor; 14 – D.J. Ramshaw; 13 – T.M. Moody and R.T. Ponting; 12 – S. Young; 11 – B.P. Julian, S.G. Law, P.C. Nobes and J.D. Siddons; 10 – G.J. Allardice, R.J. Davison, D.F. Hills, D.M. Jones, M.L. Love, N.D. Maxwell, S.K. Warne, M.E. Waugh and D.S. Webber.

SECTION B
New Zealand

Shell Cup
Shell Trophy
Pakistan tour, Test and one-day international series
Indian tour, Test and one-day international series
First-class averages
Form charts

Shane Thomson – Cricketer of the Year. (David Munden/Sports-Line)

63

The 1993–4 season saw the New Zealand Cricket Association make radical changes in the first-class competition, the Shell Trophy. Matches were played over four days, associations met each other once only, and the top four sides in the league competition qualified for the semi-finals. Unfortunately, domestic cricket was hampered by the fact that the national side was playing a Test series in Australia before Christmas and in the Benson and Hedges World Series in January. They would return to New Zealand in time to meet Pakistan in three Test matches and five one-day internationals. As the Pakistanis departed, the Indians arrived to play a Test match and four one-day internationals. It was also planned that the winners of the New Zealand one-day competition, the Shell Cup, should meet their Australian counterparts in the Trans-Tasman Challenge. A busy time lay ahead, and Canterbury prepared for the season by visiting South Africa and meeting Eastern Province in a first-class fixture.

SHELL CUP

27 December 1993 *at Basin Reserve, Wellington*

Wellington 186
Auckland 187 for 1 (J.I. Pamment 105 not out)

Auckland (2 pts.) won by 9 wickets

at Trust Bank Park, Hamilton

Northern Districts 223 for 7 (B.A. Young 64)
Central Districts 216 (S.W.J. Wilson 91)

Northern Districts (2 pts.) won by 7 runs

at Molyneux Park, Alexandra

Canterbury 288 for 5 (C.Z. Harris 94 not out, C.L. Cairns 63, R.T. Latham 53)
Otago 174 (I.S. Billcliff 56)

Canterbury (2 pts.) won by 114 runs

Yorkshire-born James Pamment hit 5 sixes and 8 fours as Auckland raced to victory over Wellington. Pamment's 116-ball innings saw Auckland win with more than 10 overs to spare. Wellington were handicapped when Larsen was forced to retire hurt at 115 for 3.

Where the Shell Trophy had, in a sense, contracted, the Shell Cup expanded. Each side was to meet the other on a home and away basis. Northern Districts celebrated by recording their first one-day victory for almost three years. Northern scored an impressive 223, with Grant Bradburn supporting Bryan Young's 64 with an innings of 42 off 45 balls. Central Districts died bravely, and

Simon Wilson took the individual award for his 91 off 113 balls.

In Alexandra, Canterbury trounced Otago. The last 10 overs of the Canterbury innings realised 118 runs, and Chris Harris, who later took 3 for 20, hit 94 off 95 balls with 2 sixes and 7 fours.

29 December 1993 *at Eden Park, Auckland*

Auckland 164 (M.F. Sharpe 4 for 30)
Canterbury 165 for 2 (B.R. Hartland 54, R.T. Latham 51)

Canterbury (2 pts.) won by 8 wickets

at Basin Reserve, Wellington

Central Districts 238 (C.D. Ingham 67, R.K. Brown 50)
Wellington 166 (R.G. Twose 4 for 25)

Central Districts (2 pts.) won by 72 runs

at Molyneux Park, Alexandra

Northern Districts 233 (S.A. Thomson 64)
Otago 119 (P.W. Dobbs 51)

Northern Districts (2 pts.) won by 114 runs

The second round of matches produced three one-sided victories. Not only were Auckland overwhelmed by Canterbury, but they also lost Morrison who retired with a groin strain after bowling just one ball. The injury was to

Blair Hartland established a record for the Shell Cup when he hit 161 for Canterbury against Northern Districts at Timaru. (Alan Cozzi)

keep him out of the second half of the one-day series in Australia.

Led by Warwickshire's Roger Twose, Central Districts beat Wellington with ease. Ingham provided the foundation to the innings, and Rodney Brown hit 50 off 51 balls. Flushed by success in the first round, Northern Districts again won with plenty to spare. Skipper Grant Bradburn gave a fine all-round performance, hitting 48 off 51 balls and taking 3 for 28.

31 December 1993 *at Hagley Park, Christchurch*

Canterbury 244 for 9 (C.L. Cairns 84)
Wellington 159 for 8

Canterbury (2 pts.) won by 85 runs

at Blake Park, Mt Maunganui

Northern Districts 193 for 7 (S.A. Thomson 57)
Auckland 190 for 9

Northern Districts (2 pts.) won by 3 runs

at Pukekura Park, New Plymouth

Otago 165 for 7 (I.S. Billcliff 52, C.J.W. Finch 51 not out)
Central Districts 168 for 5

Central Districts (2 pts.) won by 5 wickets

Chris Cairns hit 2 sixes and 7 fours in his 75-ball innings as Canterbury maintained their winning run against a woeful Wellington side who could find excuse only in the poor conditions in which they had to bat.

Northern Districts were harder pressed to maintain their one hundred per cent record. Chasing a target of 194, Auckland were going well until they lost Pamment in the 26th over and Vaughan three balls later.

Otago were trounced for the third time in three matches, but their fate could have been even worse. They were 39 for 5 and 95 for 7, and only a ferocious 51 off 33 balls by Chris Finch, ably supported by Dion Nash, gave them a hint of respectability although not enough to trouble Central Districts.

2 January 1994 *at Pukekura Park, New Plymouth*

Canterbury 200 for 7
Central Districts 201 for 5 (M.J. Greatbatch 69)

Central Districts (2 pts.) won by 5 wickets

at Basin Reserve, Wellington

Northern Districts 187
Wellington 189 for 1 (M.H. Austen 95 not out)

Wellington (2 pts.) won by 9 wickets

at Eden Park, Auckland

Otago 184 (E.J. Marshall 51)
Auckland 127

Otago (2 pts.) won by 57 runs

Canterbury suffered their first defeat in the competition when Central Districts beat them with more than six overs to spare, and Northern Districts, too, lost for the first time. They were surprisingly beaten by Wellington who had played poorly in the first three matches. Wellington owed much to skipper Michael Austen who shared an opening stand of 124 with Andrew Jones and went on to make 95 off 127 balls with 13 fours. Wellington won with 13 balls to spare.

Otago gained their first win and owed much to Man of the Match Evan Marshall. Batting at number eight, he hit 51 off 38 balls, and then took 3 for 21 in eight overs.

4 January 1994 *at Eden Park, Auckland*

Central Districts 217 for 4 (M.J. Greatbatch 56)
Auckland 112

Central Districts (2 pts.) won by 105 runs

at Aurangi Park, Timaru

Canterbury 313 for 7 (B.R. Hartland 161, L.G. Howell 59)
Northern Districts 208 for 7 (S.A. Thomson 61)

Canterbury (2 pts.) won by 105 runs

at Molyneux Park, Alexandra

Otago 254 for 9 (K.R. Rutherford 102, P.W. Dobbs 81)
Wellington 205 (L.J. Doull 68 not out)

Otago (2 pts.) won by 49 runs

Central Districts and Canterbury inflicted crushing defeats on their opponents to go level on points at the top of the table at the half-way stage. Ingham and McRae gave Central a fine start with an opening partnership of 80, and Greatbatch hit 56 off 63 balls. Auckland were never in contention, and Tony Blain had two catches and two stumpings as they crashed to 112 all out in 40.4 overs.

In Timaru, Blair Hartland established a record for the competition. He batted until the 46th over and hit 161 off 153 balls. His innings included a six and 17 fours. He and Howell added 189 for the second wicket, and Canterbury reached 313 for 7, the highest total amassed in the Shell Cup.

Ken Rutherford found form with 102 off as many balls and dominated an opening partnership of 151 with Peter Dobbs. Rutherford hit 3 sixes and 9 fours, and Otago went on to beat Wellington comfortably.

6 January 1994 *at Blake Park, Mt Maunganui*

Otago 200 for 8 (I.S. Billcliff 50)
Northern Districts 201 for 6 (B.G. Cooper 61)

Northern Districts (2 pts.) won by 4 wickets

at Queen Elizabeth II Park, Masterton

Wellington 225
Central Districts 228 for 9 (C.D. Garner 87)

Central Districts (2 pts.) won by 1 wicket

at Hagley Park, Christchurch

Auckland 175 for 6
Canterbury 178 for 2 (S.P. Fleming 74 not out)

Canterbury (2 pts.) won by 8 wickets

With six rounds of matches completed, Auckland and Wellington were virtually out of contention for a place in the semi-finals. Otago failed against Northern Districts who were revived by Cooper and Bradburn. The pair added 111 after coming together at 43 for 3, and Northern went on to win with nine balls to spare. Central Districts, too, were revived. Chasing a target of 226, they were 53 for 4 before Craig Garner and Rodney Brown added 100. The last over arrived with Central needing six to win with two wickets standing. Pawson was run out with two runs needed, but Lamason hit the fourth ball of the over for four to win the game.

Canterbury crushed Auckland with 8.4 overs to spare. Fleming and Howell shared an unbroken stand of 122 in 88 minutes. Fleming's 74 came off 65 balls.

9 January 1994 *at Basin Reserve, Wellington*

Wellington 197 for 9 (E.B. McSweeney 69)
Canterbury 157

Wellington (2 pts.) won by 40 runs

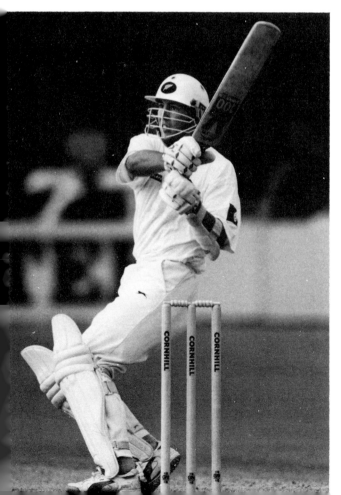

at Eden Park, Oval

Northern Districts 227 (B.G. Cooper 61, M.L. Su'a 5 for 42)
Auckland 196

Northern Districts (2 pts.) won by 31 runs

10 January 1994 *at Centennial Park, Oamaru*

Otago 188 for 6
Central Districts 133 (C.D. Garner 59)

Otago (2 pts.) won by 55 runs

The favourites lost ground, with both Canterbury and Central Districts being surprisingly beaten. Canterbury looked ready to maintain their impressive record when they reached 94 for 1 against Wellington, but six wickets then fell for 19 runs, and they never made an effective recovery. Auckland suffered their sixth defeat in succession, and Otago beat Central Districts in the first match to be played on the reserve day, the first day having been washed out.

11 January 1994 *at Basin Reserve, Wellington*

Wellington 217 for 9 (R.J. Kerr 61, D.J. Nash 4 for 25)
Otago 107 (B.R. Williams 4 for 22)

Wellington (2 pts.) won by 110 runs

at Smallbone Park, Rotorua

Canterbury 138 for 8 (N.J. Astle 60 not out)
Northern Districts 134

Canterbury (2 pts.) won by 4 runs

at Waikanae Park, Waikanae

Central Districts 123
Auckland 124 for 5 (J.I. Pamment 51 not out)

Auckland (2 pts.) won by 5 wickets

Wellington kept alive their slim hopes with a victory over Otago which brought the two sides level on points. Canterbury went clear at the top with a narrow victory over Northern Districts. Northern's bowlers did well, and only Nathan Astle showed the necessary application among the Canterbury batsmen. A second-wicket stand of 69 between Wealleans and Burnett seemed to have put Northern on the road to victory, but four wickets fell for five runs. Six runs were needed from the last two overs, but Hayes was run out, and Canterbury were the victors. Auckland's miserable run ended with a resounding win over Central Districts.

Adam Parore gave up wicket-keeping for a period to concentrate on his batting. He scored heavily for Auckland and eventually regained his Test place. (David Munden/Sports-Line)

13 January **1994** *at Eden Park, Auckland*

Auckland 155 (C.M. Spearman 66)
Wellington 131

Auckland (2 pts.) won by 24 runs

at Horton Park, Blenheim

Northern Districts 163
Central Districts 164 for 6

Central Districts (2 pts.) won by 4 wickets

at Hagley Park, Christchurch

Canterbury 137 for 9
Otago 140 for 6

Otago (2 pts.) won by 4 wickets

The penultimate round of matches saw few runs scored. Martin Crowe returned to the Wellington team and, wearing a kneebrace, he made 27 in 75 minutes against Auckland, but he deemed himself unfit to return to the national squad in Australia. Auckland's victory gave Wellington little hope of qualifying for the semi-finals. Central Districts confirmed their qualification by beating Northern Districts with three balls to spare, and Otago looked likely to become the fourth qualifiers when they surprisingly beat Canterbury.

16 January **1994** *at Hagley Park, Christchurch*

Central Districts 121 for 8 (R.G. Twose 51)
Canterbury 122 for 3

Canterbury (2 pts.) won by 7 wickets

at Harry Barker Reserve, Gisborne

Northern Districts 132 (J.D. Wells 4 for 26)
Wellington 133 for 3

Wellington (2 pts.) won by 7 wickets

17 January **1994** *at Carisbrook, Dunedin*

Otago 214 for 9 (D.J. Nash 84, M.L. Su'a 4 for 47)
Auckland 105 (E.J. Marshall 7 for 49)

Otago (2 pts.) won by 109 runs

Defending champions Canterbury finished top of the Shell Cup league when they beat Central Districts in a low-scoring match in Christchurch. Wellington, with Martin Crowe scoring 49, gained a consolation victory over Northern Districts, but failed to qualify for the semi-finals as Otago beat Auckland. Nash hit 4 sixes in his 84 as Otago made 214 from their 50 overs, and Auckland were bowled out in 15.1 overs. Evan Marshall took a remarkable 7 for 49 in 7.1 overs, and Jeff Wilson held five catches as well as taking the wicket of Vaughan.

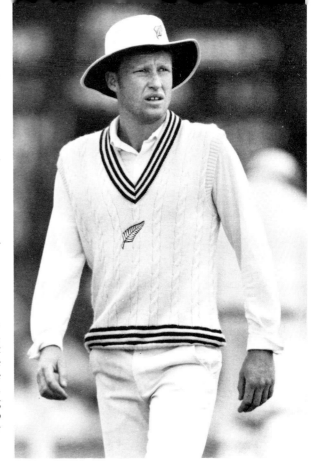

Mark Priest returned to the Canterbury side in the New Year and confirmed his standing as New Zealand's best slow left-arm bowler and a batsman of considerable talent, but he failed to gain selection for the tour of England. (David Munden/Sports-Line)

SHELL CUP FINAL TABLE

	P	W	L	Pts.
Canterbury	10	7	3	14
Central Districts	10	6	4	12
Northern Districts	10	5	5	10
Otago	10	5	5	10
Wellington	10	4	6	8
Auckland	10	3	7	6

SEMI-FINALS

23 January **1994** *at Trust Bank Park, Hamilton*

Northern Districts 240 for 5 (B.A. Young 51)
Otago 168 (I.S. Billcliff 60)

Northern Districts won by 72 runs

23 and 24 January **1994** *at Hagley Park, Christchurch*

Canterbury 151 (A.J. Alcock 5 for 31)
Central Districts 33 for 1

Match abandoned

Northern Districts qualified to meet the loser of the major semi-final when they beat Otago with some ease. Northern scored consistently and dismissed Dobbs and Rutherford with only 21 scored. Billcliff and Breen raised Otago's hopes with a stand of 81, but Otago lost their last six wickets for 35 runs.

Central Districts bowled and fielded splendidly to restrict Canterbury to 151, but rain halted play and prevented any resumption on the reserve day so that Canterbury moved into the final automatically as they had finished top of the qualifying league.

27 January 1994 *at McLean Park, Napier*

Northern Districts 179 for 7 (G.P. Burnett 76 not out)
Central Districts 181 for 7

Central Districts won by 3 wickets

In a match reduced to 47 overs, Central Districts won a place in the final by beating Northern Districts with five balls to spare. Graham Burnett's 76 off 114 balls was the backbone of the Northern innings, and he had able support from Young and Thomson. Central began slowly before Greatbatch and Blain gave the innings the required energy, and it was Dave Lamason, Man of the Match, who steered them into the final.

SHELL CUP FINAL
CANTERBURY *v.* CENTRAL DISTRICTS, at Napier

Lancaster Park had been unfit for cricket for most of the season due to damage caused to the outfield during a rock concert. The Canterbury Cricket Association deemed that it was fit for the final, but the New Zealand Board declared otherwise and, to the chagrin of Canterbury, the final was moved to Napier.

Germon won the toss and Canterbury batted. They began dreadfully. Murray was out in the eighth over, and Howell, Hartland and Chris Harris were dismissed in the space of three overs. Duff dismissed Latham with his first delivery, and Canterbury, 66 for 5, faced humiliation. Fleming joined Cairns in the 20th over, and suddenly the game was transformed. Cairns advanced down the wicket to almost every delivery. He met fire with fire, and between the 42nd and 45th overs, 50 runs came off 24 balls.

Fleming gave brave support, gathering runs all the time, but the hero was Chris Cairns. Off 106 balls, he hit 99, with 2 sixes and 7 fours. He was run out going for the second run which would have made him the first batsman to score a century in a Shell Cup final.

SHELL CUP FINAL – CENTRAL DISTRICTS *v.* CANTERBURY
29 January 1994 at McLean Park, Napier

CANTERBURY

B.R. Hartland	c Garner, **b** Alcock	14
D.J. Murray	c Greatbatch, **b** Alcock	11
L.G. Howell	lbw, **b** Blake	3
C.Z. Harris	c Blain, **b** Alcock	1
C.L. Cairns	run out	99
R.T. Latham	c Greatbatch, **b** Duff	15
S.P. Fleming	c Greatbatch, **b** Lamason	58
N.J. Astle	not out	14
*L.K. Germon (capt)	not out	7
R.M. Ford		
M.B. Owens		
Extras	b 1, lb 9, w 8	18
(50 overs)	(for 7 wickets)	240

CENTRAL DISTRICTS

C.D. Ingham	c Harris, **b** Ford	34
G.P. McRae	c Germon, **b** Cairns	21
C.D. Garner	run out	10
M.J. Greatbatch	c Hartland, **b** Cairns	44
R.G. Twose (capt)	c Hartland, **b** Harris	38
*T.E. Blain	c Fleming, **b** Harris	31
D.W. Lamason	st Germon, **b** Harris	3
S.W. Duff	c Murray, **b** Cairns	3
W.A. Wisneski	**b** Cairns	6
D.C. Blake	c Astle, **b** Owens	3
A.J. Alcock	not out	3
Extras	b 2, lb 6, w 3, nb 8	19
(49 overs)		215

	O	M	R	W
Blake	9	2	38	1
Alcock	10	1	39	3
Wisneski	5	1	23	–
Twose	9	–	50	–
Duff	10	1	32	1
Lamason	7	–	48	1

	O	M	R	W
Ford	10	2	26	1
Owens	9	–	53	1
Cairns	10	–	44	4
Harris	10	–	32	3
Astle	10	–	52	–

FALL OF WICKETS
1–20, 2–31, 3–33, 4–34, 5–66, 6–208, 7–228

FALL OF WICKETS
1–36, 2–66, 3–81, 4–139, 5–186, 6–199, 7–199, 8–206, 9–209

Umpires: B.L. Aldridge & R.S. Dunne   *Man of the Match:* C.L. Cairns   *Canterbury won by 25 runs*

Craig Ingham and Gavin McRae gave Central Districts a rapid start, being particularly severe on Michael Owens. Cairns was introduced for the eighth over, and he immediately had McRae caught behind. Garner maintained the aggression, and 50 came in the 14th over in spite of Ford's ten economic overs on the trot. In his final over, Ford dismissed Ingham, and Garner was then run out by Harris. Greatbatch and Twose still kept up Central's challenge with 50 coming off 55 balls. Cairns bowled Greatbatch with a slower ball, but Blain hit 31 off 37 balls, and still Central were chasing victory. A magnificent airborne catch by Hartland accounted for Twose, and Harris dismissed Blain and Lamason with successive deliveries. Hope had now receded for Central and, fittingly, Cairns led Canterbury to their third win in three years, a record.

 SHELL TROPHY

11, 12, 13 and **14 December 1993** *at Victoria Park, Wanganui*

Central Districts 308 (S.W.J. Wilson 105, C.D. Ingham 72, H.T. Davis 4 for 61) and 186 (R.G. Twose 81, M.C. Goodson 6 for 48)

Wellington 506 for 4 dec. (M.H. Austen 202, R.T. Hart 120, M.W. Douglas 95)

Wellington won by an innings and 12 runs

Wellington 16 pts., Central Districts 0 pts.

at Dudley Park, Rangiora

Canterbury 128 (C.M. Brown 6 for 50, J.T.C. Vaughan 4 for 27) and 146 (S.P. Fleming 57, C.M. Brown 4 for 40)

Auckland 121 (C.W. Flanagan 6 for 30) and 105 (C.W. Flanagan 5 for 37)

Canterbury won by 48 runs

Canterbury 16 pts., Auckland 0 pts.

at Trust Bank, Hamilton

Otago 233 (J.M. Allan 56) and 104 for 3 (R.A. Lawson 54 not out)

Northern Districts 82 (D.J. Nash 5 for 18) and 254 (G.E. Bradburn 61, A.J. Gale 5 for 72)

Otago won by 7 wickets

Otago 16 pts., Northern Districts 0 pts.

The first two rounds of the Shell Trophy were played before the Shell Cup without the presence of leading players who were on duty with the national side in Australia. The first round of matches produced positive results, but hardly in the manner that had been desired. The only game which lasted into the fourth day was the

one at Wanganui. Craig Ingham and Simon Wilson began with a partnership of 173 in just under five hours, but Central Districts failed to build on this start, and their last six wickets fell for 37 runs on the second morning. By the close of the day, Wellington were 169 for 0, and on the third day, Michael Austen and Ron Hart took their stand to 316 before Hart fell to Twose. Austen dominated the partnership. The Wellington captain had once hit a double century for Western Province, but he had not reached three figures since emigrating to New Zealand. Mark Douglas hit 95 off 119 balls, and Austen declared shortly before the close leaving Central an uncomfortable period during which they lost Ingham and Garner. They batted throughout the final day in an attempt to make Wellington bat again, but the leg-breaks of Matthew Goodson proved too much for them. He finished with a career best 6 for 48.

With Lancaster Park unfit, Canterbury switched their game to Rangiora, but the pitch was not up to standard, and the game finished before lunch on the third day. It was a paradise match for bowlers. Chris Brown and Chris Flanagan both returned the best figures of their careers, Brown was a newcomer, and Auckland skipper Justin Vaughan also enjoyed himself, but, batting second, his side was always trailing.

Put in to bat on a difficult pitch, Otago struggled to reach 233 in nearly 118 overs, being bowled out on the second morning. It proved to be a winning score. Northern Districts were bowled out for 82 in 34.4 overs and, following-on, were 189 for 6 at the end of the second day. Bradburn and Bailey shared a fourth-wicket stand of 108, but Otago won comfortably on the third day.

16, 17, 18 and **19 December 1993** *at Eden Park, Auckland*

Auckland 291 (A.C. Parore 87 not out, A.T. Reinholds 71, J.T.C. Vaughan 69) and 215 for 9 dec. (J.T.C. Vaughan 79, M.N. Hart 5 for 66)

Northern Districts 221 (G.P. Burnett 71) and 244 (B.G. Cooper 87, M.D. Bailey 57, S.W. Brown 5 for 56)

Auckland won by 41 runs

Auckland 16 pts., Northern Districts 0 pts.

at Basin Reserve, Wellington

Wellington 287 (E.B. McSweeney 111, D.S. McHardy 60) and 281 for 7 (E.B. McSweeney 99, M.W. Douglas 57, C.W. Flanagan 4 for 50)

Canterbury 257 (B.R. Hartland 65, L.G. Howell 60, J.D. Wells 6 for 59)

Match drawn

Wellington 4 pts., Canterbury 0 pts.

at Carisbrook, Dunedin

Central Districts 95 for 1 dec. and 116 for 3 dec. (C.D. Ingham 54)

Otago 0 for 0 dec. and 182 for 7 (P.W. Dobbs 82, D.J. Nash 51)

Match drawn

Central Districts 4 pts., Otago 0 pts.

The second round of matches in the Shell Trophy was badly hit by rain. The best of the weather was in Auckland where the match meandered along for the first three days and sprang into life. Asked to score 286 from a minimum of 83 overs, Northern Districts slumped to 79 for 4. Cooper and Bailey added 111 to restore Northern's fortunes, and with Robert Hart offering useful assistance, the visitors reached 235 for 6. Hart then fell to a spectacular catch by Adam Parore, and the tail folded quickly.

Rain prevented any play on the third day at Wellington, but the final day held interest in that Ervin McSweeney came close to hitting two centuries in a match. He had scored a fine 111 in the first innings with 2 sixes and 15 fours, and on the last afternoon he reached 99 with Canterbury now employing occasional bowlers. He drove a leg-spinner from Germon, who had abandoned the keeper's gloves, straight back to the bowler. It was Germon's first wicket in first-class cricket.

There was little play on the first day in Dunedin, and there was none at all on the second and third days. Even the forfeiture of an innings could not produce a result.

18, 19, 20 and **21 January 1994** *at Trust Bank Park, Hamilton*

Canterbury 407 (S.P. Fleming 105, D.J. Murray 95, L.K. Germon 89, M.J. Stephens 5 for 101)
Northern Districts 138 (M.W. Priest 4 for 32) and 254 (G.E. Bradburn 63, M.W. Priest 4 for 54)

Canterbury won by an innings and 15 runs

Canterbury 16 pts., Northern Districts 0 pts.

at Basin Reserve, Wellington

Wellington 330 (M.H. Austen 89, L.J. Doull 79) and 165 (E.J. Marshall 5 for 27)
Otago 272 (L.C. Breen 73, M.C. Goodson 4 for 65) and 124 (M.C. Goodson 5 for 40)

Wellington won by 99 runs

Wellington 16 pts., Otago 0 pts.

at Fitzherbert Park, Palmerston North

Central Districts 449 (R.G. Twose 99, R.K. Brown 90, M.E.L. Lane 84, C.D. Ingham 73) and 33 for 0
Auckland 151 and 330 (J.I. Pamment 98, D.N. Patel 59, S.W. Duff 4 for 111)

Central Districts 16 pts., Auckland 0 pts.

With the preliminary part of the Shell Cup programme complete, the Shell Trophy resumed, and associations were able to call upon some of their leading players. Canterbury moved closer to the final stages of the competition and virtually eliminated Northern Districts with a resounding victory in Hamilton. Batting until shortly

before lunch on the second day, Canterbury took a firm grip on the game from the outset. Darrin Murray and Blair Hartland began with a partnership of 76, and Murray batted well for his 95 which included a six and 15 fours, but the real substance of the innings was provided by Stephen Fleming and Lee Germon. The highly talented Fleming hit the second century of his career with a six and 11 fours. To his batting and excellent wicket-keeping, Germon allies shrewd leadership, and his clever use of his bowlers saw Northern Districts batting again before the end of the second day. Canterbury's varied attack was in top form, but particular honours went to Mark Priest who had been unable to play before Christmas because of business commitments. He finished the match with 8 for 86 as Canterbury won on the third day.

Wellington moved to the top of the table with victory over Otago. A shortened first day saw Wellington reach 197 for 6. Austen did not add to his score on the second morning, but Matthew Goodson and Lincoln Doull

Wellington's Heath Davis – the fastest bowler in the country and the leading wicket-taker with 31 wickets, but still wayward and inconsistent. (Alan Cozzi)

added 85. Doull hit the first fifty of his career, but it was leg-spinner Goodson who caused Otago problems with the ball, destroying their middle order in a spell which sent five wickets tumbling while 46 runs were scored. With the pitch now posing problems, Wellington were bowled out by Wixon and Marshall for 165, and Otago were left 93 overs in which to score 224. They never looked like approaching their target as Man of the Match Goodson again took control to finish with nine wickets in a match for the second time in three Trophy rounds.

Central Districts batted until 3.20 on the second day against Auckland. Ingham and Twose added 165 for the third wicket, and Rodney Brown and Mark Lane 165 for the seventh. By the close of play, Auckland were 97 for 7. Thanks to James Pamment's 98 in 245 minutes, Auckland took the game into the last day, but they never had a real hope of saving the match.

3, 4, 5 and 6 February 1994 *at Eden Park, Auckland*

Wellington 116 (M.L. Su'a 6 for 56) and 152
(M.H. Austen 58, D.N. Patel 6 for 43)
Auckland 266 (G.R. Jones 4 for 85) and 3 for 0

Auckland won by 10 wickets

Auckland 16 pts., Wellington 0 pts.

at Dudley Park, Rangiora

Otago 179 (P.W. Dobbs 63, G.R. Baker 53) and 145
(M.W. Priest 6 for 72)
Canterbury 303 (D.J. Boyle 117, N.J. Astle 69, A.J. Gale
6 for 75) and 22 for 1

Canterbury won by 9 wickets

Canterbury 16 pts., Otago 0 pts.

at Trafalgar Park, Nelson

Central Districts 272 (G.P. McRae 62, S.W. Duff 59,
J.B.M. Furlong 51 not out, R.P. de Groen 5 for 89)
and 247 for 6 dec. (T.E. Blain 50)
Northern Districts 217 (M.D. Bailey 84, M.E. Parlane 75)
and 300 for 9 (M.E. Parlane 89, G.E. Bradburn 73 not
out, D.J. Hartshorn 4 for 124)

Match drawn

Central Districts 4 pts., Northern Districts 0 pts.

Wellington suffered their first defeat and lost their place at the top of the table. They suffered at the hands of two players recently omitted from the New Zealand side, Su'a and Patel. Murphy Su'a produced the best bowling performance of his career as Wellington were bundled out on a truncated first day. Auckland, too, found runs difficult to score, but Mills, Su'a, Pringle and Morrison gave much substance to the late order, and the last three wickets realised 157 runs. Wellington fared badly when they batted for a second time. Patel's off-breaks brought him six wickets, and four of his victims fell to catches at silly mid-off by James Pamment. Auckland won inside three days.

Canterbury moved to the top of the table with their third win in four matches. Only a sixth-wicket stand of 91 between Baker and Dobbs saved Otago from total disaster on the first day. David Boyle's 8¼-hour innings put Canterbury in command in spite of Aaron Gale's career-best bowling performance. Batting again, Otago were perplexed by the left-arm spin of Priest, and the game was over before the scheduled close of the third day.

No play was possible on the first day in Nelson after which solid batting took Central Districts to 272. Northern looked as if they might take first-innings points, but they lost their last five wickets for 38 runs. Eventually, they were asked to make 303 off 65 overs to win the match. Parlane and Wealleans began with a partnership of 110, but the real spark was provided by skipper Grant Bradburn who hit 73 off 69 balls. From the last three overs, 39 runs were wanted, and, with two wickets in hand, Northern needed seven from the last two balls of the final over. Robbie Hart skied Hartshorn to Furlong, but Bradburn hit the last ball over the inner fielders for four. So Central finished one wicket short, and Northern ended three runs short and still pointless.

10, 11, 12 and 13 February 1994 *at Lancaster Park, Christchurch*

Canterbury 341 (M.W. Priest 73 not out, D.J. Murray 70)
and 400 for 4 (C.Z. Harris 140 not out, D.J. Murray
85), B.R. Hartland 55, N.J. Astle 52 not out)
Central Districts 261 (S.J. Roberts 5 for 70)

Match drawn

Canterbury 4 pts., Central Districts 0 pts.

at Carisbrook, Dunedin

Auckland 141 (J.W. Wilson 4 for 29) and 269
(A.C. Parore 133, A.T. Reinholds 61, R.P. Wixon 5 for
83)
Otago 163 (C. Pringle 7 for 63) and 173 (C. Pringle 7
for 56)

Auckland won by 74 runs

Auckland 12 pts., Otago 4 pts.

at Trust Bank Park, Hamilton

Wellington 218 (M.W. Douglas 66, R.L. Hayes 4 for 41)
and 255 (M.W. Douglas 106)
Northern Districts 312 (G.P. Burnett 131, H.T. Davis 4
for 95) and 164 for 4

Northern Districts 16 pts., Wellington 0 pts.

Canterbury adopted a policy of 'what we have we hold'. Consistent batting into the second day took them to 341 and, with Sharpe and Roberts bowling well, they took the first-innings points which ensured that they would finish top of the table and have home advantage in the semi-final. They batted for much of the third day and all the last day. Harris was in for nearly six hours for the highest score of his career, and the Canterbury batsmen took a long look at Central District's bowling.

Auckland came from behind to best Otago and clinch second place in the table. Auckland had two heroes. Chris Pringle had match figures of 14 for 119 so becoming the fourth Auckland bowler to take 14 wickets in a match while Adam Parore, relieved of wicket-keeping duties, hit 133. Otago's defeat cost them a place in the semi-finals.

Champions for the past two seasons, Northern Districts entered their final match without a point to their credit, but they bowled out Wellington on the opening day and never lost their grip on the match. Graham Burnett, formerly of Wellington, provided the substance to the Northern innings and, in spite of Mark Douglas' century, Northern ran out comfortable winners.

SHELL TROPHY TABLE

	P	W	L	D	Pts.
Canterbury	5	3	–	2	52
Auckland	5	3	2	–	44
Wellington	5	2	2	1	36
Central Districts	5	1	1	3	24
Otago	5	1	3	1	20
Northern Districts	5	1	3	1	16

SEMI-FINALS

17, 18, 19 and **20 February 1994** *at Lancaster Park, Christchurch*

Central Districts 195 (S.W. Duff 85) and 241 (R.G. Twose 70, M.W. Priest 4 for 76)

Canterbury 559 (L.K. Germon 114, G.R. Stead 113 not out, M.W. Priest 102, C.Z. Harris 70, W.A. Wisneski 5 for 115)

Canterbury won by an innings and 123 runs

at Eden Park, Auckland

Auckland 170 (A.T. Reinholds 52, H.T. Davis 4 for 48, G.R. Jonas 4 for 48) and 322 for 4 dec. (A.C. Parore 84, D.N. Patel 84)

Wellington 108 (M.L. Su'a 5 for 44, W. Watson 4 for 30)

Match drawn

The semi-finals clashed with the second Test match against Pakistan, but it is doubtful whether Blain and Greatbatch could have saved Central Districts from being overwhelmed by Canterbury. Central were 36 for 5 when Duff came to the wicket and only his defiant batting, which included a ninth-wicket stand of 89 with Leonard, saved his side from total humiliation. In spite of Harris' spirited 70, it was the Canterbury late order which placed the match firmly in the control of the home side. The last five wickets produced 400 runs with Germon, Priest and Stead, playing only his second match for the province, hitting centuries. Canterbury batted into the fourth day, and a demoralised Central Districts again capitulated before Roberts, Sharpe and Priest.

Rain in Auckland meant that the home side's first innings was stretched over the first two days. On the third day Wellington were bowled out inside three hours with Watson and Su'a causing the damage. Having qualified for the final by virtue of their first-innings lead, Auckland batted out the rest of the match.

SHELL TROPHY FINAL
CANTERBURY *v.* AUCKLAND, at Rangiora

One must question what value the New Zealand cricket authorities put upon their premier domestic competition when they schedule the final to be played at the same time as the third Test match against Pakistan. As the Test match was to be played at Lancaster Park, Canterbury were forced to move the venue for the final to Dudley Park, Rangiora.

Initially, it seemed that the pitch at Dudley Park would be as difficult as it had been when the same two sides met there at the beginning of the season. Auckland had begun confidently enough, but after Reinholds offered no shot to a ball from Owens on the stroke of lunch, their innings fell apart, and Canterbury were batting before the end of the day. At the close, they had lost Boyle, Murray and Harris to Willie Watson and Dipak Patel for 32 runs.

There was no recovery on the second morning. Three wickets fell immediately while two runs were scored, and it was only the determination of skipper Lee Germon that lifted them from 64 for 8 to 94 all out.

Leading by 85 on the first innings, Auckland now seemed to take a grip on the match. Uninhibited by the early loss of Reinholds, they prospered through the batting of Adam Parore who, since being relieved of wicket-keeping duties and promoted to number three, had shown considerable run-getting powers. He and Spearman added 56, and with Patel, Parore put on 76. At 132 for 2, Auckland had one hand on the trophy, but Mark Priest, enjoying a wonderful run of success, dismissed Patel, Pamment and Parore in quick succession. Auckland tumbled to 191 for 7 by stumps, with only Vaughan keeping his head above the wreckage.

Vaughan added only six to his overnight score on the third morning and he, like Su'a and Weston, fell victim to Sharpe. Canterbury now began their quest to score 290 to win the Shell Trophy. They batted steadily, but wickets fell at regular intervals, and when the exciting Fleming was run out third ball it seemed they must lose. The fall of Astle and Germon reduced them to 159 for 6 and defeat seemed even more assured, but David 'Barnacle' Boyle had stood firm, and now he was joined by Mark Priest. They added 78 before the end of the day, and Canterbury were within 53 runs of victory.

Nothing could dislodge Boyle and Priest on the final morning until, with the scores level, Priest was brilliantly caught in the gully off Vaughan. In anti-climax, a leg-bye produced the winning run, but Priest and Boyle, who batted for seven hours 40 minutes, had provided one of the great partnerships of New Zealand cricket. Canterbury had completed a 'double'.

AUCKLAND	FIRST INNINGS		SECOND INNINGS		CANTERBURY	FIRST INNINGS		SECOND INNINGS	
A.T. Reinholds	b Owens	32	b Owens	0	D.J. Boyle	c Mills, b Watson	7	(2) not out	92
C.M. Spearman	lbw, b Sharpe	20	c Priest, b Astle	26	D.J. Murray	c and b Patel	12	(1) c Pamment, b Patel	9
A.C. Parore	c Germon, b Sharpe	14	lbw, b Priest	91	L.G. Howell	lbw, b Watson	5	lbw, b Watson	17
D.N. Patel	b Priest	8	c Fleming, b Priest	25	C.Z. Harris	c Vaughan, b Watson	0	b Su'a	29
R.A. Jones	c Astle, b Owens	0	(7) lbw, b Sharpe	7	S.P. Fleming	run out	5	run out	0
J.T.C. Vaughan (capt)	not out	48	b Sharpe	29	N.J. Astle	c Vaughan, b Su'a	1	c Mills, b Vaughan	25
J.I. Pamment	c Germon, b Roberts	15	(5) lbw, b Priest	2	*L.K. Germon (capt)	b Patel	37	lbw, b Patel	3
*J.M. Mills	c Harris, b Sharpe	2	c Fleming, b Owens	9	M.W. Priest	c Jones, b Su'a	3	c Pamment, b Vaughan	88
M.L. Su'a	c Owens, b Harris	16	c Priest, b Sharpe	2	M.F. Sharpe	c Spearman, b Watson	1		
W. Watson	run out	12	c Boyle, b Sharpe	2	S.J. Roberts	b Vaughan	9	(9) not out	0
M.J. Haslam	c Howell, b Priest	0	not out	3	M.B. Owens	not out	0		
Extras	b 2, lb 6, nb 4	12	lb 2, nb 6	8	Extras	nb 14	14	b 3, lb 10, nb 14	27
		179		204			94	(for 7 wickets)	290

	O	M	R	W	O	M	R	W		O	M	R	W	O	M	R	W
Owens	18	5	36	2	15	5	40	2	Su'a	19	8	36	2	22	5	65	1
Roberts	12	4	16	1	14	3	47	–	Patel	18.5	9	24	2	36	9	86	2
Priest	29	9	58	2	24	9	45	3	Watson	20	7	31	4	32	10	61	1
Sharpe	14	2	42	3	18	3	59	4	Vaughan	2	–	3	1	12	4	18	2
Harris	6	2	8	1					Haslam					24	9	47	–
Astle	2	–	11	–	4	2	11	1									

FALL OF WICKETS

1–38, 2–63, 3–72, 4–75, 5–84, 6–116, 7–124, 8–153, 9–174
1–0, 2–56, 3–132, 4–134, 5–155, 6–164, 7–186, 8–197, 9–201

FALL OF WICKETS

1–18, 2–24, 3–24, 4–33, 5–34, 6–34, 7–55, 8–64, 9–92
1–23, 2–71, 3–114, 4–115, 5–152, 6–159, 7–289

Umpires: D.B. Cowie & C.E. King

Canterbury won by 3 wickets

PAKISTAN TOUR

30 January 1994 *at Trust Bank Park, Hamilton*

Pakistanis 211 for 6 (Inzamam-ul-Haq 105, Shoaib Mohammad 51 not out)
Sir Ron Brierley's XI 207 for 7 (G.E. Bradburn 83 not out)

Pakistanis won by 4 runs

Returning to top-level cricket at the age of 44, Lance Cairns led Sir Ron Brierley's XI in the 50-over match which opened the Pakistanis' tour. He dismissed both openers, Saeed Anwar and Shakeel Ahmed, and conceded only 16 runs in his seven overs, but Inzamam-ul-Haq hit 105 off 120 balls, with a six and 11 fours. Bradburn's 83 off 92 balls put the home side in a challenging position, but Cairns needed to hit the last ball of the match for six to win the contest. He managed only one.

31 January and 1, 2 February 1994 *at Trust Bank Park, Hamilton*

New Zealand Second XI 318 for 5 dec. (G.P. Burnett 59, B.A. Pocock 95, M.J. Greatbatch 65 not out) and 290 for 4 dec. (L.K. Germon 100 not out, L.G. Howell 59,

M.J. Greatbatch 50 retired hurt, B.R. Hartland 50)
Pakistanis 344 for 3 dec. (Saeed Anwar 131 retired hurt, Salim Malik 53 not out, Inzamam-ul-Haq 50 not out) and 155 for 2 (Shakeel Ahmed 68, Aamir Sohail 55)

Match drawn

The first first-class match of the Pakistan tour produced a glut of runs. Greatbatch led a New Zealand side of Test hopefuls, and they plundered runs on the first day. Pocock was caught behind after batting for just over five hours while Greatbatch himself hit 65 off 48 balls. Saeed Anwar's 131 included 2 sixes and 21 fours and came off 188 balls. Germon, whom many would like to see keeping wicket for New Zealand and even captaining the side, reached an excellent century on the last day.

1 February 1994 *at Carisbrook, Dunedin*

North Island 166 for 9
South Island 167 for 5 (C.Z. Harris 64 not out, S.P. Fleming 52)

South Island won by 6 wickets

With nine one-day internationals looming, a 'trial' match was agreed, but the selectors can have learned little from this 50-over contest.

A return to form and favour for Salim Malik and captain of Pakistan for the tour of New Zealand following the players' revolt against team selection and the leadership of Wasim Akram. (David Munden/Sports-Line)

4, 5, 6 and **7 February 1994** *at McLean Park, Napier*

New Zealand Emerging Players XI 93 and 290 for 4
  (S.P. Fleming 109 not out, S.A. Thomson 77)
Pakistanis 485 for 8 dec. (Saeed Anwar 114, Basit Ali
  100, Asif Mujtaba 76, Inzamam-ul-Haq 65, Salim
  Malik 59)

Match drawn

No play was possible on the first day, and on the second, in conditions ideal for bowling, the young New Zealanders capitulated before the Pakistan seam attack. The tourists, 80 for 1 at the close of the second day, scored heavily on the third, and Saeed Anwar, Basit Ali and Inzamam-ul-Haq all retired when they felt that they had had sufficient practice. Batting for survival on the last day, the home side were encouraged by Fleming and Thomson, two very promising cricketers, who added 138 for the fourth wicket.

9, 10, 11 and **12 February 1994** *at Smallbone Park, Rotorua*

New Zealand Academy XI 269 (S.P. Fleming 77,
  A.C. Parore 67, G.P. Burnett 63, K.P. Smith 5 for 39)
  and 203 for 8 dec. (D.J. Murray 84, M.J. Stephens 4
  for 64)
Northern Districts 120 (D.J. Nash 6 for 30) and 91
  (H.T. Davis 4 for 18)

New Zealand Academy XI won by 261 runs

In an effort to give more match practice to players of promise, the New Zealand Cricket Board arranged three first-class fixtures for the Academy XI. In the first of these, the young cricketers showed to good effect and won handsomely against Northern Districts.

FIRST TEST MATCH
NEW ZEALAND *v.* PAKISTAN, at Auckland

Captaining Pakistan for the first time, Salim Malik won the toss and asked New Zealand to bat on a grassy pitch. He was immediately rewarded for his boldness when deposed captain Wasim Akram had Pocock caught behind for 0. No other wickets fell before lunch, but Young was out to the first ball after the interval and, 37 minutes later, Rutherford dragged a ball from Waqar Younis onto his stumps.

While Andrew Jones provided solidity, Mark Greatbatch countered with aggression, hitting 48 off 34 balls in his 47-minute stay. His innings included 2 sixes and 8 fours. He had been particularly severe on Mushtaq Ahmed, but the leg-spinner had his revenge when Greatbatch skied to cover.

Jones did not survive the left-hander long and with Thomson and Blain promising more than they ultimately achieved, the late order succumbed to Waqar and Wasim with an air of inevitability. New Zealand came straight back into the match, however, by capturing four wickets before the close of play which came at 61 for 4 with Salim Malik and Basit Ali thankful to survive.

The Pakistan captain and his partner did not survive long on the second morning and although Inzamam-ul-Haq, Wasim Akram and Rashid Latif all showed spirit, Pakistan fell short of the New Zealand score by 27 runs. Doull and de Groen had swung the ball appreciably, and Young held three catches. He was to hold three more in the second innings to establish a record for New Zealand.

By the end of the second day, on which 16 wickets fell, Pakistan were batting again. Wasim Akram bowled unchanged to record the best figures of his Test career. He was ably supported in the field and, on a day full of action, umpires Bird and Dunne were guilty of some bizarre counting with regard to the number of balls to an over.

Pakistan scored three in one over before the end of the day, and although Saeed Anwar and Asif Mujtaba fell in quick succession on the third morning, Aamir Sohail batted with sense and aggression to take his side close to

Five wickets in a Test innings for the first time for Simon Doull in the match at Eden Park, but the pace bowler was to be plagued by injury. (Paul Sturgess/Sports-Line)

victory. The victory was achieved when Rashid Latif hit Shane Thomson for six shortly after lunch.

In their second innings, New Zealand had batted badly, and only some rustic shots from Cairns and Doull took the score past 100. Doull was one New Zealander who could take comfort from the match. He had his first five-wicket haul in a Test and finished with match figures of 7 for 114. Wasim Akram, of course, was Man of the Match.

SECOND TEST MATCH
NEW ZEALAND *v.* PAKISTAN, at Wellington

New Zealand made two changes from the side which lost the first Test: Morrison returned in place of Owens and Hart won his first Test cap when Cairns was ruled unfit once more. Pakistan were forced to make one change when off-spinner Akram Raza came in for Mushtaq Ahmed who had returned to Pakistan with a back injury.

Rutherford won the toss, and New Zealand batted on a pitch which offered no help to the bowlers. What help the Pakistan bowlers received came from the New Zealand batsmen who gave a woeful display. Only Jones who batted 167 minutes for his 43 showed the necessary

---

FIRST TEST MATCH – NEW ZEALAND *v.* PAKISTAN
10, 11 and 12 February 1994 at Eden Park, Auckland

NEW ZEALAND

	FIRST INNINGS		SECOND INNINGS	
B.A. Young	c Rashid, b Waqar	29	c Rashid, b Wasim	0
B.A. Pocock	c Rashid, b Wasim	0	c Asif, b Wasim	10
A.H. Jones	c Rashid, b Mushtaq	66	c Rashid, b Wasim	6
K.R. Rutherford (capt)	b Waqar	14	b Waqar	18
M.J. Greatbatch	c Salim, b Mushtaq	48	c Inzamam, b Wasim	0
S.A. Thomson	c Rashid, b Waqar	29	c Rashid, b Waqar	0
C.L. Cairns	c Salim, b Mushtaq	6	c Asif, b Ata-ur-Rehman	31
*T.E. Blain	c Mushtaq, b Wasim	26	c Rashid, b Ata-ur-Rehman	4
S.B. Doull	c and b Waqar	0	c Salim, b Wasim	29
R.P. de Groen	c Mushtaq, b Wasim	2	not out	0
M.B. Owens	not out	2	c Rashid, b Wasim	0
Extras	b 4, lb 8, w 1, nb 7	20	b 4, lb 5, nb 3	12
		242		**110**

PAKISTAN

	FIRST INNINGS		SECOND INNINGS	
Saeed Anwar	c Blain, b Cairns	16	c Young, b de Groen	7
Aamir Sohail	c Jones, b de Groen	16	c Young, b Thomson	78
Asif Mujtaba	c Blain, b Doull	8	c and b Doull	0
Mushtaq Ahmed	c Young, b Doull	0		
Salim Malik (capt)	c Young, b Doull	18	(4) c Young, b de Groen	11
Basit Ali	c Blain, b Cairns	25	(5) c and b Doull	7
Inzamam-ul-Haq	c Young, b de Groen	43	(6) not out	20
*Rashid Latif	lbw, b Doull	30	(7) not out	13
Wasim Akram	c Blain, b de Groen	35		
Waqar Younis	c Cairns, b Doull	11		
Ata-ur-Rehman	not out	2		
Extras	lb 6, nb 5	11	lb 3, nb 2	5
		215	(for 5 wickets)	**141**

	O	M	R	W	O	M	R	W
Wasim Akram	22.3	9	50	3	16.1	4	43	6
Waqar Younis	15	2	46	4	10	3	35	2
Ata-ur-Rehman	14	3	55	–	6	1	23	2
Mushtaq Ahmed	17	1	79	3				

	O	M	R	W	O	M	R	W
Cairns	18	2	75	2	6	1	15	–
Owens	7	1	28	–	2	–	10	–
Doull	15	2	66	5	16	–	48	2
Thomson					4	1	17	1
de Groen	17.4	5	40	3	13	3	48	2

FALL OF WICKETS

1–3, 2–67, 3–95, 4–170, 5–175, 6–185, 7–228, 8–228, 9–233
1–0, 2–8, 3–31, 4–35, 5–40, 6–44, 7–67, 8–103, 9–110

FALL OF WICKETS

1–17, 2–36, 3–48, 4–50, 5–87, 6–93, 7–141, 8–176, 9–207
1–21, 2–25, 3–56, 4–73, 5–119

Umpires: H.D. Bird & R.S. Dunne

Pakistan won by 5 wickets

application. Greatbatch again chose belligerence, hitting 45 off 56 balls, but a longer stay would have been of more benefit to his side.

Again, it was the Pakistani pace men who wrecked New Zealand. Wasim Akram claimed Young in the first over of the match, and Ata-ur-Rehman took the wickets of three of the top batsmen.

New Zealand had early success when Morrison trapped Aamir Sohail leg before, but Saeed Anwar was in dominant mood and had hit 30 out of 35 before the close. Night-watchman Akram Raza was soon out on the second morning, but there was little joy for New Zealand after that. Saeed Anwar was devastating, and Basit Ali joined him in a third-wicket stand which was worth 197 in 209 minutes. Having hit 13 thundering boundaries, Basit Ali was bowled when he attempted to sweep the off-spinner Thomson. The left-handed Saeed Anwar plundered for another half an hour before being run out. His spectacular 169 included 26 fours, and it was his first Test century. Salim Malik and Inzamam-ul-Haq now continued the slaughter and Pakistan ended the day on 398 for 4, with Salim on 62, and Inzamam on 63.

Both batsmen reached centuries before lunch on the third day, and when Salim Malik was caught and bowled by the left-arm spinner Hart he and Inzamam had added 258 in 251 minutes. Indeed, Pakistan's 548 had come at just under one run a minute. Inzamam hit a six and 19 fours, and Salim 20 fours. Altogether there were 79 boundaries in the Pakistan innings.

New Zealand began disastrously, losing both openers inside the first quarter of an hour of their second innings. Rutherford saw attack as the best response to the situation, and he hit 11 fours in his 97-ball innings during which he lived dangerously before being caught at slip. Greatbatch did not last long, but Thomson stayed with Jones until the close and hit 15 off Waqar's last over of the day, a rather sensational method of playing out time.

The fourth day began with New Zealand on 189 for 4. Jones was on 66, and Thomson on 37. The start was delayed by rain until after lunch, but the match was over in $3\frac{1}{2}$ hours. Jones and Thomson fell in quick succession, and Hart lasted only 34 minutes. The entertainment came in a ninth-wicket stand between Blain and Morrison who battled bravely. They added 74 in an hour, and both batsmen reached their highest scores in Test cricket. Waqar and Wasim were not to be denied, however, and Pakistan took the match and the series with a day to spare. Wasim Akram, in taking 7 for 119, bettered his best bowling figures in a Test match which he had established in the first game of the series.

SECOND TEST MATCH – NEW ZEALAND v. PAKISTAN
17, 18, 19, 20 and 21 February 1994 at Basin Reserve, Wellington

NEW ZEALAND

	FIRST INNINGS		SECOND INNINGS	
B.A. Young	lbw, b Wasim	0	(2) b Wasim	4
B.A. Pocock	b Ata-ur-Rehman	16	(1) b Waqar	0
A.H. Jones	lbw, b Ata-ur-Rehman	43	b Wasim	76
K.R. Rutherford (capt)	c Akram, b Ata-ur-Rehman	7	c Akram, b Ata-ur-Rehman	63
M.J. Greatbatch	c Rashid, b Waqar	45	c Rashid, b Wasim	10
S.A. Thomson	b Wasim	7	c Ata-ur-Rehman, b Wasim	47
*T.E. Blain	c Saeed, b Waqar	8	c Basit, b Wasim	78
M.N. Hart	not out	12	b Wasim	7
D.K. Morrison	c Rashid, b Wasim	5	(10) lbw, b Waqar	42
S.B. Doull	c Basit, b Waqar	17	(9) c Salim, b Wasim	15
R.P. de Groen	b Wasim	4	not out	1
Extras	lb 7, nb 4	11	b 1, lb 5, nb 12	18
		175		**361**

PAKISTAN

	FIRST INNINGS	
Saeed Anwar	run out	169
Aamir Sohail	lbw, b Morrison	2
Akram Raza	c Blain, b Morrison	0
Basit Ali	b Thomson	85
Salim Malik (capt)	c and b Hart	140
Inzamam-ul-Haq	not out	135
*Rashid Latif		
Wasim Akram		
Waqar Younis		
Ata-ur-Rehman		
Asif Mujtaba		
Extras	b 5, lb 6, nb 6	17
	(for 5 wickets, dec.)	**548**

	O	M	R	W	O	M	R	W
Wasim Akram	24	10	60	4	37	7	119	7
Waqar Younis	22	5	51	3	25.2	4	111	2
Ata-ur-Rehman	15	4	50	3	18	1	86	1
Akram Raza	6	4	7	–	12	4	25	–
Aamir Sohail					1	–	1	–
Salim Malik					2	–	13	–

	O	M	R	W
Morrison	31	4	139	2
de Groen	31	8	104	–
Doull	27	6	112	–
Hart	31.2	9	102	1
Thomson	17	3	80	1

FALL OF WICKETS

1–0, 2–40, 3–49, 4–100, 5–126, 6–128, 7–140, 8–149, 9–170
1–3, 2–6, 3–120, 4–143, 5–209, 6–216, 7–244, 8–276, 9–350

FALL OF WICKETS

1–34, 2–36, 3–233, 4–290, 5–548

Umpires: B.L. Aldridge & H.D. Bird

Pakistan won by an innings and 12 runs

THIRD TEST MATCH
NEW ZEALAND v. PAKISTAN, at Christchurch

With Atu-ur-Rehman and Asif Mujtaba unfit, Pakistan brought in Atif Rauf for his first match of the tour and for his first Test, and Aamir Nazir. Cairns was still unfit for New Zealand, for whom Pringle returned in place of de Groen. There were doubts as to whether Rutherford would be able to lead the side, for he had bruised a hand in practice, but, with the aid of painkillers, he took the field after winning the toss and asking Pakistan to bat first.

Morrison's first ball of the match was hit straight to mid-on by Saeed Anwar, and Rutherford dropped the catch. At lunch, Pakistan were 120 for 0. If the morning had belonged to Saeed Anwar and Aamir Sohail, the afternoon belonged to the New Zealand bowlers who had been badly served in the opening session when Aamir was dropped twice. Five wickets fell in the afternoon as 87 runs were added. Simon Doull had started the rot by dismissing both openers, and he accounted for Inzamam shortly before the interval.

New Zealand continued to attack in the final session, and when Rashid and Wasim fell it looked as if they would not reach 300, but Basit Ali, upright and regal, was in violent mood. He hit 3 sixes and 9 fours as he blasted

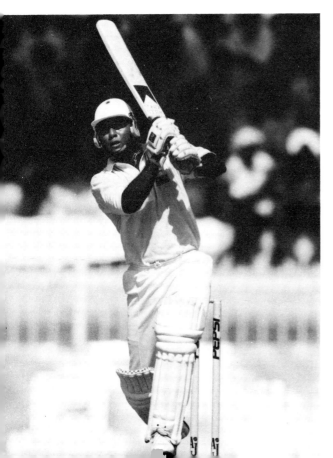

his way to reach 97 in the last over of the day. Then he square-cut the ball to Hartland who missed New Zealand's sixth chance of the match. Basit Ali moved to 98, Pakistan to 334 for 7.

The first half of the second day saw New Zealand in total charge. The last three Pakistani wickets realised only another 10 runs, but the end did not arrive before Basit Ali had deservedly completed his maiden Test century.

Hartland went cheaply, but Young gave Jones sound support in a second-wicket stand of 97 in 107 minutes. Jones, playing in what he stated would be his last Test match, was magnificent. He scored with unusual briskness, and his 81 came off 129 balls with 7 fours. Unfortunately, the New Zealand middle order again failed to cope with the pace of Waqar Younis, and the last nine wickets went down for 91 runs to leave the home side trailing by 144 runs on the first innings and facing, it seemed, another heavy defeat.

Morrison and Doull struck back encouragingly, removing both openers before the close which came with Pakistan 8 for 2. Having removed Atif Rauf on the third morning, Simon Doull was forced to withdraw from the attack with a strained back muscle but, even under this handicap, the New Zealand bowlers performed admirably. Morrison's outswing troubled all batsmen, and Hart accepted the responsibility thrust upon him through Doull's absence with a fine spell of left-arm spin bowling. Basit Ali, badly dropped by Morrison when he was 38, was again top-scorer for Pakistan.

Pakistan had batted indifferently, but New Zealand faced a target of 324 to win the match, a total they had never previously reached in winning a Test match. When bad light ended play early they were 9 for 0.

The New Zealand batting showed greater resolve than it had done in the previous matches of the series but, with Jones run out for the second time in the match and Rutherford and a subdued Greatbatch falling in quick succession, the home side stood at 133 for 4. Victory was still 199 runs away, and it seemed there was little hope.

Shane Thomson now joined Bryan Young in one of the epic partnerships in New Zealand cricket. Young was rock-like. He was in the 80s for nearly an hour and a half, but he finally completed his first Test hundred. Thomson, having got firmly behind the line to every delivery and swayed out of the way of every bouncer, was more belligerent. At the end of the day, the pair were still together, and the score was 277 for 4. New Zealand were just 47 runs away from a famous victory.

Young added only five to his overnight total before edging a delivery from Wasim Akram into his stumps. He had batted for nearly seven hours and had displayed the best of temperaments. Thomson reached his first Test hundred and his 120, which included 2 sixes and 15 fours, came off 167 balls in 233 minutes. This was a mighty effort. Not to be outdone, Tony Blain hit a six and a four, and New Zealand had risen from the ashes after four successive defeats in Test matches.

A maiden Test century for the highly talented Basit Ali in the third match of the series. (David Munden/Sports-Line)

THIRD TEST MATCH – NEW ZEALAND v. PAKISTAN

24, 25, 26, 27 and 28 February 1994 at Lancaster Park, Christchurch

PAKISTAN	FIRST INNINGS			SECOND INNINGS		
Saeed Anwar	c Young, **b** Doull	69		c Blain, **b** Morrison	0	
Aamir Sohail	c Hartland, **b** Doull	60		c Young, **b** Doull	3	
Atif Rauf	c Greatbatch, **b** Morrison	16		c Young, **b** Doull	9	
Salim Malik (capt)	**b** Hart	18		(5) c Pringle, **b** Morrison	23	
Basit Ali	c Hartland, **b** Pringle	103		(6) run out	67	
Inzamam-ul-Haq	c Greatbatch, **b** Doull	5		(7) c sub (Hastings), **b** Morrison	20	
*Rashid Latif	c Hartland, **b** Thomson	27		(8) c and **b** Hart	3	
Wasim Akram	c Greatbatch, **b** Morrison	5		(9) **b** Hart	17	
Akram Raza	not out	29		(4) st Blain, **b** Hart	26	
Waqar Younis	c Doull, **b** Morrison	2		c Blain, **b** Morrison	10	
Aamir Nazir	**b** Morrison	0		not out	0	
Extras	lb 6, w 1, nb 3	10		nb 1	1	
		344			**179**	

NEW ZEALAND	FIRST INNINGS			SECOND INNINGS		
B.R. Hartland	c Basit, **b** Waqar	3		(2) c Inzamam, **b** Wasim	10	
B.A. Young	lbw, **b** Aamir	38		(1) **b** Wasim	120	
A.H. Jones	run out	81		run out	26	
K.R. Rutherford (capt)	c Inzamam, **b** Waqar	7		lbw, **b** Wasim	13	
M.J. Greatbatch	lbw, **b** Wasim	1		c Inzamam, **b** Waqar	1	
S.A. Thomson	c Rashid, **b** Waqar	3		not out	120	
*T.E. Blain	lbw, **b** Waqar	0		not out	11	
M.N. Hart	**b** Wasim	6				
S.B. Doull	lbw, **b** Waqar	17				
D.K. Morrison	not out	6				
C. Pringle	**b** Waqar	0				
Extras	b 5, lb 9, nb 24	38		lb 5, nb 18	23	
		200		(for 5 wickets)	**324**	

	O	M	R	W	O	M	R	W
Morrison	24	3	105	4	21.3	5	66	4
Doull	25	2	93	3	5	–	13	2
Pringle	33	6	83	1	17	3	41	–
Hart	9	2	37	1	18	5	47	3
Thomson	6	–	20	1	4	–	12	–

	O	M	R	W	O	M	R	W
Wasim Akram	22	5	54	2	38	6	105	3
Waqar Younis	19	1	78	6	27	6	84	1
Aamir Nazir	15	2	54	1	16	–	59	–
Akram Raza					19	5	49	–
Aamir Sohail					2	1	5	–
Salim Malik					4	1	13	–
Saeed Anwar					1	–	4	–

FALL OF WICKETS

1–125, 2–147, 3–169, 4–195, 5–206, 6–254, 7–261, 8–339, 9–344
1–0, 2–4, 3–26, 4–53, 5–77, 6–133, 7–152, 8–154, 9–171

FALL OF WICKETS

1–12, 2–109, 3–124, 4–139, 5–147, 6–147, 7–171, 8–186, 9–198
1–22, 2–76, 3–119, 4–133, 5–287

Umpires: R.S. Dunne & K.T. Francis

New Zealand won by 5 wickets

TEST MATCH AVERAGES – NEW ZEALAND v. PAKISTAN

NEW ZEALAND BATTING

	M	Inns	NO	Runs	HS	Av	100s	50s
A.H. Jones	3	6	–	298	81	49.66	–	3
S.A. Thomson	3	6	1	206	120*	41.20	1	–
B.A. Young	3	6	–	191	120	31.83	1	–
D.K. Morrison	2	3	1	53	42	26.50	–	–
T.E. Blain	3	6	1	127	78	25.40	–	1
K.R. Rutherford	3	6	–	122	63	20.33	–	1
M.J. Greatbatch	3	6	–	105	48	17.50	–	–
S.B. Doull	3	5	–	78	29	15.60	–	–
M.N. Hart	2	3	1	25	12*	12.50	–	–
B.A. Pocock	2	4	–	26	16	6.50	–	–
R.P. de Groen	2	4	2	7	4	3.50	–	–

Played in one Test: B.R. Hartland 3 & 10; C. Pringle 0; C.L. Cairns 6 & 31; M.B. Owens 2* & 0

NEW ZEALAND BOWLING

	Overs	Mds	Runs	Wkts	Av	Best	10/m	5/inn
S.B. Doull	88	10	332	12	27.66	5-66	–	1
D.K. Morrison	76.3	12	310	10	31.00	4-66	–	–
M.N. Hart	58.2	16	186	5	37.20	3-47	–	–
R.P. de Groen	61.4	16	192	5	38.40	3-40	–	–
S.A. Thomson	31	4	129	3	43.00	1-17	–	–
C.L. Cairns	24	3	90	2	45.00	2-75	–	–
C. Pringle	50	9	124	1	124.00	1-83	–	–
M.B. Owens	9	1	38	–	–			

NEW ZEALAND FIELDING FIGURES

9 – B.A. Young; 8 – T.E. Blain (ct 7/st 1); 3 – B.R. Hartland, S.B. Doull and M.J. Greatbatch; 2 – M.N. Hart; 1 – A.H. Jones, C. Pringle, C.L. Cairns and sub (M.A. Hastings)

PAKISTAN BATTING

	M	Inns	NO	Runs	HS	Av	100s	50s
Inzamam-ul-Haq	3	5	2	223	135*	74.33	1	–
Basit Ali	3	5	–	287	103	57.40	1	2
Saeed Anwar	3	5	–	261	169	52.20	1	1
Salim Malik	3	5	–	210	140	42.00	1	–
Aamir Sohail	3	5	–	159	78	31.80	–	2
Akram Raza	2	3	1	55	29*	27.50	–	–
Rashid Latif	3	4	1	73	30	24.33	–	–
Wasim Akram	3	3	–	57	35	19.00	–	–
Waqar Younis	3	3	–	23	11	7.66	–	–
Asif Mujtaba	2	2	–	8	8	4.00	–	–

Played in two Tests: Ata-ur-Rehman 2*
Played in one Test: Atif Rauf 16 & 9; Mushtaq Ahmed 0; Aamir Nazir 0 & 0*

PAKISTAN BOWLING

	Overs	Mds	Runs	Wkts	Av	Best	10/m	5/inn
Wasim Akram	159.4	41	431	25	17.24	7-119	1	2
Waqar Younis	118.2	21	405	18	22.50	6-78	–	1
Ata-ur-Rehman	53	9	214	6	35.66	3-50	–	–
Aamir Nazir	31	2	113	1	113.00	1-54	–	–
Aamir Sohail	3	1	6	–	–			
Salim Malik	6	1	26	–	–			
Akram Raza	37	13	81	–	–			

Bowled in one innings: Saeed Anwar 1–0–4–0; Mushtaq Ahmed 17–1–79–3

PAKISTAN FIELDING FIGURES

13 – Rashid Latif; 4 – Salim Malik and Inzamam-ul-Haq; 3 – Basit Ali; 2 – Akram Raza, Asif Mujtaba and Mushtaq Ahmed; 1 – Saeed Anwar, Waqar Younis and Ata-ur-Rehman

A New Zealander hero in the historic victory over Pakistan in the third Test – Bryan Young. (Alan Cozzi)

4, 5, 6 and 7 March 1994 *at Molyneux Park, Alexandra*

New Zealand Academy XI 312 (A.C. Parore 134,
   A.J. Gale 4 for 68) and 191 for 1 dec. (D.J. Murray
   112 not out)

Otago 173 (P.W. Dobbs 50, D.J. Nash 5 for 31,
   C.M. Brown 4 for 19) and 237 (L.C. Breen 100,
   H.T. Davis 5 for 37)

New Zealand Academy XI won by 93 runs

The Academy XI triumphed for the second time in as
many matches. They owed much initially to Parore who,
coming in at 79 for 4, hit 134 in just under five hours and
furthered his claims for a recall to the Test side. Otago
collapsed before Nash and Brown, and skipper Murray
hit 112 off 211 balls when the Academy batted a second
time.

 ONE-DAY INTERNATIONAL SERIES
NEW ZEALAND v. PAKISTAN

Rain reduced the opening match of the series to a 30-over
contest. New Zealand were the side to suffer more, for
they had already used 10 overs to score 32 runs before the
rains came. On the resumption, New Zealand batted
wildly. Two men were stumped and three caught at long-
on by Asif Mujtaba. A target of 123 looked to be too much
for Pakistan when they slipped to 35 for 4, but Saeed
Anwar hit 60 off 72 balls, and Rashid Latif hit 3 sixes, two
off consecutive deliveries from Cairns. Latif's 32 came off
18 balls.

The second match was a total disaster for New Zealand. Play was halted for a while after Ata-ur-Rehman
was struck by a missile thrown by a spectator, and the
home side then capitulated in astonishing fashion when
chasing a small target. The New Zealanders' performance
was embarrassing.

Some pride was restored in the third encounter, but
Pakistan still won to take the series with a three-nil lead.
The feature of the Pakistan innings was the second-
wicket stand of 142 between Aamir Sohail and Inzamam-
ul-Haq. New Zealand looked in sight of victory with 46
runs needed from the last six overs and seven wickets
standing. Wasim Akram and Waqar Younis returned to
slow the scoring and to capture wickets. Blain also ran
himself out, and New Zealand lost by 11 runs.

There was high drama in the fourth match when tight
bowling from Larsen in particular restricted Pakistan to
161 in their 50 overs. New Zealand started wretchedly,
but Jones, Rutherford, Cairns and Thomson all lifted the
tempo. At 142 for 4, victory seemed assured, but the last
six wickets fell for 19 runs. The destroyer was Waqar
Younis, and it was he who bowled the last over. With four
balls left, New Zealand needed three to win with the last
pair together. An overthrow brought de Groen two runs

New Zealand's one-day specialist – Gavin Larsen. (Mark Leech)

and levelled the score, but the next delivery was a typical
Waqar yorker which trapped de Groen leg before to tie
the match.

The final game of the series saw New Zealand victorious at last. Batting first on a difficult pitch, Pakistan
played with a sense of bewilderment, and their first 22
runs were comprised of 15 singles and seven extras. Basit
Ali, inevitably, revived spirits with a six and 3 fours in his
85-ball 57, but Pakistan's total was still moderate. It
looked as if it might be sufficient when New Zealand
were reduced to 45 for 3, but Shane Thomson joined Blair
Hartland in a joyful stand. Hartland hit 68 off 109 balls,
and Thomson 48 off 67 balls to take New Zealand to
victory with nearly 16 overs to spare.

INDIAN TOUR

10, 11 and 12 March 1994 *at Carisbrook, Dunedin*

New Zealand Emerging Players 233 for 4 dec. (B.R.
   Hartland 98, R. A. Lawson 62) and 236 for 3 (M.W.
   Douglas 64 not out, B.R. Hartland 54, M.D. Bailey 52
   not out)

Indians 352 (M. Prabhakar 147, S.V. Manjrekar 134,
   G.E. Bradburn 4 for 99)

Match drawn

FIRST ONE-DAY INTERNATIONAL – NEW ZEALAND *v.* PAKISTAN
3 March 1994 at Carisbrook, Dunedin

NEW ZEALAND

M.J. Greatbatch	run out	14
B.A. Young	c Salim Malik, b Akram Raza	20
A.H. Jones	c Wasim Akram, b Akram Raza	15
C.L. Cairns	c Asif Mujtaba, b Akram Raza	13
K.R. Rutherford (capt)	st Rashid Latif, b Aamir Sohail	3
S.A. Thomson	st Rashid Latif, b Aamir Sohail	8
C.Z. Harris	c and b Salim Malik	19
*T.E. Blain	c Asif Mujtaba, b Salim Malik	5
G.R. Larsen	not out	9
D.K. Morrison	c Asif Mujtaba, b Salim Malik	1
C. Pringle	not out	6
Extras	lb 5, w 1, nb 3	9
(30 overs)	(for 9 wickets)	122

PAKISTAN

Saeed Anwar	not out	60
Aamir Sohail	c Blain, b Pringle	5
Inzamam-ul-Haq	c Jones, b Pringle	1
Salim Malik (capt)	lbw, b Cairns	2
Basit Ali	lbw, b Cairns	4
Asif Mujtaba	c Cairns, b Morrison	14
*Rashid Latif	not out	32
Wasim Akram		
Waqar Younis		
Akram Raza		
Ata-ur-Rehman		
Extras	lb 2, w 3	5
(26.1 overs)	(for 5 wickets)	123

	O	M	R	W
Wasim Akram	6	2	18	–
Waqar Younis	4	1	14	–
Ata-ur-Rehman	4	–	17	–
Akram Raza	6	1	18	3
Aamir Sohail	6	–	33	2
Salim Malik	4	–	17	3

	O	M	R	W
Pringle	5	–	20	2
Thomson	4	1	21	–
Larsen	5	1	15	–
Cairns	6	1	33	2
Harris	3	–	17	–
Morrison	3.1	–	15	1

FALL OF WICKETS

1–18, 2–54, 3–58, 4–72, 5–74, 6–99, 7–105, 8–109, 9–114

FALL OF WICKETS

1–17, 2–24, 3–27, 4–35, 5–74

Umpires: R.S. Dunne & C.E. King   *Man of the Match*: Saeed Anwar   *Pakistan won by 5 wickets*

SECOND ONE-DAY INTERNATIONAL – NEW ZEALAND *v.* PAKISTAN
6 March 1994 at Eden Park, Auckland

PAKISTAN

Saeed Anwar	c Blain, b Morrison	9
Aamir Sohail	c Rutherford, b Thomson	48
Inzamam-ul-Haq	lbw, b Pringle	14
Salim Malik (capt)	c Blain, b Larsen	5
Basit Ali	c Blain, b Larsen	8
Asif Mujtaba	lbw, b Morrison	1
*Rashid Latif	c Greatbatch, b Harris	3
Wasim Akram	c Greatbatch, b Thomson	33
Akram Raza	run out	3
Waqar Younis	b Thomson	7
Ata-ur-Rehman	not out	0
Extras	b 1, lb 4, w 8, nb 2	15
(43.3 overs)		146

NEW ZEALAND

M.J. Greatbatch	c Akram Raza, b Ata-ur-Rehman	23
B.A. Young	lbw, b Wasim Akram	0
A.H. Jones	c Aamir Sohail, b Wasim Akram	1
K.R. Rutherford (capt)	run out	37
S.A. Thomson	c Salim Malik, b Akram Raza	6
C.L. Cairns	b Aamir Sohail	3
C.Z. Harris	c Rashid Latif, b Waqar Younis	18
*T.E. Blain	st Rashid Latif, b Akram Raza	2
G.R. Larsen	b Wasim Akram	5
D.K. Morrison	c Rashid Latif, b Wasim Akram	0
C. Pringle	not out	4
Extras	lb 2, w 8, nb 1	11
(44.3 overs)		110

	O	M	R	W
Morrison	8	2	16	2
Pringle	8	–	31	1
Cairns	7	1	24	–
Larsen	10	–	27	2
Harris	7	–	29	1
Thomson	3.3	1	14	3

	O	M	R	W
Wasim Akram	7.3	–	23	4
Waqar Younis	8	–	18	1
Ata-ur-Rehman	9	2	25	1
Salim Malik	2	–	4	–
Akram Raza	10	1	21	2
Aamir Sohail	8	–	17	1

FALL OF WICKETS

1–10, 2–33, 3–41, 4–60, 5–61, 6–65, 7–127, 8–139, 9–139

FALL OF WICKETS

1–3, 2–8, 3–45, 4–62, 5–71, 6–86, 7–90, 8–104, 9–105

Umpires: D.B. Cowie & D.M. Quested   *Man of the Match*: Wasim Akram   *Pakistan won by 36 runs*

THIRD ONE-DAY INTERNATIONAL – NEW ZEALAND v. PAKISTAN
9 March 1994 at Basin Reserve, Wellington

PAKISTAN

Saeed Anwar	b Cairns	16
Aamir Sohail	c Young, b Morrison	76
Inzamam-ul-Haq	c Cairns, b Pringle	88
Basit Ali	b Morrison	1
Wasim Akram	b Morrison	0
Salim Malik (capt)	not out	10
*Rashid Latif	b Larsen	3
Asif Mujtaba	not out	1
Akram Raza		
Waqar Younis		
Ata-ur-Rehman		
Extras	b 4, lb 9, w 3, nb 2	18
(48 overs)	(for 6 wickets)	213

NEW ZEALAND

B.A. Young	run out	37
M.J. Greatbatch	c Aamir Sohail, b Ata-ur-Rehman	9
A.H. Jones	run out	38
K.R. Rutherford (capt)	c Salim Malik, b Waqar Younis	46
S.A. Thomson	b Wasim Akram	38
C.L. Cairns	b Wasim Akram	2
C.Z. Harris	not out	8
*T.E. Blain	run out	3
G.R. Larsen	b Waqar Younis	6
D.K. Morrison	not out	4
C. Pringle		
Extras	b 3, lb 5, w 3	11
(48 overs)	(for 8 wickets)	202

	O	M	R	W
Pringle	9	–	52	1
Morrison	10	1	32	3
Larsen	10	1	42	1
Cairns	10	–	26	1
Thomson	2	–	14	–
Harris	7	–	34	–

	O	M	R	W
Wasim Akram	10	1	41	2
Waqar Younis	10	–	43	2
Ata-ur-Rehman	6	–	15	1
Aamir Sohail	6	–	29	–
Salim Malik	10	–	37	–
Akram Raza	6	–	29	–

FALL OF WICKETS

1–29, 2–171, 3–174, 4–174, 5–206, 6–209

FALL OF WICKETS

1–32, 2–76, 3–106, 4–168, 5–176, 6–177, 7–181, 8–193

Umpires: B.L. Aldridge & D.M. Quested   *Man of the Match*: Inzamam-ul-Haq   *Pakistan won by 11 runs*

FOURTH ONE-DAY INTERNATIONAL – NEW ZEALAND v. PAKISTAN
13 March 1994 at Eden Park, Auckland

PAKISTAN

Saeed Anwar	c Blain, b Larsen	25
Aamir Sohail	c Blain, b Larsen	24
Inzamam-ul-Haq	c Young, b Larsen	7
Salim Malik (capt)	b Thomson	7
Basit Ali	run out	34
Asif Mujtaba	c Rutherford, b Hart	5
*Rashid Latif	b Thomson	5
Wasim Akram	b Larsen	15
Akram Raza	not out	11
Waqar Younis	c Hartland, b Pringle	2
Ata-ur-Rehman	not out	11
Extras	b 2, lb 8, w 5	15
(50 overs)	(for 9 wickets)	161

NEW ZEALAND

B.A. Young	b Waqar Younis	5
B.R. Hartland	b Waqar Younis	3
A.H. Jones	c Basit Ali, b Akram Raza	21
K.R. Rutherford	c Waqar Younis, b Salim Malik	47
C.L. Cairns	run out	39
S.A. Thomson	c Rashid Latif, b Waqar Younis	24
*T.E. Blain	c Rashid Latif, b Wasim Akram	0
G.R. Larsen	lbw, b Waqar Younis	1
M.N. Hart	b Waqar Younis	6
C. Pringle	not out	1
R.P. de Groen	lbw, b Waqar Younis	2
Extras	lb 5, w 7	12
(49.4 overs)		161

	O	M	R	W
Pringle	10	–	29	1
de Groen	6	2	26	–
Cairns	7	1	21	–
Larsen	10	–	24	4
Hart	10	1	29	1
Thomson	7	1	22	2

	O	M	R	W
Wasim Akram	10	1	24	1
Waqar Younis	9.4	1	30	6
Ata-ur-Rehman	4	–	22	–
Akram Raza	10	1	21	1
Aamir Sohail	9	–	29	–
Salim Malik	7	–	30	1

FALL OF WICKETS

1–38, 2–59, 3–60, 4–80, 5–85, 6–101, 7–126, 8–139, 9–146

FALL OF WICKETS

1–8, 2–9, 3–65, 4–85, 5–142, 6–144, 7–152, 8–152, 9–159

Umpires: D.B. Cowie & R.S. Dunne   *Man of the Match*: Waqar Younis   *Match tied*

FIFTH ONE-DAY INTERNATIONAL – NEW ZEALAND v. PAKISTAN
15 March 1994 at Lancaster Park, Christchurch

PAKISTAN			NEW ZEALAND		
Saeed Anwar	c Hart, b Pringle	2	B.A. Young	c Rashid Latif, b Waqar Younis	3
Aamir Sohail	c Rutherford, b Morrison	1	B.R. Hartland	not out	68
Inzamam-ul-Haq	c Young, b Pringle	4	A.H. Jones	c Rashid Latif, b Waqar Younis	1
Asif Mujtaba	b Cairns	3	K.R. Rutherford (capt)	c Akram Raza, b Ata-ur-Rehman	1
Salim Malik (capt)	c Young, b Cairns	15	S.A. Thomson	not out	48
Basit Ali	c Young, b Pringle	57	C.L. Cairns		
*Rashid Latif	c Parore, b Morrison	9	*A.C. Parore		
Wasim Akram	c Parore, b Larsen	7	M.N. Hart		
Akram Raza	not out	23	G.R. Larsen		
Waqar Younis	c Cairns, b Morrison	4	D.K. Morrison		
Ata-ur-Rehman	not out	3	C. Pringle		
Extras	lb 6, w 8, nb 3	17	Extras	lb 8, w 14, nb 3	25
(50 overs)	(for 9 wickets)	145	(34.1 overs)	(for 3 wickets)	146

	O	M	R	W		O	M	R	W
Morrison	10	2	20	3	Wasim Akram	6.3	–	17	–
Pringle	10	1	21	3	Waqar Younis	8.1	1	33	2
Cairns	10	–	36	2	Ata-ur-Rehman	9	–	44	1
Larsen	10	1	21	1	Aamir Sohail	4	–	18	–
Hart	4	–	17	–	Akram Raza	3.3	–	14	–
Thomson	6	–	24	–	Salim Malik	3	–	12	–

FALL OF WICKETS

1–3, 2–8, 3–17, 4–19, 5–45, 6–65, 7–86, 8–121, 9–136

FALL OF WICKETS

1–26, 2–34, 3–45

Umpires: B.L. Aldridge & C.E. King *Man of the Match*: B.R. Hartland *New Zealand won by 7 wickets*

A docile pitch condemned the opening match of the Indian tour to a draw. Hartland and Lawson began the game with a partnership of 167. Manoj Prabhakar hit a sparkling 147 with a six and 16 fours and shared a fourth-wicket stand of 193 with Sanjay Manjrekar. Manjrekar's 134 included a six and 15 fours.

14, 15 and 16 March 1994 *at Pukekura Park, New Plymouth*

New Zealand Academy XI 253 for 5 dec. (B.A. Pocock 139 not out)

Indians 96 for 1 (A.D. Jadeja 55 not out)

Match drawn

Rain shortened the first day and wiped out the third day of India's second match of the tour. There was sufficient time for Blair Pocock to respond to Hartland's 98 in the previous match against the tourists with an unbeaten 139 in seven hours. Pocock and Hartland were vying for the spot of Young's opening partner in the forthcoming Test match.

TEST MATCH
NEW ZEALAND v. INDIA, at Hamilton

Following the retirement of Andrew Jones, New Zealand introduced Stephen Fleming to Test cricket. India fielded their full complement of spinners, but they were without Prabhakar whose injury was to cost him his one-season contract with Warwickshire. New Zealand also included Adam Parore at the expense of Tony Blain, who had had a long, hard job behind the stumps in the national side. Parore had scored heavily in recent matches, but Blain's non-inclusion in the party to tour England was very harsh on the player.

There was an autumnal feeling about the start of the Test, and play could not begin until mid-afternoon because of drizzle. Rutherford won the toss, and New Zealand batted. In 38.5 overs, they stumbled to 81 for 3. Hartland edged a Kapil Dev outswinger to slip in the second over of the day, and Young lobbed a catch to gully shortly after. In the final session, Greatbatch moved back and held out his bat to a short-pitched delivery from Srinath who bowled well. Fleming was missed third ball, but he played resolutely thereafter, opening his account with a thunderous boundary after being scoreless for 23 minutes.

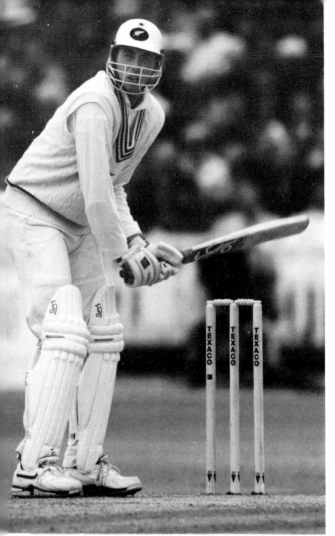

Thomson bowled Azharuddin round his legs. Manjrekar edged Morrison to slip, and the New Zealand pace bowler aided by the persevering Pringle soon mopped up the Indian tail. By the end of the day, New Zealand had reduced the gap between the two sides to 20 runs and had not lost a wicket.

Young and Hartland extended their opening partnership to 56 the next morning. It represented New Zealand's best opening stand of the summer. Hartland was caught behind off Srinath, but Young and Rutherford now added 116 on a pitch that was assisting the spinners. Rutherford was dynamic. His 59 came off 89 deliveries, and he hit Chauhan for consecutive sixes over square-leg as well as claiming 5 fours. Chauhan was to gain his revenge, bowling Rutherford and having Young caught behind when he advanced down the wicket. Greatbatch fell before tea and Thomson after the break, but Fleming remained until the close, unbeaten on 67 with New Zealand 306 for 5.

Stephen Fleming, a flamboyant left-hander, was on the verge of a making a century in his first Test, an achievement his exciting batting richly deserved, when he pushed the ball quietly to first slip. Fleming had hit 12 fours and faced 177 balls, and his innings had lasted 10 minutes over four hours. Rutherford declared half an hour before lunch, and India had 66 overs in which to score 310.

To have any chance of success, New Zealand needed a quick breakthrough, but it did not come. Mongia and Sidhu put on 102 for the first wicket. Sidhu hit 3 sixes and 8 fours in a typically aggressive 98, and when he fell to a rather impulsive stroke the game petered out to its inevitable draw.

 ## ONE-DAY SERIES
NEW ZEALAND v. INDIA

In these changing times, the main purpose of India's visit to New Zealand was a four-match one-day series. The first of these matches saw some spectacular batting from two of New Zealand's young hopefuls, Thomson and Fleming. The home side had begun moderately before this pair came together in a stand of 144 in 110 minutes. Thomson hit a six and 7 fours in his 97-ball innings while Fleming, who selflessly ran himself out at the close, made 90 off 107 balls with 8 fours. Harris hit the last ball of the innings for six, and New Zealand reached a respectable 240.

India began at four runs an over, reaching 123 for 1. Harris then dismissed Jadeja, and he turned the game in New Zealand's favour when he bowled Azharuddin. Morrison confirmed the victory when he performed the hat-trick, bowling Kapil Dev, Ankola and Mongia.

The second match showed a complete reversal of fortune. New Zealand limped to 142 and were bowled out in the 50th over. Kapil Dev claimed his 250th wicket in one-day internationals when he had Fleming caught behind. India roared to victory through an astonishing innings from Sachin Tendulkar who hit 2 sixes and 15 fours in his

A thrilling Test debut for New Zealand against India at Hamilton by Stephen Fleming. (David Munden/Sports-Line)

Rutherford and Fleming looked settled the next morning, and the New Zealand captain was particularly impressive as he moved to his 17th fifty in Test cricket. Fleming lost concentration and hooked Srinath to fine-leg, but the real disaster for New Zealand came shortly after when Rutherford edged a ball from Kumble into his stumps. His dismissal heralded a collapse as the Indian spinners took control.

There was early encouragement for the home side when Morrison knocked Sidhu's off stump out of the ground. Kambli was quickly held low at slip, but Tendulkar flourished from the outset. He hit 43 off 47 balls – 7 fours and a six – but his dazzling innings came to an end when he skied a totally unexpected 'bouncer' from off-spinner Thomson for Nash to take a splendid running catch. India closed on 104 for 3.

Mongia, the emergency opener, had batted for 227 minutes and given Azharuddin and others sound support when he was run out by Fleming's direct hit on the stumps. It was New Zealand's only success of the third morning, but they came back well in the afternoon when

TEST MATCH – NEW ZEALAND v. INDIA
19, 20, 21, 22 and 23 March 1994 at Trust Bank Park, Hamilton

NEW ZEALAND

	FIRST INNINGS		SECOND INNINGS	
B.R. Hartland	c Chauhan, b Kapil Dev	0	(2) c Mongia, b Srinath	25
B.A. Young	c Kumble, b Srinath	13	(1) c Mongia, b Chauhan	85
K.R. Rutherford (capt)	b Kumble	63	b Chauhan	59
M.J. Greatbatch	c Azharuddin, b Srinath	12	c Manjrekar, b Kumble	27
S.P. Fleming	c Kambli, b Srinath	16	c Kapil Dev, b Chauhan	92
S.A. Thomson	c Manjrekar, b Raju	12	b Venkatapathy Raju	26
*A.C. Parore	c and b Chauhan	9	c Mongia, b Kapil Dev	17
M.N. Hart	b Chauhan	17	not out	20
D.J. Nash	not out	10	not out	9
D.K. Morrison	lbw, b Srinath	3		
C. Pringle	b Venkatapathy Raju	18		
Extras	lb 9, nb 5	14	b 2, lb 1, nb 5	8
		187	(for 7 wickets, dec.)	368

INDIA

	FIRST INNINGS		SECOND INNINGS	
*N.R. Mongia	run out	45	b Hart	38
N.S. Sidhu	b Morrison	10	c Parore, b Hart	98
V.G. Kambli	c Young, b Pringle	9	b Pringle	19
S.R. Tendulkar	c Nash, b Thomson	43	not out	11
M. Azharuddin (capt)	b Thomson	63		
S.V. Manjrekar	c Young, b Morrison	29	(5) not out	8
Kapil Dev	c Fleming, b Nash	18		
A.R. Kumble	c Fleming, b Morrison	7		
R.K. Chauhan	not out	12		
Venkatapathy Raju	c Young, b Morrison	2		
J. Srinath	c Parore, b Pringle	1		
Extras	lb 6, w 1	7	lb 3	3
		246	(for 3 wickets)	177

	O	M	R	W	O	M	R	W
Srinath	31	8	60	4	33	4	104	1
Kapil Dev	9	2	29	1	16	2	43	1
Kumble	23	8	34	1	27	6	68	1
Venkatapathy Raju	13.2	5	14	2	24	6	53	1
Chauhan	21	6	41	2	29	5	97	3

	O	M	R	W	O	M	R	W
Morrison	30	9	52	4	8	1	15	–
Nash	20	5	57	1	13	6	25	–
Pringle	22.3	8	52	2	12	2	29	1
Hart	19	5	33	–	15	2	66	2
Thomson	11	1	46	2	11	1	39	–

FALL OF WICKETS

1-1, 2-21, 3-49, 4-100, 5-122, 6-124, 7-154, 8-155, 9-158
1-56, 2-172, 3-176, 4-220, 5-265, 6-317, 7-355

FALL OF WICKETS

1-25, 2-38, 3-89, 4-138, 5-183, 6-216, 7-226, 8-227, 9-237
1-102, 2-140, 3-167

Umpires: B.L. Aldridge & Khizar Hayat

Match drawn

82 which came off only 49 deliveries. It is hard to accept that this batting genius was still a month short of his 21st birthday when he played this innings.

Tendulkar was again to the fore in the third match when he and Jadeja began the Indian innings with 105 runs in 91 minutes. Tendulkar scored 63 of these runs before giving way to Sidhu who lashed 71 off 77 balls with a six and 3 fours.

Facing a formidable 255, New Zealand slipped to 131 for 5, but died bravely. Thomson and Parore added 85, and it looked as if a famous victory might be achieved. Kumble intervened, dismissing them both and finishing with 5 for 33 as New Zealand fell 13 short of winning the match.

New Zealand drew the series when they won the final match in exciting fashion. There was another ferocious assault by Tendulkar at the start of the game, 40 off 26 balls; a steadier contribution from Jadeja; and violence towards the end of the Indian innings from Mongia. New Zealand soon lost Harris, but Young and Rutherford put on 82 in 86 minutes. Fleming batted with dash, but when he and Rutherford fell to Kumble at the same score India looked to have gained control. Thomson and Parore were the heroes once again. They shared an unbroken partnership of 88 in 65 minutes to take their side to victory with a ball to spare.

Shane Thomson was named Man of the Series.

TRANS-TASMAN CHALLENGE

4 April 1994 *at Lancaster Park, Christchurch*

New South Wales 260 for 8 (M.G. Bevan 90, T.H. Bayliss 52)

Canterbury 174 (B.R. Hartland 59, R.T. Latham 57, S. Thompson 5 for 11)

New South Wales won by 86 runs

A long New Zealand season ended with the match between the one-day competition winners of Australia and the home country. The Australians chose to bat first and, with Bevan and Bayliss sharing a third-wicket stand of 119 in 82 minutes, scored an impressive 260 in their 50 overs. Canterbury began sensationally, 92 coming in 59 minutes. Latham hit 3 sixes and 6 fours in his 44-ball innings. Fleming made 29, but the last nine wickets fell for 33 runs. Off-spinner Robertson took 3 for 34 in his 10 overs, and, remarkably, Thompson had 5 for 11 in three overs.

Now the New Zealanders set off for Sharjah and England. The treadmill never stops.

FIRST ONE-DAY INTERNATIONAL – NEW ZEALAND v. INDIA
25 March 1994 at McLean Park, Napier

NEW ZEALAND		
B.R. Hartland	c Mongia, b Srinath	8
B.A. Young	c Mongia, b Srinath	11
K.R. Rutherford (capt)	c Mongia, b Ankola	23
S.P. Fleming	run out	90
S.A. Thomson	c Jadeja, b Kumble	83
C.Z. Harris	not out	18
D.J. Nash	not out	1
*A.C. Parore		
G.R. Larsen		
D.K. Morrison		
C. Pringle		
Extras	lb 2, w 3, nb 1	6
(50 overs)	(for 5 wickets)	240

INDIA		
A.D. Jadeja	c Pringle, b Harris	55
N.S. Sidhu	c Parore, b Larsen	34
V.G. Kambli	st Parore, b Thomson	37
M. Azharuddin (capt)	b Harris	9
S.R. Tendulkar	c Rutherford, b Nash	15
S.V. Manjrekar	not out	22
Kapil Dev	b Morrison	17
S.A. Ankola	b Morrison	0
J. Srinath	c Hartland, b Pringle	4
*N.R. Mongia	b Morrison	0
A.R. Kumble	not out	1
Extras	b 2, lb 10, w 5, nb 1	18
(50 overs)	(for 9 wickets)	212

	O	M	R	W
Kapil Dev	10	–	36	–
Srinath	10	1	59	2
Ankola	7	–	24	1
Jadeja	8	–	41	–
Kumble	10	–	41	1
Tendulkar	5	–	37	–

	O	M	R	W
Pringle	10	1	33	1
Morrison	9	1	35	3
Nash	9	–	34	1
Larsen	9	1	40	1
Harris	8	–	32	2
Thomson	5	–	26	1

FALL OF WICKETS

1–17, 2–26, 3–60, 4–204, 5–230

FALL OF WICKETS

1–65, 2–123, 3–150, 4–152, 5–177, 6–206, 7–206, 8–211, 9–212

Umpires: R.S. Dunne & D.M. Quested   *Man of the Match*: S.A. Thomson   *New Zealand won by 28 runs*

SECOND ONE-DAY INTERNATIONAL – NEW ZEALAND v. INDIA
27 March 1994 at Eden Park, Auckland

NEW ZEALAND		
B.A. Young	c Mongia, b Ankola	16
B.R. Hartland	c Azharuddin, b Kapil Dev	0
K.R. Rutherford (capt)	c Azharuddin, b Srinath	6
S.P. Fleming	c Mongia, b Kapil Dev	6
S.A. Thomson	c Mongia, b Ankola	1
C.Z. Harris	not out	50
*A.C. Parore	run out	23
M.N. Hart	b Chauhan	10
G.R. Larsen	st Mongia, b Chauhan	5
D.K. Morrison	st Mongia, b Chauhan	2
C. Pringle	b Srinath	17
Extras	lb 2, w 3, nb 1	6
(49.4 overs)		142

INDIA		
A.D. Jadeja	c Rutherford, b Pringle	18
S.R. Tendulkar	c and b Hart	82
V.G. Kambli	c Hart, b Harris	21
M. Azharuddin (capt)	not out	12
S.V. Manjrekar	not out	7
Kapil Dev		
*N.R. Mongia		
A.R. Kumble		
R.K. Chauhan		
J. Srinath		
S.A. Ankola		
Extras	w 2, nb 1	3
(23.2 overs)	(for 3 wickets)	143

	O	M	R	W
Kapil Dev	10	1	18	2
Srinath	7.4	2	17	2
Ankola	8	–	27	2
Jadeja	4	–	6	–
Kumble	10	2	29	–
Chauhan	10	1	43	3

	O	M	R	W
Morrison	6	–	46	–
Pringle	6	1	41	1
Larsen	2	–	24	–
Hart	5.2	–	19	1
Harris	4	1	13	1

FALL OF WICKETS

1–1, 2–11, 3–31, 4–33, 5–34, 6–86, 7–105, 8–111, 9–115

FALL OF WICKETS

1–61, 2–117, 3–126

Umpires: B.L. Aldridge & C.E. King   *Man of the Match*: S.R. Tendulkar   *India won by 7 wickets*

THIRD ONE-DAY INTERNATIONAL – NEW ZEALAND v. INDIA
30 March 1994 at Basin Reserve, Wellington

INDIA

A.D. Jadeja	b Morrison	56
S.R. Tendulkar	lbw, b Larsen	63
N.S. Sidhu	not out	71
V.G. Kambli	c Pringle, b Nash	23
M. Azharuddin (capt)	b Morrison	24
Kapil Dev	c Thomson, b Pringle	4
*N.R. Mongia	not out	3
A.R. Kumble		
R.K. Chauhan		
J. Srinath		
S.A. Ankola		
Extras	b 1, lb 4, w 6	11
(50 overs)	(for 5 wickets)	255

NEW ZEALAND

B.A. Young	b Srinath	2
C.Z. Harris	c Jadeja, b Kumble	44
B.R. Hartland	st Mongia, b Kumble	21
K.R. Rutherford (capt)	c Kapil Dev, b Srinath	35
S.P. Fleming	run out	2
S.A. Thomson	st Mongia, b Kumble	60
*A.C. Parore	b Kumble	47
G.R. Larsen	b Srinath	2
D.J. Nash	c Kapil Dev, b Kumble	6
C. Pringle	not out	8
D.K. Morrison	not out	4
Extras	b 1, lb 6, w 4, nb 1	12
(50 overs)	(for 9 wickets)	243

	O	M	R	W
Pringle	7	–	36	1
Morrison	10	–	57	2
Nash	9	–	55	1
Larsen	10	–	33	1
Harris	5	–	30	–
Thomson	9	–	39	–

	O	M	R	W
Kapil Dev	8	–	40	–
Srinath	10	3	31	3
Ankola	10	–	55	–
Kumble	10	–	33	5
Chauhan	5	–	30	–
Jadeja	5	–	35	–
Tendulkar	2	–	12	–

FALL OF WICKETS
1–105, 2–154, 3–199, 4–237, 5–248

FALL OF WICKETS
1–5, 2–65, 3–70, 4–76, 5–131, 6–216, 7–221, 8–231, 9–232

Umpires: R.S. Dunne & C.E. King   Man of the Match: A.R. Kumble   *India won by 12 runs*

FOURTH ONE-DAY INTERNATIONAL – NEW ZEALAND v. INDIA
2 April 1994 at Lancaster Park, Christchurch

INDIA

A.D. Jadeja	c Rutherford, b Pringle	68
S.R. Tendulkar	b Larsen	40
N.S. Sidhu	c Nash, b Harris	9
V.G. Kambli	run out	19
M. Azharuddin (capt)	c Larsen, b Hart	1
Kapil Dev	b Morrison	15
*N.R. Mongia	not out	40
A.R. Kumble	not out	18
J. Srinath		
S.A. Ankola		
Venkatesh Prasad		
Extras	lb 7, w 5	12
(50 overs)	(for 6 wickets)	222

NEW ZEALAND

B.A. Young	b Kumble	43
C.Z. Harris	lbw, b Kapil Dev	0
K.R. Rutherford (capt)	c and b Kumble	61
S.P. Fleming	c Venkatesh Prasad, b Kumble	25
S.A. Thomson	not out	40
*A.C. Parore	not out	47
D.J. Nash		
G.R. Larsen		
M.N. Hart		
D.K. Morrison		
C. Pringle		
Extras	lb 2, w 4, nb 1	7
(49.5 overs)	(for 4 wickets)	223

	O	M	R	W
Morrison	10	1	47	1
Pringle	6	–	43	1
Nash	5	–	33	–
Larsen	9	1	37	1
Harris	10	1	25	1
Hart	10	1	30	1

	O	M	R	W
Kapil Dev	8	3	20	1
Srinath	9.5	–	46	–
Venkatesh Prasad	9	–	49	–
Ankola	8	–	37	–
Kumble	10	–	47	3
Tendulkar	5	–	22	–

FALL OF WICKETS
1–61, 2–80, 3–114, 4–118, 5–150, 6–183

FALL OF WICKETS
1–7, 2–89, 3–135, 4–135

Umpires: B.L. Aldridge & D.B. Cowie   Man of the Match: A.C. Parore   *New Zealand won by 6 wickets*

FIRST-CLASS AVERAGES

BATTING

	M	Inns	NO	Runs	HS	Av	100s	50s
G.R. Stead	2	3	1	131	113*	65.50	1	–
C.Z. Harris	4	6	1	301	140*	60.20	1	1
R.G. Twose	6	9	2	395	99	56.42	–	3
M.W. Priest	5	6	1	279	102	55.80	1	2
M.H. Austen	6	10	–	484	202	48.40	1	2
G.E. Bradburn	6	11	3	362	73*	45.25	–	3
A.C. Parore	10	18	1	742	134	43.64	2	4
M.W. Douglas	7	12	1	472	106	42.90	1	4
D.J. Murray	10	16	1	639	112*	42.60	1	4
L.K. Germon	10	12	2	412	114	41.20	2	1
A.H. Jones	4	8	–	324	81	40.50	–	3
D.J. Boyle	5	8	1	282	117	40.28	1	1
L.J. Doull	5	7	1	240	79	40.00	–	1
S.P. Fleming	11	17	1	633	109*	39.56	2	3
S.W.J. Wilson	7	13	3	369	105	36.90	1	–
E.B. McSweeney	5	8	1	253	111	36.14	1	1
B.A. Young	5	10	–	357	120	35.70	1	1
S.A. Thomson	5	10	1	321	120*	35.66	1	1
J.T.C. Vaughan	7	13	3	330	79*	33.00	–	2
B.R. Hartland	10	17	1	489	98	32.60	–	5
M.J. Greatbatch	5	10	2	259	65*	32.37	–	2
G.P. Burnett	9	17	1	514	131	32.12	1	3
P.W. Dobbs	6	11	–	351	82	31.90	–	3
N.J. Astle	6	7	1	187	69	31.16	–	2
M.D. Bailey	6	12	1	341	84	31.00	–	3
C.D. Ingham	6	11	1	303	73	30.30	–	3
B.A. Pocock	7	12	1	331	139*	30.09	1	1
G.P. McRae	3	5	–	148	62	29.60	–	1
A.T. Reinholds	7	14	1	382	71	29.38	–	3
S.W. Duff	6	9	1	234	85	29.25	–	2
K.R. Rutherford	5	10	–	287	63	28.70	–	3
M.E. Farlane	4	8	–	229	89	28.62	–	2
R.P. Wixon	6	10	6	114	34*	28.50	–	–
R.T. Hart	3	5	–	142	120	28.40	1	–
R.K. Brown	6	8	–	227	90	28.37	–	1
R.A. Lawson	4	7	1	170	62	28.33	–	2
D.N. Patel	6	10	–	276	84	27.60	–	2
D.J. Hartshorn	6	8	2	160	35	26.66	–	–
L.C. Breen	4	8	–	204	100	25.50	1	1
T.E. Blain	4	8	1	177	78	25.28	–	2
L.G. Howell	8	12	1	259	60	23.54	–	2
B.G. Cooper	6	12	1	246	87	22.36	–	1
I.S. Billcliff	6	11	2	197	39	21.88	–	–
J.M. Mills	4	6	–	125	46	20.83	–	–
M.L. Su'a	5	8	1	143	45	20.42	–	–
D.J. Nash	9	13	3	201	51	20.10	–	1
D.S. McHardy	3	5	–	100	60	20.00	–	1
G.R. Baker	6	10	1	170	53	18.88	–	1
J.M. Allan	6	11	–	194	56	17.63	–	1
J.I. Pamment	7	13	1	204	98	17.00	–	1
A. Somani	4	7	–	118	40	16.85	–	–
M.N. Hart	7	13	3	162	26	16.20	–	–
S.B. Doull	6	9	–	141	32	15.66	–	–
J.D. Wells	6	9	–	118	43	13.11	–	–
C.M. Spearman	5	10	1	113	26	12.55	–	–
R.G. Hart	6	11	–	134	36	12.18	–	–
K.A. Wealleans	5	10	–	111	51	11.10	–	1

(Qualification – 100 runs, average 10.00)

BOWLING

	Overs	Mds	Runs	Wkts	Av	Best	10/m	5/inn
J.T.C. Vaughan	68.2	26	117	10	11.70	4-27	–	–
C.W. Flanagan	162.3	63	335	23	14.56	6-30	1	2
M.F. Sharpe	122	31	299	19	15.73	4-59	–	–
M.W. Priest	261.2	102	458	28	16.35	6-72	–	1
C.M. Brown	145.1	51	330	20	16.50	6-50	1	1
C. Pringle	176.3	50	397	22	18.04	7-56	1	2
W. Watson	134.4	40	296	16	18.50	4-30	–	–
A.J. Gale	197.5	60	445	22	20.22	6-75	–	2
D.J. Nash	220.1	63	537	26	20.65	6-30	–	3
M.C. Goodson	260.4	88	539	25	21.56	6-48	–	2
R.L. Hayes	168.3	47	415	19	21.84	4-41	–	–
G.R. Jonas	145.4	43	340	15	22.66	4-48	–	–
M.B. Owens	152	44	380	16	23.75	3-31	–	–
S.J. Roberts	170	39	454	19	23.89	5-70	–	1
D.K. Morrison	135.3	31	407	17	23.94	4-52	–	–
M.L. Su'a	134.3	33	444	18	24.66	6-56	–	2
J.D. Wells	113.2	41	297	12	24.75	6-59	–	1
D.N. Patel	141.5	48	316	12	26.33	6-43	–	1
D.J. Leonard	108	22	345	13	26.53	3-18	–	–
G.E. Bradburn	193	51	489	18	27.16	4-99	–	–
E.J. Marshall	170.2	39	469	17	27.58	5-27	–	1
H.T. Davis	287.1	68	861	31	27.77	5-37	–	1
M.J. Stephens	145.2	50	394	14	28.14	5-101	–	1
R.P. Nixon	273.3	98	471	16	29.43	5-83	–	2
S.B. Doull	168	26	553	18	30.72	5-66	–	1
S.W. Duff	270.2	70	583	18	32.38	4-111	–	–
M.N. Hart	253.2	59	738	22	33.54	5-66	–	1
R.P. de Groen	142	37	420	12	35.00	5-89	–	1
C.D. Lee	124.3	33	373	10	37.30	3-34	–	–
D.J. Hartshorn	234.3	66	585	13	45.00	4-124	–	–

(Qualification - 10 wickets)

LEADING FIELDERS

28 – L.K. Germon (ct 24/st 4); 22 – G.R. Baker (ct 18/st 4) and A.C. Parore (ct 21/st 1); 16 – S.P. Fleming, R.G. Hart (ct 13/st 3) and E.B. McSweeney (ct 15/st 1); 15 – J.M. Mills; 13 – J.T.C. Vaughan; 12 – B.A. Young; 11 – T.E. Blain (ct 10/st 1) and J.I. Pamment; 10 – M.D. Bailey

SECTION C
South Africa
Castle Cup
Benson and Hedges Series
UCBSA Bowl and limited-over competition
England 'A' Tour
Australian tour, Test and one-day international series
First-class averages

The historic match at Alexandra, England 'A' v. Transvaal Invitation XI with the shanty town as the backdrop. (Shaun Botterill/Allsport)

The emphasis on one-day cricket is nowhere more pronounced than in South Africa. The Australian tourists were to be engaged in eight limited-over internationals, the Benson and Hedges day/night matches and the UCB Bowl one-day competition overwhelmed the domestic fixture list. Large attendances at the Benson and Hedges games suggested that this is the form of cricket that South Africans most enjoy. Even Canterbury and Barbados whose tours provided the curtain-raisers to the season were involved in a plethora of one-day games while playing only one first-class match each.

 ## PRE-SEASON FRIENDLY MATCHES

14, 15 and **16** September 1993 *at Grahamstown*

Eastern Province 298 for 6 dec. (D.J. Callaghan 104, P.G. Amm 77) and 242 for 6 dec. (P.G. Amm 71, L.J. Koen 56, M.C. Venter 54)
Canterbury 270 for 6 dec. (C.Z. Harris 118 not out, L.G. Howell 94) and 167 for 4

Match drawn

11 September 1993 *at Buffalo Park, East London*

Border 162 for 9 (P.N. Kirsten 64, M.F. Sharpe 4 for 32)
Canterbury 164 for 5 (S.P. Fleming 63)

Canterbury won by 5 wickets

18 September 1993 *at Jansenville*

Canterbury 234 for 9 (S.P. Fleming 62)
Jansenville 74

Canterbury won by 160 runs

20 September 1993 *at St George's Park, Port Elizabeth*

Canterbury 243 for 6 (C.Z. Harris 57, R.T. Latham 51)
Eastern Province 219 (S.C. Pope 88 not out, L.J. Koen 55, R.M. Ford 6 for 32)

Canterbury won by 24 runs

22 September 1993 *at Vredeburg*

Canterbury 230 for 6 (C.Z. Harris 113, B.Z. Harris 55 not out)
Boland 187 (M. Erasmus 55, N.J. Astle 4 for 44)

Canterbury won by 43 runs

New Zealand's Shell Cup holders, Canterbury, enjoyed a successful pre-season tour of South Africa. They won all four one-day games, but failed to chase the target of 271 in 61 overs in the first-class match with Eastern Province.

Terence Lazard, 307 not out for Boland against his former side Western Province, a record for first-class cricket in South Africa, but only for a month.

Chris Harris scored 158 without being dismissed in the match against Eastern Province, and he averaged 62 in the one-day matches with a century against Boland.

17, 18 and **19** September 1993 *at Boland Park, Worcester*

Western Province 345 for 5 dec. (A.P. Kuiper 129 not out, D. Jordaan 63) and 151 for 4 (D. Jordaan 76 not out)
Boland 575 for 5 dec. (T.N. Lazard 307 not out, J.B. Commins 165)

Match drawn

Terry Lazard, the Boland captain, formerly of Western Province, set a record for first-class cricket in South Africa, 307 not out against his ex-team-mates. He beat by one run the record set up by Eric Rowan 54 years earlier. Lazard's record was to stand only a matter of weeks.

24, 25 and **26** September 1993 *at Centurion Park, Verwoerdburg*

Northern Transvaal 339 for 6 dec. (M.J.R. Rindel 137) and 207 for 6 dec. (A.J. Seymore 59, J.J. Strydom 50)
Barbados 246 (V.C. Drakes 100) and 303 for 4 (P.A. Wallace 76, S.L. Campbell 53, F.L. Reifer 51 not out)

Barbados won by 6 wickets

22 September 1993 *at Lenasia*

UCB Invitation XI 149 (M. Yachad 58)
Barbados 151 for 3 (S.L. Campbell 52)

Barbados won by 7 wickets

29 September 1993 *at De Beers Country Club, Kimberley*

Barbados 317 for 9 (A.F.G. Griffith 126, F.L. Reifer 82)
Griqualand West 148 for 6

Barbados won by 169 runs

1 October 1993 *at Springbok Park, Bloemfontein*

Barbados 86 for 4
v. **Orange Free State**

Match abandoned

2 October 1993 *at Harmony Ground, Virginia*

Barbados 223 for 5 (P.A. Wallace 88, S.L. Campbell 61)
Orange Free State 85 for 3

Match abandoned

3 October 1993 *at Springbok Park, Bloemfontein*

Orange Free State 190 for 9 (V.C. Drakes 4 for 26)
Barbados 191 for 6 (A.F.G. Griffith 59, S.L. Campbell 51)

Barbados won by 4 wickets

8 October 1993 *at St George's Park, Port Elizabeth*

Eastern Province 195 for 9 (K.C. Wessels 78,
    S.M. Skeete 4 for 25)
Barbados 107

Eastern Province won by 88 runs

9 October 1993 *at Buffalo Park, East London*

Barbados 178
Border 179 for 4

Border won by 6 wickets

12 October 1993 *at Kingsmead, Durban*

Barbados 143
Natal 147 for 4 (A.C. Hudson 67 not out)

Natal won by 6 wickets

13 October 1993 *at Wanderers, Johannesburg*

Barbados 137 (R.P. Snell 4 for 26, S. Jacobs 4 for 38)
Transvaal 139 for 2 (M.W. Rushmere 62 not out)

Transvaal won by 8 wickets

In a tour that was hit by some bad weather, Barbados
were beaten four times in one-day matches, but they
gained a sensational victory in the first-class fixture.
Asked to make 301 to win, they scored at more than six
runs an over. Northern Transvaal gave batsman Seymore
his first-class debut. He had won his South African
Schools cap in 1992.

 CASTLE CUP

22, 23, 24 and 25 October 1993 *at Springbok Park, Bloemfontein*

Border 323 (A.G. Lawson 110, B.M. Osborne 55,
    A.A. Donald 4 for 78) and 212 (G.C. Victor 74,
    A.A. Donald 4 for 32)
Orange Free State 277 (J.M. Arthur 91, W.J. Cronje 74,
    O.D. Gibson 4 for 50) and 262 for 5 (L.J. Wilkinson
    63 not out, G.F.J. Liebenberg 63, P.J.R. Steyn 63)

Orange Free State by 5 wickets

Orange Free State 6 pts., Border 2 pts.

*Daryll Cullinan established a record for South African cricket when he
hit 337 not out for Transvaal against Northern Transvaal in
Johannesburg. (David Munden/Sports-Line)*

at Wanderers, Johannesburg

Northern Transvaal 517 for 8 dec. (C.B. Lambert 214,
    J.J. Strydom 109, R.F. Pienaar 73, C.E. Eksteen 4 for
    144) and 159 for 4 (P.H. Barnard 89 not out)
Transvaal 602 for 9 dec. (D.J. Cullinan 337 not out,
    S.J. Cook 102, P.S. de Villiers 4 for 106)

Match drawn

Transvaal 2 pts., Northern Transvaal 0 pts.

at Coetzenburg, Stellenbosch

Western Province 366 (B.M. McMillan 116, D.B. Rundle
    81, G. Kirsten 58, P.A.J. DeFreitas 5 for 80) and 73
    for 0
Boland 139 and 296 (P.A.J. DeFreitas 54, D. MacHelm
    4 for 74)

Western Province won by 10 wickets

Western Province 6 pts., Boland 0 pts.

at Kingsmead, Durban

Natal 359 (E.L.R. Stewart 79, N.E. Wright 72) and 170
    for 5 (A.C. Hudson 90)
Eastern Province 422 (D.J. Callaghan 113, D.J.
    Richardson 67, P.G. Amm 59, K.C. Wessels 58)

Match drawn

Eastern Province 2 pts., Natal 0 pts.

South Africa's premier first-class competition began sensationally. Andy Lawson, once of Pershore CC in Worcestershire, hit the second century of his career, and Orange Free State lost their last seven wickets for 44 runs to give Border first-innings points. Donald and Stephenson bowled Free State back into the game, and the home side were left more than a day in which to score 259 to win.

In Johannesburg, the West Indian Test opener Clayton Lambert made his debut for Northern Transvaal and hit 214, sharing a second-wicket stand of 308 with skipper Strydom. Fanie de Villiers reduced the home side to 23 for 3, but Daryll Cullinan was then joined by Jimmy Cook. The pair added 283. Cullinan, 53 at the end of the second day, scored 202 on the third day, and finished on 337 when Cook declared, so beating the record that Lazard had established only a month earlier.

Boland fielded eight players making their debut in the Castle Cup. Two English professionals, Cann and DeFreitas, were among them. DeFreitas began well, dismissing openers Touzel and Jordaan, with only seven scored, and he had a fine all-round match but, with McMillan hitting a solid century and Rundle providing some fireworks, Western Province recovered. They won less than half an hour into the last day.

The cricket in Durban was rather dour with Eastern Province not being bowled out until the last morning and neither side topped 2.5 runs an over throughout the match.

29, 30, 31 October and 1 November 1993 *at*
Coetzenburg, Stellenbosch

Boland 454 (J.B. Commins 137, T.N. Lazard 110, P.A.J. DeFreitas 63, S.D. Jack 4 for 119) and 328 for 6 dec. (W.S. Truter 110 not out, C.P. Dettmer 93)

Transvaal 351 (S.J. Cook 119 not out, D.R. Laing 52, A. Newman 5 for 96)

Match drawn

Boland 2 pts., Transvaal 0 pts.

at St. George's Park, Port Elizabeth

Border 322 (P.J. Botha 124 not out, A.G. Lawson 86) and 342 for 7 (P.N. Kirsten 181, M.P. Stonier 75)

Eastern Province 457 for 9 dec. (D.J. Richardson 128, E.A.E. Baptiste 97, D.J. Callaghan 71)

Match drawn

Eastern Province 2 pts., Border 0 pts.

at Centurion Park, Verwoerdburg

Western Province 510 for 7 dec. (G. Kirsten 192, A.P. Kuiper 90, C.A. Best 71) and 67 for 3

Northern Transvaal 210 and 366 (C.B. Lambert 137, K.J. Rule 122, G. Kirsten 6 for 68, M.W. Pringle 4 for 43)

Western Province won by 7 wickets

Western Province 6 pts., Northern Transvaal 0 pts.

at Springbok Park, Bloemfontein

Orange Free State 450 for 8 dec. (W.J. Cronje 150, J.M. Arthur 99) and 317 for 4 dec. (G.F.J. Liebenberg 142, W.J. Cronje 107)

Natal 435 (J.N. Rhodes 114, N.C. Johnson 95, M.D. Marshall 59 not out) and 181

Orange Free State won by 151 runs

Orange Free State 6 pts., Natal 0 pts.

Making his debut for Boland in the Castle Cup, pace bowler Newman took five wickets for 96 runs in 27 overs, but his side failed to beat Transvaal. Lazard decided to let his team bat out the last day instead of trying to force the issue.

There was also stalemate at St George's Park. Peterus Botha hit the highest score of his career and was the main reason for Border realizing 128 runs from their last three wickets. His partners contributed 36 between them. David Richardson made his highest Castle Cup score and shared a stand of 156 with Baptiste for the sixth wicket. Skipper Peter Kirsten saved his side from defeat with a patient 181.

Orange Free State claimed their second victory and became favourites to retain the Castle Cup, and it was the variety of their attack rather than the pace of Donald and Stephenson which brought success over Natal. Cronje and Arthur shared a second-wicket stand of 222 in the first innings, and Cronje and Liebenberg, who made the highest score of his career, shared a stand of 216 for the same wicket in the second innings. Hansie Cronje, a cricketer who grows in stature daily, hit a century in each innings for the first time. Jonty Rhodes and Neil Johnson shared a brave sixth-wicket stand of 144, with Johnson, born in what is now Zimbabwe, hitting the highest score of his career. Their efforts could not save Natal who were brushed aside on the last day.

Western Province maintained pressure on the Free State with an exciting win over Northern Transvaal for whom Lambert hit another century. Northern Transvaal were forced to follow-on, but Lambert and Rule defied Western in a fourth-wicket stand of 211. Eventually, Western Province hit 67 in 14.5 overs to win the match. Their hero was skipper Gary Kirsten. He began with the highest score of his career, and when Northern Transvaal were proving obdurate on the last morning he brought about a collapse. He took 6 for 68 as the last seven wickets fell for 30 runs. He had never before taken a wicket with his off-breaks in the Castle Cup.

25, 26, 27 and 28 November 1993 *at St George's Park, Port Elizabeth*

Western Province 188 (R.E. Veenstra 4 for 60) and 294 (G. Kirsten 116, A.P. Kuiper 53, E.A.E. Baptiste 4 for 43)

Eastern Province 231 (P.G. Amm 56, E.A.E. Baptiste 58, A. Martyn 4 for 60) and 186

Western Province won by 65 runs

Western Province 6 pts., Eastern Province 2 pts.

at Centurion Park, Verwoerdburg

Northern Transvaal 274 (K.J. Rule 101 not out,
M. Erasmus 5 for 34) and 258 (K.J. Rule 92)
Boland 149 and 272 (J.B. Commins 67, W.S. Truter 62,
T. Bosch 4 for 32)

Northern Transvaal won by 111 runs

Northern Transvaal 6 pts., Boland 0 pts.

at Buffalo Park, East London

Border 392 (S.J. Palframan 123, P.N. Kirsten 73,
A.G. Lawson 60, N.C. Johnson 5 for 114) and 152 for
1 (A.G. Lawson 68 not out, B.M. Osborne 58 not out)
Natal 443 (N.C. Johnson 136, C.E.B. Rice 59,
S.M. Pollock 56, I.L. Howell 4 for 123)

Match drawn

Natal 2 pts., Border 0 pts.

Another century from skipper Gary Kirsten provided the
substance for Western Province's victory over Eastern
Province who led by 43 on the first innings. Western lost
three wickets in clearing off these arrears, but Kirsten's
determination and excellent leadership brought victory
by mid-afternoon on the last day.

Two outstanding innings by wicket-keeper Kevin Rule
brought victory for Northern Transvaal over Boland.
Rule, who had hit a career-best in the previous match,
scored 101 out of 166 while he was at the wicket in the first
innings and 92 out of 136 in the second.

Border's wicket-keeper Steve Palframan hit a maiden
first-class century, dominating a stand of 156 with Frans
Cronje for the seventh wicket. Palframan was one of Neil
Johnson's five victims in a career-best haul. Johnson then
shared a sixth-wicket stand of 150 and reached a maiden
first-class hundred to become Man of the Match.

10, 11, 12 and **13** December 1993 *at Springbok Park,
Bloemfontein*

Orange Free State 323 (P.J.R. Steyn 90, L.J. Wilkinson
72, P.A.J. DeFreitas 4 for 59) and 302 for 7 dec.
(F.D. Stephenson 95, J.F. Venter 76)
Boland 365 (K.C. Jackson 90, W.S. Truter 78,
P.A.J. DeFreitas 52, J.B. Commins 50, N. Boje 6 for
101) and 139 for 3

Match drawn

Boland 2 pts., Orange Free State 0 pts.

at Jan Smuts Ground, Pietermaritzburg

Western Province 300 (E.O. Simons 96, C.A. Best 63,
A.C. Dawson 56, P.W.E. Rawson 4 for 29) and 173
for 6
Natal 429 (M.D. Marshall 120 not out, N.E. Wright 89)

Match drawn

Natal 2 pts., Western Province 0 pts.

With the leading players having departed for Australia,
neither Free State nor Western Province could gain a
point. Slow left-arm bowler Nicky Boje did well for Free
State, but Boland took first-innings points in spite of
losing their last five wickets for 25 runs. In contrast,
Natal's tail wagged furiously, the last three wickets realising 210 runs. This was due to Malcolm Marshall. The
West Indian's 120 not out was the seventh and highest
century of his career. Marshall was captaining Natal, and
his opposing captain, Eric Simmons, also hit a career-best
96.

26, 27, 28 and **29** December 1993 *at Buffalo Park, East London*

Boland 238 for 4 (P.A.J. DeFreitas 103 not out,
T.N. Lazard 89 not out)
v. **Border**

Match abandoned

No points

*Malcolm Marshall hit the highest score of his career, 120 not out for
Natal against Western Province, 12 December 1993. (George
Herringshaw ASP)*

at Kingsmead, Durban

Natal 346 (N.E. Wright 82, D.J. Watson 57) and 91 for 2 dec.
Northern Transvaal 103 for 4 dec. and 198 (M.J.R. Rindel 75, D.N. Crookes 5 for 84)

Natal won by 136 runs
Natal 6 pts., Northern Transvaal 0 pts.

at Wanderers, Johannesburg

Eastern Province 160 (S.D. Jack 4 for 44) and 217 (E.A.E. Baptiste 60, M. Michau 52, M.R. Hobson 7 for 61)
Transvaal 126 (E.A.E. Baptiste 5 for 41) and 218 for 8 (B.M. White 59)

Match drawn
Eastern Province 2 pts., Transvaal 0 pts.

Lazard and DeFreitas shared an unbroken fourth-wicket stand of 157 at Buffalo Park, but no play was possible after the first day. There was little play on the second and third days in Durban, and the captains, Marshall and Strydom, were named jointly as Men of the Match for their efforts in keeping the game alive. Johnson took three quick wickets when Northern Transvaal went in search of 335 to win, and Derek Crookes gave Natal victory with the best bowling performance of his career as an off-spinner.

Baptiste had a fine all-round match for Eastern Province against Transvaal, and his side looked the most likely winners in Johannesburg, but time was lost to bad weather on the last day when only 42 overs were possible.

1, 2, 3 and **4** January 1994 *at St George's Park, Port Elizabeth*

Orange Free State 309 (J.F. Venter 55, F.D. Stephenson 53) and 251 for 2 dec. (J.M. Arthur 105 not out, P.J.R. Steyn 88 not out)
Eastern Province 310 for 8 dec. (S.C. Pope 67 not out, M. Michau 56) and 226 for 9 (P.G. Amm 50, F.D. Stephenson 4 for 57)

Match drawn
Eastern Province 2 pts., Orange Free State 0 pts.

at Buffalo Park, East London

Northern Transvaal 146 (A. Badenhorst 4 for 26) and 230 (K.J. Rule 69, I.L. Howell 5 for 72)
Border 475 for 4 dec. (P.N. Kirsten 271, A.G. Lawson 83, P.C. Strydom 60 not out)

Border won by an innings and 99 runs
Border 6 pts., Northern Transvaal 0 pts.

at Newlands, Cape Town

Transvaal 255 (B.M. White 108, E.O. Simons 4 for 41) and 282 for 7 dec. (S.J. Cook 85, M. Yachad 51)
Western Province 131 (C.E. Eksteen 7 for 29) and 226 (A.P. Kuiper 76, R.J. Ryall 58, C.E. Eksteen 5 for 66)

Transvaal won by 180 runs
Transvaal 6 pts., Western Province 0 pts.

Orange Free State failed to take a point in an exciting match in Port Elizabeth. Consistent batting gave Eastern Province first-innings points, but some brisk batting from Arthur and Steyn made it possible for van Zyl to declare and to set Eastern a target of 251 in 59 overs. They began well enough, but the loss of three wickets for six runs took them to a precarious 226 for 9, and the last pair just held out.

Peter Kirsten hit the 51st and highest century of his career and led Border to an innings victory against Northern Transvaal. Kirsten's 271 occupied 177.4 overs and his fine form earned him a call to join the South African side in Australia.

Transvaal won the traditional New Year match against Western Province who still topped the table, having played one more game than Orange Free State. Transvaal had two heroes; Brad White hit a maiden first-class hundred and slow left-arm bowler Clive Eksteen had a remarkable match. His 7 for 29 in the first innings was the best performance of the season as well as the best of his career, and he took 10 or more wickets in a match for the first time.

21, 22, 23 and **24** January 1994 *at Newlands, Cape Town*

Western Province 318 (L.F. Bleekers 87, S.G. Koening 64, N. Boje 4 for 96) and 220 for 9 dec. (E.O. Simons 54 not out, S.G. Koenig 52)

A career-best 271 for Peter Kirsten, Border v. Northern Transvaal, 3 January 1994. (David Munden/Sports-Line)

Orange Free State 273 (L.J. Wilkinson 105, M.W. Pringle
4 for 55, A. Martyn 4 for 65) and 49 for 1

Match drawn

Western Province 2 pts., Orange Free State 0 pts.

at Centurion Park, Verwoerdburg

Northern Transvaal 215 (K.J. Rule 63) and 201 for 7
Eastern Province 67 (G. Smith 5 for 24)

Match drawn

Northern Transvaal 2 pts., Eastern Province 0 pts.

Western Province extended their lead in the Castle Cup
to eight points, but their attritional methods won few
friends. They won the toss and scored 139 for 4 off 80.3
overs on the first day. They increased their rate of scoring
on the second day, but they barely got above two an over.
Wilkinson revived Free State after three wickets had gone
for 22, but the policy of attrition continued to the end.

The loss of the last day's play robbed Northern Transvaal of victory against Eastern Province.

28, 29, 30 and 31 January 1994 *at Springbok Park, Bloemfontein*

Orange Free State 339 (J.F. Venter 83) and 14 for 0
Northern Transvaal 159 (N. Boje 4 for 39) and 193
(B.J. Somerville 72, M.I. Gidley 5 for 48)

Orange Free State won by 10 wickets

Orange Free State 6 pts., Northern Transvaal 0 pts.

at Wanderers, Johannesburg

Border 251 (P.C. Strydom 117, M.J. Vandrau 4 for 72)
and 214 (M.P. Stonier 51, M.J. Vandrau 5 for 42)
Transvaal 272 (M. Yachad 77, M.W. Rushmere 69,
B.C. Fourie 6 for 74) and 197 for 7 (M. Yachad 100
not out)

Transvaal won by 3 wickets

Transvaal 6 pts., Border 0 pts.

Orange Free State returned to form with a resounding
victory in three days over Northern Transvaal. Former
Leicestershire bowler Gidley took five wickets in the
second innings on the occasion of his debut in the Castle
Cup.

English county players were also in evidence in Johannesburg where Derbyshire off-break bowler Matthew
Vandrau twice had the best bowling performance of his
career. There was also a career-best bowling performance
by Brenden Fourie.

11, 12, 13 and 14 February 1994 *at Wanderers, Johannesburg*

Transvaal 418 for 7 dec. (S.J. Cook 110,
M.W. Rushmere 82 not out, D.J. Cullinan 66) and 118
(J.F. Venter 5 for 14)
Orange Free State 327 for 9 dec. (F.D. Stephenson 78,
P.J.R. Steyn 64, J.F. Venter 63) and 210 for 6 (G.F.J.
Liebenberg 62)

Orange Free State won by 4 wickets

Orange Free State 6 pts., Transvaal 2 pts.

at Coetzenburg, Stellenbosch

Boland 351 (M. Erasmus 73, P.A.J. DeFreitas 68,
J.B. Commins 55, N.C. Johnson 5 for 79) and 276 for
8 dec. (K.C. Jackson 61)
Natal 306 (A.C. Hudson 92, M.D. Marshall 73) and 187
(D.N. Crookes 52, C.W. Henderson 4 for 25)

Boland won by 134 runs

Boland 6 pts., Natal 0 pts.

Cronje and Donald returned from Australia in time to
assist Orange Free State in their final match, but it was
Transvaal who took the early honours. Led by Jimmy
Cook, the middle order scored heavily, and Free State
faced a daunting 418. The loss of three wickets for 74
suggested that the visitors would struggle to save the
follow-on, but Steyn, Venter and Stephenson played well
and scored briskly. Franklyn Stephenson made early
break-throughs in Transvaal's second innings, but it was
the introduction of Jacobus Venter's off-spin into the

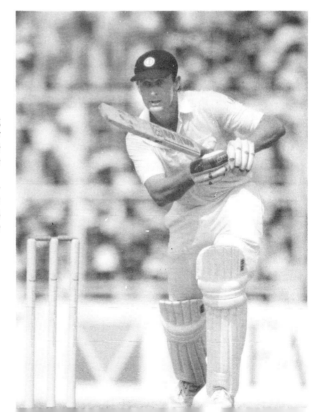

*A tower of strength for Western Province in the one-day game
Adrian Kuiper. (David Munden/Sports-Line)*

attack which turned the game in favour of Free State. In 8.4 overs, he took 5 for 14 as Transvaal lost their last five wickets for 28 runs. Orange Free State needed to score 210 at 3.5 runs an over, a feat they accomplished thanks to Liebenberg's foundation, Stephenson's hitting and contributions from all who batted. The win took Free State four points clear of Western Province at the top of the table and left them an anxious wait until Western's last match in 12 days' time.

In a game of less moment, Boland gave a fine team performance to beat Natal.

26, 27, 28 February and 1 March 1994 *at Kingsmead, Durban*

Natal 464 (N.E. Wright 102, D.M. Benkenstein 71, D.N. Crookes 59, N.C. Johnson 55) and 144 (S.D. Jack 6 for 30, C.E. Eksteen 4 for 53)

Transvaal 296 (S.J. Cook 136, P.L. Symcox 4 for 64) and 123 for 3

Match drawn

Natal 2 pts., Transvaal 0 pts.

at Newlands, Cape Town

Western Province 210 (B.M. McMillan 61, A. Badenhorst 4 for 37, P.J. Botha 4 for 45) and 327 for 7 dec. (S.G. Koening 121 not out, G. Kirsten 78)

Border 231 (I.L. Howell 52 not out) and 309 for 9 (M.P. Stonier 59, P.N. Kirsten 51)

Border won by 1 wicket

Border 6 pts., Western Province 0 pts.

at St George's Park, Port Elizabeth

Boland 307 (J.B. Commins 92, T.N. Lazard 77, L. Germishuys 58, A.G. Huckle 6 for 99) and 176 (M. Erasmus 66, T.G. Shaw 4 for 23)

Eastern Province 308 for 7 dec. (D.J. Callaghan 63, K.C. Wessels 62) and 177 for 2 (K.C. Wessels 53 not out)

Eastern Province won by 8 wickets

Eastern Province 6 pts., Boland 0 pts.

Jimmy Cook hit his fourth Castle Cup century of the season, but Transvaal were pointless against Natal, legspinner Alan Huckle produced a career-best bowling performance which helped Eastern Province to victory over Boland, their first win of the season; but all eyes were on Newlands. Put in to bat, Western Province were reduced to 93 for 6 before McMillan and skipper Matthews conjured 117 runs out of the last four wickets. It still seemed that Western would take first-innings points, but a ninth-wicket stand of 50 between Howell and Fourie thwarted them. Left-hander Sven Koening, 21 years old and in his first season in the Castle Cup, brought Western back into the game with a mature maiden century and a second-wicket stand of 153 with Gary Kirsten. Koening held the innings together, and

A maiden century in the Benson and Hedges day/night competition for Clive Rice, 44 years old. (David Munden/Sports-Line)

Matthews was able to declare and set Border a target of 307 in 129 overs. As the highest fourth-innings winning total in the Castle Cup is 313, Border faced a formidable task. In spite of skipper Peter Kirsten's 51 and some solid batting throughout the order, Border slipped to 250 for 8, and it seemed that the match and the Castle Cup would go to Western Province, but Derbyshire's Simon Base hit lustily, and he and Ian Howell, who made his two highest scores of the season in this match, 50 and 30, both unbeaten, added 54. Three runs were still needed when Simons bowled Base, but Badenhorst hit Matthews for four and won the match. Western Province had lost the Castle Cup by one wicket.

CASTLE CUP FINAL TABLE

	P	W	L	D	Pts.
Orange Free State (1)	7	4	–	3	24
Western Province (5)	7	3	2	2	20
Eastern Province (2)	7	1	1	5	16
Transvaal (4)	7	2	1	4	16
Border (6)	7	2	2	3	14
Natal (3)	7	1	2	4	12
Boland (–)	7	1	3	3	10
Northern Transvaal (7)	7	1	4	2	8
(1993 positions in brackets)					

BENSON AND HEDGES DAY/NIGHT SERIES

15 October 1993 *at St George's Park, Port Elizabeth*

Northern Transvaal 161
Eastern Province 162 for 7

Eastern Province (4 pts.) won by 3 wickets

at PAM Brink Stadium, Springs

Natal 212 for 8
Impalas 165 for 7 (D.N. Crookes 4 for 38)

Natal (4 pts.) won by 47 runs

With the cessation of the knock-out tournament, the Benson and Hedges day/night series became the senior one-day competition in South Africa. It was certainly the best supported of all forms of cricket. The eight Castle Cup sides and Impalas, a team comprised of Bowl cricketers, competed on a league basis. The matches were played in between the Castle Cup fixtures.

20 October 1993 *at Wanderers, Johannesburg*

Transvaal 275 for 6 (D.J. Cullinan 111 not out, M.W. Rushmere 54)
Impalas 181 for 5 (W.E. Schonegevel 55)

Transvaal (4 pts.) won on faster scoring rate

Five days before establishing a record for first-class cricket in South Africa, Daryll Cullinan hit his highest score in the Benson and Hedges competition.

5 November 1993 *at Springbok Park, Bloemfontein*

Orange Free State 227 for 7
Eastern Province 159 for 9 (N. Boje 4 for 18)

Orange Free State (4 pts.) won by 68 runs

at Wanderers, Johannesburg

Transvaal 166 for 5 (M. Yachad 56, S.J. Cook 52)
v. **Western Province**

Match abandoned

Transvaal 2 pts., Western Province 2 pts.

6 November 1993 *at PAM Brink Stadium, Springs*

Northern Transvaal 142 for 7
Impalas 97 for 8

Northern Transvaal (4 pts.) won by 45 runs

Bad weather caused abandonment in Johannesburg and the reduction of the match in Springs from 50 to 23 overs an innings.

10 November 1993 *at Centurion Park, Verwoerdburg*

Northern Transvaal 239 for 6 (M.J.R. Rindel 73, J.J. Strydom 51, O.D. Gibson 4 for 62)
Border 243 for 5 (P.N. Kirsten 134 not out)

Border (4 pts.) won by 5 wickets

at Springbok Park, Bloemfontein

Impalas 108 for 8 (B.T. Player 4 for 7)
Orange Free State 56 for 2

Orange Free State (4 pts.) won on faster scoring rate

Peter Kirsten hit the second-highest score ever recorded in the Benson and Hedges tournament and would surely have beaten Philip Amm's 136 had Border not reached their target with 11 balls to spare. Orange Free State's target against Impalas was reduced to 54 off 20 overs, but they won in 8.2 overs. Brad Player had the remarkable figures of 10–7–7–4 for the Free State.

12 November 1993 *at Buffalo Park, East London*

Western Province 252 for 4 (D. Jordaan 91, G. Kirsten 68, A.P. Kuiper 56 not out)
Border 231 (P.J. Botha 73, I.L. Howell 50, A. Martyn 4 for 52)

Western Province (4 pts.) won by 21 runs

at Kingsmead, Durban

Natal 154 for 7
Boland 109 for 1

Natal (4 pts.) won on faster scoring rate

Deon Jordaan made his highest Benson and Hedges score while Boland failed to reach a readjusted target of 118 in 23 overs.

17 November 1993 *at St George's Park, Port Elizabeth*

Transvaal 193 for 7
Eastern Province 197 for 4 (M. Michau 104 not out)

Eastern Province (4 pts.) won by 6 wickets

19 November 1993 *at PAM Brink Stadium, Springs*

Impalas 205 for 6 (J.E. Morris 65, W.E. Schonegevel 51)
Border 206 for 3 (A.G. Lawson 82, P.N. Kirsten 71)

Border (4 pts.) won by 7 wickets

at Springbok Park, Bloemfontein

Orange Free State 271 for 8 (C.J.P.G. van Zyl 59 not out, J.F. Venter 55)
Western Province 210 (A.P. Kuiper 66)

Orange Free State (4 pts.) won by 61 runs

Marcelle Michau hit his maiden Benson and Hedges century to steer Eastern Province to victory over Transvaal while Peter Kirsten and Andrew Lawson put on 147 for Border's first wicket against Impalas.

8 December 1993 *at Centurion Park, Verwoerdburg*

Northern Transvaal 247 for 6 (R.F. Pienaar 87)
Natal 185

Northern Transvaal (4 pts.) won by 62 runs

at Springbok Park, Bloemfontein

Orange Free State 189 for 9 (P.J.R. Steyn 55)
Transvaal 169 (J.F. Venter 5 for 21)

Orange Free State (4 pts.) won by 20 runs

at Buffalo Park, East London

Eastern Province 186 for 9
Border 187 for 5

Border (4 pts.) won by 5 wickets

Jacobus Venter returned his best figures of the competition, and Orange Free State notched their fourth win in a row.

15 December 1993 *at Centurion Park, Verwoerdburg*

Northern Transvaal 131
Orange Free State 133 for 6

Orange Free State (4 pts.) won by 4 wickets

at Newlands, Cape Town

Western Province 256 for 5 (D. Jordaan 116, A.P. Kuiper 74)
Impalas 229 for 8 (J.E. Morris 68, A.C. Dawson 4 for 45)

Western Province (4 pts.) won by 27 runs

Orange Free State virtually assured themselves of a place in the semi-finals with their fifth win in as many matches. Deon Jordaan reached his first century in the competition and shared a third-wicket stand of 155 with Adrian Kuiper. Impalas, led by John Morris of Derbyshire and Durham, were deducted one over because of their slow rate.

17 December 1993 *at Wanderers, Johannesburg*

Natal 222 for 4 (C.E.B. Rice 103)
Transvaal 125

Natal (4 pts.) won by 97 runs

at Newlands, Cape Town

Western Province 217 for 8 (E.O. Simons 67, A.P. Kuiper 52)
Boland 123 (E.O. Simons 4 for 15)

Western Province (4 pts.) won by 94 runs

18 December 1993 *at Danie Craven Stadium, Stellenbosch*

Boland 237 for 9 (T.N. Lazard 67)
Border 238 for 8 (F.J.C. Cronje 55 not out)

Border (4 pts.) won by 2 wickets

At the age of 44, Clive Rice hit his first century in the competition. Border were 142 for 7 before Frans Cronje and Ian Howell added 88 to make possible victory over Boland with two balls to spare.

20 December 1993 *at Kingsmead, Durban*

Natal 210 for 8 (N.E. Wright 80, M.L. Bruyns 55)
Orange Free State 184

Natal (4 pts.) won by 26 runs

at Buffalo Park, East London

Transvaal 235 for 8 (M. Yachad 86, B.C. Fourie 4 for 44)
Border 238 for 3 (P.N. Kirsten 86, B.M. Osborne 85 not out)

Border (4 pts.) won by 7 wickets

22 December 1993 *at Newlands, Cape Town*

Northern Transvaal 161 (M.J.R. Rindel 82, M.W. Pringle 4 for 36)
Western Province 162 for 5 (H.H. Gibbs 55 not out)

Western Province (4 pts.) won by 5 wickets

23 December 1993 *at Danie Craven Stadium, Stellenbosch*

Orange Free State 205 for 9
Boland 112 (F.D. Stephenson 4 for 11)

Orange Free State (4 pts.) won by 93 runs

at St George's Park, Port Elizabeth

Natal 192 (N.C. Johnson 61)
Eastern Province 133 (N.C. Johnson 4 for 32)

Natal (4 pts.) won by 59 runs

In the last batch of games before Christmas, Natal and Orange Free State clearly emerged as the front runners with five and six wins respectively and one defeat each.

7 January 1994 *at Buffalo Park, East London*

Border 89 for 6
Orange Free State 7 for 0

Match abandoned

Border 2 pts., Orange Free State 2 pts.

at PAM Brink Stadium, Springs

Impalas 262 for 4 (W.E. Schonegevel 103, W.R. Radford 101)
Boland 200 (J.B. Commins 52)

Impalas (4 pts.) won by 62 runs

at Newlands, Cape Town

Western Province 206 for 7 (C.A. Best 57)
Eastern Province 195 for 7 (T.G. Shaw 56 not out)

Western Province (4 pts.) won by 11 runs

Impalas gained their only win of the season in spectacular fashion. Their 262 for 4 was their highest score in the competition while the centuries by Wayne Schonegevel (Griqualand West) and Wayne Radford (Eastern Transvaal) were only the second and third centuries hit for Impalas, Charlesworth's 100 against Eastern Province, 1990–1, being the previous century. The pair put on 205 for the first wicket, a record for any Impalas wicket.

12 January 1994 *at Kingsmead, Durban*

Natal 249 for 7 (M.D. Marshall 63)
Western Province 147

Natal (4 pts.) won by 102 runs

at Wanderers, Johannesburg

Boland 230 for 7 (A.T. Holdstock 66, J.B. Commins 52)
Transvaal 232 for 7 (D.R. Laing 85, B.M. White 84)

Transvaal (4 pts.) won by 3 wickets

14 January 1994 *at Danie Craven Stadium, Stellenbosch*

Eastern Province 185 (M. Michau 59, P.A. Rayment 57)
Boland 101

Eastern Province (4 pts.) won by 84 runs

at Centurion Park, Verwoerdburg

Transvaal 208 for 9 (M. Yachad 113)
Northern Transvaal 102 for 5

Northern Transvaal (4 pts.) won on faster scoring rate

Malcolm Marshall's all-round brilliance, 3 for 19 and a whirlwind 63, assured Natal of a place in the semi-finals. Mandy Yachad scored his third and highest century in the competition, but Northern Transvaal's target was reduced to 102 off 20 overs, and they won with an over to spare.

19 January 1994 *at Danie Craven Stadium, Stellenbosch*

Northern Transvaal 138
Boland 143 for 8

Boland (4 pts.) won by 2 wickets

at St George's Park, Port Elizabeth

Eastern Province 220 for 8 (P.G. Amm 65, E.A.E. Baptiste 56)
Impalas 129

Eastern Province (4 pts.) won by 91 runs

at Kingsmead, Durban

Natal 234 for 9 (N.C. Johnson 62)
Border 219 for 8 (P.J. Botha 73, P.C. Strydom 67, D.N. Crookes 4 for 53)

Natal (4 pts.) won by 15 runs

The last round of matches made no difference to the final standings with Natal, Orange Free State, Western Province and Border qualifying for the knock-out stage.

BENSON AND HEDGES FINAL TABLE

	P	W	L	NR	Pts.
Natal	8	7	1	–	28
Orange Free State	8	6	1	1	26
Western Province	8	5	2	1	22
Border	8	5	2	1	22
Eastern Province	8	4	4	–	16
Northern Transvaal	8	3	5	–	12
Transvaal	8	2	5	1	10
Impalas	8	1	7	–	4
Boland	8	1	7	–	4

SEMI-FINALS

2 February 1994 *at Buffalo Park, East London*

Natal 134 (D.M. Benkenstein 57)
Border 139 for 7

Border won by 3 wickets

at Newlands, Cape Town

Western Province 192 for 9 (E.O. Simons 55 not out, B.T. Player 4 for 41)
Orange Free State 118 (E.O. Simons 4 for 19, A. Meyer 4 for 26)

Western Province won by 74 runs

4 February 1994 *at Kingsmead, Durban*

Border 183 for 9 (P.C. Strydom 72)
Natal 186 for 6 (M.L. Bruyns 85 not out)

Natal won by 4 wickets

at Springbok Park, Bloemfontein

Orange Free State 237 for 7 (W.J. Cronje 120)
Western Province 174 (A.P. Kuiper 52)

Orange Free State won by 63 runs

6 February 1994 *at Kingsmead, Durban*

Natal 244 for 6 (A.C. Hudson 88, M.D. Marshall 64 not out)
Border 191 (D.N. Crookes 4 for 32)

Natal won by 53 runs

at Springbok Park, Bloemfontein

Orange Free State 145
Western Province 140

Orange Free State won by 5 runs

Both semi-finals went to a third leg with the ultimate winners having lost the first match. Malcolm Marshall played a decisive part in Natal's game while Hansie Cronje's third and highest century in the competition earned Orange Free State a third match with Western

Province. That decisive leg proved to be one of the most tense encounters of the season. Free State were put in to bat and crashed to 82 for 8. Stephenson then found an able ally in Boje, and the pair added 53. Western's innings followed a similar pattern. They were reduced to 66 for 8 before Matthews and Rundle added 56. Matthews was then aided by Martyn as 18 runs were added, but Donald bowled Martyn with the first ball of the last over with Western Province still six runs short of victory.

FINAL

The final proved to be an anti-climax. Jonty Rhodes was back to lead Natal, and he won the toss and chose to bat. Hudson and Wright began solidly enough, but the advent of Allan Donald and Brad Player brought about a dramatic change. The medium-pace Player caught and bowled Wright, bowled Rhodes and took four of the first six wickets to fall. Decisively, Donald captured the sixth man, Hudson, who had faced 88 balls for 47. The Natal innings was in ruins, and the only other batsman to reach double figures was Crookes, 13 off 29 deliveries.

Orange Free State had an uneasy start against Peter Rawson who bowled a magnificent spell, but once his quota was spent, they raced to victory. Wilkinson hit 22 off 31 balls, and Venter, 37 off 32 balls, finished the match with a six off Symcox as Orange Free State won with 21.5 overs to spare and so completed the 'double'.

 UNITED CRICKET BOARD OF SOUTH AFRICA BOWL

7, 8, 9 and **10** October 1993
SECTION TWO

at PAM Brink Stadium, Springs

Western Province 'B' 244 for 6 dec. (S.G. Koening 57, T.J. Mitchell 53 not out, L.C.R. Jordaan 4 for 59) and 224 for 5 dec. (H.D. Ackerman 57)

Eastern Transvaal 207 (C.R. Norris 73 not out, W.R. Radford 68, A. Martyn 6 for 60) and 174 for 9 (C.R. Norris 68, F. Benjamin 4 for 40)

Match drawn

Western Province 'B' 2 pts., Eastern Transvaal 0 pts.

at Witrand Stadium, Potchefstroom

Griqualand West 194 (F.C. Brooker 72 not out) and 94 for 4

Western Transvaal 175 (B.E. van der Vyver 4 for 32)

Match drawn

Griqualand West 2 pts., Western Transvaal 0 pts.

BENSON AND HEDGES FINAL – NATAL *v.* ORANGE FREE STATE
11 March 1994 at Kingsmead, Durban

NATAL			ORANGE FREE STATE		
A.C. Hudson	c Radley, **b** Donald	47	J.M. Arthur	c Stewart, **b** Rawson	10
N.E. Wright	c and **b** Player	6	G.F.J. Liebenberg	lbw, **b** Rawson	6
J.N. Rhodes (capt)	**b** Player	2	W.J. Cronje (capt)	**b** Pollock	20
N.C. Johnson	c Radley, **b** Player	6	L.J. Wilkinson	not out	22
D.M. Benkenstein	c Wilkinson, **b** Donald	6	J.F. Venter	not out	37
M.D. Marshall	c Cronje, **b** Player	8	P.J.R. Steyn		
*E.L.R. Stewart	**b** Player	0	F.D. Stephenson		
D.N. Crookes	c Radley, **b** van Zyl	13	C.J.P.G. van Zyl		
P.L. Symcox	lbw, **b** Donald	1	B.T. Player		
A.G. Pollock	c Stephenson, **b** Donald	2	*P.J.L. Radley		
P.W.E. Rawson	not out	0	A.A. Donald		
Extras	lb 3, w 6, nb 3	12	Extras	lb 3, w 6, nb 4	13
(36.2 overs)		103	(28.1 overs)	(for 3 wickets)	108

	O	M	R	W		O	M	R	W
Stephenson	8	3	18	–	Marshall	8	1	31	–
van Zyl	4.2	–	20	1	Rawson	10	4	11	2
Cronje	6	2	14	–	Johnson	5	–	25	–
Player	10	–	27	5	Pollock	4	–	23	1
Donald	8	–	21	4	Symcox	1.1	–	15	–

FALL OF WICKETS
1–42, 2–48, 3–57, 4–71, 5–81, 6–83, 7–85, 8–88, 9–96

FALL OF WICKETS
1–21, 2–36, 3–53

Umpires: S.B. Lambson & K.E. Liebenberg   *Man of the Match:* B.T. Player   *Orange Free State won by 7 wickets*

The lesser of South Africa's two first-class competitions was divided into two groups with the winners of each group meeting in the final. The opening matches in Section Two were badly hit by the weather. There was no play at all on the first day in Potchefstroom. In Springs, left-arm pace bowler Aubrey Martyn, who has assisted Marlow and played for Buckinghamshire Under-25, had career-best figures of 6 for 60. Martyn quickly won promotion to the 'A' side and was chosen for the South African tour of England.

29, 30, 31 October and 1 November 1993

SECTION ONE

at Wanderers, Johannesburg

Transvaal 'B' 317 for 8 dec. (B.M. White 93, G.A. Pollock 64, W.V. Rippon 51) and 223 for 7 dec. (B.M. White 109)
Northern Transvaal 'B' 245 (B.J. Sommerville 53, P.E. Smith 4 for 60) and 241 (B.J. Sommerville 77, M.J. Vandrau 5 for 85)

Transvaal 'B' won by 54 runs

Transvaal 'B' 6 pts., Northern Transvaal 'B' 0 pts.

at Buffalo Park, East London

Natal 'B' 291 (M. Badat 54 not out, D.J. Watson 50, A.W. Schoeman 4 for 64) and 221 (M.L. Bruyns 82, Q.R. Still 5 for 53)
Border 'B' 277 (F.J.C. Cronje 85) and 39 for 4

Match drawn

Natal 'B' 2 pts., Border 'B' 0 pts.

at Harare Sports Club, Harare

Zimbabwe Board XI 275 for 9 dec. (I.P. Butchart 60, G.K. Bruk-Jackson 58, C.A. van Ee 4 for 19) and 331 for 9 dec. (G.K. Bruk-Jackson 130)
Orange Free State 'B' 343 (C.F. Craven 152, C.J. van Heerden 69, M.P. Jarvis 4 for 86, P.A. Strang 4 for 93) and 91 for 1 (C. Light 52 not out)

Match drawn

Orange Free State 'B' 2 pts., Zimbabwe Board XI 0 pts.

SECTION TWO

at Witrand Stadium, Potchefstroom

Western Transvaal 240 (A. Cilliers 56, H.M. de Vos 50 not out) and 340 (H.M. de Vos 95, A. Cilliers 56, A.J. van Deventer 55, S.M. Skeete 6 for 88)
Eastern Transvaal 336 (T. Jamaal 114, C.R. Norris 78, T.A. Marsh 50, F. Baird 5 for 72, A.H. Gray 4 for 83) and 175 for 7 (T.A. Marsh 51 not out)

Match drawn

Eastern Transvaal 2 pts., Western Transvaal 0 pts.

at Goodwood Oval, Cape Town

Eastern Province 'B' 403 for 9 dec. (C. Wait 103, P.A. Tullis 76, S.C. Pope 65, M.G. Beamish 62)
Western Province 'B' 244 (G. Roe 4 for 42) and 322 for 3 (H.H. Gibbs 152 not out, R.A. Koster 68 not out, L.F. Bleekers 55)

Match drawn

Eastern Province 'B' 2 pts., Western Province 'B' 0 pts.

at Kimberley Country Club, Kimberley

Griqualand West 120 (S.T. Jefferies 4 for 20) and 415 (W.E. Schonegevel 82, J.E. Johnson 79, M.N. Angel 52, D. Smith 5 for 80)
Boland 'B' 321 (L. Germishuys 80 not out, K.C. Jackson 51, M.N. Angel 4 for 50) and 218 for 9

Boland 'B' won by 1 wicket

Boland 'B' 6 pts., Griqualand West 0 pts.

Transvaal 'B' skipper Brad White hit 93 and 109, a maiden first-class century, to set up his side's victory over Northern Transvaal 'B'. There was also some good bowling from Derbyshire's Matthew Vandrau who had match figures of 8 for 143. In East London another to have bowling success was slow left-armer Quentin Still who

Pace bowler Aubrey Martyn showed outstanding form for Western Province 'B' in the Bowl competition. He earned promotion to the Castle Cup side and was selected for the party to tour England, only to be robbed of his chance by injury. (David Munden/Sports-Line)

took seven wickets on his debut. In the same match, Bruyns hit 82 on his debut.

In an effort to aid Zimbabwe in the development of cricket and to offer first-class experience to promising players, the UCBSA invited a Zimbabwe team to participate in the Bowl. The Zimbabwe side was led by the experienced all-rounder Butchart, but it was Bruk-Jackson, later to win Test honours, who excelled with a maiden first-class hundred. There was also a maiden century for Chris Craven.

In Section Two, Dirk de Vos established a world record by hitting two fifties and claiming 10 wicket-keeping victims, all caught, in the same match. The seven Eastern Transvaal wickets to fall in the second innings were all caught by de Vos. West Indians were well in evidence in this match, with Gray of Trinidad and Surrey opening the bowling for the West and Skeete of Barbados for the East.

Wait, on his debut, and Herschelle Gibbs reached maiden first-class hundreds, while at Kimberley there was much excitement. Trailing by 201 on the first innings, Griqualand West fought back splendidly with their last three second-innings wickets realising 153 runs. Boland 'B' had a violent race to make the required runs. They hit 218 off 33 overs, but it was left to the last pair, Roos and Drew, to score the last 17 runs.

25, 26, 27 and 28 November 1993

SECTION ONE

at Kingsmead, Durban

Transvaal 'B' 339 (M.O. Johnston 108, P.M. Boa 57) and 73 for 3

Natal 'B' 167 (D.J. Watson 57, M.J. Vandrau 4 for 29) and 243 (A.G. Pollock 4 for 57)

Transvaal 'B' won by 7 wickets

Transvaal 'B' 6 pts., Natal 'B' 0 pts.

at University of OFS Ground, Bloemfontein

Northern Transvaal 'B' 409 (L.P. Vorster 188, G. Dros 80) and 121 for 1 (P.H. Barnard 63 not out, J. Groenwald 50 not out)

Orange Free State 'B' 387 (J.F. Venter 193, G. Smith 5 for 59)

Match drawn

Northern Transvaal 'B' 2 pts., Orange Free State 'B' 0 pts.

at Bulawayo Athletic Club, Bulawayo

Zimbabwe Board XI 294 (C.B. Wishart 77, P.A.N. Emslie 5 for 103)

Border 'B' 21 for 0

Match abandoned

No points

SECTION TWO

at Brackenfell Sports Field, Brackenfell

Boland 'B' 186 and 293 (R.I. Dalrymple 85, A.V. Birrell 4 for 95)

Eastern Province 'B' 215 (A.V. Birrell 51) and 212 for 7 (A. Botha 82)

Match drawn

Eastern Province 'B' 2 pts., Boland 'B' 0 pts.

Playing in his second first-class match, M.O. Johnston of Transvaal 'B' hit 108 and took six catches and three stumpings in his side's win over Natal 'B'. In Bloemfontein, there were career-best scores for Louis Vorster and Jacobus Venter, but rain ruined the match in Zimbabwe.

10, 11, 12 and 13 December 1993

SECTION ONE

at The Feathers, East London

Transvaal 'B' 135 (A. Badenhorst 5 for 52) and 196 (P.M. Boa 57, B.C. Fourie 4 for 37)

Border 'B' 355 (B.W. Lones 104, M.P. Stonier 101, G. Cooke 4 for 68)

Border 'B' won by an innings and 24 runs

Border 'B' 6 pts., Transvaal 'B' 0 pts.

at Centurion Park, Verwoerdburg

Northern Transvaal 'B' 279 (D.J. van Zyl 77, M.P. Jarvis 6 for 74) and 220 (D. Smith 88 not out, W. Dry 75, M.P. Jarvis 5 for 51)

Zimbabwe Board XI 190 (C. van Noordwyk 5 for 51, A. Serfontein 4 for 63) and 311 for 6 (S. Carlisle 70, I.P. Butchart 60 not out, G.C. Martin 54)

Zimbabwe Board XI won by 4 wickets

Zimbabwe Board XI 6 pts., Northern Transvaal 'B' 2 pts.

SECTION TWO

at Plumstead, Cape Town

Western Province 'B' 299 for 8 dec. (T.J. Mitchell 68, M.C. de Villiers 50 not out, S.T. Jefferies 4 for 93) and 185 for 5 dec. (H.D. Ackerman 54)

Boland 'B' 207 (L. Germishuys 68, W.N. van As 62, A. Meyer 7 for 67) and 108 (F. Benjamin 4 for 41)

Western Province 'B' won by 169 runs

Western Province 'B' 6 pts., Boland 'B' 0 pts.

at St George's Park, Port Elizabeth

Eastern Transvaal 279 (B. Randall 59, T. Jamaal 53, A.G. Huckle 4 for 98) and 152 (B.N. Schultz 7 for 70)

Veteran medium-pace bowler Steve Jefferies still going strong for Boland in the Bowl competition. (Stuart D. Franklin/ASP)

Eastern Province 'B' 277 (P.A. Rayment 66, G. Miller 57, S.M. Skeete 4 for 74) and 158 for 5 (L.J. Koen 54)

Eastern Province 'B' won by 5 wickets

Eastern Province 'B' 6 pts., Eastern Transvaal 2 pts.

Transvaal's hundred per cent record came crashing when they were overwhelmed by Border 'B' for whom Stonier and Lones hit 200 for the first wicket. Zimbabwe Board XI claimed their first win with the experienced Malcolm Jarvis taking 11 wickets. Northern Transvaal 'B' were 74 for 7 in their second innings before Dry and Smith added 141. In typical fashion, Butchart hit 60 of the last 83 runs Zimbabwe XI needed for victory.

Medium-pacer Adnaan Meyer returned the best figures of his embryo career as Boland 'B' beat Western Province 'B', and Brett Schultz showed that he was on the way to recovery when he bowled Eastern Province 'B' to victory over Eastern Transvaal. Having been outstanding against Sri Lanka, Schultz had missed the tour of Australia through injury.

17, 18, 19 and 20 December 1993

SECTION ONE

at University of OFS Ground, Bloemfontein

Orange Free State 'B' 260 (C. Light 85, M.I. Gidley 60, L. Klusner 4 for 38) and 262 for 6 dec. (M.I. Gidley 82, S. Nicholson 76, R.A. Brown 55 not out)

Natal 'B' 268 for 8 dec. (D.J. Watson 71, B.A. Nash 50 not out) and 207 for 6 (D.J. Watson 70)

Match drawn

Natal 'B' 2 pts., Orange Free State 'B' 0 pts.

SECTION TWO

at Brackenfell Sports Field, Brackenfell

Boland 'B' 215 (L. Germishuys 108 not out) and 231 for 4 dec. (C.P. Dettmer 58, F. Davids 51)

Western Transvaal 146 and 185 (M.J. Cann 5 for 68, A.G. Elgar 4 for 83)

Boland 'B' won by 115 runs

Boland 'B' 6 pts., Western Transvaal 0 pts.

at PAM Brink Stadium, Springs

Griqualand West 438 for 9 dec. (F.C. Brooker 89, P. Kirsten 87, F. Viljoen 75 not out, J.E. Morris 65) and 213 for 2 dec. (J.E. Morris 109, W.E. Schonegevel 79)

Eastern Transvaal 381 (W.R. Radford 157, T.A. Marsh 106) and 224 (C.R. Norris 76, M.N. Angel 4 for 50)

Griqualand West won by 46 runs

Griqualand West 6 pts., Eastern Transvaal 0 pts.

There were two outright wins in Section Two, the most notable being Griqualand West's win over Eastern Transvaal. Inspired by skipper John Morris, Griqualand West hit 438 off 99 overs. Reduced to 99 for 4, Eastern Transvaal hit back with a stand of 109 for the fifth wicket between Wayne Radford and Terry Marsh. Both men hit maiden first-class centuries. Radford had made his debut in 1977, but had only returned to first-class cricket in 1992–3 after an 11-year absence from the game. Morris responded in even more vigorous manner, hitting 109 off 20 overs in an opening partnership of 177 with Schonegevel; and Griqualand West ran out close winners.

14, 15, 16 and 17 January 1994

SECTION ONE

at Sandringham, Queenstown

Orange Free State 'B' 230 (A. Moreby 66, D. Taljard 4 for 57) and 319 for 7 (C.J. van Heerden 126 not out)

Border 'B' 411 for 8 dec. (Q.R. Still 129 not out, M.P. Stonier 121)

Match drawn

Border 'B' 2 pts., Orange Free State 'B' 0 pts.

Quentin Still confirmed an outstanding debut season with a maiden century while Michael Stonier, having hit a maiden first-class hundred in his previous innings, completed a higher one against Free State.

21, 22, 23 and 24 January 1994

SECTION ONE

at Wanderers, Johannesburg

Zimbabwe Board XI 167 and 163 for 8 (G.A. Paterson 73)

Transvaal 'B' 387 for 5 dec. (M.W. Rushmere 188, P.M. Boa 69, N. Rhodes 67)

Match drawn

Transvaal 'B' 2 pts., Zimbabwe Board XI 0 pts.

at Jan Smuts Stadium, Pietermaritzburg

Natal 'B' 379 for 8 dec. (G.W. Bashford 100, W. Bond 75)

Northern Transvaal 'B' 68 for 2

Match drawn

No points

SECTION TWO

at Witrand Stadium, Potchefstroom

Western Province 'B' 384 for 8 dec. (T.J. Mitchell 90, A. Meyer 89, R.J. Ryall 61)

Western Transvaal 169 (A.J. van Deventer 61, D. MacHelm 6 for 31) and 116 for 3

Match drawn

Western Province 'B' 2 pts., Western Transvaal 0 pts.

at Kimberley Country Club, Kimberley

Griqualand West 142 (C. Wait 4 for 18) and 232 for 8 dec. (F. Viljoen 61)

Eastern Province 'B' 101 (J.E. Johnson 5 for 28) and 250 for 7 (M.G. Beamish 111, M.N. Angel 4 for 62)

Match drawn

Griqualand West 2 pts., Eastern Province 'B' 0 pts.

at PAM Brink Stadium, Springs

Eastern Transvaal 223 (W.R. Radford 101, R. Hoffman 5 for 26)

Boland 'B' 32 for 0

Match drawn

No points

Rain brought havoc to matches, but Mark Rushmere was able to complete the 16th and highest century of his career while Grant Bashford hit his first.

Left-arm spinner MacHelm bowled well, and Michael Beamish, in his first season, hit his first century.

Derbyshire off-spinner Matthew Vandrau bowled well for Transvaal in all competitions. (Paul Sturgess/Sports-Line)

27, 28, 29 and 30 January 1994

SECTION ONE

at Kingsmead, Durban

Zimbabwe Board XI 329 (G.C. Martin 73, G.K. Bruk-Jackson 58, M.W. Handman 4 for 94) and 236 for 3 (S. Carlisle 111 not out, G.C. Martin 68)

Natal 'B' 360 (G.W. Bashford 115, W. Bond 61, R.B. Armstrong 54)

Match drawn

Natal 'B' 2 pts., Zimbabwe Board XI 0 pts.

28, 29, 30 and 31 January 1994 *at Berea Park, Pretoria*

Border 'B' 297 (B.W. Lones 75, G.C. Victor 65, A.C. Dewar 51, A. Serfontein 5 for 50) and 221 for 5 dec. (G.W. Thompson 106)

Northern Transvaal 'B' 303 for 8 dec. (L.P. Vorster 107 not out, W. Dry 67, J. Ehrke 4 for 51) and 216 for 9 (R.F. Pienaar 56, Q.R. Still 5 for 56)

Northern Transvaal 'B' won by 1 wicket

Northern Transvaal 'B' 6 pts., Border 'B' 0 pts.

Four sides completed their programmes in Section One and could only draw consolations from individual performances. Carlisle hit Zimbabwe Board XI's second century of the season, and Bashford hit his second in succession. Vorster led by example, and Greg Thompson hit his first hundred and finished on the losing side.

11, 12, 13 and 14 February 1994

SECTION ONE

at University of OFS, Bloemfontein

Orange Free State 'B' 292 for 9 dec. (S. Nicholson 114 not out, C.J. van Heerden 60)

Transvaal 'B' 90 for 8

Match drawn

No points

SECTION TWO

at St George's Park, Port Elizabeth

Western Transvaal 246 and 135 for 3 dec.
Eastern Province 'B' 112 and 255 for 9 (J.P. Heath 120 not out)

Match drawn

Western Transvaal 2 pts., Eastern Province 'B' 0 pts.

at Kimberley Country Club, Kimberley

Western Province 'B' 284 for 4 dec. (H.D. Ackerman 154, J. Kallis 54 not out) and 259 for 1 dec. (F.B. Touzel 128 not out, D. Jordaan 105 not out)
Griqualand West 285 for 9 dec. (B.E. van der Vyver 127, W.E. Schonegevel 59, D. MacHelm 7 for 85) and 215 (K.C. Dugmore 68, D. MacHelm 4 for 82)

Western Province 'B' won by 43 runs

Western Province 'B' 6 pts., Griqualand West 2 pts.

Section Two reached an appropriate climax as victory in the match at Kimberley would give either side a place in the final. Hylton Ackerman, son of the former Northamptonshire player, chose the occasion to score his maiden first-class hundred. A career-best 127 from van der Vyver helped Griqualand West to take first-innings points in spite of the splendid bowling of MacHelm. Western Province responded with a second-wicket stand of 207 between Jordaan and Touzel, and with the spinners MacHelm and Bulbring dominant, Griqualand West found the task of scoring 259 to win just beyond them.

SECTION ONE

	P	W	L	D	Pts.
Transvaal 'B'	5	2	1	2	14
Northern Transvaal 'B'	5	1	2	2	10
Border 'B'	5	1	1	3	8
Zimbabwe Board XI	5	1	–	4	6
Natal 'B'	5	–	1	4	6
Orange Free State 'B'	5	–	–	5	0

SECTION TWO

	P	W	L	D	Pts.
Western Province 'B'	5	2	–	3	16
Boland 'B'	5	2	1	2	12
Griqualand West	5	1	2	2	12
Eastern Province 'B'	5	1	–	4	10
Eastern Transvaal	5	–	2	3	4
Western Transvaal	5	–	1	4	2

FINAL

12, 13 and 14 March 1994 *at Wanderers, Johannesburg*

Western Province 'B' 171 (R.A. Koster 54) and 314 for 6 (R.A. Koster 95, J. Kallis 69, D. Jordaan 58, H.H. Gibbs 57 not out)
Transvaal 'B' 382 for 6 dec. (W.V. Rippon 92, C. Grainger 70, P.M. Boa 63)

Match drawn

The scheduled first day of the final, 11 March, saw no play possible so that the game was virtually doomed to be drawn from the start. One must reflect on the whole recognition of this competition as first-class. Since South Africa has been welcomed back into the fold and cricket in the country is undergoing something akin to a renaissance, should a first-class tournament really be comprised of eight second elevens, a scratch side from abroad and three teams of moderate standard? At the moment, the structure of the first-class game in the Republic defies logic.

 ## UCBSA BOWL LIMITED-OVER COMPETITION

The UCBSA introduced a new one-day competition to be played alongside the four-day Bowl matches. The teams were again in two groups. The summarised results were as follows.

SECTION ONE

31 October 1993 *at Buffalo Park, East London*

Border 'B' 177 for 8
Natal 'B' 129

Border 'B' (4 pts.) won by 48 runs

at Harare Sports Club, Harare

Orange Free State 'B' 247 for 6 (J.F. Venter 109 not out, C.F. Craven 63)
Zimbabwe Board XI 227 for 8 (D.N. Erasmus 58)

Orange Free State 'B' (4 pts.) won by 20 runs

1 November 1993 *at Wanderers, Johannesburg*

Northern Transvaal 'B' 211 for 8 (B.J. Sommerville 101, M.R. Hobson 5 for 43)
Transvaal 'B' 180 (G.A. Pollock 50)

Northern Transvaal 'B' (4 pts.) won by 31 runs

27 November 1993 *at University of OFS, Bloemfontein*

Northern Transvaal 'B' 114 (C.F. Craven 4 for 25)
Orange Free State 'B' 115 for 0 (M.I. Gidley 58 not out)

Orange Free State 'B' (4 pts.) won by 10 wickets

28 November 1993 *at Kingsmead, Durban*

Transvaal 'B' 205 for 8 (G.A. Pollock 57)
Natal 'B' 209 for 4 (B.A. Nash 62, G.W. Bashford 55 not out)

Natal 'B' (4 pts.) won by 6 wickets

at Bulawayo Athletic Club, Bulawayo

Zimbabwe Board XI *v*. Border 'B'

Match abandoned

Zimbabwe Board XI 2 pts., Border 'B' 2 pts.

12 December 1993 *at Victoria Ground, King William's Town*

Border 'B' 213 for 8 (A.C. Dewar 58)
Transvaal 'B' 179 (K.G. Bauermeister 4 for 30)

Border 'B' (4 pts.) won by 34 runs

13 December 1993 *at Centurion Park, Verwoerdburg*

Northern Transvaal 'B' 202 for 9
Zimbabwe Board XI 190 for 8

Northern Transvaal 'B' (4 pts.) won by 12 runs

19 December 1993 *at Springbok Park, Bloemfontein*

Orange Free State 'B' 188 (C. Light 76)
Natal 'B' 189 for 2 (D.J. Watson 64, J. Payn 57 not out, L. Klusener 51)

Natal 'B' (4 pts.) won by 8 wickets

16 January 1994 *at Queenstown*

Border 'B' 156
Orange Free State 'B' 159 for 6 (C. Light 80)

Orange Free State 'B' (4 pts.) won by 4 wickets

24 January 1994 *at Jan Smuts Ground, Pietermaritzburg*

Northern Transvaal 'B' 166 for 8
Natal 'B' 111

Northern Transvaal 'B' (4 pts.) won by 55 runs

at Wanderers, Johannesburg

Transvaal 'B' *v*. Zimbabwe Board XI

Match abandoned

Transvaal 'B' 2 pts., Zimbabwe Board XI 2 pts.

30 January 1994 *at Kingsmead, Durban*

Zimbabwe Board XI 219 for 9
Natal 'B' 215 for 8 (C.B. Rhodes 66)

Zimbabwe Board XI (4 pts.) won by 4 runs

at Berea Park, Pretoria

Northern Transvaal 'B' 216 for 5 (P.H. Barnard 68)
Border 'B' 217 for 8 (D.O. Nosworthy 56, G.W. Thompson 52)

Border 'B' (4 pts.) won by 2 wickets

14 February 1994 *at University of OFS, Bloemfontein*

Orange Free State 'B' *v*. Transvaal 'B'

Match abandoned

Orange Free State 'B' 2 pts., Transvaal 'B' 2 pts.

Louis Vorster led by example for Northern Transvaal 'B' in the Bowl. (David Munden/Sports-Line)

The left-handed Jacobus Venter enjoyed an outstanding season in all competitions, and it was he who hit the first century of the tournament. The following day, Blaise Sommerville, skipper of Northern Transvaal 'B', hit the other century in Section One. In the same match, medium-pacer Malcolm Hobson became the only bowler to take five wickets in an innings.

Orange Free State 'B' notched a place in the final by virtue of superior run rate to Border 'B', 4.11 to 3.79.

SECTION ONE FINAL TABLE

	P	W	L	Nr	Pts.
Orange Free State 'B'	5	3	1	1	14
Border 'B'	5	3	1	1	14
Northern Transvaal 'B'	5	3	2	–	12
Zimbabwe Board XI	5	1	2	2	8
Natal 'B'	5	2	3	–	8
Transvaal 'B'	5	–	3	2	4

SECTION TWO

10 October 1993 at PAM Brink Stadium, Springs

Western Province 'B' 245 for 4 (S.G. Koening 66, H. Pangarkar 66, H.D. Ackerman 64)
Eastern Transvaal 142

Western Province 'B' (4 pts.) won by 103 runs

at Witrand Stadium, Potchefstroom

Griqualand West 195 for 7 (N.E. Alexander 62 not out)
Western Transvaal 198 for 7

Western Transvaal (4 pts.) won by 3 wickets

31 October 1993 at Kimberley Country Club, Kimberley

Griqualand West 181 for 8 (W.E. Schonegevel 69, K.C. Jackson 4 for 35)
Boland 'B' 182 for 5 (K.C. Jackson 67, J. Wahl 55 not out)

Boland 'B' (4 pts.) won by 5 wickets

at Witrand Stadium, Potchefstroom

Eastern Transvaal 211 for 8 (K.A. Moxham 69 not out)
Western Transvaal 206 (D.J.J. de Vos 52)

Eastern Transvaal (4 pts.) won by 5 runs

1 November 1993 at Northerns-Goodwood Oval, Cape Town

Eastern Province 'B' 249 for 4 (G. Miller 96 not out, M. Michau 94)
Western Province 'B' 234 for 8 (L.F. Bleekers 82)

Eastern Province 'B' (4 pts.) won by 15 runs

28 November 1993 at Brackenfell Sports Field, Brackenfell

Boland 'B' 216 (L. Germishuys 58)
Eastern Province 'B' 169 (M.J. Cann 5 for 47)

Boland 'B' (4 pts.) won by 47 runs

Former Leicestershire all-rounder Martin Gidley had a particularly successful season in limited-over cricket for Orange Free State 'B'. (David Munden/Sports-Line)

12 December 1993 at Plumstead, Cape Town

Boland 'B' 184 (W.N. van As 92 not out)
Western Province 'B' 188 for 8 (R.A. Koster 57)

Western Province 'B' (4 pts.) won by 2 wickets

13 December 1993 at St George's Park, Port Elizabeth

Eastern Transvaal 179
Eastern Province 'B' 183 for 6

Eastern Province 'B' (4 pts.) won by 4 wickets

20 December 1993 at Brackenfell Sports Field, Brackenfell

Western Transvaal 208 for 8 (H.G. Prinsloo 69 not out)
Boland 'B' 192 for 8

Western Transvaal (4 pts.) won by 16 runs

21 December 1993 at PAM Brink Stadium, Springs

Griqualand West 202 for 9 (B.E. van der Vyver 71, P. Kirsten 57)
Eastern Transvaal 203 for 5 (A. Norris 86 not out, W.R. Radford 63)

Eastern Transvaal (4 pts.) won by 5 wickets

14 January 1994 at St George's Park, Port Elizabeth

Western Transvaal 168 for 9 (A.J. van Deventer 60)
Eastern Province 'B' 170 for 4 (S.C. Pope 65 not out)

Eastern Province 'B' (4 pts.) won by 6 wickets

23 January 1994 *at Kimberley Country Club, Kimberley*

Griqualand West 239 for 8 (J.E. Morris 71, B.E. van der Vyver 67, A.V. Birrell 4 for 32)
Eastern Province 'B' 210 (J.P. Heath 65, A.J. Swanepoel 4 for 35)

Griqualand West (4 pts.) won by 29 runs

24 January 1994 *at PAM Brink Stadium, Springs*

Eastern Transvaal *v.* Boland 'B'

Match abandoned
Eastern Transvaal 2 pts., Boland 'B' 2 pts.

at Witrand Stadium, Potchefstroom

Western Transvaal 197 for 9 (H.M. de Vos 53, C. Haupt 5 for 21)
Western Province 'B' 200 for 1 (H.D. Ackerman 107 not out, F.B. Touzel 79)

Western Province 'B' (4 pts.) won by 9 wickets

13 February 1994 *at Kimberley Country Club, Kimberley*

Griqualand West *v.* Western Province 'B'

Match abandoned
Griqualand West 2 pts., Western Province 'B' 2 pts.

Former Glamorgan cricketer Michael Cann and Haupt of Western Province were the only bowlers to take five wickets in an innings, and the only centurion was Hylton Ackerman. Ackerman who, a fortnight later, was to score a maiden first-class hundred, hit 107 out out and shared an opening stand of 196 in 48 overs with Touzel as Western Province 'B' beat Western Transvaal.

SECTION TWO FINAL TABLE

	P	W	L	Nr	Pts.
Western Province 'B'	5	3	1	1	14
Eastern Province 'B'	5	3	2	–	12
Boland 'B'	5	2	2	1	10
Eastern Transvaal	5	2	2	1	10
Western Transvaal	5	2	3	–	8
Griqualand West	5	1	3	1	6

FINAL

9 March 1994 *at Newlands, Cape Town*

Western Province 'B' 111
Orange Free State 'B' 113 for 5 (A.C. Dawson 5 for 17)

Orange Free State 'B' won by 5 wickets

Bowled out in 44.2 overs, with only a seventh-wicket stand of 40 between Dawson and Mitchell saving them from total humiliation, Western Province 'B' gave a sorry showing in a disappointing final. Orange Free State 'B'

Walter Masemola bowling during the historic match at Alexandra against England 'A' (Shaun Botterill/Allsport)

reached 47 before Dawson bowled Gidley, and he continued to gnaw away at the Free State innings. A medium-pacer of limited experience, Alan Dawson finished with 5 for 17 from nine overs to add to his 25. In spite of his efforts, Free State reached their target in 27.3 overs. It is hard to justify this new tournament as a senior limited-over competition.

 ## ENGLAND 'A' TOUR

4 December 1993 *at Alexandra, Transvaal*

England 'A' 121
Transvaal Invitation XI 78 (D.G. Cork 6 for 9)

England 'A' won by 43 runs

The tour began in Alexandra, a township close to Johannesburg. England 'A' were the first representative side to play in the township, and although the English tourists won with ease, the result mattered little. In the words of Ali Bacher, England's visit was a 'beacon of hope' for all townships. An impressive spell of bowling by Dominic Cork was the highlight of the match.

6 December 1993 *at Witrand Ground, Potchefstroom*

England 'A' 260 for 6 (J.P. Crawley 88, A.P. Wells 61, H. Morris 55)
Western Transvaal 178 for 7 (A.J. van Deventer 52)

England 'A' won by 82 runs

A highly competitive and talented party most ably led by Hugh Morris won their second 50-over match with considerable ease. John Crawley was most impressive in the second victory, his innings of 88 containing strokes of the highest quality.

8 December 1993 *at PAM Brink Stadium, Springs*

England 'A' 281 for 6 (M.N. Lathwell 133)
Eastern Transvaal 204 for 3 (S.M. Skeete 77, A. Norris 55)

England 'A' won by 77 runs

A cool, damp morning delayed the start of the match in Springs for half an hour, but Mark Lathwell overcame the conditions with 2 sixes and 10 fours in his 133 which occupied 47 overs. Eastern Transvaal were without pace bowler Wikus Botha, suspended for abusive language, but Barbadian Sam Skeete kept alive their hopes of victory with an aggressive 77. He was particularly severe on Peter Such. Robert Croft and Darren Gough bowled miserly spells, however, and Eastern Transvaal fell well short of their target.

10, 11 and **12** December 1993 *at Wanderers, Johannesburg*

Transvaal 161 (M.D. Haysman 52) and 200 (M.W.
Rushmere 64 not out, M.D. Haysman 52, M.C. Ilott 6 for 61)
England 'A' 293 (M.N. Lathwell 83, M.R. Hobson 4 for 76) and 69 for 1

England 'A' won by 9 wickets

Despite losing Martin Bicknell and Martin McCague with injuries, England 'A' enjoyed an excellent start in their first first-class match of the tour. Jimmy Cook won the toss, but only Haysman, who had arrived in South Africa via Australia and Leicestershire, and Laing showed any idea of how to cope with the visiting medium-pacers. England lost Morris at 9, but Lathwell and Crawley added 102 before Crawley was run out. Lathwell survived the verbal abuse of Jack to end the day on 77 out of his side's 146 for 3. He added only six the following morning, but Rhodes and Cork played well to add 87 for the seventh wicket, and England led by 132 on the first innings. Transvaal scored 100 for 2 before the close, but once the Haysman–Rushmere partnership was broken, they collapsed before some splendid bowling by Ilott on the third day, the start of which was delayed by $2\frac{3}{4}$ hours. The reason for the delay was the illness spreading through the England party which reduced them to four fit men, and, in the circumstances, England's victory with an hour to spare was remarkable.

15 December 1993 *at Zwide Ground, Port Elizabeth*

England 'A' 189 for 7 (J.P. Crawley 58, C. Wait 4 for 34)
Eastern Province XI 86

England 'A' won by 103 runs

Mark Ilott appeals in the match between England 'A' and Transvaal, 10–12 December. Ilott, who was outstanding on the tour, took 6 for 61 in the second innings of this match. (Shaun Botterill/Allsport)

The tourists' second visit to a township was notable for the performance of medium-pacer Wait, who has played for Otley in the Leeds League. He completed the hat-trick when he sent back Dale, Croft and Cork. England had always looked winners after making 189 in their 45 overs.

17, 18, 19 and 20 December 1993 *at St George's Park, Port Elizabeth*

England 'A' 566 for 5 dec. (J.P. Crawley 286, A.P. Wells 126, H. Morris 79)

Eastern Province 192 (G. Morgan 60 not out, R.D.B. Croft 5 for 41) and 304 (A. Botha 74, E.A.E. Baptiste 58)

England 'A' won by an innings and 70 runs

After Lathwell had been dismissed for 5 with the score on 24, Morris and Crawley engaged in a stand worth 153. When Morris was caught off Baptiste, Alan Wells joined Crawley in a partnership which went into the second day and realised 261. Wells enjoyed some luck, but he hit hard and often for 86 overs to make 126. Crawley, unbeaten on 150 after the first day, was more cautious, but he batted without blemish for $9\frac{3}{4}$ hours to reach the highest score of his career and the highest score made by an Englishman in a representative match abroad since Brearley's 312 not out in Pakistan in 1966–7. Crawley hit 4 sixes and 36 fours and, with this innings and his general form on the tour, marked himself down firmly as an England batsman of the very near future. In contrast, following an opening stand of 58, the Eastern Province batting was woeful, and Croft, in particular, caused many problems which only wicket-keeper Morgan could solve. Following-on, Eastern Province lost four wickets for 84 before Baptiste's resilience took the game into the fourth day. He, Botha and Shaw also resisted stoutly, and Morgan was again undefeated, but England won by an innings.

Sadly, Martin Bicknell, a pace-bowler of immense promise, was forced to leave the tour because of injury. He was replaced by Paul Taylor of Northamptonshire.

23 December 1993 *at John Passmore Oval, Langa, Cape Town*

England 'A' 170 for 9 (A.P. Wells 65, A. Meyer 4 for 25)

Western Province Invitation XI 151 for 7 (H.D. Ackerman 68)

England 'A' won by 19 runs

A close encounter for England in the third township match. Alan Wells countered the early threat of 'Moggs' Meyer who had helped reduce the visitors to 19 for 4 with his medium pace, and accurate bowling restricted the Invitation XI. Martin Bicknell appeared in this match and seemed to bowl comfortably, but it was confirmed that he would be returning to England for medical treatment. He bowled only four first-class overs on the tour.

26, 27 and 28 December 1993 *at Newlands, Cape Town*

Western Province 177 (D. Jordaan 65) and 178 (D. Gough 4 for 57)

England 'A' 321 (M.B. Loye 68, A. Dale 64, J.P. Crawley 51, A.C. Dawson 5 for 42) and 35 for 0

England 'A' won by 10 wickets

The pace trio of Ilott, Gough and Cork undermined the Western Province batting on the opening day which ended with the visitors on 74 for the loss of openers Morris and Lathwell. Loye, with his first half-century of the tour, Crawley and Dale took England to a strong position on the second day, but the medium pace of Alan Dawson caused the later batsmen trouble, and five wickets went down for 64 runs. Ilott and Gough showed spirit in a last-wicket stand which gave England a lead of 144. With Ilott, Gough and Cork again impressing, Western Province succumbed lamely for a second time, and England won with a day to spare.

1, 2, 3 and 4 January 1994 *at Kingsmead, Durban*

Natal 458 for 9 dec. (C.R.B. Armstrong 97, D.M. Benkenstein 95, D.J. Watson 87)

England 'A' 116 (D.N. Crookes 4 for 35) and 285 (J.P. Crawley 81, M.B. Loye 68, L. Kluesner 4 for 61, D.N. Crookes 4 for 103)

Natal won by an innings and 57 runs

The ninth match of the tour was a bad one for England 'A'. They lost Martin Bicknell and they suffered their first defeat. Armstrong and Watson began Natal's innings with a partnership of 192, and the rest of the batsmen performed consistently so that Malcolm Marshall, the old enemy, was able to declare and capture the wickets of Lathwell and Crawley before the end of the second day. Particularly impressive among the Natal batsmen was Dale Benkenstein, a young player who has assisted Pudsey St Lawrence.

On the third day, England 'A' lost eight wickets for 67 runs and were forced to follow-on. Most trouble was caused by the off-spinner Crookes, and he accounted for Lathwell and Wells when England batted again. Once Crawley and Loye were separated on the last morning – they lasted just eight overs – England were hurried to defeat by a varied attack.

7, 8 and 9 January 1994 *at Centurion Park, Pretoria*

Northern Transvaal 138 (B.J. Sommerville 60, M.C. Ilott 4 for 32) and 162 (D.G. Cork 4 for 50)

England 'A' 205 (H. Morris 57, S. Elworthy 4 for 55) and 96 for 2

England 'A' won by 8 wickets

The wicket at Centurion Park was not conducive to easy batting, and the England bowlers were quick to exploit the home side's discomfort. Mark Ilott bowled splendidly, taking three wickets in the first session of the match and confirming his standing as the main strike bowler on the tour. Blaise Sommerville resisted with great good sense for 60 of the 71.1 overs that the innings lasted, but a seventh-wicket stand of 40 with Elworthy was the best that the innings could offer.

England 'A' struggled in turn and were 81 for 4 at the close, one of the wickets being that of nightwatchman Ilott, but Morris remained firm on 29. With Loye, Morris was to add an invaluable 63, and England 'A' took a first-innings lead of 67. This took on gigantic proportions when Northern Transvaal collapsed against the England seamers for a second time. At one period, four wickets fell for one run to Cork and Ilott who finished with match figures of 7 for 96. After Morris and Lathwell had fallen for 37, Crawley and Wells hit off the runs on the third morning.

12 January 1994 *at Kimberley Country Club, Kimberley*

England 'A' 216 (R.D.B. Croft 51, J.E. Johnson 5 for 33)
Griqualand West 134 for 8

England 'A' won by 82 runs

John Morris, once of Derbyshire shortly to be of Durham, won the toss on behalf of his Griqualand West side and asked England to bat. Bowled out with two balls of their 50-over quota remaining, the visitors did well to reach 216 on a sluggish pitch and a slow outfield. Medium-pacer Johan Johnson bowled with control and penetration, and, for England, Croft hit 51 and Cork 47 off 66 balls. The home side could never match England's rate.

14, 15, 16 and 17 January 1994 *at Springbok Park, Bloemfontein*

Orange Free State 370 (G.F.J. Liebenberg 82,
P.J.R. Steyn 80, M.J. McCague 4 for 84) and 262 for
9 dec. (J.M. Arthur 106)
England 'A' 180 (A.P. Wells 53) and 323 for 5
(J.P. Crawley 128, H. Morris 64)

Match drawn

A slow pitch and a hot day gave England a hard time after they had lost the toss in Bloemfontein. McCague captured an early wicket, but Liebenberg and Steyn added 130, and it was not until the last session that England clawed their way back into contention. Having ended the first day on 344 for 9, Orange Free State were all out for 370 on the second morning. Stephenson bowled Lathwell fourth ball, and Morris went in the fourth over so that England 'A' were soon in trouble. Crawley and Wells put on 67, but four wickets then fell for 31 runs, and there was no effective recovery as the tourists crumbled to 180 all out. Franklyn Stephenson did not enforce the follow-on,

Gerhadus Liebenberg's fine batting against England 'A' won him a place in the party to tour England. (David Munden/Sports-Line)

and Arthur hit a chanceless 106 in $4\frac{1}{2}$ hours. Stephenson eventually declared and asked England 'A' to score 453 in 127 overs if they were to win the match. They hit 59 for the loss of Lathwell and night-watchman Taylor before the close. Defeat was avoided on the final day thanks mainly to Crawley's second century of the tour. He and Morris, an excellent captain, added 96 and, with Wells, Crawley put on 104.

21, 22, 23 and 24 January 1994 *at Buffalo Park, East London*

England 'A' 320 (S.J. Rhodes 108, M.B. Loye 71) and
175 for 5 dec. (H. Morris 55)
Border 200 (B.M. Osborne 50) and 189 for 9 (P.M. Such
4 for 51)

Match drawn

Another slow pitch, stifling humidity and a laborious batting performance on the opening day were major reasons for England 'A' failing to win their penultimate match of the tour. Loye's innings occupied nearly five hours, and runs came at little more than two an over. The rate increased only a little on the second day when England 'A' scored another 91 runs, lost their last four wickets and saw Rhodes move to a century in $6\frac{1}{2}$ hours. Border underlined the slowness of the pitch when they moved to 125 for 4 in 66 overs before the close. Such and Croft broke resistance on the third morning, and Ilott mopped up the tail so that England 'A' led by 120 on the first innings. Providing the brightest batting of the match,

they scored 175 for 5 by the end of play and gave themselves a day in which to bowl out Border. Unfortunately, two hours' play was lost to rain on the final morning and, in spite of some fine bowling from Peter Such, Border just survived.

27, 28, 29, 30 and 31 January 1994 *at St George's Park, Port Elizabeth*

South Africa 'A' 357 (E.O. Simons 88, G.F.J. Liebenberg 79, M.C. Ilott 4 for 71) and 221 (P.J.R. Steyn 69, M.C. Ilott 5 for 43, D. Gough 5 for 81)

England 'A' 329 (A.P. Wells 130, M.B. Loye 51) and 126 for 4

Match drawn

The most meaningful of recent England 'A' tours ended with a representative match against a strong South African 'A' team led by Jimmy Cook. The England team lacked Dominic Cork who had returned home on compassionate grounds, and the eleven chosen were Lathwell, Morris, Crawley, Loye, Wells, Dale, Rhodes, Croft, Ilott, Gough and Such.

Cook won the toss, and the South African side made 173 for 4 in 91 dour overs on the opening day. There was a patient innings of 79 from opener Liebenberg who gave evidence of what is known as the Test-match temperament. The second day witnessed more enterprising cricket, and Eric Simons' all-round performance edged the game in favour of South Africa. Kuiper was out after taking more than two hours to score 12, but Simons batted positively and helped his side to reach 357. Then, after Pringle had had the unhappy Lathwell caught for 0, Simons trapped Crawley leg before, and England 'A' ended on 54 for 2.

It was Alan Wells who brought England 'A' back into the match on the third day with a flawless innings of 130. Morris and night-watchman Ilott had departed while the score reached 92 before Loye and Wells added 171 in 67 overs. Wells' masterly innings occupied 5½ hours and included 19 fours. He reached his hundred off 197 balls.

The loss of three wickets in the last six overs undid much of his good work, and England 'A' ended the day 88 runs in arrears with only three wickets standing.

Another 60 were added on the fourth morning when Croft proved obdurate so that South Africa's lead was restricted to 28. They completely failed to gain any advantage from this when their batsmen were again painfully slow, runs coming at less than two an over in the afternoon session. Jimmy Cook raised the tempo in the evening with 48 off 91 deliveries, but 156 for 3 gave little hope of either side forcing a result.

The consistently excellent bowling of Mark Ilott and Darren Gough's first five-wicket haul of the tour meant South Africa added only another 65 runs as their last seven wickets fell, but England could never approach the required run rate on a dead pitch, and the match was drawn.

From both sides, the tour was an outstanding success. Importantly cricket was taken into three townships, and South African state sides fielded their strongest available elevens in games against the tourists. England 'A' were a highly competitive party, and the group did not contain one player who did not have hopes of claiming a place in the full England side. Morris led the side admirably, and Ilott, Crawley and Wells enjoyed fine tours. The disappointments were the injury to Martin Bicknell and the form of Mark Lathwell.

 AUSTRALIAN TOUR

10 February 1994 *at Randjesfontein*

Australians 223 (D.M. Jones 60, E.A.E. Baptiste 4 for 56)

N.F. Oppenheimer's XI 141 for 5 (A.P. Kuiper 56)

Match abandoned

A thunderstorm brought an abrupt end to the first match of the Australians' tour. Nicky Oppenheimer's XI in-

---

FIRST-CLASS AVERAGES – ENGLAND 'A'

BATTING

	M	Inns	NO	Runs	HS	Av	100s	50s
J.P. Crawley	8	13	1	779	286	64.91	2	2
A.P. Wells	8	14	3	593	130	53.90	2	1
S.J. Rhodes	8	11	4	293	108	41.85	1	–
M.B. Loye	8	12	1	439	71	39.90	–	4
H. Morris	8	14	1	402	79	30.92	–	4
R.D.B. Croft	5	4	1	69	32*	23.00	–	–
A. Dale	7	11	2	196	64	21.77	–	1
D. Gough	5	6	2	75	24	18.75	–	–
M.N. Lathwell	7	13	1	215	83	17.91	–	1
D.G. Cork	4	3	–	32	16	10.66	–	–
M.C. Ilott	6	5	1	40	18*	10.00	–	–
P.M. Such	6	6	2	25	12*	6.25	–	–
M.J. McCague	5	5	–	31	14	6.20	–	–
J.P. Taylor	2	3	–	12	11	4.00	–	–

Played in one match: M.P. Bicknell 22 & 5*

BOWLING

	Overs	Mds	Runs	Wkts	Av	Best	10/m	5/inn
M.C. Ilott	229.1	60	525	37	14.18	6-61	–	2
D.G. Cork	129.1	34	333	17	19.58	4-50	–	–
D. Gough	192.1	34	589	23	25.60	5-81	–	1
R.D.B. Croft	177	52	397	14	28.35	5-41	–	1
M.J. McCague	150	32	434	15	28.93	4-84	–	–
A. Dale	120	24	333	11	30.27	3-34	–	–
P.M. Such	272.3	76	623	19	32.78	4-51	–	–
J.P. Taylor	62	8	205	5	41.00	2-65	–	–

Bowled in one innings: M.P. Bicknell 4–2–4–0

FIELDING FIGURES

33 – S.J. Rhodes (ct 30/st 3); 9 – A.P. Wells; 8 – M.N. Lathwell and H. Morris; 5 – M.B. Loye; 4 – J.P. Crawley; 3 – R.D.B. Croft and M.J. McCague; 2 – J.P. Taylor, D. Gough, P. M. Such, D.G. Cork and M.C. Ilott; 1 – A. Dale

cluded two cricketers from the townships, Jacob Malao and Jeffrey Toyana, who were the first players from the underdeveloped areas to appear in this traditional tour opener. Malao took 3 for 59 with his left-arm spin.

12, 13 and 14 February 1994 *at Centurion Park, Verwoerdburg*

Australians 363 (D.M. Jones 85, M.J. Slater 51,
    M.L. Hayden 50, S. Elworthy 4 for 85) and 281 for 4
    dec. (M.E. Waugh 134, M.A. Taylor 75)
Northern Transvaal 209 (D.J. van Zyl 63 not out,
    P.R. Reiffel 4 for 27) and 186 (P.R. Reiffel 4 for 57)

Australians won by 249 runs

The Australians made a fine start to their tour by winning their first first-class match in three days. Consistent batting took them to a good score, and the quicker bowlers, Hughes, McGrath and Reiffel bowled out the home side for 209, but Taylor did not enforce the follow-on. Mark Waugh's 134 came off as many balls and included 3 sixes and 14 fours, and he and Taylor added 165 for the second wicket. Northern Transvaal collapsed for a second time.

17 February 1994 *at Witram Stadium, Potchefstroom*

Australians 141 for 5 (M.E. Waugh 55)
v **President's XI**

Match abandoned

In their last match before the first one-day series, the Australians were restricted to 35 overs.

FIRST ONE-DAY INTERNATIONAL SERIES

So great is the obsession for one-day cricket in South Africa that two four-match series were scheduled. The first was to be played in daylight before the Test series; the second would be day/night matches after the Test series.

South Africa took a commanding lead by winning the first two matches within the space of 24 hours. Hansie Cronje was the star of both victories, hitting 112 off 120 balls in the first encounter, with 2 sixes off Shane Warne, and 97 off 102 deliveries, 3 sixes off Warne, in the second. In the match in Verwoerdburg, Adrian Kuiper hit 26 off the last over, bowled by McDermott. The last three balls were struck for sixes.

Warne reasserted himself with four wickets in Port Elizabeth, but South Africa clinched the series with an easy win in Durban. Matthews' early strikes undermined the Australian innings and even Border's battling 69 could not rally the tourists who were out with nearly seven overs of their quota unused. South Africa had something of a fright when three wickets suddenly fell for 18 runs, but Cronje was again in excellent form, and his seventh boundary won the match.

26, 27, 28 February and 1 March 1994 *at Springbok Park, Bloemfontein*

Australians 450 for 8 dec. (M.E. Waugh 154, S.R.
    Waugh 102, M.J. Slater 65, B.T. Player 4 for 107) and
    270 for 6 dec. (M.J. Slater 105, M.A. Taylor 54,
    J.F. Venter 5 for 101)
Orange Free State 264 (L.J. Wilkinson 53, J.M. Arthur 51,
    T.B.A. May 5 for 98) and 396 (W.J. Cronje 251,
    M.G. Hughes 4 for 127)

Australians won by 60 runs

The Waugh twins added 232 for the fourth wicket on the opening day. The runs were scored in just over three hours of devastating batting. Tim May bowled the tourists to a commanding lead on the second day, but there was some apprehension for the Australians when Cronje hit Warne for 16 off three deliveries in an attempt to gain dominance before the beginning of the Test series. Warne finished with 3 for 73. Slater's elegant and forceful hundred allowed Taylor to declare and set Free State a target of 457 with more than a day in which to score the runs. The Australians won, but the last day belonged to Hansie Cronje who hit a magnificent 251 off 306 balls with 28 fours and 4 sixes. It was the highest score of Cronje's career, and a knock of outstanding merit.

Craig Matthews was the most successful bowler in the one-day series, maintaining hostility and accuracy. (David Munden/Sports-Line)

FIRST ONE-DAY INTERNATIONAL – SOUTH AFRICA *v.* AUSTRALIA
19 February 1994 at Wanderers, Johannesburg

SOUTH AFRICA				AUSTRALIA			
P.N. Kirsten	c Reiffel, **b** McGrath		47	M.A. Taylor	**b** Snell		30
G. Kirsten	c Healy, **b** Reiffel		12	D.C. Boon	c Rhodes, **b** Kuiper		58
W.J. Cronje	c Reiffel, **b** McDermott		112	D.M. Jones	c Cronje, **b** Simons		42
J.N. Rhodes	not out		47	M.E. Waugh	c Richardson, **b** Simons		14
A.P. Kuiper	not out		2	S.R. Waugh	not out		46
K.C. Wessels (capt)				A.R. Border (capt)	**b** de Villiers		25
*D.J. Richardson				*I.A. Healy	not out		4
E.O. Simons				P.R. Reiffel			
R.P. Snell				S.K. Warne			
P.S. de Villiers				C.J. McDermott			
A.A. Donald				G.D. McGrath			
Extras	lb **5**, w **2**, nb **5**		12	Extras	lb **4**, w **3**, nb **1**		8
(50 overs)	(for 3 wickets)		232	(50 overs)	(for 5 wickets)		227

	O	M	R	W		O	M	R	W
McDermott	10	–	52	1	Donald	9	1	46	–
Reiffel	10	1	36	1	de Villiers	10	–	43	1
McGrath	10	1	29	1	Snell	10	–	55	1
S.R. Waugh	10	–	54	–	Simons	10	–	29	2
Warne	10	–	56	–	Kuiper	7	–	30	1
					Cronje	4	–	20	–

FALL OF WICKETS
1–39, 2–123, 3–229

FALL OF WICKETS
1–61, 2–108, 3–143, 4–155, 5–209

Umpires: S.B. Lambson & C.J. Mitchley

South Africa won by 5 runs

SECOND ONE-DAY INTERNATIONAL – SOUTH AFRICA *v.* AUSTRALIA
20 February 1994 at Centurion Park, Verwoerdburg

SOUTH AFRICA				AUSTRALIA			
P.N. Kirsten	**b** M.E. Waugh		22	D.C. Boon	c Cronje, **b** Matthews		2
G. Kirsten	c S.R. Waugh, **b** McGrath		18	M.A. Taylor	run out		21
W.J. Cronje	run out		97	D.M. Jones	**b** Matthews		5
J.N. Rhodes	lbw, **b** Warne		44	M.E. Waugh	lbw, **b** Matthews		0
K.C. Wessels (capt)	c Healy, **b** McGrath		22	S.R. Waugh	**b** Simons		86
A.P. Kuiper	not out		47	A.R. Border (capt)	run out		41
E.O. Simons	not out		2	*I.A. Healy	c G. Kirsten, **b** Kuiper		4
*D.J. Richardson				P.R. Reiffel	c Simons, **b** de Villiers		10
R.P. Snell				S.K. Warne	c Wessels, **b** Cronje		9
P.S. de Villiers				C.J. McDermott	run out		16
C.R. Matthews				G.D. McGrath	not out		0
Extras	lb **6**, w **3**, nb **4**		13	Extras	lb **12**, w **3**		15
(50 overs)	(for 5 wickets)		265	(42.4 overs)			209

	O	M	R	W		O	M	R	W
McDermott	10	3	46	–	de Villiers	8	2	20	1
Reiffel	8	–	50	–	Matthews	8	2	26	3
M.E. Waugh	9	1	52	1	Simons	7.4	–	39	1
McGrath	10	1	42	1	Snell	8	–	38	–
S.R. Waugh	5	–	28	–	Kuiper	6	–	38	1
Warne	8	1	41	1	Cronje	5	–	36	1

FALL OF WICKETS
1–45, 2–58, 3–152, 4–203, 5–229

FALL OF WICKETS
1–11, 2–19, 3–19, 4–34, 5–141, 6–145, 7–174, 8–189, 9–209

Umpires: W. Diedricks & K.E. Liebenberg

South Africa won by 56 runs

THIRD ONE-DAY INTERNATIONAL – SOUTH AFRICA v. AUSTRALIA
22 February 1994 at St George's Park, Port Elizabeth

AUSTRALIA				SOUTH AFRICA		
M.A. Taylor	c Richardson, b de Villiers	2		P.N. Kirsten	c McGrath, b Warne	27
D.C. Boon	b de Villiers	76		G. Kirsten	b McDermott	6
D.M. Jones	run out	67		W.J. Cronje	c McDermott, b S.R. Waugh	45
M.E. Waugh	c Rhodes, b Matthews	60		J.N. Rhodes	c Healy, b M.E. Waugh	36
C.J. McDermott	run out	15		K.C. Wessels (capt)	run out	5
S.R. Waugh	c Matthews, b Donald	18		A.P. Kuiper	b McDermott	33
A.R. Border (capt)	not out	40		*D.J. Richardson	not out	23
*I.A. Healy	not out	1		P.L. Symcox	c Boon, b Warne	4
P.R. Reiffel				C.R. Matthews	b Warne	0
S.K. Warne				P.S. de Villiers	b Warne	4
G.D. McGrath				A.A. Donald	b McDermott	0
Extras	lb 1, w 1	2		Extras	lb 6, nb 4	10
(50 overs)	(for 6 wickets)	281		(43 overs)		193

	O	M	R	W		O	M	R	W
de Villiers	10	1	55	2	McDermott	10	1	35	3
Matthews	10	1	46	1	McGrath	7	2	17	–
Donald	10	–	60	1	Reiffel	8	–	40	–
Cronje	10	1	62	–	Warne	10	–	36	4
Symcox	4	–	25	–	S.R. Waugh	4	–	33	1
Kuiper	6	–	32	–	M.E. Waugh	4	–	26	1

FALL OF WICKETS
1–12, 2–135, 3–180, 4–198, 5–233, 6–276

FALL OF WICKETS
1–8, 2–49, 3–115, 4–125, 5–127, 6–165, 7–178, 8–181, 9–188

Umpires: C.J. Mitchley & R.E. Koertzen
Australia won by 88 runs

FOURTH ONE-DAY INTERNATIONAL – SOUTH AFRICA v. AUSTRALIA
24 February 1994 at Kingsmead, Durban

AUSTRALIA				SOUTH AFRICA		
D.C. Boon	c de Villiers, b Simons	34		A.C. Hudson	lbw, b Reiffel	37
M.J. Slater	c Richardson, b de Villiers	1		P.N. Kirsten	c Healy, b Reiffel	15
D.M. Jones	lbw, b Matthews	8		W.J. Cronje	not out	50
M.E. Waugh	c Hudson, b Matthews	3		J.N. Rhodes	c M.E. Waugh, b Warne	3
S.R. Waugh	lbw, b Simons	2		K.C. Wessels (capt)	not out	40
A.R. Border (capt)	not out	69		A.P. Kuiper		
*I.A. Healy	c Richardson, b Kuiper	0		E.O. Simons		
P.R. Reiffel	c Wessels, b Kuiper	0		*D.J. Richardson		
S.K. Warne	b Matthews	23		R.P. Snell		
C.J. McDermott	b Matthews	0		C.R. Matthews		
G.D. McGrath	c Richardson, b Cronje	0		P.S. de Villiers		
Extras	lb 7, w 4, nb 3	14		Extras	lb 1, w 8, nb 3	12
(43.2 overs)		154		(45 overs)	(for 3 wickets)	157

	O	M	R	W		O	M	R	W
de Villiers	8	–	30	1	McDermott	10	–	35	–
Matthews	8	5	10	4	McGrath	10	4	20	–
Simons	10	4	22	2	S.R. Waugh	4	–	24	–
Snell	9	1	42	–	Reiffel	10	1	31	2
Cronje	3.2	–	19	1	Warne	8	2	32	1
Kuiper	5	–	24	2	M.E. Waugh	3	–	14	–

FALL OF WICKETS
1–3, 2–12, 3–18, 4–23, 5–91, 6–93, 7–100, 8–138, 9–138

FALL OF WICKETS
1–51, 2–55, 3–69

Umpires: W. Diedricks & K.E. Liebenberg
South Africa won by 7 wickets

FIRST TEST MATCH
SOUTH AFRICA v. AUSTRALIA,
at Johannesburg

With Mark Taylor unwell, Australia gave a first Test cap to Hayden who had worked hard for his opportunity. Wessels won the toss and batted. South Africa scored a run a minute in the first hour for the loss of Hudson, but two more wickets fell before lunch. Most unhappily for South Africa, Cronje tried to run a ball from Steve Waugh to third man, but he succeeded only in steering it into the hands of Border at first slip. On the stroke of lunch, Hughes bowled Gary Kirsten, and South Africa were 103 for 3. Sadly, the dismissal was accompanied by some invective from Hughes, and once again cricket and Australia were sullied.

Three wickets fell in quick succession after lunch, and it was left to Rhodes and Richardson to add 68 off 59 balls to save South Africa from total disaster. Rhodes, in fact, batted for 170 minutes and was ninth out. He had taken his side out of the pit, but they were still scrabbling for a foothold. Australia closed on 34 without loss.

South Africa gained their foothold on the second morning by capturing three wickets in the first hour. Hayden provided Richardson with his 50th dismissal in his 12th Test so making the South African 'keeper the quickest to reach this mark, but before this Australia had already lost Slater to the sixth ball of the day. He was brilliantly caught by Hudson who covered much ground at third man and held the ball as he leapt through the air. Boon was out hooking, but Mark Waugh and Border suggested recovery as they added 66. Incredibly, both were run out within the space of 10 balls.

Steve Waugh was now left clinging to the wreckage, but McDermott swung his bat effectively, hitting 31 off 23 balls, and 44 were added in 25 minutes for the ninth wicket.

South Africa's pace bowlers had clawed their side a lead of three runs, and Hudson and Gary Kirsten scored 42 in 19 overs before the end of the day.

Gary Kirsten was out at 76, falling to May, but Border did not call upon Warne until the 44th over in the innings. By this time, Cronje had been at the wicket for 45 minutes and had been hitting May, who bowled for the first 100 minutes of the day, cleanly and often. Warne's third ball bowled Hudson round his legs, and the bowler, perhaps frustrated at being kept out of the attack so long, hurled abuse at the departing batsman. It was an astonishing outburst. Warne and Hughes were fined by the match referee Donald Carr and, to their credit, the Australian Board added their own punishment.

Cronje inflicted his own brand of punishment on the Australians. Between lunch and tea, he and Wessels added 119 off 28 overs. In the 25 minutes just before tea, Cronje hit 33 off 21 balls, and he went to his century half an hour after the break. He was out when he cut Hughes into the hands of gully. He had faced 192 balls and hit a six and 16 fours. The Australians had paid a high price for

Hansie Cronje, South Africa's player of the season, hits out during his fine innings of 122 in the first Test. (Mike Hewitt/Allsport)

their lack of discipline. At the end of the day, South Africa were 335 for 5.

The tail wagged strongly, and Wessels' declaration left Australia a minimum of 133 overs in which to score 454 runs to win. Hayden again gave indication that the gap between state and Test level is a large one. Slater settled, but he became de Villiers' second victim, and Australia entered the last day on an uneasy 123 for 2.

In the fifth over of the final day, Mark Waugh was caught behind off Donald and, before lunch, Border was spectacularly caught by Gary Kirsten running back from backward short-leg and holding the ball as he dived; Steve Waugh was caught low down first ball; and Boon's 273-minute innings was ended by Matthews' outswinger.

Healy fell to Donald's slower ball, and McMillan quickly accounted for Warne and McDermott. This left just Hughes and May, but they held out for 66 minutes and, with tea approaching, clouds gathering and a stoppage for rain, there was a possibility that defeat would be avoided. Justice prevailed, and with his third ball of the match, Cronje had May taken at short-leg.

12, 13 and **14** March 1994 *at Coetzenburg, Stellenbosch*

Australians 254 for 7 dec. (D.M. Jones 63, D.C. Boon 52) and 228 for 6 dec. (M.A. Taylor 74, S.R. Waugh 71)

Boland 155 (G.D. McGrath 4 for 38) and 132 for 5

Match drawn

The last first-class game of the Australian tour outside the Test series ended an hour and a half early when both sides agreed to a draw in what had been a rather casual encounter.

FIRST TEST MATCH – SOUTH AFRICA v. AUSTRALIA
4, 5, 6, 7 and 8 March 1994 at Wanderers, Johannesburg

SOUTH AFRICA

	FIRST INNINGS			SECOND INNINGS	
A.C. Hudson	c Healy, b McDermott	17	b Warne		60
G. Kirsten	b Hughes	47	c Hughes, b May		35
W.J. Cronje	c Border, b S.R. Waugh	21	c S.R. Waugh, b Hughes		122
K.C. Wessels (capt)	c Hayden, b Hughes	18	c Border, b Warne		50
P.N. Kirsten	b May	12	c Boon, b May		53
J.N. Rhodes	c M.E. Waugh, b McDermott	69	c Healy, b S.R.Waugh		14
B.M. McMillan	c Boon, b May	0	(8) b Warne		24
*D.J. Richardson	lbw, b Warne	31	(9) c Border, b Warne		20
C.R. Matthews	c Boon, b, Hughes	6	(10) not out		31
P.S. de Villiers	b McDermott	16	(7) b McDermott		4
A.A. Donald	not out	0	not out		15
Extras	b 1, lb 10, nb 3	14	b 13, lb 4, nb 5		22
		251	(for 9 wickets, dec.)		**450**

AUSTRALIA

	FIRST INNINGS			SECOND INNINGS	
M.J. Slater	c Hudson, b de Villiers	26	(2) b de Villiers		41
M.L. Hayden	c Richardson, b Donald	15	(1) b de Villiers		5
D.C. Boon	c de Villiers, b Donald	17	b Matthews		83
M.E. Waugh	run out	42	c Richardson, b Donald		28
A.R. Border (capt)	run out	34	c G. Kirsten, b McMillan		14
S.R. Waugh	not out	45	c Richardson, b Matthews		0
*I.A. Healy	b Matthews	11	c and b Donald		30
M.G. Hughes	c G. Kirsten, b McMillan	7	not out		26
S.K. Warne	lbw, b Matthews	15	lbw, b McMillan		1
C.J. McDermott	lbw, b Donald	31	b McMillan		10
T.B.A. May	lbw, b de Villiers	2	c G. Kirsten, b Cronje		11
Extras	b 1, lb 1, nb 1	3	lb 5, nb 2		7
		248			**256**

	O	M	R	W	O	M	R	W
McDermott	15.2	3	63	3	35	3	112	1
Hughes	20	6	59	3	25	5	86	1
May	22	5	62	2	39	11	107	2
S.R. Waugh	9	2	14	1	10	3	28	1
Warne	14	4	42	1	44.5	14	86	4
M.E. Waugh					6	2	14	–

	O	M	R	W	O	M	R	W
Donald	19	–	86	3	23	3	71	2
de Villiers	19.3	1	74	2	30	11	70	2
McMillan	14	3	46	1	19	2	61	3
Matthews	15	4	40	2	20	6	42	2
G. Kirsten					4	–	7	–
Cronje					0.3	–	0	1

FALL OF WICKETS

1–21, 2–70, 3–103, 4–116, 5–126, 6–126, 7–194, 8–203, 9–249
1–76, 2–123, 3–258, 4–289, 5–324, 6–343, 7–366, 8–403, 9–406

FALL OF WICKETS

1–35, 2–56, 3–70, 4–136, 5–142, 6–169, 7–176, 8–201, 9–245
1–18, 2–95, 3–136, 4–164, 5–164, 6–191, 7–219, 8–225, 9–248

Umpires: S.B. Lambson & D.R. Shepherd　　　　　　　　　　　　　　　　*South Africa won by 197 runs*

SECOND TEST MATCH
SOUTH AFRICA v. AUSTRALIA,
at Cape Town

South Africa fielded an unchanged side while Australia brought in McGrath for May and had Taylor back in place of Hayden. Again Wessels won the toss, and again South Africa batted.

The pitch was slow and offered some gentle turn so that work was hard for both batsmen and bowlers. Hudson and Gary Kirsten set a good standard by scoring 71 in the first 80 minutes before Kirsten was excitingly run out by Slater. McGrath then delivered the great blow for Australia, inducing Cronje to edge the ball into his stumps after he had faced only 11 balls. Wessels, too, went cheaply, looping the ball to second slip, but Hudson found a solid partner in Peter Kirsten.

Hudson, celebrating his 29th birthday, was lucky to survive a leg-before appeal by Warne, but he batted well and was particularly severe on Hughes whose length throughout the match was erratic. Hudson hit 13 fours and faced 175 balls in reaching his second Test century. It

Michael Slater runs out Gary Kirsten in the second Test match.
(Mike Hewitt/Allsport)

May is caught off Cronje, and South Africa celebrate victory in the first Test. (Mike Hewitt/Allsport)

was an admirable effort, for he held the innings together at a difficult time. He was run out in the second over after tea when Steve Waugh hit the stumps with his throw made while sprawling on the ground. Rhodes lasted only a quarter of an hour, but Peter Kirsten and Brian McMillan steered South Africa to 237 for 5 at the close.

Warne accounted for Peter Kirsten with his third ball of the second day, but South Africa's policy of caution was soon in evidence. It was apparent that the intention was to bat as long as possible; both Peter Kirsten and Brian McMillan batted for more than 4¼ hours. Matthews was in 70 minutes for his seven. To avoid defeat and thereby ensure that the series, too, would not be lost was of paramount importance. Australia, 112 for 1 at the close, ended with honours even but much to do if they were to win the match.

By the end of the third day, a draw seemed inevitable. Border had batted 277 minutes for 45, Mark Waugh had been taken in the gully, and Steve Waugh and Healy were left at the start of an important sixth-wicket stand with South Africa 25 runs ahead. Boon's characteristic defiance and phlegm had done much to take Australia to this point.

Suddenly, on the fourth day, the game came alive. Healy and Steve Waugh extended their partnership to 108 and gave the batting some urgency. Matthews removed Healy and Hughes with successive deliveries, but Australia had seized the initiative. When South Africa began their second innings 45 minutes after lunch they were 74 runs in arrears.

There were no obvious problems for Hudson and Gary Kirsten, but the advent of Shane Warne altered matters. With his fourth ball he had Kirsten leg before, yet still, with 75 minutes of the day remaining, South Africa were only one wicket down and just five runs short of drawing level.

Driving at Steve Waugh, Cronje was well caught and bowled. Wessels responded slowly to Hudson's call for an easy single and, after reference to the third umpire and television evidence, he was adjudged run out. Three runs later, three wickets fell. Hudson was leg before to Steve Waugh, who had a wonderful day, de Villiers fell to Warne's yorker, and Peter Kirsten made a hash of an attempted sweep. In the last 18 overs of the day South Africa had lost five wickets for 31 runs, and they closed on 100 for 6, with defeat imminent.

Steve Waugh trapped McMillan leg before early on the last morning, but Richardson and Rhodes took the game into the afternoon with a stand of 61. The second new ball broke the partnership, McGrath having Richardson caught behind. Steve Waugh was kept on, and he had Rhodes taken at short mid-wicket. Two balls later, he knocked back Donald's middle stump to finish with his best bowling figures in Test cricket.

In 106 minutes, Australia knocked off the required runs, and the series was level.

Steve Waugh flattens Donald's middle stump, and South Africa are ▶
out for 164. (Patrick Eagar)

SECOND TEST MATCH – SOUTH AFRICA v. AUSTRALIA
17, 18, 19, 20 and 21 March 1994 at Newlands, Cape Town

SOUTH AFRICA

	FIRST INNINGS		SECOND INNINGS	
A.C. Hudson	run out	102	lbw, b S.R. Waugh	49
G. Kirsten	run out	29	lbw, b Warne	10
W.J. Cronje	b McGrath	2	c and b S.R. Waugh	19
K.C. Wessels (capt)	c M.E. Waugh, b McDermott	11	run out	9
P.N. Kirsten	lbw, b Warne	70	c Taylor, b Warne	3
J.N. Rhodes	lbw, b McGrath	5	c Border, b S.R. Waugh	27
B.M. McMillan	b Warne	74	(8) lbw, b S.R. Waugh	3
*D.J. Richardson	lbw, b McDermott	34	(9) c Healy, b McGrath	31
C.R. Matthews	not out	7	(10) not out	0
P.S. de Villiers	c Taylor, b Warne	7	(7) lbw, b Warne	0
A.A. Donald	c Healy, b McGrath	7	b S.R. Waugh	0
Extras	lb 6, nb 7	13	b 4, lb 6, nb 3	13
		361		**164**

AUSTRALIA

	FIRST INNINGS		SECOND INNINGS	
M.J. Slater	c P.N. Kirsten, b de Villiers	26	(2) not out	43
M.A. Taylor	c Richardson, b de Villiers	70	(1) b Donald	14
D.C. Boon	c Richardson, b de Villiers	96	not out	32
M.E. Waugh	c P.N. Kirsten, b McMillan	7		
A.R. Border (capt)	c Richardson, b Matthews	45		
S.R. Waugh	b Matthews	86		
*I.A. Healy	c de Villiers, b Matthews	61		
M.G. Hughes	lbw, b Matthews	0		
S.K. Warne	c McMillan, b de Villiers	11		
C.J. McDermott	c P.N. Kirsten, b Matthews	1		
G.D. McGrath	not out	1		
Extras	b 6, lb 17, w 1, nb 7	31	b 1, nb 2	3
		435	(for 1 wicket)	**92**

	O	M	R	W	O	M	R	W
McDermott	27	6	80	2	13	3	39	–
Hughes	20	1	80	–	5	1	12	–
McGrath	26.1	4	65	3	16	6	26	1
S.R. Waugh	9	3	20	–	22.3	9	28	5
Warne	47	18	78	3	30	13	38	3
M.E. Waugh	10	3	23	–	3	1	11	–
Border	5	2	9	–	1	1	0	–

	O	M	R	W	O	M	R	W
Donald	35	10	111	–	5	–	20	1
de Villiers	44.4	12	117	4	6	–	20	–
Matthews	36	12	80	5	6	1	14	–
McMillan	29	8	82	1	5	–	23	–
G. Kirsten	4	–	13	–	1.1	–	10	–
Cronje	11	4	9	–	2	–	4	–

FALL OF WICKETS

1–71, 2–78, 3–100, 4–189, 5–198, 6–260, 7–335, 8–339, 9–348
1–33, 2–69, 3–94, 4–97, 5–97, 6–97, 7–103, 8–164, 9–164

FALL OF WICKETS

1–40, 2–145, 3–153, 4–244, 5–310, 6–418, 7–418, 8–430, 9–434
1–30

Umpires: K.E. Liebenberg & D.R. Shepherd

Australia won by 9 wickets

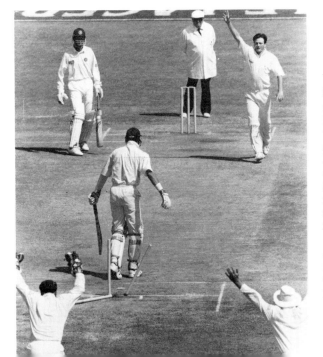

THIRD TEST MATCH
SOUTH AFRICA v. AUSTRALIA,
at Durban

South Africa were unchanged for the third match running, but Australia brought in Reiffel for Hughes who had had a dreadful match at Cape Town. Wessels won the toss again, and he asked Australia to bat. Donald quickly gained the advantage for South Africa by dismissing Taylor, and he was to claim two more wickets in the afternoon session to leave Australia struggling on 123 for 5. Healy and Steve Waugh added 92, and Australia recovered to 241 for 6 by the close, but Wessels never seemed willing to press home his advantage, content to maintain defensive fields and adopt a negative attitude.

Wessels could claim his tactics were justified when the Australian innings ended 11.2 overs into the second day for the addition of only another 28 runs. Hudson and Gary Kirsten began South Africa's reply with a century partnership in 174 minutes. Three wickets fell for 18 runs

Border pulls de Villiers during his innings of 45 in the second Test match. This was the last Test series for a great cricketer and captain.
(Patrick Eagar)

with Wessels falling fourth ball, but Cronje and Peter Kirsten took the score to 143 at stumps.

When play ended early because of bad light on the third day South Africa had reached 322 for 6. They had batted for 10½ hours, and runs had barely come at two an over. The attrition continued into the fourth day, and the cricket was dreadful. Both sides, it seemed, had abandoned hopes of victory. Australia ended on 89 for 2, and

the last day had no meaning except for Mark Waugh who hit 113 off 222 balls and Slater whose 95 came from 202 balls.

Sadly, this was the last Test match of Allan Border's career. It was his 156th Test, a record, his 93rd as captain, a record; and he scored 11,174 runs, a record, and took 156 catches, a record. That is greatness.

THIRD TEST MATCH – SOUTH AFRICA v. AUSTRALIA
25, 26, 27, 28 and 29 March 1994 at Kingsmead, Durban

AUSTRALIA

	FIRST INNINGS		SECOND INNINGS	
M.J. Slater	c Rhodes, **b** Matthews	20	(2) lbw, **b** Donald	95
M.A. Taylor	lbw, **b** Donald	1	(1) lbw, **b** de Villiers	12
D.C. Boon	c G. Kirsten, **b** Donald	37	c P.N. Kirsten, **b** Donald	12
M.E. Waugh	c Richardson, **b** Donald	43	(5) not out	113
A.R. Border (capt)	c Rhodes, **b** McMillan	17	(6) not out	42
S.R. Waugh	c Wessels, **b** Matthews	64		
*I.A. Healy	**b** Matthews	55		
P.R. Reiffel	lbw, **b** de Villiers	13		
S.K. Warne	c Wessels, **b** Matthews	2	(4) c McMillan, **b** Donald	12
C.J. McDermott	c Donald, **b** de Villiers	6		
G.D. McGrath	not out	0		
Extras	lb 1, w 1, nb 9	11	lb 6, w 1, nb 4	11
		269	(for 4 wickets)	**297**

SOUTH AFRICA

	FIRST INNINGS	
A.C. Hudson	lbw, **b** Reiffel	65
G. Kirsten	c Healy, **b** Reiffel	41
W.J. Cronje	c S.R. Waugh, **b** Warne	26
K.C. Wessels (capt)	lbw, **b** McDermott	1
P.N. Kirsten	lbw, **b** S.R. Waugh	49
J.N. Rhodes	lbw, **b** Warne	78
B.M. McMillan	c Slater, **b** S.R. Waugh	84
*D.J. Richardson	c Reiffel, **b** Warne	59
C.R. Matthews	lbw, **b** Warne	1
P.S. de Villiers	lbw, **b** S.R. Waugh	0
A.A. Donald	not out	0
Extras	b 3, lb 10, nb 5	18
		422

	O	M	R	W	O	M	R	W
Donald	18	1	71	3	28	7	66	3
de Villiers	24.2	5	55	2	24	5	69	1
Matthews	29	9	65	4	28	12	56	–
McMillan	19	5	56	1	22	6	53	–
Cronje	5	1	8	–	18	5	40	–
G. Kirsten	6	1	13	–	3	1	7	–
Rhodes					1	1	0	–

	O	M	R	W
McDermott	38	11	76	1
Reiffel	30	7	77	2
McGrath	41	11	78	–
Warne	55	20	92	4
S.R. Waugh	27.2	12	40	3
M.E. Waugh	11	3	38	–
Border	3	1	8	–

FALL OF WICKETS

1–7, 2–45, 3–81, 4–123, 5–123, 6–215, 7–250, 8–256, 9–259
1–55, 2–81, 3–109, 4–157

FALL OF WICKETS

1–100, 2–117, 3–118, 4–155, 5–256, 6–274, 7–417, 8–422, 9–422

Umpires: Mahboob Shah & C.J. Mitchley

Match drawn

TEST MATCH AVERAGES – SOUTH AFRICA v. AUSTRALIA

SOUTH AFRICA BATTING

	M	Inns	NO	Runs	HS	Av	100s	50s
A.C. Hudson	3	5	–	293	102	58.60	1	2
J.N. Rhodes	3	5	–	193	78	38.60	–	2
W.J. Cronje	3	5	–	190	122	38.00	1	–
P.N. Kirsten	3	5	–	187	70	37.40	–	2
B.M. McMillan	3	5	–	185	84	37.00	–	2
D.J. Richardson	3	5	–	175	59	35.00	–	1
G. Kirsten	3	5	–	162	47	32.40	–	–
C.R. Matthews	3	5	3	45	31*	22.50	–	–
K.C. Wessels	3	5	–	89	50	17.80	–	1
A.A. Donald	3	5	3	22	15*	11.00	–	–
P.S. de Villiers	3	5	–	27	16	5.40	–	–

AUSTRALIA BATTING

	M	Inns	NO	Runs	HS	Av	100s	50s
S.R. Waugh	3	4	1	195	86	65.00	–	2
M.E. Waugh	3	5	1	233	113*	58.25	1	–
D.C. Boon	3	6	1	277	96	55.40	–	2
M.J. Slater	3	6	1	251	95	50.20	–	1
I.A. Healy	3	4	–	157	61	39.25	–	2
A.R. Border	3	5	1	152	45	38.00	–	–
M.A. Taylor	2	4	–	97	70	24.25	–	1
M.G. Hughes	2	3	1	33	26*	16.50	–	–
C.J. McDermott	3	4	–	48	31	12.00	–	–
S.K. Warne	3	5	–	41	15	8.20	–	–

Played in two Tests: G.D. McGrath 1* & 0*; Played in one Test: M.L. Hayden 15 & 5;
T.B.A. May 2 & 11; P.R. Reiffel 13

SOUTH AFRICA BOWLING

	Overs	Mds	Runs	Wkts	Av	Best	10/m	5/inn
C.R. Matthews	134	44	297	13	22.84	5-80	–	1
A.A. Donald	128	21	425	12	35.41	3-66	–	–
P.S. de Villiers	148.3	33	405	11	36.81	4-117	–	–
B.M. McMillan	108	24	321	6	53.50	3-61	–	–
W.J. Cronje	36.3	10	61	1	61.00	1-0	–	–
G. Kirsten	18.1	2	50	–	–			

Bowled in one innings: J.N. Rhodes 1–1–0–0

AUSTRALIA BOWLING

	Overs	Mds	Runs	Wkts	Av	Best	10/m	5/inn
S.R. Waugh	77.5	29	130	10	13.00	5-28	–	1
S.K. Warne	190.5	69	336	15	22.40	4-86	–	–
T.B.A. May	61	16	169	4	42.25	2-62	–	–
G.D. McGrath	83.1	21	169	4	42.25	3-65	–	–
C.J. McDermott	128.2	26	370	7	52.85	3-63	–	–
M.G. Hughes	70	13	237	4	59.25	3-59	–	–
A.R. Border	9	4	17	–	–	–	–	–
M.E. Waugh	30	9	86	–	–	–	–	–

Bowled in one innings: P.R. Reiffel 30–7–77–2

SOUTH AFRICA FIELDING FIGURES

7 – D.J. Richardson; 4 – P.N. Kirsten; 2 – J.N. Rhodes, P.S. de Villiers, A.A. Donald,
K.C. Wessels and B.M. McMillan; 1 – A.C. Hudson

AUSTRALIA FIELDING FIGURES

5 – I.A. Healy; 4 – A.R. Border; 3 – D.C. Boon and S.R. Waugh; 2 – M.A. Taylor and
M.E. Waugh; 1 – M.L. Hayden, M.G. Hughes, P.R. Reiffel and M.J. Slater

SECOND ONE-DAY INTERNATIONAL SERIES

Kepler Wessels was not well received at East London, for there had been strong criticism of his leadership in the final Test, and it seemed that all that he did went wrong. Omitting their spinner, South Africa lost six of their own wickets to the Australian spinners, and Wessels ran out Kuiper and then himself. He then dropped Slater, and Australia won with 10 overs to spare. Steve Waugh hit 11 fours, and his 67 came off 60 balls.

At Port Elizabeth, Australia fought a losing battle under inadequate lighting. Facing a target of 228, they slipped to 77 for 7 before Warne and Reiffel established an eighth-wicket record for a one-day international by hitting 119 off 117 balls. When they were separated the end came quickly.

In the penultimate match, at Cape Town, Australia lost two quick wickets, but Taylor and Mark Waugh added 123. The partnership was broken freakishly, for Waugh was dropped by Kuiper who, nevertheless, gathered the ball and ran out Taylor. South Africa seemed on course for victory, but they were undermined by Shane Warne, their perpetual tormentor.

Australia won the day/night series 3–1, or more realistically, the one-day series was drawn 4–4 when they took the final match by the slimmest of margins. Wessels reverted to his role as opener and helped Hudson to put on 82 for the first wicket as South Africa went in search of a moderate target of 204. At 143 for 3, they were still the likely winners, but Reiffel brought about a collapse, dismissing Rhodes and the excellent Hudson within the space of three overs. Warne tempted Kuiper to disaster, and McMillan was excitingly run out by Healy's backhand flip. The last over arrived with South Africa needing six to win and Fleming, the replacement for McDermott who was again to undergo surgery, bowling. The young Victorian kept a tight line and restricted Richardson and Shaw to four runs, with Richardson run out as he attempted the impossible. In 10 overs, six wickets had fallen for 59 runs.

The tour was at an end and so was Allan Border's career at international level. He had seemed an institution in the one-day scene – 273 matches and 6,524 runs.

FIFTH ONE-DAY INTERNATIONAL – SOUTH AFRICA v. AUSTRALIA
2 April 1994 at Buffalo Park, East London

SOUTH AFRICA

Batsman	Dismissal	Runs
A.C. Hudson	c Warne, b Reiffel	14
P.N. Kirsten	c M.E. Waugh, b Warne	53
W.J. Cronje	c Warne, b May	10
J.N. Rhodes	st Healy, b May	16
A.P. Kuiper	run out	12
K.C. Wessels (capt)	run out	15
E.O. Simons	st Healy, b Border	6
B.M. McMillan	b S.R. Waugh	17
*D.J. Richardson	not out	7
C.R. Matthews	c Healy, b Border	0
P.S. de Villiers	st Healy, b Border	0
Extras	lb 4, w 1, nb 3	8
(49.5 overs)		158

AUSTRALIA

Batsman	Dismissal	Runs
M.J. Slater	c Kirsten, b Simons	31
D.C. Boon	run out	30
D.M. Jones	lbw, b Simons	8
M.E. Waugh	not out	21
S.R. Waugh	not out	67
A.R. Border (capt)		
*I.A. Healy		
P.R. Reiffel		
S.K. Warne		
T.B.A. May		
G.D. McGrath		
Extras	lb 2	2
(40 overs)	(for 3 wickets)	159

	O	M	R	W
McGrath	6	1	20	–
Reiffel	7	1	13	1
S.R. Waugh	9	1	25	1
May	10	–	35	2
Warne	10	–	34	1
Border	7.5	–	27	3

	O	M	R	W
de Villiers	8	–	31	–
Matthews	8	–	34	–
Simons	10	2	32	2
McMillan	6	–	21	–
Cronje	7	–	32	–
Kuiper	1	–	7	–

FALL OF WICKETS

1–35, 2–62, 3–87, 4–109, 5–118, 6–129, 7–139, 8–156, 9–158

FALL OF WICKETS

1–57, 2–66, 3–71

Umpires: R.E. Koertzen & K.E. Liebenberg *Man of the Match:* A.R. Border *Australia won by 7 wickets*

SIXTH ONE-DAY INTERNATIONAL – SOUTH AFRICA *v.* AUSTRALIA
4 April 1994 at St George's Park, Port Elizabeth

SOUTH AFRICA		
A.C. Hudson	c Warne, **b** May	63
P.N. Kirsten	**b** Reiffel	10
W.J. Cronje	c Healy, **b** M.E. Waugh	11
J.N. Rhodes	c Jones, **b** S.R.Waugh	66
K.C. Wessels (capt)	**b** Reiffel	27
E.O. Simons	run out	23
B.M. McMillan	run out	2
*D.J. Richardson	not out	2
T.G. Shaw		
C.R. Matthews		
P.S. de Villiers		
Extras	b **1**, lb **15**, w **5**, nb **2**	23
(50 overs)	(for 6 wickets)	227

AUSTRALIA		
D.C. Boon	c Wessels, **b** de Villiers	4
M.J. Slater	c Richardson, **b** Matthews	16
D.M. Jones	**b** Simons	13
M.E. Waugh	**b** Simons	17
S.R. Waugh	lbw, **b** McMillan	7
A.R. Border (capt)	lbw, **b** Shaw	5
*I.A. Healy	c Wessels, **b** Shaw	5
P.R. Reiffel	c Simons, **b** Matthews	58
S.K. Warne	run out	55
T.B.A. May	c and **b** de Villiers	4
G.D. McGrath	not out	0
Extras	lb **13**, w **4**	17
(49.1 overs)		201

	O	M	R	W
McGrath	10	1	41	–
Reiffel	10	1	33	2
M.E. Waugh	7	–	26	1
S.R. Waugh	10	1	48	1
May	10	–	45	1
Warne	3	–	18	–

	O	M	R	W
de Villiers	9	1	42	2
Matthews	9.1	1	35	2
McMillan	8	–	38	1
Simons	10	3	24	2
Shaw	8	2	19	2
Cronje	5	1	30	–

FALL OF WICKETS

1–18, 2–48, 3–153, 4–175, 5–216, 6–223

FALL OF WICKETS

1–4, 2–35, 3–50, 4–59, 5–65, 6–68, 7–77, 8–196, 9–201

Umpires: W. Diedricks & S.B. Lambson   *Man of the Match:* J.N. Rhodes   *South Africa won by 26 runs*

SEVENTH ONE-DAY INTERNATIONAL – SOUTH AFRICA *v.* AUSTRALIA
6 April 1994 at Newlands, Cape Town

AUSTRALIA		
M.A. Taylor	run out	63
M.L. Hayden	lbw, **b** Matthews	0
D.M. Jones	c Richardson, **b** Matthews	8
M.E. Waugh	**b** Matthews	71
S.R. Waugh	**b** Simons	23
A.R. Border (capt)	not out	40
*I.A. Healy	c Wessels, **b** Matthews	26
P.R. Reiffel	not out	0
S.K. Warne		
T.B.A. May		
G.D. McGrath		
Extras	lb **8**, w **1**, nb **2**	11
(50 overs)	(for 6 wickets)	242

SOUTH AFRICA		
A.C. Hudson	lbw, **b** Warne	62
G. Kirsten	c M.E. Waugh, **b** Reiffel	3
W.J. Cronje	c Taylor, **b** Warne	37
J.N. Rhodes	st Healy, **b** Warne	35
A.P. Kuiper	not out	38
K.C. Wessels (capt)	c Border, **b** M.E. Waugh	12
E.O. Simons	not out	9
B.M. McMillan		
*D.J. Richardson		
C.R. Matthews		
P.S. de Villiers		
Extras	b **1**, lb **8**, nb **1**	10
(50 overs)	(for 5 wickets)	206

	O	M	R	W
de Villiers	10	1	52	–
Matthews	10	–	47	4
McMillan	10	–	46	–
Simons	10	–	31	1
Cronje	5	–	40	–
Kuiper	5	–	18	–

	O	M	R	W
McGrath	10	1	38	–
Reiffel	7	2	18	1
May	10	–	38	–
S.R. Waugh	4	–	22	–
Warne	10	–	31	3
M.E. Waugh	9	1	50	1

FALL OF WICKETS

1–0, 2–10, 3–133, 4–163, 5–180, 6–242

FALL OF WICKETS

1–22, 2–101, 3–114, 4–163, 5–186

Umpires: R.E. Koertzen & C.J. Mitchley   *Man of the Match:* M.E. Waugh   *Australia won by 36 runs*

EIGHTH ONE-DAY INTERNATIONAL – SOUTH AFRICA v. AUSTRALIA
8 April 1994 at Springbok Park, Bloemfontein

AUSTRALIA			SOUTH AFRICA		
M.J. Slater	st Richardson, b Shaw	34	A.C. Hudson	c Border, b Reiffel	84
M.A. Taylor	c Wessels, b Matthews	1	K.C. Wessels (capt)	b S.R. Waugh	28
M.E. Waugh	c Wessels, b Simons	13	W.J. Cronje	b McGrath	18
D.C. Boon	c Wessels, b Matthews	45	J.N. Rhodes	c S.R. Waugh, b Reiffel	13
S.R. Waugh	c McMillan, b de Villiers	42	A.P. Kuiper	c M.E. Waugh, b Warne	6
A.R. Border (capt)	c McMillan, b Matthews	11	B.M. McMillan	run out	4
*I.A. Healy	not out	41	*D.J. Richardson	run out	18
P.R. Reiffel	not out	8	E.O. Simons	b S.R. Waugh	18
S.K. Warne			T.G. Shaw	not out	2
G.D. McGrath			C.R. Matthews		
D.W. Fleming			P.S. de Villiers		
Extras	lb 6, w 1, nb 1	8	Extras	lb 6, w 4, nb 1	11
(50 overs)	(for 6 wickets)	203	(50 overs)	(for 8 wickets)	202

	O	M	R	W		O	M	R	W
de Villiers	10	1	44	1	McGrath	10	–	44	1
Matthews	10	–	40	3	Fleming	10	2	33	–
Simons	10	2	36	1	Reiffel	10	–	34	2
Shaw	10	–	30	1	Warne	10	–	37	1
McMillan	7	–	34	–	S.R. Waugh	10	–	48	2
Kuiper	3	–	13	–					

FALL OF WICKETS

1–7, 2–31, 3–69, 4–140, 5–143, 6–184

FALL OF WICKETS

1–82, 2–111, 3–143, 4–158, 5–162, 6–164, 7–196, 8–202

Umpires: S.B. Lambson & C.J. Mitchley   *Man of the Match:* A.C. Hudson   *Australia won by 1 run*

FIRST-CLASS AVERAGES

BATTING

	M	Inns	NO	Runs	HS	Av	100s	50s		M	Inns	NO	Runs	HS	Av	100s	50s
D.J. Cullinan	4	6	2	459	337*	114.75	1	1	M.W. Rushmere	9	14	2	546	188	45.50	1	3
D.J. Callaghan	4	6	2	400	113	100.00	2	2	J.B. Commins	9	16	–	726	165	45.37	2	4
A. Meyer	4	4	2	192	89	96.00	–	1	R.B. Armstrong	7	9	1	361	97	45.12	–	2
C.J. van Heerden	6	8	3	364	126*	72.80	1	2	P.A.J. DeFreitas	7	11	–	451	103*	45.10	1	4
W. Bond	2	2	–	136	75	68.00	–	2	P.C. Strydom	6	8	1	313	117	44.71	1	1
W.J. Cronje	7	13	–	870	251	66.92	4	1	R.I. Dalrymple	3	6	2	177	85	44.25	–	1
T.N. Lazard	9	16	3	853	307*	65.61	2	2	D.J. Watson	7	11	–	486	87	44.18	–	4
P.N. Kirsten	9	14	–	872	271	62.28	2	4	A.G. Lawson	8	13	1	522	110	43.50	1	4
S.J. Cook	8	14	2	745	136	62.08	4	1	G. Morgan	6	10	5	216	60*	43.20	–	1
J.P. Heath	2	4	1	181	120*	60.33	1	–	P.M. Boa	7	11	2	380	69	42.22	–	4
M.D. Marshall	8	11	4	420	120*	60.00	1	2	L.J. Wilkinson	7	12	1	461	105	41.90	1	3
G.W. Bashford	4	6	1	291	115	58.20	2	–	G.F.J. Liebenberg	9	18	1	705	142	41.47	1	4
W.R. Radford	4	7	–	390	157	55.71	2	1	P.G. Amm	9	15	–	615	77	41.00	–	5
L.M. Germishuys	8	13	4	493	108*	54.77	1	3	J.N. Rhodes	6	11	–	450	114	40.90	1	2
C.R. Norris	5	9	1	434	78	54.25	–	4	N.R. Rhodes	3	3	–	122	67	40.66	–	1
G. Kirsten	7	12	–	650	192	54.16	2	2	K.J. Rule	9	18	4	563	122	40.21	2	3
J. Kallis	3	4	1	160	69	53.33	–	2	C.F. Craven	5	6	–	239	152	39.83	1	–
D.J. Richardson	5	7	–	370	128	52.85	1	2	W. Dry	5	7	1	238	75	39.66	–	2
B.W. Lones	5	6	1	264	104	52.80	1	1	S. Nicholson	5	8	1	275	114*	39.28	1	2
M.P. Stonier	8	13	1	596	121	49.66	2	3	F.C. Brooker	5	10	2	314	89	39.25	–	2
L.P. Vorster	6	9	1	394	188	49.25	2	–	M.I. Gidley	6	10	2	314	82	39.25	–	2
T.J. Mitchell	5	8	2	289	90	48.16	–	3	N.E. Wright	8	13	–	497	102	38.23	1	3
F. Viljoen	3	6	2	192	75*	48.00	–	2	A.P. Kuiper	10	19	3	610	129*	38.12	1	3
A.C. Hudson	7	13	–	622	102	47.84	1	4	J.E. Morris	4	8	–	304	109	38.00	1	1
R.A. Koster	6	9	2	332	95	47.42	–	3	B.E. van der Vyver	4	6	–	228	127	38.00	1	1
J.F. Venter	9	13	–	604	193	46.46	1	4	J. Payn	3	4	–	152	44	38.00	–	–
B.M. McMillan	6	9	–	414	116	46.00	1	3	K.C. Wessels	6	9	1	303	62	37.87	–	4
P.J.R. Steyn	9	18	3	688	90	45.86	–	6	J.M. Arthur	9	17	1	600	106	37.50	2	3
H.H. Gibbs	6	12	2	456	152*	45.60	1	1	H.D. Ackerman	6	11	–	408	154	37.09	1	2

FIRST-CLASS AVERAGES

BATTING

	M	Inns	NO	Runs	HS	Av	100s	50s
S.G. Koening	7	14	1	481	121*	37.00	1	3
F.B. Touzel	8	15	3	441	128*	36.75	1	–
C.B. Lambert	8	16	–	578	214	36.12	2	–
M. Michau	5	8	–	287	56	35.87	–	2
W.V. Rippon	3	4	–	143	92	35.75	–	2
T. Jamaal	5	9	–	321	114	35.66	1	1
E.A.E. Baptiste	8	12	–	421	97	35.08	–	4
P.A. Tullis	3	3	–	104	76	34.66	–	1
L. Botes	5	7	2	172	49	34.40	–	–
H.M. de Vos	5	9	1	275	95	34.37	–	2
D.J. Pryke	4	5	2	103	48	34.33	–	–
B.M. White	8	15	–	511	109	34.06	2	2
D. Jordaan	10	20	3	579	105*	34.05	1	4
A.J. van Deventer	5	9	1	272	61	34.00	–	2
A. Cilliers	5	8	1	237	56	33.85	–	2
G.C. Martin	4	7	–	237	73	33.85	–	3
D.M. Benkenstein	8	11	1	338	95	33.80	–	3
F.D. Stephenson	8	15	1	468	95	33.42	–	3
W.E. Schonegevel	5	10	–	334	82	33.40	–	3
B.J. Sommerville	8	15	–	498	77	33.20	–	4
G.W. Thompson	5	6	–	198	106	33.00	1	–
W.S. Truter	8	14	1	429	110*	33.00	1	2
R.F. Pienaar	10	19	2	554	73*	32.58	–	2
F.J.C. Cronje	6	8	1	228	85	32.57	–	1
E.O. Simons	8	16	2	454	96	32.42	–	3
C. Light	6	9	1	257	85	32.12	–	2
D.B. Rundle	3	4	–	128	81	32.00	–	1
D.J. van Zyl	7	13	2	351	77	31.90	–	2
D. Smith	4	5	1	127	88*	31.75	–	1
T.A. Marsh	5	9	1	252	106	31.50	1	2
I.L. Howell	8	11	5	189	52*	31.50	–	1
M. Yachad	8	14	1	408	100*	31.38	1	1
R.J. Ryall	10	12	4	250	61	31.25	–	2
E.L.R. Stewart	3	6	1	155	79	31.00	–	1
N.C. Johnson	8	12	1	339	136	30.81	1	4
M. Badat	4	7	2	153	54*	30.60	–	1
M.J.R. Rindel	9	17	2	451	137	30.06	1	1
J. Groenewald	3	6	1	149	50*	29.80	–	1
A. Botha	6	12	–	344	82	28.66	–	2
D.N. Crookes	8	11	–	315	59	28.63	–	2
P. Kirsten	5	9	1	227	87	28.37	–	1
P.J. Botha	8	11	1	283	124*	28.30	1	–
K.C. Dugmore	3	6	1	141	66	28.20	–	1
G.C. Victor	6	8	–	225	74	28.12	–	2
G. Grainger	6	9	–	252	70	28.00	–	1
Q.R. Still	5	8	2	167	129*	27.83	1	–
M. Erasmus	8	12	1	304	73	27.63	–	2
A. Moreby	4	5	–	138	66	27.60	–	1
L.F. Bleekers	5	10	1	243	87	27.60	–	2
M.D. Haysman	8	14	–	374	52	26.71	–	2
P.A. Rayment	5	8	1	182	66	26.00	–	1
C. Wait	5	9	1	208	103	26.00	1	–
C.P. Dettmer	5	9	–	231	93	25.66	–	2
P.L. Symcox	4	7	1	154	34*	25.66	–	–
S.C. Pope	9	15	1	357	67*	25.50	–	2
B.M. Osborne	8	13	1	304	58*	25.33	–	3
C.A. Best	8	15	–	376	71	25.06	–	2
M.G. Beamish	5	9	–	222	111	24.66	1	1
G. Dros	6	11	1	246	80	24.60	–	1
O. Henry	3	5	–	119	49	23.80	–	–
S.M. Pollock	6	8	1	166	56	23.71	–	1
W.N. van As	5	9	–	212	62	23.55	–	1
K.G. Bauermeister	4	5	–	116	47	23.20	–	–
S. Elworthy	10	18	2	371	46	23.18	–	–
C.J.P.G. van Zyl	8	12	3	208	51	23.11	–	1
P.H. Barnard	6	11	2	206	89*	22.88	–	2
M.L. Bruyns	6	9	1	182	82	22.75	–	1
B.T. Player	9	12	2	226	47	22.60	–	–
K.C. Jackson	9	16	1	334	90	22.26	–	3
B.A. Nash	5	8	1	154	50*	22.00	–	1
S.D. Jack	8	12	3	195	42	21.66	–	–
S.J. Palframan	8	11	–	231	123	21.00	1	–
A.T. Holdstock	5	9	2	146	32*	20.85	–	–
C.S.N. Marais	6	8	1	144	45	20.57	–	–
P.J.L. Radley	9	12	4	162	27	20.25	–	–
C.W. Henderson	9	11	4	141	53*	20.14	–	1
G.A. Pollock	3	6	–	120	64	20.00	–	1
M.O. Johnston	6	9	1	160	108	20.00	1	–
T.G. Shaw	9	14	4	200	42	20.00	–	–
R.E. Veenstra	8	12	1	219	31	19.90	–	–
U.H. Goedeke	6	8	1	139	28	19.85	–	–
J.J. Strydom	10	20	1	376	109	19.78	1	1
A.C. Dawson	9	16	4	231	56	19.25	–	1
J.S. Roos	5	8	1	134	40	19.14	–	–
N. Boje	9	11	4	134	36	19.14	–	–
L. Klusener	7	12	3	165	36	18.33	–	–
V.F. du Preez	4	7	–	128	36	18.28	–	–
N. Martin	5	7	–	127	49	18.14	–	–
J.E. Johnson	5	8	–	143	79	17.87	–	1
N.W. Pretorius	5	6	–	107	33	17.83	–	–
S. Jacobs	8	11	2	156	41*	17.33	–	–
B.H. Richards	3	6	–	103	43	17.16	–	–
P.W.E. Rawson	6	8	2	101	46*	16.83	–	–
L.J. Koen	6	10	–	163	56	16.30	–	2
H.G. Prinsloo	5	8	1	114	31	16.28	–	–
M.C. Venter	9	15	–	243	54	16.20	–	1
G. Miller	5	8	–	128	57	16.00	–	1
A.J. Seymore	4	8	–	128	59	16.00	–	1
A.G. Elgar	6	8	1	111	44	15.85	–	–
H.C. Bakkes	8	10	3	108	33	15.42	–	–
B. Randall	5	9	2	105	59	15.00	–	1
N. Pothas	8	11	1	149	45	14.90	–	–
A.V. Birrell	5	9	1	119	51	14.87	–	1
M.J. Vandrau	4	8	1	104	36	14.85	–	–
M.W. Pringle	8	13	2	161	33	14.63	–	–
D.R. Laing	8	12	–	167	52	13.91	–	1
H. Coetzee	4	8	–	111	46	13.87	–	–
M.J. Davis	5	8	–	108	33	13.50	–	–
M.J. Cann	6	10	1	116	45	12.88	–	–
L.D. Botha	5	8	–	102	32	12.75	–	–
R.E. Bryson	7	10	–	109	44	10.90	–	–

(Qualification – 100 runs, average 10.00)
(Played in one match – L.G. Howell 94 & 33)

BOWLING

	Overs	Mds	Runs	Wkts	Av	Best	10/m	5/inn
B.N. Schultz	57	12	158	10	15.80	7-70	–	1
M.J. Cann	91.1	26	228	13	17.53	5-68	–	1
G.P. Cooke	119.3	30	284	16	17.75	4-68	–	–
M.J. Vandrau	217.1	70	476	26	18.30	5-42	–	2
A.G. Pollock	128.5	31	298	16	18.62	4-57	–	–
T.J. Mitchell	84.4	32	189	10	18.90	3-0	–	–
A.H. Gray	122.4	30	384	19	20.21	4-83	–	–
S.M. Skeete	92	24	272	13	20.92	6-88	–	1
L. Klusener	201.4	37	567	27	21.00	4-38	–	–
M.W. Pringle	254.4	68	601	28	21.46	4-43	–	–
A.V. Birrell	121.3	30	370	17	21.76	4-95	–	–
B.C. Fourie	274.4	65	661	30	22.03	6-74	–	1
F.D. Stephenson	306	79	715	32	22.34	4-57	–	–
A.G. Elgar	195.1	77	475	21	22.61	4-83	–	–
J.E. Johnson	139	26	436	19	22.94	5-28	–	1
C.R. Matthews	195.1	56	438	19	23.05	5-80	–	1
M. Erasmus	240.1	63	554	24	23.08	5-54	–	1
M.I. Gidley	141.4	51	282	12	23.50	5-48	–	1
Q.R. Still	176.4	46	454	19	23.89	5-43	–	2
A. Badenhorst	233	46	650	27	24.07	5-52	–	1
A. Serfontein	99.4	22	315	13	24.23	5-50	–	1

FIRST-CLASS AVERAGES

BOWLING

	Overs	Mds	Runs	Wkts	Av	Best	10/m	5/inn		Overs	Mds	Runs	Wkts	Av	Best	10/m	5/inn
A. Martyn	378.2	93	961	39	24.64	6-60	–	1	S.M. Pollock	168.2	57	382	11	34.72	3-33	–	–
E.A.E. Baptiste	316.3	106	629	25	25.16	5-41	–	1	N.W. Pretorius	137	27	455	13	35.00	3-56	–	–
G. Roe	120	34	309	12	25.75	4/42	–	–	C. van Noordwyk	193.4	25	704	20	35.20	5-51	–	1
A. Meyer	95.1	11	285	11	25.90	7-67	–	1	A.A. Donald	246.1	42	780	22	35.45	4-32	–	–
S.D. Jack	304.2	57	864	33	26.18	6-30	–	1	A.G. Huckle	396.4	78	1212	34	35.64	6-99	–	1
T.G. Shaw	441.5	166	867	33	26.27	4-23	–	–	S. Abrahams	268.4	100	513	14	36.64	3-60	–	–
P.A.J. DeFreitas	200.3	44	530	20	26.50	5-80	–	1	M.D. Marshall	331	112	698	19	36.73	3-35	–	–
R.E. Veenstra	289	82	667	25	26.68	4-32	–	–	C.W. Henderson	347.2	105	885	24	36.87	4-25	–	–
E.O. Simons	228.4	66	457	17	26.88	4-41	–	–	R.A. Lyle	134.4	36	371	10	37.10	2-27	–	–
G. Smith	148	27	457	17	26.88	5-24	–	2	D.N. Crookes	367.5	97	892	23	38.78	5-84	–	1
O.D. Gibson	97.1	14	297	11	27.00	4-50	–	–	S. Elworthy	300.5	60	970	25	38.80	4-55	–	–
M.N. Angel	171.2	38	488	18	27.11	4-50	–	–	P.A.N. Emslie	166.2	33	548	14	39.14	5-103	–	1
T.A. Marsh	98	24	308	11	28.00	3-80	–	–	H. Williams	164.5	41	450	11	40.90	3-69	–	–
A. Newman	78	8	281	10	28.10	5-96	–	1	B.T. Player	252.3	60	676	15	45.06	4-107	–	–
D.R. Laing	163.5	35	426	15	28.40	3-18	–	–	F. Benjamin	179.3	32	550	12	45.83	4-40	–	–
A. Cilliers	107.1	19	372	13	28.61	3-57	–	–	L.C.R. Jordaan	161	34	464	10	46.40	4-59	–	–
D. MacHelm	320.4	84	832	29	28.68	7-85	1	2	R.E. Bryson	180.4	34	655	14	46.78	3-35	–	–
C.J.P.G. van Zyl	225.2	64	518	18	28.77	3-21	–	–	H.C. Bakkes	227	50	613	13	47.15	3-71	–	–
B.M. McMillan	207.5	50	522	18	29.00	3-32	–	–	G.D. Stevenson	148	37	489	10	48.90	3-44	–	–
P.J. Botha	187	60	409	14	29.21	4-45	–	–	B.J. Drew	176	28	599	12	49.91	3-57	–	–
M.W. Handman	139.1	38	383	13	29.46	4-94	–	–	P.L. Symcox	199.3	50	504	10	50.40	4-64	–	–
T. Bosch	236.3	56	685	23	29.78	4-32	–	–									
C.E. Eksteen	462.4	151	1014	34	29.82	7-29	1	2									
M.R. Hobson	217.5	27	780	26	30.00	7-61	–	1									
N.C. Johnson	206	57	580	19	30.52	5-79	–	2									
I.L. Howell	411.4	145	830	27	30.74	5-72	–	1									
N. Boje	475.2	152	1115	35	31.85	6-101	–	1									
S. Jacobs	273.4	81	550	17	32.35	2-23	–	–									
P.W.E. Rawson	179.5	65	389	12	32.41	4-29	–	–									
L.D. Botha	95.4	16	327	10	32.70	3-37	–	–									
A.C. Dawson	216.3	55	527	16	32.93	5-42	–	1									
F. Venter	181.4	34	661	20	33.05	5-14	–	2									
P.S. de Villiers	218.3	46	586	17	34.47	4-106	–	–									

(Qualification – 10 wickets)

Averages of Zimbabwe Board XI players will be found in the Zimbabwe section.

LEADING FIELDERS

32 – R.J. Ryall (ct 27/st 5); 31 – M.O. Johnston (ct 26/st 5); 27 – N. Pothas (ct 25/st 2); 26 – S.J. Palframan (ct 24/st 2); 24 – P.J.L. Radley (ct 21/st 3); 23 – K.J. Rule (ct 21/st 2); 22 – L.M. Germishuys (ct 16/st 6); 17 – L.F. Bleekers and C.S.N. Marais (ct 16/st 1); 16 – D.J. Richardson; 15 – G. Morgan, H.M. de Vos and B. Randall (ct 10/st 5); 14 – P. Kirsten and U.H. Goedeke; 11 – B.M. White, C. Wait and M.D. Haysman; 10 – G.W. Bashford and F.B. Touzel

SECTION D
India
Irani Cup
Duleep Trophy
Deodhar Trophy
Hero Cup
Sri Lankan tour, Test and one-day international series
Ranji Trophy
First-class averages

Kapil Dev – more wickets in Test cricket than any other bowler.
(Stuart D. Franklin/ASP)

Indian cricket enjoyed a golden period in 1993 and 1994. The total dominance in the series against England had been followed by equally emphatic victories over Zimbabwe and Sri Lanka, and Kapil Dev was closely approaching Sir Richard Hadlee's record of 431 Test wickets. Originally it was intended that Pakistan would visit India for a Test series which would rigidly examine the qualities of two of the world's outstanding sides, but political and religious tensions caused the Pakistanis to cancel their tour and to withdraw from the Hero Cup, the tournament arranged to celebrate the Diamond Jubilee of the Bengal Cricket Association. England had declined an invitation to participate in the competition, and Australia and New Zealand were engaged in a Test series in Australia and were therefore unable to compete.

As is customary, the Indian season began with the Irani Cup match.

IRANI CUP
PUNJAB v. REST OF INDIA, at Ludhiana

Punjab fielded nine of the side which had won the Ranji Trophy for the association for the first time six months earlier. Although missing several leading Test players, the Rest of India side, led by Manjrekar, was a strong one. Manjrekar won the toss, and the representative side batted. There was quick success for the medium pace of Bhupinder Singh senior who sent back Raman and Ganguly with only 16 scored, but Jadeja, who batted three hours for his 64, and Manjrekar added 104. The most entertaining cricket of the first day, however, came from Rahul Dravid and Jedhe who put on 145 in 129 minutes. Jedhe hit 12 fours in an aggressive knock.

The Rest closed on 296 for 5, but Dravid's polished innings ended early on the second day as the last five wickets went down for 51 runs. Bhupinder finished with six wickets.

Sidhu and Krishan Mohan went quickly, but Vikram Rathore and Gursharan Singh kept Punjab in contention with a stand of 122. Rathore was particularly severe on leg-spinner Anath Padmanabhan, hitting him for six and four in his opening over. At 155 for 4 at the end of the second day, Punjab still had skipper Gursharan Singh at the crease and must have hoped for a good score, but the second new ball proved to be their undoing. Gursharan drove rashly at Jadeja, and, exploiting some moisture in the pitch and a slight breeze, Prashant Vaidya mopped up the tail. Mongia held six catches behind the stumps, one more than Arun Sharma had taken for Punjab.

Still Punjab maintained an interest in the match as Bhupinder Singh senior again bowled splendidly to help reduce the Rest to 115 for 5 by the end of the third day. On the fourth day, Punjab faltered in the field, an aspect of the game which was usually one of their strengths. Santosh Jedhe attacked lustily before being caught in the covers, but Mongia thrived on missed chances and reached an unbeaten century in 211 minutes. He hit a six and 14 fours and faced 144 balls in what was his fifth first-class century. Mongia had an outstanding match, took

Ten wickets in the Irani Cup match for Bhupinder Singh senior and international recognition. (Mueen-ud-Din Hameed/Sports-Line)

ten catches, a record, and was later to win his first Test cap. He played for Dulwich in the Surrey Championship three seasons ago.

Needing 367 to win, Punjab ended the fourth day on 101 for 2, with Sidhu and Gursharan in full flow. They continued well on the last morning, but once they were separated Punjab fell apart against the off-spin of Chauhan. The last eight wickets went down for 28 runs, and Rest of India retained the trophy. Chauhan took four wickets in seven balls without a run being scored.

DULEEP TROPHY

10, 11, 12 and **13** October 1993 *at Municipal Corporation Ground, Rajkot*

West Zone 551 for 8 dec. (V.G. Kambli 151, S.V. Manjrekar 144 not out, R.J. Shastri 77, K.S. More 58, S.R. Tendulkar 52)

IRANI CUP – PUNJAB v. REST OF INDIA
1, 2, 3, 4 and 5 October 1993 at Punjab University Agricultural Ground, Ludhiana

REST OF INDIA

	FIRST INNINGS		SECOND INNINGS	
A.D. Jadeja	c A.K. Sharma, b Bhupinder	64	c A.K. Sharma, b Bhupinder	7
W.V. Raman	c A.K. Sharma, b Bhupinder	0	c A.K. Sharma, b Bhupinder	20
Saurav C. Ganguly	c Gursharan, b Bhupinder	1	lbw, b Kamal	8
S.V. Manjrekar (capt)	c Gursharan, b Bedi	49	lbw, b Bhupinder	0
R.S. Dravid	c A.K. Sharma, b Bedi	93	c Kamal, b Vij	29
S.V. Jedhe	c A.K. Sharma, b Bhupinder	76	c Rathore, b Bedi	43
*N.R. Mongia	c Mohan, b Bedi	11	not out	100
R.K. Chauhan	c A.K. Sharma, b Bhupinder	6	lbw, b Vij	19
P.S. Vaidya	c Sidhu, b Kamal	15	b Kamal	17
K.N.A. Padmanabhan	lbw, b Bhupinder	0	c A.K. Sharma, b Kamal	3
Venkatesh Prasad	not out	11	c Kapoor, b Bhupinder	0
Extras	b 5, lb 8, w 6, nb 2	21	b 6, nb 1	7
		347		253

PUNJAB

	FIRST INNINGS		SECOND INNINGS	
V. Rathore	c Mongia, b Jadeja	74	c Mongia, b Vaidya	6
N.S. Sidhu	c Mongia, b Vaidya	0	c Jedhe, b Ganguly	88
K. Mohan	c Jedhe, b Prasad	12	(6) c Mongia, b Chauhan	0
Gursharan Singh (capt)	c Mongia, b Jadeja	64	c Mongia, b Ganguly	51
Amit Sharma	c Mongia, b Prasad	1	c Mongia, b Chauhan	4
A.R. Kapoor	c Jadeja, b Vaidya	15	(3) c Jedhe, b Prasad	18
*Arun K. Sharma	c Mongia, b Ganguly	23	c Jadeja, b Chauhan	0
Bhupinder Singh snr	c Jadeja, b Ganguly	7	b Chauhan	0
O. Kamal	not out	10	lbw, b Chauhan	2
B. Vij	c Mongia, b Vaidya	9	b Padmanabhan	4
A. Bedi	c Dravid, b Vaidya	2	not out	4
Extras	lb 3, w 7, nb 7	17	lb 4, w 3, nb 1	8
		234		185

	O	M	R	W	O	M	R	W
Bhupinder Singh snr	34.2	9	103	9	34.4	6	81	4
Bedi	26	6	76	3	17	5	53	1
Kamal	25.3	9	76	1	27	4	72	3
Vij	14	2	47	–	13	2	38	2
Kapoor	8	2	32	–	3	–	3	–

	O	M	R	W	O	M	R	W
Venkatesh Prasad	29	13	44	2	20	8	33	1
Vaidya	23.3	2	69	4	16	6	40	1
Ganguly	11	5	17	2	11	6	15	2
Chauhan	20	3	58	–	12	6	29	5
Padmanabhan	4	1	15	–	4.5	1	11	1
Jedhe	4	–	7	–	12	3	34	–
Jadeja	8	–	21	2	7	1	19	–

FALL OF WICKETS

1–3, 2–16, 3–120, 4–145, 5–290, 6–310, 7–317, 8–321, 9–321
1–14, 2–40, 3–40, 4–47, 5–94, 6–149, 7–191, 8–234, 9–250

FALL OF WICKETS

1–2, 2–27, 3–149, 4–154, 5–179, 6–181, 7–206, 8–213, 9–224
1–16, 2–37, 3–157, 4–175, 5–175, 6–175, 7–175, 8–175, 9–181

Umpires: A.L. Naramasimhan & R.T. Ramachandran

Rest of India won by 181 runs

South Zone 289 (A. Vaidya 55, A. Kuruvilla 4 for 85) and 207 (R.J. Shastri 5 for 55)

West Zone won by an innings and 55 runs

West Zone 6 pts., South Zone 0 pts.

at Moti Baug Palace Grounds, Baroda

Central Zone 250 (P.K. Amre 71, A.R. Kapoor 4 for 60) and 361 (P.K. Amre 104 not out, A.R. Khurasiya 103, Yusuf Ali Khan 62, Maninder Singh 4 for 70)

North Zone 708 for 9 dec. (A.D. Jadeja 264, Ajay K. Sharma 151, A.R. Kapoor 103 not out, N.S. Sidhu 57, R.K. Chauhan 5 for 195)

North Zone won by an innings and 97 runs

North Zone 6 pts., Central Zone 0 pts.

Prolific scoring in the Duleep Trophy, 1100 runs in the season and a recall to the Test side for Sanjay Manjrekar (David Munden/Sports-Line)

The Duleep Trophy had a changed format in 1993–4. Instead of the traditional knock-out competition, a league programme was played with each zone meeting the others so increasing the number of matches from four to ten. The first two matches saw resounding victories for the West and North Zones. Shastri's return was marked by a fine all-round performance. Bhave was out first ball, but Shastri and Kambli put on 216 for the second wicket. Kambli was in dominant form and hit 4 sixes and 18 fours in his 151. Manjrekar hit 144 off 206 balls, and Tendulkar, leading a first-class side for the first time, declared late on the second day. South Zone was bowled out twice by an attack which had ample variety and in which Ankola and Kuruvilla were impressive.

North Zone, too, could field a balanced attack although Kapil Dev allowed himself only eight overs in the match. He was needed on the first day when Central Zone were bowled out for 250 with skipper Amre alone offering real resistance. North Zone lost Prabhakar for 4, but Sidhu and Jadeja added 145. Jadeja went on to reach his highest score in first-class cricket. He hit 3 sixes and 32 fours in an innings which lasted 566 minutes. He faced 441 balls and added 319 for the third wicket with Ajay Sharma. Kapoor inflicted more pain on the Central bowlers with his maiden first-class hundred off 112 balls. Chauhan bowled nobly to finish with 5 for 195 in 51 overs, but poor Hirwani, once India's first choice leg-spinner, had 1 for 225 in 53 overs.

*Opening batsman and opening bowler for India in the Hero Cup –
Manoj Prabhakar. (Sporting Pictures (UK) Ltd)*

Facing an innings defeat, Central Zone showed spirit through Yusuf Ali Khan and Khurasiya who put on 147 for the second wicket. Khurasiya scored 82 of the first hundred of this partnership. Amre then scored an unbeaten century, but he could not stave off defeat.

19, 20, 21 and **22** October 1993 *at Race Course Ground, Rajkot*

East Zone 206 (C.S. Pandit 67, Saurav Ganguly 51,
   J. Srinath 4 for 41) and 80

South Zone 333 (Robin Singh 109, V.B. Chandrasekhar
   67, J. Srinath 55, U. Chatterjee 4 for 57)

South Zone won by an innings and 47 runs

South Zone 6 pts., East Zone 0 pts.

at Moti Baugh Palace Ground, Baroda

West Zone 187 (S.V. Manjrekar 63, S.S. Bhave 55) and
   169 (S.V. Jedhe 51)

North Zone 403 (Ajay K. Sharma 110, Bhupinder Singh
   snr 50)

North Zone won by an innings and 47 runs

North Zone 6 pts., West Zone 0 pts.

Beaten by an innings in their opening match, South Zone reversed their fortunes in the second. Test bowlers Srinath and Kumble were too much for East Zone while Robin Singh's 17th first-class hundred and Srinath's 55 off 94 balls at number ten took South Zone to a winning score.

Like East Zone, West Zone chose to bat when they won the toss, but the North took a grip on the game on the first day and never relinquished it. Ajay Sharma hit 110 off 156 balls, and Bhupinder Singh senior and Obaid Kamal put on 87 for the last wicket. When West Zone batted a second time Shastri was at number seven. He had been off the field for 53 minutes with a thigh injury and, under a new experimental rule, he had to stay off the field for that length of time when his team batted.

28, 29, 30 and **31** October 1993 *at Sardar Patel Stadium, Valsad*

North Zone 170 (Venkatesh Prasad 7 for 38) and 99
   (S. Subramaniam 5 for 14, Robin Singh 4 for 30)

South Zone 200 (S. Sharath 61, Robin Singh 60,
   O. Kamal 4 for 25) and 73 for 3

South Zone won by 7 wickets

South Zone 6 pts., North Zone 0 pts.

at Wankhede Stadium, Bombay

East Zone 462 (C.S. Pandit 125, S.J. Kalyani 114,
   S.T. Banerjee 81, S.S. Karim 60, N.D. Hirwani 4 for 133)

Central Zone 197 (P.K. Dwevedi 50, P.S. Vaidya 4 for
   41) and 242 (G.K. Pandey 106 not out, U. Chatterjee
   4 for 80)

East Zone won by an innings and 23 runs

East Zone 6 pts., Central Zone 0 pts.

Anil Kumble, a master bowler in all forms of cricket. (David Munden/ Sports-Line)

Having won their first two matches by an innings, North Zone found themselves beaten inside three days by South Zone. They were put in to bat and lost seven wickets on a shortened first day. Karnataka's Venkatesh Prasad completed the best bowling performance of his career on the second morning, and a stand of 128 for the fifth wicket between Robin Singh and Sharath gave South Zone a slight advantage. Skipper Robin Singh and Subramaniam, who finished with match figures of 5 for 14 off 10.1 overs, then routed North Zone who lost their last seven wickets for nine runs.

East Zone recovered from their trauma of the previous match, and moved from 58 for 3 to reach a match-winning 462, although their last three wickets went for one run. Pandey played an heroic rearguard action for Central. His 106 came off 163 balls, the next highest score was 21.

6, 7, 8, 9 and **10** November 1993 *at Lalbhai Contractor Stadium, Vesu, Surat*

West Zone 235 (S.V. Manjrekar 113) and 103 (S.T. Banerjee 6 for 48)

East Zone 439 (S.S. Karim 79, L.S. Rajput 73, Iqbal Siddiqui 4 for 97)

East Zone won by an innings and 101 runs

East Zone 6 pts., West Zone 0 pts.

at Poona Club Ground, Pune

Central Zone 252 (M.S. Mudgal 65, G.K. Pandey 64, Robin Singh 4 for 50) and 387 (Rizwan Shamshad 141, P.V. Gandhe 80, M. Venkataramana 4 for 77)

South Zone 200 (D. Vasu 77, N.D. Hirwani 4 for 72) and 154 (N.D. Hirwani 5 for 48)

Central Zone won by 285 runs

Central Zone 6 pts., South Zone 0 pts.

East Zone batted consistently to take a commanding lead over West Zone for whom Manjrekar had been a lone hand. Bhave batted throughout West Zone's second innings, becoming the first batsman to carry his bat through an innings in the Duleep Trophy. He finished on 28.

The match in Pune was not completed until early on the fifth morning. It was a tense match in which runs never came freely. Central Zone's key figures were Rizwan Shamshad who reached his fourth first-class hundred and Hirwani who had match figures of 9 for 120 in 50 overs, a marked contrast to his figures in the opening match of the competition.

15, 16, 17, 18 and **19** November 1993 *at Wankhede Stadium, Bombay*

West Zone 407 (R.J. Shastri 87, N.R. Mongia 81, T.B. Arothe 63, H.A. Kinikar 56) and 328 for 6 dec. (R.J. Shastri 126, S.V. Manjrekar 116, N.D. Hirwani 4 for 109)

Central Zone 424 (Rizwan Shamshad 133, G.K. Pandey 104, Yusuf Ali Khan 63, A. Kuruvilla 4 for 71) and 232 (G.K. Pandey 72, Iqbal Siddiqui 5 for 55)

West Zone won by 79 runs

West Zone 6 pts., Central Zone 2 pts.

at Poona Club Ground, Pune

North Zone 415 (Rajesh Puri 151, Bhupinder Singh snr 73) and 274 for 8 dec. (Bantoo Singh 63, A.D. Jadeja 62)

East Zone 329 (S.S. Karim 78, L.S. Rajput 64, C.S. Pandit 60) and 208 for 6 (C.J. Sharma 60, S.S. Karim 52 not out, A.D. Jadeja 4 for 99)

Match drawn

North Zone 2 pts., East Zone 0 pts.

Solid batting took West Zone to an impressive score, but Central countered with century partnerships between Yusuf Ali Khan and Shamshad, and Shamshad and Pandey. Nevertheless, the eight and ninth wickets fell at 400, and it was left to Hirwani and Abhay Sharma to steer Central Zone to a first-innings lead. Manjrekar hit his third century in four matches, and he and Shastri put on 148 for the third wicket when the West batted again. Manjrekar's runs came off 132 balls, and his fast scoring helped his side claim second place. Central Zone collapsed before Iqbal Siddiqui who took five wickets in an innings in a Duleep Trophy match for the first time.

At Pune, Rajesh Puri hit his first Duleep Trophy century and added 104 for the sixth wicket with Bhupinder Singh senior who hit his highest score in first-class cricket. North Zone took a lead on the first innings on the fifth morning after rain had ruled out play on the third day. They then scored briskly and left East Zone 23 overs' batting. East Zone needed to score at 10 runs an over in order to overtake West Zone and claim second spot. They made a bold attempt. Sharma hit 60 off 40 balls, Rajput 41 off 28, and Karim 52 off 43, but they fell just short of the required rate. Jadeja had the remarkable figures of 4 for 99 in 12 overs.

DULEEP TROPHY FINAL TABLE

	P	W	L	D	Pts.	RR
North Zone	4	2	1	1	14	–
West Zone	4	2	2	–	12	3.00
East Zone	4	2	1	1	12	2.98
South Zone	4	2	2	–	12	2.81
Central Zone	4	1	3	–	8	–

 ## DEODHAR TROPHY

16 October 1993 *at Municipal Corporation Ground, Rajkot*

South Zone 220 for 2 (W.V. Raman 84, M. Azharuddin 75 not out)

West Zone 177 for 6

South Zone (4 pts.) won by 43 runs.

at Indian Petrochemical Corp. Ltd. Ground, Baroda

Central Zone 165

North Zone 168 for 3 (N.S. Sidhu 104 not out)

North Zone (4 pts.) won by 7 wickets

25 October 1993 *at Municipal Corporation Ground, Rajkot*

Match abandoned

East Zone 2 pts., South Zone 2 pts.

at Indian Petrochemical Corp. Ltd. Ground, Baroda

Match abandoned

North Zone 2 pts., West Zone 2 pts.

3 November 1993 *at Wankhede Stadium, Bombay*

Central Zone 189 (Abinash Kumar 4 for 46)

East Zone 190 for 3 (Tarun Kumar 61)

East Zone (4 pts.) won by 7 wickets

at Lalbhai Contractor Stadium, Vesu, Surat

South Zone 82 (O. Kamal 4 for 15)

North Zone 68 (Venkatesh Prasad 6 for 18)

South Zone (4 pts.) won by 14 runs

11 November 1993 *at Nehru Stadium, Pune*

South Zone 207 for 7 (V.B. Chandrasekhar 77)

Central Zone 210 for 9 (M.S. Mudgal 75, Rizwan Shamshad 50, R.A. Swaroop 4 for 37)

Central Zone (4 pts.) won by 1 wicket

at Sardar Patel Stadium, Bulsar

East Zone 283 for 5 (Saurav Ganguly 109, C.S. Pandit 58 not out, S.J. Kalyani 54)

West Zone 228 (S.V. Manjrekar 64, A.C. Bedade 53)

East Zone (4 pts.) won by 55 runs

21 November 1993 *at Wankhede Stadium, Bombay*

Central Zone 72

West Zone 74 for 0

West Zone (4 pts.) won by 10 wickets

at Nehru Stadium, Pune

Match abandoned

East Zone 2 pts., North Zone 2 pts.

The 50-over competition between the zones bears the name of the great Indian cricketer Dinkar Balwant Deodhar, who died at the age of 101 years 7 months just a few weeks before the beginning of the 1993–4 tournament which was badly hit by the weather and which produced some amazingly low scores. The opening match at Rajkot was reduced to 30 overs and three other games were abandoned. Sidhu hit his first century in the competition as North Zone beat Central Zone. Sidhu dominated the innings, for the next highest score was 17. Without Sidhu, North Zone were bowled for the lowest score in the history of the competition, 68 against South Zone. Venkatesh Prasad took 6 for 18 in 10 overs, the best figures ever recorded in the Deodhar Trophy.

The most thrilling game was at Pune where Sodhi and Majithia scored the 11 runs needed to beat South Zone. When they came together Central Zone were 197 for 9.

DEODHAR TROPHY FINAL TABLE

	P	W	L	Ab.	Pts.
East Zone	4	2	–	2	12
South Zone	4	2	1	1	10
North Zone	4	1	1	2	8
West Zone	4	1	2	1	6
Central Zone	4	1	3	–	4

The international limited-over competition to celebrate the Diamond Jubilee of the Bengal Cricket Association proved to be a great success, attracting good crowds and producing some entertaining cricket. Each country selected a party of 15 players.

For Zimbabwe, Ranchod joined the tour late and did not play in any of the matches. Rennie, Whittal and Streak were all introduced to international cricket.

Jadeja replaced Sidhu in the Indian party when the latter was injured, and R.J. Ratnayake replaced Gurusinha in the Sri Lankan party when Gurusinha was forced to return home due to injury. Sri Lanka did not call upon Dassanayake in the tournament.

West Indies used all 15 players, but South Africa did not call upon D.B. Rundle or E.L.R. Stewart.

The competition began with a comfortable win for India over Sri Lanka. Javagal Srinath returned his best figures in a one-day international and, in spite of the fact that Kapil Dev bowled seven wides, Sri Lanka were restricted to 203 and bowled out in the final over. Mahanama hit 73 off 124 balls. Raman was out first ball, but Kambli and Azharuddin put on 100 for the third wicket. Kambli's 78 came off 105 balls, and Azharuddin, who was to enjoy a splendid tournament, hit 2 sixes and 4 fours in his 75 which also came off 105 balls.

Sri Lanka were in action again two days later when Ranatunga won the toss and asked West Indies to bat first. He was rewarded with the wickets of Haynes and Simmons, but Lara hit 11 fours and Adams made 55 off as many deliveries to revive the momentum of the West Indian innings. More significantly, Anderson Cummins hit 41 off 19 balls, and the last five overs of the innings realised 50 runs. This proved to be the difference between the two sides. An opening spell of 3 for 4 in six overs from Winston Benjamin rocked Sri Lanka. Hashan Tillekeratne reached an outstanding maiden century in limited-over international cricket, his 104 coming off only 110 balls, but it was the bowling of Benjamin which won the match. He finished with his best figures in a one-day international.

Only nine overs were possible in the game between South Africa and Zimbabwe. Zimbabwe had just enjoyed the success of dismissing Hudson when the rain arrived.

Rain affected the fourth match, delaying the start by 80 minutes and reducing the contest to 40 overs each side. West Indies asked South Africa to bat first. Having lost three wickets for 52, South Africa were revived by Cullinan and Rhodes who scored 65 off 67 balls. Cullinan reached a maiden fifty in limited-over international cricket before retiring unwell with the score on 136 for 5. West Indies were restricted by some tight bowling and by the brilliant fielding of Jonty Rhodes who established a record for a one-day international when he held five catches.

Patna became the 31st ground in India to host a one-day international when the Moin-ul-Haq Stadium staged

Mohammad Azharuddin led his country to success in a Test match for the ninth time and averaged over 100 in the series against Sri Lanka. (Ben Radford/Allsport)

the match between Sri Lanka and Zimbabwe. Put in to bat, Sri Lanka owed much to de Silva and Ranatunga who hit 96 off 108 balls. Ratnayake's 32 off 15 balls boosted the score in the final stages of the innings. Campbell and Waller showed spirit for Zimbabwe, but the left-arm spinner Sanath Jayasuriya bowled well, and Sri Lanka won with ease.

Careful innings by Richardson and Arthurton restored substance to the West Indian innings against India after Lara and Simmons had gone cheaply. They added 78 in 20.3 overs. India collapsed to 55 for 6, and play was halted in the 17th over when West Indian fielders were pelted with missiles. The crowd of 50,000 was eventually quietened, but the violence and bad light resulted in a 48-minute stoppage, and India's target was reduced to 170 in 38 overs. It did not matter as they were bowled out for 100 in 28.3 overs.

India seemed to have recovered their form in the match against Zimbabwe. Raman went for 0, but Prabhakar hit 91 off 126 balls and shared a second-wicket stand of 122 off 185 balls with Kambli. The fireworks came from Azharuddin who hit 54 from 56 deliveries. Zimbabwe began badly, but consistent application kept them in touch with the required run rate. The last over arrived with 10 runs needed, and from Prabhakar's last ball, two were needed. Streak struck well, but he hesitated in going for the second run. Azharuddin's throw to Yadav was true, and the match was tied. The teams shared the points under the rules of the competition.

South Africa gained a comfortable win over Sri Lanka who were undermined by the bowling of Snell. The pace bowler returned his best figures in a one-day international. Similarly, Zimbabwe were crushed by West Indies two days later. Harper and Cummins put on 43 in 25 balls for West Indies' seventh wicket. Zimbabwe were bowled out for their lowest score in a limited-over international.

The final match in the qualifying league saw India beat South Africa with ease to claim a place in the semi-finals. A stand of 88 in 19 overs between Jadeja and Kambli gave substance to the Indian innings, and Azharuddin joined Kambli in a partnership of 51 in 11 overs. The Indian total was a moderate one, and when Rhodes and Cronje joined in a stand of 68 South Africa looked likely winners. In the 28th over, Jadeja came on to bowl. He immediately knocked back Cronje's middle stump, and from that point South Africa were a beaten side. This was the first game of cricket to be played at the Punjab Cricket Association Stadium in Mohali which is some seven miles from Chandigarh. It was therefore the 32nd ground and the 29th town or city in India to host a one-day international.

LEAGUE TABLE

	P	W	L	Ab.	Tie	Pts.
West Indies	4	3	1	–	–	6
South Africa	4	2	1	1	–	5
India	4	2	1	–	1	5
Sri Lanka	4	1	3	–	–	2
Zimbabwe	4	–	2	1	1	2

South Africa took second place on run rate differential, 0.54 as opposed to India's 0.08, while Sri Lanka were placed ahead of Zimbabwe by virtue of more victories.

SEMI-FINALS

In the first day/night match to be played in Calcutta, India beat South Africa by a very narrow margin. A crowd of 90,000 watched the game in which a third umpire, using the television monitor, was employed in a match in India for the first time. There was gloom for the crowd early on when Jadeja was the first to go, and Prabhakar and Kambli were out within two balls of each other, both given out by television umpire Bansal at the request of Bucknor. They were the first of seven run-outs in the match. When Tendulkar fell to Snell India were 53 for 4.

Azharuddin and Amre revived India with a stand of 95 in 26.1 overs. Azharuddin hit a six and 7 fours in his 90 which came off 118 balls, and he, more than anyone, took India to the reasonable score of 195.

Hudson was dropped three times as he hit 62 off 111 deliveries, and when McMillan got into his stride, hitting 48 off 54 balls, South Africa looked certain winners. They needed 45 off 30 balls, and when the last over arrived they required six with two wickets standing. Jadeja ran out Richardson, and Ankola's return to Yadav beat de Villiers. Only three runs were scored, and India snatched an astonishing victory by two runs. Tendulkar was the last-over hero.

The other semi-final provided a more decisive outcome. Put in to bat, Sri Lanka seemed likely to be bowled out cheaply before de Silva and Kalpage joined in a record sixth-wicket stand of 109 from 116 balls. Aravinda de Silva, playing his 125th one-day international, hit a six and 4 fours, and his 68 came from 78 deliveries. He hit 38 runs from the last 18 balls he received.

Sri Lanka's 188 never looked like being a winning score, but it took on massive proportions when the medium-pacer Wickramasinghe trapped Haynes leg before second ball with his in-swinger and then had Simmons magnificently caught in the slips by Mahanama. That was the end of the Sri Lankan celebrations. Arthurton joined Lara in a stand worth 163, and Lara batted effortlessly until being bowled by Muralitharan in the 38th over. Richardson came in, and the game was won with 8.1 overs to spare.

FINAL

A crowd of 100,000 saw India outplay West Indies in the final and so win a major limited-over trophy on their own soil for the first time. India were put in to bat and began steadily. Impetus was given to the innings by Kambli and Azharuddin who added 80 off 87 balls. Ambrose ran out Kambli by kicking the ball onto the stumps, and India scored only eight runs off 36 balls as three wickets fell between the 37th and 43rd overs. Tendulkar and Kapil Dev restored pride with 42 in 9.2 overs, and 225 looked a reasonable score. Simmons went quickly but by the 15th over West Indies were 57 for 1. They then lost three wickets in three overs before Holder and Hooper added 38. Kumble dismissed them both, and his final spell saw him take the last six wickets for four runs in 20 balls. His 6 for 12 represented the best figures by an Indian bowler in a one-day international.

Azharuddin was named as Player of the Tournament. He scored 311 runs, average 77.15, which was the outstanding batting performance in every respect. Winston Benjamin with 14 wickets was the leading bowler. Kumble had 13 wickets, and Srinath 12. Tillekeratne hit the only century of the competition.

HERO CUP – MATCH ONE – INDIA *v.* SRI LANKA
7 November 1993 at Green Park, Kanpur

SRI LANKA		
R.S. Mahanama	lbw, **b** Chauhan	73
A.P. Gurusinha	c Yadav, **b** Srinath	11
S.T. Jayasuriya	c Sharma, **b** Srinath	7
P.A. de Silva	run out	33
A. Ranatunga (capt)	c and **b** Tendulkar	1
H.P. Tillekeratne	c Srinath, **b** Prabhakar	35
*R.S. Kaluwitharana	c Sharma, **b** Chauhan	20
D.K. Liyanage	c Kapil Dev, **b** Srinath	4
R.S. Kalpage	c Kumble, **b** Srinath	3
C.P.H. Ramanayake	not out	3
G.P. Wickramasinghe	c Kapil Dev, **b** Srinath	0
Extras	lb **5**, w **8**	13
(49.4 overs)		203

INDIA		
M. Prabhakar	c Kalpage, **b** Wickramasinghe	20
W.V. Raman	lbw, **b** Wickramasinghe	0
V.G. Kambli	c Ramanayake, **b** Liyanage	78
M. Azharuddin (capt)	not out	75
S.R. Tendulkar	not out	26
Ajay K. Sharma		
Kapil Dev		
*V. Yadav		
A.R. Kumble		
R.K. Chauhan		
J. Srinath		
Extras	lb **4**, w **2**	6
(44.4 overs)	(for 3 wickets)	205

	O	M	R	W
Prabhakar	7	2	27	1
Kapil Dev	7	–	30	–
Srinath	6.4	1	24	5
Kumble	10	–	46	–
Tendulkar	10	2	27	1
Chauhan	6	–	28	2
Sharma	3	–	16	–

	O	M	R	W
Wickramasinghe	6	1	13	2
Ramanayake	5.4	–	31	–
Liyanage	7	–	40	1
Ranatunga	3	–	19	–
Tillekeratne	9	–	39	–
Jayasuriya	6	–	32	–
Kalpage	8	–	27	–

FALL OF WICKETS
1–43, **2**–53, **3**–116, **4**–117, **5**–147, **6**–175, **7**–188, **8**–200, **9**–202

FALL OF WICKETS
1–1, **2**–46, **3**–146

Umpires: S.U. Bucknor & I.D. Robinson   *Man of the Match:* J. Srinath   *India won by 7 wickets*

HERO CUP – MATCH TWO – WEST INDIES *v.* SRI LANKA
9 November 1993 at Wankhede Stadium, Bombay

WEST INDIES		
B.C. Lara	c Muralitharan, **b** Ranatunga	67
D.L. Haynes (capt)	c Mahanama, **b** Wickramasinghe	0
P.V. Simmons	c Mahanama, **b** Liyanage	3
C.L. Hooper	**b** Ranatunga	38
K.L.T. Arthurton	st Kaluwitharana, **b** Muralitharan	6
J.C. Adams	st Kaluwitharana, **b** Kalpage	55
R.A. Harper	lbw, **b** Kalpage	20
*J.R. Murray	not out	11
A.C. Cummins	c sub (Ramanayake), **b** Kalpage	41
W.K.M. Benjamin	not out	0
C.A. Walsh		
Extras	b **1**, lb **18** w **8**	27
(50 overs)	(for 8 wickets)	268

SRI LANKA		
R.S. Mahanama	lbw, **b** Benjamin	11
U.C. Hathurusinghe	**b** Benjamin	1
S.T. Jayasuriya	c Haynes, **b** Benjamin	2
H.P. Tillekeratne	**b** Benjamin	104
D.P. Samaraweera	c and **b** Harper	25
A. Ranatunga (capt)	st Murray, **b** Hooper	14
*R.S. Kaluwitharana	c Arthurton, **b** Hooper	10
R.S. Kalpage	not out	29
D.K. Liyanage	**b** Benjamin	3
M. Muralitharan	not out	4
G.P. Wickramasinghe		4
Extras	b **1**, lb **14**, w **2**, nb **2**	19
(50 overs)	(for 8 wickets)	222

	O	M	R	W
Wickramasinghe	10	2	54	1
Liyanage	8	–	24	1
Hathurusinghe	2	–	22	–
Ranatunga	10	1	44	2
Kalpage	10	–	64	3
Muralitharan	10	1	41	1

	O	M	R	W
Walsh	8	2	25	–
Benjamin	10	3	22	5
Cummins	8	2	37	–
Harper	5	–	36	1
Simmons	10	–	38	–
Hooper	9	–	49	2

FALL OF WICKETS
1–10, **2**–26, **3**–104, **4**–111, **5**–172, **6**–211, **7**–220, **8**–268

FALL OF WICKETS
1–10, **2**–16, **3**–21, **4**–72, **5**–118, **6**–143, **7**–204, **8**–214

Umpires: S.K. Bansal & R.T. Ramchandran   *Man of the Match:* W.K.M. Benjamin   *West Indies won by 46 runs*

HERO CUP – MATCH THREE – SOUTH AFRICA v. ZIMBABWE
10 November 1993 at M. Chinnaswamy Stadium, Bangalore

SOUTH AFRICA				ZIMBABWE	
K.C. Wessels (capt)	not out		10	*A. Flower (capt)	
A.C. Hudson	lbw, **b** Brain		5	G.W. Flower	
W.J. Cronje	not out		4	A.D.R. Campbell	
D.J. Cullinan				A.C. Waller	
J.N. Rhodes				D.L. Houghton	
D.J. Callaghan				M.H. Dekker	
B.M. McMillan				I.P. Butchart	
*D.J. Richardson				S.G. Peall	
C.R. Matthews				J. Rennie	
P.S. de Villiers				D.H. Brain	
A.A. Donald				H. Streak	
Extras	w 3		3	Extras	
(9 overs)	(for 1 wicket)		22		

	O	M	R	W
Brain	5	–	12	1
Streak	4	–	10	–

FALL OF WICKET

1–18

Umpires: P.D. Reporter & S.K. Sharma

Match abandoned

HERO CUP – MATCH FOUR – SOUTH AFRICA v. WEST INDIES
14 November 1993 at Brabourne Stadium, Bombay

SOUTH AFRICA			WEST INDIES		
A.C. Hudson	c Simmons, **b** K.C.G. Benjamin	5	B.C. Lara	c Rhodes, **b** Snell	7
K.C. Wessels (capt)	c Lara, **b** Ambrose	3	D.L. Haynes	c Rhodes, **b** Snell	28
W.J. Cronje	lbw, **b** Hooper	12	P.V. Simmons	c Rhodes, **b** Symcox	29
D.J. Cullinan	retired ill	70	K.L.T. Arthurton	st Richardson, **b** Symcox	16
J.N. Rhodes	**b** W.K.M. Benjamin	40	C.L. Hooper	lbw, **b** Cronje	17
B.M. McMillan	**b** W.K.M. Benjamin	24	R.B. Richardson (capt)	c and **b** Cronje	1
*D.J. Richardson	not out	17	*J.C. Adams	c Rhodes, **b** Symcox	4
P.L. Symcox	not out	3	A.C. Cummins	c Rhodes, **b** Donald	17
R.P. Snell			W.K.M. Benjamin	c Cronje, **b** McMillan	0
P.S. de Villiers			C.E.L. Ambrose	c Snell, **b** McMillan	0
A.A. Donald			K.C.G. Benjamin	not out	7
Extras	lb **2**, w **3**, nb **1**	6	Extras	b **4**, lb **7**, w **2**	13
(40 overs)	(for 5 wickets)	180	(37 overs)		139

	O	M	R	W			O	M	R	W
Ambrose	8	1	23	1		Donald	5	–	15	–
K.C.G. Benjamin	8	–	41	1		de Villiers	5	2	5	–
W.K.M. Benjamin	8	–	40	2		Snell	6	–	30	2
Cummins	8	1	43	–		McMillan	5	–	25	2
Hooper	8	–	31	1		Symcox	8	1	20	3
						Cronje	8	1	33	2

FALL OF WICKETS

1–9, 2–11, 3–52, 4–117, 5–176

FALL OF WICKETS

1–14, 2–50, 3–73, 4–78, 5–87, 6–95, 7–120, 8–124, 9–131

Umpires: V.K. Ramaswamy & R.C. Sharma   *Man of the Match:* J.N. Rhodes   *South Africa won by 41 runs*

HERO CUP – MATCH FIVE – SRI LANKA v. ZIMBABWE

15 November 1993 at Moin-ul-Haq Stadium, Patna

SRI LANKA				ZIMBABWE		
R.S. Mahanama	c Dekker, b Brain	16		*A. Flower (capt)	run out	11
S.T. Jayasuriya	c Waller, b Brain	23		D.H. Brain	lbw, b Ratnayake	2
H.P. Tillekeratne	lbw, b Omarshah	24		A.D.R. Campbell	c Ratnayake, b Jayasuriya	37
P.A. de Silva	c and b Omarshah	68		D.L. Houghton	b Liyanage	12
A. Ranatunga (capt)	c Rennie, b Dekker	59		A.C. Waller	c Tillekeratne, b Ranatunga	55
D.K. Liyanage	b Rennie	8		M.H. Dekker	lbw, b Ranatunga	1
R.J. Ratnayake	not out	32		G. Whittal	b Jayasuriya	36
*R.S. Kaluwitharana	not out	4		A.H. Omarshah	b Jayasuriya	14
R.S. Kalpage				S.G. Peall	c Kalpage, b Tillekeratne	12
M. Muralitharan				H. Streak	st Kaluwitharana, b Jayasuriya	5
G.P. Wickramasinghe				J. Rennie	not out	3
Extras	b 18, lb 5, w 15, nb 1	29		Extras	b 5, lb 4, w 9, nb 2	20
(50 overs)	(for 6 wickets)	263		(49 overs)		208

	O	M	R	W		O	M	R	W
Brain	10	1	45	2	Wickramasinghe	6	1	13	–
Streak	8	–	67	–	Ratnayake	7	–	12	1
Rennie	9	–	37	1	Liyanage	10	1	36	1
Peall	10	–	35	–	Muralitharan	10	–	43	–
Omarshah	10	–	50	2	Kalpage	6	–	46	–
Dekker	3	–	16	1	Jayasuriya	4	–	19	4
					Ranatunga	5	–	24	2
					Tillekeratne	1	–	6	1

FALL OF WICKETS

1–38, 2–49, 3–114, 4–210, 5–221, 6–225

FALL OF WICKETS

1–6, 2–22, 3–53, 4–130, 5–132, 6–133, 7–188, 8–189, 9–202

Umpires: K. Parthasarathy & Dr S. Chowdhury   Man of the Match: A. Ranatunga   *Sri Lanka won by 55 runs*

HERO CUP – MATCH SIX – INDIA v. WEST INDIES

16 November 1993 at Gujarat Stadium, Motera, Ahmedabad

WEST INDIES				INDIA		
B.C. Lara	b Kumble	23		M. Prabhakar	c Adams, b Walsh	11
P.V. Simmons	run out	9		Kapil Dev	lbw, b Ambrose	1
R.B. Richardson (capt)	c Kambli, b Kumble	41		V.G. Kambli	c Lara, b Benjamin	10
K.L.T. Arthurton	b Kumble	41		M. Azharuddin (capt)	c Ambrose, b Simmons	23
C.L. Hooper	c Yadav, b Srinath	8		S.R. Tendulkar	lbw, b Walsh	2
*J.C. Adams	not out	26		W.V. Raman	c Lara, b Benjamin	4
R.I.C. Holder	c Chauhan, b Srinath	10		Ajay K. Sharma	b W.K.M. Benjamin	0
R.A. Harper	run out	2		*V. Yadav	st Adams, b Hooper	20
W.K.M. Benjamin	not out	14		A.R. Kumble	c Benjamin, b Hooper	14
C.E.L. Ambrose				R.K. Chauhan	not out	3
C.A. Walsh				J. Srinath	c Harper, b Hooper	2
Extras	b 1, lb 21, w 6	28		Extras	lb 2, w 8	10
(50 overs)	(for 7 wickets)	202		(28.3 overs)		100

	O	M	R	W		O	M	R	W
Prabhakar	10	1	50	–	Ambrose	6	–	18	1
Srinath	10	1	33	2	Walsh	7	2	25	2
Kapil Dev	8	–	21	–	Simmons	5	–	19	1
Kumble	10	1	24	3	Benjamin	6	–	27	3
Chauhan	10	2	41	–	Hooper	4.3	1	9	3
Tendulkar	2	–	11	–					

FALL OF WICKETS

1–34, 2–36, 3–114, 4–128, 5–157, 6–177, 7–186

FALL OF WICKETS

1–12, 2–18, 3–37, 4–40, 5–55, 6–55, 7–77, 8–85, 9–96

Umpires: I.D. Robinson & K.E. Liebenberg   Man of the Match: W.K.M. Benjamin   *West Indies won by 69 runs (adjusted target)*

HERO CUP – MATCH SEVEN – INDIA v. ZIMBABWE
18 November 1993 at Nehru Stadium, Indore

INDIA		
M. Prabhakar	st A. Flower, b Peall	91
W.V. Raman	c Houghton, b Brain	0
V.G. Kambli	c Rennie, b Peall	55
*V. Yadav	c G.W. Flower, b Peall	0
M. Azharuddin (capt)	not out	54
S.R. Tendulkar	c and b Streak	24
P.K. Amre	not out	1
Kapil Dev		
A.R. Kumble		
R.K. Chauhan		
J. Srinath		
Extras	b 4, lb 8, w 8, nb 3	23
(50 overs)	(for 5 wickets)	248

ZIMBABWE		
*A. Flower (capt)	st Yadav, b Chauhan	56
G.W. Flower	b Prabhakar	2
A.D.R. Campbell	b Srinath	7
D.L. Houghton	lbw, b Kapil Dev	22
A.C. Waller	c Azharuddin, b Tendulkar	32
G. Whittal	run out	33
A.H. Omarshah	c Chauhan, b Srinath	37
S.G. Peall	c Yadav, b Srinath	17
D.H. Brain	c Azharuddin, b Prabhakar	1
H. Streak	run out	11
J. Rennie	not out	9
Extras	lb 10, w 11	21
(50 overs)		248

	O	M	R	W
Brain	10	–	37	1
Streak	10	2	44	1
Rennie	9	–	36	–
Omarshah	5	–	31	–
Peall	10	–	54	3
G.W. Flower	6	–	34	–

	O	M	R	W
Prabhakar	10	–	41	2
Srinath	10	–	44	3
Tendulkar	8	–	48	1
Kapil Dev	6	–	31	1
Kumble	8	–	42	–
Chauhan	8	–	32	1

FALL OF WICKETS
1–6, 2–128, 3–128, 4–197, 5–239

FALL OF WICKETS
1–10, 2–23, 3–67, 4–131, 5–143, 6–207, 7–208, 8–212, 9–237

Umpires: K.E. Leibenberg & S.U. Bucknor   *Man of the Match:* M. Prabhakar   *Match tied*

HERO CUP – MATCH EIGHT – SOUTH AFRICA v. SRI LANKA
19 November 1993 at Nehru Stadium, Guwahati

SOUTH AFRICA		
K.C. Wessels (capt)	st Kaluwitharana, b Muralitharan	53
A.C. Hudson	c Kaluwitharana, b Ratnayake	5
W.J. Cronje	b Muralitharan	28
D.J. Cullinan	b Jayasuriya	41
J.N. Rhodes	c Mahanama, b Jayasuriya	16
B.M. McMillan	not out	31
P.L. Symcox	b Jayasuriya	4
R.P. Snell	b Ratnayake	20
*D.J. Richardson	not out	1
P.S. de Villiers		
A.A. Donald		
Extras	lb 7, w 6, nb 2	15
(50 overs)	(for 7 wickets)	214

SRI LANKA		
R.S. Mahanama	c Richardson, b Donald	10
S.T. Jayasuriya	c Richardson, b Snell	27
H.P. Tillekeratne	lbw, b Snell	4
P.A. de Silva	lbw, b Snell	2
A. Ranatunga (capt)	lbw, b Symcox	6
*R.S. Kaluwitharana	c Rhodes, c Cronje	17
R.S. Kalpage	c de Villiers, b Cronje	1
R.J. Ratnayake	run out	21
D.K. Liyanage	c Cronje, b de Villiers	16
G.P. Wickramasinghe	b Snell	17
M. Muralitharan	not out	0
Extras	lb 5, w 4, nb 6	15
(40.1 overs)		136

	O	M	R	W
Wickaramasinghe	6	–	29	–
Ratnayake	8	2	24	2
Liyanage	5	1	27	–
Muralitharan	10	1	36	2
Kalpage	10	1	39	–
Jayasuriya	7	–	31	3
de Silva	4	–	21	–

	O	M	R	W
Donald	8	–	25	1
de Villiers	9	1	17	1
Snell	7.1	2	12	4
McMillan	5	–	26	–
Cronje	6	1	21	2
Symcox	5	–	30	1

FALL OF WICKETS
1–18, 2–81, 3–101, 4–132, 5–163, 6–171, 7–212

FALL OF WICKETS
1–25, 2–48, 3–50, 4–59, 5–78, 6–80, 7–81, 8–109, 9–135

Umpires: V.K. Ramaswamy & Dr S. Chowdhury   *Man of the Match:* R.P. Snell   *South Africa won by 78 runs*

HERO CUP – MATCH NINE – WEST INDIES *v.* ZIMBABWE
21 November 1993 at Lal Bahadur Shastri Stadium, Hyderabad

WEST INDIES

B.C. Lara	c Streak, b Brain	4
D.L. Haynes	run out	75
P.V. Simmons	lbw, b Streak	0
R.B. Richardson (capt)	c A. Flower, b Streak	5
R.I.C. Holder	c Brandes, b Peall	50
K.L.T. Arthurton	run out	16
R.A. Harper	b Rennie	26
A.C. Cummins	c Brain, b Rennie	26
W.K.M. Benjamin	run out	8
K.C.G. Benjamin	not out	1
*J.R. Murray		
Extras	b 2, lb 9, w 9, nb 2	22
(50 overs)	(for 9 wickets)	233

ZIMBABWE

*A. Flower (capt)	c Haynes, b K.C.G. Benjamin	22
G.W. Flower	c Simmons, b W.K.M. Benjamin	7
A.D.R. Campbell	lbw, b W.K.M. Benjamin	0
D.L. Houghton	c Murray, b Simmons	22
A.C. Waller	b Simmons	9
G. Whittal	c Cummins, b Harper	9
S.G. Peall	b Cummins	10
D.H. Brain	c Harper, b Simmons	1
H. Streak	not out	0
J. Rennie	lbw, b Cummins	0
E.A. Brandes	absent injured	–
Extras	lb 9, w 5, nb 5	19
(36.3 overs)		99

	O	M	R	W
Brain	6	1	24	1
Streak	10	2	44	2
Rennie	9	–	42	2
Brandes	9.3	–	56	–
Peall	10	–	34	1
Campbell	5	–	16	–
Whittal	0.3	–	6	–

	O	M	R	W
K.C.G. Benjamin	7	1	19	1
W.K.M. Benjamin	6	2	13	2
Cummins	5.3	–	19	2
Simmons	10	–	23	3
Harper	8	2	16	1

FALL OF WICKETS
1–10, 2–24, 3–38, 4–130, 5–156, 6–169, 7–212, 8–231

FALL OF WICKETS
1–23, 2–23, 3–43, 4–67, 5–80, 6–88, 7–91, 8–98, 9–99

Umpires: R.C. Sharma & S.K. Bansal   *Man of the Match:* D.L. Haynes   *West Indies won by 134 runs*

HERO CUP – MATCH TEN – INDIA *v.* SOUTH AFRICA
22 November 1993 at Punjab C.A. Stadium, Mohali

INDIA

M. Prabhakar	lbw, b de Villiers	1
A.D. Jadeja	run out	39
V.G. Kambli	b Cronje	86
S.R. Tendulkar	c Richardson, b Cronje	3
M. Azharuddin (capt)	run out	31
P.K. Amre	c Donald, b Cronje	2
Kapil Dev	c Wessels, b de Villiers	22
*V. Yadav	b Snell	2
A.R. Kumble	run out	2
J. Srinath	c Hudson, b Snell	1
S.A. Ankola	not out	2
Extras	b 1, lb 10, w 16, nb 3	30
(49.2 overs)		221

SOUTH AFRICA

A.C. Hudson	lbw, b Kapil Dev	27
K.C. Wessels (capt)	c Yadav, b Srinath	1
W.J. Cronje	b Jadeja	39
J.N. Rhodes	lbw, b Ankola	56
D.J. Callaghan	c Kapil Dev, b Jadeja	6
B.M. McMillan	lbw, b Kumble	2
*D.J. Richardson	not out	23
P.L. Symcox	b Prabhakar	2
R.P. Snell	c Kumble, b Ankola	2
P.S. de Villiers	c Yadav, b Ankola	1
A.A. Donald	not out	5
Extras	lb 4, w 7, nb 3	14
(50 overs)	(for 9 wickets)	178

	O	M	R	W
Donald	8	–	39	–
de Villiers	8.2	–	27	2
Snell	10	–	54	2
McMillan	10	–	45	–
Cronje	10	–	29	3
Symcox	3	–	16	–

	O	M	R	W
Prabhakar	10	–	36	1
Srinath	7	1	22	1
Ankola	10	1	33	3
Kapil Dev	8	1	32	1
Kumble	10	–	35	1
Jadeja	5	1	16	2

FALL OF WICKETS
1–6, 2–94, 3–129, 4–180, 5–188, 6–192, 7–192, 8–199, 9–211

FALL OF WICKETS
1–7, 2–40, 3–108, 4–124, 5–127, 6–144, 7–147, 8–150, 9–157

Umpires: S.U. Bucknor & I.D. Robinson   *Man of the Match:* V.G. Kambli   *India won by 43 runs*

HERO CUP – SEMI-FINAL – INDIA *v.* SOUTH AFRICA
24 November 1993 at Eden Gardens, Calcutta

INDIA				SOUTH AFRICA		
M. Prabhakar	run out	3		K.C. Wessels (capt)	lbw, **b** Srinath	5
A.D. Jadeja	lbw, **b** de Villiers	6		A.C. Hudson	**b** Kumble	62
V.G. Kambli	run out	4		W.J. Cronje	run out	13
M. Azharuddin (capt)	**c** Richardson, **b** Snell	90		D.J. Cullinan	lbw, **b** Kapil Dev	10
S.R. Tendulkar	**c** Richardson, **b** Snell	15		J.N. Rhodes	**c** Azharuddin, **b** Jadeja	16
P.K. Amre	run out	48		B.M. McMillan	not out	48
Kapil Dev	run out	7		P.L. Symcox	**c** Amre, **b** Jadeja	6
*V. Yadav	**c** Rhodes, **b** de Villiers	3		R.P. Snell	st Yadav, **b** Kumble	1
A.R. Kumble	**c** McMillan, **b** Snell	0		*D.J. Richardson	run out	15
J. Srinath	**b** de Villiers	4		P.S. de Villiers	run out	0
S.A. Ankola	not out	2		A.A. Donald	not out	1
Extras	lb **5**, w **5**, nb **3**	13		Extras	lb **9**, w **4**, nb **3**	16
(50 overs)		195		(50 overs)	(for 9 wickets)	193

	O	M	R	W			O	M	R	W
Donald	8	–	44	–		Prabhakar	8	1	30	–
de Villiers	10	1	19	3		Srinath	8	–	39	1
Snell	8	–	33	3		Kapil Dev	8	–	31	1
McMillan	9	–	41	–		Ankola	6	–	21	–
Cronje	9	–	25	–		Kumble	10	–	29	2
Symcox	6	–	28	–		Jadeja	9	–	31	2
						Tendulkar	1	–	3	–

FALL OF WICKETS

1–12, **2**–18, **3**–18, 4–53, **5**–148, **6**–173, 7–184, **8**–189, 9–192

FALL OF WICKETS

1–10, **2**–45, **3**–65, 4–106, **5**–130, **6**–141, 7–145, **8**–189, 9–191

Umpires: S.U. Bucknor & I.D. Robinson   *Man of the Match:* M. Azharuddin   *India won by 2 runs*

HERO CUP – SEMI-FINAL – WEST INDIES *v.* SRI LANKA
25 November 1993 at Eden Gardens, Calcutta

SRI LANKA				WEST INDIES		
R.S. Mahanama	lbw, **b** Cummins	31		B.C. Lara	**b** Muralitharan	82
S.T. Jayasuriya	**c** Simmons, **b** Benjamin	18		D.L. Haynes	lbw, **b** Wickramasinghe	0
H.P. Tillekeratne	lbw, **b** Cummins	11		P.V. Simmons	**c** Mahanama, **b** Wickramasinghe	0
P.A. de Silva	run out	68		K.L.T. Arthurton	not out	72
A. Ranatunga (capt)	**c** Lara, **b** Hooper	2		R.B. Richardson (capt)	not out	15
*R.S. Kaluwitharana	**b** Hooper	1		C.L. Hooper		
R.S. Kalpage	not out	41		*J.C. Adams		
R.J. Ratnayake	not out	2		A.C. Cummins		
M. Muralitharan				W.K.M. Benjamin		
C.P.H. Ramanayake				C.E.L. Ambrose		
G.P. Wickramasinghe				C.A. Walsh		
Extras	lb **11**, w **3**	14		Extras	lb **2**, w **12**, nb **7**	21
(50 overs)	(for 6 wickets)	188		(41.5 overs)	(for 3 wickets)	190

	O	M	R	W			O	M	R	W
Ambrose	10	–	59	–		Wickramasinghe	6	–	27	2
Walsh	10	3	33	–		Ramanayake	3	–	18	–
Benjamin	10	2	29	1		Ratnayake	4	–	11	–
Cummins	10	–	38	2		Kalpage	9.5	–	47	–
Hooper	10	3	18	2		Muralitharan	10	–	37	1
						Jayasuriya	2	–	14	–
						de Silva	3	–	16	–
						Ranatunga	4	–	18	–

FALL OF WICKETS

1–33, **2**–63, **3**–68, 4–73, **5**–77, **6**–186

FALL OF WICKETS

1–2, **2**–3, **3**–166

Umpires: S.K. Bansal & Dr S. Chowdhury   *Man of the Match:* B.C. Lara   *West Indies won by 7 wickets*

INDIA			WEST INDIES		
M. Prabhakar	c Adams, b Ambrose	11	B.C. Lara	b Tendulkar	33
A.D. Jadeja	c Richardson, b W.K.M. Benjamin	30	P.V. Simmons	b Prabhakar	0
V.G. Kambli	run out	68	R.B. Richardson (capt)	c and b Kapil Dev	18
M. Azharuddin (capt)	c Adams, b Cummins	38	K.L.T. Arthurton	lbw, b Kapil Dev	5
S.R. Tendulkar	not out	28	R.I.C. Holder	b Kumble	15
P.K. Amre	lbw, b Cummins	0	C.L. Hooper	lbw, b Kumble	23
Kapil Dev	c Hooper, b Cummins	24	*J.C. Adams	c Azharuddin, b Kumble	4
*V. Yadav	b Ambrose	3	A.C. Cummins	b Kumble	1
A.R. Kumble	not out	5	W.K.M. Benjamin	b Kumble	3
J. Srinath			C.E.L. Ambrose	b Kumble	0
Venkatapathy Raju			K.C.G. Benjamin	not out	0
Extras	b 2, lb 12, w 2, nb 2	18	Extras	lb 12, w 8, nb 1	21
(50 overs)	(for 7 wickets)	225	(40.1) overs		123

	O	M	R	W		O	M	R	W
Ambrose	10	1	35	2	Prabhakar	6	–	21	1
K.C.G. Benjamin	10	1	35	–	Srinath	6	–	12	–
W.K.M. Benjamin	10	1	47	1	Jadeja	1	–	18	–
Cummins	10	1	38	3	Kapil Dev	10	3	18	2
Hooper	8	–	42	–	Tendulkar	7	1	24	1
Simmons	2	–	14	–	Kumble	6.1	2	12	6
					Venkatapathy Raju	4	–	6	–

FALL OF WICKETS

1–25, 2–81, 3–161, 4–161, 5–161, 6–207, 7–218

FALL OF WICKETS

1–1, 2–57, 3–57, 4–63, 5–101, 6–113, 7–118, 8–122, 9–122

Umpires: K.E. Liebenberg & I.D. Robinson   *Man of the Match:* A.R. Kumble   *India won by 102 runs*

SRI LANKAN TOUR

13, 14 and 15 January 1994 *at Ferozeshah Kotla Ground, Delhi*

Sri Lankan XI 157 for 9 dec. (N.D. Hirwani 4 for 49)
President's XI 34 for 1

Match drawn

Sri Lanka's preparatory match before the first Test match was ruined by rain. No play was possible on days one and two.

FIRST TEST MATCH
INDIA v. SRI LANKA, at Lucknow

India gave a first Test cap to Nayan Mongia who had played club cricket for Dulwich in the Surrey Championship three years ago; Azharuddin won the toss, and India batted.

The first day's Test cricket at Lucknow for 42 years was notable for a flamboyant innings from Navjot Singh

India's new wicket-keeper Nayan Mongia enjoyed a fine debut series. (Mueen-ud-Din Hameed/Sports-Line)

Sidhu who hit his fifth and highest Test century. Always renowned for his powerful hitting, Sidhu struck 8 sixes and 9 fours. Once considered an unthinking slogger, Sidhu has learned to build an innings and to restrain himself in the early stages of his knock. At lunch, he was on 27, but he cut loose in the afternoon.

Muralitharan was hit for 30 in his first three overs, and six of Sidhu's sixes came off the off-spinner. With Tendulkar, Sidhu added 121 before being caught at long-on.

Tendulkar, unbeaten on 88 as India closed at 269 for 3, dominated a fourth-wicket stand of 142 with Azharuddin. The 20-year old soon reached his seventh Test century on the second day after fog had delayed the start for 75 minutes, and when he was dismissed the later batsmen showed style and panache.

Manjrekar celebrated his return to Test cricket with an innings of 61, and Mongia hit 44 off 55 balls. The day ended with India all out for 511.

Sri Lanka began well in reply as Mahanama and Samaraweera scored 120 for the first wicket, but an hour after lunch on the third day, Mahanama swept at Kumble and Mongia ran from behind the stumps to catch the ball in front of the wicket on the leg side. Next ball Samaraweera was leg before to Chauhan, and Sri Lanka now crumbled.

Ranatunga was out to a slog. Aravinda de Silva was brilliantly caught close to the bat by Azharuddin, and six wickets fell in the space of 20 overs with only wicket-keeper Dassanayake showing the necessary character and determination.

Having closed on 197 for 7, Sri Lanka were hustled out for the addition of 21 more runs when play resumed after the rest day. Following-on, they batted in the second innings much as they had done in the first. They reached 100 for 1, but after lunch Anil Kumble, who took the individual award, wrought havoc. He was aided by some rash batting, but his figures of 7 for 59 were the best of his career and a testament to his quality as a bowler. Once more India were victorious with more than a day to spare.

SECOND TEST MATCH
INDIA v. SRI LANKA, at Bangalore

India were unchanged for the second encounter while Sri Lanka replaced Liyanage with Jayasuriya. Once again Azharuddin won the toss, and once again India batted.

FIRST TEST MATCH – INDIA v. SRI LANKA
18, 19, 20 and 22 January 1994 at Babu Stadium, Lucknow

INDIA

FIRST INNINGS		
M. Prabhakar	lbw, b Liyanage	21
N.S. Sidhu	c Kalpage, b Muralitharan	124
V.G. Kambli	run out	5
S.R. Tendulkar	c Samaraweera, b Anurasiri	142
M. Azharuddin (capt)	c Tillekeratne, b Anurasiri	47
S.V. Manjrekar	c and b Muralitharan	61
Kapil Dev	c Wickramasinghe, b Muralitharan	42
*N.R. Mongia	c Samaraweera, b Muralitharan	44
A.R. Kumble	b Wickramasinghe	4
R.K. Chauhan	c Tillekeratne, b Muralitharan	3
Venkatapathy Raju	not out	5
Extras	lb 3, w 2, nb 8	13
		511

SRI LANKA

	FIRST INNINGS		SECOND INNINGS	
R.S. Mahanama	c Mongia, b Kumble	73	c Azharuddin, b Kumble	45
D.P. Samaraweera	lbw, b Chauhan	42	lbw, b Kumble	12
H.P. Tillekeratne	c Mongia, b Kumble	7	c Prabhakar, b Kumble	47
P.A. de Silva	c Azharuddin, b Kumble	13	b Kumble	11
A. Ranatunga (capt)	c Chauhan, b Raju	9	c Mongia, b Kumble	0
R.S. Kalpage	c Azharuddin, b Kumble	2	c Kumble, b Raju	2
*P.B. Dassanayake	st Mongia, b Raju	36	b Prabhakar	15
D.K. Liyanage	lbw, b Prabhakar	12	c Mongia, b Chauhan	23
S.D. Anurasiri	b Prabhakar	2	lbw, b Kumble	4
G.P. Wickramasinghe	lbw, b Kapil Dev	6	not out	0
M. Muralitharan	not out	9	b Kumble	0
Extras	lb 7	7	b 5, lb 6, w 4	15
		218		**174**

	O	M	R	W
Wickramasinghe	20	3	84	1
Liyanage	17	6	55	1
Ranatunga	3	2	1	–
Anurasiri	58	13	147	2
Kalpage	22	2	59	–
Muralitharan	41.3	3	162	5

	O	M	R	W	O	M	R	W
Prabhakar	16.4	7	36	2	16	3	38	1
Kapil Dev	10	3	27	1	3	–	8	–
Venkatapathy Raju	20	10	25	2	14	5	28	1
Kumble	37	10	69	4	27.3	9	59	7
Chauhan	23	7	54	1	12	2	30	1

FALL OF WICKETS

1–53, 2–84, 3–205, 4–347, 5–370, 6–446, 7–458, 8–482, 9–501

FALL OF WICKETS

1–120, 2–120, 3–132, 4–149, 5–149, 6–158, 7–191, 8–197, 9–208
1–29, 2–100, 3–109, 4–109, 5–122, 6–122, 7–162, 8–174, 9–174

Umpires: R.C. Sharma & S. Venkataraghavan

India won by an innings and 119 runs

Sri Lanka's attack was dominated by spin, but the spinners had neither the control nor the venom of their Indian counterparts, and the home side flourished.

The pitch had plenty of bounce, but the Indian batsmen showed remarkable technical ability in a thrilling display. Prabhakar was caught behind in the first session. Sidhu and Kambli responded by adding 148 in 189 minutes. Both batsmen looked certain to score centuries, yet both fell to their first errors of judgement. Kambli, believing a fielder was being moved, lofted to long-on, and Sidhu was leg before swinging across the line although he asserted he touched the ball. Tendulkar now let fly with a barrage of shots, and he moved from 50 to 90 off 26 deliveries towards the end of the day which came with India in total control on 339 for 3.

Tendulkar failed to reach his hundred on the second morning, but Azharuddin made no mistake. With 13 fours and a six, he reached his 13th Test century, and his wristy stroke-play delighted the crowd and mocked Sri Lanka's defensive field-placings. Kapil Dev entertained with a bright 53 which included a massive six off Muralitharan, and Azharuddin declared, leaving Sri Lanka 70 minutes to negotiate at the end of the second day. They failed badly, losing Samaraweera to a catch at slip and de Silva to a rash hook.

Mahanama and Ranatunga moved confidently forward on the third day, but when they had added 35 to the overnight score Ranatunga was palpably leg before to Kapil Dev who now scented Richard Hadlee's record of 431 Test wickets. Mahanama gave Kumble a return catch, and from that point only Kalpage, with his maiden fifty in Test cricket, withstood the Indian bowling for long. Inevitably, it seemed, Sri Lanka followed-on, for this was now the established pattern of Indian success. That success was within their grasp by the end of the day, for seven Sri Lankan wickets were captured for 179 runs. There was aggression from Tillekeratne, and Mahanama was unfortunate in that a hard drive ricocheted off Azharuddin's knee into the hands of the bowler. Much of the rest of the batting was very poor.

The Indian win was assured, but what now became the centre of interest was how close Kapil Dev could get to Hadlee's record. Kumble complicated matters by having Kalpage leg before, but in the next over Wickramasinghe was caught at mid-off off Kapil. Kumble now bowled wide of the stumps as Kapil made his final effort. Having failed with his yorker, he produced an outswinger which Anurasiri edged to first slip. Kapil Dev was level with Richard Hadlee and was carried from the field. Incidentally, India had won by an innings.

SECOND TEST MATCH – INDIA v. SRI LANKA
26, 27, 29 and 30 January 1994 at Chinnaswamy Stadium, Bangalore

INDIA

FIRST INNINGS		
M. Prabhakar	c Dassanayake, b Wickramasinghe	14
N.S. Sidhu	lbw, b Muralitharan	99
V.G. Kambli	c Wickramasinghe, b Muralitharan	82
S.R. Tendulkar	b Anurasiri	96
M. Azharuddin (capt)	lbw, b Muralitharan	108
S.V. Manjrekar	c Mahanama, b Muralitharan	39
Kapil Dev	not out	53
*N.R. Mongia	not out	18
A.R. Kumble		
R.K. Chauhan		
Venkatapathy Raju		
Extras	b 6, lb 6, nb 20	32
	(for 6 wickets, dec.)	541

SRI LANKA

	FIRST INNINGS		SECOND INNINGS	
R.S. Mahanama	c and b Kumble	47	c Azharuddin, b Raju	36
D.P. Samaraweera	c Prabhakar, b Kapil Dev	0	c Tendulkar, b Prabhakar	4
P.A. de Silva	c Chauhan, b Prabhakar	17	(4) lbw, b Raju	8
A. Ranatunga (capt)	lbw, b Kapil Dev	26	(5) c Sidhu, b Kumble	28
S.T. Jayasuriya	c Prabhakar, b Kumble	22	(6) c sub, b Chauhan	1
H.P. Tillekeratne	c Raju, b Kumble	0	(3) c and b Chauhan	80
R.S. Kalpage	lbw, b Kapil Dev	63	lbw, b Kumble	18
*P.B. Dassanayake	lbw, b Prabhakar	16	lbw, b Kumble	0
S.D. Anurasiri	c Tendulkar, b Prabhakar	4	c Azharuddin, b Kapil Dev	7
G.P. Wickramasinghe	c Mongia, b Prabhakar	8	c Sidhu, b Kapil Dev	1
M. Muralitharan	not out	8	not out	20
Extras	lb 12, nb 8	20	b 9, lb 3	12
		231		215

	O	M	R	W
Wickramasinghe	20	–	98	1
Jayasuriya	8	2	26	–
Muralitharan	65	11	179	4
Ranatunga	4	–	14	–
Anurasiri	45	2	158	1
Kalpage	19	1	54	–

	O	M	R	W	O	M	R	W
Prabhakar	20	4	82	4	3	–	18	1
Kapil Dev	21.1	5	73	3	8.3	1	41	2
Kumble	13	2	50	3	16	3	64	3
Venkatapathy Raju	4	–	14	–	12	2	36	2
Chauhan					16	3	44	2

FALL OF WICKETS

1–34, 2–182, 3–248, 4–372, 5–459, 6–468

FALL OF WICKETS

1–7, 2–36, 3–94, 4–116, 5–132, 6–132, 7–189, 8–196, 9–208

1–5, 2–69, 3–97, 4–164, 5–168, 6–176, 7–179, 8–188, 9–189

Umpires: S.K. Bansal & K. Parathasarathy

India won by an innings and 95 runs

3, 4 and **5** **February 1994** *at Mohali, Chandigarh*

Sri Lankan XI 341 for 7 dec. (H.P. Tillekeratne 176 not
out, D.P. Samaraweera 89, Bhupinder Singh snr 4 for
83) and 187 for 5 dec. (A. Gunawardene 61,
S.T. Jayasuriya 59)

Punjab 234 for 3 dec. (V. Rathore 143 not out,
Bhupinder Singh jnr 52) and 86 for 2

Match drawn

In the first-class match which separated the second and
third Test matches, Hashan Tillekeratne hit the highest
score of his career. Jayasuriya and Gunawardene played
well in the second innings, but neither was to feature in
the final Test. The 'floating' place rather surprisingly
went to Atapattu. For Punjab, there was an impressive
innings from Rathore and some excellent medium-pace
bowling from Bhupinder Singh senior.

THIRD TEST MATCH
INDIA *v.* SRI LANKA, at Ahmedabad

The pattern changed. Sri Lanka won the toss and batted.
What followed was more familiar. The initial attention
was entirely on Kapil Dev, and he did not disappoint. He
had Tillekeratne caught at forward short-leg to give 432
wickets in Test cricket, one more than the record established by Sir Richard Hadlee. Although Hadlee's wickets
had been taken in 86 Tests and Kapil Dev was playing in
his 130th Test, nothing should detract from the Indian's
achievement. Kapil Dev had taken 219 of his wickets in
his own country which other fast bowlers have found to
be a graveyard for their efforts.

With Kapil Dev showered in rose petals and the record
safe, the Indian spinners took over. On a doubtful pitch,
Venkatapathy Raju, in particular, thrived. He was to take
11 wickets in a Test match for the first time, and the only
effective resistance to the Indian spinners in the first
innings came from number ten Wickramasinghe who hit
22 before being lured forward, beaten and easily stumped.

Facing a total of 119, India hit 90 for 1 in 34 overs before
the close. The stroke-play of Sidhu and Kambli mocked
the efforts of the Sri Lankan batsmen.

There was encouragement for Sri Lanka on the second
morning. Kambli flashed wildly at Wickramasinghe, who
showed some promise of genuine pace, Tendulkar drove
impetuously at the same bowler, and Sidhu fell to Muralitharan without addition to the score. Azharuddin alone
played the turning ball with confidence, reaching his 14th
Test hundred, his seventh as captain, and displaying a
masterly technique, patience and utmost concentration.

Azharuddin gained great assistance from Chauhan
who batted without scoring for 71 minutes on the second
evening when India closed on 329 for 8 and who scored
his first run, a boundary, after 85 minutes at the crease.
The ninth-wicket partnership realised 67 before Azharuddin, who batted for six hours, faced 260 balls and hit a
six and 16 fours, finally fell to Muralitharan.

*Venkatapathy Raju bowled India to their sixth innings victory in eight
Test matches, 11 for 125 at Ahmedabad (David Munden/Sports-Line)*

Sri Lanka began their second innings well, but they lost
three wickets for five runs in the last half hour of the day
to slip to 154 for 5. One of those dismissed was Marvan
Atapattu who thereby recorded a 'pair' and extended his
Test record to one run in six innings.

The game was over early on the fourth day so giving
India victory in a home Test for the eighth time in
succession. Six of these wins have been by an innings.
Azharuddin, Man of the Match and Man of the Series,
equalled the record of Gavaskar and the Nawab of
Pataudi junior in leading his country to victory for the
ninth time.

In every respect, the series was one of total triumph for
India.

ONE-DAY INTERNATIONAL SERIES

Having made his Test debut, wicket-keeper Mongia, who
had an excellent start to his international career, played in
limited-over international matches for the first time as did
Vaas, Fernando, Gunawardene and Pushpakumara of Sri
Lanka. Kapil Dev was rested for two matches in the
series.

SRI LANKA

	FIRST INNINGS		SECOND INNINGS	
R.S. Mahanama	lbw, b Kumble	18	lbw, b Raju	63
D.P. Samaraweera	b Chauhan	16	run out	20
H.P. Tillekeratne	c Manjrekar, b Kapil Dev	5	c Azharuddin, b Raju	40
P.A. de Silva	lbw, b Raju	7	c Azharuddin, b Chauhan	14
A. Ranatunga (capt)	c Azharuddin, b Raju	15	c Sidhu, b Raju	29
M.S. Atapattu	b Chauhan	0	c Mongia, b Chauhan	0
R.S. Kalpage	c Azharuddin, b Chauhan	2	c Azharuddin, b Chauhan	9
*P.B. Dassanayake	c Kambli, b Raju	10	not out	21
S.D. Anurasiri	b Raju	4	c Prabhakar, b Raju	6
G.P. Wickramasinghe	st Mongia, b Raju	22	c Prabhakar, b Raju	0
M. Muralitharan	not out	5	c Mongia, b Raju	4
Extras	b 8, lb 7	15	b 4, lb 11, nb 1	16
		119		**222**

INDIA

	FIRST INNINGS	
M. Prabhakar	b Anurasiri	14
N.S. Sidhu	c Kalpage, b Muralitharan	43
V.G. Kambli	c Ranatunga, b Wickramasinghe	57
S.R. Tendulkar	b Wickramasinghe	6
M. Azharuddin (capt)	b Muralitharan	152
S.V. Manjrekar	c Ranatunga, b de Silva	16
Kapil Dev	lbw, b de Silva	4
*N.R. Mongia	lbw, b Anurasiri	14
A.R. Kumble	c Kalpage, b de Silva	15
R.K. Chauhan	b Muralitharan	9
Venkatapathy Raju	not out	1
Extras	b 17, lb 5, nb 5	27
		358

	O	M	R	W	O	M	R	W
Prabhakar	5	–	13	–	5	1	11	–
Kapil Dev	9	4	15	1	5	1	12	–
Kumble	15	3	30	1	28	9	45	–
Venkatapathy Raju	23.5	7	38	5	32.3	9	87	6
Chauhan	11	8	8	3	30	14	45	3
Tendulkar					4	1	7	–

	O	M	R	W
Wickramasinghe	36	9	108	2
Ranatunga	8	1	15	–
Anurasiri	28	3	75	2
Muralitharan	36.3	7	79	3
Kalpage	7	2	9	–
de Silva	23	5	50	3

FALL OF WICKETS

1–34, 2–39, 3–47, 4–59, 5–59, 6–71, 7–79, 8–89, 9–108
1–70, 2–98, 3–149, 4–149, 5–153, 6–167, 7–214, 8–214, 9–222

FALL OF WICKETS

1–27, 2–110, 3–123, 4–123, 5–169, 6–203, 7–249, 8–288, 9–355

Umpires: A.L. Narasimhan & V.K. Ramaswamy

India won by an innings and 17 runs

TEST MATCH AVERAGES – INDIA v. SRI LANKA

INDIA BATTING

	M	Inns	NO	Runs	HS	Av	100s	50s
M. Azharuddin	3	3	–	307	152	102.33	2	–
N.S. Sidhu	3	3	–	266	124	88.66	1	1
S.R. Tendulkar	3	3	–	244	142	81.33	1	1
Kapil Dev	3	3	1	99	52*	49.50	–	1
V.G. Kambli	3	3	–	144	82	48.00	–	1
S.V. Manjrekar	3	3	–	116	61	38.66	–	1
N.R. Mongia	3	3	1	76	44	38.00	–	–
M. Prabhakar	3	3	–	49	21	16.33	–	–
A.R. Kumble	3	2	–	19	15	9.50	–	–
R.K. Chauhan	3	2	–	12	9	6.00	–	–
Venkatapathy Raju	3	2	2	6	5*	–	–	–

INDIA BOWLING

	Overs	Mds	Runs	Wkts	Av	Best	10/m	5/inn
Venkatapathy Raju	106.2	33	228	16	14.25	6-87	1	2
A.R. Kumble	136.3	36	317	18	17.61	7-59	1	1
R.K. Chauhan	92	34	181	10	18.10	3-8	–	–
M. Prabhakar	65.4	16	198	8	24.75	4-82	–	–
Kapil Dev	56.4	14	176	7	25.14	3-73	–	–

Bowled in one innings: S.R. Tendulkar 4–1–7–0

INDIA FIELDING FIGURES

10 – M. Azharuddin; 9 – N.R. Mongia (ct 7/st 2); 5 – M. Prabhakar; 3 – N.S. Sidhu and R.K. Chauhan; 2 – S.R. Tendulkar and A.R. Kumble; 1 – Venkatapathy Raju, V.G. Kambli, S.V. Manjrekar and sub

SRI LANKA BATTING

	M	Inns	NO	Runs	HS	Av	100s	50s
R.S. Mahanama	3	6	–	282	73	47.00	–	2
H.P. Tillekeratne	3	6	–	179	80	29.83	–	1
M. Muralitharan	3	6	4	46	20*	23.00	–	–
P.B. Dassanayake	3	6	1	98	36	19.60	–	–
A. Ranatunga	3	6	–	107	29	17.83	–	–
R.S. Kalpage	3	6	–	96	63	16.00	–	1
D.P. Samaraweera	3	6	–	94	42	15.66	–	–
P.A. de Silva	3	6	–	70	17	11.66	–	–
G.P. Wickramasinghe	3	6	1	37	22	7.40	–	–
S.D. Anurasiri	3	6	–	27	7	4.50	–	–

Played in one Test: D.K. Liyanage 12 & 23; M.S. Atapattu 0 & 0; S.T. Jayasuriya 22 & 1

SRI LANKA BOWLING

	Overs	Mds	Runs	Wkts	Av	Best	10/m	5/inn
M. Muralitharan	143	21	420	12	35.00	5-162	–	1
G.P. Wickramasinghe	76	12	290	4	72.50	2-108	–	–
S.D. Anurasiri	131	18	380	5	76.00	2-75	–	–
A. Ranatunga	15	3	30	0	–	–	–	–
R.S. Kalpage	48	5	122	0	–	–	–	–

Bowled in one innings: D.K. Liyanage 17–6–55–1; P.A. de Silva 23–5–50–3; S.T. Jayasuriya 8–2–26–0

SRI LANKA FIELDING FIGURES

3 – R.S. Kalpage; 2 – G.P. Wickramasinghe, A. Ranatunga, H.P. Tillekeratne and D.P. Samaraweera; 1 – R.S. Mahanama, P.B. Dassanayake and M. Muralitharan

The first match provided a close encounter. Put in to bat, India were given a fine start by Prabhakar and Sidhu who hit a characteristic 108. Three Indian batsmen were run out in the search for quick runs, and Sri Lanka faced a daunting target of 247. Aravinda de Silva hit 69 off 85 balls to raise their hopes, but 16 were still needed when the last over arrived. Srinath won the game for India by bowling both Kalpage and Wickramasinghe.

India clinched the series by winning the second match with some ease. A hostile opening attack gave Sri Lanka great problems after they had been asked to bat first, and they were reduced to 65 for 5. A fine stand of 132 between Kalpage and Ranatunga who made his highest score in a one-day international stopped the rout, but Prabhakar followed his best figures in this type of cricket with 39 in an opening stand of 98 with Sidhu, and India went on to win with 10 balls to spare.

Rain interrupted the third match after India, having been put in to bat, had made 213 from their 50 overs. The Sri Lankan target was twice revised and, ultimately, they required 141 from 33 overs. Fifteen were needed from the last over, which was bowled by Srinath, and de Silva, Man of the Match, and Dassanayake scored the necessary runs to give Sri Lanka their only victory of the tour with one ball to spare.

RANJI TROPHY

SOUTH ZONE

3, 4, 5 and **6** December 1993 *at Panaji Gymkhana, Panaji*

Goa 204 (A. Shetty 71 not out, Suresh Kumar 4 for 64) and 11 for 0

Kerala 353 for 9 dec. (Feroze V. Rasheed 91, V. Narayanan Kutty 63, P.T. Subramaniam 53, A. Shetty 4 for 95)

Match drawn

Kerala 2 pts., Goa 0 pts.

at Indira Gandhi Stadium, Vijayawada

Karnataka 311 for 6 (P.V. Shashikanth 89, J. Arun Kumar 84, R.S. Dravid 54)

v. **Andhra**

Match drawn

Karnataka 1 pt., Andhra 1 pt.

FIRST ONE-DAY INTERNATIONAL – INDIA *v.* SRI LANKA
15 February 1994 at Municipal Ground, Rajkot

INDIA				SRI LANKA		
M. Prabhakar	run out		67	R.S. Mahanama	c and b Tendulkar	35
N.S. Sidhu	c Mahanama, b Vaas		108	D.P. Samaraweera	st Mongia, b Tendulkar	14
V.G. Kambli	run out		25	H.P. Tillekeratne	c Mongia, b Kumble	34
M. Azharuddin (capt)	run out		14	P.A. de Silva	b Kumble	69
S.R. Tendulkar	c Ranatunga, b Kalpage		1	A. Ranatunga (capt)	c Mongia, b Tendulkar	8
P.K. Amre	not out		16	S.T. Jayasuriya	c Kambli, b Kumble	31
Kapil Dev	not out		4	R.S. Kalpage	b Srinath	25
*N.R. Mongia				*U.N.K. Fernando	not out	2
A.R. Kumble				G.P. Wickramasinghe	b Srinath	1
J. Srinath				S.D. Anurasiri	not out	0
R.K. Chauhan				C. Vaas		
Extras	b 1, lb 1, w 8, nb 1		11	Extras	lb 5, w 5, nb 9	19
(50 overs)	(for 5 wickets)		246	(50 overs)	(for 8 wickets)	238

	O	M	R	W		O	M	R	W
Vaas	8	2	40	1	Prabhakar	10	–	53	–
Wickramasinghe	10	2	42	–	Srinath	7	–	37	2
Ranatunga	2	–	18	–	Kapil Dev	6	–	26	–
Anurasiri	7	–	42	–	Tendulkar	8	–	43	3
Kalpage	10	–	37	1	Kumble	10	–	41	3
Jayasuriya	10	–	47	–	Chauhan	9	–	33	–
de Silva	3	–	18	–					

FALL OF WICKETS

1–122, 2–181, 3–211, 4–214, 5–236

FALL OF WICKETS

1–46, 2–66, 3–119, 4–137, 5–200, 6–218, 7–235, 8–238

Umpires: P.D. Reporter & J. Kurishunkal   *Man of the Match:* N.S. Sidhu   *India won by 8 runs*

SECOND OND-DAY INTERNATIONAL – INDIA v. SRI LANKA
18 February 1994 at Lal Bahadur, Hyderabad

SRI LANKA		
R.S. Mahanama	c Tendulkar, b Prabhakar	15
A.A.W. Gunawardene	c Mongia, b Prabhakar	2
H.P. Tillekeratne	c Mongia, b Prabhakar	0
P.A. de Silva	c Chauhan, b Prabhakar	0
A. Ranatunga (capt)	c Mongia, b Prabhakar	98
S.T. Jayasuriya	c Mongia, b Tendulkar	9
R.S. Kalpage	c and b Srinath	51
*U.N.K. Fernando	not out	20
R. Pushpakumara	not out	3
C. Vaas		
M. Muralitharan		
Extras	b 3, lb 10, w 9, nb 6	28
(50 overs)	(for 7 wickets)	226

INDIA		
M. Prabhakar	c Jayasuriya, b Muralitharan	39
N.S. Sidhu	run out	79
V.G. Kambli	not out	56
M. Azharuddin (capt)	c Pushpakumara, b Jayasuriya	16
S.R. Tendulkar	not out	11
P.K. Amre		
Kapil Dev		
*N.R. Mongia		
A.R. Kumble		
J. Srinath		
R.K. Chauhan		
Extras	b 10, lb 7, w 6, nb 3	26
(48.2 overs)	(for 3 wickets)	227

	O	M	R	W
Prabhakar	10	–	35	5
Srinath	10	1	45	1
Kapil Dev	6	1	19	–
Tendulkar	8	–	35	1
Chauhan	9	–	40	–
Kumble	7	–	39	–

	O	M	R	W
Pushpakumara	7.2	–	30	–
Vaas	7	1	22	–
de Silva	6	–	34	–
Muralitharan	10	–	39	1
Jayasuriya	8	–	38	1
Kalpage	10	–	47	–

FALL OF WICKETS
1–3, 2–11, 3–17, 4–31, 5–65, 6–197, 7–217

FALL OF WICKETS
1–98, 2–161, 3–197

Umpires: S. Choudhury & H.K. Sharma   *Man of the Match:* M. Prabhakar   *India won by 7 wickets*

THIRD ONE-DAY INTERNATIONAL – INDIA v. SRI LANKA
20 February 1994 at Burlton Park, Jalhandar

INDIA		
A.D. Jadeja	b Kalpage	37
N.S. Sidhu	b Muralitharan	46
V.G. Kambli	c Tillekeratne, b Muralitharan	12
P.K. Amre	b Jayasuriya	3
S.R. Tendulkar	run out	52
M. Azharuddin (capt)	c Samaraweera, b de Silva	11
*N.R. Mongia	run out	3
J. Srinath	c Samaraweera, b de Silva	7
R.K. Chauhan	not out	26
S.A. Ankola	b Vaas	0
Venkatapathy Raju	not out	1
Extras	b 2, lb 1, w 8, nb 4	15
(50 overs)	(for 9 wickets)	213

SRI LANKA		
R.S. Mahanama	lbw, b Srinath	6
D.P. Samaraweera	run out	49
H.P. Tillekeratne	lbw, b Venkatapathy Raju	23
P.A. de Silva	not out	32
S.T. Jayasuriya	b Venkatapathy Raju	0
A. Ranatunga (capt)	c Mongia, b Venkatapathy Raju	0
R.S. Kalpage	st Mongia, b Tendulkar	4
*P.B. Dassanayake	not out	20
G.P. Wickramasinghe		
C. Vaas		
M. Muralitharan		
Extras	b 2, lb 3, w 2	7
(32.5 overs)	(for 6 wickets)	141

	O	M	R	W
Vaas	10	2	43	1
Wickramasinghe	9	–	34	–
Kalpage	10	–	36	1
Muralitharan	10	2	40	2
Jayasuriya	4	–	27	1
de Silva	7	–	30	2

	O	M	R	W
Srinath	7.5	–	53	1
Ankola	5	–	23	–
Venkatapathy Raju	8	–	19	3
Chauhan	8	2	18	–
Tendulkar	4	–	23	1

FALL OF WICKETS
1–83, 2–102, 3–112, 4–112, 5–136, 6–142, 7–161, 8–209, 9–209

FALL OF WICKETS
1–8, 2–72, 3–88, 4–88, 5–88, 6–99

Umpires: M.R. Singh & K.S. Gridharan   *Man of the Match:* P.A. de Silva   *Sri Lanka won on faster scoring rate at M.A. Chidambaram Stadium, Madras*

Hyderabad 78 for 3
v. **Tamil Nadu**

Match drawn

Hyderabad 1 pt., Tamil Nadu 1 pt.

A more realistic and rewarding points system was introduced in the Ranji Trophy for the 1993–4 season. The emphasis was put on winning, with six points being awarded for a win and two for a first-innings lead. Unfortunately, the first round of matches in the South Zone was ruined by rain. In Panaji, 118 minutes were lost on the third day while there was no play at all on the fourth. There were only 64 minutes' play on the second day in Vijayawada and no play at all thereafter, and Madras suffered worst of all as there were just 135 minutes' play possible on the third day.

11, 12, 13 and **14** December 1993 *at DNR College Ground, Bhimavaram*

Tamil Nadu 208 (M. Senthilnathan 54, Tanveer Jabbar 51, G.V.V. Gopalaraju 5 for 35) and 135
(H. Ramishken 4 for 28)
Andhra 109 (M. Venkataramana 4 for 20) and 112

Tamil Nadu won by 122 runs

Tamil Nadu 6 pts., Andhra 0 pts.

at M. Chinnaswamy Stadium, Bangalore

Karnataka 392 (J. Arun Kumar 141, A. Vaidya 68, S. Joshi 64 not out, P.V. Shashikanth 58, A. Shetty 4 for 113)
Goa 139 (Venkatesh Prasad 5 for 41) and 168
(J. Srinath 4 for 55, R. Ananth 4 for 56)

Karnataka won by an innings and 85 runs

Karnataka 6 pts., Goa 0 pts.

at Nehru Stadium, Kottayam

Hyderabad 176 (V. Jaisimha 57, K.N.A. Padmanabhan 5 for 35) and 268 for 6 dec. (M.V. Sridhar 124, B. Ramprakash 4 for 77, K.N.A. Padmanabhan 4 for 98)
Kerala 65 (Venkatapathy Raju 5 for 18, Arshad Ayub 5 for 28) and 210 (Venkatapathy Raju 5 for 77)

Hyderabad won by 169 runs

Hyderabad 6 pts., Kerala 0 pts.

The second round of matches produced three conclusive victories for the most powerful sides in the zone. In the first first-class match to be played on the DNR College Ground, Ramishken bowled V.B. Chandrasekhar with the first ball of the match. It was a prelude to what was to be a low-scoring game with Tamil Nadu victorious in three days.

The match at Bangalore was also over in three days. Arun Kumar hit 141 off 277 balls in what was only his

second first-class innings and shared an opening stand of 160 with Shashikanth. Dravid took six catches in the match, and Srinath claimed his 50th wicket in 15 Ranji Trophy matches.

Hyderabad's Test spinners, Venkatapathy Raju and Arshad Ayub destroyed Kerala. Arshad Ayub performed the hat-trick when he accounted for Sunder, Ramprakash and Rasheed. On a pitch which always encouraged the bowlers, Sridhar hit 124 off 225 balls with a six and 10 fours. This match, too, ended inside three days.

19, 20, 21 and **22** December 1993 *at M.A. Chidambaram Stadium, Madras*

Tamil Nadu 267 (Robin Singh 112, V.B. Chandrasekhar 62, B. Ramprakash 5 for 90)
Kerala 0 for 0

Match drawn

Tamil Nadu 1 pt., Kerala 1 pt.

at Port Trust Golden Jubilee Stadium, Salagramapuram

Andhra 301 (V. Vijayasarathi 66) and 180 (Pathak 52, S. Mahadevan 6 for 60)
Goa 251 (H. Ramishken 5 for 77) and 148 for 9
(V. Vijayasarathi 4 for 52)

Match drawn

Andhra 2 pts., Goa 0 pts.

at Gymkhana Ground, Secunderabad

Karnataka 252 (R.S. Dravid 60, Arshad Ayub 5 for 78, Venkatapathy Raju 4 for 49) and 227 (K.A. Jeshwanth 68)
Hyderabad 322 (M. Azharuddin 120, Kanwaljit Singh 50) and 158 for 2

Hyderabad won by 8 wickets

Hyderabad 6 pts., Karnataka 0 pts.

Rain returned to ruin Tamil Nadu's match in Madras. There was no play on the second and fourth days. Robin Singh, unbeaten on 99 when joined by the last batsman Sriram who was making his debut, hit 2 sixes and 7 fours in an innings which lasted 343 minutes.

The first first-class match to be staged at Port Trust Golden Jubilee Stadium ended excitingly. Needing 231 to win, Goa reached 102 for 2 before the last 15 overs arrived, but collapsed to 148 for 9 and only just avoided defeat.

The Hyderabad spinners again perplexed the opposition and bowled out Karnataka on the opening day. A captain's innings from Azharuddin, 120 off 169 balls with 11 fours, took Hyderabad to a first-innings lead. This was Azharuddin's fifth Ranji Trophy, but his first for five years so demanding have been international calls. Kanwaljit Singh, batting at number 11, hit a maiden first-class fifty off 57 balls. He then joined with Arshad Ayub and Venkatapathy Raju in bowling out Karnataka, and Hyderabad won comfortably on the last day.

27, 28, 29 and **30** December 1993 *at Nehru Stadium, Kottayam*

Andhra 169 (A. Pathak 53, V. Vijayasarathi 51 not out, K.N.A. Padmanabhan 8 for 57) and 86 (K.N.A. Padmanabhan 6 for 37, Suresh Kumar 4 for 19)

Kerala 232 (P.G. Sunder 103, G.V.V. Gopalaraju 6 for 54) and 27 for 0

Kerala won by 10 wickets

Kerala 6 pts., Andhra 0 pts.

at Dr Rajendra Prasad Stadium, Margao

Hyderabad 362 (M. Azharuddin 155, V. Jaisimha 95, R.D. Kambli 4 for 119)

Goa 88 (Venkatapathy Raju 5 for 23, Arshad Ayub 4 for 26) and 149 (A. Gaekwad 50, M. Sawkar 50, Venka Pratad 4 for 29)

Hyderabad won by an innings and 125 runs

Hyderabad 6 pts., Goa 0 pts.

at M. Chinnaswamy Stadium, Bangalore

Karnataka 148 (M. Venkataramana 5 for 29) and 376 for 7 dec. (R.S. Dravid 151 not out, J. Arun Kumar 68)

Tamil Nadu 222 (J. Srinath 5 for 62) and 171 (A. Kripal Singh 64 not out, Venkatesh Prasad 4 for 31)

Karnataka won by 131 runs

Karnataka 6 pts., Tamil Nadu 2 pts.

With the second-best figures ever recorded for Kerala in the Ranji Trophy, skipper Anantha Padmanabhan bowled Kerala to victory over Andhra with his leg-breaks and googlies. Andhra bowled tightly, but Sunder's 103 off 140 balls turned the match in Kerala's favour before Padmanabhan struck again.

Azharuddin hit 19 fours and 2 sixes in his second century in succession and shared a fourth-wicket stand of 237 with Jaisimha. Not surprisingly, Goa succumbed to Hyderabad's spinners and were beaten in three days. Hyderabad, with three wins in four matches, were assured of a place in the later stages of the competition.

In a match vital to both sides, Karnataka were bowled out for 148 on the first day which ended with Tamil Nadu on 72 for 4. Arjan Singh was out without addition on the second morning, but an eighth-wicket stand of 65 between Subramanian and Gokulkrishnan took Tamil Nadu to first-innings points. Rahul Dravid's patient century, 151 off 320 balls in 392 minutes, tilted the match in favour of Karnataka, and Jeshwant's declaration left Tamil Nadu the last day in which to score 303 to win. They never looked like succeeding against the bowling of Venkatesh Prasad and Kumble. Gokulkrishnan was twice called for throwing. This was only his second Ranji Trophy match, and he had been called for throwing on his debut.

8, 9, 10 and **11** January 1994 *at M.A. Chidambaram Stadium, Madras*

Goa 184 (P.A. Amonkar 58) and 160 (S. Subramanian 5 for 49, M. Venkataramana 4 for 45)

Tamil Nadu 295 (A. Kripal Singh 85, D. Vasu 55, U. Naik 6 for 74) and 53 for 0

Tamil Nadu won by 10 wickets

Tamil Nadu 6 pts., Goa 0 pts.

at M. Chinnaswamy Stadium, Bangalore

Karnataka 265 (R.S. Dravid 105 not out, K.N.A. Padmanabhan 4 for 89) and 136 for 2 (S. Bhat 64 not out, R.S. Dravid 56 not out)

Kerala 89 (Venkatesh Prasad 7 for 37) and 310 (S. Oasis 110, B. Ramprakash 67)

Karnataka won by 8 wickets

Karnataka 6 pts., Kerala 0 pts.

at Gymkhana Ground, Secunderabad

Andhra 263 (G.N. Srinivas 99, M.F. Rehman 73, N.P. Singh 5 for 84) and 180 for 7 (Kanwaljit Singh 4 for 53)

Hyderabad 944 for 6 dec. (M.V. Sridhar 366, V. Jaisimha 211, N. David 207 not out, Abdul Azeem 85)

Match drawn

Hyderabad 2 pts., Andhra 0 pts.

Not surprisingly, Tamil Nadu demolished Goa in three days. Goa's captain Uday Naik dismissed Vasu and Robin Singh with successive deliveries and had Senthilnathan dropped at slip off the next ball to be denied a hat-trick.

Dravid's seventh Ranji Trophy hundred set up Karnataka's victory over Kerala who were bowled out for 89 thanks to a career-best performance from medium-pacer Venkatesh Prasad. Following-on, they were saved from indignity by Sunil Oasis who hit a maiden first-class hundred in what was his fifth match.

History was made in Secunderabad. Winning the toss, Andhra reached 224 for 6 on the first day, Srinivas and Rehman having put on 153 for the second wicket. Hyderabad, without Azharuddin and Venkatapathy Raju, were 763 for 4 by the end of the third day, 467 runs having been scored for the loss of one wicket in 95 overs during the day. When Arshad Ayub finally declared on the fourth day Hyderabad had made 944 for 6, the highest total recorded in the Ranji Trophy and the fourth highest in first-class cricket. Sridhar's 366 in 699 minutes off 523 balls is the highest score made for Hyderabad. His innings included 37 fours and 5 sixes and was one of three scores over 200 in the Hyderabad innings, a world record. Jaisimha, who hit 2 sixes and 31 fours in his 211 off 234 balls shared a fourth-wicket partnership of 344 with Sridhar while Noel David, who was only in the side because Azharuddin was on international duty, shared a fifth-wicket stand of 326. David hit 3 sixes and 22 fours in his 268-ball innings. It was only his second appearance in first-class cricket. He made 15 and 1 on his first appearance. Two bowlers, Gopala Raju and Prakash, conceded 466 runs between them.

Batting a second time 681 runs in arrears, Andhra earned a draw. Former Test bowler Raghuram A. Bhat stood as umpire in this match. It was his debut in this capacity.

SOUTH ZONE FINAL TABLE

	P	W	L	D	Pts.
Hyderabad	5	3	–	2	21
Karnataka	5	3	0	1	19
Tamil Nadu	5	2	1	2	16
Kerala	5	1	2	2	9
Andhra	5	–	2	3	3
Goa	5	–	4	1	0

WEST ZONE

1, 2, 3 and **4** December 1993 *at Shastri Maidan, Vallabh Vidyanagar*

Gujarat 157 (Maqbool Malam 71) and 259
    (M.H. Parmar 69, Nisarg Patel 69, Iqbal Siddiqui 5 for 70)
Maharashtra 460 for 6 dec. (J. Narse 139 not out,
    S.S. Sugwekar 96, H.A. Kinikar 90, S.J. Jadav 50)

Maharashtra won by an innings and 44 runs

Maharashtra 6 pts., Gujarat 0 pts.

at GSFC Sports Complex, Baroda

Bombay 523 (S.V. Manjrekar 156, S.S. Dighe 102,
    V.G. Kambli 75, S.R. Tendulkar 50, T.B. Arothe 5 for 178)
Baroda 279 (A.C. Bedade 133, R.J. Shastri 6 for 73)
    and 126 (N.R. Mongia 51, S.V. Bahutule 4 for 42)

Bombay won by an innings and 118 runs

Bombay 6 pts., Baroda 0 pts.

With Iqbal Siddiqui having match figures of 8 for 135 and Narse scoring a maiden first-class century, Maharastra brushed aside Gujarat.

The might of Bombay was soon in evidence as, put in to bat, they reached 292 for 4 on the first day. Manjrekar and Dighe, who claimed seven victims behind the stumps, extended their partnership to 227 on the second day, both batsmen reaching centuries. By the close of the day, Baroda had lost two wickets to Shastri who finished with 8 for 92 in the match and captured his 100th Ranji Trophy wicket. Bombay won early on the last day.

8, 9, 10 and **11** December 1993 *at Race Course Ground, Rajkot*

Baroda 459 (K.S. Chavan 118, A.C. Bedade 81,
    R.B. Parikh 77, K.S. More 56)

Saurashtra 217 (S.S. Tanna 67, T.B. Arothe 6 for 76)
    and 214 (S. Kotak 82, N.R. Odedra 61, R.G.M. Patel 5 for 33)

Baroda won by an innings and 28 runs

Baroda 6 pts., Saurashtra 0 pts.

at Dadoji Konddev Stadium, Thane

Maharashtra 285 (J. Narse 76, S.V. Jedhe 67) and 75
    (P.L. Mhambre 5 for 35)
Bombay 344 (S.R. Tendulkar 138, Z. Bharucha 93,
    P. Kanade 4 for 77) and 17 for 1

Bombay won by 9 wickets

Bombay 6 pts., Maharashtra 0 pts.

Baroda and Bombay both crushed their opponents in the second round of West Zone matches. Baroda were well served by Chavan who hit his seventh Ranji Trophy century and shared an opening stand of 192 with Parikh, and by the spin of Arothe. The mighty batting of Tendulkar and all-round strength gave Bombay victory in three days.

16, 17, 18 and **19** December 1993 *at Race Course Ground, Rajkot*

Gujarat 380 (M.H. Parmar 138, K. Patadiwala 66,
    R.R. Garsondia 4 for 82) and 154 for 9 dec.
    (B.M. Radia 4 for 48)
Saurashtra 321 (S. Kotak 81, S.S. Tanna 71,
    N.R. Odedra 52, B.H. Mistry 4 for 73) and 163 for 7
    (N.R. Odedra 75, B. Dutta 63, D.T. Patel 4 for 55)

Match drawn

Gujarat 2 pts., Saurashtra 0 pts.

At Poona Club, Pune

Baroda 462 (J.J. Martin 134, A.C. Bedade 122,
    K.S. More 51, Iqbal Siddiqui 7 for 139) and 68 for 1
Maharashtra 451 (A.V. Kale 132, S.S. Bhave 111,
    H.A. Kinikar 65, M.S. Narula 6 for 101)

Match drawn

Baroda 2 pts., Maharashtra 0 pts.

There were five debutants in the Gujarat team, but it was skipper Parmar, who shared in two century stands, who gave the innings substance with 138 in six hours. His side came close to winning when Saurashtra chased a target of 214 in 29 overs and lost seven wickets with only Odedra and Dutta reaching double figures.

Bedade hit his sixth Ranji Trophy hundred and Jacob Martin his first as Baroda piled up a big score in spite of Iqbal Siddiqui's career-best bowling performance. Brave innings from skipper Bhave and Abhijit Kale, a century on his debut, just failed to give Maharashtra first-innings points.

24, 25, 26 and **27** December 1993 *at Sardar Patel Stadium, Ahmedabad*

Bombay 414 (S.V. Manjrekar 146, R.J. Shastri 100) and 7 for 0

Gujarat 125 (S.S. Patil 4 for 35) and 295 (K. Patadiwala 152, S.V. Bahutule 4 for 77)

Bombay won by 10 wickets

Bombay 6 pts., Gujarat 0 pts.

at Nehru Stadium, Pune

Maharashtra 589 for 3 dec. (H.A. Kinikar 184, S.S. Bhave 180, S.V. Jedhe 138 not out, A.V. Kale 58)

Saurashtra 372 (N.R. Odedra 137, S. Kotak 87, P. Kanade 4 for 57) and 193 for 2 (B.M. Jadeja 75, S.S. Tanna 57 not out)

Match drawn

Maharashtra 2 pts., Saurashtra 0 pts.

With Shastri and Manjrekar sharing a second-wicket stand of 178, Bombay moved to a commanding score against Gujarat who were forced to follow-on. That they avoided an innings defeat was entirely due to Patadiwala who hit 152 in his second first-class match. His runs came off 255 balls and included 2 sixes and 20 fours.

Kinikar and Bhave scored 325 for Maharashtra's first wicket before Kinikar was forced to retire hurt. Bhave was out at 375, but Jedhe became the third batsman to reach his century, Kinikar returning later. Odedra's century failed to save his side from having to follow-on, but they avoided defeat.

31 December 1993, **1, 2** and **3** January 1994 *at Wankhede Stadium, Bombay*

Saurashtra 335 (S. Kotak 71, B. Dutta 69) and 190 (P.L. Mhambre 6 for 47, S.A. Ankola 4 for 67)

Bombay 320 (S.V. Manjrekar 68, S.S. Dighe 51, M.P. Rana 5 for 98) and 206 for 2 (R.J. Shastri 93 not out, S.R. Tendulkar 80 not out)

Bombay won by 8 wickets

Bombay 6 pts., Saurashtra 2 pts.

at IPCL Sports Complex, Baroda

Baroda 558 for 8 dec. (J.J. Martin 152 not out, K.S. More 115, N.R. Mongia 87, A.C. Bedade 57, R.P. Parikh 54) and 124 for 6 dec.

Gujarat 216 (Nisarg Patel 55, N. Modi 50) and 163 for 6 (Nisarg Patel 59, N. Bakriwala 56)

Match drawn

Baroda 2 pts., Gujarat 0 pts.

Saurashtra won their first points of the season and astonished all by leading Bombay on the first innings. Indeed,

Atul Bedade scored freely for Baroda and won a place in India's side for the AustralAsia Cup in Sharjah. (Mueen-ud-Din Hameed/Sports-Line)

Saurashtra gave Bombay their hardest fight of the tournament, setting a target of 206 in 41 overs. Bombay won with seven balls to spare thanks to Shastri and Tendulkar who shared an unbroken third-wicket stand of 148 off 169 balls in under two hours.

A seventh-wicket partnership of 251 between Martin and More took Baroda past the 500 mark, but More did not enforce the follow-on, and Gujarat earned a draw.

WEST ZONE FINAL TABLE

	P	W	L	D	Pts.
Bombay	4	4	–	–	24
Baroda	4	1	1	2	10
Maharashtra	4	1	1	2	8
Gujarat	4	–	2	2	2
Saurashtra	4	–	2	2	2

NORTH ZONE

26, 27, 28 and **29** November 1993 *at Ferozeshah Kotla Ground, Delhi*

Delhi 114 (V. Jain 5 for 48, Dhanraj Singh 4 for 19) and 365 for 9 (A.S. Wassan 104 not out, Bantoo Singh 81, M. Nayyar 50, P. Jain 6 for 86)

Haryana 475 (N.R. Goel 166, A. Kaypee 74, Avtar Singh 53, Maninder Singh 5 for 120)

Match drawn

Haryana 2 pts., Delhi 0 pts.

Vineet Jain, making his debut, was the principal reason for the collapse of Delhi on the opening day after they had won the toss and decided to bat. He was ably supported by Dhanraj Singh whose 4 for 19 came from 16.3 overs. Haryana then made their highest score against Delhi with Goel and Avtar Singh, making his debut, putting on 162 for the second wicket. The left-handed Goel reached his second and higher century. Batting again 361 runs in arrears, Delhi were saved from defeat by Bantoo Singh and pace bowler Atul Wassan who reached the second century of his career, batting at number eight. So Haryana were denied their first ever win over Delhi.

2, 3, 4 and 5 December 1993 *at PCA Stadium, Mohali*

Punjab 169 (Bhupinder Singh snr 62, V. Rathore 54, M.V. Rao 7 for 77) and 385 for 8 dec. (A.V. Mehra 136, Bhupinder Singh jnr 100 not out, M.V. Rao 5 for 85)

Services 181 (B. Vij 6 for 67) and 170 (S. Chopra 52, Bhupinder Singh snr 4 for 37)

Punjab won by 203 runs

Punjab 6 pts., Services 2 pts.

Reigning champions Punjab succumbed to a career-best bowling performance by medium-pacer Mathiala Rao. Services' last pair gave them first-innings points, but Ajay Mehra and Bhupinder Singh junior restored order with a third-wicket partnership of 119. Punjab went on to win with ease. Punjab's wicket-keeper Manav Mehra held seven catches on his debut.

8, 9, 10 and 11 December 1993 *at Indira Stadium, Una*

Himachal Pradesh 150 (S. Subramanya 6 for 32) and 137 (R. Bittoo 83, S. Shirsat 5 for 38, P. Maitrey 4 for 30)

Services 381 (S. Chopra 129, S.R. Mohsin 99 not out, R. Vinayak 77, Jeshwant Rai 5 for 125)

Services won by an innings and 94 runs

Services 6 pts., Himachal Pradesh 0 pts.

at PCA Stadium, Mohali

Punjab 525 for 3 dec. (V. Rathore 250, Amit Sharma 97, A.V. Mehra 88, Gursharan Singh 50 not out)

Jammu & Kashmir 243 (A. Gupta 87, B. Vij 7 for 58) and 131 (A. Kapoor 5 for 57, B. Vij 4 for 32)

Punjab won by an innings and 151 runs

Punjab 6 pts., Jammu & Kashmir 0 pts.

As expected, the two minnows of the North Zone were crushed inside three days. Rashid Mohsin, making his debut for Services, was left unbeaten on 99 when the last wicket fell. Record stands of 219 for the first wicket between Rathore and Mehra, and 222 for the second between Rathore and Amit Sharma, took Punjab to their highest score against Jammu and Kashmir. Vikram Rathore hit a six and 24 fours off 334 balls in the highest score of his career. Left-arm spinner Bharti Vij had 11 wickets in the match.

14, 15, 16 and 17 December 1993 *at Punjab Agricultural University, Ludhiana*

Punjab 109 (A.S. Wassan 4 for 13) and 201 (A.S. Wassan 4 for 43)

Delhi 97 (O. Kamal 4 for 29) and 214 for 8 (M. Prabhakar 107 not out)

Delhi won by 4 wickets

Delhi 6 pts., Punjab 2 pts.

at Nahar Singh Stadium, Faridabad

Services 314 (Chinmoy Sharma 74, S. Chopra 61, R. Vinayak 55, P. Jain 5 for 112) and 120 (V. Jain 7 for 45)

Haryana 258 for 7 dec. (Rajesh Puri 143, A. Kaypee 88, Jitender Singh 71, V. Yadav 67, A.D. Jadeja 54, S. Subramanya 4 for 98)

Haryana won by an innings and 98 runs

Haryana 6 pts., Services 0 pts.

at Indira Ground, Una

Himachal Pradesh 223 (R. Bittoo 103, S. Sharma 6 for 66) and 454 for 7 dec. (R. Bittoo 150, R. Nayyar 97, Shambhunath Sharma 74)

Jammu & Kashmir 345 (Sanjay Sharma 75, S. Thakur 5 for 116) and 211 for 6 (R.A. Bali 68, V. Bhakar 52)

Match drawn

Jammu & Kashmir 2 pts., Himachal Pradesh 0 pts.

Bowlers dominated the match in Ludhiana where 19 wickets fell on the first day. Delhi were bowled out for their lowest total against Punjab, but they won the match thanks to a splendid century from Manoj Prabhakar who was leading the side for the first time.

Haryana overwhelmed Services while Ramesh Bittoo became the first Himachal Pradesh player to score a century in each innings, only for his side to be pointless against Jammu and Kashmir.

20, 21, 22 and 23 December 1993 *at PCA Stadium, Mohali*

Punjab 496 for 4 dec. (V. Rathore 155, Bhupinder Singh jnr 132, Gursharan Singh 77 not out, N.S. Sidhu 59, K. Mohan 57)

Himachal Pradesh 135 (N. Gaur 50, B. Vij 6 for 44) and 136 (B. Vij 6 for 32)

Punjab won by an innings and 225 runs

Punjab 6 pts., Himachal Pradesh 0 pts.

at Vishkarma School Ground, Rohtak

Haryana 470 (A. Kaypee 129, Jitender Singh 120,
  A. Gupta 4 for 98, S. Sharma 4 for 128)

Jammu & Kashmir 114 (P. Jain 6 for 32) and 224
  (A.S. Bhatti 69, P. Thakur 5 for 69, P. Jain 5 for 85)

Haryana won by an innings and 132 runs

Haryana 6 pts., Jammu & Kashmir 0 pts.

at Air Force Sports Complex, Palam, Delhi

Services 514 (S. Chopra 186, S. Narula 102) and 68 for
  3

Delhi 389 (S. Dogra 152 not out, V. Dahiya 64,
  P. Maitrey 4 for 89)

Match drawn

Services 2 pts., Delhi 0 pts.

With the five batsmen who went to the crease passing 50 and Vij having match figures of 12 for 76, Punjab routed Himachal Pradesh in three days. Wicket-keeper Arun Sharma had four catches and three stumpings in the match. Haryana also won in three days with Jitender Singh hitting a maiden first-class hundred.

The waning powers of Delhi were in evidence as they struggled against Services for whom Narula hit a maiden first-class century and Chopra hit a career best. Sumeet Dogra, formerly of Haryana, hit a century in his first match for Delhi.

26, 27, 28 and 29 December 1993 *at Indira Ground, Una*

Himachal Pradesh 156 (Maninder Singh 5 for 39, Shakti
  Singh 4 for 46) and 156 (Maninder Singh 6 for 51)

Delhi 432 for 3 dec. (A.K. Sharma 235 not out, Bantoo
  Singh 130)

Delhi won by an innings and 120 runs

Delhi 6 pts., Himachal Pradesh 0 pts.

at Air Force Complex, Palam, Delhi

Services 467 (R. Vinayak 97, S. Subramanya 85,
  S. Narula 64, S. Chopra 51) and 4 for 0

Jammu & Kashmir 274 (A.S. Bhatti 64, A. Gupta 59,
  M.V. Rao 4 for 68) and 194 (Sarabjit Singh 63,
  S. Shirsat 5 for 65)

Services won by 10 wickets

Services 6 pts., Jammu & Kashmir 0 pts.

at Nehru Stadium, Gurgaon

Punjab 303 (N.S. Sidhu 50) and 229 for 7 dec.
  (Gursharan Singh 69, P. Thakur 5 for 78)

Haryana 126 (Bhupinder Singh snr 7 for 46) and 129
  (B. Vij 5 for 19)

Punjab won by 277 runs

Punjab 6 pts. Haryana 0 pts.

Delhi bowled out Himachal Pradesh by mid-afternoon on the first day and, after losing two wickets for 42, took total control of the match. Bantoo Singh and Ajay Sharma added 340 for the third wicket, and Delhi moved to victory inside three days. They were still short of qualifying for the pre-quarter-finals and needed to win their last match as Services beat Jammu and Kashmir to reach 16 points.

Haryana were also left needing to win their last match for they were well beaten by Punjab who claimed the North Zone championship. In a tense match, Bhupinder Singh senior was outstanding, taking 4 for 6 in four overs in his initial spell of fast-medium-pace bowling. Haryana were reduced to 14 for 4.

1, 2, 3 and 4 January 1994 *at Ferozeshah Kotla Ground, Delhi*

Jammu & Kashmir 109 (Kanwaljit Singh 51, A.S. Wassan
  4 for 34) and 203 (R. Sharma 60)

Delhi 342 (M. Prabhakar 165, V. Dahiya 66, A. Qayum 6
  for 130)

Delhi won by an innings and 30 runs

Delhi 6 pts., Jammu & Kashmir 0 pts.

at TIT School Ground, Bhiwani

Haryana 476 for 6 dec. (N.R. Goel 112, Rajesh Puri 101
  not out, Jitender Singh 82, A. Kaypee 78, Avtar Singh
  50 not out)

Himachal Pradesh 145 (P. Jain 7 for 73) and 146
  (R. Nayyar 64, P. Jain 8 for 67)

Haryana won by an innings and 185 runs

Haryana 6 pts., Himachal Pradesh 0 pts.

Delhi and Haryana qualified for the later stages of the Ranji Trophy by beating weaker opponents as expected. Both matches were over in three days. Delhi bowled out Jammu before lunch on the first day, but they then lost six wickets before taking first-innings lead, and it was Prabhakar's 165 off 279 balls with 26 fours which finally gave them the advantage. Haryana were more conclusive as Himachal Pradesh were routed by Pradeep Jain who had match figures of 15 for 140. The left-arm spinner's second-innings haul was a career best, and it brought his total of wickets to 45 in five Ranji Trophy matches in the season.

NORTH ZONE FINAL TABLE

	P	W	L	D	Pts.
Punjab	5	4	1	–	26
Haryana	5	3	1	1	20
Delhi	5	3	–	2	18
Services	5	2	2	1	16
Jammu & Kashmir	5	–	4	1	2
Himachal Pradesh	5	–	4	1	0

C.S. Pandit of Assam. (Adrian Murrell/Allsport)

EAST ZONE

30 November, **1**, **2** and **3** December 1993 *at Eden Gardens, Calcutta*

Bengal 529 for 3 dec. (S.J. Kalyani 208, Saurav Ganguly 200 not out)

Tripura 175 (R. Deb Burman 67, P.S. Vaidya 5 for 68) and 271 (S. Das Gupta 76 not out, A. Deb Burman 63, S. Paul 56, C.M. Sharma 4 for 72)

Bengal won by an innings and 83 runs

Bengal 6 pts., Tripura 0 pts.

at Moin-ul-Haq Stadium, Patna

Assam 398 (C.S. Pandit 111, Deepak Das 76, Dhananjay Singh 5 for 100) and 240 for 5 dec. (L.S. Rajput 54 not out, Z. Zuffri 52, Deepak Das 51)

Bihar 254 (Adil Hussain 60, Javed Zaman 4 for 80) and 179 for 5 (Sanjeev Kumar 54)

Match drawn

Assam 2 pts., Bihar 0 pts.

Saurav Das Gupta must have regretted his decision to ask Bengal to bat first when he saw his opponents end the first day on 329 for 2 from 86.5 overs. The following day, Srikant Kalyani and Saurav Ganguly took their third-wicket partnership to 334. Both batsmen reached double centuries, for Ganguly it was the first of his career. In spite of some defiance from Tripura when they followed-on, there was never any doubt as to who would win the match. Prashant Vaidya and Chetan Sharma bowled with fire to share 15 wickets between them.

Slow batting and a tentative declaration lost Assam the chance of victory against Bihar. Pandit hit his 13th century on the winning day.

9, 10, 11 and **12** December 1993 *at Eden Gardens, Calcutta*

Bengal 274 (Saurav Ganguly 148, C.M. Sharma 65, Javed Zaman 5 for 68) and 441 for 3 dec. (I.B. Roy 130, C.M. Sharma 114 not out, Saurav Ganguly 100 not out)

Assam 192 (U. Chatterjee 6 for 29) and 175 (U. Chatterjee 5 for 44)

Bengal won by 348 runs

Bengal 6 pts., Assam 0 pts.

at Sports Stadium, Behrampur

Tripura 172 (R. Biswal 4 for 61) and 163 (R. Deb Burman 53, R. Biswal 5 for 46)

Orissa 284 (D.B. Mohanty 76, Ameya Roy 72) and 53 for 1

Orissa won by 9 wickets

Orissa 6 pts., Tripura 0 pts.

Bengal slipped to 96 for 6 against Assam before Saurav Ganguly and Chetan Sharma added 166 to put them in command. Saurav hit a century in each innings, his second hundred of the match coming off 94 balls. Chetan Sharma, 65 in the first innings, hit his first century in 13 seasons in the Ranji Trophy in the second. Indu Bhusan Roy also scored a hundred as Bengal moved relentlessly towards victory. Their outstanding bowler was the left-arm spinner Utpal Chatterjee.

The contest between Orissa and Tripura produced few fireworks.

18, 19, 20 and **21** December 1993 *at Government High School, Karimganj*

Assam 396 (Rajinder Singh 96 not out, L.S. Rajput 74, K.K. Baruah 50)

Tripura 188 (Javed Zaman 6 for 65) and 149 (Javed Zaman 5 for 51)

Assam won by an innings and 59 runs

Assam 6 pts., Tripura 0 pts.

19, 20, 21 and **22** December 1993 *at Ispat Stadium, Rourkela*

Bihar 426 (S.S. Karim 138, S. Banerjee 77, Sanjeev Kumar 51) and 151 for 6

Orissa 293 (Ameya Roy 65, K.G. Dube 63, K.V.P. Rao 4 for 56, Avinash Kumar 4 for 79)

Match drawn

Bihar 2 pts., Orissa 0 pts.

Tripura were beaten for the third time in as many matches and again inside three days. A seventh-wicket partnership of 152 between Karim and Banerjee was the substance of Bihar's big score against Orissa which brought them first-innings points.

26, 27, 28 and 29 December 1993 *at Sports Stadium, Behrampur*

Assam 160 (R. Biswal 7 for 45) and 157 (Gautam Dutta 52, Sushil Kumar 5 for 60)
Orissa 396 (Ameya Roy 88, P. Mohapatra 50)

Orissa won by an innings and 79 runs

Orissa 6 pts., Assam 0 pts.

at MECON, Ranchi

Bihar 150 (Indranil Bose 57, C.M. Sharma 6 for 30) and 131 (P.S., Vaidya 4 for 72)
Bengal 453 (J. Arun Lal 142, S.J. Kalyani 132, Dhananjay Singh 5 for 102, Avinash Kumar 4 for 119)

Bengal won by an innings and 172 runs

Bengal 6 pts., Bihar 0 pts.

Consistent batting to support the career-best bowling performance of Ranjib Biswal who perplexed Assam with his off-breaks gave Orissa an innings victory in three days and a place in the pre-quarter-finals. Bengal's third victory in succession was founded on the bowling of Chetan Sharma and Utpal Chatterjee and a second-wicket partnership of 162 between Arun Lal and Kalyani.

4, 5, 6 and 7 January 1994 *at Permit Field, Balasore*

Orissa 204 (C.M. Sharma 5 for 52) and 158 (C.M. Sharma 4 for 34)
Bengal 313 (Snehashish Ganguly 64) and 51 for 2

Bengal won by 8 wickets

Bengal 6 pts., Orissa 0 pts.

at PTT Ground, Agartala

Bihar 227 (Indranil Bose 50)
Tripura 62 (K.V.P. Rao 6 for 12) and 44 (Avinash Kumar 5 for 22)

Bihar won by an innings and 121 runs

Bihar 6 pts., Tripura 0 pts.

Put in to bat, Orissa batted lamely against Bengal who, although not showing their best form, won with ease to collect maximum points and the East Zone trophy.

Bihar scored only 227 against Tripura yet won by an innings. Tripura, possibly the weakest side in India, scored 62 off 52.2 overs and 44 off 40.3 overs. Slow left-armer Kashireddi Rao took 6 for 12 in 18.2 overs in the first innings and 3 for 2 in 7.3 overs in the second. In spite of this victory, Bihar failed to qualify for the knock-out stage. Assam qualified with a better run quotient.

EAST ZONE FINAL TABLE

	P	W	L	D	Pts.
Bengal	4	4	–	–	24
Orissa	4	2	1	1	12
Assam	4	1	2	1	8
Bihar	4	1	1	2	8
Tripura	4	–	4	–	0

CENTRAL ZONE

29, 30 November, 1 and 2 December 1993 *at MB College Ground, Udaipur*

Madhya Pradesh 187 (A. Vijayvargiya 68, R.K. Chauhan 52 not out) and 393 (D.K. Nilosey 123 not out, P.K. Dwevedi 99, R. Rathore 4 for 101)
Rajasthan 420 (P.K. Amre 218, R. Sanghi 108, D.K. Nilosey 4 for 74, N.D. Hirwani 4 for 79) and 161 for 6

Rajasthan won by 4 wickets

Rajasthan 6 pts., Madhya Pradesh 0 pts.

The pride of India – Sachin Tendulkar. (David Munden/Sports-Line)

Put in to bat, Madhya Pradesh fell to a varied attack, and when Pravin Amre and debutant Rajesh Sanghi shared a third-wicket partnership of 217 Rajasthan took total control. Sanghi had played for Dulwich in 1993. Rajasthan scored at five an over on the last day to clinch the match.

2, 3, 4 and 5 December 1993 *at Green Park, Kanpur*

Vidarbha 335 (M. Pandey 78, P. Hingnikar 68, G. Sharma 4 for 71, A.W. Zaidi 4 for 93) and 367 for 5 (Y.T. Ghare 107 not out, K.S.M. Iyer 89, U.I. Gani 87, M.G. Gogte 51)

Uttar Pradesh 583 for 8 dec. (R. Shamshed 160, R. Sapru 139 not out, S.S. Khandkar 121)

Match drawn

Uttar Pradesh 2 pts., Vidarbha 0 pts.

A third-wicket stand of 226 between Khandkar and Shamshed and a not-out century from Sapru took Uttar Pradesh to first-innings points against Vidarbha.

7, 8, 9 and 10 December 1993 *at Karnail Singh Stadium, Delhi*

Railways 535 for 4 dec. (Yusuf Ali Khan 215, K.B. Kala 112, Abhay Sharma 65 not out, Manvinder Singh 56)

Uttar Pradesh 472 (R. Shamshed 169, M.S. Mudgal 129, Iqbal Thakur 5 for 144)

Match drawn

Railways 2 pts., Uttar Pradesh 0 pts.

at Indira Gandhi Stadium, Alwar

Rajasthan 264 (R. Sanghi 68, M.S. Dosi 4 for 44) and 208 (V. Yadav 80, P.V. Gandhe 8 for 61)

Vidarbha 261 (U.S. Phate 63, K.S.M. Iyer 50, R. Rathore 4 for 50) and 212 for 6 (U.S. Phate 53)

Vidarbha won by 4 wickets

Vidarbha 6 pts., Rajasthan 2 pts.

The most closely contested of the five zones, Central Zone, produced its first outright winner when Vidarbha beat Rajasthan after conceding first-innings points by three runs. Vidarbha's hero was off-break bowler Pritam Gandhe who returned career-best figures of 8 for 61 in Rajasthan's second innings. Railways batted into the third day against Uttar Pradesh with skipper Yusuf Ali Khan and Kala adding 245 for the second wicket. Mudgal and Shamshed responded with 141 for Uttar Pradesh's third wicket, and 147 runs were added for the fourth by Shamshed and Gautam, but the game meandered to a tedious draw.

15, 16, 17 and 18 December 1993 *at VCA Ground, Nagpur*

Railways 179 and 221 (P.S. Rawat 63, Abhay Sharma 62, P.V. Gandhe 6 for 76)

Vidarbha 324 (P.B. Hingnikar 130, S.G. Gujar 51, Javed Alam 7 for 99) and 80 for 4

Vidarbha won by 6 wickets

Vidarbha 6 pts., Railways 0 pts.

at Bhilai Steel Plant Ground, Bhilai

Madhya Pradesh 330 (S.S. Lahore 78, M.S. Sahni 67, Jasbir Singh 4 for 58) and 291 (M.S. Sahni 71, Jasbir Singh 8 for 125)

Uttar Pradesh 303 (R. Shamshed 84, R. Sapru 61, N.D. Hirwani 5 for 82) and 26 for 1

Match drawn

Madhya Pradesh 2 pts., Uttar Pradesh 0 pts.

Praveen Hingnikar's century and some more fine bowling by Gandhe took Vidarbha to victory in three days against Railways and gave the state every chance of reaching the knock-out stage of the Ranji Trophy. Uttar Pradesh were engaged in another rather tedious draw.

23, 24, 25 and 26 December 1993 *at Karnail Singh Stadium, Delhi*

Railways 308 (Abhay Sharma 143, K.B. Kala 62, M. Aslam 4 for 75)

Rajasthan 156 (K. Bharatan 4 for 57) and 121 (Iqbal Thakur 5 for 36)

Railways won by an innings and 31 runs

Railways 6 pts., Rajasthan 0 pts.

at VCA Stadium, Nagpur

Madhya Pradesh 385 (A.R. Khurasiya 142, D.K. Nilosey 54, A.V. Vijayvargiya 53, K.K. Patel 50) and 47 for 2

Vidarbha 165 (N.D. Hirwani 8 for 52) and 266 (U.S. Gani 93, S.S. Lahore 5 for 66)

Madhya Pradesh won by 8 wickets

Madhya Pradesh 6 pts., Vidarbha 0 pts.

Railways caused a great surprise by beating Rajasthan and so leaving the issue as to who would qualify for the knock-out stage of the tournament undecided until the last round of matches. Put in to bat on a pitch of many vagaries, Railways were well served by the patient Abhay Sharma who hit his fifth Ranji Trophy century. Rajasthan's batsmen were unable to cope with the pitch, and they were beaten in three days.

Vidarbha needed just two points from their last match to make sure of qualification, but they put Madhya Pradesh in to bat and then fell foul of the left-handed Khurasiya who struck fiercely on the opening day. Worse was to come for Vidarbha as former Test leg-spinner Hirwani returned the best figures of his career and they were forced to follow-on.

1, 2, 3 and 4 January **1994** *at Roop Singh Stadium, Gwalior*

Railways 339 (Abhay Sharma 103, Yusuf Ali Khan 61, R.K. Chauhan 5 for 130) and 279 (K.B. Kala 71, Yusuf Ali Khan 55, P. Shepherd 54, N.D. Hirwani 8 for 66)

Madhya Pradesh 324 (A.R. Khurasiya 104, M.S. Sahni 59, K.K. Patel 55, M. Majithia 4 for 97) and 296 for 7 (P.K. Dwevedi 93, D.K. Nilosey 80)

Madhya Pradesh won by 3 wickets

Madhya Pradesh 6 pts., Railways 2 pts.

at Chowk Stadium, Lucknow

Uttar Pradesh 448 (S.S. Khandkar 121, R. Shamshed 83, G.K. Pandey 74, M.S. Mudgal 54, P. Krisnakumar 6 for 162, M. Aslam 4 for 115) and 188 for 2 dec. (M.S. Mudgal 58, R.N. Pal 54)

Rajasthan 403 (V. Yadav 157, G. Khoda 93, G. Sharma 6 for 122) and 235 for 8 (G. Khoda 50)

Rajasthan won by 2 wickets

Rajasthan 6 pts., Uttar Pradesh 2 pts.

Leading by 15 runs on the first innings, Railways succumbed to another fine piece of bowling by Hirwani and lost their last seven second-innings wickets for 71 runs. Scoring at four runs an over, Madhya Pradesh raced to victory and a place in the knock-out round. The foundation of their win came with a second-wicket stand of 136 between Dwevedi and Nilosey.

Leading by 45 runs on the first innings and 188 for 2 in their second innings on the last afternoon, Uttar Pradesh surprisingly declared. Rajasthan happily knocked off the required runs in 40 overs to win by two wickets. This win not only allowed them to move above Railways and qualify but alsotook them to the top of the table. Not all were happy with events, however, and Rajesh Sanghi, the newcomer, declined to play in Rajasthan's next match.

Vidarbha qualified for the knock-out stage for the first time in 19 years.

CENTRAL ZONE FINAL TABLE

	P	W	L	D	Pts.
Rajasthan	4	2	2	–	14
Madhya Pradesh	4	2	1	1	14
Vidarbha	4	2	1	1	12
Railways	4	1	2	1	10
Uttar Pradesh	4	–	1	3	4

PRE-QUARTER FINALS

12, 13, 14, 15 and **16** February **1994** *at M. Chinnaswamy Stadium, Bangalore*

Karnataka 468 (K. Jeshwant 123, P.V. Shashikanth 95, J. Arun Kumar 75, S.G. Chakraborty 5 for 128)

Assam 107 (D. Johnson 8 for 55) and 176

Karnataka won by an innings and 186 runs

at Nahar Singh Stadium, Faridabad

Bombay 718 (A.A. Muzumdar 260, R.J. Shastri 118, J.V. Paranjpe 117, S.S. Dighe 111, P. Thakur 7 for 254)

Haryana 291 (V. Yadav 131, M. Patel 5 for 80) and 226 (V. Yadav 50, Iqbal Khan 5 for 37, S.V. Bahutule 4 for 81)

Bombay won by an innings and 202 runs

at Mansarovar Ground, Jaipur

Hyderabad 272 (M.V. Sridhat 89, V. Pratap 67, P. Krishnakumar 5 for 78) and 233

Rajasthan 202 (S.V. Mudkavi 56) and 136 (Kanwaljit Singh 4 for 22)

Hyderabad won by 167 runs

at VCA Ground, Nagpur

Maharashtra 535 (S.S. Bhave 129, S.S. Sugwekar 106, J. Narse 67, A.V. Kale 61, M.S. Dosi 5 for 157) and 350 for 2 dec. (S.V. Jedhe 150 not out, S.S. Sugwekar 106 not out, H.A. Kinikar 50)

Vidarbha 356 (Y.T. Ghare 103) and 131 for 5

Match drawn

Maharashtra qualified for quarter-finals on first-innings lead

at Nehru Stadium, Indore

Orissa 437 (P.R. Mohapatra, 140, R.B. Biswal 138) and 244 (S.S. Das 98, P.S. Kumar 65, D. Parmar 6 for 105)

Madhya Pradesh 370 (A.R. Khurasiya 91, P.K. Dwevedi 64) and 230 for 9 (D.K. Nilosey 111 not out)

Match drawn

Orissa qualified for quarter-finals on first-innings lead

at Eden Gardens, Calcutta

Bengal 213 (Snehasish Ganguly 68) and 445 for 8 (J. Arun Lal 177, A.O. Malhotra 64 not out, S.J. Kalyani 51)

Delhi 178 (S. Sensharma 4 for 45)

Match drawn

Bengal qualified for quarter-finals on first-innings lead

Baroda 366 (R.P. Parikh 99, T.B. Arothe 70, J.J. Martin
54, D. Vasu 5 for 87) and 368 (P. Dave 80,
K.S. Chavan 67, S. Subramaniam 4 for 83)
Tamil Nadu 268 (Robin Singh 87, T.B. Arothe 4 for 35)
and 97 for 4 (D. Vasu 51)

Match drawn

Baroda qualified for quarter-finals on first-innings lead

Karnataka took only three of the scheduled five days to
beat Assam. Put in to bat, they were given a fine start by
Arun Kumar and Shashikanth who scored 134 for the first
wicket. The off-spin of Chakraborty checked the scoring,
but Jeshwant who hit 123 off 172 balls and reached his
century with a six reasserted the batting dominance on
the second morning. The inexperienced Assam batting
line-up was then routed by 23-year-old David Johnson
who surprised himself by bowling quicker than he had
ever done before. The game was over in under three
hours on the third day. Wicket-keeper Avinash Vaidya
had nine victims in the match, seven catches and two
stumpings.

Bombay has ever been renowned for the talent it has
produced and, following in the wake of Tendulkar and
Kambli, came Amol Muzumdar, 19-year-old commerce
student from Mithibai College. Coming to the wicket
with his side 47 for 2, he shared a stand of 150 with
Paranjpe, and then was guided through a stand of 228 by
skipper Ravi Shastri. Muzumdar displayed the finest of
temperaments. Blessed with patience, he batted for 639
minutes, faced 516 balls and hit 31 fours before being
stumped off Thakur, who sent down 73.1 overs, for 260,
the highest score ever recorded by a batsman on his first-
class debut. Faced by this astonishing record and a total of
718, Haryana slipped to defeat in four days. Another
debutant was seam bowler Manish Patel who took 5 for 80
in Haryana's first innings.

Muzumdar was educated at Shardashram School
which also numbers Tendulkar, Kambli and Amre among
its former pupils, an impressive array.

On a pitch on which the ball tended to keep low,
Hyderabad struggled to 220 for 7 on the first day, but
Rajasthan's struggle was even greater on the second day
at Jaipur, and they surrendered a significant first-innings
lead on the third. Scoring at little more than two runs an
over, Hyderabad consistently and remorselessly reached
233 to leave Rajasthan more than a day in which to score
304 to win. They were 117 for 7 at the start of the last day,
and the game was over 45 minutes later.

Vidarbha's dreams of progressing further ended when
Maharashtra won the toss in Nagpur and scored 387 for 5
on the first day, Bhave and Sugwekar sharing a third-
wicket partnership of 180. Sugwekar hit a century in each
innings, and Maharashtra's token declaration left
Vidarbha 55 overs in which to score 530.

Centuries from Biswal and Mohapatra, who shared a
fifth-wicket stand of 158 which stretched into the second
day, rescued Orissa after an uncertain start. Madhya
Pradesh began disastrously, losing two wickets for 48

*In his 13th season in the Ranji Trophy, Chetan Sharma hit a maiden
first-class century for Bengal against Assam. (Mark Leech)*

runs before the end of the second day. Khurasiya hit 12
fours and batted bravely on the third day, but Orissa's
total always looked just out of Madhya Pradesh's reach.
On the last day, 18 wickets fell, and it looked as if
Parmar's bowling might bring Madhya Pradesh a sensational victory. Nilosey, at number six, hit a whirlwind
hundred, but wickets fell around him as Madhya Pradesh
went in search of 312 for victory. Ultimately, all honours
went to Orissa.

The fading star of Delhi was eclipsed in Calcutta. They
bowled out Bengal for 213 on the opening day, but left-
arm medium-pacer Sagarmoy Sensharma then performed the hat-trick, dismissing Hitesh Sharma, Bantoo
Singh and Ajay Sharma, and Delhi closed on 14 for 3.
There was no effective recovery, and with Arun Lal
hitting 177 off 294 deliveries and no play possible on the
last day, Bengal were in the quarter-finals.

The match in Baroda followed a similar pattern, with
the home side winning through because of their determination and the failure of Tamil Nadu's front-line batsmen.

QUARTER-FINALS

26, 27 28 February, 1 and 2 March 1994 *at Eden Gardens, Calcutta*

Hyderabad 261 and 209 (C.M. Sharma 4 for 47)
Bengal 392 (Snehasish Ganguly 149, C.M. Sharma 62, Kanwaljit Singh 4 for 79) and 79 for 1

Bengal won by 9 wickets

at IPCL Sports Complex, Baroda

Baroda 592 (K.S. Chavan 190, A.C. Bedade 159, M.S. Narula 131, A.R. Kapoor 4 for 106, U. Kamal 4 for 130)
Punjab 349 (A.V. Mehra 152, Gursharan Singh 60, V. Rathore 50, S.S. Hazare 5 for 66) and 287 for 8 (K. Mohan 70, V. Rathore 54)

Match drawn

Baroda qualified for semi-finals on first-innings lead

at Poona Club, Pune

Maharashtra 645 (S.S. Sugwekar 225, S.S. Bhave 104, Iqbal Siddiqui 76, S.J. Jadhav 62, A.V. Kale 58, S.V. Jedhe 50, R.B. Biswal 5 for 172) and 176 for 7 dec. (S.S. Bhave 60)

Orissa 398 (Ameya Roy 116, S. Raul 70) and 33 for 3

Match drawn

Maharashtra qualified for semi-finals on first-innings lead

at M. Chinnaswamy Stadium, Bangalore

Karnataka 406 (S.M.H. Kirmani 139, S. Joshi 118, J. Arun Kumar 65, P. Mhambrey 4 for 86, S.V. Bahutule 4 for 103) and 305 for 5 dec. (J. Arun Kumar 105, R.S. Dravid 69, P.V. Shashikant 51)
Bombay 460 (R.J. Shastri 151, S.V. Bahutule 134 not out, S. More 66, S.K. Kulkarni 55) and 89 for 5 (S. Joshi 5 for 29)

Match drawn

Bombay qualified for semi-finals on first innings lead

Put in to bat on a pitch which always gave the bowlers some encouragement, Hyderabad were bowled out on the first day in Calcutta where Bengal's varied attack again performed well. Bengal batted with great caution, but they were 109 for 5 before Snelhasish Ganguly and Chetan Sharma came together in a decisive stand of 129. Mintoo Das also batted well, and Bengal established a commanding lead. The bowling of Sharma and

Syed Kirmani of Karnataka hit his 13th first-class century in what was his 27th year in first-class cricket. (Adrian Murrell/Allsport)

Chatterjee proved too much for Hyderabad, and Bengal won with ease.

Winning the toss, Baroda reached 305 for 3 at the end of the first day. Chavan and Bedade completed centuries on the second day and extended their partnership to 195. Three wickets fell for 11 runs, but Narula and Chavan then added 230, and the game passed beyond the reach of Punjab, winners in 1993.

Sugwekar's third century in succession became a double century on the second day, and his stand of 233 with Bhave, plus some late-order hitting, took Maharashtra to a massive score. Orissa battled on, but had little hope of reaching Maharashtra's total after losing their first five wickets for 136.

Karnataka recovered from 162 for 6 to pass 400 thanks to a partnership of 227 between Kirmani and Joshi. Syed Kirmani, 44 years old and no longer keeping wicket, hit his 13th hundred in a career which has lasted 27 years. Sunil Joshi made the first century of his career in what was his second season. With Bombay 174 for 6, it seemed that Karnataka would take the vital first-innings lead, but Ravi Shastri found a partner in the left-handed Sairaj Bahutule, and the pair added 259. Trailing by 54 runs, Karnataka made a bold attempt to keep the game alive. They scored at five runs an over, and Keshwant's declaration left his bowlers 82 overs in which to win the match. Bombay batted grimly. They were reduced to 21 for 3, but Bharucha batted through the 82 overs to finish with 44, and Bombay were saved. Sunil Joshi's 5 for 29 came from 31 overs.

SEMI-FINALS

12, 13, 14, 15 and **16** March 1994 *at Eden Gardens, Calcutta*

Baroda 249 (K.S. Chavan 75, P.S. Vaidya 4 for 49) and
123 (S. Sensharma 4 for 31)

Bengal 278 (J. Arun Lal 89, S.S. Hazare 4 for 68) and
98 for 2

Bengal won by 8 wickets

at Nehru Stadium, Pune

Bombay 509 (S. More 170, S.K. Kulkarni 139,
R.J. Shastri 65, A.A. Muzumdar 55) and 316 for 7
(A.A. Muzumdar 101 not out, Z. Bharucha 51,
S.V. Jedhe 4 for 75)

Maharashtra 338 (S.S. Sugwekar 142, H.A. Kinikar 59,
S.V. Bahutule 4 for 68, P. Mhambrey 4 for 100)

Match drawn

Bombay qualified for final on first innings lead

The uncertainties of the Eden Gardens pitch caused Malhotra to ask Baroda to bat first when he won the toss. The visitors showed extreme caution, but they were all out on the second day for 249. By the end of that day, Bengal were 124 for 2 and seemingly set for a big lead. A middle-order collapse saw five wickets go down for 29 runs, and when the ninth wicket fell Bengal were still

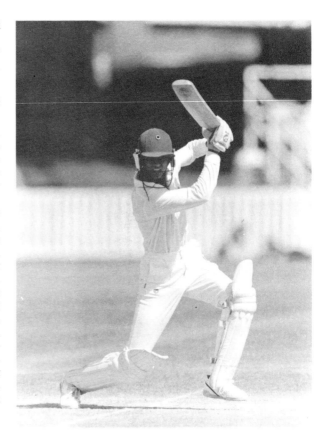

Amol Muzumdar established a world record when he scored 260 for Bombay against Haryana on the occasion of his first-class debut, Faridabad, 12–15 February 1994. (Patrick Eagar)

three runs behind. The damage had been caused by veteran leg-spinner Hazare, but Vaidya and Sensharma now attacked him and added a vital 32. Baroda fell apart in the second innings, and the match was over on the fourth day.

Bombay were 39 for 2 before Muzumdar, who had not played in the quarter-final, joined Sunil More in a stand of 113. From that point runs flowed and, in spite of Sugwekar equalling team-mate Bhave's record of four centuries in the season, Maharashtra never approached Bombay's huge total. In Bombay's second innings, Muzumdar reached his second first-class hundred in three innings.

 RANJI TROPHY FINAL
BOMBAY *v.* BENGAL, at Bombay

Once totally dominant in the competition, Bombay had not, in fact, won the Ranji Trophy since 1985 so that their success in 1993–4 was sweet to them. It was, of course, achieved without the help of leading players like Tendulkar and Kambli in the later stages.

Malhotra decided to bat first when he won the toss, but batsmen struggled against the seam of Manish Patel and the leg-spin of Sairaj Bahutule. Only the veteran Arun Lal and the promising Saurav Ganguly played with composure, and the only stand of substance was one of 69 by this pair for the sixth wicket.

The left-arm spin of Utpal Chatterjee was soon introduced into the Bengal attack, and he immediately dismissed Bharucha and Patil to leave Bombay on 18 for 2 at the end of the first day.

There was no sign of recovery on the second morning until the arrival of Muzumdar. A batsman of prodigious talent, he added 76 with Shastri and 52 with Kulkarni. The late middle order showed commendable application, and Bombay led by 63 in spite of the splendid efforts of Chatterjee.

Bengal began the third day disastrously and were 33 for 4. Malhotra and Saurav and Snedhasish Ganguly stopped the rot, but Shastri varied his bowlers intelligently, and Bombay had two days in which to score 195 to win the trophy.

Batting with good sense and determination, they needed only one.

Returned to form and fitness, Ravi Shastri led Bombay to triumph in the Ranji Trophy. (David Munden/Sports-Line)

RANJI TROPHY FINAL – BOMBAY v. BENGAL
27, 28, 29 and 30 March 1994 at Wankhede Stadium, Bombay

BENGAL

	FIRST INNINGS			SECOND INNINGS	
A. Verma	c Dighe, b Mhambrey	10	lbw, b Patel		4
*M. Das	lbw, b Patel	17	c More, b Shastri		3
J. Arun Lal	c Kulkarni, b Patel	62	c Dighe, b Patel		0
Snehasish Ganguly	c Shastri, b Patel	3	(6) c More, b Bahutule		30
A.O. Malhotra (capt)	c Kulkarni, b Bahutule	15	c Bharucha, b Bahutule		62
S.J. Kalyani	c More, b Bahutule	5	(4) c More, b Shastri		1
Saurav Ganguly	b Patel	40	c More, b Bahutule		88
C.M. Sharma	b Shastri	22	c Dighe, b Patel		35
U. Chatterjee	b Bahutule	19	b Mhambrey		17
P.S. Vaidya	c Bharucha, b Bahutule	0	not out		9
S. Sensharma	not out	0	c Patel, b Shastri		0
Extras		0	b 4, lb 3, w 1		8
		193			257

BOMBAY

	FIRST INNINGS			SECOND INNINGS	
Z. Bharucha	c Arun Lal, b Chatterjee	11	b Verma		23
S. More	b Chatterjee	16	not out		83
S.S. Patil	c Saurav Ganguly, b Chatterjee	0			
J.V. Paranjpe	run out	17	not out		44
A.A. Muzumdar	c and b Chatterjee	78			
R.J. Shastri (capt)	c Vaidya, b Sharma	29			
S.K. Kulkarni	c Sensharma, b Chatterjee	35			
*S.S. Dighe	c Saurav Ganguly, b Sharma	20			
S.V. Bahutule	not out	26	(3) c Sharma, b Sensharma		40
P. Mhambrey	c Saurav Ganguly, b Chatterjee	6			
M. Patel	c Das, b Chatterjee	1			
Extras	b 2, lb 4, nb 11	17	b 2, lb 1, nb 2		5
		256	(for 2 wickets)		195

	O	M	R	W	O	M	R	W
Mhambrey	10	3	25	1	9	2	17	1
Patel	24	7	59	4	17	3	35	3
Patil	11	2	46	–	10	1	43	–
Bahutule	19	5	49	4	32	2	108	3
Shastri	7.2	1	14	1	19.4	3	47	3

	O	M	R	W	O	M	R	W
Vaidya	13	–	57	–	7	4	3	–
Sensharma	10	2	33	–	12	3	34	1
Sharma	16	1	40	2	12.5	3	39	–
Chatterjee	39.2	11	71	7	30	6	78	–
Verma	15	1	49	–	16	2	38	1

FALL OF WICKETS
1–10, 2–34, 3–38, 4–73, 5–81, 6–150, 7–157, 8–191, 9–191
1–9, 2–9, 3–13, 4–33, 5–105, 6–110, 7–177, 8–208, 9–256

FALL OF WICKETS
1–18, 2–18, 3–41, 4–58, 5–134, 6–186, 7–223, 8–225, 9–240
1–62, 2–144

Umpires: S.K. Bansal & V.K. Ramaswamy

Bombay won by 8 wickets

FIRST-CLASS AVERAGES

BATTING

	M	Inns	NO	Runs	HS	Av	100s	50s		M	Inns	NO	Runs	HS	Av	100s	50s
A.A. Muzumdar	3	4	1	494	260	164.66	2	2	R. Vinayak	5	7	–	300	97	42.85	–	3
A.K. Sharma	5	5	1	504	235*	126.00	3	–	V.Z. Yadav	5	10	1	382	157	42.44	1	1
S.S. Sugwekar	5	8	2	728	225	121.33	4	1	M.S. Sahni	5	9	1	322	71	40.25	–	3
M. Azharuddin	8	9	1	677	155	84.62	4	–	L.S. Rajput	7	11	1	402	74	40.20	–	4
N. David	3	5	1	334	207*	83.50	1	–	M.S. Narula	8	12	4	320	131	40.00	1	–
S. Dogra	4	3	1	160	152*	80.00	1	–	Sanjay Sharma	3	6	2	159	75	39.75	–	1
R. Shamshed	8	12	1	867	169	78.81	4	2	S. Narula	3	5	–	198	102	39.60	1	1
S.S. Khandkar	4	4	–	303	121	75.75	2	–	S.S. Dighe	8	9	–	355	111	39.44	2	1
M.V. Sridhar	7	11	1	757	366	75.70	2	1	S. Bhat	3	5	2	118	64*	39.33	–	1
S.V. Manjrekar	12	18	3	1100	156	73.33	5	3	D. Das	2	4	–	152	76	38.00	–	2
R. Sapru	4	4	1	216	139*	72.00	1	1	A.R. Khurasiya	9	17	1	597	142	37.31	3	1
P.K. Amre	5	10	2	564	218	70.50	2	1	K.A. Jeshwant	7	10	–	372	123	37.20	1	1
S. Chopra	5	8	–	555	186	69.37	2	3	M.H. Parmar	5	10	1	334	138	37.11	1	1
A.V. Mehra	5	9	2	464	152*	66.28	2	1	G.N. Srinivas	2	4	–	147	99	36.75	–	1
S.K. Kulkarni	3	5	1	265	139	66.25	1	1	P.B. Hinganikar	5	10	–	359	130	35.90	1	1
Bhupinder Singh jnr	7	11	3	511	132	63.87	2	2	P.V. Shashikanth	7	11	–	392	95	35.63	–	4
J. Arun Kumar	6	9	–	566	141	62.88	2	4	Z. Barucha	7	13	3	355	93	35.50	–	2
S. More	4	7	1	374	170	62.33	1	2	R.B. Parikh	6	10	–	354	99	35.40	–	3
G.K. Pandey	7	11	2	559	106*	62.11	2	3	U.S. Phate	2	4	–	141	63	35.25	–	2
V. Rathore	11	19	2	1047	250	61.58	3	4	B. Dutta	4	8	1	246	69	35.14	–	2
D.K. Nilosey	5	9	2	428	123*	61.14	2	2	Kapil Dev	4	4	1	105	53*	35.00	–	1
K.B. Kala	4	6	–	359	112	59.83	1	2	A.O. Malhotra	8	10	2	278	64*	34.75	–	2
A.C. Bedade	7	11	–	657	159	59.72	3	2	I.B. Roy	6	10	1	311	130	34.55	1	–
S.R. Tendulkar	9	11	1	594	142	59.40	2	4	N. Mody	2	4	–	138	50	34.50	–	1
A.V. Kale	5	6	–	351	132	58.50	1	2	S.M.H. Kirmani	7	9	1	276	139	34.50	1	–
Abhay Sharma	7	12	3	525	143	58.33	2	2	A.S. Wassan	6	7	2	172	104*	34.40	1	–
R.J. Shastri	12	18	1	963	151	56.64	4	4	G.K. Khoda	5	10	1	308	93	34.22	–	2
J. Arun Lal	8	14	1	729	177	56.07	2	2	Peroze V. Rasheed	5	6	–	205	91	34.16	1	1
V.G. Kambli	6	7	–	392	151	56.00	1	3	R. Nayyar	5	10	1	304	97	33.77	–	2
N.S. Sidhu	8	10	–	558	124	55.80	1	5	I. Bose	4	7	–	234	57	33.42	–	2
Y.T. Ghare	5	10	3	371	107*	53.00	2	–	K.S.M. Iyer	5	10	–	328	89	32.80	–	2
R.S. Dravid	13	20	4	846	151*	52.87	2	5	Chinmoy Sharma	5	8	1	229	74	32.71	–	1
N.R. Mongia	9	14	4	525	100*	52.50	1	3	Amit Sharma	6	8	2	196	97	32.66	–	1
S.V. Jedhe	11	16	2	734	150*	52.42	2	4	P.K. Dwevedi	8	15	–	484	99	32.26	–	4
H.A. Kinikar	8	12	–	628	184	52.33	1	5	Robin Singh	10	13	–	413	112	31.76	2	1
Jitender Singh	5	6	–	314	120	52.33	1	2	Gursharan Singh	12	19	2	540	77*	31.76	–	6
S.H. Kotak	4	7	–	363	87	51.85	–	4	V. Dahiya	5	6	–	190	66	31.66	–	2
V.M. Jaisimha	7	9	–	466	211	51.77	1	2	Rajinder Singh	6	11	1	311	96*	31.10	–	1
N.R. Odedra	4	8	–	414	137	51.75	1	3	Bantoo Singh	9	13	–	402	130	30.92	1	2
S.S. Karim	7	12	2	510	138	51.00	1	4	A. Gaekwad	5	9	–	273	50	30.33	–	1
S. Meeraj	2	4	2	101	42*	50.50	–	–	M.F. Rehman	5	8	–	242	73	30.25	–	2
A. Kaypee	6	8	–	403	129	50.37	1	3	S.S. Lahore	5	9	1	242	78	30.25	–	2
S.S. Bhave	11	17	1	805	180	50.31	4	2	M. Senthilnathan	6	8	1	210	54	30.00	–	1
Saurav Ganguly	14	19	2	854	200*	50.23	3	2	P.S. Rawat	4	6	1	148	63	29.60	–	1
Ameya Roy	6	8	–	401	116	50.12	1	3	R.B. Biswal	7	10	–	294	138	29.40	1	–
C.S. Pandit	7	11	1	500	125	50.00	2	2	K. Narayanan	5	8	2	175	63	29.16	–	1
J.S. Narse	7	9	2	350	139*	50.00	1	2	A.S. Pathak	6	10	–	288	64	28.80	–	3
Yusuf Ali Khan	7	12	–	599	215	49.91	1	4	P.A. Amonkar	4	8	–	230	58	28.75	–	1
K. Patdiwala	3	6	1	248	152	49.60	1	1	A.R. Bali	3	6	–	172	68	28.66	–	1
S.V. Bahutule	9	12	4	393	134*	49.12	1	–	K.S. More	10	16	1	427	115	28.46	1	3
Rajesh Puri	9	13	2	536	151	48.72	3	–	N. Gaur	3	6	–	170	50	28.33	–	1
C.M. Sharma	11	16	4	584	114*	48.66	1	3	B.M. Jadeja	4	8	1	197	75	28.14	–	1
S.J. Kalyani	12	17	2	722	208	48.13	3	1	P. Shepherd	4	6	–	167	54	27.83	–	1
M. Prabhakar	9	9	1	385	165	48.12	2	1	V. Pratap	7	10	1	248	67	27.55	–	1
N.R. Goel	6	8	–	384	166	48.00	2	–	J.V. Paranjype	8	12	1	303	117	27.54	1	–
M.S. Mudgal	6	9	–	429	129	47.66	1	3	A.R. Kapoor	13	17	2	413	103*	27.53	1	–
S.R. Mohsin	3	4	1	143	99*	47.66	–	1	S. Sharath	5	7	1	165	61	27.50	–	1
K.S. Chavan	7	12	–	568	190	47.33	2	2	S.J. Jadhav	5	6	–	165	62	27.50	–	2
J.J. Martin	7	11	2	425	152*	47.22	2	1	Ashwani Gupta	5	10	–	274	87	27.40	–	2
A. Kripal Singh	4	5	1	188	85	47.00	–	2	T.B. Arothe	9	15	–	411	70	27.40	–	2
R. Bittoo	5	10	–	466	150	46.60	2	1	A. Hussain	4	7	1	164	60	27.33	–	1
Snehasish Ganguly	8	9	1	368	149	46.00	1	2	R. Sanghi	4	8	1	218	108	27.25	1	1
S. Oasis	5	6	1	228	110	45.60	1	–	A. Khatua	6	9	1	217	48	27.12	–	–
A.D. Jadeja	9	13	–	583	264	44.84	1	3	Yuvraj Singh	7	9	3	161	43	26.83	–	–
P.R. Mohapatra	5	8	1	313	140	44.71	1	1	P. Dave	4	7	1	161	80	26.83	–	2
S. Joshi	6	8	2	267	118	44.50	1	1	D. Vasu	8	12	1	293	77	26.63	–	3
V. Yadav	7	9	–	400	131	44.44	1	2	M.G. Gogte	2	4	–	106	51	26.50	–	1
V.I. Ghani	5	10	1	399	93	44.33	–	2	G. Dutta	5	8	1	185	52	26.42	–	1
S.S. Tanna	4	8	1	305	71	43.57	–	3	N.A. Patel	4	8	–	211	69	26.37	–	3
Avtar Singh	6	8	2	258	53	43.00	–	2	R. Deb Burman	4	8	–	210	67	26.25	–	1

FIRST-CLASS AVERAGES

BATTING

	M	Inns	NO	Runs	HS	Av	100s	50s
P. Maitrey	5	7	1	157	45	26.16	–	–
D.B. Mohanty	6	9	–	229	76	25.44	–	1
K. Dubey	6	8	1	178	63	25.42	–	1
S.T. Banerjee	5	8	–	201	81	25.12	–	2
R.N. Pal	4	5	–	124	54	24.80	–	1
T. Kumar	5	8	1	173	30	24.71	–	–
Vishal Sharma	4	8	–	196	49	24.50	–	–
Bhupinder Singh snr	13	16	–	390	73	24.37	–	3
A.V. Vijayvargiya	4	7	–	170	68	24.28	–	1
M. Subramaniya	5	8	1	168	85	24.00	–	1
S. Kumar	4	7	–	168	54	24.00	–	2
S.G. Gujar	5	9	–	215	51	23.88	–	1
R.K. Chauhan	9	14	3	261	52*	23.72	–	1
V. Vijayasarathy	5	8	1	166	66	23.71	–	2
V.B. Chandrasekhar	10	16	1	355	67	23.66	–	2
P.G. Sunder	5	6	–	139	103	23.16	1	–
A.S. Bhatti	3	6	–	139	69	23.16	–	2
S.V. Mudkavi	5	9	2	160	56	22.85	–	1
R.A. Swarup	8	13	–	297	48	22.84	–	–
Sushil Kumar	6	8	–	182	65	22.75	–	1
J. Srinath	6	8	1	159	55	22.71	–	1
Z. Zuffri	4	7	–	158	52	22.57	–	1
Raju Sharma	4	8	–	179	60	22.37	–	1
A. Malhotra	5	5	–	110	40	22.00	–	–
A. Vaidya	12	15	1	306	68	21.85	–	2
B. Mehta	3	6	1	109	32	21.80	–	–
G. Gautam	3	6	1	109	78*	21.80	–	1
T. Jabbar	6	8	–	172	51	21.50	–	1
P.V. Gandhe	8	14	1	277	80	21.30	–	2
S. Paul	4	8	–	167	56	20.87	–	1
Maninder Singh	10	13	3	207	39	20.70	–	–
K.V.S.D. Kamaraju	5	8	–	164	31	20.50	–	–
K.K. Patel	8	16	1	306	55	20.40	–	2
Y. Barde	3	6	–	122	36	20.33	–	–
S. Das Gupta	4	8	1	139	76*	19.85	–	1
V.V. Kumar	5	8	–	158	74	19.75	–	1
K.K. Barua	4	7	1	118	50	19.66	–	1
Kamaljit Singh (JK)	5	10	–	191	51	19.10	–	1
B. Vidya	4	8	–	152	52	19.00	–	1
Sureah Kumar	6	10	2	152	35	19.00	–	–
Shambhu Sharma	5	10	–	190	74	19.00	–	1
Parminder Singh	3	6	–	112	29	18.66	–	–
Abdul Azeem	7	11	–	201	85	18.27	–	1
P.S. Vaidya	13	16	5	199	51	18.09	–	1
A. Deb Burman	4	8	–	144	63	18.00	–	1
A.W. Zaidi	4	7	1	107	25	17.83	–	–
B. Ramprakash	6	8	–	139	67	17.37	–	1
Brijender Sharma	4	8	–	138	38	17.25	–	–
P. Thakur	6	7	1	102	28*	17.00	–	–
Kanwaljit Singh (Hy)	5	6	–	100	50	16.66	–	1
M. Nayyar	5	7	–	115	50	16.42	–	1
Sarabjit Singh	5	9	1	131	63	16.37	–	1
M. Sawkar	5	9	–	144	50	16.00	–	1
A.R. Kumble	6	7	–	111	34	15.85	–	–
K.N.A. Padmanabhan	6	8	1	104	43	14.85	–	–
N.D. Hirwani	10	17	5	178	59	14.83	–	1
S. Subramananiam	8	11	1	148	43	14.80	–	–
R. Jaswant	4	8	1	102	28	14.57	–	–
Iqbal Siddiqui	11	13	2	158	76	14.36	–	1
A.S. Shetty	5	9	1	107	71*	13.37	–	1
M.K. Obaid	10	13	3	133	40	13.30	–	–
K. Srinath	6	10	–	130	44	13.00	–	–
W.V. Raman	9	12	–	155	33	12.91	–	–
H.S. Sodhi	7	13	2	134	28	12.18	–	–
R.S.P. Rathore	8	15	1	166	34	11.85	–	–
U. Chatterjee	12	15	2	144	25	11.07	–	–

(Qualification – 100 runs, average 10.00)
(Played in one match – S.S. Das 98 & 9)

BOWLING

	Overs	Mds	Runs	Wkts	Av	Best	10/m	5/inn
K.V.P. Rao	96.5	48	138	13	10.61	6-12	–	1
Kanawaljit Singh (Hy)	189.3	64	366	24	15.25	4-22	–	–
K.N.A. Padmanabhan	258.4	80	511	33	15.48	8-57	1	3
Venkatapathy Raju	335.5	109	678	42	16.14	6-87	2	5
U. Chatterjee	362	111	811	49	16.55	7-71	1	3
D. Johnson	90	20	243	14	17.35	8-55	–	1
B. Vij	279.1	63	786	45	17.46	7-58	2	5
P. Jain	328.4	99	814	46	17.69	8-67	2	6
Javed Zaman	147.3	30	439	24	18.29	6-65	1	3
Venkatesh Prasad	411.2	124	930	50	18.60	7-37	1	3
Arshad Ayub	196.3	49	437	23	19.00	5-28	–	2
C.M. Sharma	344.5	62	1059	54	19.61	6-30	–	2
M. Venkataramana	245.2	67	594	30	19.80	5-29	–	1
S. Mahadevan	73	19	200	10	20.00	6-60	–	1
S. Subramaniam	298.3	110	562	28	20.07	5-14	–	2
Bhupinder Singh snr	431.4	127	1068	53	20.15	7.46	1	2
P.S. Vaidya	372.1	77	1081	53	20.39	5-68	–	1
M.V. Rao	157.1	29	466	22	21.18	7-77	1	2
R.B. Biswal	257	55	658	31	21.22	7-45	1	3
A.S. Wassan	160.4	33	491	23	21.34	4-13	–	–
S.T. Banerjee	129.1	31	345	16	21.56	6-48	–	1
M. Suresh Kumar	161	30	367	17	21.58	4-19	–	–
A.R. Kumble	255.2	74	654	30	21.80	7-59	1	1
Dhananjay Singh	124.4	22	349	16	21.81	5-100	–	1
S. Joshi	184.2	74	352	16	22.00	5-29	–	1
D. Vasu	238.4	76	512	23	22.26	5-87	–	1
R.J. Shastri	185.1	35	589	26	22.65	6-73	–	2
S.A. Ankola	156	42	416	18	23.11	4-67	–	–
S. Sensharma	167.5	26	534	23	23.21	4-31	–	–
N.D. Hirwani	468.1	91	1376	59	23.32	8-52	1	4
J. Srinath	173.1	30	560	24	23.33	5-62	–	1
I. Thakur	98	18	375	16	23.43	5-36	–	2
P. Mhambrey	256.4	62	712	30	23.73	6-47	–	1
Abinash Kumar	235.1	76	523	22	23.77	5-22	–	1
B. Ramprakash	209	64	381	16	23.81	5-90	–	1
K. Bharatan	126	40	312	13	24.00	5-39	–	1
S.V. Bahutule	319.2	56	958	39	24.56	4-42	–	–
Maninder Singh	290.1	79	690	28	24.64	6-51	1	3
Mohammad Aslam	87.4	10	273	11	24.81	4-75	–	–
Shakti Singh	132.4	36	399	16	24.93	4-46	–	–
M. Patel	123	20	400	16	25.00	5-80	–	1
P.K. Krishna Kumar	106.4	12	358	14	25.57	6-162	–	2
S. Shirsat	135.1	22	384	15	25.60	5-38	–	2
Javed Alam	145	38	411	16	25.68	7-99	–	1
A. Bedi	142	42	388	15	25.86	3-30	–	–
N.P. Singh	159.3	35	414	16	25.87	5-84	–	1
G. Sharma	196.4	67	446	17	26.23	6-122	–	1
V.N. Buch	148.5	40	421	16	26.31	3-17	–	–
R.S.P. Rathore	255.4	55	716	27	26.51	5-116	–	1
Jasbir Singh	181.1	47	426	16	26.62	8.125	1	1
S.S. Hazare	177.3	43	427	16	26.68	5-66	–	1
M.K. Obaid	328.4	96	783	29	27.00	4-25	–	–
Iqbal Siddiqui	355.1	61	1087	40	27.17	7-139	–	3
A.S. Shetty	194.3	44	437	16	27.31	4-95	–	–
M. Prabhakar	210.4	58	558	20	27.90	4-82	–	–
M. Subramaniya	151	28	453	16	28.31	6-32	–	1
V. Jain	133	16	460	16	28.75	7-45	–	2
M.S. Doshi	218.5	26	547	19	28.78	5-157	–	1
A.R. Kapoor	282	56	951	33	28.81	5-57	–	1
P. Thakur	309	79	810	28	28.92	7-254	–	3
G.V. Gopal Raju	171.2	42	464	16	29.00	6-54	–	2
M.S. Narula	207.1	51	496	17	29.17	6-101	–	1
B.H. Mistry	93.3	16	301	10	31.10	4-73	–	–
H. Ramkishen	179.4	44	488	16	30.50	5-77	–	1
A.D. Jadeja	90.5	13	336	11	30.54	4-99	–	–
A. Kuruvilla	257.4	54	798	26	30.69	4-71	–	–
R.K. Chauhan	348.2	83	1015	33	30.75	5-29	–	3
T.B. Arothe	343.1	77	987	32	30.84	6-76	–	2
Robin Singh	165.1	28	514	16	32.12	4-30	–	–

FIRST-CLASS AVERAGES

BOWLING

	Overs	Mds	Runs	Wkts	Av	Best	10/m	5/inn
V. Vijayasarathy	167.2	38	419	13	32.23	4-52	–	–
P. Maitrey	136.4	23	398	12	33.16	4-30	–	–
P.V. Gandhe	353.1	67	931	28	33.25	8-61	–	2
P.J. Kanade	277.4	53	735	22	33.40	4-57	–	–
S.S. Lahore	194	65	438	13	33.69	5-66	–	1
R.R. Goarsondia	125.1	20	342	10	34.20	4-82	–	–
R.G.M. Patel	195	37	549	16	34.31	5-33	–	1
Sushil Kumar	372.1	77	953	27	35.29	5-60	–	1
F. Ghayas	114.5	21	353	10	35.30	3-16	–	–
R. Ananth	228.2	63	611	17	35.94	4-56	–	–
V. Arvind	187	47	475	13	36.53	4-102	–	–
P.Y. Chitale	199.3	72	433	11	39.36	3-72	–	–
A.W. Zaidi	133.5	25	398	10	39.80	4-93	–	–
Sanjay Sharma	139.5	24	403	10	40.30	6-66	–	1
A. Qayyum	191.3	41	558	13	42.92	6-130	–	1
D.T. Patel	148	22	474	11	43.09	4-55	–	–
A. Gupta	127	15	475	11	43.18	4-98	–	–

	Overs	Mds	Runs	Wkts	Av	Best	10/m	5/inn
R.D. Kambli	143.2	19	436	10	43.60	4-119	–	–
G.K. Pandey	152	24	465	10	46.50	2-24	–	–
S. Thakur	123.5	18	467	10	46.70	5-116	–	1
S.S. Patil	234.2	49	761	15	50.73	4-35	–	–

(Qualification – 10 wickets)

LEADING FIELDERS

42 – A. Vaidya (ct 37/st 5); 37 – S.S. Dighe (ct 34/st 3); 34 – Arun K. Sharma (ct 29/st 5); 31 – V. Yadav (ct 26/st 5); 27 – S.S. Karim (ct 25/st 2) and N.R. Mongia (ct 25/st 2); 26 – K.S. More (ct 22/st 4); 22 – S.M. Kondhalkar (ct 20/st 2); 18 – R.S. Dravid and Abhay Sharma (ct 14/st 4); 17 – Yuvraj Singh (ct 16/st 1); 16 – A.R. Kapoor; 15 – M. Azharuddin, S.S. Bhave and A. Sheikh (ct 12/st 3); 14 – A.D. Jadeja, S. More and K.K. Patel (ct 10/st 4); 13 – V. Dahiya, M. Das, H.A. Kinikar, M.S. Mudgal (ct 6/st 7) and M. Sanjay (ct 12/st 1); 12 – K.S.M. Iyer and R. Puri; 11 – Saurav Ganguly, A. Roy and M.V. Sridhar; 10 – K.S. Chauhan, P.K. Dwevedi, S.V. Jedhe, Sarabjit Singh (ct 7/st 3), S.R. Tendulkar, D. Vasu and R. Vinayak.

SECTION E
Pakistan

Wills Cup

Patron's Trophy

Zimbabwe tour, Test and one-day international series

Quaid-e-Azam Trophy

First-class averages

Waqar Younis – the youngest captain of Pakistan and 27 wickets in three Test matches against Zimbabwe. (Alan Cozzi)

There always appears to be a remoteness between Pakistan at international level and domestic cricket in Pakistan, and 1993–4 was no exception although there was a home Test and one-day international series against Zimbabwe. Political and religious tensions prevented Pakistan from going to India, and India from visiting Pakistan. The inevitable cricket politics of Pakistan saw a rebellion against the captaincy of Wasim Akram and his replacement by Salim Malik for the tour to New Zealand. This display of player power did not save Javed Miandad who was omitted from the party, but it did result in the dismissal of the Board of Control by the President. Life is never dull in cricket in Pakistan, and as the 1994–5 season approached Javed seemed to be fighting his way back into contention for a place in the Test side. He had announced his retirement from Test cricket, but he was persuaded to reconsider his decision at the request of Prime Minister Benazir Bhutto. One must remember that only a year ago there was bewilderment and anger at the omission of Salim Malik from the party to tour West Indies. Now he is captain of Pakistan. A year can be a short time in politics.

Zahid Fazal – the season's leading run-scorer – outstanding form for Pakistan International Airlines and Lahore. (David Munden/Sports-Line)

 WILLS CUP

28 September 1993 *at UBL Sports Complex*

Bahawalpur 193 for 9 (Sajid Rahman 51)
HBFC 197 for 4 (Faisal Qureshi 80 not out, Munir-ul-Haq 60)

HBFC (4 pts.) won by 6 wickets

at Rawalpindi Stadium, Rawalpindi

Islamabad 99
PACO 100 for 1 (Shahid Saeed 57 not out)

PACO (4 pts.) won by 9 wickets

at Bagh-e-Jinnah Ground, Lahore

National Bank 240 (Mohammad Javed 61)
Lahore City 143

National Bank (4 pts.) won by 97 runs

at Qaddafi Stadium, Lahore

PNSC 229 for 8 (Sher Ali 78, Aamer Ishaq 58)
Railways 230 for 7 (Ijaz Ahmed 104, Mazhar Qayyum 54, Nasir Wasti 4 for 25)

Railways (4 pts.) won by 3 wickets

at Iqbal Stadium, Faisalabad

Faisalabad v. **PIA**

Match abandoned

Faisalabad 2 pts., PIA 2 pts.

Seventeen teams competed for the 50-over trophy. There were eight associations and nine departments taking part in the preliminary rounds. Divided into four groups, the teams played each other on a league basis, and the top two sides from each group qualified for the final rounds.

29 September 1993 *at Sports Stadium, Sargodha*

Sargodha 149 for 7
ADBP 150 for 5 (Atif Rauf 67 not out)

ADBP (4 pts.) won by 5 wickets

at Qaddafi Stadium, Lahore

PNSC 254 for 6 (Sohail Jaffer 101)
Karachi Blues 192 for 8 (Zahid Ali 102 not out)

PNSC (4 pts.) won by 62 runs

at UBL Sports Complex, Karachi

Karachi Whites 170 (Abdullah Khan 66, Abdul Qadir 4 for 23)
Habib Bank 171 for 2 (Salim Malik 74 not out, Shakeel Ahmed 72)

Habib Bank (4 pts.) won by 8 wickets

at Rawalpindi Stadium, Rawalpindi

Rawalpindi 241 for 8 (Raja Arshad 75, Masroor Hussain 58, Masood Anwar 4 for 45)
United Bank 224

Rawalpindi (4 pts.) won by 17 runs

A significant performance in the second round of matches came in the match between Karachi Whites and Habib Bank. The individual award went to Abdul Qadir. The former Test leg-spinner was attempting to win his way back into the Pakistan side after injury, and his performances in the one-day tournament did earn him a place in the party for the Sharjah competition.

30 September 1993 *at UBL Sports Complex, Karachi*

Bahawalpur 160 (Abdul Qadir 4 for 24, Salim Malik 4 for 39)

Habib Bank 161 for 2 (Ijaz Ahmed 59, Tahir Rasheed 57 not out)

Habib Bank (4 pts.) won by 8 wickets

at Qaddafi Stadium, Lahore

Karachi Blues 187 (Mansoor Khan 63)

National Bank 188 for 3 (Shahid Anwar 73, Saeed Azad 68 not out)

National Bank (4 pts.) won by 7 wickets

at Sports Stadium, Sargodha

PIA 251 for 9 (Rizwan-uz-Zaman 89)

Sargodha 162 for 9 (Mohammad Nawaz 58, Ayaz Jilani 4 for 24)

PIA (4 pts.) won by 89 runs

at Rawalpindi Stadium, Rawalpindi

Rawalpindi 205 for 5 (Masroor Hussain 76, Tariq Mahboob 58 not out)

PACO 135

Rawalpindi (4 pts.) won by 70 runs

Habib Bank emerged as clear favourites to take the title with their strength in bowling and the consistent batting of Ijaz Ahmed. Abdul Qadir was again effective in the match against Bahawalpur, but the individual award was won by Salim Malik.

1 October 1993 *at UBL Sports Complex, Karachi*

HBFC 219 for 6

Karachi Whites 220 for 6 (Abdullah Khan 61, Ameer-ud-Din 55)

Karachi Whites (4 pts.) won by 4 wickets

at Iqbal Stadium, Faisalabad

Faisalabad 135

ADBP 137 for 1 (Zahoor Elahi 71 not out)

ADBP (4 pts.) won by 9 wickets

at Arbab Niaz Stadium, Peshawar

Islamabad 172 for 7 (Yousuf Butt 67 not out)

United Bank 175 for 5 (Aamer Bashir 66)

United Bank (4 pts.) won by 5 wickets

at Qaddafi Stadium, Lahore

PNSC 232 for 7 (Aamer Ishaq 63, Sajjad Akbar 59, Sajjad Ali 57 not out)

Lahore City 191 (Nasir Wasti 4 for 44)

PNSC (4 pts.) won by 41 runs

United Bank, one of the strongest combinations in Pakistan cricket, gained their only victory of the tournament. United Bank had lost four of their best players – Waqar Younis, Basit Ali, Inzamam-ul-Haq and Mushtaq Ahmed – to the six-a-side competition in Hong Kong and so played throughout the Wills Cup at half strength and failed to reach the semi-final.

2 October 1993 *at UBL Sports Complex, Karachi*

Habib Bank 241 for 8 (Ijaz Ahmed 68, Shakeel Ahmed 51)

HBFC 239 (Shazhad Ilyas 103, Tariq Alam 60 not out)

Habib Bank (4 pts.) won by 2 runs

at Arbab Niaz Stadium, Peshawar

Railways 253 for 6 (Nadeem Younus 68, Mazhar Qayyum 53 not out)

National Bank 147

Railways (4 pts.) won by 106 runs

at Qaddafi Stadium, Lahore

Karachi Blues 205 for 5 (Abid Hanif 63, Aamer Iqbal 60)

Lahore City 208 for 7 (Wasim Mir 54)

Lahore City (4 pts.) won by 3 wickets

at Iqbal Stadium, Faisalabad

PIA 202 (Asif Mohammad 53)

ADBP 206 for 2 (Atif Rauf 80 not out, Saeed Anwar 69)

ADBP (4 pts.) won by 8 wickets

at Niaz Stadium, Hyderabad

United Bank 220 for 8 (Mansoor Akhtar 72, Yahya Toor 4 for 37)

PACO 223 for 8 (Shahid Nawaz 55)

PACO (4 pts.) won by 2 wickets

A fine all-round performance by Yahya Toor helped to give PACO victory over the luckless United Bank with three balls to spare. The slow left-arm bowler took four wickets and then hit 37 not out to steer his side to their narrow victory. Yahya, who bats right-handed, won the individual award.

3 October 1993 *at UBL Sports Complex, Karachi*

Bahawalpur 197 for 8

Karachi Whites 201 for 2 (Ameer-ud-Din 89, Iqbal Saleem 80 not out)

Karachi Whites (4 pts.) won by 8 wickets

at Qaddafi Stadium, Lahore

Karachi Blues 235 for 7 (Mansoor Khan 67, Abid Hanif 53, Zahid Ali 51 not out)
Railways 236 for 8 (Ijaz Ahmed 64)

Railways (4 pts.) won by 2 wickets

at Rawalpindi Stadium, Rawalpindi

Rawalpindi 183 for 9 (Nadeem Abbasi 54)
Islamabad 120 (Irfan Bhatti 4 for 25)

Rawalpindi (4 pts.) won by 63 runs

at Iqbal Stadium, Faisalabad

Faisalabad 239 for 9 (Maqbool Ahmed 57 not out)
Sargodha 215 (Tanvir Afzal 4 for 48)

Faisalabad (4 pts.) won by 24 runs

at Bagh-e-Jinnah Ground, Lahore

National Bank 248 for 9 (Sajid Ali 73)
PNSC 180

National Bank (4 pts.) won by 68 runs

The final round of preliminary matches left only three sides – Habib Bank, Rawalpindi and ADBP – unbeaten, and the final positions after the preliminary matches were as follows:

Pool A	P	W	L	Ab	Pts.	RR
Habib Bank	3	3	–	–	12	4.45
Karachi Whites	3	2	1	–	8	4.17
HBFC	3	1	2	–	4	4.42
Bahawalpur	3	–	3	–	0	3.79

Pool B	P	W	L	Ab	Pts.	RR
Rawalpindi	3	3	–	–	12	4.34
PACO	3	2	1	–	8	4.08
United Bank	3	1	2	–	4	4.24
Islamabad	3	–	3	–	0	3.22

Pool C	P	W	L	Ab	Pts.	RR
Railways	4	3	1	–	12	4.61
National Bank	4	3	1	–	12	4.24
PNSC	4	2	2	–	8	4.58
Lahore City	4	2	2	–	8	3.99
Karachi Blues	4	–	4	–	0	4.16

Pool D	P	W	L	Ab	Pts.	RR
ADBP	3	3	–	–	12	4.04
PIA	3	1	1	1	6	4.62
Faisalabad	3	1	1	1	6	3.84
Sargodha	3	–	3	–	0	3.91

FINAL ROUND

11 October 1993 *at National Stadium, Karachi*

Karachi Whites 148
Rawalpindi 148 for 9

Rawalpindi (4 pts.) won on losing fewer wickets with scores level

at Niaz Stadium, Hyderabad

National Bank 226
ADBP 229 for 2 (Saeed Anwar 105, Zahoor Elahi 89)

ADBP (4 pts.) won by 8 wickets

at Qaddafi Stadium, Lahore

Habib Bank 248 for 5 (Javed Miandad 59 not out, Salim Malik 53)
PACO 131 (Asadullah Butt 4 for 35)

Habib Bank (4 pts.) won by 117 runs

at Municipal Stadium, Gujranwala

Railways 213 for 8 (Mohammad Ramzan 57)
PIA 214 for 4 (Asif Mujtaba 78 not out, Rizwan-uz-Zaman 60)

PIA (4 pts.) won by 6 wickets

Saeed Anwar hit his first century in the Wills Cup as ADBP beat National Bank with three overs to spare. Habib Bank continued their winning ways and, in their victory over PACO, it was wicket-keeper Tahir Rasheed who took the honours. His five catches earned him the Man of the Match award.

12 October 1993 *at National Stadium, Karachi*

National Bank 182
Karachi Whites 173 for 9 (Abdullah Khan 50, Naeem Khan 4 for 33)

National Bank (4 pts.) won by 9 runs

at Niaz Stadium, Hyderabad

Rawalpindi 138 (Mohammad Asif 4 for 30)
ADBP 143 for 1 (Zahoor Elahi 60 not out)

ADBP (4 pts.) won by 9 wickets

at Qaddafi Stadium, Lahore

Habib Bank 239 for 7 (Ijaz Ahmed 103, Javed Miandad 64)
Railways 217 for 9 (Mohammad Ramzan 60)

Habib Bank (4 pts.) won by 22 runs

at Municipal Stadium, Gujranwala

PACO 214 for 9 (Mujahid Jamshed 58, Ayaz Jilani 4 for 41)

PIA 216 for 3 (Sagheer Abbas 100 not out, Asif Mohammad 64 not out)

PIA (4 pts.) won by 7 wickets

Ijaz Ahmed hit his fourth century in the Wills Cup competition and Sagheer Abbas his first as Habib Bank and PIA won for the second time in the final round of matches. PIA had another hero in off-break bowler Ayaz Jilani who returned his best figures in the tournament.

13 October 1993 *at National Stadium, Karachi*

National Bank 164

Rawalpindi 167 for 8 (Naeem Akhtar 71)

Rawalpindi (4 pts.) won by 2 wickets

at Niaz Stadium, Hyderabad

Karachi Whites 171 for 6

ADBP 172 for 1. (Saeed Anwar 101 not out)

ADBP (4 pts.) won by 9 wickets

at Qaddafi Stadium, Lahore

PIA 234 for 6 (Zahid Fazal 61)

Habib Bank 189 (Azeem Hafeez 4 for 31)

PIA (4 pts.) won by 45 runs

at Municipal Stadium, Gujranwala

PACO 173 (Kamran Khan 55, Iqbal Zahoor 5 for 31)

Railways 177 for 3 (Nadeem Younus 68)

Railways (4 pts.) won by 7 wickets

Saeed Anwar hit his second century in three days and ADBP topped group one in the final round. Habib Bank suffered their first defeat of the season while left-arm spinner Iqbal Zahoor returned his best figures for the competition with the only five-wicket haul of the season's tournament.

FINAL ROUND GROUP STANDINGS

Group One	P	W	L	Pts.	RR
ADBP	3	3	–	12	5.02
Rawalpindi	3	2	1	8	3.04
National Bank	3	1	2	4	3.83
Karachi Whites	3	–	3	0	3.82

Group Two	P	W	L	Pts.	RR
PIA	3	3	–	12	4.61
Habib Bank	3	2	1	8	4.60
Railways	3	1	2	4	4.27
PACO	3	–	3	0	3.89

SEMI-FINALS

15 October 1993 *at National Stadium, Karachi*

Habib Bank 199 for 9 (Ijaz Ahmed 64, Akram Raza 51 not out)

ADBP 187 (Atif Rauf 66, Javed Hayat 53, Asadullah Butt 4 for 32)

Habib Bank won by 12 runs

at Arbab Niaz Stadium, Peshawar

PIA 164 (Zahid Fazal 55)

Rawalpindi 164 for 7

Rawalpindi won on losing fewer wickets with scores level

Contained by the tight bowling of ADBP's Zakir Khan and Raja Afaq, Habib Bank were in deep trouble when Salim Malik, Tahir Rasheed and Javed Miandad were run out in quick succession as they strove to increase the run rate. Habib Bank were rescued by Ijaz Ahmed and Akram Raza, but the total of 199 still looked well within reach of ADBP. The Agricultural Development Bank began badly, but Atif Rauf and Javed Hayat retrieved the situation and made victory look possible. Atif Rauf was dismissed for the first time in the competition in which he scored 299 runs, but Manzoor Elahi joined Javed Hayat and took ADBP to the brink of victory. Then came collapse, and Habib Bank won by 12 runs.

Rawalpindi, the giant-killers of the tournament, gained a surprise win over the strong PIA side and so became the first association team to reach the Wills Cup final since Lahore in 1982.

FINAL

Rawalpindi began promisingly in the final, bowling tightly and fielding well, but their cricket throughout was rather subdued, and Habib Bank soon took control. Shakeel Ahmed and Ijaz Ahmed put on 129 in 78 minutes and Habib Bank did not lose the initiative after this stand. Ijaz Ahmed hit a six and 9 fours in his 71 which came in 94 minutes and, as he also fielded brilliantly, he was an obvious choice for Man of the Match.

Ijaz Ahmed also took the individual award as batsman of the tournament, 426 runs average 53.25. The bowling award went to Rawalpindi's young pace bowler Irfan Bhatti who took 17 wickets at 14.11 runs each and earned praise from the national selectors. Sajid Ali of National Bank took the fielding award while Habib Bank's Tahir Rasheed was named as best wicket-keeper.

WILLS CUP FINAL – HABIB BANK v. RAWALPINDI
22 October 1993 at Qaddafi Stadium, Lahore

HABIB BANK

Shakeel Ahmed	c Raja Arshad, b Shakeel Ahmed	83
Moin-ul-Atiq	c Nadeem Abbasi, b Mohammad Akram	16
Ijaz Ahmed	c Shakeel Ahmed, b Irfan Bhatti	71
Salim Malik (capt)	c and b Naeem Akhtar	22
Javed Miandad	not out	24
Naved Anjum	b Mohammad Akram	4
*Tahir Rasheed	not out	5
Akram Raza		
Abdul Qadir		
Asadullah Butt		
Nadeem Ghauri		
Extras	b 2, lb 9, w 11, nb 2	24
(50 overs)	(for 5 wickets)	249

RAWALPINDI

Raja Arshad	c Akram Raza, b Naved Anjum	11
Azmat Jail (capt)	c Tahir Rasheed, b Akram Raza	28
Masroor Hussain	run out	12
Maqsood Ahmed	c and b Akram Raza	25
Tariq Mahboob	lbw, b Nadeem Ghauri	0
*Nadeem Abbasi	c Salim Malik, b Akram Raza	32
Naeem Akhtar	c sub (Sohail Fazal), b Abdul Qadir	14
Mohammad Riaz	b Asadullah Butt	39
Irfan Bhatti	not out	19
Shakeel Ahmed	not out	2
Mohammad Akram		
Extras	b 4, lb 8, w 8, nb 1	21
(50 overs)	(for 8 wickets)	203

	O	M	R	W
Irfan Bhatti	10	2	38	1
Naeem Akhtar	10	2	30	1
Mohammad Akram	10	1	71	2
Mohammad Riaz	10	1	43	–
Shakeel Ahmed	10	–	56	1

	O	M	R	W
Naved Anjum	5	–	24	1
Asadullah Butt	9	–	35	1
Nadeem Ghauri	10	2	22	1
Akram Raza	10	2	32	3
Abdul Qadir	10	–	40	1
Salim Malik	6	–	38	–

FALL OF WICKETS

1–36, 2–165, 3–199, 4–221, 5–239

FALL OF WICKETS

1–17, 2–57, 3–73, 4–80, 5–116, 6–134, 7–156, 8–201

Umpires: Shakoor Rana & Khizar Hayat   *Man of the Match:* Ijaz Ahmed   *Habib Bank won by 46 runs*

PATRON'S TROPHY

24, 25, 26 and 27 October 1993 *at UBL Sports Complex, Karachi*

United Bank 368 (Mansoor Akhtar 118, Mahmood Hamid 79, Javed Sami Khan 51, Ashfaq Ahmed 5 for 123) and 111 for 4

PIA 493 (Rizwan-uz-Zaman 134, Asif Mohammad 89 not out, Zahid Fazal 73, Aamir Malik 60, Sahid Ahmed 55, Tauseef Ahmed 5 for 146)

Match drawn

PIA 4 pts., United Bank 0 pts.

at Niaz Stadium, Hyderabad

PNSC 75 (Murtaza Hussain 4 for 12, Shahid Hussain 4 for 20) and 211 (Azam Khan 74, Sher Ali 53, Shahid Hussain 5 for 57, Yahya Toor 4 for 26)

PACO 168 (Umar Rasheed 55) and 104 (Naved Nazeer 4 for 12)

PNSC won by 14 runs

PNSC 10 pts., PACO 0 pts.

at Bagh-e-Jinnah Ground, Lahore

HBFC 186 (Faisal Qureshi 50, Akram Raza 5 for 56) and 226 (Nusrat Mahboob 77, Nadeem Ghauri 5 for 70, Akram Raza 4 for 75)

Habib Bank 484 for 7 dec. (Ijaz Ahmed 92, Shahid Javed 92, Tahir Rasheed 64 not out, Asadullah Butt 51 not out, Ijaz Elahi 4 for 147)

Habib Bank won by an innings and 72 runs

Habib Bank 10 pts., HBFC 0 pts.

at Iqbal Stadium, Faisalabad

ADBP 456 (Zahoor Elahi 84, Atif Rauf 80, Mujahid Hameed 77 not out, Ghaffar Kazmi 56, Athar Laeeq 4 for 86)

National Bank 268 (Sajid Ali 107, Raja Afaq 6 for 91, Mohammad Asif 4 for 82) and 323 for 4 (Ameer Akbar 100 not out, Sajid Ali 84, Saeed Azar 61)

Match drawn

ADBP 4 pts., National Bank 0 pts.

Two days after the Wills Cup final, Pakistan's first-class competition for departments and business houses began. Inevitably, it seems, leading players were missing as they were engaged in preparations for the one-day tournament in Sharjah. The veteran Mansoor Akhtar hit the first century of the season, his 26th, but another veteran, Rizwan-uz-Zaman, led PIA to first-innings points with the 34th century of his career. In a match dominated by the bowlers, PNSC beat PACO after trailing by 93 runs on the first innings. The turning point of the game was a second-wicket stand of 120 between Azam Khan and Sher Ali when PNSC batted for a second time.

Habib Bank continued with their excellent form, trouncing HBFC by an innings. Habib Bank batted consistently, and Tahir Rasheed and Asadullah Butt shared an unbroken eighth-wicket partnership of 105. Asadullah hit the first first-class fifty of his career.

National Bank, who should have been demoted but had been reprieved by the Pakistan Board, were saved from defeat by Ameer Akbar who hit 100 off 139 balls.

30, 31 October and 1, 2 November 1993 *at Qaddafi Stadium, Lahore*

National Bank 373 (Tahir Shah 117 not out, Sajid Ali 52, Ijaz Elahi 6 for 132)

HBFC 145 (Munir-ul-Haq 50) and 153 (Athar Laeeq 5 for 38)

National Bank won by an innings and 75 runs

National Bank 10 pts., HBFC 0 pts.

at Bagh-e-Jinnah Ground, Lahore

Railways 401 (Ijaz Ahmed 126, Nadeem Younis 71, Akram Raza 4 for 127) and 42 for 2

Habib Bank 414 (Shahid Javed 131, Shakeel Ahmed 83, Ijaz Ahmed 74, Shaukat Mirza 69, Arshad Khan 6 for 109)

Match drawn

Habib Bank 4 pts., Railways 0 pts.

at National Stadium, Karachi

PIA 412 for 7 dec. (Aamir Malik 164, Asif Mohammad 104, Rizwan-uz-Zaman 57)

PACO 351 (Ghulam Ali 120, Umar Rasheed 72, Tanvir Ali 5 for 89)

Match drawn

PIA 4 pts., PACO 0 pts.

at UBL Sports Complex, Karachi

PNSC 242 (Sher Ali 93, Sajjad Akbar 63 not out, Sohail Jaffar 57, Tauseef Ahmed 6 for 90) and 185 (Azam Khan 77, Tauseef Ahmed 5 for 61, Masood Anwar 5 for 73)

United Bank 271 (Mahmood Hamid 66, Raaes Ahmed 57, Sajjad Ali 4 for 54, Mohsin Kamal 4 for 71) and 112 for 7

Match drawn

United Bank 4 pts., PNSC 0 pts.

Having lost five wickets for 122 runs, National Bank were sparked to recovery by a century from Tahir Shah, batting at number seven. HBFC twice failed against a varied attack. Ijaz Ahmed of Railways hit the second and higher century of his career, but Ijaz Ahmed of Habib Bank, the Test cricketer, shared a second-wicket stand of 145 with Shakeel Ahmed which set his side on the way to a first-innings lead. Shahid Javed built upon the work of the second-wicket pair with 131 in 348 minutes.

A game of tedium saw PIA score at less than two an over on the opening day at the National Stadium. Indeed, their innings lasted until the third morning. Aamir Malik and Asif Mohammad added 220 for the third wicket, but the partnership occupied more than six hours. Ghulam Ali reached the seventh century of his career for PACO, but he could not revitalise the match.

Off-spinner Tauseef Ahmed bowled United Bank into a winning position against PNSC, but the home side failed in their bid to score 157 in 33 overs. Three men were run out, and only Iqbal Imam, with 32 off 30 balls, came to terms with the required run rate.

6, 7, 8 and 9 November 1993 *at National Stadium, Karachi*

PIA 269 (Rizwan-uz-Zaman 96, Babar Zaman 56, Sohail Farooqi 4 for 38, Sajjad Akbar 4 for 84) and 270 for 4 (Rizwan-uz-Zaman 117 not out, Asif Mohammad 72)

PNSC 221 (Nadeem Afzal 5 for 57)

Match drawn

PIA 4 pts., PNSC 0 pts.

at Shahi Bagh Stadium, Peshawar

HBFC 179 (Masood Anwar 7 for 95)

United Bank 181 for 2 (Mansoor Akhtar 88, Aamer Bashir 69 not out)

Match drawn

United Bank 4 pts., HBFC 0 pts.

at Sargodha Stadium, Sargodha

Habib Bank 412 (Shakeel Ahmed 156, Akram Raza 66, Tahir Rasheed 52 not out, Manzoor Elahi 6 for 113)

ADBP 416 for 6 (Ghaffar Kazmi 129, Atif Rauf 100, Javed Hayat 74)

Match drawn

ADBP 4 pts., Habib Bank 0 pts.

at Municipal Stadium, Gujranwala

PACO 420 (Kamran Khan 150, Ghulam Ali 97, Aamer Wasim 4 for 84) and 242 for 5 (Shahid Saeed 115 not out)

Railways 299 (Mohammad Ramzan 110, Mohammad Aslam 4 for 123)

Match drawn

PACO 4 pts., Railways 0 pts.

An opening stand of 104 between Babar Zaman and Rizwan-uz-Zaman for PIA was followed by collapse, but the Airline still took first-innings points. Rizwan-uz-Zaman followed his first-innings 96 with 117 not out, but overs had been lost to rain, and the match meandered to a draw. Rain ruined the game in Peshawar where no play was possible on the first two days. Mansoor Akhtar and Aamer Bashir shared a second-wicket stand of 126 to give United Bank the first-innings lead.

Shakeel Ahmed's 156 and centuries by Atif Rauf and Ghaffar Kazmi who shared a fourth-wicket partnership of 132 were the highlights of a rather dreary game in Sargodha. There was also a distinct lack of urgency in Gujranwala where Kamran Khan hit the highest score of his career.

13, 14, 15 and 16 November 1993 *at Iqbal Stadium, Faisalabad*

HBFC 163 (Ashfaq Ahmed 5 for 54) and 140 (Faisal Gurashi 64, Ashfaq Ahmed 6 for 52)

PIA 97 (Kabir Khan 5 for 42, Shahzad Ilyas 4 for 33) and 210 for 1 (Aamir Malik 104 not out, Shoaib Mohammad 65)

PIA won by 9 wickets

PIA 10 pts., HBFC 0 pts.

at Rawalpindi Stadium, Rawalpindi

Habib Bank 398 (Salim Malik 103, Tahir Rasheed 97, Shahid Javed 81, Waqar Younis 5 for 134)

United Bank 121 (Basit Ali 56, Naved Anjum 9 for 56) and 150 (Naved Anjum 5 for 47)

Habib Bank won by an innings and 127 runs

Habib Bank 10 pts., United Bank 0 pts.

at Qaddafi Stadium, Lahore

National Bank 182 (Umar Rasheed 4 for 38) and 196 (Sajid Ali 50, Umar Rasheed 6 for 39)

PACO 186 (Naeem 4 for 30, Barkatullah 4 for 46) and 71 for 4

Match drawn

PACO 4 pts., National Bank 0 pts.

at Sargodha Stadium, Sargodha

Railways 241 (Mohammad Ramzan 161 not out, Mohammad Asif 5 for 71) and 225 (Ijaz Ahmed 64, Mazhar Qayyum 53, Mohammad Afaq 4 for 80)

ADBP 471 for 7 dec. (Atif Rauf 120, Zahoor Elahi 73, Mujahid Hameed 68 not out, Manzoor Elahi 67 not out, Rashid Khan 4 for 165)

ADBP won by an innings and 5 runs

The fourth round of matches welcomed the arrival of leading players who had been involved in the Sharjah Cup. Asif Mujtaba and Shoaib Mohammad were Test

players involved in the low-scoring match in Faisalabad where medium-pacer Ashfaq Ahmed took the honours. Trailing by 66 runs on the first innings, PIA recovered handsomely to win by nine wickets. The victory was founded on an opening stand of 174 between Aamir Malik and Shoaib Mohammad.

Salim Malik returned to Habib Bank with a century, and Tahir Rasheed furthered his Test claims by opening Habib's innings and scoring 97. In spite of having Waqar Younis, Inzamam-ul-Haq, Mushtaq Ahmed, Basit Ali and Rashid Latif in their side, United Bank were beaten by an innings. Tahir followed his 97 with six catches behind the stumps while poor Rashid Latif followed his three catches with 0 and 1. The star of the match was Naved Anjum with match figures of 14 for 103.

Rain disrupted play in Lahore where PACO had 26 overs in which to score 193 to beat National Bank and never came close to the target. In Sargodha, Mohammad Ramzan came to the wicket with one wicket down for six runs and batted through to the end of the innings to reach the highest score of his career, 161 out of 235 scored while he was at the wicket. His effort proved in vain, for Railways were beaten by an innings. An opening partnership of 123 by Saeed Anwar and Zahoor Elahi of ADBP was followed by a century from Atif Rauf and a sparkling unbroken eighth-wicket partnership of 105 between Mujahid Hameed and Manzoor Elahi.

20, 21, 22 and 23 November 1993 *at Rawalpindi Stadium, Rawalpindi*

Habib Bank 229 (Nadeem Afzal 4 for 70) and 287 (Akram Raza 61, Asadullah Butt 58 not out, Ashfaq Ahmed 7 for 127)

PIA 109 (Asadullah Butt 4 for 34, Naved Anjum 4 for 35) and 238 (Moin Khan 67, Zahid Fazal 61)

Habib Bank won by 168 runs

Habib Bank 10 pts., PIA 0 pts.

at LCCA Ground, Lahore

PACO 440 (Shahid Nawaz 143, Shahid Saeed 101, Javed Hayat 4 for 112, Mohammad Asif 4 for 121)

ADBP 290 (Manzoor Elahi 75, Atif Rauf 64, Murtaza Hussain 4 for 92, Mohammad Zahid 4 for 99) and 242 for 3 (Mansoor Rana 110 not out, Atif Rauf 71)

Match drawn

PACO 4 pts., ADBP 0 pts.

at Qaddafi Stadium, Lahore

National Bank 304 (Sajid Ali 122, Waqar Younis 4 for 83) and 194 (Waqar Younis 6 for 84, Salim Jaffar 4 for 51)

United Bank 258 (Mahmood Hamid 101, Athar Laeeq 4 for 79, Naeem Ashraf 4 for 71) and 87 for 3

Match drawn

National Bank 4 pts., United Bank 0 pts.

Outstanding bowling for Habib Bank in all types of cricket by Naved Anjum. (Alan Cozzi)

at Municipal Stadium, Gujranwala

PNSC 235 (Sher Ali 60, Mohammad Ali 5 for 68) and
229 (Farrukh Bari 80, Sajjad Akbar 69, Iqbal Zahoor
5 for 52)
Railways 181 (Mohammad Ramzan 50, Sajjad Akbar 4
for 48) and 131 for 6 (Ali-ud-Din 4 for 53)
Match drawn
PNSC 4 pts., Railways 0 pts.

Habib Bank took a firm grip on the first place in the table with their third win in five matches. With Ashfaq Ahmed returning the best figures of his career, PIA made a good fight-back in a game dominated by bowlers, but Akram Raza and Asadullah Butt hit fifties batting at numbers nine and ten in the second innings to put Habib Bank well in command. Naved Anjum, with match figures of 7 for 89, brought his total of wickets to 21 for 192 in two matches.

Shahid Saeed shared century stands with Ghulam Ali and Shahid Nawaz for PACO against ADBP while, in spite of Waqar Younis' ten wickets in the match, United Bank were pointless against National Bank. PNSC and Railways ran out of time.

27, 28, 29 and **30 November 1993** *at Model Town Ground, Lahore*

HBFC 196 (Wasim Ali 58, Sajjad Akbar 6 for 68) and
203 (Faisal Qureshi 57, Sajjad Akbar 5 for 49)
PNSC 310 (Mujahir Shah 68 not out, Sohail Jaffar 59,
Sajjad Akbar 53, Sher Ali 52, Kazim Mehdi 4 for 101)
and 93 for 2 (Sohail Jaffar 63 not out)
PNSC won by 8 wickets
PNSC 10 pts., HBFC 0 pts.

at LCCA Ground, Lahore

PACO 319 (Kamran Khan 69, Ghulam Ali 53) and
83 for 3
Habib Bank 287 (Shaukat Mirza 80 not out, Mohammad
Husnain 61, Mohammad Zahid 8 for 114)
Match drawn
PACO 4 pts., Habib Bank 0 pts.

at Municipal Stadium, Gujranwala

United Bank 101 (Manzoor Elahi 5 for 57) and 276 for 5
(Saifullah 80, Parvez Shah 80, Mahmood Hamid 64)
ADBP 255 (Ghaffar Kazmi 69, Masood Anwar 4 for 69)
Match drawn
ADBP 4 pts., United Bank 0 pts.

at Iqbal Stadium, Faisalabad

Railways 151 (Athar Laeeq 5 for 58) and 338 (Babar
Javed 65, Mohammad Ramzan 60, Hafeez-ur-
Rehman 5 for 75)
National Bank 111 (Mohammad Ali 6 for 37, Imran Adil 4
for 46) and 139 for 6
Match drawn
Railways 4 pts., National Bank 0 pts.

The leading cricketers were again absent because of the demands of the national side. HBFC were beaten for the fourth time in five matches and remained pointless. Railways took their first points, but they might well have beaten National Bank had Mohammad Ramzan been brave enough to declare. The match between PACO and Habib Bank was badly affected by rain, only 11 overs being possible on the last day. The slow left-arm bowler Mohammad Zahid surprised Habib Bank with the best bowling figures of his career. Rain ruined the last day of the game in Gujranwala.

5, 6, 7 and 8 December 1993 *at Bagh-e-Jinnah Ground, Lahore*

PACO 369 (Ghulam Ali 85, Kamran Khan 58, Murtaza Hussain 53) and 213 for 3 (Ghulam Ali 115 not out, Mujahid Jamshed 62)

United Bank 236 (Mohammad Javed Khan 63, Aamer Bashir 61, Shahid Hussain 4 for 30)

Match drawn

PACO 4 pts., United Bank 0 pts.

at Iqbal Stadium, Faisalabad

National Bank 480 (Shahid Tanvir 109, Ameer Akbar 100, Wasim Arif 73, Sajid Ali 66, Naved Nazir 4 for 111) and 205 for 5 (Shahid Anwar 84, Saeed Azad 67)

PNSC 352 (Sajjad Akbar 132 not out, Azam Khan 61, Sajjad Ali 50, Naeem Ashraf 4 for 112)

Match drawn

National Bank 4 pts., PNSC 0 pts.

at UBL Sports Complex, Karachi

PIA 231 (Asif Mohammad 89, Ghayyur Qureshi 5 for 71) and 343 for 9 dec. (Wasim Haider 100 not out, Zahid Fazal 64, Javed Hayat 5 for 118)

ADBP 205 (Mansoor Rana 67) and 88 for 2

Match drawn

PIA 4 pts., ADBP 0 pts.

at Multan CC Stadium, Multan

Railways 502 for 6 dec. (Ijaz Ahmed 159, Nadeem Younis 105, Naseer Ahmed 102 not out, Muhtashim Rashid 4 for 133)

HBFC 199 (Wasim Yousufi 101) and 249 (Wasim Ali 102, Iqbal Zahoor 4 for 78)

Railways won by an innings and 54 runs

Railways 10 pts., HBFC 0 pts.

The seventh round of matches coincided with the first Test match between Zimbabwe and Pakistan so that most attention was elsewhere. There was consistent scoring in Lahore as the game meandered to a draw, and there were three centuries in the run-soaked match in Faisalabad. There was some slow scoring in the early stages of the match in Karachi, and the game was only enlivened by Wasim Haider's third first-class century from number eight in the order.

Railways claimed their first win of the season and made the highest score of the season. Ijaz Ahmed of Railways hit his second hundred of the competition and the highest score of his career. There were also centuries from Nadeem Younis, his first, and Naseer Ahmed. HBFC slumped to 23 for 4 in reply and, in spite of Wasim Yousufi's maiden first-class hundred, a brilliant 101 made out of 176 while he was at the wicket, they were forced to follow-on. The left-handed Wasim Ali battled bravely, but HBFC remained pointless.

11, 12, 13 and 14 December 1993 *at Municipal Stadium, Gujranwala*

National Bank 137 (Nadeem Ghauri 8 for 51) and 385 for 7 dec. (Sajid Ali 154, Saaed Azad 61, Akram Raza 4 for 90)

Habib Bank 190 (Shahid Javed 61) and 323 for 9 (Idrees Baig 83, Nadeem Khan 5 for 80)

Match drawn

Habib Bank 4 pts., National Bank 0 pts.

at UBL Sports Complex, Karachi

Railways 328 (Nadeem Younis 68, Mazhar Qayyum 64, Rashid Khan 4 for 93) and 121 (Mazhar Qayyum 56, Zahid Ahmed 4 for 11, Asif Mohammad 4 for 40)

PIA 295 (Zahid Fazal 74, Sohail Miandad 64, Imran Adil 6 for 85) and 157 for 2 (Sohail Miandad 72, Nasir Khan 61)

PIA won by 8 wickets

PIA 10 pts., Railways 0 pts.

at Iqbal Stadium, Faisalabad

PNSC 243 (Manzoor Elahi 4 for 71) and 128 (Ghaffar Kazmi 5 for 40)

ADBP 235 (Ghaffar Kazmi 68, Mohsin Kamal 5 for 66) and 138 for 5

ADBP won by 5 wickets

ADBP 10 pts., PNSC 0 pts.

at LCCA Ground, Lahore

PACO 326 (Kamran Khan 135, Shahid Saeed 63, Mujahid Jamshed 59, Shahid Ali Khan 8 for 123)

HBFC 173 (Faisal Qureshi 51) and 142 (Aamer Hanif 7 for 71)

PACO won by an innings and 11 runs

PACO 10 pts., HBFC 0 pts.

The penultimate round of matches provided one of the best contests of the tournament. Put in to bat at Gujranwala, National Bank were bowled out for 137 thanks mainly to left-arm spinner Nadeem Ghauri who returned the best figures of his career. Habib Bank struggled to take the lead, and the difference between the two sides on the first innings was 53. Sajid Ali led the fight-back for National, and his declaration left Habib Bank more than a day in which to score 333 to win or, more positively, his bowlers time in which to bowl out the opposition. Mohammad Husnain went quickly, but a third-wicket stand of 100 kept alive Habib's chances. Nadeem Khan gnawed away at the middle order with his left-arm spin, and when the last ball had been bowled National Bank were one wicket, and Habib Bank 10 runs, short of victory.

Railways gave more evidence of recent improvement, but a second-innings collapse cost them the game against

PIA. ADBP's second win was founded on good team-work while PACO owed their first win of the season to a fine innings by Kamran Khan, 135 off 147 balls, and to a career-best bowling performance from Aamer Hanif, the right-arm medium pacer.

18, 19, 20 and **21 December 1993** *at UBL Sports Complex, Karachi*

Railways 178 (Ijaz Ahmed 61, Masood Anwar 5 for 65) and 141 (Iqbal Imam 5 for 26)

United Bank 136 (Iqbal Zahoor 5 for 57) and 187 for 7

United Bank won by 3 wickets

United Bank 10 pts., Railways 0 pts.

at LCCA Ground, Lahore

PNSC 297 (Nasir Wasti 65, Aamer Ishaq 63, Rehan Ali Khan 54, Naved Anjum 5 for 61)

Habib Bank 744 for 7 (Shakeel Ahmed 200, Shaukat Mirza ́160 not out, Idrees Baig 158, Akram Raza 145 not out, Mohsin Kamal 5 for 168)

Match drawn

Habib Bank 4 pts., PNSC 0 pts.

at Niaz Stadium, Hyderabad

PIA 540 (Sohail Miandad 142, Aamir Malik 125, Asif Mohammad 62, Zahid Fazal 53, Sagheer Abbas 51, Nadeem Khan 5 for 164)

National Bank 265 (Naeem Ashraf 104, Mohammad Javed 73) and 51 for 1

Match drawn

PIA 4 pts., National Bank 0 pts.

at Iqbal Stadium, Faisalabad

HBFC 179 (Raja Afaq 6 for 53) and 75 for 0 (Jahangir Khan 61 not out)

ADBP 303 (Ghaffar Kazmi 133, Mansoor Rana 64, Shahid Ali Khan 5 for 101)

Match drawn

ADBP 4 pts., HBFC 0 pts.

United Bank gained the sole win of the season in their final match. Their chances of success in the competition had been obliterated by the demands of the national side.

Adopting a policy of 'what we have we hold', Habib Bank batted for the last 2⅓ days of the match against PNSC and made the highest score of the tournament. Shakeel Ahmed hit the first double century of his career and shared a second-wicket stand of 342 with Idrees Baig. Shaukat Mirza and Akram Raza both hit the highest scores of their careers and combined in an unbroken eighth-wicket partnership of 249 in 129 minutes. Akram Raza's 145 came off as many deliveries, and Shaukat Mirza faced only 207 balls for his 160.

PIA also ran up a huge score with Sohail Miandad and Aamir Malik adding 203 for the second wicket against National Bank. Outplayed by ADBP, HBFC ended the competition without a single point.

FINAL TABLE

	P	W	D	L	Pts.
Habib Bank	8	3	5	–	42
PIA	8	2	5	1	40
ADBP	8	2	6	–	38
PACO	8	1	6	1	30
PNSC	8	2	5	1	24
United Bank	8	1	6	1	18
National Bank	8	1	7	–	18
Railways	8	1	4	3	14
HBFC	8	–	2	6	0

SEMI-FINALS

25, 26, 27 and **28 December 1993** *at UBL Sports Complex, Karachi*

PACO 180 (Nadeem Ghauri 6 for 55) and 255 (Shahid Nawaz 76, Nadeem Ghauri 4 for 72)

Habib Bank 285 (Sohail Fazal 82, Mohammad Zahid 5 for 68) and 151 for 2 (Idrees Baig 65 not out)

Habib Bank won by 8 wickets

at LCCA Ground, Lahore

PIA 455 (Asif Mohammad 183, Ayaz Jilani 78, Zahid Ahmed 61)

ADBP 215 for 2 (Atif Rauf 88 not out, Mansoor Rana 83 not out)

Match drawn

Bowlers dominated the match in Karachi, and it was match figures of 10 for 127 from slow left-arm spinner Nadeem Ghauri which gave Habib Bank the edge. Sohail Fazal hit 82, and he received good support from late-order batsmen Akram Raza and Naved Anjum. PACO made a spirited fight-back with nightwatchman Zulqar-nain hitting 45 and complementing the more adventur-ous Shahid Nawaz, but Habib Bank were not to be denied.

In Lahore, rain disrupted play on the first and third days. Asif Mohammad hit the highest score of his career, his patient 183 coming from 491 balls and occupying 627 minutes, but it was a mighty effort in view of the fact that his side were 17 for 3 when he came to the wicket. There was a late flourish from Ayaz Jilani at number ten, but PIA were to pay dearly for their slow start. ADBP made 215 for 2 in 67.3 overs and, with the match drawn, it was they who entered the final as they had been 101 for 2 after 40 overs as opposed to PIA's 76 for 4 at the same point.

ADBP

HABIB BANK

ADBP	FIRST INNINGS		SECOND INNINGS	
Saeed Anwar	lbw, b Asadullah	52	lbw, b Naved	6
Zahoor Elahi	c Tahir, b Shakeel	122	c Shaukat, b Naved	0
Atif Rauf	b Asadullah	118	c Tahir, b Naved	85
Mansoor Rana (capt)	lbw, b Asadullah	5	(5) lbw, b Naved	4
Ghaffar Kazmi	lbw, b Asadullah	1	(4) c Shaukat, b Naved	20
Javed Hayat	b Naved	48	c Salim, b Akram	3
Manzoor Elahi	c Tahir, b Naved	26	not out	22
*Mohammad Nadeem	lbw, b Naved	1		
Qasim Shera	c Shaukat, b Shakeel	7	(8) not out	1
Mohammad Asif	lbw, b Akram	8		
Ghayyur Qureshi	not out	20		
Extras	b 7, lb 7, w 2, nb 31	47	lb 2, nb 16	18
	penalty runs	20		
		475	(for 6 wickets)	159

HABIB BANK	FIRST INNINGS	
Shakeel Ahmed	c Mohammad, b Manzoor	1
*Tahir Rashid	lbw, b Ghayyur	4
Idrees Baig	c Mohammad, b Qasim	141
Ijaz Ahmed	c Manzoor, b Ghayyur	22
Salim Malik (capt)	lbw, b Manzoor	39
Shahid Javed	lbw, b Ghayyur	23
Shaukat Mirza	lbw, b Ghayyur	8
Asadullah Butt	lbw, b Qasim	8
Naved Anjum	lbw, b Qasim	0
Akram Raza	not out	76
Shakeel Khan	c Mohammad, b Manzoor	19
Extras	b 10, lb 22, w 2, nb 8	42
		383

	O	M	R	W	O	M	R	W
Naved Anjum	45	6	146	3	15	4	44	5
Asadullah Butt	33	6	91	4	3	–	22	–
Shakeel Khan	31	5	79	2	5	–	30	–
Ijaz Ahmed	12	–	47	–	2	–	10	–
Akram Raza	26.3	10	65	1	5	1	20	1
Salim Malik	3	–	13	–	7	1	31	–

	O	M	R	W
Manzoor Elahi	28.5	7	98	3
Ghayyur Qureshi	32	5	105	4
Qasim Shera	29	3	91	3
Mohammad Asif	7	1	21	–
Ghaffar Kazmi	8	–	36	–

FALL OF WICKETS

1–169, 2–212, 3–221, 4–229, 5–380, 6–384, 7–387, 8–414, 9–426
1–1, 2–14, 3–75, 4–83, 5–118, 6–154

FALL OF WICKETS

1–6, 2–10, 3–54, 4–122, 5–184, 6–195, 7–250, 8–250, 9–319

Umpires: Khalid Aziz & Mian Aslam

Match drawn. ADBP won the trophy by virtue of first-innings lead

FINAL

Salim Malik returned to lead Habib Bank in the final, taking over from Akram Raza who had captained the side admirably. Salim won the toss, but he must later have regretted his decision to ask ADBP to bat first, for Saeed Anwar and Zahoor Elahi opened with a partnership of 169 in 177 minutes. They were out within three-quarters of an hour of each other, but Atif Rauf batted with patience, and ADBP were 250 for 4 at the end of the day.

They were still at the crease at the close of the second day, 414 for 7 from 136 overs, and Habib Bank's tardy over rate was to cost them 20 penalty runs.

Habib Bank began disastrously, losing both openers with only 10 scored. The only serious resistance came from Idrees Baig, enjoying a patch of golden form, who batted just under 5¾ hours for his 141. By the end of the third day, Habib were struggling on 242 for 6, and they were further hampered on the fourth day when just over 38 overs were possible. Having been 319 for 9, they were grateful to be 363 without further loss at the close of play, and this was due to another brave knock by Akram Raza.

The last pair added 20 more runs on the last morning, and, with Naved Anjum continuing his sparkling bowling form, Habib Bank captured wickets quickly, but there was never any hope that they could wrest the trophy from ADBP who won by virtue of their first-innings lead.

ZIMBABWE TOUR

26, 27 and **28 November 1993** *at Arbab Niaz Stadium, Peshawar*

Zimbabwe XI 405 for 5 dec. (A.D.R. Campbell 135 retired ill, A. Flower 103 retired hurt)

Bank of Khyber XI 254 for 2 (Shoaib Mohammad 101, Shahid Javed 50 not out, Shakeel Ahmed 50)

Match drawn

The hastily arranged tour of Pakistan by Zimbabwe began with a first-class match between the visitors and a Bank of Khyber XI led by Shoaib Mohammad. The Pakistan side was not a strong one, and the batsmen on both sides enjoyed themselves with only seven wickets falling in three days. Campbell hit 135 in 422 minutes, and skipper Andy Flower's 103 included 14 boundaries. Both batsmen found reasons to retire once they had sated themselves. Shoaib's hundred was a tedious affair. This was the only match in which Zimbabwe engaged outside the Test and one-day series.

FIRST TEST MATCH
PAKISTAN *v.* ZIMBABWE, at Karachi

The Defence Stadium became the latest Test venue as Zimbabwe and Pakistan met in a Test for the first time. Zimbabwe introduced six newcomers to Test cricket: Bruk-Jackson, Dekker, Peall, Rennie, Streak and Whittal. All save Bruk-Jackson had appeared in a one-day international. With Wasim Akram deemed unfit, Waqar Younis captained Pakistan for the first time. He was the youngest player to lead Pakistan, and his devastating bowling was to make him Man of the Match. Andy Flower was leading Zimbabwe for the first time in a Test match.

Waqar won the toss, and Pakistan batted. They won few friends for their slow progress on the first two days, but it must be said that Zimbabwe fielded brilliantly. Aamir Sohail dominated the opening stand of 95 before becoming the first Test victim of off-spinner Peall. Inzamam-ul-Haq was the only other batsman to be dismissed on the first day which ended with Pakistan on 197. Shoaib

Whittal has his stumps shattered by Ata-ur-Rehman and Pakistan are close to winning the first Test match against Zimbabwe. (Mueen-ud-Din Hameed/Sports-Line)

FIRST TEST MATCH – PAKISTAN *v.* ZIMBABWE
1, 2, 3, 4 and 5 December 1993 at Defence Stadium, Karachi

PAKISTAN

	FIRST INNINGS			SECOND INNINGS	
Aamir Sohail	b Peall	63	run out		29
Shoaib Mohammad	c A. Flower, b Rennie	81			
Inzamam-ul-Haq	c A. Flower, b Brandes	21	(2) not out		57
Javed Miandad	lbw, b Brandes	70	run out		12
Basit Ali	c A. Flower, b Whittal	36	(3) c and b Brandes		13
Asif Mujtaba	c Dekker, b Brandes	4	(5) not out		10
*Rashid Latif	not out	68			
Waqar Younis (capt)	c Peall, b G.W. Flower	13			
Mushtaq Ahmed	c A. Flower, b Peall	18			
Tauseef Ahmed	not out	21			
Ata-ur-Rehman					
Extras	b 15, lb 12, nb 1	28	b 6, lb 2, w 1, nb 1		10
	(for 8 wickets, dec.)	423	(for 3 wickets, dec.)		131

ZIMBABWE

	FIRST INNINGS			SECOND INNINGS	
G.W. Flower	b Waqar	24	b Ata-ur-Rehman		25
M.H. Dekker	lbw, b Waqar	5	lbw, b Waqar		0
A.D.R. Campbell	lbw, b Mushtaq	53	c Inzamam, b Mushtaq		8
D.L. Houghton	lbw, b Waqar	46	lbw, b Waqar		18
*A. Flower (capt)	lbw, b Ata-ur-Rehman	63	c Inzamam, b Mushtaq		21
G.J. Whittal	run out	33	b Ata-ur-Rehman		2
G.K. Bruk-Jackson	b Waqar	31	lbw, b Waqar		4
S.G. Peall	c Sohail, b Waqar	0	b Waqar		0
D.H. Streak	b Waqar	0	not out		19
E.A. Brandes	not out	0	b Waqar		17
J.A. Rennie	lbw, b Waqar	3	lbw, b Waqar		0
Extras	b 5, lb 24, w 1, nb 1	31	b 12, lb 5, nb 3		20
		289			134

	O	M	R	W	O	M	R	W
Brandes	35	4	106	3	13	–	59	1
Streak	29	6	77	–	10	1	40	–
Rennie	32	6	90	1	3	–	24	–
Whittal	12	4	26	1				
Peall	41	10	89	2				
G.W. Flower	6	2	8	1				

	O	M	R	W	O	M	R	W
Waqar Younis	34.1	3	91	7	21.5	7	44	6
Ata-ur-Rehman	15	5	28	1	16	6	20	2
Mushtaq Ahmed	39	11	89	1	17	7	24	2
Tauseef Ahmed	23	7	49	–	6	2	13	–
Shoaib Mohammad	1	–	1	–				
Aamir Sohail	1	–	1	–	2	–	16	–
Asif Mujtaba	3	2	1	–				

FALL OF WICKETS

1–95, 2–134, 3–217, 4–268, 5–280, 6–305, 7–332, 8–363
1–47, 2–76, 3–108

FALL OF WICKETS

1–16, 2–71, 3–132, 4–153, 5–230, 6–280, 7–284, 8–284, 9–285
1–1, 2–17, 3–61, 4–63, 5–65, 6–78, 7–80, 8–92, 9–130

Umpires: Mahboob Shah & Shakeel Khan

Pakistan won by 131 runs

Mohammad, recalled to the Test side for the first time since the tour of England in 1992, had reached 71.

Shoaib's obdurate innings came to an end on the second day, but Javed Miandad hit 7 fours in his 175-ball innings to put Pakistan in total command. Rashid Latif reached a spirited 68, his highest score in Test cricket, before Waqar declared on the third morning. Zimbabwe faced a daunting task on a pitch of low bounce.

In spite of the early loss of Dekker, Zimbabwe battled manfully, and Campbell was particularly impressive with 7 fours in his 53. Houghton, a fine player, hit 8 fours, and Zimbabwe reached the close with 179 on the board for the loss of four wickets.

With Andy Flower still at the crease, Zimbabwe looked quite capable of drawing the match, but after Flower was leg before to Ata-ur-Rehman, Waqar Younis brushed aside the tail. The last five wickets went down for nine runs, and Waqar took four wickets in 15 balls.

Pakistan went for quick runs when they batted a second time. They reached 111 for 3 before the close and added another 20 on the last morning before Waqar declared to leave Zimbabwe 68 overs in which to score 266 to win.

Any hope of scoring the runs disappeared when Dekker and Campbell were soon out, and it soon looked as if the game would be over early when another blast from Waqar, who needs little help from his fielders, sent Zimbabwe crashing to 92 for 8. Then came unexpected resistance from Streak and Brandes. They held out for 68

minutes before Brandes had his stumps shattered by Waqar. Rennie fell almost immediately to leave Streak bravely unbeaten on 19 which had occupied 137 minutes. Rennie's wicket fell with only 31 balls remaining so that Zimbabwe had come very close to denying Pakistan. Waqar Younis could not be denied. His 13 for 135 was his best performance in Test cricket.

 SECOND TEST MATCH
PAKISTAN *v.* ZIMBABWE, at Rawalpindi

Having provided Test cricket's 70th venue in staging the first match of the series at the Defence Stadium in Karachi, Pakistan provided the 71st by scheduling the second match in Rawalpindi. Wasim Akram returned to lead Pakistan as his hand injury had healed, and a first Test cap was given to Ashfaq Ahmed. Both spinners, Mushtaq and Tauseef, were omitted. David Brain returned to the Zimbabwe side in place of Rennie. Andy Flower won the toss and asked Pakistan to bat.

From the start, the Pakistan batting looked fragile on a pitch which encouraged the seamers. In 75 overs on the first day, Pakistan made 185 for 5, and at one time, they had looked as if they might fare worse. Inzamam and Javed were bowled as they played across the line, and Basit Ali was caught when he hooked rashly. A sixth-wicket stand of 56 between Asif Mujtaba and Rashid Latif was broken early on the second morning, and the last four wickets fell rapidly. Zimbabwe had bowled very well, with Brain taking the main honours to return his best Test figures with his left-arm medium pace.

Zimbabwe started badly, losing Grant Flower to the fifth ball of the first over without a run scored. Flower edged a lifting delivery into the hands of first slip. Undaunted, Campbell attacked from the start and raced to 50 off 40 balls in 52 minutes. He hit 8 fours and a six in this first part of his innings, and 3 more fours followed off the next five balls he faced. Then, to the astonishment of the Pakistan press as well as of Campbell himself, he was given out leg before by umpire Javed Akhtar when the ball clearly hit him outside the line of the leg stump.

The Pakistan bowlers now regained control, and although Zimbabwe passed 200 with only five wickets down on the third day, they could take just a slender lead as Waqar Younis again caused havoc among the lower order. For the 15th time in Test cricket, he took five or more wickets in an innings, and once more he was to be named as Man of the Match.

Zimbabwe owed much to the dogged determination of Dekker who batted into the third day and was the backbone of the innings, but now it was the bowlers who became the heroes. In the 22 overs at the end of the day, Streak dismissed both openers and Brain accounted for nightwatchman Ata-ur-Rehman. Pakistan went nervously into the rest day on 40 for 3.

A rising star among Pakistan's pace bowlers – Ashfaq Ahmed who won his first Test cap in the match against Zimbabwe at Rawalpindi. (Mueen-ud-Din Hameed/Sports-Line)

When play resumed Brandes and Streak quickly got rid of Javed and Inzamam, and Pakistan were 58 for 5. Basit Ali countered with an aggressive innings that saw him hit six boundaries and share a stand of 74 with Asif Mujtaba. As Asif Mujtaba offered solidity so his partners provided the aggression, and Rashid Latif hit 7 fours in a fifty that came off 78 balls in 105 minutes. Asif and Rashid added 77 of which Asif's share was only 18, but his contribution to Pakistan's recovery could not be measured in runs alone.

Pakistan closed the fourth day on 221 for 8 and added another 27 on the last morning. Streak ended the innings by having Waqar caught in the gully and so completed his first five-wicket haul in Test cricket. Zimbabwe needed 240 in 67 overs to gain their first Test victory in what was their sixth Test match. They were entitled to have every confidence of success.

This confidence was drained when Grant Flower was bowled by the first ball of the innings, but Campbell, who looked a glorious player in this match, and Dekker added 135 in 178 minutes. Campbell played some exciting shots as he had done in the first innings, and he became Zimbabwe's leading run-scorer in Test cricket. While he was at the wicket Zimbabwe had scent of victory, but a

Glorious batting in the second Test match from Zimbabwe's Alistair Campbell – a thrilling player. (Mueen-ud-Din Hameed/Sports-Line)

SECOND TEST MATCH – PAKISTAN v. ZIMBABWE
9, 10, 11, 13 and 14 December 1993 at Rawalpindi Stadium, Rawalpindi

PAKISTAN

	FIRST INNINGS		SECOND INNINGS	
Aamir Sohail	c Houghton, b Streak	8	lbw, b Streak	9
Shoaib Mohammad	lbw, b Brain	18	c A. Flower, b Streak	13
Inzamam-ul-Haq	b Brain	38	b Brandes	14
Javed Miandad	b Streak	20	(5) b Streak	10
Basit Ali	c Streak, b Brandes	25	(6) lbw, b Brandes	40
Asif Mujtaba	not out	54	(7) c A. Flower, b Brain	51
*Rashid Latif	lbw, b Brain	33	(8) c Houghton, b Streak	61
Wasim Akram (capt)	c Campbell, b Brandes	11	(9) lbw, b Brandes	15
Waqar Younis	lbw, b Brandes	7	(10) c Campbell, b Streak	17
Ata-ur-Rehman	lbw, b Brain	10	(4) lbw, b Brain	0
Ashfaq Ahmed	c A. Flower, b Streak	0	not out	1
Extras	b 4, lb 12, w 2, nb 3	21	b 1, lb 11, w 3, nb 2	17
		245		**248**

ZIMBABWE

	FIRST INNINGS		SECOND INNINGS	
G.W. Flower	c Inzamam, b Wasim	0	b Wasim	0
M.H. Dekker	c Inzamam, b Waqar	68	not out	68
A.D.R. Campbell	lbw, b Ata-ur-Rehman	63	c Sohail, b Ata-ur-Rehman	75
D.L. Houghton	c Asif, b Ashfaq	5	lbw, b Waqar	4
*A. Flower (capt)	c Wasim, b Waqar	12	c Rashid, b Waqar	0
G.J. Whittal	c Inzamam, b Ashfaq	29	lbw, b Wasim	0
H.H. Streak	c Inzamam, b Waqar	2	(8) b Waqar	0
G.K. Bruk-Jackson	c Aamir, b Waqar	0	(7) c Rashid, b Wasim	4
D.H. Brain	c Rehman, b Waqar	16	b Waqar	2
E.A. Brandes	c Basit, b Wasim	18	lbw, b Wasim	1
S.G. Peall	not out	11	c Inzamam, b Wasim	10
Extras	b 9, lb 10, w 1, nb 10	30	b 1, lb 11, w 1, nb 10	23
		254		**187**

	O	M	R	W	O	M	R	W
Brandes	32	5	82	3	31	9	71	3
Brain	32	9	41	4	34	6	73	2
Streak	23.2	5	58	3	20.3	3	56	5
Whittal	17	6	39	–	4	1	10	–
Peall	6	3	9	–	8	4	13	–
G.W. Flower					4	–	13	–

	O	M	R	W	O	M	R	W
Wasim Akram	21	4	68	2	23.2	3	65	5
Waqar Younis	19	3	88	5	21	4	50	4
Ata-ur-Rehman	14	4	40	1	8	1	22	1
Ashfaq Ahmed	17	8	31	2	6	1	22	–
Aamir Sohail	3	–	8	–				
Shoaib Mohammad					4	1	16	–

FALL OF WICKETS

1–29, 2–33, 3–99, 4–101, 5–131, 6–187, 7–209, 8–225, 9–241
1–25, 2–38, 3–39, 4–54, 5–58, 6–132, 7–209, 8–219, 9–240

FALL OF WICKETS

1–0, 2–102, 3–110, 4–126, 5–131, 6–203, 7–203, 8–204, 9–225
1–0, 2–135, 3–140, 4–144, 5–147, 6–152, 7–153, 8–164, 9–168

Umpires: Javed Akhtar & Shakoor Rana

Pakistan won by 52 runs

Grant Flower is bowled by Wasim Akram with the first ball of Zimbabwe's second innings. (Mueen-ud-Din Hameed/Sports-Line)

THIRD TEST MATCH – PAKISTAN v. ZIMBABWE
16, 17, 18, 20 and 21 December 1993 at Qaddafi Stadium, Lahore

PAKISTAN

	FIRST INNINGS		SECOND INNINGS	
Aamir Sohail	c Campbell, b Brain	2	c James, b Brain	32
Shoaib Mohammad	c Brandes, b Rennie	14	not out	53
Inzamam-ul-Haq	b Brandes	33		
Javed Miandad	lbw, b Brain	31		
Basit Ali	b Brain	29		
Asif Mujtaba	c James, b Brain	0	(3) not out	65
*Rashid Latif	c Houghton, b Brandes	7		
Wasim Akram (capt)	not out	16		
Waqar Younis	b Brain	0		
Mushtaq Ahmed	b Brandes	1		
Ata-ur-Rehman	c James, b Rennie	0		
Extras	b 4, lb 6, nb 4	14	b 7, lb 13, w 1, nb 3	24
		147	(for 1 wicket)	174

ZIMBABWE

	FIRST INNINGS	
G.W. Flower	c Rashid, b Ata-ur-Rehman	30
M.H. Dekker	c Rashid, b Wasim	2
A.D.R. Campbell	c Rashid, b Waqar	6
D.L. Houghton	c Rashid, b Waqar	50
A. Flower (capt)	not out	62
G.J. Whittal	c Asif, b Wasim	2
*W.R. James	c Shoaib, b Waqar	8
H.H. Streak	b Waqar	0
D.H. Brain	c Sohail, b Wasim	28
E.A. Brandes	lbw, b Wasim	9
J.A. Rennie	c Rashid, b Waqar	2
Extras	b 10, lb 13, w 1, nb 7	31
		230

	O	M	R	W	O	M	R	W
Brandes	14	3	45	3	16	5	31	–
Brain	15	3	42	5	14	6	28	1
Streak	12	3	28	–	16	4	25	–
Rennie	10.4	3	22	2	14	6	35	–
G.W. Flower					10	2	15	–
Whittal					10.5	4	17	–
Campbell					1	–	3	–
A. Flower					0.1	–	0	–

	O	M	R	W
Wasim Akram	32	7	70	4
Waqar Younis	34.4	9	100	5
Ata-ur-Rehman	13	6	24	1
Mushtaq Ahmed	5	1	13	–

FALL OF WICKETS

1–3, 2–50, 3–54, 4–107, 5–111, 6–130, 7–130, 8–135, 9–140
1–56

FALL OF WICKETS

1–17, 2–35, 3–88, 4–121, 5–126, 6–141, 7–141, 8–187, 9–215

Umpires: Khizar Hayat & Athar Zaidi

Match drawn

TEST MATCH AVERAGES – PAKISTAN *v.* ZIMBABWE

PAKISTAN BATTING

	M	Inns	NO	Runs	HS	Av	100s	50s
Asif Mujtaba	3	6	3	184	65*	61.33	–	3
Rashid Latif	3	4	1	169	68*	56.33	–	2
Shoaib Mohammad	3	5	1	179	81	44.75	–	2
Inzamam-ul-Haq	3	5	1	163	57*	40.75	–	1
Javed Miandad	3	5	–	143	70	28.60	–	1
Basit Ali	3	5	–	143	40	28.60	–	–
Aamir Sohail	3	6	–	143	63	23.83	–	1
Wasim Akram	2	3	1	42	16*	21.00	–	–
Mushtaq Ahmed	2	2	–	19	18	9.50	–	–
Waqar Younis	3	4	–	37	17	9.25	–	–
Ata-ur-Rehman	3	3	–	10	10	3.33	–	–

Played in one Test: Tauseef Ahmed 21*; Ashfaq Ahmed 0 & 1*

ZIMBABWE BATTING

	M	Inns	NO	Runs	HS	Av	100s	50s
A.D.R. Campbell	3	5	–	205	75	41.00	–	3
A. Flower	3	5	1	158	63	39.50	–	2
M.H. Decker	3	5	1	143	68*	35.75	–	2
D.L. Houghton	3	5	–	123	50	24.60	–	1
G.W. Flower	3	5	–	79	30	15.80	–	–
D.H. Brain	2	3	–	46	28	15.33	–	–
G.J. Whittal	3	5	–	66	33	13.20	–	–
E.A. Brandes	3	5	1	45	18	11.25	–	–
G.K. Bruk-Jackson	2	4	–	39	31	9.75	–	–
S.G. Peall	2	4	1	21	11*	7.00	–	–
H.H. Streak	3	5	1	21	19*	5.25	–	–
J.A. Rennie	2	3	–	5	3	1.66	–	–

Played in one Test: W.R. James 8

PAKISTAN BOWLING

	Overs	Mds	Runs	Wkts	Av	Best	10/m	5/inn
Waqar Younis	130.4	31	373	27	13.81	7-91	1	4
Wasim Akram	76.2	14	203	11	18.45	5-65	–	1
Ata-ur-Rehman	66	22	134	6	22.33	2-20	–	–
Ashfaq Ahmed	23	9	53	2	26.50	2-31	–	–
Mushtaq Ahmed	61	19	126	3	42.00	2-24	–	–
Shoaib Mohammad	5	1	17	–	–	–	–	–
Aamir Sohail	6	–	26	–	–	–	–	–
Tauseef Ahmed	29	9	62	–	–	–	–	–

Bowled in one innings: Asif Mujtaba 3-2-1-0

ZIMBABWE BOWLING

	Overs	Mds	Runs	Wkts	Av	Best	10/m	5/inn
D.H. Brain	95	24	184	12	15.33	5-42	–	1
E.A. Brandes	141	26	394	13	30.30	3-45	–	–
H.H. Streak	110.5	22	284	8	35.50	5-56	–	1
G.W. Flower	20	4	36	1	36.00	1-8	–	–
S.G. Peall	55	17	111	2	55.50	2-89	–	–
J.A. Rennie	59.4	15	171	3	57.00	2-22	–	–
G.J. Whittal	43.5	15	92	1	92.00	1-26	–	–

Bowled in one innings: A. Flower 0.1-0-0-0; A.D.R. Campbell 1-0-3-0

PAKISTAN FIELDING FIGURES

7 – Rashid Latif and Inzamam-ul-Haq; 4 – Aamir Sohail; 2 – Asif Mujtaba; 1 – Shoaib Mohammad, Basit Ali, Wasim Akram and Ata-ur-Rehman

ZIMBABWE FIELDING FIGURES

7 – A. Flower; 3 – A.D.R. Campbell, G.W. Flower and W.R. James; 2 – E.A. Brandes; 1 – M.H. Dekker, S.G. Peall and H.H. Streak

reckless pull resulted in a top edge to extra cover half an hour before tea, and that, sadly, marked the end of Zimbabwe.

Waqar dismissed Houghton, and Andy Flower was brilliantly caught left-handed by Rashid diving in front of first slip. The wicket-keeper flung himself backwards and to his left. The floodgates were now open, and only last man Peall gave Dekker any help in trying to stem the flow. Inzamam equalled the Pakistan record when he held an edge from Peall at first slip to claim his fifth catch of the innings, and Pakistan were victors by 52 runs.

Once again Zimbabwe had lost a match, and the series, which they might have saved. Dekker became the first Zimbabwean and the 27th opener in Test cricket to carry his bat through a completed innings. He had survived for 289 minutes.

This was Wasim Akram's first Test victory as captain of Pakistan. As it transpired, it was likely to be his last for some time.

Brave batting from opener Mark Dekker who became the first Zimbabwean to carry his bat through a Test innings. (Mueen-ud-Din Hameed/Sports-Line)

Five wickets for David Brain in the first innings of the third Test match. (Mueen-ud-Din Hameed/Sports-Line)

day during which Houghton reached his fifty and 11 runs were scored.

Houghton was immediately out on the fourth morning, and when Whittal was caught at short-leg, James at third slip, and Streak bowled first ball, Zimbabwe were 141 for 7. Brain, 28 off 26 balls and Man of the Match, helped to add 46 for the eighth wicket, and Brandes and Rennie also gave useful assistance to Andy Flower who scored 62 in $2\frac{1}{2}$ hours and took his side to a commendable first-innings lead of 83.

Pakistan scored 37 runs in 27 overs before the close, and the final day provided a tedium which is best forgotten.

Waqar Younis was undeniably Man of the Series for his 27 wickets, but Zimbabwe had surprised Pakistan and many others with the quality and determination of their cricket. They were learning fast. Pakistan, on the other hand, were still in search of some batting stability to complement the best pace-bowling attack in the world.

Wicket-keeping of the highest order from Rashid Latif. (David Munden/Sports-Line)

THIRD TEST MATCH
PAKISTAN *v.* ZIMBABWE, at Lahore

Mushtaq Ahmed returned in place of Ashfaq Ahmed while James came in as wicket-keeper for Zimbabwe, so releasing Andy Flower to concentrate on the duties of captaincy, and Peall was omitted. Rennie came in for Bruk-Jackson. James was making his Test debut.

Zimbabwe won the toss, and Pakistan were asked to bat on a pitch which encouraged the seam bowlers. In Brain's first over, Aamir Sohail was caught in the gully. Shoaib and Inzamam suggested few difficulties until Shoaib was caught at long-leg hooking a bouncer. Inzamam played on, as did Basit Ali, and when Asif Mujtaba was well caught down the leg side Pakistan were 111 for 5. There was to be no effective recovery, and with David Brain taking 5 for 42, his best figures in Test cricket, Pakistan were all out for 147, and Zimbabwe ended a most satisfactory first day on 15 without loss.

Three wickets fell on the second day which was reduced by more than two hours because of mist and bad light. All three batsmen fell to excellent catches by Rashid Latif, but Houghton found form, and the score moved to 110 for 3. Only 21 minutes' play was possible on the third

ONE-DAY SERIES
PAKISTAN v. ZIMBABWE

QUAID-E-AZAM TROPHY

Not surprisingly, Pakistan totally dominated the one-day series. Wasim Akram destroyed the visitors in the opening match to leave his batsmen with the easiest of tasks, and when Zimbabwe's batsmen found some form on Christmas Day Pakistan replied with an opening stand of 88 between Asif Mujtaba and Saeed Anwar. Asif showed the other side of his character from the one he had displayed in the final Test with a flowing innings.

The third match witnessed two newcomers to one-day international cricket, Glen Bruk-Jackson and Irfan Bhatti who many thought should have played at Rawalpindi in the second Test. Inzamam-ul-Haq played a blistering innings, and Zimbabwe batted poorly. In the left-handed Alistair Campbell, however, they have a batsman of world class, and much will be heard of him.

Led by former Test wicket-keeper Moin Khan, Karachi Whites sought to retain the Quaid-e-Azam Trophy which they had won for the past three seasons. The senior first-class competition has lost some of its lustre in recent years since it has been restricted to regional sides and departments have been allowed entry only to the Patron's Trophy. The tournament's importance was reduced further in 1994 when the Test players were unable to take part in the earlier rounds because of Pakistan's tour of New Zealand. The party to New Zealand was led by Salim Malik following the player revolt which had caused changes to the original selection and the removal of Wasim Akram from the captaincy.

8, 9, 10 and 11 January 1994 *at National Stadium, Karachi*

Karachi Whites 141 (Zahid Ahmed 6 for 15) and 201 for 7 (Zahid Ahmed 4 for 65)

Faisalabad 274 (Zahid Ahmed 58, Saadat Gul 58, Athar Laeeq 4 for 44)

Match drawn

Faisalabad 4 pts., Karachi Whites 0 pts.

FIRST ONE-DAY INTERNATIONAL – PAKISTAN v. ZIMBABWE
24 December 1993 at National Stadium, Karachi

ZIMBABWE			PAKISTAN		
*A. Flower (capt)	c Rashid Latif, b Wasim Akram	0	Saeed Anwar	b Streak	68
G.W. Flower	b Aqib Javed	6	Asif Mujtaba	b Brain	11
A.D.R. Campbell	b Wasim Akram	8	Inzamam-ul-Haq	b Streak	12
D.L. Houghton	c Basit Ali, b Salim Malik	52	Basit Ali	not out	41
M.H. Dekker	run out	33	*Rashid Latif	not out	10
G.J. Whittal	run out	18	Javed Miandad		
D.H. Brain	b Aqib Javed	4	Salim Malik		
E.A. Brandes	lbw, b Wasim Akram	2	Wasim Akram (capt)		
S.G. Peall	b Wasim Akram	0	Waqar Younis		
H.H. Streak	c Javed Miandad, b Wasim Akram	2	Mushtaq Ahmed		
J.A. Rennie	not out	3	Aqib Javed		
Extras	b 1, lb 9, w 3, nb 2	15	Extras	lb 2, w 3, nb 1	5
(38 overs)		143	(33.5 overs)	(for 3 wickets)	147

	O	M	R	W		O	M	R	W
Wasim Akram	7	1	15	5	Brandes	5	–	31	–
Aqib Javed	8	1	21	2	Brain	7	–	30	1
Waqar Younis	7	–	43	–	Peall	7	1	30	–
Mushtaq Ahmed	8	1	21	–	Streak	8	2	15	2
Salim Malik	5	–	19	1	Rennie	6	–	32	–
Asif Mujtaba	3	–	14	–	Dekker	0.5	–	7	–

FALL OF WICKETS
1–0, 2–19, 3–22, 4–92, 5–117, 6–128, 7–131, 8–131, 9–139

FALL OF WICKETS
1–18, 2–48, 3–126

Umpires: Amanullah Khan & Ferozuddin Butt *Man of the Match*: Wasim Akram *Pakistan won by 7 wickets*

SECOND ONE-DAY INTERNATIONAL – PAKISTAN v. ZIMBABWE
25 December 1993 at Rawalpindi Stadium, Rawalpindi

ZIMBABWE

A. Flower (capt)	lbw, **b** Wasim Akram	14
M.H. Dekker	**b** Aamer Nazir	23
A.D.R. Campbell	**b** Wasim Akram	74
D.L. Houghton	c Basit Ali, **b** Waqar Younis	58
D.H. Brain	c Asif Mujtaba, **b** Waqar Younis	0
G.J. Whittal	not out	3
G.W. Flower		
*W.R. James		
E.A. Brandes		
H.H. Streak		
J.A. Rennie		
Extras	lb **12**, w **9**, nb **2**	23
		——
(40 overs)	(for 5 wickets)	195

PAKISTAN

Saeed Anwar	**b** Dekker	45
Asif Mujtaba	c Whittal, **b** Streak	61
Basit Ali	**b** Dekker	5
Javed Miandad	c Rennie, **b** Brandes	19
Inzamam-ul-Haq	not out	44
Wasim Akram (capt)	not out	6
Salim Malik		
*Rashid Latif		
Waqar Younis		
Aqib Javed		
Aamer Nazir		
Extras	b **1**, lb **7**, w **8**	16
		——
(39.4 overs)	(for 4 wickets)	196

	O	M	R	W
Wasim Akram	8	–	32	2
Waqar Younis	8	–	46	2
Aamer Nazir	8	–	30	1
Aqib Javed	8	–	31	–
Salim Malik	7	–	37	–
Asif Mujtaba	1	–	7	–

	O	M	R	W
Brandes	8	1	40	1
Brain	7	1	30	–
Rennie	7.4	–	38	–
Streak	7	–	31	1
G.W. Flower	3	–	15	–
Dekker	4	–	16	2
Campbell	2	–	9	–
A. Flower	1	–	9	–

FALL OF WICKETS
1–30, 2–87, 3–189, 4–190, 5–195

FALL OF WICKETS
1–88, 2–98, 3–121, 4–188

Umpires: Khalid Aziz & Siddiq Khan   *Man of the Match*: Asif Mujtaba   *Pakistan won by 6 wickets*

THIRD ONE-DAY INTERNATIONAL – PAKISTAN v. ZIMBABWE
27 December 1993 at Qaddafi Stadium, Lahore

PAKISTAN

Saeed Anwar	c James, **b** Brandes	25
Asif Mujtaba	c James, **b** Rennie	12
Inzamam-ul-Haq	not out	80
Basit Ali	**b** Streak	9
Javed Miandad	lbw, **b** Streak	55
Wasim Akram (capt)	not out	17
Salim Malik		
*Rashid Latif		
Mushtaq Ahmed		
Aqib Javed		
Irfan Bhatti		
Extras	b **1**, lb **3**, w **10**, nb **4**	18
		——
(40 overs)	(for 4 wickets)	216

ZIMBABWE

A. Flower (capt)	c Aqib Javed, **b** Irfan Bhatti	15
M.H. Dekker	c Mushtaq Ahmed, **b** Irfan Bhatti	4
A.D.R. Campbell	st Rashid Latif, **b** Mushtaq Ahmed	26
D.L. Houghton	lbw, **b** Mushtaq Ahmed	9
G.J. Whittal	c Rashid Latif, **b** Mushtaq Ahmed	7
G.K. Bruk-Jackson	st Rashid Latif, **b** Salim Malik	12
*W.R. James	not out	14
D.H. Brain	c and **b** Salim Malik	1
E.A. Brandes	c Irfan Bhatti, **b** Salim Malik	7
H.H. Streak	c Asif Mujtaba, **b** Basit Ali	7
J.A. Rennie	not out	13
Extras	b **4**, lb **8**, w **11**, nb **3**	26
		——
(40 overs)	(for 9 wickets)	141

	O	M	R	W
Brandes	8	–	44	1
Brain	6	–	33	–
Rennie	8	–	53	1
Streak	8	1	32	2
Dekker	5	–	27	–
Whittal	4	–	18	–
Campbell	1	–	5	–

	O	M	R	W
Wasim Akram	5	–	29	–
Irfan Bhatti	8	–	23	2
Aqib Javed	4	–	8	–
Mushtaq Ahmed	8	1	19	3
Salim Malik	8	1	22	3
Asif Mujtaba	4	–	11	–
Basit Ali	3	–	17	1

FALL OF WICKETS
1–41, 2–42, 3–61, 4–188

FALL OF WICKETS
1–21, 2–21, 3–61, 4–66, 5–79, 6–88, 7–91, 8–101, 9–117

Umpires: Iftikhar Malik & Ikram Rabbani   *Man of the Match*: Inzamam-ul-Haq   *Pakistan won by 75 runs*

Lahore 430 (Mansoor Rana 115, Shahid Saeed 92, Aamir Malik 54, Murtaza Hussain 5 for 118)

Bahawalpur 262 (Mazhar Qayyum 64, Saifullah 50, Mohammad Ali 5 for 87) and 7 for 2

Match drawn

Lahore 4 pts., Bahawalpur 0 pts.

at Margazhar, Islamabad

Sargodha 291 for 8 dec. (Akram Raza 67, Mohammad Nawaz 57, Ayaz Jilani 4 for 92)

Islamabad 279 (Zahid Umar 57, Sajjad Ali 50, Sajjad Akbar 6 for 82)

Match drawn

Sargodha 4 pts., Islamabad 0 pts.

at Rawalpindi Stadium, Rawalpindi

Rawalpindi 150 (Ali Gohar 5 for 63, Shakeel Sajjad 4 for 34) and 256 (Mohammad Riaz 59 not out, Sher Ali 52, Ali Gohar 5 for 90)

Karachi Blues 406 for 8 dec. (Ata-ur-Rehman 103, Mohammad Javed 76, Iqbal Imam 58, Mohammad Akram 4 for 112) and 4 for 0

Karachi Blues 10 pts., Rawalpindi 0 pts.

Little play was possible on the last day in Karachi so depriving Faisalabad of an unexpected victory. Slow left-arm bowler Zahid Ahmed took ten wickets in a match for the first time in his career.

Rain restricted play on the first day in Lahore where the home side scored heavily. Mansoor Rana hit 115 off 205 balls after Shahid Saeed and Shahid Anwar had put on 90 for the first wicket. A third-wicket stand of 83 between wicket-keeper Saifullah and Mazhar Qayyum was the core of Bahawalpur's response, but it could not save them from having to follow-on on the last day.

There was no play possible on the first two days in Islamabad, and Ata-ur-Rehman, Karachi's right-handed batsman (not the Lahore Test bowler), hit the first century of his career to set up Karachi Blues' win over Rawalpindi in Rawalpindi.

15, 16, 17 and **18 January 1994** *at National Stadium, Karachi*

Lahore 260 (Babar Zaman 72, Shahid Anwar 58, Haaris A. Khan 4 for 72) and 225 for 2 (Shahid Saeed 80, Zahid Fazal 67 not out)

Karachi Whites 501 for 9 dec. (Mahmood Hamid 202 not out, Athar Laeeq 80, Ghulam Ali 59, Shahid Ali Khan 4 for 140)

Match drawn

Karachi Whites 4 pts., Lahore 0 pts.

Shahid Saeed, 229 for Lahore against Faisalabad and a prime reason for his side's success in the Quaid-e-Azam Trophy. (David Munden/Sports-Line)

at Iqbal Stadium, Faisalabad

Bahawalpur 12 for 0

v. **Faisalabad**

Match abandoned

No points

at Margazhar, Islamabad

Islamabad 255 for 9 dec. (Tanvir Razzaq 86)

Karachi Blues 256 for 3 (Sohail Miandad 142, Sohail Jaffar 63 not out)

Match drawn

Karachi Blues 4 pts., Islamabad 0 pts.

at Rawalpindi Stadium, Rawalpindi

Sargodha 239 for 6 (Asad Malik 100 not out, Akram Raza 58)

v. **Rawalpindi**

Match abandoned

No points

Rain ruined the second round of matches in three centres, but not in Karachi where Mahmood Hamid hit his first double century and Athar Laeeq the highest score of his career. There was also a career-best for Sohail Miandad and a maiden first-class century for Asad Malik in the matches affected by the weather.

22, 23, 24 and 25 January 1994 *at National Stadium, Karachi*

Bahawalpur 319 (Mohammad Khalid 93 not out, Tariq Mahmood 79) and 228 (Mazhar Qayyum 74, Haaris A. Khan 4 for 82)

Karachi Whites 384 (Mahmood Hamid 102, Moin Khan 97, Mohammad Zahid 5 for 126, Murtaza Hussain 4 for 134) and 65 for 5

Match drawn

Karachi Whites 4 pts., Bahawalpur 0 pts.

at Lahore CA Ground, Lahore

Faisalabad 460 (Shahid Nawaz 267, Ijaz Ahmed 105, Mohammad Ali 5 for 142)

Lahore 485 for 4 (Shahid Saeed 229, Zahid Fazal 152)

Match drawn

Lahore 4 pts., Faisalabad 0 pts.

at Sargodha Sports Stadium, Sargodha

Karachi Blues 198 (Sohail Mehdi 60, Sajjad Akbar 4 for 64) and 415 for 5 (Mohammad Javed 116 not out, Manzoor Akhtar 115 not out, Sohail Miandad 69, Amiruddin 64)

Sargodha 301 (Akram Raza 97, Mohammad Husnain 78)

Match drawn

Sargodha 4 pts., Karachi Blues 0 pts.

at Rawalpindi Stadium, Rawalpindi

Islamabad 92 (Raja Afaq 5 for 37, Mohammad Riaz 4 for 30) and 171 (Raja Afaq 6 for 84)

Rawalpindi 281 (Nadeem Younis 95, Shahid Nasi 72, Ghaffar Kazmi 66, Ayaz Jilani 8 for 104)

Rawalpindi won by an innings and 17 runs

Rawalpindi 10 pts., Islamabad 0 pts.

Mahmood Hamid hit his second century in succession and shared a sixth-wicket stand of 189 with skipper Moin Khan as Karachi Whites drew with Bahawalpur, but the feast of runs was in Lahore. Shahid Nawaz hit the highest score of his career and the highest score of the season as he and Ijaz Ahmed who, in the Patron's Trophy had prospered for Railways, added 311 for Faisalabad's fourth wicket. Shahid Nawaz faced 346 balls. Lahore countered by taking first-innings points through Shahid Saeed who hit the first double century of his career and Zahid Fazal who hit the highest score of his career. Manzoor Akhtar and Mohammad Javed shared an unbroken sixth-wicket stand of 224 in the drawn game at Sargodha while off-break bowler Ayaz Jilani returned the best figures of his career for Islamabad and still finished on the losing side.

29, 30, 31 January and 1 February 1994 *at National Stadium, Karachi*

Karachi Whites 344 (Mahmood Hamid 157, Ayaz Jilani 4 for 72) and 196 for 6 (Sajid Ali 50)

Islamabad 155 (Aamer Ishaq 56, Haaris A. Khan 4 for 21, Humayun Fida Hussain 4 for 63) and 382 (Aamer Ishaq 93, Mujahid Jamshed 71)

Karachi Whites won by 4 wickets

Karachi Whites 10 pts., Islamabad 0 pts.

at Bahawal Stadium, Bahawalpur

Bahawalpur v. **Rawalpindi**

Match postponed

at Lahore CA Ground, Lahore

Lahore 499 for 9 dec. (Zahid Fazal 199, Shahid Anwar 65, Aamir Malik 63, Sohail Mehdi 4 for 120, Manzoor Akhtar 4 for 147)

Karachi Blues 329 (Manzoor Akhtar 124 not out, Mohammad Asif 4 for 110) and 387 for 5 (Iqbal Saleem 101 not out, Mohammad Javed 93, Amiruddin 82)

Match drawn

Lahore 4 pts., Karachi Blues 0 pts.

at Bohran Wali Ground, Faisalabad

Faisalabad 321 (Shahid Nawaz 54, Amanullah 4 for 86) and 194 (Nadeem Arshad 59, Mohammad Ramzan 54, Mohammad Husnain 4 for 8)

Sargodha 262 (Mohammad Nawaz 140 not out, Tanvir Afzal 4 for 85)

Match drawn

Faisalabad 4 pts., Sargodha 0 pts.

Mahmood Hamid hit his third century in successive matches as Karachi Whites gained their first win of the season. Forced to follow-on, Islamabad fought back well, but Karachi Whites hit 196 at nearly five an over to win.

The stadium at Bahawalpur was not available so the game with Rawalpindi was postponed until early April. At Lahore, Zahid Fazal bettered the career-best score he had established in the previous match, but splendid all-round cricket from Manzoor Akhtar and a maiden first-class hundred from Iqbal Saleem who shared a fifth-wicket partnership of 184 with Mohammad Javed saved Karachi Blues from defeat.

In Faisalabad, Mohammad Nawaz carried his bat through Sargodha's innings. He faced 265 balls and batted for 331 minutes.

6, 7, 8 and 9 February 1994 *at National Stadium, Karachi*

Rawalpindi 190 (Nadeem Younis 74, Shahid Javed 52, Nadeem Khan 4 for 66, Haaris A. Khan 4 for 68) and 206 (Nadeem Khan 5 for 84, Haaris A. Khan 5 for 93)

Karachi Whites 206 (Ghulam Ali 64, Shakeel Ahmed 7 for 69) and 194 for 7 (Aaley Haider 93 not out, Shakeel Ahmed 4 for 65)

Karachi Whites won by 3 wickets

Karachi Whites 10 pts., Rawalpindi 0 pts.

at Lahore CA Ground, Lahore

Bahawalpur 154 (Azhar Mahmood 6 for 68) and 156 for 5 (Mazhar Qayyum 66)

Islamabad 244 (Ayaz Jilani 51, Imran Adil 5 for 104)

Match drawn

Islamabad 4 pts., Bahawalpur 0 pts.

at Iqbal Stadium, Faisalabad

Karachi Blues 212 (Sohail Jaffar 67, Naved Nazeer 5 for 38) and 291 for 5 (Sohail Mehdi 102 not out, Manzoor Akhtar 100 not out, Sohail Miandad 50)

Faisalabad 154 (Shahid Nawaz 66, Ali Gohar 4 for 64)

Match drawn

Karachi Blues 4 pts., Faisalabad 0 pts.

at Sargodha Stadium, Sargodha

Sargodha 361 (Sajjad Akbar 143, Mohammad Nawaz 75, Ashraf Bashir 68, Tahir Shah 4 for 69)

Lahore 465 for 3 (Aamir Malik 200 not out, Mansoor Rana 100 not out, Zahid Fazal 80)

Match drawn

Lahore 4 pts., Sargodha 0 pts.

Karachi Whites notched up their second win in succession, but they were hard pressed to beat Rawalpindi in a low-scoring game. Needing 191 to win, they were 126 for 5, and the match was in the balance, but Aaley Haider hit the highest score of his career to steer them to victory.

The game in Lahore was abandoned on the last day, and Manzoor Akhtar hit another century for Karachi Blues as he and Sohail Mehdi shared an unbroken partnership of 205 for the sixth wicket on a rather meaningless last day. Mansoor Rana and Aamir Malik, who hit the first double century of his career, also shared a big stand, an unbroken 248 for Lahore's fourth wicket against Sargodha.

19, 20, 21 and **22 February 1994** at National Stadium, Karachi

Karachi Blues 130 (Haaris A. Khan 4 for 41) and 241 (Munir-ul-Haq 61, Haaris A. Khan 5 for 71)

Karachi Whites 304 (Mahmood Hamid 70, Nadeem Khan 62 not out, Mohammad Husnain 4 for 48) and 71 for 0 (Ghulam Ali 53 not out)

Karachi Whites won by 10 wickets

Karachi Whites 10 pts., Karachi Blues 0 pts.

at Lahore CA Ground, Lahore

Lahore 405 (Zahid Fazal 94, Aamir Manzoor 63, Ali Kamran 54 not out, Mohammad Asif 53, Aamir Nazir 4 for 136) and 295 for 9 (Aamir Malik 107, Mohammad Asif 50, Ali Kamran 50, Aqib Javed 4 for 92)

Islamabad 297 (Atif Rauf 100, Rameez Raja 80, Afzaal Haider 4 for 77)

Match drawn

Lahore 4 pts., Islamabad 0 pts.

at Iqbal Stadium, Faisalabad

Rawalpindi 385 (Mujahid Hameed 110, Nadeem Younis 71)

Faisalabad 140 (Shahid Nawaz 54, Raja Afaq 4 for 32) and 126 for 4 (Ijaz Ahmed 73 not out)

Match drawn

Rawalpindi 4 pts., Faisalabad 0 pts.

Aamir Malik 200 not out and 107 in successive matches for Lahore and outstanding success as captain. (Ben Radford/Allsport)

at Sargodha Stadium, Sargodha

Sargodha 277 (Idrees Baig 128 not out, Mohammad Altaf 5 for 91)

Bahawalpur 215 (Tariq Mahmood 87, Mohammad Sarfraz 4 for 89)

Match drawn

Sargodha 4 pts., Bahawalpur 0 pts.

Karachi Whites claimed top spot in the Quaid-e-Azam table with a comfortable victory over their local rivals. The Whites' last two wickets realised 116 runs with Nadeem Khan at number ten the principal run-getter. Off-break bowler Haaris Ahmed Khan had another fine match, taking 9 for 112.

Aamir Malik hit his second century in successive matches in the match at Lahore, and there were centuries also for Mujahid Hameed at Faisalabad, and at Sargodha for Idrees Baig who was being considered as a possible Test opener. There was no play on the first two days in Sargodha.

26, 27, 28 February and 1 March 1994 *at National Stadium, Karachi*

Sargodha 265 (Sajjad Akbar 138)

Karachi Whites 444 for 7 (Zafar Iqbal 115, Asif Rizvi 110 not out, Moin Khan 94)

Match drawn

Karachi Whites 4 pts., Sargodha 0 pts.

at Margazhar, Islamabad

Faisalabad 309 for 4 (Mohammad Ramzan 103, Shahid Nawaz 78 not out, Nadeem Afzal 52 not out)

v. **Islamabad**

Match abandoned

No points

at Rawalpindi Stadium, Rawalpindi

Lahore 458 (Zahid Fazal 133, Babar Zaman 80, Aslam Raza 57 not out, Shahid Anwar 55, Naeem Akhtar 5 for 115) and 28 for 3

Rawalpindi 280 (Maqsood Ahmed 68, Nadeem Abbasi 53, Naeem Ashraf 4 for 95, Mohammad Ali 4 for 115) and 301 (Nadeem Younis 103, Pervez Iqbal 52, Naeem Ashraf 5 for 79)

Match drawn

Lahore 4 pts., Rawalpindi 0 pts.

at Defence Stadium, Karachi

Karachi Blues *v.* **Bahawalpur**

Walk-over

Karachi Blues 10 pts., Bahawalpur 0 pts.

The last round of matches reduced the competition to something bordering on farce. Bahawalpur failed to arrive at the Defence Stadium in Karachi, and the Blues were given a walk-over. Bahawalpur still had their postponed match against Rawalpindi to arrange, but the governing body of the tournament decided to scratch them from the tournament which brought a slight re-arrangement in the top four places. Lahore, Karachi Blues, Karachi Whites, Islamabad and Sargodha all lost points that they had gained against Bahawalpur.

QUAID-E-AZAM TROPHY – FINAL TABLE

	P	W	L	D	Ab	Pts.
Karachi Whites	6	3	–	3	–	32
Lahore	6	–	–	6	–	20
Karachi Blues	6	1	1	4	–	18
Rawalpindi	6	1	2	2	1	14
Faisalabad	6	–	–	5	1	8
Sargodha	6	–	–	5	1	8
Islamabad	6	–	2	3	1	0

SEMI-FINALS

14, 15, 16 and 17 April 1994 *at Qaddafi Stadium, Lahore*

Rawalpindi 244 (Naeem Akhtar 56) and 253 for 8 (Nadeem Younis 74, Ihsan Butt 53 not out)

Lahore 294 (Naeem Ashraf 68, Shahid Anwar 60, Naeem Akhtar 6 for 98)

Match drawn

15, 16, 17 and 18 April 1994 *at National Stadium, Karachi*

Karachi Whites 560 (Ghulam Ali 138, Irfanullah 128, Zafar Iqbal 128, Mohammad Husnain 5 for 62) and 175 for 5 (Asim Rizvi 77 not out)

Karachi Blues 242 (Nadeem Khan 6 for 72, Haaris A. Khan 4 for 85)

Match drawn

In a competition rapidly losing credibility, Lahore and Karachi Whites reached the final by means of leading on the first innings in matches which were drawn. After a blank first day, Rawalpindi were put in to bat and struggled to 244 in 58 overs. Their score was boosted only by Naeem Akhtar's 56 off 41 balls at number nine. Lahore struggled in reply and were 211 for 8 before Naeem Ashraf and Mohsin Kamal added 83 in 79 minutes to give their side a first-innings lead and a place in the final.

Karachi Whites batted first when Moin Khan won the toss and batted well into the second day to build up a massive score which the Blues were never likely to approach.

QUAID-E-AZAM TROPHY FINAL
KARACHI WHITES *v.* LAHORE

The Test players had finished their travels to New Zealand and Sharjah and were available for the Quaid-e-Azam final. Basit Ali took over as captain of Karachi Whites, but lost the toss to Aamir Malik who asked Karachi to bat first on a pitch which looked likely to help the seamers. So it proved, as Karachi were bowled out in 37.2 overs by Mohsin Kamal and Naeem Ashraf. Only Basit Ali, with a ferocious 68 off 85 deliveries in under an hour and a half, offered real resistance.

Lahore finished the day in a strong position, 115 for 1, but the middle order collapsed on the second day as medium-pacer Zafar Iqbal produced the best bowling performance of his career. Some late hitting by Mohammad Ali, 33 off 44 balls in 49 minutes, restored Lahore's advantage, and from that point on, they always looked to be the winners. Basit Ali hastened the end with his declaration, and Naeem Ashraf whose left-arm medium pace had brought him the best figures of his career was named Man of the Match.

The structure and value of the first-class competitions in Pakistan is in urgent need of reappraisal.

Mohsin Kamal took eight wickets in the Quaid-e-Azam Trophy final as Lahore beat Karachi Whites. (David Munden/Sports-Line)

QUAID-E-AZAM TROPHY FINAL – LAHORE *v.* KARACHI WHITES
25, 26, 27 and 28 April 1994 at Qaddafi Stadium, Lahore

KARACHI WHITES

	FIRST INNINGS			SECOND INNINGS	
Ghulam Ali	c Ashraf, b Naeem	22	lbw, b Mohsin	11
Azam Khan	c Sohail, b Mohsin	2	c Ashraf, b Mohsin	3
Irfanullah	c Tahir, b Mohsin	10	c Ashraf, b Mohammad	0
Mahmood Hamid	c Tahir, b Naeem	6	c Shahid b Mohsin	33
Basit Ali (capt)	c Mohsin, b Naeem	68	c sub (Tanvir), b Mohsin	13
Asim Rizvi	c Ashraf, b Naeem	0	not out	25
Zafar Iqbal	c Shahid, b Sohail	23	c Shahid, b Naeem	29
*Rashid Latif	c Ashraf, b Mohsin	29	c Ashraf, b Mohsin	36
Athar Laeeq	c Ashraf, b Naeem	0		
Haaris A. Khan	not out	5		
Humayun Fida	lbw, b Naeem	0		
Extras	lb 1, nb 6	7	lb 2, nb 4	6
	penalty runs	20		
		192	(for 7 wickets, dec.)	156

LAHORE

	FIRST INNINGS			SECOND INNINGS	
Babar Zaman	b Zafar	68	(2) c Azam, b Humayun	19
Aamir Manzoor	c Ghulam, b Athar	33	(1) not out	45
Shahid Anwar	b Zafar	21		
Aamir Malik (capt)	b Zafar	14		
Tahir Shah	c Mahmood, b Zafar	0	(3) not out	27
Sohail Fazal	b Zafar	4		
Naeem Ashraf	b Ghulam	28		
*Ashraf Ali	c Rashid, b Zafar	16		
Mohsin Kamal	b Zafar	17		
Shahid Ali Khan	b Humayun	10		
Mohammad Ali	not out	33		
Extras	lb 2, w 1, nb 8	11	lb 2, w 1	3
		255	(for 1 wicket)	94

	O	M	R	W	O	M	R	W
Mohsin Kamal	15	1	84	3	11.5	–	84	5
Mohammad Ali	6	–	33	–	9	–	34	1
Naeem Ashraf	14.2	1	45	6	12	–	36	1
Sohail Fazal	1	–	9	1				
Shahid Ali Khan	1	1	0	–				
Aamir Malik					1	1	0	–

	O	M	R	W	O	M	R	W
Humayun Fida	13.4	1	55	1	3	–	28	1
Athar Laeeq	25	4	83	1	3	–	26	–
Zafar Iqbal	20	4	65	7	2	–	4	–
Haaris A. Khan	7	–	19	–	1	–	5	–
Ghulam Ali	6	1	31	1				
Rashid Latif					4	–	29	–

FALL OF WICKETS

1–4, 2–34, 3–36, 4–48, 5–48, 6–89, 7–137, 8–138, 9–172
1–13, 2–14, 3–14, 4–50, 5–67, 6–113, 7–156

FALL OF WICKETS

1–81, 2–119, 3–136, 4–136, 5–146, 6–147, 7–188, 8–203, 9–210
1–55

Umpires: Khizar Hayat & Riaz-ud-Din

Lahore won by 9 wickets

FIRST-CLASS AVERAGES

BATTING

	M	Inns	NO	Runs	HS	Av	100s	50s
Rizwan-uz-Zaman (PIA)	4	5	2	426	134	142.00	2	2
Manzoor Akhtar (KB)	6	7	3	389	124*	97.25	3	–
Atif Rauf (ADBP/I)	12	15	1	934	120	66.71	4	5
Idrees Baig (HB/S)	10	13	2	719	158	65.36	3	2
Aamir Malik (PIA/L)	17	21	2	1159	200*	61.00	5	3
Shaukat Mirza (HB)	9	10	2	488	160*	61.00	1	2
Mansoor Rana (ADBP/L)	14	18	5	767	115	59.00	3	3
Zahid Fazal (PIA/L)	17	23	2	1205	199	57.38	3	8
Akram Raza (HB/S)	13	15	3	657	145*	54.75	1	4
Mujahid Hameed (ADBP/R)	10	12	4	425	110	53.12	1	2
Shakeel Ahmed (HB/I)	11	12	–	628	200	52.33	2	2
Sajjad Akbar (PNSC/S)	13	17	2	775	143	51.66	3	3
Shahid Saeed (PACO/L)	14	21	2	939	229	49.42	3	3
Shahid Nawaz (PACO/F)	15	21	2	891	267	46.89	2	5
Manzoor Elahi (ADBP)	10	11	4	324	75	46.28	–	2
Asif Mohammad (PIA/R)	11	15	1	637	183	45.50	2	4
Mahmood Hamid (UB/KW)	17	28	4	1088	202*	45.33	4	4
Sohail Miandad (PIA/KB)	10	17	1	695	142	43.43	2	4
Ghaffar Kazmi (ADBP/R)	13	17	1	694	133	43.37	2	4
Zafar Iqbal (NB/KW)	6	8	–	344	128	43.00	2	1
Ijaz Ahmed (Ry/F)	13	20	3	725	159	42.64	3	3
Nadeem Younis (Ry/R)	14	21	–	894	105	42.57	2	6
Sajid Ali (NB/KW)	12	22	–	895	154	40.68	3	5
Shoaib Mohammad (PIA)	6	10	1	364	101	40.44	1	–
Ameer Akbar (NS)	8	14	2	481	100*	40.08	2	–
Shahid Javed (HB/R)	17	23	2	800	131	38.09	1	5
Ghulam Ali (PACO/KW)	18	30	2	1048	138	37.43	3	6
Mohammad Ramzan (Ry/F)	14	22	2	748	161*	37.40	3	3
Mohammad Nawaz (Ry/S)	9	12	1	403	140*	36.63	1	2
Mohammad Javed (NB/KB)	12	17	2	542	116*	36.13	1	3
Tahir Shah (NB/L)	11	16	4	424	117*	35.33	1	–
Tahir Rasheed (HB/KW)	14	15	3	423	97	35.25	–	3
Mazhar Qayyum (Ry/B)	11	18	–	634	74	35.22	–	7
Aamer Bashir (UB)	7	12	3	312	69*	34.66	–	2
Basit Ali (UB/KW)	6	11	1	332	68	33.20	–	2
Shahid Anwar (NB/L)	15	23	2	683	84	32.52	–	5
Moin Khan (PIA/KW)	15	20	2	569	97	31.61	–	3
Sher Ali (PNSC/R)	9	15	1	434	93	31.00	–	5
Mansoor Akhtar (UB)	8	12	–	371	118	30.91	1	1
Zahoor Elahi (ADBP)	10	14	–	426	122	30.42	1	2
Aamer Ishaq (PNSC/I)	9	13	–	390	93	30.00	–	3
Kamran Khan (PACO/L)	12	20	–	582	150	29.10	2	2
Naeem Ashraf (NB/L)	11	14	–	407	104	29.07	1	1
Sohail Jaffar (PNSC/KB)	12	19	2	494	67	29.05	–	5
Babar Zaman (PIA/L)	9	14	1	372	80	28.61	–	4
Zahid Ahmed (PIA/F)	11	14	2	341	61	28.41	–	3
Aamer Hanif (PACO/KW)	14	20	1	523	47	27.52	–	–
Wasim Ali (HBFC)	8	14	–	355	102	25.35	1	1
Iqbal Imam (UB/KB)	12	15	2	325	58	25.00	–	1
Mujahid Jamshed (PACO/I)	11	17	–	422	71	24.82	–	3
Mohammad Husnain (HB/S)	14	17	–	413	78	24.29	–	2
Saeed Azad (NB/KW)	10	19	2	409	67	24.05	–	3
Faisal Qureshi (HBFC)	8	14	–	333	64	23.78	–	4
Azam Khan (PNSC/KW)	11	20	1	440	77	23.15	–	3
Tariq Alam (HBFC)	8	14	–	321	49	22.92	–	–
Wasim Yousufi (HBFC)	8	14	–	321	101	22.92	1	–
Athar Laeeq (NB/KW)	16	22	6	320	80	20.00	–	1
Saifullah (UB/B)	10	17	–	332	80	19.52	–	2
Naseer Ahmed (Ry/R)	12	18	1	312	102*	18.35	1	–

(Qualification – 300 runs)

BOWLING

	Overs	Mds	Runs	Wkts	Av	Best	10/m	5/inn
Umar Rasheed (PACO)	100	25	215	15	14.33	6-39	1	1
Naved Anjum (HB)	216	45	664	42	15.80	9-56	1	4
Waqar Younis (UB)	224.3	46	674	42	16.04	7-91	2	6
Zafar Iqbal (NB/KW)	116.3	24	336	18	18.67	7-65	–	2
Haaris A. Khan (KW)	408.3	114	919	45	20.42	5-71	–	2
Aamir Hanif (PACO/KW)	128	15	395	19	20.78	7-71	–	1
Iqbal Zahoor (Ry)	192.3	47	440	21	20.95	5-57	–	2
Tauseef Ahmed (UB)	226.5	67	487	22	22.13	6-90	1	3
Naeem Ashraf (NB/L)	340.3	49	1064	48	22.16	6-45	–	2
Raja Afaq (ADBP/R)	376.5	71	985	44	22.38	6-53	1	4
Ashfaq Ahmed (PIA)	219.2	40	697	31	22.48	7-127	1	4
Manzoor Elahi (ADBP)	251	62	720	32	22.50	6-113	–	2
Masood Anwar (UB)	278.5	59	752	33	22.78	7-95	–	3
Sajjad Akbar (PNSC/S)	436	79	1234	54	22.85	6-68	1	3
Zahid Ahmed (PIA/F)	313	98	719	31	23.19	6-15	1	1
Iqbal Imam (UB/KB)	121	17	365	15	24.33	5-26	–	1
Hafeez-ur-Rehman (NB)	174.2	25	432	17	25.41	5-75	–	1
Ayaz Jilani (PIA/I)	192.5	27	603	23	26.21	8-104	–	1
Nadeem Ghauri (NB/L)	322.3	77	895	34	26.32	8-51	1	3
Athar Laeeq (NB/KW)	427.4	89	1324	50	26.48	5-38	–	2
Asadullah Butt (HB/R)	258.5	57	851	32	26.59	4-34	–	–
Mohammad Zahid (PACO/B)	361.4	76	931	35	26.60	8-114	–	3
Ali Gohar (KB)	167.3	26	613	23	26.65	5-63	1	2
Imran Adil (Ry/B)	266.1	41	922	34	27.11	6-85	–	2
Mohsin Kamal (PNSC/L)	291.1	33	1147	42	27.30	5-66	–	3
Arshad Khan (Ry)	274.4	49	765	28	27.32	6-109	–	1
Shahid Hussain (PACO)	277.4	71	621	22	28.22	5-57	–	1
Mohammad Ali (Ry/L)	433.3	59	1600	56	28.57	6-37	–	4
Nadeem Khan (NB/KW)	493.5	127	1231	41	30.02	6-72	–	4
Nadeem Afzal (PIA/F)	262.5	46	825	27	30.55	5-57	–	1
Wasim Haider (PIA)	151	34	466	15	31.06	4-40	–	–
Azhar Mahmood (I)	143	17	467	15	31.13	6-68	–	1
Akram Raza (HB/S)	431.3	97	1188	37	32.10	5-56	–	1
Javed Hayat (ADBP/L)	356	69	964	30	32.13	5-118	–	1
Murtaza Hussain (PACO/B)	406.2	92	1013	31	32.67	5-118	–	1
Kabir Khan (HBFC)	147	24	529	16	33.06	5-42	–	1
Shahid A. Khan (HBFC/L)	213.2	34	670	20	33.50	8-123	–	2
Naved Nazir (PNSC/F)	300.4	64	885	25	35.40	5-38	–	1
Mohammad Asif (ADBP/L)	526.2	105	1312	31	42.32	5-71	–	1
Sajjad Ali (PNSC/1)	281	43	942	22	42.81	4-54	–	–

(Qualification – 15 wickets)

LEADING FIELDERS

38 – Tahir Rasheed (HB/KW) (ct 31/st 7); 35 – Moin Khan (PIA/KW) (ct 32/st 3); 30 – Wasim Arif (NB) (ct 28/st 2); 28 – Saifullah (UB/B) (ct 23/st 5); 22 – Zulqarnain (PACO) (ct 19/st 3); 21 – Iqbal Saleem (KB) (ct 19/st 2); 20 – Bilal Ahmed (ADBP) (ct 19/st 1) and Mutahir Shah (PNSC) (ct 19/st 1); 18 – Naseer Ahmed (Ry/R) (ct 16/st 2); 14 – Wasim Yousufi (HBFC) (ct 13/st 1); 13 – Aslam Raza (L) (ct 12/st 1) and Rashid Latif (KW) (ct 12/st 1); 12 – Ashraf Ali (L), Sajid Ali (NB/KW), Ijaz Ahmed (Ry/F) and Zahid Fazal (PIA/L); 11 – Abid Rafiq (S) (ct 9/st 2), Iqbal Imam (UB/KB), Mohammad Ramzan (Ry/F) and Aamir Malik (PIA/L); 10 – Sanaullah (PACO/L) ct 9/st 1) and Nadeem Abbasi (R)

ABBREVIATIONS USED FOR TEAM NAMES

ADBP – Agricultural Development Bank of Pakistan; B – Bahawalpur; F – Faisalabad; HB – Habib Bank; HBFC – House Building Finance Corporation; I – Islamabad; KB – Karachi Blues; KW – Karachi Whites; L – Lahore; NB – National Bank; PACO – Pakistan Automobile Corporation; PIA – Pakistan International Airlines; PNSC – Pakistan National Shipping Corporation; R – Rawalpindi; Ry – Railways; S – Sargodha; UB – United Bank

SECTION F
The ICC Trophy in Kenya
United Arab Emirates, Kenya and Holland qualify for the World Cup in 1996

*Sultan Zarawani – captain of United Arab Emirates and the only
native-born player in the side. (Mueen-ud-Din Hameed/Sports-Line)*

The growing popularity of cricket throughout the world was never better exemplified than in the ICC Trophy of 1994 which was staged in Kenya. This was the first time that the competition had been held outside Europe, and it was also the first time that three countries would qualify to participate in the World Cup finals. The elevation of Zimbabwe to Test status and the decision to extend the World Cup to 12 nations provided the opportunity for three sides to gain places in India, Pakistan and Sri Lanka in 1996.

The decision to hold the competition in Kenya was an outstanding success, with the sides all housed in one hotel helping to achieve a feeling of cricketing brotherhood.

GROUP A

12 February 1994 *at Nairobi Club*

Malaysia 118 for 9
Holland 119 for 1 (N.E. Clarke 64 not out)

Holland won by 9 wickets

12 and **13** February 1994 *at Jaffreys*

Papus New Guinea 248 for 5 (V. Pala 66 not out,
   C. Amini 63)
Gibraltar 113 (F. Arua 5 for 31)

Papua New Guinea won by 135 runs

14 February 1994 *at Premier*

Gibraltar 80
Holland 85 for 0

Holland won by 10 wickets

14 and **15** February 1994 *at Ngara*

Ireland 230 for 8 (D.A. Lewis 50)
Papus New Guinea 88 for 7

Ireland won on faster scoring rate

16 and **17** February 1994 *at Gymkhana*

Papua New Guinea 165 (G. Rarua 50, V. Muniabdi 4 for
   28)
Malaysia 121

Papua New Guinea won by 44 runs

at Sir Ali

Gibraltar 136 for 9 (C. McCrum 4 for 16)
Ireland 138 for 4

Ireland won by 6 wickets

18 February 1994 *at Ruaraka*

Holland 235 for 8 (N.E. Clarke 119)
Ireland 165

Holland won by 70 runs

at Ngara

Malaysia 253 for 4 (D. Talla 112 not out, E. Seah 62)
Gibraltar 119 for 9

Malaysia won by 134 runs

20 February 1994 *at Simba Union*

Malaysia 110 (C. Hoey 4 for 18)
Ireland 111 for 1 (J.D.R. Benson 74 not out)

Ireland won by 9 wickets

at Aga Khan

Holland 212 for 5 (R. Scholte 90 not out)
Papua New Guinea 113 (H. Visse 4 for 22)

Holland won by 99 runs

As expected, Holland won all four matches in Group A to top the league and qualify for the quarter-finals along with Ireland. Ireland's victory over Papua New Guinea was greeted with protests as the beaten side pointed out that the tournament regulations made no provision for a team to win on faster run rate. Ireland were dogged with bad luck as Stephen Warke, the skipper, broke his elbow and leg-spinner Hoey was also injured. Decker Curry was forced to return home following the death of his father.

GROUP A – FINAL TABLE

	P	W	L	Pts.
Holland	4	4	–	16
Ireland	4	3	1	12
Papua New Guinea	4	2	2	8
Malaysia	4	1	3	4
Gibraltar	4	–	4	0

GROUP B

13 and **14** February 1994 *at Simba Union*

Argentina 120
Bangladesh 123 for 3

Bangladesh won by 7 wickets

at Sir Ali

East Africa 92 (J. Samarasekera 4 for 14)
United Arab Emirates 93 for 3

United Arab Emirates won by 7 wickets

15 and **16** February 1994 *at Aga Khan*

United States 206 (D. Renny 61, Azhar Saeed 4 for 24)
United Arab Emirates 209 for 6

United Arab Emirates won by 4 wickets

at Impala

East Africa 98 (G.M. Nowsher 4 for 36)
Bangladesh 99 for 3

Bangladesh won by 7 wickets

17 **February 1994** *at Jaffreys*

Argentina 128
United Arab Emirates 130 for 2

United Arab Emirates won by 8 wickets

at Nairobi Club

East Africa 105
United States 106 for 1 (E. Lewis 68 not out)

United States won by 9 wickets

19 **February 1994** *at Jaffreys*

United States 145 (P. Singh 69)
Bangladesh 147 for 7 (M. Akram Khan 64 not out)

Bangladesh won by 3 wickets

at Premier

Argentina 220
East Africa 143 (C. Tunon 5 for 37)

Argentina won by 77 runs

21 **February 1994** *at Sir Ali*

United States 337 for 6 (R. Latchman 75 not out,
    S. Skeete 67, D.I. Kallicharran 58)
Argentina 226 for 6 (G. Kirshbaum 57)

United States won by 111 runs

at Ngara

Bangladesh 233 for 7 (Jahangir Alam 117 not out, Salim
    Shahzad 56)
United Arab Emirates 236 for 4 (Saleem Raza 61 not out,
    R. Poonawala 54, V. Mehra 50)

United Arab Emirates won by 6 wickets

United Arab Emirates' squad of 16 was comprised of nine
Pakistanis, five Indians, a Sri Lankan and Sultan Zarawani, the captain and the only player from the Emirates in
the side. This imported team proved a very strong batting
combination with Riaz Poonawala, well known for his
feats in the Ranji Trophy, an admirable opener. They won
each of their four matches, but their win over United
States brought protests. The Americans complained that
the pitch had been rolled overnight contrary to regulations. A glance at the United States side revealed names
familiar for their prowess in the Shell Shield and the Red
Stripe Cup in the West Indies. In their match against
Bangladesh, United States collapsed from 80 for 0 to 145
all out, and the pitch was reported.

*Prolific scorer for UAE – Mazhar Hussain (Mueen-ud-Din Hameed/
Sports-Line)*

GROUP B – FINAL TABLE

	P	W	L	Pts.
United Arab Emirates	4	4	–	16
Bangladesh	4	3	1	12
United States	4	2	2	8
Argentina	4	1	3	4
East Africa	4	–	4	0

GROUP C

12 **February 1994** *at Premier*

Israel 99 (R. Ali 4 for 26, D. Tikolo 4 for 30)
Kenya 100 for 1

Kenya won by 9 wickets

at Impala

Canada 159 for 8
Singapore 50 for 8 (T. Gardner 5 for 12)

No result

14 February 1994 *at Nairobi Club*

Namibia 51 (Bhowan Singh 7 for 21)
Canada 52 for 0

Canada won by 10 wickets

at Ruaraka

Singapore 76 (A. Karim 5 for 20, R. Ali 4 for 9)
Kenya 77 for 1

Kenya won by 9 wickets

16 February 1994 *at Ngara*

Singapore 116
Namibia 117 for 5 (D. Karg 50)

Namibia won by 5 wickets

16 and **17** February 1994 *at Ruaraka*

Israel 89 (D. Joseph 5 for 19)
Canada 90 for 2

Canada won by 8 wickets

18 February 1994 *at Simba Union*

Kenya 198
Namibia 169 for 9 (D. Karg 51)

Kenya won by 29 runs

at Gymkhana

Singapore 120
Israel 121 for 8

Israel won by 2 wickets

20 February 1994 *at Impala*

Namibia 257 for 9 (G. Murgatroyd 93, M. Martins 56)
Israel 198 (N. Wald 92)

Namibia won by 59 runs

at Gymkhana

Canada 210 for 9 (P. Prashad 84)
Kenya 213 for 7 (D. Chudasma 62)

Kenya won by 3 wickets

Kenya, the host nation, set a high standard in Group C winning their first two matches with some furious hitting. They scored 100 for 1 in 15 overs against Israel and 77 for 1 in 9.2 overs against Singapore. Namibia were rather unlucky, for, in their first match, they were caught on a damp pitch and were victims of some inspired bowling by seamer Bhowan Singh of Canada who performed the hat-trick.

GROUP C – FINAL TABLE

	P	W	L	NR	Pts.
Kenya	4	4	–	–	16
Canada	4	2	1	1	10
Namibia	4	2	2	–	8
Israel	4	1	3	–	4
Singapore	4	–	3	1	2

GROUP D

13 and **14** February 1994 *at Aga Khan*

West Africa 93
Bermuda 94 for 2 (D. Smith 54 not out)

Bermuda won by 8 wickets

at Gymkhana

Denmark 192 (A. Ahmed 61, S. Brew 4 for 43)
Hong Kong 192 for 8 (J.O.D. Orders 63 not out,
  O.H. Mortensen 4 for 21)

*Hong Kong won by losing fewer wickets with scores
  level*

15 and **16** February 1994 *at Simba Union*

Denmark 219 (J. Gregerson 50, A. From 50)
Fiji 126 (S. Henriksen 5 for 56)

Denmark won by 93 runs

at Jaffreys

Hong Kong 154 (J. Fordham 79, A. Edwards 5 for 27)
Bermuda 154 for 8 (D. Minors 56 not out)

Bermuda won by losing fewer wickets with scores level

*Former Leicestershire cricketer Justin Benson represented Ireland in
the tournament. (David Munden/Sports-Line)*

17 February **1994** *at Premier*

West Africa 146 (S. Henriksen 4 for 10)
Denmark 148 for 6 (D. Orgle 4 for 39)

Denmark won by 4 wickets

at Aga Khan

Fiji 126 (S. Brew 4 for 16)
Hong Kong 127 for 3 (J. Fordham 50 not out)

Hong Kong won by 7 wickets

19 February **1994** *at Nairobi Club*

Fiji 84 (C. Wade 4 for 28)
Bermuda 85 for 1 (D. Smith 56 not out)

Bermuda won by 9 wickets

at Sir Ali

Hong Kong 355 for 8 (S. Brew 124, S. Atkinson 68,
    J. Fordham 58, S. Kpundeh 4 for 65)
West Africa 110

Hong Kong won by 245 runs

21 February **1994** *at Jaffreys*

Fiji 232 for 9 (L. Sorovakatini 84)
West Africa 88 (S. Campbell 4 for 17)

Fiji won by 144 runs

at Ruaraka

Denmark 183 for 7 (A. Butt 70, J. Gregerson 53)
Bermuda 185 for 4 (C. Smith 51)

Bermuda won by 6 wickets

Defeat at the hands of Hong Kong in their opening match proved disastrous for Denmark who many had thought would reach the last stages of the competition. Coached by Dermot Reeves, Hong Kong fought fiercely, and Stewart Brew's hat-trick was really the turning point of the match. Later, with Brew hitting a century, Hong Kong reached the highest score of the tournament. Denmark could still have won a place in the last eight with Henriksen and the ever-lively Mortensen bowling well, but they gave a poor batting display against the consistent and accomplished Bermudans.

QUARTER-FINALS

GROUP ONE

23 February **1994** *at Gymkhana*

Hong Kong 86 (A. Nijuguna 5 for 24)
Kenya 90 for 2

Kenya won by 8 wickets

at Premier

Holland 205 (R. van Oosterom 64)
Bangladesh 158 (H. Visee 4 for 32)

Holland won by 47 runs

25 February **1994** *at Simba Union*

Kenya 295 for 6 (M. Odumbe 119, D. Chudasma 75)
Bangladesh 282 for 8 (A. Islam 74, Minhazul Abedin 68,
    J. Aslam 57)

Kenya won by 13 runs

at Nairobi Club

Holland 288 for 8 (N.E. Clarke 113, S.W. Lubbers 63)
Hong Kong 154 (S. Brew 61)

Holland won by 134 runs

27 February **1994** *at Ruaraka*

Holland 250 for 8 (S.W. Lubbers 67, T. de Leede 51)
Kenya 251 for 8 (S. Tikolo 95)

Kenya won by 2 wickets

at Aga Khan

Bangladesh 238 for 8 (Minhazul Abedin 66)
Hong Kong 181 (J.O.D. Orders 58, Minhazul Abdein 4
    for 40)

Bangladesh won by 57 runs

A crushing defeat by Kenya in their first match in the quarter-finals virtually ended Hong Kong's hopes of progressing further in the competition. More surprising, perhaps, was that Kenya won a high-scoring game against Bangladesh who had already been beaten by Holland and therefore passed out of the tournament. Bangladesh had reached the semi-final stage of the trophy in 1982 and 1990 and had started the 1994 competition as second favourites.

SECTION D – FINAL TABLE

	P	W	L	Pts.
Bermuda	4	4	–	16
Hong Kong	4	3	1	12
Denmark	4	2	2	8
Fiji	4	1	3	4
West Africa	4	–	4	0

GROUP ONE – FINAL TABLE

	P	W	L	Pts.
Kenya	3	3	–	12
Holland	3	2	1	8
Bangladesh	3	1	2	4
Hong Kong	3	–	3	0

GROUP TWO

23 February 1994 *at Ruaraka*

United Arab Emirates 295 for 4 (Mazhar Hussain 122, Azhar Saeed 58)
Ireland 236 for 9 (Arshad Laiq 4 for 49)

United Arab Emirates won by 59 runs

at Simba Union

Canada 149 for 9 (N. Gibbons 4 for 31)
Bermuda 151 for 2

Bermuda won by 8 wickets

25 February 1994 *at Aga Khan*

Canada 278 for 7 (I. Liburd 87, T. Gardner 76)
United Arab Emirates 279 for 9 (Azhar Saeed 126 not out)

United Arab Emirates won by 1 wicket

at Gymkhana

Ireland 202 (C. McCrum 54)
Bermuda 206 for 3 (C. Smith 89, C. Marshall 62 not out)

Bermuda won by 7 wickets

27 February 1994 *at Nairobi Club*

Bermuda 329 for 9 (D. Smith 110, A. Steede 76, C. Smith 71)
United Arab Emirates 330 for 9 (Saleem Raza 78, R. Poonawala 53)

United Arab Emirates won by 1 wicket

at Premier

Ireland 212 for 7 (M.F. Cohen 74)
Canada 213 for 5

Canada won by 5 wickets

The power of the UAE side was never more apparent than in the quarter-finals. They crushed Ireland in a high-scoring game in which Mazhar Hussain hit 122 off 121 balls. They then reached the target of 330 set by Bermuda with two balls and one wicket to spare even though they had been penalised one over for bowling a slow over-rate. They had already scored 279 for 9 to beat Canada.

GROUP TWO – FINAL TABLE

	P	W	L	Pts.
United Arab Emirates	3	3	–	12
Bermuda	3	2	1	8
Canada	3	1	2	4
Ireland	3	–	3	0

Opening batsman Poonawalla – a tower of strength for UAE – hit 71 in the final against Kenya. (Mueen-ud-Din Hameed/Sports-Line)

SEMI-FINALS

1 March 1994 *at Aga Khan*

Kenya 318 for 5 (M. Odumbe 158 not out, S. Tikolo 67)
Bermuda 254 for 9 (C. Smith 108)

Kenya won by 64 runs

3 March 1994 *at Nairobi Club*

Holland 194 (T. de Leede 52)
United Arab Emirates 195 for 4 (M. Ishaq 72 not out, Saleem Raza 64 not out)

United Arab Emirates won by 6 wickets

Maurice Odumbe hit the highest score of the competition, and his innings gave Kenya victory over Bermuda and a place in the World Cup finals in 1996. Clay Smith hit 108 off 96 balls in reply before being adjudged leg before by umpire van Reenen of Namibia with whom he had a prolonged argument. United Arab Emirates beat Holland with 5.2 overs to spare. Saleem Raza, 65 off 55 balls, and Mohammad Ishaq shared an unbroken fifth-wicket partnership of 123 in 20 overs.

THIRD PLACE PLAY-OFF

5 March 1994 *at Simba Union*

Holland 306 for 2 (N.E. Clarke 121 not out,
 S.W. Lubbers 81, G.J.A.F. Aponso 53)

Bermuda 203

Holland won by 103 runs

Put in to bat, Holland began with a stand of 114 in 26 overs between Clarke and Aponso. West-Indian born Noel Clarke hit his third century of the competition, 121 off 141 balls, with a six and 10 fours. Skipper Steve Lubbers scored 81 from 55 balls, and Bermuda conceded more than 300 runs for the third time in a week. Lubbers, who also bowled a tidy spell of off-spin, took the individual award. Most importantly, Holland won a place in the World Cup finals.

FINAL

Zarawani won the toss and asked Kenya to bat. Chudasma was out in the second over, caught at mid-on, but Otieno and Odumbe added 98. Odumbe was again his side's top scorer, hitting 87 off 115 balls and adding 102 with Steve Tikolo, one of three brothers in the Kenyan party. A feature of the Kenyan innings was the exciting running between the wickets.

Having shown their strength in chasing big totals, UAE always looked to be favourites. Poonawala and Azhar Saeed gave them a fine start with a stand of 141. Poonawala began the innings with two boundaries and his 71 came off 92 balls. There was an uncertain period, but Ishaq and Mehra added 56, and Mohammed Ishaq's 51 off 36 balls earned the Man of the Match award from Clyde Walcott. In effect, the UAE won with more ease than the final score suggests.

This was not a popular win. Basheer Mauladad, Chairman of the Kenyan Cricket Association, called for a change in the ICC's residential regulations so that mercenaries could not be imported and a side could not buy its way into the World Cup finals as UAE had done. Sir Clyde Walcott denounced Mauladad's statement, but most people were on the Kenyan's side, and there is an investigation into the residential qualifications of members of the Emirates' winning side.

ICC TROPHY FINAL – KENYA *v.* UNITED ARAB EMIRATES

6 March 1994 at Ruaraka, Nairobi

KENYA			UNITED ARAB EMIRATES		
D. Chudasma	c Azhar Saeed, b Sohail Butt	0	R. Poonawala	lbw, b Tito	71
*K. Otieno	c and b Azhar Saeed	49	Azhar Saeed	c Odumbe, b Tito	59
M. Odumbe	b Samarasekera	87	Mazhar Hussain	b Suji	9
S. Tikolo	b Saleem Raza	54	M. Ishaq	c Chudasma, b Suji	51
S. Kassamali	c Imtiaz Abbasi, b Saleem Raza	0	V. Mehra	run out	34
T. Tikolo (capt)	not out	42	Saleem Raza	c T. Tikolo, b Suji	6
E. Tito	run out	25	J. Samarasekera	run out	4
M. Orewa	not out	1	Arshad Laiq	c T. Tikolo, b Suji	20
A. Karim			*Imtiaz Abbasi	not out	1
A. Suji			Sohail Butt	not out	0
R. Ali			Sultan Zarawan (capt)		
Extras	b 1, lb 16, w 6	23	Extras	b 1, lb 13, w 12, nb 1	27
(50 overs)	(for 6 wickets)	281	(49.1 overs)	(for 8 wickets)	282

	O	M	R	W		O	M	R	W
Samarasekera	9	1	38	1	Suji	10	–	61	4
Sohail Butt	10	–	59	1	Ali	6	–	27	–
Arshad Laiq	9	–	50	–	Orewa	2	–	14	–
Azhar Saeed	9	–	46	1	Odumbe	10	–	44	–
Saleem Raza	10	–	48	2	Karim	9	–	56	–
Sultan Zarawani	3	–	23	–	S. Tikolo	3	–	14	–
					Tito	9.1	–	52	2

FALL OF WICKETS
1–1, 2–99, 3–201, 4–202, 5–211, 6–268

FALL OF WICKETS
1–141, 2–148, 3–177, 4–233, 5–242, 6–254, 7–276, 8–281

Umpires: W. Molenaar & P. P'Hara   *Man of the Match:* M. Ishaq   *United Arab Emirates won by 2 wickets*

SECTION G
Sharjah
The Champions Trophy:

Pakistan, Sri Lanka and West Indies

The AustralAsia Cup:

Pakistan, India, Sri Lanka, Australia, New Zealand and the United Arab Emirates

West Indies with the Pepsi Cola Champions Trophy after their victory in the final against Pakistan who had won the competition for six years in succession. (David Munden/Sports-Line)

Two factors have tended to lessen the importance and prestige of the Sharjah tournaments in recent years. The first is the proliferation of one-day internationals throughout the world which has made some nations unwilling or unable to compete in the United Arab Emirates: the second is the refusal of India to participate because of what they see as bias in favour of Pakistan in the conduct of earlier competitions. Happily, the second of these difficulties was resolved early in 1994 when the Indian Board made peace with the organisers in Sharjah.

The Champions Trophy 1993, sponsored by Pepsi Cola, brought together Pakistan, Sri Lanka and West Indies who had failed to reach the final of the competition when they last competed in 1991. The team that Richie Richardson now led, however, was a tighter, stronger unit than that with which he had begun his captaincy of West Indies two years previously. They showed their strength in the opening match when they brushed aside Sri Lanka whose skipper Arjuna Ranatunga played virtually a lone hand in taking his side to 172. The early dismissal of Lara may have given the Sri Lankans some encouragement, but a stand of 137 between Simmons and Richardson took West Indies to the point of victory.

West Indies began their second match rather shakily, losing four wickets for 82 runs, but Adams and Arthurton led a belligerent revival, and 83 runs were plundered from the last 10 overs of the innings. Both Basit Ali and Asif Mujtaba batted well, but Pakistan, the reigning champions, never looked like reaching their target.

The following day, Saeed Anwar and Asif Mujtaba put on 171 for Pakistan's first wicket against Sri Lanka. Saeed's 107 came off 109 balls and included 2 sixes and 11 fours; Asif Mujtaba batted throughout the 50 overs for his first century in a one-day international. It was immediately apparent that a target of 314 was well beyond the reach of Sri Lanka.

A second century in successive matches from Saeed Anwar took Pakistan to victory in their return match with West Indies. West Indies omitted wicket-keeper Murray in order to accommodate Desmond Haynes who had recovered from a throat infection, but it was a third-wicket partnership of 132 between Simmons and Arthurton which gave the West Indian innings substance. The runs came off 140 balls. Saeed carried Pakistan to victory with a stunning knock. His 131 came from 141 balls and included 3 sixes and 12 fours. He was out in the 48th over when he lofted Hooper to mid-off, and when just 10 runs were required for victory. His 131 was the highest score made by a Pakistani batsman in a limited-over international.

Saeed Anwar's aggressive left-handed batting brought more honours to Pakistan in the fifth match when he hit his third century in succession. Sri Lanka batted as well as at any time in the tournament. Jayasuriya made his first 32 runs off 12 balls, and his fifty came off 27 balls. In all, he hit a six and 6 fours in his 65 which came from 56 deliveries. He and Mahanama put on 105 for the second

wicket. Saeed equalled the record of Zaheer Abbas in reaching his third century in succession, and he hit 3 sixes and 11 fours in an innings which occupied 104 balls. With Inzamam-ul-Haq, he added 109 for the second wicket, but Pakistan needed 17 from the last two overs with only three wickets standing. The penultimate over of the innings, bowled by Aravinda de Silva, produced 15 runs, however, and Pakistan won with two balls to spare.

As West Indies beat Sri Lanka with ease in the last game of the qualifying round, Pakistan's problems mounted. Wasim Akram broke a bone in his right hand while batting against Sri Lanka and was unfit for the final as was Javed Miandad. Abdul Qadir and Aqib Javed had already broken down, and Aamir Hanif, somewhat surprisingly for primarily he is a batsman, had flown out to bolster the side. There was a hostile reaction to the loss of Qadir and Aqib, for they were accused of having duped 'their way into the team by declaring themselves fit', only to reveal their true condition once the tour was under way.

Aamir Hanif was one of three players to make their debuts in limited-over internationals during the tour. The other two were Samaraweera of Sri Lanka and Holder of West Indies.

Man of the Series – Phil Simmons, the West Indian all-rounder.
(David Munden/Sports-Line)

CHAMPIONS TROPHY – MATCH ONE – SRI LANKA v. WEST INDIES
28 October 1993 at Sharjah C.A. Stadium

SRI LANKA		
R.S. Mahanama	c Lara, b Cummins	27
U.C. Hathurusinghe	run out	2
A.P. Gurusinha	b Cummins	8
P.A. de Silva	c Lara, b Benjamin	1
H.P. Tillekeratne	c Murray, b Benjamin	1
A. Ranatunga (capt)	not out	83
S.T. Jayasuriya	c Ambrose, b Benjamin	23
*R.S. Kaluwitharana	c Simmons, b Hooper	0
R.S. Kalpage	c Murray, b Cummins	7
C.P.H. Ramanayake	c Richardson, b Ambrose	9
G.P. Wickramasinghe	c and b Ambrose	0
Extras	b 1, lb 6, w 3, nb 1	11
(48.5 overs)		172

WEST INDIES		
P.V. Simmons	b Jayasuriya	92
B.C. Lara	c Ranatunga, b Gurusinha	5
R.B. Richardson (capt)	not out	69
K.L.T. Arthurton	not out	1
C.L. Hooper		
J.C. Adams		
*J.R. Murray		
A.C. Cummins		
K.C.G. Benjamin		
C.E.L. Ambrose		
C.A. Walsh		
Extras	w 4, n 2	6
(46 overs)	(for 2 wickets)	173

	O	M	R	W
Ambrose	7.5	1	20	2
Walsh	7	4	10	–
Benjamin	9	1	34	3
Cummins	10	1	32	3
Simmons	5	–	17	–
Hooper	10	1	52	1

	O	M	R	W
Wickramasinghe	7	1	27	–
Ramanayake	8	2	22	–
Gurusinha	3	–	14	1
Kalpage	10	–	25	–
Jayasuriya	9	–	41	1
de Silva	6	–	34	–
Hathurusinghe	2	–	10	–
Tillekeratne	1	1	0	–

FALL OF WICKETS

1–6, 2–24, 3–27, 4–29, 5–71, 6–117, 7–119, 8–138, 9–171

FALL OF WICKETS

1–34, 2–171

Umpires: H.D. Bird & D.R. Shepherd   Man of the Match: P.V. Simmons   West Indies won by 8 wickets

CHAMPIONS TROPHY – MATCH TWO – PAKISTAN v. WEST INDIES
29 October 1993 at Sharjah C.A. Stadium

WEST INDIES		
P.V. Simmons	c Rashid Latif, b Waqar Younis	25
B.C. Lara	c Rashid Latif, b Wasim Akram	14
R.B. Richardson (capt)	c Saeed Anwar, b Aqib Javed	2
K.L.T. Arthurton	c Aamir Sohail, b Mushtaq Ahmed	84
C.L. Hooper	c Rashid Latif, b Mushtaq Ahmed	6
J.C. Adams	not out	81
*J.R. Murray	lbw, b Wasim Akram	6
A.C. Cummins	b Wasim Akram	18
W.K.M. Benjamin	not out	2
C.E.L. Ambrose		
K.C.G. Benjamin		
Extras	b 1, lb 19, w 7, nb 2	29
(50 overs)	(for 7 wickets)	267

PAKISTAN		
Aamir Sohail	lbw, b K.C.G. Benjamin	3
Saeed Anwar	c Lara, b Cummins	22
Inzamam-ul-Haq	c K.C.G. Benjamin, b Hooper	25
Javed Miandad	b K.C.G. Benjamin	0
Basit Ali	run out	46
Asif Mujtaba	not out	60
Wasim Akram (capt)	c Adams, b Ambrose	28
*Rashid Latif	c Lara, b Ambrose	0
Mushtaq Ahmed	c Murray, b Hooper	2
Waqar Younis	c Lara, b Hooper	15
Aqib Javed	not out	6
Extras	b 6, w 14, nb 1	21
(50 overs)	(for 9 wickets)	228

	O	M	R	W
Wasim Akram	10	–	36	3
Aqib Javed	10	–	38	1
Waqar Younis	7.1	–	57	1
Mushtaq Ahmed	10	1	44	2
Aamir Sohail	4.5	–	31	–
Asif Mujtaba	8	–	41	–

	O	M	R	W
Ambrose	9	1	29	2
K.C.G. Benjamin	9	1	37	2
W.K.M. Benjamin	6	–	40	–
Cummins	10	1	44	1
Hooper	10	–	33	3
Simmons	6	–	39	–

FALL OF WICKETS

1–32, 2–35, 3–57, 4–82, 5–201, 6–225, 7–263

FALL OF WICKETS

1–4, 2–47, 3–48, 4–59, 5 147, 6–185, 7–190, 8–194, 9–213

Umpires: D.R. Shepherd & J.W. Holder   Man of the Match: J.C. Adams   West Indies won by 39 runs

CHAMPIONS TROPHY – MATCH THREE – PAKISTAN *v.* SRI LANKA
30 October 1993 at Sharjah C.A. Stadium

PAKISTAN

Saeed Anwar	c Muralitharan, b Ranatunga	107
Asif Mujtaba	not out	113
Inzamam-ul-Haq	b Ramanayake	37
Wasim Akram (capt)	b Ramanayake	15
Basit Ali	not out	29
Javed Miandad		
Salim Malik		
*Rashid Latif		
Mushtaq Ahmed		
Ata-ur-Rehman		
Aqib Javed		
Extras	lb 4, w 4, nb 4	12
(50 overs)	(for 3 wickets)	313

SRI LANKA

R.S. Mahanama	lbw, b Wasim Akram	1
A.P. Gurusinha	lbw, b Wasim Akram	6
S.T. Jayasuriya	c Inzamam-ul-Haq, b Mushtaq Ahmed	58
P.A. de Silva	run out	14
H.P. Tillekeratne	c Saeed Anwar, b Salim Malik	20
A. Ranatunga (capt)	c Rashid Latif, b Mushtaq Ahmed	24
*R.S. Kaluwitharana	c Wasim Akram, b Asif Mujtaba	31
R.S. Kalpage	not out	16
C.P.H. Ramanayake	not out	14
M. Muralitharan		
G.P. Wickramasinghe		
Extras	b 2, lb 5, w 7, nb 1	15
(50 overs)	(for 7 wickets)	199

	O	M	R	W
Wickramasinghe	10	2	59	–
Ramanayake	10	1	54	2
Gurusinha	4	1	22	–
Kalpage	10	–	63	–
Jayasuriya	3	–	31	–
Muralitharan	6	–	42	–
Ranatunga	7	–	38	1

	O	M	R	W
Wasim Akram	8	1	21	2
Aqib Javed	3	–	15	–
Ata-ur-Rehman	8	1	35	–
Salim Malik	10	–	44	1
Mushtaq Ahmed	10	1	45	2
Asif Mujtaba	9	–	28	1
Basit Ali	2	–	4	–

FALL OF WICKETS

1–171, 2–247, 3–270

FALL OF WICKETS

1–4, 2–26, 3–53, 4–103, 5–114, 6–145, 7–173

Umpires: H.D. Bird & J.W. Holder   Man of the Match: Asif Mujtaba   *Pakistan won by 114 runs*

CHAMPIONS TROPHY – MATCH FOUR – PAKISTAN *v.* WEST INDIES
1 November 1993 at Sharjah C.A. Stadium

WEST INDIES

B.C. Lara	c Rashid Latif, b Mushtaq Ahmed	14
D.L. Haynes	c Mushtaq Ahmed, b Wasim Akram	6
P.V. Simmons	b Ata-ur-Rehman	81
K.L.T. Arthurton	c Saeed Anwar, b Mushtaq Ahmed	63
R.B. Richardson (capt)	c Salim Malik, b Mushtaq Ahmed	7
C.L. Hooper	c Asif Mujtaba, b Wasim Akram	18
*J.C. Adams	not out	18
R.A. Harper	b Wasim Akram	2
A.C. Cummins	st Rashid Latif, b Abdul Qadir	10
K.C.G. Benjamin	b Wasim Akram	4
C.A. Walsh	not out	2
Extras	b 3, lb 10, w 20, nb 2	35
(50 overs)	(for 9 wickets)	260

PAKISTAN

Saeed Anwar	c Lara, b Hooper	131
Asif Mujtaba	c Arthurton, b Cummins	15
Inzamam-ul-Haq	run out	20
Javed Miandad	c Adams, b Benjamin	20
Basit Ali	run out	16
Salim Malik	not out	34
Wasim Akram (capt)	not out	5
Mushtaq Ahmed		
*Rashid Latif		
Abdul Qadir		
Ata-ur-Rehman		
Extras	b 1, lb 9, w 9, nb 1	20
(49 overs)	(for 5 wickets)	261

	O	M	R	W
Wasim Akram	10	1	40	4
Ata-ur-Rehman	10	1	59	1
Mushtaq Ahmed	10	1	46	3
Abdul Qadir	10	–	43	1
Salim Malik	7	–	35	–
Asif Mujtaba	3	–	24	–

	O	M	R	W
Walsh	10	1	39	–
Benjamin	10	1	54	1
Cummins	10	–	69	1
Hooper	9	–	43	1
Harper	8	–	36	–
Simmons	2	–	10	–

FALL OF WICKETS

1–26, 2–57, 3–189, 4–201, 5–204, 6–222, 7–234, 8–251, 9–256

FALL OF WICKETS

1–42, 2–86, 3–143, 4–186, 5–251

Umpires: J.W. Holder & D.R. Shepherd   Man of the Match: Saeed Anwar   *Pakistan won by 5 wickets*

CHAMPIONS TROPHY – MATCH FIVE – PAKISTAN v. SRI LANKA
2 November 1993 at Sharjah C.A. Stadium

SRI LANKA		
R.S. Mahanama	st Rashid Latif, b Mushtaq Ahmed	59
A.P. Gurusinha	lbw, b Aamir Hanif	7
S.T. Jayasuriya	c Mushtaq, b Salim Malik	65
A. Ranatunga (capt)	st Rashid Latif, b Salim Malik	35
P.A. de Silva	run out	62
*R.S. Kaluwitharana	c Inzamam-ul-Haq, b Ata-ur-Rehman	23
R.S. Kalpage	not out	1
H.P. Tillekeratne		
D.K. Liyanage		
C.P.H. Ramanayake		
G.P. Wickramasinghe		
Extras	lb 5, w 10, nb 3	18
(50 overs)	(for 6 wickets)	270

PAKISTAN		
Saeed Anwar	c Mahanama, b Liyanage	111
Asif Mujtaba	c Kaluwitharana, b Liyanage	34
Inzamam-ul-Haq	c Wickramasinghe, b Liyanage	53
Basit Ali	run out	13
Salim Malik	c and b Ramanayake	14
Aamir Hanif	not out	17
Wasim Akram (capt)	run out	5
*Rashid Latif	c Mahanama, b Wickramasinghe	2
Mushtaq Ahmed	run out	6
Abdul Qadir	not out	7
Ata-ur-Rehman		
Extras	lb 1, w 1, nb 7	9
(49.4 overs)	(for 8 wickets)	271

	O	M	R	W
Wasim Akram	10	1	42	–
Ata-ur-Rehman	10	1	53	1
Aamir Hanif	3.4	–	27	1
Mushtaq Ahmed	10	1	56	1
Abdul Qadir	7.2	–	35	–
Salim Malik	9	–	52	2

	O	M	R	W
Wickramasinghe	9.4	–	35	1
Ramanayake	8	–	62	1
Liyanage	10	–	49	3
Kalpage	10	–	37	3
Jayasuriya	5	–	37	–
Ranatunga	2	–	17	–
de Silva	5	1	33	–

FALL OF WICKETS

1–26, 2–131, 3–153, 4–197, 5–263, 6–270

FALL OF WICKETS

1–86, 2–195, 3–209, 4–225, 5–233, 6–244, 7–254, 8–260

Umpires: H.D. Bird & J.W. Holder   *Man of the Match:* Saeed Anwar   *Pakistan won by 2 wickets*

CHAMPIONS TROPHY – MATCH SIX – WEST INDIES v. SRI LANKA
3 November 1993 at Sharjah C.A. Stadium

SRI LANKA		
R.S. Mahanama	c Murray, b Simmons	23
D.P. Samaraweera	c Hooper, b Walsh	3
S.T. Jayasuriya	c Murray, b W.K.M. Benjamin	27
P.A. de Silva	c and b Harper	14
H.P. Tillekeratne	c Walsh, b Hooper	26
A. Ranatunga (capt)	c Haynes, b Harper	17
*R.S. Kaluwitharana	c Holder, b Harper	0
R.S. Kalpage	c W.K.M. Benjamin, b K.C.G. Benjamin	30
D.K. Liyanage	c Harper, b K.C.G. Benjamin	14
C.P.H. Ramanayake	not out	9
G.P. Wickramasinghe	not out	6
Extras	lb 9, w 2, nb 2,	13
(50 overs)	(for 9 wickets)	182

WEST INDIES		
B.C. Lara	c Kaluwitharana, b Kalpage	42
D.L. Haynes (capt)	b Wickramasinghe	0
P.V. Simmons	not out	90
C.L. Hooper	not out	47
R.I.C. Holder		
J.C. Adams		
R.A. Harper		
*J.R. Murray		
W.K.M. Benjamin		
K.C.G. Benjamin		
C.A. Walsh		
Extras	nb 4	4
(38.4 overs)	(for 2 wickets)	183

	O	M	R	W
Walsh	10	2	34	1
K.C.G. Benjamin	8	–	30	2
Simmons	4	–	19	1
W.K.M. Benjamin	8	–	32	1
Harper	10	1	31	3
Hooper	10	–	27	1

	O	M	R	W
Wickramasinghe	8	1	37	1
Ramanayake	7	–	33	–
Liyanage	5	–	30	–
Kalpage	7.4	1	32	1
Jayasuriya	10	–	48	–
Tillekeratne	1	–	3	–

FALL OF WICKETS

1–16, 2–50, 3–62, 4–74, 5–110, 6–110, 7–132, 8–167, 9–167

FALL OF WICKETS

1–1, 2–87

Umpires: J.W. Holder & D.R. Shepherd   *Man of the Match:* P.V. Simmons   *West Indies won by 8 wickets*

CHAMPIONS TROPHY – FINAL – PAKISTAN *v.* WEST INDIES
5 November 1993 at Sharjah C.A. Stadium

PAKISTAN			WEST INDIES		
Saeed Anwar	b Cummins	16	D.L. Haynes	c Rashid Latif, b Ata-ur-Rehman	3
Aamir Sohail	c Lara, b Benjamin	10	B.C. Lara	c Rashid Latif, b Mushtaq Ahmed	153
Inzamam-ul-Haq	c Haynes, b Walsh	30	P.V. Simmons	c and b Salim Malik	42
Salim Malik	c Walsh, b Ambrose	84	K.L.T. Arthurton	c sub (Aamir Hanif), b Ata-ur-Rehman	44
Basit Ali	not out	127	R.B. Richardson (capt)	not out	15
*Rashid Latif	not out	2	C.L. Hooper	not out	5
Asif Mujtaba			*J.C. Adams		
Mushtaq Ahmed			A.C. Cummins		
Waqar Younis (capt)			K.C.G. Benjamin		
Ata-ur-Rehman			C.E.L. Ambrose		
Aamir Nazir			C.A. Walsh		
Extras	b 1, lb 5, w 4, nb 5	15	Extras	lb 10, w 8, nb 5	23
(50 overs)	(for 4 wickets)	284	(45.3 overs)	(for 4 wickets)	285

	O	M	R	W		O	M	R	W
Ambrose	10	2	64	1	Waqar Younis	8	–	65	–
Walsh	10	4	33	1	Ata-ur-Rehman	8	–	43	2
Cummins	9	–	57	1	Aamir Nazir	8.3	–	54	–
Benjamin	8	–	37	1	Mushtaq Ahmed	10	1	46	1
Hooper	10	1	65	–	Salim Malik	9	1	47	1
Simmons	3	–	22	–	Aamir Sohail	2	–	20	–

FALL OF WICKETS

1–28, **2**–30, **3**–87, **4**–259

FALL OF WICKETS

1–29, **2**–140, **3**–213, **4**–273

Umpires: H.D. Bird & D.R. Shepherd   *Man of the Match*: B.C. Lara   *West Indies won by 6 wickets*

LEAGUE TABLE

	P	W	L	Pts.
West Indies	4	3	1	6
Pakistan	4	3	1	6
Sri Lanka	4	–	4	0

FINAL

Put in to bat, Pakistan struggled as the West Indian bowlers exploited the early morning moisture in the pitch. Only 11 runs came from the first 10 overs, and by the end of the 20th, Pakistan were 51 for 2. Ten overs later, they were 94 for 3, but Basit Ali had begun his remarkable partnership with Salim Malik. From 126 balls, they scored 172 runs. Salim hit a six and 6 fours in his 96-ball innings, but he was overshadowed by the brilliance of Basit Ali who looked set to score the fastest century in limited-over cricket before taking six balls to reach 100 after coming to 96 in 61 deliveries. His 127 not out came off 79 balls and included 5 sixes and 12 fours. It was a magnificent innings.

Richie Richardson with the trophy. (David Munden/Sports-Line)

OPPOSITE: *Asanka Gurusinha – a lone hero for troubled Sri Lanka in the AustralAsia Cup. (David Munden/Sports-Line)*

Brian Lara, Man of the Match in the final, is congratulated by Keith Arthurton on reaching his century. (David Munden/Sports-Line)

Facing a daunting target of 285, West Indies had early discomfort when Haynes was caught behind at 29, but by then Lara was already into his stride. He dominated the West Indian innings, hitting 153 off 138 balls with 21 fours. This was the highest score ever made in a Sharjah tournament, and it helped West Indies to victory with 27 balls to spare.

Lara was named man of the match, and, controversially, Simmons was named man of the series ahead of Saeed Anwar. Haynes had a poor series, but he was one of the three beneficiaries – Shoaib Mohammad and Nazir Mohammad were the other two – and received $35,000.

West Indies' victory broke Pakistan's run of six successive triumphs in Sharjah. It was the fourth time that West Indies had won the trophy.

AUSTRALASIA CUP

For the first time in four years, Sharjah staged two tournaments, with the AustralAsia Cup being revived in 1994. As in 1990, there were six competing nations, but United Arab Emirates, who had just won a place in the finals of the World Cup, competed in a Sharjah tournament for the first time, replacing Bangladesh who had been in the AustralAsia Cup in 1990. Many of the United Arab Emirates' side had played first-class cricket in Pakistan.

Pakistan were the only leading nation at full strength. India, Australia and New Zealand introduced new faces while Sri Lanka had been ravaged by controversy. Aravinda de Silva had been omitted by the selectors who considered him to be unfit. In protest, skipper Arjuna Ranatunga had withdrawn from the party along with other leading players, and Mahanama had taken over the captaincy. Sri Lanka could ill afford such dissension.

There was sadness and concern for India at the start of the tournament when manager Ajit Wadekar suffered a mild heart attack. With Wadekar confined to hospital, Gavaskar took over the management of the Indian side. The Indians, with their leading batsmen in top form and Bhupinder Singh making an impressive debut, had no difficulty in winning their opening match against United Arab Emirates and thereby they virtually assured themselves of a place in the semi-finals.

In the second match, Australia enjoyed an equally convincing victory over Sri Lanka. Tillekeratne hit 64 off 95 balls, but he had little support. Sri Lanka's only bowling success was when Chaminda Vaas accounted for Slater as he swung across the line. Taylor and Mark Waugh added 133 off 162 balls, and Waugh's 64 off 83 balls included a six and 6 fours.

India failed to bat out their 50 overs against Pakistan who won comfortably with 5.3 overs to spare. Australia gained their second win when they beat the inexperienced New Zealand side with 13 balls to spare. The Australians fielded well, and Mark Taylor took two fine catches in the deep. Slater was out second ball, but Hayden and Boon added 123 in 30 overs before Hayden fell to a diving catch at point. Boon hit 10 fours and a six, but Warne's bowling was the telling factor for Australia, not for the first time.

United Arab Emirates batted first against Pakistan when they won the toss, but they floundered against a varied attack. Pakistan raced to victory. Aamir Sohail hit 51 off 67 balls, Saeed Anwar 39 off 28, and Inzamam-ul-Haq made 50 off 47 deliveries.

New Zealand scraped into the semi-finals with victory over Sri Lanka in their final match. Sri Lanka were 41 for 4 inside 12 overs, but Asanka Gurusinha and Upal Chandana put on 88 before Chandana was caught at long-off. The required run rate climbed to eight an over, and New Zealand looked to be winning with ease. Sixteen were needed from the last over with the last pair together, and 10 were needed from the last two balls. Gurusinha hit Nash for six over long-off, but his attempt to hit the last delivery for four was thwarted and produced only a single. His consolation was to win the individual award, but his worries continued. In Sri Lanka, his home and that of Mahanama were under police guard following the arguments over team selection and the withdrawal of Ranatunga and others. New Zealand's innings owed much to Shane Thomson who made 50 off 41 balls with 3 fours and a six.

Aamir Sohail . . . (Alan Cozzi)

The second semi-final was dominated by Aamir Sohail and Inzamam-ul-Haq who established a world record with a second-wicket stand of 263 off 251 balls. This was the highest partnership ever recorded in a one-day international. Inzamam-ul-Haq made 137 off 129 balls with 15 fours and took the individual award.

The final was a more sedate affair than has been usual in matches between Pakistan and India. Pakistan had always looked to be the strongest side in the tournament, and they were given an excellent start by Saeed Anwar and Aamir Sohail. There was a brisk innings from Basit Ali, and once India had been reduced to 83 for 4, the match was as good as over. Kambli and Bedade made a spirited effort at recovery, but Salim Malik's bowling was again very effective.

. . . and Inzaman-ul-Haq established a new world record with a partnership of 263 for Pakistan against New Zealand. (David Munden/Sports-Line)

GROUP A

	P	W	L	Pts.
Pakistan	2	2	–	4
India	2	1	1	2
United Arab Emirates	2	–	2	0

GROUP B

	P	W	L	Pts.
Australia	2	2	–	4
New Zealand	2	1	1	2
Sri Lanka	2	–	2	0

In the first semi-final, Australia batted consistently against India, and when Tendulkar was caught at midwicket in the third over Australia seemed well in charge. Jadeja and Sidhu turned the game with a partnership of 130 and, after Jadeja had fallen to Warne, Sidhu and Azharuddin added 69. When Sidhu was out 35 were needed from 7.2 overs. Warne had again bowled admirably, but Kambli hit him for 2 sixes and 2 fours in his ninth over which cost 22 runs in all, and India won with 4.2 overs to spare.

AUSTRALASIA CUP – MATCH ONE – UNITED ARAB EMIRATES *v.* INDIA
13 April 1994 at Sharjah C.A. Stadium

INDIA

A.D. Jadeja	c Arshad Laiq, b Sohail Butt	25
S.R. Tendulkar	c Imtiaz Abbasi, b Sultan Zarawani	63
N.S. Sidhu	b Sohail Butt	0
M. Azharuddin (capt)	c Samarasekera, b Salim Raza	81
V.G. Kambli	not out	82
A.C. Bedade	c Imtiaz Abbasi, b Samarasekera	7
*N.R. Mongia	not out	4
A.R. Kumble		
Bhupinder Singh snr		
Venkatapathy Raju		
J. Srinath		
Extras	b 1, lb 2, w 6, nb 2	11
(50 overs)	(for 5 wickets)	273

UNITED ARAB EMIRATES

Riaz Poonawalla	c Mongia, b Bhupinder Singh snr	22
Azhar Saeed	c Mongia, b Srinath	3
Mazhar Hussain	c Jadeja, b Bhupinder Singh snr	70
Vijay Mehra	c Mongia, b Bhupinder Singh snr	43
Mohammad Ishaque	c Jadeja, b Srinath	23
Salim Raza	c Mongia, b Srinath	6
J. Samarasekera	c Tendulkar, b Venkatapathy Raju	3
Arshad Laiq	b Kumble	4
Sultan Zarawani (capt)	b Kumble	4
*Imtiaz Abbasi	not out	6
Sohail Butt	not out	6
Extras	lb 4, w 5, nb 3	12
(50 overs)	(for 9 wickets)	202

	O	M	R	W
Samarasekera	10	–	48	1
Sohail Butt	10	–	52	2
Arshad Laiq	10	–	56	–
Azhar Saeed	10	1	38	–
Sultan Zarawani	3	–	22	1
Salim Raza	7	–	54	1

	O	M	R	W
Srinath	10	1	48	3
Bhupinder Singh snr	10	1	34	3
Jadeja	5	–	32	–
Tendulkar	5	–	22	–
Venkatapathy Raju	10	–	32	1
Kumble	10	–	30	2

FALL OF WICKETS
1–49, 2–55, 3–130, 4–230, 5–254

FALL OF WICKETS
1–26, 2–26, 3–120, 4–161, 5–169, 6–182, 7–183, 8–188, 9–191

Umpires: K. Kanjee & S.B. Lambson   *Man of the Match:* V.G. Kambli   *India won by 71 runs*

AUSTRALASIA CUP – MATCH TWO – SRI LANKA *v.* AUSTRALIA
14 April 1994 at Sharjah C.A. Stadium

SRI LANKA

R.S. Mahanama (capt)	lbw, b Reiffel	10
M.A.R. Samarasekera	c Langer, b S.R. Waugh	24
A.P. Gurusinha	run out	1
S.T. Jayasuriya	run out	8
H.P. Tillekeratne	c Taylor, b S.R. Waugh	64
R.S. Kalpage	c Bevan, b Warne	4
U. Chandana	c Bevan, b Reiffel	18
*P.B. Dassanayake	lbw, b Warne	7
C.P.H. Ramanayake	lbw, b Warne	2
M. Manasinghe	b Fleming	2
C. Vaas	not out	0
Extras	lb 10, w 1, nb 3	14
(49.3 overs)		154

AUSTRALIA

M.A. Taylor (capt)	not out	68
M.J. Slater	b Vaas	15
M.E. Waugh	not out	64
M.L. Hayden		
*J.L. Langer		
S.R. Waugh		
M.G. Bevan		
P.R. Reiffel		
S.K. Warne		
T.B.A. May		
D.W. Fleming		
Extras	b 1, lb 7, w 3	11
(36.5 overs)	(for 1 wicket)	158

	O	M	R	W
Reiffel	10	1	28	2
Fleming	9.3	1	27	1
S.R. Waugh	6	–	17	2
May	10	–	25	–
Warne	10	1	29	3
M.E. Waugh	4	–	18	–

	O	M	R	W
Ramanayake	8	1	15	–
Vaas	10	1	35	1
Manasinghe	6.5	–	28	–
Jayasuriya	4	–	22	–
Kalpage	5	–	29	–
Chandana	3	–	21	–

FALL OF WICKETS
1–30, 2–38, 3–40, 4–61, 5–91, 6–124, 7–136, 8–142, 9–153

FALL OF WICKET
1–25

Umpires: K. Kanjee & K.E. Liebenberg   *Man of the Match:* M.E. Waugh   *Australia won by 9 wickets*

AUSTRALASIA CUP – MATCH THREE – INDIA v. PAKISTAN
15 April 1994 at Sharjah C.A. Stadium

INDIA		
A.D. Jadeja	c Rashid Latif, **b** Aqib Javed	19
S.R. Tendulkar	c Basit Ali, **b** Akram Raza	73
N.S. Sidhu	c Rashid Latif, **b** Ata-ur-Rehman	47
M. Azharuddin (capt)	c Inzamam-ul-Haq, **b** Salim Malik	29
A.C. Bedade	**st** Rashid Latif, **b** Salim Malik	1
V.G. Kambli	c Akram Raza, **b** Ata-ur-Rehman	4
*N.R. Mongia	run out	5
A.R. Kumble	**b** Wasim Akram	6
Bhupinder Singh snr	run out	6
R.K. Chauhan	c Saeed Anwar, **b** Aqib Javed	13
J. Srinath	not out	1
Extras	lb **2**, w **10**, nb **3**	15
(46.3 overs)		219

PAKISTAN		
Saeed Anwar	lbw, **b** Chauhan	72
Aamir Sohail	**b** Chauhan	20
Inzamam-ul-Haq	c Mongia, **b** Chauhan	1
Salim Malik (capt)	c Azharuddin, **b** Srinath	25
Basit Ali	not out	75
Asif Mujtaba	not out	16
Wasim Akram		
*Rashid Latif		
Akram Raza		
Aqib Javed		
Ata-ur-Rehman		
Extras	lb **4**, w **7**, nb **3**	14
(44.3 overs)	(for 4 wickets)	223

	O	M	R	W
Wasim Akram	8.3	1	36	1
Aqib Javed	9	1	41	2
Ata-ur-Rehman	9	–	50	2
Salim Malik	10	–	49	2
Akram Raza	10	–	41	1

	O	M	R	W
Srinath	9.3	–	58	1
Bhupinder Singh snr	7	1	44	–
Kumble	9	–	27	–
Chauhan	10	–	47	3
Tendulkar	8	–	34	–
Jadeja	1	–	9	–

FALL OF WICKETS

1–62, **2**–111, **3**–156, 4–164, **5**–179, **6**–187, **7**–187, **8**–197, **9**–218

FALL OF WICKETS

1–76, **2**–89, **3**–106, 4–171

Umpires: K.E. Liebenberg & S.B. Lambson   *Man of the Match:* Saeed Anwar   *Pakistan won by 6 wickets*

AUSTRALASIA CUP – MATCH FOUR – AUSTRALIA v. NEW ZEALAND
16 April 1994 at Sharjah C.A. Stadium

NEW ZEALAND		
B.A. Young	c and **b** Fleming	63
B.R. Hartland	lbw, **b** Warne	23
M.W. Douglas	lbw, **b** Warne	0
S.P. Fleming	c Taylor, **b** Fleming	35
S.A. Thomson	c Taylor, **b** Fleming	32
*A.C. Parore	c and **b** Warne	12
C.Z. Harris	lbw, **b** Warne	14
G.R. Larsen (capt)	not out	9
M.N. Hart	c Hayden, **b** Fleming	2
D.K. Morrison	**b** McGrath	2
C. Pringle	not out	2
Extras	b **1**, lb **6**, w **2**, nb **4**	13
(50 overs)	(for 9 wickets)	207

AUSTRALIA		
M.J. Slater	**b** Morrison	0
M.L. Hayden	c Harris, **b** Pringle	67
D.C. Boon	c sub (Nash), **b** Thomson	68
M.G. Bevan	not out	39
*J.L. Langer	not out	20
M.A. Taylor (capt)		
S.R. Waugh		
S.K. Warne		
P.R. Reiffel		
D.W. Fleming		
G.D. McGrath		
Extras	lb **11**, w **3**	14
(47.5 overs)	(for 3 wickets)	208

	O	M	R	W
Reiffel	10	–	35	–
McGrath	10	–	44	1
Waugh	10	1	48	–
Warne	10	–	34	4
Fleming	10	–	39	4

	O	M	R	W
Morrison	6	2	22	1
Pringle	9.5	1	43	1
Larsen	9	–	42	–
Harris	6	–	25	–
Hart	7	–	26	–
Thomson	10	2	39	1

FALL OF WICKETS

1–75, **2**–75, **3**–125, 4–134, **5**–169, **6**–183, **7**–191, **8**–201, 9 203

FALL OF WICKETS

1–0, **2**–123, **3**–166

Umpires: K. Kanjee & S.B. Lambson   *Man of the Match:* S.K. Warne   *Australia won by 7 wickets*

AUSTRALASIA CUP – MATCH FIVE – UNITED ARAB EMIRATES *v.* PAKISTAN
17 April 1994 at Sharjah C.A. Stadium

UNITED ARAB EMIRATES					
Riaz Poonawalla	c Rashid Latif, b Ata-ur-Rehman				22
Azhar Saeed	c Akram Raza, b Wasim Akram				0
Mazhar Hussain	c Rashid Latif, b Ata-ur-Rehman				10
Vijay Mehra	c Aamir Sohail, b Salim Malik				5
Mohammad Ishaq	c Rashid Latif, b Salim Malik				4
Salim Raza	c Akram Raza, b Wasim Akram				16
J. Samarasekera	not out				31
Arshad Laiq	c Wasim Akram, b Salim Malik				31
Sultan Zarawani (capt)	run out				6
*Imtiaz Abbasi	b Wasim Akram				2
Sohail Butt	b Ata-ur-Rehman				2
Extras	lb 2, w 10, nb 4				16
(49.5 overs)					145

PAKISTAN					
Saeed Anwar	c Poonawalla, b Salim Raza				39
Aamir Sohail	not out				51
Inzamam-ul-Haq	not out				50
Salim Malik (capt)					
Basit Ali					
Asif Mujtaba					
Wasim Akram					
*Rashid Latif					
Akram Raza					
Ata-ur-Rehman					
Aqib Javed					
Extras	lb 2, w 4				6
(23.1 overs)	(for 1 wicket)				146

	O	M	R	W			O	M	R	W
Wasim Akram	10	1	19	3		J. Samarasekera	5	–	31	–
Aqib Javed	10	2	29	–		Sohail Butt	3	–	27	–
Ata-ur-Rehman	9.5	–	32	3		Arshad Laiq	4	–	25	–
Salim Malik	10	1	42	3		Salim Raza	3	1	17	1
Akram Raza	10	3	21	–		Azhar Saeed	4.1	–	18	–
						Sultan Zarawani	4	–	26	–

FALL OF WICKETS
1–7, 2–40, 3–45, 4–45, 5–65, 6–68, 7–125, 8–138, 9–141

FALL OF WICKET
1–76

Umpires: K. Kanjee & K.E. Liebenberg   *Man of the Match:* Ata-ur-Rehman   *Pakistan won by 9 wickets*

AUSTRALASIA CUP – MATCH SIX – SRI LANKA *v.* NEW ZEALAND
18 April 1994 at Sharjah C.A. Stadium

NEW ZEALAND					
B.R. Hartland	run out				5
B.A. Young	c Jayasuriya, b Gurusinha				34
*A.C. Parore	c Dassanayake, b Jayasuriya				37
M.W. Douglas	run out				30
S.P. Fleming	c Tillekeratne, b Kalpage				14
S.A. Thomson	c Chandana, b Vaas				50
C.Z. Harris	c Chandana, b Ramanayake				22
D.J. Nash	run out				2
G.R. Larsen (capt)	run out				14
C. Pringle	not out				0
H.T. Davis					
Extras	b 1, lb 5, nb 3				9
(50 overs)	(for 8 wickets)				217

SRI LANKA					
R.S. Mahanama (capt)	lbw, b Pringle				18
M.A.R. Samarasekera	c Fleming, b Nash				4
A.P. Gurusinha	not out				117
S.T. Jayasuriya	c Davis, b Nash				5
H.P. Tillekeratne	run out				0
V. Chandana	c Young, b Nash				26
R.S. Kalpage	c Harris, b Thomson				6
*P.B. Dassanayake	c Parore, b Larsen				5
H.C.P. Ramanayake	b Pringle				21
A. Weerakkody	c Nash, b Pringle				2
C. Vaas	not out				1
Extras	b 1, lb 6, w 3				10
(50 overs)	(for 9 wickets)				215

	O	M	R	W			O	M	R	W
Ramanayake	10	1	41	1		Pringle	10	1	46	3
Vaas	10	1	31	1		Davis	2	–	14	–
Weerakkody	6	–	41	–		Larsen	10	1	34	1
Gurusinha	10	1	30	1		Harris	9	–	33	–
Jayasuriya	7	–	37	1		Thomson	9	1	38	1
Kalpage	7	–	31	1		Nash	10	1	43	3

FALL OF WICKETS
1–12, 2–68, 3–94, 4–121, 5–135, 6–194, 7–198, 8–206

FALL OF WICKETS
1–24, 2–24, 3–30, 4–41, 5–129, 6–147, 7–152, 8–189, 9–202

Umpires: S.B. Lambson & K.E. Liebenberg   *Man of the Match:* A.P. Gurusinha   *New Zealand won by 2 runs*

AUSTRALASIA CUP – SEMI-FINAL – INDIA *v.* AUSTRALIA
19 April 1994 at Sharjah C.A. Stadium

AUSTRALIA				INDIA		
M.A. Taylor (capt)	b Srinath	11		A.D. Jadeja	c Boon, b Warne	87
D.C. Boon	b Kumble	21		S.R. Tendulkar	c Taylor, b McGrath	6
M.E. Waugh	run out	16		N.S. Sidhu	st Langer, b Warne	80
S.R. Waugh	c Mongia, b Srinath	53		M. Azharuddin (capt)	not out	36
M.G. Bevan	c Jadeja, b Kumble	25		V.G. Kambli	not out	28
M.L. Hayden	c Jadeja, b Kumble	48		A.C. Bedade		
*J.L. Langer	run out	36		*N.R. Mongia		
P.R. Reiffel	c Tendulkar, b Srinath	7		A.R. Kumble		
S.K. Warne	run out	4		Venkatesh Prasad		
D.W. Fleming	not out	2		R.K. Chauhan		
G.D. McGrath	not out	0		J. Srinath		
Extras	lb 14, w 6, nb 1	21		Extras	lb 4, w 2, nb 2	8
(50 overs)	(for 9 wickets)	244		(45.4 overs)	(for 3 wickets)	245

	O	M	R	W		O	M	R	W
Srinath	9	1	32	3	McGrath	8	–	35	1
Venkatesh Prasad	8	1	39	–	Reiffel	8	–	32	–
Kumble	10	1	50	3	S.R. Waugh	8	–	52	–
Chauhan	10	2	37	–	Fleming	9.4	–	59	–
Tendulkar	8	–	39	–	Warne	9	–	40	2
Jadeja	5	–	33	–	M.E. Waugh	3	–	23	–

FALL OF WICKETS
1–29, 2–53, 3–62, 4–115, 5–158, 6–222, 7–227, 8–242, 9–244

FALL OF WICKETS
1–11, 2–141, 3–210

Umpires: K. Kanjee & S.B. Lambson   *Man of the Match*: A.D. Jadeja   *India won by 7 wickets*

AUSTRALASIA CUP – SEMI-FINAL – PAKISTAN *v.* NEW ZEALAND
20 April 1994 at Sharjah C.A. Stadium

PAKISTAN				NEW ZEALAND		
Saeed Anwar	c Parore, b Nash	37		B.A. Young	c Saeed Anwar, b Ata-ur-Rehman	36
Aamir Sohail	c Douglas, b Pringle	134		B.R. Hartland	c Rashid Latif, b Wasim Akram	11
Inzamam-ul-Haq	not out	137		*A.C. Parore	c sub, b Salim Malik	82
Wasim Akram	not out	7		S.A. Thomson	run out	62
Salim Malik (capt)				S.P. Fleming	b Aamir Sohail	1
Basit Ali				M.W. Douglas	b Salim Malik	3
Asif Mujtaba				C.Z. Harris	not out	34
*Rashid Latif				D.J. Nash	b Wasim Akram	2
Akram Raza				G.R. Larsen (capt)	not out	18
Ata-ur-Rehman				C. Pringle		
Aqib Javed				H.T. Davis		
Extras	b 1, lb 2, w 8, nb 2	13		Extras	lb 6, w 7, nb 4	17
(50 overs)	(for 2 wickets)	328		(50 overs)	(for 7 wickets)	266

	O	M	R	W		O	M	R	W
Pringle	10	–	57	1	Wasim Akram	10	–	50	2
Davis	4	–	37	–	Aqib Javed	10	–	56	–
Nash	9	–	60	1	Ata-ur-Rehman	5	–	35	1
Larsen	10	–	71	–	Akram Raza	10	–	42	–
Thomson	7	–	44	–	Salim Malik	10	–	55	2
Harris	10	–	56	–	Aamir Sohail	5	–	22	1

FALL OF WICKETS
1–57, 2–320

FALL OF WICKETS
1–19, 2–66, 3–199, 4–202, 5 201, 6–207, 7–218

Umpires: K. Kanjee & K.E. Liebenberg   *Man of the Match*: Inzamam-ul-Haq   *Pakistan won by 62 runs*

AUSTRALASIA CUP – FINAL – PAKISTAN *v.* INDIA
22 April 1994 at Sharjah C.A. Stadium

PAKISTAN		
Saeed Anwar	c Prasad, b Chauhan	47
Aamir Sohail	b Srinath	69
Inzamam-ul-Haq	st Mongia, b Chauhan	12
Salim Malik (capt)	c Azharuddin, b Chauhan	1
Basit Ali	b Srinath	57
Asif Mujtaba	not out	34
Wasim Akram	c Azharuddin, b Srinath	2
*Rashid Latif	not out	17
Akram Raza		
Ata-ur-Rehman		
Aqib Javed		
Extras	lb 3, w 3, nb 5	11
(50 overs)	(for 6 wickets)	250

INDIA		
A.D. Jadeja	c Basit Ali, b Wasim Akram	0
S.R. Tendulkar	c Aamir Sohail, b Ata-ur-Rehman	24
N.S. Sidhu	c and b Akram Raza	36
M. Azharuddin (capt)	c Rashid Latif, b Aqib Javed	3
V.G. Kambli	c Akram Raza, b Salim Malik	56
A.C. Bedade	c Asif Mujtaba, b Aamir Sohail	44
*N.R. Mongia	c and b Aamir Sohail	3
A.R. Kumble	c Rashid Latif, b Salim Malik	12
R.K. Chauhan	run out	5
J. Srinath	not out	6
Venkatesh Prasad	lbw, b Wasim Akram	0
Extras	lb 4, w 10, nb 8	22
(47.4 overs)		211

	O	M	R	W
Srinath	10	–	56	3
Venkatesh Prasad	9	1	44	–
Kumble	10	–	56	–
Chauhan	9	–	29	3
Tendulkar	8	–	45	–
Jadeja	4	–	17	–

	O	M	R	W
Wasim Akram	8	–	39	2
Aqib Javed	7	1	27	1
Ata-ur-Rehman	8	–	27	1
Akram Raza	10	–	47	1
Salim Malik	9	–	45	2
Aamir Sohail	5	–	22	2

FALL OF WICKETS

1–96, 2–125, 3–127, 4–149, 5–215, 6–219

FALL OF WICKETS

1–1, 2–60, 3–63, 4–83, 5–163, 6–180, 7–182, 8–203, 9–209

Umpires: S.B. Lambson & K.E. Liebenberg   *Man of the Match:* Aamir Sohail   *Pakistan won by 39 runs*

SECTION H
Sri Lanka
Test and one-day international series *v.* India, South Africa and West Indies

The splendid Khetterama Stadium in Colombo. (Michael King/Allsport)

With near success over Australia and success against England fresh in the memory, Sri Lanka greeted the arrival of the Indian touring side, in July 1993, with some optimism. It was apparent, however, that the Indians now offered the very strongest opposition. They had totally overwhelmed England, were full of confidence, and were arguably able to field the strongest side in their history.

12,13 and 14 July 1993 *at Welageedra Stadium, Kurunegala*

Indians 342 for 6 dec. (M. Azharuddin 100, K.S. More 60 not out, M. Prabhakar 53) and 148 for 1 (P K. Amre 70 not out, N.S. Sidhu 66 not out)

Sri Lankan Board President's XI 415 (S.T. Jayasuriya 151, H.P. Tillekeratne 101, R.S. Kalpage 69 not out, Venkatapathy Raju 4 for 101)

Match drawn

Indian skipper Azharuddin began the short tour with an accomplished century and was able to declare his side's innings closed after most of his batsmen had shown to advantage. The President's XI slipped to 97 for 4, but Test players Tillekeratne and Jayasuriya hit centuries and shared a stand of 192 for the fifth wicket. The left-handed Kalpage also batted well.

FIRST TEST MATCH
SRI LANKA *v.* INDIA, at Kandy

The decision to play a Test match in Kandy during the monsoon season proved to be a complete disaster. No play was possible on the first day, and only 10 overs could be bowled in 50 minutes after lunch on the second day. Sri Lanka, having been put in to bat, lost three wickets.

FIRST ONE-DAY INTERNATIONAL
SRI LANKA *v.* INDIA, at Colombo

The first and second Test matches were punctuated by the first of three one-day internationals. Put in to bat, India found runs difficult to get on a slow wicket which was particularly well exploited by the young off-spinner Ruwan Kalpage. Kalpage was foiled, however, by the Indian captain Mohammad Azharuddin who batted magnificently to reach 53 in 23 overs and so put his side in a reasonable position.

FIRST TEST MATCH – SRI LANKA *v.* INDIA
17, 18, 19, 21 and 22 July 1993 at Asgiriya Stadium, Kandy

SRI LANKA			INDIA
R.S. Mahanama	c More, b Kapil Dev	0	M. Prabhakar
U.C. Hathurusinghe	c Kumble, b Prabhakar	4	N.S. Sidhu
A.P. Gurusinha	not out	10	V.G. Kambli
P.A. de Silva	c Kumble, b Prabhakar	1	S.R. Tendulkar
A. Ranatunga (capt)	not out	7	M. Azharuddin (capt)
H.P. Tillekeratne			P.K. Amre
*A.M. de Silva			Kapil Dev
C.P.H. Ramanayake			*K.S. More
D.K. Liyanage			A.R. Kumble
M. Muralitharan			R.K. Chauhan
K.P.J. Warnaweera			J. Srinath
Extras	1b **1**, nb **1**	2	
	(for 3 wickets)	24	

	O	M	R	W
Kapil Dev	5	1	10	1
Prabhakar	6	1	13	2
Srinath	1	1	0	–

FALL OF WICKETS
1–0, 2–6, 3–8

Umpires: K.T. Francis & T.M. Samarasinghe

Match drawn

Needing 213 to win, Sri Lanka were given a good start by Mahanama and Hathurusinghe. Hathurusinghe, who was hobbling from a knee injury, was the backbone of the innings, and, with the aggressive Aravinda de Silva, he added 115 for the third wicket. This was welcome relief for Sri Lanka after Kumble had dismissed Mahanama and Gurusinha with successive deliveries in his opening over.

Aravinda de Silva twice in one over put Srinath over the ropes for six, and at 161 for 2 in the 40th over, Sri Lanka looked to be heading for an easy win. Then de Silva was brilliantly caught at mid-wicket attempting a third six. Sri Lanka collapsed as this was the first of eight wickets to fall for 50 runs. When Prabhakar bowled Wickramasinghe with the second ball of the final over India had snatched an amazing victory by one run.

SECOND TEST MATCH
SRI LANKA v. INDIA, at Colombo

Sri Lanka gave a first Test cap to Kalpage who had performed impressively in two matches against the Indians. There were no other surprises, nor was it a surprise when India batted on winning the toss. There was help for the bowlers during the first session as the ball bounced appreciably and moved off the seam. Prabhakar struggled for 74 minutes before falling to Gurusinha, but thereafter Sidhu and Kambli took control.

Four Test centuries in five innings for the remarkable Vinod Kambli. (David Munden/Sports-Line)

FIRST ONE-DAY INTERNATIONAL – SRI LANKA v. INDIA
25 July 1993 at Khetterama Stadium, Colombo

INDIA				SRI LANKA		
M. Prabhakar	c and b Gurusinha	39		R.S. Mahanama	st Yadav, b Kumble	24
N.S. Sidhu	b Kalpage	39		U.C. Hathurusinghe	lbw, b Chauhan	64
V.G. Kambli	b Kalpage	9		A.P. Gurusinha	c Kapil Dev, b Kumble	0
M. Azharuddin (capt)	c Hathurusinghe, b Ramanayake	53		P.A. de Silva	c Amre, b Srinath	62
S.R. Tendulkar	c Gurusinha, b Jayasuriya	21		A. Ranatunga (capt)	lbw, b Chauhan	2
P.K. Amre	b Kalpage	7		H.P. Tillekeratne	c Kambli, b Prabhakar	5
Kapil Dev	c Tillekeratne, b Wickramasinghe	27		S.T. Jayasuriya	c Amre, b Kapil Dev	17
*V. Yadav	c Kalpage, b Ramanayake	6		R.S. Kalpage	not out	9
A.R. Kumble	not out	0		*A.M. de Silva	run out	4
R.K. Chauhan				C.P.H. Ramanayake	b Srinath	0
J. Srinath				G.P. Wickramasinghe	b Prabhakar	0
Extras	1b 1, w 5, nb 5	11		Extras	1b 5, w 15, nb 4	24
(50 overs)	(for 8 wickets)	212		(49.2 overs)		211

	O	M	R	W		O	M	R	W
Ramanayake	10	–	50	2	Kapil Dev	10	3	29	1
Wickramasinghe	9	–	41	1	Prabhakar	9.2	–	50	2
Hathurusinghe	4	–	24	–	Srinath	10	–	64	2
Gurusinha	7	–	21	1	Kumble	10	2	22	2
Jayasuriya	10	–	33	1	Chauhan	10	–	41	2
Kalpage	10	–	42	3					

FALL OF WICKETS
1–77, 2–92, 3–97, 4–139, 5–148, 6–200, 7–210, 8–212

FALL OF WICKETS
1–46, 2–46, 3–161, 4–172, 5–173, 6–186, 7–196, 8–207, 9–208

Umpires: K.T. Francis & T.M. Samarasinghe   *Man of the Match*: M. Azharuddin   *India won by 1 run*

The pair added 126 with Sidhu the dominant partner. He drove impressively before being brilliantly caught at short-leg by Tillekeratne. Kambli, dropped at the wicket off Kalpage when 41, played with great responsibility and followed his double centuries against England and Zimbabwe with 125. He was out on the second morning when India collapsed from 300 for 4 overnight to 366 all out, the last five wickets falling for 14 runs.

Sri Lanka were censured by referee Burge for their slow over rate, but they batted briskly enough and got off to a reasonable start. Then came a collapse as four wickets fell for 48 runs, de Silva being the fourth man out shortly after becoming the second Sri Lankan to complete 2,000 runs in Test cricket. Ranatunga and Tillekeratne halted the slide, and Sri Lanka closed on 200 for 4, with the captain 82 not out.

Sadly, Sri Lanka suffered a more disastrous collapse on the third morning as leg-spinner Kumble and pace bowler Srinath undermined the middle-order. Ranatunga was one of Kumble's victims as five wickets went down for 11 runs. Wickramasinghe and Warnaweera added 36 for the last wicket, but Sri Lanka conceded a lead of 112 on the first innings.

India now took complete control of the game as Prabhakar and Sidhu scored 171 for the first wicket. Prabhakar equalled his highest Test score, hitting 11 fours and facing 183 balls before being taken at short-leg off the deserving Kalpage. Kambli was given out caught behind to his obvious displeasure, which brought him a reprimand from the referee, and India closed on 205 for 2, with Sidhu on 85.

He completed his fourth Test century on the fourth day, and Tendulkar moved serenely and purposefully to his sixth. Azharuddin's declaration left Sri Lanka a day and a half in which to score 472. They reached a grim 86 for 2 by the close.

SECOND TEST MATCH – SRI LANKA v. INDIA
27, 28, 29, 31 July and 1 August 1993 at Sinhalese Sports Club, Colombo

INDIA

	FIRST INNINGS		SECOND INNINGS	
M. Prabhakar	lbw, b Gurusinha	4	c Tillekeratne, b Kalpage	95
N.S. Sidhu	c Tillekeratne, b Warnaweera	82	c A.M. de Silva, b Hathurusinghe	104
V.G. Kambli	c Mahanama, b Hathurusinghe	125	c A.M. de Silva, b Warnaweera	4
S.R. Tendulkar	c Tillekeratne, b Kalpage	28	not out	104
M. Azharuddin (capt)	lbw, b Wickramasinghe	26	c Tillekeratne, b Kalpage	21
P.K. Amre	c Kalpage, b Warnaweera	21	not out	15
Kapil Dev	lbw, b Gurusinha	35		
*K.S. More	c Mahanama, b Warnaweera	4		
A.R. Kumble	lbw, b Wickramasinghe	1		
R.K. Chauhan	c A.M. de Silva, b Wickramasinghe	2		
J. Srinath	not out	0		
Extras	b 9, lb 3, w 10, nb 16	38	b 5, lb 1, w 2, nb 8	16
		366	(for 4 wickets, dec.)	359

SRI LANKA

	FIRST INNINGS		SECOND INNINGS	
R.S. Mahanama	c More, b Prabhakar	22	lbw, b Kapil Dev	9
U.C. Hathurusinghe	b Kumble	37	c Azharuddin, b Prabhakar	43
A.P. Gurusinha	lbw, b Prabhakar	4	c Chauhan, b Kumble	39
P.A. de Silva	c Azharuddin, b Kumble	22	c Azharuddin, b Kumble	93
A. Ranatunga (capt)	c Srinath, b Kumble	88	c More, b Prabhakar	14
H.P. Tillekeratne	c More, b Srinath	28	c sub (Raman), b Prabhakar	2
*A.M. de Silva	c Amre, b Kumble	0	b Kapil Dev	1
R.S. Kalpage	c More, b Srinath	1	c Amre, b Srinath	5
D.K. Liyanage	lbw, b Kumble	2	c Azharuddin, b Chauhan	8
G.P. Wickramasinghe	not out	11	lbw, b Kumble	4
K.P.J. Warnaweera	b Prabhakar	20	not out	2
Extras	b 9, lb 5, w 4, nb 1	19	b 6, lb 6, w 2, nb 2	16
		254		236

	O	M	R	W	O	M	R	W		O	M	R	W	O	M	R	W
Liyanage	19	3	64	–	10	2	31	–	Kapil Dev	11	4	26	–	26	13	34	2
Wickramasinghe	27	6	83	3	22	4	58	–	Prabhakar	15.5	5	43	3	18	4	49	3
Hathurusinghe	17	2	48	1	12	1	35	1	Srinath	17	5	42	2	15	2	36	1
Gurusinha	16	2	49	2	7	–	24	–	Kumble	24	3	87	5	38.1	14	85	3
Warnaweera	20.1	1	76	3	20	1	86	1	Chauhan	10	1	42	–	24	18	20	1
Kalpage	8	1	34	1	38	3	97	2									
Ranatunga					2	1	5	–									
P.A. de Silva					7	–	17	–									

FALL OF WICKETS

1–25, 2–151, 3–219, 4–282, 5–311, 6–352, 7–362, 8–363, 9–366
1–171, 2–176, 3–263, 4–316

FALL OF WICKETS

1–48, 2–58, 3–85, 4–96, 5–207, 6–208, 7–209, 8–218, 9–218
1–44, 2–59, 3–127, 4–180, 5–182, 6–191, 7–198, 8–221, 9–229

Umpires: I. Anandappa & S. Ponnadurai

India won by 235 runs

Gurusinha and de Silva offered stubborn resistance, but Gurusinha was splendidly caught by Chauhan in the first session, and four wickets fell in the second when Prabhakar dismissed Ranatunga and Tillekeratne in successive overs with the second new ball. Aravinda de Silva batted with style and resolution, but India were not to be denied, and the game was over shortly after tea.

This was India's first Test victory on foreign soil since Headingley in 1986, 27 overseas Tests previously. It was also their fifth victory in six Tests, but it was marred by the complaints as to their on-field behaviour. Both sides were warned by referee Burge, and new umpires were chosen for the third Test of the series. Manoj Prabhakar was named Man of the Match.

THIRD TEST MATCH
SRI LANKA v. INDIA, at Colombo

Sri Lanka made three changes for the final Test, bringing back Jayasuriya, Kaluwitharana and Muralitharan in place of Liyanage, Ashley de Silva and Kalpage. Ranatunga won the toss, and the home side batted. They endured early problems as both openers fell to the new-ball attack. Mahanama was leg before to Prabhakar, and Kapil Dev moved closer to Richard Hadlee's record when he had Hathurusinghe taken at short-leg.

Gurusinha began shakily, but he showed in character in reaching fifty, hitting a six and 8 fours in his 199-ball innings. He and Aravinda de Silva added 136 in 58 overs to give the Sri Lankan innings some substance, but the home side again faced a crisis when Gurusinha and Ranatunga were dismissed within five overs of each other. Aravinda de Silva remained and reached his sixth Test century, his first in Sri Lanka. He showed the greatest concentration allied to his rich array of strokes, and by the end of the first day he had batted for 306 minutes and hit 12 fours and a six in his 118 not out. It was a towering hit over mid-wicket off Kumble for six which brought up his century.

Beginning the second day on 226 for 4, Sri Lanka again lost their way as they failed to capitalise on the splendid work of de Silva and Tillekeratne. They did not force the pace, and the total of 351 from 142.1 overs was disappointing. India closed on 84 for 0, but the day was most marked by the unpleasant gamesmanship that developed between the two sides who were again warned by referee Burge and restrained by some firm umpiring.

On the third day, India added 300 runs to their score for the loss of five wickets. Remarkably, in his seventh Test, Kambli hit his fourth century in his last five innings, and with Tendulkar and Azharuddin showing panache, India moved into a strong position. On the fourth day, they lost their last five wickets for 62 runs, mainly because of some splendid off-spin bowling by Muralitharan. Sri Lanka closed on 132 for 1, and the game looked certain to be drawn.

So it proved. Sri Lanka slumped to 157 for 4, but Mahanama and Tillekeratne added 132. Mahanama faced

A first Test century in Sri Lanka for Aravinda de Silva, and an excellent series against India. (David Munden/Sports-Line)

362 balls and hit 19 fours for his third Test century. He was out when he skied an attempted hook off Prabhakar to Chauhan. Prabhakar's first eight overs of the day had been maidens.

Mahanama took the individual award, and India took the series, their first overseas since winning in England in 1986.

SECOND AND THIRD ONE-DAY INTERNATIONALS
SRI LANKA v. INDIA

Sri Lanka had regained some pride with their performance in the final Test, and they gained further comfort from their victories in the second and third one-day internationals, victories which gave them the limited-over series.

In the second one-day international, in Colombo, India seemed set for a comfortable victory. They had restricted Sri Lanka to 204 in 50 overs, and, having lost their first two wickets for 16 runs, were taken to the brink of victory by Prabhakar and Azharuddin who added 136 in 29.1 overs. They were the only batsmen to master a slow-paced wicket and a sluggish outfield, and victory seemed assured, but an incredible collapse took place, the last seven wickets falling for 21 runs in nine overs. Amre and Yadav went to rash and unnecessary big hits while Tendulkar was stupidly run out going for a needless second run. Sri Lanka snatched a totally unexpected victory to the delight of the biggest crowd ever to watch a cricket match in the island.

A capacity crowd of 10,000 saw Sri Lanka clinch the series in Moratuwa. A magnificent innings of 85 off 101 deliveries by Azharuddin was the highlight of the Indian

THIRD TEST MATCH – SRI LANKA *v.* INDIA
4, 5, 7, 8 and 9 August 1993 at P. Saravanamuttu Stadium, Colombo

SRI LANKA

	FIRST INNINGS		SECOND INNINGS	
R.S. Mahanama	lbw, b Prabhakar	6	c Chauhan, b Prabhakar	151
U.C. Hathurusinghe	c Amre, b Kapil Dev	6	c sub (Raman), b Raju	22
A.P. Gurusinha	c Tendulkar, b Kumble	56	c sub (Raman), b Kumble	35
P.A. de Silva	c Raju, b Kumble	148	c Kambli, b Kumble	2
A. Ranatunga (capt)	c Kapil Dev, b Raju	9	c Tendulkar, b Prabhakar	13
H.P. Tillekeratne	b Chauhan	51	c and b Kumble	86
S.T. Jayasuriya	lbw, b Chauhan	0	not out	31
*R.S. Kaluwitharana	b Prabhakar	40		
G.P. Wickramasinghe	c Tendulkar, b Chauhan	0		
M. Muralitharan	b Kapil Dev	7		
K.P.J. Warnaweera	not out	1		
Extras	b 3, lb 20, w 1, nb 3	27	b 6, lb 4, w 1, nb 1	12
		351	(for 6 wickets)	352

INDIA

	FIRST INNINGS	
M. Prabhakar	c Jayasuriya, b Wickramasinghe	55
N.S. Sidhu	c Kaluwitharana, b Wickramasinghe	39
V.G. Kambli	lbw, b Warnaweera	120
S.R. Tendulkar	c Ranatunga, b Hathurusinghe	71
M. Azharuddin (capt)	c Wickramasinghe, b Muralitharan	50
P.K. Amre	c Kaluwitharana, b Wickramasinghe	21
A.R. Kumble	b Muralitharan	9
Kapil Dev	lbw, b Warnaweera	27
*K.S. More	c and b Muralitharan	4
R.K. Chauhan	not out	15
Venkatapathy Raju	c Jayasuriya, b Muralitharan	1
Extras	b 5, lb 12, w 1, nb 16	34
		446

	O	M	R	W	O	M	R	W
Kapil Dev	27.1	10	56	2	24	11	33	–
Prabhakar	21	7	59	2	31	14	59	2
Venkatapathy Raju	25	5	55	1	27	5	66	1
Tendulkar	3	–	4	–				
Kumble	40	12	95	2	38.2	7	108	3
Chauhan	26	7	59	3	33	5	76	–

	O	M	R	W
Wickramasinghe	38	8	95	3
Gurusinha	11	1	27	–
Warnaweera	23	2	86	2
Hathurusinghe	20	6	53	1
Ranatunga	4	2	2	–
Muralitharan	47.1	12	136	4
Jayasuriya	8	2	30	–

FALL OF WICKETS

1–13, 2–29, 3–165, 4–182, 5–281, 6–286, 7–309, 8–309, 9–347
1–75, 2–142, 3–144, 4–157, 5–289, 6–352

FALL OF WICKETS

1–86, 2–109, 3–271, 4–334, 5–384, 6–388, 7–397, 8–409, 9–437

Umpires: B.C. Cooray & P. Manuel

Match drawn

Roshan Mahanama scored heavily for Sri Lanka against India in all types of cricket. (Patrick Eagar)

innings, but Sri Lanka always seemed in control after Mahanama and Gurusinha had added 85 for the second wicket. Aravinda de Silva helped Mahanama to maintain the pace in a stand of 66, but Mahanama was handicapped by an injured toe and was in considerable pain. With Sri Lanka 15 runs short of victory, he was forced to retire. He received a thunderous reception. There was a tremor of wickets, but the left-handed Kalpage hit the third ball of the last over to the third-man boundary to win the match for Sri Lanka.

SECOND ONE-DAY INTERNATIONAL – SRI LANKA v. INDIA
11 August 1993 at Khetterama Stadium, Colombo

SRI LANKA		
U.C. Hathurusinghe	run out	38
A.P. Gurusinha	c Chauhan, b Prabhakar	9
H.P. Tillekeratne	lbw, b Chauhan	23
P.A. de Silva	c Azharuddin, b Kapil Dev	16
A. Ranatunga (capt)	c Tendulkar, b Prabhakar	50
S.T. Jayasuriya	lbw, b Chauhan	17
*R.S. Kaluwitharana	run out	9
R.S. Kalpage	not out	17
G.P. Wickramasinghe	not out	1
C.P.H. Ramanayake		
M. Muralitharan		
Extras	b 1, lb 8, w 13, nb 2	24
(50 overs)	(for 7 wickets)	204

	O	M	R	W
Kapil Dev	10	1	36	1
Prabhakar	8	1	33	2
Srinath	8	1	34	–
Tendulkar	6	1	20	–
Chauhan	9	–	37	2
Kumble	9	–	35	–

INDIA		
M. Prabhakar	c Kalpage, b Jayasuriya	86
N.S. Sidhu	c Tillekeratne, b Wickramasinghe	0
V.G. Kambli	lbw, b Wickramasinghe	7
M. Azharuddin (capt)	c Gurusinha, b Wickramasinghe	62
S.R. Tendulkar	run out	15
P.K. Amre	b Muralitharan	1
Kapil Dev	lbw, b Jayasuriya	0
*V. Yadav	b Kalpage	1
A.R. Kumble	lbw, b de Silva	10
R.K. Chauhan	c and b Kalpage	4
J. Srinath	not out	0
Extras	lb 6, w 4	10
(49.2 overs)		196

	O	M	R	W
Ramanayake	7	2	23	–
Wickramasinghe	8	–	34	3
Gurusinha	2	–	10	–
Hathurusinghe	5	1	14	–
Muralitharan	10	–	38	1
Jayasuriya	10	–	45	2
Kalpage	6	–	22	2
de Silva	1.2	–	4	1

FALL OF WICKETS

1–27, 2–82, 3–103, 4–109, 5–142, 6–158, 7–202

FALL OF WICKETS

1–0, 2–16, 3–152, 4–175, 5–178, 6–179, 7–180, 8–189, 9–196

Umpires: B.C. Cooray & B.M. Pathirana   *Man of the Match:* A. Ranatunga   *Sri Lanka won by 8 runs*

THIRD ONE-DAY INTERNATIONAL – SRI LANKA v. INDIA
15 August 1993 at Tyronne Fernando Stadium, Moratuwa

INDIA		
M. Prabhakar	c Gurusinha, b Wickramasinghe	17
N.S. Sidhu	c Kalpage, b Wickramasinghe	7
V.G. Kambli	c Mahanama, b Muralitharan	19
M. Azharuddin (capt)	c Jayasuriya, b Ramanayake	85
S.R. Tendulkar	c Muralitharan, b Jayasuriya	25
A.K. Sharma	st Kaluwitharana, b Jayasuriya	20
Kapil Dev	c de Silva, b Ramanayake	4
*V. Yadav	run out	27
A.R. Kumble	not out	4
R.K. Chauhan	b Wickramasinghe	0
J. Srinath	not out	5
Extras	lb 8, w 3, nb 3	14
(50 overs)	(for 9 wickets)	227

	O	M	R	W
Ramanayake	10	1	42	2
Wickramasinghe	10	1	54	3
Hathurusinghe	3	–	12	–
Gurusinha	2	–	7	–
Muralitharan	5	1	21	1
Jayasuriya	10	1	38	2
Kalpage	10	–	45	–

SRI LANKA		
R.S. Mahanama	retired hurt	92
U.C. Hathurusinghe	c Kumble, b Prabhakar	12
A.P. Gurusinha	run out	43
P.A. de Silva	b Chauhan	30
A. Ranatunga (capt)	c Kumble, b Prabhakar	22
S.T. Jayasuriya	lbw, b Prabhakar	2
*R.S. Kaluwitharana	c Kapil Dev, b Srinath	1
R.S. Kalpage	not out	5
C.P.H. Ramanayake	not out	4
G.P. Wickramasinghe		
M. Muralitharan		
Extras	lb 15, w 5	20
(49.3 overs)	(for 6 wickets)	231

	O	M	R	W
Kapil Dev	7	1	22	–
Prabhakar	9	1	38	3
Srinath	9.3	1	46	1
Tendulkar	4	–	15	–
Chauhan	10	–	39	1
Kumble	7	–	37	–
Sharma	3	–	19	–

FALL OF WICKETS

1–22, 2–43, 3–65, 4–112, 5–165, 6–181, 7–217, 8–218, 9–219

FALL OF WICKETS

1–27, 2–112, 3–178, 4–216, 5–217, 6–222

Umpires: B.C. Cooray & P. Manuel   *Man of the Match:* R.S. Mahanama   *Sri Lanka won by 4 wickets*

An outstanding all-round success for India for whom he opened both the batting and the bowling, Manoj Prabhakar. (USPA)

13, 14 and 15 August 1993 *at Galle*

Sri Lankan Board XI 90 (B.N. Schultz 4 for 18, C.E. Eksteen 4 for 28) and 182 (C.E. Eksteen 4 for 55)
South Africans 285 (D.J. Cullinan 92, S.J. Cook 88)

South Africans won by an innings and 13 runs

With Sri Lanka engaged in their one-day series against India, their next Test opponents were already in the country. South Africa's feverish return to international cricket maintained its momentum with the Test and one-day series in Sri Lanka preluding their visit to India for the Hero Cup and their trip to Australia for another Test series and the Benson and Hedges one-day series. Then they would be back to South Africa to entertain the Australians for more Tests and one-day internationals.

They could not have hoped for a better start to their short tour of Sri Lanka. They totally outplayed an inexperienced Board XI. Left-arm spinner Clive Eksteen pressed hard for his first Test cap with match figures of 8 for 83 while another left-arm bowler, Brett Schultz, disturbed the home side with his pace and claimed seven wickets in the match. Cook and Cullinan shared a fourth-wicket stand of 170.

FIRST ONE-DAY INTERNATIONAL – SRI LANKA *v.* SOUTH AFRICA
22 August 1993 at Asgiriya Stadium, Kandy

SRI LANKA				SOUTH AFRICA		
R.S. Mahanama	run out		49	A.C. Hudson	b de Silva	6
U.C. Hathurusinghe	c Cullinan, b Symcox		51	K.C. Wessels (capt)	c Ranatunga, b de Silva	4
P.A. de Silva	c Rhodes, b Symcox		2	W.J. Cronje	c Mahanama, b Muralitharan	22
A. Ranatunga (capt)	c Snell, b Donald		29	D.J. Cullinan	b Muralitharan	0
S.T. Jayasuriya	run out		3	J.N. Rhodes	not out	8
A.P. Gurusinha	not out		22	B.M. McMillan	not out	3
*R.S. Kaluwitharana	not out		1	*D.J. Richardson		
H.P. Tillekeratne				P.L. Symcox		
R.S. Kalpage				R.P. Snell		
G.P. Wickramasinghe				P.S. de Villiers		
M. Muralitharan				A.A. Donald		
Extras	lb 7, w 15		22	Extras	lb 5, w 4	9
			—			—
(41.3 overs)	(for 5 wickets)		179	(14 overs)	(for 4 wickets)	52

	O	M	R	W		O	M	R	W
Donald	7	–	23	1	Wickramasinghe	3	1	6	–
de Villiers	5	–	23	–	de Silva	5	–	23	2
Snell	6.3	–	33	–	Kalpage	1	–	3	–
McMillan	5	–	33	–	Muralitharan	3	–	6	2
Symcox	9	1	28	2	Jayasuriya	2	–	9	–
Cronje	9	–	32	–					

FALL OF WICKETS
1–110, **2**–116, **3**–121, **4**–127, **5**–171

FALL OF WICKETS
1–9, **2**–26, **3**–39, **4**–40

Umpires: B.C. Cooray & P. Manuel

Match abandoned

18, 19 and **20 August 1993** *at Welagedera Stadium, Kurunegala*

South Africans 333 for 9 dec. (A.C. Hudson 91,
P.L. Symcox 77 not out, K.C. Wessels 62,
H.D.P.K. Dharmasena 5 for 91) and 156 for 4
(J.N. Rhodes 50)

Sri Lankan Board President's XI 291 (A.H. Wickremaratne
82, D.P. Samaraweera 72, S.T. Jayasuriya 54,
P.S. de Villiers 5 for 68, R.P. Snell 4 for 75)

Match drawn

Both sides could take comfort from the second and final
first-class match before the international series. Batsmen
on both sides showed good form, and off-break bowler
Dharmasena impressed for the Sri Lankans. It was evi-
dent from the early matches that the South Africans had a
strong advantage with their pace attack.

FIRST ONE-DAY INTERNATIONAL
SRI LANKA *v.* SOUTH AFRICA
at Kandy

Once more the weather in Kandy proved inappropriate
for cricket and brought the abandonment of the first of
the three one-day internationals. South Africa, who won
the toss, gave an international debut to off-spinner Symcox, and he performed well, proving to be the most
successful of the bowlers.

Mahanama, who reached 2,000 runs in limited-over
internationals, and Hathurusinghe brought the hundred
up in 24 overs and put on 110 for the first wicket, but rain
interrupted the Sri Lankan innings. South Africa were
given a reduced target of 107 in 25 overs, but the game
was evenly balanced when the rain returned.

FIRST TEST MATCH
SRI LANKA *v.* SOUTH AFRICA, at Moratuwa

The inaugural Test match between Sri Lanka and South
Africa saw Brian Aldridge of New Zealand officiate as the
first ICC sponsored neutral umpire and brought first Test
caps to the South African spinners Eksteen and Symcox,
and to the slow left-arm spinner Wijetunge of Sri Lanka,
who also introduced yet another wicket-keeper to Test
cricket in Pubudu Dassanayake.

Ranatunga won the toss, and Sri Lanka batted, but they
soon lost Hathurusinghe to a sharply rising delivery in
Donald's third over. Gurusinha fell in the same manner,
and Schultz bowled Mahanama round his legs after he
had reached 50 off 124 deliveries. Ranatunga became the
third victim of the Donald–Richardson combination, and
when de Silva was taken at slip Sri Lanka were struggling
on 168 for 5. Kalpage and Tillekeratne eased fears by
taking their side to the end of a fascinating first day on 241
for 5. The South African spinners had disappointed, but

*Saviour of the first Test for South Africa – Jonty Rhodes. (David
Munden/Sports-Line)*

Cronje had given the pace bowlers admirable support
with his accurate medium-pace bowling, conceding only
18 runs in 19 overs.

He captured the wicket of Kalpage early on the second
day, the left-hander having added only three to his
overnight score before giving Richardson his fourth
catch. Tillekeratne went on to reach his third 90 in Test
cricket, and Sri Lanka scored 331, but they failed to take
a wicket in 42 overs before the close as Hudson and
Wessels took the score to 81.

Eight overs into the third day, Wessels swept Muralitharan into the hands of backward square-leg, and the off-
spinner also claimed Cronje. Had Gurusinha not
dropped Hudson off Muralitharan, South Africa would
have been in some trouble, but the opener survived for
another two hours and hit a six and 10 fours in a dour
innings which lasted just under five hours. When he
became Wijetunge's first victim in Test cricket South

Africa began to crumble, the last eight wickets tumbling for 88 runs in 29 overs. Muralitharan finished with 5 for 104, his first five-wicket haul in Test cricket.

Sri Lanka led by 64, but they lost Mahanama and night-watchman Wijetunge in Symcox's first over, and they closed at 26 for 2, the game very much in the balance.

The balance moved very much in favour of South Africa when Donald and Schultz quickly claimed Hathurusinghe and Gurusinha, but then came some spectacular batting from Ranatunga in particular. He and de Silva, who hooked lavishly and reached 50 off 67 balls, added 121 in 23 overs. Ranatunga's fifty came off 43 balls, and with Tillekeratne, 103 were added in another 23 overs. Ranatunga had to summon the aid of a runner after being hit on the toe by a Brett Schultz yorker. It slowed his rate of scoring only a little, and his hundred came off 114 balls, the fastest by a Sri Lankan in Test cricket. He was finally bowled by Schultz after scoring 131 from 140 balls. He hit a six and 18 fours. His magnificent innings took him to

2,500 runs in Test cricket, the first Sri Lankan to reach this mark, and it had set up the possibility of a Sri Lankan victory. This possibility came closer to reality when Hathurusinghe and Wickramasinghe captured the wickets of Hudson and Cronje before the close which came with South Africa reeling on 25 for 2.

Wessels went early on the final morning, but Cook and Cullinan defended doggedly for two hours. Their dismissals and the quick departure of Richardson put Sri Lanka on the brink of victory. They were denied by Jonty Rhodes who reached a maiden Test century in 4½ hours when great pressure was on him. He faced 193 balls, and although he benefited from being faced with attacking fields which left him scoring opportunities, he did not give a chance. He was given fine support by Symcox in a stand which virtually saved the match, and by Eksteen who stayed 92 minutes for his four runs.

Ranatunga's only consolation was that he was named Man of the Match.

FIRST TEST MATCH – SRI LANKA v. SOUTH AFRICA
25, 26, 28, 29 and 30 August 1993 at Tyronne Fernando Stadium, Moratuwa

SRI LANKA

	FIRST INNINGS		SECOND INNINGS	
R.S. Mahanama	b Schultz	53	lbw, b Symcox	17
U.C. Hathurusinghe	c Richardson, b Donald	1	b Donald	9
A.P. Gurusinha	c Richardson, b Donald	26	(4) b Schultz	27
P.A. de Silva	c Wessels, b Schultz	27	(5) c Richardson, b Symcox	68
A. Ranatunga (capt)	c Richardson, b Donald	44	(6) b Schultz	131
H.P. Tillekeratne	lbw, b Schultz	92	(7) not out	33
R.S. Kalpage	c Richardson, b Cronje	42	(8) not out	0
*P.B. Dassanayake	b Schultz	7		
P.K. Wijetunge	b Donald	10	(3) c Hudson, b Symcox	0
G.P. Wickramasinghe	c Rhodes, b Donald	11		
M. Muralitharan	not out	2		
Extras	lb 11, w 1, nb 4	16	b 3, lb 6, nb 6	15
		331	(for 6 wickets, dec.)	300

SOUTH AFRICA

	FIRST INNINGS		SECOND INNINGS	
K.C. Wessels (capt)	c Tillekeratne, b Muralitharan	47	(2) c Wickramasinghe, b Muralitharan	16
A.C. Hudson	c Gurusinha, b Wijetunge	90	(1) c Dassanayake, b Hathurusinghe	4
W.J. Cronje	b Muralitharan	17	c sub (Jayasuriya), b Wickramasinghe	1
D.J. Cullinan	lbw, b Hathurusinghe	33	lbw b Wickramasinghe	46
S.J. Cook	b Wickramasinghe	7	c Tillekeratne, b Wijetunge	24
J.N. Rhodes	c Tillekeratne, b Muralitharan	8	not out	101
*D.J. Richardson	c and b Wickramasinghe	2	c Tillekeratne, b de Silva	4
P.L. Symcox	c Mahanama, b Muralitharan	48	c Hathurusinghe, b de Silva	21
C.E. Eksteen	b Muralitharan	1	not out	4
A.A. Donald	not out	0		
B.N. Schultz	lbw, b Kalpage	0		
Extras	lb 4, w 1, nb 9	14	b 10, lb 4, w 1, nb 15	30
		267	(for 7 wickets)	251

	O	M	R	W	O	M	R	W
Donald	28	5	69	5	22	5	73	1
Schultz	31.2	12	75	4	20	2	82	2
Eksteen	14	4	44	–	9	2	34	–
Cronje	26	14	32	1	8	2	27	–
Symcox	28	3	100	–	21	2	75	3

	O	M	R	W	O	M	R	W
Wickramasinghe	19	4	58	2	22	6	59	2
Gurusinha	3	–	3	–				
Kalpage	17.5	6	23	1	8	2	21	–
Wijetunge	29	2	58	1	23	3	60	1
Muralitharan	39	8	104	5	31	11	48	1
de Silva	1	–	3	–	17	3	35	2
Hathurusinghe	4	–	14	1	9	5	9	1
Tillekeratne					2	–	5	–

FALL OF WICKETS

1–5, 2–77, 3–100, 4–157, 5–168, 6–258, 7–273, 8–285, 9–313
1–26, 2–26, 3–34, 4–75, 5–196, 6–299

FALL OF WICKETS

1–104, 2–152, 3–179, 4–203, 5–203, 6–206, 7–240, 8–262, 9–267
1–13, 2–15, 3–47, 4–92, 5–126, 6–138, 7–199

Umpires: B.L. Aldridge & K.T. Francis

Match drawn

SECOND AND THIRD ONE-DAY INTERNATIONALS
SRI LANKA v. SOUTH AFRICA

In the first match, South Africa achieved their biggest victory in a one-day international since their return to the fold. The batting was consistent rather than inspired. Wessels, who won the toss, took 24 overs to score 28. He and Hudson, who hit 48 off 80 balls, scored 90 for the first wicket. Rhodes hit 43 off 63 deliveries, and McMillan batted well, but a total of 222 did not look too daunting. It became huge when Sri Lanka lost their first seven wickets in 70 balls for 36 runs. Tillekeratne hit two boundaries, but there was never any likelihood of Sri Lanka avoiding their heaviest defeat in 34 home internationals. McMillan added three wickets and three catches to his brisk batting to take the individual award.

Sri Lanka drew the series by winning the final match comfortably. Choosing to bat first, they were indebted to Mahanama, who hit 41 off 58 balls, and de Silva who batted for 30 overs to score 61 and to lead his side to 198. In reply, South Africa were reduced to 77 for 7, mainly by Ramanayake who bowled himself back into the Test side. Snell hit 51 off 60 balls, and he and de Villiers added a record 51 for the last wicket, but Sri Lanka never looked as though they would be denied.

Hashan Tillekeratne – bedevilled in the nineties. (David Munden/ Sports-Line)

SECOND ONE-DAY INTERNATIONAL – SRI LANKA v. SOUTH AFRICA
2 September 1993 at Khetterama Stadium, Colombo

SOUTH AFRICA

Batsman	Dismissal	Runs
K.C. Wessels (capt)	c Tillekeratne, b Jayasuriya	28
A.C. Hudson	c Mahanama, b Ranatunga	48
D.J. Cullinan	st Dassanayake, b Jayasuriya	5
J.N. Rhodes	c Mahanama, b Kalpage	43
S.J. Cook	c Dassanayake, b Wickramasinghe	15
B.M. McMillan	c Tillekeratne, b Jayasuriya	35
P.L. Symcox	c Mahanama, b Jayasuriya	12
R.P. Snell	not out	12
*D.J. Richardson	not out	1
P.S. de Villiers		
A.A. Donald		
Extras	lb 12, w 8, nb 3	23
(50 overs)	(for 7 wickets)	222

SRI LANKA

Batsman	Dismissal	Runs
R.S. Mahanama	c Richardson, b de Villiers	11
U.C. Hathurusinghe	c McMillan, b Donald	10
S.T. Jayasuriya	lbw, b McMillan	3
P.A. de Silva	c Richardson, b McMillan	8
A. Ranatunga (capt)	c de Villiers, b McMillan	6
A.P. Gurusinha	c McMillan, b Snell	1
H.P. Tillekeratne	c Richardson, b de Villiers	20
R.S. Kalpage	c Richardson, b Symcox	0
*P.B. Dassanayake	c McMillan, b Donald	11
G.P. Wickramasinghe	b de Villiers	4
M. Muralitharan	not out	0
Extras	lb 7, w 16, nb 1	24
(34 overs)		98

	O	M	R	W
Wickramasinghe	7	–	28	1
Hathurusinghe	3	–	14	–
de Silva	4	1	14	–
Kalpage	10	1	42	1
Muralitharan	6	–	28	–
Jayasuriya	10	–	53	4
Ranatunga	10	1	31	1

	O	M	R	W
Donald	7	1	18	2
de Villiers	10	4	15	3
Snell	5	–	15	1
McMillan	5	1	12	3
Symcox	5	–	20	1
Wessels	2	–	11	–

FALL OF WICKETS
1–90, 2–92, 3–102, 4–138, 5–174, 6–198, 7–214

FALL OF WICKETS
1–24, 2–24, 3–34, 4–39, 5–43, 6–52, 7–60, 8–92, 9–92

Umpires: D.N. Pathirana & T.M. Samarasinghe   *Man of the Match:* B.M. McMillan   *South Africa won by 124 runs*

THIRD ONE-DAY INTERNATIONAL – SRI LANKA *v.* SOUTH AFRICA
4 September 1993 at Khetterama Stadium, Colombo

SRI LANKA

R.S. Mahanama	st Richardson, **b** Symcox	41
U.C. Hathurusinghe	**c** Richardson, **b** Donald	2
H.P. Tillekeratne	**c** Richardson, **b** McMillan	15
P.A. de Silva	not out	61
A. Ranatunga (capt)	**c** Donald, **b** Snell	30
S.T. Jayasuriya	**b** Donald	5
H. Wickremaratne	st Richardson, **b** Symcox	1
R.S. Kalpage	**c** and **b** Snell	9
*P.B. Dassanayake	run out	14
G.P. Wickramasinghe	**b** de Villiers	0
C.P.H. Ramanayake		
Extras	b **1**, lb **5**, w **14**	20
		—
(50 overs)	(for 9 wickets)	198

SOUTH AFRICA

A.C. Hudson	**c** Dassanayake, **b** Wickramasinghe	1
K.C. Wessels (capt)	lbw, **b** Ramanayake	16
W.J. Cronje	**c** Dassanayake, **b** Ramanayake	2
D.J. Cullinan	**b** Ramanayake	3
J.N. Rhodes	**b** Kalpage	27
B.M. McMillan	**c** Mahanama, **b** Hathurusinghe	7
*D.J. Richardson	run out	5
P.L. Symcox	**c** Kalpage, **b** Hathurusinghe	3
R.P. Snell	**c** Kalpage, **b** Ramanayake	51
A.A. Donald	**b** Kalpage	0
P.S. de Villiers	not out	12
Extras	lb **3**, w **19**, nb **5**	27
		—
(46.1 overs)		154

	O	M	R	W
Donald	10	–	35	2
de Villiers	10	1	31	1
Snell	10	–	52	2
McMillan	10	–	41	1
Symcox	10	1	33	2

	O	M	R	W
Ramanayake	8.1	–	17	4
Wickramasinghe	6	2	24	1
Hathurusinghe	10	2	18	2
Ranatunga	6	–	24	–
Kalpage	10	–	36	2
Jayasuriya	6	–	32	–

FALL OF WICKETS

1–7, **2**–53, **3**–73, **4**–127, **5**–136, **6**–141, **7**–156, **8**–191, **9**–198

FALL OF WICKETS

1–2, **2**–10, **3**–18, **4**–38, **5**–56, **6**–72, **7**–77, **8**–101, **9**–103

Umpires: K.T. Francis & P. Manuel   *Man of the Match*: P.A. de Silva   *Sri Lanka won by 44 runs*

SECOND TEST MATCH – SRI LANKA v. SOUTH AFRICA
6, 7, 8 and 10 September 1993 at Sinhalese Sports Club, Colombo

SRI LANKA

	FIRST INNINGS			SECOND INNINGS	
R.S. Mahanama	c Richardson, b Schultz	7	b Schultz		0
U.C. Hathurusinghe	c McMillan, b Donald	34	c Cronje, b Donald		0
H.P. Tillekeratne	c Cronje, b McMillan	9	c Richardson, b Snell		9
P.A. de Silva	c Richardson, b Schultz	34	c and b Donald		24
A. Ranatunga (capt)	c Cullinan, b Snell	11	(6) c Richardson, b Schultz		14
S.T. Jayasuriya	b Schultz	44	(7) b Schultz		16
*P.B. Dassanayake	c Richardson, b Donald	0	(8) c Richardson, b Snell		10
H.D.P.K. Dharmasena	c Richardson, b Schultz	5	(9) c Richardson, b Schultz		2
C.P.H. Ramanayake	not out	3	(5) lbw, b McMillan		0
G.P. Wickramasinghe	b Schultz	17	c Donald, b Snell		21
M. Muralitharan	c Rhodes, b Snell	0	not out		14
Extras	lb 3, nb 1	4	lb 4, nb 5		9
		168			**119**

SOUTH AFRICA

	FIRST INNINGS	
K.C. Wessels (capt)	c Dassanayake, b Muralitharan	92
A.C. Hudson	lbw, b Wickramasinghe	58
W.J. Cronje	b de Silva	122
D.J. Cullinan	c and b Muralitharan	52
J.N. Rhodes	run out	10
B.M. McMillan	b Muralitharan	0
*D.J. Richardson	c Jayasuriya, b Muralitharan	11
P.L. Symcox	st Dassanayake, b de Silva	50
R.P. Snell	st Dassanayake, b de Silva	48
A.A. Donald	not out	4
B.N. Schultz	st Dassanayake, b Muralitharan	6
Extras	b 5, lb 20, w 1, nb 16	42
		495

	O	M	R	W	O	M	R	W
Donald	12	4	22	2	10	7	6	2
Schultz	20	8	48	5	16	4	58	4
Snell	19	3	57	2	12	4	32	3
McMillan	9	1	38	1	4	–	11	1
Symcox	2	2	0	–	1	–	8	–

	O	M	R	W
Ramanayake	20	5	63	–
Wickramasinghe	31	6	111	1
Hathurusinghe	7	4	12	–
Dharmasena	45	12	91	–
Muralitharan	54	17	101	5
Jayasuriya	9	1	47	–
de Silva	13	1	39	3
Ranatunga	2	–	6	–

FALL OF WICKETS

1–7, 2–27, 3–72, 4–85, 5–117, 6–119, 7–145, 8–147, 9–167
1–1, 2–1, 3–30, 4–31, 5–49, 6–54, 7–69, 8–76, 9–101

FALL OF WICKETS

1–137, 2–179, 3–284, 4–306, 5–307, 6–333, 7–401, 8–480, 9–487

Umpires: B.L. Aldridge & T.M. Samarasinghe

South Africa won by an innings and 208 runs

SECOND TEST MATCH
SRI LANKA v. SOUTH AFRICA, at Colombo

Sri Lanka, without the injured Gurusinha, gave a first Test cap to Kumara Dharmasena, a right-handed batsman and off-break bowler. Jayasuriya and Ramanayake returned to the exclusion of Wijetunge and Kalpage. South Africa brought in pace bowler Snell for spinner Eksteen, and McMillan returned for Cook. Ranatunga won the toss, and Sri Lanka batted, but the early omens were bad for them. Schultz, bowling his left-arm at a lively pace and deriving considerable life from the pitch, had both openers dropped by Cullinan at third slip in his first two overs.

South African wicket-keeper Dave Richardson enjoyed a good series against Sri Lanka. (David Munden/Sports-Line)

The misses mattered little as Schultz induced Mahanama to glove the ball to the wicket-keeper, and McMillan aided by Cronje accounted for Tillekeratne. In the afternoon session, five wickets fell for 75 runs, and the South Africans took a grip on the game which they were never to relinquish. Jayasuriya played an innings of panache, hitting 7 fours as he scored 44 off 79 balls, but the Sri Lankans found no substance and were dismissed for a miserable 168. Brett Schultz was outstanding, troubling all batsmen and finishing with the best figures of his career.

Having ended the first day on 48 for 0, South Africa consolidated their strong position on the second day which produced only 232 runs and two wickets. Hudson faced 177 balls for his 58, and Wessels batted for $5\frac{1}{4}$ hours and faced 220 deliveries before falling to a perfect off-break from Muralitharan.

Cronje, too, was in defensive mood, but he ended the day on 54, and the next morning, having lost Cullinan who did not add to his overnight score, he moved to his second Test hundred. It was an innings of labour, 412 minutes of relentless concentration and discipline.

Restraint was forced upon him when, in addition to Cullinan, Rhodes, McMillan and Richardson fell in the morning session. Symcox and Snell stopped the rot, and South Africa reached 495. Muralitharan took his second five-wicket haul in successive Tests, bettering his first Test figures by three runs.

By close of play on the third day, South Africa virtually had the Test won. Both Sri Lankan openers went without scoring, and Tillekeratne and Ramanayake also fell before the close which came with the home side on 49 for 4.

There was to be no reprieve for Sri Lanka, and Schultz and Snell assured South Africa of their first overseas Test win since 1965 shortly before lunch on the fourth day. It was the biggest victory in their Test history, and for Sri Lanka, whose batting was a shambles, it was a worst-ever Test defeat.

Not surprisingly, Schultz took the individual award, but there was some consolation for the diminutive Dassanayake who, in his second Test, stumped the last three South African batsmen and so equalled the Sri Lankan record for stumpings in Test cricket.

THIRD TEST MATCH
SRI LANKA *v.* SOUTH AFRICA, at Colombo

South Africa fielded an unchanged side for the final Test of the series while Sri Lanka made one change, Liyanage replacing Wickramasinghe. Wessels won the toss, and South Africa batted.

On a heavily watered pitch, they lost half their side for 128 before tea on the first afternoon and looked in dire trouble, but they were saved by Cullinan and Richardson who added 103 by the close without being separated.

The lateral movement provided by Liyanage and Ramanayake had caused particular trouble, but Richardson and Cullinan played with great good sense and were not separated until the second morning when Richardson hit Muralitharan into the hands of mid-on. Cullinan reached his first Test hundred after 358 minutes at the crease and almost immediately, seemingly exhausted, he was out. Cullinan hit 17 fours in his first innings and

THIRD TEST MATCH – SRI LANKA *v.* SOUTH AFRICA
14, 15, 16, 18 and 19 September 1993 at P. Saravanamuttu Stadium, Colombo

SOUTH AFRICA

	FIRST INNINGS		SECOND INNINGS	
A.C. Hudson	c Tillekeratne, b Dharmasena	22	(2) b Ramanayake	28
K.C. Wessels (capt)	b Liyanage	26	(1) c Mahanama, b Hathurusinghe	7
W.J. Cronje	b Ramanayake	24	not out	73
D.J. Cullinan	c Ramanayake, b Jayasuriya	102	c sub (Samaraweera), b Dharmasena	4
J.N. Rhodes	st Dassanayake, b Muralitharan	7	b Muralitharan	19
B.M. McMillan	c Jayasuriya, b Muralitharan	2	not out	0
*D.J. Richardson	c de Silva, b Muralitharan	62		
P.L. Symcox	c Tillekeratne, b Ramanayake	30		
R.P. Snell	not out	13		
A.A. Donald	lbw, b Ramanayake	1		
B.N. Schultz	c de Silva, b Muralitharan	0		
Extras	b 6, lb 10, nb 11	27	b 4, lb 17, nb 7	28
		316	(for 4 wickets)	**159**

SRI LANKA

	FIRST INNINGS	
R.S. Mahanama	c McMillan, b Schultz	25
U.C. Hathurusinghe	c Richardson, b Donald	1
*P.B. Dassanayake	run out	8
P.A. de Silva	lbw, b Symcox	82
A. Ranatunga (capt)	c Richardson, b Schultz	50
H.P. Tillekeratne	c Richardson, b Schultz	37
S.T. Jayasuriya	c Cronje, b Schultz	65
H.D.P.K. Dharmasena	c Richardson, b Schultz	5
D.K. Liyanage	b Donald	0
C.P.H. Ramanayake	not out	0
M. Muralitharan		
Extras	b 7, lb 9, nb 7	23
	(for 9 wickets, dec.)	**296**

	O	M	R	W	O	M	R	W		O	M	R	W
Ramanayake	25	4	75	3	10	1	26	1	Donald	30	12	62	2
Liyanage	21	4	58	1	4	1	17	–	Schultz	36.5	9	63	5
Hathurusinghe	6	4	6	–	8	4	7	1	McMillan	30	8	64	–
Dharmasena	28	5	79	1	18	8	29	1	Snell	25	8	44	–
Muralitharan	35.1	8	64	4	15	3	39	1	Symcox	18	5	47	1
de Silva	1	–	9	–	3	1	3	–					
Jayasuriya	5	1	9	1	3	1	17	–					

FALL OF WICKETS

1–51, 2–53, 3–96, 4–108, 5–128, 6–250, 7–281, 8–311, 9–315
1–11, 2–58, 3–65, 4–159

FALL OF WICKETS

1–1, 2–27, 3–55, 4–156, 5–202, 6–263, 7–273, 8–294, 9–296

Umpires: B.L. Aldridge & B.C. Cooray

Match drawn

ABOVE: *Mighty work throughout the season by off-spinner Muttiah Muralitharan. He took 24 Test wickets in five matches at the end of 1993. (Chris Cole/Allsport)*

RIGHT: *Sri Lankan skipper Arjuna Ranatunge reached 2,500 runs in Test cricket, scored the fastest century made by a Sri Lankan batsman in a Test match and played some blazing innings against the South Africans. (David Munden/Sports-Line)*

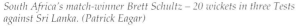

South Africa's match-winner Brett Schultz – 20 wickets in three Tests against Sri Lanka. (Patrick Eagar)

faced 222 balls. Symcox saw South Africa past 300, and Muralitharan was once again the best of the Sri Lankan bowlers.

Before the close of the second day, Hathurusinghe again fell to Donald, and Dassanayake was brilliantly run out by Jonty Rhodes. Mahanama fended a rising ball from Schultz to second slip, and Sri Lanka were 55 for 3. Ranatunga and de Silva steadied the innings and added 62 before the end of the day.

The third morning brought the most bitter of disappointments as two of the world's most entertaining batsmen, Ranatunga and de Silva, scored a meagre 36 runs in the first session. Both men appeared to disregard any attempt to play the shots on which their exciting reputations had been founded, and Ranatunga took 124 balls to reach his half century. He remained static for the next half hour during which time he faced 25 deliveries, and he then edged Schultz to the wicket-keeper.

Aravinda de Silva reached 50 on the stroke of lunch and then scored four singles in the next 80 minutes. The afternoon session produced 44 runs from 29 overs. The final session, shortened because of bad light, saw 48 runs come from 17 overs. The acceleration towards the end of the day was due to Jayasuriya who showed what could have been achieved with 35 off 44 deliveries. De Silva was finally out when he offered no shot to an off-break from Symcox. He had batted for 384 minutes, hit 8 fours and faced 263 deliveries.

There was more spirit on the fourth morning, with Jayasuriya continuing to bat fluently, but the Sri Lankan innings had occupied 628 minutes, 139.5 overs, before Ranatunga declared 20 runs short of the South African total. The home side's hopes were lifted when they captured three South African wickets quite cheaply, but Cronje remained unbeaten, and heavy overnight rain ended all speculation, no play being possible on the final day. So South Africa took the series one-nil.

The Sri Lankan national side endured one of the busiest periods in the country's cricket history. Following the departure of the South Africans, Sri Lanka competed in the one-day tournaments in Sharjah and India. Then came the much-awaited meeting with West Indies, the first time that the two sides had played Test cricket against each other. Unfortunately, the brief tour by West Indies turned out to be a bitter disappointment, ruined by bad weather and by the decision to play the historic Test match at Moratuwa rather than at the Sinhalese Sports Club or the Khetterama Stadium.

FIRST ONE-DAY INTERNATIONAL
SRI LANKA v. WEST INDIES, at Colombo

Rain delayed the start of the first match of West Indies' tour, the first of three games in the one-day series, and bad light brought it to an early close. The match was reduced to 39 overs a side, and West Indies, who decided to bat first, reached an impressive 197 for 3 thanks mainly to Lara's 89 from 119 balls.

Sri Lanka found batting difficult against the hostility of Walsh and Ambrose, and the home side were further handicapped when Jayasuriya was carried off with cramp in the ninth over. Aravinda de Silva fell in Walsh's next over, but shortly after Ranatunga had hit Hooper for six and four, the game was brought to an end.

3, 4 and 5 December 1993 *at Galle*

West Indians 279 for 6 (C.L. Hooper 89, R.I.C. Holder 71 not out, R.A. Harper 57)
Sri Lankan Board President's XI

Match drawn

Rain destroyed the West Indians' one first-class match outside the Test. No play at all was possible on the last day.

FIRST ONE-DAY INTERNATIONAL – SRI LANKA v. WEST INDIES
1 December 1993 at P. Saravanamuttu Stadium, Colombo

WEST INDIES			SRI LANKA		
B.C. Lara	c and b Jayasuriya	89	R.S. Mahanama	not out	10
P.V. Simmons	c Kalpage, b Ratnayake	11	S.T. Jayasuriya	retired hurt	4
R.B. Richardson (capt)	b Anurasiri	21	P.A. de Silva	c Simmons, b Walsh	2
K.L.T. Arthurton	not out	37	A. Ranatunga (capt)	not out	11
C.L. Hooper	not out	13	H.P. Tillekeratne		
J.C. Adams			H. Wickremaratne		
R.A. Harper			R.S. Kalpage		
*J.R. Murray			*R.S. Kaluwitharana		
K.C.G. Benjamin			R.J. Ratnayake		
C.A. Walsh			G.P. Wickramasinghe		
C.E.L. Ambrose			S.D. Anurasiri		
Extras	lb **15**, w **9**, nb **2**	26	Extras	lb **6**, w **1**, nb **1**	8
		—			—
(39 overs)	(for 3 wickets)	197	(12.1 overs)	(for 1 wicket)	35

	O	M	R	W			O	M	R	W
Wickramasinghe	7	1	22	–	Ambrose		5	2	4	–
Ratnayake	7	1	37	1	Walsh		5	1	10	1
Kalpage	8	–	37	–	Benjamin		1.1	–	5	–
Ranatunga	1	–	10	–	Hooper		1	–	10	–
Anurasiri	8	1	26	1						
Jayasuriya	7	1	40	1						
de Silva	1	–	10	–						

FALL OF WICKETS
1–33, **2**–121, **3**–154

FALL OF WICKET
1–16

Umpires: B.C. Cooray & P. Manuel

Match abandoned

TEST MATCH
SRI LANKA *v.* WEST INDIES, at Moratuwa

The inaugural Test match between Sri Lanka and West Indies, almost 12 years after Sri Lanka's elevation to the top rank, was blighted by bad weather, bad drainage and controversy. The choice of the Tyronne Fernando Stadium at Moratuwa as the venue for such a prestigious match aroused considerable criticism in all quarters. The ground is the least of Sri Lanka's Test centres. It is situated on the outskirts of Colombo, and it is said to have once been a rice paddy-field. The fact that the ground remains soggy when others have dried supports this assertion.

The stadium is named after Tyronne Fernando, President of the Cricket Board of Control of Sri Lanka, Minister of Information and Broadcasting, and the parliamentary representative for Moratuwa – a man of influence. Many suggested that this was the reason that the venue was selected for what was Sri Lanka's 50th, and West Indies' 350th, Test match. The politician himself argued that Sri Lanka had never been beaten at Moratuwa, and that the wicket there would nullify the West Indian pace attack. The lack of adequate drainage certainly nullified the cricket.

No play was possible on the scheduled first day, and the two sides agreed to forgo the rest day, but even then, the waterlogged outfield prevented any play until lunch on the second day. For the first time in nearly five years, West Indies included two spinners in their side, recalling Roger Harper to partner Carl Hooper, while Sri Lanka played only one seamer, Wickramasinghe, and gave a first Test cap to opening batsman Dulip Samaraweera.

Samaraweera struggled for two hours for 16 before being third out at 57, caught at short-leg off Hooper who, with Harper, did most of the bowling and restricted the scoring. On the second day, de Silva and Ranatunga extended their partnership to 49 before Winston Benjamin bowled the aggressive de Silva off an inside edge. Jayasuriya went first ball, and Sri Lanka were in great trouble.

Kalpage saved the hat trick, but he was involved in a controversial· decision when umpire Samarasinghe turned down an appeal for a bat-and-pad catch by Harper off Hooper. The left-handed Kalpage and the courageous Dassanayake added 51 for the seventh wicket in just under 2½ hours, but the stand was broken when Dassanayake was caught behind off the second new ball, and the later Sri Lankan batsmen surrendered meekly.

In all, 11 wickets fell on the second day, for after a few perfunctory overs with the new ball, Ranatunga brought

TEST MATCH – SRI LANKA *v.* WEST INDIES
9, 10, 11, 12 and 13 December 1993 at Tyronne Fernando Stadium, Moratuwa

SRI LANKA

	FIRST INNINGS		SECOND INNINGS	
R.S. Mahanama	c Murray, b Benjamin	11	c Simmons, b Benjamin	11
D.P. Samaraweera	c Harper, b Hooper	16	run out	5
H.P. Tillekeratne	c Lara, b Harper	0	not out	9
P.A. de Silva	b Benjamin	53	not out	15
A. Ranatunga (capt)	c Lara, b Walsh	31		
S.T. Jayasuriya	lbw, b Benjamin	0		
R.S. Kalpage	c Richardson, b Ambrose	39		
*P.B. Dassanayake	c Murray, b Benjamin	18		
G.P. Wickramasinghe	c Lara, b Ambrose	0		
S.D. Anurasiri	b Ambrose	1		
M. Muralitharan	not out	1		
Extras	b 1, lb 9, nb 10	20	lb 2, nb 1	3
		190	(for 2 wickets)	43

WEST INDIES

	FIRST INNINGS	
D.L. Haynes	lbw, b Anurasiri	20
P.V. Simmons	c Dassanayake, b Kalpage	17
R.B. Richardson (capt)	c Dassanayake, b Kalpage	51
B.C. Lara	c Dassanayake, b Muralitharan	18
K.L.T. Arthurton	c Jayasuriya, b Anurasiri	0
C.L. Hooper	c Samaraweera, b Muralitharan	62
R.A. Harper	lbw, b Jayasuriya	3
*J.R. Murray	lbw, b Anurasiri	7
W.K.M. Benjamin	b Muralitharan	2
C.E.L. Ambrose	not out	7
C.A. Walsh	c Kalpage, b Muralitharan	0
Extras	b 4, lb 1, nb 12	17
		204

	O	M	R	W	O	M	R	W
Ambrose	12.2	5	14	3	6	2	13	–
Walsh	21	6	40	1	9.1	4	20	–
Harper	24	12	36	1	1	–	3	–
Hooper	20	5	44	1				
Benjamin	20	8	46	4	6	5	5	1
Arthurton	1	1	0	–				

	O	M	R	W
Wickramasinghe	11	–	35	–
Ranatunga	4	1	6	–
Anurasiri	35	6	77	3
Kalpage	10	2	27	2
Muralitharan	15.5	4	47	4
Jayasuriya	3	–	7	1

FALL OF WICKETS

1–18, 2–30, 3–57, 4–106, 5–106, 6–130, 7–181, 8–182, 9–188
1–17, 2–18

FALL OF WICKETS

1–42, 2–42, 3–78, 4–84, 5–168, 6–178, 7–191, 8–191, 9–204

Umpires: K.T. Francis & T.M. Samarasinghe

Match drawn

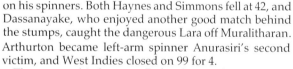

Two spinners who returned to Test cricket after long absences:
LEFT: *Don Anurasiri of Sri Lanka. (David Munden/Sports-Line) and*
RIGHT: *Roger Harper of West Indies (Stuart D. Franklin/ASP)*

on his spinners. Both Haynes and Simmons fell at 42, and Dassanayake, who enjoyed another good match behind the stumps, caught the dangerous Lara off Muralitharan. Arthurton became left-arm spinner Anurasiri's second victim, and West Indies closed on 99 for 4.

The partnership between Richardson and Hooper was eventually worth 84, and it was ended in rather bizarre circumstances. Richardson moved out to drive Kalpage and was beaten in the flight. Dassanayake fumbled the ball, but broke the wicket and appealed for the stumping. Umpire Samarasinghe refused the appeal, but umpire Francis gave Richardson out caught off an inside edge. Television replays suggested that two wrongs had made a right.

In the space of ten balls after lunch, Muralitharan took three wickets, and West Indies' lead was restricted to 14. In 83 minutes' batting, Sri Lanka scored 43 for 2, and the game was finely balanced on a pitch that was giving increasing encouragement to spinners, but then there was rain, and the last two days were lost. Even though the weather was dry, the ground remained soggy, and an important and potentially fascinating game was ruined because of poor facilities and bad judgement.

SECOND AND THIRD ONE-DAY INTERNATIONALS
SRI LANKA v. WEST INDIES, at Colombo

The second one-day international was the only match of the three-week tour which was not ruined by rain. In front of a crowd of 30,000, Sri Lanka became the first side to win batting second under the lights of the magnificent Khetterama Stadium. Haynes and Lara gave West Indies a splendid platform with an opening partnership of 128, but the later batsmen failed to capitalise on this advantage. Sri Lanka's victory owed much to de Silva and Ranatunga who added 60 brisk runs for the fourth wicket. Ranatunga hit 66 off 79 balls, but he was involved in an unfortunate incident eight overs from the end when, in completing a single, he diverted a throw from Lara with his foot and, against the spirit of the game, took two extra runs. The West Indians were also upset by what they saw as eccentric calls for above-the-shoulder no-balls and wides. Sri Lanka won when Liyanage hit the first ball of the final over over mid-off for a single.

Inevitably, the final match of the series was shortened by rain. Put in to bat, Sri Lanka made only 103 in 23 overs. With Haynes and Lara again providing a sound start, West Indies were never really in trouble, and Arthurton finished the match by pulling the first ball of the last over for a mighty six.

SECOND ONE-DAY INTERNATIONAL – SRI LANKA v. WEST INDIES
16 December 1993 at Khetterama Stadium, Colombo

WEST INDIES

D.L. Haynes	c and b Anurasiri	51
B.C. Lara	c Mahanama, b Jayasuriya	65
P.V. Simmons	c Wickramasinghe, b Kalpage	10
K.L.T. Arthurton	not out	50
R.B. Richardson (capt)	b Kalpage	15
C.L. Hooper	c Tillekeratne, b Kalpage	4
A.C. Cummins	run out	1
*J.C. Adams	lbw, b Kalpage	0
W.K.M. Benjamin	b Liyanage	11
C.E.L. Ambrose	not out	2
C.A. Walsh		
Extras	lb 9, w 9, nb 2	20
(49 overs)	(for 8 wickets)	229

SRI LANKA

R.S. Mahanama	c Lara, b Cummins	18
S.T. Jayasuriya	c Adams, b Walsh	11
H.P. Tillekeratne	b Hooper	26
P.A. de Silva	c Hooper, b Cummins	51
A. Ranatunga (capt)	not out	66
R.S. Kalpage	lbw, b Cummins	1
*R.S. Kaluwitharana	lbw, b Cummins	2
H. Wickremaratne	b Ambrose	3
D.K. Liyanage	not out	11
G.P. Wickramasinghe		
S.D. Anurasiri		
Extras	b 4, lb 9, w 18, nb 10	41
(48.1 overs)	(for 7 wickets)	230

	O	M	R	W
Wickramasinghe	8	–	40	–
Liyanage	8	–	36	1
Kalpage	10	–	45	4
Anurasiri	10	–	32	1
Ranatunga	2	–	16	–
Jayasuriya	10	–	41	1
de Silva	1	–	10	–

	O	M	R	W
Ambrose	9	–	49	1
Walsh	8.1	–	31	1
Cummins	10	–	33	4
Benjamin	10	–	50	–
Hooper	7	–	33	1
Arthurton	4	–	21	–

FALL OF WICKETS

1–128, 2–136, 3–155, 4–184, 5–194, 6–195, 7–195, 8–223

FALL OF WICKETS

1–26, 2–40, 3–120, 4–180, 5–187, 6–189, 7–208

Umpires: K.T. Francis & B.C. Cooray   *Man of the Match:* A. Ranatunga   *Sri Lanka won by 3 wickets*

THIRD ONE-DAY INTERNATIONAL – SRI LANKA v. WEST INDIES
18 December 1993 at Sinhalese Sports Club, Colombo

SRI LANKA

R.S. Mahanama	c Richardson, b Walsh	10
S.T. Jayasuriya	c Arthurton, b Walsh	1
H.P. Tillekeratne	b Walsh	6
P.A. de Silva	c Ambrose, b Simmons	34
A. Ranatunga (capt)	c Adams, b Simmons	7
R.S. Kalpage	not out	26
*R.S. Kaluwitharana	not out	6
D.P. Samaraweera		
D.K. Liyanage		
S.D. Anurasiri		
G.P. Wickramasinghe		
Extras	b 1, lb 6, w 5, nb 1	13
(23 overs)	(for 5 wickets)	103

WEST INDIES

D.L. Haynes	c Jayasuriya, b Anurasiri	23
B.C. Lara	b Jayasuriya	29
R.B. Richardson (capt)	c Samaraweera, b Jayasuriya	2
C.L. Hooper	run out	4
P.V. Simmons	not out	15
K.L.T. Arthurton	not out	24
*J.C. Adams		
C.E.L. Ambrose		
A.C. Cummins		
W.K.M. Benjamin		
C.A. Walsh		
Extras	lb 5, w 4, nb 1	10
(22.1 overs)	(for 4 wickets)	107

	O	M	R	W
Ambrose	5	2	12	–
Walsh	5	–	24	3
Benjamin	4	–	21	–
Cummins	4	–	15	–
Simmons	5	–	24	2

	O	M	R	W
Wickramasinghe	4.1	–	20	–
Liyanage	3	1	16	–
Anurasiri	5	–	17	1
Kalpage	5	–	21	–
Jayasuriya	5	–	28	2

FALL OF WICKETS

1–2, 2–14, 3–25, 4–49, 5–82

FALL OF WICKETS

1–42, 2–58, 3–65, 4–67

Umpires: P. Manuel & W.A. Wickramasinghe   *Man of the Match:* K.L.T. Arthurton   *West Indies won by 6 wickets*

TEST MATCH AVERAGES – SRI LANKA v. SOUTH AFRICA

SRI LANKA BATTING

	M	Inns	NO	Runs	HS	Av	100s	50s
A. Ranatunga	3	5	–	250	131	50.00	1	1
P.A. de Silva	3	5	–	235	82	47.00	–	2
H.P. Tillekeratne	3	5	1	180	92	45.00	–	1
S.T. Jayasuriya	2	3	–	125	65	41.66	–	1
R.S. Mahanama	3	5	–	102	53	20.40	–	1
G.P. Wickramasinghe	2	3	–	49	21	16.33	–	–
M. Muralitharan	3	3	2	16	14*	16.00	–	–
U.C. Hathurusinghe	3	5	–	45	34	9.00	–	–
P.B. Dassanayake	3	4	–	25	10	6.25	–	–
H.D.P.K. Dharmasena	2	3	–	12	5	4.00	–	–
C.P.H. Ramanayake	2	3	2	3	3*	3.00	–	–

Played in one Test: D.K. Liyanage 0; A.P. Gurusinha 26 & 27; R.S. Kalpage 42 & 0*; P.K. Wijetunge 10 & 0

SRI LANKA BOWLING

	Overs	Mds	Runs	Wkts	Av	Best	5/inn
U.C. Hathurusinghe	34	17	48	3	16.00	1-7	–
P.A. de Silva	35	5	89	5	17.80	3-39	–
M. Muralitharan	174.1	47	356	16	22.25	5-101	2
C.P.H. Ramanayake	55	10	164	4	41.00	3-75	–
R.S. Kalpage	25.5	8	44	1	44.00	1-23	–
G.P. Wickramasinghe	72	16	228	5	45.60	2-58	–
P.K. Wijetunge	52	5	118	2	59.00	1-58	–
S.T. Jayasuriya	17	3	73	1	73.00	1-9	–
D.K. Liyanage	25	5	75	1	75.00	1-58	–
H.D.P.K. Dharmasena	91	25	199	2	99.50	1-29	–

Bowled in one innings: A.P. Gurusinha 3–0–3–0; H.P. Tillekeratne 2–0–5–0; A. Ranatunga 2–0–6–0

SRI LANKA FIELDING FIGURES

6–H.P. Tillekeratne and P.B. Dassanayake (ct 2-st 4); 2 – S.T. Jayasuriya (plus one as sub), R.S. Mahanama, P.A. de Silva and G.P. Wickramasinghe; 1 – U.C. Hathurusinghe, C.P.H. Ramanayake, A.P. Gurusinha, M. Muralitharan and D.P. Samaraweera

SOUTH AFRICA BATTING

	M	Inns	NO	Runs	HS	Av	100s	50s
R.P. Snell	2	2	2	61	48	61.00	–	–
W.J. Cronje	3	5	1	237	122	59.25	1	1
D.J. Cullinan	3	5	–	237	102	47.40	1	1
A.C. Hudson	3	5	–	202	90	40.40	–	2
K.C. Wessels	3	5	–	188	92	37.60	–	1
P.L. Symcox	3	4	–	149	50	37.25	–	1
J.N. Rhodes	3	5	1	145	101*	36.25	1	–
D.J. Richardson	3	4	–	79	62	19.75	–	1
A.A. Donald	3	3	2	5	4*	5.00	–	–
B.N. Schultz	3	3	–	6	6	2.00	–	–
B.M. McMillan	2	3	1	2	2	1.00	–	–

Played in one Test: S.J. Cook 7 & 24; C.E. Eksteen 1 & 4*

SOUTH AFRICA BOWLING

	Overs	Mds	Runs	Wkts	Av	Best	5/inn
B.N. Schultz	124.1	35	326	20	16.30	5-48	2
A.A. Donald	102	33	232	12	19.35	5-69	1
R.P. Snell	56	15	133	5	26.60	3-32	–
B.M. McMillan	43	9	113	2	56.50	1-11	–
P.L. Symcox	70	12	230	4	57.50	3-75	–
W.J. Cronje	34	16	59	1	59.00	1-32	–

Bowled in one innings: C.E. Eksteen 23–6–78–0

SOUTH AFRICA FIELDING FIGURES

17 – D.J. Richardson; 3 – W.J. Cronje; 2 – J.N. Rhodes and B.M. McMillan; 1 – A.C. Hudson, K.C. Wessels and D.J. Cullinan

TEST MATCH AVERAGES – SRI LANKA v. INDIA

SRI LANKA BATTING

	M	Inns	NO	Runs	HS	Av	100s	50s
P.A. de Silva	3	5	–	266	148	53.20	1	1
H.P. Tillekeratne	3	4	–	167	86	41.75	–	2
R.S. Mahanama	3	5	–	188	151	37.60	1	–
A.P. Gurusinha	3	5	1	144	56	36.00	–	1
A. Ranatunga	3	5	1	131	88	32.75	–	1
K.P.J. Warnaweera	3	3	2	23	20	23.00	–	–
U.C. Hathurusinghe	3	5	–	112	43	22.40	–	–
G.P. Wickramasinghe	2	3	1	15	11*	7.50	–	–
M. Muralitharan	2	1	–	7	7	7.00	–	–
D.K. Liyanage	2	2	–	10	8	5.00	–	–
A.M. de Silva	2	2	–	1	1	0.50	–	–

Played in one Test: S.T. Jayasuriya 0 & 31*; R.S. Kalpage 1 & 5; R.S. Kaluwitharana 40; C.P.H. Ramanayake did not bat

SRI LANKA BOWLING

	Overs	Mds	Runs	Wkts	Av	Best
G.P. Wickramasinghe	87	18	236	6	39.33	3-83
K.P.J. Warnaweera	63.1	4	248	6	41.33	3-76
R.S. Kalpage	46	4	131	3	43.66	2-97
U.C. Hathurusinghe	49	9	136	3	45.33	1-35
A.P. Gurusinha	34	3	100	2	50.00	2-49
A. Ranatunga	6	3	7	–	–	–
D.K. Liyanage	29	5	95	–	–	–

Bowled in one innings: M. Muralitharan 47.1–12–136–4; P.A. de Silva 7–0–17–0; S.T. Jayasuriya 8–2–30–0

SRI LANKA FIELDING FIGURES

4 – H.P. Tillekeratne; 3 – A.M. de Silva; 2 – R.S. Mahanama, S.T. Jayasuriya and R.S. Kaluwitharana; 1 – A. Ranatunga, G.P. Wickramasinghe, R.S. Kalpage and M. Muralitharan

INDIA BATTING

	M	Inns	NO	Runs	HS	Av	100s	50s
S.R. Tendulkar	3	3	1	203	104*	101.50	1	1
V.G. Kambli	3	3	–	249	125	83.00	2	–
N.S. Sidhu	3	3	–	225	104	75.00	1	1
M. Prabhakar	3	3	–	154	95	51.33	–	2
M. Azharuddin	3	3	–	97	50	32.33	–	1
Kapil Dev	3	2	–	62	35	31.00	–	–
P.K. Amre	3	3	1	57	21	28.50	–	–
R.K. Chauhan	2	2	1	17	15*	17.00	–	–
A.R. Kumble	3	2	–	10	9	5.00	–	–
K.S. More	3	2	–	8	4	4.00	–	–

Played in two Tests: J. Srinath 0*
Played in one Test: Venkatapathy Raju 1

INDIA BOWLING

	Overs	Mds	Runs	Wkts	Av	Best	5/inn
M. Prabhakar	91.5	31	223	12	18.58	3-43	–
J. Srinath	33	8	78	3	26.00	2-42	–
A.R. Kumble	140.3	36	375	13	28.84	5-87	1
Kapil Dev	93.1	39	159	5	31.80	2-56	–
R.K. Chauhan	93	31	197	4	49.25	3-59	–
Venkatapathy Raju	52	10	121	2	60.50	1-55	–

Bowled in one innings: S.R. Tendulkar 3–0–4–0

INDIA FIELDING FIGURES

5 – K.S. More; 4 – M. Azharuddin; 3 – S.R. Tendulkar, P.K. Amre, A.R. Kumble and sub (W.V. Raman); 2 – R.K. Chauhan; 1 – V.G. Kambli, Kapil Dev, Venkatapathy Raju and J. Srinath

SECTION I
Zimbabwe
Logan Cup

Matches with Western Province, Worcestershire and Warwickshire

First-class averages

Wayne James hit the highest score ever made by a Zimbabwe-born batsman on home soil, 215 for Matabeleland against Mashonaland Country Districts. (USPA)

For the first time since Independence in 1980, there was no international cricket in Zimbabwe in 1993–4. The Zimbabwe national side played a Test series in Pakistan, thanks to the cancellation of that country's tour of India, and competed in the limited-over competitions in Sharjah and in India, but international cricket in Zimbabwe itself was restricted to visits by Worcestershire, Warwickshire and Western Province.

In spite of this void at Test and one-day international level, Zimbabwe saw more first-class cricket than ever before with the inter-provincial Logan Cup competition, sponsored by Lonrho, elevated to first-class status.

12, 13 and 14 October 1993 *at Harare Sports Club*

Western Province 310 for 6 dec. (G. Kirsten 75, D.B. Rundle 59 not out, F.B. Touzel 57) and 143 for 4 dec.

Mashonaland 116 (D.B. Rundle 4 for 14) and 246 (G.W. Flower 71, A.D.R. Campbell 64, A.C. Dawson 4 for 49)

Western Province won by 91 runs

Western Province became the first South African side to play first-class cricket in Zimbabwe since Independence when they took on Mashonaland who were playing their inaugural match. Mashonaland had seven players who had, or who were to gain, international experience in their side, and they were boosted by the inclusion of James of Glamorgan and the West Indian Colin Joseph. In spite of this, they gave a disappointing display. Western Province were 214 for 6, but Rundle and Matthews added 96 in 77 minutes. Rundle then became the scourge of the home side who were tumbled out on the second day. Matthews' declaration left Mashonaland more than a day in which to score 338 to win. Campbell and Grant Flower gave their side hope with a third-wicket stand of 80, but

the last eight wickets fell for 80 runs as Western Province claimed an easy win in spite of losing Matthews through injury. Remarkably, Gary Kirsten took the first first-class wickets of his career, finishing with 3 for 26.

There were more links with South Africa when a Zimbabwe Board XI was invited to compete in the UCBSA Bowl. The side played five first-class games in the competition, and details of these matches will be found in the South African section.

 ## LONRHO LOGAN CUP

Four sides were awarded first-class status – Mashonaland, Mashonaland Under-24, Mashonaland Country Districts and Matabeleland. Originally scheduled to be played at intervals throughout the season, the Logan Cup fixtures were redrafted to enable the leading players to participate once dates for the Pakistan tour were known.

Each side was to play each other once in the Logan Cup, with the two top sides in the league meeting in the final. Each team was allowed two overseas players, but there was considerable criticism that the status and ability of some of these players did not justify their inclusion in the competition at the expense of young local players. Steve James of Glamorgan and Trevor Penney of Warwickshire (born in Zimbabwe) were exceptions, but other 'overseas' cricketers were Justin Inglis, Richard Halsell and James Jordan whose experiences were limited to second-eleven matches for Warwickshire, Lancashire and Sussex and for MCC. There was also concern that, on return from Pakistan, Zimbabwe's leading players failed to show adequate commitment to the tournament.

No charge was made for admission to the matches, and they were poorly advertised. However, a start has been made, and Zimbabwe's first first-class domestic competition has been launched.

14, 15 and 16 October 1993 *at Harare South*

Mashonaland Country Districts 210 and 203 for 6 (A.C. Waller 62, G.K. Bruk-Jackson 59)
Mashonaland 140 (R.A. Strang 4 for 45)

Match drawn

Mashonaland Country Districts 14 pts., Mashonaland 9 pts.

at Queens Sports Club, Bulawayo

Matabeleland 296 (W.R. James 66, B.A. Clark 55, D.J. Rowett 4 for 65) and 200 (G.J. Whittal 73)
Mashonaland Under-24 251 (G.W. Flower 66, J.A. Rennie 5 for 47) and 137 for 5

Match drawn

Matabeleland 17.5 pts., Mashonaland Under-24 14 pts.

An inspiring captain for Mashonaland Under-24 team, winners of the Lonrho Logan Cup, Grant Flower. (David Munden/Sports-Line)

Rain ended play shortly after mid-day on both the second and third days at Harare. Mashonaland lost their last five wickets without a run being scored. Leg-spinner Paul Strang took three wickets in four balls.

In Bulawayo, James and Clark added 131 for Matabeleland's fifth wicket, and eventually Mashonaland Under-24 were set to score 246 in 35 overs. They were 7 for 3, but they recovered to save the match.

11, 12 and **13** February 1994 *at Harare Sports Club*

Mashonaland Under-24 284 (G.W. Flower 55, S.G. Davies 50) and 45 for 0

Mashonaland 75 and 253 (A. Flower 59, M.G. Burmester 52)

Mashonaland Under-24 won by 10 wickets

Mashonaland Under-24 21 pts., Mashonaland 8 pts.

at Bulawayo Athletic Club

Matabeleland 433 (W.R. James 215, B.A. Clark 56, G.J. Crocker 6 for 84)

Mashonaland Country Districts 220 for 7 dec. and 179 (A.C. Waller 51, J.A. Rennie 6 for 34)

Matabeleland won by an innings and 34 runs

Matabeleland 21.5 pts., Mashonaland Country Districts 10 pts.

Put in to bat, Mashonaland Under-24 were given a good start by Grant Flower and Gavin Rennie who scored 109 in difficult conditions. In response to their opponents' determined display, the senior Mashonaland side gave a limp performance. They fared better when they followed-on, but the Under-24 side were very deserving winners.

History was made in Bulawayo where Wayne James hit 215 off 337 balls, the highest score ever made by a Zimbabwe-born batsman on home soil. Again he had good support from Clark with whom he shared a fifth-wicket partnership of 148. James' wonderfully determined display put his side in total command in spite of Gary Crocker's six wickets, and his leadership was invaluable in the field. Country Districts declared with seven wickets down in order to prevent Matabeleland from gaining further bowling points. It mattered little, for John Rennie's splendidly aggressive bowling took Matabeleland to a resounding victory.

4, 5 and **6** March 1994 *at Harare Sports Club*

Mashonaland 358 (A. Flower 85) and 160 for 3 dec. (D.L. Houghton 80)

Matabeleland 214 (M.D. Abrams 64, D.H. Brain 5 for 56) and 253 for 9 (M.P. Jarvis 4 for 41)

Match drawn

Mashonaland 25.5 pts., Matabeleland 11.5 pts.

Malcolm Jarvis – leading wicket-taker with 33 wickets. (David Munden/Sports-Line)

at Alexandra Sports Club, Harare

Mashonaland Under-24 283 (G.W. Flower 96, C.B. Wishart 66) and 292 (G.W. Flower 96, D.N. Erasmus 76, G.J. Rennie 57, P.A. Strang 4 for 97)

Mashonaland Country Districts 249 (K.J. Arnott 51) and 296 for 8 (A.D.R. Campbell 73)

Match drawn

Mashonaland Under-24 21 pts., Mashonaland Country Districts 16 pts.

Smarting from their defeat at the hands of the Under-24 side, Mashonaland showed great determination against Matabeleland but were unable to force victory. Andy Flower and Houghton were the men who gave substance to both Mashonaland innings, and Jarvis bowled his side to the brink of victory, but John Rennie and debutant Henry Olonga played out the final 10 balls of the match to earn a draw.

Two splendid innings from Grant Flower gave the Under-24s the edge against Country Districts although the Districts side believed they had Flower caught at the wicket off the first ball of the match. Needing 337 to win in 49 overs, Country Districts made a very bold bid for victory but failed bravely.

FINAL TABLE

	P	W	L	D	Pts.
Mashonaland Under-24	3	1	–	2	56
Matabeleland	3	1	–	2	50.5
Mashonaland	3	–	1	2	42.5
Mashonaland Co Districts	3	–	1	2	40

FINAL

18, 19 and 20 March 1994 *at Harare Sports Club*

Mashonaland Under-24 286 (G.J. Rennie 76) and 245
(S.V. Carlisle 54, G.J. Whittal 6 for 34)
Matabeleland 140 (W.R. James 52 not out, D.D.
Standard 4 for 23)

Match drawn

*Mashonaland Under-24 won the Logan Cup by virtue of
first-innings lead*

The final proved a disappointing anticlimax to the competition as the Under-24 side had only to bat out their second innings without risk or enterprise to win the trophy. Put in to bat, the Under-24s reached a solid total in spite of a rare failure from Grant Flower. In response, Matabeleland narrowly managed to save the follow-on, but their inept batting display cost them the cup.

6, 7 and 8 April 1994 *at Harare Sports Club*

Worcestershire 279 for 6 dec. (T.S. Curtis 68) and 169
for 4 dec. (D.A. Leatherdale 54)
Zimbabwe 'B' 187 (W.R. James 59, R.K. Illingworth 6 for
56) and 152 (R.K. Illingworth 5 for 38)

Worcestershire won by 109 runs

With Richard Illingworth taking 11 for 94, Worcestershire won a low-scoring match which was most marked for some poor batting.

13, 14 and 15 April 1994 *at Bulawayo Athletic Club*

Matabeleland Invitation XI 224 (H.H. Streak 62) and 291
(W.R. James 96, L.P. Vorster 83)
Worcestershire 322 (G.R. Haynes 83, D.B. D'Oliveira 66)
and 27 for 0

Match drawn

Strengthened by Louis Vorster of Northern Transvaal, Matabeleland were reduced to 104 for 7 by the Worcestershire seam attack, but they were revived by Streak's maiden first-class fifty. With strength in the middle order, Worcestershire took a first-innings lead of 98, but their victory bid was thwarted by James and Vorster.

12, 13 and 14 April 1994 *at Old Hararians Sports Club*

Warwickshire 396 for 5 dec. (Asif Din 217, R.G. Twose
101 retired hurt) and 165 (S.G. Peall 4 for 39)
Mashonaland XI 296 for 9 dec. (A. Flower 113) and 138
for 4 (G.K. Bruk-Jackson 67)

Match drawn

Batting for most of the first day, Asif Din and Twose established a second-wicket record partnership in Zimbabwe cricket, but the perfection of the pitch inevitably doomed the game to a draw.

Shortly after the end of the season the Zimbabwe Cricket Union appointed Don Arnott, the former national wicket-keeper, as their chief executive.

The first-class averages include matches played by Zimbabwe Board XI in the South African Bowl competition.

FIRST-CLASS AVERAGES

BATTING

	M	Inns	NO	Runs	HS	Av	100s	50s
W.R. James	6	10	1	620	215	68.88	1	4
A. Flower	5	8	1	392	113	56.00	1	2
D.L. Houghton	2	3	–	157	80	52.33	–	1
G.W. Flower	6	12	1	534	96	48.54	–	5
G.K. Bruk-Jackson	6	12	1	496	130	45.09	1	4
S.V. Carlisle	6	11	1	385	111*	38.50	1	2
I.P. Butchart	4	7	1	209	60*	34.83	–	2
A.C. Waller	3	6	–	206	62	34.33	–	2
G.A. Paterson	5	8	–	250	73	31.25	–	1
S.G. Davies	4	7	1	187	50	31.16	–	1
A.D.R. Campbell	5	10	1	279	73	31.00	–	2
H.H. Streak	4	6	1	154	62	30.80	–	1
C.M. Robertson	2	4	–	116	43	29.00	–	–
U. Ranchod	7	11	4	201	48	28.71	–	–
G.J. Rennie	6	12	1	309	76	28.09	–	2
D.N. Erasmus	10	18	1	441	76	25.94	–	1
B.A. Clark	4	6	–	150	56	25.00	–	2
G.C. Martin	9	14	–	342	73	24.42	–	3
K.J. Arnott	4	8	–	188	51	23.50	–	1
M.H. Dekker	5	8	–	177	48	22.12	–	–
S.G. Peall	4	7	1	130	44	21.66	–	–
H.J. Hira	6	11	4	133	46	19.00	–	–
N.R. van Rensburg	7	11	1	190	40	19.00	–	–
G.J. Whittal	4	7	–	133	73	19.00	–	1
D.J.R. Campbell	9	15	–	274	41	18.26	–	–
P.A. Strang	8	12	–	219	45	18.25	–	–
G.J. Crocker	6	10	4	108	31*	18.00	–	–
C.B. Wishart	10	18	–	323	77	17.94	–	1
M.P. Jarvis	9	13	5	137	25	17.12	–	–
S.P. James	4	7	–	106	28	15.14	–	–
M.D. Adams	5	10	–	145	64	14.50	–	1
J.R. Craig	5	8	–	102	26	12.75	–	–

(Qualification – 100 runs, average 10.00)

BOWLING

	Overs	Mds	Runs	Wkts	Av	Best	10/m	5/inn
G.J. Whittal	135	35	323	16	20.18	6-34	–	1
D. Matambanadzo	92.5	15	286	13	22.00	3-43	–	–
M.P. Jarvis	357.3	119	753	33	22.81	6-74	1	2
E. Matambanadzo	78	17	241	10	24.10	3-20	–	–
J.A. Rennie	222.5	54	651	23	28.30	6-34	–	2 •
H.J. Hira	121.1	36	322	11	29.27	3-43	–	–
S.G. Peall	165	36	453	14	32.35	4-39	–	–
G.J. Crocker	127.2	33	337	10	33.70	6-84	–	1
P.A. Strang	250	55	775	21	36.90	4-45	–	–
G.C. Martin	231	67	522	10	52.20	3-44	–	–

(Qualification – 10 wickets)

LEADING FIELDERS

17 – D.J.R. Campbell (ct 12/st 5); 16 – W.R. James (ct 15/st 1) and B. Ngondo;
9 – P.A. Strang; 8 – M.H. Dekker and A. Flower (ct 7/st 1)

SECTION J
West Indies
Red Stripe Cup
Geddes Grant Shield
England Tour, one-day international and Test series
First-class averages

Keith Arthurton on his way to a century in the first Test match against England at Sabina Park, Kingston, Jamaica. (Patrick Eagar)

The leading West Indian cricketers returned to the Caribbean exhausted after competing in tournaments in Sharjah, India and Sri Lanka. Indeed, West Indies and Leeward Islands captain Richie Richardson was ordered by his doctor to rest for a month such was the concern as to Richardson's health after a non-stop round of cricket and travel. He missed the first three matches in the Red Stripe Cup, and Arthurton led Leeward Islands during that time.

Two former Test cricketers to miss the season in the Caribbean were the left-handed opening batsman of Guyana, Clayton Lambert, and the Trinidad pace bowler Tony Gray. Both men had accepted contracts to play cricket in South Africa. Lambert was sorely missed, for Guyana's highest opening stand of the Red Stripe Cup was 31 in the second innings of the first match of the season. Ian Bishop again missed the season because of his back injury, and Carl Hooper was to be troubled by a similar complaint.

RED STRIPE CUP

7, 8, 9 and **10 January 1994** *at Sabina Park, Kingston, Jamaica*

Guyana 316 (K.F. Semple 142, C.A. Walsh 4 for 65) and 216 (R.C. Haynes 4 for 67)

Jamaica 314 (J.C. Adams 112, R.C. Haynes 50, C.G. Butts 4 for 63, B.S. Browne 4 for 84) and 124 for 4 (J.C. Adams 58 not out)

Match drawn

Guyana 8 pts., Jamaica 4 pts.

at Kensington Oval, Bridgetown, Barbados

Leeward Islands 384 (S.C. Williams 157, K.L.T. Arthurton 58, V.C. Drakes 4 for 63) and 282 (R.D. Jacobs 68, S.C. Williams 60, W.E. Reid 4 for 56)

Barbados 343 (S.L. Campbell 141, D.L. Haynes 61) and 80 for 2

Match drawn

Leeward Islands 8 pts., Barbados 4 pts.

at Mindoo Phillip Park, Castries, St Lucia

Windward Islands 143 and 253 (J.R. Murray 79, D.A. Joseph 57, R. Dhanraj 4 for 37)

Trinidad and Tobago 241 (A. Balliram 76, P.V. Simmons 69) and 158 for 9 (C.E. Cuffy 4 for 24)

Trinidad and Tobago won by 1 wicket

Trinidad and Tobago 16 pts., Windward Islands 0 pts.

The start of the season was delayed in a bizarre manner. At Sabina Park, the groundstaff had rolled a glove into the pitch without noticing, and the resultant repairs put back the beginning of the match for half an hour. When play did start Courtney Walsh immediately accounted for Sudesh Dhaniram, but the 23-year-old Keith Semple hit the first century of his career and helped Guyana to a good score. In reply, Jamaica lost their first four wickets for 37 runs. Robert Haynes, Redwood and Rose all offered spirited resistance, but it was Jimmy Adams' magnificent effort which took Jamaica close to first innings points. Walsh and Haynes bowled manfully, but a draw became inevitable.

Leeward Islands held the advantage in the drawn match with Barbados. They were given a magnificent start by Stuart Williams, the right-handed opening batsman, who hit the highest score of his career and played two innings of high quality. He was matched by the powerful Sherwin Campbell whose 141 was his best score in first-class cricket. Particularly strong on the off side, Campbell, like Williams, looked to be pressing strong claims for a place in the West Indian side.

In Castries, the newly erected floodlight pylons cast a shadow across the pitch which held up play for a short period each day. The game could not recommence until shadow covered the whole pitch. In light or shadow, batsmen did not find it easy to score on a pitch of doubtful quality. Electing to bat, Windwards struggled against a varied attack. Trinidad moved into the lead thanks mainly to a fifth-wicket partnership of 102 between Balliram and Simmons who batted in the middle order. Anil Balliram, making his first-class debut a month before his 20th birthday, was impressive in technique and temperament. Junior Murray, awarded the MBE for his services to sport in Grenada, led a Windwards revival, and Trinidad were set 155 to win. At 146 for 6, they looked certain winners, but then three wickets fell for one run. Marlon Black and Surujdath Mahabir, both making their first-class debuts, kept their nerve and took Trinidad to their first victory for two seasons.

Centuries for Jimmy Adams in the first two Red Stripe Cup games, but his island, Jamaica, was unable to force victory in either match. (Patrick Eagar)

A maturing all-rounder of outstanding ability, Shivnarine Chanderpaul of Guyana. (Ben Radford/Allsport)

14, 15, 16 and 17 January 1994 *at Kensington Oval, Bridgetown, Barbados*

Jamaica 406 (J.C. Adams 133, R.G. Samuels 68,
F.R. Redwood (62 not out) and 118

Barbados 232 (D.L. Haynes 84, R.C. Haynes 4 for 82)
and 250 for 8 (V.C. Drakes 91 not out, C.A. Walsh 6
for 109)

Match drawn

Jamaica 8 pts., Barbados 4 pts.

at Queen's Park, St George's, Grenada

Guyana 286 (K.F. Semple 58, S. Chanderpaul 57,
L.A. Joseph 52, C.E. Cuffy 5 for 50) and 109 for 3
dec. (C.L. Hooper 54 not out)

Windward Islands 186 (J.R. Murray 83) and 63 for 6

Match drawn

Guyana 8 pts., Windward Islands 4 pts.

at Sturge Park, Plymouth, Montserrat

Trinidad and Tobago 99 (K.C.G. Benjamin 5 for 19,
C.E.L. Ambrose 4 for 12) and 183 (B.C. Lara 84,
W.D. Phillip 4 for 55)

Leeward Islands 392 (K.L.T. Arthurton 93, C.W. Walwyn
80, L.L. Lawrence 56, L.A. Harrigan 51)

Leeward Islands won by an innings and 110 runs

Leeward Islands 16 pts., Trinidad and Tobago 0 pts.

In spite of a second century of the season from Jimmy
Adams and a Herculean bowling effort on the last day by
Courtney Walsh, Jamaica failed to beat Barbados. Barbados needed 293 to win when they began their second
innings on the evening of the third day. Desmond
Haynes scored 25 and in the course of his innings became
the highest run-scorer in inter-territorial cricket in the
Caribbean. In his 50th match, he passed the record of
3,887 runs scored by Maurice Foster of Jamaica between
1966 and 1978. When he was out, at 61, Vasbert Drakes
was sent in as nightwatchman. Drakes, a fast bowler,
generally batted at number nine and had not made a fifty
in the Red Stripe Cup although he had scored a century
against Northern Transvaal during Barbados' tour of
South Africa. He was one not out at the close of the third
day against Jamaica and batted throughout the last day,
facing 255 balls and surviving 353 minutes for his 91. It
was estimated that he was dropped seven times, much to
the chagrin of Walsh, the Jamaican captain, who sent
down 33 of the 44 overs he bowled in the second innings
on the last day, adding five more wickets to that of
Haynes.

The drawn match in Grenada was most notable for the
achievement of Clyde Butts, the Guyana off-spinner,
who, when bowling Dawnley Joseph, passed Ranjie
Nanan's record of 256 wickets in inter-territorial cricket.
Like Butts, Nanan, who played for Trinidad between 1973
and 1990, was also an off-spinner. Butts announced that
this was to be his last season in the Red Stripe Cup.

Leeward Islands surged to the top of the Red Stripe
table with a three-day victory over Trinidad and Tobago.
Choosing to bat first, Trinidad were routed on the opening day by Ambrose and the Benjamins. Consistent batting took Leewards to a commanding lead, with Clifford
Walwyn hitting 80 in his second first-class match. When
Trinidad batted again Brian Lara alone offered serious
resistance to the left-arm spin of Warrington Phillip and
of Keith Arthurton whose 2 for 10 was his best performance in the Red Stripe Cup.

21, 22, 23 and 24 January 1994 *at Queen's Park Oval, Port-of-Spain, Trinidad*

Jamaica 206 (D. Ramnarine 5 for 48) and 217
(F.R. Redwood 57, R. Dhanraj 4 for 40)

Trinidad and Tobago 257 (B.C. Lara 180, R.C. Haynes 6
for 82, F.A. Rose 4 for 74) and 167 for 7 (K. Mason
52 not out)

Trinidad and Tobago won by 3 wickets

Trinidad and Tobago 16 pts., Jamaica 0 pts.

at Bourda, Georgetown, Guyana

Barbados 292 (S.L. Campbell 103, C.L. Hooper 5 for
77)

Junior Murray fought almost a lone hand for Windward Islands. (Ben Radford/Allsport)

Guyana 174 for 4 (P.D. Persaud 52, K.F. Semple 51 not out)

Match abandoned

Guyana 4 pts., Barbados 4 pts.

at Warner Park, Basseterre, St Kitts

Windward Islands 267 (J.R. Murray 95, K.C.G. Benjamin 4 for 96) and 162

Leeward Islands 323 (S.C. Williams 107, R.D. Jacobs 71 not out, C.E. Cuffy 4 for 49) and 110 for 3

Leeward Islands won by 7 wickets

Leeward Islands 16 pts., Windward Islands 0 pts.

The match at Port-of-Spain will always be remembered as the occasion on which Brian Lara played one of the most remarkable innings ever seen in West Indian cricket. In the words of Tony Cozier, 'For statistical domination, its effect on the outcome of the match and its impact on the morale of the team, it might well be the greatest (innings) of all.'

Lara won the toss and asked Jamaica to bat. Dinanath Ramnarine, who toured England with the West Indian Young Cricketers in 1993 and who was playing in his third Red Stripe Cup match, took five wickets in an innings for the first time, and Jamaica were bowled out for 206. Trinidad, without the injured Ken Williams and Phil Simmons, were 38 for 2 when Lara came to the wicket at seven minutes past four on the first afternoon. By the end of the day, they were 103 for 6, and Lara was on 49. He completely dominated the remainder of the Trinidad innings, and when he was last out, caught at long-off as he attempted to hit Robert Haynes for a second successive six, he had scored 180 of the 219 runs made while he

was at the wicket. Of these 219 runs, 18 were extras, so that Lara scored 89.5 per cent of the runs made from the bat while he was at the crease. He made 131 runs on the second day while his partners made 12 between them. He faced 249 balls, hit 24 fours and 2 sixes, and his innings lasted 249 minutes. Here, indeed, was one of the truly great innings, and it turned possible defeat into victory. Leg-spinner Dhanraj troubled Jamaica when they batted a second time, and Keno Mason steered Trinidad to their second win of the season with his maiden first-class fifty. In style and stature, the 21-year-old Mason was looked upon as another Gus Logie.

There was no play possible on the second and third days in Guyana where Sherwin Campbell hit his second century of the season.

Another batsman in fine form was Stuart Williams who also hit his second century of the season and played a significant part in Leewards' comfortable victory over Windwards whose batting looked increasingly suspect. Windwards suffered a further blow when all-rounder Casper Davis, who scored 25 and 43 not out, had his arm broken by a ball from Winston Benjamin.

28, 29, 30 and **31** January **1994** *at Kensington Oval, Bridgetown, Barbados*

Windward Islands 273 and 194 for 8 (D.A. Joseph 88, O.D. Gibson 4 for 40)

Barbados 321 for 7 dec. (S.L. Campbell 100 not out, P.A. Wallace 72, C.O. Browne 55, R.N. Lewis 5 for 103)

Match drawn

Barbados 8 pts., Windward Islands 4 pts

at Guaracara Park, Pointe-a-Pierre, Trinidad

Trinidad and Tobago 178 (B.S. Browne 5 for 27) and 382 (B.C. Lara 169, S. Ragoonath 74, C.G. Butts 4 for 115)

Guyana 282 (S. Chanderpaul 101) and 200 (S. Chanderpaul 64, E.C. Antoine 4 for 36)

Trinidad and Tobago won by 78 runs

Trinidad and Tobago 16 pts., Guyana 5 pts.

29, 30 and **31** January and **1** February **1994**

Leeward Islands 439 (R.B. Richardson 151, K.L.T. Arthurton 118) and 26 for 1

Jamaica 249 (N.O. Perry 60, F.R. Redwood 59, C.E.L. Ambrose 4 for 40, W.K.M. Benjamin 4 for 44) and 215 (C.E.L. Ambrose 4 for 40)

Leeward Islands won by 9 wickets

Leeward Islands 16 pts., Jamaica 0 pts.

A third century in four matches for Sherwin Campbell was the highlight in Bridgetown where Barbados again failed to press home their advantage and clinch victory.

The Bajan pace bowlers, in particular, seemed unable to recapture their form of the previous season. Skipper Joseph led Windwards by example, and they clung on grimly in their second innings to force a draw.

Another magnificient innings from Brian Lara kept alive Trinidad's hopes of winning the Red Stripe Cup. Shivnarine Chanderpaul, a prodigious left-handed talent, hit his first Red Stripe century, and Guyana took a first-innings lead of 104. When Lara came to the wicket in the second innings Trinidad were 26 for 1. He proceeded to hit 169 out of 298 before he was fourth out, run out. He had turned the course of the match, and once Trinidad had dismissed Roger Harper and Chanderpaul, victory was theirs. This third win brought Trinidad to 48 points, and it left them as Leewards' only contenders for the title.

Leewards moved to 56 points following their destruction of Jamaica. Returning to the side after his enforced rest, Richie Richardson hit 151 and batted for nearly eight hours. He and Arthurton added 178 for the third wicket to put Leewards in total command. Against Ambrose and the Benjamins, Jamaica showed little evidence of saving the follow-on and were 87 for 6 at one time. The determination of Freddie Redwood and Nehemiah Perry raised the spirits, but defeat was inevitable.

Richie Richardson was forced to miss the opening stages of the Red Stripe Cup competition through exhaustion, but he returned to hit 151 against Jamaica and to lead Leeward Islands to triumph in both domestic competitions. (Ben Radford/Allsport)

4, 5, 6 and **7 February 1994** *at Queen's Park Oval, Port-of-Spain, Trinidad*

Trinidad and Tobago 435 (B.C. Lara 206, K. Mason 63, P.V. Simmons 62, A.C. Cummins 4 for 92)

Barbados 198 (A.F.G. Griffith 50, R. Dhanraj 8 for 51) and 240 for 5 (R.I.C. Holder 116 not out, L.K. Puckerin 55)

Match drawn

Trinidad and Tobago 8 pts., Barbados 4 pts.

5, 6, 7 and **8 February 1994** *at Sabina Park, Kingston, Jamaica*

Windward Islands 122 (C.A. Walsh 5 for 21) and 159

Jamaica 417 (N.O. Perry 160, J.C. Adams 81, C.E. Cuffy 6 for 81)

Jamaica won by an innings and 136 runs

Jamaica 16 pts., Windward Islands 0 pts

Sharing stands of 108 with Simmons and 216 with Mason, Brian Lara played another mighty innings for Trinidad, hitting 206 while 129 runs came from the other end. It seemed that Trinidad would climb into first place in the Red Stripe Cup table when leg-spinner Rajindra Dhanraj returned the best figures of his career and the best figures in the competition in the season, and Barbados had to follow-on 237 runs in arrears. The loss of almost a complete day to rain and a defiant century by the Barbados skipper Roland Holder, who had not had the best of seasons, denied Trinidad who temporarily drew level at the top of the table with Leewards.

A listless Windwards side was totally outplayed by Jamaica for whom Nehemiah Perry hit a sparkling maiden first-class century. There was considerable concern as to Windwards' inept performances in the competition, and St Lucia's sports minister Desmond Braithwaite called for a full investigation. Manager Irving Shillingford cited lack of pre-tournament preparation and lack of commitment on the part of the players. One who could claim exemption from this criticism was Cameron Cuffy, the giant fast bowler, who took 24 wickets at under 15 runs each during the competition.

The final individual honours went to Brian Lara who, in scoring 715 runs, average 79.44, reclaimed the record for the most runs scored in the West Indian domestic competition.

10, 11, 12 and **13 February 1994** *at Blairmont, Berbice, Guyana*

Guyana 241 (R.A. Harper 79, Sunil Dhaniram 57, J.C.G. Benjamin 4 for 50) and 222 (S. Chanderpaul 73, K.F. Semple 67, L.C. Weekes 4 for 54, W.D. Phillip 4 for 67)

Leeward Islands 289 (W.K.M. Benjamin 71, L.A. Harrigan 61, R.A. Harper 5 for 61) and 134 (R.A. Harper 5 for 38, C.G. Butts 4 for 38)

Guyana won by 40 runs

Guyana 16 pts., Leeward Islands 5 pts.

A key factor in Leeward Islands' success in the Red Stripe Cup and Geddes Grant Shield – Kenny Benjamin. (David Munden/Sports-Line)

Leeward Islands lost for the first time in the season, but they gained the first-innings points that they needed to give them the Red Stripe Cup. Roger Harper won an important toss, but Guyana lost five wickets for 71 runs before Harper and Sunil Dhaniram added 141. At 167 for 6, Leewards were in danger of trailing on the first innings, but a typically aggressive 71 from Winston Benjamin gave them the vital points and the title. Guyana lost two wickets before clearing the arrears of 48, but Chanderpaul and Semple added 85 before the spin of Weekes and Phillip brought about a collapse. On a rapidly deteriorating pitch, Leewards floundered against the off-spin of Harper and Butts. Harper's 10 for 99 were the best match figures of the season, and Clyde Butts, appropriately, ended a great career on a high note.

RED STRIPE CUP – FINAL TABLE

	P	W	L	D	Pts.
Leeward Islands (2)	5	3	1	1	61
Trinidad & Tobago (6)	5	3	1	1	56
Guyana (1)	5	1	1	3*	41
Jamaica (4)	5	1	2	2	28
Barbados (3)	5	–	–	5*	24
Windward Islands (5)	5	–	3	2	8

*Includes one no-result   (1993 positions in brackets)

GEDDES GRANT SHIELD

5 January 1994 *at Sabina Park, Kingston, Jamaica*

Jamaica 229 for 3 (R.G. Samuels 103, D.S. Morgan 53)
Guyana 201 for 6
Jamaica (2 pts.) won by 28 runs
(Man of the Match – R.G. Samuels)

at Mindoo Phillip Park, Castries, St Lucia

Trinidad and Tobago 114
Windward Islands 115 for 6 (R. Dhanraj 4 for 41)
Windward Islands (2 pts.) won by 4 wickets
(Man of the Match – C.A. Davis)

at Kensington Oval, Bridgetown, Barbados

Leeward Islands 138 (A.C. Cummins 5 for 16)
Barbados 139 for 2
Barbados (2 pts.) won by 8 wickets
(Man of the Match – A.C. Cummins)

12 January 1994 *at Recreation Ground, St John's, Antigua*

Leeward Islands 194 (S.C. Williams 55, R. Dhanraj 4 for 41)
Trinidad and Tobago 193 for 7 (B.C. Lara 84, K.A. Williams 61 retired hurt)
Leeward Islands (2 pts.) won by 1 run
(Man of the Match – B.C. Lara)

at Kensington Oval, Bridgetown, Barbados

Jamaica 194 for 9
Barbados 178 for 1 (S.L. Campbell 80 not out)
Barbados (2 pts.) won on faster scoring rate
(Man of the Match – S.L. Campbell)

at Queen's Park, St George's, Grenada

Windward Islands 104 (L.A. Joseph 4 for 27)
Guyana 105 for 4
Guyana (2 pts.) won by 6 wickets
(Man of the Match – L.A. Joseph)

19 January 1994 *at Queen's Park Oval, Port-of-Spain, Trinidad*

Jamaica 266 for 5 (J.C. Adams 75, R.W. Staple 57, T.O. Powell 54 not out)
Trinidad and Tobago 155 (D. Williams 53)
Jamaica (2 pts.) won by 111 runs
(Man of the Match – J.C. Adams)

at Hampton Court, Essequibo, Guyana

Barbados 140
Guyana 143 for 6

Guyana (2 pts.) won by 4 wickets

(Man of the Match – C.L. Hooper)

at Grove Park, Charlestown, Nevis

Leeward Islands 220 (R.D. Jacobs 80, C.A. Davis 4 for 22, C.E. Cuffy 4 for 57)
Windward Islands 161 (D. Thomas 54)

Leeward Islands (2 pts.) won by 59 runs

(Man of the Match) – R.D. Jacobs

26 January 1994 *at Kensington Oval, Bridgetown, Barbados*

Windward Islands 161
Barbados 164 for 5 (C.O. Browne 51 not out)

Barbados (2 pts.) won by 5 wickets

(Man of the Match – C.O. Brown)

at Guaracara Park, Pointe-à-Pierre, Trinidad

Guyana 206 for 9 (S. Chanderpaul 51 not out, R. Dhanraj 5 for 26)
Trinidad and Tobago 210 for 7 (B.C. Lara 86 not out)

Trinidad and Tobago (2 pts) won by 3 wickets

(Man of the Match – R. Dhanraj)

27 January 1994 *at Sabina Park, Kingston, Jamaica*

Leeward Islands 201 (F.R. Redwood 4 for 30)
Jamaica 195 (J.C. Adams 69)

Leeward Islands (2 pts.) won by 6 runs

(Man of the Match – W.K.M. Benjamin)

2 February 1994 *at Queen's Park Oval, Port-of-Spain, Trinidad*

Trinidad and Tobago 131 (K. Mason 68, O.D. Gibson 5 for 25)
Barbados 133 for 1 (P.A. Wallace 70 not out)

Barbados (2 pts.) won by 9 wickets

(Man of the Match – O.D. Gibson)

3 February 1994 *at Sabina Park, Kingston, Jamaica*

Windward Islands 200 for 6 (R.A. Marshall 77 not out, R.C. Haynes 4 for 27)
Jamaica 201 for 3 (R.G. Samuels 99 not out, F.R. Redwood 52 not out)

Jamaica (2 pts.) won by 7 wickets

(Man of the Match – R.G. Samuels)

8 February 1994 *at Blairmont, Berbice, Guyana*

Leeward Islands 159 for 7 (S.C. Williams 50)
Guyana 129 for 5

Leeward Islands (2 pts.) won on faster scoring rate

(Man of the Match – S.C. Williams)

Leeward Islands, somewhat fortuitously, added the Geddes Grant Shield to the Red Stripe Cup and so completed the domestic double. They were well beaten in the opening encounter when Anderson Cummins established a new record for the competition, taking 5 for 16 in 8.5 overs. Barbados had comfortable wins in four of their five matches and quickly earned a place in the final.

Leewards, on the other hand, had a succession of narrow victories which owed much to the panic of their opponents. Following their defeat by Barbados, they met Trinidad in Antigua, and their 194 scarcely looked to be a winning score when Trinidad were 169 for 3 with Brian Lara and Ken Williams in full flow. Williams was struck in the left eye by a ball from Winston Benjamin, and it was later learned that he had lost most of the sight in the injured eye. Panic set in when Lara was out although only seven were needed from the last two overs, and four from the last, bowled by Winston Benjamin. Two were needed from the last ball to level the scores, but Lara, acting as runner for the injured Ramnarine, was run out as he attempted the second run.

There was a similar situation in the match against Jamaica who, chasing a target of 202, reached 187 for 4, only for their last six wickets to tumble for eight runs in an unnecessary scramble. Even in their final game, Leewards had some fortune when Guyana, needing to score 139 in 27 overs, saw Percival and Sattaur add 63 but never establish the right run rate.

Sherwin Campbell was the leading run-scorer in the tournament, and, as he was in the Red Stripe Cup, Rajindra Dhanraj, Trinidad and Tobago's leg-spinner, was the leading wicket-taker. Jamaica's left-handed opener Robert Samuels hit the only century of the tournament, and he might well have had another had not Cuffy deliberately bowled a wide to give Jamaica the match against Windwards when Samuels was on 99. Clyde Butts took only four wickets in the 44 overs he bowled, but he was by far the most economical bowler in the tournament, conceding just 2.34 runs an over.

GEDDES GRANT PRELIMINARY TABLE

	P	W	L	Pts.	NRR
Barbados	5	4	1	8	0.6162
Leeward Islands	5	4	1	8	0.1451
Jamaica	5	3	2	6	0.4170
Guyana	5	2	3	4	0.1449
Windward Islands	5	1	4	2	−0.3473
Trinidad and Tobago	5	1	4	2	−1.0328

GEDDES GRANT FINAL

The commitments of the England tour meant that the 50-over competition final could not be played until five weeks after the completion of the preliminary matches. Holder won the toss and asked Leewards to bat on a perfect pitch. The quality of the pitch can be seen from the fact that 43 fours and 8 sixes were hit in the match.

Stuart Williams and Lanville Harrigan began Leewards' innings with a stand of 172, a record for the competition. Harrigan hit 2 sixes and 7 fours in his 68 off 81 balls. Richardson kept up the momentum with 43 off 35 balls.

Barbados had been forced to omit left-arm spinner Winston Reid who sustained an eye injury during practice, and they opted for batsman Horace Waldron and his occasional off-spin as replacement. Waldron conceded 17 runs in his first two overs, and Holder was forced to turn to five overs of gentle medium from Desmond Haynes. Clifford Walwyn took four boundaries off Vasbert Drake's last over, and Barbados faced the daunting task of having to score at 5.78 runs an over to win the match.

They were not without hope. Philo Wallace hit 3 massive sixes in Kenneth Benjamin's first two overs, all on the leg side, and Sherwin Campbell, who had enjoyed an outstanding season at all levels, made 61 off 62 balls with

10 fours. Thereafter, Barbados began to crumble against the unlikely left-arm bowling of Keith Arthurton who took four of the last six wickets to give Leewards their first Shield victory since 1982.

ENGLAND TOUR

The England selectors had bravely broken with the old guard and chosen a party in which only four of the 17 – Smith, Russell, Malcolm and Stewart – had reached 30 years of age. Atherton had led England in two Tests against Australia and had shown that he was an imaginative captain who embraced responsibility eagerly. He had also revealed that he was tough and resolute, a man who refused to be riled or intimidated. There were technical imperfections in his batting, and his Test record was moderate, but Atherton suggested a youthful revitalisation of English cricket.

Inevitably, there were controversial selections in the England side. It was difficult to understand why Salisbury was chosen ahead of Such, and why Igglesden won a place ahead of Bicknell or Ilott although, as it transpired, Bicknell's fitness was once again in doubt. The continued presence of Lewis in an England party owed more to lack of an alternative all-rounder than to merit.

GEDDES GRANT SHIELD FINAL – BARBADOS v. LEEWARD ISLANDS
12 March 1994 at Kensington Oval, Bridgetown, Barbados

LEEWARD ISLANDS			BARBADOS		
S.C. Williams	c Campbell, b Cummins	85	D.L. Haynes	b Lawrence	35
L.A. Harrigan	c Browne, b Cummins	68	P.A. Wallace	c and b W.K.M. Benjamin	38
R.B. Richardson (capt)	c Maynard, b Drakes	43	S.L. Campbell	c Jacobs, b Arthurton	61
K.L.T. Arthurton	c Cummins, b Gibson	18	R.I.C. Holder (capt)	c Jacobs, b K.C.G. Benjamin	16
*R.D. Jacobs	c Browne, b Gibson	17	L.K. Puckerin	b Ambrose	43
C.W. Walwyn	not out	21	H.R. Waldron	c Jacobs, b Arthurton	3
W.K.M. Benjamin	c Puckerin, b Drakes	9	*C.O. Browne	run out	2
L.L. Lawrence	not out	0	V.C. Drakes	b Arthurton	22
C.E.L. Ambrose			A.C. Cummins	b Arthurton	18
L.C. Weekes			O.D. Gibson	not out	3
K.C.G. Benjamin			D.R. Maynard	c Jacobs, b Ambrose	0
Extras	b 1, lb 10, w 13, nb 4	28	Extras	lb 8, w 4, nb 2	14
		—			—
(50 overs)	(for 6 wickets)	289	(46.1 overs)		255

	O	M	R	W		O	M	R	W
Cummins	8	–	51	2	Ambrose	8.1	–	36	2
Gibson	10	–	49	2	K.C.G. Benjamin	9	–	61	1
Maynard	10	–	38	–	W.K.M. Benjamin	8	1	43	1
Drakes	10	–	65	2	Weekes	9	2	42	–
Waldron	7	–	45	–	Lawrence	4	–	30	1
Haynes	5	–	30	–	Arthurton	8	1	35	4

FALL OF WICKETS

1–172, 2–181, 3–224, 4–248, 5–259, 6–277

FALL OF WICKETS

1–61, 2–109, 3–137, 4–169, 5–179, 6–181, 7–222, 8–245, 9–254

Umpires: C.E. Cumberbatch & D. Holder   *Man of the Match:* S.C. Williams   *Leeward Islands won by 34 runs*

23, 24, 25 and **26 January 1994** *at Recreation Ground, Antigua*

England XI 419 (M.A. Atherton 108, A.J. Stewart 100 retired hurt, A.R. Caddick 77, H.A.G. Anthony 4 for 130) and 265 for 3 dec. (G.A. Hick 111, G.P. Thorpe 80)

Antigua XI 360 (M.V. Simon 129, A.R. Caddick 5 for 106) and 121 (I.D.K. Salisbury 4 for 10, S.L. Watkin 4 for 32)

England XI won by 203 runs

29, 30 and **31 January 1994** *at Warner Park, Basseterre, St Kitts*

England XI 308 for 6 dec. (M.R. Ramprakash 136, R.A. Smith 71, A.J. Stewart 67) and 184 for 7 dec. (C.C. Lewis 65)

St Kitts and Nevis 258 (H.W. Williams 53) and 22 for 4

Match drawn

England began their tour with two matches which, although of four- and three-day duration, were not accorded first-class status. The principal West Indian cricketers were still engrossed in the Red Stripe Cup. Centuries from Atherton and Stewart, captain and vice-captain, and an opening stand of 183 gave the tour a hearty beginning in Antigua. England did lose four wickets in seven balls, three in one over to Anthony, but they went on to win handsomely, and with Hick getting a second-innings hundred, there was encouragement for nearly all.

The second match produced encouragement of a different kind, with Ramprakash staking a claim for recognition with a century, and Atherton quickly controlling Tufnell when the Middlesex firebrand showed dissent after two appeals for leg before had been rejected.

3, 4, 5 and **6 February 1994** *at Recreation Ground, Antigua*

Leeward Islands 181 (C.W. Walwyn 65) and 173 (I.D.K. Salisbury 4 for 59)

England XI 312 (M.A. Atherton 77, R.C. Russell 56) and 44 for 3

England XI won by 7 wickets

The tour began in earnest with a resounding victory over the Red Stripe Cup champions Leeward Islands, but before England became too enthusiastic about this win, they needed to reflect that Leewards had omitted their five Test players, Ambrose, Arthurton, Richardson and the Benjamins. Batting first, Leewards succumbed on the first day to an attack which offered pace, accuracy and variety. Having negotiated a difficult period at the end of the first day, Atherton and Ramprakash put together an opening stand of 105. Atherton again led by example, showing infinite patience on a pitch which increasingly displayed uneven bounce. Thereafter, Hick, Thorpe and Hussain perished through self-inflicted wounds, and it

was left to Russell and Caddick to establish a worthwhile lead with a ninth-wicket stand of 68. Batting again, Leewards struggled to take the game into the fourth day as Ian Salisbury found help from the pitch and from the approach of the batsmen. England's win on the last morning was accomplished with some discomfort and with the news that Caddick had suffered an injured knee.

10, 11, 12 and **13 February 1994** *at Kensington Oval, Bridgetown, Barbados*

Barbados 348 (R.I.C. Holder 85, S.L. Campbell 83, P.A. Wallace 57, D.E. Malcolm 7 for 134) and 192 for 5 dec. (S.L. Campbell 54)

England XI 302 (M.A. Atherton 108, R.A. Smith 59, O.D. Gibson 5 for 87) and 48 for 0

Match drawn

The game against Barbados was England's last chance to decide upon their best selections before the first Test match and the five one-day internationals. Barbados won the toss and scored 289 for 6 on the opening day. Five of the wickets went to Devon Malcolm whose bowling was erratic and expensive but productive. There were three notable innings of contrasting styles. Philo Wallace batted with briskness and panache; Campbell gave further evidence of his quality and belligerence; and Holder played handsomely before falling in the penultimate over of the day. There was rain at the start of the second morning's play, and Barbados then lost three wickets in four overs. This early success for England was followed by a glut of missed chances, and the last Barbados wicket realised 49 runs. In compensation, Atherton and Stewart began briskly and scored 87 in two hours before Stewart had his middle stump knocked back. Atherton continued in total command, and the day ended with England 144 for 2, and Atherton 71.

Atherton duly completed his second century of the tour on the third morning, but, Robin Smith apart, the rest of the batting offered little comfort as Gibson ripped through the late order. The loss of two wickets early in their second innings gave Barbados some cause for concern, but Holder and Campbell added 77 in 102 minutes, and the game moved inevitably to a draw. England's worry now was over Fraser who had a cracked bone in his left hand.

Chris Lewis bowls Phil Simmons for 0 as England win the first one-day international. (Ben Radford/Allsport)

FIRST ONE-DAY INTERNATIONAL
WEST INDIES *v.* ENGLAND, at Bridgetown

FIRST TEST MATCH
WEST INDIES *v.* ENGLAND, at Kingston

Following their shabby fielding display against Barbados, England showed a marked improvement in the first one-day international. Atherton decided to bat first when he won the toss, and if there was a lack of boundaries, the England captain never allowed the score to stagnate. He held the innings together, hitting 6 fours in his 86 which came off 147 deliveries. Later impetus came from Hick and Maynard. Hick helped Atherton in a stand of 93 in 20 overs while Maynard made 22 off 16 balls through some sensible running.

A target of 203 seemed well within West Indies' reach, and Lara suggested menace with two resounding fours. Then he scooped to mid-wicket, and when Haynes was caught at mid-wicket by Malcolm who had to run back to take the catch, England's spirits lifted. Haynes' shot was a careless one, and it gave Igglesden his first wicket in a one-day international with the second ball he bowled in this form of cricket.

Aided by some extraordinarily bad strokes, Chris Lewis took three wickets in 11 balls, and the West Indian innings was in shreds. Lewis showed fire and accuracy, and he moved the ball appreciably, but one could not believe that the West Indian batsmen would be as irresponsible in the Test series as they were in this first one-day international.

England preferred Thorpe and Maynard to Ramprakash or Hussain, lost Fraser through injury and went into the Test without a spinner. The West Indian team followed a similar pattern, with four pace men chosen ahead of Harper and, with Hooper absent with an aching back, the spin was left to Adams, a most versatile cricketer. Kenny Benjamin won preference over Anderson Cummins.

At first, all seemed well for England. Atherton won the toss, and, in 192 minutes, he and Stewart scored 121. Slow to get under way, they reached 50 by the 20th over, and the only sign of a mishap was when Atherton edged Ambrose to slip where Simmons and Lara could not hold the chance when it rebounded from one to the other.

By mid-afternoon, both batsmen seemed assured, and Stewart had hit 10 fours. He had been dropped by Winston Benjamin at long-leg, but he was out rather surprisingly when he essayed an unwise pull and was caught behind. Quite suddenly, all the good work of the openers was undone. Atherton chased a widish delivery to give Murray his second catch, and Smith was bowled by Walsh through a wide gap between bat and pad. Hick and Thorpe batted for 20 overs without ever suggesting permanence, and Hick was out when he was bowled off an inside edge. Without addition to the score, Thorpe was out playing across the line, and Russell was leg before

FIRST ONE-DAY INTERNATIONAL – WEST INDIES *v.* ENGLAND
16 February 1994 at Kensington Oval, Bridgetown, Barbados

ENGLAND

M.A. Atherton (capt)	c Richardson, b Cummins	86
*A.J. Stewart	c Lara, b Benjamin	11
G.P. Thorpe	c Adams, b Benjamin	4
R.A. Smith	c and b Harper	12
G.A. Hick	c Simmons, b Cummins	47
M.P. Maynard	not out	22
C.C. Lewis	not out	6
S.L. Watkin		
A.P. Igglesden		
P.C.R. Tufnell		
D.E. Malcolm		
Extras	b 4, lb 7, nb 3	14
(50 overs)	(for 5 wickets)	202

WEST INDIES

D.L. Haynes	c Malcolm, b Igglesden	17
B.C. Lara	c Igglesden, b Malcolm	9
R.B. Richardson (capt)	c Maynard, b Lewis	12
K.L.T. Arthurton	b Lewis	6
P.V. Simmons	b Lewis	0
*J.C. Adams	c Thorpe, b Igglesden	29
R.A. Harper	lbw, b Watkin	11
A.C. Cummins	c Thorpe, b Malcolm	24
W.K.M. Benjamin	c Thorpe, b Tufnell	0
C.E.L. Ambrose	c Smith, b Malcolm	10
C.A. Walsh	not out	1
Extras	b 1, lb 10, w 11	22
(40.4 overs)		141

	O	M	R	W
Ambrose	10	2	35	–
Walsh	10	–	42	–
Benjamin	10	2	38	2
Cummins	10	1	28	2
Harper	10	–	48	1

	O	M	R	W
Malcolm	8.4	1	41	3
Watkin	8	1	27	1
Lewis	8	2	18	3
Igglesden	8	2	12	2
Tufnell	8	–	32	1

FALL OF WICKETS

1–35, 2–45, 3–73, 4–166, 5–176

FALL OF WICKETS

1–17, 2–43, 3–48, 4–48, 5–55, 6–82, 7–121, 8–122, 9–136

Umpires: L.H. Barker & C. Duncan   *Man of the Match:* M.A. Atherton   *England won by 61 runs*

A brave beginning to the series for England skipper Mike Atherton as he hooks Kenny Benjamin for four. (Patrick Eagar)

Hick is bowled by Adams for 23. (David Munden/Sports-Line)

fourth ball to a shooter. Lewis was caught at square-leg by Adams, and England closed on an unhappy 209 for 7, with Maynard on 24 and Caddick on 3.

There was no addition to the overnight score when Caddick was caught by Adams off Kenny Benjamin. Adams was to take four more catches in the match to equal Sobers' record of six in a Test for West Indies against England. It was also the first time that Kenny Benjamin had taken five wickets in a Test innings, and he added a sixth when he trapped Maynard leg before.

Dismissed for a very disappointing 234, England quickly lifted their spirits. In the third over of the West Indian innings, Haynes pushed at a ball from Malcolm on his off stump and was caught at first slip. In the next over, Simmons drove late at an outswinger and was caught behind. Only another five overs had elapsed when Richardson hooked Malcolm into the hands of deep square-leg. West Indies were 23 for 3, and England were elated.

The elation proved premature. Uneasy against the pace of Malcolm initially because of eye trouble, which was rectified with the application of drops, Lara began to force the pace. Arthurton was assured from the start and, as his confidence grew, he began to feed greedily on some untidy bowling. The pair added 144 before Lara swept ill-advisedly at Hick's first delivery and was bowled behind his legs. Adams, who received a reception fitting to a local hero, quickly settled, and by the end of the day, West Indies were four runs ahead, and Arthurton, 113, had reached his second Test century.

Arthurton's fine innings came to an end on the third morning when he fell to the second new ball. His 126, an innings of great character and considerable charm, had occupied 323 minutes, and he faced 232 balls. He hit 11 fours and 2 sixes, both off Hick. His dismissal left West Indies on 256 for 5, and England had a chance to claw

their way back into the game. Jimmy Adams thought otherwise. Murray played a brisk innings, and 63 were added in 73 minutes. Winston Benjamin was equally aggressive, and with Adams showing patience, determination and style, the West Indian lead grew and grew. The rapid departure of Ambrose fourth ball and Kenny Benjamin first ball threatened to leave Adams marooned, short of his maiden Test hundred. So it proved, for when Walsh missed a straight delivery Adams was on 95. Correct in technique, dignified in approach, Adams had faced 226 balls and batted for 342 minutes. He hit 10 fours, and, most importantly, he had put West Indies in a winning position.

Courtney Walsh emphasised that position with a torrid opening spell at the start of the England second innings. Atherton and Stewart survived 10 very hostile overs, and the England captain, in particular, suffered some painful knocks with apparent calm. Stewart drove Walsh towards the sight-screen where Kenny Benjamin overtook the ball, picked up and threw on the turn to hit the stumps while Stewart was short of a rather ambitious third run.

A rare sight for England – Lara is out, bowled Hick for 83. (David Munden/Sports-Line)

Thorpe was having his hand examined because of an injury sustained while fielding, and Smith came in to last for four unhappy overs before being caught at short-leg off his glove. He had ducked to a short delivery and taken his eye off the ball. Atherton, too, was caught at short-leg after a brave and bruising 113 minutes, and Maynard succumbed almost immediately to a rearing delivery. Hick battled on commendably, and Russell partnered him sensibly for the last seven overs of the day which ended with England 80 for 4.

The contemplations of the rest-day allowed Hick and Russell to continue sensibly when play resumed. They extended their stand to 63 in 75 minutes before Russell chipped into the hands of square-leg. England also lost Thorpe before lunch. The Surrey left-hander was yorked by Winston Benjamin.

Hick had batted admirably, showing both courage and a greater technical awareness against the pace attack. He continued in a positive manner after the interval, but the second new ball inevitably proved decisive. Lewis was leg-before to Ambrose, and Hick was very well caught at second slip four runs short of what would have been a much-deserved century. He had batted for 310 minutes, faced 187 balls, hit 12 fours and played an innings of great quality.

Igglesden gave Adams the catch to equal the record, and there followed a theatrical last-wicket stand of 39 in which both Caddick and Malcolm reached their highest Test scores. Unfortunately, this stand brought forth a spell of bowling from Walsh which sullied the match. Presumably enraged by the obstinacy of Malcolm's batting, Walsh subjected the Derbyshire 'rabbit' to a stream of short-pitched deliveries which battered Malcolm about the ribs and left him needing on-field treatment on three occasions. Haynes was leading West Indies as Richardson was off the field with a headache, but neither he nor umpire Robinson of Zimbabwe spoke to Walsh regarding his intimidatory tactics, not even when Walsh chose to sharpen his attack on the body by bowling round the wicket. Walsh finally bowled Malcolm as the batsman backed away to square-leg, but one would prefer to remember Walsh's first spell in England's second innings when he set up his side's victory rather than this disgraceful finale.

Needing 95 to win, West Indies lost Simmons and Lara before the close, but ended the day on 87, and the game was over after half an hour on the last morning.

Jimmy Adams was named Man of the Match, and England's problems multiplied when it was announced that Malcolm was to fly home for treatment on his injured knee.

Disaster for England as Stewart is run out by Kenny Benjamin's direct hit on the stumps. (David Munden/Sports-Line)

Atherton is caught by Adams off Walsh. Adams held six catches in the match to equal the West Indian Test record. (David Munden/Sports-Line)

Thorpe's stumps are shattered by Winston Benjamin and England move closer to defeat. (Adrian Murrell/Allsport)

FIRST TEST MATCH – WEST INDIES v. ENGLAND
19, 20, 21, 23 and 24 February 1994 at Sabina Park, Kingston, Jamaica

ENGLAND

Batsman	FIRST INNINGS		SECOND INNINGS	
M.A. Atherton (capt)	c Murray, b K. Benjamin	55	c Adams, b Walsh	28
A.J. Stewart	c Murray, b K. Benjamin	70	run out	19
G.P. Thorpe	b K. Benjamin	16	(7) b W. Benjamin	14
R.A. Smith	b Walsh	0	(3) c Adams, b Walsh	2
G.A. Hick	b Adams	23	(4) c sub (Harper), b K. Benjamin	96
M.P. Maynard	lbw, b K. Benjamin	35	(5) c Murray, b W. Benjamin	0
*R.C. Russell	lbw, b K. Benjamin	0	(6) c Adams, b W. Benjamin	32
C.C. Lewis	c Adams, b Ambrose	8	lbw, b Ambrose	21
A.R. Caddick	c Adams, b K. Benjamin	3	not out	29
A.P. Igglesden	not out	3	c Adams, b K. Benjamin	0
D.E. Malcolm	run out	6	b Walsh	18
Extras	b 2, lb 5, w 4, nb 4	15	b 1, lb 3, w 2, nb 2	8
		234		**267**

WEST INDIES

Batsman	FIRST INNINGS		SECOND INNINGS	
D.L. Haynes	c Thorpe, b Malcolm	4	not out	43
P.V. Simmons	c Russell, b Caddick	8	lbw, b Igglesden	12
R.B. Richardson (capt)	c Maynard, b Malcolm	5	(4) not out	4
B.C. Lara	b Hick	83	(3) b Caddick	28
K.L.T. Arthurton	c Lewis, b Malcolm	126		
J.C. Adams	not out	95		
*J.R. Murray	lbw, b Igglesden	34		
W.K.M. Benjamin	b Caddick	38		
C.E.L. Ambrose	b Caddick	0		
K.C.G. Benjamin	b Lewis	0		
C.A. Walsh	lbw, b Lewis	0		
Extras	lb 10, w 1, nb 3	14	b 5, lb 3	8
		407	(for 2 wickets)	**95**

	O	M	R	W	O	M	R	W
Ambrose	22	8	46	1	24	4	67	1
Walsh	23	6	41	1	24.5	6	67	3
K.C.G. Benjamin	24	7	66	6	18	2	60	2
W.K.M. Benjamin	19.1	7	43	–	20	3	56	3
Adams	10	1	31	1	2	–	9	–
Simmons					3	1	4	–

	O	M	R	W	O	M	R	W
Malcolm	23	3	113	3	5	1	19	–
Caddick	29	5	94	3	6	1	19	1
Lewis	26	4	82	2	3	–	6	–
Igglesden	24	5	53	1	7	–	36	1
Hick	21	4	55	1	3	1	2	–
Stewart					2.2	–	5	–

FALL OF WICKETS

1–121, 2–133, 3–134, 4–172, 5–172, 6–172, 7–194, 8–209, 9–227
1–34, 2–39, 3–58, 4–63, 5–126, 6–155, 7–213, 8–226, 9–228

FALL OF WICKETS

1–12, 2–12, 3–23, 4–167, 5–256, 6–319, 7–389, 8–389, 9–390
1–38, 2–87

Umpires: S.U. Bucknor & I.D. Robinson

West Indies won by 8 wickets

 ONE-DAY INTERNATIONAL SERIES
Matches Two to Five

England began very well in the second one-day international. Atherton and Stewart hit 112 in 25 overs and threatened to reduce the West Indian pace men to impotence. Stewart hit Walsh for 3 fours off successive deliveries, and Walsh limped off the field with an injured ankle after bowling five overs. Stewart's 66 came off 88 balls, and his innings included a six and 9 fours and was ended when he was needlessly run out when Atherton responded too eagerly to his partner's sweep to short-leg. The England skipper was out four overs later, but Hick and Smith scored 81 off 85 balls. There followed the usual cascade of catches in the deep and wild swipes from the later batsmen as 62 runs came from the last 10 overs.

Lara was soon out, but Simmons and Haynes quickly asserted superiority, and West Indies were 111 for 1 after 25 overs. England then regained the initiative. Haynes smashed Hick straight, but the bowler stuck out his right hand and held a stinging catch. Simmons chopped Fraser

into his stumps, and Arthurton danced down the wicket and missed.

Rain interrupted play when West Indies were 158 for 4 off 36 overs. With three overs lost, their readjusted target allowed them 11 more overs in which to score 80 runs. Richardson responded vigorously to this new challenge, but the great hero was Jimmy Adams who hit 52 off 46 balls and took his side to victory with seven balls to spare.

The third one-day international provided an ominous sign of the shape of things to come. Atherton won the toss and asked West Indies to bat first. The general belief was that moisture in the pitch would give early assistance to the bowlers. This could have been true had the England bowlers been able to maintain any consistency of line or length. As it was, Haynes and Simmons attacked Igglesden and Watkin from the start, and when Lewis came into the attack Simmons hoisted him over square-leg for six. From the first 10 overs, 32 were scored. After 20 overs, the score was 86; and by the end of the 30th, it was 140. Haynes swept Tufnell for six, and then hit him out of the ground. The dismissal of the two openers brought no respite to the England bowlers. Lara batted effortlessly, but he scored an astonishing 60 off 41 balls and hit only 5 fours. From the last 10 overs, 95 runs were plundered, 55 of them came from the last four overs. Richardson hit

Watkin for six over mid-wicket, and there were 23 runs in an over from Igglesden. The last four balls of that over saw Richardson hit 4, 4, 4 and 6. When the innings was closed Richardson had made 52 off 26 balls, and England had conceded more runs in a one-day international than they had ever done before.

What followed was anti-climax. Lewis was promoted to open in a gesture aimed at displaying that England would make a positive attempt to reach their target. Lewis could make nothing of Kenny Benjamin and Cummins, and he was leg before after 10 balls. There followed a series of dismissals which, not unnaturally, had a hint of despair about them. The batsmen were held in a vice-like grip by some tight bowling, and even the occasional leg-spin of Lara earned two wickets as England suffered their heaviest defeat in a one-day international.

West Indies took a winning lead in the one-day series when they won comfortably in Trinidad. Again Atherton won the toss and, with rain forecast, he asked West Indies to bat first. Igglesden retired from the attack after three overs, leaving the field through heat exhaustion. With the exception of Fraser, the England bowling was once more lacking in discipline, and the plunder started anew. Haynes and Simmons made 45 in eight overs, but there was a ray of hope for England when Fraser sent back Lara and Arthurton in the 13th over. Richardson could not repeat his fireworks of the previous match, but Adams provided Haynes with the assistance he needed, and 124

Anderson Cummins appeals for leg before against Chris Lewis in the third one-day international. (Ben Radford/Allsport)

Desmond Haynes on the way to his 17th century in limited-over international cricket in the fourth match of the series. (Ben Radford/Allsport)

runs came in 21 overs. Haynes hit 14 fours in his 196-ball innings and was particularly severe on Salisbury as he moved to his 17th century in limited-over internationals. The West Indian innings was interrupted by a shower, and it was ended by a second, heavier, shower. This meant that England's target was reduced to 209 in 36 overs.

Stewart was out in the fifth over, but Atherton and Smith kept hopes alive with a partnership of 63 in 14 overs. Atherton jabbed at Kenny Benjamin and was bowled through the gap between bat and pad. Five overs later, Smith was bowled as he essayed a cut at Harper. Six overs later, the off-spinner claimed his fourth wicket, and the England innings was in tatters.

The Queen's Park Oval was again the venue when the final match of the series was played the following day. The England bowling looked better than it had done in the earlier matches, but Simmons launched an attack on Caddick which produced 14 off three successive balls. Simmons made 84 off 104 deliveries, and there were useful contributions from all batsmen. Roger Harper, in particular, hit hard and often, and his 37 came from 33 balls.

Heavy rain in the third over of England's innings brought England's target down to 201 in 40 overs which looked more within their capabilities. Stewart began with a flourish and hit 9 fours in his 38-ball innings. His innings gave Atherton and Hick ample time to steer

Angus Fraser traps Brian Lara leg before in the fourth one-day international. (Ben Radford/Allsport)

England towards their target in a third-wicket stand worth 68. The quick demise of Maynard and Ramprakash caused a little flutter of concern, but it was not serious. For England, the victory was welcome if of little significance.

SECOND ONE-DAY INTERNATIONAL – WEST INDIES v. ENGLAND
26 February 1994 at Sabina Park, Kingston, Jamaica

ENGLAND			WEST INDIES		
M.A. Atherton (capt)	c Arthurton, b Harper	46	D.L. Haynes	c and b Hick	53
*A.J. Stewart	run out	66	B.C. Lara	lbw, b Watkin	8
R.A. Smith	c Harper, b K.C.G. Benjamin	56	P.V. Simmons	b Fraser	39
G.A. Hick	c Cummins, b Arthurton	31	K.L.T. Arthurton	st Stewart, b Hick	12
M.P. Maynard	b Cummins	22	R.B. Richardson (capt)	c Fraser, b Watkin	32
N. Hussain	c Richardson, b Cummins	10	*J.C. Adams	not out	52
C.C. Lewis	b K.C.G. Benjamin	0	R.A. Harper	lbw, b Watkin	0
S.L. Watkin	b K.C.G. Benjamin	0	A.C. Cummins	c Smith, b Watkin	16
A.P. Igglesden	not out	2	W.K.M. Benjamin	not out	9
P.C.R. Tufnell	not out	2	K.C.G. Benjamin		
A.R.C. Fraser			C.A. Walsh		
Extras	lb 9, w 7, nb 2	18	Extras	b 3, lb 7, w 6, nb 3	19
(50 overs)	(for 8 wickets)	253	(45.5 overs)	(for 7 wickets)	240

	O	M	R	W		O	M	R	W
Walsh	5	1	26	–	Igglesden	7	1	29	–
K.C.G. Benjamin	10	1	44	3	Watkin	9.5	1	49	4
Cummins	8	1	42	2	Fraser	9	–	50	1
W.K.M. Benjamin	8	–	33	–	Lewis	9	–	48	–
Harper	8	–	45	1	Tufnell	4	–	22	–
Simmons	7	–	32	–	Hick	7	–	32	2
Arthurton	4	–	22	1					

FALL OF WICKETS
1–112, **2**–128, **3**–209, **4**–214, **5**–247, **6**–248, **7**–248, **8**–249

FALL OF WICKETS
1–13, **2**–111, **3**–128, **4**–130, **5**–186, **6**–186, **7**–223

Umpires: L.H. Barker & S.U. Bucknor   *Man of the Match:* J.C. Adams   *West Indies won on faster scoring rate*

THIRD ONE-DAY INTERNATIONAL – WEST INDIES v. ENGLAND
1 March 1994 at Arnos Vale, St Vincent

WEST INDIES				ENGLAND		
D.L. Haynes	c Lewis, b Tufnell	83		C.C. Lewis	lbw, b Cummins	2
P.V. Simmons	c Hussain, b Tufnell	63		*A.J. Stewart	c Adams, b K.C.G. Benjamin	13
B.C. Lara	c Stewart, b Fraser	60		R.A. Smith	b Ambrose	18
K.L.T. Arthurton	c Smith, b Watkin	28		G.A. Hick	c Cummins, b Harper	32
R.B. Richardson (capt)	not out	52		M.P. Maynard	c Simmons, b Cummins	6
*J.C. Adams	c Smith, b Watkin	6		N. Hussain	c and b Harper	16
R.A. Harper	run out	15		M.A. Atherton (capt)	not out	19
A.C. Cummins	not out	0		S.L. Watkin	c Lara, b Arthurton	4
W.K.M. Benjamin				A.P. Igglesden	c Ambrose, b Lara	18
K.C.G. Benjamin				A.C.R. Fraser	st Adams, b Lara	1
C.E.L. Ambrose				P.C.R. Tufnell	not out	0
Extras	lb 4, w 2	6		Extras	b 1, lb 12, w 6	19
		—				—
(50 overs)	(for 6 wickets)	313		(50 overs)	(for 9 wickets)	148

	O	M	R	W		O	M	R	W
Igglesden	10	1	65	–	K.C.G. Benjamin	6	–	21	1
Watkin	9	–	61	2	Cummins	8	1	22	2
Lewis	9	–	67	–	W.K.M. Benjamin	5	1	15	–
Fraser	10	1	46	1	Ambrose	6	2	13	1
Hick	3	–	18	–	Simmons	7	1	18	–
Tufnell	9	–	52	2	Harper	10	–	29	2
					Arthurton	6	1	12	1
					Lara	2	–	5	2

FALL OF WICKETS

1–142, 2–156, 3–230, 4–242, 5–256, 6–300

FALL OF WICKETS

1–7, 2–24, 3–41, 4–64, 5–98, 6–105, 7–119, 8–144, 9–148

Umpires: L.H. Barker & G.T. Johnson   *Man of the Match:* D.L. Haynes   *West Indies won by 165 runs*

FOURTH ONE-DAY INTERNATIONAL – WEST INDIES v. ENGLAND
5 March 1994 at Queen's Park Oval, Port-of-Spain, Trinidad

WEST INDIES				ENGLAND		
D.L. Haynes	b Lewis	115		M.A. Atherton (capt)	b K.C.G. Benjamin	41
P.V. Simmons	c Hick, b Lewis	16		*A.J. Stewart	b K.C.G. Benjamin	2
B.C. Lara	lbw, b Fraser	19		R.A. Smith	b Harper	45
K.L.T. Arthurton	c Stewart, b Fraser	0		G.A. Hick	c and b Harper	10
R.B. Richardson (capt)	c Ramprakash, b Caddick	13		M.P. Maynard	b Harper	8
*J.C. Adams	c Caddick, b Fraser	40		M.R. Ramprakash	b Ambrose	31
R.A. Harper	b Lewis	23		C.C. Lewis	c Lara, b Harper	4
A.C. Cummins	not out	13		A.R. Caddick	not out	20
W.K.M. Benjamin	not out	0		I.D.K. Salisbury	b Cummins	5
C.E.L. Ambrose				A.P. Igglesden	run out	0
K.C.G. Benjamin				A.R.C. Fraser	not out	4
Extras	b 4, lb 4, w 13, nb 5	26		Extras	b 1, lb 9, w 11, nb 2	23
		—				—
(45.4 overs)	(for 7 wickets)	265		(36 overs)	(for 9 wickets)	193

	O	M	R	W		O	M	R	W
Igglesden	3	–	16	–	K.C.G. Benjamin	8	–	37	2
Caddick	10	–	60	1	Cummins	6	–	34	1
Fraser	10	–	31	3	Ambrose	8	–	34	1
Lewis	9.4	1	59	3	W.K.M. Benjamin	7	–	38	–
Salisbury	9	–	58	–	Harper	7	–	40	4
Hick	4	–	33	–					

FALL OF WICKETS

1–45, 2–75, 3–75, 4–98, 5–222, 6–238, 7–265

FALL OF WICKETS

1–23, 2–86, 3–110, 4–121, 5–130, 6–145, 7–177, 8–184, 9–185

Umpires: S.U. Bucknor & C.E. Cumberbatch   *Man of the Match:* D.L. Haynes   *West Indies won on faster scoring rate*

FIFTH ONE-DAY INTERNATIONAL – WEST INDIES v. ENGLAND
6 March 1994 at Queen's Park Oval, Port-of-Spain, Trinidad

WEST INDIES				ENGLAND		
P.V. Simmons	b Salisbury		84	M.A. Atherton (capt)	b K.C.G. Benjamin	51
*J.C. Adams	c Atherton, b Salisbury		23	*A.J. Stewart	b Cummins	53
B.C. Lara	c Stewart, b Caddick		16	R.A. Smith	lbw, b Cummins	4
K.L.T. Arthurton	c Ramprakash, b Lewis		17	G.A. Hick	not out	47
R.B. Richardson (capt)	c Stewart, b Salisbury		15	M.P. Maynard	c Adams, b K.C.G. Benjamin	1
R.I.C. Holder	run out		26	M.R. Ramprakash	c Adams, b Walsh	10
R.A. Harper	c and b Lewis		37	C.C. Lewis	not out	16
A.C. Cummins	c Smith, b Lewis		11	A.R. Caddick		
W.K.M. Benjamin	c Ramprakash, b Lewis		8	I.D.K. Salisbury		
K.C.G. Benjamin	not out		0	S.L. Watkin		
C.A. Walsh				A.R.C. Fraser		
Extras	b 1, lb 10, w 1, nb 1		13	Extras	b 2, lb 9, w 4, nb 4	19
			—			—
(50 overs)	(for 9 wickets)		250	(36.4 overs)	(for 5 wickets)	201

	O	M	R	W		O	M	R	W
Fraser	10	2	41	–	W.K.M. Benjamin	8	1	33	–
Watkin	10	–	56	–	Walsh	10	–	58	1
Lewis	10	–	35	4	Cummins	7.4	–	36	2
Caddick	10	2	66	1	K.C.G. Benjamin	9	–	55	2
Salisbury	10	–	41	3	Harper	2	–	8	–

FALL OF WICKETS
1–89, 2–126, 3–135, 4–164, 5–164, 6–230, 7–232, 8–248, 9–250

FALL OF WICKETS
1–62, 2–83, 3–151, 4–156, 5–174

Umpires: S.U. Bucknor & C.E. Cumberbatch   *Man of the Match:* A.J. Stewart   *England won on faster scoring rate*

10, 11, 12 and **13 March 1994** *at Bourda, Georgetown, Guyana*

England XI 308 for 2 dec. (M.R. Ramprakash 154 not out, G.P. Thorpe 84) and 170 for 1 dec. (N. Hussain 103 not out)

West Indian Board President's XI 181 for 7 dec. (K.F. Semple 76) and 170 for 3 (R.G. Samuels 56)

Match drawn

England's preparations for the second Test match suffered a blow when the second day of the game in Bourda was lost to bad weather. Faced mainly by spin, Mark Ramprakash batted throughout the first day to score an impressive 154. He and Thorpe shared a second-wicket stand of 158 after Robin Smith had again gone cheaply. Both Atherton and Stewart had stood down, and Smith opened and led the side, but again he displayed a total lack of confidence. Rain delayed the start of the third day, but England made good progress with Salisbury taking three wickets and Fraser bowling well. Hooper, leading the West Indian side, was out for 7 and ruled himself out of the rest of the series on account of his back injury. Semple and Mason added 91 for the President's XI's fifth wicket. Hussain excelled on the last day, batting with freedom and splendour, but his innings failed to win him a place in the Test side.

SECOND TEST MATCH
WEST INDIES v. ENGLAND,
at Bourda, Georgetown

A contracts dispute involving the West Indian players was resolved before the start of the second Test for which the home side made one change. The 19-year-old all-rounder Chanderpaul took the place of Phil Simmons. Richardson moved up to open the innings with Haynes. England were without the injured Malcolm, but Fraser returned while Salisbury replaced Caddick who was not fully fit, and Ramprakash was preferred to Maynard. Smith and Thorpe, somewhat fortuitously, retained their places.

There was considerable surprise when, having won the toss, Richardson returned to the dressing room for consultation and then asked England to bat on what appeared to be a good surface. There seemed to be method in his madness when, with the fourth ball of his first over, Walsh bowled Stewart off a bottom edge. Ramprakash came in at number three and was leg before in Walsh's next over to leave England 2 for 2 inside 20 minutes. The situation demanded thought and the utmost concentration, and Atherton and Smith provided these qualities. They ignored anything wide of the off stump and gradually came to terms with the pace of the pitch.

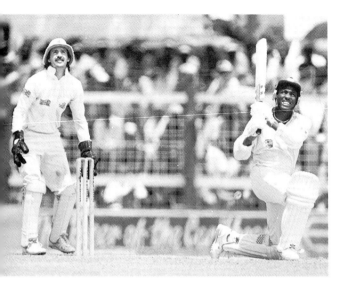

Brian Lara's memorable season continues with an innings of 167 in the second Test match. (Ben Radford/Allsport)

ball Lara hooked him for six. It must be remembered that this was only Lara's second Test hundred – the first had been an innings of 277 against Australia – and he was comparatively new to international cricket. His destruction of the England attack gave no hint of the novice, and when he finally clipped Lewis to square-leg he had made 167 off 210 balls with 25 fours and 2 sixes. A genius is among us.

Adams now enjoyed another fruitful partnership, this time with the rising star and local hero, Shivnarine Chanderpaul, the fourth left-hander in the top half of the West Indian order. Wristy, eager, temperamentally sound, Chanderpaul remained calm as he began to crack the ball around the ground. In 38 overs, he helped Adams to add 126 before he tried to pull a dreadful long-hop and, perhaps too excited for once, missed. Murray went immediately, but Adams reached his first Test century in his sixth appearance for West Indies. He might have been stumped on 97 off Hick's bowling, but Russell was below par, and with Winston Benjamin in violent mood, West Indies ended the day in total control, 487 for 6. Adams had made 102.

He extended his score to 137 on the fourth morning and, when he was last out, he had hit 21 fours and faced 262 balls. Moreover, West Indies led by 234 runs, having

Their application was rewarded. They added 171 before, with tea nearing, Smith hit Kenny Benjamin off his toes into the hands of square-leg. Smith had hit a six and 11 fours and had shown a glimpse of his old power and confidence. He had offered one chance when he was 27. The second new ball accounted for Hick. He hooked Winston Benjamin for 2 fours, but Ambrose found the shoulder of his bat with a ball which lifted and moved away, and he was taken at second slip. Ambrose bowled Thorpe eight runs later, and England closed on 258 for 5, with their captain unbeaten on 131. It was a masterly innings, secure, yet peppered with some fine shots, particularly on the off side. He had given his side the firmest of bases.

Sadly, England completely lost the initiative on the second day. In two hours, they lost their last five wickets for 46 runs. Once Atherton had gone, there was little resistance. Ambrose, showing more fire and purpose than he had done in his previous encounters with the tourists, beat him with a beautiful delivery that pitched just outside the off stump and straightened slightly to take the outside edge. Atherton's had been a monumental innings – 412 minutes, and 17 fours off 296 deliveries.

Scoring with a freedom that England could not hope to emulate, West Indies raced to 152 for the loss of Richardson by the close by which time, Lara, having given Haynes 100 minutes' start, had already overtaken the elder statesman, 57 to 53.

In the first hour of the third day, Salisbury dismissed Haynes and Arthurton, but Lara was unperturbed. He dealt savagely with anything that was remotely loose from Salisbury, and in truth, there were too many presents on offer from the leg-spinner. In 29 overs, Lara and Adams added 112. Lara took 14 runs from an over by Igglesden, but he might have been stumped off Ramprakash when he was 120. As it was, he hit a full toss from Hick for six, and when Lewis was given the second new

Thorpe is bowled by Ambrose for 0. (Ben Radford/Allsport)

SECOND TEST MATCH – WEST INDIES v. ENGLAND
17, 18, 19, 20 and 22 March 1994 at Bourda, Georgetown, Guyana

ENGLAND

	FIRST INNINGS			SECOND INNINGS	
M.A. Atherton (capt)	c Murray, b Ambrose	144	b Ambrose		0
A.J. Stewart	b Walsh	0	b K. Benjamin		79
M.R. Ramprakash	lbw, b Walsh	2	b Ambrose		5
R.A. Smith	c Lara, b K. Benjamin	84	c Richardson, b Ambrose		24
G.A. Hick	c Richardson, b Ambrose	33	b K. Benjamin		5
G.P. Thorpe	b Ambrose	0	b Walsh		20
I.D.K. Salisbury	lbw, b W. Benjamin	8	(9) b Walsh		19
*R.C. Russell	c Richardson, b Ambrose	13	(7) c Murray, b Ambrose		6
C.C. Lewis	c Richardson, b K. Benjamin	17	(8) c Adams, b K. Benjamin		24
A.R.C. Fraser	not out	0	b K. Benjamin		0
A.P. Igglesden	b K. Benjamin	0	not out		1
Extras	lb 14, nb 7	21	b 2, lb 2, w 1, nb 2		7
		322			**190**

WEST INDIES

	FIRST INNINGS	
D.L. Haynes	c Russell, b Salisbury	63
R.B. Richardson (capt)	c Lewis, b Fraser	35
B.C. Lara	c Atherton, b Lewis	167
K.L.T. Arthurton	c Thorpe, b Salisbury	5
J.C. Adams	lbw, b Igglesden	137
S. Chanderpaul	b Salisbury	62
*J.R. Murray	lbw, b Salisbury	0
W.K.M. Benjamin	b Fraser	44
C.E.L. Ambrose	c Russell, b Lewis	10
K.C.G. Benjamin	c Russell, b Lewis	1
C.A. Walsh	not out	10
Extras	b 2, lb 6, w 1, nb 13	22
		556

	O	M	R	W	O	M	R	W		O	M	R	W
Ambrose	30	8	58	4	23	5	37	4	Lewis	28	1	110	3
Walsh	26	7	69	2	25	4	71	2	Igglesden	24.3	3	94	1
K.C.G. Benjamin	23.5	5	60	3	19	6	34	4	Fraser	29	5	85	2
W.K.M. Benjamin	26	9	62	1	16	4	44	–	Salisbury	37	4	163	4
Adams	3	1	10	–	2	2	0	–	Hick	20	1	61	–
Chanderpaul	16	2	49	–					Ramprakash	15	1	35	–

FALL OF WICKETS

1–0, 2–2, 3–173, 4–245, 5–253, 6–276, 7–281, 8–322, 9–322

1–0, 2–30, 3–91, 4–96, 5–129, 6–140, 7–150, 8–185, 9–186

FALL OF WICKETS

1–63, 2–177, 3–203, 4–315, 5–441, 6–441, 7–505, 8–520, 9–532

Umpires: C. Duncan & S. Venkataraghavan

West Indies won by an innings and 44 runs

made their highest score against England at Bourda. Rain delayed the start of the England innings which again began disastrously. Atherton was bowled by Ambrose's fourth ball, a fine delivery which came off the England skipper's bat and which gave the giant fast bowler his 200th Test wicket. Ramprakash was bowled by a shooter 10 overs later, and Ambrose returned after tea to have Smith taken at second slip.

Kenny Benjamin struck Hick on the elbow and then bowled him, but throughout all this, Stewart had responded with belligerent defiance to be 72 not out at the close as England were on the brink of defeat on 119 for 4.

Five overs into the last day, Stewart was bowled by a shooter. Thorpe played and missed with monotonous regularity before being bowled by Walsh, and Russell, incredibly, survived for 56 minutes before Ambrose put him out of his misery. Lewis and Salisbury played with calm and sense for 107 minutes as the cricket became rather lethargic, but eventually Lewis lost concentration and was caught at short square-leg. Fraser survived a wide and was then bowled, statistically first ball, and Salisbury's brave two-hour innings was ended with another shooter. England had been outplayed and had suffered their fifth innings defeat in their last 11 Tests.

THIRD TEST MATCH
WEST INDIES v. ENGLAND, at Port-of-Spain

Caddick for Igglesden was the only change in an England side which had to win in Port-of-Spain in order to keep the series and their hopes alive. West Indies were unchanged. Richardson won the toss, and West Indies batted.

Haynes and Richardson negotiated the first session with calm and some fortune. Both were dropped off straightforward chances, but immediately after lunch Haynes offered a wretched pull shot at a ball from Salisbury which came through low and quickly and he was bowled. Lara and Richardson now engaged in a second-wicket stand which realised 92. Richardson, having batted for 267 minutes, fell leg before to a full toss from Salisbury. This was the first of four wickets to fall in 21 balls for six runs. Lara offered no shot at a delivery from Lewis which cut back sharply. In his next over, Lewis, bowling round the wicket, had Adams taken at silly mid-off. One run later, Arthurton was leg before.

An all-too-familiar sight. Hick looks at his hands after putting down a chance at slip. (Ben Radford/Allsport)

Chanderpaul and Murray steadied the innings, but Fraser returned to take two well deserved wickets, and West Indies closed on 227 for 7.

Fraser, who had bowled so well early in the innings without success, quickly ended the West Indians' first knock on the second morning. Ambrose was taken at slip, Kenny Benjamin was bowled between bat and pad, and Lewis had Walsh leg before first ball. England were batting before lunch. They soon lost Stewart who played back to a ball of full length which kept low, but Ramprakash and Atherton added 66 in 85 minutes. Ramprakash was out when he skied the ball as he attempted a hook, and four overs later, Atherton was caught behind off a low inside edge.

Smith again looked anything but happy, and he was leg before when he played back to Ambrose, but the West Indies now became lethargic. They bowled without fire, and catches went down. Hick was missed at slip by Richardson who diverted the ball into Lara's face. Trinidad's captain had to leave the field for repairs. Hick, somewhat frenetic, was eventually trapped in front by Walsh, but Thorpe and Russell, both a little fortunate to be in the side, survived against some moderate bowling, and England closed on 236 for 5.

Thorpe, Russell and Lewis all fell to Ambrose on the third morning but, once he was rested, Salisbury was able to prosper, and England took a lead of 76. This lead took on immense proportions when, inspired by some fine attacking bowling from Caddick and some safer fielding, England captured three wickets before the deficit was wiped off. Caddick took a splendid reflex catch off his own bowling to dispose of Richardson, and Lara was very well caught at mid-off by Salisbury. Haynes was bowled shortly after tea, but Arthurton and Adams added 80 brisk runs. Arthurton, who should have been stumped off Salisbury when 21, miscued to mid-on, and 12 runs later Adams smote a high full toss from Salisbury against Smith at short-leg. The ball looped up from the fielder's arm and was caught by Russell who ran round from behind the stumps. Smith, felled by the blow, was later diagnosed as bruised but not broken. West Indies closed

Ambrose traps Atherton leg before with the first ball of England's second innings, and the debacle is under way. (Ben Radford/Allsport)

Ramprakash is stranded, run out in the first over, and England face misery. (Ben Radford/Allsport)

at 143 for 5, and England had the scent of a famous victory.

That sweet smell of success turned sour on the fourth day. The pattern was determined early in the day when Chanderpaul, on four, was dropped at slip by Hick off the easiest of chances. Hick was to repeat the offence when the same batsman was on 29. Caddick again bowled very

The scoreboard at the end of the England innings. (Ben Radford/Allsport)

THIRD TEST MATCH – WEST INDIES *v.* ENGLAND
25, 26, 27, 29 and 30 March 1994 at Queen's Park Oval, Port-of-Spain, Trinidad

WEST INDIES

	FIRST INNINGS			SECOND INNINGS	
D.L.Haynes	b Salisbury	38	b Lewis	19
R.B. Richardson (capt)	lbw, b Salisbury	63	c and b Caddick	3
B.C. Lara	lbw, b Lewis	43	c Salisbury, b Caddick	12
K.L.T. Arthurton	lbw, b Lewis	1	c Stewart, b Caddick	42
J.C. Adams	c Smith, b Lewis	2	c Russell, b Salisbury	43
S. Chanderpaul	b Fraser	19	c Fraser, b Caddick	50
*J.R. Murray	not out	27	c Russell, b Caddick	14
W.K.M. Benjamin	b Fraser	10	c Fraser, b Lewis	35
C.E.L. Ambrose	c Thorpe, b Fraser	13	b Caddick	12
K.C.G. Benjamin	b Fraser	9	not out	5
C.A. Walsh	lbw, b Lewis	0	lbw, b Lewis	1
Extras	b 1, lb 13, w 1, nb 12	27	b 8, lb 13, nb 12	33
		252		269

ENGLAND

	FIRST INNINGS			SECOND INNINGS	
M.A. Atherton (capt)	c Murray, b W. Benjamin	48	lbw, b Ambrose	0
A.J. Stewart	b Ambrose	6	b Ambrose	18
M.R. Ramprakash	c and b W. Benjamin	23	run out	1
R.A. Smith	lbw, b Ambrose	12	b Ambrose	0
G.A. Hick	lbw, b Walsh	40	c Murray, b Ambrose	6
G.P. Thorpe	c Lara, b Ambrose	86	b Ambrose	3
*R.C. Russell	b Ambrose	23	(8) c sub (Simmons), b Ambrose	4
C.C. Lewis	b Ambrose	9	(9) c W. Benjamin, b Walsh	6
I.D.K. Salisbury	c Lara, b Walsh	36	(7) c Lara, b Walsh	0
A.R. Caddick	c Lara, b W. Benjamin	6	c Lara, b Walsh	1
A.R.C. Fraser	not out	8	not out	0
Extras	b 10, lb 9, w 1, nb 11	31	lb 6, nb 1	7
		328		46

	O	M	R	W	O	M	R	W		O	M	R	W	O	M	R	W
Fraser	24	9	49	4	25	6	71	–	Ambrose	29	6	60	5	10	1	24	6
Caddick	19	5	43	–	26	5	65	6	Walsh	27.2	3	77	2	9.1	1	16	3
Lewis	25.2	3	61	4	27.5	6	71	3	K.C.G. Benjamin	20	5	70	–				
Salisbury	22	4	72	2	9	1	41	1	W.K.M. Benjamin	24	3	66	3				
Ramprakash	2	1	8	–					Adams	4	–	18	–				
Hick	3	1	5	–					Chanderpaul	5	–	13	–				
									Arthurton	3	–	5	–				

FALL OF WICKETS

1–66, 2–158, 3–158, 4–163, 5–164, 6–201, 7–212, 8–241, 9–251
1–15, 2–37, 3–51, 4–131, 5–143, 6–167, 7–227, 8–247, 9–267

FALL OF WICKETS

1–16, 2–82, 3–87, 4–115, 5–167, 6–249, 7–273, 8–281, 9–294
1–0, 2–1, 3–5, 4–21, 5–26, 6–27, 7–37, 8–40, 9–45

Umpires: S. Venkataraghavan & S.U. Bucknor

West Indies won by 147 runs

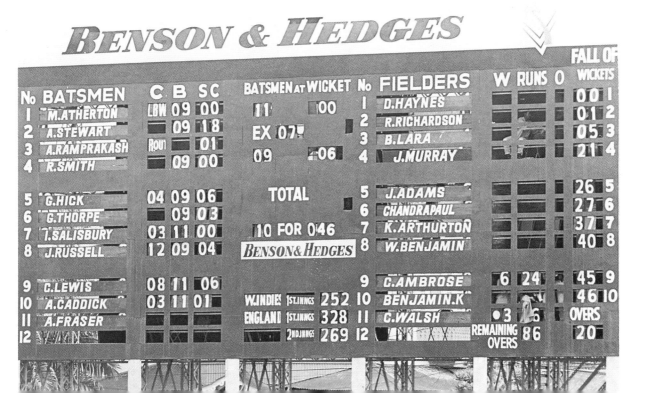

well, but Chanderpaul played with sense, Winston Benjamin hit with gusto, 35 off 51 balls, and England were left with a day and a half in which to score 194 runs to win the match. Rain interrupted the afternoon's play so that England had 15 overs of the fourth day remaining in which to begin their quest for victory. By the close of play, they were, but for a miracle or a monsoon, a beaten team.

With his first ball, Ambrose caught Atherton plumb in front, and on the fifth ball of the over, Ramprakash turned the ball to long-leg, attempted a second run, hesitated, and was run out with ease. A schoolboy would have been ashamed at such a dismissal. After one over, England were 1 for 2. The second ball of Ambrose's second over came back sharply to beat Smith's forward defensive prod, find the gap between bat and pad and uproot his off stump. Stewart and Hick survived for five overs before Hick hung out his bat to one of Ambrose's lesser deliveries and was caught behind. With the fifth ball of his next over, Ambrose sent Stewart's off stump reeling. Walsh at last got a deserved wicket when he had Salisbury caught at slip, and Russell was taken at second slip two overs later to give Ambrose his fifth wicket. It became six when the tall Antiguan bowled Thorpe with the last ball of the day. England were 40 for 8, humiliated by bowling of unrelenting pace and accuracy.

Walsh finished the job on the last morning, but Caddick, Lewis and Fraser did see England past their lowest score in Test history, by one run.

To no one's surprise, Ambrose was Man of the Match.

2, 3, 4 and 5 April 1994 *at Queen's Park, St George's, Grenada*

England XI 319 (M.R. Ramprakash 91, A.J. Stewart 65, G.A. Hick 59, R.N. Lewis 5 for 95) and 165 (G.A. Hick 74, M.R. Ramprakash 67, R.N. Lewis 4 for 51)

West Indies Board XI 313 (R.I.C. Holder 116, D.E. Malcolm 4 for 81, P.C.R. Tufnell 4 for 87) and 172 for 2 (S.C. Williams 102 not out)

West Indies Board XI won by 8 wickets

For England, the defeat at the hands of the Board XI in Grenada was almost as great a humiliation as the defeat that they suffered in the third Test match. They reached 206 before losing their second wicket, Ramprakash making a painstaking 91, and then lost their last seven wickets for 42 runs. Hussain and Maynard batted at numbers seven and eight, an indication that they had no hope of being selected for the fourth Test, an incredible decision.

The ground at St George's, Grenada, where England suffered further humiliation. (Ben Radford/Allsport)

A rampant Angus Fraser has Adams caught by Thorpe. (Ben Radford/ Allsport)

Alec Stewart drives to the boundary on his way to his second century of the match. (Ben Radford/Allsport)

Hussain entered the match at the head of England's first-class averages for the tour. Having been defeated by pace in Trinidad, England were now perplexed by the leg-spin of Rawle Lewis. Holder kept his side in contention with an admirable century, and Devon Malcolm, returning to the England XI, took four wickets and looked ready for a recall to the Test side. Batting again, England lost Smith for 0, but then saw Ramprakash and Hick add 140. The last eight wickets fell for 25 runs, Thorpe being absent ill. In fact, the last five wickets fell for three runs. Williams and Wallace hit 47 runs in the last eight overs of the day, and the match was over before lunch on the last day. The first wicket realised 81 in 17 overs, and Williams finished the match by hitting Tufnell for 5 fours in succession. His 102 had come from 103 balls. England were broken.

FOURTH TEST MATCH
WEST INDIES *v.* ENGLAND, at Bridgetown

Few Test sides could have entered the fourth match of a series with their fortunes at a lower ebb than England's in the Caribbean in 1994. The shattering defeat in Trinidad had been followed by a humiliating trouncing in Grenada, and they faced an unchanged, triumphant West Indies side, three up in the series. Surprisingly, England made no changes to their batting line-up, choosing only to bring in Tufnell for Salisbury. Malcolm was considered to be not fully fit for a five-day Test match.

Richardson won the toss and decided to bowl first on a ground where West Indies had won their last 12 Test matches. There seemed to be no logic in his decision when Atherton, a wonderful leader by example, and Stewart hit 171 in 222 minutes for the first wicket. They tamed the West Indian attack, and 83 unblemished runs came in 27 overs before lunch. Stewart began to unleash a series of pleasing shots in the afternoon, and Atherton hit Kenny Benjamin for 2 fours in succession only to lose concentration and edge to slip. He deserved a century, but he had confirmed that the greatest benefit for England to emerge from the so-far disastrous tour was that he and Stewart had established a highly successful opening partnership.

Ramprakash made 20 in just over an hour before being caught behind pushing at Winston Benjamin, but in the next over, Stewart completed his fifth Test century. It came in seven minutes under four hours and was full of positive strokeplay. Smith's misery continued when he was caught behind off a brutal delivery from Winston Benjamin who then accounted for Stewart. The Surrey man played a tired shot and was bowled off an inside edge, but he had batted nobly, hitting 18 fours. It was a marvellous way to celebrate a 31st birthday. Thorpe fell to a careless shot against the second new ball, and England closed on 299 for 5, the initiative slipping away from them.

Hick began the second day in the grand manner, despatching two of the first three balls for four. The fourth – or third as one of Hick's fours came from a no-ball – was edged to the keeper. Two balls later, Lewis was dismissed in a similar fashion. Ambrose, for it was he who was the bowler, also yorked Caddick and had Russell caught off a skier at square-leg to claim four of the last five England wickets.

West Indies did not lose a wicket before lunch although there was a rumpus over a run out, which was resolved when it was revealed that the ball had reached the boundary even though only three runs were allowed. Haynes was forced to retire hurt with an injured finger when he had scored 35, and shortly West Indies were in some trouble. Richardson played back to Fraser and prodded at the ball for Atherton to take a low catch at third slip. In the same over, Arthurton drove loosely and was caught behind.

Lara played in his usual expansive manner and hit 5 fours but, with Fraser off the field, he was dismissed by Lewis, magnificently caught by the substitute Hussain at cover-point.

In the session after tea, Fraser and Tufnell bowled in tandem for 20 overs. This proved the turning point for England as, at one point, four wickets fell to Fraser in 18 balls at a personal cost of one run. Adams edged to slip, the returning Haynes clipped a catch to mid-off, and both Murray and Winston Benjamin were taken at slip as, unbelievably, West Indies struggled to avoid the follow-on. They were saved by the two left-handers, Chanderpaul and Ambrose, who batted with a mixture of coolness and belligerence. West Indies closed on 188 for 7.

On the third morning, Chanderpaul led West Indies' riposte. He hit 7 fours and showed that he had an attacking panache to complement his sound defence. Kenny Benjamin hit 4 fours and a six, and the last wicket produced 41 runs as Walsh was dropped on the boundary by Ramprakash. West Indies had come within 51 runs of England before Fraser accounted for Walsh, and much of the initiative that Fraser's wonderful bowling had gained was lost, not least because of some sloppy fielding. Fraser finished with 8 for 75, his best bowling figures in any form of cricket. He is a likeable and dedicated man who has suffered cruelly through injury, and, in the present climate, England function best only when he is at his fittest and in form.

England lost both Atherton and Ramprakash to catches close to the wicket before the tea break. Smith flattered to deceive and was leg before when he padded up to a

straight ball. Stewart and Hick responded with vigour, and they lifted England's spirits and revived hopes of victory by taking their side to 171 for 3 by the end of play. Stewart was on 62, and Hick on 52.

In 25 overs before lunch on the fourth day, England added 49 runs to their score for the loss of Hick. In the afternoon, the runs began to flow. Thorpe, an enigma still unsure of a regular place in the side, began smoothly, and Stewart, his base secure, scored with exhilarating freedom so that runs came at five an over. At lunch Stewart was 75, but after the break he moved serenely to his sixth Test hundred in just under seven hours. It was his second hundred of the match, and he became the seventh English batsman to score two hundreds in a Test, the first to accomplish the feat against West Indies. Thorpe gave him admirable, confident, fluent support, and the pair added 150. Atherton became the first England captain for 10 years to declare against West Indies, and the home side had more than a day in which to score 446 if they wanted to win the match.

Such hopes disappeared by the close of play. Caddick, finding a fire and accuracy which he had lacked totally in the first innings, had deputy opener Adams caught behind and Kenny Benjamin taken at slip. With Richardson being forced to retire hurt, and Haynes low in the order nursing his injured finger, West Indies ended the day on a perilous 47 for 2.

In the first hour of the last day, Lara and Arthurton scored 63 runs in a manner which betrayed no hint of crisis. Tufnell probed intelligently, but it was Caddick who gained the vital third wicket. Lara pulled hard, but he got underneath the ball, and Tufnell, running back from mid-on, took a fine catch.

The two left-handers, Arthurton and Chanderpaul, frustrated England until the stroke of lunch. For the last over of the morning session, Atherton introduced Hick into the attack and, with his first ball, the occasional off-spinner had Chanderpaul well caught at slip by the substitute Hussain. This was the lift that England needed and, half an hour into the afternoon, Tufnell claimed a deserved wicket, Arthurton edging the ball into his stumps as he played back when he should have played forward. Murray steered Caddick to first slip, and Richardson, greatly handicapped by his hamstring injury, drove the same bowler into the hands of cover. Winston Benjamin slogged himself to destruction, and Haynes was caught bat and pad. Walsh hit Tufnell out of the ground three times in one over, but, with two hours remaining, Lewis scattered Ambrose's stumps, and England had gained a famous victory.

Fraser had, in the first innings, produced the best figures by an England bowler against West Indies. Stewart had hit a century in each innings. But the remarkable achievement was that a side who had been humiliated, and subsequently ridiculed and castigated, only days earlier had risen from the ashes to outplay their adversaries. They deserved the highest possible praise.

England scent victory as Tufnell bowls Arthurton for 52. (Ben Radford/Allsport)

FOURTH TEST MATCH – WEST INDIES v. ENGLAND
8, 9, 10, 12 and 13 April 1994 at Kensington Oval, Bridgetown, Barbados

ENGLAND

	FIRST INNINGS		SECOND INNINGS	
M.A. Atherton (capt)	c Lara, b K. Benjamin	85	c Lara, b Walsh	15
A.J. Stewart	b W. Benjamin	118	b Walsh	143
M.R. Ramprakash	c Murray, b W. Benjamin	20	c Chanderpaul, b Walsh	3
R.A. Smith	c Murray, b W. Benjamin	10	lbw, b K. Benjamin	13
G.A. Hick	c Murray, b Ambrose	34	c Lara, b Walsh	59
G.P. Thorpe	c sub (Simmons), b K. Benjamin	7	c Arthurton, b Walsh	84
*R.C. Russell	c Chanderpaul, b Ambrose	38	not out	17
C.C. Lewis	c Murray, b Ambrose	0	c Walsh, b Adams	10
A.R. Caddick	b Ambrose	8		
A.R.C. Fraser	c Chanderpaul, b Walsh	3		
P.C.R. Tufnell	not out	0		
Extras	lb 8, nb 24	32	b 8, lb 6, nb 36	50
		355	(for 7 wickets, dec.)	394

WEST INDIES

	FIRST INNINGS		SECOND INNINGS	
D.L. Haynes	c Atherton, b Fraser	35	(8) c Thorpe, b Tufnell	15
R.B. Richardson (capt)	c Atherton, b Fraser	20	(1) c Ramprakash, b Caddick	33
B.C. Lara	c sub (Hussain), b Lewis	26	c Tufnell, b Caddick	64
K.L.T. Arthurton	c Russell, b Fraser	0	(5) b Tufnell	52
J.C. Adams	c Thorpe, b Fraser	26	(2) c Russell, b Caddick	12
S. Chanderpaul	c Ramprakash, b Tufnell	77	c sub (Hussain), b Hick	5
*J.R. Murray	c Thorpe, b Fraser	0	c Thorpe, b Caddick	5
W.K.M. Benjamin	c Hick, b Fraser	8	(9) c Stewart, b Tufnell	3
C.E.L. Ambrose	c Hick, b Fraser	44	(10) b Lewis	12
K.C.G. Benjamin	not out	43	(4) c Hick, b Caddick	0
C.A. Walsh	c Tufnell, b Fraser	13	not out	18
Extras	lb 1, nb 11	12	b 1, lb 7, nb 10	18
		304		237

ENGLAND

	O	M	R	W	O	M	R	W
Ambrose	24.2	5	86	4	22	4	75	–
Walsh	24	3	88	1	28	5	94	5
W.K.M. Benjamin	22	4	76	3	22	3	58	–
K.C.G. Benjamin	20	5	74	2	22	1	92	1
Chanderpaul	10	4	23	–	10	3	30	–
Adams					6.5	–	31	1

WEST INDIES

	O	M	R	W	O	M	R	W
Fraser	28.5	7	75	8	17	7	40	–
Caddick	24	2	92	–	17	3	63	5
Lewis	17	2	60	1	8.2	1	23	1
Tufnell	32	12	76	1	36	12	100	3
Hick					4	2	3	1

FALL OF WICKETS

1–171, 2–223, 3–242, 4–265, 5–290, 6–307, 7–307, 8–327, 9–351
1–33, 2–43, 3–79, 4–194, 5–344, 6–382, 7–394

FALL OF WICKETS

1–55, 2–55, 3–95, 4–126, 5–126, 6–126, 7–134, 8–205, 9–263
1–43, 2–43, 3–128, 4–150, 5–164, 6–179, 7–195, 8–199, 9–216

Umpires: L.H. Barker & D.B. Hair

England won by 208 runs

FIFTH TEST MATCH
WEST INDIES v. ENGLAND, at Antigua

Brian Lara crashes another boundary in his record innings of 375. (Ben Radford/Allsport)

The series has been won. England had tasted triumph and euphoria to ease the earlier pain. The first-class season in England was under way. But still there was one Test in the Caribbean to be played. England made no changes although Hussain for Ramprakash might have been a realistic consideration; but West Indies brought in Williams, winning his first Test cap, and Simmons for the injured Haynes and Richardson. Walsh led West Indies for the first time, won the toss, and West Indies batted on a benign surface.

Both openers were out within eight overs. Williams was caught on the boundary hooking Fraser, and Simmons was leg before to Caddick a few balls later. That was England's last success for four hours, although they might have had more pleasure had Hick held simple chances at slip. Adams was the beneficiary, and he made Hick suffer, hitting him for successive sixes. In 244 minutes, Adams and Lara added 179. By the end of the day, Lara was in total control. At lunch, his score was 23;

An historic setting. The Recreation Ground, Antigua, where Brian Lara established a new Test record. (Ben Radford/Allsport)

at tea, 92. At the close, he was 164, and West Indies were 274 for 3.

On the second day, Lara's dominance was even more complete. Only one wicket fell, that of Arthurton half an hour after lunch. He had contributed 47 to a stand of 183, but he had given Lara brave support as he was nursing an injured hand. Chanderpaul, in his turn, supported Lara, but it was Lara himself who earned all the plaudits. In spite of showers which halted play and could have affected the concentration of a lesser man, he became only the 12th batsman in history to hit a triple century in

Test cricket. At the end of the day, he was 320 not out, and West Indies were 502 for 4.

Cricket history was made on Monday, 18 April 1994. With his score on 361, Brian Lara cover-drove Caddick for four to equal Garry Sobers' Test record of 365. In the next over, bowled by Lewis, he pulled a short ball viciously for four, and the ground was invaded by hordes clamouring to congratulate a master batsman on the mightiest of achievements. Among the first to congratulate Lara was Sir Garfield Sobers whose record he had beaten.

Lara was out in the last over of the morning, driving

FIFTH TEST MATCH – WEST INDIES v. ENGLAND
16, 17, 18, 20 and 21 April 1994 at Recreation Ground, St John's, Antigua

WEST INDIES

	FIRST INNINGS		SECOND INNINGS	
P.V. Simmons	lbw, b Caddick	8	not out	22
S.C. Williams	c Caddick, b Fraser	3	not out	21
B.C. Lara	c Russell, b Caddick	375		
J.C. Adams	c sub (Hussain), b Fraser	59		
K.L.T. Arthurton	c Russell b Caddick	47		
S. Chanderpaul	not out	75		
*J.R. Murray				
W.K.M. Benjamin				
C.E.L. Ambrose				
K.C.G. Benjamin				
C.A. Walsh (capt)				
Extras	lb 3, nb 23	26		0
	(for 5 wickets, dec.)	593	(for no wicket)	43

ENGLAND

	FIRST INNINGS	
M.A. Atherton (capt)	c Murray, b Ambrose	135
A.J. Stewart	c Ambrose, b K. Benjamin	24
M.R. Ramprakash	lbw, b K. Benjamin	19
R.A. Smith	lbw, b K. Benjamin	175
G.A. Hick	b K. Benjamin	20
G.P. Thorpe	c Adams, b Chanderpaul	9
*R.C. Russell	c Murray, b W. Benjamin	62
C.C. Lewis	not out	75
A.R. Caddick	c W. Benjamin, b Adams	22
A.R.C. Fraser	b Adams	0
P.C.R. Tufnell	lbw, b W. Benjamin	0
Extras	b 9, lb 20, nb 23	52
		593

	O	M	R	W	O	M	R	W
Fraser	43	4	121	2	2	1	2	–
Caddick	47.2	8	158	3	2	1	11	–
Tufnell	39	8	110	–	6	4	5	–
Lewis	33	1	140	–				
Hick	18	3	61	–	8	2	11	–
Ramprakash					3	1	5	–
Thorpe					2	1	1	–
Stewart					1	–	8	–

	O	M	R	W
Ambrose	40	18	66	1
Walsh	40	9	123	–
W.K.M. Benjamin	41.1	15	93	2
K.C.G. Benjamin	37	7	110	4
Chanderpaul	24	1	94	1
Adams	22	4	74	2
Arthurton	2	1	4	–

FALL OF WICKETS
1–11, 2–12, 3–191, 4–374, 5–593

FALL OF WICKETS
1–40, 2–70, 3–373, 4–393, 5–401, 6–417, 7–535, 8–585, 9–589

Umpires: S.U. Bucknor & D.B. Hair

Match drawn

tiredly at Caddick, and he left the field beneath an arch of bats held on high by his team-mates.

The statistics of Lara's unblemished, marvellous innings cannot depict the grace and majesty of his batting. He came to the wicket at 10.31 a.m. on the Saturday, with West Indies 11 for 1, and he was out at 12.30 p.m. on the Monday, with his side 593 for 5. He faced 536 balls, batted 766 minutes and hit 45 fours. These figures can tell nothing of the glory.

England lost Stewart after nearly an hour's play, and just over half an hour later, Ramprakash was leg before to Kenny Benjamin. Atherton and Smith both moved past 60, and England closed on 185 for 2.

When the game resumed after the rest day there was an air of anti-climax and unreality, which was inevitable after Lara's innings and in a match which seemed certain to be drawn. Atherton, who had done a fine job as captain and opener on a difficult tour, reached his fifth Test hundred before lunch, and Smith soon followed him.

Smith went on to hit the highest of his nine Test hundreds, but it really came too late to erase the opinion that he had endured a disastrous tour. Atherton and Smith scored 303 for the third wicket, a record for England against West Indies, but four wickets fell for 44 runs and, although England were 442 for 6 at the close, they were not as comfortable as they might have been.

The West Indies team erupts as Lara passes Sobers' record. (Ben Radford/Allsport)

Russell and Lewis ended all doubts the next morning when they came safely through the new ball barrage at the start of play. Thereafter, the game moved quietly to the draw which the pitch had deemed inevitable. England gained consolation from achieving parity, but the lasting memory of the West Indian season will ever be the batting of Brian Lara.

TEST MATCH AVERAGES – WEST INDIES v. ENGLAND

WEST INDIES BATTING

	M	Inns	NO	Runs	HS	Av	100s	50s
B.C. Lara	5	8	–	798	375	99.75	2	2
J.C. Adams	5	7	1	374	137	62.33	1	2
S. Chanderpaul	4	6	1	288	77	57.60	–	4
K.L.T. Arthurton	5	7	–	273	126	39.00	1	1
D.L. Haynes	4	7	1	217	63	36.16	–	1
R.B. Richardson	4	7	2	163	63	32.60	–	1
W.K.M. Benjamin	5	6	–	138	44	23.00	–	–
P.V. Simmons	2	4	1	50	22*	16.66	–	–
J.R. Murray	5	6	1	80	34	16.00	–	–
C.E.L. Ambrose	5	6	–	91	44	15.16	–	–
K.C.G. Benjamin	5	6	2	58	43*	14.50	–	–
C.A. Walsh	5	6	2	42	18*	10.50	–	–

Played in one Test: S.C. Williams 3 & 21*

ENGLAND BATTING

	M	Inns	NO	Runs	HS	Av	100s	50s
M.A. Atherton	5	9	–	510	144	56.66	2	2
A.J. Stewart	5	9	–	477	143	53.00	2	2
R.A. Smith	5	9	–	320	175	35.55	1	1
G.A. Hick	5	9	–	316	96	35.11	–	2
G.P. Thorpe	5	9	–	239	86	26.55	–	2
R.C. Russell	5	9	1	195	62	24.37	–	1
C.C. Lewis	5	9	1	170	75*	21.25	–	1
I.D.K. Salisbury	2	4	–	63	36	15.75	–	–
A.R. Caddick	4	6	1	69	29*	13.80	–	–
M.R. Ramprakash	4	7	–	73	23	10.42	–	–
A.R.C. Fraser	4	6	3	11	8*	3.66	–	–
A.P. Igglesden	2	4	2	4	3*	2.00	–	–
P.C.R. Tufnell	2	2	1	0	0*	0.00	–	–

Played in one Test: M.P. Maynard 35 & 0; D.E. Malcolm 6 & 18

WEST INDIES BOWLING

	Overs	Mds	Runs	Wkts	Av	Best	10/m	5/inn
C.E.L. Ambrose	224.2	59	519	26	19.96	6-24	1	2
K.C.G. Benjamin	183.5	38	566	22	25.72	6-66	–	1
C.A. Walsh	227.2	44	646	19	34.00	5-94	–	1
W.K.M. Benjamin	190.2	48	498	12	41.50	3-56	–	–
J.C. Adams	49.5	8	173	4	43.25	2-74	–	–
S. Chanderpaul	65	10	209	1	209.00	1-94	–	–
K.L.T. Arthurton	5	1	9	–	–	–	–	–

Bowled in one innings: P.V. Simmons 3–1–4–0

ENGLAND BOWLING

	Overs	Mds	Runs	Wkts	Av	Best	10/m	5/inn
A.R.C. Fraser	168.5	39	443	16	27.68	8-75	–	1
A.R. Caddick	170.2	30	545	18	30.27	6-65	–	2
I.D.K. Salisbury	68	9	276	7	39.42	4-163	–	–
C.C. Lewis	168.3	18	553	14	39.50	4-61	–	–
D.E. Malcolm	28	4	132	3	44.00	3-113	–	–
A.P. Igglesden	55.3	8	183	3	61.00	1-36	–	–
P.C.R. Tufnell	113	36	291	4	72.75	3-100	–	–
G.A. Hick	77	14	198	2	99.00	1-3	–	–
A.J. Stewart	3.2	–	13	–	–	–	–	–
M.R. Ramprakash	20	3	48	–	–	–	–	–

Bowled in one innings: G.P. Thorpe 2–1–1–0

WEST INDIES FIELDING FIGURES

13 – J.R. Murray; 9 – B.C. Lara; 8 – J.C. Adams; 4 – R.B. Richardson; 3 – W.K.M. Benjamin and S. Chanderpaul; 2 – sub (P.V. Simmons); 1 – K.L.T. Arthurton, C.E.L. Ambrose, C.A. Walsh and sub (R.A. Harper).

ENGLAND FIELDING FIGURES

10 – R.C. Russell; 7 – G.P. Thorpe; 3 – M.A. Atherton, G.A. Hick and sub (N. Hussain); 2 – A.J. Stewart, C.C. Lewis, A.R. Caddick, M.R. Ramprakash, A.R.C. Fraser and P.C.R. Tufnell; 1 – R.A. Smith, M.P. Maynard and I.D.K. Salisbury.

FIRST-CLASS AVERAGES

BATTING

	M	Inns	NO	Runs	HS	Av	100s	50s
B.C. Lara	10	17	–	1513	375	89.00	5	3
J.C. Adams	10	16	2	810	137	57.85	3	4
S.L. Campbell	7	12	2	547	141	54.70	3	2
K.F. Semple	6	11	2	489	142	54.33	1	4
S.C. Williams	8	15	3	626	157	52.16	3	1
S. Chanderpaul	10	17	3	708	101	50.57	1	7
R.I.C. Holder	7	11	2	450	116*	50.00	2	1
K.L.T. Arthurton	10	15	1	662	126	47.28	2	3
N.O. Perry	6	9	1	357	160	44.62	1	1
R.A. Harper	5	7	–	287	79	41.00	–	1
R.B. Richardson	6	11	2	348	151	38.66	1	1
V.C. Drakes	6	8	3	192	91*	38.40	–	1
F.R. Redwood	5	8	1	265	62*	37.85	–	3
D.L. Haynes	9	15	2	489	84	37.61	–	3
C.W. Walwyn	4	7	–	255	80	36.42	–	2
D.A. Joseph	6	12	1	395	88	35.90	–	2
P.A. Wallace	6	10	–	347	72	34.70	–	2
C.A. Davis	3	6	2	135	43*	33.75	–	–
K. Mason	6	10	1	297	63	33.00	–	2
R.D. Jacobs	7	11	2	276	71*	30.66	–	2
J.R. Murray	10	16	1	438	95	29.20	–	3
C.O. Browne	7	10	1	259	55	28.77	–	1
P.V. Simmons	6	11	1	281	69	28.10	–	2
C.L. Hooper	5	8	1	195	54*	27.85	–	1
W.D. Phillip	5	7	3	103	41*	25.75	–	–
R.G. Samuels	6	11	–	282	68	25.63	–	2
F.A. Rose	4	6	2	101	47*	25.25	–	–
A.F.G. Griffith	3	5	–	126	50	25.20	–	1
P.D. Persaud	3	5	–	123	52	24.60	–	1
L.A. Harrigan	6	11	–	267	61	24.27	–	2
R.W. Staple	5	9	–	211	42	23.44	–	–
S. Ragoonath	3	5	–	114	74	22.80	–	1
R.C. Haynes	5	9	–	205	50	22.77	–	1
W.K.M. Benjamin	10	13	–	279	71	21.46	–	1
L.K. Puckerin	3	5	–	105	55	21.00	–	1
Sunil Dhaniram	5	7	–	147	57	21.00	–	1
A. Balliram	5	9	–	176	76	19.55	–	1
L.A. Joseph	4	6	–	115	52	19.16	–	1
G. Cupid	5	10	–	188	49	18.80	–	–
D. Williams	5	9	–	160	46	17.77	–	–
T.O. Powell	3	6	–	102	49	17.00	–	–
K.K. Sylvester	5	9	–	140	44	15.55	–	–
L.L. Lawrence	5	7	–	107	56	15.28	–	1
K.C.G. Benjamin	10	13	3	152	43*	15.20	–	–
C.E.L. Ambrose	9	12	–	164	44	13.66	–	–
R.A. Marshall	5	10	–	100	40	10.00	–	–

(Qualification – 100 runs, average 10.00)

BOWLING

	Overs	Mds	Runs	Wkts	Av	Best	10/m	5/inn
C.E.L. Ambrose	336	96	741	45	16.46	6-24	1	2
R.A. Harper	88.2	19	214	12	17.83	5-38	1	2
C.E. Cuffy	172	45	431	24	17.95	6-81	–	2
R. Dhanraj	202.3	33	609	31	19.64	8-51	1	1
W.D. Phillip	149.2	39	359	16	22.43	4-55	–	–
B. St A. Browne	140	23	555	24	23.12	5-27	–	1
C.A. Walsh	403.4	87	1048	45	23.28	6-109	–	3
R.C. Haynes	205.5	39	499	21	23.76	6-82	–	1
O.D. Gibson	145.1	24	405	17	23.82	5-87	–	1
L.C. Weekes	74.3	13	246	10	24.60	4-54	–	–
K.C.G. Benjamin	339.4	70	1056	42	25.14	6-66	–	2
D. Ramnarine	125.4	23	379	15	25.26	5-48	–	1
C.G. Butts	194.3	44	481	18	26.72	4-38	–	–
A.C. Cummins	141.5	21	483	17	28.41	4-92	–	–
S.M. Skeete	88.2	12	318	11	28.90	3-13	–	–
R.N. Lewis	194	30	625	21	29.76	5-95	–	2
W.E. Reid	124	23	337	11	30.63	4-56	–	–
N.O. Perry	187.2	43	460	15	30.66	3-39	–	–
V.A. Walsh	109	28	339	11	30.81	3-22	–	–
F.A. Rose	122.1	16	470	15	31.33	4-74	–	–
S. Chanderpaul	151.5	27	424	13	32.61	3-26	–	–
V.C. Drakes	155.5	18	568	17	33.41	4-63	–	–
W.K.M. Benjamin	324.4	80	909	27	33.66	4-44	–	–
E.C. Antoine	124.5	21	413	12	34.41	4-36	–	–

(Qualification – 10 wickets)

LEADING FIELDERS

30 – R.O. Jacobs (ct 27/st 3); 23 – B.C. Lara; 18 – C.O. Browne (ct 17/st 1) and J.R. Murray; 17 – D. Williams (ct 12/st 5); 16 – J.C. Adams; 14 – S.L. Campbell; 13 – R.A. Harper and K.A. Wong (ct 10/st 3); 12 – K.F. Semple

SECTION K
England
Benson and Hedges Cup
Britannic Assurance County Championship
AXA Equity & Law Sunday League
New Zealand tour, Tetley Challenge, Texaco Trophy, Cornhill Test Series
NatWest Trophy
South African tour, Tetley Challenge, Cornhill Test Series, Texaco Trophy
First-class form charts
First-class averages

The Walker Ground at Southgate where the New Zealanders began their tour. (Patrick Eagar)

English cricket lost three good men in the winter months with the deaths of Reg Hayter, Tom Pearce and Brian Johnston. In their different ways, they each contributed much to the game, and the present writer will remain ever grateful for the wisdom, encouragement and humour that he received from each. They will be much missed.

It had been generally expected that M.J.K. Smith, managing the England side in the Caribbean, would accede to the position lately held by Ted Dexter as England's supremo, but a late challenge, motivated, one felt, by those who felt that the Oxbridge dominance had lasted long enough, saw the post go to Ray Illingworth. Ian Botham was not the only one to suggest that the appointment of Illingworth had come 20 years too late; and it was unfortunate that the Yorkshireman saw fit to make critical remarks about some of the players appearing against West Indies before he had really taken up his post. While that tour of the Caribbean was still in progress the season in England began.

13, 14 and 15 April *at Oxford*

Durham 270 (P. Bainbridge 68, C.W. Scott 64, P.W. Trimby 5 for 84) and 0 for 0 dec.
Oxford University 20 for 1 dec. and 73 (S.J.E. Brown 5 for 8)

Durham won by 177 runs

at Cambridge

Cambridge University 144
Nottinghamshire 36 for 1

Match drawn

Rain and cold greeted the players at Oxford and Cambridge. Only two balls were bowled on the second day at Fenner's, and none on the third. There was some impressive leg-spin bowling by Patrick Trimby in The Parks, but rain produced declaration and forfeiture, and Oxford fell well short of reaching a target of 251 in three hours.

16, 17 and 18 April *at Cambridge*

Cambridge University *v.* **Northamptonshire**

Match abandoned

16, 18 and 19 April *at Oxford*

Hampshire 353 for 6 dec. (V.P. Terry 112, T.C. Middleton 102) and 61 for 4
Oxford University 162 (R.R. Montgomerie 50, C.A. Connor 4 for 37)

Match drawn

While Brian Lara was breaking Sobers' Test record rain prevented play at Cambridge and cut the first day away from the match at Oxford where Middleton and Terry put on 189 for Hampshire's first wicket. Paul Terry, in his benefit year, scored the season's first century.

David Constant muffled against the weather as the England season opens, Oxford University v. Durham, 14 April. (David Munden/ Sports-Line)

20, 21 and 22 April *at Cambridge*

Kent 446 for 5 dec. (N.R. Taylor 129, D.R. Fulton 109, T.R. Ward 86) and 100 for 5 dec. (C.M. Pitcher 4 for 37)
Cambridge University 84 (M.M. Patel 5 for 33) and 122 (M.M. Patel 5 for 44, N.J. Llong 5 for 63)

Kent won by 340 runs

at Oxford

Glamorgan 355 for 5 dec. (S.P. James 150, P.A. Cottey 109, D.L. Hemp 51) and 211 for 4 dec. (O.D. Gibson 61, D.L. Hemp 50 not out)
Oxford University 257 for 9 dec. (R.R. Montgomerie 80, G.I. Macmillan 50) and 110 for 2

Match drawn

David Fulton hit a maiden first-class century and shared a first-wicket partnership of 144 with Trevor Ward at Fenner's. Nigel Llong had a career-best bowling performance with his off-breaks, but it was Min Patel, slow left-arm, who took the eye with match figures of 10 for 77.

James and Cottey scored 197 for Glamorgan's first wicket at Oxford, and Montgomerie and Macmillan responded with 126 for the university's first wicket.

21, 22, 23 and **24** April *at Lord's*

England 'A' 357 (D.J. Bicknell 80, K.J. Shine 4 for 79)
and 48 for 0
Middlesex 156 (M.W. Gatting 58, M.C. Ilott 4 for 31)
and 394 for 4 dec. (M.W. Gatting 224 not out,
J.D. Carr 102)

Match drawn

23 April *at Oxford*

Combined Universities *v.* **Gloucestershire**

Match abandoned

24 April *at Oxford (Christchurch)*

Kent 231
Combined Universities 209 for 6 (G.I. Macmillan 71)

Kent won by 22 runs

England 'A', who had done so well in every respect in
South Africa and who had the benefit of the addition of
Darren Bicknell to their side, performed well for the first
two days against the county champions, but found that
lightning did not strike twice when Gatting and Carr
added 288 for the county's fourth wicket after they had
been asked to follow-on.

*The season's first centurion, Paul Terry 112, Hampshire v. Oxford
University, 16 April. (David Munden/Sports-Line)*

BENSON AND HEDGES CUP

ROUND ONE

26 April *at Oxford*

Combined Universities 191 for 3 (R.R. Montgomerie 52)
Lancashire 193 for 3 (J.P. Crawley 73)

Lancashire won by 7 wickets

(Gold Award – J.P. Crawley)

at Leicester

Ireland 160 for 9 (S.J.S. Warke 53)
Leicestershire 164 for 1 (N.E. Briers 70 not out,
P.V. Simmons 64)

Leicestershire won by 9 wickets

(Gold Award – P.V. Simmons)

at Lord's

Northamptonshire 232 for 7 (M.B. Loye 71 not out)
Middlesex 236 for 4 (M.R. Ramprakash 119 not out)

Middlesex won by 6 wickets

(Gold Award – M.R. Ramprakash)

at Trent Bridge

Minor Counties 191 for 4 (I. Cockbain 54 not out)

Nottinghamshire 195 for 7

Nottinghamshire won by 3 wickets

(Gold Award – I. Cockbain)

at The Oval

Surrey 288 for 3 (A.J. Stewart 167 not out, D.M. Ward
50)
Somerset 253 (M.N. Lathwell 120, M.P. Bicknell 4 for
49)

Surrey won by 35 runs

(Gold Award – A.J. Stewart)

at Hove

Scotland 157 for 7 (J.D. Love 53)
Sussex 161 for 2 (D.M. Smith 65 not out, A.P. Wells 51
not out)

Sussex won by 8 wickets

(Gold Award – D.M. Smith)

The season proper began with the first round of the
Benson and Hedges Cup. Minor Counties, Scotland,
Combined Universities and Ireland were despatched as
expected, and Phil Simmons took the Gold Award on the
occasion of his debut for Leicestershire. Two ties brought
together counties all of whom had confident aspirations
of reaching the later stages of the competition.

Northamptonshire were handicapped by the absence
of Curtly Ambrose who had failed to arrive from the
Caribbean following the end of the Test series. His

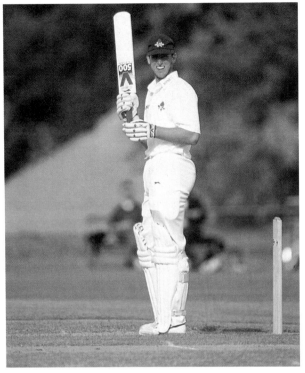

Gold Award and a bright future for Lancashire's John Crawley, 73 for the county in the first round of the Benson and Hedges Cup. (Chris Cole/Allsport)

absence certainly tilted the balance in favour of Middlesex. Northamptonshire began steadily, but they found it difficult to accelerate against the bowling of Tufnell and Emburey who, between them, conceded only 69 runs from 22 overs and captured six of the seven wickets that fell. Mal Loye, 71 off 65 balls, added 76 in nine overs with Penberthy towards the end of the innings, but Northamptonshire still looked short of a winning score.

Taylor and Penberthy held the early Middlesex batsmen in check, and when Gatting was second out at 80 nearly 29 overs had elapsed. The Middlesex hero was Mark Ramprakash who paced his innings splendidly to reach his second and higher hundred in the competition and who took his side to victory with seven balls to spare. His 119 came off 150 balls and, most importantly, he was the prime reason for Middlesex plundering the 70 runs they needed from the last 10 overs in the gathering gloom. Ambrose would have made that task harder.

Surrey took the field without an overseas cricketer for the match against Somerset. The great Waqar Younis would not be returning because of an operation for appendicitis, and his replacement, West Indian Cameron Cuffy, had yet to arrive. Surrey were also playing in the wake of a controversial AGM which had brought about a restructuring of the club and had aired many grievances. Winning the toss and batting first, Surrey soon lost Darren Bicknell, but Alec Stewart hit 18 fours and a six and reached the highest score recorded by a Surrey batsman in limited-over cricket. On the attack, he looks as

good as any player in the world. David Ward gave him fine support with 50 off 68 balls, and Somerset faced a massive target of 289. They had not been well served by some petulant bowling from Caddick and van Troost and by the strange under-use of Mushtaq Ahmed.

Stewart had made his 167 off 187 balls, and Lathwell, a noted quick scorer, responded for Somerset with 120 off 136 deliveries, but he never suggested the regality of Stewart, and when he was out his side fell apart. Surrey had bowlers, Martin Bicknell, Joey Benjamin and Mark Butcher in particular, who displayed a discipline and control that Somerset could well envy.

28, 29, 30 April and 1 May *at Chesterfield*

Durham 625 for 6 dec. (M. Saxelby 181, J.I. Longley 100 not out, J.E. Morris 90, W. Larkins 83, S. Hutton 78, P.A.J. DeFreitas 4 for 150) and 162 for 3

Derbyshire 341 (K.J. Barnett 69, M. Azharuddin 55, P.A.J. DeFreitas 52) and 442 (M. Azharuddin 205, C.J. Adams 94, S.J.E. Brown 5 for 93)

Durham won by 7 wickets

Durham 24 pts., Derbyshire 4 pts.

at Bristol

Gloucestershire 203 (A.R. Caddick 4 for 40, Mushtaq Ahmed 4 for 88) and 284 (S.G. Hinks 68, R.C. Russell 66 not out, T.H.C. Hancock 55, Mushtaq Ahmed 4 for 104)

Somerset 229 (N.A. Folland 79 not out, C.A. Walsh 5 for 71) and 175 (C.A. Walsh 6 for 72)

Gloucestershire won by 83 runs

Gloucestershire 20 pts., Somerset 5 pts

at Southampton

Hampshire 321 (V.P. Terry 130, M.C.J. Nicholas 68, M.C. Ilott 4 for 74) and 191 (S.D. Udal 59, P.M. Such 7 for 66)

Essex 243 (N. Shahid 91) and 270 for 2 (G.A. Gooch 123 not out, N. Hussain 115 not out)

Essex won by 8 wickets

Essex 21 pts., Hampshire 7 pts.

at Leicester

Leicestershire 482 (P.V. Simmons 261, P.A. Nixon 106, J.J. Whitaker 55) and 9 for 0

Northamptonshire 224 (A.J. Lamb 70) and 266 (A. Fordham 102)

Leicestershire won by 10 wickets

Leicestershire 24 pts., Northamptonshire 3 pts.

at The Oval

Worcestershire 205 (S.J. Rhodes 59 not out, M.A. Butcher 4 for 31, M.P. Bicknell 4 for 41) and

343 (W.P.C. Weston 62, T.M. Moody 60,
M.A. Butcher 4 for 67

Surrey 470 (G.P. Thorpe 190, A.J. Hollioake 123,
J.E. Brinkley 6 for 98) and 79 for 1

Surrey won by 9 wickets

Surrey 24 pts., Worcestershire 5 pts.

at Edgbaston

Glamorgan 365 (D.L. Hemp 127, O.D. Gibson 61,
T.A. Munton 4 for 57) and 189 (S.P. James 61,
G.C. Small 5 for 46)

Warwickshire 657 for 7 dec. (R.G. Twose 277 not out,
B.C. Lara 147)

Warwickshire won by an innings and 103 runs

Warwickshire 22 pts., Glamorgan 4 pts.

28, 29 and 30 April *at Oxford*

Nottinghamshire 252 for 8 dec. (J.C. Adams 117,
P. Johnson 69, C.J. Hollins 4 for 64) and 278 for 6
dec. (P. Johnson 107, J.C. Adams 52 not out)

Oxford University 238 for 3 dec. (S.C. Ecclestone 80 not
out, R.R. Montgomerie 53) and 103 for 2

Match drawn

28, 29, 30 April and 2 May *at Old Trafford*

Lancashire 354 (N.J. Speak 105, J.E.R. Gallian 57,
D. Gough 5 for 75) and 225 for 4 dec. (J.P. Crawley
77, J.E.R. Gallian 71)

Yorkshire 275 and 305 for 3 (M.D. Moxon 161 not out)

Yorkshire won by 7 wickets

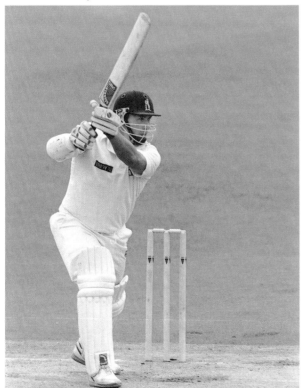

*Exciting debuts in county cricket for two West Indian Test players –
Phil Simmons, a record 261 for Leicestershire against
Northamptonshire, and Brian Lara, 147 for Warwickshire against
Glamorgan with more to follow. (David Munden/Sports-Line)*

29 April *at Southgate*

New Zealanders 288 for 4 (B.A. Pocock 109, M.D. Crowe
56)

England Amateur XI 149

New Zealanders won by 139 runs

30 April and 1, 2 May *at Cambridge*

Middlesex 257 for 7 dec. (K.R. Brown 61, J.D. Carr 55
not out, R.L. Johnson 50 not out) and 163 for 2 dec.
(J.E. Emburey 78 not out)

Cambridge University 121 (P.N. Weekes 5 for 12) and
221 (J.P. Carroll 90, J.E. Emburey 4 for 59,
P.N. Weekes 4 for 83)

Middlesex won by 78 runs

1 May *at Arundel*

New Zealanders 229 for 5 (S.P. Fleming 86 not out)

Lavinia, Duchess of Norfolk's XI 160 (G.R. Larsen 4 for
17)

New Zealanders won by 69 runs

at Old Trafford

Yorkshire 169 for 7 (C. White 50 not out)

Lancashire 130 (C. White 5 for 12)

Yorkshire won by 39 runs

*Overshadowed by Lara, but not outscored – Roger Twose began an
outstanding season for Warwickshire with 277 not out against
Glamorgan. (David Munden/Sports-Line)*

2 May *at The Oval*

New Zealanders 259 for 8 (S.A. Thomson 90 not out)

Surrey 261 for 4 (D.M. Ward 88 not out, A.J. Hollioake 86 not out)

Surrey won by 6 wickets

The Britannic Assurance County Championship began in rousing fashion. Each of the six matches produced a result, and there were some mighty and memorable performances.

At Chesterfield, Durham made their highest score in first-class cricket. They paraded their now traditional array of close-season imports – Saxelby, Morris and Longley – and all three came good. The left-handed Mark Saxelby from Nottinghamshire opened the innings with Larkins, and the pair put on 169. John Morris, playing against his old county, then shared a second-wicket stand of 190 with Saxelby whose 181 off 238 balls with 26 fours and 2 sixes was not only his maiden first-class hundred, but the highest score ever made for Durham.

The second day belonged to Jonathan Longley, formerly of Kent, who hit his first championship hundred, needing only 124 balls to reach the mark. Derbyshire's own debutant, Phillip DeFreitas, now with his third county, claimed four wickets, but on the third morning Derbyshire had to follow-on. Chris Adams responded with a typically blazing 94, but it was Azharuddin, playing his first game for the county for three years, who came close to transforming the game. He hit a hundred before lunch on the last morning and moved to 200 off 188 balls by hitting his sixth six shortly after lunch. He also hit 21 exquisite fours, and his 205 was made out of 256 in four hours, an astonishing performance which deserved better reward than defeat by seven wickets.

Somerset gave a first-class debut to leg-spinner Vincent Clarke and took a first-innings lead over Gloucestershire. They seemed set for victory when the home side were reduced to 149 for 5 in their second innings, but Russell and Hancock added 93. Walsh, an inspiring captain, took 4 for 1 in 18 balls as Somerset plummeted to 17 for 4. There was no effective recovery, and Gloucestershire won early on the last day.

Hampshire did not have Gower who had moved to the press and commentary boxes, but they welcomed a new opening attack in Winston Benjamin and Norman Cowans. Essex included pace bowler Michael Kasprowicz of Queensland and Ronnie Irani from Lancashire. Irani really owed his place to the fact that Stephenson had suffered a damaged hand in practice against Kasprowicz. Gooch must have doubted the wisdom of his decision to ask Hampshire to bat first when Paul Terry went doggedly to his second century of the season, his first against Essex in his 17-year career, and the home side ended the day on 282 for 7. Ilott, continuing his fine form of South Africa, finished with four wickets, but Essex looked certain to have to follow-on when they slumped to 97 for 6. Shahid found an able partner in the big-hitting Kasprowicz, and the pair added 64. Ilott also made a useful contribution, but Hampshire led by 78. Peter Such, who had bowled well for England 'A' at Lord's, was primarily

Worcestershire pace-bowler James Brinkley took six wickets on his first-class debut against Surrey at The Oval, but finished on the losing side. (Tom Morris)

responsible for Hampshire's second-innings demise, but Essex still faced a target of 270. They lost Lewis and Garnham for 71 before Gooch and Hussain took total command and steered them to victory with more than half a day to spare.

Leicestershire's new acquisition, West Indian opener Phil Simmons, established a county record by hitting 261 on his debut. His innings included 34 fours and 4 sixes and occupied 450 minutes. He and wicket-keeper Nixon added 253 for the sixth wicket. Northamptonshire, still without Ambrose, were beaten in three days. Simmons became the first batsman to score a double century on his championship debut.

At The Oval, James Brinkley, fast medium pace, took 6 for 98 on the occasion of his first-class debut, but Worcestershire were well beaten by the home side. Brinkley reduced Surrey to 83 for 5, but Graham Thorpe was joined by Adam Hollioake in a partnership of 220. Martin Bicknell and Mark Butcher, with a career-best bowling performance, had shot out Worcestershire on the opening day, and although the visitors showed sterner character in their second innings, Surrey were not to be denied.

Warwickshire had contracted Manoj Prabhakar as their overseas player for 1994, but when the Indian all-rounder was reported to have fitness problems the county moved quickly to sign Brian Lara. The West Indian left-hander promptly broke Sobers' Test record by scoring 375 in Antigua, and the applications for membership at Edgbaston multiplied. He did not bat on the first day against Glamorgan, for the visitors had won the toss, and David

Hemp, a less well-known left-hander, hit an admirable maiden first-class hundred. The Friday saw the crowd witness what they had anticipated. Lara hit 2 sixes and 23 fours in his 147 which came off 160 balls. His runs came in a second-wicket stand of 215 with Roger Twose. The quality of Lara's stroke-play was thrilling and enchanting; and it must be remembered that this was his first innings since his 375. Twose went on to play the longest innings recorded for Warwickshire, 606 minutes, and the second highest in the county's history. He hit 34 fours and a six and led Warwickshire to a score equal to the record they established against Hampshire in 1899. Not surprisingly, Glamorgan wilted when they batted a second time.

Nottinghamshire had sacked Mike Hendrick in the winter months and replaced him as manager/coach by Alan Ormrod. They had also signed Jimmy Adams as overseas player in place of Chris Cairns, and the versatile West Indian responded with a hundred on his debut. Oxford University's Hollins, son of the former Chelsea and Arsenal footballer, took four wickets.

Yorkshire won the friendly matches against Lancashire when Moxon hit 161 off 216 balls in the first-class match and Craig White produced an impressive all-round performance in the one-day encounter. The New Zealanders arrived quietly but not too impressively, for against Surrey their bowling looked very ragged.

4, 5 and 6 May *at Worcester*

Worcestershire 343 for 7 dec. (S.J. Rhodes 100 not out, G.R. Haynes 82, G.A. Hick 67) and 103 for 6 dec. (G.R. Larsen 4 for 13)

New Zealanders 194 for 7 dec. (K.R. Rutherford 84) and 153 for 4 (K.R. Rutherford 52)

Match drawn

5, 6, 7 and 9 May *at Stockton-on-Tees*

Essex 423 (P.J. Prichard 108, N. Hussain 101, R.C. Irani 58 not out, J. Wood 6 for 110) and 36 for 0

Durham 175 (M. Saxelby 63, M.S. Kasprowicz 6 for 61) and 281 (M. Saxelby 131, J.E. Morris 64, P.M. Such 4 for 61)

Essex won by 10 wickets

Essex 24 pts., Durham 2 pts.

at Bristol

Gloucestershire 319 for 8 dec. (B.C. Broad 128, R.C. Russell 79, P.W. Jarvis 4 for 78) and 159 for 9 dec.

Sussex 178 (A.P. Wells 51, C.A. Walsh 5 for 66) and 85 for 2

Match drawn

Gloucestershire 6 pts., Sussex 2 pts.

at Southampton

Hampshire 271 (S.D. Udal 83, R.A. Smith 58, P.A.J. DeFreitas 5 for 59) and 119 for 1 dec.

Derbyshire 76 for 2 dec. and 199 for 5 (A.S. Rollins 81, S.D. Udal 4 for 83)

Match drawn

Derbyshire 4 pts., Hampshire 2 pts.

at Canterbury

Nottinghamshire 185 (P. Johnson 70, A.P. Igglesden 5 for 38) and 178 (R.T. Robinson 52, M.J. McCague 6 for 50)

Kent 125 and 229 (C.L. Hooper 66, C.C. Lewis 5 for 55)

Nottinghamshire won by 9 runs

Nottinghamshire 20 pts., Kent 4 pts.

at Old Trafford

Lancashire 129 (Wasim Akram 50, J.E. Benjamin 5 for 48) and 342 (J.E.R. Gallian 171, C.E. Cuffy 4 for 70)

Surrey 301 for 9 dec. (A.J. Stewart 126, A.D. Brown 65, D.M. Ward 51) and 171 for 0 (A.J. Stewart 88 not out, D.J. Bicknell 67 not out)

Surrey won by 10 wickets

Surrey 23 pts., Lancashire 4 pts.

Jason Gallian hit 171 for Lancashire on his debut in the county championship. (Paul Sturgess/Sports-Line)

Adrian Pierson – a career-best 8 for 42 for Leicestershire against Warwickshire, 5 May. (David Munden/Sports-Line)

at Lord's

Yorkshire 297 for 8 dec. (M.D. Moxon 72, C. White 62, A.P. Grayson 61) and 0 for 0 dec.

Middlesex 0 for 0 dec. and 224 for 7 (M.W. Gatting 65)

Match drawn

Middlesex 3 pts., Yorkshire 2 pts.

at Northampton

Northamptonshire 338 for 4 dec. (A. Fordham 129, N.A. Felton 62, R.J. Bailey 58) and 0 for 0 dec.

Glamorgan 38 for 0 dec. and 89 for 7 (C.E.L. Ambrose 4 for 53)

Match drawn

Northamptonshire 3 pts., Glamorgan 1 pt.

at Edgbaston

Leicestershire 403 (N.E. Briers 154, B.F. Smith 78) and 135 for 5 dec.

Warwickshire 254 (B.C. Lara 106, R.G. Twose 51, A.R.K. Pierson 8 for 42) and 206 for 7 (B.C. Lara 120 not out, D.J. Millns 4 for 54)

Match drawn

Leicestershire 8 pts., Warwickshire 5 pts.

Gavin Larsen took four wickets in 11 balls for the New Zealanders in their match at Worcester, but that was in the second innings, and the tourists, generally, did not acquit themselves well. Davis conceded 113 runs off 14 overs on the truncated first day, and only the fielding was of an acceptable quality. Rhodes and Haynes batted into the second day to add 172 for Worcestershire's fifth wicket, but the match always seemed to be heading for a draw.

Rain restricted the first day at Stockton-on-Tees to 52 overs. Prichard and Hussain, who hit his second century of the season, shared a third-wicket stand of 185, and Irani hit an unbeaten maiden first-class fifty. Kasprowicz produced a fine spell of bowling, and Durham were forced to follow-on. Saxelby claimed his second century for his new county, but the last six wickets went down for 67 runs, and Essex asserted early championship rights with their second win in as many matches.

Play was lost on the first two days at Bristol where Chris Broad hit his 50th first-class century and, having retired with a migraine early in his innings, returned to share a stand of 185 with Russell for the sixth wicket. Walsh bowled Gloucestershire to a first-innings lead of 141, but Sussex reduced them to 94 for 8 in their second innings before Smith and Russell added 65. In the circumstances, Walsh's decision to ask Sussex to score 301 in 51 overs was unrealistic, and the match was drawn. Moores, the Sussex wicket-keeper, equalled the county record with eight catches in the match.

With no play possible on the first and third days, the match at Southampton was destined to be drawn, but it was not without incident. DeFreitas performed the hat-trick when he had Middleton caught in the gully, bowled Nicholas and had Aymes leg before; Shaun Udal hit the highest score of his career; and Kim Barnett tore a knee cartilage while fielding.

Only 39 overs were possible on the first day at Canterbury, but Nottinghamshire lost seven wickets for 167 runs. The relaid wicket took its toll on the second day when 23 wickets fell, and extras were abundant in all four innings. In spite of Hooper donning a helmet and battling bravely, Nottinghamshire beat Kent in three days.

Surrey made the most of a restricted first day at Old Trafford by capturing nine Lancashire wickets for 129 runs. Wasim Akram hit 50 off 56 balls, but it was Cuffy, playing his first match for Surrey, and Joey Benjamin who took the honours. On the second day, the Surrey batsmen made a mockery of Lancashire's efforts. Runs came at nearly five an over, with Alec Stewart reaching his century off 114 balls, and Ward his 50 off 49 balls. Alistair Brown compounded the home side's misery as he moved to 50 off 39 deliveries. In all, he hit Watkinson for 5 sixes. Jason Gallian marked his championship debut with an outstanding innings of 171 off 392 balls. It was the highest innings by a Lancashire championship debutant since 1867, and it included 22 fours. It seemed that it might even save Lancashire from humiliation, but Darren Bicknell and Alec Stewart hit the 171 that Surrey needed for victory in under 46 overs.

There was no play on the third day and little on the first at Lord's, and even forfeitures could not bring a result.

The same applied at Northampton where no play was possible on the first day, and Fordham and Felton scored 142 for the home side's first wicket on the second. North-amptonshire welcomed back Ambrose, and he nearly bowled his side to a sensational victory on the last day. Needing 301 at 3.5 runs an over, Glamorgan were shattered by Ambrose and Taylor. Croft hit 35, but a storm was what saved them.

At Edgbaston, the first and third days saw only 44 balls in total. On the second, Nigel Briers hit 154. Inevitably, he was overshadowed. Brian Lara lashed 102 off 136 balls and almost alone withstood the career-best bowling performance of off-spinner Adrian Pierson who took 8 for 11 in 58 balls. Asked to make 285 in 57 overs, Warwickshire slipped to 120 for 6, but Lara hit his fourth century in consecutive first-class innings.

7, 8 and 9 May *at Taunton*

Somerset 364 for 8 dec. (R.J. Turner 104 not out, A.N. Hayhurst 84, I. Fletcher 51)

New Zealanders 182 (B.A. Pocock 61, M.D. Crowe 56, Mushtaq Ahmed 5 for 57) and 247 for 2 (M.D. Crowe 102 not out, B.A. Pocock 51 retired hurt)

Match drawn

at Cambridge

Worcestershire 324 for 3 dec. (G.R. Haynes 102 not out, T.M. Moody 64, D.B. D'Oliveira 61) and 108 for 3 dec.

Cambridge University 203 (R.D. Mann 53)

Match drawn

Plagued by injuries and inept batting form, the New Zealanders were forced to follow-on at Taunton when they lost their last nine wickets for 41 runs. Martin Crowe showed class and character with a fine second-innings century. Robert Turner, inexplicably preferred to Neil Burns as Somerset's wicket-keeper, hit the second and higher century of his career. Gavin Haynes also hit the second century of his career in the drawn match at Fenner's.

 ## AXA EQUITY & LAW LEAGUE

8 May *at Stockton-on-Tees*

Essex 158 for 7 (N. Hussain 57 not out)

Durham 159 for 5

Durham (4 pts.) won by 5 wickets

at Bristol

Sussex 233 for 6 (A.P. Wells 61, N.J. Lenham 58 not out, M.P. Speight 56)

Gloucestershire 187 (M.W. Alleyne 81)

Sussex (4 pts.) won by 46 runs

at Southampton

Hampshire 174 for 8 (R.A. Smith 64, A.E. Warner 4 for 33)

Derbyshire 178 for 3 (M. Azharrudin 71 not out)

Derbyshire (4 pts.) won by 7 wickets

at Canterbury

Kent 162 for 8 (K.P. Evans 4 for 26)

Nottinghamshire 164 for 6

Nottinghamshire (4 pts.) won by 4 wickets

at Old Trafford

Surrey 179 for 7

Lancashire 178 for 6 (G.D. Lloyd 77, N.H. Fairbrother 59 retired hurt)

Surrey (4 pts.) won by 1 run

at Lord's

Middlesex 157 for 9 (M.W. Gatting 51)

Yorkshire 158 for 4 (C. White 54 not out)

Yorkshire (4 pts.) won by 6 wickets

at Northampton

Northamptonshire 148 for 8 (A.L. Penberthy 69 not out)

Glamorgan 151 for 6 (M.P. Maynard 54)

Glamorgan (4 pts.) won by 4 wickets

at Edgbaston

Warwickshire 173 for 4 (D.A. Reeve 65 not out, Asif Din 54 not out)

Leicestershire 151 (M.A.V. Bell 5 for 19)

Warwickshire (4 pts.) won by 22 runs

Dominic Cork won the Gold Award for his astonishing innings for Derbyshire in their victory over Lancashire at Derby, 10 May. (Gary M. Price/Allsport)

Glamorgan began their attempt to retain the Sunday League title with victory at Northampton, Ottis Gibson ending the match with six off Ambrose. Azharuddin hit 5 sixes, and Karl Krikken took five catches in Derbyshire's victory at Southampton. Kevin Evans of Nottinghamshire and Michael Bell of Warwickshire, five wickets in 18 balls, had their best Sunday bowling performances, and Lancashire suffered four run outs and just failed to score 13 off the last over against Surrey.

BENSON AND HEDGES CUP

ROUND TWO

10 May *at Canterbury*

Gloucestershire 189 for 9 (A.J. Wright 55)

Kent 193 for 6

Kent won by 4 wickets

(Gold Award – M.V. Fleming)

at Chelmsford

Leicestershire 241 for 9 (P.V. Simmons 57, J.J. Whitaker 53)

Essex 246 for 2 (G.A. Gooch 130 not out, N. Hussain 59)

Essex won by 8 wickets

(Gold Award – G.A. Gooch)

at Derby

Lancashire 280 for 5 (M.A. Atherton 100, J.P. Crawley 73)

Derbyshire 282 for 6 (A.S. Rollins 70, D.G. Cork 63 not out)

Derbyshire won by 4 wickets

(Gold Award – D.G. Cork)

at Lord's

Middlesex 150

Warwickshire 151 for 7

Warwickshire won by 3 wickets

(Gold Award – T.A. Munton)

at The Oval

Glamorgan 236 for 6 (H. Morris 55)

Surrey 240 for 7 (D.J. Bicknell 90, G.P. Thorpe 51)

Surrey won by 3 wickets

(Gold Award – D.J. Bicknell)

at Southampton

Yorkshire 178 for 6

Hampshire 182 for 2 (T.C. Middleton 63 not out, R.A. Smith 58)

Hampshire won by 8 wickets

(Gold Award – T.C. Middleton)

at Stockton-on-Tees

Durham 190 for 8

Worcestershire 191 for 2 (G.A. Hick 104 not out, T.M. Moody 65 not out)

Worcestershire won by 8 wickets

(Gold Award – P.J. Newport)

at Trent Bridge

Sussex 239 for 9 (A.P. Wells 51, M.A. Crawley 4 for 43)

Nottinghamshire 241 for 3 (R.T. Robinson 91 not out, J.C. Adams 86)

Nottinghamshire won by 7 wickets

(Gold Award – R.T. Robinson)

A spate of wides and no-balls provided 27 runs for Gloucestershire against Kent after Walsh had chosen to bat on a sporty pitch and seen his side reduced to 16 for 3. Wright and Russell led a revival, but it was never enough to present Kent with a daunting target.

Gooch dropped Simmons at slip off the fourth ball of the match at Chelmsford, and the West Indian reached 50 off 88 balls. Topley dismissed Simmons after Leicestershire had reached 92 in 26 overs, and when Kasprowicz sent back Briers and Wells in the space of six balls Essex were gaining the ascendancy. Facing a target of 242, lower than expected, Essex lost Prichard at 81, but Hussain played splendidly for 59 off 64 balls. Gooch, uncertain at first, was soon driving freely and he finished the match by hitting Parsons out of the ground. His 130 came off 153 balls. It was his 12th hundred in the competition and it took him to his 21st Gold Award.

At Derby, there was a replay of the 1993 final. With England skipper Michael Atherton making his first Benson and Hedges century and sharing a second-wicket stand of 131 in 26 overs with the promising John Crawley, Lancashire, without Fairbrother and Wasim Akram, reached a challenging 280 in their 55 overs. Derbyshire, lacking Kim Barnett, lost Bowler at 12, but Adams and Rollins added 104 in 26 overs. Thereafter, Derbyshire lost their way and, at 192 for 6, they needed 89 off eight overs. Colin Wells, recently of Sussex, and Dominic Cork reduced the target to 59 off five, and 29 off two. With Austin conceding 18 in the 54th over and Cork failing to score from the first ball of the last over, 11 were needed from Watkinson's last five balls. Two twos and a pull to the square-leg boundary meant that three were needed from two deliveries. Cork thrust forward and swung the ball high over mid-wicket for six, and Derbyshire were home. Astonishingly, Cork had hit 63 off 34 balls while Wells had been no slouch with 47 off 54 deliveries.

The game at Lord's disappointed. Middlesex made a meagre 150, and Warwickshire won with 16 balls to spare. Lara hit 34 off 47 balls, and there was a mild collapse when he fell to Johnson, but from the time that Munton had caused Middlesex early embarrassment there had only looked to be one winner.

Ottis Gibson hit 37 off 33 balls as Glamorgan's innings against Surrey had begun to dwindle, but the home side seemed set for victory when Darren Bicknell and Graham Thorpe joined in a second-wicket stand of 104. Alistair Brown gave one of his dynamic displays, 38 off 25 balls, and looked to have settled the issue until Gibson took two wickets in the 51st over. Smith settled the nerves, and Surrey won with two balls to spare, leaving Glamorgan to reflect on errors in the field.

Hampshire and Worcestershire won with considerable ease as did Nottinghamshire. Mark Crawley's medium pace earned him his best figures in the competition, and Robinson and Adams added 163 after Sussex, who missed catches, had taken two wickets for 13 runs.

12, 13 and 14 May at Lord's

New Zealanders 249 for 6 dec. (S.P. Fleming 118 not out) and 101 for 9

Middlesex 156 for 4 dec. (J.D. Carr 57 not out)

Match drawn

12, 13, 14 and 16 May at Chelmsford

Kent 191 (T.R. Ward 67, R.C. Irani 4 for 27) and 399 (C.L. Hooper 160, T.R. Ward 50, P.M. Such 5 for 133, J.H. Childs 4 for 127)

Essex 541 for 5 dec. (G.A. Gooch 236, P.J. Prichard 109) and 50 for 6

Essex won by 4 wickets

Essex 24 pts., Kent 1 pt.

at Cardiff

Yorkshire 339 (R.J. Blakey 87, R.B. Richardson 59, D. Gough 54, S.L. Watkin 4 for 64, O.D. Gibson 4 for 86) and 170 for 3 dec. (M.D. Moxon 88 not out)

Glamorgan 208 (R.D. Stemp 4 for 48) and 26 for 0

Match drawn

Yorkshire 7 pts., Glamorgan 5 pts.

at Leicester

Somerset 288 (A.N. Hayhurst 79 not out, D.J. Millns 4 for 62) and 230 (N.A. Folland 91, M.N. Lathwell 86, D.J. Millns 5 for 65)

Leicestershire 409 (B.F. Smith 95, P.N. Hepworth 60, A.R. Caddick 5 for 92) and 110 for 5

Leicestershire won by 5 wickets

Leicestershire 23 pts., Somerset 5 pts.

at Trent Bridge

Durham 242 (W. Larkins 91) and 155 (J.A. Afford 5 for 48)

Nottinghamshire 285 (P. Johnson 101, J.C. Adams 60,

Chris Adams of Derbyshire hit centuries against Surrey on successive days and twice finished on the losing side. (Alan Cozzi)

P.R. Pollard 50, D.A. Graveney 6 for 80) and 113 for 2

Nottinghamshire won by 8 wickets

Nottinghamshire 22 pts., Durham 5 pts.

at The Oval

Derbyshire 208 (J.E. Benjamin 4 for 55, M.P. Bicknell 4 for 56) and 224 (C.J. Adams 109 not out)

Surrey 570 for 6 dec. (D.M. Ward 294 not out, G.P. Thorpe 114, A.D. Brown 92)

Surrey won by an innings and 138 runs

Surrey 24 pts., Derbyshire 3 pts.

at Hove

Hampshire 267 (R.A. Smith 124, W.K.M. Benjamin 51, F.D. Stephenson 5 for 41, I.D.K. Salisbury 4 for 90) and 167 (F.D. Stephenson 6 for 55)

Sussex 279 (M.P. Speight 126) and 156 for 8

Sussex won by 2 wickets

Sussex 22 pts., Hampshire 6 pts.

at Worcester

Gloucestershire 390 (A.J. Wright 82, B.C. Broad 76, T.H.C. Hancock 58, N.V. Radford 4 for 70) and 203

for 7 dec. (S.G. Hinks 74, R.K. Illingworth 4 for 51)
Worcestershire 329 for 9 dec. (G.A. Hick 150) and 180 for 9

Match drawn

Gloucestershire 7 pts., Worcestershire 5 pts.

14, 15 and 16 May *at Cambridge*

Lancashire 293 for 2 dec. (N.J. Speak 102 not out, M.A. Atherton 86, J.P. Crawley 81) and 201 for 6 dec. (G. Yates 53 not out)
Cambridge University 227 for 6 dec. (J. Ratledge 79, R.Q. Cake 77) and 118 for 2 (R.Q. Cake 70 not out)

Match drawn

14, 16 and 17 May *at Oxford*

Warwickshire 303 for 5 dec. (D.P. Ostler 149, P.A. Smith 50 not out)
Oxford University 47 for 2

Match drawn

There was encouragement for the New Zealanders when Fleming, who got off the mark with a six off Shine, hit a century against Middlesex at Lord's. There was even some success for the New Zealand bowlers but, with the Texaco Trophy and Test series looming, the form of the tourists was far from satisfactory.

At Chelmsford, Essex made it three wins in three matches. On the opening day, they bowled out Kent with Irani claiming four wickets, the best performance of his budding career. On the second, Gooch and Prichard took their opening stand to 316, a county record. Gooch hit 26 fours and 3 sixes in his 332-ball innings of 236 while Prichard faced 224 balls for his 109. Only 40 overs were possible on the third day, but the last day saw some sensational cricket with, it seemed, every delivery either being hit to the boundary or claiming a wicket. Carl Hooper played a brilliant innings, reaching a century before lunch off 79 balls and finishing with 160 off 149 balls. In an exhilarating display, he added 123 in 24 overs for the third wicket with Trevor Ward and, suitably, fell to a brilliant running catch by Hussain. The spinners, Childs and Such, finally took their revenge, and the last five Kent wickets fell for 30. Needing 50 to win in the final session, Essex got into a terrible mess against Hooper and Patel who claimed three wickets each before the home county finally claimed victory.

Only 14 overs were possible on the last day at Cardiff where, in their first innings, Glamorgan collapsed, eight wickets falling for 58, before Lefebvre, Metson and Watkin realised 74 from the last two wickets.

Hayhurst's patience could not save Somerset at Leicester where David Millns, once regarded as an England fast bowler and now seemingly forgotten, had match figures of 9 for 127. He was mainly responsible for Somerset losing their last five second-innings wickets for 26 runs. Van Troost was absent, visiting his sick mother in Holland.

Nottinghamshire beat Durham in three days on a Trent Bridge pitch which encouraged the spinners. Thanks to a fourth-wicket stand of 125 between Adams and Johnson, Nottinghamshire took control, but they lost their last five wickets for 18 runs as David Graveney returned his best bowling figures for Durham. With Afford finding form and Durham sliding from 102 for 3 to 155 all out, the home county won with ease on the Saturday evening.

Rain restricted play on the first day at The Oval where Derbyshire, hit by their annual crop of injuries, floundered against the pace of Benjamin and Martin Bicknell. Harris, a debutant, and Warner sent back the Surrey openers with only 10 scored, but Thorpe and Ward added 301, and Brown then joined Ward in a stand of 173 in 37 overs for the sixth wicket. David Ward is an uplifting sight when he is in full flow. No man hits the ball farther, harder or more often, and when rain ended play on the Saturday he had hit 32 fours and 5 sixes in a faultless innings of 294. Stewart had no option but to declare on the Monday, and Surrey moved to their win and the top of the table in spite of Chris Adams' belligerent century at number seven. It was his second century against Surrey in successive days, and both times he finished on the losing side. He reached his hundred off 95 balls.

Sussex turned the drift of the game against Hampshire on the Friday afternoon. Facing a total of 267, they were 73 for 6, but Speight hit 107 between lunch and tea as 172 runs were scored in the session. Speight faced 147 balls and hit 5 sixes and 16 fours. He had able support from Salisbury, and Sussex took a slender lead. Stephenson and Giddins wrecked Hampshire's second innings, but Sussex, needing 156 to win, struggled, losing three wickets for one at one time before Moores, 47, and later Jarvis and Hemmings steered them home.

There was an exciting finish at Worcester where play was limited to 64 overs on the first day. Some solid batting down the order – Wright and Hancock added 120 for the sixth wicket, Smith and Russell 64 for the ninth – took Gloucestershire to a good score which Worcestershire did well to match. They were indebted to Hick, who hit his 73rd first-class hundred. Eventually, they were set a target of 265 in 54 overs. They never looked like reaching the target, and Ball had Radford caught off the penultimate ball of the match, but Brinkley survived the last delivery to save the game for Worcestershire.

Lancashire gave first-class debuts to Derbyshire and Fielding in the rain-affected match at Cambridge. The match at Oxford was also ruined by rain, and there was no play at all on the last day.

 AXA EQUITY & LAW LEAGUE

15 May *at Chelmsford*
Essex 122
Kent 123 for 2
Kent (4 pts.) won by 8 wickets

at Cardiff

Glamorgan 137 (S.P. James 51, D. Gough 4 for 20, A.P. Grayson 4 for 25)

Yorkshire 139 for 1 (D. Byas 71, M.D. Moxon 55 not out)

Yorkshire (4 pts.) won by 9 wickets

at Leicester

Somerset 168 for 7

Leicestershire 170 for 2 (P.V. Simmons 72)

Leicestershire (4 pts.) won by 8 wickets

at Trent Bridge

Nottinghamshire *v.* **Durham**

Match abandoned

Nottinghamshire 2 pts., Durham 2 pts.

at The Oval

Derbyshire 247 for 3 (C.J. Adams 119 not out, P.D. Bowler 67)

Surrey 253 for 4 (A.J. Stewart 92, G.P. Thorpe 60)

Surrey (4 pts.) won by 6 wickets

at Hove

Sussex 161 for 9 (K. Greenfield 61)

Hampshire 150 for 1 (R.A. Smith 82 not out, V.P. Terry 52 not out)

Hampshire (4 pts.) won on faster scoring rate

at Worcester

Gloucestershire 135 for 7

Worcestershire 141 for 0 (T.M. Moody 78 not out)

Worcestershire (4 pts.) won by 10 wickets

Darren Gough celebrated his selection for the England Texaco squad by combining with Grayson to inflict defeat upon Glamorgan who lost their last eight wickets for 42 runs. Chris Adams' 86-ball innings of 119 not out failed to bring success to Derbyshire against Surrey who awarded Brown his county cap. Thorpe and Stewart added 134 in 18 overs for Surrey's second wicket. Worcestershire's Moody and Curtis hit 141 in 23.2 overs to beat Gloucestershire.

15 May *at Northampton*

Northamptonshire 188 for 5

New Zealanders 192 for 2 (B.A. Young 90, A.C. Parore 60 not out)

New Zealanders won by 8 wickets

17 May *at Leicester*

Leicestershire 169

New Zealanders 170 for 3

New Zealanders won by 7 wickets

Young and Parore hit 136 in 33 overs at Northampton, and Fleming ended the match at Leicester with consecutive sixes off Pierson. The tourists seemed in good heart for the Texaco Trophy.

18, 19 and 20 May *at Oxford*

Leicestershire 303 for 7 dec. (B.F. Smith 75) and 165 for 2 dec. (V.J. Wells 87 not out, N.E. Briers 51 not out)

Oxford University 139 (C.J. Hollins 68, D.J. Millns 6 for 44) and 229 for 4 (R.R. Montgomerie 101 not out, G.I. Macmillan 64)

Match drawn

Leicestershire included B.C. Fourie, the South African, in their side and gave a first-class debut to left-arm medium pace bowler Sheriyar. Oxford, who looked the better of the two university sides at this early stage of the season, were 76 for 9 before Hollins and Maclay added 63. Montgomerie and Macmillan began their second innings with a stand of 118.

 TEXACO TROPHY
ENGLAND *v.* NEW ZEALAND

The new Illingworth regime recalled Dermot Reeve to one-day international service, preferred Rhodes to Russell and gave international debuts to the Hampshire off-spinner Shaun Udal and the Yorkshire pace bowler Darren Gough. Gough had done well on the 'A' tour of South

Gooch is bowled by Thomson. (Patrick Eagar)

Chris Pringle wrecks Hick's stumps with an inswinging yorker.
Pringle took five wickets in the match. (David Munden/Sports-Line)

Africa, although nowhere near as well as Ilott, while, if one had spoken to Illingworth in the period when he was a commentator, one had the impression that Udal was the only off-spinner of whom he was aware. In the event, neither Udal nor Gough let the new chairman down.

New Zealand, who won the toss and asked England to bat, had infinite problems. Doull had returned home injured, Greatbatch was out of form, Crowe was plagued by illness and injury, and the problems were to mount as the game progressed. The weather was unkind, the pitch was not conducive to stroke-play and the game was to fade into insignificance.

Alec Stewart began aggressively, hitting 24 off 30 balls, but he casually pulled Pringle into the hands of long-leg after 38 minutes at the crease in which he had monopolised the scoring. The pitch was no help to Smith who stuttered and left. Gooch, recalled to the colours, was rapturously received. He responded by pushing the score along as rapidly as he could before being bowled by a ball from off-spinner Thomson which turned massively. He had already been dropped by Parore off Hart, and the New Zealand wicket-keeper had an untidy day behind the stumps.

The substance of the England innings was provided by Mike Atherton who batted most sensibly, never attempting extravagance on this pitch, but consistently working the ball away through the leg side. He was run out by Crowe's direct throw from backward point, and Chris

TEXACO TROPHY – ENGLAND v. NEW ZEALAND
19 May 1994 at Edgbaston, Birmingham

ENGLAND			NEW ZEALAND		
M.A. Atherton (capt)	run out	81	B.A. Young	b Gough	65
A.J. Stewart	c Nash, b Pringle	24	M.D. Crowe	c Stewart, b Gough	0
R.A. Smith	c Parore, b Thomson	15	*A.C. Parore	b Udal	42
G.A. Gooch	b Thomson	23	K.R. Rutherford (capt)	lbw, b Udal	0
G.A. Hick	b Pringle	18	S.P. Fleming	c and b Hick	17
D.A. Reeve	c Fleming, b Pringle	16	S.A. Thomson	c Lewis, b Hick	7
*S.J. Rhodes	c Thomson, b Pringle	12	G.R. Larsen	c and b Lewis	13
C.C. Lewis	b Pringle	19	D.J. Nash	b Lewis	0
S.D. Udal	not out	3	M.N. Hart	c Stewart, b Lewis	13
D. Gough			C. Pringle	c Hick, b Fraser	3
A.R.C. Fraser			D.K. Morrison	not out	17
Extras	b 1, lb 5, w 7	13	Extras	lb 4, w 1	5
		—			—
(55 overs)	(for 8 wickets)	224	(52.5 overs)		182

	O	M	R	W		O	M	R	W
Morrison	6	–	31	–	Fraser	10	–	37	1
Pringle	11	1	45	5	Gough	11	1	36	2
Nash	6	1	20	–	Udal	11	–	39	2
Larsen	10	1	43	–	Reeve	4	–	15	–
Hart	11	–	45	–	Lewis	9.5	2	20	3
Thomson	11	–	34	2	Hick	7	–	31	2

FALL OF WICKETS
1–33, 2–84, 3–140, 4–161, 5–180, 6–199, 7–199, 8–224

FALL OF WICKETS
1–2, 2–78, 3–81, 4–110, 5–134, 6–136, 7–136, 8–149, 9–152

Umpires: R. Palmer & N.T. Plews   *Man of the Match:* M.A. Atherton   *England won by 42 runs*

Pringle took four more wickets with his full length, varied space and constant accuracy.

New Zealand were grossly handicapped when Morrison limped off after bowling six overs, and, although it was not realised at the time, he was limping out of the tour.

With his sixth ball in international cricket, Darren Gough, showing pace and hostility, had Crowe caught at first slip. In the next 20 overs, Young and Parore added 76, and the game seemed in the balance. Shortly before tea, Udal bowled Parore, and from that point on New Zealand surrendered tamely with none of their leading batsmen giving Young the support his capable innings deserved.

The second match scheduled for Lord's two days later was abandoned without a ball being bowled because of heavy rain.

19, 20, 21 and 23 May *at Derby*

Derbyshire 188 (T.M. Moody 4 for 24) and 178 for 6
Worcestershire 302 (C.M. Tolley 84)

Match drawn

Worcestershire 7 pts., Derbyshire 4 pts.

at Gateshead Fell

Durham 305 (W. Larkins 158 not out, C.A. Walsh 5 for 88, M.W. Alleyne 4 for 70) and 173 (J.I. Longley 71 not out, A.M. Smith 5 for 40)
Gloucestershire 169 and 201 (T.H.C. Hancock 61, J. Wood 5 for 48)

Durham won by 108 runs

Durham 23 pts., Gloucestershire 4 pts.

at Southampton

Middlesex 387 (M.R. Ramprakash 83, J.D. Carr 79, N.F. Williams 63, M.W. Gatting 51, M.J. Thursfield 6 for 130)
Hampshire 203 (M. Keech 57, N.F. Williams 6 for 49) and 230 for 3 (T.C. Middleton 72, K.D. James 52 not out)

Match drawn

Middlesex 7 pts., Hampshire 3 pts.

at Canterbury

Kent 556 (M.R. Benson 90, C.L. Hooper 83, M.V. Fleming 72, S.A. Marsh 72, N.R. Taylor 54, M. Watkinson 4 for 101)
Lancashire 261 (N.J. Speak 57 not out, M.M. Patel 8 for 96) and 279 for 4 (G.D. Lloyd 93 not out, M. Watkinson 62 not out)

Match drawn

Kent 8 pts., Lancashire 4 pts.

Adam Hollioake – exciting all-round cricket in Surrey's early season success. (David Munden/Sports-Line)

at Trent Bridge

Nottinghamshire 368 for 7 dec. (J.C. Adams 121, K.P. Evans 104) and 0 for 0 dec.
Sussex 81 for 4 dec. and 278 for 9 (C.W.J. Athey 94, J.W. Hall 56, J.A. Afford 5 for 87, J.C. Adams 4 for 80)

Match drawn

Nottinghamshire 5 pts., Sussex 2 pts.

at Taunton

Somerset 355 (A.N. Hayhurst 111 not out, M.N. Lathwell 86) and 22 for 0 dec.
Warwickshire 57 for 0 dec. and 322 for 4 (B.C. Lara 136, D.P. Ostler 51)

Warwickshire won by 6 wickets

Warwickshire 18 pts., Somerset 2 pts.

at The Oval

Surrey 181 (C.E.L. Ambrose 5 for 38) and 322 for 8 dec. (A.D. Brown 90, D.M. Ward 80, A.J. Hollioake 66 not out)
Northamptonshire 188 (R.J. Bailey 59, J.E. Benjamin 6 for 57) and 316 for 7 (N.A. Felton 87, M.B. Loye 66)

Northamptonshire won by 3 wickets

Northamptonshire 20 pts., Surrey 4 pts.

Mike Atherton, Man of the Match, with the Texaco Trophy and the newcomers to the England side, Darren Gough and Shaun Udal. (Adrian Murrell/Allsport)

at Leeds

Yorkshire 307 (C. White 108 not out, D. Byas 59, M.C. Ilott 5 for 89, J.P. Stephenson 4 for 74) and 203 for 4 dec. (M.D. Moxon 80)

Essex 188 (P.J. Prichard 50, C. White 5 for 40) and 131 for 4 (M.A. Garnham 53 not out, J.J.B. Lewis 52 not out)

Match drawn

Yorkshire 7 pts., Essex 4 pts.

The rain took its toll of matches. There was no play at all at Derby and Trent Bridge on the Friday or Saturday, and none at Southampton, Canterbury, Taunton and The Oval on the Saturday. Elsewhere play was limited. Tom Moody produced his best bowling performance for Worcestershire, and Derbyshire had to thank Krikken and Griffith for earning a draw.

Durham won their second championship match of the season and climbed to fourth place in the table. They claimed the extra half-hour on the third day, but the game went 13 balls into the fourth day. Wayne Larkins became the first Durham batsman to carry his bat through a first-class innings as he hit his highest score for the county. He hit a six and 28 fours and faced 265 balls on a bitterly cold day. Left-arm medium-pacer Michael Smith took five wickets in an innings for the first time when Durham batted for a second time, but the Gloucestershire batsmen failed again.

Although there were valuable contributions right down the order, Middlesex laboured against Hampshire who included five ex-Middlesex players in their side. One of them, Martin Thursfield, returned the best bowling figures of his career while Keech made his highest score for his new county. Kevan James helped to save the game for Hampshire, and Maru and Cowans bowled most economically. The Middlesex hero was beneficiary Neil

Williams who followed an aggressive 63 with a devastating spell of bowling.

Wonderfully consistent batting took Kent to a big score against Lancashire, and Patel was most impressive with his left-arm spin, claiming his second 10-wicket haul in a match in the season, taking 4 for 4 in 22 balls on the fourth morning. Lancashire followed-on, and they looked likely to be beaten when they slipped to 135 for 4, but Lloyd and Watkinson stood firm and shared an unbroken stand of 144.

In spite of the loss of two days, Nottinghamshire came close to beating Sussex at Trent Bridge. Their first-day saviours were Adams and Evans who came together with the score on 142 for 5. They added 178 in 48 overs, earning four batting points which had not looked possible. Forfeiture and arrangement allowed Sussex 84 overs in which to try to score 288 runs to win the match. They were given a splendid start by Athey and Hall who scored 159 for the first wicket. There was no indication of the drama to come as Sussex reached 272 for 5 with two overs remaining. Afford dismissed Remy and Moores with successive balls, the last two of his last over. Off the second ball of the final over of the match, Stephenson was caught at deep extra-cover, and with his next ball Adams scattered Salisbury's stumps. This left the veteran Eddie Hemmings, so recently a Trent Bridge favourite, to survive the last three balls. Incredibly, Sussex had lost four wickets in five deliveries and had nearly lost the match.

There were sensations of a different kind at Taunton where Somerset gave a first-class debut to medium-pacer Paul Bird and batted grimly on the first day. Richard Davis, formerly of Kent, took five catches in the Somerset innings, but the loss of the third day meant discussions and agreements which left Warwickshire with a target of 321 in 95 overs. Rain reduced this to 234 from 33 overs after they had reached 87 for 1 with Lara at the crease. Having scored five off 10 balls, he returned after the stoppage to hit 131 from 84, with 14 fours and 2 sixes. The sixes came off Rose who received terrible punishment and was warned for bowling two beamers. Lara's hundred came off 72 balls, the fastest of the season to date, and was his fifth in succession. With Asif Din, he added 126 in 14 overs for the fourth wicket, and Warwickshire won with 20 balls to spare – superlatives exhausted.

At The Oval, Surrey suffered their first defeat of the season. Bowled out on the first day by Ambrose and Curran, they recovered through Joey Benjamin to finish the first innings on almost equal terms. Their batsmen then refound their form and Martin Bicknell, leading Surrey for the first time, was able to set Northamptonshire a target of 316 in 89 overs. They needed 169 in 34 overs after tea and, with intelligent batting, won with two balls to spare.

Essex, too, lost their hundred per cent record. They were victims of a fine all-round performance by Craig White who returned the best bowling figures of his career after hitting his second first-class century. Rain interrupted the match, and Essex were finally asked to make 323 in 71 overs. They were 49 for 4 before, with Hussain absent injured, Garnham and Lewis batted out for a draw.

AXA EQUITY & LAW LEAGUE

22 May *at Derby*

Derbyshire *v.* Worcestershire

Match abandoned

Derbyshire 2 pts., Worcestershire 2 pts.

at Gateshead Fell

Durham *v.* Gloucestershire

Match abandoned

Durham 2 pts., Gloucestershire 2 pts.

at Southampton

Middlesex 158 for 5 (J.D. Carr 59 not out)

Hampshire 159 for 0 (V.P. Terry 91 not out,
T.C. Middleton 57 not out)

Hampshire (4 pts.) won by 10 wickets

at Canterbury

Kent 166 for 9

Lancashire 170 for 2 (J.P. Crawley 91, G.D. Lloyd 55
not out)

Lancashire (4 pts.) won by 8 wickets

at Trent Bridge

Nottinghamshire *v.* Sussex

Match abandoned

Nottinghamshire 2 pts., Sussex 2 pts.

at Taunton

Somerset 105 for 7

Warwickshire 106 for 5

Warwickshire (4 pts.) won by 5 wickets

at The Oval

Northamptonshire 53 for 7 (M.P. Bicknell 5 for 12)
v. **Surrey**

Match abandoned

Surrey 2 pts., Northamptonshire 2 pts.

at Leeds

Yorkshire *v.* Essex

Match abandoned

Yorkshire 2 pts., Essex 2 pts.

A 40-over match was possible only at Canterbury and Southampton where Hampshire won with three overs to spare. Lancashire won with 19 balls to spare after Crawley and Lloyd had put on 157 for the second wicket against Kent. Warwickshire beat Somerset in a 20-over

thrash, and Martin Bicknell had his best Sunday League bowling figures only for the match to be abandoned.

24, 25 and **26 May** *at Leeds*

Yorkshire 408 for 5 dec. (R.J. Blakey 84 not out,
D. Byas 68, R.B. Richardson 63, C. White 59,
M.B. Owens 4 for 89)

New Zealanders 173 (C. White 5 for 42) and 202
(B.R. Hartland 60)

Yorkshire won by an innings and 33 runs

Michael Owens, the replacement for Simon Doull who had returned home injured, was the best of the New Zealand bowlers on the opening day at Headingley, but it was Yorkshire who took all the honours. They batted consistently, scored at four runs an over and twice bowled out the tourists with ease. White had another fine all-round match, but for the New Zealanders there was total gloom. Crowe was unable to bat in the second innings because of illness, and their display throughout the match was abysmal. Yorkshire gave a first-class debut to fast bowler Weekes from Montserrat.

Chris White's fine all-round performance against Essex did much to earn him his first Test cap. (David Munden/Sports-Line)

BENSON AND HEDGES CUP

QUARTER-FINALS

24 May *at Derby*

Derbyshire 98 (S.R. Lampitt 6 for 26)
Worcestershire 100 for 1

Worcestershire won by 9 wickets

(Gold Award – S.R. Lampitt)

24 and 25 May *at Trent Bridge*

Nottinghamshire 275 for 8 (P.R. Pollard 104)
Surrey 278 for 4 (D.J. Bicknell 109, D.M. Ward 73)

Surrey won by 6 wickets

(Gold Award – D.M. Ward)

25 May *at Southampton*

Essex 124 for 3
Hampshire 127 for 1 (R.A. Smith 73 not out)

Hampshire won by 9 wickets

(Gold Award – R.A. Smith)

at Edgbaston

Warwickshire *v.* Kent

Match abandoned

Warwickshire won bowl-out 5–4

Derbyshire, the holders, were knocked out of the Benson and Hedges Cup in emphatic fashion. Barnett was again absent and Cork was still feeling the after-effects of knee surgery, but there could be little excuse for Derbyshire who were bowled out for their lowest score in the competition. They lost their last five wickets for seven runs, and Lampitt took six wickets in 30 deliveries. Worcestershire quickly lost D'Oliveira, but there were few problems as they strolled to victory in 18.2 overs with the aid of 34 extras.

Rain allowed only the Nottinghamshire innings on the first day at Trent Bridge, and it seemed that the home side had posted a winning score. Mark Crawley and Paul Pollard, who made his first century in the competition, scored 130 for the first wicket. When rain interrupted play Nottinghamshire were 195 for 3 with 15 overs remaining, and on the restart they somewhat lost their way, finishing well short of a score of above 300 that looked possible.

Darren Bicknell gave Surrey's challenge solidity after Stewart, controversially given out caught behind, and Thorpe had fallen for 125. The man who provided the impetus to the innings was David Ward. He hit 6 sixes and 3 fours to reach 73 off 57 balls. The knock earned him his first Gold Award. Alistair Brown ended the match by hitting Afford for six, six and four.

At Southampton, play could not start until 4.25 on the Wednesday which meant that only a 19-over thrash was

possible. Put in to bat, Essex scored 44 in eight overs, but the introduction of Udal accounted for Gooch and, in the next over, Prichard. Stephenson hit 47, and there was some late hitting by Hussain, but 124 did not look a winning target. Hampshire lost Terry at 13, but Smith and Nicholas hit off the remaining runs in 13 overs to take their side to victory with 10 balls to spare.

If this was seen as an unsatisfactory way to decide a place in the semi-final of such an important tournament, it was far superior to what happened at Edgbaston. Warwickshire failed to use the 'Brumbrella' to guard their pitch against the rain, and play was not possible. Kent complained bitterly at the lapse on Warwickshire's part, but the game went to a bowl-out in the indoor nets, and the home side won.

26, 27, 28 and 30 May *at Ilkeston*

Derbyshire 230 (R.A. Pick 6 for 62) and 222
  (T.J.G. O'Gorman 55, G.W. Mike 4 for 71)
Nottinghamshire 199 (G.F. Archer 52, D.E. Malcolm 5
  for 59) and 255 for 9 (P. Johnson 62, P.R. Pollard 53,
  P.A.J. DeFreitas 4 for 61)

Nottinghamshire won by 1 wicket

Nottinghamshire 19 pts., Derbyshire 5 pts.

at Gloucester

Gloucestershire 319 for 7 dec. (A.J. Wright 87,
  T.H.C. Hancock 75, R.I. Dawson 55, J.E. Benjamin 4
  for 51) and 106 for 4 dec.
Surrey 72 for 3 dec. and 354 for 9 (D.J. Bicknell 129)

Surrey won by 1 wicket

Surrey 19 pts., Gloucestershire 4 pts.

at Southport

Lancashire 521 (J.P. Crawley 281 not out, N.J. Speak
  87, J.E.R. Gallian 53, Mushtaq Ahmed 6 for 156)
Somerset 273 (G.D. Rose 79, M.N. Lathwell 50, Wasim
  Akram 5 for 117) and 160 (M.N. Lathwell 61,
  R.J. Harden 51 not out, Wasim Akram 8 for 30)

Lancashire won by an innings and 88 runs

Lancashire 22 pts., Somerset 3 pts.

at Leicester

Leicestershire 204 (P.A. Nixon 51, D.J. Spencer 4 for
  31) and 281 for 5 dec. (N.E. Briers 82, P.E. Robinson
  78)
Kent 157 (C.L. Hooper 56, A.D. Mullally 4 for 38) and
  189 (D.P. Fulton 50, G.J. Parsons 4 for 34)

Leicestershire won by 139 runs

Leicestershire 21 pts., Kent 4 pts.

at Lord's

Warwickshire 211 (N.F. Williams 4 for 71) and 306 for 5
  dec. (B.C. Lara 140, P.A. Smith 65)

A Gold Award for Stuart Lampitt for his 6 for 26 which helped Worcestershire to victory over Derbyshire in the Benson and Hedges Cup quarter-final. (Mark Leech)

Middlesex 249 (M.A. Roseberry 119, M.W. Gatting 52, G.C. Small 4 for 70) and 245 for 9 (M.A. Roseberry 73, T.A. Munton 5 for 76)

Match drawn

Middlesex 5 pts., Warwickshire 5 pts.

at Hove

Glamorgan 432 for 6 dec. (A. Dale 131, H. Morris 106, D.L. Hemp 55) and 187 for 4 dec. (H. Morris 53)

Sussex 300 for 5 dec. (D.M. Smith 74, P. Moores 70 not out) and 260 for 6 (F.D. Stephenson 71 not out, J.W. Hall 70, A.P. Wells 64)

Match drawn

Glamorgan 6 pts., Sussex 5 pts.

at Worcester

Northamptonshire 112 (N.V. Radford 4 for 48) and 357 for 6 dec. (M.B. Loye 107 not out, A.L. Penberthy 69, K.M. Curran 61, A. Fordham 58)

Worcestershire 256 (J.P. Taylor 5 for 62) and 57 for 2

Match drawn

Worcestershire 6 pts., Northamptonshire 4 pts.

28, 29 and **30 May** *at Chelmsford*

New Zealanders 428 for 5 dec. (K.R. Rutherford 129, B.A. Young 122, S.A. Thomson 52 not out) and 108 for 3 dec.

Essex 334 (R.C. Irani 83, N. Hussain 71, M.N. Hart 4 for 106)

Match drawn

28, 30 and **31 May** *at Oxford*

Yorkshire 254 (D. Byas 71, M.J. Foster 63, R.S. Yeabsley 4 for 75) and 224 for 4 dec. (M.P. Vaughan 106 not out)

Oxford University 212 for 3 dec. (R.R. Montgomerie 80, C.M. Gupte 72) and 166 (R.S. Yeabsley 52 not out, M.P. Vaughan 4 for 39)

Yorkshire won by 100 runs

Ilkeston was one of only two grounds where play was possible on the first day, but Derbyshire, having been put in, struggled for runs, reaching 211 for 7 off 117 overs. They were indebted to O'Gorman for this score. He had been summoned from the Second XI because Warner was injured in pre-match practice and Azharuddin was ill. O'Gorman finished unbeaten on 44 which occupied 74 overs. Malcolm and DeFreitas bowled Derbyshire to a 31-run lead on the second day, but it was the final day which produced an excitement which could not have been anticipated earlier in the match. With Pick again bowling very well and Mike making early, valuable inroads, Derbyshire were bowled out for 222 on the Saturday evening, leaving Nottinghamshire ample time in which to score 254 to win. DeFreitas bowled with great commitment and with Griffith capturing two quick wickets in the middle order, Nottinghamshire slipped to 214 for 8. Noon found a good partner in Pick, who had an excellent match, and they added 31 before Pick was leg before to DeFreitas. Afford managed a single, and Noon drove Devon Malcolm to the cover boundary to win the match.

The only other ground on which play was possible on the Thursday was Southport. John Crawley chose to make it the occasion of his highest score in the championship, 281 not out off 515 balls. He shared a fourth-wicket stand of 168 with Speak and ended the first day unbeaten on 119. In all, Crawley hit 30 fours and 8 sixes, and his sixes were hit during a last-wicket stand of 122 with Barnett. Crawley's contribution to the stand was 107. Somerset were forced to follow-on on the Saturday, and they were routed by Wasim Akram on the Monday. They collapsed from 120 for 3 to 160 all out, the last five wickets going down in 28 balls from Wasim Akram who finished with his career-best figures of 8 for 30. This was Somerset's fourth defeat in as many championship matches.

Rain restricted play on the second day at Gloucester as well as causing total abandonment on the first day. The inevitable negotiations left Surrey with a target of 354 in 90 overs. Darren Bicknell and Alec Stewart put on 121 for the first wicket, but the big guns, Thorpe, Ward and

Brown, all failed. Darren Bicknell kept calm through these disasters, reaching his hundred off 163 balls, and when he was caught at point Surrey needed 72 off 14 overs. When the last over arrived Surrey needed eight to win with two wickets standing. With two balls to go, the scores were level, and Benjamin was caught behind. Cuffy joined Butcher who had shown great maturity in making 43 not out, and they ran a bye to wicket-keeper Russell off the last ball of the match. It was a fine victory which took Surrey 18 points clear at the top of the table, but Gloucestershire could reflect on the fact that they conceded 42 runs from no-balls towards Surrey's victory.

Leicestershire, second to Surrey, had a comfortable win in a low-scoring game against Kent. Kent needed only 239 in 80 overs to win, but Benson, Ward, Hooper and Llong were all back in the pavilion with just 47 scored. Fulton, Fleming and Marsh offered resistance, but Peter Hepworth's 3 for 30, the best bowling performance of the occasional off-break bowler's career, took Leicestershire to victory.

Brian Lara failed to equal the record of six centuries in successive innings when he was caught behind by Keith Brown off Middlesex's young medium-pace bowler Richard Johnson. Warwickshire were bowled out for 211, but Middlesex, having reached 156 for 2 in reply, lost five wickets for 29 runs and ended with a meagre lead of 38 on the first innings. Lara then became the eighth batsman to hit six hundreds in seven innings. His 140 came from 157 balls with a six and 22 fours, and his every visit to the crease was being greeted with an excitement and expectation recalling the days of Compton and Edrich, or, more recently, Ian Botham. Munton set Middlesex a target of 269 in 50 overs. Again Roseberry was in fine form, but he, Gatting and Ramprakash fell while three runs were scored. Brown and Haynes, batting at number seven, revived matters, but Munton and Small struck, and Emburey and Fraser had to survive the last nine balls to save the match. Middlesex were without Tufnell who had been given leave of absence in order to sort out his domestic problems.

Glamorgan scored 384 for 5 in 110 overs when play started on the Friday at Hove. Morris and James began with 125 for the first wicket, and Dale and Hemp hit 140 in 36 overs for the third wicket, Dale going to his century with a six off Salisbury. Sussex responded with equally brisk scoring, with Moores, 70 off 74 balls, and Salisbury adding an unbeaten 103 for the sixth wicket. In the end, Morris was able to set Sussex a target of 320 in 62 overs although Glamorgan eventually bowled 74. Athey and Smith went cheaply, but Hall and Wells took the score to 148. At that point, two wickets fell for 22 runs, and Greenfield's defence and Stephenson's aggression were the contrasting qualities that took Sussex to a draw.

Fifteen wickets fell in a day when play finally got under way on the Friday at Worcester, and when the home county's tail batted solidly on the Saturday to claim a first-innings lead of 144 it seemed that Northamptonshire, recent conquerors of Surrey, were heading for defeat. When play ended on Saturday evening they had lost their first four batsmen and were still six runs in arrears. Determined batting by Curran, Loye and Penberthy on

the Monday, by which time the pitch had lost its moisture, was followed by a token declaration which gave Worcestershire 50 overs in which to score 214.

The New Zealand batsmen gained some confidence in their last match before the first Test. Young and Rutherford scored 191 in 48 overs for the second wicket, and Irani made his highest first-class score, but the match was a meaningless exercise. It did not please the paying customer.

At Oxford, Richard Yeabsley, the university's medium-pacer, returned career-best bowling figures and followed with a maiden first-class fifty. He was overshadowed by Yorkshire's Michael Vaughan who reached his first century in first-class cricket and then produced the best bowling performance of his career.

AXA EQUITY & LAW LEAGUE

29 May *at Ilkeston*

Derbyshire 227 for 7 (P.D. Bowler 61, M. Azharuddin 52)

Nottinghamshire 233 for 3 (P. Johnson 90, J.C. Adams 72 not out)

Nottinghamshire (4 pts.) won by 7 wickets

at Gloucester

Surrey 191 for 7 (D.M. Ward 76)

Gloucestershire 181 for 9 (R.C. Russell 70)

Surrey (4 pts.) won by 10 runs

at Old Trafford

Lancashire 207 for 9 (J.P. Crawley 60, A. Payne 4 for 37)

Somerset 192 for 6 (G.D. Rose 68)

Lancashire (4 pts.) won by 15 runs

at Leicester

Kent 254 for 6 (M.R. Benson 74, T.R. Ward 50)

Leicestershire 194 (C.L. Hooper 4 for 37)

Kent (4 pts.) won by 60 runs

at Lord's

Middlesex 155 for 7

Warwickshire 157 for 7

Warwickshire (4 pts.) won by 3 wickets

at Hove

Glamorgan 139 for 9

Sussex 118 for 3

Sussex (4 pts.) won on faster scoring rate

Worcestershire 178 for 8
Northamptonshire 160 for 7 (K.M. Curran 75 not out)

Worcestershire (4 pts.) won by 18 runs

An uneventful Sunday saw Adams hit Colin Wells for six to end the match at Ilkeston. Nottinghamshire won with 4.2 overs to spare. Johnson and Adams put on 115 for the winners' second wicket. Gloucestershire were beaten by Surrey and had Ball suffering a broken hand while fielding. Crawley celebrated the award of his county cap with a winning innings for Lancashire who also awarded Peter Martin his county cap.

2, 3, 4 and 6 June *at Chelmsford*

Essex 362 (P.J. Prichard 119, J.J.B. Lewis 109) and 183 for 4 dec. (J.J.B. Lewis 78, P.J. Prichard 62)
Gloucestershire 266 for 8 dec. and 279 for 8 (T.H.C. Hancock 123, B.C. Broad 63, J.H. Childs 6 for 71)

Match drawn

Gloucestershire 14 pts., Essex 7 pts.

at Swansea

Surrey 429 (A.J. Hollioake 101 not out, G.P. Thorpe 65, M.A. Butcher 62, D.J. Bicknell 54, S.L. Watkin 4 for 115)
Glamorgan 77 for 2

Match drawn

Surrey 4 pts., Glamorgan 2 pts.

at Tunbridge Wells

Sussex 319 (C.W.J. Athey 169 not out, A.P. Igglesden 4 for 42) and 237 for 8 dec. (P. Moores 68, D.M. Smith 50, M.M. Patel 6 for 91)
Kent 336 for 6 dec. (C.L. Hooper 79, M.V. Fleming 63, T.R. Ward 60, M.R. Benson 55) and 152 for 5 (M.V. Fleming 66)

Match drawn

Kent 7 pts., Sussex 5 pts.

at Lord's

Worcestershire 557 (S.R. Lampitt 122, T.S. Curtis 117, T.M. Moody 83, J.E. Emburey 4 for 101) and 0 for 0 dec.
Middlesex 209 for 3 dec. (M.A. Roseberry 97, M.R. Ramprakash 59 not out) and 304 for 8 (D.L. Haynes 125, M.R. Ramprakash 62)

Match drawn

Worcestershire 5 pts., Middlesex 4 pts.

Brian Lara raises his bat on high. Keith Piper runs to congratulate him. Lara, 501 not out. (Clive Brunskill/Allsport)

at Northampton

Northamptonshire 330 (A.L. Penberthy 79 not out, K.M. Curran 68, P.J. Martin 5 for 61) and 120 for 3 dec. (R.J. Bailey 54 not out)
Lancashire 190 for 4 dec. (J.P. Crawley 69 not out) and 215 for 8 (N.J. Speak 63, G.D. Lloyd 52)

Match drawn

Northamptonshire 4 pts., Lancashire 4 pts.

at Taunton

Somerset 332 for 3 dec. (R.J. Harden 103 not out, M.E. Trescothick 81, A.N. Hayhurst 76 not out) and 0 for 0 dec.
Hampshire 0 for 0 dec. and 245

Somerset won by 87 runs

Somerset 19 pts., Hampshire 1 pt.

at Edgbaston

Durham 556 for 8 dec. (J.E. Morris 204, P. Bainbridge 67, D.A. Graveney 65 not out, A.C. Cummins 62, S. Hutton 61)
Warwickshire 810 for 4 dec. (B.C. Lara 501 not out, K.J. Piper 116 not out, R.G. Twose 51)

Match drawn

Warwickshire 6 pts., Durham 5 pts.

at Middlesbrough

Yorkshire 181 (S.A. Kellett 50, G.W. Mike 5 for 44) and
121 (R.A. Pick 5 for 29)

Nottinghamshire 159 and 145 for 5

Nottinghamshire won by 5 wickets

Nottinghamshire 20 pts., Yorkshire 4 pts.

Prichard and Lewis added 192 for Essex's second wicket against Gloucestershire, and with Kasprowicz producing some fierce hitting towards the end of the innings, Essex reached a satisfactory score. Consistent batting by the later order kept Gloucestershire in contention, but the pattern of the game was altered when only 35 balls could be bowled on the Saturday. Scoring at six runs an over on the last morning, Essex declared and set the visitors a target of 280 in 71 overs. This was a generous declaration, and with Hancock, who reached his highest score in first-class cricket, and Broad adding 138 for the second wicket, Gloucestershire looked to be sure winners. With 10 overs remaining, they needed only 47 with eight wickets standing. Childs then took a wicket in each of his next five overs. With the second ball of the last over Pearson, who was making his debut for Essex, had Russell caught at cover, and Davies' drive off the final ball could only produce two which levelled the scores. By virtue of being the side batting second, Gloucestershire earned eight points which their collapse hardly deserved.

Adam Hollioake hit the second century of his brief career for Surrey against Glamorgan. His innings included 10 fours and 3 sixes, and he reached both fifty and a hundred with sixes, but there was restricted play on the second day, six overs on the third and none on the fourth.

At Tunbridge Wells, Bill Athey carried his bat through the 106.5 overs of the Sussex innings. Kent lost Fulton with no score, but consistent batting from that point took them to a first-innings lead. No play was possible on the third day, and on the last, there was more impressive bowling by Min Patel. Kent were set to make 221 in 25 overs, which they looked upon as an unrealistic task in spite of Fleming's initial burst. He reached 50 off 36 balls.

Stuart Lampitt hit a maiden first-class hundred after Curtis, Haynes and Moody had put Worcestershire in a commanding position at 309 for 5. Lampitt faced 204 balls, hitting 11 fours and 3 sixes, and shared two stands of 74 for the seventh and eighth wickets. With no play on the third day, Middlesex declared and Worcestershire forfeited so that Middlesex were left with 80 overs in which to score 349 to win. Desmond Haynes hit a superlative century, and he and Ramprakash added 118 in 23 overs for the third wicket. Illingworth went on the defensive and frustrated both batsmen. Four wickets fell for 14 runs, but Brown and Williams had no troubles in saving the game.

In an attempt to produce a result and keep the game alive, declarations were in evidence at Northampton where Allan Lamb generously offered Lancashire 69

overs in which to score 261. Three wickets fell for 77, but Lloyd and Speak doubled the score. Then, in 11 deliveries, three wickets fell, and Lancashire were happy to settle for a draw.

Trescothick hit his highest score and Harden and Hayhurst shared an unbroken fourth-wicket stand of 136 to take Somerset to 332 for 3. The loss of most of the second day and all of the third led to forfeitures of innings by both sides, and left Hampshire the last day in which to score 333. Three wickets in nine balls by van Troost undermined Hampshire's challenge, and in spite of late heroics from Udal and Benjamin, they never looked like preventing Somerset from registering their first win of the season.

At Edgbaston, Durham scored 365 for 3 on the first day. On the second, John Morris was dismissed without adding to his overnight score of 204. This innings, which included 24 fours and 5 sixes, was the highest score made for Durham in first-class cricket. Cummins and Graveney added a record 134 for the eighth wicket and, when Cummins was leg before to Twose, Bainbridge declared. Warwickshire ended the day on 210 for 2, Lara not out 111. There was no play on the third day. It is believed that the captains, Reeve and Bainbridge, could come to no agreement regarding declarations and target, so Warwickshire batted on on the last day. Lara scored 174 in the pre-lunch session and a famous record was scented. He and Penney added 314 for the third wicket of which Penney's share was a totally unselfish 44. For the fifth wicket with Piper, who hit the highest score of his career, Lara shared an unbroken record partnership of 322. Warwickshire reached 810 for 4, their highest score in first-class cricket.

Brian Lara faced 427 balls in the 474 minutes he was at the wicket. He hit 62 fours and 10 sixes so beating the record of 68 boundaries hit by Perrin of Essex against Derbyshire in 1904. Dropped at the wicket by Scott when 18, and at mid-off when 238, Lara scored 501 to establish a record for the highest score ever made in first-class cricket. The record had previously been held by Hanif Mohammad with 499 for Karachi against Bahawalpur 35 years earlier. In scoring 390 runs in a day, Lara had established another record. By scoring seven centuries in eight innings, Lara had beaten Fry, Tyldesley and Bradman, and he equalled Bradman's record of reaching 1,000 runs in a season in seven innings. Spare a thought for Durham's slow left-arm bowler David Cox who took 0 for 163 on the occasion of his debut. So Lara holds the two most significant batting records the game has to offer – the highest score in first-class cricket and the highest in Test cricket – and they had been established within the space of two months. Nevertheless, in the context of the match at Edgbaston, the only result and meaning was Warwickshire 6 points, Durham 5 points.

In contrast, neither side reached 200 in the match at Middlesbrough where Nottinghamshire beat Yorkshire in three days. Gregory Mike returned his best bowling figures for the winners.

AXA EQUITY & LAW LEAGUE

5 June *at Chelmsford*

Essex 175 for 9 (J.P. Stephenson 60, C.A. Walsh 4 for 20)

Gloucestershire 148

Essex (4 pts.) won by 27 runs

at Swansea

Glamorgan 220 for 1 (H. Morris 127 not out)

Surrey 46 for 1

Match abandoned

Glamorgan 2 pts., Surrey 2 pts.

at Tunbridge Wells

Sussex 208 for 6 (A.P. Wells 63)

Kent 212 for 5 (C.L. Hooper 74, E.S.H. Giddins 4 for 23)

Kent (4 pts.) won by 5 wickets

at Lord's

Middlesex 174 for 6 (M.R. Ramprakash 80)

Worcestershire 153

Middlesex (4 pts.) won by 21 runs

at Northampton

Lancashire 191 for 9 (C.E.L. Ambrose 4 for 20)

Northamptonshire 183 (A.J. Lamb 78, Wasim Akram 5 for 41)

Lancashire (4 pts.) won by 8 runs

at Taunton

Somerset 221 for 8 (M.N. Lathwell 55)

Hampshire 181 (T.C. Middleton 62, N.A. Mallender 4 for 38)

Somerset (4 pts.) won on faster scoring rate

at Edgbaston

Warwickshire 236 for 8 (D.P. Ostler 83)

Durham 152

Warwickshire (4 pts.) won by 84 runs

at Leeds

Nottinghamshire 190 for 7

Yorkshire 192 for 3 (D. Byas 101 not out, S.A. Kellett 58)

Yorkshire (4 pts.) won by 7 wickets

Hugh Morris hit his highest Sunday League score, but rain brought the match at Swansea to an abrupt end. Ed Giddins, Curtly Ambrose and Wasim Akram all had best

Sunday bowling performances, but only Wasim finished on the winning side.

FIRST TEST MATCH
ENGLAND *v.* NEW ZEALAND, at Trent Bridge

With Pringle unfit and Morrison virtually out of the tour, New Zealand had few selection problems, for their 11 fit men picked themselves. This meant a first Test cap for vice-captain Gavin Larsen who had appeared in 55 one-day internationals, and for Heath Davis, fast and wild. England brought Gooch and DeFreitas back to Test cricket, gave first caps to Rhodes and White, the Yorkshire all-rounder reared in Australia, and omitted Ilott and Stemp, an astonishing choice, from the chosen 13. Ilott has not been blessed with fortune in his relationship with selectors and their whims. Gough was unfit and could not be considered while Such, insanely omitted from the party that toured the Caribbean, was rightly restored.

New Zealand, rapidly being regarded as the worst side to tour England in recent years, won the toss and batted on a pitch that was good and became better. The weather was less than friendly. There was rain in mid-afternoon which meant that play was extended and finished in evening sunshine.

After four muted overs from Devon Malcolm, Phillip DeFreitas was brought on and, with his sixth ball, he had Hartland taken at second slip. Young went in the same manner and when, on the stroke of lunch, Crowe, who had looked a class above any other batsman, carelessly flicked at White's 13th ball in Test cricket to give Rhodes a leg-side catch, New Zealand were 66 for 3. The match was already tilted heavily in England's favour.

Rutherford should have been caught in the gully by Smith who dislocated a finger instead of catching the ball, but he fell to DeFreitas who bowled admirably throughout the match. He maintained an excellent line of attack on and just outside the off-stump, and his outswinger proved lethal.

Thomson slashed at a rare wide delivery from Fraser to give Hick his third catch and, at 108 for 5, New Zealand were sinking fast. Stephen Fleming provided the one bright batting spot of the day. He played without inhibition, striking the ball with a full flow of the bat. He and Parore added 61 before Fleming, who hit 9 fours, was caught in the gully, a spectacular effort by White. Parore went 30 runs later, and Larsen lofted the accurate Such to mid-off. Hart and Nash shamed the specialist batsmen with some positive cricket which took New Zealand to 236 for 8 at the close.

Seven overs into the second day, Hart nudged Fraser to second slip where Hick took his fourth catch of the innings. In the next over, Nash was caught behind off Malcolm, and Atherton and Stewart went out to open the England innings at 11.45.

Davis' first ball in Test cricket was the most extravagant of wides. The ball swung ferociously down the leg-side, beat Parore's frantic dive by yards and crashed into the boundary fence. Stewart may have believed, with some

Uninhibited batting from Stephen Fleming during his innings of 54. (Ben Radford/Allsport)

220 balls with 23 fours. England were 277 for 1, and Atherton, a batsman of sound temperament and exemplary determination, was on 101. The New Zealand attack was weak, but runs still have to be scored, and Gooch and Atherton were masterly. For the most part, the weather was cold and dark. Only the batting brightened the gloom and warmed the soul.

Without adding to his overnight score, Atherton edged a ball from Larsen to the wicket-keeper to give the New Zealand vice-captain his first Test wicket. Hick hit 3 fours, but he was beaten by Nash's yorker and bowled. Gooch continued to dominate. He reached 200 in just over 6½ hours, and at lunch he was on 210. There seemed no reason why he should not double his score, but the first ball he faced after the break he edged to slip. He had hit 29 fours, faced 317 balls and batted for 417 minutes. There could now be no argument as to the justification for recalling him.

The tempo slowed as Hart and Thomson found some rhythm, but White showed confidence and belligerence before driving impatiently to mid-off. Smith was less convincing against the spinners, but he battled on for 223

justification, that there were easy pickings to be had, but he played lazily at Davis and clipped the ball into the hands of mid-on. For the rest of the day, he had to sit and watch Gooch and Atherton claim the spoils.

To recall Gooch to the England side at the age of 40 was controversial, especially when it meant the omission of promising, younger batsmen like Thorpe, Hussain and Crawley who might well have established themselves and gained confidence against New Zealand, but England have won few Tests in recent years, and Gooch remains the best batsman in the country. This, he clearly demonstrated. At the end of the day, he had made 152 off

FIRST CORNHILL TEST MATCH – ENGLAND v. NEW ZEALAND
2, 3, 4, 5 and 6 June 1994 at Trent Bridge, Nottingham

NEW ZEALAND

	FIRST INNINGS			SECOND INNINGS	
B.A. Young	c Hick, b DeFreitas	15	(2) c Rhodes, b Fraser	53
B.R. Hartland	c Hick, b DeFreitas	6	(1) lbw, b DeFreitas	22
K.R. Rutherford (capt)	lbw, b DeFreitas	25	c Atherton, b Such	14
M.D. Crowe	c Rhodes, b White	16	lbw, b DeFreitas	28
S.P. Fleming	c White, b DeFreitas	54	c White, b Hick	11
S.A. Thomson	c Hick, b Fraser	14	c White, b Such	6
*A.C. Parore	c Rhodes, b Malcolm	38	c Rhodes, b DeFreitas	42
G.R. Larsen	c Fraser, b Such	8	c Stewart, b DeFreitas	2
M.N. Hart	c Hick, b Fraser	36	lbw, b Fraser	22
D.J. Nash	c Rhodes, b Malcolm	19	c Rhodes, b DeFreitas	5
H.T. Davis	not out	0	not out	0
	lb 6, nb 14	20	lb 1, nb 20	21
		251		**226**

ENGLAND

	FIRST INNINGS	
M.A. Atherton (capt)	c Parore, b Larsen	101
A.J. Stewart	c Larsen, b Davis	8
G.A. Gooch	c Crowe, b Thomson	210
G.A. Hick	b Nash	18
R.A. Smith	run out	78
C. White	c Larsen, b Hart	19
*S.J. Rhodes	c Thomson, b Nash	49
P.A.J. DeFreitas	not out	51
A.R.C. Fraser	c Fleming, b Larsen	8
P.M. Such		
D.E. Malcolm		
	lb 9, w 6, nb 10	25
	(for 8 wickets, dec.)	**567**

	O	M	R	W	O	M	R	W
Malcolm	17.4	5	45	2	10	2	39	–
Fraser	21	10	40	2	23	8	53	2
DeFreitas	23	4	94	4	22.3	4	71	5
Such	19	7	28	1	34	12	50	2
White	13	3	38	1	3	3	0	–
Hick					14	6	12	1

	O	M	R	W
Davis	21	–	93	1
Nash	36	5	153	2
Larsen	44.4	11	116	2
Hart	35	7	123	1
Thomson	38	6	73	1

FALL OF WICKETS

1–13, 2–37, 3–66, 4–78, 5–108, 6–169, 7–188, 8–194, 9–249
1–59, 2–95, 3–95, 4–122, 5–141, 6–141, 7–147, 8–201, 9–224

FALL OF WICKETS

1–16, 2–279, 3–314, 4–375, 5–414, 6–482, 7–528, 8–567

Umpires: H.D. Bird & S.U. Bucknor

England won by an innings and 90 runs

Gooch and Atherton leave the field having added 263 for England's second wicket. (Patrick Eagar)

minutes although he was missed when 34. He was run out when Rhodes sent him back, the decision coming via the television umpire. England ended the day on 516 for 6.

Rhodes, who had supplied the runs for which he had been chosen, went early on the Sunday morning, but DeFreitas, enjoying a wonderful match, hit 51 off 59 balls, and when Fraser was out Atherton declared.

New Zealand's second innings began with a flurry of defiant boundaries. Malcolm conceded 25 runs in three overs, and 50 was on the board off 53 balls. In the 11th over, Hartland was harshly leg before to DeFreitas, and New Zealand lunched at 73 for 1.

Rutherford fell to a brilliant reflex catch at silly point by Atherton off the impressive and economical Such, and the first ball of the next over saw Young, who had batted very well, edge to the wicket-keeper.

Crowe looked the class batsman that he is, but he lost Fleming shortly before tea, and perished himself after the interval when he played across the line at DeFreitas. Thomson went in the next over, and when Larsen was caught at slip the end was nigh. Parore and Hart believed otherwise, and they survived the extra half-hour to take New Zealand to 184 for 7.

In his fourth over of the last day, Fraser broke the brave stand by having Hart leg before. DeFreitas claimed the last two wickets to justify his being given yet another chance to prove himself by finishing with match figures of 9 for 165, the best of his chequered Test career.

 BENSON AND HEDGES CUP

SEMI-FINALS

7 June *at The Oval*

Surrey 267 for 7 (G.P. Thorpe 87, D.M. Ward 61)
Warwickshire 270 for 6 (B.C. Lara 70)

Warwickshire won by 4 wickets

(Gold Award – D.A. Reeve)

7 and 8 June *at Worcester*

Hampshire 244 for 6 (R.A. Smith 108)
Worcestershire 245 for 7 (G.R. Haynes 65, T.M. Moody 56, N.G. Cowans 4 for 36)

Worcestershire won by 3 wickets

(Gold Award – G.R. Haynes)

Dermot Reeve steers Warwickshire into the Benson and Hedges Cup final and takes the Gold Award, v. Surrey, The Oval, 7 June. (Ben Radford/Allsport)

Put in to bat, Surrey began cautiously against the bowling of Small and Munton. Obviously feeling the need to accelerate, Stewart drove wildly at an outswinger in Twose's first over, the 20th, and was caught behind for 24. Seven overs later, Bicknell was neatly caught and bowled by Reeve, but Thorpe and Ward began to score briskly from the start. Their efforts to increase the run rate led to some bizarre incidents in search of a leg-bye on the eve of lunch, which came at 127 for 2 from 35 overs.

Runs flowed in the post-lunch period although Ward was badly dropped by Neil Smith in the 43rd over. Smith gained some revenge when he bowled Ward six overs later as the batsman tried to cut a ball that was too close to him. In 22 overs, Ward and Thorpe had added 118. In the next 4½ overs, 32 runs were scored, mainly through some excellent running aided by limp fielding, but three wickets fell, including that of Thorpe to a smart return catch by Neil Smith. The last three overs of the innings realised 24 runs, yet one had the feeling that Surrey were short of a winning score.

Lara had been off the field for the latter part of the Surrey innings, exhausted, it was said, by his efforts in reaching 501 the previous day. He dropped down the order to number six and, initially, he was not missed. Burns, preferred to Piper who had hit a century the day before, was out in the sixth over having made 18 out of 28. In 15 overs, Ostler and Twose scored 78, but Pigott dismissed them both, and Paul Smith. In 16 balls, the former Sussex bowler had taken 3 for 11, and Surrey were on top. Lara was active from the start, but he offered a hard chance to Boiling early on, driving the ball straight back to the bowler who failed to cling on to the catch. That was the nearest Surrey got to victory. Lara hit 70 off 73 balls and added 93 in 20 overs with Reeve before he swung tiredly at Hollioake and was bowled. The Warwickshire captain, ever a contributor, steered his side to victory with five balls remaining.

Robin Smith hit his fourth hundred in the Benson and Hedges Cup competition, but he finished on the losing side. He went to three figures with a six and a four off Haynes, and he shared stands of 69 in 21 overs with Nicholas and 88 in 12 with Keech. Smith lived with uncertainty, but he might well have caused havoc in the closing overs had he not been run out by his partner Winston Benjamin. Hampshire's 244 looked a winning total when Cowans dismissed Curtis and D'Oliveira for 22, and when Hick was run out by Middleton the balance was very much in favour of the visitors. The weather declined, and the match went into a second day with Worcestershire on 118 for 3, 127 needed from 22 overs.

Moody completed his fifty off 84 balls on the second day, but he was out six runs later, and Worcestershire were 141 for 4, their big guns departed. Haynes was joined by Leatherdale, and in a devastating display of hitting these two won the game. They added 77 in nine overs. The three overs between the 45th and 47th produced 43 runs, and when Haynes skied to cover he had hit 6 fours and made 65 off 62 balls. Leatherdale was caught at gully to give Cowans his fourth wicket, but the task was now easy, and although Rhodes went with the scores level, Worcestershire won with 14 balls to spare.

8, 9 and 10 June *at Swansea*

Glamorgan 361 (O.D. Gibson 85, H. Morris 84, C. Pringle 5 for 58) and 226 for 6 dec. (P.A. Cottey 90 not out)

New Zealanders 282 for 5 dec. (S.P. Fleming 151) and 306 for 2 (K.R. Rutherford 115 retired hurt, B.A. Young 95, S.A. Thomson 50 not out)

New Zealanders won by 8 wickets

Ken Rutherford hit the fastest century of the season, reaching 100 off 71 balls, and the New Zealanders won their first Tetley Challenge match of the tour. Glamorgan were 171 for 6 before Gibson hit 4 sixes in his 115-ball innings of 85. Chris Pringle showed a welcome return to fitness with five wickets. On the second day, Stephen Fleming showed his talent with a flowing 151. He hit 21 fours and 4 sixes and shared a fourth-wicket stand of 191 in 50 overs with Greatbatch who made only 34 off 143 balls. Cottey's brisk knock enabled Morris to set a target of 306 in 70 overs. Rutherford, Young and Thomson reached the target with four overs to spare.

9, 10, 11 and 13 June *at Derby*

Derbyshire 392 (P.A.J. DeFreitas 108, C.J. Adams 94, T.J.G. O'Gorman 75) and 143

Leicestershire 273 (J.J. Whitaker 75, N.E. Briers 59, C.M. Wells 4 for 61) and 263 for 3 (J.J. Whitaker 79 not out, P.V. Simmons 62, V.J. Wells 59 not out)

Leicestershire won by 7 wickets

Leicestershire 22 pts., Derbyshire 8 pts.

at Hartlepool

Durham 545 for 8 dec. (J.E. Morris 186, S. Hutton 101, W. Larkins 77, G. Fowler 60)

Northamptonshire 156 (M.B. Loye 62, R.J. Bailey 51, A. C. Cummins 5 for 32, S.J.E. Brown 4 for 49) and 302 (K.M. Curran 91 not out, A Fordham 56, A. C. Cummins 5 for 72)

Durham won by an innings and 87 runs

Durham 24 pts., Northamptonshire 0 pts.

at Basingstoke

Nottinghamshire 435 (G.F. Archer 100, R.T. Robinson 66, K.P. Evans 50) and 253 for 8 dec. (R.T. Robinson 63, G.F. Archer 57, W.M. Noon 55 not out)

Hampshire 403 for 6 dec. (R.S.M. Morris 174, A.N. Aymes 69) and 285 for 8 (R.A. Smith 111, R.S.M. Morris 63)

Match drawn

Hampshire 14 pts., Nottinghamshire 5 pts.

at Canterbury

Kent 418 for 8 dec. (C.L. Hooper 89, N.R. Taylor 86,

T.R. Ward 52) and 280 (T.R. Ward 63, J.E. Emburey 4 for 48)

Middlesex 454 (D.L. Haynes 104, M.R. Ramprakash 99, J.D. Carr 64, D.W. Headley 4 for 108, M.M. Patel 4 for 117) and 204 for 7 (D.L. Haynes 104)

Match drawn

Kent 6 pts., Middlesex 6 pts.

Left-hander Stewart Hutton hit a maiden first-class hundred for Durham against Northamptonshire, at Hartlepool, 10 June. (David Munden/Sports-Line)

at Horsham

Sussex 355 (F.D. Stephenson 107, J.W. Hall 55, M. Watkinson 4 for 40) and 381 for 9 dec. (N.J. Lenham 102, A.P. Wells 61, F.D. Stephenson 57)

Lancashire 286 (M. Watkinson 68 not out, N.J. Speak 62, P.J. Martin 57, E.S.H. Giddins 5 for 81) and 390 (Wasim Akram 98, G.D. Lloyd 65, N.J. Speak 50, I.D.K. Salisbury 5 for 109)

Sussex won by 60 runs

Sussex 24 pts., Lancashire 6 pts.

at Worcester

Worcestershire 381 (S.J. Rhodes 76 not out, G.A. Hick 65, G.R. Haynes 55, T.M. Moody 51, R.C. Irani 4 for 91) and 285 for 3 dec. (T.M. Moody 108 not out, G.A. Hick 101)

Essex 262 (G.A. Gooch 101, R.C. Irani 50 not out, S.R. Lampitt 5 for 75) and 405 for 6 (G.A. Gooch 205, R.C. Irani 119)

Essex won by 4 wickets

Essex 22 pts., Worcestershire 8 pts.

at Bradford

Yorkshire 424 (M.P. Vaughan 105, D. Byas 102, R.J. Blakey 84, M. Dimond 4 for 73, G.D. Rose 4 for 78) and 273 for 5 dec. (C. White 71 not out, D. Byas 62, R.J. Blakey 50)

Somerset 332 (G.D. Rose 121, M.E. Trescothick 54, R.D. Stemp 4 for 67) and 224 for 4 (R.J. Harden 71 not out, N.A. Folland 56)

Match drawn

Yorkshire 8 pts., Somerset 7 pts.

11, 12 and 13 June *at Bristol*

Gloucestershire 286 for 9 dec. (M.W. Alleyne 70, D.J. Nash 4 for 59) and 368 for 7 dec. (M.G.N. Windows 106, R.I. Dawson 87)

New Zealanders 295 for 5 dec. (B.A. Pocock 103 not out, B.A. Young 87, M.D. Crowe 73) and 222 for 9 (M.J. Greatbatch 53, A.M. Smith 4 for 59)

Match drawn

at Cambridge

Glamorgan 307 for 2 dec. (S.P. James 138 not out, A. Dale 109) and 197 for 4 dec. (A. Roseberry 94, P.A. Cottey 59, N.J. Haste 4 for 69)

Cambridge University 244 for 8 dec. (R.Q. Cake 107) and 104 for 4 (R.Q. Cake 66)

Match drawn

at The Oval

Surrey 397 for 8 dec. (A.W. Smith 202 not out) and 184 for 7 dec. (S.C. Ecclestone 4 for 66)

Oxford University 314 for 6 dec. (C.M. Gupte 105, H.S. Malik 53 not out) and 210 for 7 (W.S. Kendall 113 not out)

Match drawn

at Glasgow (Hamilton Crescent)

Ireland 316 for 5 dec. (S.G. Smyth 70, D.J.S. Warke 60) and 281 for 3 dec. (D.A. Lewis 113 not out, G.D. Harrison 105 not out)

Scotland 279 for 2 dec. (B.M.W. Patterson 114, A.C. Storie 102 not out) and 169 for 3 (A.C. Storie 64 not out)

Match drawn

In spite of the fact that Phillip DeFreitas hit his first first-class century for four years, Derbyshire were beaten in three days by Leicestershire. Leicestershire were 231 for 9, the follow-on looming, but Malcolm, who conceded 121 in 18 overs, was wayward, and Millns and Pierson added 42 for the last wicket. Derbyshire collapsed in their second innings, losing their last six wickets for 30 runs. Simmons romped to 62, and Whitaker and Vince Wells shared an unbroken stand of 117 to win the match on the Saturday evening.

Durham were again in high-scoring mood. Fowler and Larkins began the innings with a stand of 100, and Larkins then shared a partnership of 152 with Morris. On the second day, the left-handed Stewart Hutton reached a maiden first-class hundred, but the great sensation was the disintegration of Northamptonshire who lost their last eight wickets for 24 runs. Following-on, Northamptonshire fared better in their second innings, but Cummins took 10 wickets in a match for the first time, and the visitors ended pointless. This was Durham's third championship win of the season, and so, at the beginning of June, they had already bettered their record of their first two seasons.

There was a thrilling finish and some fine individual performances at Basingstoke. Sean Morris hit the first century of his first-class career, and batted splendidly in the second innings, too, when he and Smith added 144 for the second wicket. Needing 286 in 60 overs, Hampshire were 209 for 2 with 13 overs remaining, but wickets tumbled. The last ball arrived with the injured Middleton having to hit three to win the match, but he managed just two.

Runs were plentiful at Canterbury where Desmond Haynes hit a century in each innings and finished with a runner after jarring a knee. Middlesex needed 244 in 44 overs to win, and with Haynes and Ramprakash hitting 81 in 17 overs after Roseberry had been run out without facing a ball, they looked likely to succeed. Patel bowled a mean spell and dismissed Gatting, and once Haynes had fallen to Headley, Middlesex were content to survive.

Stephenson and Jarvis scored 107 for Sussex's seventh wicket against Lancashire who were in grave danger of having to follow-on when their ninth wicket fell at 169. Martin and Watkinson combined to add 115, the highest stand of the innings, to take their side to within 69 of Sussex. The home county again hit hard with Lenham making 102 which included 19 fours. Lancashire had the last day in which to score 451 to win. They began cautiously, but with middle-order consistency they reached 219 for 5 at tea. The onslaught came in the final session when Wasim Akram hit 98 off 76 balls with 10 fours and 8 sixes. Alan Wells persevered with Salisbury and Hemmings, and it was Hemmings who bowled Wasim with only three overs remaining to give Sussex victory.

At Worcester, the home side won the toss and made 254 for 6 on the shortened first day. They accelerated on the Friday, but Gooch led the Essex response sharing an opening partnership of 105 with John Stephenson and reaching a patient century which was vitally important in view of the fact that Prichard was forced to retire hurt with a broken thumb. Essex fell apart, and it was left to the impressive Irani to ward off the fear of the follow-on. Hick and Moody then plundered, adding 167 in 34 overs

A budding all-rounder of the highest quality, Ronnie Irani, captured by Essex from Lancashire, took four wickets and shared a fourth-wicket stand of 245 with Gooch to take Essex to a memorable win over Worcestershire. (Paul Sturgess/Sports-Line)

for Worcestershire's third wicket. Curtis declared, and Essex had five overs and a day in which to score an improbable 405 to win. Stephenson fell at 89, Lewis at 132, and when Hussain fell without scoring it seemed Worcestershire would win quickly. Ronnie Irani now joined Gooch and, in 60 overs, they added 245. Gooch played an innings that was as meaningful as it was magnificent. In its context, it surpassed Lara's 501 at Edgbaston a week earlier, for this was an innings for which every run had to be fought and which, eventually, won a match where reason had suggested defeat. The pitch was untrustworthy and Essex's second-best batsman was nursing a broken thumb, but Gooch mastered pitch and bowlers. He did not need to nurse Irani, for the 22-year-old from Lancashire, the capture of the season, batted with the utmost confidence and maturity, keeping the score moving when Gooch slumbered for a while in the nineties. This was a maiden first-class hundred of great character. Gooch became the sixth player to score two centuries in a match on five or more occasions, and he reached 1,000 runs for the season, but he and Irani fell in successive overs to Newport, and with Garnham going cheaply there was still work to be done. Nine runs were needed from the last over, and it was not until the last ball that Shahid scored the single which won the match. It was the third time in three seasons that Essex had scored more than 400 in the fourth innings to win a game, and there have only been 12 instances in the history of the championship. Worcestershire did not come out of the game well on the last day. Illingworth resorted to negative bowling outside the leg stump; Lampitt indulged in bouncers; and Rhodes was reported for constant, distracting chatter. There are laws of the game, and there is a spirit of the game. Both should be adhered to.

There was dissension at Bradford where Stemp was fined for his response when an appeal for a catch at the wicket against Lathwell was rejected. Silverwood was the bowler. Vaughan and Byas scored 216 for Yorkshire's second wicket with Vaughan making his first championship hundred. Somerset were 173 for 8 still 102 short of avoiding the follow-on before Rose, first with Mallender, then with Dimond, conjured 159 from the last two wickets. Eventually, Somerset had a day in which to score 366. They declined the offer.

Windows was given a maiden first-class hundred off 71 balls by some friendly bowling in search of a declaration at Bristol. Morrison survived the last three overs of the match to save the game for the New Zealanders and then returned to New Zealand because of injury. Andrew Roseberry hit the highest score of his career at Cambridge, and at The Oval there were three maiden first-class hundreds. Gupte and Kendall hit hundreds for Oxford University, and Andrew Smith turned his three-figured innings into 202, an innings which included 26 fours and 6 sixes.

AXA EQUITY & LAW LEAGUE

12 June *at Derby*

Leicestershire 190 for 9 (P.A. Nixon 57)
Derbyshire 191 for 4 (M. Azharuddin 91 not out)

Derbyshire (4 pts.) won by 6 wickets

at Hartlepool

Durham 266 for 6 (W. Larkins 108)
Northamptonshire 266 for 3 (A. Fordham 111, K.M. Curran 88 not out)

Match tied

Durham 2 pts., Northamptonshire 2 pts.

at Basingstoke

Nottinghamshire 219 for 8 (C.A. Connor 4 for 34)
Hampshire 222 for 7

Hampshire (4 pts.) won by 3 wickets

at Canterbury

Middlesex 213 for 7 (M.A. Roseberry 105)
Kent 202

Middlesex (4 pts.) won by 11 runs

at Horsham

Sussex 229 for 9 (J.W. Hall 69)
Lancashire 232 for 3 (M.A. Atherton 101 not out, J.E.R. Gallian 58 not out)

Lancashire (4 pts.) won by 7 wickets

at Worcester

Essex 119 (N.V. Knight 61 not out)
Worcestershire 122 for 6

Worcestershire (4 pts.) won by 4 wickets

at Leeds

Somerset 226 for 5 (M.E. Trescothick 74)
Yorkshire 224 for 8 (D. Byas 58, N.A. Mallender 4 for 45)

Somerset (4 pts.) won by 2 runs

There were two centuries at Hartlepool, and Fordham's was his first in the Sunday League. Northamptonshire needed six off the last ball, but Walker was no-balled for a high full toss. This meant that four were now needed from the last ball, and Longley made a scrambling stop to prevent a boundary so that the match was tied. Knight of Essex and Trescothick of Somerset both made their highest Sunday scores.

15, 16 and 17 June *at Cambridge*

Essex 323 for 4 dec. (N.V. Knight 150, N. Hussain 62) and 132 for 6 dec. (J.S. Hodgson 4 for 14)
Cambridge University 181 (G.W. Jones 74, D.M. Cousins 6 for 35) and 144 for 5

Match drawn

Nick Knight hit the fourth and highest century of his career, and Darren Cousins had career-best bowling figures for Essex. Thanks to left-hander Garri Jones who hit the highest score of his career, Cambridge avoided the follow-on. Hodgson produced the remarkable figures of 19–12–14–4 with his off-breaks, a career-best performance, but Cambridge never pursued the target of 275 in 73 overs.

16, 17, 18 and 20 June *at Cardiff*

Glamorgan 402 (M.P. Maynard 118, D.L. Hemp 51, D.E. Malcolm 4 for 109) and 196 (A. Dale 75)
Derbyshire 470 (T.J.G. O'Gorman 128, M. Azharuddin 109, K.M. Krikken 85 not out, K.J. Barnett 51, S.L. Watkin 6 for 143) and 129 for 2 (C.J. Adams 58)

Derbyshire won by 8 wickets

Derbyshire 23 pts., Glamorgan 6 pts.

at Old Trafford

Lancashire 176 (S.D. Udal 6 for 79) and 349 (M. Watkinson 117, S.P. Titchard 99, C.A. Connor 4 for 86)

Mike Watkinson, the Lancashire captain, a century and 11 wickets against Hampshire, 16–20 June. (David Munden/Sports-Line)

Hampshire 100 (M. Watkinson 8 for 30) and 162 (M.C.J. Nicholas 72 not out, G. Yates 5 for 34)

Lancashire won by 263 runs

Lancashire 20 pts., Hampshire 4 pts.

at Leicester

Leicestershire 397 (N.E. Briers 147, P.A. Nixon 95, J.E. Emburey 5 for 95) and 237 (N.E. Briers 85, J.E. Emburey 4 for 86)

Middlesex 623 for 9 dec. (M.W. Gatting 225, K.R. Brown 102 not out, J.D. Carr 88, M.R. Ramprakash 74) and 12 for 0

Middlesex won by 10 wickets

Middlesex 23 pts., Leicestershire 4 pts.

at Luton

Northamptonshire 151 and 481 for 7 dec. (M.B. Loye 132, K.M. Curran 114, R.J. Warren 91, P.J. Hartley 4 for 119)

Yorkshire 148 (D. Byas 56, C.E.L. Ambrose 5 for 16) and 324 (M.P. Vaughan 117, R.B. Richardson 76, A.L. Penberthy 4 for 87)

Northamptonshire won by 160 runs

Northamptonshire 20 pts., Yorkshire 4 pts.

at Trent Bridge

Nottinghamshire 318 (P. Johnson 129, C.A. Walsh 5 for 60) and 110 (C.A. Walsh 7 for 42)

Gloucestershire 223 (R.C. Russell 63 not out, M. Davies 54, G.W. Mike 4 for 49) and 206 for 7

Gloucestershire won by 3 wickets

Gloucestershire 21 pts., Nottinghamshire 7 pts.

at Bath

Somerset 428 (M.N. Lathwell 206, A.N. Hayhurst 79, J.E. Benjamin 5 for 100) and 329 for 6 dec. (M.E. Trescothick 121, N.A. Folland 72, A.W. Smith 5 for 103)

Surrey 288 (A.D. Brown 97, G.D. Rose 4 for 58) and 152 (D.M. Ward 59)

Somerset won by 317 runs

Somerset 24 pts., Surrey 5 pts.

at Hove

Durham 278 (W. Larkins 78, C.W. Scott 51, M. Saxelby 50, I.D.K. Salisbury 4 for 93) and 241 (W. Larkins 71, J.E. Morris 58, J.I. Longley 57, E.E. Hemmings 5 for 53)

Sussex 411 (C.W.J. Athey 166, A.C. Cummins 5 for 84) and 109 for 2 (A.P. Wells 52 not out)

Sussex won by 8 wickets

Sussex 24 pts., Durham 6 pts.

at Edgbaston

Warwickshire 417 (R.G. Twose 142, D.P. Ostler 94) and 288 for 6 dec. (D.P. Ostler 87, C.L. Hooper 4 for 77)

Kent 359 (C.L. Hooper 136, M.V. Fleming 73, T.R. Ward 63) and 270 (M.V. Fleming 61, M.A. Ealham 52, N.M.K. Smith 7 for 133)

Warwickshire won by 76 runs

Warwickshire 23 pts., Kent 6 pts.

17, 18 and 19 June *at Worcester*

Worcestershire 340 for 7 dec. (D.A. Leatherdale 138, K.R. Spiring 56, R.K. Illingworth 53 not out) and 233 for 6 dec. (A.C.H. Seymour 87, K.R. Spiring 52)

Oxford University 95 (Parvaz Mirza 4 for 29, J.E. Brinkley 4 for 33) and 252 (C.J. Hollins 76, R.R. Montgomerie 51, D.B. D'Oliveira 4 for 67)

Worcestershire won by 226 runs

Matthew Maynard returned to the Glamorgan side after injury and hit 118 on the opening day. It seemed that the home county had established a strong position, but Azharuddin hit 16 fours in his stylish 109, and on the third morning, O'Gorman, who had played with uncharacteristic restraint, added 145 for the eighth wicket with Krikken, who hit the highest score of his career. Glamorgan floundered against the Derbyshire pace men when they batted a second time, and the visitors claimed their first championship win of the season shortly after lunch on the last day. Adams and Barnett hit 101 in 15 overs to bring a swift victory.

Lancashire, too, won early on the last day. Udal had given Hampshire the advantage on the first day taking six wickets on a dry, uneven pitch. Lancashire were also handicapped by an injury to Gallian who was run out when he twisted an ankle and collapsed in the middle of the pitch. The second day was a disaster for Hampshire who saw their last seven wickets fall for 38 runs. Their destroyer was Mike Watkinson who bowled his off-breaks to take a career-best 8 for 30, so equalling Wasim Akram's best of the season figures. Watkinson's part in the match was far from finished. Titchard had held steady when Lancashire batted a second time, but when Watkinson came to the wicket his side was 136 for 6. He added 119 with Titchard, and 86 with Wasim Akram. He hit 117, and then took three more wickets to give him 11 wickets and a century in the same match. Hampshire faded feebly before Watkinson and Yates who had the best bowling figures of his career.

Having batted well on the first day, Leicestershire were savaged by Middlesex. Gatting reached the seventh double century of his career with 33 fours and 2 sixes and added 162 in 36 overs for the third wicket with Ramprakash. Carr and Brown then piled on the agony for a tired attack, and Leicestershire had no hope of saving the game.

On the first day, 18 wickets fell at Luton where Yorkshire lost their first three wickets for one run. Sanity returned when Northamptonshire batted again. Warren, who hit the highest score of his career, and Loye added 121 for the third wicket, and Loye and Curran added 165 for the fifth. Yorkshire battled well, with Vaughan hitting the highest score of his young career, but defeat was inevitable.

The bowling of Courtney Walsh took Gloucestershire to victory over Nottinghamshire in three days. Johnson and Mike hit 103 in 23 overs for the home side's seventh wicket on the opening day, and Gloucestershire trailed by 95 on the first innings. Walsh's magnificent bowling revived his side's hopes, but, needing 206 to win, they were 129 for 5. Dawson and Russell added 72, and although two wickets fell for three runs, Gloucestershire gained their second win of the season.

Surrey's championship hopes received a severe setback at Bath. Mark Lathwell, with 33 fours, hit the first double century of his career on the opening day, sharing a fourth-wicket stand of 216 with Hayhurst. Brown hit 97 off 108 balls to help Surrey avoid the follow-on, but Trescothick then hit a maiden first-class century to put the game out of the visitors' reach. Surrey disintegrated before a mixture of pace and spin on the last day, and they led the table by one point from Essex and Leicestershire,

having played one more game than both of those counties.

Durham's run of success came to an end when they were beaten in three days by Sussex. Bill Athey hit the 49th century of his career, and there was consistent batting throughout the order. Hemmings and Salisbury proved too much for Durham in their second innings, and although Athey was out first ball, Sussex won with ease.

An opening partnership of 192 between Ostler and Twose set Warwickshire on the path to victory over Kent for whom Hooper responded with a typically stylish hundred. Ostler and Twose shared their second century stand of the match, 126, and Reeve eventually asked Kent to make 347 in 93 overs. With off-break bowler Neil Smith returning the best bowling figures of his career, Warwickshire had another championship win and remained unbeaten in all competitions, and this with Lara contributing only 19 and 31.

While Hollins and D'Oliveira had best batting and bowling performances in the match at Worcester, the sad story was that Kendall, who in the previous match had hit a maiden first-class hundred, broke his hand and so lost his place in the side for the Varsity match.

 ## AXA EQUITY & LAW LEAGUE

19 June *at Swansea*

Derbyshire 203 for 5 (M. Azharuddin 81 not out)
Glamorgan 204 for 5 (M.P. Maynard 65, H. Morris 62)
Glamorgan (4 pts.) won by 5 wickets

at Old Trafford

Hampshire 113
Lancashire 115 for 4
Lancashire (4 pts.) won by 6 wickets

at Leicester

Leicestershire 301 for 7 (P.V. Simmons 140, V.J. Wells 112)
Middlesex 240 (M.A. Feltham 75, G.J. Parsons 4 for 50)
Leicestershire (4 pts.) won by 61 runs

at Luton

Yorkshire 204 for 6 (R.B. Richardson 55)
Northamptonshire 194 (R.J. Bailey 58)
Yorkshire (4 pts.) won by 10 runs

at Trent Bridge

Nottinghamshire 248 for 8 (J.C. Adams 70, P. Johnson 67)
Gloucestershire 180
Nottinghamshire (4 pts.) won by 68 runs

at Bath

Somerset 239 for 6 (N.A. Folland 75, G.D. Rose 62)
Surrey 221 for 9 (D.M. Ward 54, G.D. Rose 4 for 35)

Somerset (4 pts.) won by 18 runs

at Hove

Sussex 188 (P. Bainbridge 4 for 32)
Durham 190 for 1 (M. Saxelby 79 not out, J.E. Morris 77 not out)

Durham (4 pts.) won by 9 wickets

at Edgbaston

Kent 210 for 7 (T.R. Ward 63)
Warwickshire 211 for 4 (Asif Din 86 not out, B.C. Lara 63)

Warwickshire (4 pts.) won by 6 wickets

The four leading sides – Lancashire, Warwickshire, Yorkshire and Nottinghamshire – were all victorious, and only four points separated them, and Surrey who, like Nottinghamshire, had 16 points. Simmons and Wells set up a Leicestershire Sunday League record by adding 241 for the second wicket against Middlesex. Both batsmen hit their first Sunday League centuries. Lara hit his first Sunday League fifty.

 SECOND TEST MATCH
ENGLAND *v.* NEW ZEALAND, at Lord's

England made one change from the side that won at Trent Bridge, Taylor replacing Malcolm. Even allowing for the fact that Ilott and Gough were unfit, this was a strange selection, for the Northamptonshire left-arm bowler had shown only moderate form in the early part of the season. New Zealand had Pringle fit again in place of Larsen, and Owens was chosen ahead of Davis. Pocock opened with Young instead of Hartland. Rutherford won the toss, and New Zealand batted on a sunny day and a dry, flat pitch.

Initially, they failed to take advantage of the benefits that weather and wicket had bestowed upon them. Young was leg before to the last ball of the first over of the match, and the first boundary did not come until Rutherford cover-drove DeFreitas in the eighth over. This brought the score to 12, and six of these runs were extras. Pocock opened his account in DeFreitas' next over with a leg-glance for four, but after an hour, New Zealand had scored 24 from 14 overs.

The introduction of Such for the 20th over of the innings brought immediate results, for Pocock prodded forward to the last ball of the over and was caught high at silly mid-off. Rutherford might have also fallen to Such, for he offered a chance to White at mid-on, but lunch

Martin Crowe square-cuts a ball to the boundary during his magnificent innings of 142. (Adrian Murrell/Allsport)

came with the score on 65 for 2 of which the New Zealand captain had made 37.

In the second over after lunch, Rutherford was suddenly all at sea to DeFreitas. He got a thick edge which fell just short of Hick in the slips, and then, bat away from his body, steered the ball low to Stewart at first slip. In that immediate post-lunch period, one longed for someone to hit the ball hard, but then Fleming got into his stride and 52 runs came in 63 minutes. Of the 71 runs scored for the fourth wicket, Fleming hit 41, with 7 fours, before he fell to an inswinger from Fraser who was bowling from the Nursery end. At tea, New Zealand were 160 for 4 from 55 overs.

In the final session of the day, 156 runs were scored from 35 overs. Martin Crowe, who took sixes off three different bowlers, hit 85 of these runs, and Shane Thomson 63. White was made to look the raw and inexperienced bowler he is, and the England attack was pounded. Crowe was magnificent. He passed 5,000 runs in Test cricket and scored his 16th Test hundred. It was his fourth against England and his second at Lord's. The quality of his strokeplay was of the very highest, and although he was obviously troubled at times by his

Hick's eager hands await the catch offered by Bryan Young off Such. Young had made 94. (David Munden/Sports-Line)

Deeper trouble as Gooch is leg before first ball to Nash. (Patrick Eagar)

damaged knee, the certainty and speed of his footwork still marked him as one of the world's very greatest batsmen. Thomson gave him wonderful support and was positive in all he did. His innings included 12 fours.

Only two runs had been added to the overnight score when Thomson was run out by Taylor's direct hit on the stumps from cover off the 15th ball of the second morning. The stand of 180 between Crowe and Thomson was a new record for New Zealand's fifth wicket against England.

At 12.15, Martin Crowe mishooked DeFreitas and was caught at mid-wicket. His 142 had come off 255 balls in 365 minutes and included 20 fours as well as the 3 sixes hit on the first evening. Not only did this innings confirm that Crowe remained a great batsman in spite of the illness and injury he had suffered, but also it revitalised a series that was in danger of a premature death. It had instilled confidence and belief into the New Zealand side and at lunch they were 389 for 6.

In the first over after lunch, Hart was badly dropped at first slip by Stewart off Taylor, but two balls later, Parore was caught by Rhodes diving in front of first slip. Six runs and seven overs later, Hart, frustrated by the accuracy of

Such, swung lavishly and was bowled. This brought no relief to England, for the last two New Zealand wickets produced 79 runs. This was thanks to a splendidly sensible and aggressive innings from Nash who hit 7 fours in his 56 which was only two short of his aggregate number of runs for his previous four Tests.

Alec Stewart began the England innings at a furious rate. He hit 45 off 44 balls with 9 fours before touching a lifting ball from Nash to the wicket-keeper. England were 65 for 1 in 13 overs, but in the next 13, Gooch and

SECOND CORNHILL TEST MATCH – ENGLAND v. NEW ZEALAND
16, 17, 18, 19 and 20 June 1994 at Lord's

NEW ZEALAND

	FIRST INNINGS			SECOND INNINGS	
B.A. Young	lbw, b Fraser	0	(2) c Hick, b Such	94
B.A. Pocock	c Smith, b Such	10	(1) lbw, b DeFreitas	2
K.R. Rutherford (capt)	c Stewart, b DeFreitas	37	lbw, b DeFreitas	0
M.D. Crowe	c Smith, b DeFreitas	142	b DeFreitas	9
S.P. Fleming	lbw, b Fraser	41	lbw, b Taylor	39
S.A. Thomson	run out	69	not out	38
*A.C. Parore	c Rhodes, b Taylor	40	not out	15
M.N. Hart	b Such	25		
D.J. Nash	b White	56		
C. Pringle	c Hick, b DeFreitas	14		
M.B. Owens	not out	2		
Extras	b 3, lb 15, w 1, nb 21	40	lb 4, nb 10	14
		476	(for 5 wickets, dec.)	**211**

ENGLAND

	FIRST INNINGS			SECOND INNINGS	
M.A. Atherton (capt)	lbw, b Hart	28	c Young, b Nash	33
A.J. Stewart	c Parore, b Nash	45	c Crowe, b Nash	119
G.A. Gooch	lbw, b Nash	13	lbw, b Nash	0
R.A. Smith	c and b Nash	6	c Parore, b Nash	23
G.A. Hick	c Young, b Pringle	58	lbw, b Pringle	37
C. White	run out	51	c Thomson, b Nash	9
*S.J. Rhodes	not out	32	not out	24
P.A.J. DeFreitas	c Parore, b Thomson	11	lbw, b Owens	3
A.R.C. Fraser	c and b Nash	10	lbw, b Hart	2
J.P. Taylor	c Parore, b Nash	0	not out	0
P.M. Such	c Parore, b Nash	4		
Extras	b 4, lb 12, nb 7	23	b 2, lb 1, nb 1	4
		281	(for 8 wickets)	**254**

	O	M	R	W	O	M	R	W		O	M	R	W	O	M	R	W
Fraser	36	9	102	2	15	–	50	–	Owens	7	–	34	–	10	3	35	1
DeFreitas	35	8	102	3	16	–	63	3	Nash	25	6	76	6	29	8	93	5
Taylor	20	4	64	1	6	2	18	1	Pringle	23	5	65	1	16	5	41	1
Such	30	8	84	2	25	5	55	1	Hart	44	21	50	1	41	23	55	1
White	21.1	5	84	1	4	1	21	–	Thomson	22	8	40	1	12	4	27	–
Gooch	5	1	13	–													
Hick	2	–	9	–	2	2	0	–									

FALL OF WICKETS

1–0, 2–39, 3–67, 4–138, 5–318, 6–350, 7–391, 8–397, 9–434
1–9, 2–9, 3–29, 4–144, 5–170

FALL OF WICKETS

1–65, 2–95, 3–95, 4–101, 5–193, 6–225, 7–241, 8–265, 9–271
1–60, 2–60, 3–136, 4–210, 5–217, 6–240, 7–244, 8–250

Umpires: N.T. Plews & S.U. Bucknor

Match drawn

A spectacular catch high at slip by Young off Man of the Match Nash ends Atherton's second innings, and England are in trouble. (Patrick Eagar)

Atherton scored 29 and moved sedately to the close.

The third ball of the third day accounted for Gooch. He offered no stroke to the first ball he received and was palpably lbw. In the next over, Atherton was leg before to Hart, and England were 95 for 3. Smith was like an animal in pain. To be twice dropped before mis-hooking a short ball straight up in the air suggests neither the confidence nor the judgement required of an England number four. Hick was little better. He and White added 92, yet one cannot remember seeing Hick bat worse in a Test match. As with his bowling, so with his batting, White was raw and inexperienced, often frenetic, and he eventually fell to a run out which needed a recourse to the television monitor, and even then brought much debate.

If lacking the scars of years of Test encounters, the New Zealand attack offered more variety then England's had done. Nash was wonderful, a revelation. He bowled with pace and fire and in one innings doubled his number of Test wickets. England were in grave danger of being forced to follow-on, nor was that danger past until the last pair were together. Rhodes' batting gave more reason for his inclusion in an England side than his wicket-keeping had done, but he failed to shield Fraser, in particular, from as much of the bowling as he should have done. The last session, in which England lost their last four wickets, produced a meagre 43 runs. New Zealand were so far ahead on points that a referee might have stopped the contest.

New Zealand began the fourth day with a lead of 195 runs, and there was a hint that they would squander this advantage as they pressed for quick runs. Pocock and Rutherford fell off successive deliveries from DeFreitas who also bowled Crowe with a ball that came back sharply. Bryan Young and Stephen Fleming soon ended England's dream of an early reprieve by taking New Zealand to 87 for 3 at lunch. In 29 overs in the afternoon, another 81 were added for the loss of Fleming. The

wicket-taker was Taylor who, from the little he was used, had lost the confidence of his captain because of his first innings waywardness.

Young went shortly after tea, well caught at slip off Such who laboured long, hard and honestly. Young had hit 15 fours and faced 168 balls. He had held New Zealand together at a crucial time, and he was unlucky not to be rewarded with the century that his batting so richly deserved.

Rutherford declared, setting England a target of 407. He was not rewarded with a wicket before the close, for Stewart was again punishing, and 56 came from 14 overs.

In the third over of the last morning, Nash had Atherton caught high at second slip and trapped Gooch leg before first ball. New Zealand scented victory more strongly than ever, but Stewart was decisive in all he did, and England went to lunch at 130, with Stewart on 78.

Smith, never in form but grittily determined, was out three overs after lunch when he top-edged a square-cut to the wicket-keeper. Hick played positively for 20 overs before falling to Pringle, but it was the dismissal of Stewart with tea just two overs away that gave fresh impetus to New Zealand's cause. He had hit 20 fours and was facing his 229th delivery when he steered the ball into the hands of gully. It was a fine innings, as much as any batsman could be expected to do, but England were not safe yet.

In the second over with the second new ball, Nash whose bowling throughout the match was quick, accurate, hostile and varied and well worthy of the individual award, had White caught at fourth slip off a massive away-swinger. Owens, badly underused in the second innings when he bowled well, trapped DeFreitas leg before with a ball that kept low, and New Zealand had ample time in which to capture the two remaining wickets.

Rhodes was obdurate and so, too, was Fraser, but Hart finally got a wicket when the Middlesex bowler was adjudged leg before by umpire Steve Bucknor, the first overseas umpire to officiate in Test matches in England. Gloom gathered for England, but the skies darkened and for the last 25 minutes Rhodes and Taylor stood firm against Hart and Thomson. With four lights showing, Nash, the man who had brought New Zealand to the brink of victory, could not be risked.

A top-class spinner might have won the game for New Zealand, but for all his accuracy, Hart seems not to be a wicket-taker, and he lacks variety and imagination.

 NATWEST TROPHY

21 June *at Finchampstead*

Kent 384 for 4 (C.L. Hooper 136 not out, T.R. Ward 120, P.J. Oxley 5 for 87)

Berkshire 241 for 5 (J.R. Wood 88, D.A. Shaw 57)

Kent won by 143 runs

(Man of the Match – C.L. Hooper)

at March

Cambridgeshire 107 (C.A. Connor 4 for 11)
Hampshire 110 for 1 (R.A. Smith 59 not out)

Hampshire won by 9 wickets

(Man of the Match – C.A. Connor)

21 and **22 June** *at Exmouth*

Devon 242 for 5 (P.M. Roebuck 83)
Yorkshire 246 for 6 (C. White 65 not out)

Yorkshire won by 4 wickets

(Man of the Match – P.M. Roebuck)

at Northop Hall, Mold

Minor Counties Wales 104
Middlesex 108 for 1 (D.L. Haynes 64 not out)

Middlesex won by 9 wickets

(Man of the Match – K.R. Brown)

at Lakenham

Worcestershire 309 for 8 (G.R. Haynes 98, T.S. Curtis
  78)
Norfolk 172 (S.G. Plumb 57)

Worcestershire won by 137 runs

(Man of the Match – G.R. Haynes)

at Northampton

Ireland 182 for 6 (S.G. Smyth 61)
Northamptonshire 183 for 3 (R.J. Warren 100 not out)

Northamptonshire won by 7 wickets

(Man of the Match – R.J. Warren)

at Aston Rowant

Somerset 349 for 4 (M.E. Trescothick 116, R.J. Harden
  105 not out, M.N. Lathwell 64)
Oxfordshire 130 (A.P. van Troost 5 for 22)

Somerset won by 219 runs

(Man of the Match – M.E. Trescothick)

at The Oval

Staffordshire 165 for 8 (S.D. Myles 71)
Surrey 166 for 1 (G.P. Thorpe 84 not out, D.J. Bicknell
  56 not out)

Surrey won by 9 wickets

(Man of the Match – J.E. Benjamin)

at Hove

Essex 272 for 5 (G.A. Gooch 86, J.P. Stephenson 55)
Sussex 256 (N.J. Lenham 82 not out, D.M. Smith 64,
  R.C. Irani 4 for 59)

Essex won by 16 runs

(Man of the Match – R.C. Irani)

at Edgbaston

Warwickshire 361 for 8 (R.G. Twose 110, D.P. Ostler 81)
Bedfordshire 164 (J.D. Robinson 67)

Warwickshire won by 197 runs

(Man of the Match – R.G. Twose)

22 June *at Bowdon*

Cheshire 107 for 9 (J.D. Gray 51 not out, S.J.E. Brown 5
  for 22)
Durham 108 for 5

Durham won by 5 wickets

(Man of the Match – S.J.E. Brown)

at Netherfield

Cumberland 188 for 7
Leicestershire 192 for 3 (J.J. Whitaker 73 not out,
  B.F. Smith 63 not out)

Leicestershire won by 7 wickets

(Man of the Match – B.F. Smith)

*Middlesex wicket-keeper Keith Brown equalled the NatWest Trophy
record with six dismissals in the match against Minor Counties
Wales. (David Munden/Sports-Line)*

at Swansea

Glamorgan 344 for 5 (S.P. James 123, A. Dale 110,
M.P. Maynard 75)
Lincolnshire 184 for 9

Glamorgan won by 160 runs

(Man of the Match – S.P. James)

at Bristol

Gloucestershire 228 for 8 (R.I. Dawson 60)
Derbyshire 229 for 7 (K.J. Barnett 113 not out,
C.J. Adams 52)

Derbyshire won by 3 wickets

(Man of the Match – K.J. Barnett)

at Old Trafford

Scotland 178 for 9 (G.N. Reifer 72)
Lancashire 179 for 5 (M.A. Atherton 50)

Lancashire won by 5 wickets

(Man of the Match – G.N. Reifer)

at Jesmond

Nottinghamshire 344 for 6 (P. Johnson 146, C.C. Lewis
89, R.T. Robinson 62)
Northumberland 116 (K.P. Evans 6 for 10)

Nottinghamshire won by 228 runs

(Man of the Match – P. Johnson)

The weather was not kind to the NatWest Trophy, and
only two of the 16 matches could be completed on the
scheduled day. There were no successes for the Minor
Counties although there were some fine individual performances.

Kent and Nottinghamshire both recorded their highest
scores in the competition and in the match at Jesmond,
Kevin Evans produced the remarkable figures of 6 for 10
in seven overs, a Nottinghamshire record, and his best
performance in any competition.

Peter Roebuck batted, bowled and captained well as his
Devon side lost to Yorkshire with just four balls remaining. Keith Brown took the individual award at Northop
Hall for his five catches and a stumping which equalled
the competition record held by Bob Taylor and Terry
Davies. Having gained his first Gold Award in the Benson
and Hedges Cup a few weeks earlier, Gavin Haynes took
his first NatWest Trophy award for Man of the Match.
Warren of Northamptonshire and Trescothick of Somerset won the individual awards on the occasion of their
first appearances in the competition. Essex all-rounder
Irani was also playing in his first NatWest match, and he
took the individual award as Sussex slid to defeat more
easily than the scores suggest.

Roger Twose confirmed his fine all-round form of the
season with 110 and 2 for 30 for Warwickshire against
Bedfordshire.

22, 23 and **24 June** *at Cambridge*

New Zealanders 256 (M.J. Greatbatch 68, S.A. Thomson
66 not out) and 196 (P.W. Trimby 4 for 58)
Combined Universities 320 (G.W. White 104, I.G. Steer
67, J.C. Hallett 52, M.B. Owens 5 for 74, S.J. Roberts
4 for 60) and 122 for 8 (G.R. Larsen 5 for 24)

Match drawn

23 June *at Highclere*

Earl of Carnavon's XI 223 (G.I. Macmillan 78)
South Africans 224 for 3 (J.N. Rhodes 111,
K.C. Wessels 68 not out)

South Africans won by 7 wickets

The New Zealanders had a hard time against the stu-
dents. They were uneasy against Trimby, the Oxford leg-
spinner, who had match figures of 7 for 97 in 48 overs,
and, having reduced the Universities to 23 for 4, they
were subjected to a fifth-wicket stand of 153 between
White and Steer. Needing 133 in 50 overs to win, the
Universities slumped to 80 for 8 with Larsen taking 5 for 7
in 41 balls, but they survived to draw.

The Queen and the Duke of Edinburgh welcomed the
South Africans at Highclere Castle where £30,000 was
raised for the National Playing Fields Association.

23, 24, 25 and **27 June** *at Ilford*

Nottinghamshire 409 (R.T. Robinson 182, G.F. Archer
67, W.M. Noon 62 not out) and 167 for 8 (P.R. Pollard
53 not out, P.M. Such 4 for 71)
Essex 153 (R.C. Irani 61, J.A. Afford 4 for 30) and 422
(J.P. Stephenson 144, G.A. Gooch 66, M.A. Garnham
62, J.C. Adams 4 for 63)

Nottinghamshire won by 2 wickets

Nottinghamshire 24 pts., Essex 3 pts.

at Colwyn Bay

Lancashire 359 (M. Watkinson 155, S.L. Watkin 4 for 59)
and 264 for 6 dec. (J.P. Crawley 83)
Glamorgan 238 (D.L. Hemp 56, H. Morris 52,
G. Chapple 5 for 79) and 165 (G. Yates 4 for 31,
M. Watkinson 4 for 73)

Lancashire won by 220 runs

Lancashire 23 pts., Glamorgan 5 pts.

at Lord's

Middlesex 511 (M.A. Roseberry 152, M.R. Ramprakash
135, M.A. Feltham 51, S.J.E. Brown 5 for 113)
Durham 283 (A.C. Cummins 63, R.L. Johnson 4 for 64)
and 194

Middlesex won by an innings and 34 runs

Middlesex 24 pts., Durham 4 pts.

Warwickshire 463 (B.C. Lara 197, J.P. Taylor 4 for 139) and 230 for 6 (D.P. Ostler 87)

Northamptonshire 267 (A.J. Lamb 81, R.J. Bailey 54, T.A. Munton 5 for 53) and 423 (M.B. Loye 113, R.J. Warren 94 not out, K.M. Curran 56, T.A. Munton 5 for 79)

Warwickshire won by 4 wickets

Warwickshire 24 pts., Northamptonshire 6 pts.

at The Oval

Leicestershire 263 (V.J. Wells 70, P.A. Nixon 58, J.E. Benjamin 6 for 81) and 188 (T.J. Boon 66, J.E. Benjamin 4 for 51)

Surrey 501 (A.J. Stewart 142, A.J. Hollioake 138, G.P. Thorpe 64, D.J. Bicknell 59)

Surrey won by an innings and 50 runs

Surrey 24 pts., Leicestershire 5 pts.

at Worcester

Sussex 295 (F.D. Stephenson 95, N.J. Lenham 70) and 257 (M.D. Speight 81, C.W.J. Athey 57, S.R. Lampitt 4 for 37)

Worcestershire 317 (W.P.C. Weston 70, S.R. Lampitt 57, I.D.K. Salisbury 5 for 79) and 238 for 9 (G.A. Hick 73, F.D. Stephenson 4 for 78)

Worcestershire won by 1 wicket

Worcestershire 23 pts., Sussex 6 pts.

at Leeds

Hampshire 305 (V.P. Terry 141 not out, R.S.M. Morris 56, D. Gough 6 for 70) and 325 for 8 dec.

The South Africans return – taking the field at Highclere, 23 June. (Adrian Murrell/Allsport)

(R.A. Smith 134, R.S.M. Morris 82, M.C.J. Nicholas 65 not out)

Yorkshire 257 (R.J. Blakey 73 not out, C.A. Connor 4 for 75) and 275 for 7 (C. White 51)

Match drawn

Hampshire 6 pts., Yorkshire 5 pts.

25, 26 and 27 June at Derby

Derbyshire 424 for 9 dec. (T.J.G. O'Gorman 143, M.E. Cassar 66)

New Zealanders 210 (M.J. Greatbatch 84, A.C. Parore 50, S.J. Base 4 for 58) and 196 (B.R. Hartland 65)

Derbyshire won by an innings and 18 runs

at Canterbury

Kent 292 (G.R. Cowdrey 114, S.A. Marsh 57, W.J. Cronje 4 for 47) and 0 for 0 dec.

South Africans 0 for 0 dec. and 258 (D.J. Richardson 88, T.G. Shaw 66, D.W. Headley 5 for 60)

Kent won by 34 runs

at Bristol

Gloucestershire 357 for 2 dec. (R.J. Cunliffe 177 not out, M.W. Alleyne 101 not out, G.D. Hodgson 51) and 218 for 0 dec. (R.I. Dawson 127 not out, A.J. Wright 84 not out)

Cambridge University 129 (R.C. Williams 4 for 28) and 134 (V.J. Pike 6 for 41)

Gloucestershire won by 312 runs

Essex suffered their first championship defeat of the season, but, having been forced to follow-on by Nottinghamshire, they came close to pulling off a remarkable victory. Nottinghamshire survived the early loss of

An outstanding season for Joey Benjamin who took 10 wickets in Surrey's victory over Leicestershire, 23–5 June. (Mike Hewitt/ Allsport)

Pollard and the insane run out of Johnson for one to score 333 for 5 on the opening day. Tim Robinson played his first big innings of the season, but he was out early on the second morning, having hit 22 fours and a six. Essex bowlers threatened to bring an abrupt end to the innings, but Noon, a valuable acquisition in place of the sick Bruce French, and Field-Buss added 48 for the ninth wicket. Essex were reduced to 81 for 7 by a varied attack, and only the sparkling batting of Irani saved them from total humiliation. It could not save them from having to bat again before the end of the second day, handicapped by Knight suffering from a strained thigh muscle. Gooch and Stephenson began with a flourish but, just before the close, Gooch fell to Adams. Stephenson, whose season had begun late through injury, played splendidly until falling to the second new ball shortly after tea on the third day. Garnham batted purposefully, and Nottinghamshire were left with more than a day in which to score 167 to win. In the one over they faced on the Saturday evening, they lost Robinson. Night-watchman Mike was soon out on the Monday, but Essex were further handicapped by the loss of Ilott through injury. Such and Childs gnawed away at the Nottinghamshire batting. Pollard alone stood firm, batting through 62.4 overs to take his side to victory by two wickets shortly after tea.

In his first season as captain of Lancashire, Mike Watkinson continued with his outstanding all-round form. His side were 96 for 6 against Glamorgan before he shared stands of 124 with Martin and 99 with Hegg. Watkinson hit 6 sixes and 19 fours in what was the highest score of his career, and the last four Lancashire wickets realised 263 runs. Glamorgan, too, recovered, for they were 123 for 6 at one time, and only the efforts of Lefebvre and Metson took them past the point of having to follow on as Glen Chapple had the first five-wicket haul of his career. Watkinson's declaration eventually left Glamorgan a target of 386 in 80 overs. They reached 121 for 3 before collapsing to Watkinson and Yates.

Middlesex demolished Durham in three days. Their massive total was founded upon a third-wicket stand of 179 between Ramprakash and Roseberry and the late hitting of Feltham. Durham, handicapped by an injury to Wood in his first over which prevented him from bowling again in the match, twice succumbed to a varied attack.

Lara equalled Bradman's record by hitting his eighth century in 11 first-class innings, scoring 140 between lunch and tea and sharing a fourth-wicket stand of 168 in 31 overs with Trevor Penney. He hit 30 fours and 3 sixes, but he had his helmet split by a ball from Ambrose. Northamptonshire were bowled out by Munton and Welch and, following-on, were 83 for 4 in their second innings. Loye, Curran and Warren offered defiance, and Warwickshire were left the considerable task of scoring 228 in 38 overs to win the match. Moles, playing his first game of the season after illness and injury, dropped down the order, and Twose and Ostler began the challenge with 107 in 17 overs. At 190 for 2, victory looked certain, but four wickets, including that of Lara, batting at number seven, fell for 23 runs, and it was left to Dermot Reeve, batting with a runner, to hit the third ball of the last over for four to bring victory.

Surrey clung to the top of the table with a five-point lead over Nottinghamshire by dismantling Leicestershire in three days. Alec Stewart took 4 fours in one over off Millns as he raced to 142 off 171 balls, adding 169 with Thorpe at four runs an over. Adam Hollioake scorched to a hundred off 121 balls, and he hit 5 sixes and 16 fours in the highest score of his so promising career. Joey Benjamin had his first 10-wicket haul in first-class cricket and became the first bowler to reach 50 wickets in the season. The Oval was, for a time at least, a happy place.

Worcestershire led Sussex by 22 runs on the first innings at Worcester, but Speight's 81 out of 123 off 107 balls gave their second innings some glamour and left the home side with a target of 236. Curtis and Weston began briskly on the Saturday evening, but Curtis fell to Stephenson who also had Hick dropped at slip. This proved a costly miss, for Hick hit 15 fours and took the score to 170 for 3. The next five wickets went down for 43 runs, and when Illingworth fell to Salisbury Worcestershire were still two runs short of victory. Radford settled the issue with a boundary, and Rhodes was left unbeaten on 37 which had occupied 35 overs.

Hampshire slumped from 91 for 0 to 96 for 5 as Darren Gough took three wickets in 11 balls to prove his fitness to the England selectors. Paul Terry saved Hampshire by carrying his bat through the innings for the first time. Having lost Moxon for 0, Yorkshire batted with caution but trailed by 48 runs on the first innings. Morris and Smith hit 214 for Hampshire's third wicket in the second innings, and the home side were left 106 overs in which to score 374. They slipped to 144 for 5 and settled for a draw.

The New Zealanders gave a limp display against Derbyshire for whom O'Gorman hit 26 fours after being dropped before he had scored. There was no play on the first day at Canterbury where the South Africans began their tour proper, and this meant the forfeiture of Kent's second innings. South Africa's first innings lasted seven balls. Kent were 52 for 5 before Cowdrey rallied them. Richardson and Shaw did the same for the tourists, adding 157 after six wickets had fallen for 64. Dean Headley had inspired the early collapse, and he returned to dismiss Shaw and ultimately win the match.

Gloucestershire gave a first-class debut to leg-spinner Vyvyan Pike, and he began his career with match figures of 9 for 69. His team-mates also enjoyed themselves against a weak Cambridge side. Cunliffe and Dawson hit maiden centuries, and Ricardo Williams returned the best bowling figures of his career.

 ## AXA EQUITY & LAW LEAGUE

26 June *at Ilford*

Essex 184 for 7

Nottinghamshire 188 for 3 (P. Johnson 82, J.C. Adams 60 not out)

Nottinghamshire (4 pts.) won by 7 wickets

Glamorgan 198 for 4 (H. Morris 99 not out)
Lancashire 171 for 9 (W.K. Hegg 52, S.R. Barwick 4 for 38)

Glamorgan (4 pts.) won by 27 runs

Middlesex 249 for 6 (M.R. Ramprakash 97, D.L. Haynes 52)
Durham 250 for 9 (M. Saxelby 54)

Durham (4 pts.) won by 1 wicket

Warwickshire 218 for 6 (D.P. Ostler 78)
Northamptonshire 104 (N.M.K. Smith 4 for 19)

Warwickshire (4 pts.) won by 114 runs

Leicestershire 263 (P.V. Simmons 72)
Surrey 141 (V.J. Wells 5 for 10)

Leicestershire (4 pts.) won by 122 runs

Worcestershire 242 for 4 (G.A. Hick 103, A.C.H. Seymour 57)
Sussex 145 (M.P. Speight 57, R.K. Illingworth 4 for 23)

Worcestershire (4 pts.) won by 97 runs

Yorkshire 191 for 6 (M.D. Moxon 58)
Hampshire 122

Yorkshire (4 pts.) won by 69 runs

Essex included Diwan in their side against Nottinghamshire. He had scored heavily in the Second XI. Another debutant was wicket-keeper Dawood who had arrived at Northamptonshire via Yorkshire in rather controversial circumstances. Dawood had an untidy time as Warwickshire maintained their unbeaten start to the season. Phil Tufnell played his first game for Middlesex since April. Durham won with two balls and a wicket to spare, but it was hoped that Tufnell's personal problems were behind him. Vince Wells had his best Sunday bowling figures as Leicestershire trounced Surrey for whom de la Pena, once of Gloucestershire, made his debut.

29, 30 June and **1** July *at Hove*

Sussex 358 for 7 dec. (N.J. Lenham 76, P.W. Jarvis 70 not out) and 91 for 6 (P.L. Symcox 5 for 29)
South Africans 613 for 6 dec. (B.M. McMillan 132, P.N. Kirsten 130, W.J. Cronje 94, K.C. Wessels 77, G.F.J. Liebenberg 64 not out)

Match drawn

Oxford University 453 for 9 dec. (C.J. Hollins 131, C.M. Gupte 122, G.I. Macmillan 69)
Cambridge University 253 (R.S. Yeabsley 6 for 54) and 243 for 8 (A.R. Whittall 91 not out, J.S. Hodgson 54, R.S. Yeabsley 4 for 50)

Match drawn

The pitch on the opening day at Hove seemed lifeless, but the South Africans proved otherwise on the second day with a third-wicket stand of 133 between Cronje and Wessels. Peter Kirsten and McMillan took their sixth-wicket stand of 173 into the last morning, and the South Africans reached their highest-ever score against a county side. Then, as Sussex juggled with their order, off-spinner Pat Symcox took five wickets and came close to bowling his side to a surprise win.

The 149th Varsity Match provided the 47th draw. Oxford started as firm favourites and, when Montgomerie won the toss, batted and shared an opening stand of 104 with Macmillan the odds in favour of the dark blues seemed fully justified. By the end of the first day, Cambridge were virtually out of the match. Chris Hollins had reached a maiden first-class hundred off 123 balls, Chinmay Gupte had scored his second century in three matches. Oxford were 379 for 3. Hollins and Gupte were finally separated when they had added 240 for the fourth wicket. The remaining batsmen perished in the search for quick runs. There were problems for Oxford when Ecclestone was forced to withdraw from the attack with an injured back, but Richard Yeabsley steadily began to work his way through the Cambridge batting, and they were reduced to 186 for 9. Pitcher and Cooke held out for the last hour, but Pitcher gave Macmillan his fourth slip catch with only one run added the following morning, and Yeabsley finished with a career-best 6 for 54. Following-on, Cambridge were 27 for 4, and then 105 for 6 before Hodgson, who reached a maiden first-class fifty, and Whittall added 65. Haste also gave Whittall good support, but it was the Zimbabwean who was the hero, batting for $2\frac{1}{2}$ hours, hitting 13 fours and 2 sixes in the highest score of his career and saving the match for Cambridge.

30 June, **1**, **2** and **4** July *at Derby*

Derbyshire 344 (K.J. Barnett 148, A.S. Rollins 53 not out, M.A. Feltham 5 for 69) and 105 (R.L. Johnson 10 for 45)
Middlesex 545 (M.W. Gatting 147, M.R. Ramprakash 131, J.D. Carr 108 not out, C.M. Wells 4 for 52)

Middlesex won by an innings and 96 runs

Middlesex 23 pts., Derbyshire 5 pts.

Surrey 236 (S.J.E. Brown 4 for 62) and 538 for 6 dec. (D.J. Bicknell 190, A.D. Brown 172)

Durham 335 (C.W. Scott 108, J.I. Longley 51) and 149 (A.C.S. Pigott 4 for 22)

Surrey won by 290 runs

Surrey 21 pts., Durham 7 pts.

at Bristol

Glamorgan 302 (D.L. Hemp 136, M.P. Maynard 69, M.C.J. Ball 5 for 69) and 39 for 1

Gloucestershire 149 (S.R. Barwick 4 for 28) and 191 (R.C. Russell 85 not out, S.R. Barwick 5 for 44)

Glamorgan won by 9 wickets

Glamorgan 23 pts., Gloucestershire 4 pts.

at Maidstone

Kent 377 (N.R. Taylor 139, M.V. Fleming 66) and 407 for 5 dec. (C.L. Hooper 183, N.R. Taylor 83)

Yorkshire 331 (M.P. Vaughan 81, D. Byas 58, R.B. Richardson 54, D.W. Headley 5 for 128) and 278 (M.D. Moxon 122, M.M. Patel 5 for 68)

Kent won by 175 runs

Kent 24 pts., Yorkshire 7 pts.

at Leicester

Essex 218 (J.P. Stephenson 83) and 195 (R.C. Irani 64, D.J. Millns 4 for 78)

Leicestershire 462 (P.A. Nixon 115, P.V. Simmons 86, G.J. Parsons 70, M.S. Kasprowicz 5 for 120)

Leicestershire won by an innings and 49 runs

Leicestershire 24 pts., Essex 5 pts.

at Trent Bridge

Nottinghamshire 538 (P. Johnson 132, P.R. Pollard 110, W.M. Noon 75, R.A. Pick 65 not out, C.C. Lewis 51) and 153 for 3 dec. (R.T. Robinson 94)

Northamptonshire 417 for 7 dec. (R.J. Bailey 113, R.J. Warren 66) and 88 for 1

Match drawn

Nottinghamshire 6 pts., Northamptonshire 5 pts.

at Taunton

Somerset 349 (A.N. Hayhurst 98, M.E. Trescothick 55) and 297 for 7 dec. (R.J. Harden 131 not out)

Worcestershire 315 (D.A. Leatherdale 139, R.K. Illingworth 59, Mushtaq Ahmed 5 for 66) and 278 (W.P.C. Weston 83, T.M. Moody 79, Mushtaq Ahmed 7 for 94)

Somerset won by 53 runs

Somerset 22 pts., Worcestershire 6 pts.

at Edgbaston

Lancashire 392 (J.P. Crawley 141, N.H. Fairbrother 76) and 194 (J.P. Crawley 54, N.M.K. Smith 7 for 42)

All 10 wickets in Derbyshire's second innings for Middlesex's fast medium-pace bowler Richard Johnson, Derby, 2 July. (Paul Sturgess/ Sports-Line)

Warwickshire 407 (T.L. Penney 111, A.J. Moles 87, J.D. Ratcliffe 69, G. Chapple 4 for 52, Wasim Akram 4 for 82) and 183 for 4 (R.G. Twose 90)

Warwickshire won by 6 wickets

Warwickshire 24 pts., Lancashire 6 pts.

2, 3 and **4 July** *at Southampton*

Hampshire 300 for 8 dec. (V.P. Terry 75, A.A. Donald 5 for 58) and 198 for 5 (R.S.M. Morris 101 not out)

South Africans 264 for 9 dec. (J.N. Rhodes 77, G. Kirsten 50, S.D. Udal 5 for 63)

Match drawn

Phil Tufnell played his first championship match of the season, but was not among the wicket-takers as Derbyshire lurched from slump to slump to reach 313 for 7 on the opening day. By the end of the second day, Middlesex had raced to 394 for 3 in 96 overs. Gatting and Ramprakash added 202 for the third wicket, and Carr completed the destruction of the home county's attack with a delightful 108 on the third day. Middlesex finally reached 545 which included a record 81 extras, 54 of them from 27 no-balls. Beginning their second innings soon after lunch, Derbyshire lost Barnett in Richard Johnson's first over. In his third over, Johnson bowled Vandrau. Johnson then had five wickets in five successive overs, and Derbyshire were all out on the fifth ball of the 41st over. Johnson's final figures were 18.5–6–45–10. He had become the first bowler for 30 years to take all ten wickets in a championship match, and, at the age of 19 years 185 days, the youngest to accomplish the feat in England.

When Surrey were bowled out for 236 on the first day at Darlington it seemed their championship aspirations would receive a severe setback. Durham struggled to take a lead until Chris Scott hit the first century of his career and shared a ninth-wicket stand of 88 with David Graveney. On the Saturday, Durham were eclipsed. Darren Bicknell laid the foundation with a technically accomplished 190 in 6½ hours. He and Alistair Brown added 222 in 38 overs for the fourth wicket, and 211 runs came in the afternoon session. Brown hit Graveney for 5 sixes, and there were 18 fours in his 152-ball innings. Four times, Brown cleared the football stand with his hits. Durham dissolved on the last day, being all out before lunch.

Glamorgan notched their first championship win of the season when they beat Gloucestershire in three days. Maynard and the ever-improving and impressive Hemp added 152 for the fourth wicket, but others contributed little. Gloucestershire, losing six wickets for 40 runs at one period, were forced to follow-on, and they fared little better against Barwick in their second innings than they had done in their first.

Kent recovered from 88 for 5 to 377 all out on the opening day against Yorkshire. This was due mainly to a brutal innings from Fleming, 66 off 46 balls, and a steadying innings of 139 from Taylor who shared a ninth-wicket stand of 107 with Patel. Yorkshire, who gave a first-class debut to Scots-born pace bowler Hamilton, batted solidly in reply to keep the game evenly balanced. The match tilted violently in favour of Kent on the Saturday when Hooper established a county record with 10 sixes. There are few sights as lovely in cricket as when the nonchalant Carl Hooper is at the crease in full flow. A target of 454 was always too much for the young Yorkshire side. In spite of Moxon's century, they bowed to Patel as most sides were doing, and Yorkshire were left bottom of the table.

Hit by injuries and Test calls, Essex fielded only four capped players at Leicester where they gave a first-class debut to Diwan who, unfortunately, 'bagged a pair'. Leicestershire also gave a debut to off-break bowler Mason. Mason's first wicket in first-class cricket was that of Pearson as Essex were tumbled out on the first day. With Leicestershire 246 for 6, Essex were still in the match, but Nixon then hit the highest score of his career and added 152 in 38 overs with Parsons. The defiant batting of Irani, Cousins and Childs could not avert the inevitable, and Leicestershire won in three days.

Johnson and Pollard shared a fourth-wicket stand of 213 on the first day for Nottinghamshire against Northamptonshire, and with the last three wickets realising 125 runs, the home county batted until the Friday afternoon. Bailey hit his first century of the season after a run of fifties, and there was substance to all the Northamptonshire innings so that a result was always going to be

David Hemp, a young batsman of exciting promise, and a shining light for Glamorgan in a disappointing season. (Mike Hewitt/Allsport)

difficult to achieve. Rain on the last day ended all speculation.

Somerset, who had begun the season badly, recorded their third championship victory. Mushtaq Ahmed, in his last game for the county before joining the Pakistan side for the tour of Sri Lanka, had match figures of 12 for 160 and was mainly instrumental for the Somerset victory. The home county had batted dourly on the opening day, circumspect after four middle-order wickets had gone for 63. The late order offered a more positive approach, and when, facing a total of 349, Worcestershire were 105 for 7, an early finish looked likely. Leatherdale and Illingworth added 183 for the eighth wicket so that the first innings was eventually close to parity. Somerset showed no more urgency in their second innings than they had done in their first, but Harden batted well on the last morning and had excellent support from Mallender and Mushtaq. Needing 332 to win, Worcestershire reached 209 for 2 before Mushtaq brought about a collapse. The last eight wickets went down for 69 runs, and Somerset won with seven balls to spare.

Even without Lara, Warwickshire were too strong for Lancashire. Lancashire romped away on the first day with Crawley, further pressing his claims for an England cap, and Fairbrother adding 164 for the third wicket.

Warwickshire responded with characteristic determination and self-belief. Moles and Twose put on 111 for the first wicket, and Moles anchored the innings. Penney, awarded his county cap, and Ratcliffe added 136 for the fourth wicket, and although the home county lost their last seven wickets for 28 runs, four of them in a 37-ball spell to Chapple, they took a first-innings lead of 15. Lancashire then collapsed before the off-breaks of Neil Smith, who returned the best figures of his career. Seventeen wickets fell on the Saturday. With Twose and Penney again in fine form, Warwickshire strolled to victory on the Monday and climbed to fourth place in the championship.

G.W. White, who had played one game for Somerset in 1991 and who had scored a century for Combined Universities against the New Zealanders a fortnight earlier, appeared for Hampshire against the South Africans. There was some impressive bowling from Udal and Donald, and some good batting by Rhodes, Terry and Morris, but rain was the winner.

AXA EQUITY & LAW LEAGUE

3 July *at Derby*

Middlesex 175 for 8
Derbyshire 177 for 2 (T.J.G. O'Gorman 63 not out, C.J. Adams 56 not out)

Derbyshire (4 pts.) won by 8 wickets

at Darlington

Surrey 222 for 8 (A.W. Smith 50 not out, A. Walker 4 for 43)
Durham 220 for 9 (A.C. Cummins 67)

Surrey (4 pts.) won by 2 runs

at Bristol

Gloucestershire 184 for 9
Glamorgan 187 for 6 (H. Morris 52, S.P. James 50)

Glamorgan (4 pts.) won by 4 wickets

at Maidstone

Yorkshire 165 for 8 (A.P. Grayson 55)
Kent 166 for 2 (T.R. Ward 59, C.L. Hooper 52 not out)

Kent (4 pts.) won by 8 wickets

at Leicester

Leicestershire 171 (P.V. Simmons 57)
Essex 147 (P.V. Simmons 4 for 19)

Leicestershire (4 pts.) won by 24 runs

at Trent Bridge

Nottinghamshire 231 for 6 (J.C. Adams 66, C.C. Lewis 53 not out)

Northamptonshire 232 for 9 (M.B. Loye 64, G.W. Mike 4 for 41)

Northamptonshire (4 pts.) won by 1 wicket

at Taunton

Somerset 194 for 9 (G.D. Rose 69, R.J. Harden 59)
Worcestershire 195 for 5 (T.S. Curtis 55)

Worcestershire (4 pts.) won by 5 wickets

at Edgbaston

Lancashire 204 for 7 (N.H. Fairbrother 70)
Warwickshire 111 (G. Yates 4 for 34)

Lancashire (4 pts.) won by 93 runs

Warwickshire suffered their final defeat in any competition during the season when they were crushed by Lancashire at Edgbaston. The visitors lost two wickets in Munton's first over, but Fairbrother hit 70, and Hegg took 24 off five consecutive balls in Munton's last over. With Yates returning his best Sunday League figures, Warwickshire were bowled out in 29.4 overs. Durham recovered from 77 for 6 to reach 220 through the efforts of Cummins and Scott, but were eventually beaten by two runs while Gibson hit six off Walsh's last ball of the match to give Glamorgan victory at Bristol. Northamptonshire also beat Nottinghamshire off the last ball at Trent Bridge. Capel, batting at number nine through injury, hit a six off the second ball of the last over and four off the final delivery to win the match. Radford's 23 off 13 balls took Worcestershire to victory after 31 had been needed from three overs at Taunton.

THIRD TEST MATCH
ENGLAND *v.* NEW ZEALAND, at Old Trafford

Darren Gough earned his first Test cap in place of Taylor while Greatbatch became Young's third opening partner of the series in the New Zealand side. Atherton won the toss, and England batted on a pitch which proved to have far less pace than anticipated.

Stewart began with his customary flourish. In 45 minutes, off 31 balls, he reached 24 with 5 fours before pulling the ball into the hands of mid-on. Next ball, Nash found the outside edge of Gooch's bat, and Young held the catch at second slip. On the stroke of lunch, Smith edged the ball down into his stumps, and England were 68 for 3. Nash had bowled splendidly, and had Owens and Pringle not maintained a line too far outside the off stump, England may well have been in worse trouble.

Hick started sensibly and comfortably and, in 95 minutes, added 36 grinding runs with his captain. He perished as had Stewart, lifting a pull shot and being caught at mid-wicket. White was most uncertain, but he stayed to the end of the day by which time he had made 42, Atherton had reached 96, and England were 199 for 4.

Atherton's determination and concentration was never more needed, nor more in evidence. He had come to terms with the limitations that the pitch imposed, and he had grafted relentlessly to take himself and his side to a position of some strength.

White did not add to his overnight score, being caught low at slip early on the second morning after an invaluable stand of 99 with Atherton. The England skipper's reward for his immense application came when he drove Nash regally through the covers to reach his seventh Test century. It had taken him 384 minutes, but it had come close to putting England in an impregnable position. He was adjudged leg before when he was on 111, a hasty and harsh decision by the South African umpire Lambson, for the ball from Nash struck Atherton high. His innings included 14 fours, and he faced 307 balls. Suddenly, when Rhodes was out 11 runs later, England were 235 for 7, and the position which had seemed impregnable about half an hour earlier looked decidedly uncertain.

Certainty was provided by DeFreitas and Gough. Off 70 balls, DeFreitas reached 50; Gough, in his first Test, moved to 50 off 95 balls. In 34 overs, they added 130 highly entertaining and very hard-hit runs. For DeFreitas, it was the occasion of his highest Test score; for Gough, it was a debut with some thundering drives and pulls which raised memories of Ian Botham.

Mark Greatbatch had fractured a thumb while fielding, but he still opened the New Zealand innings and in the second over he spooned a catch to slip to give Gough a wicket with his fifth ball in Test cricket. Rutherford pushed a ball from DeFreitas into the hands of mid-off where Gooch almost spilled the catch, his 100th in Test cricket. Fleming was dropped by Fraser at cover, but almost immediately he was caught behind off Gough. This brought in Crowe who had been off the field unwell for much of the day and had been ill before the match. Shortly before the close, at 84 for 4, he lost Young, and Gough and DeFreitas had built upon their captain's work to give England total command.

Nightwatchman Hart was caught by Atherton at point with nine runs added to the overnight score, and wickets fell regularly. New Zealand were all out at lunch on the third day for 151. Only Crowe, eighth out, had displayed the necessary technique and application. His 70 had come off 91 balls and included a six and 11 fours. He was a class above and apart from his colleagues, and he was batting again before tea.

In the third over of the afternoon, Young was leg before to DeFreitas. Rutherford was caught behind off Gough who bounced and yorked with an enthusiasm that was infectious. Fleming again disappointed, caught at second slip, and Greatbatch's innings, just short of two hours, ended when he was caught at backward square-leg off White, a useful seamer capable of some very quick deliveries.

Crowe at last found a partner in Thomson, and they added 59 in 17 overs before Thomson drove a catch into the covers. Crowe was less belligerent than he had been

THIRD CORNHILL TEST MATCH – ENGLAND v. NEW ZEALAND
30 June, 1, 2, 4 and 5 July 1994 at Old Trafford, Manchester

ENGLAND

FIRST INNINGS			
M.A. Atherton (capt)	lbw, b Nash		111
A.J. Stewart	c Pringle, b Nash		24
G.A. Gooch	c Young, b Nash		0
R.A. Smith	b Owens		13
G.A. Hick	c Nash, b Owens		20
C. White	c Hart, b Owens		42
*S.J. Rhodes	c Parore, b Nash		12
P.A.J. DeFreitas	b Owens		69
D. Gough	c sub (Davis), b Pringle		65
A.R.C. Fraser	c Thomson, b Hart		10
P.M. Such	not out		5
Extras	lb 8, w 1, nb 2		11
			382

NEW ZEALAND

FIRST INNINGS			SECOND INNINGS	
B.A. Young	c Rhodes, b DeFreitas	25	lbw, b DeFreitas	8
M.J. Greatbatch	c Hick, b Gough	0	c DeFreitas, b White	21
K.R. Rutherford (capt)	c Gooch, b DeFreitas	7	c Rhodes, b Gough	13
S.P. Fleming	c Rhodes, b Gough	14	c Hick, b Fraser	11
M.D. Crowe	c Gooch, b White	70	c Hick, b DeFreitas	115
M.N. Hart	c Atherton, b Gough	0	(8) not out	16
S.A. Thomson	c Rhodes, b DeFreitas	9	(6) c Smith, b Gough	21
*A.C. Parore	c Rhodes, b White	7	(7) c Gooch, b DeFreitas	71
D.J. Nash	not out	8	not out	6
C. Pringle	b White	0		
M.B. Owens	c Stewart, b Gough	4		
Extras	nb 7	7	b 8, lb 13, nb 5	26
		151	(for 7 wickets)	308

	O	M	R	W
Nash	39	9	107	4
Owens	34	12	99	4
Pringle	39	12	95	1
Hart	27.3	9	50	1
Thomson	7	1	23	–

	O	M	R	W	O	M	R	W
Fraser	12	3	17	–	19	7	34	1
Gough	16.3	2	47	4	31.2	5	105	2
DeFreitas	17	2	61	3	30	6	60	3
Such	5	2	8	–	10	2	39	–
White	7	1	18	3	14	3	36	1
Gooch					2	–	13	–

FALL OF WICKETS

1–37, 2–37, 3–68, 4–104, 5–203, 6–224, 7–235, 8–365, 9–372

FALL OF WICKETS

1–2, 2–12, 3–47, 4–82, 5–93, 6–113, 7–125, 8–140, 9–140

1–8, 2–34, 3–48, 4–73, 5–132, 6–273, 7–287

Umpires: D.R. Shepherd & S.B. Lambson

Match drawn

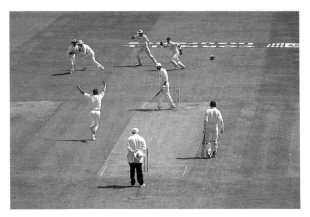

ABOVE: *Gooch falls caught at slip for 0. (Patrick Eagar)*

RIGHT: *Robin Smith is bowled by Owens who shows his delight. (Patrick Eagar)*

in the first innings, but Parore balanced Crowe's watchful defence with uninhibited aggression, lashing 9 fours and reaching 50 off 65 balls. New Zealand closed on 205 for 5, Crowe on 65.

Only 82 minutes' play was possible between lunch and tea on the fourth day, and England seemed to lose their sense of purpose as Crowe and Parore added 48 runs in that time. Crowe moved on to 94, Parore to 66, his highest Test score.

Rain also ruined the final day of the third Test match. Crowe and Parore took their stand to 141, a record for New Zealand's sixth wicket against England. Parore was caught in the covers. Crowe was caught at second slip after he had hit 15 fours and faced 237 balls in scoring his

17th Test century. It was another admirable innings, and a match-saving one. Never fully fit, hampered by an injured knee, he remained one of the world's greatest batsmen. He was a giant in the series although the adjudicators chose to give the awards to DeFreitas and Nash.

England had won their first home series for four years, and New Zealand ended with hope for a better future. They had been deprived of the presence of their three main strike bowlers, Cairns, Doull and Morrison, but they had battled on, and Nash is good.

TEST MATCH AVERAGES – ENGLAND v. NEW ZEALAND

ENGLAND BATTING

	M	Inns	NO	Runs	HS	Av	100s	50s
M.A. Atherton	3	4	–	273	111	68.25	2	–
S.J. Rhodes	3	4	2	117	49	58.50	–	–
G.A. Gooch	3	4	–	223	210	55.75	1	–
A.J. Stewart	3	4	–	196	119	49.00	1	–
P.A.J. DeFreitas	3	4	1	134	69	44.66	–	2
G.A. Hick	3	4	–	133	58	33.25	–	1
C. White	3	4	–	121	51	30.25	–	1
R.A. Smith	3	4	–	120	78	30.00	–	1
P.M. Such	3	2	1	9	5*	9.00	–	–
A.R.C. Fraser	3	4	–	30	10	7.50	–	–

Played in one Test: D. Gough 65; J.P. Taylor 0 & 0*; D.E. Malcolm did not bat

NEW ZEALAND BATTING

	M	Inns	NO	Runs	HS	Av	100s	50s
M.D. Crowe	3	6	–	380	142	63.33	2	1
A.C. Parore	3	6	1	213	71	42.60	–	1
B.A. Young	3	6	–	195	94	32.50	–	2
S.A. Thomson	3	6	1	157	69	31.40	–	1
D.J. Nash	3	5	2	94	56	31.33	–	1
S.P. Fleming	3	6	–	170	54	28.33	–	1
M.N. Hart	3	5	1	99	36	24.75	–	–
K.R. Rutherford	3	6	–	96	37	16.00	–	–
C. Pringle	2	2	–	14	14	7.00	–	–
M.B. Owens	2	2	1	6	4	6.00	–	–

Played in one Test: H.T. Davis 0* & 0*; M.J. Greatbatch 0 & 21; B.R. Hartland 6 & 22; G.R. Larsen 8 & 2; B.A. Pocock 10 & 2

ENGLAND BOWLING

	Overs	Mds	Runs	Wkts	Av	Best	10/m	5/inn
G.A. Hick	18	8	21	1	21.00	1-12	–	–
P.A.J. DeFreitas	143.5	24	451	21	21.47	5-71	–	1
D. Gough	47.5	7	152	6	25.33	4-47	–	–
C. White	62.1	15	197	6	32.83	3-18	–	–
J.P. Taylor	26	6	82	2	41.00	1-18	–	–
D.E. Malcolm	27.4	7	84	2	42.00	2-45	–	–
A.R.C. Fraser	126	37	296	7	42.28	2-40	–	–
P.M. Such	123	36	264	6	44.00	2-50	–	–
G.A. Gooch	7	1	26	–	–			

NEW ZEALAND BOWLING

	Overs	Mds	Runs	Wkts	Av	Best	10/m	5/inn
D.J. Nash	129	28	429	17	25.23	6-76	1	2
M.B. Owens	51	15	168	5	33.60	4-99	–	–
C. Pringle	78	22	201	3	67.00	1-41	–	–
M.N. Hart	147.3	60	278	4	69.50	1-50	–	–
S.A. Thomson	79	19	163	2	81.50	1-40	–	–

Bowled in one innings: H.T. Davis 21–0–93–1; G.R. Larsen 44.4–11–116–2

ENGLAND FIELDING FIGURES

12 – S.J. Rhodes; 9 – G.A. Hick; 3 – G.A. Gooch, A.J. Stewart, C. White and R.A. Smith; 2 – M.A. Atherton; 1 – P.A.J. DeFreitas and A.R.C. Fraser

NEW ZEALAND FIELDING FIGURES

7 – A.C. Parore; 3 – B.A. Young, S.A. Thomson and D.J. Nash; 2 – M.D. Crowe and G.R. Larsen; 1 – S.P. Fleming, M.N. Hart, K.R. Rutherford and sub (H.T. Davis)

NATWEST TROPHY

ROUND TWO

6 July *at Southampton*

Hampshire 187 (M.C.J. Nicholas 62)
Kent 188 for 6

Kent won by 4 wickets

(Man of the Match – M.C.J. Nicholas)

at Uxbridge

Middlesex 259 for 6 (M.A. Roseberry 67)
Northamptonshire 262 for 3 (A.J. Lamb 129 not out, R.J. Bailey 52)

Northamptonshire won by 7 wickets

(Man of the Match – A.J. Lamb)

at The Oval

Surrey 343 for 6 (G.P. Thorpe 145 not out, D.M. Ward 87)
Lancashire 218 (I.D. Austin 57, Wasim Akram 50, C.E. Cuffy 4 for 43)

Surrey won by 125 runs

(Man of the Match – G.P. Thorpe)

6 and 7 July *at Darlington*

Durham 278 (P. Bainbridge 85, J.E. Morris 67, D.G. Cork 5 for 43)
Derbyshire 280 for 6 (T.J.G. O'Gorman 89, M. Azharuddin 74 not out, A.C. Cummins 4 for 48)

Derbyshire won by 4 wickets

(Man of the Match – T.J.G. O'Gorman)

at Cardiff

Glamorgan 316 for 8 (M.P. Maynard 78, P.A. Cottey 57, R.D.B. Croft 50, M.S. Kasprowicz 5 for 60)
Essex 240 for 9 (N. Shahid 85 not out)

Glamorgan won by 76 runs

(Man of the Match – O.D. Gibson)

at Leicester

Warwickshire 296 for 6 (T.L. Penney 65 not out, P.A. Smith 50)
Leicestershire 168 (T.J. Boon 55)

Warwickshire won by 128 runs

(Man of the Match – T.L. Penney)

at Worcester

Worcestershire 263 for 6 (G.A. Hick 97)

Nottinghamshire 174

Worcestershire won by 89 runs

(Man of the Match – G.A. Hick)

at Leeds

Yorkshire 215 (D. Byas 71, A.N. Hayhurst 4 for 29)
Somerset 216 for 7 (R.J. Harden 64)

Somerset won by 3 wickets

(Man of the Match – A.N. Hayhurst)

Once again the weather was less than kind to the NatWest Trophy, and only three of the eight ties could be completed on the scheduled day. Kent brushed aside Hampshire with considerable ease. Nicholas and Aymes scored 76 in 22 overs, but either side of this stand the Hampshire skipper was a lone survivor on a rapidly sinking ship. Kent needed only 46.5 overs to knock off the required runs.

Northamptonshire without Ambrose had been beaten by Middlesex in the Benson and Hedges Cup; with him, they reversed the result. Choosing to bat first, Middlesex showed consistency on an Uxbridge wicket that oozed runs, but 259 did not look to be an unbeatable score. So it proved. Warren and Felton went for 62, but Bailey and Lamb then added 163. Lamb dominated the stand, reaching his fourth hundred in the competition off 88 balls, and taking 25 off an over from Tufnell. Northamptonshire won with six overs to spare.

Surrey, apprehensive about playing Lancashire at The Oval after traumatic experiences in recent years, recorded their highest score in limited-over cricket as Thorpe, again reminding the England selectors of his talent, hit his first hundred in the NatWest Trophy. He and David Ward, that glorious hitter of the ball, added 180 in 32 overs for the third wicket. In reply, Lancashire subsided to 56 for 6 before the later order offered some respectability.

Durham appeared to have established a strong position when, having made 278 in their 60 overs, they dismissed both Derbyshire openers for 19. O'Gorman and Adams shared a stand of 108, and Azharuddin was the partner in a stand of 109. DeFreitas was out for 0, but Azharuddin and Cork took Derbyshire to the brink of a victory which O'Gorman had made possible. Another contributory factor to the Derbyshire victory was 62 extras, which included 21 wides and 21 no balls!

Only 36.4 overs were possible on the Wednesday at Cardiff, and Glamorgan reached 162 for 3. Some ill-disciplined Essex bowling – 11 wides and 18 no-balls were conceded – and some adventurous batting took the home county to 316. Essex disintegrated to 139 for 7, and although Shahid and Ilott added 73, the issue had long since been decided.

Reeve and Penney shared a sixth-wicket partnership of 123, a record for the 60-over competition, for Warwickshire against Leicestershire. The runs came in 19 overs, and Warwickshire scored 100 runs from their last 10 overs. Leicestershire surrendered feebly.

Worcestershire brushed aside Nottinghamshire with

equal ease while a desultory game at Headingley saw Somerset win with a ball to spare. Byas apart, Yorkshire did not bat well, particularly as van Troost was in wretched form. Hayhurst pressed himself into service and took four wickets. The last seven Yorkshire wickets fell for 45 runs. Somerset reached 202 for 4, but panic set in and victory came in a desperate last over.

6, 7 and 8 July *at Bristol*

Gloucestershire 278 for 9 dec. (M.W. Alleyne 75, R.I. Dawson 71, P.S. de Villiers 5 for 118) and 201 for 7 (M.W. Alleyne 86)

South African 129 for 6 dec. (K.C. Wessels 52)

Match drawn

8 July *at Comber, County Down*

New Zealanders 233 for 6 (S.P. Fleming 58)

Ireland 227 for 9 (S.J.S. Warke 82, C. Pringle 4 for 27)

New Zealanders won by 6 runs

10 July *at Dublin (Malahide)*

Ireland 147 for 9 (S.A. Thomson 4 for 28)

New Zealanders 148 for 1 (B.R. Hartland 80 not out)

New Zealanders won by 9 wickets

at Glasgow (Titwood)

South Africans 7 for 0

***v.* Scotland**

Match abandoned

Rain prevented any play after lunch on the first day at Bristol. The South Africans declared early on the final day, but were upset that Russell failed to respond and attempt to keep the game alive.

 BENSON AND HEDGES CUP FINAL
WARWICKSHIRE *v.* WORCESTERSHIRE, at Lord's

It must be admitted that 1994 did not produce one of the more memorable Benson and Hedges Cup finals. The pitch was more damp than expected, giving an advantage to the side bowling first that disturbs the balance of a one-day game. Warwickshire, by far the better organised and better led of the two sides on the day, were quick to gain from the advantage that winning the toss gave them.

Worcestershire did not enter the final as the most popular of counties. Their attitude when beaten by Essex at the beginning of June had caused adverse comment, and when beating Nottinghamshire in the NatWest Trophy two days before the final Illingworth and Rhodes had been involved in the run out of Crawley which, if not against the law of the game, was certainly against the spirit.

Casting aside these criticisms, Worcestershire began

positively, with nine runs coming in Small's opening over. It was virtually their last crumb of joy. Seymour had started with a splendid straight drive towards the Nursery End boundary. Incomprehensibly, the left-hander, controversially preferred to Weston, swung wildly across the line in Munton's first over, aiming in the direction of mid-wicket, and was bowled. It was a grotesque dismissal. Curtis and Hick were now full of apprehension, and in the 11th over, Curtis dabbed at a good ball from Small, and Piper, a far better wicket-keeper than his England counterpart on this showing, dived in front of first slip to take a splendid catch.

Hick, inhibited, failed to play his natural game. Circumspection dominated, and he played back to the bubbling Paul Smith, missed, and paid the price. The score was 55, and it was already the 25th over.

Hopes rested with Moody, and he and Haynes added 45 in 13 overs, but Moody was never allowed enough of the strike, nor was he ever allowed to dictate to Warwickshire's eager attack. When Haynes was caught behind off Neil Smith's slower ball the game was practically decided.

In the 44th over, Leatherdale skied Paul Smith to long-leg. In the next over, Rhodes fell to Twose second ball, and one more over and Lampitt was gone, caught at backward point. One run had been added when Illingworth hit the ball to Penney and ran. Moody, who had hit 47 off 84 balls and might have conjured something from the closing overs, was run out by yards. Inside four overs, Worcestershire had lost four wickets for two runs. Illingworth and Radford added 42 in eight overs, but the match had long since been over as a contest. All concerned deserved a better surface than was provided here on which to play a major final.

Ostler and Twose hurried and bustled from the start, and Worcestershire could not stem them. Curtis' tactics were unfathomable. With 80 on the board and less than half of Warwickshire's overs used, he persisted in posting long-on and long-off to Hick and offered singles aplenty. A study of the history of the competition might have led him to have followed Gatting's example in the 1983 final. The Middlesex captain turned the tables on Essex by abandoning the one-day concept and setting close fields to attacking bowling. Such courage and wisdom was lacking here.

Worcestershire's fielding generally lacked energy as exemplified by Illingworth's half-hearted attempt to accept a chance offered by Ostler, yet it was through fielding that the opening stand was finally broken in the 24th over. Twose declined the offer of a single, and Leatherdale's return to Hick left Ostler stranded. Twose then ran himself out, beaten by Haynes' hit on the stumps from mid-off. Man of the Moment Lara contributed eight smooth runs off 17 balls before clipping Newport to mid-wicket, and three wickets had fallen for 12 runs in three overs.

There were no more alarms. Paul Smith batted with sense and vigour. Asif Din threw his wicket away when haste was unnecessary, but Reeve joined Man of the Match Smith to take the side he leads so well to the easiest of victories.

One of the features of Warwickshire's victory was the outstanding and effervescent wicket-keeping of Keith Piper. (Adrian Murrell/Allsport)

Meagre success for Worcestershire in the field, Ostler is run out by Hick for 55. (David Munden/Sports-Line)

AXA EQUITY & LAW LEAGUE

10 July at Derby

Durham 144 for 8 (P.A.J. DeFreitas 4 for 9)
Derbyshire 148 for 2 (C.J. Adams 65 not out)

Derbyshire (4 pts.) won by 8 wickets

at Bristol

Gloucestershire 232 for 6 (M.G.N. Windows 72, A.J. Wright 50)
Somerset 194

Gloucestershire (4 pts.) won by 38 runs

at Southampton

Essex 183 (G.A. Gooch 99)
Hampshire 184 for 4 (R.A. Smith 74)

Hampshire (4 pts.) won by 6 wickets

at Leicester

Northamptonshire 210 for 4
Leicestershire 202 (P.A. Nixon 60)

Northamptonshire (4 pts.) won by 8 runs

12 July at The Oval

Surrey 221 for 6 (D.J. Bicknell 95 not out, D.M. Ward 63)
Worcestershire 223 for 1 (T.M. Moody 107, T.S. Curtis 99 not out)

Worcestershire (4 pts.) won by 9 wickets

at Edgbaston

Glamorgan 155 (P.A. Smith 5 for 38)
Warwickshire 156 for 6 (D.A. Reeve 52 not out)

Warwickshire (4 pts.) won by 4 wickets

Worcestershire must have rued the fact that they had not batted at Lord's in the Benson and Hedges Cup final as they did at The Oval against Surrey three days later. Facing a target of 222 in the rescheduled Sunday League game, they won with 21 balls to spare as Moody and Curtis hit 219 for the first wicket. Ward and Darren Bicknell had scored 157 in 27 overs for Surrey's fifth wicket earlier in the match. Warwickshire, with Paul Smith again producing a lively pace and hitting hard, beat Glamorgan to stay top of the table. Reeve, batting with a runner for much of his innings, hit 52 off 73 balls.

COSTCUTTER CUP
at Harrogate

SEMI-FINALS

11 July

Nottinghamshire 233 for 8 (W.M. Noon 60 not out)
Gloucestershire 236 for 4 (T.H.C. Hancock 129 not out)

Gloucestershire won by 6 wickets

12 July

Yorkshire 193 for 7 (R.J. Blakey 55 not out)
Sussex 197 for 7 (C.W.J. Athey 71)

Sussex won by 3 wickets

PRIZE STRUCTURE

£97,680 of the £622,629 Benson and Hedges sponsorship of this event will go in prize money for teams or individuals.

The breakdown is as follows:

- The Champions will win £31,000 (and hold, for one year only, the Benson and Hedges Cup)
- For the Runners-up £15,500
- For the losing Semi-finalists £7,750
- For the losing Quarter-finalists £3,875
- For the Second round winners £1,250
- For the First round winners £925.

INDIVIDUAL GOLD AWARDS

There will be a Benson and Hedges Gold Award for the outstanding individual performance at all matches throughout the Cup.

These will be:

In the First round	£140
In the Second round	£170
In the Quarter-finals	£280
In the Semi-finals	£330
In the Final	£650

The playing conditions and Cup records are on the reverse.

HOLDERS:
DERBYSHIRE COUNTY CRICKET CLUB

BENSON and HEDGES CUP 1994

MARYLEBONE CRICKET CLUB

50p   50p

FINAL

WARWICKSHIRE v. WORCESTERSHIRE

at Lord's Ground, Saturday, July 9th 1994

Any alterations to teams will be announced over the public address system

WARWICKSHIRE		
1 D. P. Ostler	run out	55
2 R. G. Twose	run out	37
3 B. C. Lara	c Hick b Newport	8
4 P. A. Smith	not out	42
5 Asif Din	c Rhodes b Moody	15
†6 D. A. Reeve	not out	9
7 T. L. Penney		
*8 K. J. Piper		
9 N. M. K. Smith		
10 G. C. Small		
11 T. A. Munton		
B , l-b 1, w 5, n-b		6
	Total...	172

WORCESTERSHIRE		
†1 T. S. Curtis	c Piper b Small	13
2 A. C. H. Seymour	b Munton	3
3 G. A. Hick	l b w b P. Smith	27
4 T. M. Moody	run out	47
5 G. R. Haynes	c Piper b N. Smith	22
6 D. A. Leatherdale	c Ostler b P. Smith	4
*7 S. J. Rhodes	l b w b Twose	0
8 S R. Lampitt	c Penney b P. Smith	1
9 R. K. Illingworth	l b w b Reeve	18
10 N. V. Radford	not out	23
11 P. J. Newport	not out	1
B , l-b 2, w 5, n-b 4,		11
	Total...	170

FALL OF THE WICKETS

1...91 2...98 3...103 4...117 5... 6... 7... 8... 9... 10...

Bowling Analysis	O.	M.	R.	W.	Wd.	N-b
Moody	11	2	31	1	...	...
Newport	8	0	29	1	2	...
Lampitt	9.2	1	38	0	...	...
Illingworth	6	0	22	0	...	...
Radford	8	0	39	0	3	...
Hick	2	0	12	0	...	...
					...	...

FALL OF THE WICKETS

1...10 2...28 3...55 4...100 5...124 6...124 7...125 8...126 9...168 10...

Bowling Analysis	O.	M.	R.	W.	Wd.	N-b
Small	11	4	26	1	...	...
Munton	11	3	29	1	1	2
P. Smith	11	1	34	3	1	...
Reeve	9	1	38	1	1	...
N. Smith	5	0	16	1	1	...
Twose	8	1	25	1	1	...

† Captain   * Wicket-keeper

Umpires—H. D. Bird & K. E. Palmer

Scorers—A. E. Davis, J. W. Sewter & E. Solomon

Toss won by—Warwickshire who elected to field

RESULT—Warwickshire won by 6 wickets

The playing conditions for the Benson & Hedges Cup Competition are printed on the back of this score card.

Total runs scored at end of each over :—

Warwickshire

1	2	3	4	5	6	7	8	9	10	11	12	13	14	15	16	17	18	19	20
21	22	23	24	25	26	27	28	29	30	31	32	33	34	35	36	37	38	39	40
41	42	43	44	45	46	47	48	49	50	51	52	53	54	55					

Worcestershire

1	2	3	4	5	6	7	8	9	10	11	12	13	14	15	16	17	18	19	20
21	22	23	24	25	26	27	28	29	30	31	32	33	34	35	36	37	38	39	40
41	42	43	44	45	46	47	48	49	50	51	52	53	54	55					

Reproduced by kind permission of MCC

FINAL

13 July

Sussex 218 for 9
Gloucestershire 220 for 8

Gloucestershire won by 2 wickets

12, 13 and 14 July *at Chester-le-Street*

Durham 228 (G. Fowler 68, C.W. Scott 53,
B.M. McMillan 4 for 47, P.S. de Villiers 4 for 80) and
301 for 7 (G. Fowler 61, P. Bainbridge 50)
South Africans 428 for 4 dec. (G. Kirsten 201 retired
hurt, A.C. Hudson 64, K.C. Wessels 53)

Match drawn

South Africans could be well pleased with their batting
form again Durham, but they were still denied victory as
the injured Larkins proved defiant. Gary Kirsten, who hit
a most competent double century, and Hudson shared an
opening stand of 118.

14, 15, 16 and 18 July *at Southend*

Essex 274 (N. Hussain 82 not out, J.P. Stephenson 58,
G.A. Gooch 53, S.L. Watkin 4 for 63) and 181
(M.A. Garnham 61 not out, R.D.B. Croft 4 for 78)
Glamorgan 248 (P.A. Cottey 54, P.M. Such 5 for 78) and
189 (O.D. Gibson 55, J.H. Childs 5 for 58)

Essex won by 18 runs

Essex 22 pts., Glamorgan 5 pts.

at Portsmouth

Hampshire 192 (K.E. Cooper 4 for 38) and 220
(W.K.M. Benjamin 54)
Gloucestershire 132 (W.K.M. Benjamin 5 for 31) and
115 (S.D. Udal 5 for 46)

Hampshire won by 165 runs

Hampshire 20 pts., Gloucestershire 4 pts.

at Canterbury

Worcestershire 202 (M.A. Ealham 4 for 12) and 422
(G.A. Hick 159, R.K. Illingworth 59 not out, M.M. Patel
4 for 106)
Kent 166 and 318 (S.A. Marsh 67, G.R. Cowdrey 58,
R.K. Illingworth 4 for 79, P.J. Newport 4 for 100)

Worcestershire won by 140 runs

Worcestershire 21 pts., Kent 4 pts.

at Blackpool

Derbyshire 490 for 8 dec. (T.J.G. O'Gorman 145,
A.S. Rollins 97, K.J. Barnett 83) and 186 for 7
Lancashire 83 (P.A.J. DeFreitas 6 for 39, D.E. Malcolm 4
for 43) and 589 (N.H. Fairbrother 136, J.E.R. Gallian

118, G. Yates 54 not out, M.A. Atherton 51,
D.G. Cork 4 for 135)

Derbyshire won by 3 wickets

Derbyshire 21 pts., Lancashire 2 pts.

at Taunton

Somerset 246 (R.J. Turner 56, M.E. Trescothick 53,
K.P. Evans 4 for 46, C.C. Lewis 4 for 65) and 412
(R.J. Harden 68, M.E. Trescothick 59, G.D. Rose 54,
R.A. Pick 4 for 100)
Nottinghamshire 157 (C.C. Lewis 52, A.R. Caddick 6 for
70) and 390 (J.C. Adams 144 not out, K.P. Evans 77,
R.T. Robinson 55, G.D. Rose 4 for 78)

Somerset won by 111 runs

Somerset 21 pts., Nottinghamshire 4 pts.

at Guildford

Warwickshire 246 (G. Welch 59, D.R. Brown 54) and
399 for 9 dec. (A.J. Moles 203 not out, N.M.K. Smith
57)
Surrey 143 (A.J. Stewart 56, R.G. Twose 6 for 28,
T.A. Munton 4 for 41) and 246 (T.A. Munton 5 for 96,
N.M.K. Smith 4 for 71)

Warwickshire won by 256 runs

Warwickshire 21 pts., Surrey 4 pts.

at Arundel

Sussex 228 (C.W.J. Athey 70, R.L. Johnson 4 for 40)
and 238 (M.P. Speight 97, P.C.R. Tufnell 4 for 61)
Middlesex 87 (F.D. Stephenson 5 for 25, J. Lewry 4 for
40) and 231 (M.A. Roseberry 76, I.D.K. Salisbury 6
for 55)

Sussex won by 148 runs

Sussex 21 pts., Middlesex 4 pts.

at Harrogate

Yorkshire 331 (D. Byas 91, A.P. Grayson 60,
M.D. Moxon 53, G.J. Parsons 4 for 67) and 319
(R.B. Richardson 63)
Leicestershire 373 (J.J. Whitaker 148, V.J. Wells 83,
T.J. Boon 56, P.J. Hartley 4 for 110) and 163

Yorkshire won by 114 runs

Yorkshire 21 pts., Leicestershire 7 pts.

16, 17 and 18 July *at Northampton*

South Africans 296 for 7 dec. (K.C. Wessels 70,
J.N. Rhodes 59, B.M. McMillan 50) and 216 for 3
dec. (G. Kirsten 102)
Northamptonshire 250 for 5 dec. (K.M. Curran 81,
M.B. Loye 50) and 131 for 4

Match drawn

Essex ended an horrendous period by beating Glamorgan at Southend and thereby keeping their season alive. Batting first, they were given a good start by Gooch and Stephenson, but both batsmen perished as they attempted to force the pace on a sluggish pitch. The accuracy of the Glamorgan attack took its toll as the last six Essex wickets went down for 25 runs. Hussain alone stood firm amid the wreckage. Where Glamorgan had relied primarily on medium pace to undermine the Essex innings, the home county turned to spinners Such and Childs. Once Cottey and Croft had been separated, the last six wickets fell for 42 runs. Essex had gained a lead of 26, but this mattered little when they tumbled to 90 for 6. Garnham revived optimism, but Glamorgan faced a target of 208 which, on a pitch increasingly aiding the spinners, gave hope to both sides. Gibson, promoted to number three in the absence of the injured Hemp, struck violent blows to tilt the game very much in favour of Glamorgan, but two wickets late on Saturday evening left the visitors on 149 for 5. Croft and Metson progressed happily on the Monday morning and took the score to 181 before Irani, in his one over of the day, trapped Metson leg before as he tried to pull. This preluded a collapse as the last five wickets fell for eight runs, four of the wickets going to Childs.

There were no such dramatics at Portsmouth where the game was all over in three days. Fifteen wickets fell on the first day and 18 on the second on a pitch which offered considerable bounce to bowlers of the calibre of Walsh and Winston Benjamin. Hampshire had a valuable lead of 60 on the first innings, but they lost Morris with a broken finger and four wickets for 78 when they batted a second time. Udal and Benjamin hit well, and a target of 281 was always going to be too much for Gloucestershire on a pitch on which only one batsman had reached 50.

Worcestershire lost their last five wickets for 16 runs at Canterbury, destroyed by Ealham's 4 for 12 in 5.4 overs. Kent succumbed to a mixture of seam and spin, and the advantage passed to the visitors. It was enhanced by an innings of natural forcefulness from Graeme Hick, always at his best when attacking. Patel's left-arm spin dented the middle order, but Illingworth and Parvaz Mirza grasped the game for Worcestershire with a last-wicket stand of 102. By the time Marsh came to the wicket on the last day and batted sensibly and positively, Kent's cause was already lost.

Derbyshire finally beat Lancashire on the last afternoon of an astonishing game in Blackpool. Derbyshire were 41 for 2 before Barnett and O'Gorman added 119. O'Gorman, displaying more patience than one usually associates with him, took his side to a strong position. Adrian Rollins hit the highest score of his career and, to the consternation of the crowd, Derbyshire did not declare until tea-time on the second day. In the next two hours, 24 overs, Lancashire were all out for 83. They followed on and lost only three wickets on the Saturday when Gallian and Fairbrother added 207 for the third wicket. Gallian batted 8¼ hours for his 118, facing 357 balls before being yorked by DeFreitas. Derbyshire faced more frustration when Yates and Chapple, Lancashire's last-wicket pair, added 83. This meant that the visitors had 43

overs in which to score 183, a feat they accomplished for the loss of seven wickets with an over to spare. There were 81 extras in Lancashire's second innings.

Mushtaq Ahmed was not missed at Taunton where the pitch was most helpful to the quicker bowlers. Put in to bat, Somerset were 108 for 5, but Rob Turner and the later order played with sense, and from the time that Turner and Rose added 75, Somerset were in charge. Nottinghamshire crumpled before Caddick on the second day, and Somerset consolidated their position with consistent batting in their second innings. Nottinghamshire lost four wickets on the Saturday evening and, in spite of Adams' fine knock, they never looked like avoiding defeat.

In contrast, Surrey had seemed to have done well in the important clash with Warwickshire at Guildford. They won the toss, asked the visitors to bat and reduced them to 131 for 8. Then, against expectation, Douglas Brown, in his first championship match, and Graeme Welch, playing his third, added 100 good, crisp runs. Warwickshire's 246 was still a moderate total, and although Surrey lost Darren Bicknell for 0, Stewart and Thorpe put on 107. Munton introduced Twose into the attack. He took three wickets in eight balls and finished the day with 5 for 22 from nine overs. Surrey, in disarray at 129 for 6, did not recover on the second morning when Twose completed the best bowling performance of his career as a gentle medium pacer. Reprieved, Warwickshire now moved to an impregnable position as Andy Moles carried his bat through their second innings, and Surrey lost five wickets before the close of play on Saturday. The home side died bravely on the Monday, but the battle had already been lost.

Middlesex, 35 for 7, never recovered from the shock of being bowled out for 87 on the second day at Arundel. They were demolished by Franklyn Stephenson and Jason Lewry, a left-arm pace bowler who was appearing in his first championship match. With Speight accepting the positive role which makes him such an attractive batsman, Sussex took an unassailable position in spite of some fine and encouraging bowling by Tufnell. There was sterner resistance from Middlesex when they batted a second time, but Salisbury produced his best figures of the season, and the game was over in three days.

It looked as if Leicestershire would establish a massive lead over Yorkshire when they reached 302 for 2 in reply to the home county's 331. Whitaker, who scored 100 runs in boundaries, Wells and Boon, who had to retire hurt for a time, had added 260, and Leicestershire were rampant. They were subdued by White who had 3 for 28 in nine overs, and their lead was restricted to 42. From then on, the game moved in favour of Yorkshire. Richardson and White added 96 for their fourth wicket, and the late order made substantial contributions. Needing 278 to win, Leicestershire, without the injured Simmons, fell to Hartley, Gough and Stemp, and Yorkshire moved off the bottom with their first win of the season.

The South Africans settled for gentle batting practice on the eve of the first Test match. Donald and de Villiers did not play against Northamptonshire.

AXA EQUITY & LAW LEAGUE

17 July *at Southend*

Essex 214 for 7 (G.A. Gooch 101)
Glamorgan 214 (P.A. Cottey 70)

Match tied

Essex 2 pts., Glamorgan 2 pts.

at Portsmouth

Gloucestershire 149
Hampshire 152 for 5

Hampshire (4 pts.) won by 5 wickets

at Canterbury

Worcestershire 144 (M.J. McCague 4 for 19,
M.V. Fleming 4 for 36)
Kent 145 for 6

Kent (4 pts.) won by 4 wickets)

at Old Trafford

Lancashire 211 for 6 (J.P. Crawley 64, N.H. Fairbrother
51)
Derbyshire 203 for 9

Lancashire (4 pts.) won by 8 runs

at Taunton

Somerset 319 for 4 (M.N. Lathwell 117, G.D. Rose 61
not out, N.A. Folland 61)
Nottinghamshire 193 for 9 (J.C. Adams 86,
A.P. van Troost 4 for 23)

Somerset (4 pts.) won by 126 runs

at Guildford

Warwickshire 249 for 7 (R.G. Twose 96 not out,
D.P. Ostler 55)
Surrey 236 for 8 (A.D. Brown 69, D.M. Ward 63)

Warwickshire (4 pts.) won by 13 runs

at Arundel

Sussex 225 for 5 (A.P. Wells 103)
Middlesex 208 (F.D. Stephenson 4 for 24)

Sussex (4 pts.) won by 17 runs

at Scarborough

Leicestershire 182 for 9 (P.V. Simmons 85)
Yorkshire 186 for 5 (D. Byas 63)

Yorkshire (4 pts.) won by 5 wickets

Gooch established a Sunday League record by hitting his
12th century in the competition. Glamorgan needed 10

*Alamgir Sheriyar performed the hat-trick for Leicestershire against
Durham on 23 July; Vince Wells accomplished the same feat in the
same match.*

off the last over to win, and two off the last ball with
Barwick facing Irani. Knight's throw from the covers beat
Barwick's dive, and the match was tied. Alan Wells hit
103 off 101 balls as Sussex staged the first Sunday League
game to be played at Arundel, and Richie Richardson hit a
four off the last ball to give Yorkshire victory over Leicestershire. Lancashire kept up their challenge by beating
Derbyshire, but Warwickshire remained top with a fine
win over Surrey. They were languishing on 96 for 5 before
Roger Twose hit 7 sixes in an innings of 96 off 67 balls.

21, 22, 23 and **25 July** *at Durham University*

Durham 225 (S.J.E. Brown 69, W. Larkins 53,
M. Saxelby 53, V.J. Wells 5 for 50) and 196
(J.A. Daley 57, A. Sheriyar 4 for 44)
Leicestershire 428 (J.J. Whitaker 107, V.J. Wells 77,
B.F. Smith 59, S.J.E. Brown 4 for 111)

Leicestershire won by an innings and 5 runs

Leicestershire 24 pts., Durham 5 pts.

at Abergavenny

Kent 408 (T.R. Ward 110, C.L. Hooper 87, M.R. Benson 66, R.P. Lefebvre 4 for 63) and 330 (T.R. Ward 125, S.R. Barwick 4 for 79)

Glamorgan 266 (S.P. James 67, O.D. Gibson 67) and 378 (D.L. Hemp 133, P.A. Cottey 80, M.M. Patel 4 for 88)

Kent won by 94 runs

Kent 24 pts., Glamorgan 5 pts.

at Cheltenham

Gloucestershire 291 (M.G.N. Windows 73, R.I. Dawson 71, P.J. Hartley 4 for 77) and 484 (M.W. Alleyne 109, A.J. Wright 85, T.H.C. Hancock 58, M.A. Robinson 4 for 92)

Yorkshire 247 (M.P. Vaughan 74, C.A. Walsh 4 for 75) and 204 (R.J. Blakey 82, C.A. Walsh 6 for 85)

Gloucestershire won by 324 runs

Gloucestershire 22 pts., Yorkshire 5 pts.

at Old Trafford

Lancashire 163 (M.A. Feltham 4 for 50) and 484 for 9 dec. (N.H. Fairbrother 204, N.J. Speak 82, S.P. Titchard 76)

Middlesex 101 (I.D. Austin 5 for 23, M. Watkinson 4 for 26) and 185 (I.D. Austin 5 for 37)

Lancashire won by 361 runs

Lancashire 20 pts., Middlesex 4 pts.

at Northampton

Northamptonshire 529 (R.R. Montgomerie 151, R.J. Bailey 93, M.B. Loye 79, K.M. Curran 69) and 8 for 0

Derbyshire 211 (K.J. Barnett 77, A.S. Rollins 52, C.E.L. Ambrose 7 for 48) and 324 (K.M. Krikken 54, T.J.G. O'Gorman 51, K.J. Barnett 50)

Northamptonshire won by 10 wickets

Northamptonshire 24 pts., Derbyshire 2 pts.

at Trent Bridge

Nottinghamshire 125 and 248 (R.T. Robinson 60 not out, A.C.S. Pigott 6 for 46)

Surrey 604 for 4 dec. (D.J. Bicknell 235 not out, A.D. Brown 134 not out, D.M. Ward 81, G.P. Thorpe 70)

Surrey won by an innings and 231 runs

Surrey 23 pts., Nottinghamshire 1 pt.

at Hove

Somerset 360 (M.N. Lathwell 124, R.J. Harden 79, A.R. Caddick 58 not out, E.E. Hemmings 7 for 66)

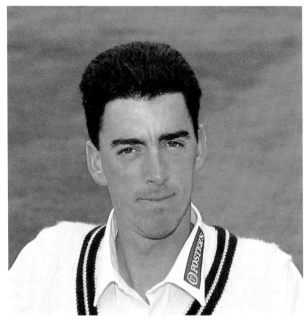

A career-best 235 not out for Darren Bicknell as Surrey beat Nottinghamshire by an innings at Trent Bridge, 21–5 July. (Mike Hewitt/Allsport)

and 302 for 8 dec. (M.N. Lathwell 92, M.E. Trescothick 87, P.W. Jarvis 7 for 58)

Sussex 280 (N.J. Lenham 68, J.W. Hall 59, H.R.J. Trump 6 for 68) and 314 (N.J. Lenham 73, J.W. Hall 54, H.R.J. Trump 6 for 127, G.D. Rose 4 for 45)

Somerset won by 68 runs

Somerset 24 pts., Sussex 5 pts.

at Edgbaston

Warwickshire 361 (B.C. Lara 70, N.M.K. Smith 65, A.J. Moles 57) and 268 (R.G. Twose 92, J.H. Childs 4 for 63)

Essex 215 (N.V. Knight 56, N. Hussain 53, T.A. Munton 6 for 89) and 211 (N.V. Knight 113, D.R. Brown 4 for 25, T.A. Munton 4 for 41)

Warwickshire won by 203 runs

Warwickshire 24 pts., Essex 5 pts.

at Worcester

Hampshire 228 (M.C.J. Nicholas 84 not out, S.R. Lampitt 5 for 33, P.J. Newport 4 for 50) and 336 (R.A. Smith 162, S.R. Lampitt 4 for 49)

Worcestershire 193 (W.K.M. Benjamin 6 for 46) and 315 (T.S. Curtis 95, S.D. Udal 6 for 85)

Hampshire won by 56 runs

Hampshire 21 pts., Worcestershire 4 pts.

Only four of the nine matches went into the fourth day. One of the matches to finish in three days was the remarkable encounter in Durham. In his first championship match, left-arm pace bowler Alamgir Sheriyar dismissed both Fowler and Morris before Larkins began to attack the bowling. The medium pace of Vince Wells was then introduced, and he immediately accounted for Larkins and Daley. Four overs later, he performed the first hat-trick of his career, having Bainbridge and Cummins caught at slip by Simmons and trapping Scott leg before. Wells enjoyed a fine match as he partnered Whitaker in a fourth-wicket stand of 184. Simon Brown followed his career-best 69 with four wickets, but Leicestershire led by 203 on the first innings. This proved to be enough for victory. When Durham batted again Wells took another three wickets, Millns captured three and Sheriyar finished the innings with the second hat-trick of the match. Scott was caught by Nixon after the ball had jumped out of Simmons' hands; Graveney was also caught behind, in more orthodox fashion; and Lugsden was bowled. For Sheriyar, deputising for the injured Mullally, it was a sensational end to a dramatic debut in the championship.

The game at Abergavenny was one of those that did last four days. Kent began with a stand of 143 between Ward and Benson, and runs came briskly. Hooper added only three to his overnight score on the Friday, and the last seven wickets went down for 20 runs. Glamorgan, too, suffered a collapse. They reached 153 for 2, and then lost five wickets for 27 runs. Gibson and Metson added 85, but Glamorgan trailed by 142. Ward was again in belligerent mood and reached his second hundred of the match. It was the second occasion on which he had scored a century in each innings against Glamorgan. Needing 473 to win, Glamorgan lost James on the Saturday evening. A fifth-wicket partnership of 186 in 49 overs between the increasingly impressive Hemp and the tenacious Cottey gave Glamorgan hopes of an improbable victory. Once they were separated, however, the innings quickly ended, the last four wickets going down for 17 runs.

A third-wicket stand of 134 between Windows and Dawson gave substance to the Gloucestershire innings against Yorkshire. Moxon and Vaughan scored 142 for Yorkshire's first wicket, but thereafter only Grayson offered resistance to the Gloucestershire pace bowlers. By Saturday evening, the home county had taken complete control of the match with Mark Alleyne hitting his first championship hundred of the summer. Needing 529 to win, Yorkshire stumbled to 154 for 5 and succumbed to Walsh, an admirable and inspiring captain and a very fine fast bowler.

Middlesex gave a first-class debut to pace bowler Marc, but this event was overshadowed by the other happenings at Old Trafford. At the end of the first day, Lancashire had been bowled out for 163, and Middlesex were 62 for 3. Middlesex succumbed for 101 on the Friday and, led by a blistering innings from Fairbrother, Lancashire reached 414 for 4 at nearly five runs an over. Fairbrother and Speak added 135, and Fairbrother ended the day with 198 off 188 balls. His innings included 21 fours and 7 sixes.

He completed his double century on the Saturday morning, and Middlesex again batted poorly as Ian Austin took 10 wickets in a match for the first time. The game had produced 933 runs and a deserved and resounding victory for Lancashire, but the men from the ministry deemed that the pitch had been inadequately prepared and was too damp on the first day and, accordingly, Lancashire were deducted 25 points. The reasoning of those entrusted with the care of a lovely game defies comprehension, but one fears that the path they have chosen leads to the extinction of county cricket.

With his highest score in first-class cricket, his first championship century, Richard Montgomerie set Northamptonshire on the road to a huge score against Derbyshire. He shared an opening stand of 105 with Warren and a second-wicket stand of 189 with Bailey. There were later flourishes from Loye and Curran who added 115 for the fifth wicket, taking their stand into the second day, and Northamptonshire were in an impregnable position. Only Barnett offered serious resistance to the hostility of Ambrose but, following-on, Derbyshire showed consistent application and determination. It was still not enough to save them, and the game ended in three days.

Surrey held on to their place at the head of the table with a three-day victory at Trent Bridge. Nottinghamshire fell to Joey Benjamin on the opening day, and Darren Bicknell and Thorpe quickly added 156 after Smith had gone for 0. Nightwatchman Pigott was soon out on the Friday, but Ward and Bicknell added 172. Brown and Bicknell continued their stand into the third morning, and when Thorpe declared at 604 for 4, they had added 253, with Bicknell having reached the highest score of his career. Nottinghamshire duly fell with Pigott returning his best figures for Surrey.

Jarvis also had his best return for his new county, Sussex, but the consistency of the Somerset batting proved decisive. Lathwell played two fine innings, and Trump took 12 wickets in the match to take his side to victory. Trump was aided in the second innings by Graham Rose who bowled off-cutters instead of his usual seamers.

Warwickshire demolished Essex in three days at Edgbaston to keep close to Surrey in the championship. They scored 361 in 100.2 overs on the opening day with Lara hitting 70 off 81 balls and Neil Smith taking them to maximum batting points with 65 at number eight. Nick Knight held five catches. Essex had six overs before the close and lost Stephenson and Such for 43. Knight and Hussain both made fifties, but Warwickshire took the honours. Acting skipper Tim Munton was in top form, and Keith Piper established a county record with seven catches behind the stumps. Warwickshire's approach, batting, bowling or fielding, was always positive and, in spite of Nick Knight's championship-best 113, Essex never looked likely to approach the 415 they needed for victory. Four wickets in five overs from Dougie Brown undermined their efforts, and they went from 151 for 2 to 211 all out to give Warwickshire their fifth championship win in succession.

A stand of 100 between Nicholas and Aymes was the only batting of substance on the first day for Hampshire against Worcestershire. Winston Benjamin's hostility and a splendidly belligerent innings from Robin Smith turned the game in favour of Hampshire on the second day. Smith went on to make 162 in nearly five hours, and Udal bowled Hampshire to victory on the last day although resistance was stern.

AXA EQUITY & LAW LEAGUE

24 July at Durham University

Leicestershire 244 for 6 (V.J. Wells 100, P.V. Simmons 88)

***v.* Durham**

Match abandoned

Leicestershire 2 pts., Durham 2 pts.

at Ebbw Vale

Kent 155 for 7 (C.L. Hooper 60)

Glamorgan 147 for 7

Kent (4 pts.) won by 8 runs

at Cheltenham

Yorkshire 260

Gloucestershire 261 for 7 (M.W. Alleyne 102 not out)

Gloucestershire (4 pts.) won by 3 wickets

at Old Trafford

Lancashire 48 for 1

***v.* Middlesex**

Match abandoned

Lancashire 2 pts., Middlesex 2 pts.

at Northampton

Derbyshire 233 for 4 (M. Azharuddin 111 not out)

Northamptonshire 140 for 5

Northamptonshire (4 pts.) won on faster scoring rate

at Trent Bridge

Nottinghamshire 223 for 5 (J.C. Adams 93 not out)

Surrey 143 for 1 (D.J. Bicknell 61 not out, A.D. Brown 55)

Match abandoned

Nottinghamshire 2 pts., Surrey 2 pts.

at Hove

Somerset 157 for 6

Sussex 158 for 3 (D.M. Smith 55 not out)

Sussex (4 pts.) won by 7 wickets

at Edgbaston

Essex 147

Warwickshire 148 for 7

Warwickshire (4 pts.) won by 3 wickets

at Worcester

Worcestershire 201 for 5 (G.R. Haynes 83, T.S. Curtis 69)

Hampshire 159

Worcestershire (4 pts.) won by 42 runs

Azharuddin hit 111 off 81 balls, with 2 fours and 8 sixes, for Derbyshire against Northamptonshire. He and Rollins added 142 in 19 overs, but the home side, well behind the required run rate at the time, were given a lease of life by a thunderstorm which reduced their target and gave them an unexpected victory. Rain was also an advantage to Warwickshire, for the game at Old Trafford was abandoned, and Warwickshire's win over Essex put them six points clear of the field. Alleyne hit his second century of the weekend for Gloucestershire against Yorkshire, but there was sad news from Cheltenham. It was announced, that at his own request, Richie Richardson was being released from his contract with Yorkshire. There had been great concern over Richardson's health, and a London specialist had diagnosed acute fatigue syndrome. Richardson was the first to be destroyed by the endless, thoughtless round of Test cricket. One fears this likeable man and very fine cricketer will not be the last.

FIRST TEST MATCH
ENGLAND *v.* SOUTH AFRICA, at Lord's

Lord's was bathed in sunshine to welcome the return of South Africa to Test cricket in England after an absence of 29 years. England left out Robin Smith and replaced him with John Crawley while Such gave way to Salisbury. The Hampshire off-spinner Udal had also been named in the England party, but he was omitted on the morning of the match. South Africa did not include a regular spin bowler in their side. Wessels won the toss, and South Africa batted.

Hudson, who had arrived in England with the reputation of being the most consistent of the South African batsmen and, along with Cronje, probably the best, had not enjoyed a happy tour, and he did nothing to brighten his form before the Lord's capacity crowd. In the 10th over, he hooked Gough's bouncer, and Gooch ran several yards in front of the Mound Stand to take an excellent catch. The veteran was applauded wherever he fielded from that time on.

Cronje went six overs later, caught high at short-leg off an inside edge onto his pad. Wessels now joined the impressive and confident Gary Kirsten, and crisis faded as lunch came with 76 scored from 28 overs.

The third-wicket pair played sensibly, adding 106, with Kirsten hitting 12 fours, mainly on the off side. They had

just begun to accelerate and take control when Hick, who had earlier bowled one over, returned and deceived Gary Kirsten with a ball that turned from the rough so that the batsman spooned gently to cover. Peter Kirsten replaced his half-brother, but he never settled. A controversial selection for the tour, because he is not the fluent batsman that he was in his Derbyshire days, he fell in the second over after tea, prodding at Gough and edging thinly to the keeper.

England, having removed four of South Africa's top five batsmen for 164 on a good pitch, could well claim the advantage, but Rhodes, in a fashion all his own, gave Wessels the assistance he required, and, in 26 overs, 75 runs were added. The pitch was a little slow, but this may have suited Wessels who pushed and stroked for 298 minutes and occasionally produced a savage cover-drive to reach an historic century. He and his side could not conceal their joy, and the crowd rose to him. His innings seemed to symbolise South Africa's endeavours to be welcomed back into the fold.

Rhodes played across the line to White and lost his off

FIRST CORNHILL TEST MATCH – ENGLAND v. SOUTH AFRICA
21, 22, 23 and 24 July 1994 at Lord's

SOUTH AFRICA

	FIRST INNINGS		SECOND INNINGS	
A.C. Hudson	c Gooch, b Gough	6	(2) lbw, b Fraser	3
G. Kirsten	c DeFreitas, b Hick	72	(1) st Rhodes, b Hick	44
W.J. Cronje	c Crawley, b Fraser	7	c Fraser, b Gough	32
K.C. Wessels (capt)	c Rhodes, b Gough	105	c Crawley, b Salisbury	28
P.N. Kirsten	c Rhodes, b Gough	8	b Gough	42
J.N. Rhodes	b White	32	b Gough	32
B.M. McMillan	c Rhodes, b Fraser	29	not out	39
*D.J. Richardson	lbw, b Gough	26	c Rhodes, b Fraser	3
C.R. Matthews	b White	41	b Gough	25
P.S. de Villiers	c Rhodes, b Fraser	8		
A.A. Donald	not out	5		
Extras	lb 9, nb 9	18	b 8, lb 10, nb 12	30
		357	(for 8 wickets, dec.)	278

ENGLAND

	FIRST INNINGS		SECOND INNINGS	
M.A. Atherton (capt)	c Wessels, b Donald	20	c McMillan, b de Villiers	8
A.J. Stewart	b Donald	12	c Richardson, b Matthews	27
J.P. Crawley	c Hudson, b de Villiers	9	c Hudson, b McMillan	7
G.A. Hick	c Richardson, b de Villiers	38	lbw, b McMillan	11
G.A. Gooch	lbw, b de Villiers	20	lbw, b Donald	28
C. White	c Richardson, b Donald	10	c Wessels, b Matthews	0
*S.J. Rhodes	b McMillan	15	not out	14
I.D.K. Salisbury	not out	6	(10) lbw, b Donald	0
P.A.J. DeFreitas	c Wessels, b Donald	20	(8) c G. Kirsten, b Matthews	1
D. Gough	c and b Donald	12	(9) retired hurt	0
A.R.C. Fraser	run out	3	lbw, b McMillan	1
Extras	b 2, lb 5, nb 8	15	b 1, lb 1	2
		180		99

	O	M	R	W	O	M	R	W		O	M	R	W	O	M	R	W
DeFreitas	18	5	67	–	14	3	43	–	Donald	19.3	5	74	5	12	5	29	2
Gough	28	6	76	4	19.3	5	46	4	De Villiers	16	5	28	3	12	4	26	1
Salisbury	25	2	68	–	19	4	53	1	Matthews	16	6	46	–	14	6	25	3
Fraser	24.5	7	72	3	23	5	62	2	McMillan	10	1	25	1	6.5	2	16	3
Hick	10	5	22	1	24	14	38	1	Cronje					1	–	1	–
White	13	2	43	2	3	–	18	–									

FALL OF WICKETS

1–18, 2–35, 3–141, 4–164, 5–239, 6–241, 7–281, 8–334, 9–348
1–14, 2–73, 3–101, 4–141, 5–208, 6–209, 7–220, 8–278

FALL OF WICKETS

1–19, 2–41, 3–68, 4–107, 5–119, 6–136, 7–141, 8–161, 9–176
1–16, 2–29, 3–45, 4–74, 5–74, 6–82, 7–85, 8–88, 9–99

Umpires: H.D. Bird & S.G. Randell

South Africa won by 356 runs

stump, and three overs later, Wessels drove loosely and tiredly at a wideish ball from Gough and was caught by England's Rhodes, diving to his left. South Africa were 244 for 6 at the close, and England could still claim the advantage. Wessels had hit 15 fours and faced 217 balls.

England's advantage was quickly eroded on the Friday morning. The new ball was due, but Salisbury bowled a couple of meaningless overs, and DeFreitas bowled a line outside the off stump that was wide and very hittable. He was plundered for 31 runs in five overs. Richardson, having hit 26 off 35 balls, was leg before to Gough's inswinger, but Matthews scored more freely and more merrily than Richardson had done. In the first hour of the day, 67 runs were scored. Of the 53 runs scored in 12 overs for the eighth wicket, Matthews was responsible for 41. He was out when he tried to turn White to leg and was bowled off his pad.

McMillan, who had stood firm for 131 minutes, was ninth out, caught down the leg side off Fraser, and it was Fraser, the most consistent of the England bowlers who brought the innings to a close. By then, South Africa had taken 113 runs from the morning's play.

Two boundaries came in Donald's opening over, but the fifth ball of his second kept low, and Stewart was bowled off an inside edge. Crawley's first Test runs were four through mid-wicket off Donald, and he looked good off his legs, clipping de Villiers to the boundary. After eight overs England were 35 for 1, but in the tenth over, Crawley, yearning too often to hit to leg, was taken at slip off de Villiers.

Atherton had begun well, but he became becalmed and he had been batting for 89 minutes when he played at a ball from Donald with bat well away from his body and was caught at slip. Hick had survived an early, close appeal for leg before to Donald and had settled to play with authority. Two fours off the back foot were regal shots, but the loss of Gooch seemed to sap his confidence. He remained static on 38 for nearly 40 minutes before pushing timidly at de Villiers and paying the price. This left England crippled on 119 for 5.

Rhodes had somehow survived leg before appeals by McMillan, but he had no answer to the same bowler's inswinger which went through bat and pad; and White then fell to Donald's outswinger. England were 141 for 7, and the day had belonged totally to South Africa and to their all-pace attack.

There was defiance on the Saturday morning – briefly. DeFreitas hit 4 fours and made 20 off 10 balls in his nine-minute innings. Donald had him taken at slip and then took a fine, tumbling one-handed caught-and-bowled to remove Gough. The end, perhaps, typified the difference between the two sides. Gary Kirsten ran from short-leg towards the long-on boundary in pursuit of the ball. He picked up, turned and threw in one movement to run out Fraser who was attempting a third run. In 39 minutes, England had lost their last three wickets for 39 runs. South Africa led by 177 runs.

Fraser and Gough opened the bowling, and Hudson was out in the third over as he played back to Fraser. The rest of the day was something of a grind as South Africa failed to reach three runs an over and scored 195 for 4 in

Gary Kirsten sweeps Salisbury as Rhodes and Hick look on attentively. (David Munden/Sports-Line)

315 minutes. Gary Kirsten played some handsome shots before jumping out to Hick, who seemed to mesmerise the batsmen with slowness rather than spin. Cronje had already gone, hooking at Gough, and Wessels was taken at short-leg off Salisbury.

The inclusion of Salisbury in the England side raises debate. It is a wonderful weapon to have a leg-spinner of quality in one's side, but is it right to include a leg-spinner if there is no leg-spinner of Test standard available? At present, Salisbury is not a Test match bowler.

Such considerations were overwhelmed by the news that television, which was now the major authority in the rationale, organisation and judgement of cricket, had discovered Atherton, the England captain, ball tampering. Atherton was shown rubbing the ball after taking his hand from his pocket. It was later revealed to the referee, though not in the initial enquiry, that Atherton had dust in his pocket on which to dry his hands. Although this had not been told to Peter Burge in the first instance, the public was informed that the England captain had offered his trousers to the referee for inspection. This tedious affair resulted in Atherton being twice fined, and in a wealth of newsprint being wasted over the next few days with charge, countercharge, judgement and execution. The whole sorry affair obscured the ridiculous punishment of the deduction of 25 points imposed upon Lancashire at Old Trafford and tended to minimise the dreadful defeat inflicted upon England by a hard-working but far from great side.

Wessels declared at lunch on the Sunday by which time South Africa were 455 runs ahead of England. There were some strange factors to be considered in the composition and deployment of the England side. The left-handed qualities of Thorpe or Darren Bicknell or several others had once again been ignored; and if White was a Test all-rounder, why did he bowl only one spell of three overs while South Africa made 278 in 102.3 overs? In contrast, Hick bowled 24 overs although he bowls little for Worces-tershire and cannot be considered as a front-line Test off-spinner. Why, too, was Rhodes preferred as wicket-keeper when he was so obviously inferior to several others in the country, Piper and Marsh among them? England were again wandering rudderless, and Sunday afternoon gave terrible evidence of this.

Atherton was the victim of a fine ball from de Villiers, an outswinger which the batsman edged low to McMillan at second slip. Crawley, too, perished at slip although with less excuse, and when Hick was instantly and cruelly adjudged leg before by Umpire Randell after two fine back-foot boundaries England were 35 for 3.

Stewart had shown restraint, and he and Gooch added 29 in 44 minutes to suggest that the crisis was passing. It had not yet begun. Stewart was caught behind off a good ball from Matthews, and next ball, White, all at sea, was caught at slip. Donald was recalled and had Gooch leg before, falling to leg in a manner not unfamiliar. Gough was struck and retired hurt, and soon Procter was waving the South African flag from the team balcony. It was a thoroughly merited and historic victory, and it deserved to be celebrated. It was, for Mike Atherton, the low point of his career, but he is a determined young man, and England need him badly as captain and opener.

NATWEST TROPHY

QUARTER-FINALS

26 July at Derby

Derbyshire 128 (D.G. Cork 62, M.A. Ealham 4 for 10)
Kent 129 for 5
Kent won by 5 wickets
(Man of the Match – M.A. Ealham)

at Taunton

Somerset 124 (N.M.K. Smith 4 for 26)
Warwickshire 125 for 2
Warwickshire won by 8 wickets
(Man of the Match – N.M.K. Smith)

at Northampton

Northamptonshire 128 (P.J. Newport 4 for 30)
Worcestershire 129 for 8
Worcestershire won by 2 wickets
(Man of the Match – S.J. Rhodes)

27 July at Swansea

Glamorgan 161 (A.J. Murphy 6 for 26)
Surrey 165 for 5 (G.P. Thorpe 56)
Surrey won by 5 wickets
(Man of the Match – A.J. Murphy)

Only two batsmen reached 50 and 165 was the highest score by any side in the quarter-finals of the NatWest

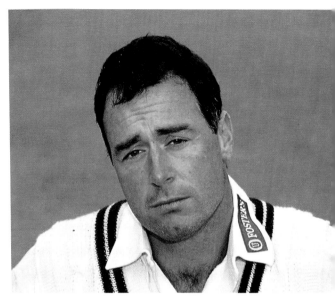
Six wickets for Tony Murphy and the Man of the Match award as Surrey crush Glamorgan. (Mike Hewitt/Allsport)

Trophy. On a damp pitch at Derby, the winning stand of 44 between Cowdrey and Ealham occupied 20 overs, which says much about the difficulties of batting. Barnett was bowled in the opening over, and, in spite of Cork's 62 off 74 balls, a marvellous effort, Derbyshire never recovered. Ealham pipped Cork for the individual award, for he followed his 4 for 10 with 26 not out.

Warwickshire continued to look unstoppable and to stay on course to win all four trophies when they humiliated Somerset, winning with nearly 36 overs to spare.

Steve Rhodes took four catches and a stumping as Worcestershire tumbled out Northamptonshire for 128. Victory seemed a formality, but Worcestershire were shattered by Curtly Ambrose and reduced to 96 for 7. Rhodes, who batted for an hour and a half, found an ally in Newport, and through sheer determination, the pair added 32, Newport being out when the scores were level.

The match at Swansea could not be played until the Wednesday. Stewart won the toss and asked Glamorgan to bat in conditions which aided the seam bowlers. Cuffy and Benjamin began with the meanest of spells. Indeed, Cuffy's first 10 overs cost only six runs and brought him the wickets of both openers. Cottey alone seemed capable of dealing with the moving ball, but his innings of 36 was ended by a fine leaping catch behind the stumps by Alec Stewart who set up a record for the competition with seven catches in the innings. Four of his catches were off the bowling of Tony Murphy who maintained a relentless length and moved the ball consistently and considerably. This was an outstanding performance, and he was well worthy of his six wickets and his award. Darren Bicknell was bowled sweeping and Stewart was well caught low at mid-on by Lefebvre, but Surrey never looked like losing. Thorpe hit a brisk 56, and Brown clouted. Both fell to the deserving Croft, but Surrey won with 11.2 overs to spare.

27, 28 and 29 July *at Trent Bridge*

South Africans 327 for 6 dec. (W.J. Cronje 108, J.N. Rhodes 71 not out, P.N. Kirsten 57) and 164 for 3 dec. (D.J. Cullinan 61 not out)

Nottinghamshire 218 (R.T. Robinson 82) and 139 (P.L. Symcox 5 for 44, T.G. Shaw 4 for 29)

South Africans won by 134 runs

Relying on the spinners not wanted in the Tests, the South Africans won their first victory over a county side. Cronje hit his first hundred of the tour, reaching three figures off 148 balls.

28, 29, 30 July and 1 August *at Chesterfield*

Warwickshire 280 (B.C. Lara 142, S.J. Base 5 for 92) and 259 (D.P. Ostler 68, A.J. Moles 63, B.C. Lara 51, K.J. Barnett 5 for 31)

Derbyshire 198 (T.A. Munton 7 for 52) and 202 (N.M.K. Smith 5 for 69)

Warwickshire won by 139 runs

Warwickshire 22 pts., Derbyshire 4 pts.

at Durham University

Yorkshire 405 (R.J. Blakey 94 not out, B. Parker 52, S.J.E. Brown 5 for 131) and 230 for 8 dec. (R.J. Blakey 67, A.P. Grayson 62 not out)

Durham 357 (C.W. Scott 107 not out, J.A. Daley 84, C.E.W. Silverwood 4 for 67) and 162 (J.I. Longley 54, R.D. Stemp 6 for 37)

Yorkshire won by 116 runs

Yorkshire 22 pts., Durham 6 pts.

at Swansea

Somerset 372 (A.N. Hayhurst 121, R.J. Harden 90, R.J. Turner 64 not out, O.D. Gibson 5 for 79) and 302 (M.E. Trescothick 115, A.N. Hayhurst 65, O.D. Gibson 6 for 80)

Glamorgan 533 (P.A. Cottey 191, O.D. Gibson 81, D.L. Hemp 77) and 84 for 7

Match drawn

Somerset 6 pts., Glamorgan 5 pts.

at Cheltenham

Kent 360 (M.R. Benson 159, T.R. Ward 98, M.W. Alleyne 5 for 78) and 195 (M.A. Ealham 68 not out, C.A. Walsh 4 for 82)

Gloucestershire 271 (M.W. Alleyne 96, R.I. Dawson 53, M.J. McCague 5 for 89) and 234 (M.W. Alleyne 80, C.A. Walsh 66, M.J. McCague 4 for 65)

Kent won by 50 runs

Kent 24 pts., Gloucestershire 6 pts.

at Southampton

Northamptonshire 164 (A.L. Penberthy 56 not out, C.A. Connor 7 for 47) and 358 (A.J. Lamb 131, S.D. Udal 5 for 119)

Hampshire 229 (M.C.J. Nicholas 53, J.G. Hughes 5 for 69) and 269 (M.C.J. Nicholas 107, C.E.L. Ambrose 7 for 44)

Northamptonshire won by 24 runs

Northamptonshire 20 pts., Hampshire 5 pts.

at Uxbridge

Middlesex 527 for 7 dec. (M.R. Ramprakash 123 not out, M.W. Gatting 108, M.A. Roseberry 88, D.L. Haynes 63) and 277 for 3 dec. (D.L. Haynes 123, M.W. Gatting 81 not out)

Essex 422 for 6 dec. (G.A. Gooch 140, R.C. Irani 102 not out, N.V. Knight 59) and 307 for 7 (N. Hussain 86, J.J.B. Lewis 76 not out)

Match drawn

Middlesex 6 pts., Essex 6 pts.

at The Oval

Surrey 195 (G.P. Thorpe 71, F.D. Stephenson 6 for 50) and 115 (F.D. Stephenson 5 for 32)

Sussex 344 (J.W. Hall 85, P. Moores 66, C. Remy 55 not out, A.J. Hollioake 4 for 48)

Sussex won by an innings and 34 runs

Sussex 22 pts., Surrey 3 pts.

30, 31 July and 1 August *at Leicester*

South Africa 270 for 8 dec. (D.J. Cullinan 66, G.F.J. Liebenberg 59) and 163 for 5 dec. (G. Kirsten 62, W.J. Cronje 54)

Leicestershire 167 (P.S. de Villiers 6 for 67) and 216 for 7 (J.J. Whitaker 59)

Match drawn

Warwickshire moved to the top of the table with a three-day victory over Derbyshire. On the first day, when 16 wickets fell, Lara hit a hundred before lunch off 94 balls, but once he and Penney had been separated after adding 160 for the fourth wicket, Warwickshire's last seven wickets went down for 56 runs. Munton wrecked Derbyshire, taking 4 for 23 in seven overs at one stage, but the key factor in Warwickshire's continuing success was their effervescent team work. Neil Smith bowled his side to victory in three days, and with three of his five victims he had the aid of Keith Piper. The Warwickshire wicket-keeper had six catches and a stumping in the innings, which brought his total dismissals for the match to a record 11, 10 catches and a stumping.

After Yorkshire had batted into the second day and reached a daunting score Durham slipped to 38 for 4. They were rescued by Daley and Scott who added 130 for the sixth wicket. Scott, who made his first-class debut in 1981, had hit a maiden first-class century earlier in the season, and he now reached his second. Silverwood returned his best bowling figures for Yorkshire, but Durham's fighting tail restricted the Yorkshire lead to 48. When Cummins and Brown reduced Yorkshire to 44 for 4 in their second innings Durham were on top, but Blakey and Grayson revived the visitors' chances. Set a target of 279 in 60 overs, Durham were beaten with 14 balls to spare, Stemp producing the best bowling figures of his career.

There was considerable tedium on the first day at Swansea. Somerset were 43 for 3 before Harden and Hayhurst added 143 in 62 overs. Turner, still inexplicably preferred to Burns, batted 78 overs for his 64, and Steve Barwick ended with a Glamorgan record for overs and maidens – 65.2–29–109–1. Glamorgan shamed Somerset by reaching 350 in 88 overs. Hemp, who reached a thousand runs for the season, and Cottey, who made the highest score of his career, led the charge, and Gibson followed with his highest score for Glamorgan. Gibson was also to return his best bowling figures for the county. Glamorgan's 533 included 81 extras, 65 of them no-balls. Andre van Troost finished with the unenviable figures of 29–3–172–3. Even though Glamorgan were without Watkin in their attack when Somerset batted again, the visitors still laboured. Turner faced 42 balls for 0. Needing 142 in 22 overs to win, Glamorgan lost their way completely, and were thankful to hang on for a draw in a match in which their earlier cricket deserved victory.

Benson and Ward scored 209 for Kent's first wicket against Gloucestershire, but Kent's last eight wickets fell for 64 with Alleyne completing his best bowling performance. On the second day, Dawson and Alleyne added 121 for Gloucestershire's fourth wicket, but with McCague finding form and fitness after his absence and Marsh holding catches, Kent took an 89-run lead. They were slipped to 84 for 6 against the magnificent Walsh before Ealham, Marsh and Patel rallied them. Gloucestershire had the better part of two days in which to score 285, but McCague and Ealham reduced them to 94 for 7. Walsh and Alleyne retaliated with a vigorous assault which brought 127 for the eighth wicket, but Kent won in three days.

At Southampton, 14 wickets fell on the first day. Seven of them went to Cardigan Connor, and John Hughes replied with a career-best bowling performance for Northamptonshire. In spite of Mark Nicholas' effort, the Hampshire lead was restricted to 65. Northamptonshire lost three wickets in erasing the arrears, but Lamb's 100 off 158 balls gave the visitors new life. The tail wagged furiously, and the last four wickets produced 136 runs. Needing 294 to win, Hampshire were 44 for 4. Mark Nicholas played a fighting innings, reaching his first first-class hundred for three years in the most difficult circumstances against some very hostile bowling. It was a fine knock, but when he went so did Hampshire's hopes, and the strength and power of Ambrose was the deciding factor.

The Uxbridge pitch provided five centuries, 1533 runs, and only 23 wickets in four days. You won't lose 25 points

for that although some feel that you should. The oddities of the match were that Ramprakash hit a six through his own car window, and that Irani, unable to bowl because of a back injury, was attacked on the second evening by what was described as a drunken member of Uxbridge Rugby Club. He received a black eye, but hit a century the following day. There were 67 extras in Middlesex's first innings, 52 of them were no-balls. Essex were set a target of 381 in 92 overs, but the early loss of Gooch and Stephenson made them lose interest.

Surrey were knocked off the top of the table when Sussex beat them in three days at The Oval. They were twice shattered by the Sussex pace trio of Stephenson, Jarvis and Giddins. The loss of three wickets for 52 and the temporary retirement of Speight left Sussex in some trouble, but Moores and Hall added 132. Jamie Hall entered the record books, for it took him 304 minutes to reach 50, the slowest recorded fifty in the county championship. Remy hit a brisker, maiden fifty, and Sussex won with a day to spare.

In the tourists' match, Wessels was hit on the arm and went to hospital for X-ray and treatment. There was a first-class debut for Maddy, and Cullinan and Liebenberg added 121 for the South Africans' fourth wicket.

 ## AXA EQUITY & LAW LEAGUE

31 July *at Chesterfield*

Warwickshire 239 for 8 (R.G. Twose 74, N.M.K. Smith 56, D.G. Cork 4 for 44)

***v.* Derbyshire**

Match abandoned

Warwickshire 2 pts., Derbyshire 2 pts.

at Durham University

Yorkshire 174

Durham 165 for 4 (W. Larkins 55, M. Saxelby 54)

Durham (4 pts.) won on faster scoring rate

at Swansea

Somerset 107

Glamorgan 111 for 5

Glamorgan (4 pts.) won by 5 wickets

at Cheltenham

Kent 227 for 4 (M.V. Fleming 79, C.L. Hooper 61)

Gloucestershire 177 for 6 (A.J. Wright 69)

Kent (4 pts.) won by 50 runs

at Southampton

Northamptonshire 191 for 8

Hampshire 185 for 7 (V.P. Terry 95)

Northamptonshire (4 pts.) won by 6 runs

at Uxbridge

Essex 135 (R.S. Yeabsley 5 for 32)
Middlesex 136 for 3

Middlesex (4 pts.) won by 7 wickets

at The Oval

Sussex 185 for 7
Surrey 187 for 4 (A.J. Hollioake 72 not out)

Surrey (4 pts.) won by 6 wickets

Larkins and Saxelby hit 120 for Durham's first wicket, and then three wickets fell for 0. Rain gave Durham victory. Kent provided some phenomenal hitting at Cheltenham where the match was reduced to 20 overs. Fleming hit 70 off 35 balls. He hit 6 sixes, three in succession off Babington who conceded 50 runs in three overs. Hooper's 61 came off 33 balls. Yeabsley produced his best bowling figures in one-day cricket as Essex tumbled to Middlesex, and Hollioake had a one-day highest score for Surrey who beat Sussex.

4, 5, 6 and 8 August *at Chesterfield*

Derbyshire 247 (A.S. Rollins 79, D.G. Cork 55) and 366 for 8 dec. (K.J. Barnett 77 not out, C.J. Adams 68)
Gloucestershire 195 (A.J. Wright 65, A.E. Warner 4 for 39) and 263 (D.E. Malcolm 6 for 95)

Derbyshire won by 155 runs

Derbyshire 21 pts., Gloucestershire 4 pts.

at Chelmsford

Essex 216 (R.C. Irani 61, G. Chapple 4 for 86) and 138 (N.V. Knight 53)
Lancashire 414 (N.H. Fairbrother 103, J.E.R. Gallian 98, S.P. Titchard 61, P.M. Such 4 for 66)

Lancashire won by an innings and 60 runs

Lancashire 24 pts., Essex 4 pts.

at Canterbury

Hampshire 298 (M.C.J. Nicholas 108, R.A. Smith 69, M.J. McCague 5 for 89) and 182 (M.A. Ealham 7 for 53)
Kent 273 (C.L. Hooper 138, C.A. Connor 4 for 73, K.D. James 4 for 78) and 189 (M.R. Benson 71 not out, C.A. Connor 6 for 59)

Hampshire won by 18 runs

Hampshire 22 pts., Kent 6 pts.

at Lord's

Middlesex 267 (M.W. Gatting 73) and 368 for 4 dec. (D.L. Haynes 134, J.D. Carr 78 not out)
Glamorgan 285 (O.D. Gibson 70, M.A. Feltham 4 for 51) and 270 (P.A. Cottey 79, H. Morris 69, A. Dale 52, J.E. Emburey 6 for 89, P.N. Weekes 4 for 79)

Middlesex won by 80 runs

Middlesex 22 pts., Glamorgan 6 pts.

at Northampton

Sussex 273 (F.D. Stephenson 64, C.C. Remy 60) and 270 (M.P. Speight 81, A.P. Wells 62, F.D. Stephenson 54)
Northamptonshire 144 (F.D. Stephenson 5 for 22) and 182 (M.B. Loye 53, R.R. Montgomerie 52, E.S.H. Giddins 5 for 20)

Sussex won by 217 runs

Sussex 22 pts., Northamptonshire 4 pts.

at Trent Bridge

Leicestershire 318 (T.J. Boon 70, N.E. Briers 58, P.V. Simmons 54, G.W. Mike 4 for 50) and 188 (J.J. Whitaker 91, J.A. Afford 4 for 73)
Nottinghamshire 337 (C.C. Lewis 95, R.T. Robinson 55, A.D. Mullally 5 for 85) and 170 for 4 (P.R. Pollard 61, G.F. Archer 58)

Nottinghamshire won by 6 wickets

Nottinghamshire 23 pts., Leicestershire 7 pts.

at Taunton

Durham 171 (G.D. Rose 4 for 40) and 203 (A.R. Caddick 6 for 51, A.P. van Troost 4 for 81)
Somerset 234 (M.N. Lathwell 67, A.C. Cummins 6 for 64) and 141 for 1 (M.N. Lathwell 69, I. Fletcher 54 not out)

Somerset won by 9 wickets

Somerset 21 pts., Durham 4 pts.

at Worcester

Warwickshire 216 (S.R. Lampitt 4 for 32) and 346 for 5 (T.L. Penney 84 not out, A.J. Moles 67, G. Welch 66, B.C. Lara 57)
Worcestershire 473 for 4 dec. (T.S. Curtis 180, W.P.C. Weston 94, D.A. Leatherdale 71 not out, S.R. Lampitt 56 not out, N.M.K. Smith 4 for 141)

Match drawn

Worcestershire 6 pts., Warwickshire 1 pt.

Derbyshire were always in control of the match at Chesterfield where Gloucestershire were without Walsh. The conditions were not easy for batsmen, and Rollins played a solid innings which occupied 71 overs. Barnett and Adams batted with more flair in the home county's second innings, and when Malcolm struck to reduce Gloucestershire to 67 for 4 on the Saturday evening the game was as good as over.

Essex gave one of their worst displays of recent years in losing to Lancashire. They won the toss and decided to bat first in a steamy atmosphere where the ball was moving in all directions. After two overs they came off for bad light which made one wonder why they chose to bat. Irani and Garnham apart, they batted wretchedly, and Garnham was forced to retire for a period after being struck by a ball from Martin. Gallian and Titchard hit 144 in 43 overs for Lancashire's first wicket, and Fairbrother hit 103 off 177 balls. Garnham, who had received 16 stitches, left the field with double vision, and when he returned he was hit by a delivery from Childs and needed more stitches. Amid all this, Lancashire pressed on in a highly professional manner and won inside three days.

Mark Nicholas hit his second century in successive matches, and with Cardigan Connor again in good form, Hampshire won a keen contest at Canterbury. Ealham, enjoying a fine run of form, returned the best bowling figures of his career, but, set to make 207 in 106 overs, Kent slid from 30 for 0 to 60 for 6. The ever-reliable Marsh shared a stand of 48 with Benson, and McCague then helped Benson to add 57, but, in spite of the gallant Benson carrying his bat through an innings for the first time in his career, Kent failed to reach their target.

Plagued by injuries to pace bowlers, Middlesex gave a debut to emergency signing Harris of Teddington C.C. He had appeared for Leicestershire in 1986. Glamorgan gave a first-class debut to medium-pacer Parkin. Glamorgan took a narrow first-innings lead, but the batting of Haynes and Carr put Middlesex in a strong position. Needing 351 to win, Glamorgan were given an excellent start by Morris and Dale who put on 119, but then came collapse, and only Cottey offered resistance to the off-spin of Weekes and Emburey.

Sussex again won in three days. Remy hit his highest score and added 102 in 23 overs for the sixth wicket after Sussex had slipped to 147 for 5. Speight and Wells added 146 for Sussex's third wicket in the second innings after Northamptonshire had just managed to save the follow-on. As they had done in the first innings, the Sussex pace attack proved too much for Northamptonshire, and the game was over with more than a day to spare.

Having been on level terms with Nottinghamshire for the first two days, Leicestershire collapsed against the spin of Afford on the Saturday and were beaten comfortably on the Monday.

Somerset, who gave a championship debut to Ecclestone of Oxford University, beat Durham in two days. Durham lost their last eight second-innings wickets for 48 runs.

Warwickshire's championship hopes received a severe setback when they took only one point from the game at Worcester. Rain shortened the first day, and Curtis and Weston put on 208 for the home county's first wicket. Curtis' hundred took 350 minutes, 302 deliveries. Lampitt and Leatherdale were speedier in an unbroken fifth-wicket stand of 133 and, with the game out of their reach, Warwickshire could only bat for survival. Moles and nightwatchman Welch shared a third-wicket stand of 135, Welch hitting the highest score of his career.

AXA EQUITY & LAW LEAGUE

7 August *at Chesterfield*

Derbyshire 226 for 3 (P.D. Bowler 56, K.J. Barnett 50 not out)

Gloucestershire 193 for 8

Derbyshire (4 pts.) won by 33 runs

at Chelmsford

Lancashire 221 for 4 (S.P. Titchard 96, J.E.R. Gallian 84)

Essex 222 for 5 (J.P. Stephenson 73)

Essex (4 pts.) won by 5 wickets

at Canterbury

Hampshire 169 for 7 (T.C. Middleton 65)

Kent 170 for 4 (C.L. Hooper 56)

Kent (4 pts.) won by 6 wickets

at Lord's

Middlesex 151 for 5 (K.R. Brown 52 not out)

Glamorgan 152 for 3 (D.L. Hemp 73)

Glamorgan (4 pts.) won by 7 wickets)

at Northampton

Sussex 152 for 7

Northamptonshire 156 for 4 (R.J. Warren 55)

Northamptonshire (4 pts.) won by 6 wickets

Trent Bridge

Leicestershire 168 (P.A. Nixon 72)

Nottinghamshire 142 (P.R. Pollard 53, V.J. Wells 4 for 31)

Leicestershire (4 pts.) won by 26 runs

at Taunton

Somerset 233 for 6 (G.D. Rose 91 not out, S.C. Ecclestone 66)

Durham 234 for 4 (J.I. Longley 88, M. Saxelby 52)

Durham (4 pts.) won by 6 wickets

at Edgbaston

Worcestershire 182 for 8 (G.R. Haynes 76)

Warwickshire 179 for 8 (N.V. Radford 4 for 36)

Worcestershire (4 pts.) won by 3 runs

Gloucestershire introduced two new cricketers to the Sunday League, bowlers Averis and Sheeraz, but Derbyshire won comfortably at Chesterfield. An opening stand of 159 between Gallian and Titchard appeared to have put Lancashire on the way to victory at Chelmsford, but

Essex surprisingly won with a ball to spare. Durham hit 43 off the last 3.2 overs to beat Somerset, but the astonishing result was at Edgbaston where the largest crowd for 14 years gathered for a Sunday League match. Warwickshire's costly failure to bowl their overs in the required time meant that the match became a 38-over contest. Facing a target of 183, Ostler and Neil Smith hit 105 in 14 overs. Worcestershire appeared beaten, but the introduction of Radford saw both openers caught at deep square-leg by Seymour. Radford also dismissed Paul Smith and Twose, and Leatherdale ran out Asif Din, whose benefit match it was, for 0. Lara, who made 37, fell to Lampitt in the penultimate over, and Warwickshire needed eight from the final over bowled by Leatherdale. He kept his head, bowled Piper, conceded only four runs, and Worcestershire moved to within four points of Warwickshire and had a game in hand.

SECOND TEST MATCH
ENGLAND v. SOUTH AFRICA, at Leeds

An injury to Craig White denied him a Test match on his home ground and kept him out of cricket for the rest of the season. He was replaced by Graham Thorpe while Phil Tufnell, who had only slight success since his return to cricket, came in for Ian Salisbury. The philosophy that proclaimed that if a cricketer did well in county cricket he would be rewarded had quickly disappeared.

South Africa were unchanged, and it was they who had to take the field when Atherton won the toss. The first day belonged undeniably to England. The batsmen countered the pace of Donald, and the off-side theory of the other bowlers, to such an extent that the South Africans looked decidedly careworn by the end of the day. This was due mostly to an innings of panache and confidence from Thorpe who gave greater variety to the England batting and an innings of utmost character by Atherton who set a magnificent example to his side and won back any respect he might have lost with the public after the incidents at Lord's.

Gooch went off with a great flourish, but he drove at a wideish ball in the 11th over and was caught low at second slip. Hick was to be caught in the same position shortly after lunch, but this time McMillan held the ball high to his right. In the next 37 overs, Atherton and Thorpe added 142 runs. Thorpe injected a sense of urgency into the batting, driving and hooking with certainty. He hit 13 fours in his 112-ball innings, and he played with such authority as to leave all bemused as to why this was his first Test of the season. He was out when he drove McMillan to cover without, for once, moving his feet.

Atherton, felled once by a bouncer from McMillan, worked the ball off his legs to great effect and played some exquisite cover drives. He had scored only 19 in 27 overs at lunch, but his assurance, his determination and his calm were warming characteristics. He exuded the air of a leader who was determined to succeed. He richly deserved a century, but having faced 224 balls, batted for

320 minutes and hit a six (a hook off de Villiers) and 9 fours, he was splendidly caught and bowled by McMillan who enjoyed a very good day. Stewart and Crawley took England to 288 for 4 at the close.

Stewart and Crawley consolidated England's position of superiority the next morning, with Crawley holding out until the stroke of lunch, and Stewart playing with the freedom and strength on the off-side which makes him such an attractive batsman. He was bowled by McMillan some 40 minutes after lunch having hit 15 fours and faced 171 balls. Rhodes again proved his worth as a batsman, and DeFreitas and Gough made positive contributions. Atherton was happy to declare and leave South Africa 36 minutes' batting at the end of the day. In the fifth of the nine overs possible, Gough found the edge of Hudson's bat, and Atherton took the catch at third slip. With South Africa 31 for 1 at the close, England were well on top.

The first over of the third day was all that England could have hoped for. At DeFreitas' third ball, Gary Kirsten nibbled unnecessarily outside the off stump, and Rhodes took the catch. The next ball bowled Hansie Cronje. Richardson played with sensible aggression, but he was bowled by Fraser, and three overs before lunch, Fraser struck again, having Wessels taken at short-leg off a ball that lifted sharply in contrast to the shooter which had bowled Richardson. At lunch, South Africa were 122 for 5, the follow-on looming.

In the afternoon session, South Africa scored 83 runs and lost, in the penultimate over before the break, Jonty Rhodes who was adjudged caught behind off Gough although the batsman vigorously demonstrated that the ball had touched his arm, not bat or glove, a gesture which Mr Burge overlooked.

In 32 overs in the final session of the day, South Africa made 113, and the follow-on was avoided far more easily than had looked possible at the lunch interval. This was mainly due to Peter Kirsten who, at the age of 39 years 84 days, became the second oldest player to score a maiden Test century. He had been something of a controversial choice for the tour, for many believed that his best years were behind him and that a younger batsman should have been chosen. Certainly he has not the fluency of his Derbyshire days, but he showed the greatest possible resolve for 295 minutes, faced 226 balls, hit 13 fours and saved his side. He was caught in the gully off DeFreitas just before the close, but by then McMillan was gaining control. He hit one more boundary to prove the point, and South Africa closed on 318 for 7.

If England had been in charge for most of the first three days, the fourth saw South Africa come close to parity. The eighth-wicket stand between McMillan and Matthews became worth 77 in 15 overs. Matthews hit a six and 10 fours in an innings which brought South Africa to within 30 of the England score. He had splendid support from de Villiers and Donald. DeFreitas finished with four wickets, deservedly, and Tufnell had two of the last three wickets. Gough was disappointing. Perhaps over-reacting and over-responsive to the acclaim of the local crowd, he indulged too frequently in the short-pitched delivery or the intended yorker and suffered in consequence.

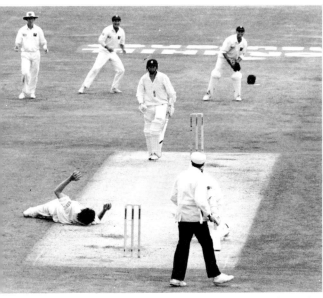

Atherton, on 99, is caught and bowled by McMillan. (Patrick Eagar)

England lost Atherton at 39 and Gooch at 57 in the 25th over, but Hick and, in particular, Thorpe played positive cricket. England closed on 144 for 2, and the game looked destined to be drawn.

The last morning was notable for the fact that Thorpe again batted splendidly, hitting 10 fours before being run out by Richardson after an unwise run from a Hick mis-hit, and Hick reached his first Test century in England. The three figures came just after 12.30 off 184 balls. It was a vital innings for Hick. At last the sound barrier had been broken, the four-minute mile had been run. He was relaxed and aggressive, natural, the Hick of county cricket.

He had hit 3 sixes, 9 fours and faced 192 balls when he tried to swing a full toss to leg and was lbw. Crawley, meaninglessly, was sent in for five minutes before lunch and was caught at deep square-leg second ball. Atherton declared.

England had four hours in which to bowl out South Africa, but this never looked likely. Hudson was again uncertain, Gary Kirsten positive, and Cronje fretted. Tufnell bowled adequately without suggesting he would win the match. There were numerous appeals, but the game meandered to a draw.

SECOND CORNHILL TEST MATCH – ENGLAND *v.* SOUTH AFRICA
4, 5, 6, 7 and 8 August 1994 at Headingley, Leeds

ENGLAND

	FIRST INNINGS		SECOND INNINGS	
G.A. Gooch	c McMillan, b de Villiers	23	c Richardson, b Matthews	27
M.A. Atherton (capt)	c and b McMillan	99	c sub (Cullinan), b de Villiers	17
G.A. Hick	c McMillan, b de Villiers	25	lbw, b McMillan	110
G.P. Thorpe	c Rhodes, b McMillan	72	run out	73
A.J. Stewart	b McMillan	89	not out	36
J.P. Crawley	lbw, b Matthews	38	c Cronje, b McMillan	0
*S.J. Rhodes	not out	65		
P.A.J. DeFreitas	b Donald	15		
D. Gough	run out	27		
A.R.C. Fraser	c Cronje, b de Villiers	6		
P.C.R. Tufnell				
Extras	b 1, lb 5, nb 12	18	lb 1, nb 3	4
	(for 9 wickets, dec.)	477	(for 5 wickets, dec.)	267

SOUTH AFRICA

	FIRST INNINGS		SECOND INNINGS	
A.C. Hudson	c Atherton, b Gough	9	(2) c and b Tufnell	12
G. Kirsten	c Rhodes, b DeFreitas	7	(1) c Rhodes, b DeFreitas	65
*D.J. Richardson	b Fraser	48		
W.J. Cronje	b DeFreitas	0	(3) not out	13
K.C. Wessels (capt)	c Crawley, b Fraser	25	(4) b Tufnell	7
P.N. Kirsten	c Stewart, b DeFreitas	104	(5) not out	8
J.N. Rhodes	c Rhodes, b Gough	46		
B.M. McMillan	b Tufnell	78		
C.R. Matthews	not out	62		
P.S. de Villiers	st Rhodes, b Tufnell	13		
A.A. Donald	c Crawley, b DeFreitas	27		
Extras	b 8, lb 7, nb 13	28	b 2, lb 2, nb 7	11
		447	(for 3 wickets)	116

	O	M	R	W	O	M	R	W		O	M	R	W	O	M	R	W
Donald	29	2	135	1					Gough	37	3	153	2	10	5	15	–
de Villiers	39.3	12	108	3	25	3	98	1	DeFreitas	29.1	6	89	4	14	3	41	1
Matthews	39	7	97	1	24	8	53	1	Fraser	31	5	92	2	7	2	19	–
McMillan	37	12	93	2	15.3	–	66	2	Tufnell	32	13	81	2	23	8	31	2
Cronje	16	3	38	–	12	3	39	–	Gooch	3	–	9	–				
G. Kirsten					2	1	10	–	Hick	1	–	8	–	6	3	6	–

FALL OF WICKETS

1–34, 2–84, 3–226, 4–235, 5–350, 6–367, 7–394, 8–447, 9–477
1–39, 2–57, 3–190, 4–267, 5–267

FALL OF WICKETS

1–13, 2–31, 3–31, 4–91, 5–105, 6–199, 7–314, 8–391, 9–410
1–43, 2–93, 3–104

Umpires: R.S. Dunne & D.R. Shepherd

Match drawn

NATWEST TROPHY

SEMI-FINALS

9 August *at The Oval*

Worcestershire 357 for 2 (T.M. Moody 180 not out,
  T.S. Curtis 136 not out)
Surrey 350 (D.J. Bicknell 89, A.J. Hollioake 60,
  A.D. Brown 52, G.A. Hick 4 for 54)

Worcestershire won by 7 runs

at Edgbaston

Warwickshire 265 for 8 (A.J. Moles 105 not out)
Kent 257 (T.R. Ward 80, N.R. Taylor 64)

Warwickshire won by 8 runs

Rarely can the NatWest Trophy have produced two more
exciting semi-finals although in one case, perhaps, the
small margin of victory is deceiving. At The Oval, world
records for one-day cricket were established. Put in to bat,
Worcestershire lost Seymour at 41 when he edged
Pigott's first ball, a delivery of no great merit, into his
stumps. More seriously, Hick was caught at second slip
off Benjamin seven runs later, and Surrey, temporarily,
were on top. By lunch, however, Curtis and Moody had
advanced the score to 125 for 2 from 34 overs. In the
afternoon, they tore Surrey apart. The remaining 26 overs
produced 232 runs. The stand between Curtis and Moody
was worth 309, a record for any wicket in one-day cricket
between first-class sides. Curtis, who hit his highest score
in the NatWest Trophy, batted admirably, his innings
occupied 155 balls and he hit 10 fours, giving Worcestershire necessary substance, but it was Tom Moody who
was the star performer. His 180 was a record for the
competition and came off 161 balls. He hit 3 sixes and 25
fours and went from 50 to 150 in 51 balls. This was
phenomenal stuff, but one must question Surrey's tactics.
The omission of Murphy, the hero of the quarter-final,
was a dreadful mistake, and one cannot conceive how
Pigott or even Martin Bicknell was preferred to him on
this occasion. For Surrey, the dropping of Murphy had
sad consequences as the bowler quit the club. It was also
apparent that leading the side from behind the stumps, as
Stewart does in one-day matches, was a handicap in an
encounter such as this. The Surrey fielding, usually good,
wilted badly, and Stewart could do little about it from
where he was positioned. None of this should detract
from Worcestershire's wonderful batting. The ferocity of
Moody's hitting on this mighty ground was incredible.
From their last 20 overs, Worcestershire plundered 201
runs.

A target of 358 seemed well beyond the reach of any
side, even one so blessed with fine hitters as Surrey, yet,
at tea, with 122 from 25 overs for the loss of Stewart,
Surrey were in touch. Disastrously, two overs after the

break, Thorpe ran himself out. Ward could not find his
form and departed quickly, but Brown was soon striking
the ball vehemently, and 75 came in 11 overs. Brown hit
his maiden NatWest fifty off 39 balls before being caught
at long-off off Moody. Darren Bicknell went in the next
over, and Martin Bicknell and Pigott followed swiftly so
that Surrey seemed well beaten, but still they fought.

Hollioake hit 4 sixes and 4 fours, and his 60 came off 36
balls. Boiling, too, made a useful and vigorous contribution, and, in the last over, Joey Benjamin smote 2 sixes
off Lampitt. On the penultimate ball of the match, he hit
Lampitt high again to the long-off boundary where
Moody held the ball above his head. Moody is six feet six
and a half inches tall, and had he not pulled off this fine
catch, the ball would have gone for six. Worcestershire
had won by seven runs, and, not surprisingly, Moody
was Man of the Match.

There were fewer fireworks at Edgbaston where Warwickshire's splendid team-work snatched victory from
Kent. Put in to bat, Warwickshire soon lost Ostler, but
Lara was beginning to look dangerous when Ealham
failed to hold a return catch. It proved not to be a disaster,
for Ealham did accept a similar chance eight runs later.
Paul Smith, like Reeve fit only for one-day encounters,
was soon out, but there followed a crucial stand of 74
between Moles and the eager Twose who was angry with
himself when he played rashly at Headley to be caught
behind. There was energy from Reeve, but three wickets
from Fleming halted the home side's advance, and it was
Andy Moles, who batted throughout the 60 overs, who
was the ultimate hero.

Kent began slowly, but Ward and Taylor added 124 in
30 overs for the second wicket to make victory seem
highly probable. With 15 overs to go, Kent needed 81 to
win with eight wickets in hand. The loss of three wickets
in four overs, the inability of the Kent batsmen to cope
with Reeve's slower ball and some more spectacular
wicket-keeping from Piper turned the game, and
although Marsh brought Kent to within eight runs of the
Warwickshire total, the home side had long taken a grip
on the match. Andy Moles was the individual award-
winner.

10, 11 and 12 August *at Torquay*

South Africans 249 (D.J. Cullinan 68) and 173 for 7 dec.
Minor Counties 153 for 2 dec. (R.J. Evans 59) and 173
  for 9 (S.D. Myles 59 not out, P.L. Symcox 4 for 60)

Match drawn

11, 12, 13 and 15 August *at Colchester*

Essex 378 (N.V. Knight 115, M.A. Garnham 55,
  J.J.B. Lewis 52)
Surrey 88 (M.C. Ilott 6 for 24, M.S. Kasprowicz 4 for 51)
  and 203 (D.J. Bicknell 72, P.M. Such 6 for 46)

Essex won by an innings and 87 runs

Essex 24 pts., Surrey 4 pts.

at Bristol

Gloucestershire 296 (R.I. Dawson 93, M.G.N. Windows 77) and 254 (M.W. Alleyne 81, A.J. Wright 66, C.E.L. Ambrose 4 for 51, K.M. Curran 4 for 65)

Northamptonshire 349 (K.M. Curran 92, A.L. Penberthy 62, A.J. Lamb 61, M.W. Alleyne 4 for 76) and 203 for 2 (R.R. Montgomerie 90, A. Fordham 75)

Northamptonshire won by 8 wickets

Northamptonshire 22 pts., Gloucestershire 5 pts.

at Canterbury

Kent 385 (S.A. Marsh 85 not out, M.J. McCague 56, P. Bainbridge 4 for 72) and 96 for 1

Durham 196 (M. Saxelby 62, C.L. Hooper 5 for 52, M.M. Patel 4 for 68) and 284 (J.E. Morris 94, P. Bainbridge 63, M.M. Patel 6 for 84)

Kent won by 9 wickets

Kent 24 pts., Durham 4 pts.

at Leicester

Leicestershire 283 and 283 for 9 dec. (D.J. Millns 64 not out, G.J. Parsons 52)

Worcestershire 278 (G.R. Haynes 53, G.J. Parsons 5 for 34) and 191 (D.A. Leatherdale 61, D.J. Millns 6 for 84)

Leicestershire won by 97 runs

Leicestershire 22 pts., Worcestershire 6 pts.

at Lord's

Somerset 248 (A.N. Hayhurst 62, R.J. Harden 61, P.C.R. Tufnell 4 for 41) and 110 (P.C.R. Tufnell 4 for 17)

Middlesex 388 for 8 dec. (J.D. Carr 171 not out, P.N. Weekes 117, A.R. Caddick 4 for 84)

Middlesex won by an innings and 30 runs

Middlesex 24 pts., Somerset 4 pts.

at Eastbourne

Sussex 171 (D.M. Smith 63, P.A.J. DeFreitas 5 for 73, D.E. Malcolm 4 for 37) and 127 (D.G. Cork 6 for 29)

Derbyshire 123 (E.S.H. Giddins 5 for 38, I.D.K. Salisbury 4 for 20) and 176 for 9 (P.D. Bowler 52)

Derbyshire won by 1 wicket

Derbyshire 20 pts., Sussex 4 pts.

at Edgbaston

Nottinghamshire 597 for 8 dec. (C.C. Lewis 220 not out, P.R. Pollard 134, P. Johnson 63, K.P. Evans 55)

Warwickshire 321 (G. Welch 84 not out, K.J. Piper 57, K.P. Evans 4 for 71) and 233 (R.G. Twose 80, C.C. Lewis 4 for 86)

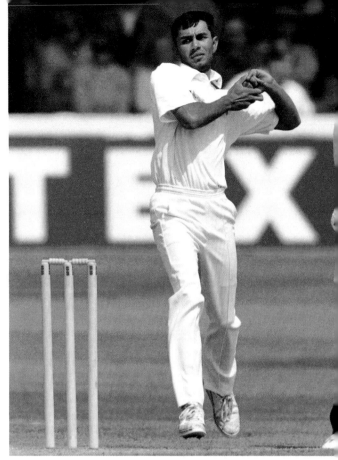

Bowler of the year, left-arm spinner Min Patel, 10 wickets in Kent's victory over Durham, 11–15 August. (Alan Cozzi)

Nottinghamshire won by an innings and 43 runs

Nottinghamshire 24 pts., Warwickshire 5 pts.

at Leeds

Yorkshire 214 (M.D. Moxon 69, A.P. Grayson 51 not out, G. Chapple 4 for 51, P.J. Martin 4 for 87) and 314 (D. Byas 104, A.P. Grayson 95, B. Parker 50, P.J. Martin 5 for 68)

Lancashire 404 (N.J. Speak 143, I.D. Austin 50, D. Gough 4 for 126) and 125 for 3 (J.E.R. Gallian 50)

Lancashire won by 7 wickets

Lancashire 24 pts., Yorkshire 5 pts.

13, 14 and 15 August *at Pontypridd*

Glamorgan 336 for 5 dec. (D.L. Hemp 126, P.A. Cottey 84, A.J. Dalton 51 not out) and 222 for 9 dec. (M.P. Maynard 101)

South Africans 288 for 6 dec. (R.P. Snell 94, W.J. Cronje 78) and 140 for 3 (G. Kirsten 76 not out)

Match drawn

Suddenly, the championship race became wide open. At Colchester, only 5.2 overs were possible on the first day, but on the second, led by an opening stand of 116

between Nick Knight and Darren Robinson, Essex scored
at a brisk pace. The left-handed Knight reached his third
hundred of the season, and there were valuable and
positive contributions from Lewis and Garnham. Surrey
had chosen, most surprisingly, to omit Ward and play
seven bowlers in their side. It proved a sad tactic as,
before lunch on the Saturday, they were bowled out for
88. Ilott and Kasprowicz bowled unchanged, maintaining
a good line and moving the ball off the seam. Three
Surrey men surrendered without playing a shot. Darren
Bicknell attempted to hold the innings together when
Surrey followed-on, but although he was unbeaten on the
Saturday evening, five wickets were down for 187 at the
close. Even without Childs, who had injured a foot while
batting, Essex soon completed the rout on the last morning as Such began to extract some turn from the pitch.

At Bristol, Gloucestershire, without Walsh, were well
beaten by Northamptonshire. Wright and Windows began with a stand of 110, and there was some fine batting
by Dawson, but Gloucestershire were punished by
Northamptonshire's late order. The visitors' last five
wickets realised 201 runs. In contrast, Gloucestershire's
last six second-innings wickets produced only 18 runs,
and with Montgomerie and Fordham beginning Northamptonshire's challenge for victory with a partnership of
129, only one result seemed possible.

Kent trounced Durham at Canterbury with similar
decisive contributions from their late-order batsmen. On
the second day, Marsh and McCague, who hit a career-
best 56, added 131 for the eighth wicket. Kent gained
further advantage by capturing three Durham wickets in
the last 18 balls of the day, and with the middle order
collapsing to the spin of Patel and Hooper on the Saturday, it was inevitable that Durham would have to follow-
on. Hooper and Patel again caused problems, but Morris
and Bainbridge added 165 for the third wicket. They were
both dismissed on the Saturday evening, and Durham's
last eight wickets went down for 47 runs.

Leicestershire moved to within nine points of Warwickshire at the top of the table, and had a game in hand,
when they won a close struggle with Worcestershire.
Even batting by both sides brought the first innings to
near parity, and the game was very much in the balance
on the Saturday evening when Leicestershire were 171
for 8. At this point, Millns joined Parsons, who had
bowled well, and the pair batted into the Monday morning, adding 103 in 37 overs. Millns followed his career-
best batting performance with his best bowling performance of the season, and Leicestershire romped to victory.
Worcestershire were without the injured Phil Weston in
their second innings.

Phil Tufnell returned his best bowling figures of the
season as Middlesex crushed Somerset. Middlesex had
not been without problems of their own, for they were
123 for 6 when Weekes joined Carr. The pair transformed
the match, adding 264 in 63 overs. Carr, whose deeds so
often go unsung and seemingly unnoticed, was unbeaten
on 171 while Weekes, who hit 15 fours and 2 sixes,
reached the first century of his career. Somerset subsided
meekly on the Monday.

There was a tense struggle and scarcity of runs at
Eastbourne. Only 93 balls were possible on the first day
when Sussex lost Athey to Malcolm. On the second day,
19 wickets fell. Apart from Smith, still a good player of fast
bowling, Sussex wilted against Malcolm and DeFreitas
while Derbyshire surrendered to a combination of pace
and spin in the guise of Giddins and Salisbury. On the
Saturday, Cork and Malcolm were the Sussex destroyers,
and Derbyshire, needing 176 to win, ended the day on 94
for 5. They were soon 99 for 6 on the Monday, and in spite
of some brave blows from DeFreitas and Cork, they
slipped to 148 for 9 and imminent defeat when Warner
fell for 0. Vandrau had kept cool while those around him
perished, and now he was joined by Malcolm who carved
one ball over long-on for six. This shot off Stephenson
brought Derbyshire to within five runs of victory, and a
cover-drive to the boundary by Vandrau followed by a
scrambled single saw the game won.

Warwickshire's grip on the title was loosened when
they suffered an innings defeat at the hands of Nottinghamshire. Pollard scored a century on the first day,
and the second witnessed a stop-start 220 from Chris
Lewis. He faced 318 balls and hit 6 sixes and 21 fours.
Warwickshire were 91 for 3 at the end of the second day,
and, in spite of battling cricket from Piper, Welch and Neil
Smith, they were forced to follow-on on the Saturday.
Welch, an increasingly effective all-rounder, hit a career-
best 84 while, in the follow-on, Lara was bowled by fellow
West Indian Jimmy Adams for his first championship
'duck'. There was no recovery for the home side on the
Monday, and their championship lead was cut to nine
points and some half a dozen sides were still capable of
winning the championship.

Yorkshire failed to take good advantage of first use of
the pitch at Headingley and fell apart against the bowling
of Martin and Chapple in the Roses match. By the end of
the second day, Lancashire had recovered from 85 for 4
through good middle-order batting and had taken a first-
innings lead. Speak was the architect of Lancashire's
recovery, and the last four wickets produced 179 runs.
Byas, a most accomplished batsman who needs only
consistency to make him a candidate for the England
side, hit a fine century to take Yorkshire into a narrow
lead, and he and Grayson added 142 for the fifth wicket.
Six wickets then fell for 44 runs, and Lancashire ran out
easy winners.

In their last Tetley Challenge match, the South Africans
were harshly punished by Maynard, Hemp and Cottey.
Snell hit a career-best 94, but the tourists did not respond
to Maynard's declaration which left them 57 overs in
which to score 272.

 AXA EQUITY & LAW LEAGUE

14 August *at Colchester*

Essex 217 for 5 (G.A. Gooch 63, N. Hussain 61)
Surrey 219 for 4 (D.M. Ward 91)

Surrey (4 pts.) won by 6 wickets

at Bristol

Northamptonshire 159 (T.C. Walton 72)
Gloucestershire 162 for 2 (A.J. Wright 61 not out)

Gloucestershire (4 pts.) won by 8 wickets

at Canterbury

Kent 264 for 6 (C.L. Hooper 77, M.V. Fleming 68)
Durham 196 for 8 (J.A. Daley 98 not out)

Kent (4 pts.) won by 68 runs

at Leicester

Worcestershire 203 for 8 (G.A. Hick 65, T.S. Curtis 52,
   P.N. Hepworth 5 for 51)
Leicestershire 201 for 9 (B.F. Smith 56, D.L. Maddy 53,
   S.R. Lampitt 4 for 25)

Worcestershire (4 pts.) won by 2 runs

at Lord's

Somerset 159 for 7
Middlesex 161 for 2 (J.C. Pooley 59, M.A. Roseberry 50)

Middlesex (4 pts.) won by 8 wickets

at Eastbourne

Sussex 152 for 6 (C.W.J. Athey 58 not out)
Derbyshire 156 for 3 (D.G. Cork 66)

Derbyshire (4 pts.) won by 7 wickets

at Edgbaston

Warwickshire 294 for 6 (B.C. Lara 75, D.P. Ostler 59)
Nottinghamshire 222 for 9 (R.T. Robinson 76)

Warwickshire (4 pts.) won by 72 runs

at Leeds

Lancashire 183 for 6 (N.H. Fairbrother 58 not out)
Yorkshire 140 for 9 (A.A. Metcalfe 65 not out)

Lancashire (4 pts.) won by 43 runs

Gooch proved his fitness for the final Test with 63 off 67
balls, but Essex were beaten by Surrey. Gooch had been
suffering from a hamstring injury which kept him out of
the championship match with Surrey. Daley hit his
highest score in any competition, but Durham lost to
Kent who, along with other winners, Worcestershire and
Lancashire, were the main challengers to Warwickshire's
supremacy.

18, 19, 20 and 22 August *at Derby*

Kent 392 (S.A. Marsh 88, T.R. Ward 86, M.A. Ealham
   64, D.G. Cork 6 for 80) and 247 (C.L. Hooper 82,
   M.J. Vandrau 4 for 53, A.E. Warner 4 for 95)
Derbyshire 288 (P.D. Bowler 88, D.G. Cork 56,
   M.J. McCague 9 for 86) and 282 (K.J. Barnett 69,
   M.J. Vandrau 66, A.S. Rollins 52, M.J. McCague 6 for
   61)

Kent won by 69 runs

Kent 24 pts., Derbyshire 6 pts.

at Hartlepool

Glamorgan 206 (S.J.E. Brown 6 for 68) and 282
   (M.P. Maynard 71, R.D.B. Croft 53, A. Walker 4 for
   59)
Durham 230 (J.E. Morris 57, J.I. Longley 52,
   R.D.B. Croft 4 for 76) and 262 for 7 (J.E. Morris 123
   not out, O.D. Gibson 6 for 88)

Durham won by 3 wickets

Durham 21 pts., Glamorgan 5 pts.

at Southampton

Surrey 150 (A.D. Brown 78, S.D. Udal 5 for 26) and 385
   (M.A. Butcher 134, A.J. Hollioake 65, M.A. Lynch 60,
   S.D. Udal 5 for 137)
Hampshire 603 for 7 dec. (M.C.J. Nicholas 145,
   V.P. Terry 135, A.N. Aymes 76, R.A. Smith 75,
   G.W. White 57)

Hampshire won by an innings and 68 runs

Hampshire 24 pts., Surrey 2 pts.

at Old Trafford

Lancashire 172 and 356 (N.H. Fairbrother 120,
   G.D. Lloyd 112, C.A. Walsh 5 for 91)
Gloucestershire 298 (M.G.N. Windows 85, P.J. Martin 4
   for 53, I.D. Austin 4 for 85) and 231 for 8
   (M.G.N. Windows 77, M. Watkinson 4 for 82)

Gloucestershire won by 2 wickets

Gloucestershire 22 pts., Lancashire 4 pts.

at Leicester

Leicestershire 192 and 90 (F.D. Stephenson 4 for 23,
   P.W. Jarvis 4 for 50)
Sussex 247 (N.J. Lenham 51) and 37 for 1

Sussex won by 9 wickets

Sussex 21 pts., Leicestershire 4 pts.

at Northampton

Middlesex 398 (J.D. Carr 136, M.A. Roseberry 72,
   P.N. Weekes 50, J.G. Hughes 4 for 60) and 368 for 3
   dec. (M.W. Gatting 201 not out, J.D. Carr 106 not
   out)
Northamptonshire 462 (A. Fordham 158, A.J. Lamb 88
   not out, R.J. Bailey 88) and 308 for 4 (R.J. Bailey 129
   not out, A.J. Lamb 54)

Northamptonshire won by 6 wickets

Northamptonshire 24 pts., Middlesex 6 pts.

at Weston-super-Mare

Somerset 226 (M.N. Lathwell 61, M.C. Ilott 4 for 87) and
243 (M.E. Trescothick 92, M.S. Kasprowicz 7 for 83)

Essex 140 (A.P. van Troost 4 for 50) and 193

Somerset won by 136 runs

Somerset 21 pts., Essex 4 pts.

at Kidderminster

Nottinghamshire 331 (C.C. Lewis 77, R.T. Robinson 67,
N.V. Radford 5 for 93) and 315 for 7 dec.
(R.T. Robinson 134)

Worcestershire 285 (G.R. Haynes 98, C.C. Lewis 5 for
71) and 365 for 5 (G.R. Haynes 141, T.S. Curtis 118
not out)

Worcestershire won by 5 wickets

Worcestershire 22 pts., Nottinghamshire 7 pts.

at Scarborough

Yorkshire 310 (B. Parker 62, P.J. Hartley 61, D. Byas
57, G. Welch 4 for 74) and 347 (M.D. Moxon 116,
R.J. Blakey 77, R.P. Davis 6 for 94)

Warwickshire 459 (D.P. Ostler 186, A.J. Moles 65,
G. Welch 60, R.D. Stemp 4 for 107) and 200 for 2
(R.G. Twose 86 not out)

Warwickshire won by 8 wickets

Warwickshire 24 pts., Yorkshire 5 pts.

Derbyshire, the most unpredictable of counties, were
beaten by Kent after a good fight. On the opening day,
Kent, having won the toss, batted and reached 97 before
Benson edged Cork to the wicket-keeper. With his next
two balls, Cork had Walker and Hooper leg before to
perform the first hat-trick of his career. Cork, in top form,
finished with six wickets, but a seventh-wicket stand of
139 between Ealham and Marsh took Kent to a strong
position. Like Kent's, Derbyshire's middle order fell
apart, and not even Cork's late flourish could bring his
side to within 100 runs of Kent. The Derbyshire innings
was totally ravaged by Martin McCague who, after a
season marred by injury, took a career-best 9 for 86. When
Kent batted a second time there was an exciting 82 off 55
balls from Hooper, but there was also another middle-
order collapse, and it needed a positive innings of 47 from
McCague to lift the visitors from the worrying position of
151 for 7. Needing 352 to win, Derbyshire were 27 for 3
before Rollins and Barnett added 121. There was also
spirited resistance from Wells and Vandrau, but, with
McCague returning the best match figures of the season,
Kent were not to be denied.

The game at Hartlepool was over in the three days.
Durham's slender first-innings lead was nullified by a
Maynard gem, 71 off 61 balls and, with Croft coming into
some kind of all-round form late in the season, Glamorgan were able to set a target of 259. Three wickets in four
balls by Ottis Gibson reduced Durham to 100 for 5.
Hutton and Morris then added 94, and Morris, mixing

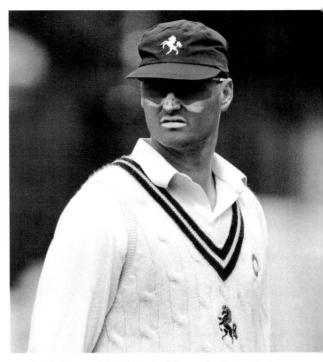

*Martin McCague took 15 wickets for 147 runs for Kent against
Derbyshire, 18–22 August, and, after a long period absent through
injury, he bowled himself into the party to tour Australia. (David
Munden/Sports-Line)*

sound defence with some exciting stroke-play, took Durham to a worthy victory. He hit a six and 18 fours and
played with supreme confidence to end Durham's run of
seven defeats.

Surrey's lingering hopes of winning the championship
were extinguished when they lost by an innings at Southampton. Hampshire were in the lead by the end of the
first day. Connor, Udal and James destroyed the visitors,
and although Middleton was out for 0, Terry and White
engaged in a stand which was worth 162 by the end of the
day. It added only one more run on the Friday, but Terry
and Smith added 116. Terry hit 18 fours and a six, and
Mark Nicholas reached his third century in four innings
and 1,000 runs for the season. Surrey were quite dreadful,
and Nicholas and Aymes extended their sixth-wicket
stand to 184 on the third day. Mark Butcher hit a career-
best 134 and batted with considerable panache, but the
Surrey cause had long since been lost and defeat came
early on the Monday.

The return of Walsh brought victory to Gloucestershire
over Lancashire, for he played a significant part in his
side's win, performing well with both bat and ball. Lancashire chose to bat and were bowled out for 172 in 59.3
overs. Mark Harvey, making his debut for Lancashire,
was Walsh's first victim of the day, caught behind by
Russell. Matthew Windows hit his highest championship
score and helped Gloucestershire to a significant first-
innings lead. Batting again, Lancashire were 54 for 3
before Lloyd and Fairbrother, back to form and fitness,
added 231. Both fell to ugly shots after batting well, and

seven wickets fell for 71 runs to leave Gloucestershire a target of 231. Windows again batted well, and the visitors were 126 for 1 and well set when four wickets fell for 23 runs. The Gloucestershire slide continued on the Monday, and, at 200 for 8, they looked in danger of defeat. Walsh thought otherwise. He hit 3 sixes, 2 fours, broke a window in the pavilion and scored 31 runs off 17 balls to win the match.

Like Surrey, Leicestershire timidly surrendered their title aspirations. They gave two abject batting performances against Sussex, who were only required to play adequately, and were beaten in two days.

John Carr's masterly run of form continued with a century in each innings against Northamptonshire. This meant that he had scored centuries in three successive innings, but his efforts proved to be in vain. Sparked by Fordham, who shared a third-wicket stand of 209 with Bailey, Northamptonshire surprisingly took a first-innings lead. Gatting who, like Tufnell, had not been wanted by England at The Oval hit his third double century of the season and shared an unbroken third-wicket partnership of 282 with Carr. His declaration left Northamptonshire a target of 305 in 64 overs. At tea, with Northamptonshire 59 for 1 from 24 overs, a draw looked the most likely result, but when Lamb and Bailey came together the atmosphere changed. Lamb made 54 from 46 balls, but 169 were needed from 20 overs, and 81 from eight. After the loss of Lamb, Bailey had good assistance from Curran. It was Bailey's outstanding innings which brought the home county victory off the last ball. He hit 5 sixes and 12 fours, and his 129 came off 116 deliveries.

Essex's lingering hopes of winning the championship dissolved with a miserable batting performance at Weston-super-Mare where they were beaten in three days. They won the toss, asked Somerset to bat and bowled them out for 226, 29 of the runs coming in a last-wicket stand. Before the close, Essex lost both openers for 5, and there was no real recovery on the second day when only Kasprowicz offered positive retaliation to Caddick, van Troost and Rose. Kasprowicz then bowled splendidly to return career-best figures, but Trescothick shamed his elders with a masterly innings on a pitch which was assisting the seam bowlers, and he put the game out of the reach of Essex who showed little appetite for a target of 330.

Like other counties challenging Warwickshire, Nottinghamshire saw their hopes dwindle, yet they had seemed in a strong position until the last afternoon. With Lewis showing his late season all-round revitalisation, Nottinghamshire led Worcestershire by 46 runs on the first innings in spite of Haynes' excellent 98 with 19 fours. Tim Robinson also hit 19 fours on the Saturday when his 134 off 243 balls put his side in a commanding position. He declared on the Saturday evening so leaving Worcestershire the last day in which to score 362 to win or the Nottinghamshire bowlers three sessions in which to bowl their side to victory. After an hour, two wickets had fallen, those of Church and Moody, and 28 runs had been scored. Haynes, however, was as strong and confident as he had been in the first innings. He hit 26 fours and a six in his first championship century of the summer and shared

a stand of 200 with Tim Curtis who contributed 49 to the partnership. If Haynes and D'Oliveira provided fireworks, Curtis gave the essential stability to the innings, and he was unbeaten for 118 off 295 balls when the match was won with 7.4 overs to spare.

With their challengers floundering, Warwickshire had a comprehensive victory over Yorkshire and moved 29 points clear at the top of the table. Yorkshire won the toss and scored quite consistently on the opening day, but the balanced Warwickshire attack gnawed away throughout 103 overs and claimed the four bowling points. The Yorkshire innings was over 11 balls into the second day, but Warwickshire suffered early shocks when Twose fell to Hartley for 1 and Lara provided debutant Alex Wharf with a most notable first first-class wicket by edging to the wicket-keeper. That was really the end of Yorkshire's joy. Moles and Ostler added 191, and Ostler scored his first championship hundred of the season. He hit a seven by virtue of a throw that struck a fielding helmet, a six and 21 fours, and with Welch, Piper and Neil Smith making useful contributions, Warwickshire led by 149 on the first innings. Moxon showed true Yorkshire spirit with a fine century, and by Saturday evening, with only three wickets down, the arrears had been wiped out and a 52-run lead had been established. Moxon fell early on the Monday, but Blakey and Wharf continued the resistance before left-arm spinner Davis whittled away at the Yorkshire batting to claim six wickets in the innings. Warwickshire needed 199 from 49 overs, and when Moles and Twose scored 89 for the first wicket at six runs an over victory was as much as assured. Indeed, Warwickshire required just 40.3 overs to win the match.

 AXA EQUITY & LAW LEAGUE

21 August *at Derby*

Kent 295 for 4 (C.L. Hooper 113, M.J. Walker 69 not out)

Derbyshire 219 (C.L. Hooper 4 for 50)

Kent (4 pts.) won by 76 runs

at Hartlepool

Glamorgan 241 for 4 (S.P. James 102, P.A. Cottey 66 not out)

Durham 222 for 9 (A.C. Cummins 66, J.A. Daley 54, R.P. Lefebvre 4 for 23)

Glamorgan (4 pts.) won by 19 runs

at Southampton

Surrey 261 for 8 (A.D. Brown 99, K.D. James 5 for 42)

Hampshire 262 for 3 (R.A. Smith 110 not out, T.C. Middleton 73)

Hampshire (4 pts.) won by 7 wickets

at Old Trafford

Gloucestershire 198 for 8 (M.W. Alleyne 83 not out)
Lancashire 199 for 5 (N.H. Fairbrother 63)

Lancashire (4 pts.) won by 5 wickets

at Leicester

Sussex 205 for 9 (A.P. Wells 51)
Leicestershire 163 (C.C. Remy 4 for 43)

Sussex (4 pts.) won by 42 runs

at Northampton

Middlesex 269 for 4 (J.C. Pooley 77, M.R. Ramprakash 73)
Northamptonshire 235 (A.J. Lamb 69, T.C. Walton 54, G.A.R. Harris 5 for 26)

Middlesex (4 pts.) won by 34 runs

at Weston-super-Mare

Somerset 204 for 8 (M.E. Trescothick 60)
Essex 119 (S.C. Ecclestone 4 for 31)

Somerset (4 pts.) won by 85 runs

at Worcester

Worcestershire 169 for 9 (J.E. Hindson 4 for 19)
Nottinghamshire 148 (C.C. Lewis 75, S.R. Lampitt 4 for 22)

Worcestershire (4 pts.) won by 21 runs

at Scarborough

Yorkshire 209 for 3 (D. Byas 55, R.J. Blakey 55 not out)
Warwickshire 155

Yorkshire (4 pts.) won by 54 runs

Leading Kent for the first time, Carl Hooper gave a magnificent all-round performance in the victory at Derby. He hit his highest Sunday League score, 113 off 83 balls, and captured four wickets. Kent retained third place. Surrey slipped out of contention with defeat at Southampton while Trump and Ecclestone recorded best Sunday bowling figures as Somerset beat bottom of the table Essex. Hindson took four wickets on his Sunday debut for Nottinghamshire, but Worcestershire won to draw level on points with Warwickshire who were beaten by Yorkshire. Remarkably, Middlesex's emergency signing, seam bowler Harris, took five wickets against Northamptonshire.

THIRD TEST MATCH
ENGLAND *v.* SOUTH AFRICA, at The Oval

South Africa made one change, Cullinan replacing Hudson who had been unable to find form on the tour.

Donald, hampered by injury at Headingley, reported fit. England omitted Fraser from their party and, on the day of the match, preferred Joey Benjamin who was in the party at Leeds to Tufnell. Malcolm returned in place of Fraser. Gooch was deemed fit, and Gatting, who had been on stand-by, left to play for Middlesex.

The omission of Tufnell was widely criticised, for it left England without a front line spin bowler on a pitch where it was believed he could be a match-winner, but the inclusion of the 33-year old Joey Benjamin who had had an outstanding season for Surrey gave credibility to the stated intention of rewarding those who performed well in county cricket. Nor was Benjamin to let England down. He was soon in action as Wessels won the toss, and South Africa batted.

England had quick success. In the third over, Gary Kirsten, half-forward, was late to judge a ball that lifted and left him and was caught behind. In his second spell, Malcolm was far too fast for Peter Kirsten, an unwise choice as an opener, and shattered his stumps with a yorker.

With his 14th ball in Test cricket, Joey Benjamin had an appeal for leg before against Hansie Cronje upheld, and South Africa were 73 for 3. Cronje had seemed in no trouble against Benjamin who tended to bowl too wide of the off stump at an undemanding pace, yet the Surrey bowler was to become the star of the first day.

On the stroke of lunch, Cullinan was caught behind off DeFreitas' away swinger. A very lively first session had brought four wickets and 85 runs, which, from an England point of view, was some 20 too many. Wicket-balls had been punctuated by a large number of loose deliveries.

Wessels, dropped in the gully by Gooch off Malcolm, was not happy against the unexpected bounce, but he batted doggedly for two hours before shuffling across his stumps to Benjamin and being clearly leg before. When Rhodes ducked into a delivery from Malcolm which he completely misread and was hit on the helmet above the left ear, South Africa were effectively 136 for 6. Rhodes was led from the field, pale and unsteady, and spent the night in hospital.

McMillan and Richardson now responded in typical South African fashion, hitting 124 in 30 overs, and the England out-cricket was not impressive. Benjamin returned to account for Richardson, and in his next over he had Matthews taken at slip. McMillan, having fathered a useful stand with de Villiers, remained unbeaten for 91 at the end of the day when South Africa were 326 for 8.

The second day started late because of rain, and although play was extended until seven o'clock, South Africa bowled their overs so slowly that a capacity crowd who had paid a considerable amount of money for their seats lost some 14 overs, but then the paying customer has little consideration these days – television will provide. McMillan added only two to his overnight score before edging to slip. He had deserved a hundred for his fine effort on the first day which had brought him 9 fours. He reacted to a crisis in a positive manner, and he did

THIRD CORNHILL TEST MATCH – ENGLAND v. SOUTH AFRICA
18, 19, 20 and 21 August 1994 at The Oval, Kennington

SOUTH AFRICA

	FIRST INNINGS			SECOND INNINGS	
G. Kirsten	c Rhodes, b DeFreitas	2	(2) c and b Malcolm		0
P.N. Kirsten	b Malcolm	16	(1) c DeFreitas,		
			b Malcolm		1
W.J. Cronje	lbw, b Benjamin	38	b Malcolm		0
K.C. Wessels (capt)	lbw, b Benjamin	45	c Rhodes, b Malcolm	28
D.J. Cullinan	c Rhodes, b DeFreitas	7	c Thorpe, b Gough	94
J.N. Rhodes	retired hurt	8	(9) c Rhodes, b Malcolm	10
B.M. McMillan	c Hick, b DeFreitas	93	(6) c Thorpe, b Malcolm	25
*D.J. Richardson	c Rhodes, b Benjamin	58	(7) lbw, b Malcolm	3
C.R. Matthews	c Hick, b Benjamin	0	(8) c Rhodes, b Malcolm	0
P.S. de Villiers	c Stewart, b DeFreitas	14	not out		0
A.A. Donald	not out	14	b Malcolm		0
Extras	b 8, lb 10, w 1, nb 18	37	lb 5, nb 9		14
		332			175

ENGLAND

	FIRST INNINGS			SECOND INNINGS	
G.A. Gooch	c Richardson, b Donald	8	b Matthews		33
M.A. Atherton (capt)	lbw, b de Villiers	0	c Richardson, b Donald	63
G.A. Hick	b Donald	39	not out		81
G.P. Thorpe	b Matthews	79	not out		15
A.J. Stewart	b de Villiers	62			
J.P. Crawley	c Richardson, b Donald	5			
*S.J. Rhodes	lbw, b de Villiers	11			
P.A.J. DeFreitas	run out	37			
D. Gough	not out	42			
J.E. Benjamin	lbw, b de Villiers	0			
D.E. Malcolm	c sub (Shaw), b				
	Matthews	4			
Extras	b 1, w 1, nb 15	17	lb 6, nb 7		13
		304	(for 2 wickets)		205

	O	M	R	W	O	M	R	W
DeFreitas	26.2	5	93	4	12	3	25	–
Malcolm	25	5	81	1	16.3	2	57	9
Gough	19	1	85	–	9	1	39	1
Benjamin	17	2	42	4	11	1	38	–
Hick	5	1	13	–	2	–	11	–

	O	M	R	W	O	M	R	W
Donald	17	2	76	3	17	4	96	1
de Villiers	19	3	62	4	12	–	66	–
Matthews	20.5	4	82	2	11.3	4	37	1
McMillan	12	1	67	–				
Cronje	8	3	16	–				

FALL OF WICKETS

1–2, 2–43, 3–73, 4–85, 5–136, 6–260, 7–266, 8–301, 9–332
1–0, 2–1, 3–1, 4–73, 5–137, 6–143, 7–143, 8–175, 9–175

FALL OF WICKETS

1–1, 2–33, 3–93, 4–145, 5–165, 6–219, 7–222, 8–292, 9–293
1–56, 2–180

Umpires: K.E. Palmer & R.S. Dunne

England won by 8 wickets

TEST MATCH AVERAGES – ENGLAND v. SOUTH AFRICA

ENGLAND BATTING

	M	Inns	NO	Runs	HS	Av	100s	50s
G.P. Thorpe	2	4	1	239	79	79.66	–	3
G.A. Hick	3	6	1	304	110	60.80	1	1
A.J. Stewart	3	5	1	226	89	56.50	–	2
S.J. Rhodes	3	4	2	105	65*	52.50	–	1
D. Gough	3	4	2	81	42*	40.50	–	–
M.A. Atherton	3	6	–	207	99	34.50	–	2
G.A. Gooch	3	6	–	139	33	23.16	–	–
P.A.J. DeFreitas	3	4	–	73	37	18.25	–	–
J.P. Crawley	3	5	–	59	38	11.80	–	–
A.R.C. Fraser	2	3	–	10	6	3.33	–	–

Played in one Test: C. White 10 & 0; I.D.K. Salisbury 6* & 0; D.E. Malcolm 4;
P.C.R. Tufnell did not bat; J.E. Benjamin 0

SOUTH AFRICA BATTING

	M	Inns	NO	Runs	HS	Av	100s	50s
B.M. McMillan	3	5	1	264	93	66.00	–	2
K.C. Wessels	3	6	–	238	105	50.50	1	–
P.N. Kirsten	3	6	–	179	104	35.80	1	–
J.N. Rhodes	3	5	1	128	46	32.00	–	–
C.R. Matthews	3	5	1	128	62*	32.00	–	1
G. Kirsten	3	6	–	190	72	31.66	–	2
D.J. Richardson	3	5	–	138	58	27.60	–	1
A.A. Donald	3	4	2	46	27	23.00	–	–
W.J. Cronje	3	6	1	90	38	18.00	–	–
P.S. de Villiers	3	4	1	35	14	11.66	–	–
A.C. Hudson	2	4	–	30	12	7.50	–	–

Played in one Test: D.J. Cullinan 7 & 94

ENGLAND BOWLING

	Overs	Mds	Runs	Wkts	Av	Best	10/m	5/inn
D.E. Malcolm	41.3	7	138	10	13.80	9-57	1	1
J.E. Benjamin	28	3	80	4	20.00	4-42	–	–
P.C.R. Tufnell	55	21	112	4	28.00	2-31	–	–
C. White	16	2	61	2	30.50	2-43	–	–
A.R.C. Fraser	85.5	19	245	7	35.00	3-72	–	–
D. Gough	122.3	21	414	11	37.63	4-46	–	–
P.A.J. DeFreitas	113.3	25	358	9	39.77	4-89	–	–
G.A. Hick	47	23	98	2	49.00	1-22	–	–
I.D.K. Salisbury	44	6	121	1	121.00	1-53	–	–

Bowled in one innings: G.A. Gooch 3–0–9–0

SOUTH AFRICA BOWLING

	Overs	Mds	Runs	Wkts	Av	Best	10/m	5/inn
B.M. McMillan	81.2	16	267	9	29.66	3-16	–	–
P.S. de Villiers	123.3	27	388	12	32.33	4-62	–	–
A.A. Donald	89.3	15	410	12	34.16	5-74	–	1
C.R. Matthews	125.2	35	340	8	42.50	3-25	–	–
W.J. Cronje	37	9	94	–	–	–	–	–

Bowled in one innings: G. Kirsten 2–1–10–0

SOUTH AFRICA FIELDING FIGURES
7 – D.J. Richardson; 4 – B.M. McMillan; 3 – K.C. Wessels; 2 – W.J. Cronje and
A.C. Hudson; 1 – G. Kirsten, J.N. Rhodes, A.A. Donald, sub (D.J. Cullinan) and sub
(T.G. Shaw)

ENGLAND FIELDING FIGURES
16 – S.J. Rhodes (ct 14/st 2); 4 – J.P. Crawley; 2 – G.A. Hick, G.P. Thorpe, A.J. Stewart
and P.A.J. DeFreitas; 1 – G.A. Gooch, M.A. Atherton, A.R.C. Fraser, P.C.R. Tufnell
and D.E. Malcolm

generally sluggish day, with South Africa bowling mainly defensively and at a wretchedly slow over-rate in the Wessels' custom of 'what we have we hold'. The last 23 minutes of the day confounded this policy. DeFreitas and Gough hit 59 runs, 38 of them in boundaries. It was heady stuff, and it brought the game back into balance.

Mr Burge's decision to fine Atherton had a dramatic effect upon the match, for it seemed that more than ever the England side were united behind their captain, and it was quite apparent that the nation felt that the Lancastrian had been badly treated.

Gough and DeFreitas extended their partnership to 70 in 11 overs before DeFreitas was run out by Cullinan's underarm throw. DeFreitas hit a six and 4 fours, and his runs came off 31 balls. Gough, who stands tall to hit the ball with venom, hit a six and 6 fours and faced 47 balls. These two brought England a chance of victory and, in the process, they tamed Donald, meeting fire with fire.

Fire was apparent when England took the field. Rarely in recent years has one seen an England side so determined, so committed. DeFreitas bowled a maiden to the elder Kirsten, and then Devon Malcolm began his assault. He had been hit on the head by de Villiers when he batted, and whether or not this had any galvanising effect on the Derbyshire bowler we cannot tell, but he was to produce three spells of bowling during the day of such pace and menace that they electrified the crowd, destroyed the South Africans and gave him an indelible place in the history of Test cricket. His first ball to Gary Kirsten reared from a length to such an extent that the batsman must have sniffed the ball as it flew past him. Malcolm's third delivery was short. Completely undermined and shattered by the pace of the first two deliveries he had received, Gary Kirsten turned his back on the ball and it looped in the air off his glove. Following through, Malcolm beat short-leg to the catch.

much to make South Africa feel that they were safe from defeat.

Umpire Ken Palmer adjudged Mike Atherton leg before first ball although most onlookers felt that the England captain had touched the ball with his bat. Atherton left the crease immediately, made no gesture to the umpire although he shook his head ruefully and looked at his bat on the way to the pavilion. Referee Burge fined the England captain 50% of his match fee for dissent. The spectators were certainly aware of disappointment although not of the clear dissent that Jonty Rhodes had shown at Headingley. As Mr Burge had threatened Atherton publicly after the events at Lord's, it seemed to most of us that the referee was exacting some kind of revenge. Such an act is, in effect, an abuse of power, and it would seem that Mr Burge is not a man who should be refereeing Test matches.

Gooch was caught behind 11 overs later, and Hick, who had looked in good form, was yorked by Donald's devastating in-swinger, England were 93 for 3. Thorpe had been wonderfully positive. His 79 came in 158 minutes, and he had hit 11 fours before being bowled through the gate. Stewart, too, was in glowing form, but he lost Crawley whose tendency to play across the line had been cruelly exposed in the glare of the Test match arena. Stewart was bowled by de Villiers after a confident innings which, perhaps once again, promised a little more than it achieved. Rhodes was another de Villiers victim, and at 222 for 7, the game was slipping away from England. In spite of Stewart and Thorpe, it had been a

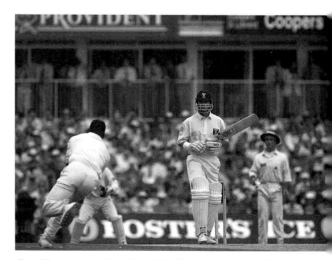

Gary Kirsten is caught and bowled by Devon Malcolm, and South Africa are 0 for 1. (Patrick Eagar)

Peter Kirsten took a single off DeFreitas which brought him to face Malcolm's second over. He essayed a hook at a short delivery, was never in control of the shot, and DeFreitas took a good catch at long-leg. The batsmen had crossed, and Cronje, paralysed by Malcolm's pace, had his middle stump knocked back as he pushed forward. After four overs, South Africa were 1 for 3, and Malcolm had taken all three wickets without conceding a run.

Having bowled five overs, Malcolm was rested, and a period of calm ensued. Wessels and Cullinan added 72 in 20 overs, but when Malcolm returned for his second spell in the afternoon he accounted for Wessels. The South African captain played two wild shots, the second of which ended up in the wicket-keeper's gloves.

McMillan was badly dropped by Gooch at slip, and he and Cullinan added 64 in 17 overs. Malcolm was recalled for his third spell shortly before tea, and McMillan fended a lifting ball to Thorpe at first slip. Two overs later, Richardson was comprehensively beaten by a ball of full length, and Matthews gloved the third ball he received to Rhodes who accepted his chance well. At last Cullinan was removed. He alone had shown the technical ability and physical determination to cope with the demands made by the England attack. He had faced 134 balls and hit 12 fours when he was caught at slip as he tried to force Gough off the back foot. None would have begrudged him a century. For South Africa, he was a beacon in the gloom.

Malcolm soon finished the innings. The courageous Jonty Rhodes slashed to the keeper, and Donald was bowled off his pads. England needed 204 to win, and Malcolm, whose last spell had brought him 5 for 17 in 33 balls, had finished with figures of 16.3 overs, two maidens, 57 runs, and nine wickets. Only two English bowlers have bettered these figures in a Test match – Laker, twice at Old Trafford in 1956; and Lohmann against the embryo South Africans at Johannesburg in 1896.

The aggression and positivity that England had shown in the field were now shown with the bat. In 78 minutes, 16 overs, before the close, they scored 107 for the loss of Gooch. Gooch might have been caught by McMillan at second slip in the first over, but by then he had already scored eight. The first five overs of the innings produced 56 runs, and it was in this over that Gooch was bowled by Matthews. There was no respite for the South Africans as Hick joined the fray, reaching 27 off 29 balls before the end of the day. The South African pace attack was totally destroyed and was exposed as being limited in variation. Atherton, 42 not out, left the field to a tumultuous ovation.

The England captain was the only man dismissed on the fourth, the last, day. He touched a Donald lifter to Richardson, but by then he and Hick had added 124 in 28 overs. Hick, whose 81 not out included 13 fours and was an even better innings than his century at Headingley, and Thorpe, 15 off 14 balls, took England to the sweetest of victories. It was a victory which may well have changed the course of England's fortunes, for there was substance and character here, a vitality that has long been missing.

DeFreitas bowls Wessels in the first of the two matches. (David Munden/Sports-Line)

Malcolm was Man of the Match, and he and McMillan were Men of the Series. There should have been a word for Atherton. He had made his mistakes, endured much and been unduly punished, but he had shown qualities of leadership at the end which augur well for the future of English cricket.

TEXACO TROPHY
ENGLAND v. SOUTH AFRICA

It is probable that any international match would have been an anti-climax after The Oval Test, but, inevitably, after a long summer containing the one-day match against New Zealand and six Tests, the Texaco Trophy matches against South Africa became a superfluity. Both matches were very much in England's favour. Donald and McMillan were unfit for South Africa. Snell and Shaw came in – a spinner at last. Fairbrother, Lewis, Cork and Udal became part of England's squad, and Malcolm and Fraser, in the party, played in neither match.

Choosing to bat first at Edgbaston, South Africa could not get started. Rhodes, Cullinan and Cronje were out just as they promised to accelerate, and it was Shaw and Richardson who provided the late impetus with 33 off the last five overs. Stewart and Atherton scored 57 in 19 overs, and when Atherton was out 90 were needed from 20 overs. Hick was again in majestic form, and with Fairbrother and Thorpe hustling, this became a simple task. Hick was out with the scores level, and Rhodes did not, in fact, face a ball.

Unfortunately, the second match went into a second day because of rain. Donald returned in place of Snell, but again it was Shaw who seemed to pose most problems. An opening stand of 43 by Gary Kirsten and Wessels was soon nullified when three wickets fell for four runs. In spite of Cullinan's 54, there was no effective recovery.

TEXACO TROPHY – FIRST ONE-DAY INTERNATIONAL – ENGLAND v. SOUTH AFRICA
24 August at Edgbaston, Birmingham

SOUTH AFRICA				ENGLAND		
K.C. Wessels (capt)	b DeFreitas	4		M.A. Atherton (capt)	run out	49
G. Kirsten	c DeFreitas, b Lewis	30		A.J. Stewart	c de Villiers, b Shaw	32
P.N. Kirsten	c Rhodes, b DeFreitas	8		G.A. Hick	c Shaw, b Snell	81
J.N. Rhodes	c Thorpe, b Cork	35		G.P. Thorpe	run out	26
D.J. Cullinan	b DeFreitas	45		N.H. Fairbrother	not out	19
W.J. Cronje	b Lewis	36		*S.J. Rhodes	not out	0
*D.J. Richardson	not out	20		C.C. Lewis		
R.P. Snell	c Gough, b Lewis	2		D.G. Cork		
T.G. Shaw	not out	17		P.A.J. DeFreitas		
C.R. Matthews				D. Gough		
P.S. de Villiers				S.D. Udal		
Extras	lb 6, w 10, nb 2	18		Extras	b 9, w 2, nb 1	12
		—				—
(55 overs)	(for 7 wickets)	215		(54 overs)	(for 4 wickets)	219

	O	M	R	W		O	M	R	W
DeFreitas	9	1	38	3	de Villiers	11	2	27	–
Gough	11	2	40	–	Matthews	11	1	42	–
Lewis	8	–	32	3	Shaw	11	–	34	1
Udal	11	–	34	–	Snell	11	–	49	1
Cork	11	–	46	1	Cronje	9	–	50	–
Hick	5	1	19	–	G. Kirsten	1	–	8	–

FALL OF WICKETS

1–5, 2–30, 3–58, 4–103, 5–174, 6–176, 7–182

FALL OF WICKETS

1–57, 2–126, 3–181, 4–215

Umpires: J.C. Balderstone & H.D. Bird   *Man of the Match:* G.A. Hick   *England won by 6 wickets*

TEXACO TROPHY – SECOND ONE-DAY INTERNATIONAL – ENGLAND v. SOUTH AFRICA
27 and 28 August at Old Trafford, Manchester

SOUTH AFRICA				ENGLAND		
G. Kirsten	c Lewis, b Cork	30		M.A. Atherton (capt)	c Wessels, b Matthews	19
K.C. Wessels (capt)	lbw, b DeFreitas	21		A.J. Stewart	c Cullinan, b Donald	11
W.J. Cronje	run out	0		G.A. Hick	lbw, b Donald	0
J.N. Rhodes	lbw, b Cork	0		G.P. Thorpe	c Cullinan, b Shaw	55
D.J. Cullinan	run out	54		N.H. Fairbrother	run out	3
B.M. McMillan	st Rhodes, b Udal	0		*S.J. Rhodes	run out	56
*D.J. Richardson	c Lewis, b Gough	14		C.C. Lewis	not out	17
T.G. Shaw	b Gough	6		P.A.J. DeFreitas	not out	7
C.R. Matthews	b Cork	26		D.G. Cork		
P.S. de Villiers	not out	14		D. Gough		
A.A. Donald	not out	2		S.D. Udal		
Extras	lb 6, w 4, nb 4	14		Extras	w 4, nb 10	14
		—				—
(55 overs)	(for 9 wickets)	181		(48.2 overs)	(for 6 wickets)	182

	O	M	R	W		O	M	R	W
DeFreitas	11	4	12	1	Donald	10.2	1	47	2
Gough	10	1	39	2	de Villiers	8	1	29	–
Lewis	9	–	44	–	McMillan	10	1	53	–
Udal	11	2	17	1	Matthews	9	2	20	1
Cork	11	1	49	3	Shaw	11	–	33	1
Hick	3	–	14	–					

FALL OF WICKETS

1–43, 2–47, 3–47, 4–64, 5–68, 6–113, 7–121, 8–163, 9–163

FALL OF WICKETS

1–27, 2–28, 3–42, 4–60, 5–130, 6–171

Umpires: M.J. Kitchen & K.E. Palmer   *Man of the Match:* S.J. Rhodes   *England won by 4 wickets*

England slipped to 60 for 4, but Thorpe and Rhodes oozed self-belief, and victory came with nearly seven overs to spare.

England had ended the season in the highest state of optimism. Certainly they had found unity and a passionate desire to succeed. South Africa had been brought closer to reality. Since their readmission to international cricket their enthusiasm and commitment had carried them along with some success, but in England, their weaknesses had become apparent. They were a team of great character, but they lacked personality. There was a desperate need for a Ken McEwan in the middle order, and an even greater need for a spin bowler of high quality.

25, 26, 27 and 29 August *at Cardiff*

Glamorgan 295 (P.A. Cottey 142, D.J. Millns 4 for 83) and 360 for 9 dec. (R.D.B. Croft 80, C.P. Metson 51, D.L. Hemp 50)

Leicestershire 244 (P.E. Robinson 86, T.J. Boon 74) and 261 (V.J. Wells 56, R.D.B. Croft 5 for 80)

Glamorgan won by 150 runs

Glamorgan 22 pts., Leicestershire 5 pts.

at Portsmouth

Hampshire 512 (V.P. Terry 164, K.D. James 53, J. Wood 5 for 141) and 215 for 3 dec. (G.W. White 73 not out)

Durham 386 (J.E. Morris 149, A.C. Cummins 65, P. Bainbridge 64, C.A. Connor 4 for 122) and 285 for 7 (J.A. Daley 159 not out, N.G. Cowans 4 for 76)

Match drawn

Hampshire 8 pts., Durham 6 pts.

at Northampton

Kent 165 (N.R. Taylor 67 not out, M.A. Ealham 52, A.L. Penberthy 5 for 54) and 248 (C.E.L. Ambrose 6 for 31)

Northamptonshire 260 (R.J. Bailey 115, R.J. Warren 57, M.J. McCague 4 for 60) and 156 for 2 (A. Fordham 70, R.R. Montgomerie 50 not out)

Northamptonshire won by 8 wickets

Northamptonshire 22 pts., Kent 4 pts.

at Trent Bridge

Nottinghamshire 242 (G. Yates 4 for 55) and 177 (G.W. Mike 60 not out, M. Watkinson 4 for 36, G. Chapple 4 for 64)

Lancashire 567 (J.P. Crawley 250, W.K. Hegg 66)

Lancashire won by an innings and 148 runs

Lancashire 23 pts., Nottinghamshire 3 pts.

at The Oval

Surrey 425 (D.J. Bicknell 89, A.W. Smith 68 not out, M.A. Feltham 4 for 94) and 313 for 3 dec.

(A.D. Brown 83 not out, D.M. Ward 79, M.A. Butcher 70)

Middlesex 350 for 5 dec. (M.R. Ramprakash 124, D.L. Haynes 53) and 392 for 8 (M.W. Gatting 103, M.R. Ramprakash 90, J.D. Carr 62 not out)

Middlesex won by 2 wickets

Middlesex 24 pts., Surrey 6 pts.

at Hove

Sussex 131 (T.A. Munton 4 for 22) and 127 (T.A. Munton 4 for 52)

Warwickshire 183 (D.F. Ostler 50, P.W. Jarvis 4 for 68) and 79 for 0

Warwickshire won by 10 wickets

Warwickshire 20 pts., Sussex 4 pts.

at Worcester

Worcestershire 355 (W.P.C. Weston 72, P.J. Hartley 5 for 89) and 73 (M.A. Robinson 5 for 48, P.J. Hartley 4 for 20)

Yorkshire 489 for 5 dec. (M.D. Moxon 274 not out, A.P. Grayson 100)

Yorkshire won by an innings and 61 runs

Yorkshire 24 pts., Worcestershire 3 pts.

Glamorgan gained their second victory of the season and virtually ended Leicestershire's challenge for the title. Glamorgan were 149 for 7 before Metson joined Cottey in a stand that was worth 116. Cottey, as determined and resolute as ever, batted for five hours and hit 19 fours and confirmed his position as his side's perpetual saviour from humiliation. A fourth-wicket stand of 132 between Boon and Robinson took Leicestershire to 170 for 3, but their last seven wickets fell for 74. In their second innings, Glamorgan recovered from 64 for 3 through some good batting from the middle order. Croft was in particularly fluent form, scoring 80 out of 132 while he was at the wicket. He then captured one of the four Leicestershire wickets which fell on the Saturday evening, and he finished with 5 for 80 after the visitors had offered sterner resistance on the Monday.

Hampshire continued with their prolific run-scoring, batting into the second day and showing consistency as they made 512. Terry provided the disciplined backbone to the innings, batting 6¼ hours and hitting 23 fours. Durham avoided the follow-on, not only because of John Morris' 149, but through some excellent later work by Bainbridge, Cummins and Scott. Eventually, Durham were asked to make 342 in 78 overs. Losing Longley and Morris in Cowans' first over, Durham looked beaten at 56 for 3, but Jimmy Daley hit a sparkling maiden first-class century which not only saved Durham but gave them a scent of victory. In the end, the match was drawn, but young Daley could draw much comfort from his 159 off 249 balls in 296 minutes. He hit 26 fours.

Northamptonshire confirmed recent improvement in

form with a three-day victory over Kent. Put in to bat, Kent collapsed to 39 for 5 before Taylor and Ealham added 103. Then the last five wickets fell for 23. Bailey's bubbling century took the home county to a substantial first-innings lead, and Ambrose then brought about the demolition of Kent's second innings. Marsh and Ealham added 65 for the seventh wicket, but the last three Kent wickets fell for four runs. Montgomerie and Fordham hit 113 for the first wicket as Northamptonshire sought 154 for victory, and the game was over on the Saturday evening.

Like Leicestershire, Nottinghamshire saw their challenge to Warwickshire fade as they were overwhelmed by Lancashire who clinched victory on the last morning. Choosing to bat first when they won the toss, Nottinghamshire occupied 125.3 overs in scoring 242. In 91 overs by the end of the second day, Lancashire had established a 23-run lead, and on the Saturday, Crawley, omitted from England's Texaco Cup squad, and Hegg extended their seventh-wicket partnership to 235. Crawley, in devastating form, hit his third double century in eight months. He destroyed the Nottinghamshire attack, and his 250 came off 398 balls with 33 fours and 2 sixes. A dispirited Nottinghamshire side sunk to 82 for 6 on the Saturday evening. They lasted 40 more overs on Monday, Gregory Mike showing commendable defiance.

At The Oval, play could not begin until 3 p.m. on the first day, but consistent and aggressive batting took Surrey to 425 at more than four runs an over. Middlesex responded with a century from Ramprakash and a declaration 75 runs in arrears once they had captured the fourth batting point. Again Surrey scored at more than four runs an over, and Martin Bicknell's declaration left Middlesex a target of 389 in 89 overs. Gatting opened, and he and Ramprakash put on 180 in 44 overs for the second wicket. Weekes hit 46 off 39 balls, and Middlesex needed 104 off the last 24 overs with seven wickets in hand. Surrey fought back, and the eighth wicket went down with 14 still needed. Gordon Harris survived, and Carr, as he had done throughout the month, batted with glory and intelligence to take his side to a very fine victory. Gatting's 103 off 143 balls which, with Ramprakash's 90 from 157 deliveries, had provided the platform for the Middlesex victory, had also furthered his claim for a place in the party to tour Australia.

Warwickshire's hold on the Britannic Assurance County Championship became vice-like when, with their nearest challengers faltering, they beat Sussex in three days on a pitch at Hove which was much enjoyed by the seamers. Sussex lost their last six wickets for 29 runs on the opening day as Twose, Munton and Small took complete control, but Warwickshire closed unhappily on 9 for 2. They were soon 9 for 3, but that incomparable spirit and determination which had served them so well all season saw Ostler, Piper, Penney and Welch fight back against Giddins, Stephenson and Jarvis and claim a vital first-innings lead of 52. By the close of play on the second day, Sussex had crashed to 107 for 8. A last-wicket stand of 16 between Hemmings and Giddins delayed the inevitable for only a short time, and Moles and Twose romped to victory at four runs an over.

Worcestershire batted somewhat dourly against Yorkshire, and a last-wicket stand of 81 between Illingworth and Edwards was particularly irritating to the visitors. Yorkshire, 98 for 2 at the end of the second day, were also rather laboured in their approach, but Moxon and Grayson cut loose on the Saturday. They added 200, with Grayson reaching a maiden first-class century off 157 balls. Moxon, who hit 40 fours and faced 490 deliveries, gave a masterly display to hit the highest score made for Yorkshire since the Second World War. He declared when his side had a lead of 134, and Hartley then captured three wickets before the close as Worcestershire scored just one run. This became 11 for 6 on the Monday, and the game was over before lunch with the ninth-wicket stand of 38 between Radford and Leatherdale being the best of the innings.

AXA EQUITY & LAW LEAGUE

28 August *at Neath*

Glamorgan 210 for 5
Leicestershire 177 (D.L. Maddy 54, S.R. Barwick 5 for 36)
Glamorgan (4 pts.) won by 33 runs

at Portsmouth

Hampshire 217 for 6 (A.N. Aymes 54)
Durham 220 for 0 (W. Larkins 131 not out, J.I. Longley 72 not out)
Durham (4 pts.) won by 10 wickets

at Northampton

Kent 273 for 6 (C.L. Hooper 122, G.R. Cowdrey 82, C.E.L. Ambrose 4 for 20)
Northamptonshire 233 for 9 (T.C. Walton 57)
Kent (4 pts.) won by 40 runs

at Trent Bridge

Lancashire 226 for 7 (J.P. Crawley 66)
Nottinghamshire 227 for 2 (R.T. Robinson 119 not out, P. Johnson 54)
Nottinghamshire (4 pts.) won by 8 wickets

at The Oval

Middlesex 261 for 4 (M.A. Roseberry 119 not out)
Surrey 262 for 3 (A.D. Brown 142 not out, D.J. Bicknell 57)
Surrey (4 pts.) won by 7 wickets

at Hove

Sussex 157 for 7 (A.P. Wells 60)
Warwickshire 161 for 5 (D.P. Ostler 84 not out)
Warwickshire (4 pts.) won by 5 wickets

A Warwickshire hero, Tim Munton led the side admirably in the absence of Reeve, took wickets consistently and was named the Players' Player of the Year. (Alan Cozzi)

Yorkshire 188 for 6
Worcestershire 169 for 9 (T.S. Curtis 81 not out)

Yorkshire (4 pts.) won by 19 runs

As Lancashire and Worcestershire lost ground, Glamorgan and Kent kept alive their hopes of overhauling Warwickshire in the final stretch of the Sunday League. With Hooper again in marvellous form, 122 off 112 balls, and Cowdrey plundering 82 off 72 balls, Kent savaged 109 from their last 10 overs to set up victory over Northamptonshire. Larkins and Longley hit 220 in 34.4 overs to record Durham's best Sunday victory, and there were centuries for Robinson and Roseberry, but Warwickshire, without the injured Lara, beat Sussex with five overs to spare and held on to the top place.

29 August *at Scarborough*

South Africans 151 (W.J. Cronje 53, K.C.G. Benjamin 4 for 36)
President's XI 155 for 6

President's XI won by 4 wickets

30 and 31 August, 1 and 2 September *at Chelmsford*

Sussex 246 (M.P. Speight 73, M.C. Ilott 6 for 72) and 277 (J.W. Hall 56, P.M. Such 6 for 116, M.C. Ilott 4 for 57)
Essex 418 (N.V. Knight 157, G.A. Gooch 79, R.C. Irani 67, E.S.H. Giddins 5 for 83) and 106 for 3

Essex won by 7 wickets
Essex 24 pts., Sussex 5 pts.

at Bristol

Gloucestershire 350 for 4 dec. (A.J. Wright 184 not out, T.H.C. Hancock 59 not out) and 143 for 2 dec.
Leicestershire 167 for 3 dec. (J.J. Whitaker 81 not out) and 224 (P.A. Nixon 87, C.A. Walsh 5 for 47)

Gloucestershire won by 102 runs
Gloucestershire 21 pts., Leicestershire 1 pt.

at Old Trafford

Lancashire 267 (M. Watkinson 87) and 311 (G.D. Lloyd 56, W.K. Hegg 52 not out)
Worcestershire 591 (G.A. Hick 215, T.M. Moody 109, S.J. Rhodes 67, G. Chapple 5 for 149, P.J. Martin 4 for 93)

Worcestershire won by an innings and 13 runs
Worcestershire 24 pts., Lancashire 4 pts.

at Worksop

Nottinghamshire 476 for 6 dec. (G.F. Archer 168, R.T. Robinson 99, C.C. Lewis 68 not out, P. Johnson 51)
Glamorgan 221 (M.P. Maynard 69) and 218 (M.P. Maynard 58, H. Morris 51, J.E. Hindson 5 for 53)

Nottinghamshire won by an innings and 37 runs
Nottinghamshire 24 pts., Glamorgan 2 pts.

at Taunton

Somerset 346 (A.N. Hayhurst 72, P.C.L. Holloway 50, C.E.L. Ambrose 5 for 59) and 25 for 0 dec.
Northamptonshire 71 for 1 dec. and 304 for 8 (A.L. Penberthy 88 not out, C.E.L. Ambrose 78, R.J. Warren 53, A.R. Caddick 4 for 92)

Northamptonshire won by 2 wickets
Northamptonshire 20 pts., Somerset 3 pts.

at Edgbaston

Hampshire 278 (V.P. Terry 71, S.D. Udal 64, T.A. Munton 4 for 44) and 163 (N.M.K. Smith 5 for 65)
Warwickshire 536 (B.C. Lara 191, R.G. Twose 137, C.A. Connor 4 for 124)

Warwickshire won by an innings and 95 runs

Warwickshire 24 pts., Hampshire 4 pts.

at Sheffield

Yorkshire 235 (M.P. Vaughan 86, D. Byas 53,
D.E. Malcolm 4 for 63) and 222 for 9 dec. (B. Parker
54 not out)

Derbyshire 200 for 7 dec. (C.J. Adams 66, D.G. Cork
50) and 73 (D. Gough 4 for 24, M.A. Robinson 4 for
35)

Yorkshire won by 184 runs

Yorkshire 20 pts., Derbyshire 5 pts.

31 August, **1** and **2** September *at Scarborough*

President's XI 343 for 6 dec. (P.R. Sleep 79 not out,
B.A. Young 66, K.L.T. Arthurton 60, J.E. Morris 57)
and 0 for 0 dec.

South Africans 0 for 0 dec. and 270 for 6 (A.C. Hudson
116)

Match drawn

 Northern Electric Trophy

3 September *at Scarborough*

Durham 222 for 8 (S. Hutton 68, J.A. Daley 57,
D. Gough 4 for 29)

Yorkshire 210 (D. Byas 53, J. Wood 4 for 32)

Durham won by 12 runs

Warwickshire won the Britannic Assurance County
Championship when they bowled out Hampshire on
Friday, 2 September, to win by an innings while, at the
same time, Leicestershire were falling to Gloucestershire.
There had seemed little chance of any county catching
Warwickshire over the last weeks of the season so that
their fourth championship, their first for 22 years, came as
no surprise. They were unquestionably the best side in
the competition by a good margin. They scored runs
quickly, had a balanced attack and played with a corporate spirit which gave joy to all who watched them. They
bowled out Hampshire on the first day at Edgbaston, the
visitors losing five middle-order wickets for 10 runs. Udal
and Maru halted the slide, and the last four wickets
added 139 runs. The second day was restricted to 45
overs, but Twose and Lara showed splendid form, and
Warwickshire scored 210 for 1. Runs continued to flow at
four an over on the third day when Twose and Lara
extended their partnership to a thrilling 295 in 61 overs.
Lara passed 2,000 runs, hitting 191 from 222 balls, while
Twose, who had enjoyed a marvellous season and was in
no way overshadowed, faced 215 for his 137. Munton
decided to bat into the last morning, and, when Hampshire struggled to avoid an innings defeat, he made early

inroads before allowing spinners Neil Smith and Richard
Davis to take over. Hampshire's last seven wickets fell for
43 runs, and Warwickshire were champions. If Reeve had
imbued spirit into the side and Lara had provided inspiration, Munton's role must not be forgotten. With Reeve
fit enough only for the limited-over games, Munton had
led the side for much of the season, and he did a magnificent job. He was a worthy recipient of the trophy.

Leicestershire's hopes were extinguished at Bristol
where Gloucestershire scored 350 for 4 in 100 overs on the
first day after Leicestershire had captured three wickets
in the first 18 overs. The Gloucestershire revival was
mainly due to Tony Wright who reached the highest
score of his career, hit a six and 22 fours, and shared an
unbroken fifth-wicket partnership of 145 with Hancock.
With only 42 overs play on the third day after a blank
second day, declarations were negotiated which left Leicestershire a target of 327. Walsh quickly sent back both
openers, and, at 110 for 6, Leicestershire were submerg-
ing fast. Nixon, rightly chosen for a place in the England
'A' side to tour India, offered positive resistance, but
Gloucestershire, the wooden spoon threat of 1993 long
forgotten, were not to be denied.

Northamptonshire climbed into third place with a
sensational victory over Somerset. There was a rain-
restricted first day, and no play at all on the second at
Taunton. The third day saw Somerset complete their first
innings and declare their second innings closed after 17
balls so leaving Northamptonshire, who had ended their
first innings after 15 overs, the last day in which to score
301 to win. The pitch was lively, and the Somerset seam
attack appeared to have set up victory when they reduced
the visitors to 73 for 5. There was some resolution from
Bailey and Warren, but at 152 for 7, all looked lost for
Northamptonshire. Ambrose and Penberthy had other
ideas. Ambrose, a massive batsman of rustic style when
the mood takes him, hit 2 sixes and 9 fours in an innings of
78 which came off 96 balls. The more correct Penberthy
hit a six and 14 fours and was unbeaten on 88 which came
off 118 balls. He took his side to victory with nearly 27
overs to spare and was awarded his county cap for his
wonderful efforts.

A career-best 168 by Graeme Archer took Nottinghamshire to a commanding position after two days against
Glamorgan. The third day saw the visitors fall to a varied
attack and forced to follow on. Maynard and Morris
began their second innings with a partnership of 114, but
five wickets then fell for 16 runs. All five wickets, four of
them in 21 balls, went to James Hindson, the left-arm
spinner, who took five wickets in a championship match
for the first time. Cottey and Croft suggested a recovery,
but the last five Glamorgan wickets went down for 17
runs.

Fielding Gooch, Stephenson, Ilott and Prichard in the
same side for only the second time in the season, Essex
gained a decisive and encouraging victory over Sussex.
Choosing to bat first, Sussex adopted tactics which re-
sembled a 10-over slog and were bowled out in under 63
overs. Only Speight and Moores showed sense and
correctness in a fifth-wicket stand of 68. Mark Ilott, fully
recovered from injury, had six wickets although he had

considerable help from the batsmen. Gooch and Knight scored 128 for Essex's first wicket, and Knight and Irani 132 for the fourth in 36 overs. Nick Knight, a beautifully compact left-hander, hit 23 fours and 2 sixes in making the highest score of his career, and he produced some exquisite strokes. Sussex showed far greater purpose when they batted again, with Hall proving obdurate, and Giddins and Salisbury frustrating in a last-wicket stand of 51. Giddins made 24, the highest score of his career, and hit Such, who finished with six wickets, for 2 sixes. Ilott had match figures of 10 for 129, and one felt that but for missing so much of the season through injury, he would have been in the party to tour Australia. Salisbury caused a minor panic by taking three wickets, but Knight and Irani saw Essex to a comfortable win.

Lancashire continued their lop-sided season with an innings defeat at the hands of Worcestershire. Hick, batting with the exuberance of a man reprieved from the scaffold, hit 215, his ninth double century, and shared a stand of 265 for the fourth wicket with Tom Moody. There was a useful late contribution from Rhodes who continued to enjoy a fine year with the bat, and Lancashire had little hope of avoiding defeat once they had lost their first four wickets on the Thursday evening.

Rain disrupted the game at Sheffield and brought a declaration from Derbyshire when they were 35 in arrears on the first innings. The last afternoon was sensational as Gough and Robinson reduced Derbyshire to 17 for 6. DeFreitas hit 27, and there were 11 extras, but there was no salvation for Derbyshire.

Rain wiped out play on the second day at Scarborough, and even forfeitures could not bring a result for South Africa in their final match of the tour. Andrew Hudson scored a hundred, a sad epitaph for one of whom much had been expected.

NATWEST TROPHY FINAL
WARWICKSHIRE *v.* WORCESTERSHIRE at Lord's

The NatWest Trophy had been plagued by rain throughout the season, nor was the competition reprieved at the final stage. The same two counties who had featured in the Benson and Hedges Cup final were on duty at Lord's again, but Worcestershire won the toss and, on this occasion, Warwickshire batted first. Curtis' judgement was correct, for there was moisture in the pitch, and the ball moved appreciably.

Worcestershire had reached the final by virtue of a marvellous innings from Tom Moody at The Oval, but it was the Australian's bowling which now gave his county an early advantage. Bowling a gentle medium pace, but bringing the ball down from a considerable height, he maintained accuracy and wobbled the ball both ways. It was not easy for batting and, having hit Newport to the cover boundary for four, Ostler was deceived by a slower ball and offered a straightforward catch to gully. This wicket came in Newport's first over so that Lara was soon at the crease and was immediately confronted by two vociferous appeals. The second ball he received was down the leg side, and there was a unanimous appeal for

County Champions – Warwickshire County Cricket Club.
BACK ROW *(l. to r.): Mulraine, Powell, Giles and Altree*
MIDDLE ROW *(l. to r.): Dennis Amiss, Burns, Penney, Wasim Khan, Ratcliffe, Davis, Bell and Welch*
FRONT ROW *(l. to r.): Neal Abberley, Moles, Ostler, Bob Woolmer, Munton, Reeve (capt), Small, Asif Din, Paul Smith, Twose, Neil Smith and Piper*
One important batsman is missing from this photograph – Brian Lara. (Paul Sturgess/Sports-Line)

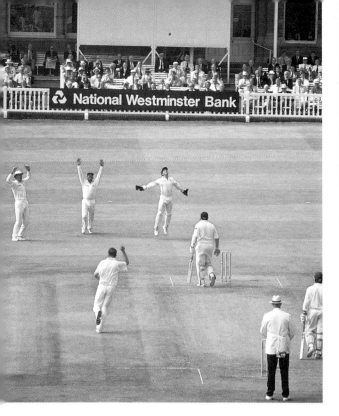

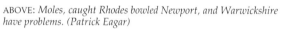

ABOVE: *Moles, caught Rhodes bowled Newport, and Warwickshire have problems. (Patrick Eagar)*

BELOW: *Gladstone Small is run out as the Warwickshire innings draws to its close. (Patrick Eagar)*

RIGHT: *Tim Curtis holds the NatWest Trophy. (Patrick Eagar)*

a catch at the wicket. Umpire Plews pondered dramatically and signalled a wide. This was followed by an equally vehement appeal for leg before which was also rejected and which caused Rhodes to become so excited as to earn a word of rebuke from umpire Shepherd – thankfully there are no referees in the NatWest Trophy. Rhodes remained so excited that he dived in front of D'Oliveira and caused a slip catch offered by Moles to be missed.

Moles perished in the tenth over, touching a splendid delivery from the admirable Newport to the wicket-keeper. The score was 17. Lara had taken 26 balls to get off the mark, and he was far from comfortable in the early stages of his innings. A more athletic and alert fielder than Illingworth might well have caught him at square-leg, but he survived, and gradually the ball began to sizzle past those square of the wicket. The man plays the ball so late that it is a difficult task for the fielder to judge the pace and placement from the bat.

Paul Smith clouted 2 fours, and the fifty went up in the 19th over, but his wicket went down in the same over. He slogged once too often and was easily taken at mid-on. Moody completed his immaculate spell, 1 for 17 in 12 overs, and Radford and Lampitt were now the bowlers. The third and fourth balls of the 28th over, Twose, compact and assured, put through mid-wicket for four. At the end of the next over, rain ended play for the day; Warwickshire 88 for 3, Lara 36, Twose 20; honours slightly in favour of Worcestershire.

There is an inevitable anticlimax when a limited-over match goes into a second day. There are fewer people, a less tense atmosphere. Perhaps Twose felt a sense of anticlimax, for he fell almost immediately on the Sunday,

Brian Lara began uncertainly, but his brilliant timing and positive approach breathed life into the Warwickshire innings. (David Munden/Sports-Line)

mishitting to extra cover. Lara, however, was soon flowing sweetly in spite of Radford's niggling accuracy which brought him the wicket of Penney and the concession of only 11 runs from the five overs that remained to him on the second day.

Reeve could not find his touch, and Lara's magnificence came to an end in the 46th over when he swung Haynes to deep square-leg. Haynes had been pressed into service when Lara had punished Illingworth severely, and now he had captured the major prize. A six and 7 fours were Lara's main hits, and his 81 had occupied 117 balls. Without him Warwickshire would have long since vanished, for Reeve, obviously unwell for all his enthusiasm, could not push the score along at the rate demanded. He was caught behind off the splendid Newport, and but for Neil Smith's lusty blows and the scampering of Piper, the innings would have fizzled out miserably. As it was, the last seven overs produced a meagre 35 runs.

Munton's opening spell – like Moody he bowled his 12 overs through – was the equal of Newport's and Moody's in quality, but Curtis and D'Oliveira were determined to lay a firm base. In the 14th over, D'Oliveira, in his last fortnight as a Worcestershire player, was caught at slip, and in the next over, Curtis was deceived by a low bounce. Warwickshire's spirits rose, but they were soon

The Avengers – Hick and Moody. (David Munden/Sports-Line)

NATWEST TROPHY FINAL – WARWICKSHIRE v. WORCESTERSHIRE
3 and 4 September 1994 at Lord's

WARWICKSHIRE

A.J. Moles	c Rhodes, b Newport	8
D.P. Ostler	c Lampitt, b Newport	4
B.C. Lara	c Hick, b Haynes	81
P.A. Smith	c Haynes, b Moody	13
R.G. Twose	c Leatherdale, b Newport	22
T.L. Penney	lbw, b Radford	18
D.A. Reeve (capt)	c Rhodes, b Newport	13
N.M.K. Smith	c Illingworth, b Lampitt	20
*K.J. Piper	not out	16
G.C. Small	run out	5
T.A. Munton	not out	0
Extras	b 1, lb 8, w 10 nb 4	23
(60 overs)	(for 9 wickets)	223

WORCESTERSHIRE

T.S. Curtis (capt)	b Reeve	11
D.B. D'Oliveira	c Lara, b Munton	12
G.A. Hick	not out	93
T.M. Moody	not out	88
G.R. Haynes		
D.A. Leatherdale		
*S.J. Rhodes		
S.R. Lampitt		
P.J. Newport		
R.K. Illingworth		
N.V. Radford		
Extras	lb 6, w 11, nb 6	23
(49.1 overs)	(for 2 wickets)	227

	O	M	R	W
Moody	12	4	17	1
Newport	12	2	38	4
Radford	12	1	45	1
Lampitt	11	1	45	1
Illingworth	6	–	35	–
Haynes	7	–	34	1

	O	M	R	W
Small	12	2	40	–
Munton	12	3	23	1
Reeve	6	1	30	1
P.A. Smith	7	1	54	–
Twose	5	–	36	–
N.M.K. Smith	7	–	34	–
Penney	0.1	–	4	–

FALL OF WICKETS
1–8, 2–17, 3–50, 4–90, 5–150, 6–171, 7–188, 8–215, 9–222

FALL OF WICKETS
1–29, 2–29

Umpires: N.T. Plews & D.R. Shepherd   *Man of the Match*: T.M. Moody   *Worcestershire won by 8 wickets*

dampened. Hick survived a confident appeal for caught behind and, born again as a cricketer, he soon began crashing the ball to all parts of the field. Moody joined him in exultation. In 34 overs, the pair hit off the runs needed for victory and three for good measure, 198 in all. Hick hit a six and 12 fours and faced 101 balls; Moody had 2 sixes and 10 fours and faced 112 balls. It was a time of glorious stroke-play, beautiful to watch. The Warwickshire dream of the Grand Slam was shattered, but perhaps it had been shattered when they lost the toss on a September morning.

AXA EQUITY & LAW LEAGUE

4 September *at Chelmsford*

Essex 207 for 8 (N. Hussain 76, J.P. Stephenson 68)
Sussex 174 (M.P. Speight 66, M.C. Ilott 4 for 25)

Essex (4 pts.) won by 33 runs

at Moreton-in-Marsh

Leicestershire 256 for 4 (N.E. Briers 105, V.J. Wells 65 not out)

Gloucestershire 155 (A.R.K. Pierson 4 for 29, V.J. Wells 4 for 46)

Leicestershire (4 pts.) won on faster scoring rate

at Trent Bridge

Glamorgan 178 for 9 (A. Dale 61, K.P. Evans 5 for 29)
Nottinghamshire 138 for 2 (J.C. Adams 65, M.P. Dowman 52 not out)

Nottinghamshire (4 pts.) won on faster scoring rate

at Taunton

Somerset 228 for 7 (M.N. Lathwell 83)
Northamptonshire 231 for 3 (R.J. Bailey 94 not out, R.R. Montgomerie 74)

Northamptonshire (4 pts.) won by 7 wickets

at Leeds

Derbyshire 160 for 4
Yorkshire 162 for 6 (D. Byas 87 not out)

Yorkshire (4 pts.) won by 4 wickets

Derbyshire

K.J. Barnett 113*, 4 & 0 (ct 2); M. Azharuddin 7, 74* & 7; D.G. Cork 19 & 62, 23–4–67–7; T.J.G. O'Gorman 0, 89 & 5 (ct 1); C.J. Adams 52, 3 & 26 (ct 2); M.J. Vandrau 0* & 27, 21–1–81–4; P.A.J. DeFreitas 0, 28 & 7, 35–8–112–5; P.D. Bowler 9 (ct 1); A.S. Rollins 6 (ct 2); F.A. Griffith did not bat, 0 & 8 (ct 2), 21–6–73–2; D.E. Malcolm did not bat twice & 0, 36–4–132–3; A.E. Warner 0, 12–2–57–1; C.M. Wells 0 (ct 1), 8.3–2–22–0; K.M. Krikken 8* & 6* (ct 2); S.J. Base 0, 11–0–63–1

Durham

P. Bainbridge 17* & 105 (ct 1), 21–2–67–2; J.E. Morris 67 & 25 (ct 1); W. Larkins 34 & 30 (ct 1); A.C. Cummins 11 & 6*, 22–4–73–5; A. Walker 13, 12–1–61–0; J.I. Longley 5 & 9; M. Saxelby 13 & 0; S. Hutton 10 & 1 (ct 1); C.W. Scott did not bat & 2 (ct 2); S.J.E. Brown did not bat & 0, 21.1–3–85–5; D.A. Graveney did not bat & 16* (ct 1), 20–6–51–2; J. Wood 0, 9–2–29–1

Essex

G.A. Gooch 86 & 10 (ct 2); J.P. Stephenson 55 & 19 (ct 1), 19–1–118–2; N. Hussain 47 & 26 (ct 2); M.C. Ilott did not bat & 26 (ct 1), 23.2–3–87–2; J.J.B. Lewis 24* & 1 (ct 1); N.V. Knight 23; R.C. Irani 30 & 11, 24–2–121–4; M.S. Kasprowicz 13, 12–2–60–5; P.M. Such did not bat & 6 (ct 1), 19–1–72–1; M.A. Garnham 1 & 2* (ct 1/st 1); N. Shahid 85* (ct 1); D.M. Cousins 0 & 1*, 10–1–57–1; R.M. Pearson 0, 12–0–47–1

Glamorgan

S.P. James 123 & 18; A. Dale 110 & 17, 3–0–27–1; M.P. Maynard 78, 75 & 13 (ct 5); P.A. Cottey 57, 7* & 36, 6–0–30–1; R.D.B. Croft 50, 2* & 0 (ct 1), 32.4–5–108–6; O.D. Gibson 23, 44 & 1 (ct 1), 27–3–116–5; R.P. Lefebvre did not bat, 0* & 15 (ct 3), 35–7–89–4; H. Morris 24, 4 & 4, 2–0–12–0; D.L. Hemp 6 & 13; S.L. Watkin did not bat twice & 9, 29–4–92–2; C.P. Metson did not bat, 4 & 7 (ct 4); S.R. Barwick did not bat twice & 0* (ct 1), 34–5–97–4

Gloucestershire

R.I. Dawson 60; B.C. Broad 44; M.G.N. Windows 33; T.H.C. Hancock 29, 5–0–32–0; M.W. Alleyne 24, 11.2–0–59–1; R.C. Russell 10 (ct 1); C.A. Walsh 9, 12–1–32–2; A.J. Wright 2*, 7–0–32–0; A.M. Smith 1*, 12–1–41–1; K.E. Cooper 0, 12–1–30–2

Hampshire

R.A. Smith 59* & 7 (ct 1); R.S.M. Morris 29 & 34*; M.C.J. Nicholas did not bat & 62; A.N. Aymes did not bat & 34 (ct 4); S.D. Udal did not bat & 14 (ct 1), 22–2–60–3; K.D. James did not bat & 11 (ct 1), 22–7–50–5; V.P. Terry 1 & 11 (ct 1); W.K.M. Benjamin did not bat & 5 (ct 1), 22–3–53–2; C.A. Connor did not bat & 5, 20–5–61–4; G.W. White 1; N.G. Cowans did not bat & 6*, 17–2–53–2; M. Keech 0 (ct 2), 1–0–3–0

Kent

C.L. Hooper 136*, 44, 27 & 21 (ct 5), 35–1–113–1; T.R. Ward 0, 80, 120 & 42, 6–0–29–0; G.R. Cowdrey 32*, 1 & 35; N.R. Taylor 17, 14, 64 & 24 (ct 1), 8–0–38–3; S.A. Marsh did not bat, 2*, 22 & 4* (ct 6/st 1); M.A. Ealham 26*, 1, 7 & 18* (ct 2), 33.5–3–107–7; D.P. Fulton 18; M.R. Benson 5, 44, 6 & 5 (ct 1); M.V. Fleming 7, 22, 1 & 22 (ct 4), 21.1–0–97–6; M.J. McCague did not bat & 1 (ct 1), 22–1–73–4; T.N. Wren 0, 10–0–41–0; D.W. Headley did not bat three times & 7*, 37–2–155–5; A.P. Igglesden did not bat three times, 24–5–67–5; M.M. Patel did not bat twice (ct 2), 24–4–71–1

Lancashire

I.D. Austin 62 & 5*, 24–2–97–2; Wasim Akram 50, 12–1–70–0; M. Watkinson 15 & 25* (ct 1), 18–2–91–2; W.K. Hegg did not bat & 32 (ct 1/st 1); M.A. Atherton 10 & 50 (ct 1); G.D. Lloyd 19; P.J. Martin did not bat & 16, 24–2–96–2; J.P. Crawley 22 & 9 (ct 1); N.H. Fairbrother 14 & 14 (ct 1); N.J. Speak 11 & 10 (ct 1); J.E.R. Gallian 1, 6–1–21–0; G. Yates 7* & did not bat, 24–2–89–3; Chapple did not bat, 12–2–35–1

Leicestershire

J.J. Whitaker 73* & 5; B.F. Smith 63* & 6 (ct 1); T.J. Boon 55; V.J. Wells 19 & 31, 24–3–104–1; P.V. Simmons 18 & 19 (ct 2), 23–2–118–4; N.E. Briers 25 & 2 (ct 3); P.A. Nixon did not bat & 2 (ct 1/st 1); G.J. Parsons did not bat & 2 (ct 1), 24–4–65–2; A.R.K. Pierson 0, 1–0–6–0; A.D. Mullally did not bat & 0, 24–5 70–2; D.J. Millns did not bat & 7*, 24–3–92–3; P.N. Hepworth 0; P.E. Robinson 0

Middlesex

D.L. Haynes 64* & 37; M.A. Roseberry 67 & 36; K.R. Brown did not bat & 34 (ct 5/st 1); J.C. Pooley 33; J.D. Carr did not bat & 16; M.W. Gatting did not bat & 11 (ct 2); M.A. Feltham did not bat & 25* (ct 1), 22–3–68–3; R.L. Johnson did not bat & 12*, 20–2–68–1; J.E. Emburey did not bat twice, 20.3–8–55–3; A.R.C. Fraser did not bat twice (ct 1), 22–5–63–2; M.R. Ramprakash 0* (ct 1); K.J. Shine did not bat, 12–3–31–3; P.C.R. Tufnell did not bat (ct 1), 11–0–71–1

Northamptonshire

A.J. Lamb 129*, 12 & 1 (ct 1); R.J. Warren 36, 100* & 2 (ct 1); M.B. Loye 17*, 11 & 34 (ct 1); N.A. Felton 20 & 37 (ct 1); R.J. Bailey 52, 25 & 7 (ct 2), 18–4–47–2; K.M. Curran did not bat twice & 26 (ct 1), 32–6–119–2; A.L. Penberthy did not bat twice & 18 (ct 1), 24–3–100–1; C.E.L. Ambrose did not bat twice & 7 (ct 2), 36–12–59–7; N.G.B. Cook did not bat twice & 1, 25.1–0–93–2; D. Ripley did not bat twice & 0 (ct 2); J.P. Taylor did not bat twice & 3*, 30–1–130–4

Nottinghamshire

P. Johnson 146 & 37 (ct 1); C.C. Lewis 23 & 89 (ct 1), 18–2–68–1; W.M. Noon did not bat & 34 (ct 2/st 1); R.T. Robinson 5 & 62; K.P. Evans did not bat & 21, 17–4–37–4; P.R. Pollard 10 & 13; R.A. Pick did not bat & 10, 18–1–70–4; G.W. Mike 3 & 5*, 18–2–84–1; M.A. Crawley 4 and 9 (ct 1), 15–3–48–1; J.C. Adams 11 & 1; M.G. Field-Buss did not bat & 4*, 13–1–62–0

Somerset

A.N. Hayhurst 29*, 38* & 24 (ct 1), 10.5–0–49–5; R.J. Harden 105*, 9 & 64 (ct 3); M.E. Trescothick 116, 10 & 48 (ct 1); M.N. Lathwell 64, 6 & 28 (ct 1); G.D. Rose 19*, 7 & 0, 23–3–68–2; N.A. Folland 18, 3 & 15; R.J. Turner did not bat, 15 & 6 (ct 7); A.P. van Troost did not bat twice & 7, 22–1–111–6; H.R.J. Trump 4, 6.1–2–41–1; A.R. Caddick did not bat twice & 4 (ct 1), 26–5–68–3; Mushtaq Ahmed did not bat & 0, 21–7–60–3; J.I.D. Kerr 0; N.A. Mallender did not bat & 0*, 17–3–52–1

Surrey

G.P. Thorpe 84*, 145*, 56 & 49 (ct 2); D.J. Bicknell 9, 56*, 89 & 32; A.J. Hollioake did not bat, 14*, 60 & 42 (ct 3), 21.4–1–116–4; D.M. Ward did not bat, 87, 10 & 9; A.D. Brown did not bat, 39, 1 & 52 (ct 2); J. Boiling (ct 1) did not bat twice, 5* & 24, 29–1–109–1; J.E. Benjamin did not bat three times & 25, 44.3–7–156–5; A.J. Stewart 24, 17, 21 & 4 (ct 10); M.P. Bicknell 2 & 7 (ct 1), 22–2–110–1; A.C.S. Pigott did not bat twice, 0 & 4*, 46–4–189–7; C.E. Cuffy did not bat three times & 3* (ct 1), 42–11–133–6; A.J. Murphy did not bat, 12–3–26–6; A.W. Smith did not bat, 8–1–31–0

Sussex

D.M. Smith 64; M.P. Speight 29; C.W.J. Athey 20; E.S.H. Giddins 13, 12–1–56–2; P. Moores 11 (ct 3); F.D. Stephenson 8, 12–0–57–2; E.E. Hemmings 6, 12–1–53–0; P.W. Jarvis 1, 12–1–53–0; A.P. Wells 1; I.D.K. Salisbury 0, 12–1–44–1; N.J. Lenham 82*

Warwickshire

R.G. Twose 110, 40, did not bat, 49 & 22 (ct 1), 25–1–111–3; T.L. Penney 18, 65*, 12*, 3 & 18 (ct 2), 1.4–0–12–1; D.P. Ostler 81, 19, 47, 12 & 4 (ct 2); D.A. Reeve 37, 34, did not bat, 23 & 13, 48–8–153–8; P.A. Smith 30, 50, 5 & 13, 27.5–2–107–4; Asif Din 28 & 18, 5–0–11–0; B.C. Lara 23, 16, 9, 29 & 81 (ct 3); N.M.K. Smith 12, 6*, did not bat, 15 & 20 (ct 2), 48.5–5–181–10; G.C. Small did not bat, 1 & 5 (ct 1), 31–7–86–2; A.J. Moles 41*, 105* & 8; K.J. Piper did not bat twice, 7*, 6* & 16* (ct 7/st 2); R.P. Davis did not bat, 6–1–20–1; T.A. Munton did not bat four times & 0*, 54–13–138–8; G. Welch did not bat & 0*, 16–4–41–0

Worcestershire

T.M. Moody 7, 35, 0, 180* & 88* (ct 4), 52–12–141–7; T.S. Curtis 78, 20, 0, 136* & 11 (ct 2); S.J. Rhodes 36, 6*, 24*, did not bat twice (ct 8/st 1); G.R. Haynes 98, 46, 10, did not bat twice (ct 1), 20–2–63–3; G.A. Hick 6, 97, 2, 5 & 93* (ct 6), 23–0–88–5; A.C.H. Seymour 25, 20 & 10, 2–0–5–1; S.R. Lampitt 14, 16*, 4, did not bat twice (ct 3), 37.3–4–192–6; P.J. Newport 14, did not bat four times (ct 1), 37.1–4–143–11; D.A. Leatherdale 7, 21, 0, did not bat twice (ct 2), 8.4–1–37–3; W.P.C. Weston 7 (ct 1); R.K. Illingworth 0* & did not bat four times (ct 2), 48–6–163–3; N.V. Radford 0* & did not bat three times (ct 3), 40–9–135–5; C.M. Tolley did not bat, 7–0–36–2

Yorkshire

C. White 5 & 65* (ct 1), 10.5–0–57–1; D. Byas 36 & 71; M.D. Moxon 23 & 49; A.P. Grayson 22 & 27 (ct 1), 17–1–75–2; R.B. Richardson 15 & 27; R.J. Blakey 13 & 18 (ct 2); P.J. Hartley 5 & 7*, 21–3–80–0; M.P. Vaughan 9 & 10; D. Gough did not bat & 2, 24–1–101–4; M.A. Robinson did not bat & 0, 24–4–65–2; C.E.W. Silverwood 8*, 11–2–38–1; R.D. Stemp did not bat (ct 1), 12–1–31–1

Glen Chapple bowled Lancashire to victory in two days against Durham and was chosen for the England 'A' tour of India. (David Munden/Sports-Line)

6 September *at Old Trafford*

Lancashire 148 for 7
Worcestershire 137 for 1 (G.A. Hick 63 not out, T.M. Moody 55 not out)
Worcestershire (4 pts.) won on faster scoring rate

at Edgbaston

Hampshire 197 for 4 (R.A. Smith 68)
Warwickshire 147 for 4 (B.C. Lara 56)
Warwickshire (4 pts.) won on faster scoring rate

With the two main contenders engaged in the NatWest Trophy final, there was a sense of unreality in the Sunday fixtures. Briers had a marvellous day for Leicestershire, hitting a century and taking four catches as his side beat Gloucestershire. This defeat put Gloucestershire bottom of the table, for Essex beat Sussex. Hussain hit his highest Sunday League score. Kevin Evans performed the hat-trick for Nottinghamshire against Glamorgan when he bowled Lefebvre, Metson and Watkin with the last three balls of his spell. The games involving Warwickshire and Worcestershire were played on the Tuesday and both were hit by rain. Hick and Moody were again in form with a partnership of 102 which took their side to victory after the target had been reduced. Warwickshire also won and, with one game to play, led Worcestershire by four points and Kent by six. Both of these sides had two matches remaining, but victory for Warwickshire over Gloucestershire on the last day of the season would ensure them of the title on faster run rate.

 JOSHUA TETLEY TROPHY
at Scarborough

SEMI-FINALS

5 September

Lancashire 234 for 7 (N.H. Fairbrother 60)
Durham 237 for 7 (J.E. Morris 124, G. Yates 5 for 28)
Durham won by 3 wickets

6 September

Gloucestershire 196
Yorkshire 199 for 7 (R.J. Blakey 52, A.P. Grayson 52)
Yorkshire won by 3 wickets

Nick Knight was promoted to open the Essex innings, awarded his county cap, hit the highest score of his career in the victory over Sussex at Chelmsford and was selected for the England 'A' tour of India. (Alan Cozzi)

FINAL

7 September

Durham 282 for 9 (J.E. Morris 83, S. Hutton 57)
Yorkshire 283 for 7 (S.A. Kellett 130, M.D. Moxon 52)

Yorkshire won by 3 wickets

Morris, 100 off 72 balls in the semi-final, and Kellett, 130 off 157 balls to help win the trophy, were the star batsmen of the tournament.

8, 9, 10 and **12** September *at Derby*

Derbyshire 241 (D.G. Cork 94, M.C. Ilott 4 for 65) and 52 for 1
Essex 180 (G.A. Gooch 76, S.J. Base 4 for 57)

Match drawn

Derbyshire 5 pts., Essex 4 pts.

at Stockton-on-Tees

Durham 159 (J. Wood 51, I.D. Austin 5 for 30) and 111 (G. Chapple 6 for 48)
Lancashire 202 (S.J.E. Brown 5 for 56, J. Wood 4 for 67) and 70 for 0

Lancashire won by 10 wickets

Lancashire 21 pts., Durham 4 pts.

at Cardiff

Worcestershire 265 (T.M. Moody 66, W.P.C. Weston 59, O.D. Gibson 6 for 64) and 123 for 3 dec. (D.A. Leatherdale 54 not out)
Glamorgan 134 for 3 dec. and 243 for 5 (S.P. James 116, M.P. Maynard 72)

Match drawn

Glamorgan 4 pts., Worcestershire 3 pts.

at Canterbury

Somerset 108 (T.N. Wren 6 for 48) and 227 (A.N. Hayhurst 64 not out, M.N. Lathwell 52)
Kent 392 (C.L. Hooper 127, N.R. Taylor 120, J.C. Hallett 4 for 59)

Kent won by an innings and 57 runs

Kent 24 pts., Somerset 4 pts.

at Leicester

Hampshire 225 (R.A. Smith 123, D.J. Millns 5 for 59) and 243 (P.R. Whitaker 94, P.V. Simmons 4 for 68)
Leicestershire 353 (P.A. Nixon 131, J.N.B. Bovill 5 for 108, C.A. Connor 4 for 87) and 117 for 3

Leicestershire won by 7 wickets

Leicestershire 24 pts., Hampshire 5 pts.

at Lord's

Middlesex 513 for 7 dec. (J.D. Carr 261 not out, P.N. Weekes 94, M.A. Roseberry 59)
Gloucestershire 199 (J.E. Emburey 4 for 57) and 251 (A.J. Wright 79, R.I. Dawson 57, P.C.R. Tufnell 6 for 35)

Middlesex won by an innings and 63 runs

Middlesex 24 pts., Gloucestershire 3 pts.

at Scarborough

Yorkshire 379 (B. Parker 127, A.P. Grayson 85, A.C.S. Pigott 4 for 85) and 219 for 8 (A.P. Grayson 75, R.J. Blakey 55 not out, M.P. Bicknell 5 for 44)
Surrey 307 (D.J. Bicknell 79, M.A. Butcher 76, A.J. Hollioake 68, D. Gough 6 for 66)

Match drawn

Yorkshire 8 pts., Surrey 7 pts.

Put in to bat, Derbyshire crashed to 15 for 4, losing two wickets in the first over. Gary Steer, called up from the Second XI at the last minute to make his first appearance of the season, and Dominic Cork revived the home side. Cork went to fifty with four successive boundaries off Kasprowicz, and his 94 included 17 fours. Rain brought an early close, but Simon Base bolstered the score on the second morning and then played a major part in the destruction of Essex on a green wicket. Only Gooch, ninth out, defied the accurate Derbyshire attack as Essex gave another wretched batting performance; but for 41 extras, their total would have been humiliating. With an unexpected lead of 61, Derbyshire scored 52 for 1 before the close, and rain prevented any play on the third and fourth days.

Lancashire needed only two days in which to beat Durham who were bowled out inside two hours on the first morning. The skidding seamers of Ian Austin, no longer just a limited-over cricketer, had them in total disarray, and only a last-wicket stand of 41 between the aggressive Wood and Jason Searle, an off-spinner making his first-class debut, raised spirits. Lancashire reached 154 for 4 by the close mainly through Watkinson who sustained a broken thumb but hit vigorously. Chapple's career-best bowling performance accounted for Durham for a second time, and Atherton and Speak hit off the required runs in 20 overs.

At Cardiff, Gibson bowled at a lively pace after Worcestershire had been put in to bat. Moody and Weston put on 118 in 24 overs for the third wicket, but both fell to Gibson within the space of four balls. Worcestershire ended a shortened day on 206 for 5. The tail offered little resistance on the second morning, and Gibson, who exploited a seamer's pitch well, finished with his best figures for Glamorgan. The home side were 134 for 3 when rain ended play, and the third day was washed out. Declarations left Glamorgan a target of 255, and a thrilling third-wicket partnership of 113 between Maynard and James took them to within 53 of their target. James hit his

Batsman of the month of August – John Carr of Middlesex. (David Munden/Sports-Line)

first championship century of the season, but rain curtailed the play and, frustrated by the weather, Glamorgan finished 12 runs short.

Only 31.4 overs were possible on the first day at Canterbury, and Somerset scored 88 for 1. On the second day, they were routed by Wren and McCague, the last nine wickets falling for 19 runs. Wren took five wickets in 44 balls and finished with a career best 6 for 48. Kent were 84 for 3, but Carl Hooper, who had enjoyed a wonderful season, was again in masterly form. He hit 15 fours and 2 sixes, and Kent closed on 293 for 3. He was quickly out on the Saturday morning, but Neil Taylor established a record with his 13th hundred on the St Lawrence Ground. It was, in effect, the 41st century of his career, and when he was ninth out he had hit 18 fours and faced 221 deliveries. Hallett returned the best bowling figures of his career, but Somerset finished on 111 for 4 facing an innings defeat. In spite of Hayhurst's defiance, defeat could not be avoided on the Monday.

Having suffered three successive defeats, Leicestershire bounced back to beat Hampshire and climb to second in the table. Millns, dominant and menacing, reduced Hampshire to 54 for 4, but Robin Smith batted magnificently for his 123 which saved his side from total disintegration. Leicestershire lost Simmons and Boon before the close and slipped to 90 for 5 on the second day. They were rescued by wicket-keeper Nixon who added 102 with Wells. Nixon, a positive, enthusiastic and supremely confident left-hander, became the first Leicestershire wicket-keeper since 1928 to reach 1,000 runs in a season, and he took his side to a commanding lead. Hampshire nearly saved the game through rain and a remarkable debut innings of 94 by Paul Whitaker. The left-hander did not bat faultlessly, but he showed plenty of determination and a sound temperament. Eventually, the all-round cricket of Phil Simmons took Leicestershire to victory before the rain returned.

The astonishing run of John Carr continued. Middlesex were 45 for 3 when he came to the wicket against Gloucestershire and by the end of the day they were 513 for 7 declared. With Weekes, he added 270 in 47 overs for the sixth wicket to establish a Middlesex record. An ugly, idiosyncratic stance is forgotten as Carr's delightful footwork and elegance of stroke dominates. In the highest score of his career, he hit 43 fours, and he brought his total for his last seven innings to 854 runs for once out. Once Neil Williams had made early inroads, Emburey and Tufnell destroyed Gloucestershire on a wearing pitch. Emburey took the 1,500th wicket of his career. When Gloucestershire followed-on there was defiance from Dawson and Wright in a fifth-wicket stand of 115 but, with Tufnell in top form, the last six wickets fell for 38 runs, and Middlesex won in three days.

The loss of the last day's play at Scarborough ruined a good contest. A maiden first-class century from Brad Parker who added 148 for the fifth wicket with Grayson revived Yorkshire after early losses. Darren Bicknell and

Mark Butcher began Surrey's innings with a partnership of 159, but Darren Gough took 5 for 5 in 29 balls, and the visitors were 185 for 7. Hollioake and Boiling saved the follow-on, and Yorkshire's lead was restricted to 72. Martin Bicknell made early strikes before Kellett and Grayson added 113 in 40 overs. Grayson confirmed his growing confidence and reached 1,000 runs for the season.

 AXA EQUITY & LAW LEAGUE

11 September *at Derby*

Derbyshire 170 for 9
Essex 171 for 8

Essex (4 pts.) won by 2 wickets

at Stockton-on-Tees

Durham 170 (J.I. Longley 53, P.J. Martin 5 for 32)
Lancashire 172 for 5

Lancashire (4 pts.) won by 5 wickets

at Cardiff

Glamorgan 168
Worcestershire 139 (R.D.B. Croft 6 for 20)

Glamorgan (4 pts.) won by 29 runs

at Canterbury

Kent 172 (N.J. Llong 55)
Somerset 106 (M.J. McCague 4 for 25)

Kent (4 pts.) won by 66 runs

at Leicester

Leicestershire 156
Hampshire 148

Leicestershire (4 pts.) won by 8 runs

at Lord's

Gloucestershire 175 for 7 (M.G.N. Windows 69)
Middlesex 122

Gloucestershire (4 pts.) won by 53 runs

at Scarborough

Surrey 375 for 4 (A.D. Brown 133, G.P. Thorpe 102 not out, A.J. Hollioake 59)
Yorkshire 170 (S.G. Kenlock 4 for 30, M.P. Bicknell 4 for 50)

Surrey (4 pts.) won by 205 runs

Worcestershire lost their chance of winning the Sunday League when they were beaten by Glamorgan at Cardiff. Their destroyer was off-spinner Robert Croft who had not enjoyed the best of seasons, but who returned the best figures by a Glamorgan bowler in limited-over cricket. Chasing a target of 169, Worcestershire were 63 for 0 when Croft came on for the 14th over. In his second over, he dismissed Moody, Hick and Haynes, and he took 6 for 6 in 26 balls. Worcestershire lost 10 wickets for 76 runs in 24.2 overs, and they left Kent as Warwickshire's only challengers for the title.

A very large crowd at the St Lawrence Ground saw Somerset surrender rather meekly, and Kent were left to ponder their final fixture, versus Surrey at The Oval. At Scarborough, Surrey established a Sunday League record by scoring 375 in their 40 overs. Alistair Brown hit 133 off 84 balls with 5 sixes and 13 fours, and Graham Thorpe scored 102 off 81 balls with 3 sixes and 8 fours. Hollioake's 57 came off 19 balls. The runs came at 9.375 an over.

 AXA EQUITY & LAW LEAGUE

18 September *at Chelmsford*

Northamptonshire 227 for 7 (D.J. Sales 70 not out)
Essex 226 for 4 (N. Hussain 74, P.J. Prichard 65 not out)

Northamptonshire (4 pts.) won by 1 run

at Bristol

Warwickshire 183 for 8 (T.L. Penney 55, D.A. Reeve 50)

Phenomenal hitting by Alistair Brown, 133 off 84 balls, as Surrey established a Sunday League record at Scarborough. (David Munden/ Sports-Line)

Gloucestershire 137

Warwickshire (4 pts.) won by 46 runs

at Southampton

Glamorgan 145
Hampshire 146 for 3 (V.P. Terry 78 not out)

Hampshire (4 pts.) won by 7 wickets

at Old Trafford

Lancashire 210 for 9
Leicestershire 163 (M. Watkinson 4 for 34)

Lancashire (4 pts.) won by 47 runs

at Trent Bridge

Nottinghamshire 180 for 8
Middlesex 184 for 4 (J.C. Pooley 55, P.N. Weekes 50)

Middlesex (4 pts.) won by 6 wickets

at Taunton

Somerset 190 for 8 (R.J. Harden 57)
Derbyshire 191 for 3 (P.D. Bowler 66 not out, K.J. Barnett 56 not out)

Derbyshire (4 pts.) won by 7 wickets

BENSON AND HEDGES CUP STATISTICS 1994

Derbyshire
P.D. Bowler 0 & 15; C.J. Adams 34 & 9; A.S. Rollins 70; M. Azharuddin 4 & 5; T.J.G. O'Gorman 24 & 2; C.M. Wells 48* & 25, 11–0–57–1; P.A.J. DeFreitas 9 & 16 (ct 1), 15–2–75–1; D.G. Cork 64* & 7, 16–0–86–1; K.M. Krikken did not bat & 0 (st 1); A.E. Warner did not bat & 1*, 16–0–81–2; O.H. Mortensen did not bat, 11–1–50–0; F.A. Griffith 4, 0.2–0–5–0; D.E. Malcolm 2, 4–1–14–0

Durham
W. Larkins 19; M. Saxelby 12; J.E. Morris 23; S. Hutton 8; P. Bainbridge 28, 8–0–49–0; J.I. Longley 33; A.C. Cummins 21, 11–0–37–1; C.W. Scott 11 (ct 1); D.A. Graveney 4*, 11–0–36–0; A Walker 9*, 6–0–20–1; S.J.E. Brown did not bat, 9.4–0–47–0

Essex
G.A. Gooch 130* & 21; P.J. Prichard 23 & 6 (ct 1); N. Hussain 59 & 30* (ct 1); N.V. Knight 26* & did not bat; N. Shahid did not bat twice; T.D. Topley did not bat, 11–0–46–1; M.A. Garnham did not bat & 14* (ct 2); R.C. Irani did not bat twice, 14–1–89–1; M.S. Kasprowicz did not bat twice (ct 1), 15–0–76–2; M.C. Ilott did not bat twice, 15–3–45–3; P.M. Such did not bat twice (ct 1), 15–1–68–2; J.P. Stephenson 47, 2.2–0–27–0

Glamorgan
S.P. James 12; H. Morris 55 (ct 1); A. Dale 23, 5–0–40–0; M.P. Maynard 19; P.A. Cottey 43; O.D. Gibson 37, 8.4–0–50–2; R.D.B. Croft 23*, 11–2–29–2; R.P. Lefebvre 6*, 11–0–43–1; C.P. Metson did not bat (ct 1/st 1); S.L. Watkin did not bat, 10–2–45–1; S.R. Barwick did not bat, 9–1–24–0

Gloucestershire
B.C. Broad 1; G.D. Hodgson 3; S.G. Hinks 4; M.W. Alleyne 18, 11–1–63–0; A.J. Wright 55; T.H.C. Hancock 13; R.C. Russell 31 (ct 2); M.C.J. Ball 20*, 11–1–33–2; C.A. Walsh 0, 10–1–33–1; A.M. Smith 8, 11–0–40–2; K.E. Cooper 0*, 11–3–19–1

Hampshire
V.P. Terry 10, 2 & 6 (ct 1); T.C. Middleton 63* & 17 (ct 2); R.A. Smith 58, 73* & 108 (ct 1); M.C.J. Nicholas 36*, 46* & 37 (ct 1); M. Keech did not bat & 37 (ct 2), 3–0–10–0; A.N. Aymes did not bat twice & 4* (ct 2); S.D. Udal did not bat three times, 25–1–99–3; W.K.M. Benjamin did not bat twice & 18, 25.4–2–101–2; K.D. James did not bat twice & 5* (ct 1), 21–1–76–0; C.A. Connor did not bat three times (ct 1), 24–3–115–3; N.G. Cowans did not bat three times, 26–3–97–7; R.M.F. Cox did not bat; M. Jean-Jacques did not bat, 2–0–20–0

Kent
T.R. Ward 14; M.R. Benson 37 (ct 1); N.R. Taylor 30 (ct 1); C.L. Hooper 4 (ct 1); G.R. Cowdrey 14; M.A. Ealham 10, 9–0–38–0; M.V. Fleming 36* (ct 1), 11–0–39–2; S.A. Marsh 15* (ct 1); D.W. Headley did not bat, 10.4–0–36–2; M.J. McCague did not bat, 2.2–0–10–0; A.P. Igglesden did not bat, 11–1–26–3

Lancashire
J.P. Crawley 73 & 73; J.E.R. Gallian 9 & 39, 9–0–53–0; N.J. Speak 15 & 17; N.H. Fairbrother 41* (ct 1); G.D. Lloyd 31* & 8; Wasim Akram did not bat, 10–0–30–0; M. Watkinson did not bat & 53; V.J. Wells did not bat & 0, 9–0–48–0; W.K. Hegg did not bat twice (ct 1); P.J. Martin did not bat twice, 20–4–66–1; G. Yates did not bat twice (ct 1), 21–1–77–3; I.D. Austin did not bat & 3*, 22–1–112–1; M.A. Atherton 100 (ct 2); G. Chapple did not bat, 11–1–30–2

Leicestershire
P.V. Simmons 64 & 57 (ct 1), 15–2–71–1; N.E. Briers 70* & 29 (ct 1); T.J. Boon 19*; J.J. Whitaker did not bat & 53; V.J. Wells did not bat & 0, 9–0–48–0; B.F. Smith did not bat & 22; P.A. Nixon did not bat & 5 (ct 1); G.J. Parsons did not bat & 1, 20.5–5–66–1; A.R.K. Pierson did not bat & 3* (ct 2), 22–4–70–3; D.J. Millns did not bat & 10, 19–1–76–2; A.D. Mullally did not bat & 0*, 21–7–59–2; P.E. Robinson 57

Middlesex
M.A. Roseberry 4 & 17 (ct 2); M.R. Ramprakash 119* & 42; M.W. Gatting 28 & 0; J.D. Carr 14 & 27 (ct 3); P.N. Weekes 33 & 11 (ct 1), 17–2–83–3; K.R. Brown 15* & 24; P.C.R. Tufnell did not bat, 11–1–32–3; J.E. Emburey did not bat & 0, 22–6–56–4; N.F. Williams did not bat & 5, 16.2–1–71–1; A.R.C. Fraser did not bat & 1*, 22–7–58–2; R.L. Johnson did not bat & 1, 20–4–62–1; D.L. Haynes 6

Northamptonshire
A. Fordham 38 (ct 1); N.A. Felton 25; R.J. Bailey 19, 6–0–25–0; A.J. Lamb 25; M.B. Loye 68*; K.M. Curran 5, 10.5–0–65–0; A.L. Penberthy 24, 11–1–40–1; M.N. Bowen 0, 10–1–39–1; D. Ripley 1* (ct 2); K. J. Innes did not bat, 6–1–25–1; J.P. Taylor did not bat, 10–3–28–1

Nottinghamshire
P.R. Pollard 18, 3 & 104 (ct 1); M.A. Crawley 35, 1 & 37 (ct 1), 25–3–101–5; J.C. Adams 40, 86 & 7 (ct 2), 3–0–21–0; P. Johnson 2, 35* & 26; R.T. Robinson 23, 91* & 15; C.C. Lewis 48* & did not bat (ct 1), 17–2–76–2; W.M. Noon 3, did not bat & 9 (ct 3/st 1); G.W. Mike 6, did not bat & 15* (ct 1), 26–1–121–3; R.A. Pick 10*, did not bat & 16* (ct 1), 31–2–134–0; M.G. Field-Buss did not bat, 11–0–21–0; J.A. Afford did not bat three times, 32.4–2–120–4; K.P. Evans did not bat & 8 (ct 1), 16–2–84–1; G.F. Archer 9

Somerset
M.N. Lathwell 120; A.N. Hayhurst 7, 8–0–38–0; R.J. Harden 34; N.A. Folland 38; G.D. Rose 0, 9–1–42–1; Mushtaq Ahmed 3, 7–0–33–0; V.P. Clarke 22; R.J. Turner 6 (ct 2); A.P. van Troost 5, 9–0–64–1; N.A. Mallender 2, 11–0–44–0; A.R. Caddick 4*, 10–0–62–0

Surrey
A.J. Stewart 167*, 2, 11 & 24 (ct 2); D.J. Bicknell 8, 90, 109 & 39; G.P. Thorpe 34, 51, 24 & 87 (ct 5); D.M. Ward 50, 13, 73 & 61 (ct 2); A.D. Brown 19*, 38, 26* & 8 (ct 1); A.J. Hollioake did not bat, 6, 5* & 3 (ct 1), 23–0–123–4; M.A. Butcher did not bat twice, 5 & 4 (ct 1), 34.1–1–176–4; M.P. Bicknell did not bat twice & 2*, 32.2–4–117–6; A.J. Murphy did not bat, 11–0–67–2; J. Boiling did not bat & 9*, 22–1–79–1; J.E. Benjamin did not bat four times, 43–5–191–5; A.W. Smith 15* & did not bat (ct 1), 14–2–61–3; C.E. Cuffy did not bat three times (ct 1), 27–1–154–0; A.C.S. Pigott 13*, 11–0–43–3

Sussex
D.M. Smith 65* & 20; C.W.J. Athey 23 & 32 (ct 1); M.P. Speight 1 & 16; A.P. Wells 51* & 51; N.J. Lenham did not bat & 44, 11–0–58–0; P. Moores did not bat & 6 (ct 2); F.D. Stephenson did not bat & 4, 22–3–65–3; I.D.K. Salisbury did not bat, 9–0–41–1; E.S.H. Giddins did not bat twice (ct 1), 20.2–2–88–1; P.W. Jarvis did not bat & 21*, 20–3–63–3; E.E. Hemmings did not bat & 0 (ct 1), 22–1–67–0; K. Greenfield 27

Warwickshire
T.L. Penney 39, 12* & did not bat (ct 3); R.G. Twose 0, 46 & 37 (ct 1), 13–1–58–2; B.C. Lara 34, 70 & 8; P.A. Smith 12, 8 & 42* (ct 1), 20–1–81–3; D.P. Ostler 11, 44 & 55 (ct 2); D.A. Reeve 23*, 46* & 9* (ct 1), 31–4–114–5; M. Burns 0 & 18 (ct 3/st 1); N.M.K. Smith 4 & did not bat twice (ct 2), 23.3–0–99–7; G.C. Small 5* & did not bat twice, 33–9–86–2; M.A.V. Bell did not bat (ct 1), 11–1–34–2; K.J. Piper did not bat (ct 2); T.A. Munton did not bat three times (ct 1), 33–8–92–4; Asif Din 15 & 19

Worcestershire
T.S. Curtis 0, 25*, 5 & 13 (ct 2); D.B. D'Oliveira 11, 1 & 10; G.A. Hick 104*, 40*, 40 & 27 (ct 3), 4–0–23–0; T.M. Moody 65*, did not bat, 56 & 47 (ct 2), 44–13–84–5; G.R. Haynes did not bat, 65 & 22 (ct 1), 2–0–26–0; D.A. Leatherdale did not bat twice, 30 & 4 (ct 1), 7–0–39–0; S.J. Rhodes did not bat twice, 12 & 0 (ct 7); P.J. Newport did not bat three times & 1*, 33–8–98–6; R.K. Illingworth did not bat twice, 0* & 18, 31–1–128–3; S.R. Lampitt did not bat twice, 6* & 1, 42.2–4–158–9; N.V. Radford did not bat three times & 23* (ct 1), 30–5–123–2; A.C.H. Seymour 3; C.M. Tolley did not bat

Yorkshire
M.D. Moxon 40; M.P. Vaughan 0, 3–0–13–0; D. Byas 10; R.B. Richardson 7; R.J. Blakey 40 (ct 2); C. White 12, 3–0–10–0; A.P. Grayson 22*, 9–1–30–1; P.J. Hartley 19*, 9–1–31–0; M.A. Robinson did not bat, 7–0–12–1; D. Gough did not bat, 9–1–34–0; R.D. Stemp did not bat, 11–2–47–0

at The Oval

Surrey 205 for 8 (D.J. Bicknell 79, G.P. Thorpe 60)
Kent 181 (M.V. Fleming 65)

Surrey (4 pts.) won by 24 runs

at Hove

Yorkshire 214 for 6 (A.A. Metcalfe 55 not out, D. Byas 54)

Sussex 177 (A.P. Wells 64, D. Gough 5 for 13)

Yorkshire (4 pts.) won by 37 runs

at Worcester

Worcestershire 172 for 7
Durham 146

Worcestershire (4 pts.) won by 26 runs

Warwickshire achieved a unique cricketing treble when they added the AXA Equity & Law League title to their earlier successes in the Benson and Hedges Cup and the Britannic Assurance County Championship. They needed only to win at Bristol to be assured of the title, but they started horrendously with Ostler, Neil Smith and Twose being dismissed without scoring. Lara and Penney added 68, and Penney and Reeve, who improvised in his usual exciting fashion, added 75. A total of 183 did not look too demanding, but Warwickshire's thrilling out-cricket overwhelmed Gloucestershire, and only Windows and Dawson offered resistance. It would be an understatement to describe Warwickshire as an outstanding team. They have individuals of quality – Lara, Twose, Piper, Munton and Reeve among them – but they also have a corporate passion for the game and, in Reeve, they have a leader of wit, intelligence, vision, commitment and self-belief. In the one-day game, he has no tactical superior.

Kent were Warwickshire's only threat, but they asked Surrey to bat first at The Oval, saw Darren Bicknell and Thorpe add 115 for the second wicket, and then chased a target of 206 in semi-darkness. Elsewhere, Byas became Yorkshire's top scorer in Sunday League cricket with 702 runs for the season, and Gough recorded his best Sunday League figures on his birthday. Still short of his 17th birthday, David Sales hit 70 off 56 balls as Northamptonshire beat Essex, and Gregory Mike was out 'handled ball' in the match at Trent Bridge.

15, 16, 17 and **19** September *at Chelmsford*

Northamptonshire 404 (A.J. Lamb 114, K.M. Curran 62, A.R. Roberts 51, M.S. Kasprowicz 4 for 92, J. H. Childs 4 for 104)

Essex 197 for 9 (R.C. Irani 57, G.A. Gooch 50, R.J. Bailey 5 for 59)

Match drawn

Northamptonshire 8 pts., Essex 4 pts.

AXA EQUITY & LAW LEAGUE – FINAL TABLE

	P	W	L	Tie	NR	Pts.
Warwickshire (10)	17	13	3	–	1	54
Worcestershire (16)	17	12	4	–	1	50
Kent (2)	17	12	5	–	–	48
Lancashire (6)	17	11	5	–	1	46
Yorkshire (9)	17	10	6	–	1	42
Surrey (3)	17	9	5	–	3	42
Glamorgan (1)	17	9	6	1	1	40
Derbyshire (11)	17	8	7	–	2	36
Durham (7)	17	6	7	1	3	32
Leicestershire (14)	17	7	9	–	1	30
Nottinghamshire (17)	17	6	8	–	3	30
Hampshire (15)	17	7	10	–	–	28
Northamptonshire (5)	17	6	9	1	1	28
Middlesex (8)	17	6	10	–	1	26
Sussex (4)	17	5	11	–	1	22
Somerset (18)	17	5	12	–	–	20
Essex (12)	17	4	11	1	1	20
Gloucestershire (13)	17	4	12	–	1	18

(1993 positions in brackets)

at Bristol

Gloucestershire 372 for 9 dec. (G.D. Hodgson 113, T.H.C. Hancock 70, M.G.N. Windows 63, R.P. Davis 6 for 128)

Warwickshire 24 for 0

Match drawn

Gloucestershire 4 pts., Warwickshire 4 pts.

at Southampton

Hampshire 331 (S.D. Udal 94, S.L. Watkin 5 for 98)

Glamorgan 197 for 4 (A. Roseberry 65, D.L. Hemp 61)

Match drawn

Hampshire 4 pts., Glamorgan 4 pts.

at Old Trafford

Leicestershire 206 (P.E. Robinson 54, G. Chapple 5 for 58) and 67 for 1

Lancashire 358 for 9 dec. (N.J. Speak 70, J.P. Crawley 70, G.D. Lloyd 51)

Match drawn

Lancashire 8 pts., Leicestershire 5 pts.

at Trent Bridge

Nottinghamshire 350 for 7 dec. (C.C. Lewis 108 not out)
Middlesex 52 for 0

Match drawn

Nottinghamshire 4 pts., Middlesex 3 pts.

at Taunton

Somerset 228 for 4 (R.J. Harden 95, A.N. Hayhurst 52 not out, M.E. Trescothick 51)

***v.* Derbyshire**

Match drawn

Somerset 1 pt., Derbyshire 1 pt.

at The Oval

Kent 445 (T.R. Ward 109, M.J. Walker 107, G.R. Cowdrey 69)

Surrey 70 for 1

Match drawn

Surrey 4 pts., Kent 4 pts.

at Hove

Sussex 226 (A.P. Wells 84, M.A. Robinson 4 for 44) and 181 for 8 (A.P. Wells 55, P. Moores 55, D. Gough 4 for 69)

Yorkshire 246 (M.D. Moxon 66, R.J. Blakey 61 not out, E.S.H. Giddins 4 for 77)

Match drawn

Sussex 5 pts., Yorkshire 5 pts.

at Worcester

Worcestershire 351 for 7 dec. (T.M. Moody 159, S.J. Rhodes 55 not out, A.C. Cummins 4 for 70)

Durham 193 for 2 (S. Hutton 81 not out, J.A. Daley 60 not out)

Match drawn

Worcestershire 4 pts., Durham 3 pts.

There was no thrilling end to the Britannic Assurance County Championship, no catches on the boundary as the sun set. All was wet and gloom, and 14 overs at Old Trafford was all the cricket that the last day of the season had to offer. The first day of the last round of matches had seen six overs at Hove and none elsewhere.

At Chelmsford, the rain thwarted Northamptonshire's hopes of finishing second in the table. Their early batsmen were mesmerised by John Childs, but Allan Lamb hit 3 sixes and 13 fours in his second century of the season and Kevin Curran scored 62 off 84 balls. Roberts added to Essex's discomfort, and with Bailey's off-breaks perplexing the home batsmen, Northamptonshire were looking as if they would be able to enforce the follow-on when the rains came.

There was no play on the first two days at Bristol, and some spirited Gloucestershire batting on the Saturday saw Hodgson, making a rare appearance, hit his only century of the summer. Then the rain returned.

Shaun Udal hit a career-best 94 to rescue Hampshire after Robert Croft's off-breaks had undermined the middle order while Chapple continued his success by demolishing Leicestershire at Old Trafford. He produced an opening burst which saw him take five wickets in 14 overs either side of lunch. Leicestershire were 105 for 7, but their last three wickets realised 101 runs with Pierson unbeaten on 43. Lancashire, without Fairbrother and Watkinson, lost Titchard before the close on Friday, but Speak and Crawley added 138, and they were in a commanding position before rain intervened.

Put in to bat on a greenish pitch, Nottinghamshire scored 127 for 4 on the Friday. A hard-hit century by Lewis, who finished the season strongly, was the substance of a seventh-wicket stand of 112 with Dowman, and Nottinghamshire collected four batting points. Rain ended their ambitions of finishing as runners-up.

There was no play on the first two days at Taunton and only 71 overs on the third, and only 32 overs were possible on the second day at The Oval, but Kenlock captured his first first-class wicket. On the third, Matthew Walker reached a maiden first-class century. Walker and Ward added 185 for Kent's third wicket.

The game at Hove reached a more advanced stage than any other before rain washed out the last day. Alan Wells hit his highest score of the season on a pitch which encouraged the pace men.

Play did not start until after tea on the second day at Worcester, and the home side, put in to bat, were 56 for 3. Moody then reached a hundred off 99 balls, and runs came at 5.28 an over. Worcestershire reached the 350 mark in 71.2 overs, but Durham responded well. Hutton and Daley had added 129 for their third wicket before the rain arrived, and the season came to a soggy end.

BRITANNIC ASSURANCE COUNTY CHAMPIONSHIP – FINAL TABLE

	P	W	L	D	Bonus Pts. Bat.	Bowl	Pts.
Warwickshire (16)	17	11	1	5	41	55	272
Leicestershire (9)	17	8	7	2	42	60	230
Nottinghamshire (7)	17	8	5	4	39	51	218
Middlesex (1)	17	7	3	7	43	57	212
Northamptonshire (4)	17	8	4	5	28	53	209
Essex (11)	17	7	5	5	32	63	207
Surrey (6)	17	7	7	3	32	57	201
Sussex (10)	17	7	5	5	28	60	200
Kent (8)	17	6	7	4	44	58	198
Lancashire (13)	17	8	6	3	32	59	194
Somerset (5)	17	7	7	3	32	47	191
Gloucestershire (17)	17	5	8	4	28	56	172
Yorkshire (12)	17	4	6	7	38	57	159
Hampshire (13)	17	4	7	6	32	55	159
Worcestershire (2)	17	4	6	7	42	52	158
Durham (18)	17	4	10	3	32	57	153
Derbyshire (15)	17	4	9	4	25	54	143
Glamorgan (3)	17	2	8	7	29	50	111

Gloucestershire and Hampshire each gained 8 points for batting last in matches where scores finished level. Lancashire deducted 25 points for unsuitable pitch. (1993 positions in brackets)

FIRST-CLASS AVERAGES

BATTING

	M	Inns	NO	Runs	HS	Av	100s	50s
J.D. Carr	20	27	10	1542	261*	90.70	6	7
B.C. Lara	15	25	2	2066	501*	89.82	9	3
I.G. Steer	3	3	1	142	67	71.00	–	1
M.W. Gatting	19	27	3	1671	225	69.62	6	6
G.A. Gooch	17	29	2	1747	236	64.70	6	5
C.C. Lewis	12	19	4	881	220*	58.73	2	5
M.D. Moxon	17	30	4	1458	274*	56.07	4	6
S.J. Rhodes	18	27	11	896	100*	56.00	1	5
G.A. Hick	17	29	1	1538	215	54.92	5	5
C.L. Hooper	16	29	–	1579	183	54.44	5	7
R.G. Twose	18	31	5	1411	277*	54.26	3	6
G.P. Thorpe	16	25	4	1136	190	54.09	2	7
M.R. Ramprakash	18	26	2	1271	135	52.95	4	6
A.N. Hayhurst	18	30	6	1250	121	52.08	2	10
D.J. Bicknell	18	30	4	1354	235*	52.07	3	7
C.J. Hollins	8	10	2	415	131	51.87	1	2
P.A. Cottey	19	33	6	1393	191	51.59	3	6
A.J. Moles	11	20	3	863	203*	50.76	1	5
J.P. Crawley	20	34	3	1570	281*	50.64	3	6
N.H. Fairbrother	12	22	2	1002	204	50.10	4	1
R.S.M. Morris	9	17	3	686	174	49.00	2	3
K.M. Curran	15	25	5	973	114	48.65	1	8
M.E. Trescothick	11	20	1	924	121	48.63	2	8
A.D. Brown	17	24	2	1049	172	47.68	2	6
N.V. Knight	12	21	1	944	157	47.20	4	3
A.J. Stewart	16	23	3	936	142	46.80	3	4
N.J. Speak	19	34	6	1304	143	46.57	3	7
T.M. Moody	18	28	3	1160	159	46.40	3	6
R.J. Blakey	20	36	9	1236	94*	45.77	–	11
M.C.J. Nicholas	19	32	6	1186	145	45.61	3	5
D.A. Leatherdale	17	25	3	987	139	44.86	2	3
P.R. Whitaker	2	3	–	134	94	44.66	–	1
M. Azharuddin	9	17	1	712	205	44.50	2	1
A. Fordham	11	20	1	844	158	44.42	3	4
D.M. Ward	16	22	1	921	294*	43.85	1	5
J.E.R. Gallian	12	20	–	874	171	43.70	2	5
N.R. Taylor	16	27	3	1049	139	43.70	3	4
P.E. Robinson	5	7	–	305	86	43.57	–	3
R.A. Smith	17	29	–	1263	162	43.55	5	4
R.J. Bailey	18	33	5	1214	129*	43.35	3	7
P. Johnson	17	29	2	1170	132	43.33	4	5
A.J. Lamb	15	22	1	908	131	43.23	2	5
D.P. Ostler	18	29	2	1161	186	43.00	2	6
T.R. Ward	19	33	1	1368	125	42.75	3	10
R.I. Dawson	16	30	4	1111	127*	42.73	1	7
D.L. Hemp	21	38	4	1452	136	42.70	4	8
R.T. Robinson	19	31	1	1276	182	42.53	2	10
J.E. Morris	20	35	1	1433	204	42.14	4	6
R.C. Irani	18	29	6	965	119	41.95	2	8
R.J. Harden	18	31	5	1061	131*	40.80	2	7
W. Larkins	16	27	3	976	158*	40.66	1	6
K.R. Brown	20	25	9	639	102*	39.93	1	1
M.B. Loye	15	26	3	914	132	39.73	3	5
M.N. Lathwell	18	32	1	1230	206	39.67	2	9
M.A. Lynch	4	7	1	238	60	39.66	–	1
V.P. Terry	19	34	1	1286	164	38.96	5	2
D.L. Haynes	17	27	2	973	134	38.92	5	2
A.P. Grayson	19	31	4	1046	100	38.74	1	7
P.A. Nixon	19	30	3	1046	131	38.74	3	4
K.J. Barnett	15	24	2	847	148	38.50	1	7
S.P. James	16	28	5	877	150	38.13	3	1
R.Q. Cake	10	18	1	648	107	38.11	1	3
T.L. Penney	16	24	3	798	111	38.00	1	1
N.E. Briers	19	35	3	1216	154	38.00	2	5
P.J. Prichard	11	17	2	569	119	37.93	3	2
G. Welch	12	15	3	446	84*	37.16	–	4
D. Byas	20	36	1	1297	104	37.05	2	9
C. White	13	20	2	663	108*	36.83	1	5
M.P. Vaughan	16	30	1	1066	117	36.75	3	3
M.A. Roseberry	20	32	2	1097	152	36.56	2	6
A.J. Wright	19	36	3	1203	184*	36.45	1	7
V.J. Wells	16	28	4	871	87*	36.29	–	6
W.S. Kendall	9	10	3	253	113*	36.14	1	–
B. Parker	10	18	2	578	127	36.12	1	4
A.J. Hollioake	17	23	3	722	138	36.10	3	3
M.P. Maynard	16	28	1	974	118	36.07	2	5
C.M. Gupte	10	17	2	541	122	36.06	2	1
M.A. Butcher	12	19	2	613	134	36.05	1	3
M.A. Atherton	16	27	2	899	111	35.95	2	4
A.C.H. Seymour	3	5	–	179	87	35.80	–	1
Asif Din	3	4	1	107	42*	35.66	–	–
A. Roseberry	6	8	1	249	94	35.57	–	2
J.C. Adams	18	32	5	950	144*	35.18	3	2
M.G.N. Windows	11	21	–	730	106	34.76	1	5
R.C. Russell	19	34	8	901	85*	34.65	–	4
R.B. Richardson	9	16	–	551	76	34.43	–	5
M. Saxelby	17	32	–	1102	181	34.43	2	4
R.R. Montgomerie	19	34	3	1062	151	34.25	2	8
M. Watkinson	18	28	2	889	155	34.19	2	3
M.P. Speight	17	29	–	991	126	34.17	1	4
M.J. Walker	5	7	–	239	107	34.14	1	–
P.N. Weekes	16	21	2	648	117	34.10	1	2
G.R. Haynes	20	32	2	1021	141	34.03	2	4
G.F. Archer	16	26	–	878	168	33.76	2	4
T.J.G. O'Gorman	16	28	2	872	145	33.53	3	3
C.J. Adams	18	32	3	969	109*	33.41	1	5
A.L. Penberthy	17	25	5	658	88*	32.90	–	5
M.W. Alleyne	20	37	1	1184	109	32.88	2	6
A.W. Smith	14	21	5	524	202*	32.75	1	1
A.R. Roberts	9	12	4	261	51	32.62	–	1
G. Fowler	4	7	–	227	68	32.42	–	3
S.A. Marsh	19	31	6	807	88	32.28	–	5
J.A. Daley	10	18	2	513	159*	32.06	1	3
N.A. Folland	13	22	1	671	91	31.95	–	4
J.J. Whitaker	18	32	2	958	148	31.93	2	6
M.J. Foster	4	6	1	159	63*	31.80	–	1
N. Hussain	19	31	2	922	115*	31.79	2	5
P.V. Simmons	17	30	–	953	261	31.76	1	3
B.F. Smith	14	23	3	628	95	31.30	–	4
G.R. Cowdrey	10	16	1	470	114	31.33	1	2
D.B. D'Oliveira	3	5	–	156	61	31.20	–	1
N.J. Lenham	14	27	1	809	102	31.11	1	5
C.W.J. Athey	18	34	1	1022	169*	30.96	2	3
T.S. Curtis	18	32	1	960	180	30.96	3	1
F.A. Griffith	3	5	1	123	36	30.75	–	–
H. Morris	16	31	2	885	106	30.51	1	6
W.P.C. Weston	17	28	1	818	94	30.29	–	6
K.P. Evans	16	21	4	514	104	30.23	1	3
P.R. Pollard	18	31	1	905	134	30.16	2	4
S. Hutton	14	24	2	662	101	30.00	1	3
N.A. Mallender	8	12	3	270	43*	30.00	–	–
R.J. Warren	12	21	2	566	94*	29.78	–	5
S.R. Lampitt	17	26	5	624	122	29.71	1	2
D.M. Smith	7	14	3	326	74	29.63	–	3
R.J. Cunliffe	7	13	1	354	177*	29.50	1	–
A.P. Wells	19	35	4	909	84	29.32	–	7
J.W. Hall	14	27	–	789	85	29.22	–	7
T. Edwards	9	11	7	116	47	29.00	–	–
M.V. Fleming	16	29	1	810	73	28.92	–	6
J.J.B. Lewis	16	29	3	751	109	28.88	1	4
M. Davies	4	8	2	173	54	28.83	–	1
P.A.J. DeFreitas	14	21	2	545	108	28.68	1	3
G.D. Lloyd	16	27	3	684	112	28.50	1	5
D.R. Brown	3	6	2	113	54	28.25	–	1
G.I. MacMillan	10	17	3	395	69	28.21	–	3
F.D. Stephenson	17	28	1	752	107	27.85	1	5
M.R. Benson	16	28	1	737	159	27.29	1	4
D.P. Fulton	10	16	–	433	109	27.06	1	1
N.F. Williams	10	9	4	134	63	26.80	–	1
M.A. Ealham	15	26	2	638	68*	26.58	–	4
S.D. Udal	17	30	4	684	94	26.30	–	4
O.D. Gibson	20	31	4	710	85	26.29	–	7
A.S. Rollins	16	29	2	708	97	26.22	–	6
T.C. Middleton	13	23	3	524	102	26.20	1	3
S.P. Titchard	13	21	–	549	99	26.14	–	3
R.D.B. Croft	19	25	2	600	80	26.08	–	2
P.A. Smith	12	17	3	363	65	25.92	–	2
G.J. Parsons	16	25	6	491	70	25.84	–	2
J.I. Longley	14	25	2	594	100*	25.82	1	5
I.D. Austin	11	15	–	386	50	25.73	–	1

BATTING

	M	Inns	NO	Runs	HS	Av	100s	50s
W.M. Noon	18	30	6	617	75	25.70	–	3
N.M.K. Smith	18	21	4	435	65	25.58	–	2
T.H.C. Hancock	20	37	1	920	123	25.55	1	7
P. Moores	18	32	2	766	70*	25.53	–	4
A. Dale	18	29	1	711	131	25.39	2	2
K.M. Krikken	15	27	10	426	85*	25.05	–	2
G.D. Rose	16	24	2	548	121	24.90	1	2
B.C. Broad	10	20	–	496	128	24.80	1	2
N.A. Felton	10	19	1	445	87	24.72	–	2
G.W. White	11	20	1	467	104	24.57	1	2
G.D. Hodgson	9	16	1	367	113	24.46	1	1
Wasim Akram	6	10	–	244	98	24.40	–	2
R.J. Turner	18	27	5	537	104*	24.40	1	2
S.G. Hinks	5	10	–	242	74	24.20	–	2
M.J. Vandrau	13	23	5	435	66	24.16	–	1
D.G. Cork	13	21	–	507	94	24.14	–	4
A.N. Aymes	19	32	3	697	76	24.03	–	2
P.D. Bowler	13	23	–	546	88	23.73	–	2
A.J. Dalton	6	10	2	188	51*	23.50	–	1
T.J. Boon	16	28	2	606	74	23.30	–	4
A.C. Cummins	17	29	2	629	65	23.29	–	3
N. Shahid	10	18	4	326	91	23.28	–	1
R.K. Illingworth	20	25	6	438	59*	23.05	–	3
K.J. Piper	17	24	4	454	116*	22.70	1	1
C.M. Tolley	7	11	3	180	84	22.50	–	1
C.W. Scott	20	33	3	670	108	22.33	2	3
A.R.K. Pierson	15	20	5	334	43*	22.26	–	–
S.C. Ecclestone	13	19	4	334	80*	22.26	–	1
M.P. Dowman	3	5	–	111	38	22.20	–	–
D. Gough	13	19	3	355	65	22.18	–	2
C.P. Metson	18	22	4	398	51	22.11	–	1
P. Bainbridge	18	31	1	660	68	22.00	–	5
M.J. McCague	10	16	3	285	56	21.92	–	1
R.P. Lefebvre	12	14	3	240	33	21.81	–	–
M.A. Garnham	18	30	5	542	62	21.68	–	4
A.R. Whittall	9	11	2	193	91*	21.44	–	1
G. Yates	13	20	7	272	54*	20.92	–	2
K.D. James	13	22	2	417	53	20.85	–	2
J.P. Stephenson	16	27	1	535	144	20.57	1	2
R.L. Johnson	11	13	3	205	50*	20.50	–	1
D.J. Millns	19	27	10	348	64*	20.47	–	1
W.K. Hegg	19	30	4	518	66	19.92	–	2
I. Fletcher	6	10	1	179	54*	19.88	–	2
D.A. Graveney	13	22	6	315	65*	19.68	–	1
C.C. Remy	6	11	1	194	60	19.40	–	2
W.A. Dessaur	5	9	1	154	35	19.25	–	–
P.C.L. Holloway	4	6	–	114	50	19.00	–	1
N.J. Llong	7	11	–	209	44	19.00	–	–
R.M.F. Cox	4	7	1	114	46	19.00	–	–
J.P. Carroll	9	15	2	246	90	18.92	–	1
R.J. Maru	9	15	4	207	38*	18.81	–	–
D. Ripley	16	23	9	263	36*	18.78	–	–
M.C.J. Ball	17	28	3	468	45	18.72	–	–
R.P. Davis	12	9	2	131	35*	18.71	–	–
C.E.L. Ambrose	14	16	2	257	78	18.35	–	1
H.S. Malik	5	7	1	110	53*	18.33	–	1
J.S. Hodgson	9	15	1	256	54	18.28	–	1
P.J. Newport	17	24	5	345	41	18.15	–	–
S.J.E. Brown	19	25	10	268	69	17.86	–	1
M.C. Ilott	14	16	5	194	45*	17.63	–	–
W.K.M. Benjamin	9	14	1	227	54	17.46	–	2
I.D.K. Salisbury	16	25	6	331	49	17.42	–	–
H.R.J. Trump	14	20	4	276	45*	17.25	–	–
P.J. Hartley	16	23	3	343	61	17.15	–	1
M.A. Feltham	13	16	1	256	71	17.06	–	1
G.W. Jones	8	14	1	220	74	16.92	–	1
C.M. Wells	11	20	2	303	42	16.83	–	–
D.W. Headley	9	13	5	134	46*	16.75	–	–
S.A. Kellett	9	16	–	266	50	16.62	–	1
P.W. Jarvis	17	27	6	347	70*	16.52	–	1
M.S. Kasprowicz	17	24	4	326	44	16.30	–	–
P.J. Martin	18	27	3	383	57	15.95	–	1
G.W. Mike	17	26	3	365	60*	15.86	–	1
M. Keech	5	9	–	141	57	15.66	–	1
M.P. Bicknell	9	11	2	140	41	15.55	–	–
R.D. Mann	9	16	–	248	53	15.50	–	1
Mushtaq Ahmed	9	14	3	168	38	15.27	–	–
C.A. Walsh	15	24	6	274	66	15.22	–	1
R.A. Pick	16	22	7	227	65*	15.13	–	1
N.F. Sargeant	9	13	2	166	46	15.09	–	–
G. Chapple	15	21	11	150	26*	15.00	–	–
S.J. Base	8	12	1	160	33	14.54	–	–
A.C.S. Pigott	8	11	–	160	40	14.54	–	–
J.E. Emburey	15	19	5	203	78*	14.50	–	1
V. Pike	9	12	4	114	27	14.25	–	–
R.C. Williams	10	14	2	171	38	14.25	–	1
J. Ratledge	9	16	–	227	79	14.18	–	1
G.J. Kersey	7	11	2	127	39	14.11	–	–
A.R. Caddick	12	18	2	219	58*	13.68	–	1
A.M. Smith	12	14	2	162	29	13.50	–	–
M.A. Crawley	8	14	1	172	45	13.23	–	–
D.A. Reeve	9	10	1	116	33	12.88	–	–
N.M. Kendrick	7	11	2	112	25	12.44	–	–
C.M. Pitcher	10	14	4	116	43	11.60	–	–
C.A. Connor	15	22	3	215	25	11.31	–	–
P.N. Hepworth	5	10	–	113	60	11.30	–	1
N.J. Haste	9	12	2	112	22	11.20	–	–
T.A. Munton	18	17	7	106	36	10.60	–	–
C.E.W. Silverwood	9	15	3	127	26	10.58	–	–
M.M. Patel	18	27	2	256	39	10.24	–	–
J. Wood	15	22	3	194	51	10.21	–	1
R.D. Stemp	20	28	2	263	28	10.11	–	–
N.V. Radford	15	20	4	161	25	10.06	–	–

(Qualification – 100 runs, average 10.00)

(A.C. Storie 64* & 102*; D.A. Lewis 113* & 39; G.D. Harrison 105* & 43; B.M.W. Patterson 114 & 22)

BOWLING

	Overs	Mds	Runs	Wkts	Av	Best	10/m	5/inn
K.J. Barnett	54.2	5	173	13	13.30	5-31	–	1
C.E.L. Ambrose	540	159	1113	77	14.45	7-44	2	6
C.A. Walsh	504	119	1530	89	17.19	7-42	3	9
M.J. McCague	341.1	67	1084	57	19.01	9-86	1	5
I.D. Austin	251.4	72	662	33	20.06	5-23	1	3
F.D. Stephenson	480.4	111	1345	67	20.07	6-50	2	6
J.E. Benjamin	590.3	130	1658	80	20.72	6-27	1	5
T.A. Munton	699.4	181	1748	81	21.58	7-52	2	6
M.M. Patel	811.2	202	2057	90	22.85	8-96	3	6
C. White	235.2	53	760	33	23.03	5-40	–	1
S.R. Lampitt	511.4	127	1484	64	23.18	5-33	–	2
A.R. Caddick	373.1	73	1186	51	23.25	6-51	–	3
C.C. Lewis	345.2	69	1082	46	23.52	5-55	–	2
M.C. Ilott	497.5	115	1391	59	23.57	6-24	1	3
Wasim Akram	213.2	44	646	27	23.92	8-30	1	2
W.K.M. Benjamin	281	97	585	24	24.37	6-46	–	2
E.S.H. Giddins	450.4	89	1463	60	24.38	5-38	–	3
C.A. Connor	574.4	131	1764	72	24.50	7-47	2	2
D. Gough	479.2	100	1527	62	24.62	6-66	–	3
P.A.J. DeFreitas	530.5	108	1621	65	24.93	6-39	–	4
D.J. Millns	532	99	1901	76	25.01	6-44	–	4
V.J. Wells	301.5	78	1053	42	25.07	5-50	–	1
A.C.S. Pigott	268.3	72	737	29	25.41	6-46	–	1
P.V. Simmons	300.5	81	769	30	25.63	4-68	–	–
J.E. Emburey	675	205	1514	59	25.66	6-89	–	2
G.D. Rose	344.1	70	1136	44	25.81	4-40	–	–
D.M. Cousins	112	21	337	13	25.92	6-35	–	1
R.A. Pick	507.2	122	1413	54	26.16	6-62	–	2
G.C. Small	339	79	946	36	26.27	5-46	–	1
R.L. Johnson	350.4	85	1059	40	26.47	10-45	1	1
Mushtaq Ahmed	404	114	1196	45	26.57	7-94	1	4
G. Chapple	458.4	111	1474	55	26.80	6-48	–	4
A.R.C. Fraser	531.5	141	1343	50	26.86	3-16	–	–
M.W. Alleyne	351.3	68	1103	41	26.90	5-78	–	1
R.S. Yeabsley	171.4	27	567	21	27.00	6-54	1	1
S.D. Udal	678	174	1872	69	27.13	6-79	1	7
G. Yates	321.3	70	1013	37	27.37	5-34	–	1
G.J. Parsons	462.2	131	1208	44	27.45	5-34	–	1

BOWLING

	Overs	Mds	Runs	Wkts	Av	Best	10/m	5/inn
D.W. Headley	295.1	48	990	36	27.50	5-60	–	2
P.W. Trimby	243.3	48	718	26	27.61	5-84	–	1
I.D.K. Salisbury	474	143	1336	48	27.83	6-55	–	3
P.J. Hartley	562.1	116	1701	61	27.88	5-89	–	1
S.J.E. Brown	579.1	87	2108	75	28.10	6-68	–	1
M.A. Ealham	266.4	62	762	27	28.22	7-53	–	1
P.C.R. Tufnell	463.5	128	1107	39	28.38	6-35	–	1
K.E. Cooper	418.2	99	1095	38	28.81	4-38	–	–
M. Watkinson	631.1	173	1823	63	28.93	8-30	1	1
E.E. Hemmings	422	140	959	33	29.06	7-66	–	2
D.E. Malcolm	551.3	97	2014	69	29.18	9-57	1	3
V. Pike	200	51	584	20	29.20	6-41	–	1
P.J. Martin	613.4	175	1580	54	29.25	5-61	–	2
R.C. Irani	249.4	42	834	28	29.78	4-27	–	–
K.P. Evans	411.5	105	1141	38	30.02	4-46	–	–
D.G. Cork	329.1	55	1112	37	30.05	6-29	–	2
C.E. Cuffy	389	107	1082	36	30.05	4-70	–	–
J.N.B. Bovill	119.4	23	421	14	30.07	5-108	–	1
R.D. Stemp	669.1	252	1493	49	30.46	6-37	–	2
J.G. Hughes	137.2	38	428	14	30.57	5-69	–	1
R.K. Illingworth	679	212	1499	49	30.59	4-51	–	–
D.A. Reeve	144	48	308	10	30.80	2-9	–	–
M.J. Thursfield	162.4	41	524	17	30.82	6-130	–	1
P.M. Such	670	183	1757	57	30.82	7-66	–	5
S.L. Watkin	613.4	144	1708	55	31.05	6-143	–	2
M.S. Kasprowicz	527.3	92	1869	60	31.15	7-83	–	3
P.J. Newport	516.2	103	1654	53	31.20	4-50	–	–
J.C. Adams	340.5	115	720	23	31.30	4-63	–	–
T.N. Wren	164.5	30	533	17	31.35	6-48	–	1
A.M. Smith	297.4	59	1004	32	31.37	5-40	–	1
S.R. Barwick	549.4	208	1131	36	31.41	5-44	–	1
A.C. Cummins	520.3	92	1768	56	31.57	6-64	1	4
G.W. Mike	405.5	92	1422	45	31.60	5-44	–	1
J.P. Taylor	333.4	56	1141	36	31.69	5-62	–	1
R.P. Davis	342	93	986	31	31.80	6-94	–	2
J.H. Childs	464.5	122	1254	39	32.15	6-71	–	2
C.E.W. Silverwood	248.5	47	883	27	32.70	4-67	–	–
R.C. Williams	245.5	46	856	26	32.92	4-28	–	–
P.A. Smith	182	40	594	18	33.00	3-24	–	–
J. Wood	347.4	37	1501	45	33.35	6-110	–	3
M.A. Feltham	382.3	83	1140	34	33.52	5-69	–	1
H.R.J. Trump	268.4	76	873	26	33.57	6-68	1	2
M.P. Bicknell	319.4	75	977	29	33.68	5-44	–	1
P.N. Weekes	484.2	91	1383	41	33.73	5-12	–	1
S.J. Base	199	30	782	23	34.00	5-92	–	1
A.R.K. Pierson	500.4	131	1267	37	34.24	8-42	–	2
J.A. Afford	541.3	165	1376	40	34.40	5-48	–	2
N.M.K. Smith	582	103	1693	49	34.55	7-42	–	4
K.D. James	280.1	56	900	26	34.61	4-78	–	–
D.J. Spencer	85.5	12	347	10	34.70	4-31	–	–
P.W. Jarvis	496.2	89	1773	51	34.76	7-58	–	1
R.P. Lefebvre	365.2	108	896	25	35.84	4-63	–	–
C.M. Wells	153.3	31	469	13	36.07	4-52	–	–
N.V. Radford	459.1	106	1408	39	36.10	5-93	–	1
O.D. Gibson	579.4	100	2169	60	36.15	6-64	1	4
R.G. Twose	190.5	41	544	15	36.26	6-28	–	1
A. Sheriyar	98	14	400	11	36.36	4-44	–	–
C.L. Hooper	414.1	93	1055	29	36.37	5-52	–	1
J.E.R. Gallian	95	10	368	10	36.80	2-27	–	–
A.J. Hollioake	264.1	44	958	26	36.84	4-48	–	–
M.A. Robinson	619	171	1658	45	36.84	5-48	–	1
M.J. Vandrau	290.5	63	965	26	37.11	4-53	–	–
A.L. Penberthy	400.1	83	1374	37	37.13	5-54	–	1
S.C. Ecclestone	298.3	70	825	22	37.50	4-66	–	–
N.A. Mallender	193.3	50	602	16	37.62	3-23	–	–
N.G. Cowans	349.3	89	986	26	37.92	4-76	–	–
A.P. van Troost	345.5	59	1329	35	37.97	4-50	–	–
A.D. Mullally	448.1	121	1255	33	38.03	5-85	–	1
T.M. Moody	195	48	572	15	38.13	4-24	–	–
A.P. Igglesden	316.1	75	929	24	38.70	5-38	–	1
K.J. Shine	332.4	76	1156	29	39.86	4-79	–	–
D.A. Graveney	456	121	1247	31	40.22	6-80	–	1
J.P. Stephenson	332	75	1066	26	41.00	4-74	–	–
R.J. Maru	254.1	76	621	15	41.40	3-61	–	–
N.F. Williams	326	71	1088	26	41.84	6-49	–	1
M.A. Butcher	206.4	50	670	16	41.87	4-31	–	–
G.A. Hick	173.2	55	462	11	42.00	3-64	–	–
N.G.B. Cook	288.3	92	715	17	42.05	3-46	–	–
A. Dale	277	65	975	23	42.39	2-7	–	–
A.E. Warner	256	53	817	19	43.00	4-39	–	–
J.E. Brinkley	233	40	779	18	43.27	6-98	–	1
G. Welch	267	63	970	22	44.09	4-74	–	–
M.G. Field-Buss	245.1	71	540	12	45.00	2-23	–	–
C.M. Pitcher	258.5	57	902	20	45.10	4-37	–	–
M.G.J. Ball	326.1	78	957	21	45.57	5-69	–	1
C.J. Hollins	236.3	32	890	19	46.84	4-64	–	–
K.M. Curran	423.5	86	1463	31	47.19	4-65	–	–
A.W. Smith	374	66	1340	28	47.85	5-103	–	1
M.P. Vaughan	228.3	52	678	14	48.42	4-39	–	–
J.S. Hodgson	272	85	732	15	48.80	4-14	–	–
A.R. Roberts	242	49	870	17	51.17	3-106	–	–
R.J. Bailey	166.1	33	568	11	51.63	5-59	–	1
R.D.B. Croft	715.3	158	2166	41	52.82	5-80	–	1
A.A. Barnett	191.4	39	627	10	62.70	2-35	–	–
N.J. Haste	233	47	910	13	70.00	4-69	–	–
P. Bainbridge	315.4	69	1082	14	77.28	4-72	–	–
A.R. Whittall	294.5	59	1060	11	96.36	2-34	–	–

(Qualification – 10 wickets)

LEADING FIELDERS

74 – S.A. Marsh (ct 69/st 5); 69 – K.J. Piper (ct 64/st 5); 67 – R.J. Blakey (ct 63/st 4) and S.J. Rhodes (ct 59/st 8); 62 – P. Moores (ct 61/st 1) and P.A. Nixon (ct 60/st 2); 61 – C.P. Metson (ct 54/st 7); 60 – R.C. Russell (ct 59/st 1); 58 – C.W. Scott (ct 56/st 2); 57 – K.R. Brown (ct 56/st 1); 52 – R.J. Turner (ct 46/st 6); 49 – W.K. Hegg (ct 46/st 3); 46 – D. Ripley (ct 40/st 6); 43 – W.M. Noon (ct 38/st 5); 39 – A.N. Aymes (ct 35/st 4); 38 – M.A. Garnham (ct 33/st 5); 34 – N. Hussain; 33 – A.J. Wright; 31 – M.C.J. Ball and J.D. Carr; 29 – T.R. Ward; 28 – M.W. Gatting and K.M. Krikken (ct 26/st 2); 26 – C.L. Hooper; 25 – J.P. Crawley and N.R. Taylor; 24 – D. Byas; 23 – P.V. Simmons; 22 – G.A. Hick and N.V. Knight; 21 – D.A. Leatherdale and M.A. Roseberry; 20 – M.A. Butcher, T. Edwards and T.M. Moody

English Counties Form Charts

The games covered are:

Britannic Assurance County Championship
Matches against touring and representative sides

In the batting table a blank indicates that a batsman did not play in a game, a dash (–) that he did not *bat*. A dash (–) is placed in the batting averages if a player had 2 innings or less, and in the bowling figures if no wicket was taken.

NEW ZEALANDERS IN ENGLAND, 1994 — BATTING

Batting averages

Player	M	Inns	NO	Runs	HS	Av
B.R. Hartland	8	16	1	337	65	21.05
B.A. Pocock	7	14	2	374	103*	31.16
M.D. Crowe	9	16	2	654	142	46.71
K.R. Rutherford	9	17	1	603	129	37.68
M.J. Greatbatch	9	18	3	528	84	35.20
S.A. Thomson	10	19	2	408	69	34.00
A.C. Parore	11	18	4	399	71	28.50
G.E. Larsen	9	11	3	168	40*	21.00
M.N. Hart	8	11	3	146	36	18.25
C. Pringle	7	8	0	88	24	11.00
H.T. Davis	9	7	4	9	3*	3.00
B.A. Young	8	17	1	622	122	36.58
S.P. Fleming	8	15	2	591	151	39.40
D.J. Nash	8	11	6	177	56	35.40
D.K. Morrison	6	8	6	10	10*	10.00
M.B. Owens	2	6	2	8	4	1.33
S.J. Roberts	2	4	1	32	24	8.00
M.W. Douglas	1	2	1	28	24	12.00

Match totals and results

Match	Venue	Dates	Totals	Wickets	Result
v. Worcestershire	Worcester	4–6 May	194 & 153	7 & 4	D
v. Somerset	Taunton	7–9 May	182 & 247	10 & 2	D
v. Middlesex	Lord's	12–14 May	249	6	D
v. Yorkshire	Leeds	24–6 May	173 & 202	10 & 9	L
v. Essex	Chelmsford	28–30 May	428 & 108	5 & 3	D
FIRST TEST MATCH	Trent Bridge	2–6 June	251 & 226	10 & 10	L
v. Glamorgan	Swansea	8–10 June	282 & 306	5 & 2	W
v. Gloucestershire	Bristol	11–13 June	295 & 222	5 & D	D
SECOND TEST MATCH	Lord's	16–20 June	476 & 211	10 & 5	D
v. Combined Universities	Cambridge	22–4 June	256 & 196	10 & 10	D
v. Derbyshire	Derby	25–7 June	210 & 196	9 & 9‡	L
THIRD TEST MATCH	Old Trafford	30 June–5 July	151 & 308	10 & 7	D

BOWLING

	H.T. Davis	C. Pringle	G.R. Larsen	M.N. Hart	S.A. Thomson	D.K. Morrison	D.J. Nash	M.B. Owens	B.A. Young	M.D. Crowe	A.C. Parore	S.J. Roberts	Byes	Leg-byes	Wides	No-balls	Total	Wkts
v. Worcestershire (Worcester) 4–6 May	15–0–121–1	27.5–9–64–3	23–6–64–2	14–2–51–1	8–0–40–0								5	3	1	28	343	7
v. Somerset (Taunton) 7–9 May	11–2–63–1 / 28–2–127–3	5–1–21–1 / 21–7–58–0	5–1–13–4 / 32–7–63–2	26–7–88–3	15–3–33–0									1 / 15	4	12 / 12	103 / 364	6 / 8
v. Middlesex (Lord's) 12–14 May			16–5–28–2	12–2–36–0	4–1–9–0	13–2–40–2	14–6–34–0							9		8	156	4
v. Yorkshire (Leeds) 24–6 May	20.4–1–107–1	26–8–87–0	21–9–39–1	44–12–106–4	24–8–37–0		23–4–106–0						2	17	1	38	408	5
v. Essex (Chelmsford) 28–30 May	12–0–72–1			35–7–123–1	38–6–73–1		25–4–77–3	22–3–89–4						3		14	334	10
FIRST TEST MATCH (Trent Bridge) 2–6 June	21–0–93–1		44.4–11–116–2	34–6–133–3 / 25–5–76–2	26–8–75–1 / 21–5–75–2		36–5–153–2	9–3–29–1 / 4–1–7–0						9	6	10	567	8
v. Glamorgan (Swansea) 8–10 June	8–1–50–0 / 5–0–27–1	23.3–9–58–5 / 11.4–2–38–1	16–5–35–1 / 13–2–38–1										4 / 3	12 / 3	3 / 1	8 / 10	361 / 226	10 / 6
v. Gloucestershire (Bristol) 11–13 June		19–3–74–1 / 14–5–40–2		44–21–50–1 / 41–23–55–1	20–5–50–2 / 11–4–40–0	17–2–64–1 / 6–2–13–1	20.4–7–59–4 / 5–0–16–0		8–0–76–1		5–0–55–0		1 / 5	3 / 4	1	10 / 2	286 / 368	9 / 7
SECOND TEST MATCH (Lord's) 16–20 June		23–5–65–1 / 16–5–41–1	23–11–44–1 / 20–10–24–5		22–8–40–1 / 12–4–27–0		25–6–76–6 / 29–8–93–5	7–0–34–0 / 10–3–35–1		12–0–81–2			4 / 9	12 / 14	2	7 / 1	281 / 254	10 / 8
v. Combined Universities (Cambridge) 22–4 June	11–3–59–0				22–6–60–0 / 17–2–51–1			21–4–74–5 / 5–3–12–0				21–5–60–4 / 8–2–16–2	2 / 5	1 / 8	11	24 / 4	320 / 122	10 / 8
v. Derbyshire (Derby) 25–7 June		32–8–98–2	13–3–30–0	33–11–102–1			12–2–54–1	15–2–45–2						14	1	4	424	9
THIRD TEST MATCH (Old Trafford) 30 June–5 July		39–12–95–1		27.3–9–50–1	7–1–23–0		39–9–107–4	34–12–99–4				18.2–0–87–2		8	1	2	382	10
Bowler's average	131.4–9– 719–9 79.88	258–74– 739–18 41.05	226.4–73– 494–21 23.52	335.5–105– 850–18 47.22	247–61– 633–8 79.12	36–6– 117–4 29.25	228.4–51– 775–25 31.00	127–31– 424–17 24.94	8–0– 76–1 76.00	12–0– 81–2 40.50	5–0– 55–0 –	47.2–7– 163–8 20.37						

SOUTH AFRICANS IN ENGLAND

FIELDING FIGURES

- 24 – D.J. Richardson (ct 23/st 1)
- 17 – K.C. Wessels
- 13 – G.F.J. Liebenberg (ct 10/st 3)
- 11 – W.J. Cronje
- 10 – B.M. McMillan
- 8 – J.N. Rhodes
- 7 – A.C. Hudson
- 5 – P.N. Kirsten, G. Kirsten and D.J. Cullinan
- 4 – T.G. Shaw and A.A. Donald
- 3 – Subs
- 2 – P.S. de Villiers, P.L. Symcox and C.R. Matthews

†J.N. Rhodes retired hurt

BATTING

Batting	v. Kent (Canterbury) 25–7 June	v. Sussex (Hove) 29 June–1 July	v. Hampshire (Southampton) 2–4 July	v. Gloucestershire (Bristol) 6–8 July	v. Durham (Chester-le-Street) 12–14 July	v. Northamptonshire (Northampton) 1–18 July	FIRST TEST MATCH (Lord's) 21–5 July	v. Nottinghamshire (Trent Bridge) 27–9 July	v. Leicestershire (Leicester) 30 July–1 August	SECOND TEST MATCH (Leeds) 4–8 August	v. Minor Counties (Torquay) 10–12 August	v. Glamorgan (Pontypridd) 13–15 August	M	Inns	NO	Runs	HS	Av
A.C. Hudson	0*, 0*		27	0	64	13, 102	6, 72	37, 10	9	12	22, 10	4, 23	12	19	1	382	116	21.22
G. Kirsten	2, 26		50		201*, 27	20, 41	72, 7	108	12, 62	65, 13*	1	0, 76*	11	19	3	751	201*	46.93
W.J. Cronje	8	94		4		70	105, 32		30, 54	0	47, 36	78, 1	13	20	1	661	108	34.78
D.J. Cullinan	5, 0		18	52	53, 15	59, 21*	26	71*	66, 1		68, 9	17, 29*	9	14	3	428	94	38.90
K.C. Wessels	26	77	31	6*			26		18	25, 48	16, 8	45*, 37*	12	18	2	679	105	42.43
J.N. Rhodes	20		77	1			41, 8		17, 2*		5	7	12	16	3	477	77	36.69
D.J. Richardson	88		12				5*, 5*			62*, 13			10	12	3	286	88	31.77
T.G. Shaw	66								2*				5	5	3	82	66	41.00
C.R. Matthews	15*		8*	31	42*	9	8	1*		27, 104		37, 7*	9	6	2	143	62*	35.75
P.S. de Villiers	8		18*	6		17	5*	21*, 40	59		15, 27		8	5	1	43	14	10.75
A.A. Donald	4						8*		7	78			8	6	0	68	27	22.66
P.N. Kirsten		130											10	16	5	549	130	49.90
G.F.J. Liebenberg		64*									22, 12*		7	11	1	226	64*	22.60
P.L. Symcox		37*	0			11*							7	5	3	104	39*	52.00
R.P. Snell		5	0, 1	1*		50	29, 39*	15				94	8	8	3	143	94	28.60
B.M. McMillan		132			4*						14*, 0		9	11	3	467	132	58.37
Byes	3, 5	4	4, 2	4	5, 7	1, 2	9, 8	6, 6	16, 8	8, 2	9, 1	4, 1						
Leg-byes	5, 7	2	2, 1		7	9, 9	9, 10	4, 4	8, 7	7, 1		4						
Wides						2												
No-balls	9	34	14	24	10	14	9, 12	20, 2	22, 2	13, 7	8, 8	2						
Total	258	613	264	129	428	296, 216	357, 278	327, 164	270, 163	447, 116	249, 173	288, 140						
Wickets	0/10	8	9	6	4	7, 3	10, 8	6, 3	8, 5	10, 3	10, 7	6, 3						
Result	L	D	D	D	D	D	W	W	D	D	D	D						

BATTING

Batting	THIRD TEST MATCH (The Oval) 18–22 August	v. President's XI (Scarborough) 31 August–2 September	M	Inns	NO	Runs	HS	Av
A.C. Hudson	2, 0	116	12	19	1	382	116	21.22
G. Kirsten	0, —	—	11	19	3	751	201*	46.93
W.J. Cronje	38, 94	36	13	20	1	661	108	34.78
D.J. Cullinan	45, 28	14	9	14	3	428	94	38.90
K.C. Wessels	8, 10	21	12	18	2	679	105	42.43
J.N. Rhodes	58, 3		12	16	3	477	77	36.69
D.J. Richardson		82	10	12	3	286	88	31.77
T.G. Shaw			5	5	3	82	66	41.00
C.R. Matthews	14, 0*		9	6	2	143	62*	35.75
P.S. de Villiers	14*, —		8	5	1	43	14	10.75
A.A. Donald	16, 1	32	8	6	0	68	27	22.66
P.N. Kirsten			10	16	5	549	130	49.90
G.F.J. Liebenberg		17	7	11	1	226	64*	22.60
P.L. Symcox		6*	7	5	3	104	39*	52.00
R.P. Snell		1*	8	8	3	143	94	28.60
B.M. McMillan	93, 25		9	11	3	467	132	58.37
Byes	8, 10	3, 8						
Leg-byes	10, 5							
Wides	1							
No-balls	18, 9	16						
Total	332, 175	270						
Wickets	9+, 10	0/6						
Result	L	D						

BOWLING

	A.A. Donald	P.S. de Villiers	C.R. Matthews	T.G. Shaw	W.J. Cronje	B.M. McMillan	P.L. Symcox	R.P. Snell	C. Kirsten	P.N. Kirsten	K.C. Wessels	J.N. Rhodes	Byes	Leg-byes	Wides	No-balls	Total	Wkts
v. Kent (Canterbury) 25–7 June	19-9-34-0		19-6-36-0	29-2-115-1	14.5-2-47-4								8	2		8	292	10
																		0
v. Sussex (Hove) 29 June–1 July	13-2-50-3													13	1	4	358	7
v. Hampshire (Southampton) 2–4 July	24.5-7-58-5		26-8-57-2 / 6-2-10-0	19-4-56-0 / 17-2-59-2	9-4-33-1	28-5-68-3	36-11-102-0 / 12-4-29-5	19-5-65-1 / 12-3-46-1	5-1-20-0 / 2.5-1-5-0				1	1	2	12	91	6
v. Gloucestershire (Bristol) 6–8 July	9-3-21-0	33-6-118-5 / 12-2-42-2		27-9-45-2 / 21-7-49-1	13-6-13-1 / 11-4-19-2	27-7-86-0 / 2-1-6-0	23-7-45-1 / 25-7-92-3	19-3-49-2 / 3-0-15-0	1-0-1-0				1	5	2	2	300	8
														3		12	198	5
v. Durham (Chester-le-Street) 12–14 July	15-3-49-1 / 28-3-118-2	20-3-80-4 / 22-6-69-2	13-3-34-1	15-5-37-0 / 19-7-49-1	5-1-13-0 / 7-3-8-1	18.2-2-47-4 / 16-5-44-1	17-4-63-0 / 15-3-46-0			2-1-1-0 / 7-2-23-1	2-1-7-0		11 / 4	1	6 / 3	7	278	9
														9	1	12	201	7
																	228	9 A
v. Northamptonshire (Northampton) 16–18 July	19.3-5-74-5 / 12-5-29-2	16-5-28-3 / 12-4-26-1	22-6-67-1 / 6-3-6-0		15-7-22-1	17-4-46-0 / 5-1-18-0	13-0-13-0						4 / 2	9 / 2		10	301	7
													1	5		2	250	5
FIRST TEST MATCH (Lord's) 21–5 July			16-6-46-0 / 14-6-25-3		1-0-1-0	10-1-25-1 / 6.5-2-16-3	18-6-36-3	19-5-66-3 / 8-0-21-1	6-1-31-0 / 6-1-30-0	2-1-8-0		1-0-10-0	2 / 1	2 / 1	1	8	131	4
																	180	10
v. Nottinghamshire (Trent Bridge) 27–9 July	14-2-40-1 / 13-0-45-2	20-4-67-6 / 15-3-53-2		28-9-58-2 / 22-10-29-4	7-3-9-0 / 5-2-10-0	9-4-19-2 / 8-2-17-0	22-6-56-3 / 17.4-7-44-5	20.1-8-51-1 / 5-0-22-0					1 / 4	5			99	9 B
															1		218	10
v. Leicestershire (Leicester) 30 July–1 August	29-2-135-1	39.3-12-108-3	11-5-25-1 / 8-3-24-1	1-1-0-0 / 22-5-60-3	16-3-38-0 / 12-3-39-0			15.1-4-38-3 / 9-0-35-0					8 / 5	5 / 8	4	2 / 4	139	10
													1	5			167	10
SECOND TEST MATCH (Leeds) 4–8 August		25-3-98-1	39-7-97-1 / 24-8-53-1	13-7-23-0 / 21-8-63-2	3-1-12-0 / 5-1-18-0	37-12-93-1 / 15.3-0-66-2			2-1-10-0		2-1-7-0		1	1		12 / 3	216	5
																	477	9
v. Minor Counties (Torquay) 10–12 August							15-3-49-1 / 21-4-60-4	15-2-69-1 / 5-0-24-0					5 / 9	3 / 9			267	5
																	153	2
v. Glamorgan (Pontypridd) 13–15 August			15-0-94-1 / 12-0-56-2	21-5-49-0 / 17.4-6-37-2	17-2-53-2	12-1-67-0	32.1-11-63-1 / 14-3-63-2	18-3-59-1 / 14-1-61-3							1		173	9
													2 / 1				336	5
THIRD TEST MATCH (The Oval) 18–22 August	17-2-76-3 / 12-1-96-1	19-3-62-4 / 12-0-66-0	20.5-4-82-2 / 11.3-4-37-1	20-3-99-1	8-3-16-0			18-4-45-1		7-0-44-1				6	1	15	222	10
																7	304	2
v. President's XI (Scarborough) 31 August–2 September		19-6-55-2			11-0-44-1	11-2-44-0							2	10		10	205	6
																	343	0
Bowler's average	212.2-42-775-25 / 31.00	277.3-59-922-38 / 24.26	263.2-74-749-17 / 44.05	312.4-90-828-21 / 39.42	159.5-45-395-13 / 30.38	222.4-49-662-19 / 34.84	280.5-86-761-28 / 27.17	199.2-38-666-18 / 37.00	22.5-5-97-0 / –	18-4-76-2 / 38.00	2-0-7-0 / –	1-0-10-0 / –						

A W. Larkins retired hurt
B D. Gough retired hurt

CAMBRIDGE UNIVERSITY

BATTING

	v. Nottinghamshire (Cambridge) 13–15 April	v. Northamptonshire (Cambridge) 16–18 April	v. Kent (Cambridge) 20–2 April	v. Middlesex (Cambridge) 30 April–2 May	v. Worcestershire (Cambridge) 7–9 May	v. Lancashire (Cambridge) 14–16 May	v. Glamorgan (Cambridge) 11–13 June	v. Essex (Cambridge) 15–17 June	v. Gloucestershire (Bristol) 25–7 June	v. Oxford University (Lord's) 29 June–1 July	M	Inns	NO	Runs	HS	Av
G.W. Jones	35	—	5 8	4 24	0*	77 70*	9 22	74 41	3 25	21 2	8	14	1	220	74	16.92
R.Q. Cake	21	—	26 3	40 23	21 16	6	107 66	42 11	48 5	27 27	9	16	1	645	107	43.00
J. Ratledge	6	—	4 3	23 21	18 6	12*	0 0	25 11	8 5	0 0	9	16	0	227	79	14.18
J.S. Hodgson	0	—	16 0	26 90	41 —	—	0 5	11 23	0 10	29 54	9	15	1	256	54	18.28
J.P. Carroll	17	—	19 0	13 13	53 —	17	48 3*	0 6*	5 30	31 7	9	15	2	246	90	18.92
R.D. Mann	0	—	18 6	8 9	0 —	—	8* 0	10 15	5 5	43 0*	9	16	1	248	53	15.50
C.M. Pitcher	0	—	9 3	9 1	9* —	—	1 —	— 1	1* 5	40 91*	9	11	1	103	43	10.30
A.E. Whittall	0	—	3 34	11 0*	5 —	—	— —	4 4	21* 21	10 22	9	12	3	193	91*	21.44
N.J. Haste	3	—	10 20	11 4	2 —	—	2 —	2* —	6 —	34* —	9	12	2	112	22	11.20
F.J. Cooke	24*	—	0* 4*	4 0*	— —	—	— —	— —	— —	— —	3	5	3	80	34*	13.33
M.C. Bashforth												5	3	13	9*	6.50
M.A.T. Hall											2	2	1	5	4	2.50
D.E. Stanley					4		48	6	9	0 8	5	8	2	91	48	15.16
Byes	6		1 3	2 5	4 16	2 7	3 1	8 8	2 6	7 10						
Leg-byes	5		3	6 3	1 8	7 6	4 —	14 1	1 6	10 1						
Wides	1															
No-balls			2		8	8	4	—	2	8 8						
Total	144	Ab.	84 122	121 221	203	227 118	244 104	181 144	129 134	253 243						
Wickets	10		10 10	10 10	9*	6 2	8 4	10 5	10 10	10 8						
Result	D		L	L	D	D	D	D	L	D						

BOWLING

	C.M. Pitcher	N.J. Haste	A.R. Whittall	M.C. Bashforth	J.S. Hodgson	J. Ratledge	M.A.T. Hall	J.P. Carroll
v. Nottinghamshire (Cambridge) 13–15 April								
v. Northamptonshire (Cambridge) 16–18 April	9–2–21–1	6.2–1–14–0	2–1–1–0					
v. Kent (Cambridge) 20–2 April	36–6–123–3		31–8–94–0	12–5–48–0	24–11–52–1			
v. Middlesex (Cambridge) 30 April–2 May	12.5–1–37–4		13–3–31–1		16.3–6–39–3			
v. Worcestershire (Cambridge) 7–9 May	19–7–33–2		19–8–41–1	10–2–32–0	6–0–25–0			
	14–5–42–1		24–4–7–93–2	6–2–28–0				
v. Lancashire (Cambridge) 14–16 May	17–3–55–0		8–2–27–0		26–16–25–1	3–0–7–0		
	12–4–31–2		27.5–5–95–1		11–9–39–1			
v. Glamorgan (Cambridge) 11–13 June	21–3–81–0		17–2–71–0		11–2–37–2			
	16–5–46–2		14.3–2–62–1		21–2–81–0			
v. Essex (Cambridge) 15–17 June	20–8–39–0		18.3–1–74–1		15–1–48–0			
	9–2–41–0		15.4–1–69–4		21.5–75–2	7–0–35–0		
v. Gloucestershire (Bristol) 25–7 June	19–2–86–2		22–8–50–0		19–12–14–1	6–0–24–0		
	14–3–54–0		26–2–136–1		31–7–75–0			6–1–22–0
v. Oxford University ((Lord's) 29 June–1 July	14–1–80–0		11–2–35–0		8–0–69–0		2–0–2–0	
	20–2–95–3		33–6–123–1		32–7–85–1			
	252.5–54–	233–39–	295.3–59–	28–9–	272.3–85–	16–0–	2–0–	6–1–
	864–20	910–13	1060–11	108–0	732–15	66–0	2–0	22–0
Bowler's average	43.20	70.00	96.36	—	48.80	—	—	—

Opponents' innings totals

Byes	Leg-byes	Wides	No-balls	Total	Wkts
	2			38	1 Ab.
5	12	2	2	446	5
	6		2	100	5
5	8	1	6	257	7
	4			163	2
4	11		8	324	3
1	2			108	3
9	3		14	293	6
	7			201	2
9	5	2		307	6
8	3			197	4
	3	1	2	323	4
5	4			132	6
4		2	2	357	2
3	27	6		218	2
				453	9

FIELDING FIGURES

10 – F.J. Cooke (ct 9/st 1)
8 – J.S. Hodgson
4 – C.M. Pitcher
3 – A.R. Whittall and R.Q. Cake
2 – J.P. Carroll, R.D. Mann, D.E. Stanley and N.J. Haste
1 – M.C. Bashforth and J. Ratledge
†G.W. Jones retired hurt

OXFORD UNIVERSITY

BATTING

Fixtures (in order):
- v. Durham (Oxford) 13–15 April
- v. Hampshire (Oxford) 16–19 April
- v. Glamorgan (Oxford) 20–2 April
- v. Nottinghamshire (Oxford) 28–30 April
- v. Warwickshire (Oxford) 14–17 May
- v. Leicestershire (Oxford) 18–20 May
- v. Yorkshire (Oxford) 28–31 May
- v. Surrey (The Oval) 11–13 June
- v. Worcestershire (Worcester) 17–19 June
- v. Cambridge University (Lord's) 29 June–1 July

Batting Averages

Player	M	Inns	NO	Runs	HS	Av
R.R. Montgomerie	10	17	1	541	101*	33.81
G.I. Macmillan	10	17	3	395	69	28.21
C.M. Gupte	10	17	1	529	122	33.06
A.C. Ridley	3	4	1	65	36*	21.66
W.S. Kendall	9	14	7	253	113*	36.14
S.C. Ecclestone	10	14	4	292	80*	29.20
H.S. Malik	5	7	1	110	53*	18.33
N.F.C. Martin	5	10	1	74	26	8.22
C.J. Townsend	10	9	3	61	22	10.16
A.W. Maclay	5	8	4	16	6*	4.00
P.W. Trimby	5	4	1	21	11	7.00
I.J. Sutcliffe	5	4	1	18	8*	6.00
C.J. Hollins	8	10	2	415	131	51.87
R.S. Yeabsley	6	3	1	53	52*	26.50

Team totals and results

Match	1st inns	2nd inns	Result
v. Durham	20	73	L
v. Hampshire	162	—	D
v. Glamorgan	257	110	D
v. Nottinghamshire	238	103	D
v. Warwickshire	47	—	D
v. Leicestershire	139	229	D
v. Yorkshire	212	166	L
v. Surrey	314	210	D
v. Worcestershire	95	252	L
v. Cambridge University	453	—	D

BOWLING

Bowling Averages

Bowler	Overs–Mdns–Runs–Wkts	Average
S.C. Ecclestone	281.3–66–768–22	34.90
A.W. Maclay	204.4–35–669–9	74.33
P.W. Trimby	195–33–621–19	32.68
N.F.C. Martin	144.4–27–480–7	68.57
G.I. Macmillan	94–17–324–7	46.28
H.S. Malik	68–14–241–7	34.42
C.J. Hollins	236.3–32–890–19	46.84
R.R. Montgomerie	3–0–18–0	–
R.S. Yeabsley	174.1–27–567–21	27.00
C.M. Gupte	1–0–16–0	–

DERBYSHIRE CCC

BATTING

FIELDING FIGURES

28 – K.M. Krikken (ct 26/st 2)
18 – A.S. Rollins
17 – C.J. Adams
15 – D.G. Cork
12 – T.J.G. O'Gorman
11 – P.D. Bowler
9 – M.J. Vandrau
7 – K.J. Barnett
6 – S.J. Base and subs
5 – M. Azharuddin
4 – C.M. Wells
2 – P.A.J. DeFreitas and F.A. Griffith
1 – A.E. Warner and D.E. Malcolm

†C.J. Adams retired hurt
‡M.J. Vandrau absent

AXA EQUITY AND LAW LEAGUE – AVERAGES

BATTING

	M	Inns	NO	Runs	HS	Av	100s	50s	Ct/st
M. Azharuddin	11	7	4	436	111*	145.33	1	4	1
C.J. Adams	14	13	3	485	119*	48.50	1	–	9
K.J. Barnett	13	12	2	379	56*	47.37	–	4	6
P.D. Bowler	12	11	1	354	67	35.40	–	2	4
P.A.J. DeFreitas	11	5	2	105	33	35.00	–	–	2
T.J.G. O'Gorman	16	15	6	309	63*	34.33	–	1	2
D.G. Cork	12	9	–	275	66	30.55	–	1	6
K.M. Krikken	13	4	3	30	15	30.00	–	–	22
A.E. Warner	11	5	4	27	27*	27.00	–	–	1
C.M. Wells	12	5	2	49	28*	24.50	–	–	1
F.A. Griffith	7	5	2	68	31	22.66	–	–	2
A.S. Rollins	9	3	–	122	35	17.42	–	–	10
M.J. Vandrau	8	3	–	19	10	6.33	–	–	6
S.J. Base	10	1	–	3	3	3.00	–	–	–
I.G. Steer	2	1	–	1	1	1.00	–	–	1

also – D.E. Malcolm 11 matches; O.H. Mortensen 3 matches;
R.W. Sladdin and A.J. Harris each one match

BOWLING

	Overs	Mds	Runs	Wkts	Av	Best	5/inn
S.J. Base	72	1	274	14	19.57	3-20	–
A.J. Harris	8	–	49	2	24.50	2-49	–
A.E. Warner	78.5	3	410	16	25.62	4-33	–
D.E. Malcolm	75.2	1	419	16	26.18	3-41	–
P.A.J. DeFreitas	83	6	314	11	28.54	4-9	–
C.M. Wells	85.5	5	431	14	30.78	3-55	–
F.A. Griffith	46	2	246	7	35.14	2-27	–
D.G. Cork	86.2	2	412	11	37.45	4-44	–
K.J. Barnett	6	–	50	1	50.00	1-13	–
M.J. Vandrau	38	2	226	4	56.50	3-25	–
O.H. Mortensen	21	1	122	2	61.00	2-53	–
R.W. Sladdin	4	–	24	–	–	–	–
C.J. Adams	4	–	46	–	–	–	–

BOWLING

BOWLING	D.E. Malcolm	D.G. Cork	C.M. Wells	P.A.J. DeFreitas	R.W. Sladdin	A.E. Warner	O.H. Mortensen	A.J. Harris	C.J. Adams	M. Azharuddin	P.D. Bowler	F.A. Griffith	M.J. Vandrau	M. Taylor	K.J. Barnett	S.J. Base	Byes	Leg-byes	Wides	No-balls	Total	Wkts
v. Durham (Chesterfield)	28–3–108–0	23–3–96–2	22–6–85–0	37–1–150–4	43.5–8–180–0												2	4	2	32	625	6
28 April–1 May	10–1–62–1	10–1–47–1		11–1–41–1	1.2–0–10–0												2	6		20	162	3
v. Hampshire (Southampton)	17–4–85–2	7–2–31–0		16.5–1–59–3		16–3–68–2	7–2–18–1										4		2	46	271	10
5–9 May	9–2–19–1			8–0–32–0		7–0–31–0														20	119	1
v. Surrey (The Oval)			17–0–73–0		50–8–155–2	25–2–85–2		20–4–125–2									1	7	4	28	570	6
12–16 May																						
v. Worcestershire (Derby)	23–7–111–2					22–6–72–1		12–1–40–3	12–1–61–0			15–1–58–3	2–1–3–0				13	5	2	16	302	9 A
19–23 May																						
v. Nottinghamshire (Ilkeston)	24.4–7–59–5		12–2–29–1	22–7–39–3	9.2–3–4–1							13–4–35–0					2	1		6	199	10
26–30 May	24.3–2–91–1	18.5–4–61–4		25–8–6–1	11.2–4–8–1							8–1–19–2	8–1–25–1					11		22	255	9
v. Leicestershire (Derby)	18–0–121–3			17.4–7–2		18–7–42–1											3	2		23	273	10
9–13 June				17–4–40–1		9–0–45–0											3			7	263	3
v. Glamorgan (Cardiff)	16–1–89–1					32–7–94–2						18–1–66–0	17.4–4–77–1	27–9–43–1		16–4–58–4	7	28	2	12	402	10
16–20 June	35.3–7–109–4											13.4–3–32–3	28–11–55–2	11.1–6–25–3		7–0–31–2		5		4	196	10
v. New Zealanders (Derby)	21–6–71–3	12–1–42–2				19–4–53–0	16–3–30–1						11–1–59–1		1–0–1–0	20–2–88–2	4	5	1	10	210	9 B
25–7 June																	11	3		54	196	10
v. Middlesex (Derby)	25–4–102–2	22–4–108–1	22–5–52–4										18–2–58–0	10–1–57–0				16			545	10
30 June–4 July																						
v. Lancashire (Blackpool)	12–2–43–4		7–2–8–3	12.4–3–39–6									38.5–10–102–3			31.5–8–115–2	21	1		12	83	10
14–18 July	37–7–119–0		21–6–47–0										32–6–97–3				7	9	1	50	589	10
v. Northamptonshire	28–1–98–2	35–1–135–4		29.5–128–2			0.5–0–8–0							28–8–67–1	23–2–91–3			13		7	529	9
(Northampton) 21–5 July		19–5–61–0																			8	0 C
v. Warwickshire (Chesterfield)	11–2–38–2	19.2–1–79–2	4.4–2–12–1			15–6–39–4							5–0–59–0		12.3–2–31–5	17.5–2–92–5		6		26	280	10
28 July–1 August	11–2–58–0	12–2–31–0				9–1–30–0							24–1–87–3			11–2–41–2		6	1	16	259	10
v. Gloucestershire (Chesterfield)	16–1–57–2	15–4–30–2				19–6–34–0							3–2–10–0		9–1–39–0	15–1–63–2		8	2	18	195	10
4–8 August		26–3–81–4														9–1–39–0	2	9	1	2	263	10
v. Sussex (Eastbourne)	29.5–8–95–6	24.5–8–29–6		27.5–7–73–5									10–2–26–1			26.2–4–105–0		7	2	4	171	10
11–15 August	15.3–4–37–4	30–9–80–6		6.2–1–16–0									22–3–84–1			10–1–39–0		8	1	27	127	9 D
v. Kent (Derby)	19–4–49–3	15–2–52–2	11–0–48–1			17–5–50–1							21–0–53–4		2–0–5–0		6	14	5	8	392	10
18–22 August		16–4–49–0				21–2–95–4							23.2–6–68–3					8		3	247	10
v. Yorkshire (Sheffield)	22.5–6–63–4	15–2–52–2	11–3–23–2						11–1–35–1						3.5–1–3–2		2	3	2	8	235	10
30 August–2 September	7–2–14–1	16–4–49–0	7–1–31–0						6–1–16–2						12–0–42–3			6		34	222	9
v. Essex (Derby)	9.2–0–51–3	10–0–58–2		23–11–47–1												16–1–57–4		7	2	8	180	10
8–12 September				9.2–1–12–0						8–0–40–0	1–0–17–0											
v. Somerset (Taunton)	13–2–43–1	15–2–50–2		14–4–28–1		16–3–49–1			1–0–2–0				19–4–54–0			19–4–54–0	4	4	1	2	228	4 E
15–19 September																						
Bowler's average	482.2–83–1792–57 31.43	329.1–55–1112–37 30.05	153.1–31–469–13 36.07	273.5–59–812–35 23.20	115.1–20–427–4 106.75	256–53–817–19 43.00	23–5–48–2 24.00	32–1–165–5 33.00	30–3–114–3 38.00	8–0–40–0 –	1–0–17–0 –	67.4–12–210–8 26.25	290.5–63–965–26 37.11	82.1–24–205–7 29.28	54.2–5–173–13 13.30	194–30–782–23 34.00						

A W.P.C. Weston retired hurt
B M.D. Crowe retired ill, absent ill
C T.J.G. O'Gorman 0.5–0–8–0
D A.S. Rollins 4–1–32–0
E I.G. Steer 2–0–12–0

M.E. Cassar 9–2–29–0, 15.2–1–65–3

FIELDING FIGURES

56 – C.W. Scott (ct 54/st 2)
13 – P. Bainbridge
11 – W. Larkins
10 – S. Hutton
8 – S.J.E. Brown and J.E. Morris
7 – J.I. Longley
5 – D.A. Graveney
4 – M. Saxelby
3 – J. Wood, J.A. Daley and A.C. Cummins
2 – G. Fowler
1 – S.D. Birbeck, P.J. Berry, A. Walker and D.M. Cox
†W. Larkins retired hurt

AXA EQUITY AND LAW LEAGUE – AVERAGES

BATTING

	M	Inns	NO	Runs	HS	Av	100s	50s	Ct/st
J.A. Daley	8	6	2	218	98*	54.50	–	2	1
D.A. Graveney	12	6	5	54	25*	54.00	–	–	1
A.C. Cummins	14	10	2	337	67	42.15	–	2	1
W. Larkins	12	11	1	421	131*	42.10	–	4	4
M. Saxelby	11	10	0	329	79*	36.55	–	3	3
J.I. Longley	13	12	2	342	88	34.20	–	3	–
P. Bainbridge	14	10	1	196	32	21.77	–	–	4
C.W. Scott	15	11	3	147	45	18.37	–	–	15/5
S. Hutton	9	7	–	121	42	17.28	–	1	1
J.E. Morris	15	13	1	189	77	15.75	–	1	5
A. Walker	15	9	3	75	15	12.50	–	–	4
J. Wood	9	6	1	44	9	8.80	–	–	–
G. Fowler	5	2	–	9	9	4.50	–	–	–
S.D. Birbeck	2	1	1	0	0*	0.00	–	–	1
D.A. Blenkiron	5	2	1	39	39*	–	–	–	–
S.J.E. Brown	6	2	2	5	5*	–	–	–	–

also – S. Lugsden one match; D.M. Cox three matches

BOWLING

	Overs	Mds	Runs	Wkts	Av	Best	5/inn
A. Walker	111.5	3	658	25	26.32	4-43	–
A.C. Cummins	110	3	571	20	28.55	3-32	–
P. Bainbridge	92.2	3	493	14	35.21	4-32	–
D.A. Graveney	89	5	388	10	38.80	3-49	–
J. Wood	66.3	5	340	8	42.50	2-26	–
S. Lugsden	8	–	55	1	55.00	1-55	–
S.J.E. Brown	46.4	2	282	4	70.50	2-35	–
D.M. Cox	20	–	89	1	89.00	1-25	–
S.D. Birbeck	26	–	166	1	166.00	1-47	–
D.A. Blenkiron	3	–	25	–	–	–	–

DURHAM CCC

BATTING

The full match-by-match batting and bowling scorecard tables for Durham CCC (opponents from Oxford University, Derbyshire, Essex, Nottinghamshire, Gloucestershire, Warwickshire, Northamptonshire, Sussex, Middlesex, Surrey, South Africans, Leicestershire, Yorkshire, Somerset, Kent, Glamorgan, Hampshire, Lancashire and Worcestershire) with season averages columns (M, Inns, NO, Runs, HS, Av).

BOWLING	S.J.E. Brown	J. Wood	S.D. Birbeck	P. Bainbridge	D.A. Graveney	A.C. Cummins	S. Lugsden	P.J. Berry	D.M. Cox	W. Larkins	J.E. Morris	A. Walker	J.P. Searle	J.A. Daley	Byes	Leg-byes	Wides	No-balls	Total	Wkts
v. Oxford University (Oxford)	5.2–1–11–1	4–0–9–0	1–1–0–0																20	0
13–15 April	9.3–6–8–5	8–3–15–3	6–1–13–2	8–2–18–0	9–4–12–0										5	2	1		73	10
v. Derbyshire (Chesterfield)	24–2–96–3	22–3–96–2		14–4–34–1	11.1–4–19–1	26–5–87–3									5	4	1	22	341	10
28 April–1 May	22–7–93–5	11–0–49–0		16–4–61–1	42–11–144–3	23–4–72–1									4	19	4	14	442	10
v. Essex (Stockton)	15–2–50–1	26.2–0–110–6		29–9–90–0	29–8–63–1	30–7–94–1										16	5	22	423	10
5–9 May		2.1–0–20–0		1–0–8–0		2–0–8–0												2	36	0
v. Nottinghamshire		14–1–48–1			31.5–7–80–6	16–2–58–2	18–4–58–0	4–0–32–0							2	7		18	285	10
(Trent Bridge) 12–16 May		2–0–12–0			12–5–29–0	7–1–19–1	8.2–0–15–1	11–2–26–0							3	9		2	113	2
v. Gloucestershire	20–6–49–3	14–5–30–3		5–1–18–1	1–0–2–0	18.3–6–59–3									4	7	7	10	169	10
(Gateshead Fell) 19–23 May	18.4–4–43–3	18–5–48–5		8–1–27–0	27–10–45–0	17–5–26–2									1	11	1	19	201	10
v. Warwickshire (Edgbaston)	27–1–164–1			33–6–169–1	7–1–34–0	28–1–158–2			30–5–163–0	5–0–39–0	5.5–1–33–0				28	22	2	26	810	4
2–6 June																				
v. Northamptonshire	18.1–3–49–4	9–1–31–0		2–0–8–1		14–5–32–5	8–1–34–0									2	2	4	156	10
(Hartlepool) 9–13 June	23–5–72–2	15.2–4–57–2		3–0–5–0		23–4–72–5	20–2–84–1				4–2–4–0				4	4	8	20	302	10
v. Sussex (Hove)	23–5–79–1	19–1–102–3			26–5–57–0	24–5–84–5						21–4–76–1			3	10	1	39	411	10
16–20 June	4–0–15–0	3–1–10–1			9.1–1–49–0	5–0–11–1						6–0–24–0					1		109	2
v. Middlesex (Lord's)	33.5–5–113–5	0.5–0–5–0		32.1–8–116–1	44–6–128–2	30–10–95–1					9–0–37–1				5	12	2	18	511	10
23–7 June																				
v. Surrey (Darlington)	20.4–5–62–4	13–2–46–2		16–5–37–1	8–4–21–2	21–6–47–1					3–0–9–0				3	11	1	28	236	10
30 June–4 July	25.3–2–101–3	23–4–115–1		13–2–62–0	21–2–99–1	26–3–102–1					6–0–42–0				9	8	3	8	538	6
v. South Africans	25–1–97–2	30–1–110–0		15.5–3–60–1			21–5–64–0		22–4–92–1							5	7	10	428	4
(Chester-le-Street) 12–14 July																				
v. Leicestershire (Durham)	27–2–111–4			15–4–37–0	29–5–87–3	24–4–71–2	19–4–89–0								7	26	6	12	428	10
21–5 July																				
v. Yorkshire (Durham)	33.3–3–131–5			16–5–48–0	31–12–53–2	31–7–89–2						27–9–76–1			1	7	6	14	405	10
28 July–1 August	18–2–48–2			3–1–8–0	40–17–64–3	18–0–55–3						17–3–48–0				7	1	18	230	8
v. Somerset (Taunton)	18–2–56–1	10.2–2–59–1		2–0–6–0		18–3–64–6						16–3–35–1			8	6	1	24	234	10
4–8 August	4–0–35–0	6–0–47–1		1.5–0–6–0		5–0–38–0						3–0–14–0				1		4	141	1
v. Kent (Canterbury)	22–1–111–1			24–4–72–4	17.3–5–66–3	24–6–67–2			13–1–54–0						3	12	1	22	385	10
11–15 August	3–0–15–1				9–1–34–0	3–0–7–0			9.5–1–36–0							4		4	96	1
v. Glamorgan (Hartlepool)	18–4–68–6	5–0–31–1		0.5–0–4–1		14–2–62–1						9–2–37–1				4	2	28	206	10
18–22 August	17–2–80–3	11.2–0–53–2		12–2–29–0		10–0–59–1						17–2–59–4				2	2	10	282	10
v. Hampshire (Portsmouth)	27–3–92–1	30–0–141–5		15–3–58–1	34.5–6–126–3	27–1–91–0										4	6	56	512	10
25–9 August	15–3–37–1	15–1–63–1		14–1–55–0	16.3–7–35–1	5–1–22–0									1	2		6	215	3
v. Lancashire (Stockton)	19–5–56–5	13–2–67–4		9–2–18–0		12–1–49–1							1–0–7–0		2	3	9	16	202	10
8–12 September	8–1–21–0	8–1–37–0		2–2–0–0										2–0–9–0		3	1	6	70	0
v. Worcestershire (Worcester)	21–3–81–1	14.2–0–90–1		5–0–28–0		19–3–70–4	12–0–68–1									14	2	18	351	7
15–19 September																				
	565.1–86–	347.4–37–	7–2–	315.4–69–	456–121–	520.3–92–	106.2–16–	15–2–	74.5–11–	5–0–	27.5–3–	116–23–	1–0–	2–0–						
	2044–74	1501–45	23–2	1082–14	1247–31	1768–56	412–3	58–0	345–1	39–0	125–1	369–8	7–0	9–0						
Bowler's average	27.62	33.35	11.50	77.28	40.22	31.57	137.33	–	345.00	–	125.00	45.12	–	–						

AXA EQUITY AND LAW LEAGUE – AVERAGES

BATTING	M	Inns	NO	Runs	HS	Av	100s	50s	Ct/st
G.A. Gooch	11	11	0	415	101	37.72	1	2	1
N. Hussain	16	16	1	504	76	33.60	–	4	8
J.P. Stephenson	15	15	2	391	73	30.07	–	3	5
P.J. Prichard	7	7	1	154	65*	25.66	–	1	5
M.A. Garnham	9	9	3	186	39	23.25	–	–	10
R.M. Pearson	9	6	5	23	7	23.00	–	–	–
N.V. Knight	13	13	1	275	61*	22.91	–	1	3
J.J.B. Lewis	6	5	1	70	23	17.50	–	–	1
N. Shahid	7	7	1	113	41	16.14	–	–	2
M.C. Ilott	9	5	2	43	24	14.33	–	–	2
R.C. Irani	16	16	–	185	33	11.56	–	–	2
M. Diwan	5	4	–	31	14	7.75	–	–	–
T.D. Topley	5	5	1	23	14*	7.66	–	–	3
R.J. Rollins	9	8	4	27	9*	6.75	–	–	8/3
M.S. Kasprowicz	15	12	4	61	19*	5.08	–	–	2
P.M. Such	13	8	2	29	4	4.83	–	–	2
S.J.W. Andrew	13	4	3	4	4	4.00	–	–	1
D.M. Cousins	11	5	1	9	6	2.25	–	–	–

BOWLING	Overs	Mds	Runs	Wkts	Av	Best	5inn
D.M. Cousins	73.3	5	351	18	19.50	3-18	–
R.C. Irani	58.2	6	248	11	22.54	3-22	–
M.C. Ilott	66.2	5	303	12	25.25	4-25	–
J.P. Stephenson	104.4	3	476	18	26.44	2-21	–
R.M. Pearson	55.2	2	259	8	32.37	2-33	–
P.M. Such	100	4	372	10	37.20	2-27	–
N.V. Knight	6	–	41	1	41.00	1-41	–
M.S. Kasprowicz	94.4	6	458	11	41.63	2-38	–
T.D. Topley	17.1	1	129	3	43.00	2-45	–
S.J.W. Andrew	3	1	23	–	–	–	–

ESSEX CCC — BATTING (first table)

BATTING	M	Inns	NO	Runs	HS	Av
G.A. Gooch	11	19	2	1385	236	81.47
P.J. Prichard	11	17	2	569	119	37.93
J.J.B. Lewis	16	29	2	751	109	28.88
N. Hussain	15	31	2	922	115*	31.79
N. Shahid	10	18	4	326	91	23.28
M.A. Garnham	18	30	5	542	62	21.68
R.C. Irani	18	29	6	965	119	41.95
M.S. Kasprowicz	17	24	4	326	44	16.30
M.C. Ilott	15	20	9	149	30*	13.54
P.M. Such	16	15	12	149	29	7.84
J.H. Childs	16	17	12	96	42*	19.20
J.P. Stephenson	12	27	1	535	144	20.57
N.V. Knight	21	1	–	9	9	47.20
R.J. Rollins	1	1	–	9	9	9.00
D.M. Cousins	3	4	1	45	11	11.25
R.M. Pearson	4	5	1	24	11	4.80
T.D. Topley	2	2	–	2	2	2.00
S.J.W. Andrew	6	8	7	37	11	5.28
M. Diwan	1	2	–	0	0	0.00
D.D.J. Robinson	1	1	–	38	38	38.00

ESSEX CCC — BATTING (second table)

BATTING	M	Inns	NO	Runs	HS	Av
G.A. Gooch	11	19	2	1385	236	81.47
P.J. Prichard	11	17	2	569	119	37.93
J.J.B. Lewis	16	29	2	751	109	28.88
N. Hussain	15	31	2	922	115*	31.79
N. Shahid	10	18	4	326	91	23.28
M.A. Garnham	18	30	5	542	62	21.68
R.C. Irani	18	29	6	965	119	41.95
M.S. Kasprowicz	17	24	4	326	44	16.30
M.C. Ilott	15	20	9	149	30*	13.54
P.M. Such	16	15	12	149	29	7.84
J.H. Childs	16	17	12	96	42*	19.20
J.P. Stephenson	12	27	1	535	144	20.57
N.V. Knight	21	1	–	944	157	47.20
R.J. Rollins	1	1	–	9	9	9.00
D.M. Cousins	3	4	1	45	11	11.25
R.M. Pearson	4	5	1	24	11	4.80
T.D. Topley	2	2	–	2	2	2.00
S.J.W. Andrew	6	8	7	37	11	5.28
M. Diwan	1	2	–	0	0	0.00
D.D.J. Robinson	1	1	–	38	38	38.00

BOWLING

	M.C. Ilott	M.S. Kasprowicz	R.C. Irani	G.A. Gooch	P.M. Such	J.H. Childs	N. Shahid	J.P. Stephenson	P.J. Prichard	R.M. Pearson	D.M. Cousins	S.J.W. Andrew	T.D. Topley	N. Hussain	N.V. Knight	J.J.B. Lewis	Byes	Leg-byes	Wides	No-balls	Total	Wkts
v. Hampshire (Southampton) 28 April–1 May	34.5-7-74-4	29-6-69-3	19-4-64-0	3-2-1-0	20-9-49-1	8-2-30-0	5-1-20-2										1	13			321	10
v. Durham (Stockton) 5–9 May	21.5-5-60-2 21-2-87-1	22-10-44-1 21-7-61-6	2-1-6-0 8-2-17-2	 1.3-1-0-1	28.5-9-66-7 7-4-7-0	2-0-9-0	 2-0-10-0											6 3	 2	 4	191 175	10 10
v. Kent (Chelmsford) 12–16 May	21.5-5-80-3 17-2-60-3	13.5-2-55-2 18-3-90-3	 12.2-2-27-4		47-21-61-4	30-9-65-1	 5-1-25-0										1	9 2	 1	 2	281 191	10 10
v. Yorkshire (Leeds) 19–23 May	6-2-22-0 29.5-7-89-5	14-0-67-1 30-11-75-1	14-2-48-0 7-0-47-2		39-8-133-5 4-1-10-0	 27.4-5-127-4											6	11 13	4	 14	399 307	10 10
v. New Zealanders (Chelmsford) 28–30 May	18-3-46-1 27-5-69-1	17-1-56-1 21-2-77-2	 21-4-66-2	 2-1-1-0	17-4-75-0	7-3-24-0 19-7-33-1		25-9-74-4 10-2-37-0									4 2	13 9		10 20	203 428	4 5
v. Gloucestershire (Chelmsford) 2–6 June	1-0-5-0 21.4-4-53-1	9-1-40-1 24-4-63-3	3-0-11-0		7-0-23-0 11-0-48-0	24-2-71-6		16-1-63-0 9-1-26-2	1-0-11-0								1 6	1 13	 2	14 16	108 266	3 8
v. Worcestershire (Worcester) 9–13 June	6.2-1-19-0	12.4-0-51-1 23-3-80-2	4-0-12-0 9-0-45-0					30-11-82-2 21-6-95-2									7	8 20	 2	12 22	279 381	3 8
v. Cambridge University (Cambridge) 15–17 June		2-0-12-0				14-5-20-1 11-4-16-1	12-4-25-1	16-2-38-2 6-0-26-0		27-10-54-1 13-1-53-1	24.5-5-78-2 16-2-67-1		7-1-25-0 9-2-22-1	1-0-1-0			5	5 5	1 1	14 4	285 181	3 10
v. Nottinghamshire (Ilford) 23–7 June	21-5-56-2 4.1-1-7-1	31-4-120-5	29-6-91-4 17-2-53-0		39-10-99-2 30-9-71-4	24.2-5-60-1 24.3-12-55-4		11-1-44-0		14-4-39-1 13-3-42-1	18.2-3-35-6 21-3-65-2						7	8 7	1	16 2	144 409	10 10
v. Leicestershire (Leicester) 30 June–4 July			22-5-77-2 4-1-11-1 23.2-2-99-3			16-6-45-0	6-0-26-0	19-5-50-1		7-1-38-0	14-5-26-1 18-3-66-1						16 11	7 7	 2	 20	167 462	8 10
v. Glamorgan (Southend) 14–18 July		7-1-28-0 3-0-14-0	7-4-11-1 7-0-27-2		28-8-78-5 29-9-77-3	27.3-4-65-3 29.2-8-58-5		6-2-22-0 1-0-4-0				16-6-31-1 2-1-1-0					6	7 8	1 1	11 6	248 189	10 10
v. Warwickshire (Edgbaston) 21–5 July		13.2-1-62-1 15-0-59-1	24-3-77-3		10-1-46-1 18-1-74-1	19-2-63-4		15-5-57-2				18-3-58-1 12-4-28-2					4	5 1	1 1	20 14	361 268	10 10
v. Middlesex (Uxbridge) 28 July–1 August		31-7-112-2 7-1-24-0	8-3-19-2	12-6-14-1 3-0-9-1	24-1-105-0 5-0-31-0	29-4-75-1 13-1-66-1		6-1-20-0 30-7-95-2				25.3-2-114-1 10-0-53-0					2	8 1	5	52	525 277	7 3
v. Lancashire (Chelmsford) 4–8 August	22-5-73-0	16-1-101-2			43.1-12-66-4	41-13-95-3		18-2-65-1							11.4-0-61-1	8-1-32-0	8	6		10	414	10
v. Surrey (Colchester) 11–15 August	12.4-6-24-6 15-7-32-2	13-3-51-4 12-1-44-0						19-3-50-2 17-5-37-3									 2	13 3	2 3	 16	88 203	10 10
v. Somerset (Weston-super-Mare) 18–22 August	28-8-87-4 14-2-56-0	19.2-2-57-2 27.2-2-83-7	9-1-26-0		32-14-46-6 5-1-14-0							13-3-27-0 19-5-29-2						4 10	 1	10 14	226 243	10 10
v. Sussex (Chelmsford) 30 August–2 September	22-5-72-6 26-5-57-4	15.2-4-72-2 11-5-19-0			4-0-19-1 10-1-38-1	25-7-62-0		15-2-46-0 15-2-54-1									13	10 10	 2	16 2	246 277	10 10
v. Derbyshire (Derby) 8–12 September	22-6-65-4 7-1-25-1	18.4-4-68-3 7-3-23-0			35-8-116-6 5-1-14-0			14-4-51-2 5-3-3-0				8-0-33-0						1 1		4 8	241 52	10 1
v. Northamptonshire (Chelmsford) 15–19 September	29-3-62-2	24-3-92-4			33-8-94-0	31.3-12-104-4		8-1-27-0									12	13	1	6	404	10
Bowler's average	447.3-97- 1280-53 24.15	527.3-92- 1869-60 31.15	249.4-42- 834-28 29.78	21.3-10- 25-3 8.33	538-143- 1472-51 28.86	464.5-122- 1254-39 32.15	30-6- 106-3 35.33	332-75- 1066-26 41.00	1-0- 11-0 –	74-19- 226-4 56.50	112-21- 337-13 25.92	150.3-33- 425-9 47.22	16-3- 47-1 47.00	1-0- 1-0 –	11.4-0- 61-1 61.00	8-1- 32-0 –						

AXA EQUITY AND LAW LEAGUE – AVERAGES

BATTING

	M	Inns	NO	Runs	HS	Av	100s	50s	Ct/st
H. Morris	13	13	2	530	127*	48.18	1	3	2
S.P. James	15	15	1	452	102	30.13	1	3	4
O.D. Gibson	17	15	7	206	33	25.75	–	1	4
A. Dale	13	13	1	304	61	25.33	–	1	2
M.P. Maynard	15	15	1	349	65	24.92	–	2	10
D.L. Hemp	11	10	3	253	73	23.00	–	–	1
P.A. Cottey	17	16	3	288	70	22.15	–	2	5
R.P. Lefebvre	17	10	3	102	29*	14.57	–	–	5
C.P. Metson	17	13	4	125	26*	13.88	–	–	19/5
S.R. Barwick	16	8	8	60	26*	12.00	–	–	2
S.L. Watkin	14	7	4	17	8*	5.66	–	–	–
		4	2	17		2.83	–	–	–

also – A.D. Shaw one match; G.P. Butcher three matches

BOWLING

	Overs	Mds	Runs	Wkts	Av	Best	5/inn
R.P. Lefebvre	117	5	438	24	18.25	4-23	–
R.D.B. Croft	101.4	1	470	21	22.38	6-20	1
S.R. Barwick	120	3	483	21	23.00	5-36	–
A. Dale	34	1	198	6	33.00	2-21	–
G.P. Butcher	10	–	66	2	33.00	2-8	–
S.L. Watkin	101	8	379	11	34.45	3-19	–
O.D. Gibson	92.5	5	446	12	37.16	2-35	–
P.A. Cottey	6	–	42	1	42.00	1-17	–
D.L. Hemp	0.2	–	1	–	–	–	–

GLAMORGAN CCC

BATTING

Season aggregate (first-class):

	M	Inns	NO	Runs	HS	Av
S.P. James	16	28	5	877	150	38.13
P.A. Cottey	19	33	3	1393	191	51.59
D.L. Hemp	21	38	4	1452	136	42.70
A.J. Dalton	6	10	2	188	51*	23.50
O.D. Gibson	20	31	4	710	85	26.29
G.P. Butcher	3	3	–	50	41	16.66
R.P. Lefebvre	12	14	3	240	33	21.81
C.P. Metson	18	22	4	398	51	22.11
S.D. Thomas	3	3	1	15	15*	2.33
S. Bastien	1	1	–	7	6	3.50
S.R. Barwick	16	31	2	885	106	30.51
H. Morris	17	28	1	676	131	25.03
A. Dale	18	24	1	974	118	36.07
M.P. Maynard	18	21	1	569	80	25.86
R.D.B. Croft	6	8	1	92	14	9.20
S.L. Watkin	3	4	1	249	94	35.57
A. Roseberry	2	2	–	18	14	9.00
A.D. Shaw				18	14	9.00
B.S. Phelps				2	2*	6.00
O.T. Parkin						–

First half of season matches (in column order):
v. Oxford University, 20–2 April (Oxford); v. Warwickshire, 28 April–1 May (Edgbaston); v. Northamptonshire, 5–9 May (Northampton); v. Yorkshire, 12–16 May (Cardiff); v. Sussex, 26–30 May (Hove); v. Surrey, 2–6 June (Swansea); v. New Zealanders, 8–10 June (Swansea); v. Cambridge University, 11–13 June (Cambridge); v. Derbyshire, 16–20 June (Cardiff); v. Lancashire, 23–27 June (Colwyn Bay); v. Gloucestershire, 30 June–4 July (Bristol); v. Essex, 14–18 July (Southend)

Second half of season matches (in column order):
v. Kent, 21–25 July (Abergavenny); v. Somerset, 28 July–1 August (Swansea); v. Middlesex, 4–8 August (Lord's); v. South Africans, 13–15 August (Pontypridd); v. Durham, 18–22 August (Hartlepool); v. Leicestershire, 25–9 August (Cardiff); v. Nottinghamshire, 30 August–2 September (Worksop); v. Worcestershire, 8–12 September (Cardiff); v. Hampshire, 15–19 September (Southampton)

BOWLING

BOWLING	O.D. Gibson	S. Bastien	S.D. Thomas	R.P. Lefebvre	S.R. Barwick	G.P. Butcher	P.A. Cottey	S.L. Watkin	R.D.B. Croft	A. Dale	D.L. Hemp	B.S. Phelps	O.T. Parkin	M.P. Maynard	Byes	Leg-byes	Wides	No-balls	Total	Wks
v. Oxford University (Oxford) 20-2 April	9-0-31-0	19-9-27-0	21-2-80-2	23-5-48-3	22-12-24-2	7-0-36-2									4	11	2	10	257	9
		9-3-12-1	9-1-28-1	6-3-13-0	8-2-26-0	3-0-18-0	1-0-8-0										1	2	110	2
v. Warwickshire (Edgbaston) 28 April-1 May	30-4-134-2			39-11-122-0											7	9	1	14	657	7
v. Northamptonshire (Northampton) 5-9 May	22.5-3-73-1			25-7-59-1				32-7-99-1	51-17-173-2	14-3-57-1					12	7	1	12	338	4
																			0	0
v. Yorkshire (Cardiff) 12-16 May	26.2-6-86-4			26-12-65-1				24-9-58-0	32-9-72-1	14-4-58-0					9	14	1	8	339	3
	12-3-40-0			11-4-28-0				27-3-64-4	18-5-52-0	18-5-49-1						4		6	170	5
v. Sussex (Hove) 26-30 May		16.4-4-55-1					4-4-0-23-0	12-3-20-1	16-3-44-1	8-0-34-1					2	8	2	29	300	5
		14.3-5-47-2		32-10-74-2				20-5-59-0	17-4-48-2	17-4-48-2						8	2	2	260	6
v. Surrey (Swansea) 2-6 June								14-2-44-1	22-5-71-2	8-2-29-0						8		2	429	10
								29-1-115-4	33-4-103-1	14-4-40-1					7	9		14		
v. New Zealanders (Swansea) 8-10 June	10-0-54-0	18-4-58-2		22-7-49-1	22-11-30-0			13-5-18-1	33-9-98-1	12-4-41-1					5	8		11	282	5
	10-0-61-0	8-0-53-0		7-3-9-1	15-10-16-0		6-1-16-1	18-9-31-1	26-2-120-1	12-4-41-2					4	5	1	4	306	5
v. Cambridge University (Cambridge) 11-13 June		12-4-25-0							37-11-100-1	10-4-14-2					3	7			244	8
		8-6-3-1							14.2-5-47-2	4-2-6-0	3-0-15-0				3	4	1		104	4
v. Derbyshire (Cardiff) 16-20 June	26-2-117-2	30.5-5-87-1		25-10-39-2	31.5-11-67-0			31.2-3-143-6	33-12-67-0	14-1-47-1					5	9		20	470	10
	4-0-32-1	3.2-0-17-0		21.5-5-64-3	20-11-28-4			8-0-39-0	24-6-91-1						1	1		20	129	2
v. Lancashire (Colwyn Bay) 23-7 June	29-4-91-2			1-1-0-0	28.2-14-44-5		3-1-7-0	30-10-59-4	9-1-43-1	4-1-25-1					4	12	2	16	359	6
v. Gloucestershire (Bristol) 30 June-4 July	13-4-46-1			2-9-19-2	29-10-50-1			12-6-26-2	10-1-37-0						6	9	4	10	264	6
				15-6-24-0				18.1-5-36-3								1		17	149	10
v. Essex (Southend) 14-18 July	17-4-45-2			8-1-27-1	7.4-1-15-2			17-4-45-1	19-5-58-4						3	3		13	191	10
	24-8-47-2			25.2-6-63-4	29-7-73-2			29-6-63-4	25-4-77-1							1		4	274	10
v. Kent (Abergavenny) 14-18 July	14-2-50-2			9-0-47-0				30-13-85-2		5-2-7-2					8	6		2	181	10
	19-1-90-1							14-5-25-1		6-3-3-1					5	5	8	10	408	10
v. Somerset (Swansea) 21-5 July	12-0-73-0							15-5-38-2	34-5-88-3	15-4-44-2					2	3		6	330	10
	32-9-79-5				34-1-10-79-4		4-1-16-0	19-8-29-1		20-3-58-1		28-5-80-2	12-2-45-2		5	12		6	372	10
v. Middlesex (Lord's) 28 July-1 August	28-7-92-3				65.2-29-109-1					25-9-76-1		31-14-70-2	16-4-50-0		5	12	1	12	302	6
	21-2-87-0				19-10-44-1					11-3-42-1		6-1-16-0	20-2-56-2		4	7	2	12	267	10
v. South Africans (Pontypridd) 4-8 August	12-4-46-1				21-1-4-63-3					4-1-19-0		16-2-75-0	6-1-19-0		2	8		16	368	4
					40-11-113-2			16-2-60-1	34-6-102-2	3-0-9-0					12	4	1		288	6
v. Durham (Hartlepool) 13-15 August	7-2-18-3				14-5-41-2			12-2-36-0	17-2-41-1	3-0-17-0	2-0-2-0				6	6	2		140	8
	20-2-88-6				19-6-40-0			22-8-66-2	29-6-76-4						4	2	3		230	6
v. Leicestershire (Cardiff) 18-22 August	18-3-72-3				19.4-9-32-1	6-1-28-0		18-1-70-1	21-6-40-0	5-2-7-2					2	6	5	6	262	10
	18-4-67-1				9.5-6-13-2	10-3-24-0		24-8-58-3	26-8-80-5	6-3-3-1					1	1	1	22	244	10
v. Nottinghamshire (Worksop) 25-9 August	20-7-79-1				38-8-122-2	11-1-42-0		21-4-53-1	21-6-40-0	7-1-14-2					7	14	1	16	261	7
								35-5-107-1	24-6-64-0	15-4-41-2					1	17	6	14	476	6
v. Worcestershire (Cardiff) 30 August-2 September	19-2-64-6			29-10-67-2	25.4-8-64-2		6-0-36-1	17.1-1-48-2	5-0-30-0	6-1-44-0				1-0-10-0		12		8	265	10
v. Hampshire (Southampton) 8-12 September	8-2-25-0			8-2-11-1				6-1-16-0		5-0-25-1	3-0-24-0				2	1			123	3
15-19 September				24-3-68-1				30-3-98-5	30-7-65-2						2	7	1	2	331	10
Bowler's average	579.4-100-2169-60 36.15	138.3-40-384-8 48.00	30-3-108-3 36.00	365.2-10-896-25 35.84	549.4-208-1131-36 31.41	37-5-148-2 74.00	24.4-3-106-2 53.00	613.4-144-1708-55 31.05	689.3-156-2076-40 51.90	258.6-62-906-22 41.18	8-0-41-0 —	86-22-241-4 60.25	54-9-170-4 42.50	1-0-10-0 —						

AXA EQUITY AND LAW LEAGUE – AVERAGES

BATTING

	M	Inns	NO	Runs	HS	Av	100s	50s	Ct/st
M.W. Alleyne	16	16	3	588	102*	45.23	1	—	14
M.G.N. Windows	12	12	—	347	72	28.91	—	2	1
A.J. Wright	16	15	—	394	69	26.26	—	3	7
R.I. Dawson	16	16	1	268	45	17.86	—	—	2
M.C.J. Ball	11	9	4	81	28*	16.20	—	—	3
S.G. Hinks	8	6	—	95	31	15.83	—	—	1
T.H.C. Hancock	16	16	—	253	43	15.81	—	—	3
R.C. Russell	15	14	5	139	31	15.44	—	—	10/1
G.D. Hodgson	3	3	—	42	29	14.00	—	—	3
C.A. Walsh	14	13	2	196	70	15.07	—	1	3
M. Davies	9	5	—	121	30	12.10	—	—	2
A.M. Smith	10	7	4	40	14	10.00	—	—	3
K.E. Cooper	4	3	—	24	5*	8.00	—	—	1
R.M. Wight	4	3	—	14	10	4.66	—	—	—
A.M. Babington	6	2	—	14	4*	4.00	—	—	1
R.C.J. Williams	2	1	—	13	13*	—	—	—	—
J.M.M. Averis	2	1	—	2	2*	—	—	—	—

also – K.P. Sheeraz one match (ct 1)

BOWLING

	Overs	Mds	Runs	Wkts	Av	Best	5/inn
R.M. Wight	23	—	97	5	19.40	2-28	—
C.A. Walsh	83.1	10	352	18	19.55	4-20	—
R.C. Williams	106	3	548	19	28.84	3-33	—
A.M. Babington	41	3	232	7	33.14	3-9	—
T.H.C. Hancock	15	—	105	3	35.00	2-31	—
M. Davies	57.2	2	285	8	35.62	2-23	—
A.M. Smith	69	5	354	9	39.33	2-24	—
M.W. Alleyne	86.4	4	497	11	45.18	2-25	—
K.E. Cooper	27	—	156	3	52.00	1-19	—
M.C.J. Ball	63.3	1	368	7	52.57	2-26	—
K.P. Sheeraz	6	—	30	0	—	—	—
J.M.M. Averis	6	—	44	0	—	—	—

GLOUCESTERSHIRE CCC — BATTING

Season summary (both match-by-match tables share these aggregate columns):

	M	Inns	NO	Runs	HS	Av
B.C. Broad	10	20	1	496	128	24.80
G.D. Hodgson	10	16	1	367	113	24.46
S.G. Hinks	5	10	—	242	74	24.20
M.W. Alleyne	19	37	1	1184	109	32.88
A.J. Wright	20	37	3	1203	184*	36.45
T.H.C. Hancock	19	34	1	920	123	34.65
R.C. Russell	20	37	8	901	85*	25.55
M.C.J. Ball	17	28	4	468	45	18.72
C.A. Walsh	15	24	6	274	66	15.22
A.M. Smith	8	14	9	162	29	13.50
K.E. Cooper	12	16	4	84	18*	12.00
R.J. Cunliffe	12	13	1	354	127*	42.73
R.I. Dawson	16	30	4	1111	177*	29.50
R.M. Wight	4	8	2	53	22	26.50
M. Davies	11	21	1	173	54	28.83
M.G.N. Windows	10	14	2	730	106	34.76
R.C.J. Williams	10	14	2	171	38	14.25
V. Pike	9	12	4	114	27	14.25
A.M. Babington	1	2	2	1	1*	—
K.P. Sheeraz	1	2	2	1	1*	—

First-innings matches covered (table 1): v. Somerset (Bristol) 28 April–1 May; v. Sussex (Bristol) 5–9 May; v. Worcestershire (Worcester) 12–16 May; v. Durham (Gateshead Fell) 19–23 May; v. Surrey (Gloucester) 26–30 May; v. Essex (Chelmsford) 2–6 June; v. New Zealanders 11–13 June; v. Nottinghamshire (Trent Bridge) 16–20 June; v. Cambridge University (Bristol) 25–7 June; v. Glamorgan (Bristol) 30 June–1 July; v. South Africans (Bristol) 6–8 July; v. Hampshire (Portsmouth) 14–18 July.

Matches covered (table 2): v. Yorkshire (Cheltenham) 21–5 July; v. Kent (Cheltenham) 28 July–1 August; v. Derbyshire (Chesterfield) 4–8 August; v. Northamptonshire (Bristol) 11–15 August; v. Lancashire (Old Trafford) 18–22 August; v. Leicestershire (Bristol) 30 August–2 September; v. Middlesex (Lord's) 8–12 September; v. Warwickshire (Bristol) 15–19 September.

BOWLING

BOWLING	C.A. Walsh	K.E. Cooper	A.M. Smith	M.W. Alleyne	M.C.J. Ball	T.H.C. Hancock	R.M. Wight	M. Davies	R.C. Williams	A.M. Babington	V. Pike	R.I. Dawson	K.P. Sheeraz	Byes	Leg-byes	Wides	No-balls	Total	Wkts
v. Somerset (Bristol) 28 April–1 May	24–6–71–5 / 29.4–11–72–6	18.5–5–42–2 / 30–11–51–2	18.5–1–68–3 / 8–0–17–0	6–1–23–0 / 5–1–17–2	7–2–16–0 / 5–0–15–0	2–1–3–0								— / 1	6 / 2		24 / 8	229 / 175	10 / 10
v. Sussex (Bristol) 5–9 May	18.5–2–66–5 / 10–5–17–0	16–5–43–1 / 11–2–24–1	14–6–31–3 / 7–2–23–0	4–1–6–1	12–2–34–0 / 5–1–11–0	1–1–0–0 / 3–0–10–0								2 / 4	4 / —	1	16 / 8	180 / 85	10 / 2
v. Worcestershire (Worcester) 12–16 May	26.3–4–98–3 / 15–4–31–2	28.5–5–78–3 / 16–2–57–1	15–1–69–0 / 9–1–6–2	11–3–34–3 / 4–2–6–2	7–0–36–0	3–0–11–0 / 1–0–9–0								1 / —	3 / 6	1 / 1	46 / 8	329 / 180	9 / 9
v. Durham (Gateshead Fell) 19–23 May	28–9–88–5 / 26–7–52–3	17–3–45–0 / 28–8–66–2	16–4–50–0 / 18.5–4–40–5	16.3–2–70–4 / 5–0–11–0	10–4–15–2 / 12–5–38–1									5 / 2	12 / 4		16 / 8	305 / 173	10 / 10
v. Surrey (Gloucester) 26–30 May	7–1–36–0 / 27–4–83–3	9.2–2–24–2 / 25.3–9–99–3	8–6–2–0 / 17–3–80–1	1–0–4–0 / 16–3–51–0	5.5–3–6–0 / 5–0–30–1									1 / —	1 / 9	— / 3	2 / 6	73 / 354	3 / 9
v. Essex (Chelmsford) 2–6 June	22–6–43–3	25–6–60–1 / 4–0–18–0	9.3–3–34–1 / 7–0–40–1	12.3–1–55–1	9–3–16–0	5–2–35–0	19–2–76–3 / 8–0–63–0	18–2–74–0 / 10–0–53–3						2 / 2	7 / —	— / 1	42 / 14	362 / 183	10 / 3
v. New Zealanders (Bristol) 11–13 June				15–4–32–1 / 9–1–29–1	21–12–19–2 / 26–2–69–5		12–2–48–0 / 16–5–43–2	12.3–3–33–0 / 20–4–55–1 / 3–0–8–0						— / 2	3 / 6	— / 2	8 / 22	295 / 222	4 / 5
v. Nottinghamshire (Trent Bridge) 16–20 June	17–2–60–5 / 16.3–4–42–7	19–6–45–0 / 5–1–14–0	19.5–5–57–2 / 18–6–59–4	23–9–47–2 / 10–2–19–2					19–1–87–1 / 5–1–28–1					4 / —	2 / 1	— / 1	14 / 34	318 / 110	5 / 10
v. Cambridge University (Bristol) 25–7 June			24–4–82–1 / 20–5–44–3	4–1–9–0 / 4–0–22–0	3–1–6–0	6–1–15–1				18.5–6–27–1 / 5–1–15–0	17–8–28–3 / 27.3–12–41–6			— / 2	11 / —	— / 2	16 / 2	129 / 134	10 / 10
v. Glamorgan (Bristol) 30 June–4 July	19–5–63–3 / 7–3–10–1			8–2–19–0	17–5–55–1 / 4–0–21–0						27–5–71–1			4 / —	6 / 7		19 / 4	302 / 39	10 / 1
v. South Africans (Bristol) 6–8 July		15–4–26–3			8–1–33–0				18–9–28–4		7–3–14–0			4	—		24	129	6
v. Hampshire (Portsmouth) 14–18 July	20–7–46–3 / 17–3–60–3	17.4–6–38–4 / 20.1–2–57–3	16–3–66–1 / 8–1–25–0	7–0–32–2 / 11.5–3–29–3					12–3–27–1		3–0–18–0 / 10–6–11–1			— / —	6 / 9	2 / 2	16 / 8	192 / 220	10 / 9 (A)
v. Yorkshire (Cheltenham) 21–5 July	17–1–75–4 / 18–4–85–6	13–2–46–3 / 18–2–62–2	18.2–1–79–3	4–1–9–0 / 14.2–2–78–5	2–1–1–0 / 21–1–85–1				7–0–40–0 / 6–0–26–1		9–0–46–0			— / 4	6 / 6		28 / 4	247 / 204	10 / 10
v. Kent (Cheltenham) 28 July–1 August	21–6–46–2 / 22–2–82–4			7–0–27–0 / 16–2–50–1	3–0–6–0 / 2–2–0–0				14–2–62–1 / 5.5–0–13–3		6–3–26–0 / 15–4–34–1			4 / —	5 / 4	2 / 1	6 / 4	360 / 195	10 / 10
v. Derbyshire (Chesterfield) 4–8 August		18–3–63–2 / 29.3–12–44–3	14–3–28–2 / 9–0–40–0	2–2–0–0 / 23–5–71–2	36–12–84–2 / 35–11–85–1	5–0–16–2 / 8–1–20–0		15–2–38–0 / 8–1–31–0	23–3–82–3 / 21–4–66–1			18–6–38–2 / 4–0–20–0		1 / 1	6 / 15	1 / —	15 / 25	366 / 349	10 / 8
v. Northamptonshire (Bristol) 11–15 August	17–7–27–3	20–4–59–0		36.2–10–76–4	18–1–76–2	3–0–21–0			35–8–82–3			3–1–6–0	15–2–34–2	—	8	1	4	203	2
v. Lancashire (Old Trafford) 18–22 August	26.5–1–91–5 / 11–2–72–2			13–4–28–3 / 17–0–49–2	3–1–20–0 / 7–2–31–0	4–0–31–0			10–0–32–0 / 15–4–40–2		7.3–1–23–2 / 31–6–109–3			— / 4	3 / 12		8 / 12	172 / 356	10 / 10
v. Leicestershire (Bristol) 30 August–2 September				8–2–21–0	7–0–11–1				13–3–60–0 / 6–0–24–0		10–0–34–0	5–2–9–0		3	2		16	167	3
v. Middlesex (Lord's) 8–12 September	17–3–54–1			7–0–39–0	13–4–36–1				13–5–35–2		15–3–35–2			1	11		13	224	10
v. Warwickshire (Bristol) 15–19 September	3.4–1–13–0		3–0–10–0	23–6–98–0	21–2–98–1	6–1–36–0			23–3–124–3		15–0–74–1			4 / —	16 / 1	5	18 / 4	513 / 24	7 / 0
Bowler's average	504.1–19–1530–89 17.19	418.2–99–1095–38 28.81	297.3–65–1004–32 31.37	351.3–68–1103–41 26.90	326.1–78–957–21 45.57	47–7–207–3 69.00	55–9–230–5 46.00	104.3–14–370–6 61.66	245.5–46–856–26 32.92	23.5–7–42–1 42.00	200–51–584–20 29.20	30–9–73–2 36.50	15–2–34–2 17.00						

A R.S.M. Morris retired hurt

AXA EQUITY AND LAW LEAGUE – AVERAGES

BATTING	M	Inns	NO	Runs	HS	Av	100s	50s	Ct/st
R.A. Smith	15	14	2	676	110*	56.33	1	4	5
A.N. Aymes	17	13	7	289	54	48.16	–	1	21/5
T.C. Middleton	11	11	1	334	53	33.40	–	4	3
V.P. Terry	16	16	1	428	95	32.92	–	4	7
G.W. White	5	5	1	130	49*	32.50	–	–	3
M.C.J. Nicholas	17	16	3	285	47	23.75	–	–	8
R.S.M. Morris	4	4	–	55	34	13.75	–	–	2
K.D. James	16	11	2	122	39*	13.55	–	–	3
W.K.M. Benjamin	7	3	1	39	35	13.00	–	–	3
M. Jean-Jacques	3	2	1	12	8	12.00	–	–	–
R.M.F. Cox	6	5	1	46	23*	11.50	–	–	2
M. Keech	9	7	2	80	35	11.42	–	–	1
S.D. Udal	16	10	2	83	35	10.37	–	–	5
P.R. Whitaker	2	2	–	12	7	6.00	–	–	3
C.A. Connor	17	5	2	17	17*	5.75	–	–	1
M.J. Thursfield	6	3	2	2	1*	2.00	–	–	1
J.N.B. Bovill	2	1	1	1	1*	1.00	–	–	–
N.G. Cowans	12	3	1	1	1*	0.50	–	–	2
R.J. Maru	5	4	2	13	7	–	–	–	2

BOWLING	Overs	Mds	Runs	Wkts	Av	Best	5/inn
W.K.M. Benjamin	55.1	7	227	12	18.91	3-19	–
C.A. Connor	129.3	7	567	26	21.80	4-34	–
K.D. James	112	6	508	21	24.19	5-42	1
M. Jean-Jacques	24	–	122	5	24.40	3-44	–
R.J. Maru	28.4	2	188	7	26.85	3-33	–
M.J. Thursfield	43	1	170	6	28.33	3-31	–
N.G. Cowans	89	7	394	10	39.40	2-21	–
S.D. Udal	109.3	3	588	13	45.23	2-28	–
J.N.B. Bovill	27.3	1	117	2	58.50	2-25	–
P.R. Whitaker	2	–	8	–	–	–	–
M. Keech	6.2	–	43	–	–	–	–

HAMPSHIRE CCC — BATTING (season averages)

Player	M	Inns	NO	Runs	HS	Av
T.C. Middleton	13	23	3	524	102	26.20
V.P. Terry	13	34	1	1286	164	38.96
K.D. James	13	22	2	417	53	20.85
M.C.J. Nicholas	19	32	6	1186	145	45.61
R.M.F. Cox	4	8	1	114	46	19.00
M. Keech	5	9	–	141	57	15.66
A.N. Aymes	19	32	11	697	94	24.03
S.D. Udal	17	30	4	684	94	26.30
M.J. Thursfield	3	12	1	106	47	9.63
D.P.J. Flint	3	3	–	25	21	11.31
C.A. Connor	15	21	3	215	25	11.31
R.A. Smith	14	25	4	1143	162	45.72
W.K.M. Benjamin	9	14	1	227	54	17.46
N.G. Cowans	12	15	6	51	19	5.66
R.S.M. Morris	9	17	3	686	174	49.00
R.J. Maru	10	18	5	207	38*	18.81
G.W. White	10	18	7	362	73*	21.29
J.N.B. Bovill	5	7	5	25	10*	13.50
M. Jean-Jacques	5	5	1	52	22	13.00
P.R. Whitaker	2	3	–	134	94	44.66

BOWLING

Match	C.A. Connor	M.J. Thursfield	S.D. Udal	K.D. James	D.P.J. Flint	W.K.M. Benjamin	N.G. Cowans	M. Keech	R.J. Maru	J.N.B. Bovill	M. Jean-Jacques	G.W. White	M.C.J. Nicholas	P.R. Whitaker	Byes	Leg-byes	Wides	No-balls	Total	Wks
v. Oxford University (Oxford) 16–19 April	16.4–7–37–4	15–9–26–1	26–8–54–2	10–3–20–2	8–3–12–1										3	10			162	10
v. Essex (Southampton) 28 April–1 May	20.3–7–54–3	17–8–31–2	21–7–34–0			22–4–71–3	13–2–42–2								2	9		2	243	10
	11–0–48–1	6–2–26–0	30–4–100–1			16–6–46–0	9–3–26–0	2.3–0–15–0								9			270	2
v. Derbyshire (Southampton) 5–9 May		7–2–16–1	12–4–30–1		1–0–1–0	11–5–9–0	11.1–5–18–0								1	1			76	2
		5–1–14–0	30.2–7–83–4		29–8–86–0		4–1–12–0									4			199	5
v. Sussex (Hove) 12–16 May	14.2–3–61–3		14–2–70–1	12–1–51–1		21–4–49–2	15–4–41–3								2	7	1	2	279	10
	6–2–14–1		12–5–20–1	9–2–32–1		16.2–7–52–3	10–4–29–2									9	5		156	8
v. Middlesex (Southampton) 19–23 May	30.3–3–130–6		25–4–79–1	25–4–79–1		31–12–55–2	28–10–46–1	5–2–16–0							2	16		2	387	10
v. Somerset (Taunton) 2–6 June	22.5–4–83–1		32–10–67–1	17–4–42–0		24–7–48–0	22–2–81–1	2–0–8–0	16–4–45–0						3	8	1	6	332	3
																			0	0
v. Nottinghamshire (Basingstoke) 9–13 June	29–7–95–2		45–8–146–2			33–14–59–2	24–10–69–1		25.4–6–61–3						5	5	3	2	435	10
	23–4–66–3		19–2–61–2			8–3–23–0	19–4–51–2		18–4–51–2						5	7			253	8
v. Lancashire (Old Trafford) 16–20 June	16–7–26–1		30.4–7–79–6	10–4–19–1		20–8–23–0	10–2–32–0		11–7–8–1						5	7		2	176	10
	31–7–86–4		42–10–120–2	1–0–1–0		19–5–48–0	17–5–53–1		37.1–12–75–3						5	6		6	349	10
v. Yorkshire (Leeds) 23–7 June	19–7–75–4		24–10–40–1	18–3–64–2			15–5–35–3								5	15		4	257	10
	21–5–52–2		32–10–79–3	16–6–31–0			15.4–3–50–2								4	3		10	275	7
v. South Africans (Southampton) 2–5 July	17–3–64–1	13–1–44–1	27–7–63–5	14–4–46–2	11–2–30–0					9–2–41–0					4	3	2	14	264	9
v. Gloucestershire (Portsmouth) 14–18 July	18–5–60–3		8–1–23–1			21.5–7–31–5	16–4–41–1		3–2–2–1	6–3–12–1					4	2		6	132	10
	12.5–3–41–3		19.5–4–46–5			13–3–25–1	22–7–55–1									1		12	115	10
v. Worcestershire (Worcester) 21–5 July	18–3–60–1		10–3–31–3			24.5–12–46–6	19–4–40–0				12–2–53–0					3		33	193	10
v. Northamptonshire (Southampton) 28 July–1 August	37–11–105–2		36.5–11–85–6	11–4–36–1			9–1–25–0		30–10–50–1		17–0–67–1	3–1–3–0			4	4		24	315	10
	26–8–47–7		15–4–27–0	9–1–32–0					0.5–0–4–1							9			164	10
v. Kent (Canterbury) 4–8 August	27–8–79–3		40–12–119–5	17–2–78–4			12–4–44–0		29–9–66–1		11.5–0–70–1					4	3	8	358	10
	26–4–73–4		1–0–9–0	10–1–32–1			9–3–23–0				11.5–2–44–3					3		24	273	10
v. Surrey (Southampton) 18–22 August	21–6–59–6		5–2–22–0	6.1–0–18–2			30–5–97–2		4–2–8–0							7		22	189	10
	19–5–49–3		24–14–26–5	14–4–28–2			19.4–5–76–1		26–5–82–2							5		10	150	10
v. Durham (Portsmouth) 25–9 August	26–1–105–1		44.1–12–137–5	29–7–90–3					23.3–6–43–1						4	6	1	14	385	10
	32.4–6–122–4		28–1–142–3	21–4–70–2					16–3–58–0		0.3–0–8–0	2–0–10–0	4–2–7–0			8		12	386	10
v. Warwickshire (Edgbaston) 30 August–2 September	21–5–70–0		26–5–70–0	19–1–86–0					14–1–74–0	27–4–99–3					1	11		6	285	7
	31–3–124–4		11–2–25–2							24.4–5–108–5				0.1–0–4–0	1	10		14	536	10
v. Leicestershire (Leicester) 8–12 September	30–7–87–4	14–4–32–0	13–1–64–2	12–1–42–1						5–0–21–0		5–1–13–0			1	13		8	353	10
	7–0–44–1	4–1–19–0								13–2–34–0						4		6	117	3
v. Glamorgan (Southampton) 15–19 September	8.2–36–1	8–2–28–1													2	3		10	197	4
Bowler's average	574.4–131–1764–72 — 24.50	162.4–41–524–17 — 30.82	678–174–1872–69 — 27.13	280.1–56–900–26 — 34.61	49–13–129–1 — 129.00	281–97–585–24 — 24.37	349.3–93–986–26 — 37.92	9.3–2–39–0 —	254.1–76–621–15 — 41.40	84.4–16–315–9 — 35.00	53.1–4–242–5 — 48.40	5–1–13–0 —	4–2–7–0 —	0.1–0–4–0 —						

FIELDING FIGURES
74 – S.A. Marsh (ct 69/st 5)
29 – T. R. Ward
26 – C.L. Hooper
17 – D.P. Fulton
12 – M.M. Patel
9 – M.R. Benson and M.A. Ealham
5 – D.W. Headley
4 – G.R. Cowdrey, N.R. Taylor and M.J. McCague
3 – N.J. Llong, M.V. Fleming and subs
2 – A.P. Igglesden, M.J. Walker and T.N. Wren
1 – D.J. Spencer

AXA EQUITY AND LAW LEAGUE – AVERAGES

BATTING

	M	Inns	NO	Runs	HS	Av	100s	50s	Ct/st
C.L. Hooper	17	17	2	773	122	51.53	2	6	5
N.J. Llong	16	12	6	211	55	35.16	–	1	5
G.R. Cowdrey	12	10	2	266	82	33.25	–	1	3
M.R. Benson	8	8	2	256	74	32.00	–	2	–
S.A. Marsh	16	11	7	125	28	31.25	–	–	16/3
M.V. Fleming	17	15	–	458	79	30.53	–	3	7
T.R. Ward	17	17	–	435	63	25.58	–	3	3
N.R. Taylor	8	8	2	143	36	23.83	–	–	6
M.J. Walker	9	9	1	187	69*	23.37	–	1	3
M.A. Ealham	15	14	4	179	34	17.90	–	–	4
D.J. Spencer	9	3	1	18	12	9.00	–	–	3
M.M. Patel	9	5	3	13	7	6.50	–	–	2
D.W. Headley	10	4	2	6	5	3.00	–	–	4
T.N. Wren	10	2	2	4	1*	1.33	–	–	1
A.P. Igglesden	9	4	–	–	–	–	–	–	–
J.B. Thompson	3	3	–	3	3*	–	–	–	–

also – S.C. Willis one match (ct 3)

BOWLING

	Overs	Mds	Runs	Wkts	Av	Best	5inn
M.J. McCague	55.5	4	223	18	12.38	4-19	–
N.J. Llong	13	–	67	4	16.75	2-25	–
M.V. Fleming	79	2	411	21	19.57	4-36	–
D.W. Headley	64.4	5	342	15	22.80	3-27	–
A.P. Igglesden	68.2	5	244	10	24.40	3-22	–
C.L. Hooper	122.4	5	558	20	27.90	4-37	–
M.A. Ealham	86	4	412	13	31.69	2-11	–
M.M. Patel	29.2	1	191	6	31.83	3-50	–
D.J. Spencer	33	2	130	4	32.50	2-16	–
T.N. Wren	65	5	272	8	34.00	3-29	–
J.B. Thompson	10	1	45	–	–	–	–

KENT CCC

BATTING (season summary)

	M	Inns	NO	Runs	HS	Av
D.P. Fulton	10	16	–	433	109	27.06
T.R. Ward	19	33	–	1368	125	42.75
N.J. Llong	7	11	1	209	44	19.00
N.R. Taylor	16	27	–	1049	139	43.70
G.R. Cowdrey	10	16	1	470	114	31.33
M.V. Fleming	16	29	2	810	73	28.92
M.A. Ealham	15	26	3	638	68*	26.58
M.R. Benson	15	28	1	737	159	27.29
D.W. Headley	13	13	5	134	46*	16.75
S.A. Marsh	19	31	6	807	88	32.28
M.M. Patel	18	27	2	256	39	10.24
C.L. Hooper	18	29	1	1579	183	54.44
D.J. Spencer	4	6	1	46	13	9.20
M.J. McCague	9	15	2	265	56	22.08
A.P. Igglesden	11	16	8	61	15*	7.62
J.B. Thompson	2	1	1	3	3*	3.00
C. Penn	1	2	–	0	0	0.00
T.N. Wren	7	11	4	31	18*	4.42
M.J. Walker	5	7	–	239	107	34.14

First half of season – match by match

	v. Cambridge University (Cambridge) 20–22 April	v. Nottinghamshire (Canterbury) 5–9 May	v. Essex (Chelmsford) 12–16 May	v. Lancashire (Canterbury) 19–23 May	v. Leicestershire (Leicester) 26–30 May	v. Sussex (Tunbridge Wells) 2–6 June	v. Middlesex (Canterbury) 9–13 June	v. Warwickshire (Edgbaston) 16–20 June	v. South Africans (Canterbury) 25–7 June	v. Yorkshire (Maidstone) 30 June–4 July	v. Worcestershire (Canterbury) 14–18 July	v. Glamorgan (Abergavenny) 21–5 July
Byes	5	16	0	6	5	15	13	4	8	4	–	8
Leg-byes	12	9	2	8	4	8	6	9	2	6	6	5
Wides	2	2	1	4	1	3	10	2	–	1	1	8
No-balls	2	20	–	–	2	1	19	2	8	18	6	6
Total	446	125 / 229	191 / 399	556	157 / 189	336 / 152	418 / 280	359 / 270	292	377 / 407	166 / 318	408 / 330
Wickets	5	10 / 10	10 / 10	–	10 / 10	6 / 5	8 / 10	10 / 10	10	10 / 10	10 / 10	10 / 10
Result	W	L	L	D	L	D	D	L	W	W	L	W
Points	5	4	8	8	4	7	4	6	–	24	4	24

Second half of season – match by match

	v. Gloucestershire (Cheltenham) 28 July–1 August	v. Hampshire (Canterbury) 4–8 August	v. Durham (Canterbury) 11–15 August	v. Derbyshire (Derby) 18–22 August	v. Northamptonshire (Northampton) 25–9 August	v. Somerset (Canterbury) 8–12 September	v. Surrey (The Oval) 15–19 September
Byes	4	3	3	6	5	5	14
Leg-byes	5	7	12	14	4	5	6
Wides	2	3	1	8	12	5	–
No-balls	4	22	4	27	8	24	–
Total	360 / 195	273 / 189	385 / 96	392 / 247	165 / 248	392	445
Wickets	10 / 10	10 / 10	10 / 10	10 / 10	10 / 10	10	10
Result	W	L	W	W	L	W	D
Points	24	6	24	24	4	24	4

BOWLING

	D.W. Headley	M.A. Ealham	M.V. Fleming	N.J. Llong	M.M. Patel	M.J. McCague	A.P. Igglesden	D.J. Spencer	C.L. Hooper	J.B. Thompson	D.P. Fulton	C. Penn	T.N. Wren	G.R. Cowdrey	Byes	Leg-byes	Wides	No-balls	Total	Wkts
v. Cambridge University (Cambridge) 20–2 April	11-5-10-3 / 5-1-11-0	9-4-15-0	9-5-9-0	9-3-13-1 / 22.3-6-63-5	21-7-33-5 / 27-9-44-5										1 / 2	3 / 2			84 / 122	10 / 10
v. Nottinghamshire (Canterbury) 5–9 May	14.2-1-71-4 / 14-3-39-1	4-0-11-0				9-2-35-1 / 15.1-3-50-6		5-0-30-0 / 1-0-7-0							2 / 5	9 / 5	12 / 14	2 / 20	185 / 178	10 / 5
v. Essex (Chelmsford) 12–16 May	34-5-120-2		29-5-104-0		34-3-116-1 / 7-2-29-3		16-4-38-5 / 13-4-61-3 / 24-1-92-1								4 / 2	21 / 3	1	12 / 20	541 / 50	6 / 0
v. Lancashire (Canterbury) 19–23 May			6-5-4-0	10-2-37-0	38-10-96-8 / 34-6-105-2										5	4		18	261	10
v. Leicestershire (Leicester) 26–30 May	19-4-49-2 / 19-2-76-1		9-2-27-0 / 5-1-21-0		12-4-21-3		17-5-41-0 / 5-1-13-0	17.4-3-69-2 / 8-1-35-0	21-1-84-1 / 7-0-19-3 / 24-6-46-0 / 22-2-83-2						9 / 4	16 / 22	2	2 / 14	282 / 204	4 / 10
v. Sussex (Tunbridge Wells) 2–6 June	25-5-81-2		12-4-34-0		29-8-65-3		17-4-49-1 / 17-5-35-0 / 22.5-6-42-4	14.1-3-31-1 / 10-1-34-1 / 12-1-79-1 / 18-3-62-2	8-1-35-0 / 1-0-2-0 / 12-2-21-0						7 / 16	9 / 12		8 / 27	281 / 319	5 / 10
v. Middlesex (Canterbury) 9–13 June	11-2-31-0 / 26-2-108-4		1-0-1-0 / 27-5-85-2		39-9-91-6 / 42.3-8-117-4		16-0-63-0 / 14-0-60-0		6-0-14-0 / 15-5-36-0						4 / 1	8 / 7		2 / 4	237 / 454	10 / 8
v. Warwickshire (Edgbaston) 16–20 June	11-0-51-2	20-6-54-0 / 8-2-18-0	4-0-19-1		14-2-56-3 / 42-12-106-3		36.2-10-83-2 / 8-2-31-0		14-0-53-0 / 0.4-0-6-0 / 4-1-13-0 / 20-4-77-4	25-4-89-1 / 8-2-31-0					12	16	4	6 / 4	204 / 417	10 / 7
v. South Africans (Canterbury) 25–7 June	22.2-2-60-5 / 32.3-3-128-5	9-3-17-0 / 6-1-33-0	3-0-13-0		30-6-90-2 / 1-1-0-0						0.1-0-0-0	13-4-51-1				5			288 / 0	10 / 6
v. Yorkshire (Maidstone) 30 June–4 July	22.2-6-75-2		13-1-36-2		23-4-71-1 / 27-9-49-0		19-8-51-3 / 22-8-44-1 / 20-3-74-2		8-0-32-2 / 18-6-56-1 / 15-3-27-0 / 34-3-82-2						3 / 1	8 / 5	1	9 / 12	258 / 331	0 / 10
v. Worcestershire (Canterbury) 14–18 July	17-3-50-2 / 12-4-30-1	5.4-1-12-4 / 26-6-75-2	7-1-17-0 / 20-1-65-0		26-7-68-5 / 27-11-55-3								7-0-32-1		4 / 4	6 / 6		6	278 / 202	10 / 10
v. Glamorgan (Abergavenny) 21–5 July		10-2-24-3 / 11-0-45-1	2-0-21-0 / 3-0-16-0		42-11-106-4 / 23-7-49-3	18-1-87-2 / 23.4-1-15-3			9.2-1-21-1 / 36-12-62-0				19.5-6-53-1 / 9-1-58-1 / 9-2-39-1		5 / 3	10 / 5	4	6 / 10	422 / 266	10 / 10
v. Gloucestershire (Cheltenham) 28 July–1 August		13-2-27-3 / 15-2-69-2	11-3-22-0 / 10-1-27-0		30-6-88-4 / 29.5-6-92-2	26-3-89-5 / 24-8-65-4	3-0-11-0		8-1-23-0 / 9-2-23-2						2 / 8	7 / 13		24 / 18	378 / 271	10 / 10
v. Hampshire (Canterbury) 4–8 August		22-6-47-1 / 24-8-53-7	7-1-39-1 / 8-2-19-0		2.5-0-6-1 / 3-1-2-0	29-6-85-5 / 19-4-50-3	24-7-94-2 / 22-7-47-0								10 / 2	9 / 5			234 / 298	10 / 10
v. Durham (Canterbury) 11–15 August		7-0-20-4 / 12-2-40-0			26.5-4-68-4 / 37.5-12-84-6	6-2-17-0 / 8-0-36-0			26-10-52-5 / 37-13-73-3				8-1-30-0 / 6-1-21-0		4 / 7	7 / 17		6 / 2	182 / 196	10 / 10
v. Derbyshire (Derby) 18–22 August		18-7-51-0 / 9-3-19-0	5-1-19-1		25-7-46-1	25.5-4-86-9 / 23.3-7-61-6			10-3-24-0				17-4-41-0 / 20-4-67-3		1 / 2	9 / 8	2	4	284 / 288	10 / 10
v. Northamptonshire (Northampton) 25–9 August		9-1-43-0	5-2-10-0		17-6-29-0 / 10-2-29-1	24-7-63-4 / 5-1-11-0			25-7-51-1 / 7-3-17-1				21-2-78-2 / 5-1-11-0		9	3 / 2	4	2 / 8	282 / 260	10 / 10
v. Somerset (Canterbury) 8–12 September		6-2-21-0 / 8-2-15-0	4-1-14-0		16-1-53-1 / 3-1-3-0	16-2-40-3 / 23-4-56-3			14.1-5-34-0				19-4-48-6 / 20-4-41-2		3	13	3		156 / 108	10 / 2
v. Surrey (The Oval) 15–19 September		10-3-29-0 / 5-1-17-1			32.1-15-58-3 / 6-0-29-0	5-3-6-0			11-3-27-0				4-0-14-0	0.2-0-4-0			7	8	227 / 70	10 / 1
Bowler's average	295.3-48-990-36 / 27.50	266.4-62-762-27 / 28.22	239.5-48-746-9 / 82.88	41.3-11-113-6 / 18.83	811.2-202-2057-90 / 22.85	300.1-60-953-54 / 17.64	316.1-75-929-24 / 38.70	85.5-12-347-10 / 34.70	414.1-93-1055-29 / 36.37	33-6-120-1 / 120.00	0.1-0 / 0-0 / —	13-4 / 51-1 / 51.00	164.5-30-533-17 / 31.35	0.2-0 / 4-0 / —						

LANCASHIRE CCC

AXA EQUITY AND LAW LEAGUE – AVERAGES

BATTING

	M	Inns	NO	Runs	HS	Av	100s	50s	Ct/st
N.H. Fairbrother	14	13	2	522	70	47.45	–	4	4
S.P. Titchard	5	5	1	189	96	47.25	–	1	1
W.K. Hegg	17	12	8	164	52	41.00	–	1	16
J.E.R. Gallian	9	9	2	260	84	37.14	–	2	1
J.P. Crawley	13	13	2	414	91	31.84	–	2	4
M.A. Atherton	10	10	1	264	101*	29.33	1	1	–
G.D. Lloyd	17	16	3	351	77	27.00	–	2	5
M. Watkinson	16	13	4	231	35*	25.66	–	–	5
N.J. Speak	13	12	1	251	39	22.81	–	2	2
I.D. Austin	16	10	2	120	27	15.00	–	–	3
G. Yates	17	4	2	26	14	13.00	–	–	6
Wasim Akram	8	6	1	57	33	11.40	–	–	2
P.J. Martin	17	5	2	14	8*	4.66	–	–	3
G. Chapple	12	2	–	3*	3*	–	–	–	–

also – D.J. Shadford three matches (ct 1)

BOWLING

	Overs	Mds	Runs	Wkts	Av	Best	5/inn
Wasim Akram	54.5	7	273	17	16.05	5-41	1
J.E.R. Gallian	32.4	–	172	9	19.11	2-10	–
P.J. Martin	117.4	11	288	25	19.52	5-32	1
G. Yates	91.4	–	491	19	25.84	4-34	–
I.D. Austin	104.3	–	488	15	32.53	4-34	–
G. Chapple	82	6	329	10	32.90	3-29	–
M. Watkinson	93.4	–	440	12	36.66	4-34	–
D.J. Shadford	8	–	42	–	–	–	–

BATTING — Season Averages

	M	Inns	NO	Runs	HS	Av
J.E.R. Gallian	12	20	–	874	171	43.70
J.P. Crawley	16	27	2	1472	281*	58.88
N.J. Speak	22	34	6	1304	143	46.57
N.H. Fairbrother	12	23	2	1002	204	50.10
G.D. Lloyd	13	22	3	684	112	28.50
S.P. Titchard	13	21	0	549	99	26.14
M. Watkinson	19	28	2	889	155	34.19
W.K. Hegg	19	30	4	518	66	19.92
P.J. Martin	21	27	11	383	57	15.95
G. Chapple	5	5	–	150	35*	15.00
A.A. Barnett	6	10	2	14	10	3.50
M.A. Atherton	10	17	2	419	86	27.93
Wasim Akram	11	20	0	244	98	24.40
I.D. Austin	15	15	0	386	50	25.73
G. Yates	20	10	7	272	54*	20.92
N.A. Derbyshire	2	1	1	5	5	5.00
J.M. Fielding	2	1	–	27	27*	–
M.E. Harvey	2	3	–	44	23	14.66

BOWLING

BOWLING	P.J. Martin	C. Chapple	M. Watkinson	A.A. Barnett	J.E.R. Gallian	Wasim Akram	N.A. Derbyshire	I.D. Austin	J.M. Fielding	C. Yates	M.A. Atherton	N.J. Speak	J.P. Crawley	N.H. Fairbrother	Byes	Leg-byes	Wides	No-balls	Total	Wkts
v. Yorkshire (Old Trafford) 28 April–2 May	31-11-53-2 / 17-3-63-1	25.1-9-52-3 / 12-2-42-0	25.5-5-64-3 / 12-0-50-0	47-17-87-2 / 20-2-100-1	4-0-10-0 / 10-1-46-0										– / 1	9 / 3			275 / 305	10 / 3
v. Surrey (Old Trafford) 5–9 May	11.5-2-47-2 / 10-2-35-0	11-5-37-0 / 7-2-19-0	14-3-86-3 / 11-1-37-0	10-1-46-1 / 15.4-3-56-0	2-0-12-0 / 4-0-13-0	19-3-81-3									9 / 2	3 / 7	– / 1	6 / 4	301 / 171	9 / 0
v. Cambridge University (Cambridge) 14–16 May		32.3-5-120-2	17-2-43-1 / 14-4-27-0	34-2-124-2			16-3-48-1 / 7-1-13-0	10-3-27-0 / 5-1-12-0	10.4-3-38-1 / 9-3-15-1		7-2-10-0				2 / 6	7 / 5		8 / 6	227 / 118	6 / 2
v. Kent (Canterbury) 19–23 May	38-11-90-1		29-6-101-4		2-1-1-0	33-5-117-5 / 16.4-6-30-8	21-1-107-1	3-1-5-0							6	8	4	2	556	10
v. Somerset (Southport) 26–30 May	26-9-47-3 / 6-1-26-0	13-1-62-0	23-6-67-1 / 25-9-61-1	15-7-29-1 / 19-4-41-1	6-0-34-1 / 5-0-10-1	23-6-71-3		10.1-3-32-2							8	4	3	24	273	10
v. Northamptonshire (Northampton) 2–6 June	19.3-4-61-5 / 6-3-5-0	6-2-8-0	11-0-50-1 / 10-0-40-0	12-1-48-0 / 6-1-35-2	15-2-42-1 / 12-2-48-1							1-0-12-0	1-0-4-0			4 / 4	3	10 / 16	160 / 330	10 / 10
v. Sussex (Horsham) 9–13 June	32-13-78-1		15.2-4-40-4 / 22.3-10-30-8			21-2-71-1 / 19-2-84-2				31-4-112-3 / 30-4-123-3						6 / 8	4 / 1	2 / 12	120 / 355	3 / 9
v. Hampshire (Old Trafford) 16–20 June	20.5-4-63-2 / 7-4-9-0		24.3-6-57-3			19-3-36-0				13-6-21-2 / 13-3-34-5					4 / 13	13	1	4	381 / 100	10 / 10
v. Glamorgan (Colwyn Bay) 23–7 June	10-5-11-1 / 27-9-57-0	28-7-79-5 / 8-2-29-1	14-3-34-0 / 21-7-73-4			10-2-35-1				11-3-33-2 / 11.5-4-31-1					14 / 4	6 / 4	4 / 1	4 / 8	162 / 238	10 / 10
v. Warwickshire (Edgbaston) 30 June–4 July	10-2-28-0 / 22-5-57-0	22-5-52-4 / 8-1-33-1	25-5-88-0 / 58-26-126-3							24-3-98-2 / 2-0-26-1					10	20		22	165	10
v. Derbyshire (Blackpool) 14–18 July	5-1-21-0 / 35-6-85-2	35-6-85-2	19.2-5-58-2		12-4-41-2 / 5-0-27-2	36.4-10-82-4 / 16-5-39-0				53-14-132-0 / 8-1-36-1					10 / 5	1 / 11	2	12	407 / 183	10 / 4
v. Middlesex (Old Trafford) 21–5 July	8-2-42-0 / 8-3-12-0	3-0-26-1 / 10-3-21-1	18-2-53-2 / 14-2-54-1					12.2-5-23-5 / 18.2-8-37-5							5 / 1	2 / 2		4 / 4	490 / 186	7 / 8
v. Essex (Chelmsford) 4–8 August	18-3-44-2 / 17-4-41-2	27-6-86-4 / 6-4-11-2	7.3-1-16-1 / 9-0-42-2		5-0-23-1			22-7-57-3 / 4-0-17-0		5.2-0-32-3					4 / 1	8 / 2	5	2 / 2	101 / 185	10 / 10
v. Yorkshire (Leeds) 11–15 August	23.5-3-87-4	16-4-51-4	6-1-18-0					20-9-38-1 / 24-6-57-2							1 / 2	1 / 1			216 / 138	10 / 10
v. Gloucestershire (Old Trafford) 18–22 August	24.4-10-68-5 / 23-5-53-4	22-9-58-1 / 24-3-80-0	15.1-6-37-2 / 24-8-82-4		7-0-17-1 / 6-0-44-0			33-11-85-4 / 9.5-1-40-0		10-3-28-0 / 6-0-23-1				1-0-3-0	2	1 / 15	1 / 3	6	214 / 314	10 / 8
v. Nottinghamshire (Trent Bridge) 25–9 August	24-7-55-3 / 27-12-57-1	23-9-50-1 / 21-7-64-4	26.3-9-56-2 / 26-15-36-4					15-7-21-1 / 7-1-27-0		34-12-55-4 / 7-3-10-0					4 / 4	3 / 2	1	8	298 / 231	10 / 8
v. Worcestershire (Old Trafford) 30 August–2 September	15-4-33-1 / 36-11-93-4	31-5-149-5	30-6-108-0					27.3-4-104-1		22.4-0-107-0					8	3 / 22		4	242 / 177 / 591	10 / 10 / 4
v. Durham (Stockton) 8–12 September	13-5-29-1 / 10-2-37-2	15-4-59-3 / 16-2-48-6	7.2-1-39-0	9-0-46-0				16-3-30-5 / 6.3-1-24-2							1	2 / 10		2	159 / 111	10 / 10
v. Leicestershire (Old Trafford) 15–19 September	12-1-36-1 / 10-4-20-1	21-6-58-5 / 7-1-24-0		4-1-15-0				8-1-26-1		13.4-5-29-3					3	5	1		206 / 67	10 / 1
Bowler's average	613.4-175-1580-54 / 29.25	458.4-111-1474-55 / 26.80	631.1-173-1823-63 / 28.93	191.4-39-627-10 / 62.70	95-10-368-10 / 36.80	213.2-44-646-27 / 23.92	44-5-168-2 / 84.00	251.4-72-662-33 / 20.06	19.4-6-53-2 / 26.50	321.3-70-1013-37 / 27.37	7-2-10-0 / –	1-0-12-0 / –	1-0-4-0 / –	1-0-3-0 / –						

AXA EQUITY AND LAW LEAGUE – AVERAGES

BATTING	M	Inns	NO	Runs	HS	Av	100s	50s	Ct/st
P.V. Simmons	17	17	1	660	140	38.82	1	5	7
V.J. Wells	15	15	1	422	101	30.14	2	1	1
G.I. MacMillan	4	4	–	113	48	28.25	–	–	1
P.E. Robinson	11	10	2	220	39*	24.44	–	–	8
N.E. Briers	8	7	–	171	105	24.42	1	–	4
P.A. Nixon	17	16	2	318	72	22.71	–	1	13/4
D.L. Maddy	11	11	–	213	54	21.30	–	2	9
B.F. Smith	16	16	1	298	56	19.86	–	1	5
J.J. Whitaker	8	8	–	133	44*	19.00	–	–	1
P.N. Hepworth	12	12	1	152	49	13.81	–	1	2
A.R.K. Pierson	11	10	6	55	29*	13.75	–	–	5
G.J. Parsons	10	10	2	101	38	12.62	–	–	3
J.M. Dakin	15	12	3	109	29	12.11	–	–	4
D.J. Millns	14	12	4	96	41	8.00	–	–	2
I.M. Stanger	9	6	3	10	6	3.33	–	–	4
A.F. Haye	1	1	1	0	0*	–	–	–	–
A.I. Ditta	1	1	1	0	0*	–	–	–	–
A. Sheriyar	2	1	–	0	0	0.00	–	–	–

also – T.J. Boon one match

BOWLING	Overs	Mds	Runs	Wkts	Av	Best	5/inn
V.J. Wells	95	7	435	25	17.40	5-10	1
J.M. Dakin	33.3	1	198	10	19.80	3-32	–
P.N. Hepworth	42	–	255	10	25.50	5-51	1
A.D. Mullally	76.2	8	336	13	25.84	3-9	–
G.J. Parsons	113	5	415	16	25.93	4-50	–
P.V. Simmons	89.4	2	444	17	26.11	4-19	–
A.R.K. Pierson	72.1	1	302	11	27.45	4-29	–
D.J. Millns	24	–	107	3	35.66	2-11	–
I.M. Stanger	54	1	294	8	36.75	3-34	–
A. Sheriyar	8	–	44	–	–	–	–

LEICESTERSHIRE CCC — BATTING

(First table: matches v. Northamptonshire 28 April–1 May, v. Warwickshire 5–9 May, v. Somerset 12–16 May, v. Oxford University 18–20 May, v. Kent 26–30 May, v. Middlesex 16–20 June, v. Derbyshire 9–13 June, v. Surrey 23–27 June, v. Essex 30 June–4 July, v. Yorkshire 14–18 July, v. Durham 21–5 July, v. South Africans 30 July–1 August)

	M	Inns	ON	Runs	HS	Av
P.V. Simmons	17	30	1	953	261	31.76
N.E. Briers	19	35	3	1216	154	38.00
T.J. Boon	16	28	2	606	74	23.30
J.J. Whitaker	18	32	2	958*	148	31.93
V.J. Wells	18	28	4	871	87*	36.29
B.F. Smith	14	23	5	628	95	31.40
P.A. Nixon	19	30	6	1046	131	38.74
G.J. Parsons	16	25	9	491	70	25.84
A.R.K. Pierson	15	20	5	334	43*	22.26
D.J. Millns	19	21	10	348	64*	20.47
A.D. Mullally	14	19	5	114	23	7.60
P.N. Hepworth	5	10	1	113	60	11.30
M.T. Brimson	5	9	3	45	17*	7.50
B.C. Fourie	4	5	1	28	16*	28.00
A.G. Sheriyar	5	7	2	305	86	43.57
P.E. Robinson	1	1	–	3	3	3.00
T. Mason	3	6	1	80	34	3.00
D.L. Maddy	3	6	–	80	34	13.33
J.M. Dakin	2	3	–	29	18	9.66

(Second table: matches v. Nottinghamshire 4–8 August, v. Worcestershire 11–15 August, v. Sussex 18–22 August, v. Glamorgan 25–9 August, v. Gloucestershire 30 August–2 September, v. Hampshire 8–12 September, v. Lancashire 15–19 September)

	M	Inns	ON	Runs	HS	Av
P.V. Simmons	17	30	1	953	261	31.76
N.E. Briers	19	35	3	1216	154	38.00
T.J. Boon	16	28	2	606	74	23.30
J.J. Whitaker	18	32	2	958*	148	31.93
V.J. Wells	18	28	4	871	87*	36.29
B.F. Smith	14	23	5	628	95	31.40
P.A. Nixon	19	30	6	1046	131	38.74
G.J. Parsons	16	25	9	491	70	25.84
A.R.K. Pierson	15	20	5	334	43*	22.26
D.J. Millns	19	21	10	348	64*	20.47
A.D. Mullally	14	19	5	114	23	7.60
P.N. Hepworth	5	10	1	113	60	11.30
M.T. Brimson	5	9	3	45	17*	7.50
B.C. Fourie	4	5	1	28	16*	28.00
A.G. Sheriyar	5	7	2	305	86	43.57
P.E. Robinson	1	1	–	3	3	3.00
T. Mason	3	6	1	80	34	3.00
D.L. Maddy	3	6	–	80	34	13.33
J.M. Dakin	2	3	–	29	18	9.66

BOWLING

Match	D.J. Millns	A.D. Mullally	G.J. Parsons	V.J. Wells	A.R.K. Pierson	P.V. Simmons	P.N. Hepworth	A.C. Sheryar	B.C. Fourie	M.T. Brimson	T. Mason	J.M. Dakin	Byes	Leg-byes	Wides	No-balls	Total	Wkts
v. Northamptonshire (Leicester) 28 April–1 May	10-1-45-0	18-4-57-3	13.4-5-30-3	7-2-28-0	15-3-57-3	1-0-5-0							1	1		8	224	10
v. Warwickshire (Edgbaston) 5–9 May	13-3-40-3	22-8-56-2	19-7-33-2	11-6-22-1	33-10-78-1	10-4-18-1							6	13		4	266	10
v. Somerset (Leicester) 12–16 May	13-3-52-1	20-6-55-0	15-3-57-1	6-1-29-0	17.5-5-42-8	3.4-1-21-1	1-0-8-0						14	5	4	2	254	10
	15-4-54-4	12-1-57-0	13-4-41-0	8.5-1-25-3	13-2-23-1	10-5-20-0							7	3		10	206	7
v. Oxford University (Oxford) 18–20 May	25-6-62-4	30-9-85-0	31-11-50-2	7-1-33-0	17-8-28-1	12-5-22-2							6	12		28	288	10
	21-9-65-5	7-4-20-0	15-5-37-0	11-4-22-1	22-10-39-1								4	7	4	8	230	9 (A)
v. Kent (Leicester) 26–30 May	13-3-44-6	23-11-38-4	16-9-23-1	5-0-30-0	26-7-41-1	12-1-28-1							1	7		4	139	10
	3-0-6-0	11-2-37-0	14.1-4-34-1		9-5-8-1								6	4	1	2	229	10
v. Derbyshire (Derby) 9–13 June	16.2-4-51-3	18-4-51-0	21-0-75-0	15-3-68-3	14-5-47-2	12-1-28-1	11-3-30-3	13.3-34-0					5	4	1		157	10
	16-5-34-1	21-8-32-2	9.3-4-17-3	17-5-49-3	18.1-1-53-3	10-1-37-2		12-0-35-1					2	15		14	189	10
v. Middlesex (Leicester) 16–20 June	19-3-91-2	29-6-82-0	31-5-93-2		21-4-68-1	4-2-6-0	25-2-14-3			24.4-1-109-3			2	6	10	6	392	10
	10-2-34-0	2-0-4-0				21-4-68-1				2-0-8-0			9	22		14	143	9
v. Surrey (The Oval) 23–7 June	13-3-81-1	21-1-108-1	27-4-75-1	19-5-84-1		14.1-4-38-3	35-9-101-3						9	5	1	16	623	10
v. Essex (Leicester) 30 June–4 July	17.2-5-36-3	20-3-60-0	12-4-34-0	16-8-29-3	25-8-63-1	10-3-33-3		16-4-51-2			7-0-22-1		1	3	1	12	501	10
	19-3-78-4	11-6-20-1	14.4-1-64-3	5-1-23-2	32-6-106-2	19-8-40-1		14-3-44-1					6	4	2		218	10
v. Yorkshire (Harrogate) 14–18 July	13.2-4-45-1		33-10-67-4	16-2-85-2	4-0-13-0	6-1-24-0		5-3-63-2		10-4-25-1			5	12		6	195	10
			4-0-19-0	14-4-35-3	16-6-29-0	4-0-9-0		4-0-29-0		11-3-28-0			1	5	10	4	331	10
v. Durham (Durham) 21–5 July	18-4-65-3	21-8-43-3		18-7-50-5	17.3-2-61-1	14-3-30-0							6	8	2	2	319	10
	16.1-2-57-3	14-3-38-2		13-3-39-3	13-2-35-1								5	8	4	12	225	10
v. South Africans (Leicester) 30 July–1 August	16-2-64-3	34-9-85-5	19-6-53-1	22-6-56-2	27-6-60-1	13-5-16-1			8-1-19-3	9-3-12-0		11-1-36-1	16	8	2	12	198	8
	17-3-43-0	14-6-23-1	15-3-54-1	7-2-23-1	22.1-5-70-1	4-1-6-0			20-1-54-1	24.3-7-55-1			8	1	4	22	270	5
v. Nottinghamshire (Trent Bridge) 4–8 August	11-2-52-2	13-3-56-2	20.2-6-34-5	9-2-44-0	3-2-2-0	19.5-45-2							9	6		4	163	10
	9-0-52-0	13-4-35-1	9-2-31-1		12-6-26-1	12.3-26-3							9	9	2	14	337	10
v. Worcestershire (Leicester) 11–15 August	18-1-81-1	17-2-62-2	4-1-12-0	10-2-33-2	6-2-9-0	6-2-43-0							6	10	1	12	170	10 (B)
v. Sussex (Leicester) 18–22 August	16.2-2-84-6	4-1-20-1			17-4-54-1	13-1-31-2							1	3	1	14	278	10
					22-4-55-0	10-3-22-0							8	1		14	191	10
v. Glamorgan (Cardiff) 25–9 August	22.3-7-79-2	24-1-83-4	27.1-10-67-3	10-4-42-2		15-7-45-3		19-1-91-1		17-1-42-1			4	4		18	247	10
	17-3-74-1	22-1-80-2	16-1-69-1	8-0-42-1		28-9-68-4		5-0-53-1		23-9-68-0			5	1	1	8	37	1
v. Gloucestershire (Bristol) 30 August–2 September		20-3-51-2		13-1-55-0	24-2-55-0	13-1-31-2							7			30	295	10
v. Hampshire (Leicester) 8–12 September		26-8-61-1	12-8-27-1	6-1-27-1	10-2-33-0	13-3-22-0							6	9		15	360	4
		8-1-27-0	10-3-17-1	6-2-15-0	24-2-76-1	15-7-45-3							2	1			350	4
v. Lancashire (Old Trafford) 15–19 September		18.3-3-43-2	22-6-56-1	6-0-29-0	26-3-89-2	28-9-68-4							1	3	1	2	243	10
				16-5-36-3		13-2-42-0							10	8	4	4	358	9
Bowler's average	532-99-1901-76 / 25.01	448.1-121-1255-33 / 38.03	462.2-131-1208-44 / 27.45	301.5-74-1053-42 / 25.07	500.4-131-1267-37 / 34.24	300.5-81-769-30 / 25.63	72-14-253-9 / 28.11	98-14-400-11 / 36.36	28-2-73-4 / 18.25	121.1-31-347-5 / 69.40	7-0-22-1 / 22.00	11-1-36-1 / 36.00						

A A.P. van Troost absent
B W.P.C. Weston absent injured

AXA EQUITY AND LAW LEAGUE – AVERAGES

BATTING

	M	Inns	NO	Runs	HS	Av	100s	50s	Ct/st
K.R. Brown	17	15	7	355	52*	44.37	–	3	11/4
M.R. Ramprakash	17	16	2	561	97	37.40	–	3	3
M.A. Roseberry	14	13	2	424	119*	35.33	1	–	7
J.C. Pooley	9	8	1	228	77	32.57	–	3	1
J.D. Carr	14	14	5	291	59*	32.33	–	–	4
D.L. Haynes	12	11	0	320	52	29.09	–	2	5
M.A. Feltham	13	7	2	118	75	23.60	–	1	3
P.N. Weekes	15	12	2	209	50	20.90	–	1	4
M.W. Gatting	16	10	1	180	51	20.00	–	1	5
A.R.C. Fraser	9	3	2	14	14*	14.00	–	–	2
R.L. Johnson	11	7	3	52	11*	13.00	–	–	2
A. Habib	1	1	–	11	11	11.00	–	–	–
J.E. Emburey	7	3	–	23	16	7.66	–	–	1
J.C. Harrison	1	1	–	2	2	2.00	–	–	–
P.C.R. Tufnell	10	2	1	2	1	1.00	–	–	2
N.F. Williams	6	3	1	2	2*	1.00	–	–	2
C.W. Taylor	2	1	–	1	1*	–	–	–	–
K.J. Shine	1	1	1	–	1*	–	–	–	1

also – R.S. Yeabsley three matches; G.A.R. Harris three matches

BOWLING

	Overs	Mds	Runs	Wkts	Av	Best	5inn
R.S. Yeabsley	17	6	76	5	15.20	5-32	1
G.A.R. Harris	21.1	8	101	6	16.83	5-26	1
N.F. Williams	42.2	8	123	5	24.60	2-17	–
P.C.R. Tufnell	71	12	319	12	26.58	3-28	–
A.R.C. Fraser	69	9	262	9	29.11	3-31	–
R.L. Johnson	84.5	3	458	14	32.71	3-32	–
M.A. Feltham	92	2	477	13	36.69	3-28	–
P.N. Weekes	100.4	2	553	15	36.86	3-37	–
K.J. Shine	50.5	2	303	7	43.28	2-23	–
J.E. Emburey	53	5	212	4	53.00	2-46	–
M.W. Gatting	6.2	–	58	1	58.00	1-58	–
D.L. Haynes	0.4	–	3	–	–	–	–
M.A. Roseberry	0.4	–	–	–	–	–	–
M.R. Ramprakash	4	–	21	–	–	–	–
C.W. Taylor	1	–	21	–	–	–	–
J.D. Carr	6	–	30	–	–	–	–

MIDDLESEX CCC — BATTING (season summary)

	M	Inns	NO	Runs	HS	Av
M.A. Roseberry	20	32	2	1097	152	36.56
J.C. Pooley	8	4	–	77	40	19.25
M.W. Gatting	19	27	3	1671	225	69.62
J.D. Carr	20	27	10	1542	261*	90.70
P.N. Weekes	16	21	2	648	117	34.10
K.R. Brown	20	25	9	639	102*	39.93
T.A. Radford	1	1	–	4	4	4.00
M.A. Feltham	13	16	9	256	71	17.06
N.F. Williams	10	9	4	134	63	26.80
C.W. Taylor	3	1	1	0	0*	0.00
K.J. Shine	13	8	5	39	14*	13.00
J.E. Emburey	15	19	5	203	78*	14.50
J.C. Harrison	3	3	1	4	2	2.00
R.L. Johnson	11	13	3	205	50*	20.50
D.L. Haynes	17	27	2	973	134	38.92
M.R. Ramprakash	18	26	8	1271	135	52.95
A.R.C. Fraser	8	8	1	40	16*	5.71
P.C.R. Tufnell	9	6	1	17	9*	2.80
K. Marc	1	2	1	17	9*	8.50
G.A.R. Harris	2	2	1	16	11*	16.00

BOWLING

	K.L. Shine	N.F. Williams	P.N. Weekes	M.A. Feltham	C.W. Taylor	J.E. Emburey	R.L. Johnson	A.R.C. Fraser	M.W. Gatting	M.R. Ramprakash	P.C.R. Tufnell	D.L. Haynes	K. Marc	M.A. Roseberry	G.A.R. Harris	Byes	Leg-byes	Wides	No-balls	Total	Wkts
v. England 'A' (Lord's) 21–24 April	24.1-5-79-1 / 5-1-15-1	27.8-8-72-2 / 5-2-16-0	19-8-27-1	25-4-75-1 / 3-1-7-0	25-5-90-2 / 3-0-10-0												14		8	357 / 48	10 / 0
v. Cambridge University (Cambridge) 30 April–2 May	14-6-19-0 / 5-2-4-0		14.1-7-12-5 / 9-0-37-0	4-0-16-0 / 5-1-18-1	17-6-29-2 / 8-2-14-0	16-8-21-3 / 19-5-32-1	7-1-16-0 / 12-3-30-1									2	6		18	121	0
v. Yorkshire (Lord's) 5–9 May	23-0-48-1	36-12-96-3	19-4-52-0	30.4-10-83-4 / 5-1-18-1					1-0-4-0							5	16	3	6	221 / 297	10 / 8
v. New Zealanders (Lord's) 12–14 May	19-5-74-3 / 13-5-34-2		6-1-9-1	19-8-26-2 / 5-2-9-1	17-4-55-1 / 9-5-19-2	16-3-19-1 / 19-2-58-1	16-5-36-0 / 16-8-33-3									6	6	1	2	249 / 101	9 / 9
v. Hampshire (Southampton) 19–23 May	20-4-60-1	20.3-6-49-6 / 19-5-37-1	16-3-34-1			29-13-64-0 / 14-5-37-1	19-2-58-1	29-11-58-3								1	7	1	20	203	6
v. Warwickshire (Lord's) 26–30 May	13-5-33-0	24-4-71-1 / 10-0-55-0	11-1-43-1			20-3-79-1	15-4-46-0 / 14-5-37-1	24-10-43-2 / 17-4-60-2	5-2-10-1 / 5-1-5-0							4	2		10	230 / 211	10 / 3
v. Worcestershire (Lord's) 2–6 June	24-1-109-2	29-2-109-1	39-6-109-3			34.3-5-101-4 / 25-4-118-0	17-2-64-1			1-0-4-0						2	3		4	306 / 357	10 / 5
v. Kent (Canterbury) 9–13 June		28-8-86-2 / 25-4-103-1	19-4-54-1 / 16.4-2-53-1	40-5-131-2 / 9.3-1-19-2		38-5-105-1 / 34-6-48-4	26-7-97-2 / 9-1-40-1	31-5-77-2 / 20-10-20-3								13	9		10	418 / 280	8 / 8
v. Leicestershire (Leicester) 16–20 June		15-3-38-0	25-7-54-0 / 27-4-70-2	15-2-61-0		44.3-13-95-5 / 43-18-86-4	29-7-72-3 / 23-5-50-2	17-3-51-3 / 15-5-23-2								2	10	5	19	397 / 237	10 / 10
v. Durham (Lord's) 23–7 June			14-6-18-1 / 7-0-15-1	14-4-55-2		34-10-77-2	18.5-4-64-1 / 14-3-49-3	17-4-39-2 / 23.1-4-78-3								2	7		5	283	10
v. Derbyshire (De-by) 30 June–4 July	17-0-93-1 / 6-2-15-0			29.5-8-69-5 / 12-4-37-0		24-8-42-2 / 30-14-43-2	20-5-65-1				30-9-57-0 / 2-1-2-0	2-2-0-0				6	5		20	344 / 194	10 / 6
v. Sussex (Arundel) 14–18 July				6-0-28-0 / 13-3-28-1		23-9-32-2 / 16-1-43-2	15-1-40-4 / 10-5-16-0				33-7-78-2 / 34-5-61-4					2	17		18	105 / 228	10 / 6
v. Lancashire (Old Trafford) 21–5 July	12.3-7-16-3 / 19-1-100-1			15-2-50-4 / 20-4-70-1		4-2-8-0			7-1-31-1 / 4-0-27-0 / 1-0-4-0				16-3-52-2 / 13-1-81-1	1-0-5-0		6	4		2	238	10
v. Essex (Uxbridge) 28 July–1 August	25-5-93-3 / 12-2-71-2		22-3-64-1 / 13-2-35-1	20-6-47-0 / 7-1-30-0		19-2-70-0 / 24-9-66-1					41-12-126-3 / 44-10-125-2 / 35.4-7-88-3					1	9	8	6	163 / 484	9 / 9
v. Glamorgan (Lord's) 4–8 August	10-4-35-1 / 6-1-25-0		21-4-55-2 / 30-5-79-4	17.3-4-55-1 / 10-1-38-0		33-10-73-2 / 43-11-89-6		18-3-35-3 / 11.5-5-16-3							16-3-61-1 / 11-4-37-0	3	5	2	4	422 / 307	10 / 7
v. Somerset (Lord's) 11–15 August	14-2-48-2 / 12-2-48-2		24-4-71-3 / 10-3-23-1	14-3-36-0				31-4-114-3 / 12-2-58-1	3-0-16-0		24.4-9-41-4 / 26-14-17-4					1	1		22	285 / 270	10 / 10
v. Northamptonshire (Northampton) 18–22 August	14-4-50-0 / 2-1-1-0		27-1-73-1 / 19-1-112-2	25.4-5-75-3 / 4-2-12-0						1-0-2-0	42-7-121-3 / 26-4-111-1					3	3	1	18	248 / 110	10 / 4
v. Surrey (The Oval) 25–9 August	20-2-78-3 / 3-0-15-0	25-6-113-1 / 15-2-83-0	8.5-1-46-2	28-6-94-4 / 21-4-58-1		28-12-57-4 / 30-10-60-2		13-6-22-1 / 17-4-55-0 / 24-5-53-3			26.4-6-62-3 / 28.5-13-35-6 / 25-3-71-0				19-4-83-0 / 5-0-34-0	4	7		10	462 / 308	10 / 4
v. Gloucestershire (Lord's) 8–12 September		11-5-33-2 / 12-0-45-2	3-0-11-0													4	11		12	425 / 313	3 / 3
v. Nottinghamshire (Trent Bridge) 15–19 September		24.3-4-102-1	6-2-15-0			18-7-42-2	18-3-73-1	24-5-53-3			25-3-71-0					8 / 8	21 / 9	7	32 / 14 / 14 / 28	199 / 251 / 350	10 / 10 / 7
Bowler's average	332.4-76-1156-29 / 39.86	326-71-1088-26 / 41.84	484.2-91-1383-41 / 33.73	382.3-83-1140-34 / 33.52	79-22-217-7 / 31.00	675-205-1514-59 / 25.66	350.4-85-1059-40 / 26.47	320-85-802-36 / 22.27	26-4-97-2 / 48.50	2-1-6-0	408.5-107-995-35 / 28.42	2-2-0-0	29-4-133-3 / 44.33	1-0-5-0	51-11-215-1 / 215.00						

AXA EQUITY AND LAW LEAGUE – AVERAGES

BATTING

	M	Inns	NO	Runs	HS	Av	100s	50s	Ct/st
M.N. Bowen	8	5	–	49	27*	49.00	–	–	3
T.C. Walton	9	9	1	267	72	38.14	–	3	6
R.J. Bailey	15	15	1	421	94*	35.08	–	2	6
K.M. Curran	14	14	4	414	88*	34.50	–	2	7
R.R. Montgomerie	4	4	–	136	74	34.00	–	1	1
A.J. Lamb	12	11	1	304	59	30.40	–	2	4
J.N. Snape	3	3	1	59	31*	29.50	–	–	1
D.J. Capel	3	3	1	42	29*	21.00	–	–	2
A. Fordham	13	13	–	262	111	20.15	1	–	1
M.B. Love	13	13	–	225	64	17.30	–	1	2
A.L. Penberthy	16	13	2	181	69*	16.45	–	1	2
C.E.L. Ambrose	11	7	1	92	37	15.33	–	–	4
R.J. Warren	11	11	–	98	55	10.88	–	1	7/1
D. Ripley	11	7	1	65	21	10.83	–	–	9/2
A.R. Roberts	2	2	–	20	20	10.00	–	–	1
J.G. Hughes	2	1	–	9	9	9.00	–	–	1
J.P. Taylor	12	6	2	17	11*	8.50	–	–	1
N.G.B. Cook	16	7	4	33	21*	8.25	–	–	7
N.A. Felton	4	4	–	33	17	8.25	–	–	1
K.J. Innes	5	2	–	8	4	4.00	–	–	1
I. Dawood	1	1	–	2	2	2.00	–	–	1
D.J. Sales	1	1	1	70	70*	–	–	1	–

BOWLING

	Overs	Mds	Runs	Wkts	Av	Best	5inn
A.R. Roberts	8	–	51	3	17.00	2-40	–
C.E.L. Ambrose	78.1	13	264	13	20.30	4-20	–
J.N. Snape	14	–	77	3	25.66	2-38	–
R.J. Bailey	55.1	1	295	11	26.81	3-33	–
D.J. Capel	9.5	–	54	2	27.00	1-20	–
A.L. Penberthy	92	4	532	16	33.25	3-48	–
K.M. Curran	85.1	6	423	12	35.25	3-26	–
T.C. Walton	22	–	108	3	36.00	1-18	–
J.P. Taylor	80	3	470	10	47.00	3-30	–
N.G.B. Cook	100	5	480	10	48.00	3-19	–
M.N. Bowen	43	3	256	3	85.33	1-28	–
K.J. Innes	26	1	187	2	93.50	1-35	–
J.G. Hughes	11	–	40	–	–	–	–

NORTHAMPTONSHIRE CCC BATTING — Season Averages

	M	Inns	NO	Runs	HS	Av
A. Fordham	11	20	1	844	158	44.42
N.A. Felton	10	19	1	445	87	24.72
R.J. Bailey	18	33	5	1214	129*	43.35
A.J. Lamb	15	22	5	908	131	43.23
M.B. Love	15	25	3	658	132	32.90
A.L. Penberthy	17	23	5	263	88*	18.78
D. Ripley	16	23	9	263	36*	18.78
K.J. Innes				0	0	0.00
A.R. Roberts	9	12	4	261	51	32.62
M.N. Bowen	9	12		18	13	3.60
J.P. Taylor	5	12	6	68	12	11.33
C.E.L. Ambrose	14	16	2	257	78	18.35
K.M. Curran	14	25	4	973	114	48.65
N.G.B. Cook	11	21		98	43*	8.90
R.J. Warren	12	21		566	69*	29.78
D.J. Capel	2	3		54	29	14.33
J.N. Snape	2	3		54		
R.R. Montgomerie	8	15		513	151	39.46
J.G. Hughes	4	6		47	17	7.83
T.C. Walton	4	2		16	11*	8.00
I. Dawood	1	1		2	2*	–

BOWLING

Match	J.P. Taylor	M.N. Bowen	K.J. Innes	A.L. Penberthy	A.R. Roberts	R.J. Bailey	C.E.L. Ambrose	K.M. Curran	N.G.B. Cook	D.J. Capel	J.N. Snape	I.G. Hughes	T.C. Walton	R.R. Montgomerie	Byes	Leg-byes	Wides	No-balls	Total	Wkts
v. Cambridge University (Cambridge) 16–18 April	29-9-82-3			24-3-78-2	30-3-147-3	11-2-45-0									2	5		8	482	10
v. Leicestershire (Leicester) 28 April–1 May	15-0-8-0	28.4-7-90-2	10-3-33-0	3.4-0-9-0	2-0-13-0														9	0
v. Glamorgan (Northampton) 5–9 May	3-1-5-0	1-0-1-0 / 4-1-10-0				3-0-13-0									4	1	1	2	38	0
v. Surrey (The Oval) 19–23 May	13.4-4-30-3 / 11-3-37-0			16-5-54-2 / 15-1-74-3	17-2-72-0	3-0-13-0	14-4-53-4 / 18-8-38-5	9.1-1-49-3 / 7-1-34-0	3-1-8-0 / 3-1-2-0						4	2		20	89	7
v. Worcestershire (Worcester) 26–30 May	18-1-85-2			15-3-39-1			19-6-38-0 / 29-9-67-2	28.4-9-69-1	20.3-7-47-2						4	3		2	181	10
v. Lancashire (Northampton) 2–6 June	24-4-62-5 / 5-0-32-0			10-2-36-0			6-3-8-2		9-2-26-1						4	7	1	22	322	8
v. Durham (Hartlepool) 9–13 June	13-6-16-1 / 17-3-55-3			3-0-21-0		19-6-47-3	16-4-37-1	17-3-50-0	3-1-2-0						5	4		4	256	10
v. Yorkshire (Luton) 16–20 June	36-6-121-1	25-4-83-1		27-6-98-1		19-2-55-0	11-2-21-1	9-2-26-1	26.3-3-86-1						1	5		4	57	4
v. Warwickshire (Northampton) 23–7 June	32-4-139-4 / 3-0-20-0	3-0-27-0 / 25.3-2-99-2		8-1-33-3 / 24-7-87-4		3-0-12-0 / 2-1-1-0	12.5-4-16-5 / 29-9-53-3	13-7-36-2 / 19-6-57-1	5-3-8-0 / 8-1-19-0	4-1-14-0					1	15		10	190	4
v. Nottinghamshire (Trent Bridge) 30 June–4 July				19-2-105-2 / 6-0-39-0	33.1-8-106-3	6-0-28-0 / 9-0-38-0	27.4-10-49-2 / 35.4-9-77-1	18-4-53-1 / 6-4-52-1	13-3-69-1 / 9.3-2-51-3						6	2 / 14	1	8 / 6	215	8
v. South Africans (Northampton) 16–18 July						17.2-4-64-1 / 2-1-1-0	8-3-16-0	32-4-134-1	37-7-111-1	26-6-65-0 / 3-0-10-0	12-3-44-1 / 15-4-47-0				1	11		10	545	10
v. Derbyshire (Northampton) 21–5 July	17-2-55-2 / 12-3-33-2	14-4-53-1 / 12-3-32-0		16-5-32-2 / 6-0-17-0		10-2-26-0 / 1-1-1-0	19.4-5-48-3 / 29-9-44-3	18-1-63-1 / 4-1-25-0	22-4-57-2 / 20-8-38-0						1 / 2	5 / 9	2	14	148	10 (A)
v. Hampshire (Southampton) 28 July–1 August	20-0-75-2			10-2-35-1 / 19-8-36-1	15-5-44-1 / 16-5-51-1	12.2-4-41-2 / 7-3-14-0	28.3-11-41-7	19-3-76-1	11-3-25-1 / 9.4-1-11-0			25-8-69-5 / 13-3-46-0			8	16	1	2	324	10
v. Sussex (Northampton) 4–8 August	11-C-54-1			20-6-29-0 / 19-4-50-2	18-5-55-2	3-0-20-0		22-6-70-3 / 22-7-47-1	21-11-45-1 / 19-8-26-1			21.4-7-66-2 / 13-3-31-1			9	3		4	463	6
v. Gloucestershire (Bristol) 11–15 August				12-3-37-0 / 13-2-46-3	24.4-4-79-2 / 20-5-50-2	2-1-6-0 / 5-0-18-0	28-7-50-3	23-3-90-3	21-6-40-0			16-2-63-2			8	9	1	2	230	10
v. Middlesex (Northampton) 18–22 August				12-5-24-0 / 10-3-28-0	22.1-8-50-2	2-0-4-0 / 5-0-25-0	28-8-48-4	19-4-65-4	1-1-1-0			20-6-51-0			6	6			538	10
v. Kent (Northampton) 25–9 August	10-2-39-3			24-4-97-1 / 20-1-80-1	15-2-71-0		25-5-73-3	23-5-67-2				17.4-2-60-4	10-1-52-1		1 / 4	1 / 5	2	2	153	3
v. Somerset (Taunton) 30 August–2 September	8-4-37-1 / 20.1-2-62-1			13.3-3-54-5 / 16-3-65-1	16-0-85-0	4-0-40-0	22.2-9-31-6	12-0-77-0 / 10-1-41-2 / 17-4-47-1				20-6-51-0 / 11-7-22-0	10-0-46-1		4 / 5	7 / 1	9 / 8	9 / 4	296	7
v. Essex (Chelmsford) 15–19 September	3-0-9-0			19-4-71-2	13-2-47-1	1.5-0-11-0 / 22-8-59-5	29-4-59-5	28-7-80-1 / 5-0-16-0	25-10-46-3					1-0-10-0	12	8	5	6	197	9
Bowler's average	307.4-50-1059-34 · 31.14	113.1-21-395-6 · 65.83	10-3-33-0 · —	400.1-83-1374-37 · 37.13	242-49-870-17 · 51.17	166.1-33-568-11 · 51.63	540-159-1113-77 · 14.45	423.5-86-1463-31 · 47.19	283.3-85-715-17 · 42.05	33-7-89-0 · —	27-7-91-1 · 91.00	137.2-35-428-14 · 30.57	20-1-98-2 · 49.00	1-0-10-0 · —						

A C.J. Adams retired hurt

AXA EQUITY AND LAW LEAGUE – AVERAGES

BATTING	M	Inns	NO	Runs	HS	Av	100s	50s	Ct/st
J.C. Adams	15	15	1	674	93*	61.27	–	7	5
K.P. Evans	15	12	7	108	25*	54.00	–	–	4
R.T. Robinson	12	12	1	381	119*	38.10	1	1	2
P. Johnson	13	13	1	436	90	36.33	–	4	3
C.C. Lewis	8	7	1	190	75	31.66	–	2	3
M.A. Crawley	12	11	2	222	42	24.66	–	–	5
J.E. Hindson	14	12	1	24	21	24.00	–	–	1
P.R. Pollard	14	12	–	274	53	22.83	–	1	5
M.P. Dowman	6	6	1	86	52*	17.20	–	1	1
G.F. Archer	8	8	1	114	49	16.28	–	–	1
R.T. Bates	8	8	1	16	16	16.00	–	–	–
R.A. Pick	15	9	3	27	17*	13.50	–	–	3
G.W. Mike	15	9	2	61	29*	8.71	–	–	–
W.M. Noon	14	10	4	71	27	7.85	–	–	9/3
M.G. Field-Buss	9	4	3	5	5	5.00	–	–	–
R.J. Chapman	5	2	1	2	2*	2.00	–	–	2
also – D.B. Pennett eight matches (ct 2)									

BOWLING	Overs	Mds	Runs	Wkts	Av	Best	5/inn
K.P. Evans	81	3	381	20	19.05	5-29	1
J.E. Hindson	26		112	5	22.40	4-19	–
G.W. Mike	96.3		555	20	27.75	4-41	–
C.C. Lewis	57		317	10	31.70	3-29	–
R.T. Bates	21		96	3	32.00	2-34	–
D.B. Pennett	47		229	7	32.71	2-26	–
J.C. Adams	49.2		199	6	33.16	2-26	–
R.A. Pick	48.3		292	8	36.50	3-24	–
M.G. Field-Buss	55		333	7	47.57	2-27	–
R.J. Chapman	29.3		156	3	52.00	2-44	–
M.A. Crawley	43.4		241	3	80.33	1-25	–
M.P. Dowman	4		23	–	–	–	–

NOTTINGHAMSHIRE CCC — BATTING

(Season summary — rightmost columns)

	M	Inns	NO	Runs	HS	Av
P.R. Pollard	18	31	1	905	134	30.16
M.A. Crawley	8	14	1	172	45	13.23
W.A. Dessaur	5	9	4	154	35	19.25
R.T. Robinson	19	31	1	1276	182	42.53
G.F. Archer	16	26	4	878	168	33.76
K.P. Evans	16	21	4	514	104	30.23
B.N. French	1	1	–	–	–	–
M.G. Field-Buss	8	9	2	72	23	14.40
R.A. Pick	16	22	7	227	65*	15.13
R.J. Chapman	3	4	–	36	25	9.00
J.A. Afford	15	17	6	36	10	3.27
J.C. Adams	18	32	5	950	144*	35.18
P. Johnson	17	29	2	1170	132	43.33
W.M. Noon	18	30	6	617	75	25.70
D.J. Pipes	1	2	1	12	11*	12.00
S.A. Sylvester	1	1	–	6*	6*	–
C.C. Lewis	12	19	4	881	220*	58.73
G.W. Mike	17	26	3	365	60*	15.86
M.P. Dowman	2	5	–	111	38	22.20
R.T. Bates	2	4	1	15	8	5.00
J.E. Hindson	4	4	–	1	1	0.50
D.B. Pennett	4	3	–	20	11	6.66

BOWLING

Match	R.A. Pick	K.P. Evans	R.T. Chapman	J.A. Afford	M.G. Field-Buss	S.A. Sylvester	M.A. Crawley	J.C. Adams	D.J. Pipes	C.C. Lewis	G.W. Mike	R.T. Robinson	P.R. Pollard	R.T. Bates	M.P. Dowman	J.E. Hindson	Byes	Leg-byes	Wides	No-balls	Total	Wkts
v. Cambridge University (Cambridge) 13–15 April	15-4-36-1	17-6-29-2	15-6-23-2	16-8-22-3	14-6-23-2												6	5	1		144	10
v. Oxford University (Oxford) 28–30 April	21-4-48-1			19-8-46-1	16-4-43-0		7-3-16-0	5-0-21-0	4-0-13-0								5	8		4	238	3
	6-2-13-1			16-5-24-1	12-2-24-0		8-3-15-0		4-3-6-0									2	1	6	103	2
v. Kent (Canterbury) 5–9 May	11-5-17-1	5-1-22-2		12-3-39-1		17-3-38-1				17-5-43-3	8.3-2-29-3						5	9	2	10	125	10
	18-4-40-2	5-1-18-0				5-0-19-0				24.2-8-55-5	11-2-55-1						16	4	2	20	229	10
v. Durham (Trent Bridge) 12–16 May	16-2-45-3	14.3-3-39-3		32-12-62-2	16-9-24-1			1-1-0-1		20-2-67-1							1	4		12	242	10
	14-5-29-2			27.3-13-48-5	9-2-9-1					13-1-51-1		2.1-0-31-1					7	11		6	155	10
v. Sussex (Trent Bridge) 19–23 May	5-2-9-0	7-3-16-1						23-2-80-4			3-0-5-1						5	8		4	81	4
	8-1-35-0	10-4-19-0		30-6-87-5	9-0-26-0			17-0-19-2			4-1-18-0		2-0-20-1				4	15		8	278	9
v. Derbyshire (Ilkeston) 26–30 May	35.4-12-62-6			19-6-45-0			33-16-48-1				15-5-26-1									8	230	10
	22.5-6-53-3			24-8-49-2			11-7-12-0	32-15-37-1		6-0-11-0	21-6-71-4									6	222	10
v. Yorkshire (Middlesbrough) 2–6 June	18-2-40-1	21-6-62-2		6-4-10-1			6-0-18-0	13-6-18-1			18-5-44-5							7		6	181	10
	15-8-29-5	11-3-26-1		7-2-15-0				6-2-13-0			11-3-30-3							3		2	121	10
v. Hampshire (Basingstoke) 9–13 June	25-5-94-1	33-14-80-2		22-5-84-0	23.2-8-44-1			7-0-33-1			22-4-78-2						1	10	1	16	403	6
											8-1-40-3							5	1		285	8
v. Gloucestershire (Trent Bridge) 16–20 June	5-0-34-1	17-1-69-3		8-0-42-0	15-1-61-0						18-6-49-4							6		8	223	10
	16-8-38-1			16-7-43-3	10-4-17-0			6-1-17-0			8-2-21-0						12	7	2	14	208	7
v. Essex (Ilford) 23–7 June	14-2-41-3	26-6-80-3		20-5-49-1	27.5-11-50-2			20-9-29-1		11-2-56-3	12-2-54-2						2	7		20	155	10
		17-3-47-0		17.2-8-30-4	3-1-4-1					20-2-80-1	5-0-34-0						11	5		24	422	10
v. Northamptonshire (Trent Bridge) 30 June–4 July	18-2-69-1			16-3-60-0	41-14-89-2			29-13-63-4		25-5-65-3	22-4-56-0							6		2	411	7
	7-2-17-0				42-9-105-2			21-5-69-0		5-1-18-1	4-1-12-0						1	2		8	88	1
v. Somerset (Taunton) 14–18 July	23-3-53-0	23.2-9-46-4					9-2-20-0	9-1-17-0		25-7-65-4	20-6-54-2							6	1	2	246	10
	24.2-5-100-4	29-9-89-2			7-0-21-0		3-2-3-0	3-1-2-0		25-7-58-3	15-3-78-0						12	9		10	412	10
v. Surrey (Trent Bridge) 21–5 July	36-6-125-1			61-19-145-0				27-12-63-1		2-0-6-1	27-4-131-0			26-6-74-1	7-1-22-0		14	35		24	604	4
								33-13-52-1														
v. South Africans (Trent Bridge) 27–9 July	18-3-54-3		13.4-1-74-1								21.2-3-92-1			15-2-52-1	5-1-23-0			6		20	327	6
	10-2-29-2		5-2-12-0								7-0-21-0			6-0-21-0				4		2	164	3
v. Leicestershire (Trent Bridge) 4–8 August	20.3-2-65-2	27-7-65-1								21-2-67-0	24-9-50-4							9	2	12	318	10
	10-4-21-1	5-0-18-1								9-2-22-2	20-3-87-3						8	11		10	188	10
v. Warwickshire (Edgbaston) 11–15 August	24-8-71-1	23-6-71-4						22.5-11-27-2		16-2-61-2	20-3-87-3					6-0-20-0	4	7		11	321	10
v. Worcestershire (Kidderminster) 18–22 August	14-5-41-2	17-5-49-1						29-12-41-3		26.1-7-86-4	19-4-61-1					11-5-29-1	6	8		6	233	10
	20-4-58-3	19-5-48-1						11-5-24-0		18.5-3-71-5	16-2-82-0					9-2-21-0		2		10	235	10
v. Lancashire (Trent Bridge) 25–9 August	17-4-47-2	31-5-104-2	17-1-80-1	50-13-131-1				6-0-29-1		19-2-63-1	26-3-101-3					16-2-82-0	2	10	2	8	365	5
																34-9-111-2	6	5		24	567	10
v. Glamorgan (Worksop) 30 August–2 September		21-3-39-2		19-4-57-3				5-2-11-0		22-4-75-3	6-1-16-1					9-3-28-0		6	1	16	221	9 A
		6-2-19-0		29-9-56-0						14-4-51-3	4-0-21-0					21-6-53-5	4	3	1	7	218	9
v. Middlesex (Trent Bridge) 15–19 September		8.1-3-16-0								6-3-11-0	5.3-1-12-0						4	4	1		52	0 B
Bowler's average	507.2-122-1413-54 26.16	411.5-105-1141-38 30.02	50.4-10-189-4 47.25	541.3-165-1376-40 34.40	245.1-71-540-12 45.00	22-3-57-1 57.00	77-33-132-1 132.00	340.5-115-720-23 31.30	8-3-19-0 —	345.2-69-1082-46 23.52	405.5-92-1422-45 31.60	2.1-0-31-1 31.00	2-0-20-1 20.00	47-8-147-2 73.50	12-2-45-0 —	106-27-344-8 43.00						

A G.P. Butcher absent injured
B D.B. Pennett 3-1-9-0

AXA EQUITY AND LAW LEAGUE – AVERAGES

BATTING

	M	Inns	NO	Runs	HS	Av	100s	50s	Ct/st
G.D. Rose	13	13	2	451	91*	41.00	—	5	3
R.J. Turner	15	13	8	179	37*	35.80	—	1	16
S.C. Ecclestone	8	8	1	218	66	31.14	—	1	—
M.E. Trescothick	12	12	—	370	74	30.83	—	2	4
N.A. Folland	11	11	—	309	75	28.09	—	2	4
M.N. Lathwell	17	17	—	472	117	27.76	1	2	3
A.N. Hayhurst	15	15	3	309	49	25.75	—	—	4
R.J. Harden	14	14	1	331	59	25.46	—	2	7
N.A. Mallender	9	5	3	42	19*	21.00	—	—	2
K.A. Parsons	7	1	1	18	18	18.00	—	—	1
P.C.L. Holloway	7	7	1	90	29	15.00	—	—	1
A. Payne	7	7	1	44	32*	14.66	—	—	3
J.C. Hallett	3	3	—	37	16	12.33	—	—	1
Mushtaq Ahmed	7	6	3	29	12*	9.66	—	—	2
V.P. Clarke	6	6	—	52	26	8.66	—	—	2
I. Fletcher	5	3	—	15	10	5.00	—	—	3
P.J. Bird	5	4	—	4	4	4.00	—	—	2
J.I.D. Kerr	15	5	4	4	3	3.00	—	—	—
H.R.J. Trump	6	4	1	8	6	2.66	—	—	1
A.R. Caddick	6	4	1	8	7	2.66	—	—	8
A.P. van Troost	4	4	3	12	9*	2.41	—	—	2

also – M. Dimond three matches

BOWLING

	Overs	Mds	Runs	Wkts	Av	Best	5inn
S.C. Ecclestone	45.2	11	238	11	21.63	4-31	—
G.D. Rose	83.1	4	356	15	23.73	4-35	—
A. Payne	13.1	—	95	4	23.75	4-37	—
N.A. Mallender	67.2	4	381	16	23.81	4-38	—
A.P. van Troost	52.1	1	258	9	28.66	4-23	—
A.R. Caddick	43	4	176	6	29.33	3-41	—
A.N. Hayhurst	52.5	2	320	10	32.00	2-15	—
Mushtaq Ahmed	47	—	225	6	37.50	2-41	—
J.I.D. Kerr	29.2	—	158	4	39.50	1-45	—
P.J. Bird	28	4	129	3	43.00	1-18	—
H.R.J. Trump	96.2	4	393	9	43.66	3-19	—
J.C. Hallett	14.5	—	93	2	46.50	2-40	—
V.P. Clarke	17.2	—	100	2	50.00	1-15	—
M. Dimond	10	—	76	—	—	—	—

SOMERSET CCC

BATTING — Season summary

	M	Inns	NO	Runs	HS	Av
A.N. Hayhurst	18	30	6	1250	121	52.08
M.N. Lathwell	18	32	1	1230	206	39.67
R.J. Harden	18	31	5	1061	131*	40.80
N.A. Mallender	8	12	3	270	43*	30.00
N.A. Folland	13	22	1	671	129	31.95
G.D. Rose	16	24	2	548	121	24.90
Mushtaq Ahmed	9	14	3	168	38	15.27
V.P. Clarke	2	4	—	46	38	11.50
R.J. Turner	18	27	5	537	104*	24.40
A.P. van Troost	14	18	6	108	33	9.00
A.R. Caddick	12	18	2	219	58*	13.68
I. Fletcher	10	10	1	179	54*	19.88
H.R.J. Trump	14	20	4	276	45*	17.25
A. Payne	2	1	—	12	12	6.00
P.J. Bird	3	3	—	34	16	—
M.E. Trescothick	11	20	1	924	121	48.63
K.A. Parsons	3	5	1	38	16	9.50
M. Dimond	3	2	1	34	25*	34.00
B.T.P. Donelan	1	1	—	0	0	0.00
J.C. Hallett	2	6	2	21	10	4.20
J.I.D. Kerr	3	5	1	10	4	2.50
S.C. Ecclestone	1	4	—	42	24	8.40
P.C.L. Holloway	4	6	—	114	50	19.00

BATTING — match by match (first part)

Matches (left to right):
- v. Gloucestershire (Bristol) 28 April–1 May — Total 229 / 175; Wickets 10 / 10; Result L; Points 5
- v. New Zealanders (Taunton) 7–9 May — Total 364; Wickets 8; Result D
- v. Leicestershire (Leicester) 12–16 May — Total 288 / 230; Wickets 10 / 9*; Result L; Points 5
- v. Warwickshire (Taunton) 19–23 May — Total 355 / 22; Wickets 9 / 1; Result L; Points 3
- v. Lancashire (Southport) 26–30 May — Total 273 / 160; Wickets 10 / 10; Result L; Points 3
- v. Hampshire (Taunton) 2–6 June — Total 332; Wickets 3; Result W; Points 19
- v. Yorkshire (Bradford) 9–13 June — Total 332 / 224; Wickets 10 / 4; Result D; Points 7
- v. Surrey (Bath) 16–20 June — Total 428 / 329; Wickets 10 / 9; Result W; Points 24
- v. Worcestershire (Taunton) 30 June–4 July — Total 349 / 297; Wickets 10 / 7; Result W; Points 22
- v. Nottinghamshire (Taunton) 14–18 July — Total 246 / 412; Wickets 10 / 10; Result W; Points 21
- v. Sussex (Hove) 21–25 July — Total 360 / 302; Wickets 10 / 8; Result W; Points 23
- v. Glamorgan (Swansea) 28 July–1 August — Total 372 / 302; Wickets 10 / 10; Result D; Points 6

BATTING — match by match (second part)

Matches (left to right):
- v. Durham (Taunton) 4–8 August — Total 234 / 141; Wickets 10 / 10; Result W; Points 21
- v. Middlesex (Lord's) 11–15 August — Total 248 / 110; Wickets 10 / 4; Result L; Points 4
- v. Essex (Weston-super-Mare) 18–22 August — Total 226 / 243; Wickets 10 / 10; Result W; Points 21
- v. Northamptonshire (Taunton) 13 August–2 September — Total 346 / 108; Wickets 10 / 3; Result L; Points 10
- v. Kent (Canterbury) 8–12 September — Total 108 / 227; Wickets 10 / 10; Result L; Points 3
- v. Derbyshire (Taunton) 15–19 September — Total 228; Result D

BOWLING

	A.R. Caddick	N.A. Mallender	G.D. Rose	A.P. van Troost	Mushtaq Ahmed	A.N. Hayhurst	M.N. Lathwell	H.R.J. Trump	P.J. Bird	A. Payne	K.A. Parsons	M. Diamond	B.T.P. Donelan	J.C. Hallett	S.C. Ecclestone	V.P. Clarke	Byes	Leg-byes	Wides	No-balls	Total	Wks
v. Gloucestershire (Bristol) 28 April–1 May	20.1–6–40–4 19–3–44–2	14–5–19–0 14–6–34–1		7–2–23–0 27.4–7–51–2	25–4–88–4 36–8–104–4	7–4–10–0	4–0–10–1										6 13	3 11	 2	2	203 284	10 10
v. New Zealanders (Taunton) 7–9 May	6–1–16–0			15–4–18–1 5–1–13–0	16–2–57–5 11–4–38–0		5–2–32–0										 11	6 3		6	182 247	6 2
v. Leicestershire (Leicester) 12–16 May	29–7–92–5 18–2–60–2		14–1–30–0 21–8–58–2 14–2–36–2 19–1–73–1	21–3–87–1	40–16–91–2 17.2–6–42–3 6–3–9–0	9.5–2–47–2		2–1–8–0 16–2–76–0 15–5–48–0									6	6 3	2	22	409 110	2 5
v. Warwickshire (Taunton) 19–23 May			2–2–0–0		14–0–65–2	4–0–41–1 13–2–48–0		2–2–0–0	7–1–32–0 9–0–53–0	4–1–13–0 8–1–41–0							1	2 3			57 322	0 4
v. Lancashire (Southport) 26–30 May		18.4–1–117–0 31–8–96–3		35–10–72–0	60–17–156–6	13–2–48–0		42.3–11–115–1			4–0–21–0						1 6	4 7	1 1	6 2	521	10
v. Hampshire (Taunton) 2–6 June		13.5–5–28–3 20–3–71–0	13–0–51–0 23–5–78–4	11–1–34–3	26–7–77–3 37–9–129–1	13.5–5–23–0 11–5–18–1						14–2–44–1 15.3–2–73–4	8–0–32–0				2 9	9 9		22	245 424	0 10
v. Yorkshire (Bradford) 9–13 June		18–4–53–2	12–1–63–1		13–1–72–0							7–1–38–0	7–2–27–1				9	2		10	273	10
v. Surrey (Bath) 16–20 June		9.5–0–51–1 12–4–23–3	15.2–3–58–4 11–6–18–1	15.5–5–56–1 16–8–36–3	19–7–46–0 21–6–62–3	6–2–13–2		12–4–53–2									4 3	7 2	6 8	8	288	10
v. Worcestershire (Taunton) 30 June–4 July	14–3–47–3 23–5–80–2	21–6–56–0 6–1–25–0	8–1–31–0 3–0–15–0	21–1–88–1 11–0–59–1	30.5–13–66–5 31.5–11–94–7	1–0–5–0											4 8	14 3	1	8 14	152 315	10 10
v. Nottinghamshire (Taunton) 14–18 July	18.2–3–70–6 35–10–98–2	17–6–57–2 12.5–3–31–2	6–1–16–1 21.1–4–78–4					2–1–8–1 23–7–59–1 32.4–16–68–6 42.3–9–127–6 27–6–89–1	5–3–7–0								2 1	3 13		9 4	278 157	10 10
v. Sussex (Hove) 21–5 July	20–0–90–1 21–4–56–0		15–3–45–4 22–4–69–3				5–1–32–0 8–3–21–2 2–0–9–0 3–0–8–0		23.5–5–78–0			13–2–36–0 6–1–25–0		5–0–25–0 10–3–28–0			7	8 17	7 4	2 16	390 280	10 10
v. Glamorgan (Swansea) 28 July–1 August				29–3–172–3 8.3–1–45–1		0.4–0–2–1		4–2–5–2 1–1–0–0								20–3–93–1 3–1–12–0	4	4		65	314 533	10 A 7
v. Durham (Taunton) 4–8 August	16–2–47–1 17.4–5–51–6		6–0–14–3 18–6–40–4 5–1–20–0	17.4–2–64–3 12–0–81–4		3–1–5–2 4–0–15–0 5–2–8–0									3–1–8–0 4–0–31–0 8–3–13–0		4 1	4 7	4	32	84 171	10 10
v. Middlesex (Lord's) 11–15 August	29.4–5–84–4			19–1–100–2			2–0–7–0	23–3–103–2						14–2–69–0			1	4 3	1 3	30	203	10
v. Essex (Weston-super-Mare) 18–22 August	22.2–7–58–3 16–4–47–3		7–1–27–3 15–5–39–2	16–3–50–4 15–2–61–2		1–0–7–0		7–2–34–3							2–0–5–0			5		19	388	8
v. Northamptonshire (Taunton) 30 August–2 September	7–1–24–1 25–5–92–4	5–0–31–0 16–4–62–1	1–1–0–0	2–0–15–0				8–2–41–1									1	1	1	4	140 193	10 10
v. Kent (Canterbury) 8–12 September	16–0–90–2	14–3–61–1	5–2–10–1	20.1–4–89–1 21–1–115–2		9–2–23–0		9–2–39–0						24.2–10–59–4			10 5	10 5	1 5	6 24	71 304	1 8
v. Derbyshire (Taunton) 15–19 September																						Ab.
Bowler's average	373.1–73–1186–51 23.25	193.3–50–602–16 37.62	344.1–70–1136–44 25.81	345.5–59–1329–35 37.97	404–114–1196–45 26.57	87.3–25–265–9 29.44	29–6–119–3 39.66	268.4–76–873–26 33.57	44.5–9–166–0 –	12–2–54–0 –	4–0–21–0 –	55.3–8–216–5 43.20	15–2–59–1 59.00	53.2–15–181–4 45.25	17–4–57–0 –	23–4–105–1 105.00						

A J.I.D. Kerr 21–3–91–0

AXA EQUITY AND LAW LEAGUE – AVERAGES

BATTING

	M	Inns	NO	Runs	HS	Av	100s	50s	Ct/st
D.J. Bicknell	12	12	3	459	95*	51.00	–	4	3
A.D. Brown	17	15	1	688	142*	45.86	2	5	3
D.M. Ward	17	15	1	582	91	41.57	–	5	10
G.P. Thorpe	13	11	2	331	102*	36.77	1	2	6
A.J. Stewart	10	8	–	273	92	34.12	–	2	7/1
A.W. Smith	13	10	4	203	50*	33.83	–	1	5
A.J. Hollioake	17	14	3	329	72*	29.09	–	2	5
M.A. Butcher	12	11	–	45	17	22.50	–	2	7
G.J. Kersey	5	5	2	37	15	18.50	–	–	7
J. Boiling	14	6	4	52	16*	17.33	–	–	4
A.C.S. Pigott	15	8	3	59	15	14.75	–	–	4
M.P. Bicknell	4	4	1	14	11*	14.00	–	–	1
J.E. Benjamin	10	4	2	11	9	5.50	–	–	4
M.A. Lynch	3	2	–	11	7	5.50	–	–	1
N.M. Kendrick	2	2	1	14	13*	14.00	–	–	1
A.J. Murphy	11	1	1	0	0*	0.00	–	–	–
J.M. de la Penna	1	1	1	–	–	–	–	–	–
also – C.E. Cuffy one match. S.G. Kenlock five matches (ct 3)									

BOWLING

	Overs	Mds	Runs	Wkts	Av	Best	5/inn
S.G. Kenlock	36.2	3	171	10	17.10	4-30	1
M.P. Bicknell	75	6	358	15	23.86	5-12	1
A.C.S. Pigott	107.2	8	478	17	28.11	3-48	–
N.M. Kendrick	12.3	–	86	3	28.66	2-48	–
J. Boiling	89	–	482	15	32.13	3-27	–
A.J. Murphy	78.3	7	391	10	39.10	3-35	–
A.J. Hollioake	98.4	2	650	14	46.42	3-39	–
J.E. Benjamin	60	5	283	5	56.60	3-40	–
M.A. Butcher	47	–	313	4	78.25	2-47	–
A.W. Smith	25	–	175	2	87.50	2-28	–
J.M. de la Penna	3	–	34	–	–	–	–
C.E. Cuffy	6	–	43	–	–	–	–

SURREY CCC

BATTING

(first-class matches – first half)

	v. Worcestershire (The Oval) 28 April–1 May	v. Lancashire (Old Trafford) 5–9 May	v. Derbyshire (The Oval) 12–16 May	v. Northamptonshire (The Oval) 19–23 May	v. Gloucestershire (Gloucester) 26–30 May	v. Glamorgan (Swansea) 2–6 June	v. Oxford University (The Oval) 11–13 June	v. Somerset (Bath) 16–20 June	v. Leicestershire (The Oval) 23–7 June	v. Durham (Darlington) 30 June–4 July	v. Warwickshire (Guildford) 14–18 July	v. Nottinghamshire (Trent Bridge) 21–5 July	M	Inns	NO	Runs	HS	Av
D.J. Bicknell	12 24	36 67*		10 3	11 129	54		41 5	59	11 190	0 27	235*	17	28	3	1261	235*	49.04
A.J. Stewart	3 33*	126 88*	2 0					47 4	142	22 47	56 1	70	14	24	2	514	142	42.83
G.P. Thorpe	190 7	8	114	80	28* 6	65 35	5 5	4 59	64 21	24 23	38 17	81	14	22	2	897	294*	49.83
D.M. Ward	3	51*	294*	32	10					34* 1			16	21	1	921	294*	43.85
J. Boiling	2	2*				21	3 36	97 0	20	26 172	29 6	134*	6	6	2	75	34*	18.75
A.D. Brown	21	65	92	18 90	5 26	101* 62	29	0 1	138	46			17	24	2	1049	172	47.68
A.J. Hollioake	123	0	18	41*	43*		202* 9	16		1	31 2*		17	23	1	722	138	36.10
M.A. Butcher	6	0	10*	4 4	5* 15	5 6	32 17	8 11	0* 4*	25 26	0 0		17	19	2	613	134	36.05
M.P. Bicknell	0	0	0	3 1*	5* 15	2 22	23	5* 12		39 6*	0 2*		8	13	3	99	46	15.09
N.F. Sargeant	27	0		17*	0*		17 22	7	6		45 2		9	16	1	166	50*	39.66
J.E. Benjamin	33*	3*		25 37		22	10*			10			7	15	8	148	33*	15.09
C.E. Cuffy				2									5	7	5	42	10	6.00
N.M. Kendrick			10*			24		27 10*	6		4 3*	0 1	7	11	2	112	25	12.44
M.A. Lynch							11 30				45 2		5	7	1	238	202*	32.75
A.W. Smith										25 39			21	11	2	524	202*	14.11
G.J. Kersey							23 18			1			4	5	–	127	23	20.50
G.J. Kennis							17 22				8		3	3	1	41	39	19.50
D.J. Thompson							10*	7 5	6				1	1	–	39		
A.J. Murphy													2	2	1	10	10*	
S.G. Kenlock													2	–	–			
A.C.S. Pigott	34			30	6		–	7 5	17	1	8 40	11 23	8	11	–	160	40	14.54
Byes	1	4		25 37		7	22	4 3	9	3 9	2 3	14						
Leg-byes	14 2	9 3	1 7	11 2	2 1	9 2	6 1	7 10	5	11 3	5 11	35						
Wides	10 1	2 6	7 0	7 1	3 0	2 4	22 4	1		3 8	8 2							
No-balls	25 12	6 4	28	32 12	6 42	14		6 8	16	28	8 40	24						
Total	470 79	301 171	570	181 322	73 354	429	397 184	288 152	501	236 538	143 246	604						
Wickets	W 10	W 10	W 6	10 L	W 9	10 D	8 7	10 10	10	10 W	10 10	W 4						
Result	W	W	W	L	W	D		L	W	W	L	W						
Points	24	23	24	4	19	4		5	24	21	4	23						

BATTING

(first-class matches – second half)

	v. Sussex (The Oval) 28 July–1 August	v. Essex (Colchester) 11–15 August	v. Hampshire (Southampton) 18–22 August	v. Middlesex (The Oval) 25–9 August	v. Yorkshire (Scarborough) 8–12 September	v. Kent (The Oval) 15–19 September	M	Inns	NO	Runs	HS	Av
D.J. Bicknell	14 13	0 72	2 15	89 26	79	35*	17	28	3	1261	235*	49.04
A.J. Stewart	0 2	2 15			4 3	15*	14	24	2	514	142	42.83
G.P. Thorpe	71 6	24 5	0 38	47 79	7 27		14	22	2	897	294*	49.83
D.M. Ward	6						16	21	1	921	294*	43.85
J. Boiling							6	6	2	75	34*	18.75
A.D. Brown	40 18	9 43	78	0 27	68 76	20	17	24	2	1049	172	47.68
A.J. Hollioake	5	9* 0	2 65	70	7		17	23	1	722	138	36.10
M.A. Butcher		0 0	12 134	27 38			17	19	2	613	134	36.05
M.P. Bicknell		35 0	11 29				8	13	3	99	46	15.09
N.F. Sargeant							9	16	1	166	50*	39.66
J.E. Benjamin	8	7 1		23			7	15	8	148	33*	15.09
C.E. Cuffy	1	8* 0	1* 2				5	7	5	42	10	6.00
N.M. Kendrick		9	15* 60	27 68*			7	11	2	112	25	12.44
M.A. Lynch		4	6 1	24			5	7	1	238	202*	32.75
A.W. Smith	16* 2		4 9		0		21	11	2	524	202*	14.11
G.J. Kersey	8 0						4	5	–	127	23	20.50
G.J. Kennis							3	3	1	41	39	19.50
D.J. Thompson							1	1	–	39		
A.J. Murphy				30	6		2	2	1	10	10*	
S.G. Kenlock	2	4					2	–	–			
A.C.S. Pigott							8	11	–	160	40	14.54
Byes	4 4	13	5 4	11 4	10 7	70						
Leg-byes	4 4	2 3	5 6	7 2	7 1							
Wides	4 4	2 1	2 1	1 1	1							
No-balls		24	14	32 12	10							
Total	195 115	88 203	150 385	425 313	307	70						
Wickets	10 10	10 10	10 10	10 3	10 D	D						
Result	W	L	L	L	D	D						
Points	3	4	4	6	4	4						

BOWLING

Cricket bowling averages. Figures are given as Overs–Maidens–Runs–Wickets. Where a match has two innings, the two sets of figures are separated by " / ". (Some cell alignments in this dense rotated table are approximate.)

Match (and dates)	M.P. Bicknell	J.E. Benjamin	M.A. Butcher	A.J. Hollioake	J. Boiling	C.E. Cuffy	A.D. Brown	A.J. Stewart	N.M. Kendrick	A.W. Smith	A.J. Murphy	D.J. Thompson	S.G. Kenlock	A.C.S. Pigott	G.P. Thorpe	M.A. Lynch	Byes	Leg-byes	Wides	No-balls	Total	Wkts
v. Worcestershire (The Oval) 28 April–1 May	21.3-8-41-4 / 27-8-84-1	23-5-69-1 / 30-5-87-3	20-9-31-4 / 26.4-7-67-4	18-2-53-0 / 15-2-73-1	7-4-5-1 / 16-5-23-1												3 / 7	3 / 2	1 / 6	20 / 18	205 / 343	10 / 10
v. Lancashire (Old Trafford) 5–9 May		15.5-3-48-5	10-1-32-3 / 34-11-66-1	/ 29-6-101-2		14-3-42-2 / 41.3-19-70-4	/ 4-0-10-0	/ 1-0-8-0										2 / 1		18 / 4	129 / 342	10 / 10
v. Derbyshire (The Oval) 12–16 May	21-7-56-4 / 13-3-49-2	32-7-87-3 / 23-7-55-4	10-1-33-0 / 7-1-30-0	6-0-19-0 / 12-5-38-2		18.3-4-78-1 / 16-5-53-3			9-5-9-1 / 14-1-65-1								/ 10			20 / 8	208 / 224	10 / 10
v. Northamptonshire (The Oval) 19–23 May	20-9-27-2 / 23-4-74-1	12.4-3-37-3 / 21.4-6-57-6		6-2-26-2		29-8-80-2 / 8.3-1-16-3			9-2-23-0 / 25-4-96-0								5 / 8	5 / 12	1 / 2	10 / 12	188 / 316	7 / 7
v. Gloucestershire (Gloucester) 26–30 May		21.4-4-55-3 / 31.3-10-51-4	4-1-9-0	9-2-26-0		13-5-23-0			27-6-63-0 / 10-1-30-1	6-0-15-0							2	3 / 3	/ 4	24 / 2	319 / 106	4 / 4
v. Glamorgan (Swansea) 2–6 June		10-2-26-2	4-1-10-0	11-3-37-0				1-0-2-0	4-2-4-0	1-0-5-0								9		4	77	2
v. Oxford University (The Oval) 11–13 June			11-4-33-1	10-0-41-1 / 10-2-44-0	13-5-28-0 / 16-4-38-2				27-6-81-1 / 5-0-25-1	2-1-2-1 / 10-0-55-2	14-4-42-2 / 8-4-8-0	13-0-86-1 / 14-4-37-2	12-3-38-0 / 13-2-44-0				1 / 4	2 / 5	5 / 6	10 / 6	314 / 428	6 / 7
v. Somerset (Bath) 16–20 June		31-6-100-5 / 13-1-63-1	9-1-56-0 / 7-3-19-0			32-11-72-3 / 12-1-49-0	1-0-3-0			29-4-95-0 / 33-8-103-5				17.4-1-52-1 / 7-1-18-0	5-0-23-0		4	6 / 3	3	38 / 15	329 / 263	10 / 6
v. Leicestershire (The Oval) 23–27 June		23.5-5-81-6 / 19-3-51-4				17-7-45-1 / 16-4-40-3				28-10-85-3 / 25-5-72-3				13-2-49-0 / 5-0-18-0			4	3		6 / 2	188 / 335	10 / 10
v. Durham (Darlington) 30 June–4 July		31.5-10-86-3 / 15-3-43-2	3-1-7-0	3-1-7-0	7-3-16-0	21-3-85-3 / 15-4-39-3				18-3-67-0 / 10-3-41-1				26-8-65-3 / 9-2-22-4			/ 1	9 / 10		32 / 22	149 / 246	10 / 10
v. Warwickshire (Guildford) 14–18 July		18-3-79-3 / 32-10-70-3		13-3-29-2 / 29.2-6-84-2		17-3-74-3 / 24-7-63-0				6-2-32-0 / 24-5-76-2				13.2-7-21-2 / 32-9-92-2			4	4	5	12	399	9
v. Nottinghamshire (Trent Bridge) 21–25 July		15.2-5-27-6 / 18-7-31-0		10-2-35-3	5-2-16-0	12-2-34-1 / 20-8-53-0	1-1-0-0			2-0-9-0				8-3-16-0			2	4 / 4	3 / 1	10 / 25	125 / 248	10 / 10
v. Sussex (The Oval) 28 July–1 August		31-10-72-2		5-0-22-1 / 17.5-5-48-4		27-6-60-1				21-4-68-3 / 26-5-82-1				19.2-7-46-6 / 30-15-73-2			5	10			344	10
v. Essex (Colchester) 11–15 August	21-5-81-2	24-5-62-2		15-3-54-3		22-3-69-2			15-3-51-1	9-1-49-0							5	12	1	32	378	10
v. Hampshire (Southampton) 18–22 August	23-4-92-1			16-4-70-1		14-3-38-1	9-0-34-0		40.3-6-159-3	17-0-98-1						10-2-35-0	14		4	58	603	7 A
v. Middlesex (The Oval) 25–29 August	24.1-6-48-0 / 25-1-116-3	23-6-62-3 / 22-2-97-2	14-3-75-0 / 3-0-17-0	5-0-43-0						14-1-55-0 / 8-4-49-0			23-6-54-2 / 26-2-101-3				13 / 12		8 / 1	38 / 12	350 / 392	5 / 8
v. Yorkshire (Scarborough) 8–12 September	28-3-88-1	19-1-72-0	4-0-14-0 / 9-2-25-2	7-0-32-0 / 15-1-70-2	17-3-55-0 / 26-7-56-2					34-7-110-3 / 29-5-77-1				28.1-6-85-4 / 11-3-25-0				9 / 2		2 / 4	379	10
v. Kent (The Oval) 15–19 September	21-7-44-5 / 13-2-65-1									22-2-95-2			28-5-104-3				1				219	8
Bowler's average	280.4-67 / 865-27 / 32.03	563.2-128 / 1578-76 / 20.76	206.4-50 / 670-16 / 41.87	264.1-44 / 958-26 / 36.84	107-33 / 237-6 / 39.50	389.3-107 / 1082-36 / 30.05	15-1 / 47-0 / –	2-0 / 10-0 / –	185.3-36 / 606-9 / 67.33	374-66 / 1340-28 / 47.85	22-8 / 50-2 / 25.00	27-4 / 123-3 / 41.00	53-10 / 186-3 / 62.00	268.3-72 / 737-29 / 25.41	5-0 / 23-0 / –	10-2 / 35-0 / –						

A   D.J. Bicknell: –0–1–0

AXA EQUITY AND LAW LEAGUE – AVERAGES

BATTING	M	Inns	NO	Runs	HS	Av	100s	50s	Ct/st
A.P. Wells	15	14	1	618	103	47.57	1	5	5
D.M. Smith	7	7	2	211	55*	35.16	–	5	1
J.W. Hall	4	4	–	120	69	30.00	–	1	1
K. Greenfield	16	16	2	372	61	26.57	–	1	1
I.D.K. Salisbury	8	7	5	49	13*	24.50	–	–	1
N.J. Lenham	7	7	2	120	58*	24.00	–	1	–
N.G. Phillips	6	4	3	22	11*	22.00	–	–	3
M.P. Speight	10	10	1	299	66	21.35	–	3	3
C.W.J. Athey	14	13	–	183	58*	20.33	–	1	6
F.D. Stephenson	16	14	5	237	46	18.23	–	–	11
P. Moores	16	14	5	164	41*	18.22	–	1	–
K. Newell	1	1	1	10	10	10.00	–	–	–
P.W. Jarvis	12	9	–	78	17	9.75	–	–	2
C.C. Remy	13	10	1	57	14	6.33	–	–	4
M.T.E. Peirce	1	1	–	6	6	6.00	–	–	–
J.A. North	6	6	3	17	7	2.83	–	–	1
E.E. Hemmings	15	4	1	6	6*	1.66	–	–	3
J.D. Lewry	5	1	1	1	1*	–	–	–	1

BOWLING	Overs	Mds	Runs	Wkts	Av	Best	5/inn
N.J. Lenham	2	–	17	1	17.00	1-17	–
E.E. Hemmings	32	2	127	5	25.40	3-23	–
E.S.H. Giddins	102	6	522	20	26.10	4-23	–
P.W. Jarvis	83.5	3	381	14	27.21	3-40	–
C.W.J. Athey	16.2	–	90	3	30.00	2-28	–
C.C. Remy	92	2	426	14	30.42	4-43	–
F.D. Stephenson	109.2	6	463	14	33.07	4-24	–
N.C. Phillips	33.3	–	154	4	38.50	2-19	–
J.D. Lewry	52	3	159	4	39.75	2-43	–
I.D.K. Salisbury	52	3	300	5	60.00	2-24	–
A.D. Edwards	5	–	24	–	–	–	–
K. Newell	4	–	25	–	–	–	–
J.A. North	20.1	1	80	–	–	–	–
K. Greenfield	12	–	103	–	–	–	–

also – A.D. Edwards one match

SUSSEX CCC — BATTING

(County Championship match-by-match scorecard and season averages. Season averages columns: M, Inns, NO, Runs, HS, Av)

	M	Inns	NO	Runs	HS	Av
N.J. Lenham	14	27	1	809	102	31.11
C.W.J. Athey	18	34	3	1022	169*	30.96
D.M. Smith	7	14	4	326	74	29.63
A.P. Wells	18	34	4	893	84	29.76
M.P. Speight	17	29	2	991	126	25.53
P. Moores	18	32	5	766	70*	34.17
F.D. Stephenson	17	23	1	752	107	27.85
I.D.K. Salisbury	15	24	5	325	49	18.05
P.W. Jarvis	14	24	6	347	70*	16.52
E.E. Hemmings	17	24	12	88	14*	7.33
E.S.H. Giddins	14	22	11	83	24	4.61
J.W. Hall	17	27	1	789	85	29.22
C.C. Remy	6	11	1	194	60	19.40
K. Greenfield	1	1	–	61	35*	–
N.C. Phillips	2	2	1	37	37*	37.00
J. Lewry	4	6	4	14	6*	7.00

BOWLING

Match	F.D. Stephenson	P.W. Jarvis	E.S.H. Giddins	E.E. Hemmings	I.D.K. Salisbury	N.J. Lenham	C.C. Remy	K. Greenfield	C.W.J. Athey	A.P. Wells	N.C. Phillips	J. Lewry	Byes	Leg-byes	Wides	No-balls	Total	Wks
v. Gloucestershire (Bristol) 5–9 May	33-14-74-1 / 15-4-28-2	32-8-78-4 / 19-7-48-2	20-6-41-1 / 13-3-35-2	20-4-40-0 / 19.4-7-28-3	14-3-51-0 / 5-1-14-0	9-0-24-0							4 / 2	7 / 4	9	6	319 / 159	8 / 9
v. Hampshire (Hove) 12–16 May	16.1-5-41-5	15-2-63-0	15-2-64-1		28-7-90-4									5	2		267	10
v. Nottinghamshire (Trent Bridge) 19–23 May	24-7-55-6 / 13-2-52-0	27-5-117-1	12.5-2-21-4	1-0-4-0 / 35-11-64-2	21-3-49-0 / 18-4-60-2		17-3-67-2						3	15	5 / 3	6 / 12	167 / 368 / 0	10 / 7 / 0
v. Glamorgan (Hove) 26–30 May	29-5-73-1	30-7-102-2	26-4-88-1	29-5-87-1	24-5-108-2 / 19.3-6-55-1		16-3-54-1	8-1-32-0 / 8-0-44-0	4-0-19-0 / 6-1-13-0				15 / 1	10 / 3	3 / 2	2 / 6	432 / 187	6 / 4
v. Kent (Tunbridge Wells) 2–6 June	15.5-2-53-2 / 9-0-62-2	24-1-80-2 / 5-1-37-1	12-1-45-3 / 13-3-39-0		21-7-43-0 / 31.2-12-93-4				1-0-6-0	7-2-27-0			8	5		4	336 / 152	6 / 5
v. Lancashire (Horsham) 9–13 June	18-3-65-2	23.4-7-62-3 / 16-5-40-1	5-0-43-1 / 24-5-81-5	19-8-28-0 / 30.1-8-120-3	26-11-64-3									10 / 7			286 / 390	10 / 10
v. Durham (Hove) 16–20 June	7-0-25-0 / 5-0-32-0	11-1-50-0	14-0-84-0 / 22-6-51-3	20-4-46-2	37.2-18-79-5				1-0-1-1				1 / 8	4 / 5	1	6	278 / 241	10 / 10
v. Worcestershire (Worcester) 23–7 June	12-3-23-1 / 12-0-63-0	18-2-77-1 / 13-2-49-1	3-0-15-0 / 21-7-43-2	29.2-8-53-5 / 28-11-70-3	29-12-53-1									10 / 7		2	317 / 238	10 / 9
v. South Africans (Hove) 29 June–1 July	31-10-78-4	34-4-125-2	13-2-41-2 / 26-1-106-0	8-5-10-1	2-0-4-0		20-0-89-2			7-0-48-1	36-5-127-2	31-7-106-1	5	7	1	34	613	8
v. Middlesex (Arundel) 14–18 July	16.1-5-25-5 / 8-1-23-2	26-6-92-0	7-4-12-0 / 14-3-34-0	29-7-99-2	17.5-2-55-6							21-7-40-4 / 5-0-19-0		6 / 1	1	8	87 / 231	10 / 10
v. Somerset (Hove) 21–5 July	25.4-8-81-1	22.5-2-58-7 / 11-2-49-1	21-3-87-1 / 15-1-62-0	46.5-19-66-7 / 9-2-51-0	2-0-5-0							15-3-59-1	4 / 3	2 / 3	4	6	360 / 302	10 / 8
v. Surrey (The Oval) 28 July–1 August	22-6-50-6 / 14-1-32-5	9-1-52-3	16-4-52-2		11-5-39-2 / 13-4-30-4		8-0-31-0					9-2-36-0	4 / 5	4	4	4 / 2	195 / 115	10 / 10
v. Northamptonshire (Northampton) 4–8 August	16-5-28-2	15-2-57-1 / 18-2-58-2	4.3-0-29-2 / 12-4-23-3	1-1-0-0	25-13-33-2							7-0-25-1	5 / 1	12 / 6	1	6	144 / 182	10 / 10
v. Derbyshire (Eastbourne) 11–15 August	16.2-2-55-1	5-1-10-1	13.4-4-38-5 / 16-2-38-3	18-9-20-2	4-2-3-1							8-1-30-0	2 / 12	5 / 8			123 / 176	9 / 10
v. Leicestershire (Leicester) 18–22 August	15-4-27-2	20-3-71-3	16-5-64-3	15-9-18-1 / 9-4-11-1	2-1-8-0 / 4-1-28-0								1 / 1	11 / 10	1	4	192 / 90	10 / 10
v. Warwickshire (Hove) 25–9 August	14.2-4-50-3	9.5-1-50-4 / 3-0-3-0	17-6-35-3 / 2.4-0-7-0	2-0-8-0 / 4-0-24-0	17-2-61-0								4		1	10	183 / 79	10 / 10
v. Essex (Chelmsford) 30 August–2 September	18-4-70-2	25-3-113-3	18-1-83-5	27-11-63-0	11-4-41-3				2-0-11-0 / 1-0-18-0				6 / 5	4 / ?	1	6	418 / 106	10 / 3
v. Yorkshire (Hove) 15–19 September	14-3-50-1	3-0-20-0 / 18.3-4-64-2	3-2-5-0 / 23-6-77-4	11-2-34-0 / 3-1-4-0	15-3-40-2									11	2	10	246	10
Bowler's average	480.4-111-1345-67 20.07	496.2-89-1773-51 34.76	450.4-89-1463-60 24.38	422-140-959-33 29.06	430-137-1215-47 25.85	9-0-24-0 –	61-6-241-5 48.20	16-1-76-0 –	18-1-78-1 78.00	14-2-75-1 75.00	36-5-127-2 63.50	96-20-315-7 45.00						

FIELDING FIGURES

69 – K.J. Piper (ct 64/st 5)
18 – D.A. Reeve
15 – R.P. Davis
14 – D.P. Ostler
13 – T.L. Penney
10 – B.C. Lara
7 – R.G. Twose
6 – G. Welch
5 – A.J. Moles
4 – T.A. Munton
3 – N.M.K. Smith
2 – P.A. Smith, G.C. Small and subs
1 – Asif Din, M.A.V. Bell and J.D. Ratcliffe

AXA EQUITY AND LAW LEAGUE – AVERAGES

BATTING

	M Inns	NO	Runs	HS	Av	100s	50s	Ct/st
T.L. Penney	15 13	9	229	55	57.25	–	1	4
D.P. Ostler	17 17	4	530	84*	33.12	1	5	5
D.A. Reeve	16 16	4	378	65*	31.50	–	2	2
R.G. Twose	17 16	4	397	96*	30.53	–	2	7
Asif Din	12 12	–	265	75	29.44	–	3	2
B.C. Lara	14 14	–	364	116*	26.00	1	3	6
A.J. Moles	2 2	–	51	31	25.50	–	–	3
P.A. Smith	14 14	–	252	45	18.00	–	1	4
N.M.K. Smith	17 17	3	211	56	18.00	–	–	6
G.C. Small	14 3	–	15	7	15.00	–	–	2
G. Welch	7 6	2	57	26	14.25	–	–	3
M. Burns	7 6	–	68	37	11.33	–	–	11/3
R.P. Davis	10 7	4	31	13*	10.33	–	–	11/4
K.J. Piper	12 5	1	5	5	6.00	–	–	3
D.R. Brown	17 2	2	16	15*	1.00	–	–	4

also – M.A.V. Bell one match

BOWLING

	Overs	Mds	Runs	Wkts	Av	Best	5inn
M.A.V. Bell	8	–	19	5	3.80	5-19	1
N.M.K. Smith	103.1	5	412	26	15.84	4-19	–
R.P. Davis	42.2	1	175	10	17.50	3-19	–
P.A. Smith	74.2	2	376	20	18.80	5-38	1
G. Welch	37	–	163	7	23.28	2-30	–
G.C. Small	86.2	7	397	14	28.35	3-25	–
R.G. Twose	35.4	–	199	7	28.42	3-36	–
T.A. Munton	117	12	501	16	31.31	3-57	–
D.A. Reeve	91.3	8	328	10	32.80	2-16	–
Asif Din	3	–	22	–	–	–	–

WARWICKSHIRE CCC — BATTING

Matches (April–August)

Match columns: v. Glamorgan (Edgbaston) 28 April–1 May · v. Leicestershire (Edgbaston) 5–9 May · v. Oxford University (Oxford) 14–17 May · v. Somerset (Taunton) 19–23 May · v. Middlesex (Lord's) 26–30 May · v. Durham (Edgbaston) 2–6 June · v. Kent (Edgbaston) 16–20 June · v. Northamptonshire (Northampton) 23–27 June · v. Lancashire (Edgbaston) 30 June–4 July · v. Surrey (Guildford) 14–18 July · v. Essex (Edgbaston) 21–5 July · v. Derbyshire (Chesterfield) 28 July–1 August

	M	Inns	NO	Runs	HS	Av
D.P. Ostler	18	29	2	1161	186	43.00
R.G. Twose	18	31	5	1411	277*	54.26
B.C. Lara	15	25	2	2066	501*	89.82
Asif Din	9	4	1	107	42*	35.66
D.A. Reeve	9	10	3	116	33	12.88
P.A. Smith	17	17	4	363	65	25.92
K.J. Piper	24	21	4	454	116*	22.70
N.M.K. Smith	12	9	2	435	65	25.58
R.P. Davis	18	10	7	131	35*	18.71
G.C. Small	18	17	1	78	23	8.66
T.A. Munton	16	24	7	106	36	10.60
M.A.C. Bell	1	1	1	4	4*	38.00
T.L. Penney	16	24	—	798	111	—
J.D. Ratcliffe	1	1	1	36	36*	38.00
M. Burns	12	15	3	446	84*	17.40
G. Welch	12	20	3	863	203*	37.16
A.J. Moles	11	—	3	446	84*	50.75
D.R. Brown	3	6	2	113	54	28.25

	Byes	Leg-byes	Wides	No-balls	Total	Wickets	Result	Points
v. Glamorgan	7	9	–	14	657	W	W	22
v. Leicestershire	14/7	5/3	2/10	11/–	254 / 206	10 / D	D	5
v. Oxford University	2	1	11	–	303	D	D	–
v. Somerset	3	4	1	6	57 / 322	0 / W	W	18
v. Middlesex	2/3	10/10	4	10	211 / 306	10 / 5	D	5
v. Durham	28/22	2/2	–	26	810	D	D	6
v. Kent	1/4	12/7	4/4	16/6	417 / 288	10 / 6	W	23
v. Northamptonshire	6/14	11/1	1/6	6/10	463 / 230	10 / 6	W	24
v. Lancashire	10/20	5/1	2/2	22/4	407 / 183	10 / 4	W	24
v. Surrey	4/10	10/5	5/3	22/32	246 / 399	W / 4	W	21
v. Essex	5/1	1/1	20/14	–	361 / 268	10 / 10	W	24
v. Derbyshire	5	6	26	12	280 / 259	10 / 10	W	22

Matches (August–September)

Match columns: v. Worcestershire (Worcester) 4–8 August · v. Nottinghamshire (Edgbaston) 11–15 August · v. Yorkshire (Scarborough) 18–22 August · v. Sussex (Hove) 25–9 August · v. Hampshire (Edgbaston) 30 August–2 September · v. Gloucestershire (Bristol) 15–19 September

	M	Inns	ON	Runs	HS	Av
D.P. Ostler	18	29	2	1161	186	43.00
R.G. Twose	18	31	5	1411	277*	54.26
B.C. Lara	15	25	2	2066	501*	89.82
Asif Din	9	4	1	107	42*	35.66
D.A. Reeve	9	10	3	116	33	12.88
P.A. Smith	17	17	4	454	116*	25.92
K.J. Piper	24	21	4	435	65	22.70
N.M.K. Smith	12	9	2	435	65	25.58
R.P. Davis	18	10	7	131	35*	18.71
G.C. Small	18	17	1	78	23	8.66
T.A. Munton	16	24	7	106	36	10.60
M.A.C. Bell	1	1	1	4	4*	38.00
T.L. Penney	16	24	—	798	111	17.40
J.D. Ratcliffe	1	1	1	36	36*	38.00
M. Burns	12	15	3	446	84*	37.16
G. Welch	12	20	3	863	203*	50.75
A.J. Moles	11	—	3	446	84*	50.75
D.R. Brown	3	6	2	113	54	28.25

	Byes	Leg-byes	Wides	No-balls	Total	Wickets	Result	Points
v. Worcestershire	2/3	13/7	–	16	216 / 346	10 / 5	D	1
v. Nottinghamshire	4/6	3/7	–	11	321 / 233	10 / 10	L	5
v. Yorkshire	4/6	9/3	6	22	459 / 200	10 / W	W	24
v. Sussex	4	1	–	10	183 / 79	10 / W	W	20
v. Hampshire	1	10	–	14	536	10	W	24
v. Gloucestershire	24	2	–	4	—	0	D	4

BOWLING	G.C. Small	T.A. Munton	N.M.K. Smith	D.A. Reeve	R.P. Davis	P.A. Smith	B.C. Lara	R.G. Twose	M.A.C. Bell	G. Welch	Asif Din	D.P. Ostler	D.R. Brown	Byes	Leg-byes	Wides	No-balls	Total	Wkts
v. Glamorgan (Edgbaston)	27–6–75–1	23.4–5–57–4	18–3–46–1	23–5–61–2	21–7–51–0	12–2–35–2	1–0–7–0	5–1–11–0						9	13	1	4	365	10
28 April–1 May	17.3–3–46–5	21–5–73–2	15–4–25–0		13–8–24–3	2–0–14–0								4	3			189	10
v. Leicestershire (Edgbaston)	27–3–77–3	27.2–6–78–1	13–3–35–0	14–5–43–1		16–2–67–2			26–5–89–3					8	6		10	403	10
5–9 May		11–3–25–0	17–5–52–3			9–2–27–2			5–0–19–0					4	8	1		135	5
v. Oxford University		6–4–3–0	1–0–3–0	6–4–9–2	4–3–2–0			5–3–9–0		4–0–21–0							6	47	2
(Oxford) 14–17 May																			
v. Somerset (Taunton)	36.2–6–104–1	42–17–77–3	15–6–24–0		25–9–59–2	16–7–24–3		13–1–42–0						6	19	1	2	355	9
19–23 May											2–0–9–0	1.1–0–13–0						22	0
v. Middlesex (Lord's)	28–5–70–4	35–12–68–2	3–1–15–0	17–4–31–2		12–2–35–1		5–0–19–1						1	10	2	2	249	10
26–30 May	14–2–41–2	17–3–76–5	8–0–33–0		4–0–19–0	5–0–36–2	2–0–31–0							3	6			245	9
v. Durham (Edgbaston)	22–8–80–2	28–4–103–1	32–6–97–2	5–2–12–0	36–12–105–1	15–5–51–1	11–1–47–0	9.5–1–42–1						2	17	3	6	556	8
2–6 June																			
v. Kent (Edgbaston)	17–4–40–3	27.4–5–80–2	32–7–95–1	14–1–35–1	19–3–83–1	6–1–13–1								4	9		2	359	10
16–20 June	2–0–7–0	9–0–37–0	31–4–133–7		27.1–7–68–3	4–1–16–0									9		2	270	10
v. Northamptonshire		25.1–4–53–5	12–3–33–0	20–8–29–1		14–2–53–1		9–0–28–0		12–1–58–3				9	4	5	34	267	10
(Northampton) 23–7 June		41.4–12–79–5	51–18–118–2	17–8–24–0		30–8–90–2		10–5–13–0		26–8–81–1				7	11	1	32	423	10
v. Lancashire (Edgbaston)	15.5–3–45–2	17–3–52–2	25–4–84–1		30–8–99–2			12–2–32–0		15–3–72–3					8		16	392	10
30 June–4 July	5–3–7–1	26–7–62–2	20–9–42–7		1–0–8–0			4–0–16–0		10–2–44–0				9	6	4	10	194	10
v. Surrey (Guildford)		18.5–5–41–4	7–4–6–0					13–3–28–6		7–0–39–0			4–1–22–0	2	5		8	143	10
14–18 July		28–6–96–5	33.4–13–71–4				2–0–10–0	9–3–22–0		9–3–16–1			6–1–17–0	3	11		2	246	10
v. Essex (Edgbaston)		23–4–89–6	21–5–64–2		6–3–6–0					11–4–38–2			7–1–17–0		1		20	215	10
21–5 July		21–6–41–4	23–7–57–2		22–8–60–0					8–2–26–0			9–1–25–4		2		10	211	10
v. Derbyshire (Chesterfield)		25.2–5–52–7	2–1–2–0					14–3–31–2		21–4–83–0			6–1–26–0		4		23	198	10
28 July–1 August		22–6–57–2	28–6–69–5				1–0–4–0			20–9–49–2			3–0–11–1	6	6		7	202	10
v. Worcestershire (Worcester)		35–8–72–0	41–6–141–4	20–10–26–0		17–4–59–0	4–0–13–0	19–0–79–0		20–2–69–0					14	2	16	473	4
4–8 August																			
v. Nottinghamshire (Edgbaston)	29–4–113–1	39–12–80–2	25–4–119–0			20–3–63–1		26–8–87–1		27–3–111–2				10	14	5	8	597	8
11–15 August																			
v. Yorkshire (Scarborough)	18–5–52–2	27.5–12–56–2	18–3–51–1		15–6–53–1			5–1–15–0		21–8–74–4					9	1	8	310	10
18–22 August	22–6–59–3	18.1–3–55–1	24–6–69–0		40–9–94–6					9–0–53–0				8	9		4	347	10
v. Sussex (Hove)	12–3–41–2	15.2–4–22–4	3–0–6–1					13–4–23–3		11–3–30–0				1	8		8	131	10
25–9 August	20–7–38–3	20.4–7–52–4						6–3–11–1		7–1–25–2					1	5	6	127	10
v. Hampshire (Edgbaston)	20.2–7–49–1	23–5–44–4	18–5–36–1		26–7–77–3			5–1–19–0		16–6–45–1					8		2	278	10
30 August–2 September	6–4–2–0	14–5–34–2	19.2–4–65–5		11–1–50–3									5	7			163	10
v. Gloucestershire (Bristol)		11–3–34–0	26–4–102–0	8–1–38–1	41.5–12–128–6	4–1–11–0		8–2–17–0		13–4–36–1					6			372	9
15–19 September																			
Bowler's average	339–79– 946–36 26.27	699.4–181– 1748–81 21.58	582–141– 1693–49 34.55	144–48– 308–10 30.80	342–103– 986–31 31.80	182–40– 594–18 33.00	21–1– 112–0 –	190.5–41– 544–15 36.26	31–5– 108–3 36.00	267–63– 970–22 44.09	2–0– 9–0 –	1.1–0– 13–0 –	35–5– 118–5 23.60						

WORCESTERSHIRE CCC

AXA EQUITY AND LAW LEAGUE – AVERAGES

BATTING	M	Inns	NO	Runs	HS	Av	100s	50s	Ct/st
G.A. Hick	10	9	2	356	103	50.85	1	2	11
T.S. Curtis	16	15	3	521	99*	43.41	-	5	8
T.M. Moody	16	16	2	448	107	32.00	1	2	5
S.R. Lampitt	16	12	4	197	35*	24.62	-	-	3
G.R. Haynes	16	13	-	306	83	23.53	-	2	6
A.C.H. Seymour	5	5	-	111	57	22.20	-	1	3
S.J. Rhodes	10	7	3	85	46*	21.25	-	-	17/4
D.A. Leatherdale	16	13	-	208	41	17.33	-	-	12
N.V. Radford	15	11	6	78	27	15.60	-	-	4
D.B. D'Oliveira	8	6	2	68	27	11.33	-	-	2
R.K. Illingworth	16	8	2	62	31	10.33	-	-	2
M.J. Church	15	5	1	37	18	9.25	-	-	5
P.J. Newport	15	5	2	23	17	7.66	-	-	1
C.M. Tolley	3	1	-	1	1	1.00	-	-	-
Parvaz Mirza	3	3	3	20	16*	-	-	-	6
T. Edwards	-	-	-	-	-	-	-	-	-

BOWLING	Overs	Mds	Runs	Wkts	Av	Best	5/inn
D.A. Leatherdale	11.3	-	46	4	11.50	2-15	-
P.J. Newport	114.2	9	453	25	18.12	3-21	-
S.R. Lampitt	99.2	7	435	23	18.91	4-22	-
N.V. Radford	101.3	5	491	24	20.45	4-36	-
T.M. Moody	119	11	362	17	21.29	3-18	-
C.M. Tolley	8	-	24	1	24.00	1-24	-
R.K. Illingworth	111	6	444	18	24.66	4-23	-
G.R. Haynes	15	1	79	3	26.33	1-10	-
Parvaz Mirza	17	-	82	3	27.33	2-41	-
G.A. Hick	19	-	109	-	-	-	-

BATTING — Season totals

First-class match columns (left table):
v. Surrey (The Oval) 28 April–1 May; v. New Zealanders (Worcester) 4–6 May; v. Cambridge University (Cambridge) 7–9 May; v. Gloucestershire (Worcester) 12–16 May; v. Derbyshire (Derby) 19–23 May; v. Northamptonshire (Worcester) 26–30 May; v. Middlesex (Lord's) 2–6 June; v. Essex (Worcester) 9–13 June; v. Oxford University (Oxford) 17–19 June; v. Sussex (Worcester) 23–7 June; v. Somerset (Taunton) 30 June–4 July; v. Kent (Canterbury) 14–18 July

Match columns (right table):
v. Hampshire (Worcester) 21–5 July; v. Warwickshire (Worcester) 4–8 August; v. Leicestershire (Leicester) 11–15 August; v. Nottinghamshire (Kidderminster) 18–22 August; v. Yorkshire (Worcester) 25–9 August; v. Lancashire (Old Trafford) 29 August–2 September; v. Glamorgan (Cardiff) 8–12 September; v. Durham (Worcester) 15–19 September

BATTING	M	Inns	NO	Runs	HS	Av
T.S. Curtis	18	32	1	960	180	30.96
W.P.C. Weston	17	28	1	818	94	30.29
G.A. Hick	11	19	2	1101	215	57.94
T.M. Moody	20	28	3	1160	159	46.40
G.R. Haynes	17	28	2	1021	141	34.03
P.J. Newport	17	18	7	628	100*	57.09
S.J. Rhodes	20	24	5	345	41	18.15
S.R. Lampitt	17	26	6	624	122	29.71
R.K. Illingworth	20	25	5	438	59*	23.05
N.V. Radford	15	20	4	161	25	10.06
J.E. Brinkley	10	5	3	16	16	2.00
D.B. D'Oliveira	15	11	3	156	61	31.20
D.A. Leatherdale	17	25	3	987	84	44.86
C.M. Tolley	7	11	3	180	47	22.50
T. Edwards	9	5	1	116	87	29.00
A.C.H. Seymour	5	5	-	179	56	35.80
K.R. Spring	1	3	1	108	40	54.00
Parvaz Mirza	3	5	1	47	40	11.75
M.J. Church	3	5	-	66	38	13.20

Innings extras and result rows: Byes, Leg-byes, Wides, No-balls, Total, Wickets, Result, Points.

BOWLING

	N.V. Radford	J.E. Brinkley	P.J. Newport	S.R. Lampitt	T.M. Moody	R.K. Illingworth	G.A. Hick	W.P.C. Weston	C.M. Tolley	D.B. D'Oliveira	D.A. Leatherdale	G.R. Haynes	Parvaz Mirza	T.S. Curtis	M.J. Church	Byes	Leg-byes	Wides	No-balls	Total	wks
v. Surrey (The Oval) 28 April–1 May	26-3-84-1	31-5-98-6	18-2-82-0	16-1-69-2	15-5-52-0	17-3-43-1	5-0-12-0	2-0-10-0								1	14	10	25	470	10
v. New Zealanders (Worcester) 4–6 May	21-6-46-1	9-2-33-0	7-2-15-0	7-0-29-0	2-1-6-0	3-2-4-0											4	2	12	79	1
	11-3-39-3	16-4-58-2	15-3-49-2	8.3-2-25-2		3-1-12-0										2	4	1	16	194	7
v. Cambridge University (Cambridge) 7–9 May		7-0-20-0	4-0-16-0	4-0-16-0	5-0-17-0	31-12-43-0	6-0-29-1		12-6-22-0		7-4-11-2					4	3	2		153	4
		10-1-22-1	16-4-50-0	2.2-1-1-2	5-1-16-1											4	16	1	8	203	9 (A)
v. Gloucestershire (Worcester) 12–16 May	31-8-70-4	25-3-83-0	26-7-69-2	30-8-79-2	15-6-23-0	18-6-35-1	5.1-1-10-1	2-0-10-0		12-5-18-1							11		18	390	10
	6-2-12-1	14-0-69-0	14-3-45-2	7-3-13-0		18-5-51-4	2-0-8-0									4	4		6	203	7
v. Derbyshire (Derby) 19–23 May	17-3-55-0	3-0-7-0	11-1-20-2		9-3-24-4	2-1-4-0			17-5-52-3		9-3-14-1					4	4	3	2	188	10
	14-2-34-0	5-2-13-1	6-1-9-3	16.4-9-16-3	10-1-36-1				9-0-43-1		1-0-7-0					6	3	1	20	178	6
v. Northamptonshire (Worcester) 26–30 May	18-5-48-4		28-4-83-1	29-6-72-0	7-3-27-0	18.5-7-45-1	5-1-20-1		10-2-29-0		9-1-30-0	6-2-10-0					8			112	6
	21-6-57-3		11-4-31-1	7.5-0-41-0	7-1-23-0	14.1-3-21-1			13-3-20-0		3-1-7-0	5-0-21-0				6	3		12	357	3
v. Middlesex (Lord's) 2–6 June	7-0-47-1		14-2-61-1	13-1-54-3	3-0-10-0	30-7-75-3	1-0-7-0		5-0-15-0			7-2-28-1				1	14	1	2	209	8
	8-1-31-1		12.1-3-42-2	32-9-75-5	7-3-21-0	19-6-32-1	5-2-21-0		7-1-37-0			9-0-42-0				1	9			304	9
v. Essex (Worcester) 9–13 June	18-5-48-0		22-4-96-3	23-1-84-2	6-1-23-0	25-8-66-1										1	8	2	10	262	6
	17-2-64-0					31.1-12-39-1			10-5-27-1	3-2-5-0	21-6-50-1	4-0-14-0	11.4-1-29-4			3	2		6	405	9 (B)
v. Oxford University (Worcester) 17–19 June	9-2-33-4		15-4-37-1	18-6-35-2	11-2-42-2	18-6-52-3	4.1-0-19-1	8-2-38-0	8-2-24-0	36-13-67-4	4-1-15-0	8-2-16-0	2-0-2-1				3	1	6	95	6
	4-1-9-1		26-6-100-1	15.5-4-37-4	16-1-42-2	31-12-75-2	10.2-34-0		28-8-74-2		8-1-26-1	6-1-12-0					3	3	8	252	9
v. Sussex (Worcester) 23–7 June	15-5-64-1		19-3-50-4	30-10-81-2	22-7-38-3	22-7-50-0			15-1-56-1		10.1-2-38-0					6	9	1	8	295	9
	15-6-28-1		16-2-68-0	21-4-58-1	12-4-20-1	28-17-55-3										6	7	3	8	257	6
v. Somerset (Taunton) 30 June–4 July	23-7-53-2		23-6-81-3	15.3-6-37-3	3-0-9-0	20-8-28-3	2-0-10-0										6	1	12	349	10
	16-2-57-1		21-6-71-2		7-0-25-0	45-20-79-4	14-1-46-0				4-0-15-0						7	3	8	297	7
v. Kent (Canterbury) 14–18 July	19-3-46-1		27-3-99-3	19.4-7-33-5		7-4-3-0						6.3-2-19-3	12-3-48-3			2	6	1	6	166	10
	19-0-66-1		22-9-41-2	19-4-49-4	7-0-25-0	27-5-71-2						3-1-5-0	16-4-39-1			9	3		18	318	10
v. Hampshire (Worcester) 21–5 July	23-8-42-0		16-2-68-0	21.5-7-32-4	6-2-27-0	12-3-30-3										9	13		32	228	10
	17-2-57-1		13-2-37-2	14-2-59-1	9-5-11-0	11-3-17-0					13-1-46-0					3	7		20	336	10
v. Warwickshire (Worcester) 4–8 August	13-4-40-3	23-4-68-1		30-9-81-3		1-0-8-0		7-4-12-0				14.5-5-31-1	11-2-51-0	8-1-43-0			10	2	16	216	5
	21.1-7-93-5	14-1-57-1		16-4-40-3	10-1-33-1	14-2-45-1	20-7-37-1					9-0-45-1	9.4-2-24-0			4	15	2	24	346	10
v. Leicestershire (Leicester) 11–15 August	13-4-45-0	18-5-75-0				29-9-61-2						3-0-7-0					17	1	20	283	9
	20-8-50-0		28-10-76-2			44-9-107-2											2	2	8	331	10
v. Nottinghamshire (Kidderminster) 18–22 August				11.3-0-72-3	10.1-33-1	42-13-101-2	16-5-64-3		14-3-87-0	5-1-18-0	7-2-24-0	17-5-31-1				4	2	4	7	315	7
				14-5-46-2	4-1-17-0	7-0-28-1				18-1-67-2	12-0-56-0						9		4	489	5
v. Yorkshire (Worcester) 25–9 August	14-4-56-2	10-3-22-1	16-2-54-3	15-6-48-2		42-12-98-3		2-0-10-0			4-2-14-0	4-2-14-0				8	10		16	267	10
v. Lancashire (Old Trafford) 30 August–2 September	6-0-31-0		11.1-2-34-2			2-1-3-0						4-1-12-0					3		28	311	10
v. Glamorgan (Cardiff) 8–12 September	11-2-39-0		11-2-31-1	15.6-4-82-1		17.5-1-68-3						3-0-12-0				4	4	1	2	134	3
	5-0-24-0		15-2-59-1	11-1-72-1		19-7-50-1	12-5-26-0										4	5	5	243	5
v. Durham (Worcester) 15–19 September		10-3-22-1	13-3-43-0	12-1-45-0											1-0-4-0	4	3		16	193	2
Bowler's average	459.1-106-1408-39 36.10	233-40-779-18 43.27	516.2-103-1654-53 31.20	511.4-127-1484-64 23.18	195-48-572-15 38.13	679-212-1499-49 30.59	107.2-24-343-8 42.87	21-6-85-0 —	148-36-486-8 60.75	74-22-175-7 25.00	108.1-22-339-5 67.80	108.1-23-319-7 45.57	61.4-14-193-9 21.44	8-1-43-0 —	1-0-4-0 —						

A G.W. Jones retired hurt
B W.S. Kendal retired hurt, absent hurt

YORKSHIRE CCC

FIELDING FIGURES

69 – R.J. Blakey (ct 65/st 4)
24 – D. Byas
19 – A.P. Grayson
11 – S.A. Kellett
9 – R.B. Richardson
8 – M.P. Vaughan and R.D. Stemp
7 – M.D. Moxon
6 – B. Parker
5 – C. White, M.A. Robinson and M.J. Foster
3 – P.J. Hartley and J.D. Batty
2 – G.M. Hamilton, C.E.W. Silverwood and subs
1 – D. Gough, A.A. Metcalfe and L.C. Weekes

AXA EQUITY AND LAW LEAGUE – AVERAGES

BATTING

	M	Inns	NO	Runs	HS	Av	100s	50s	Ct/st
D. Byas	16	16	2	702	101*	50.14	1	6	5
A.A. Metcalfe	9	8	3	230	65*	46.00	–	2	1
G.M. Hamilton	6	3	2	41	16*	41.00	–	–	–
C. White	6	5	1	162	54*	40.50	–	1	1
S.A. Kellett	2	2	–	74	58	37.00	–	1	–
R.B. Richardson	8	8	2	203	55	33.83	–	1	1
R.A. Kettleborough	12	12	1	32	28	32.00	–	–	2
M.D. Moxon	12	12	–	331	58	30.09	1	2	5
D. Gough	10	5	2	74	39	24.66	–	–	2
R.J. Blakey	15	15	2	314	55*	24.15	–	1	15/2
B. Parker	10	9	1	164	36	20.50	–	–	2
P.J. Hartley	13	13	2	213	40*	19.36	–	–	3
C.E.W. Silverwood	8	3	2	16	9	16.00	–	–	8
A.P. Grayson	16	12	3	123	55	13.66	–	1	8
R.D. Stemp	9	3	1	17	14*	8.50	–	–	1
M.P. Vaughan	9	6	3	19	12	6.33	–	–	3
M.A. Robinson	2	2	1	2	1*	2.00	–	–	1

also – A.G. Wharf one match (ct 1)

BOWLING

	Overs	Mds	Runs	Wkts	Av	Best	5/inn
A.G. Wharf	8	2	39	3	13.00	3-39	–
C.E.W. Silverwood	58.3	3	260	15	17.33	3-29	–
D. Gough	76.3	5	309	15	20.60	5-13	1
C. White	38	7	176	7	25.14	3-25	–
M.A. Robinson	119	17	451	17	26.52	3-28	–
R.A. Kettleborough	5	–	29	1	29.00	1-17	–
R.D. Stemp	58	2	321	11	29.18	3-31	–
G.M. Hamilton	40.1	2	242	8	30.25	2-27	–
A.P. Grayson	67	3	370	12	30.83	4-25	–
P.J. Hartley	113.2	10	541	15	36.06	2-21	–
M.J. Foster	22	1	161	2	80.50	2-74	–
D. Byas	1	–	18	–	–	–	–

Batting scorecard tables (two sections) for Yorkshire CCC, with match-by-match innings for each player and totals (M, Inns, NO, Runs, HS, Av).

BOWLING

	D. Gough	M.A. Robinson	C. White	P.J. Hartley	R.D. Stemp	M.J. Foster	M.P. Vaughan	A.P. Grayson	C.E.W. Silverwood	L.C. Weekes	M. Broadhurst	R.A. Kettleborough	G.M. Hamilton	D. Byas	J.D. Batty	A.G. Wharf	Byes	Leg-byes	Wides	No-balls	Total	Wks
v. Lancashire (Old Trafford) 28 April–2 May	23.5-5-75-5	20-2-65-0	9-1-26-1	18-3-43-0	39-19-59-3	7-2-28-0	18-4-52-1										10	6		2	354	10
	15-4-38-0	15-5-21-0		7-2-25-0	18.2-3-48-2	6-2-15-0	11-1-38-0	11-4-28-1										2		8	225	4
v. Middlesex (Lord's) 5–9 May																		13	1	18	0	0
	19.4-3-75-3	16-4-36-1	8-0-27-0	19-1-59-3	6-2-9-0		2-1-5-0											9	3	6	224	7
v. Glamorgan (Cardiff) 12–16 May	20-6-57-3	11-3-44-0	5-1-17-0	15.2-5-33-2	29-12-48-5													1			208	10
	5-1-11-0	3-2-2-0		6-2-12-0														1	1		26	0
v. Essex (Leeds) 19–23 May		18-6-33-1	13-3-40-5	19-4-59-0	6-2-15-1				14.5-6-33-3								2	6		4	188	10
		13-6-11-0	11-4-28-2	13-7-17-2	10-5-13-0		5-1-14-0		11-0-43-0									5	1	2	131	4
v. New Zealanders (Leeds) 24–6 May		17-5-29-1	15-5-42-5	14-5-26-2	10-2-28-0												1	4		14	173	10
		15-7-23-1	15-3-30-2	18-3-49-2						9.4-1-43-2								6	2	22	202	9 A
v. Oxford University (Oxford) 28–31 May		11-2-23-0		16.4-3-53-3	25-15-39-0	6-2-12-0	1-0-2-1	5-1-13-1	13-2-45-0	14.4-1-92-2	8-0-45-1							2	1	16	212	9
		11-1-54-0		16-6-36-3	30-12-50-3	3.5-1-4-2	17.3-3-33-1	2-1-1-0	5-2-7-1		3-0-7-0						2	2	2	10	166	10
v. Nottinghamshire (Middlesbrough) 2–6 June		11-3-21-0	7-1-24-0	22-5-80-1	20-8-34-2		4-1-3-1		10-3-28-3								6	7	4	22	159	10
		17.3-5-30-1	15-3-59-0		28-10-67-4		2-0-7-0		9-2-31-1								1	2		8	145	5
v. Somerset (Brad'ord) 9–13 June		23-9-75-1	173-6-43-3	22.5-8-80-1	28-14-57-1	2-1-5-0	5-2-4-0	1-0-4-0	16-2-56-1								1	2	2	12	332	10
		15-9-31-1	4-1-12-0	14-2-33-2	7-2-11-1		18-8-47-0	9-5-6-0	8-3-26-0								4	8		2	224	4
v. Northamptonshire (Luton) 16–20 June		17.1-3-51-3	13.4-1-53-2	21-5-39-3	32-12-73-0		30-10-55-0	2-0-9-0	16-4-49-3			6-2-18-0						1		14	151	10
v. Hampshire (Leeds) 23–7 June	30-5-70-0	32-9-95-1		41-6-119-4	32-10-123-1		7-1-23-0	20-7-47-2	24-1-101-2								2	11	2	16	481	7
	20-5-57-2	15-6-33-0	7-1-24-0	24.1-7-50-1	7-2-27-0		7-1-33-0	14.3-3-43-2										5		4	305	10
v. Kent (Maidstone) 30 June–4 July		16-3-54-1	15-3-59-0	15-1-47-3	7-2-27-0		8-2-24-1	7-4-7-1	20-3-101-2				17-5-76-2	3-1-16-1			4	6	1	18	325	8
		18.2-3-94-1			32-10-123-1			3-0-19-0	18-5-63-1				17-1-77-1	7-2-21-1			2	8		18	377	10
v. Leicestershire (Harrogate) 14–18 July	30-7-81-1		9-2-28-3	32-2-110-4	6.5-2-22-3		9-3-19-0	8-1-20-0	19-5-57-3						33-9-79-2		1	6	1	11	373	9 B
	13-4-30-2		6-0-32-1	14-3-51-3	15-7-29-0				20-1-93-0					3-1-8-0	4-0-16-0			8		2	163	9
v. Gloucestershire (Cheltenham) 21–5 July		11-1-28-0		21.3-3-77-4	18-6-48-1	8-1-62-2	8.1-1-62-2	2-1-5-0	26-6-67-4									11		16	291	10
v. Durham (Durham) 28 July–1 August		34.1-10-92-4	11-3-41-1	25-3-114-0	40-16-84-3	8-3-23-0	18.2-84-2	9.5-10-1	9-1-35-1					3-0-7-0			8	12		16	484	10
		31-10-72-2	13.4-1-53-2		16-2-51-2		21-3-60-0											18		16	357	10
v. Lancashire (Leeds) 11–15 August	27-4-126-4	6-0-17-1		25-4-94-1	22.9-3-37-6		7-1-17-0	1-0-1-0					8-0-45-0					18		34	162	10
	7-2-14-0	24-6-71-2		8-1-35-1	25-11-53-2								6.2-3-16-1				4	10		22	404	10
v. Warwickshire (Scarborough) 18–22 August		31-12-63-0		34-10-122-1	46-11-107-4										14.4-3-59-2	23-4-78-1					125	3
		7-0-24-0		8-1-35-1	7-1-18-0		3-0-21-0								12-2-57-2			9	2	22	459	10
v. Worcestershire (Worcester) 25–9 August		33-11-73-2		34.5-11-89-5	35-21-30-1		5.3-0-22-0	7-2-18-0					19-4-56-0				5	10	1	12	355	10
v. Derbyshire (Sheffield) 30 August–2 September	20.4-5-87-2	10-1-48-5		10-1-20-4	1-1-0-0		3-1-7-1										1	1		4	73	10 C
	11.3-3-24-4	12-2-35-4			3-0-21-0		2-1-7-0		10-1-48-2									6		8	200	10
v. Surrey (Scarborough) 8–12 September		18-4-47-1	11-3-41-1	14.4-2-50-2	3-2-4-1			2-0-5-0						3-0-7-0	14-4-48-0		2	1	1	10	73	9 D
			13.4-1-53-2		29-11-74-1												10	7			307	10
v. Sussex (Hove) 15–19 September	22.4-6-81-3	24-9-4?-4		21-4-72-2	9-4-20-1												1	8		8	226	10
	14-2-69-4	16-3-54-1		15-4-42-3	6-3-15-0													1	1	8	181	8
Bowler's average	309-72-961-45 21.35	619-171-1658-45 36.84	159.1-31-502-25 20.08	562.1-116-1701-61 27.88	669.1-252-1493-49 30.46	37.4-12-100-3 33.33	228.3-52-678-14 48.42	103.3-34-236-8 29.50	248.5-47-883-27 32.70	24.2-2-135-4 33.75	11-0-52-1 52.00	6-2-18-0 —	67.2-13-270-4 67.50	16-4-52-2 26.00	77.4-18-259-6 43.16	23-4-78-1 78.00						

A M.D. Crowe absent ill
B P.V. Simmons absent hurt
C S.M. Milburn 23-4-74-2; 1.2-0-3-1
D M.J. Vandrau absent